ACCOUNTING TRENDS & TECHNIQUES

U.S. GAAP Financial Statements

Best Practices in Presentation and Disclosure

13632-359

SIXTY-SEVENTH EDITION

1 2 3 4 5 6 7 8 9 0 AAP 1 9 8 7 6 5 4 3

ISSN 1531-4340

ISBN 978-1-93735-271-4

Director, Content and Product Development: Linda Cohen
Senior Technical Manager: Doug Bowman
Technical Manager: Liese Faircloth
Content Development Specialist: David Cohen
Production Administrator: Charlotte Ingles

Recognition

The 2013 edition of *U.S. GAAP Financial Statements—Best Practices in Presentation and Disclosure* was developed by

RAYMOND J. PETRINO, CPA
CONTENT MATTER EXPERT

DAVID J. COHEN
CONTENT DEVELOPMENT SPECIALIST
AICPA OPERATIONS AND PRODUCT
DEVELOPMENT

LIESE FAIRCLOTH, CPA
TECHNICAL MANAGER
AICPA ACCOUNTING AND AUDITING CONTENT
DEVELOPMENT

Special acknowledgment and sincere thanks are due to the following individuals for their efforts, without whom this book would not be possible:

Mark Bond
Lisa Hopson

Keira Kraft
Kathy Keough

About This Edition of *U.S. GAAP Financial Statements—Best Practices in Presentation and Disclosure*

For over 60 years, *U.S. GAAP Financial Statements—Best Practices in Presentation and Disclosure* has been the best source for reporting and disclosure examples from real world financial statements, providing accounting professionals with an invaluable resource for incorporating new and existing accounting and reporting guidance into financial statements using presentation techniques adopted by companies across numerous industries, all of which are headquartered in the United States.

Organization and Content

This 2013 edition surveyed annual reports of 350 entities of various sizes representing over 100 industries with fiscal periods ending between January and December 2012. The industry classifications of survey entities were obtained from Morningstar, Inc.

To provide you with the most useful and comprehensive look at current financial reporting presentation and disclosure, this book is topically organized and offers the following:
- Descriptive guidance that includes current reporting requirements under U.S. generally accepted accounting principles (GAAP). U.S. GAAP is generally considered to be the requirements of the Financial Accounting Standards Board (FASB) *Accounting Standards Codification*™ (ASC). Select Securities and Exchange Commission (SEC) guidance is also included.
- Examples taken from the surveyed annual reports illustrating financial statement presentation and virtually every required U.S. GAAP disclosure.
- Detailed indexes.

GUIDANCE

Discerning, plain English guidance covers the significant U.S. GAAP accounting and financial statement reporting requirements in narrative form. These narratives use common headings (recognition and measurement, presentation, and disclosure) to achieve a consistent presentation throughout all the sections. Although not a substitute for the authoritative accounting and reporting standards, the reporting guidance herein encapsulates the complex requirements to facilitate your understanding of the content. The related authoritative sources for each requirement are cited within the narratives (for example, FASB ASC 310, *Receivables*, or Regulation S-K).

SEC rules and interpretative releases may expand, modify, or decrease accounting and disclosure requirements for foreign private issuers, regardless of whether they file their annual financial statements with the SEC in Forms 10-K, 20-F, or 40-F (Canadian issuers). Therefore, it is critical to consider SEC requirements, as well as those of FASB ASC, when reviewing the financial statements of SEC registrants. A general reference to FASB ASC in this publication does not include the SEC materials. When requirements are taken from an SEC rule or regulation, that rule or regulation will be cited directly.

ILLUSTRATIVE REPORTING EXAMPLES

AICPA leverages its decades of experience as the CPA national membership organization to select the most useful, comprehensive presentation and disclosure examples, which comprise the majority of this book. Every edition of *Best Practices in Presentation and Disclosure* includes all new annual report excerpts that were chosen to be particularly relevant and useful to financial statement preparers in illustrating current reporting practices.

Because survey entities may present disclosures on specific topics within different footnotes in their annual filings, including those ostensibly about a separate accounting topic, the excerpts presented herein to illustrate a given topic may have been taken from footnotes about other topics.

INDEXES

Indexes in this edition include the "Appendix of 350 Entities," which alphabetically lists each of the 350 survey entities included in the current edition and notes where in the text excerpts from their annual reports can be found; the "Index of Authoritative Accounting & Auditing Guidance," which provides for easy cross-referencing of pronouncements to the applicable descriptive narratives; and a detailed "Subject Index," which is fully cross-referenced to all significant topics included throughout the narratives.

FASB ASC

Because FASB ASC is the source of authoritative U.S. GAAP for nongovernmental entities, in addition to guidance issued by the SEC, the guidance herein refers only to the appropriate FASB ASC reference for all standards.

Note that the effective dates of recently released guidance affect the timing of its inclusion in the financial statements of the survey entities, thereby affecting the availability of illustrative excerpts for potential inclusion in each edition of *Best Practices in Presentation and Disclosure*. This 2013 edition includes survey entities having fiscal years ending within calendar year 2012. Technical guidance for which this edition supplies illustrative annual report excerpts includes the following, among other recently issued guidance:
- ASU No. 2011-12, *Comprehensive Income (Topic 220): Deferral of the Effective Date for Amendments to the Presentation of Reclassifications of Items Out of Accumulated Other Comprehensive Income in ASU No. 2011-05*
- ASU No. 2011-11, *Balance Sheet (Topic 210): Disclosures about Offsetting*
- ASU No. 2011-10, *Property, Plant, and Equipment (Topic 360): Derecognition of in Substance Real Estate-a Scope Clarification*

Related Products

U.S. GAAP Financial Statements—Best Practices in Presentation and Disclosure is the flagship product in the AICPA's *Accounting Trends & Techniques* series; it is also available in an online format. Other titles in the *Accounting Trends & Techniques* series include
- *IFRS Financial Statements—Best Practices in Presentation and Disclosure*
- *Employee Benefit Plans Financial Statements—Best Practices in Presentation and Disclosure*
- *Not-for-Profit Entities Financial Statements—Best Practices in Presentation and Disclosure*

Notice

This book is a nonauthoritative practice aid and is not designed to provide a comprehensive understanding of all the requirements contained in U.S. GAAP. The guidance provided herein may not discuss all relevant accounting guidance on a given topic and should not be relied upon for its completeness. Users are encouraged to consult FASB ASC for complete, authoritative discussion of U.S. GAAP. Users are also encouraged to consult the complete body of SEC rules and regulations for regulatory requirements. In addition, this book does not include reporting requirements relating to other matters such as internal control or agreed-upon procedures.

Authoritative guidance on accounting treatments in accordance with U.S. GAAP can be made only by reference to the FASB ASC, which is copyright of the FAF and can be acquired directly from FASB.

This book has not been reviewed, approved, disapproved, or otherwise acted on by any senior technical committee of the AICPA and does not represent official positions or pronouncements of the AICPA.

The use of this publication requires the exercise of individual professional judgment. It is not a substitute for the original authoritative accounting and auditing guidance. Users are urged to refer directly to applicable authoritative pronouncements, when appropriate. As an additional resource, users may call the AICPA Technical Hotline at 1.877.242.7212.

Feedback

We hope that you find this edition to be informative and useful. Please let us know! What features do you like? What do you think can be improved or added? We encourage you to submit your comments and questions to Liese Faircloth, using the following contact information. All feedback is greatly appreciated and kept strictly confidential.

Liese Faircloth—Content and Product Development
AMERICAN INSTITUTE OF CERTIFIED PUBLIC ACCOUNTANTS
220 Leigh Farm Road
Durham, NC 27707-8110
Telephone: 919.402.4819
E-mail: lfaircloth@aicpa.org

You can also contact the Accounting and Auditing Content Development team of the AICPA directly via e-mail at

A&Apublications@aicpa.org

TABLE OF CONTENTS

Survey Entities

1.01 All 350 entities included in the survey are registered with the Securities and Exchange Commission (SEC). All of the survey entities have securities traded on one of the major stock exchanges: 83 percent on the New York Stock Exchange and 17 percent on NASDAQ.

1.02 Each year, entities are selected across various industry classifications with the purpose of highlighting those entities that exhibit the best practices.

General Financial Statement Considerations

RECOGNITION AND MEASUREMENT

1.03 Financial Accounting Standards Board (FASB) *Accounting Standards Codification* (ASC) 105-10-05-2 explains that if the necessary guidance for a transaction or event is not specified within a source of authoritative generally accepted accounting principles (GAAP), an entity should first consider accounting principles for similar transactions or events within a source of authoritative GAAP for that entity and then consider nonauthoritative guidance from other sources. When those accounting principles either prohibit the application of the accounting treatment to the particular transaction or event or indicate that the accounting treatment should not be applied by analogy, an entity should not follow those accounting principles.

1.04 FASB ASC 105-10-05-3 explains that accounting and financial reporting practices not included in FASB ASC are nonauthoritative. FASB Concept Statements are not considered authoritative sources of GAAP, and no preference is given to the FASB Concept Statements over other nonauthoritative sources. FASB ASC does not state that consistency with the FASB Concept Statements in connection with an entity's application of an accounting treatment is necessary. Sources of nonauthoritative accounting guidance include the following:
- Practices that are widely recognized and prevalent, either generally or in the industry
- FASB Concept Statements
- AICPA Issues Papers
- International Financial Reporting Standards (IFRSs) of the International Accounting Standards Board
- Pronouncements of professional associations or regulatory agencies
- Technical Questions and Answers included in AICPA *Technical Practice Aids*
- Accounting textbooks, handbooks, and articles

The appropriateness of other sources of accounting guidance depends on its relevance to particular circumstances, the specificity of the guidance, the general recognition of the issuer or author as an authority, and the extent of its use in practice.

1.05 As discussed in FASB ASC 105-10-05-1, GAAP, as codified in FASB ASC, includes the rules and interpretive releases of the SEC as sources of authoritative GAAP as a convenience to SEC registrants. In addition to SEC rules and interpretive releases, the SEC staff issues Staff Accounting Bulletins that represent practices that the staff follows when administering SEC disclosure requirements. SEC staff announcements and observer comments made at meetings of the Emerging Issues Task Force publicly announce the staff's views on certain accounting issues for SEC registrants.

1.06 In June 2009, FASB issued the last FASB statement referenced in that form: FASB Statement No. 168, *The* FASB Accounting Standards Codification™ *and the Hierarchy of Generally Accepted Accounting Principles—a replacement of FASB Statement No. 162.* This standard established FASB ASC as the source of authoritative U.S. accounting and reporting standards for nongovernmental companies, in addition to guidance issued by the SEC, and was effective for financial statements issued for interim and annual periods ending after September 15, 2009.

1.07 In FASB ASC's Notice to Constituents (NTC), FASB suggests the use of plain English references to describe broad FASB ASC topics going forward in financial statements and related footnote disclosures. FASB provides the following example of plain English references in the NTC when referring to the requirements of FASB ASC 815, *Derivatives and Hedging*: "as required by the Derivatives and Hedging Topic of the FASB Accounting Standards Codification."

1.08 A natural business year is the period of 12 consecutive months that end when the business activities of an entity have reached the lowest point in their annual cycle. In many instances, the natural business year of an entity ends December 31.

PRESENTATION

1.09 Rule 14a-3 of the Securities Exchange Act of 1934 states that annual reports furnished to stockholders in connection with the annual meetings of stockholders should include audited financial statements: balance sheets as of the end of the two most recent fiscal years and statements of income and cash flows for each of the three most recent fiscal years. Rule 14a-3 also states that the following information, as specified in SEC Regulation S-K should be included in the annual report to stockholders:

- Selected quarterly financial data
- Changes in, and disagreements with, accountants on accounting and financial disclosure
- Summary of selected financial data for the last five years
- Description of business activities
- Segment information
- Listing of company directors and executive officers
- Market price of, and dividends on, the company's common stock for each quarterly period within the two most recent fiscal years
- Management's discussion and analysis (MD&A) of financial condition and results of operations
- Quantitative and qualitative disclosures about market risk

1.10 FASB ASC 205-10-45-2 states only that it is ordinarily desirable for an entity to present the statement of financial position; the income statement; and the statement of changes in equity for one or more preceding years, in addition to those of the current year.

1.11 Paragraphs 3–4 of FASB ASC 205-10-45 require these statements to be comparable, and any exceptions to comparability should be described as required by FASB ASC 250, *Accounting Changes and Error Corrections*. An entity is required to repeat, or at least refer to, any notes to financial statements, other explanations, or accountants' reports that contain qualifications for prior years that appeared in the comparative statements when originally issued, to the extent this information remains significant. Multiple rules set forth in SEC Regulation S-X provide guidance to SEC registrants on the form and ordering of financial statements, the presentation of amounts, the omission of certain items, and requirements for supplemental schedules. Rule 14a-3 requires that annual reports to stockholders should include comparative balance sheets and statements of income and cash flows for each of the three most recent fiscal years. All the survey entities are SEC registrants and conformed to the aforementioned requirements of Rule 14a-3.

1.12 FASB ASC permits an entity to offset a liability with an asset only when the following certain conditions discussed in FASB ASC 210-20-45-1 are met:
- Each of two parties owes the other determinable amounts.
- The reporting party has the right to set off the amount owed with the amount owed by the other party.
- The reporting party intends to set off.
- The right of setoff is enforceable by law.

Author's Note

In December 2011, FASB issued Accounting Standards Update (ASU) No. 2011-11, *Balance Sheet (Topic 210): Disclosures about Offsetting Assets and Liabilities*, to enhance comparability of financial statements prepared in accordance with GAAP and IFRS. The amendments in this update will enhance disclosures by requiring improved information about financial instruments and derivative instruments that are either (*a*) offset in accordance with either FASB ASC 210-20-45 or 815-10-45 or (*b*) subject to an enforceable master netting arrangement or similar agreement, irrespective of whether they are offset in accordance with either of the aforementioned FASB ASC sections. The additional disclosures will enable financial statement users to better understand the effect of such arrangements on their financial position. Entities are required to apply the amendments in this ASU for annual reporting periods beginning on or after January 1, 2013, and interim periods within those annual periods. As a result of the effective date of this ASU, the excerpts appearing later in this section may not reflect all or some of these revisions.

DISCLOSURE

1.13 SEC Regulations S-X and S-K and paragraphs .19–.20 and .A22–.A23 of AU-C section 705, *Modifications to the Opinion in the Independent Auditor's Report* (AICPA, *Professional Standards*), state the need for adequate disclosure in financial statements. Normally, the financial statements alone cannot present all information necessary for adequate disclosure without considering appended notes that disclose information. All surveyed entities provided footnote disclosures to their financial statements.

1.14 FASB ASC 235, *Notes to Financial Statements*, sets forth guidelines about the content and format of disclosures of accounting policies. FASB ASC 235-10-50-1 requires that the significant accounting policies of an entity be presented as an integral part of the financial statements of the entity. FASB ASC 235-10-50-6 states that the preferable format is to present a summary of significant accounting policies preceding notes to financial statements or as the initial note under the same or a similar title.

1.15 FASB ASC 205-10-50-1 requires an entity to provide information explaining changes due to reclassifications or other reasons that affect the manner of, or basis for, presenting corresponding items for two or more periods. FASB ASC 250-10 does not require an entity to present an opening balance sheet of the earliest period presented when an entity retrospectively applies a change in accounting policy or restates to correct an error.

1.16 FASB ASC 275, *Risks and Uncertainties*, requires reporting entities to disclose information about the risks and uncertainties resulting from the nature of their operations, the use of estimates in preparing financial statements, and significant concentrations in certain aspects of the entity's operations.

PRESENTATION AND DISCLOSURE EXCERPTS

QUARTERLY FINANCIAL DATA

1.17 INTERNATIONAL PAPER COMPANY (DEC)
FINANCIAL STATEMENTS AND SUPPLEMENTARY DATA (in part)

Interim Financial Results (Unaudited)

(In millions, except per share amounts and stock prices)	1st Quarter	2nd Quarter	3rd Quarter	4th Quarter	Year
2012					
Net sales	$ 6,655	$ 7,077	$ 7,026	$ 7,075	$ 27,833
Gross margin[a]	1,671	1,807	1,886	1,882	7,246
Earnings (loss) from continuing operations before income taxes and equity earnings	213[b]	204[c]	320[d]	287[e]	1,024[b-e]
Gain from discontinued operations	5	16	14	10	45
Net earnings (loss) attributable to International Paper Company	188[b]	134[c]	237[d]	235[e,f]	794[b f]
Basic earnings (loss) per share attributable to International Paper Company common shareholders:					
Earnings (loss) from continuing operations	$ 0.42[b]	$ 0.27[c]	$ 0.51[d]	$ 0.52[e]	$ 1.72[b-e]
Gain from discontinued operations	0.01	0.04	0.03	0.02	0.10
Net earnings (loss)	0.43[b]	0.31[c]	0.54[d]	0.54[e,f]	1.82[b-f]
Diluted earnings (loss) per share attributable to International Paper Company common shareholders:					
Earnings (loss) from continuing operations	0.42[b]	0.27[c]	0.51[d]	0.51[e]	1.70[b-e]
Gain from discontinued operations	0.01	0.04	0.03	0.02	0.10
Net earnings (loss)	0.43[b]	0.31[c]	0.54[d]	0.53[e,f]	1.80[b-f]
Dividends per share of common stock	0.2625	0.2625	0.2625	0.3000	1.0875
Common stock prices					
High	$ 36.50	$ 35.59	$ 37.25	$ 39.88	$ 39.88
Low	29.45	27.29	28.29	32.95	27.29
2011					
Net sales	$ 6,387	$ 6,648	$ 6,632	$ 6,367	$ 26,034
Gross margin[a]	1,762	1,768	1,839	1,705	7,074
Earnings (loss) from continuing operations before income taxes and equity earnings	368[g]	293[j]	381[k]	416[m]	1,458[g,j,k,m]
Gain from discontinued operations	49[h]	—	—	—	49[h]
Net earnings (loss) attributable to International Paper Company	354[g-i]	219[j]	468[k,l]	281[m,n]	1,322[g-n]
Basic earnings (loss) per share attributable to International Paper Company common shareholders:					
Earnings (loss) from continuing operations	$ 0.71[g,i]	$ 0.51[j]	$ 1.08[k,l]	$ 0.65[m,n]	$ 2.95[g,i,j,k,l,m,n]
Gain from discontinued operations	0.11[h]	—	—	—	0.11[h]
Net earnings (loss)	0.82[g-i]	0.51[j]	1.08[k,l]	0.65[m,n]	3.06[g-n]
Diluted earnings (loss) per share attributable to International Paper Company common shareholders:					
Earnings (loss) from continuing operations	0.70[g,i]	0.51[j]	1.08[k,l]	0.65[m,n]	2.92[g,i,j,k,l,m,n]
Gain from discontinued operations	0.11[h]	—	—	—	0.11[h]
Net earnings (loss)	0.81[g-i]	0.51[j]	1.08[k,l]	0.65[m,n]	3.03[g-n]
Dividends per share of common stock	0.1875	0.2625	0.2625	0.2625	0.9750

(continued)

(In millions, except per share amounts and stock prices)	1st Quarter	2nd Quarter	3rd Quarter	4th Quarter	Year
2011					
Common stock prices					
High	$ 30.44	$ 33.01	$ 31.57	$ 29.85	$ 33.01
Low	24.88	26.25	22.90	21.55	21.55

Note: Since basic and diluted earnings per share are computed independently for each period and category, full year per share amounts may not equal the sum of the four quarters.

Footnotes to Interim Financial Results

(a) Gross margin represents net sales less cost of products sold, excluding depreciation, amortization and cost of timber harvested.

(b) Includes a pre-tax charge of $20 million ($12 million after taxes) related to the write-up of the Temple-Inland inventories to fair value, a pre-tax charge of $21 million ($16 million after taxes) for an inventory write-off, severance and other charges related to the restructuring of the Company's xpedx operations, a pre-tax charge of $43 million ($33 million after taxes) for integration costs associated with the acquisition of Temple-Inland, a pre-tax charge of $16 million ($10 million after taxes) for early debt extinguishment costs, a pre-tax gain of $7 million ($6 million after taxes) for adjustments related to the sale of the Shorewood business, and a gain of $1 million (before and after taxes) for other items.

(c) Includes a pre-tax charge of $12 million ($8 million after taxes) for an inventory write-off, severance and other charges related to the restructuring of the Company's xpedx operations, a pre-tax charge of $35 million ($22 million after taxes) for integration costs associated with the acquisition of Temple-Inland, a pre-tax charge of $10 million ($6 million after taxes) for debt extinguishment costs, a pre-tax charge of $62 million ($38 million after taxes) to adjust the long-lived assets of the Hueneme mill in Oxnard, California to their fair value in anticipation of its divestiture, a pre-tax charge of $9 million ($5 million after taxes) for costs associated with the third-quarter 2012 divestiture of the Hueneme mill and two other containerboard mills, a pre-tax charge of $6 million ($4 million after taxes) for an adjustment related to the sale of Shorewood, and charges of $2 million (before and after taxes) for other items.

(d) Includes a pre-tax charge of $9 million ($5 million after taxes) for an inventory write-off, severance and other charges related to the restructuring of the Company's xpedx operations, a pre-tax charge of $58 million ($34 million after taxes) for integration costs associated with the acquisition of Temple-Inland, a pre-tax charge of $13 million ($8 million after taxes) for debt extinguishment costs, a pre-tax charge of $16 million ($11 million after taxes) for costs associated with the restructuring of the Company's Packaging business in Europe, a pre-tax charge of $19 million ($49 million after taxes) for costs associated with the containerboard mill divestitures and a pre-tax gain of $5 million ($0 million after taxes) for other items.

(e) Includes a pre-tax charge of $28 million ($19 million after taxes) for integration costs associated with the acquisition of Temple-Inland, a pre-tax charge of $9 million ($6 million after taxes) for debt extinguishment costs, a pre-tax charge of $7 million ($4 million after taxes) for costs associated with the restructuring of our xpedx operations, a gain of $2 million (before and after taxes) for proceeds associated with the 2010 sale of the Arizona Chemical business, a gain of $2 million (before and after taxes) for adjustments related to the sale of the Company's Shorewood operations, a charge of $1 million (before and after taxes) for costs associated with the containerboard mill divestitures, and pre-tax charges of $5 million ($4 million after taxes) for other items.

(f) Includes a net expense of $14 million related to internal restructurings and a $5 million expense to adjust deferred tax assets related to post-retirement prescription drug coverage (Medicare Part D reimbursements).

(g) Includes a pre-tax charge of $32 million ($19 million after taxes) for early debt extinguishment costs, a pre-tax charge of $7 million ($4 million after taxes) for costs associated with the restructuring of the Company's xpedx operations, and a charge of $8 million (before and after taxes) for asset impairment costs associated with the Inverurie, Scotland mill which was closed in 2009.

(h) Includes a pre-tax gain of $50 million ($30 million after taxes) for an earnout provision related to the sale of the Company's Kraft Papers business completed in January 2007. Also, the Company sold its Brazilian Coated Paper business in the third quarter 2006. Local country tax contingency reserves were included in the business' operating results in 2005 and 2006 for which the related statute of limitations has expired. The reserves were reversed and a tax benefit of $15 million plus associated interest income of $6 million ($4 million after taxes) was recorded.

(i) Includes a gain of $7 million (before and after taxes) related to a bargain price adjustment on an acquisition by our joint venture in Turkey.

(j) Includes a pre-tax charge of $27 million ($17 million after taxes) for an environmental reserve related to the Company's property in Cass Lake, Minnesota, a pre-tax gain of $21 million ($13 million after taxes) related to the reversal of environmental reserves due to the announced repurposing of a portion of the Franklin mill, a pre-tax charge of $10 million ($6 million after taxes) for costs associated with the restructuring of the Company's xpedx operations, and a pre-tax charge of $129 million ($104 million after taxes) for a fixed-asset impairment of the North American Shorewood business.

(k) Includes a pre-tax charge of $16 million ($10 million after taxes) for costs associated with the acquisition of a majority share of Andhra Pradesh Paper Mills Limited in India, a pre-tax charge of $18 million ($13 million after taxes) for costs associated with the restructuring of the Company's xpedx operations, a pre-tax charge of $8 million ($5 million after taxes) for costs associated with signing an agreement to acquire Temple-Inland, a pre-tax charge of $6 million ($4 million after taxes) for costs associated with the sale of the Company's Shorewood operations, and a pre-tax charge of $82 million (a gain of $140 million after taxes) to reduce the carrying value of the Shorewood business based on the terms of the definitive agreement to sell this business.

(l) Includes a tax benefit of $222 million related to the reduction of the carrying value of the Shorewood business and the write-off of a deferred tax liability associated with Shorewood, and noncontrolling interest income of $8 million (before and after taxes) associated with the fixed asset impairment of Shorewood Mexico.

(m) Includes a pre-tax charge of $17 million ($13 million after taxes) for an inventory write-off, severance and other costs associated with the restructuring of the Company's xpedx operations, a pre-tax charge of $12 million ($7 million after taxes) for costs associated with the signing of an agreement to acquire Temple-Inland, a pre-tax gain of $4 million ($3 million after taxes) for an adjustment to the previously recorded loss to reduce the carrying value of the Company's Shorewood business, a charge of $3 million (before and after taxes) for asset impairment charges at our Inverurie, Scotland mill which was closed in 2009, and a gain of $6 million (before and after taxes) for interest associated with a tax claim.

(n) Includes a $24 million expense related to internal restructurings, a $9 million expense for costs associated with our acquisition of a majority interest in Andhra Pradesh Paper Mills Limited, a $13 million tax benefit related to the release of a deferred tax asset valuation allowance, and a $2 million expense for other items.

SELECTED INFORMATION FOR FIVE YEARS

1.18 AMERICAN INTERNATIONAL GROUP, INC. (DEC)
SELECTED FINANCIAL DATA

The Selected Consolidated Financial Data should be read in conjunction with Management's Discussion and Analysis of Financial Condition and Results of Operations and the Consolidated Financial Statements and accompanying notes included elsewhere herein.

(In millions, except per share data)	Years Ended December 31,				
	2012	2011	2010(a)	2009(a)	2008
Revenues:					
Premiums	$38,011	$38,990	$45,319	$48,583	$60,147
Policy fees	2,791	2,705	2,710	2,656	2,990
Net investment income	20,343	14,755	20,934	18,992	10,453
Net realized capital gains (losses)	929	701	(716)	(3,787)	(50,426)
Other income	3,582	2,661	4,582	3,729	(34,941)
Total revenues	65,656	59,812	72,829	70,173	(11,777)

(continued)

(In millions, except per share data)	Years Ended December 31,				
	2012	2011	2010[a]	2009[a]	2008
Benefits, claims and expenses:					
Policyholder benefits and claims incurred	31,977	33,450	41,392	45,314	45,447
Interest credited to policyholder account balances	4,362	4,467	4,487	4,611	5,582
Amortization of deferred acquisition costs	5,709	5,486	5,821	6,670	6,425
Other acquisition and insurance expenses	9,235	8,458	10,163	9,815	14,783
Interest expense	2,319	2,444	6,742	13,237	14,440
Net loss on extinguishment of debt	9	2,847	104	—	—
Net (gain) loss on sale of properties and divested businesses	2	74	(19,566)	1,271	—
Other expenses	2,721	2,470	3,439	5,282	5,842
Total benefits, claims and expenses	56,334	59,696	52,582	86,200	92,519
Income (loss) from continuing operations before income taxes[b]	9,322	116	20,247	(16,027)	(104,296)
Income taxes expense (benefit)	1,570	(19,424)	6,993	(2,551)	(8,097)
Income (loss) from continuing operations	7,752	19,540	13,254	(13,476)	(96,199)
Income (loss) from discontinued operations, net of taxes	(4,052)	1,790	(969)	3,750	(6,683)
Net income (loss)	3,700	21,330	12,285	(9,726)	(102,882)
Net income (loss) attributable to AIG	3,438	20,622	10,058	(8,362)	(101,784)
Income (loss) per common share attributable to AIG common shareholders					
Basic and diluted					
Income (loss) from continuing operations	4.44	10.03	16.50	(98.52)	(725.89)
Income (loss) from discontinued operations	(2.40)	0.98	(1.52)	27.15	(49.91)
Net income (loss) attributable to AIG	2.04	11.01	14.98	(71.37)	(775.80)
Dividends declared per common share	—	—	—	—	8.40
Year-end balance sheet data:					
Total investments	375,824	410,438	410,412	601,165	636,912
Total assets	548,633	553,054	675,573	838,346	848,552
Long-term debt	48,500	75,253	106,461	136,733	177,485
Total liabilities	449,630	442,138	568,363	748,550	797,692
Total AIG shareholders' equity	98,002	101,538	78,856	60,585	40,844
Total equity	98,669	102,393	106,776	88,837	48,939
Book value per share[a]	66.38	53.53	561.40	448.54	303.71
Book value per share, excluding Accumulated other comprehensive income (loss)[a][c]	57.87	50.11	498.25	400.90	353.97
AIG Property Casualty combined ratio[d]	108.6	108.8	116.8	108.4	102.1
Other data (from continuing operations):					
Other-than-temporary impairments	1,167	1,280	3,039	6,696	41,867
Adjustment to federal and foreign deferred tax valuation allowance	(1,907)	(18,307)	1,361	2,986	22,172
Amortization of prepaid commitment fee	—	49	3,471	8,359	9,279
Catastrophe-related losses	$ 2,652	$ 3,307	$ 1,076	$ 53	$ 1,840

[a] Comparability between 2010 and 2009 data is affected by the deconsolidation of AIA in the fourth quarter of 2010. Book value per share, excluding Accumulated other comprehensive income (loss) is a non-GAAP measure. See Item 7. MD&A—Use of Non-GAAP Measures for additional information. Comparability of 2010, 2009 and 2008 is affected by a one for twenty reverse stock split.

[b] Reduced by fourth quarter reserve strengthening charges of $4.2 billion and $2.2 billion in 2010 and 2009, respectively, related to the annual review of AIG Property Casualty loss and loss adjustment reserves.

[c] Amounts for periods after December 31, 2008 have been revised to reflect reclassification of income taxes from AOCI to additional paid in capital to correct the presentation of components of AIG Shareholders' Equity. See Note 1 to the Consolidated Financial Statements for additional information on the reclass.

[d] See Item 7. MD&A—Results of Operations—AIG Property Casualty Operations for a reconciliation of the adjusted combined ratio.

Changes In Accounting For Acquisition Costs

Reflects changes from the adoption of the new accounting standard related to deferred acquisition costs for 2009 and 2008, as set out in further detail below. See Note 2 to the Consolidated Financial Statements for a description of the effect of the adoption of the new accounting standards on 2011 and 2010 periods, which is also reflected in the data presented above.

(Dollars in millions, except per share data)	Year Ended December 31, 2009		
	As Previously Reported[a]	Effect of Change	As Currently Reported
Income (loss) from continuing operations	$ (13,907)	$ 431	$ (13,476)
Income (loss) from discontinued operations, net of income tax [b]	1,594	2,156	3,750
Net income (loss)	(12,313)	2,587	(9,726)
Net income (loss) attributable to AIG	$ (10,949)	$ 2,587	$ (8,362)
Net income (loss) attributable to AIG common shareholders	$ (12,244)	$ 2,587	$ (9,657)
Income (loss) per share attributable to AIG common shareholders:			
Basic and diluted:			
Income (loss) from continuing operations	$ (100.70)	$ 3.18	$ (98.52)
Income from discontinued operations	$ 11.22	$ 15.93	$ 27.15
Income (loss) attributable to AIG	$ (90.48)	$ 19.11	$ (71.37)
December 31, 2009 balance sheet data:			
Total assets	$847,585	$(9,239)	$838,346
Total liabilities	748,550	—	748,550
Total AIG shareholders' equity	69,824	(9,239)	60,585
Total equity	98,076	(9,239)	88,837
Other data (from continuing operations):			
Adjustment to federal and foreign deferred tax valuation allowance	$ 3,137	$ (151)	$ 2,986

(continued)

(In millions, except per share data)	Year Ended December 31, 2008		
	As Previously Reported[a]	Effect of Change	As Currently Reported
Loss from continuing operations	$ (94,022)	$ (2,177)	$ (96,199)
Loss from discontinued operations, net of tax	(6,365)	(318)	(6,683)
Net loss	(100,387)	(2,495)	(102,882)
Net loss attributable to AIG	$ (99,289)	$ (2,495)	$(101,784)
Net loss attributable to AIG common shareholders	$ (99,689)	$ (2,495)	$(102,184)
Loss per common share attributable to AIG common shareholders:			
Basic and diluted:			
Loss from continuing operations	$ (709.35)	$ (16.54)	$ (725.89)
Loss from discontinued operations	$ (47.50)	$ (2.41)	$ (49.91)
Net loss attributable to AIG	$ (756.85)	$ (18.95)	$ (775.80)
December 31, 2008 balance sheet data:			
Total assets	$860,418	$(11,866)	$ 848,552
Total liabilities	797,692	—	797,692
Total AIG shareholders' equity	52,710	(11,866)	40,844
Total equity	60,805	(11,866)	48,939
Other data (from continuing operations):			
Adjustment to federal and foreign deferred tax valuation allowance	$ 20,121	$ 2,051	$ 22,172

[a] Includes the effect of the reclassification of ILFC as discontinued operations.
[b] Includes an adjustment to the loss accrual related to the sale of Nan Shan of $2.3 billion.

Items Affecting Comparability Between Periods

The following are significant developments that affected multiple periods and financial statement captions. Other items that affected comparability are included in the footnotes to the table presented immediately above.

Market Events in 2008 and 2009

AIG was significantly affected by the market turmoil in late 2008 and early 2009 and recognized other-than-temporary impairment charges in 2008 related primarily to collateralized mortgage-backed securities, other structured securities and securities of financial institutions; losses related to the change in AIG's intent and ability to hold to recovery certain securities; and losses related to AIG's securities lending program.

In 2008, AIG also recognized unrealized market valuation losses representing the change in fair value of its super senior credit default swap portfolio, established a deferred tax valuation allowance and experienced an unprecedented strain on liquidity. This strain led to several transactions with the FRBNY and the Department of the Treasury. See Note 25 to the Consolidated Financial Statements for further discussion of these transactions and relationships.

FRBNY Activity and Effect on Interest Expense in 2008, 2009 and 2010

The decline in interest expense in 2010 was due primarily to a reduced weighted-average interest rate on borrowings, a lower average outstanding balance and a decline in amortization of the prepaid commitment fee asset related to the partial repayment of the FRBNY Credit Facility. On January 14, 2011, AIG repaid the remaining $20.7 billion and terminated this facility, resulting in a net $3.3 billion pretax charge in the first quarter of 2011, representing primarily the accelerated amortization of the remaining prepaid commitment fee asset included in Net loss on extinguishment of debt. See Note 25 to the Consolidated Financial Statements for further discussion of the Recapitalization.

As a result of the closing of the Recapitalization on January 14, 2011, the preferred interests (the SPV Preferred Interests) in the special purpose vehicles that held remaining AIA shares and the proceeds of the AIA initial public offering and the ALICO sale (the SPVs) were transferred to the Department of the Treasury. After such closing, the SPV Preferred Interests were not considered permanent equity on AIG's Consolidated Balance Sheet and were classified as redeemable non-controlling interests.

Asset Dispositions in 2010, 2011 and 2012

On December 9, 2012, we announced the agreement to sell up to 90% of ILFC and executed multiple asset dispositions in 2010 and 2011, as further discussed in Note 4 to the Consolidated Financial Statements, including the completion of an initial public offering of AIA in 2010 for which AIG recognized an $18.1 billion gain.

Adjustment to Federal Deferred Tax Valuation Allowance in 2008, 2009, 2010, 2011 and 2012

As further discussed in Note 24 to the Consolidated Financial Statements, AIG concluded that $18.4 billion of the deferred tax asset valuation allowance for the U.S. consolidated income tax group should be released through the Consolidated Statement of Operations in 2011. The valuation allowance resulted primarily from losses subject to U.S. income taxes recorded from 2008 through 2010.

Capitalization and Book Value Per Share

As a result of the closing of the Recapitalization on January 14, 2011, the remaining SPV Preferred Interests held by the FRBNY of approximately $26.4 billion were purchased by AIG and transferred to the Department of the Treasury. The SPV Preferred Interests were no longer considered permanent equity on AIG's Consolidated Balance Sheet, and were classified as redeemable non-controlling interests. See Note 18 to the Consolidated Financial Statements for further discussion.

The following table presents pro forma ratios as if the Recapitalization had been consummated in 2008 and a reconciliation of book value per share to book value per share, excluding Accumulated other comprehensive income (loss), which is a non-GAAP measure. See Item 7. MD&A—Use of Non-GAAP Measures for additional information. *

					Years Ended December 31,				
(In millions, except per share data)		2012		2011		2010		2009	2008
Total AIG shareholders' equity	$	98,002	$	101,538	$	78,856	$	60,585	$ 40,844
Recapitalization		—		—		(3,328)		—	—
Value on conversion of equity units		—		—		2,169		5,880	5,880
Pro forma shareholders' equity		98,002		101,538		77,697		66,465	46,724
Accumulated other comprehensive income (loss)		12,574		6,481		8,871		6,435	(6,759)
Total AIG shareholders' equity, excluding Accumulated other comprehensive income (loss)	$	85,428	$	95,057	$	69,985	$	54,150	$ 47,603
Total common shares outstanding		1,476,321,935		1,896,821,482		140,463,159		135,070,907	134,483,454
Issuable for equity units		—		—		2,854,069		7,736,904	7,736,904
Shares assumed converted		—		—		1,655,037,962		1,655,037,962	1,655,037,962
Pro forma common shares outstanding		1,476,321,935		1,896,821,482		1,798,355,190		1,797,845,773	1,797,258,320
Pro forma book value per share		N/A		N/A	$	43.20	$	36.97	$ 26.00
Pro forma book value per share, excluding accumulated other comprehensive income (loss)		N/A		N/A	$	38.27	$	33.39	$ 29.76

* Amounts for periods after December 31, 2008 have been revised to reflect reclassification of income taxes from AOCI to additional paid in capital to correct the presentation of components of AIG Shareholders' Equity. See Note 1 to the Consolidated Financial Statements for additional information on the reclass.

FORWARD-LOOKING INFORMATION

1.19 THE MOSAIC COMPANY (MAY)
MANAGEMENT'S DISCUSSION AND ANALYSIS OF FINANCIAL CONDITION AND RESULTS OF OPERATIONS (in part)

Forward-Looking Statements

Cautionary Statement Regarding Forward Looking Information

All statements, other than statements of historical fact, appearing in this report constitute "forward-looking statements" within the meaning of the Private Securities Litigation Reform Act of 1995. These statements include, among other things, statements about our expectations, beliefs, intentions or strategies for the future, including statements about the Cargill Transaction and its nature, impact and benefits, statements concerning our future operations, financial condition and prospects, statements regarding our expectations for capital expenditures, statements concerning our level of indebtedness and other information, and any statements of assumptions regarding any of the foregoing. In particular, forward-looking statements may include words such as "anticipate," "believe," "could," "estimate," "expect," "intend," "may," "potential," "predict," "project" or "should." These statements involve certain risks and uncertainties that may cause actual results to differ materially from expectations as of the date of this filing.

Factors that could cause reported results to differ materially from those expressed or implied by the forward-looking statements include, but are not limited to, the following:
- business and economic conditions and governmental policies affecting the agricultural industry where we or our customers operate, including price and demand volatility resulting from periodic imbalances of supply and demand;
- changes in farmers' application rates for crop nutrients;
- changes in the operation of world phosphate or potash markets, including continuing consolidation in the crop nutrient industry, particularly if we do not participate in the consolidation;
- pressure on prices realized by us for our products;
- the expansion or contraction of production capacity or selling efforts by competitors or new entrants in the industries in which we operate, including the effects of test runs by members of Canpotex to prove the production capacity of potash expansion projects;
- build-up of inventories in the distribution channels for our products that can adversely affect our sales volumes and selling prices;
- seasonality in our business that results in the need to carry significant amounts of inventory and seasonal peaks in working capital requirements, and may result in excess inventory or product shortages;
- changes in the costs, or constraints on supplies, of raw materials or energy used in manufacturing our products, or in the costs or availability of transportation for our products;

- rapid drops in the prices for our products and the raw materials we use to produce them that can require us to write down our inventories to the lower of cost or market;
- the effects on our customers of holding high cost inventories of crop nutrients in periods of rapidly declining market prices for crop nutrients;
- the lag in realizing the benefit of falling market prices for the raw materials we use to produce our products that can occur while we consume raw materials that we purchased or committed to purchase in the past at higher prices;
- customer expectations about future trends in the selling prices and availability of our products and in farmer economics;
- disruptions to existing transportation or terminaling facilities;
- shortages of railcars, barges and ships for carrying our products and raw materials;
- the effects of and change in trade, monetary, environmental, tax and fiscal policies, laws and regulations;
- foreign exchange rates and fluctuations in those rates;
- tax regulations, currency exchange controls and other restrictions that may affect our ability to optimize the use of our liquidity;
- other risks associated with our international operations, including any potential adverse effects on us of anti-mining protests in Peru;
- adverse weather conditions affecting our operations, including the impact of potential hurricanes or excess rainfall;
- difficulties or delays in receiving, challenges to, increased costs of obtaining or satisfying conditions of, or revocation or withdrawal of required governmental and regulatory approvals including permitting activities;
- changes in the environmental and other governmental regulation that applies to our operations, including the possibility of further federal or state legislation or regulatory action affecting greenhouse gas emissions or of restrictions, liabilities related to elevated levels of naturally-occurring radiation that arise from disturbing the ground in the course of mining activities or efforts to reduce the flow of nutrients into the Gulf of Mexico or the Mississippi River basin;
- the potential costs and effects of implementation of the U.S Environmental Protection Agency's numeric water quality standards for the discharge of nitrogen and/or phosphorus into Florida lakes and streams;
- the financial resources of our competitors, including state-owned and government-subsidized entities in other countries;
- the possibility of defaults by our customers on trade credit that we extend to them or on indebtedness that they incur to purchase our products and that we guarantee;
- any significant reduction in customers' liquidity or access to credit that they need to purchase our products;
- rates of return on, and the investment risks associated with, our cash balances;
- the effectiveness of our risk management strategy;
- the effectiveness of the processes we put in place to manage our significant strategic priorities, including the expansion of our Potash business;
- actual costs of various items differing from management's current estimates, including, among others, asset retirement, environmental remediation, reclamation or other environmental obligations, or Canadian resource taxes and royalties;
- the costs and effects of legal and administrative proceedings and regulatory matters affecting us including environmental and administrative proceedings, permitting matters and financial assurance requirements;
- the success of our efforts to attract and retain highly qualified and motivated employees;
- strikes, labor stoppages or slowdowns by our work force or increased costs resulting from unsuccessful labor contract negotiations;
- accidents involving our operations, including brine inflows at our Esterhazy, Saskatchewan potash mine as well as potential inflows at our other shaft mines, and potential fires, explosions, seismic events or releases of hazardous or volatile chemicals;
- terrorism or other malicious intentional acts;
- other disruptions of operations at any of our key production and distribution facilities, particularly when they are operating at high operating rates;
- changes in antitrust and competition laws or their enforcement;
- actions by the holders of controlling equity interests in businesses in which we hold a noncontrolling interest;
- the adequacy of our property, business interruption and casualty insurance policies to cover potential hazards and risks incident to our business, and our willingness and ability to maintain current levels of insurance coverage as a result of market conditions, our loss experience and other factors;
- restrictions on our ability to execute certain actions and potential liabilities imposed on us by the agreements relating to the Cargill Transaction; and
- other risk factors reported from time to time in our Securities and Exchange Commission reports.

Material uncertainties and other factors known to us are discussed in Item 1A, "Risk Factors," of our annual report on Form 10-K for the fiscal year ended May 31, 2012 and incorporated by reference herein as if fully stated herein.

We base our forward-looking statements on information currently available to us, and we undertake no obligation to update or revise any of these statements, whether as a result of changes in underlying factors, new information, future events or other developments.

1.20 ALLIANCE ONE INTERNATIONAL, INC. (MAR)

MANAGEMENT'S DISCUSSION AND ANALYSIS OF FINANCIAL CONDITION AND RESULTS OF OPERATIONS (in part)

Liquidity and Capital Resources

Overview

Historically we have needed capital in excess of cash flow from operations to finance accounts receivable, inventory and advances to suppliers for tobacco crops in certain foreign countries. Purchasing, processing and selling activities of our business are seasonal and our need for capital fluctuates with corresponding peaks where outstanding indebtedness may be significantly greater or less as a result. Our long-term borrowings consist of unsecured senior and convertible senior subordinated notes as well as a senior secured revolving credit facility. We also have short-term lines of credit available with a number of banks throughout the world to provide needed seasonal working capital to correspond with regional peaks of our business. Over the last twelve months, as a result of the shift in our sales patterns from shipping larger volumes in the first half of our fiscal year to the second half, we increased debt, net of cash, by $10.2 million from $1,073.1 million as of March 31, 2011 to $1,083.3 million as of March 31, 2012. Our debt is longer term in nature with a significant portion of the maturities extending out to 2016. On June 13, 2012, we entered into the Fifth Amendment to our $290.0 million revolving credit facility, which incorporates provisions that eliminate Restricted Payments, including distributions, Company Common Stock repurchases, and purchases of our public Senior Notes and Convertible Senior Subordinated Debt prior to the revolving credit facility's new extended maturity of April 15, 2014.

At March 31, 2012, we had $119.7 million in cash on our balance sheet, $462.7 million outstanding under short-term and long-term foreign lines with an additional $303.4 million available under those lines and $4.1 million outstanding of other debt for a total of $713.4 million of debt availability and cash on hand around the world, excluding $7.2 million in issued but unfunded letters of credit with $6.7 million available. Another source of liquidity as of March 31, 2012 was $155.6 million funded under our accounts receivable sale programs. Additionally, customer advances were $14.9 million in 2012 compared to $17.6 million in 2011. To the extent that these customers do not provide this advance funding, we must provide financing for their inventories. Should customers pre-finance less in the future for committed inventories, this action could negatively affect our short-term liquidity. We believe that the sources of capital we possess, or have access to, will be sufficient to fund our anticipated needs for fiscal year 2013. No cash dividends were paid to stockholders during the twelve months ended March 31, 2012. On July 28, 2010, our board of directors authorized the purchase up to $40.0 million of our common stock over the next two years and we purchased 2.4 million shares of our common stock at a weighted average price paid per share of $3.78 through March 31, 2012. Effective March 31, 2012, we did not satisfy the fixed charge coverage ratio of 2.0 to 1.0 required under the indenture governing our senior notes to permit us to access the restricted payments basket for the purchase of common stock and other actions under that basket. From time to time we may not satisfy the required ratio. Effective June 13, 2012, the Fifth Amendment to our revolving credit facility eliminates Restricted Payments, including Company Common Stock repurchases prior to its extended maturity of April 15, 2014. See Note 7 "Short-term Borrowing Arrangements" and Note 17 "Sale of Receivables" to the "Notes to Consolidated Financial Statements" for further information.

Seasonal liquidity beyond cash flow from operations is provided by our revolving credit facility, seasonal working capital lines throughout the world, advances from customers and sale of accounts receivable. For the years ended March 31, 2012 and 2011, our average short-term borrowings, aggregated peak short-term borrowings outstanding and weighted-average interest rate on short-term borrowings were as follows:

(Dollars in millions)	2012	2011
Average short-term borrowings	$448.9	$373.4
Aggregated peak short-term borrowings outstanding	$680.7	$619.3
Weighted-average interest rate on short-term borrowings	2.91%	3.47%

Aggregated peak borrowings for 2012 and 2011 were during the second quarter as we reach our seasonally adjusted high for our South American crop lines as we are shipping inventory and collecting receivables. Peak borrowings for 2012 and 2011 were repaid with cash provided by operating activities.

As of March 31, 2012, we are in our working capital build. In South America we are in the process of purchasing and processing the most recent crop, while the peak tobacco sales season for South America is at its beginning stages. Africa is also in the middle of its buying, processing and selling season and is utilizing working capital funding as well. North America and Europe are still selling and planning for the next crop that is now being grown.

Working Capital

Our working capital decreased from $846.9 million at March 31, 2011 to $828.6 million at March 31, 2012. Our current ratio was 2.3 to 1 at March 31, 2012 compared to 2.8 to 1 at March 31, 2011. The decrease in working capital is primarily related to the shift in our sales patterns and timing of shipments from larger volumes shipping in the first part of our fiscal year to the second half of the fiscal year. The volumes and timing of fourth quarter shipments resulted in increased notes payable to banks partially offset by increased accounts receivable and cash balances compared to the prior year.

The following table is a summary of items from the Consolidated Balance Sheet and Consolidated Statements of Cash Flows. Approximately $17.6 million of our outstanding cash balance at March 31, 2012 was held in foreign jurisdictions. As a result of our cash needs abroad, it is our intention to permanently reinvest these funds in foreign jurisdictions regardless of the fact that, due to the valuation allowance on foreign tax credit carryovers, the cost of repatriation would not have a material financial impact.

(In millions except for current ratio)	2012	Change $	Change %	2011	Change $	Change %	2010
		As of March 31,					
Cash and cash equivalents	$ 119.7	$ 76.2	175.2	$ 43.5	$ (86.2)	(66.5)	$ 129.7
Net trade receivables	303.1	23.2	8.3	279.9	72.5	35	207.4
Inventories and advances to tobacco suppliers	929.3	54.4	6.2	874.9	(20.0)	(2.2)	894.9
Total current assets	1,477.8	160.5	12.2	1,317.3	(65.6)	(4.7)	1,382.9
Notes payable to banks	374.5	143.1	61.8	231.4	42.4	22.4	189.0
Accounts payable	120.1	34.0	39.5	86.1	(60.3)	(41.2)	146.4
Advances from customers	14.9	(2.7)	(15.3)	17.6	(84.7)	(82.8)	102.3
Total current liabilities	649.2	178.8	38.0	470.4	(117.3)	(20)	587.7
Current ratio	2.3 to 1			2.8 to 1			2.4 to 1
Working capital	828.6	(18.3)	(2.2)	846.9	51.7	6.5	795.2
Total long term debt	821.5	(62.9)	(7.1)	884.4	95.5	12.1	788.9
Stockholders' equity attributable to Alliance One International, Inc.	327.5	14.7	4.7	312.8	(77.6)	(19.9)	390.4
Net cash provided (used) by:							
Operating activities	59.0	242.0		(183.0)	(294.3)		111.3
Investing activities	(65.1)	(49.2)		(15.9)	(6.6)		(9.3)
Financing activities	80.9	(32.1)		113.0	172.3		(59.3)

Operating Cash Flows

Net cash provided by operating activities increased $242.0 million in 2012 compared to 2011 which decreased $294.3 million compared to 2010. The increase in 2012 compared to 2011 is primarily due to less cash used for receivables and customer funding for the current crop compared to the prior year as well as increased payables and accrued expenses compared to the prior year. Partially offsetting these increases are higher levels of inventories and advances to tobacco suppliers. The decrease in 2011 compared to 2010 is primarily due to the negative impact of JTI's vertical integration initiatives on earnings, less customer funding for the current crop and the related increase in cash used for receivables. Partially offsetting these decreases are reduced levels of inventories and advances to tobacco suppliers compared to the prior year.

Investing Cash Flows

Net cash used by investing activities increased $49.2 million in 2012 compared to 2011 which increased $6.6 million compared to 2010. The increase in cash used in 2012 compared to 2011 is primarily a result of prior year events that didn't recur in the current year. In the prior year, proceeds from the sale of assets primarily related to the assets sold to PMI in Brazil are partially offset by decreased capital expenditures primarily due to the construction of our new processing facility in Brazil last year. Net cash used by investing activities also increased in 2012 compared to 2011 due to restricted cash deposits in accordance with long-term foreign seasonal lines of credit agreements entered into this year. The increase in cash used in 2011 compared to 2010 is a result of increased capital expenditures of $53.7 million primarily related to the construction of our new processing facility in Brazil. Partially offsetting the increase in cash used are increased proceeds from the sale of assets of $44.1 million primarily related to the assets sold to PMI in Brazil last year. Reductions in the purchase of foreign currency derivatives and less costs incurred for internally developed software were offset by less proceeds from notes receivable.

Financing Cash Flows

Net cash provided by financing activities was $80.9 million in 2012 compared to $113.0 million in 2011 and net cash used of $59.3 million in 2010. The decrease in cash provided in 2012 compared to 2011 is primarily related to the repayment of our revolver balance that was outstanding in the prior year partially offset by the net change in short-term borrowings as a result of the timing and volumes of our fourth quarter shipments. The increase in cash provided in 2011 compared to cash used in 2010 is primarily related to the impact of our debt refinancing on 2010 cash flows that did not recur in 2011. Partially offsetting these increases in cash provided are the purchase of $58.6 million of our 8.5% senior notes and 10% senior notes in 2011 as well as the purchase 2.4 million shares of our common stock last year.

The following table summarizes our debt financing as of March 31, 2012:

	Outstanding March 31, 2011	Outstanding March 31, 2012	Lines and Letters Available	Interest Rate	2013	2014	2015	2016	2017	Later
			March 31, 2012		**Long Term Debt Repayment Schedule**					
Senior secured credit facility:										
Revolver[1]	$ 148.0	$ —	$290.0	6.0%	$—	$ —	$ —	$ —	$ —	$—
Senior notes:										
10% senior notes due 2016[4]	611.8	615.2	—	10.0%	—	—	—	—	615.2	—
8 1/2% senior notes due 2012	6.0	6.0	—	8.5%	6.0	—	—	—	—	—
	617.8	621.2	—		6.0	—	—	—	615.2	—

(continued)

| | Outstanding | | Lines and | | Long Term Debt Repayment Schedule | | | | | |
	March 31, 2011	March 31, 2012	Letters Available	Interest Rate	2013	2014	2015	2016	2017	Later
5 1/2% convertible senior subordinated notes due 2014	115.0	115.0	—	5.5%	—	—	115.0	—	—	—
Long-term foreign seasonal borrowings	—	88.2	36.8	3.7%[2]	—	88.2	—	—	—	—
Other long-term debt	4.4	4.1	0.3	6.6%[2]	1.1	1.3	0.9	0.5	—	0.3
Notes payable to banks[3]	231.4	374.5	266.6	2.9%[2]	—	—	—	—	—	—
Total debt	$1,116.6	$1,203.0	593.7		$7.1	$89.5	$115.9	$ 0.5	$615.2	$0.3
Short-term	$ 231.4	$ 374.5								
Long-term:										
Long-term debt current	$ 0.8	$ 7.0								
Long-term debt	884.4	821.5								
	$ 885.2	$ 828.5								
Letters of credit	$ 4.9	$ 7.2	6.7							
Total credit available			$600.4							

(1) As of March 31, 2012, pursuant to Section 2.1 (A) (iv) of the Credit Agreement, the full Revolving Committed Amount was available based on the calculation of the lesser of the Revolving Committed Amount and the Working Capital Amount.

(2) Weighted average rate for the twelve months ended March 31, 2012.

(3) Primarily foreign seasonal lines of credit.

(4) Repayment of $615.2 is net of original issue discount of $19.8. Total repayment will be $635.0.

Senior Secured Credit Facility

On July 2, 2009, the Company replaced its previous credit agreement by entering into a Credit Agreement (the "Credit Agreement") with a syndicate of banks that provided for a senior secured credit facility (the "Credit Facility") of a three and one-quarter year $270.0 million revolver (the "Revolver") which initially accrued interest at a rate of LIBOR plus 2.50%. The interest rate for the Revolver may increase or decrease according to a consolidated interest coverage ratio pricing matrix as defined in the Credit Agreement, plus an applicable percentage. As of April 7, 2010, the Company increased the Revolver to $290.0 million.

First Amendment. On August 24, 2009, the Company closed the First Amendment to the Credit Agreement which included allowing the issuance of up to an additional $100.0 million of Senior Notes due 2016 within 90 days of the First Amendment Effective Date, amending the definition of Consolidated Total Senior Debt to exclude the Existing Senior Notes 2005, amending the definition of applicable percentage to clarify the effective date of the change in the applicable percentage and modifications to several schedules within the Credit Agreement.

Second Amendment. On June 9, 2010, the Company closed the Second Amendment to the Credit Agreement, which included adding back the Foreign Corrupt Practices Act estimate of $19.45 million to Consolidated Net Income for the period ended March 31, 2010 and increasing the Maximum Consolidated Leverage Ratio to 5.25 to 1.00 for the period ending September 30, 2010 and to 5.00 to 1.00 for the period ending March 31, 2011. The Second Amendment also allowed a subsidiary of the Company to incur indebtedness of up to $25.0 million after ceasing to be a wholly owned subsidiary, a guarantee by the Company of that indebtedness, the issuance of up to 30% equity interests in the subsidiary to officers, employees, directors, advisory boards and/or its third parties investors and allow certain restricted payments by the subsidiary.

Third Amendment. On June 6, 2011, the Company closed the Third Amendment to the Credit Agreement whereby the lenders agreed to extend the term of the facility to March 31, 2013. In addition, the Third Amendment modified certain financial covenants under the Credit Agreement, including establishing the financial maximum consolidated leverage ratio for each fiscal quarter through maturity, reducing the minimum consolidated interest coverage ratio for the quarter ended March 31, 2011 and the first three quarters of the fiscal year ending March 31, 2012, permitting the exclusion of the effect of specified levels of restructuring and impairment charges for the fiscal year ended March 31, 2011 and the fiscal year ending March 31, 2012 for the financial covenants impacted by the Company's EBIT, and excluding the effect of noncash deferred compensation expense up to $2.2 million for the quarter ended March 31, 2011 for these same covenants. The Third Amendment also increased the basket for capital expenditures for the year ending March 31, 2012 by $15.0 million and permitted the Company to form a subsidiary for a specified business purpose to be funded by up to $1.0 million in equity and $30.0 million in subordinated note investments by the Company, provided the subsidiary receives either revolving credit financing of up to $200.0 million from third parties or issues subordinated notes for an aggregate not to exceed $100.0 million. The Third Amendment increased the interest rates on base rate and LIBOR loans by 1.0 percentage point and the commitment fee on unborrowed amounts under the facility by 0.25 of a percentage point. In addition, pursuant to the Third Amendment, the Company agreed to grant the lenders a security interest on certain U.S. real estate.

Fourth Amendment. On November 3, 2011, the Company closed the Fourth Amendment to the Credit Agreement that expires March 31, 2013. The amendment permitted the exclusion of specified levels of restructuring and impairment charges from the financial covenants impacted by the Company's EBIT for fiscal quarters ending on or prior to March 31, 2012 and permitted the exclusion of specified levels of costs and expenses associated with the commercialization, sale or dissolution of the Company's Alert business from the financial covenants impacted by the Company's EBIT for fiscal quarters ending on or prior to December 31, 2011. The amendment also extended to April 30, 2012 the period in which the Company is permitted to form one or more subsidiaries for a specified business purpose to be funded by up to $1.0 million in equity and $30.0 million in subordinated note investments by the Company, provided the subsidiary or subsidiaries receive revolving credit financing of up to $200.0 million from third parties and issue subordinated notes for an aggregate of up to $100.0 million.

Fifth Amendment. Effective June 13, 2012, the Company closed the Fifth Amendment to the Credit Agreement. See Note 21 "Subsequent Event" to the "Notes to Consolidated Financial Statements" and Item 9B "Other Information" for further information.

Financial Covenants. Certain financial covenants and required financial ratios adjust over time in accordance with schedules in the Credit Agreement. After giving effect to the Third Amendment to the Credit Agreement, the requirements of those covenants and financial ratios at March 31, 2012 are as follows:

- a minimum consolidated interest coverage ratio of not less than 1.90 to 1.00 (1.65 for the quarters ending June and September 30, 2011 and 1.80 for the quarter ending December 31, 2011);
- a maximum consolidated leverage ratio in an amount not more than a ratio specified for each fiscal quarter as set forth in a schedule, which ratio is 5.50 for the quarter ended March 31, 2012 (6.70 for the quarter ending June 30, 2011, 7.50 for the quarter ending September 30, 2011 and 6.10 for the quarter ending December 31, 2011);
- a maximum consolidated total senior debt to working capital amount ratio of not more than 0.80 to 1.00; and
- maximum annual capital expenditures of $55.0 million during fiscal year ending March 31, 2012 and $40.0 million during any fiscal year thereafter, in each case with a one-year carry-forward for capital expenditures in any fiscal year below the maximum amount.

The Company continuously monitors its compliance with the covenants. At March 31, 2012 and during the fiscal year, the Company was in compliance with the covenants (as revised by the Third Amendment). For the third quarter ended December 31, 2011, had the Company not received a waiver which waived the testing of the maximum consolidated leverage covenant for the period October 1, 2011 through and including December 31, 2011, the Company would not have been in compliance for that period end. Significant changes in market conditions could adversely affect the Company's business. As a result, there can be no assurance that the Company will be able to maintain compliance with its financial covenants in the future. The Company records all fees and third-party costs associated with the Credit Agreement, including amendments thereto, in accordance with accounting guidance for changes in line of credit or revolving debt arrangements.

Senior Notes

On July 2, 2009, the Company issued $570.0 million of 10% Senior Notes due 2016 (the "Senior Notes") at a price of 95.177% of the face value. On August 26, 2009, the Company issued an additional $100.0 million tranche of 10% Senior Notes due 2016 at a price of 97.500% of the face value. These additional notes form part of the same series as the Senior Notes issued on July 2, 2009. The Senior Notes are required to be guaranteed by any "material domestic subsidiaries" of the Company as defined in the indenture governing the Senior Notes. The Company does not have a "material domestic subsidiary" at March 31, 2012.

During fiscal 2011, the Company purchased $35.0 million of these notes on the open market. All purchased securities were cancelled leaving $635.0 million of the 10% senior notes outstanding at March 31, 2011. Associated cash premiums and other costs paid were $1.6 million. Deferred financing costs and amortization of original issue discount of $2.0 million were accelerated.

Convertible Senior Subordinated Notes

On July 2, 2009, the Company issued $100.0 million of 5 $1/2$% Convertible Senior Subordinated Notes due 2014 (the "Convertible Notes"). The initial purchasers of the Convertible Notes were granted an option to purchase up to an additional $15.0 million of Convertible Notes solely to cover over-allotments which was exercised on July 15, 2009. Holders may surrender their Convertible Notes, in integral multiples of $1,000 principal amount, for conversion into shares of the Company's common stock at the then-applicable conversion rate until the close of business on the second scheduled trading day immediately preceding the maturity date. The initial conversion rate for the Convertible Notes is 198.8862 shares of common stock per $1,000 principal amount of Convertible Notes. The conversion rate is subject to adjustments based on certain events as described in the indenture governing the Convertible Notes. In addition, holders of these notes have certain rights and entitlements upon the occurrence of certain fundamental changes (as defined in the indenture governing the Convertible Notes).

Other Senior Notes and Senior Subordinated Notes

The Company applied a portion of the net proceeds from the issuance of the Senior Notes and Convertible Notes to fund the purchase of $120.4 million of its previously existing 8 $1/2$% Senior Notes due 2012 and the purchase, defeasance and redemption of all of its previously existing 11% Senior Notes due 2012, 12 $3/4$% Senior Subordinated Notes due 2012, 9 $5/8$% Senior Notes due 2011, 7 $3/4$% Senior Notes due 2013 and 8% Senior Notes due 2012, Series B pursuant to an early settlement of a cash tender offer.

As a result of the repurchase, defeasance and redemption of these existing notes, the Company accelerated approximately $5.6 million of deferred financing costs and $5.6 million of amortization of original issue discount during the year ended March 31, 2010.

During fiscal 2011, the Company purchased $23.6 million of the remaining 8 $3/4$% Senior Notes due 2012 on the open market. All purchased securities were cancelled leaving $6.0 million of the 8 $3/4$% senior notes outstanding at March 31, 2011. Associated cash premiums and other costs paid were $0.7 million. Deferred financing costs and amortization of original issue discount of $0.3 million were accelerated.

Convertible Note Hedge and Warrant Transactions

In connection with the offering of the Convertible Notes, the Company entered into privately negotiated convertible note hedge transactions with three counterparties ("hedge counterparties") to cover, subject to customary anti-dilution adjustments, the number of shares of the Company's common stock that initially underlie the Convertible Notes and expire on the last day that any Convertible Notes remain outstanding. The Company also entered separately into privately negotiated warrant transactions relating to the same number of shares of the Company's common stock with the hedge counterparties. The convertible note hedge transactions are expected to reduce the potential dilution with respect to the common stock of the Company upon conversion of the Convertible Notes in the event that the value per share of common stock, as measured under the convertible note hedge transactions, during the applicable valuation period, is greater than the strike price of the convertible note hedge transactions, which corresponds to the $5.0280 per share initial conversion price of the Convertible Notes and is similarly subject to customary anti-dilution adjustments. If, however, the price per share of the Company's common stock, as measured under the warrants, exceeds the strike price of the warrant transactions during the applicable valuation period, there would be dilution from the issuance of common stock pursuant to the warrants. The warrants have a strike price of $7.3325 per share, which is subject to customary anti-dilution adjustments and the maximum number of shares that could be issued under the warrant transactions is 45,743,836. The warrants expire in daily installments commencing on October 15, 2014 and ending on April 8, 2015. Both the convertible note hedge transactions and the warrant transactions require physical net-share settlement and are accounted for as equity instruments.

Foreign Seasonal Lines of Credit

The Company has typically financed its non-U.S. operations with uncommitted unsecured short-term seasonal lines of credit at the local level. These operating lines are seasonal in nature, normally extending for a term of 180 to 270 days corresponding to the tobacco crop cycle in that location. These facilities are typically uncommitted in that the lenders have the right to cease making loans and demand repayment of loans at any time. These loans are typically renewed at the outset of each tobacco season. As of March 31, 2012, the Company had approximately $374.5 million drawn and outstanding on foreign seasonal lines with maximum capacity totaling $655.2 million subject to limitations as provided for in the Credit Agreement. Additionally, against these lines there was $14 million available in unused letter of credit capacity with $7.2 million issued but unfunded.

Long-Term Foreign Seasonal Borrowings

As of March 31, 2012, the Company had foreign seasonal borrowings with maturity greater than one year. Approximately $88.2 million was drawn and outstanding with maximum capacity totaling $125.0 million. Certain of these foreign seasonal borrowings are secured by certain of the subsidiary borrowers' accounts receivable and inventories and restrict the payment of dividend by the subsidiary borrower during the term of the agreement. The Company records outstanding borrowings under its foreign seasonal revolver agreement as long-term as the Company intends to extend repayment terms to the maturity date in accordance with the agreement.

Dividends

The Fifth Amendment to the Credit Agreement eliminated the basket for restricted payments for the term of the Credit Agreement and accordingly, we may not pay any dividends under the Credit Agreement for its remaining term. In addition, the indenture governing our senior notes contains similar restrictions and also prohibits the payment of dividends and other distributions if we fail to satisfy a ratio of consolidated EBITDA to fixed charges of at least 2.0 to 1.0. At March 31, 2012, we did not satisfy this fixed charge coverage ratio. We may from time to time not satisfy this ratio.

Aggregate Contractual Obligations and Off-Balance Sheet Arrangements

We have summarized in the table below our contractual cash obligations and other commercial commitments as of March 31, 2012.

(In millions)	Total	2013	Years 2014–2015	Years 2016–2017	After 2017
			Payments/Expirations by Period		
Long-Term Debt Obligations*	$1,141.9	$ 84.0	$352.8	$704.8	$ 0.3
Capital Lease Obligations*	0.2	0.1	0.1	—	—
Other Long-Term Obligations**	58.0	10.5	10.4	9.8	27.3
Operating Lease Obligations	39.2	10.2	14.5	6.8	7.7
Capital Expenditure Commitments	2.9	2.9	—	—	—
Tobacco Purchase Obligations	742.3	742.3	—	—	—
Beneficial Interest in Receivables Sold	25.9	25.9	—	—	—
Amounts Guaranteed for Tobacco Suppliers	127.1	119.7	7.4	—	—
Total Contractual Obligations and Other Commercial Commitments	$2,137.5	$995.6	$385.2	$721.4	$35.3

* Long-Term Debt Obligations and Capital Lease Obligations include projected interest for both fixed and variable rate debt. We assume that there will be no drawings on the senior secured revolving credit facility in these calculations. The variable rate used in the projections is the rate that was being charged on our variable rate debt as of March 31, 2012. These calculations also assume that there is no refinancing of debt during any period. These calculations are on Long-Term Debt Obligations and Capital Lease Obligations only.

** Other long-term obligations consist of accrued pension and postretirement costs. Contributions for funded pension plans are based on the Pension Protection Act and tax deductibility and are not reasonably estimable beyond one year. Contributions for unfunded pension plans and postretirement plans captioned under "After 2017" include obligations during the next five years only. These obligations are not reasonably estimable beyond tens years. In addition, the following long-term liabilities included on the consolidated balance sheet are excluded from the table above: accrued postemployment costs, income taxes and tax contingencies, and other accruals. We are unable to estimate the timing of payments for these items.

We do not have any other off-balance sheet arrangements that are reasonably likely to have a current or future effect on our financial condition, results of operations, liquidity, capital expenditures or capital resources, as defined under the rules of SEC Release No. FRR-67, *Disclosure in Management's Discussion and Analysis about Off-Balance Sheet Arrangements and Aggregate Contractual Obligations*.

Lease Obligations

We have both capital and operating leases. In accordance with accounting principles generally accepted in the United States, operating leases are not reflected in the accompanying Consolidated Balance Sheet. The operating leases are for land, buildings, automobiles and other equipment; the capital leases are primarily for production machinery and equipment. The capitalized lease obligations are payable through 2015. Operating assets that are of long-term and continuing benefit are generally purchased.

Tobacco Purchase Obligations

Tobacco purchase obligations result from contracts with suppliers, primarily in the United States, Brazil and Turkey, to buy either specified quantities of tobacco or the supplier's total tobacco production. Amounts shown as tobacco purchase obligations are estimates based on projected purchase prices of the future crop tobacco. Payment of these obligations is net of our advances to these suppliers. Our tobacco purchase obligations do not exceed our projected requirements over the related terms and are in the normal course of business.

Beneficial Interest in Receivables Sold

We sell accounts receivable in a revolving trade accounts receivable securitization. Under the agreement, we receive 90% of the face value of the receivable sold, less contractual dilutions which limit the amount that may be outstanding from any one particular customer and insurance reserves that also have the effect of limiting the risk attributable to any one customer. Our 10% beneficial interest is subordinate to the purchaser of the receivables. See Note 17 "Sale of Receivables" to the "Notes to Consolidated Financial Statements" for further information.

Amounts Guaranteed for Tobacco Suppliers

In Brazil and Malawi, we provide guarantees to ensure financing is available to our tobacco suppliers. In the event these suppliers should default, we would be responsible for repayment of the funds provided to these suppliers. We also provide guarantees for financing by certain unconsolidated subsidiaries in Asia and Zimbabwe. See Note 1 "Significant Accounting Policies—Advances to Tobacco Suppliers" to the "Notes to Consolidated Financial Statements" for further information.

Planned Capital Expenditures

We have projected a total of $75.1 million in capital investments for our 2013 fiscal year of which $2.9 million is under contract at March 31, 2012. We forecast our capital expenditure needs for routine replacement of equipment as well as investment in assets that will add value to the customer or increase efficiency.

Tax and Repatriation Matters

We are subject to income tax laws in each of the countries in which we do business through wholly owned subsidiaries and through affiliates. We make a comprehensive review of the income tax requirements of each of our operations, file appropriate returns and make appropriate income tax planning analyses directed toward the minimization of our income tax obligations in these countries. Appropriate income tax provisions are determined on an individual subsidiary level and at the corporate level on both an interim and annual basis. These processes are followed using an appropriate combination of internal staff at both the subsidiary and corporate levels as well as independent outside advisors in review of the various tax laws and in compliance reporting for the various operations.

We consider unremitted earnings of certain subsidiaries operating outside the United States to be invested indefinitely. No U.S. income taxes or foreign withholding taxes are provided on such permanently reinvested earnings, in accordance with ASC 740. We regularly review the status of the accumulated earnings of each of our foreign subsidiaries and reassess this determination as part of our overall financing plans. Following this assessment, we provide deferred income taxes, net of any foreign tax credits, on any earnings that are determined to no longer be indefinitely invested. We did not record any deferred income taxes for 2012. See Note 12 "Income Taxes" to the "Notes to Consolidated Financial Statements" for further information.

NEW ACCOUNTING STANDARDS

1.21 DEERE & COMPANY (OCT)
NOTES TO CONSOLIDATED FINANCIAL STATEMENTS

3. New Accounting Standards

New Accounting Standards Adopted

In the first quarter of 2012, the company adopted the remaining provisions of Financial Accounting Standards Board (FASB) Accounting Standards Update (ASU) No. 2010-06, Improving Disclosures about Fair Value Measurements, which amends Accounting Standards Codification (ASC) 820, Fair Value Measurements and Disclosures. This ASU requires disclosures of transfers into and out of Levels 1 and 2, more detailed roll forward reconciliations of Level 3 recurring fair value measurements on a gross basis, fair value information by class of assets and liabilities, and descriptions of valuation techniques and inputs for Level 2 and 3 measurements. The effective date was the second quarter of fiscal year 2010 except for the roll forward reconciliations, which were required in the first quarter of fiscal year 2012. The adoption in 2010 and the adoption in the first quarter of 2012 did not have a material effect on the company's consolidated financial statements.

In the second quarter of 2012, the company adopted FASB ASU No. 2011-04, Amendments to Achieve Common Fair Value Measurement and Disclosure Requirements in U.S. GAAP and IFRSs, which amends ASC 820, Fair Value Measurement. This ASU requires the categorization by level for items that are required to be disclosed at fair value and information about transfers between Level 1 and Level 2 and additional disclosure for Level 3 measurements. In addition, the ASU provides guidance on measuring the fair value of financial instruments managed within a portfolio and the application of premiums and discounts on fair value measurements. The adoption did not have a material effect on the company's consolidated financial statements.

New Accounting Standards to be Adopted

In June 2011, the FASB issued ASU No. 2011-05, Presentation of Comprehensive Income, which amends ASC 220, Comprehensive Income. This ASU requires the presentation of total comprehensive income, total net income and the components of net income and comprehensive income either in a single continuous statement or in two separate but consecutive statements. The requirements do not change how earnings per share is calculated or presented. The effective date will be the first quarter of fiscal year 2013 and must be applied retrospectively. The adoption will not have a material effect on the company's consolidated financial statements.

In September 2011, the FASB issued ASU No. 2011-08, Testing Goodwill for Impairment, which amends ASC 350, Intangibles—Goodwill and Other. This ASU gives an entity the option to first assess qualitative factors to determine if goodwill is impaired. The entity may first determine based on qualitative factors if it is more likely than not that the fair value of a reporting unit is less than its carrying amount, including goodwill. If that assessment indicates no impairment, the first and second steps of the quantitative goodwill impairment test are not required. The effective date will be the first quarter of fiscal year 2013. The adoption will not have a material effect on the company's consolidated financial statements.

In December 2011, the FASB issued ASU No. 2011-11, Disclosures about Offsetting Assets and Liabilities, which amends ASC 210, Balance Sheet. This ASU requires entities to disclose gross and net information about both instruments and transactions eligible for offset in the statement of financial position and those subject to an agreement similar to a master netting arrangement. This would include derivatives and other financial securities arrangements. The effective date will be the first quarter of fiscal year 2014 and must be applied retrospectively. The adoption will not have a material effect on the company's consolidated financial statements.

In July 2012, the FASB issued ASU No. 2012-02, Testing Indefinite-Lived Intangible Assets for Impairment, which amends ASC 350, Intangibles—Goodwill and Other. This ASU gives an entity the option to first assess qualitative factors to determine if indefinite-lived intangible assets are impaired. The entity may first determine based on qualitative factors if it is more likely than not that the fair value of indefinite-lived intangible assets are less than their carrying amount. If that assessment indicates no impairment, the quantitative impairment test is not required. The effective date will be the first quarter of fiscal year 2013. The adoption will not have a material effect on the company's consolidated financial statements.

MARKET RISK INFORMATION

1.22 BERKSHIRE HATHAWAY INC. (DEC)
MANAGEMENT'S DISCUSSION AND ANALYSIS OF FINANCIAL CONDITION AND RESULTS OF OPERATIONS (in part)

Market Risk Disclosures

Our Consolidated Balance Sheets include a substantial amount of assets and liabilities whose fair values are subject to market risks. Our significant market risks are primarily associated with interest rates, equity prices, foreign currency exchange rates and commodity prices. The fair values of our investment portfolios and equity index put option contracts remain subject to considerable volatility. The following sections address the significant market risks associated with our business activities.

Interest Rate Risk

We regularly invest in bonds, loans or other interest rate sensitive instruments. Our strategy is to acquire such securities that are attractively priced in relation to the perceived credit risk. Management recognizes and accepts that losses may occur with respect to assets. We also strive to maintain high credit ratings so that the cost of our debt is minimized. We rarely utilize derivative products, such as interest rate swaps, to manage interest rate risks.

The fair values of our fixed maturity investments and notes payable and other borrowings will fluctuate in response to changes in market interest rates. In addition, changes in interest rate assumptions used in our equity index put option contract models cause changes in reported liabilities with respect to those contracts. Increases and decreases in prevailing interest rates generally translate into decreases and increases in fair values of those instruments. Additionally, fair values of interest rate sensitive instruments may be affected by the creditworthiness of the issuer, prepayment options, relative values of alternative investments, the liquidity of the instrument and other general market conditions. The fair values of fixed interest rate instruments may be more sensitive to interest rate changes than variable rate instruments.

The following table summarizes the estimated effects of hypothetical changes in interest rates on our assets and liabilities that are subject to interest rate risk. It is assumed that the interest rate changes occur immediately and uniformly to each category of instrument containing interest rate risk, and that there are no significant changes to other factors used to determine the value of the instrument. The hypothetical changes in interest rates do not reflect what could be deemed best or worst case scenarios. Variations in interest rates could produce significant changes in the timing of repayments due to prepayment options available. For these reasons, actual results might differ from those reflected in the table. Dollars are in millions.

| | | Estimated Fair Value after Hypothetical Change in Interest Rates (bp=basis points) | | | |
	Fair Value	100 bp Decrease	100 bp Increase	200 bp Increase	300 bp Increase
December 31, 2012					
Assets:					
Investments in fixed maturity securities	$32,291	$33,095	$31,456	$30,653	$29,937
Other investments[1]	14,740	15,241	14,206	13,683	13,189
Loans and finance receivables	11,991	12,410	11,598	11,229	10,883
Liabilities:					
Notes payable and other borrowings:					
Insurance and other	14,284	14,794	13,815	13,398	13,018
Railroad, utilities and energy	42,074	46,268	38,519	35,495	32,902
Finance and financial products	14,005	14,597	13,432	12,950	12,519
Equity index put option contracts	7,502	8,980	6,226	5,131	4,198
December 31, 2011					
Assets:					
Investments in fixed maturity securities	$32,188	$32,966	$31,371	$30,569	$29,859
Other investments[1]	13,927	14,501	13,382	12,863	12,374
Loans and finance receivables	13,126	13,584	12,696	12,292	11,913
Liabilities:					
Notes payable and other borrowings:					
Insurance and other	14,334	14,810	13,908	13,525	13,176
Railroad, utilities and energy	38,257	42,023	35,096	32,403	30,097
Finance and financial products	14,959	15,541	14,513	14,106	13,732
Equity index put option contracts	8,499	10,238	7,007	5,733	4,655

[1] Includes other investments that are subject to a significant level of interest rate risk.

Equity Price Risk

Historically, we have maintained large amounts of invested assets in exchange traded equity securities. Strategically, we strive to invest in businesses that possess excellent economics, with able and honest management and at sensible prices and prefer to invest a meaningful amount in each investee. Consequently, equity investments are concentrated in relatively few investees. At December 31, 2012, approximately 63% of the total fair value of equity investments was concentrated in five investees.

We often hold equity investments for long periods of time so we are not troubled by short-term price volatility with respect to our investments provided that the underlying business, economic and management characteristics of the investees remain favorable. We strive to maintain above average levels of shareholder capital to provide a margin of safety against short-term price volatility.

Market prices for equity securities are subject to fluctuation and consequently the amount realized in the subsequent sale of an investment may significantly differ from the reported market value. Fluctuation in the market price of a security may result from perceived changes in the underlying economic characteristics of the investee, the relative price of alternative investments and general market conditions.

We are also subject to equity price risk with respect to our equity index put option contracts. While our ultimate potential loss with respect to these contracts is determined from the movement of the underlying stock index between the contract inception date and expiration date, fair values of these contracts are also affected by changes in other factors such as interest rates, expected dividend rates and the remaining duration of the contract. These contracts expire between 2018 and 2026 and may not be unilaterally settled before their respective expiration dates.

The following table summarizes our equity and other investments and derivative contract liabilities with equity price risk as of December 31, 2012 and 2011. The effects of a hypothetical 30% increase and a 30% decrease in market prices as of those dates are also shown. The selected 30% hypothetical changes do not reflect what could be considered the best or worst case scenarios. Indeed, results could be far worse due both to the nature of equity markets and the aforementioned concentrations existing in our equity investment portfolio. Dollar amounts are in millions.

	Fair Value	Hypothetical Price Change	Estimated Fair Value after Hypothetical Change in Prices	Hypothetical Percentage Increase (Decrease) in Shareholders' Equity
December 31, 2012				
Assets:				
Equity securities	$87,662	30% increase	$113,961	9.1
		30% decrease	61,363	(9.1)
Other investments[1]	10,820	30% increase	15,171	1.5
		30% decrease	7,709	(1.1)
Liabilities:				
Equity index put option contracts	7,502	30% increase	5,009	0.9
		30% decrease	11,482	(1.4)
December 31, 2011				
Assets:				
Equity securities	$76,991	30% increase	$100,088	9.1
		30% decrease	53,894	(9.1)
Other investments[1]	7,432	30% increase	9,679	0.9
		30% decrease	5,708	(0.7)
Liabilities:				
Equity index put option contracts	8,499	30% increase	6,156	0.9
		30% decrease	11,949	(1.4)

[1] Includes other investments that possess significant equity price risk.

Foreign Currency Risk

We generally do not use derivative contracts to hedge foreign currency price changes primarily because of the natural hedging that occurs between assets and liabilities denominated in foreign currencies in our Consolidated Financial Statements. In addition, we hold investments in major multinational companies that have significant foreign business and foreign currency risk of their own, such as The Coca-Cola Company. Our net assets subject to translation are primarily in our insurance and utilities and energy businesses, and to a lesser extent in our manufacturing and services businesses. The translation impact is somewhat offset by transaction gains or losses on net reinsurance liabilities of certain U.S. subsidiaries that are denominated in foreign currencies as well as the equity index put option liabilities of U.S. subsidiaries relating to contracts that would be settled in foreign currencies.

Commodity Price Risk

Our diverse group of operating businesses use commodities in various ways in manufacturing and providing services. As such, we are subject to price risks related to various commodities. In most instances, we attempt to manage these risks through the pricing of our products and services to customers. To the extent that we are unable to sustain price increases in response to commodity price increases, our operating results will likely be adversely affected. We utilize derivative contracts to a limited degree in managing commodity price risks, most notably at MidAmerican. MidAmerican's exposures to commodities include variations in the price of fuel required to generate electricity, wholesale electricity that is purchased and sold and natural gas supply for customers. Commodity prices are subject to wide price swings as supply and demand are impacted by, among many other unpredictable items, weather, market liquidity, generating facility availability, customer usage, storage and transmission and transportation constraints. To mitigate a portion of the risk, MidAmerican uses derivative instruments, including forwards, futures, options, swaps and other agreements, to effectively secure future supply or sell future production generally at fixed prices. The settled cost of these contracts is generally recovered from customers in regulated rates. Financial results would be negatively impacted if the costs of wholesale electricity, fuel or natural gas are higher than what is permitted to be recovered in rates. MidAmerican also uses futures, options and swap agreements to economically hedge gas and electric commodity prices for physical delivery to non-regulated customers. The table that follows summarizes our commodity price risk on energy derivative contracts of MidAmerican as of December 31, 2012 and 2011 and shows the effects of a hypothetical 10% increase and a 10% decrease in forward market prices by the expected volumes for these contracts as of each date. The selected hypothetical change does not reflect what could be considered the best or worst case scenarios. Dollars are in millions.

	Fair Value Net Assets (Liabilities)	Hypothetical Price Change	Estimated Fair Value after Hypothetical Change in Price
December 31, 2012	$(235)	10% increase	$(187)
		10% decrease	(285)
December 31, 2011	$(445)	10% increase	$(348)
		10% decrease	(542)

CRITICAL ACCOUNTING POLICIES AND ESTIMATES

1.23 AGCO CORPORATION (DEC)

MANAGEMENT'S DISCUSSION AND ANALYSIS OF FINANCIAL CONDITION AND RESULTS OF OPERATIONS (in part)

Critical Accounting Estimates

We prepare our Consolidated Financial Statements in conformity with U.S. generally accepted accounting principles. In the preparation of these financial statements, we make judgments, estimates and assumptions that affect the reported amounts of assets and liabilities, the disclosure of contingent assets and liabilities at the date of the financial statements, and the reported amounts of revenues and expenses during the reporting period. The significant accounting policies followed in the preparation of the financial statements are detailed in Note 1 to our Consolidated Financial Statements. We believe that our application of the policies discussed below involves significant levels of judgment, estimates and complexity.

Due to the level of judgment, complexity and period of time over which many of these items are resolved, actual results could differ from those estimated at the time of preparation of the financial statements. Adjustments to these estimates would impact our financial position and future results of operations.

Allowance for Doubtful Accounts

We determine our allowance for doubtful accounts by actively monitoring the financial condition of our customers to determine the potential for any nonpayment of trade receivables. In determining our allowance for doubtful accounts, we also consider other economic factors, such as aging trends. We believe that our process of specific review of customers combined with overall analytical review provides an effective evaluation of ultimate collectability of trade receivables. Our loss or write-off experience was approximately 0.1% of net sales in 2012.

Discount and Sales Incentive Allowances

We provide various volume bonus and sales incentive programs with respect to our products. These sales incentive programs include reductions in invoice prices, reductions in retail financing rates, dealer commissions and dealer incentive allowances. In most cases, incentive programs are established and communicated to our dealers on a quarterly basis. The incentives are paid either at the time of invoice (through a reduction of invoice price), at the time of the settlement of the receivable, at the time of retail financing, at the time of warranty registration, or at a subsequent time based on dealer purchases. The incentive programs are product line specific and generally do not vary by dealer. The cost of sales incentives associated with dealer commissions and dealer incentive allowances is estimated based upon the terms of the programs and historical experience, is based on a percentage of the sales price, and is recorded at the later of (a) the date at which the related revenue is recognized, or (b) the date at which the sales incentive is offered. The related provisions and accruals are made on a product or product-line basis and are monitored for adequacy and revised at least quarterly in the event of subsequent modifications to the programs. Volume discounts are estimated and recognized based on historical experience, and related reserves are monitored and adjusted based on actual dealer purchases and the dealers' progress towards achieving specified cumulative target levels. We record the cost of interest subsidy payments, which is a reduction in the retail financing rates, at the later of (a) the date at which the related revenue is recognized, or (b) the date at which the sales incentive is offered. Estimates of these incentives are based on the terms of the programs and historical experience. All incentive programs are recorded and presented as a reduction of revenue due to the fact that we do not receive an identifiable benefit in exchange for the consideration provided. Reserves for incentive programs that will be paid either through the reduction of future invoices or through credit memos are recorded as "accounts receivable allowances" within our Consolidated Balance Sheets. Reserves for incentive programs that will be paid in cash, as is the case with most of our volume discount programs, as well as sales incentives associated with accounts receivable sold to our U.S. and Canadian retail finance joint ventures, are recorded within "Accrued expenses" within our Consolidated Balance Sheets.

At December 31, 2012, we had recorded an allowance for discounts and sales incentives of approximately $165.2 million, primarily related to allowances in our North America geographical segment that will be paid either through a reduction of future invoices, through credit memos to our dealers or through reductions in retail financing rates. If we were to allow an additional 1% of sales incentives and discounts at the time of retail sale, for those sales subject to such discount programs, our reserve would increase by approximately $7.0 million as of December 31, 2012. Conversely, if we were to decrease our sales incentives and discounts by 1% at the time of retail sale, our reserve would decrease by approximately $7.0 million as of December 31, 2012.

Inventory Reserves

Inventories are valued at the lower of cost or market using the first-in, first-out method. Market is current replacement cost (by purchase or by reproduction, dependent on the type of inventory). In cases where market exceeds net realizable value (i.e., estimated selling price less reasonably predictable costs of completion and disposal), inventories are stated at net realizable value. Market is not considered to be less than net realizable value reduced by an allowance for an approximately normal profit margin. Determination of cost includes estimates for surplus and obsolete inventory based on estimates of future sales and production. Changes in demand and product design can impact these estimates. We periodically evaluate and update our assumptions when assessing the adequacy of inventory adjustments.

Deferred Income Taxes and Uncertain Income Tax Positions

We recorded an income tax provision of $137.9 million in 2012 compared to $24.6 million in 2011. Our tax provision is impacted by the differing tax rates of the various tax jurisdictions in which we operate, permanent differences for items treated differently for financial accounting and income tax purposes, and losses in jurisdictions where no income tax benefit is recorded. Our 2012 income tax rate provision (as reconciled in Note 6 to our Consolidated Financial Statements) includes the usage of approximately $54.7 million of valuation allowance resulting from income generated in the United States during 2012. The 2012 income tax provision also includes a reversal of approximately $13.8 million of the remaining valuation allowance previously established against our U.S. deferred tax assets and the recognition of certain U.S. research and development tax credits of approximately $13.1 million. We assessed the likelihood that our remaining U.S. deferred tax assets would be recovered from estimable future taxable income and determined the reversal was appropriate during the fourth quarter of 2012 as a result of improved profitability during 2012 of our core equipment business, the inclusion of the GSI business that was acquired at the end of 2011, and recently completed forecasts projecting future profitability of the combined businesses.

A valuation allowance is established when it is more likely than not that some portion or all of a company's deferred tax assets will not be realized. We assessed the likelihood that our deferred tax assets would be recovered from estimated future taxable income and available income tax planning strategies. At December 31, 2012 and 2011, we had gross deferred tax assets of $478.0 million and $498.2 million, respectively, including $94.9 million and $181.6 million, respectively, related to net operating loss carryforwards. At December 31, 2012 we had total valuation allowances as an offset to the gross deferred tax assets of $74.5 million primarily related to net operating loss carryforwards in Brazil, Switzerland, China, and Russia. At December 31, 2011, we had total valuation allowances as an offset to the gross deferred tax assets of approximately $145.8 million primarily related to net operating loss carryforwards in Brazil, Switzerland, China, Russia and the United States. Realization of the remaining deferred tax assets as of December 31, 2012 will depend on generating sufficient taxable income in future periods, net of reversing deferred tax liabilities. We believe it is more likely than not that the remaining net deferred tax assets will be realized.

As of December 31, 2012 and 2011, we had approximately $94.5 million and $71.1 million, respectively, of unrecognized tax benefits, all of which would impact our effective tax rate if recognized. As of December 31, 2012 and 2011, we had approximately $23.5 million and $23.0 million, respectively, of current accrued taxes related to uncertain income tax positions connected with ongoing tax audits in various jurisdictions that we expect to settle or pay in the next 12 months. We recognize interest and penalties related to uncertain income tax positions in income tax expense. As of December 31, 2012 and 2011, we had accrued interest and penalties related to unrecognized tax benefits of approximately $11.9 million and $7.6 million, respectively. See Note 6 to our Consolidated Financial Statements for further discussion of our uncertain income tax positions.

Warranty and Additional Service Actions

We make provisions for estimated expenses related to product warranties at the time products are sold. We base these estimates on historical experience of the nature, frequency and average cost of warranty claims. In addition, we take into consideration the number and magnitude of additional service actions expected to be approved and policies related to additional service actions. Due to the uncertainty and potential volatility of these estimated factors, changes in our assumptions could materially affect net income.

Our estimate of warranty obligations is reevaluated on a quarterly basis. Experience has shown that initial data for any product series line can be volatile; therefore, our process relies upon long-term historical averages until sufficient data is available. As actual experience becomes available, it is used to modify the historical averages to ensure that the forecast is within the range of likely outcomes. Resulting balances are then compared with present spending rates to ensure that the accruals are adequate to meet expected future obligations.

See Note 1 to our Consolidated Financial Statements for more information regarding costs and assumptions for warranties.

Insurance Reserves

Under our insurance programs, coverage is obtained for significant liability limits as well as those risks required by law or contract. It is our policy to self-insure a portion of certain expected losses related primarily to workers' compensation and comprehensive general, product liability and vehicle liability. We provide insurance reserves for our estimates of losses due to claims for those items for which we are self-insured. We base these estimates on the expected ultimate settlement amount of claims, which often have long periods of resolution. We closely monitor the claims to maintain adequate reserves.

Pensions

We sponsor defined benefit pension plans covering certain employees principally in the United States, the United Kingdom, Germany, Finland, Norway, France, Switzerland, Australia and Argentina. Our primary plans cover certain employees in the United States and the United Kingdom.

In the United States, we sponsor a funded, qualified pension plan for our salaried employees, as well as a separate funded qualified pension plan for our hourly employees. Both plans are frozen, and we fund at least the minimum contributions required under the Employee Retirement Income Security Act of 1974 and the Internal Revenue Code to both plans. In addition, we sponsor an unfunded, nonqualified pension plan for our executives.

In the United Kingdom, we sponsor a funded pension plan that provides an annuity benefit based on participants' final average earnings and service. Participation in this plan is limited to certain older, longer service employees and existing retirees. No future employees will participate in this plan.

See Note 8 to our Consolidated Financial Statements for more information regarding costs and assumptions for employee retirement benefits.

Nature of Estimates Required. The measurement date for all of our benefit plans is December 31. The measurement of our pension obligations, costs and liabilities is dependent on a variety of assumptions provided by management and used by our actuaries. These assumptions include estimates of the present value of projected future pension payments to all plan participants, taking into consideration the likelihood of potential future events such as salary increases and demographic experience. These assumptions may have an effect on the amount and timing of future contributions.

Assumptions and Approach Used. The assumptions used in developing the required estimates include the following key factors:
- Discount rates
- Inflation
- Salary growth
- Expected return on plan assets
- Retirement rates
- Mortality rates

For the years ended December 31, 2012, 2011 and 2010, we used a globally consistent methodology to set the discount rate in the countries where our largest benefit obligations exist. In the United States, the United Kingdom and the Euro Zone, we constructed a hypothetical bond portfolio of high-quality corporate bonds and then applied the cash flows of our benefit plans to those bond yields to derive a discount rate. The bond portfolio and plan-specific cash flows vary by country, but the methodology in which the portfolio is constructed is consistent. In the United States, the bond portfolio is large enough to result in taking a "settlement approach" to derive the discount rate, where high-quality corporate bonds are assumed to be purchased and the resulting coupon payments and maturities are used to satisfy our largest U.S. pension plan's projected benefit payments. In the United Kingdom and the Euro Zone, the discount rate is derived using a "yield curve approach," where an individual spot rate, or zero coupon bond yield, for each future annual period is developed to discount each future benefit payment and, thereby, determine the present value of all future payments. Under the settlement and yield curve approaches, the discount rate is set to equal the single discount rate that produces the same present value of all future payments.

The other key assumptions were set as follows:
- Our inflation assumption is based on an evaluation of external market indicators.
- The salary growth assumptions reflect our long-term actual experience, the near-term outlook and assumed inflation.
- The expected return on plan asset assumptions reflects asset allocations, investment strategy, historical experience and the views of investment managers.
- Retirement and termination rates primarily are based on actual plan experience and actuarial standards of practice.
- The mortality rates for the U.S. and U.K. plans were updated in 2012 to reflect expected improvements in the life expectancy of the plan participants.

The effects of actual results differing from our assumptions are accumulated and amortized over future periods and, therefore, generally affect our recognized expense in such periods.

Our U.S. and U.K. pension plans comprised approximately 86% of our consolidated projected benefit obligation as of December 31, 2012. If the discount rate used to determine the 2012 projected benefit obligation for our U.S. pension plans was decreased by 25 basis points, our projected benefit obligation would have increased by $2.6 million at December 31, 2012, and our 2013 pension expense would increase by $0.1 million. If the discount rate used to determine the 2012 projected benefit obligation for our U.S. pension plans was increased by 25 basis points, our projected benefit obligation would have decreased by approximately $2.5 million at December 31, 2012, and our 2013 pension expense would decrease by approximately $0.1 million. If the discount rate used to determine the projected benefit obligation for our U.K. pension plan was decreased by 25 basis points, our projected benefit obligation would have increased by approximately $24.9 million at December 31, 2012, and our 2013 pension expense would increase by approximately $0.6 million. If the discount rate used to determine the projected benefit obligation for our U.K. pension plan was increased by 25 basis points, our projected benefit obligation would have decreased by approximately $23.7 million at December 31, 2012, and our 2013 pension expense would decrease by approximately $0.6 million.

Unrecognized actuarial losses related to our qualified pension plans were $321.5 million as of December 31, 2012 compared to $299.3 million as of December 31, 2011. The increase in unrecognized losses between years primarily resulted from a decrease in our discount rates. The unrecognized actuarial losses will be impacted in future periods by actual asset returns, discount rate changes, currency exchange rate fluctuations, actual demographic experience and certain other factors. For some of our qualified defined benefit pension plans, these losses will be amortized on a straight-line basis over the average remaining service period of active employees expected to receive benefits. For our U.S. salaried, U.S. hourly and U.K. pension plans, the population covered is predominantly inactive participants, and losses related to those plans will be amortized over the average remaining lives of those participants while covered by the respective plan. As of December 31, 2012, the average amortization period was 19 years for our U.S. qualified pension plans and 20 years for our non-U.S. pension plans. The estimated net actuarial loss for qualified defined benefit pension plans expected to be amortized from our accumulated other comprehensive loss during the year ended December 31, 2013 is approximately $11.3 million compared to approximately $9.5 million during the year ended December 31, 2012.

Investment Strategy and Concentration of Risk

The weighted average asset allocation of our U.S. pension benefit plans at December 31, 2012 and 2011 are as follows:

Asset Category	2012	2011
Large and small cap domestic equity securities	45%	37%
International equity securities	14%	13%
Domestic fixed income securities	21%	21%
Other investments	20%	29%
Total	100%	100%

The weighted average asset allocation of our non-U.S. pension benefit plans at December 31, 2012 and 2011 are as follows:

Asset Category	2012	2011
Equity securities	42%	40%
Fixed income securities	34%	36%
Other investments	24%	24%
Total	100%	100%

All tax-qualified pension fund investments in the United States are held in the AGCO Corporation Master Pension Trust. Our global pension fund strategy is to diversify investments across broad categories of equity and fixed income securities with appropriate use of alternative investment categories to minimize risk and volatility. The primary investment objective of our pension plans is to secure participant retirement benefits. As such, the key objective in the pension plans' financial management is to promote stability and, to the extent appropriate, growth in funded status.

The investment strategy for the plans' portfolio of assets balances the requirement to generate returns with the need to control risk. The asset mix is recognized as the primary mechanism to influence the reward and risk structure of the pension fund investments in an effort to accomplish the plans' funding objectives. The overall investment strategy for the U.S.-based pension plans is to achieve a mix of approximately 20% of assets for the near-term benefit payments and 80% for longer-term growth. The overall U.S. pension funds invest in a broad diversification of asset types. Our U.S. target allocation of retirement fund investments is 45% large- and small-cap domestic equity securities, 15% international equity securities, 20% broad fixed income securities and 20% in alternative investments. We have noted that over long investment horizons, this mix of investments would achieve an average return in excess of 7.1%. In arriving at the choice of an expected return assumption of 7.0% for our U.S.-based plans for the year ended December 31, 2013, we have tempered this historical indicator with lower expectations for returns and equity investment in the future as well as the administrative costs of the plans. The overall investment strategy for the non-U.S. based pension plans is to achieve a mix of approximately 35% of assets for the near-term benefit payments and 65% for longer-term growth. The overall non-U.S. pension funds invest in a broad diversification of asset types. Our non-U.S. target allocation of retirement fund investments is 40% equity securities, 30% broad fixed income investments and 30% in alternative investments. The majority of our non-U.S. pension fund investments are related to our pension plan in the United Kingdom. We have noted that over very long periods, this mix of investments would achieve an average return in excess of 7.4%. In arriving at the choice of an expected return assumption of 7.0% for our U.K.-based plans for the year ended December 31, 2013, we have tempered this historical indicator with lower expectations for returns and equity investment in the future as well as the administrative costs of the plans.

Equity securities primarily include investments in large-cap and small-cap companies located across the globe. Fixed income securities include corporate bonds of companies from diversified industries, mortgage-backed securities, agency mortgages, asset-backed securities and government securities. Alternative and other assets include investments in hedge fund of funds that follow diversified investment strategies. To date, we have not invested pension funds in our own stock, and we have no intention of doing so in the future.

Within each asset class, careful consideration is given to balancing the portfolio among industry sectors, geographies, interest rate sensitivity, dependence on economic growth, currency and other factors affecting investment returns. The assets are managed by professional investment firms. They are bound by precise mandates and are measured against specific benchmarks. Among asset managers, consideration is given, among others, to balancing security concentration, issuer concentration, investment style and reliance on particular active investment strategies.

As of December 31, 2012, our unfunded or underfunded obligations related to our qualified pension plans were approximately $265.6 million, primarily due to our pension plan in the United Kingdom. In 2012, we contributed approximately $36.1 million towards those obligations, and we expect to fund approximately $40.1 million in 2013. Future funding is dependent upon compliance with local laws and regulations and changes to those laws and regulations in the future, as well as the generation of operating cash flows in the future. We currently have an agreement in place with the trustees of the U.K. defined benefit plan that obligates us to fund approximately £15.4 million per year (or approximately $25.0 million) towards that obligation for the next 11 years. The funding arrangement is based upon the current underfunded status and could change in the future as discount rates, local laws and regulations, and other factors change.

Other Postretirement Benefits (Retiree Health Care and Life Insurance)

We provide certain postretirement health care and life insurance benefits for certain employees, principally in the United States and Brazil. Participation in these plans has been generally limited to older employees and existing retirees. See Note 8 to our Consolidated Financial Statements for more information regarding costs and assumptions for other postretirement benefits.

Nature of Estimates Required. The measurement of our obligations, costs and liabilities associated with other postretirement benefits, such as retiree health care and life insurance, requires that we make use of estimates of the present value of the projected future payments to all participants, taking into consideration the likelihood of potential future events such as health care cost increases and demographic experience, which may have an effect on the amount and timing of future payments.

Assumptions and Approach Used. The assumptions used in developing the required estimates include the following key factors:
- Health care cost trends
- Inflation
- Discount rates
- Medical coverage elections
- Retirement rates
- Mortality rates

Our health care cost trend assumptions are developed based on historical cost data, the near-term outlook, efficiencies and other cost-mitigating actions, including further employee cost sharing, administrative improvements and other efficiencies, and an assessment of likely long-term trends. For the years ended December 31, 2012, 2011 and 2010, as previously discussed, we used a globally consistent methodology to set the discount rate in the countries where our largest benefit obligations exist. In the United States, we constructed a hypothetical bond portfolio of high-quality corporate bonds and then applied the cash flows of our benefit plans to those bond yields to derive a discount rate. In the United States, the bond portfolio is large enough to result in taking a "settlement approach" to derive the discount rate, where high-quality corporate bonds are assumed to be purchased and the resulting coupon payments and maturities are used to satisfy our largest U.S. pension plan's projected benefit payments. After the bond portfolio is selected, a single discount rate is determined such that the market value of the bonds purchased equals the discounted value of the plan's benefit payments. For our Brazilian plan, we based the discount rate on government bond indices within that country. The indices used were chosen to match our expected plan obligations and related expected cash flows. Our inflation assumptions are based on an evaluation of external market indicators. Retirement and termination rates are based primarily on actual plan experience and actuarial standards of practice. The mortality rates for the U.S. plans were updated during 2012 to reflect expected improvements in the life expectancy of the plan participants. The effects of actual results differing from our assumptions are accumulated and amortized over future periods and, therefore, generally affect our recognized expense in such future periods.

Our U.S. postretirement health care and life insurance plans represent approximately 85% of our consolidated projected benefit obligation. If the discount rate used to determine the 2012 projected benefit obligation for our U.S. postretirement benefit plans was decreased by 25 basis points, our projected benefit obligation would have increased by approximately $0.8 million at December 31, 2012, and our 2013 postretirement benefit expense would increase by a nominal amount. If the discount rate used to determine the 2012 projected benefit obligation for our U.S. postretirement benefit plans was increased by 25 basis points, our projected benefit obligation would have decreased by approximately $0.8 million, and our 2013 pension expense would decrease by a nominal amount.

Unrecognized actuarial losses related to our U.S. and Brazilian postretirement benefit plans were $10.8 million as of December 31, 2012 compared to $9.4 million as of December 31, 2011, of which $10.0 million and $9.1 million, respectively, related to our U.S. postretirement benefit plans. The increase in losses primarily reflects the decrease in the discount rate during 2012. The unrecognized actuarial losses will be impacted in future periods by discount rate changes, actual demographic experience, actual health care inflation and certain other factors. These losses will be amortized on a straight-line basis over the average remaining service period of active employees expected to receive benefits, or the average remaining lives of inactive participants, covered under the postretirement benefit plans. As of December 31, 2012, the average amortization period was 14 years for our U.S. postretirement benefit plans. The estimated net actuarial loss for postretirement health care benefits expected to be amortized from our accumulated other comprehensive loss during the year ended December 31, 2013 is approximately $0.5 million, compared to approximately $0.4 million during the year ended December 31, 2012.

As of December 31, 2012, we had approximately $37.0 million in unfunded obligations related to our U.S. and Brazilian postretirement health and life insurance benefit plans. In 2012, we made benefit payments of approximately $1.8 million towards these obligations, and we expect to make benefit payments of approximately $1.8 million towards these obligations in 2013.

For measuring the expected U.S. postretirement benefit obligation at December 31, 2012 and 2011, we assumed an 8.0% health care cost trend rate for 2013 and 2012, respectively, decreasing to 5.0% by 2019 and 2018, respectively. For measuring the Brazilian postretirement benefit plan obligation at December 31, 2012, we assumed a 10.7% health care cost trend rate for 2013, decreasing to 6.2% by 2022. For measuring the Brazilian postretirement benefit plan obligation at December 31, 2011, we assumed a 10.0% health care cost trend rate for 2012, decreasing to 5.5% by 2021. Changing the assumed health care cost trend rates by one percentage point each year and holding all other assumptions constant would have the following effect to service and interest cost for 2013 and the accumulated postretirement benefit obligation at December 31, 2012 (in millions):

	One Percentage Point Increase	One Percentage Point Decrease
Effect on service and interest cost	$0.3	($0.2)
Effect on accumulated benefit obligation	$5.5	($4.4)

Litigation

We are party to various claims and lawsuits arising in the normal course of business. We closely monitor these claims and lawsuits and frequently consult with our legal counsel to determine whether they may, when resolved, have a material adverse effect on our financial position or results of operations and accrue and/or disclose loss contingencies as appropriate.

Goodwill, Other Intangible Assets and Long-Lived Assets

We test goodwill and other indefinite-lived intangible assets for impairment on an annual basis or on an interim basis if an event occurs or circumstances change that would reduce the fair value of a reporting unit below its carrying value. Our annual qualitative or quantitative assessments involve determining an estimate of the fair value of our reporting units in order to evaluate whether an impairment of the current carrying amount of goodwill and other indefinite-lived intangible assets exists. A qualitative assessment evaluates whether it is more likely than not that a reporting unit's fair value is less than its carrying amount before applying the two-step quantitative goodwill impairment test. The first step of a quantitative goodwill impairment test, used to identify potential impairment, compares the fair value of a reporting unit with its carrying amount, including goodwill. If the fair value of a reporting unit exceeds its carrying amount, goodwill of the reporting unit is not considered impaired, and, thus, the second step of the quantitative impairment test is unnecessary. If the carrying amount of a reporting unit exceeds its fair value, the second step of the quantitative goodwill impairment test is performed to measure the amount of impairment loss, if any. Fair values are derived based on an evaluation of past and expected future performance of our reporting units. A reporting unit is an operating segment or one level below an operating segment, for example, a component. A component of an operating segment is a reporting unit if the component constitutes a business for which discrete financial information is available and our executive management team regularly reviews the operating results of that component. In addition, we combine and aggregate two or more components of an operating segment as a single reporting unit if the components have similar economic characteristics. Our reportable segments are not our reporting units.

The second step of the quantitative goodwill impairment test, used to measure the amount of impairment loss, compares the implied fair value of the reporting unit goodwill with the carrying amount of that goodwill. If the carrying amount of the reporting unit goodwill exceeds the implied fair value of that goodwill, an impairment loss is recognized in an amount equal to that excess. The loss recognized cannot exceed the carrying amount of goodwill. The implied fair value of goodwill is determined in the same manner as the amount of goodwill recognized in a business combination; that is, we allocate the fair value of a reporting unit to all of the assets and liabilities of that unit (including any unrecognized intangible assets) as if the reporting unit had been acquired in a business combination and the fair value of the reporting unit was the price paid to acquire the reporting unit. The excess of the fair value of a reporting unit over the amounts assigned to its assets and liabilities is the implied fair value of goodwill.

We utilize a combination of valuation techniques, including a discounted cash flow approach and a market multiple approach, when making quantitative goodwill assessments. As stated above, goodwill is tested qualitatively or quantitatively for impairment on an annual basis and more often if indications of impairment exist.

We review our long-lived assets, which include intangible assets subject to amortization, for impairment whenever events or changes in circumstances indicate that the carrying amount of an asset may not be recoverable. An impairment loss is recognized when the undiscounted future cash flows estimated to be generated by the asset to be held and used are not sufficient to recover the unamortized balance of the asset. An impairment loss would be recognized based on the difference between the carrying values and estimated fair value. The estimated fair value is determined based on either the discounted future cash flows or other appropriate fair value methods with the amount of any such deficiency charged to income in the current year. If the asset being tested for recoverability was acquired in a business combination, intangible assets resulting from the acquisition that are related to the asset are included in the assessment. Estimates of future cash flows are based on many factors, including current operating results, expected market trends and competitive influences. We also evaluate the amortization periods assigned to its intangible assets to determine whether events or changes in circumstances warrant revised estimates of useful lives. Assets to be disposed of by sale are reported at the lower of the carrying amount or fair value, less estimated costs to sell.

We make various assumptions, including assumptions regarding future cash flows, market multiples, growth rates and discount rates, in our assessments of goodwill, other indefinite-lived intangible assets and long-lived assets for impairment. The assumptions about future cash flows and growth rates are based on the current and long-term business plans of the reporting unit or related to the long-lived assets. Discount rate assumptions are based on an assessment of the risk inherent in the future cash flows of the reporting unit or long-lived assets. These assumptions require significant judgments on our part, and the conclusions that we reach could vary significantly based upon these judgments.

During the fourth quarter of 2012, we recorded a non-cash impairment charge of approximately $22.4 million related to goodwill and certain other identifiable assets associated with our Chinese harvesting business in accordance with ASC 350. The operating results of our Chinese harvesting business from the date of acquisition in November 2011, combined with recently completed forecasts, resulted in our conclusion that it was more likely than not that the fair value of the Chinese harvesting reporting unit was less than its carrying amount. See Note 1 to our Consolidated Financial Statements for further discussion.

The results of our goodwill impairment analysis conducted as of October 1, 2012 indicated that no other reduction in the carrying amount of goodwill was required. The results of our goodwill impairment analyses conducted as of October 1, 2011 and 2010 indicated that no reduction in the carrying amount of goodwill was required.

As of December 31, 2012, we had approximately $1,192.4 million of goodwill. While our annual impairment testing in 2012 supported the carrying amount of this goodwill, we may be required to reevaluate the carrying amount in future periods, thus utilizing different assumptions that reflect the then current market conditions and expectations, and, therefore, we could conclude that an impairment has occurred.

SUMMARY OF SIGNIFICANT ACCOUNTING POLICIES

1.24 CISCO SYSTEMS, INC. (JUL)
NOTES TO CONSOLIDATED FINANCIAL STATEMENTS

2. Summary of Significant Accounting Policies

(a) Cash and Cash Equivalents—The Company considers all highly liquid investments purchased with an original or remaining maturity of less than three months at the date of purchase to be cash equivalents. Cash and cash equivalents are maintained with various financial institutions.

(b) Available-for-Sale Investments—The Company classifies its investments in both fixed income securities and publicly traded equity securities as available-for-sale investments. Fixed income securities primarily consist of U.S. government securities, U.S. government agency securities, non-U.S. government and agency securities, corporate debt securities, and asset-backed securities. These available-for-sale investments are primarily held in the custody of a major financial institution. A specific identification method is used to determine the cost basis of fixed income and public equity securities sold. These investments are recorded in the Consolidated Balance Sheets at fair value. Unrealized gains and losses on these investments, to the extent the investments are unhedged, are included as a separate component of accumulated other comprehensive income ("AOCI"), net of tax. The Company classifies its investments as current based on the nature of the investments and their availability for use in current operations.

(c) Other-than-Temporary Impairments on Investments—When the fair value of a debt security is less than its amortized cost, it is deemed impaired, and the Company will assess whether the impairment is other than temporary. An impairment is considered other than temporary if (i) the Company has the intent to sell the security, (ii) it is more likely than not that the Company will be required to sell the security before recovery of the entire amortized cost basis, or (iii) the Company does not expect to recover the entire amortized cost basis of the security. If impairment is considered other than temporary based on condition (i) or (ii) described earlier, the entire difference between the amortized cost and the fair value of the debt security is recognized in earnings. If an impairment is considered other than temporary based on condition (iii), the amount representing credit losses (defined as the difference between the present value of the cash flows expected to be collected and the amortized cost basis of the debt security) will be recognized in earnings, and the amount relating to all other factors will be recognized in other comprehensive income ("OCI").

The Company recognizes an impairment charge on publicly traded equity securities when a decline in the fair value of a security below the respective cost basis is judged to be other than temporary. The Company considers various factors in determining whether a decline in the fair value of these investments is other than temporary, including the length of time and extent to which the fair value of the security has been less than the Company's cost basis, the financial condition and near-term prospects of the issuer, and the Company's intent and ability to hold the investment for a period of time sufficient to allow for any anticipated recovery in market value.

Investments in privately held companies are included in other assets in the Consolidated Balance Sheets and are primarily accounted for using either the cost or equity method. The Company monitors these investments for impairments and makes appropriate reductions in carrying values if the Company determines that an impairment charge is required based primarily on the financial condition and near-term prospects of these companies.

(d) Inventories—Inventories are stated at the lower of cost or market. Cost is computed using standard cost, which approximates actual cost, on a first-in, first-out basis. The Company provides inventory write-downs based on excess and obsolete inventories determined primarily by future demand forecasts. The write-down is measured as the difference between the cost of the inventory and market based upon assumptions about future demand and charged to the provision for inventory, which is a component of cost of sales. At the point of the loss recognition, a new, lower cost basis for that inventory is established, and subsequent changes in facts and circumstances do not result in the restoration or increase in that newly established cost basis. In addition, the Company records a liability for firm, noncancelable, and unconditional purchase commitments with contract manufacturers and suppliers for quantities in excess of the Company's future demand forecasts consistent with its valuation of excess and obsolete inventory.

(e) Allowance for Doubtful Accounts—The allowance for doubtful accounts is based on the Company's assessment of the collectibility of customer accounts. The Company regularly reviews the allowance by considering factors such as historical experience, credit quality, age of the accounts receivable balances, economic conditions that may affect a customer's ability to pay, and expected default frequency rates. Trade receivables are written off at the point when they are considered uncollectible.

(f) Financing Receivables—The Company provides financing arrangements, including leases, financed service contracts, and loans, for certain qualified end-user customers to build, maintain, and upgrade their networks. Lease receivables primarily represent sales-type and direct-financing leases. Leases have on average a four-year term and are usually collateralized by a security interest in the underlying assets, while loan receivables generally have terms of up to three years. Financed service contracts typically have terms of one to three years and primarily relate to technical support services.

The Company determines the adequacy of its allowance for credit loss by assessing the risks and losses inherent in its financing receivables by portfolio segment. The portfolio segment is based on the types of financing offered by the Company to its customers: lease receivables, loan receivables, and financed service contracts and other. Effective in the second quarter of fiscal 2012, the Company combined its financing receivables into a single class as the two prior classes, Established Markets and Growth Markets, now exhibit similar risk characteristics as reflected by the Company's historical losses. See Note 7.

The Company assesses the allowance for credit loss related to financing receivables on either an individual or a collective basis. The Company considers various factors in evaluating lease and loan receivables and the earned portion of financed service contracts for possible impairment on an individual basis. These factors include the Company's historical experience, credit quality and age of the receivable balances, and economic conditions that may affect a customer's ability to pay. When the evaluation indicates that it is probable that all amounts due pursuant to the contractual terms of the financing agreement, including scheduled interest payments, are unable to be collected, the financing receivable is considered impaired. All such outstanding amounts, including any accrued interest, will be assessed and fully reserved at the customer level. Typically, the Company also considers receivables with a risk rating of 8 or higher to be impaired and will include them in the individual assessment for allowance. The Company evaluates the remainder of its financing receivables portfolio for impairment on a collective basis and records an allowance for credit loss at the portfolio segment level. Effective at the beginning of the second quarter of fiscal 2012, the Company refined its methodology for determining the portion of its allowance for credit loss that is evaluated on a collective basis. The refinement consists of more systematically giving effect to economic conditions, concentration of risk, and correlation. The Company also began to use expected default frequency rates published by a major third-party credit-rating agency as well as its own historical loss rate in the event of default. Previously the Company used only historical loss rates published by the same third-party credit-rating agency. These refinements are intended to better identify changes in macroeconomic conditions and credit risk. There was not a material change to the Company's total allowance for credit loss related to financing receivables as a result of these methodology refinements.

Expected default frequency rates are published quarterly by a major third-party credit-rating agency, and the internal credit risk rating is derived by taking into consideration various customer-specific factors and macroeconomic conditions. These factors, which include the strength of the customer's business and financial performance, the quality of the customer's banking relationships, the Company's specific historical experience with the customer, the performance and outlook of the customer's industry, the customer's legal and regulatory environment, the potential sovereign risk of the geographic locations in which the customer is operating, and independent third-party evaluations, are updated regularly or when facts and circumstances indicate that an update is deemed necessary. The Company's internal credit risk ratings are categorized as 1 through 10, with the lowest credit risk rating representing the highest quality financing receivables.

Financing receivables are written off at the point when they are considered uncollectible and all outstanding balances, including any previously earned but uncollected interest income, will be reversed and charged against earnings. The Company does not typically have any partially written-off financing receivables.

Outstanding financing receivables that are aged 31 days or more from the contractual payment date are considered past due. The Company does not accrue interest on financing receivables that are considered impaired or more than 90 days past due unless either the receivable has not been collected due to administrative reasons or the receivable is well secured. Financing receivables may be placed on nonaccrual status earlier if, in management's opinion, a timely collection of the full principal and interest becomes uncertain. After a financing receivable has been categorized as nonaccrual, interest will be recognized when cash is received. A financing receivable may be returned to accrual status after all of the customer's delinquent balances of principal and interest have been settled and the customer remains current for an appropriate period.

The Company facilitates third-party financing arrangements for channel partners, consisting of revolving short-term financing, generally with payment terms ranging from 60 to 90 days. In certain instances, these financing arrangements result in a transfer of the Company's receivables to the third party. The receivables are derecognized upon transfer, as these transfers qualify as true sales, and the Company receives a payment for the receivables from the third party based on the Company's standard payment terms. These financing arrangements facilitate the working capital requirements of the channel partners, and, in some cases, the Company guarantees a portion of these arrangements. The Company also provides financing guarantees for third-party financing arrangements extended to end-user customers related to leases and loans, which typically have terms of up to three years. The Company could be called upon to make payments under these guarantees in the event of nonpayment by the channel partners or end-user customers. Deferred revenue relating to these financing arrangements is recorded in accordance with revenue recognition policies or for the fair value of the financing guarantees.

(g) Depreciation and Amortization—Property and equipment are stated at cost, less accumulated depreciation or amortization, whenever applicable. Depreciation and amortization expenses for property and equipment were approximately $1.1 billion, $1.1 billion, and $1.0 billion for fiscal 2012, 2011 and 2010, respectively. Depreciation and amortization are computed using the straight-line method, generally over the following periods:

Asset Category	Period
Buildings	25 years
Building improvements	10 years
Furniture and fixtures	5 years
Leasehold improvements	Shorter of remaining lease term or 5 years
Computer equipment and related software	30 to 36 months
Production, engineering, and other equipment	Up to 5 years
Operating lease assets	Based on lease term generally up to 3 years

(h) Business Combinations—The Company allocates the fair value of the purchase consideration of its acquisitions to the tangible assets, liabilities, and intangible assets acquired, including in-process research and development ("IPR&D"), based on their estimated fair values. The excess of the fair value of purchase consideration over the fair values of these identifiable assets and liabilities is recorded as goodwill. IPR&D is initially capitalized at fair value as an intangible asset with an indefinite life and assessed for impairment thereafter. When a project underlying reported IPR&D is completed, the corresponding amount of IPR&D is reclassified as an amortizable purchased intangible asset and is amortized over the asset's estimated useful life. Acquisition-related expenses and restructuring costs are recognized separately from the business combination and are expensed as incurred.

(i) Goodwill and Purchased Intangible Assets—Goodwill is tested for impairment on an annual basis in the fourth fiscal quarter and, when specific circumstances dictate, between annual tests. When impaired, the carrying value of goodwill is written down to fair value. The goodwill impairment test involves a two-step process. The first step, identifying a potential impairment, compares the fair value of a reporting unit with its carrying amount, including goodwill. If the carrying value of the reporting unit exceeds its fair value, the second step would need to be conducted; otherwise, no further steps are necessary as no potential impairment exists. The second step, measuring the impairment loss, compares the implied fair value of the reporting unit goodwill with the carrying amount of that goodwill. Any excess of the reporting unit goodwill carrying value over the respective implied fair value is recognized as an impairment loss. Purchased intangible assets with finite lives are carried at cost, less accumulated amortization. Amortization is computed over the estimated useful lives of the respective assets, generally two to seven years. See "Long-Lived Assets," following, for the Company's policy regarding impairment testing of purchased intangible assets with finite lives. Purchased intangible assets with indefinite lives are assessed for potential impairment annually or when events or circumstances indicate that their carrying amounts might be impaired.

(j) Long-Lived Assets—Long-lived assets that are held and used by the Company are reviewed for impairment whenever events or changes in circumstances indicate that the carrying amount of such assets may not be recoverable. Determination of recoverability of long-lived assets is based on an estimate of the undiscounted future cash flows resulting from the use of the asset and its eventual disposition. Measurement of an impairment loss for long-lived assets that management expects to hold and use is based on the difference between the fair value of the asset and its carrying value. Long-lived assets to be disposed of are reported at the lower of carrying amount or fair value less costs to sell.

(k) Derivative Instruments—The Company recognizes derivative instruments as either assets or liabilities and measures those instruments at fair value. The accounting for changes in the fair value of a derivative depends on the intended use of the derivative and the resulting designation. For a derivative instrument designated as a fair value hedge, the gain or loss is recognized in earnings in the period of change together with the offsetting loss or gain on the hedged item attributed to the risk being hedged. For a derivative instrument designated as a cash flow hedge, the effective portion of the derivative's gain or loss is initially reported as a component of AOCI and subsequently reclassified into earnings when the hedged exposure affects earnings. The ineffective portion of the gain or loss is reported in earnings immediately. For a derivative instrument designated as a net investment hedge of the Company's foreign operations, the gain or loss is recorded in the cumulative translation adjustment within AOCI together with the offsetting loss or gain of the hedged exposure of the underlying foreign operations. Any ineffective portion of the net investment hedges is reported in earnings during the period of change. For derivative instruments that are not designated as accounting hedges, changes in fair value are recognized in earnings in the period of change. The Company records derivative instruments in the statements of cash flows to operating, investing, or financing activities consistent with the cash flows of the hedged item.

(l) Foreign Currency Translation—Assets and liabilities of non-U.S. subsidiaries that operate in a local currency environment, where that local currency is the functional currency, are translated to U.S. dollars at exchange rates in effect at the balance sheet date, with the resulting translation adjustments directly recorded to a separate component of AOCI. Income and expense accounts are translated at average exchange rates during the year. Remeasurement adjustments are recorded in other income, net. The effect of foreign currency exchange rates on cash and cash equivalents was not material for any of the fiscal years presented.

(m) Concentrations of Risk—Cash and cash equivalents are maintained with several financial institutions. Deposits held with banks may exceed the amount of insurance provided on such deposits. Generally, these deposits may be redeemed upon demand and are maintained with financial institutions with reputable credit and therefore bear minimal credit risk. The Company seeks to mitigate its credit risks by spreading such risks across multiple counterparties and monitoring the risk profiles of these counterparties.

The Company performs ongoing credit evaluations of its customers and, with the exception of certain financing transactions, does not require collateral from its customers. The Company receives certain of its components from sole suppliers. Additionally, the Company relies on a limited number of contract manufacturers and suppliers to provide manufacturing services for its products. The inability of a contract manufacturer or supplier to fulfill supply requirements of the Company could materially impact future operating results.

(n) Revenue Recognition—The Company recognizes revenue when persuasive evidence of an arrangement exists, delivery has occurred, the fee is fixed or determinable, and collectibility is reasonably assured. In instances where final acceptance of the product, system, or solution is specified by the customer, revenue is deferred until all acceptance criteria have been met. For hosting arrangements, the Company recognizes subscription revenue ratably over the subscription period, while usage revenue is recognized based on utilization. Technical support services revenue is deferred and recognized ratably over the period during which the services are to be performed, which is typically from one to three years. Advanced services transactional revenue is recognized upon delivery or completion of performance.

The Company uses distributors that stock inventory and typically sell to systems integrators, service providers, and other resellers. In addition, certain products are sold through retail partners. The Company refers to this as its two-tier system of sales to the end customer. Revenue from distributors and retail partners is recognized based on a sell-through method using information provided by them. Distributors and retail partners participate in various cooperative marketing and other programs, and the Company maintains estimated accruals and allowances for these programs. The Company accrues for warranty costs, sales returns, and other allowances based on its historical experience. Shipping and handling fees billed to customers are included in net sales, with the associated costs included in cost of sales.

Many of the Company's products have both software and nonsoftware components that function together to deliver the products' essential functionality. The Company's product offerings fall into the following categories:

Switching, Next-Generation Network ("NGN") Routing, Collaboration, Service Provider Video, Wireless, Security, Data Center, and Other Products. The Company also provides technical support and advanced services. The Company has a broad customer base that encompasses virtually all types of public and private entities, including enterprise businesses, service providers, commercial customers, and consumers. The Company and its salesforce are not organized by product divisions, and the Company's products and services can be sold standalone or together in various combinations across the Company's geographic segments or customer markets. For example, service provider arrangements are typically larger in scale with longer deployment schedules and involve the delivery of a variety of product technologies, including high-end routing, video and network management software, and other product technologies along with technical support and advanced services. The Company's enterprise and commercial arrangements are unique for each customer and smaller in scale and may include network infrastructure products such as routers and switches or collaboration technologies such as unified communications and Cisco TelePresence systems products along with technical support services.

The Company enters into revenue arrangements that may consist of multiple deliverables of its product and service offerings due to the needs of its customers. For example, a customer may purchase routing products along with a contract for technical support services. This arrangement would consist of multiple elements, with the products delivered in one reporting period and the technical support services delivered across multiple reporting periods. Another customer may purchase networking products along with advanced service offerings, in which all the elements are delivered within the same reporting period. In addition, distributors and retail partners purchase products or technical support services on a standalone basis for resale to an end user or for purposes of stocking certain products, and these transactions would not result in a multiple-element arrangement.

In many instances, products are sold separately in standalone arrangements as customers may support the products themselves or purchase support on a time-and-materials basis. Advanced services are sometimes sold in standalone engagements such as general consulting, network management, or security advisory projects, and technical support services are sold separately through renewals of annual contracts. The Company determines its Vendor-Specific Objective Evidence ("VSOE") based on its normal pricing and discounting practices for the specific product or service when sold separately. VSOE determination requires that a substantial majority of the historical standalone transactions have the selling prices for a product or service that fall within a reasonably narrow pricing range, generally evidenced by approximately 80% of such historical standalone transactions falling within plus or minus 15% of the median rates. In addition, the Company considers the geographies in which the products or services are sold, major product and service groups and customer classifications, and other environmental or marketing variables in determining VSOE.

When the Company is not able to establish VSOE for all deliverables in an arrangement with multiple elements, which may be due to the Company infrequently selling each element separately, not pricing products within a narrow range, or only having a limited sales history, such as in the case of certain newly introduced product categories, the Company attempts to determine the selling price of each element based on third-party evidence of selling price ("TPE"). TPE is determined based on competitor prices for similar deliverables when sold separately. Generally, the Company's go-to-market strategy differs from that of its peers, and its offerings contain a significant level of differentiation such that the comparable pricing of products with similar functionality cannot be obtained. Furthermore, the Company is unable to reliably determine what similar competitor products' selling prices are on a standalone basis. Therefore, the Company is typically not able to determine TPE.

When the Company is unable to establish fair value using VSOE or TPE, the Company uses estimated selling prices ("ESP") in its allocation of arrangement consideration. The objective of ESP is to determine the price at which the Company would transact a sale if the product or service were regularly sold on a standalone basis. ESP is generally used for new or highly proprietary offerings and solutions, or for offerings not priced within a reasonably narrow range. The Company determines ESP for a product or service by considering multiple factors, including, but not limited to, geographies, market conditions, competitive landscape, internal costs, gross margin objectives, and pricing practices. The determination of ESP is made through consultation with and formal approval by the Company's management, taking into consideration the go-to-market strategy.

The Company regularly reviews VSOE, TPE, and ESP and maintains internal controls over the establishment and updates of these estimates. There were no material impacts during the fiscal year, nor does the Company currently expect a material impact in the near term from changes in VSOE, TPE, or ESP.

The Company's arrangements with multiple deliverables may have a standalone software deliverable that is subject to the software revenue recognition guidance. In these cases, revenue for the software is generally recognized upon shipment or electronic delivery and granting of the license. The revenue for these multiple-element arrangements is allocated to the software deliverable and the nonsoftware deliverables based on the relative selling prices of all of the deliverables in the arrangement using the hierarchy in the applicable accounting guidance. In the limited circumstances where the Company cannot determine

VSOE or TPE of the selling price for all of the deliverables in the arrangement, including the software deliverable, ESP is used for the purposes of performing this allocation.

(o) Advertising Costs—The Company expenses all advertising costs as incurred. Advertising costs included within sales and marketing expenses were approximately $218 million, $325 million, and $290 million for fiscal 2012, 2011, and 2010, respectively.

(p) Share-Based Compensation Expense—The Company measures and recognizes the compensation expense for all share-based awards made to employees and directors, including employee stock options, stock grants, stock units, and employee stock purchases related to the Employee Stock Purchase Plan ("Employee Stock Purchase Rights") based on estimated fair values. The fair value of employee stock options is estimated on the date of grant using a lattice-binomial option-pricing model ("Lattice-Binomial Model"), and for employee stock purchase rights the Company estimates the fair value using the Black-Scholes model. The fair value for time-based stock awards and stock awards that are contingent upon the achievement of financial performance metrics is based on the grant date share price reduced by the present value of the expected dividend yield prior to vesting. The fair value of market-based stock awards is estimated using an option-pricing model on the date of grant. Because share-based compensation expense is based on awards ultimately expected to vest, it has been reduced for forfeitures.

(q) Software Development Costs—Software development costs required to be capitalized for software sold, leased, or otherwise marketed have not been material to date. Software development costs required to be capitalized for internal use software have also not been material to date.

(r) Income Taxes—Income tax expense is based on pretax financial accounting income. Deferred tax assets and liabilities are recognized for the expected tax consequences of temporary differences between the tax bases of assets and liabilities and their reported amounts. Valuation allowances are recorded to reduce deferred tax assets to the amount that will more likely than not be realized.

The Company accounts for uncertainty in income taxes using a two-step approach to recognizing and measuring uncertain tax positions. The first step is to evaluate the tax position for recognition by determining if the weight of available evidence indicates that it is more likely than not that the position will be sustained on audit, including resolution of related appeals or litigation processes, if any. The second step is to measure the tax benefit as the largest amount that is more than 50% likely of being realized upon settlement. The Company classifies the liability for unrecognized tax benefits as current to the extent that the Company anticipates payment (or receipt) of cash within one year. Interest and penalties related to uncertain tax positions are recognized in the provision for income taxes.

(s) Computation of Net Income per Share—Basic net income per share is computed using the weighted-average number of common shares outstanding during the period. Diluted net income per share is computed using the weighted-average number of common shares and dilutive potential common shares outstanding during the period. Diluted shares outstanding include the dilutive effect of in-the-money options, unvested restricted stock, and restricted stock units. The dilutive effect of such equity awards is calculated based on the average share price for each fiscal period using the treasury stock method. Under the treasury stock method, the amount the employee must pay for exercising stock options, the amount of compensation cost for future service that the Company has not yet recognized, and the amount of tax benefits that would be recorded in additional paid-in capital when the award becomes deductible are collectively assumed to be used to repurchase shares.

(t) Consolidation of Variable Interest Entities—The Company uses a qualitative approach in assessing the consolidation requirement for variable interest entities. The approach focuses on identifying which enterprise has the power to direct the activities that most significantly impact the variable interest entity's economic performance and which enterprise has the obligation to absorb losses or the right to receive benefits from the variable interest entity. In the event that the Company is the primary beneficiary of a variable interest entity, the assets, liabilities, and results of operations of the variable interest entity will be included in the Company's Consolidated Financial Statements.

(u) Use of Estimates—The preparation of financial statements and related disclosures in conformity with accounting principles generally accepted in the United States requires management to make estimates and judgments that affect the amounts reported in the Consolidated Financial Statements and accompanying notes. Estimates are used for the following, among others:
- Revenue recognition
- Allowances for accounts receivable, sales returns, and financing receivables
- Inventory valuation and liability for purchase commitments with contract manufacturers and suppliers
- Warranty costs
- Share-based compensation expense
- Fair value measurements and other-than-temporary impairments
- Goodwill and purchased intangible asset impairments
- Income taxes
- Loss contingencies

The actual results experienced by the Company may differ materially from management's estimates.

(v) New Accounting Update Recently Adopted—In May 2011, the Financial Accounting Standards Board ("FASB") issued an accounting standard update to provide guidance on achieving a consistent definition of and common requirements for measurement of and disclosure concerning fair value as between U.S. GAAP and International Financial Reporting Standards ("IFRS"). This accounting standard update became effective for the Company beginning in the third quarter of fiscal 2012. As a result of the application of this accounting standard update, the Company has provided additional disclosures in Note 9.

(w) Recent Accounting Standards or Updates Not Yet Effective—In June 2011, the FASB issued an accounting standard update to provide guidance on increasing the prominence of items reported in other comprehensive income. This accounting standard update eliminates the option to present components of other comprehensive income as part of the statement of equity and requires that the total of comprehensive income, the components of net income, and the components of other comprehensive income be presented either in a single continuous statement of comprehensive income or in two separate but consecutive statements. This accounting standard update is effective for the Company beginning in the first quarter of fiscal 2013, and it will result in changes in the Company's financial statement presentation.

In August 2011, the FASB approved a revised accounting standard update intended to simplify how an entity tests goodwill for impairment. The amendment will allow an entity to first assess qualitative factors to determine whether it is necessary to perform the two-step quantitative goodwill impairment test. An entity no longer will be required to calculate the fair value of a reporting unit unless the entity determines, based on a qualitative assessment, that it is more likely than not that its fair value is less than its carrying amount. This accounting standard update will be effective for the Company beginning in the first quarter of fiscal 2013, and the adoption is not expected to have any impact on the Company's Consolidated Financial Statements.

In December 2011, the FASB issued an accounting standard update requiring enhanced disclosures about certain financial instruments and derivative instruments that are offset in the statement of financial position or that are subject to enforceable master netting arrangements or similar agreements. This accounting standard update will be effective for the Company beginning in the first quarter of fiscal 2014, at which time the Company will include the required disclosures.

In July 2012, the FASB issued an accounting standard update intended to simplify how an entity tests indefinite-lived intangible assets other than goodwill for impairment by providing entities with an option to perform a qualitative assessment to determine whether further impairment testing is necessary. This accounting standard update will be effective for the Company beginning in the first quarter of fiscal 2014, and early adoption is permitted. The Company is currently evaluating the impact of this accounting standard update in its Consolidated Financial Statements.

NATURE OF OPERATIONS

1.25 PARKER-HANNIFIN CORPORATION (JUN)
NOTES TO CONSOLIDATED FINANCIAL STATEMENTS

(Dollars in thousands, except per share amounts)

1. Significant Accounting Policies (in part)

The significant accounting policies followed in the preparation of the accompanying consolidated financial statements are summarized below.

Nature of Operations—The Company is a leading worldwide diversified manufacturer of motion and control technologies and systems, providing precision engineered solutions for a wide variety of mobile, industrial and aerospace markets. The Company evaluates performance based on segment operating income before corporate and administrative expenses, interest expense and income taxes.

The Company operates in three business segments: Industrial, Aerospace and Climate & Industrial Controls. The Industrial Segment is an aggregation of several business units, which manufacture motion-control and fluid power system components for builders and users of various types of manufacturing, packaging, processing, transportation, agricultural, construction, and military vehicles and equipment. Industrial Segment products are marketed primarily through field sales employees and independent distributors. The Industrial North American operations have manufacturing plants and distribution networks throughout the United States, Canada and Mexico and primarily service North America. The Industrial International operations provide Parker products and services to 45 countries throughout Europe, Asia Pacific, Latin America, the Middle East and Africa.

The Aerospace Segment produces hydraulic, fuel, pneumatic and electro-mechanical systems and components, which are utilized on virtually every domestic commercial, military and general aviation aircraft and also performs a vital role in naval vessels and land-based weapons systems. This Segment serves original equipment and maintenance, repair and overhaul customers worldwide. Aerospace Segment products are marketed by field sales employees and are sold directly to manufacturers and end users.

The Climate & Industrial Controls Segment manufactures motion-control systems and components for use primarily in the refrigeration and air conditioning and transportation industries. The products in the Climate & Industrial Controls Segment are marketed primarily through field sales employees and independent distributors.

See the table of Business Segment Information "By Industry" and "By Geographic Area" on pages 13-13 and 13-14 for further disclosure of business segment information.

There are no individual customers to whom sales are more than three percent of the Company's consolidated sales. Due to the diverse group of customers throughout the world the Company does not consider itself exposed to any concentration of credit risks.

The Company manufactures and markets its products throughout the world. Although certain risks and uncertainties exist, the diversity and breadth of the Company's products and geographic operations mitigate the risk that adverse changes with respect to any particular product and geographic operation would materially affect the Company's operating results.

DESCRIPTION OF BUSINESS

1.26 THE COCA-COLA COMPANY (DEC)
NOTES TO CONSOLIDATED FINANCIAL STATEMENTS

Note 1: Business and Summary of Significant Accounting Policies (in part)

Description of Business

The Coca-Cola Company is the world's largest beverage company. We own or license and market more than 500 nonalcoholic beverage brands, primarily sparkling beverages but also a variety of still beverages such as waters, enhanced waters, juices and juice drinks, ready-to-drink teas and coffees, and energy and sports drinks. We own and market four of the world's top five nonalcoholic sparkling beverage brands: Coca-Cola, Diet Coke, Fanta and Sprite. Finished beverage products bearing our trademarks, sold in the United States since 1886, are now sold in more than 200 countries.

We make our branded beverage products available to consumers throughout the world through our network of Company-owned or -controlled bottling and distribution operations, bottling partners, distributors, wholesalers and retailers—the world's largest beverage distribution system. Of the approximately 57 billion beverage servings of all types consumed worldwide every day, beverages bearing trademarks owned by or licensed to us account for more than 1.8 billion servings.

On October 2, 2010, we acquired the former North America business of Coca-Cola Enterprises Inc. ("CCE"), one of our major bottlers, consisting of CCE's production, sales and distribution operations in the United States, Canada, the British Virgin Islands, the United States Virgin Islands and the Cayman Islands, and a substantial majority of CCE's corporate segment. Upon completion of the CCE transaction, we combined the management of the acquired North America business with the management of our existing foodservice business; Minute Maid and Odwalla juice businesses; North America supply chain operations; and Company-owned bottling operations in Philadelphia, Pennsylvania, into a unified bottling and customer service organization called Coca-Cola Refreshments ("CCR"). In addition, we reshaped our remaining Coca-Cola North America ("CCNA") operations into an organization that primarily provides franchise leadership and consumer marketing and innovation for the North American market.

Our Company markets, manufactures and sells:
- beverage concentrates, sometimes referred to as "beverage bases," and syrups, including fountain syrups (we refer to this part of our business as our "concentrate business" or "concentrate operations"); and
- finished sparkling and still beverages (we refer to this part of our business as our "finished product business" or "finished product operations").

Generally, finished product operations generate higher net operating revenues but lower gross profit margins than concentrate operations.

In our concentrate operations, we typically generate net operating revenues by selling concentrates and syrups to authorized bottling and canning operations (to which we typically refer as our "bottlers" or our "bottling partners"). Our bottling partners either combine the concentrates with sweeteners (depending on the product), still water and/or sparkling water, or combine the syrups with sparkling water to produce finished beverages. The finished beverages are packaged in authorized containers bearing our trademarks or trademarks licensed to us—such as cans and refillable and nonrefillable glass and plastic bottles—and are then sold to retailers directly or, in some cases, through wholesalers or other bottlers. Outside the United States, we also sell concentrates for fountain beverages to our bottling partners who are typically authorized to manufacture fountain syrups, which they sell to fountain retailers such as restaurants and convenience stores which use the fountain syrups to produce beverages for immediate consumption, or to fountain wholesalers who in turn sell and distribute the fountain syrups to fountain retailers.

Our finished product operations consist primarily of the production, sales and distribution operations managed by CCR and our Company-owned or -controlled bottling and distribution operations. CCR is included in our North America operating segment, and our Company-owned or -controlled bottling and distribution operations are included in our Bottling Investments operating segment. Our finished product operations generate net operating revenues by selling sparkling beverages and a variety of still beverages, such as juices and juice drinks, energy and sports drinks, ready-to-drink teas and coffees, and certain water products, to retailers or to distributors, wholesalers and bottling partners who distribute them to retailers. In addition, in the United States, we manufacture fountain syrups and sell them to fountain retailers, such as restaurants and convenience stores who use the fountain syrups to produce beverages for immediate consumption, or to authorized fountain wholesalers or bottling partners who resell the fountain syrups to fountain retailers. In the United States, we authorize wholesalers to resell our fountain syrups through nonexclusive appointments that neither restrict us in setting the prices at which we sell fountain syrups to the wholesalers nor restrict the territories in which the wholesalers may resell in the United States.

USE OF ESTIMATES

1.27 SPX CORPORATION (DEC)
NOTES TO CONSOLIDATED FINANCIAL STATEMENTS

(In millions, except per share data)

(2) Use of Estimates

The preparation of our consolidated financial statements in conformity with GAAP requires us to make estimates and assumptions. These estimates and assumptions affect the reported amounts of assets and liabilities, the disclosure of contingent assets and liabilities at the date of the consolidated financial statements, and the reported amounts of revenues (e.g., our percentage-of-completion estimates described above) and expenses during the reporting period. We evaluate these estimates and judgments on an ongoing basis and base our estimates on experience, current and expected future conditions, third-party evaluations and various other assumptions that we believe are reasonable under the circumstances. The results of these estimates form the basis for making judgments about the carrying values of assets and liabilities as well as identifying and assessing the accounting treatment with respect to commitments and contingencies. Actual results may differ from the estimates and assumptions used in the consolidated financial statements and related notes.

Listed below are certain significant estimates and assumptions used in the preparation of our consolidated financial statements. Certain other estimates and assumptions are further explained in the related notes.

Accounts Receivable Allowances—We provide allowances for estimated losses on uncollectible accounts based on our historical experience and the evaluation of the likelihood of success in collecting specific customer receivables. In addition, we maintain allowances for customer returns, discounts and invoice pricing discrepancies, with such allowances primarily based on historical experience. Summarized below is the activity for these allowance accounts.

	Year Ended December 31,		
	2012	2011	2010
Balance at beginning of year	$41.3	$44.3	$44.6
Acquisitions	2.8	1.2	1.1
Allowances provided	28.0	17.8	18.9
Write-offs, net of recoveries and credits issued	(21.5)	(22.0)	(20.3)
Balance at end of year	$50.6	$41.3	$44.3

Inventory—We estimate losses for excess and/or obsolete inventory and the net realizable value of inventory based on the aging of the inventory and the evaluation of the likelihood of recovering the inventory costs based on anticipated demand and selling price.

Impairment of Long-Lived and Intangible Assets Subject to Amortization—We continually review whether events and circumstances subsequent to the acquisition of any long-lived assets, or intangible assets subject to amortization, have occurred that indicate the remaining estimated useful lives of those assets may warrant revision or that the remaining balance of those assets may not be recoverable. If events and circumstances indicate that the long-lived assets should be reviewed for possible impairment, we use projections to assess whether future cash flows on an undiscounted basis related to the assets are likely to exceed the related carrying amount to determine if a write-down is appropriate. We will record an impairment charge to the extent that the carrying value of the assets exceed their fair values as determined by valuation techniques appropriate in the circumstances, which could include the use of similar projections on a discounted basis.

In determining the estimated useful lives of definite-lived intangibles, we consider the nature, competitive position, life cycle position, and historical and expected future operating cash flows of each acquired asset, as well as our commitment to support these assets through continued investment and legal infringement protection.

Goodwill and Indefinite-Lived Intangible Assets—We test goodwill and indefinite-lived intangible assets for impairment annually during the fourth quarter and continually assess whether a triggering event has occurred to determine whether the carrying value exceeds the implied value. The fair value of reporting units is based generally on discounted projected cash flows, but we also consider factors such as comparable industry price multiples. We employ cash flow projections that we believe to be reasonable under current and forecasted circumstances, the results of which form the basis for making judgments about the carrying values of the reported net assets of our reporting units. Many of our businesses closely follow changes in the industries and end markets that they serve. Accordingly, we consider estimates and judgments that affect the future cash flow projections, including principal methods of competition, such as volume, price, service, product performance and technical innovations, as well as estimates associated with cost improvement initiatives, capacity utilization and assumptions for inflation and foreign currency changes. Actual results may differ from these estimates under different assumptions or conditions. See Note 8 for further information, including discussion of impairment charges recorded in 2012, 2011 and 2010.

Accrued Expenses—We make estimates and judgments in establishing accruals as required under GAAP. Summarized in the table below are the components of accrued expenses at December 31, 2012 and 2011.

	December 31,	
	2012	2011
Employee benefits	$187.9	$181.3
Unearned revenue [1]	476.4	481.7
Warranty	50.5	46.2
Other [2]	281.8	268.1
Total	$996.6	$977.3

[1] Unearned revenue includes billings in excess of costs and estimated earnings on uncompleted contracts accounted for under the percentage-of-completion method of revenue recognition, customer deposits and unearned amounts on service contracts.

[2] Other consists of various items, including legal, interest, restructuring and dividends payable, none of which individually require separate disclosure.

Legal—It is our policy to accrue for estimated losses from legal actions or claims when events exist that make the realization of the losses probable and they can be reasonably estimated. We do not discount legal obligations or reduce them by anticipated insurance recoveries.

Environmental Remediation Costs—We expense costs incurred to investigate and remediate environmental issues unless they extend the economic useful life of related assets. We record liabilities and report expenses when it is probable that an obligation has been incurred and the amounts can be reasonably estimated. Our environmental accruals cover anticipated costs, including investigation, remediation and operation and maintenance of clean-up sites. Our estimates are based primarily on investigations and remediation plans established by independent consultants, regulatory agencies and potentially responsible third parties. We generally do not discount environmental obligations or reduce them by anticipated insurance recoveries.

Self-Insurance—We are self-insured for certain of our workers' compensation, automobile, product, general liability, disability and health costs, and we maintain adequate accruals to cover our retained liabilities. Our accruals for self-insurance liabilities are based on claims filed and an estimate of claims incurred but not yet reported, and generally are not discounted. We consider a number of factors, including third-party actuarial valuations, when making these determinations. We maintain third-party stop-loss insurance policies to cover certain liability costs in excess of predetermined retained amounts; however, this insurance may be insufficient or unavailable (e.g., because of insurer insolvency) to protect us against potential loss exposures. The key assumptions considered in estimating the ultimate cost to settle reported claims and the estimated costs associated with incurred but not yet reported claims include, among other things, our historical and industry claims experience, trends in health care and administrative costs, our current and future risk management programs, and historical lag studies with regard to the timing between when a claim is incurred and reported.

Warranty—In the normal course of business, we issue product warranties for specific products and provide for the estimated future warranty cost in the period in which the sale is recorded. We provide for the estimate of warranty cost based on contract terms and historical warranty loss experience that is periodically adjusted for recent actual experience. Because warranty estimates are forecasts that are based on the best available information, claims costs may differ from amounts provided. In addition, due to the seasonal fluctuations at certain of our businesses, the timing of warranty provisions and the usage of warranty accruals can vary period to period. We make adjustments to initial obligations for warranties as changes in the obligations become reasonably estimable. The following is an analysis of our product warranty accrual for the periods presented:

	Year Ended December 31,		
	2012	2011	2010
Balance at beginning of year	$56.3	$47.4	$49.0
Acquisitions	3.7	7.7	1.7
Provisions	25.3	21.5	20.3
Usage	(24.7)	(20.3)	(23.6)
Balance at end of year	60.6	56.3	47.4
Less: Current portion of warranty	50.5	46.2	38.9
Non-current portion of warranty	$10.1	$10.1	$ 8.5

Income Taxes—We perform reviews of our income tax positions on a continuous basis and accrue for potential uncertain tax positions in accordance with the Income Taxes Topic of the Codification. Accruals for these uncertain tax positions are classified as "Income taxes payable" and "Deferred and other income taxes" in the accompanying consolidated balance sheets based on an expectation as to the timing of when the matter will be resolved. As events change or resolution occurs, these accruals are adjusted, such as in the case of audit settlements with taxing authorities. These reviews also entail analyzing the realization of deferred tax assets. When we believe that it is more likely than not that we will not realize a benefit for a deferred tax asset, we establish a valuation allowance against it. For tax positions where it is more likely than not that a tax benefit will be sustained, we record the largest amount of tax benefit with a greater than 50% likelihood of being realized upon ultimate settlement with a taxing authority, assuming such authority has full knowledge of all relevant information.

Employee Benefit Plans—Defined benefit plans cover a portion of our salaried and hourly employees, including certain employees in foreign countries. We derive pension expense from an actuarial calculation based on the defined benefit plans' provisions and our assumptions regarding discount rate, rate of increase in compensation levels and expected long-term rate of return on plan assets. We determine the expected long-term rate of return on plan assets based upon historical actual asset returns and the expectations of asset returns over the expected period to fund participant benefits based on the current investment mix of our plans. When determining the market-related value of plan assets, changes in the market value of all plan assets are amortized over five years rather than recognizing the changes immediately. As a result, the value of plan assets that is used to calculate the expected return on plan assets differs from the current fair value of the plan assets. We determine the discount rate by matching the expected projected benefit obligation cash flows for each of the plans to a yield curve that is representative of long-term, high-quality (rated AA or higher) fixed income debt instruments as of the measurement date. The rate of increase in compensation levels is established based on our expectations of current and foreseeable future increases in compensation. We also consult with independent actuaries in determining these assumptions. See Note 10 to the consolidated financial statements for more information.

VULNERABILITY DUE TO CERTAIN CONCENTRATIONS

1.28 VISHAY INTERTECHNOLOGY, INC. (DEC)
NOTES TO THE CONSOLIDATED FINANCIAL STATEMENTS

(Dollars in thousands, except per share amounts)

Note 14—Current Vulnerability Due to Certain Concentrations

Market Concentrations

While no single customer comprises greater than 10% of net revenues, a material portion of the Company's revenues are derived from the worldwide industrial, telecommunications, and computing markets. These markets have historically experienced wide variations in demand for end products. If demand for these end products should decrease, the producers thereof could reduce their purchases of the Company's products, which could have a material adverse effect on the Company's results of operations and financial position.

Credit Risk Concentrations

Financial instruments with potential credit risk consist principally of cash and cash equivalents, short-term investments, accounts receivable, and notes receivable. Concentrations of credit risk with respect to receivables are generally limited due to the Company's large number of customers and their dispersion across many countries and industries. As of December 31, 2012, one customer comprised 14.7% of the Company's accounts receivable balance. This customer comprised 10.9% of the Company's accounts receivable balance as of December 31, 2011. No other customer comprised greater than 10% of the Company's accounts receivable balance as of December 31, 2012 or December 31, 2011. The Company continually monitors the credit risks associated with its accounts receivable and adjusts the allowance for uncollectible accounts accordingly. The credit risk exposure associated with the accounts receivable is limited by the allowance and is not considered material to the financial statements.

The Company maintains cash and cash equivalents and short-term investments with various major financial institutions. The Company is exposed to credit risk related to the potential inability to access liquidity in financial institutions where its cash and cash equivalents and short-term investments are concentrated. As of December 31, 2012, the following financial institutions held over 10% of the Company's combined cash and cash equivalents and short-term investments balance:

UniCredit*	20.8%
HSBC*	15.9%
Bank Leumi*	13.3%
Bank Hapoalim*	12.6%
KBC*	12.6%
* Participant in Credit Facility	

Sources of Supplies

Many of the Company's products require the use of raw materials that are produced in only a limited number of regions around the world or are available from only a limited number of suppliers. The Company's consolidated results of operations may be materially and adversely affected if there are significant price increases for these raw materials, the Company has difficulty obtaining these raw materials, or the quality of available raw materials deteriorates. For periods in which the prices of these raw materials are rising, the Company may be unable to pass on the increased cost to the Company's customers, which would result in decreased margins for the products in which they are used. For periods in which the prices are declining, the Company may be required to write down its inventory carrying cost of these raw materials which, depending on the extent of the difference between market price and its carrying cost, could have a material adverse effect on the Company's net earnings.

Vishay is a major consumer of the world's annual production of tantalum. Tantalum, a metal purchased in powder or wire form, is the principal material used in the manufacture of tantalum capacitors. There are few suppliers that process tantalum ore into capacitor grade tantalum powder.

From time to time, there have been short-term market shortages of raw materials utilized by the Company. While these shortages have not historically adversely affected the Company's ability to increase production of products containing these raw materials, they have historically resulted in higher raw material costs for the Company. The Company cannot assure that any of these market shortages in the future would not adversely affect the Company's ability to increase production, particularly during periods of growing demand for the Company's products.

Certain raw materials used in the manufacture of the Company's products, such as gold, copper, palladium, and other metals, are traded on active markets and can be subject to significant price volatility. To ensure adequate supply and to provide cost certainty, the Company's policy is to enter into short-term commitments to purchase defined portions of annual consumption of the raw materials utilized by the Company if market prices decline below budget. If after entering into these commitments, the market prices for these raw materials decline, the Company must recognize losses on these adverse purchase commitments.

Recently enacted rules in the U.S. on conflict minerals, which include tantalum, tungsten, tin, and gold, all of which are used in the Company's products, could result in increased prices and decreased supply of conflict minerals, which could negatively affect the Company's consolidated results of operations.

Geographic Concentration

The Company has operations outside the United States, and approximately 74% of revenues earned during 2012 were derived from sales to customers outside the United States. Additionally, as of December 31, 2012, $974,323 of the Company's cash and cash equivalents and short-term investments were held in countries outside of the United States. Some of the Company's products are produced and cash and cash equivalents and short-term investments are held in countries which are subject to risks of political, economic, and military instability. This instability could result in wars, riots, nationalization of industry, currency fluctuations, and labor unrest. These conditions could have an adverse impact on the Company's ability to operate in these regions and, depending on the extent and severity of these conditions, could materially and adversely affect the Company's overall financial condition, operating results, and ability to access its liquidity when needed. As of December 31, 2012 the Company's cash and cash equivalents and short-term investments were concentrated in the following countries:

Germany	37.9%
Israel	26.0%
Singapore	9.5%
People's Republic of China	7.8%
United States	1.8%
Other Asia	9.3%
Other Europe	7.1%
Other	0.6%

Vishay has been in operation in Israel for 42 years. The Company has never experienced any material interruption in its operations attributable to these factors, in spite of several Middle East crises, including wars.

1.29 TELEFLEX INCORPORATED (DEC)
NOTES TO CONSOLIDATED FINANCIAL STATEMENTS

Note 10—Financial Instruments (in part)

Concentration of Credit Risk

Concentrations of credit risk with respect to trade accounts receivable are generally limited due to the Company's large number of customers and their diversity across many geographic areas. A portion of the Company's trade accounts receivable outside the United States, however, include sales to government-owned or supported healthcare systems in several countries which are subject to payment delays. Payment is dependent upon the financial stability and creditworthiness of those countries' economies.

In the ordinary course of business, the Company grants non-interest bearing trade credit to its customers on normal credit terms. In an effort to reduce its credit risk, the Company (i) establishes credit limits for all of its customer relationships, (ii) performs ongoing credit evaluations of its customers' financial condition, (iii) monitors the payment history and aging of its customers' receivables, and (iv) monitors open orders against an individual customer's outstanding receivable balance.

An allowance for doubtful accounts is maintained for accounts receivable based on the Company's historical collection experience and expected collectability of the accounts receivable, considering the period an account is outstanding, the financial position of the customer and information provided by credit rating services. The adequacy of this allowance is reviewed each reporting period and adjusted as necessary.

In light of the disruptions in global economic markets, the Company instituted enhanced measures to facilitate customer-by-customer risk assessment when estimating the allowance for doubtful accounts. Such measures included, among others, monthly credit control committee meetings, at which customer credit risks are identified after review of, among other things, accounts that exceed specified credit limits, payment delinquencies and other customer problems. In addition, for some of the Company's non-government customers, the Company instituted measures designed to reduce its risk exposures, including issuing dunning letters, reducing credit limits, requiring that payments accompany orders and instituting legal action with respect to delinquent accounts. With respect to government customers, the Company evaluates receivables for potential collection risks associated with the availability of government funding and reimbursement practices.

Some of the Company's customers, particularly in Europe, have extended or delayed payments for products and services already provided. Collectability concerns regarding the Company's accounts receivable from these customers, for the most part in Greece, Italy, Spain and Portugal resulted in an increase in the allowance for doubtful accounts related to these countries. If the financial condition of these customers or the healthcare systems in these countries continue to deteriorate such that the ability of an increasing number of customers to make payments is uncertain, additional allowances may be required in future periods. The Company's aggregate accounts receivable, net of the allowance for doubtful accounts, in Spain, Italy, Greece and Portugal as a percent of the Company's total accounts receivable at the end of the period are as follows:

	December 31, 2012	December 31, 2011
	(Dollars in thousands)	
Accounts receivable (net of allowances of $6.3 million and $4.9 million in 2012 and 2011, respectively) in Spain, Italy, Greece and Portugal	$101,009	$108,545
Percentage of total accounts receivable, net	34%	38%

For the years ended December 31, 2012, December 31, 2011 and December 31, 2010, net revenues to customers in Spain, Italy, Greece and Portugal were $132.5 million, $138.4 million and $128.1 million, respectively. In the second quarter of 2012, the Company collected approximately $17.5 million from the Spanish government related to past due receivables. In the third quarter of 2012, the Company collected approximately $6.5 million from the Italian government related to past due receivables.

Segment Reporting

PRESENTATION

1.30 FASB ASC 280, *Segment Reporting*, requires that a public business enterprise report a measure of segment profit or loss, certain specific revenue and expense items, and segment assets. FASB ASC 280-10-05-1 requires that all public business enterprises report information about the revenues derived from the enterprise's products or services or groups of similar products and services; about the countries in which the enterprise earns revenues and holds assets; and about major customers, regardless of whether that information is used in making operating decisions. Even if a public company has only one operating segment, FASB ASC 280 requires that it report information about geographic areas and major customers. However, FASB ASC does not require an enterprise to report information that is impracticable to present because the necessary information is not available, and the cost to develop it would be excessive.

1.31 According to FASB ASC 280-10-50-1, an operating segment of a public entity has all of the following characteristics:
- It engages in business activities from which it may earn revenues and incur expenses, including revenues and expenses relating to transactions with other components of the same public entity.
- Its operating results are regularly reviewed by the public entity's chief operating decision maker to make decisions about resources to be allocated to the segment and assess its performance.
- Its discrete financial information is available.

1.32 FASB ASC 280 uses the management approach to identify operating segments and measure the financial information disclosed based on information reported internally to the Chief Operating Decision Maker (CODM) to make resource allocation and performance assessment decisions. However, according to FASB ASC 280-10-50-9, entities that have a matrix organization should identify operating segments based on products and services when more than one type of component is reviewed by the CODM.

1.33 FASB ASC 280-10-50-30 requires reconciliations of total segment revenues, total segment profit or loss, total segment assets, and other amounts disclosed for segments to corresponding amounts in the enterprise's general-purpose financial statements. FASB ASC 350-20-50-1 states that entities that report segment information should provide information about the changes in the carrying amount of goodwill during the period for each reportable segment.

SEGMENT INFORMATION

1.34 ALCOA INC. (DEC)
NOTES TO THE CONSOLIDATED FINANCIAL STATEMENTS

(Dollars in millions, except per-share amounts)

Q. Segment and Geographic Area Information

Alcoa is primarily a producer of aluminum products. Aluminum and alumina represent more than 80% of Alcoa's revenues. Nonaluminum products include precision castings and aerospace and industrial fasteners. Alcoa's segments are organized by product on a worldwide basis. Segment performance under Alcoa's management reporting system is evaluated based on a number of factors; however, the primary measure of performance is the after-tax operating income (ATOI) of each segment. Certain items such as the impact of LIFO inventory accounting; interest expense; noncontrolling interests; corporate expense (general administrative and selling expenses of operating the corporate headquarters and other global administrative facilities, along with depreciation and amortization on corporate-owned assets); restructuring and other charges; discontinued operations; and other items, including intersegment profit eliminations and other metal adjustments, differences between tax rates applicable to the segments and the consolidated effective tax rate, the results of the soft alloy extrusions business in Brazil, and other nonoperating items such as foreign currency transaction gains/losses and interest income are excluded from segment ATOI. Segment assets exclude, among others, cash and cash equivalents; deferred income taxes; goodwill not allocated to businesses for segment reporting purposes; corporate fixed assets; LIFO reserves; and other items, including the assets of the soft alloy extrusions business in Brazil and assets classified as held for sale related to discontinued operations.

The accounting policies of the segments are the same as those described in the Summary of Significant Accounting Policies (see Note A). Transactions among segments are established based on negotiation among the parties. Differences between segment totals and Alcoa's consolidated totals for line items not reconciled are in Corporate.

Alcoa's products are used worldwide in transportation (including aerospace, automotive, truck, trailer, rail, and shipping), packaging, building and construction, oil and gas, defense, and industrial applications. Total export sales from the U.S. included in continuing operations were $2,107 in 2012, $1,988 in 2011, and $1,543 in 2010.

Alcoa's operations consist of four worldwide reportable segments as follows:

Alumina. This segment represents a portion of Alcoa's upstream operations and consists of the Company's worldwide refinery system, including the mining of bauxite, which is then refined into alumina. Alumina is mainly sold directly to internal and external smelter customers worldwide or is sold to customers who process it into industrial chemical products. A portion of this segment's third-party sales are completed through the use of agents, alumina traders, and distributors. Slightly more than half of Alcoa's alumina production is sold under supply contracts to third parties worldwide, while the remainder is used internally by the Primary Metals segment.

Primary Metals. This segment represents a portion of Alcoa's upstream operations and consists of the Company's worldwide smelter system. Primary Metals receives alumina, mostly from the Alumina segment, and produces primary aluminum used by Alcoa's fabricating businesses, as well as sold to external customers, aluminum traders, and commodity markets. Results from the sale of aluminum powder, scrap, and excess power are also included in this segment, as well as the results of aluminum derivative contracts and buy/resell activity. Primary aluminum produced by Alcoa and used internally is transferred to other segments at prevailing market prices. The sale of primary aluminum represents more than 90% of this segment's third-party sales. Buy/resell activity refers to when this segment purchases metal from external or internal sources and resells such metal to external customers or the midstream and downstream segments in order to maximize smelting system efficiency and to meet customer requirements.

Global Rolled Products. This segment represents Alcoa's midstream operations, whose principal business is the production and sale of aluminum plate and sheet. A small portion of this segment's operations relate to foil produced at one plant in Brazil. This segment includes rigid container sheet (RCS), which is sold directly to customers in the packaging and consumer market and is used to produce aluminum beverage cans. Seasonal increases in RCS sales are generally experienced in the second and third quarters of the year. This segment also includes sheet and plate used in the aerospace, automotive, commercial transportation, and building and construction markets (mainly used in the production of machinery and equipment and consumer durables), which is sold directly to customers and through distributors. Approximately one-half of the third-party sales in this segment consist of RCS, while the other one-half of third-party sales are derived from sheet and plate and foil used in industrial markets. While the customer base for flat-rolled products is large, a significant amount of sales of RCS, sheet, and plate is to a relatively small number of customers.

Engineered Products and Solutions. This segment represents Alcoa's downstream operations and includes titanium, aluminum, and super alloy investment castings; forgings and fasteners; aluminum wheels; integrated aluminum structural systems; and architectural extrusions used in the aerospace, automotive, building and construction, commercial transportation, and power generation markets. These products are sold directly to customers and through distributors. Additionally, hard alloy extrusions products, which are also sold directly to customers and through distributors, serve the aerospace, automotive, commercial transportation, and industrial products markets.

The operating results and assets of Alcoa's reportable segments were as follows:

	Alumina	Primary Metals	Global Rolled Products	Engineered Products and Solutions	Total
2012					
Sales:					
Third-party sales	$ 3,092	$ 7,432	$ 7,378	$ 5,525	$ 23,427
Intersegment sales	2,310	2,877	163	—	5,350
Total sales	$ 5,402	$ 10,309	$ 7,541	$ 5,525	$ 28,777
Profit and loss:					
Equity income (loss)	$ 5	$ (27)	$ (6)	$ —	$ (28)
Depreciation, depletion, and amortization	455	532	229	158	1,374
Income taxes	(27)	106	167	297	543
ATOI	90	309	358	612	1,369
2011					
Sales:					
Third-party sales	$ 3,462	$ 8,240	$ 7,642	$ 5,345	$ 24,689
Intersegment sales	2,727	3,192	218	—	6,137
Total sales	$ 6,189	$ 11,432	$ 7,860	$ 5,345	$ 30,826
Profit and loss:					
Equity income (loss)	$ 25	$ (7)	$ (3)	$ 1	$ 16
Depreciation, depletion, and amortization	444	556	237	158	1,395
Income taxes	179	92	104	260	635
ATOI	607	481	266	539	1,893
2010					
Sales:					
Third-party sales	$ 2,815	$ 7,070	$ 6,277	$ 4,584	$ 20,746
Intersegment sales	2,212	2,597	180	—	4,989
Total sales	$ 5,027	$ 9,667	$ 6,457	$ 4,584	$ 25,735
Profit and loss:					
Equity income	$ 10	$ 1	$ —	$ 2	$ 13
Depreciation, depletion, and amortization	406	571	238	154	1,369
Income taxes	60	96	92	195	443
ATOI	301	488	220	415	1,424
2012					
Assets:					
Capital expenditures	$ 374	$ 318	$ 258	$ 200	$ 1,150
Equity investments	658	917	188	—	1,763
Goodwill	10	997	214	2,677	3,898
Total assets	9,709	11,709	4,603	5,891	31,912
2011					
Assets:					
Capital expenditures	$ 371	$ 463	$ 157	$ 173	$ 1,164
Equity investments	450	925	123	—	1,498
Goodwill	11	991	208	2,666	3,876
Total assets	9,782	11,867	4,559	5,831	32,039

The following tables reconcile certain segment information to consolidated totals:

	2012	2011	2010
Sales:			
Total segment sales	$28,777	$30,826	$25,735
Elimination of intersegment sales	(5,350)	(6,137)	(4,989)
Corporate*	273	262	267
Consolidated sales	$23,700	$24,951	$21,013

* For all periods presented, the Corporate amount includes third-party sales of three soft alloy extrusion facilities located in Brazil.

	2012	2011	2010
Net income attributable to Alcoa:			
Total segment ATOI	$1,369	$1,893	$1,424
Unallocated amounts (net of tax):			
Impact of LIFO	20	(38)	(16)
Interest expense	(319)	(340)	(321)
Noncontrolling interests	29	(194)	(138)
Corporate expense	(282)	(290)	(291)
Restructuring and other charges	(75)	(196)	(134)
Discontinued operations	—	(3)	(8)
Other	(551)	(221)	(262)
Consolidated net income attributable to Alcoa	$ 191	$ 611	$ 254

December 31,	2012	2011
Assets:		
Total segment assets	$31,912	$32,039
Elimination of intersegment receivables	(444)	(483)
Unallocated amounts:		
Cash and cash equivalents	1,861	1,939
Deferred income taxes	4,061	3,738
Corporate goodwill	1,272	1,281
Corporate fixed assets, net	961	935
LIFO reserve	(770)	(801)
Other	1,326	1,472
Consolidated assets	$40,179	$40,120

Sales by major product grouping were as follows:

Sales:	2012	2011	2010
Alumina	$ 2,962	$ 3,350	$ 2,740
Primary aluminum	7,121	7,907	6,842
Flat-rolled aluminum	7,378	7,642	6,277
Investment castings	1,747	1,700	1,521
Fastening systems	1,414	1,313	1,070
Architectural aluminum systems	970	973	884
Aluminum wheels	692	656	475
Other extruded aluminum and forged products	955	1,010	930
Other	461	400	274
	$23,700	$24,951	$21,013

Geographic information for sales was as follows (based upon the country where the point of sale occurred):

Sales:	2012	2011	2010
U.S.*	$12,361	$12,295	$10,560
Australia	3,222	3,587	2,842
Brazil	1,244	1,371	1,182
Spain	1,203	1,487	1,234
Netherlands**	949	1,025	940
Norway	820	927	809
France	807	825	662
Russia	713	761	584
Hungary	492	665	505
United Kingdom	438	412	331
Italy	379	537	418
China	326	283	188
Germany	216	229	231
Other	530	547	527
	$23,700	$24,951	$21,013

* Sales that occurred in the U.S. include a portion of alumina from Alcoa's refineries in Suriname, Brazil, Australia, and Jamaica and aluminum from the Company's smelters in Canada.
** Sales that occurred in the Netherlands include aluminum from Alcoa's smelter in Iceland.

Geographic information for long-lived assets was as follows (based upon the physical location of the assets):

December 31,	2012	2011
Long-lived assets:		
U.S.	$ 4,621	$ 4,439
Brazil	4,318	4,844
Australia	3,548	3,390
Iceland	1,571	1,615
Canada	1,399	1,447
Norway	898	894
Russia	494	531
Spain	445	451
Jamaica	414	417
China	395	424
Other	844	830
	$18,947	$19,282

1.35 CATERPILLAR INC. (DEC)
NOTES TO CONSOLIDATED FINANCIAL STATEMENTS

22. Segment Information

A. Basis for Segment Information

In the first quarter of 2011, we implemented revised internal financial measurements in line with changes to our organizational structure that were announced during 2010. Our previous structure used a matrix organization comprised of multiple profit and cost center divisions. There were twenty-five operating segments, twelve of which were reportable segments. These segments were led by vice-presidents that were managed by Caterpillar's Executive Office (comprised of our CEO and Group Presidents), which served as our Chief Operating Decision Maker. As part of the strategy revision, Group Presidents were given accountability for a related set of end-to-end businesses that they manage, a significant change for the company. The CEO allocates resources and manages performance at the Group President level. As such, the CEO now serves as our Chief Operating Decision Maker and operating segments are primarily based on the Group President reporting structure.

Three of our operating segments, Construction Industries, Resource Industries and Power Systems, are led by Group Presidents. One operating segment, Financial Products, is led by a Group President who has responsibility for Corporate Services. Corporate Services is a cost center primarily responsible for the performance of certain support functions globally and to provide centralized services; it does not meet the definition of an operating segment. One Group President leads the All Other operating segment.

In 2012, a portion of goodwill assets, related to recent acquisitions, that was allocated to Machinery and Power Systems operating segments is now a methodology difference between segment and external reporting. The segment information for 2011 has been retrospectively adjusted to conform to the 2012 presentation. The segment information for 2010 was not affected by this methodology change.

B. Description of Segments

We have five operating segments, of which four are reportable segments. Following is a brief description of our reportable segments and the business activities included in the All Other operating segment:

Construction Industries: A segment primarily responsible for supporting customers using machinery in infrastructure and building construction applications. Responsibilities include business strategy, product design, product management and development, manufacturing, marketing, and sales and product support. The product portfolio includes backhoe loaders, small wheel loaders, small track-type tractors, skid steer loaders, multi-terrain loaders, mini excavators, compact wheel loaders, select work tools, small, medium and large track excavators, wheel excavators, medium wheel loaders, medium track-type tractors, track-type loaders, motor graders, pipelayers and related parts. In addition, Construction Industries has responsibility for Power Systems and components in Japan and an integrated manufacturing cost center that supports Machinery and Power Systems businesses. Inter-segment sales are a source of revenue for this segment.

Resource Industries: A segment primarily responsible for supporting customers using machinery in mining and quarrying applications. Responsibilities include business strategy, product design, product management and development, manufacturing, marketing and sales and product support. The product portfolio includes large track-type tractors, large mining trucks, underground mining equipment, tunnel boring equipment, large wheel loaders, off-highway trucks, articulated trucks, wheel tractor scrapers, wheel dozers, compactors, select work tools, forestry products, paving products, machinery components and electronics and control systems. In addition, Resource Industries manages areas that provide services to other parts of the company, including integrated manufacturing, research and development and coordination of the Caterpillar Production System. During the third quarter of 2011, the acquisition of Bucyrus was completed. This added the responsibility for business strategy, product design, product management and development, manufacturing, marketing and sales and product support for electric rope shovels, draglines, hydraulic shovels, drills, highwall miners and electric drive off-highway trucks to Resource Industries. In addition, segment profit includes Bucyrus acquisition-related costs and the impact from divestiture of a portion of the Bucyrus distribution business. During the second quarter of 2012, the acquisition of Siwei was completed. Siwei primarily designs, manufactures, sells and supports underground coal mining equipment in China. See Note 23 for information on these acquisitions. Inter-segment sales are a source of revenue for this segment.

Power Systems: A segment primarily responsible for supporting customers using reciprocating engines, turbines and related parts across industries serving electric power, industrial, petroleum and marine applications as well as rail-related businesses. Responsibilities include business strategy, product design, product management, development, manufacturing, marketing, sales and product support of reciprocating engine powered generator sets, integrated systems used in the electric power generation industry, reciprocating engines and integrated systems and solutions for the marine and petroleum industries; reciprocating engines supplied to the industrial industry as well as Caterpillar machinery; the business strategy, product design, product management, development, manufacturing, marketing, sales and product support of turbines and turbine-related services; the development, manufacturing, remanufacturing, maintenance, leasing and service of diesel-electric locomotives and components and other rail-related products and services. Inter-segment sales are a source of revenue for this segment.

Financial Products Segment: Provides financing to customers and dealers for the purchase and lease of Caterpillar and other equipment, as well as some financing for Caterpillar sales to dealers. Financing plans include operating and finance leases, installment sale contracts, working capital loans and wholesale financing plans. The segment also provides various forms of insurance to customers and dealers to help support the purchase and lease of our equipment.

All Other: Primarily includes activities such as: the remanufacturing of Cat engines and components and remanufacturing services for other companies as well as the business strategy, product management, development, manufacturing, marketing and product support of undercarriage, specialty products, hardened bar stock components and ground engaging tools primarily for Caterpillar products; logistics services; the product management, development, marketing, sales and product support of on-highway vocational trucks for North America (U.S. and Canada only); distribution services responsible for dealer development and administration, dealer portfolio management and ensuring the most efficient and effective distribution of machines, engines and parts; and the 50/50 joint venture with Navistar (NC 2) until it became a wholly owned subsidiary of Navistar effective September 29, 2011. On July 31, 2012, we sold a majority interest in Caterpillar's third party logistics business. Inter-segment sales are a source of revenue for this segment. Results for the All Other operating segment are included as a reconciling item between reportable segments and consolidated external reporting.

C. Segment Measurement and Reconciliations

There are several methodology differences between our segment reporting and our external reporting. The following is a list of the more significant methodology differences:

- Machinery and Power Systems segment net assets generally include inventories, receivables, property, plant and equipment, goodwill, intangibles and accounts payable. Liabilities other than accounts payable are generally managed at the corporate level and are not included in segment operations. Financial Products Segment assets generally include all categories of assets.
- Segment inventories and cost of sales are valued using a current cost methodology.
- Goodwill allocated to segments is amortized using a fixed amount based on a 20 year useful life. This methodology difference only impacts segment assets; no goodwill amortization expense is included in segment profit.
- The present value of future lease payments for certain Machinery and Power Systems operating leases is included in segment assets. The estimated financing component of the lease payments is excluded.
- Currency exposures for Machinery and Power Systems are generally managed at the corporate level and the effects of changes in exchange rates on results of operations within the year are not included in segment profit. The net difference created in the translation of revenues and costs between exchange rates used for U.S. GAAP reporting and exchange rates used for segment reporting are recorded as a methodology difference.
- Postretirement benefit expenses are split; segments are generally responsible for service and prior service costs, with the remaining elements of net periodic benefit cost included as a methodology difference.
- Machinery and Power Systems segment profit is determined on a pretax basis and excludes interest expense, gains and losses on interest rate swaps and other income/expense items. Financial Products Segment profit is determined on a pretax basis and includes other income/expense items.

Reconciling items are created based on accounting differences between segment reporting and our consolidated external reporting. Please refer to pages A-82 to A-86 for financial information regarding significant reconciling items. Most of our reconciling items are self-explanatory given the above explanations. For the reconciliation of profit, we have grouped the reconciling items as follows:

- *Corporate costs*: These costs are related to corporate requirements and strategies that are considered to be for the benefit of the entire organization.
- *Methodology differences*: See previous discussion of significant accounting differences between segment reporting and consolidated external reporting.
- *Timing*: Timing differences in the recognition of costs between segment reporting and consolidated external reporting.

Table IV — Segment Information

(Millions of dollars)

Reportable Segments

	External Sales and Revenues	Inter-Segment Sales and Revenues	Total Sales and Revenues	Depreciation and Amortization	Segment Profit	Segment Assets at December 31	Capital Expenditures
2012							
Construction Industries	$19,334	$ 470	$19,804	$ 565	$ 1,789	$10,393	$1,045
Resource Industries	21,158	1,117	22,275	694	4,318	13,455	1,143
Power Systems	21,122	2,407	23,529	604	3,434	9,323	960
Machinery and Power Systems	$61,614	$3,994	$65,608	$1,863	$ 9,541	$33,171	$3,148
Financial Products Segment	3,090	—	3,090	708	763	36,563	1,660
Total	$64,704	$3,994	$68,698	$2,571	$10,304	$69,734	$4,808
2011							
Construction Industries	$19,667	$ 575	$20,242	$ 526	$ 2,056	$ 7,942	$ 915
Resource Industries	15,629	1,162	16,791	463	3,334	12,292	717
Power Systems	20,114	2,339	22,453	544	3,053	8,748	834
Machinery and Power Systems	$55,410	$4,076	$59,486	$1,533	$ 8,443	$28,982	$2,466
Financial Products Segment	3,003	—	3,003	710	587	31,747	1,191
Total	$58,413	$4,076	$62,489	$2,243	$ 9,030	$60,729	$3,657
2010							
Construction Industries	$13,572	$ 674	$14,246	$ 515	$ 783	$ 6,927	$ 576
Resource Industries	8,667	894	9,561	281	1,789	3,892	339
Power Systems	15,537	1,684	17,221	502	2,288	8,321	567
Machinery and Power Systems	$37,776	$3,252	$41,028	$1,298	$ 4,860	$19,140	$1,482
Financial Products Segment	2,946	—	2,946	715	429	30,346	960
Total	$40,722	$3,252	$43,974	$2,013	$ 5,289	$49,486	$2,442

Reconciliation of Sales and Revenues:

(Millions of dollars)	Machinery and Power Systems	Financial Products	Consolidating Adjustments	Consolidated Total
2012				
Total external sales and revenues from reportable segments	$61,614	$3,090	$ —	$64,704
All other operating segment	1,501	—	—	1,501
Other	(47)	70	(353)[1]	(330)
Total sales and revenues	$63,068	$3,160	$(353)	$65,875
2011				
Total external sales and revenues from reportable segments	$55,410	$3,003	$ —	$58,413
All other operating segment	2,021	—	—	2,021
Other	(39)	54	(311)[1]	(296)
Total sales and revenues	$57,392	$3,057	$(311)	$60,138
2010				
Total external sales and revenues from reportable segments	$37,776	$2,946	$ —	$40,722
All other operating segment	2,156	—	—	2,156
Other	(65)	40	(265)[1]	(290)
Total sales and revenues	$39,867	$2,986	$(265)	$42,588

[1] Elimination of Financial Products revenues from Machinery and Power Systems.

Reconciliation of Consolidated Profit Before Taxes:

(Millions of dollars)	Machinery and Power Systems	Financial Products	Consolidated Total
2012			
Total profit from reportable segments	$ 9,541	$763	$10,304
All other operating segment	1,014	—	1,014
Cost centers	17	—	17
Corporate costs	(1,517)	—	(1,517)
Timing	(298)	—	(298)
Methodology differences:			
Inventory/cost of sales	43	—	43
Postretirement benefit expense	(696)	—	(696)
Financing costs	(474)	—	(474)
Equity in profit of unconsolidated affiliated companies	(14)	—	(14)
Currency	108	—	108
Interest rate swap	2	—	2
Other income/expense methodology differences	(251)	—	(251)
Other methodology differences	(19)	17	(2)
Total consolidated profit before taxes	$ 7,456	$780	$ 8,236

(continued)

(Millions of dollars)	Machinery and Power Systems	Financial Products	Consolidated Total
2011			
Total profit from reportable segments	$ 8,443	$587	$ 9,030
All other operating segment	837	—	837
Cost centers	14	—	14
Corporate costs	(1,174)	—	(1,174)
Timing	(203)	—	(203)
Methodology differences:			
Inventory/cost of sales	21	—	21
Postretirement benefit expense	(670)	—	(670)
Financing costs	(408)	—	(408)
Equity in profit of unconsolidated affiliated companies	24	—	24
Currency	(315)	—	(315)
Interest rate swap	(149)	—	(149)
Other income/expense methodology differences	(273)	—	(273)
Other methodology differences	(42)	33	(9)
Total consolidated profit before taxes	$ 6,105	$620	$ 6,725
2010			
Total profit from reportable segments	$ 4,860	$429	$ 5,289
All other operating segment	720	—	720
Cost centers	(11)	—	(11)
Corporate costs	(987)	—	(987)
Timing	(185)	—	(185)
Methodology differences:			
Inventory/cost of sales	(13)	—	(13)
Postretirement benefit expense	(640)	—	(640)
Financing costs	(314)	—	(314)
Equity in profit of unconsolidated affiliated companies	24	—	24
Currency	6	—	6
Interest rate swap	(10)	—	(10)
Other income/expense methodology differences	(131)	—	(131)
Other methodology differences	(16)	18	2
Total consolidated profit before taxes	$ 3,303	$447	$ 3,750

Reconciliation of Assets:

(Millions of dollars)	Machinery and Power Systems	Financial Products	Consolidating Adjustments	Consolidated Total
2012				
Total assets from reportable segments	$33,171	$36,563	$ —	$69,734
All other operating segment	1,499	—	—	1,499
Items not included in segment assets:				
Cash and short-term investments	3,306	—	—	3,306
Intercompany receivables	303	—	(303)	—
Investment in Financial Products	4,433	—	(4,433)	—
Deferred income taxes	3,926	—	(516)	3,410
Goodwill, intangible assets and other assets	3,813	—	—	3,813
Operating lease methodology difference	(329)	—	—	(329)
Liabilities included in segment assets	11,293	—	—	11,293
Inventory methodology differences	(2,949)	—	—	(2,949)
Other	(182)	(107)	(132)	(421)
Total assets	$58,284	$36,456	$(5,384)	$89,356
2011				
Total assets from reportable segments	$28,982	$31,747	$ —	$60,729
All other operating segment	2,035	—	—	2,035
Items not included in segment assets:				
Cash and short-term investments	1,829	—	—	1,829
Intercompany receivables	75	—	(75)	—
Investment in Financial Products	4,035	—	(4,035)	—
Deferred income taxes	4,109	—	(533)	3,576
Goodwill, intangible assets and other assets	4,461	—	—	4,461
Operating lease methodology difference	(511)	—	—	(511)
Liabilities included in segment assets	12,088	—	—	12,088
Inventory methodology differences	(2,786)	—	—	(2,786)
Other	362	(194)	(143)	25
Total assets	$54,679	$31,553	$(4,786)	$81,446

(continued)

(Millions of dollars)	Machinery and Power Systems	Financial Products	Consolidating Adjustments	Consolidated Total
2010				
Total assets from reportable segments	$19,140	$30,346	$ —	$49,486
All other operating segment	2,472	—	—	2,472
Items not included in segment assets:				
Cash and short-term investments	1,825	—	—	1,825
Intercompany receivables	618	—	(618)	—
Investment in Financial Products	4,275	—	(4,275)	—
Deferred income taxes	3,745	—	(519)	3,226
Goodwill, intangible assets and other assets	1,511	—	—	1,511
Operating lease methodology difference	(567)	—	—	(567)
Liabilities included in segment assets	8,758	—	—	8,758
Inventory methodology differences	(2,913)	—	—	(2,913)
Other	627	(233)	(172)	222
Total assets	$39,491	$30,113	$(5,584)	$64,020

Reconciliation of Depreciation and Amortization:

(Millions of dollars)	Machinery and Power Systems	Financial Products	Consolidated Total
2012			
Total depreciation and amortization from reportable segments	$1,863	$708	$2,571
Items not included in segment depreciation and amortization:			
All other operating segment	168	—	168
Cost centers	89	—	89
Other	(38)	23	(15)
Total depreciation and amortization	$2,082	$731	$2,813
2011			
Total depreciation and amortization from reportable segments	$1,533	$710	$2,243
Items not included in segment depreciation and amortization:			
All other operating segment	172	—	172
Cost centers	77	—	77
Other	20	15	35
Total depreciation and amortization	$1,802	$725	$2,527
2010			
Total depreciation and amortization from reportable segments	$1,298	$715	$2,013
Items not included in segment depreciation and amortization:			
All other operating segment	194	—	194
Cost centers	97	—	97
Other	(16)	8	(8)
Total depreciation and amortization	$1,573	$723	$2,296

Reconciliation of Capital Expenditures:

(Millions of dollars)	Machinery and Power Systems	Financial Products	Consolidating Adjustments	Consolidated Total
2012				
Total capital expenditures from reportable segments	$3,148	$1,660	$ —	$4,808
Items not included in segment capital expenditures:				
All other operating segment	359	—	—	359
Cost centers	175	—	—	175
Timing	(71)	—	—	(71)
Other	(176)	136	(155)	(195)
Total capital expenditures	$3,435	$1,796	$(155)	$5,076
2011				
Total capital expenditures from reportable segments	$2,466	$1,191	$ —	$3,657
Items not included in segment capital expenditures:				
All other operating segment	343	—	—	343
Cost centers	146	—	—	146
Timing	(211)	—	—	(211)
Other	(98)	163	(76)	(11)
Total capital expenditures	$2,646	$1,354	$ (76)	$3,924
2010				
Total capital expenditures from reportable segments	$1,482	$ 960	$ —	$2,442
Items not included in segment capital expenditures:				
All other operating segment	285	—	—	285
Cost centers	105	—	—	105
Timing	(180)	—	—	(180)
Other	(29)	32	(69)	(66)
Total capital expenditures	$1,663	$ 992	$ (69)	$2,586

Enterprise-Wide Disclosures:

Information about Geographic Areas:

(Millions of dollars)	External Sales and Revenues[1]			Property, Plant and Equipment—Net December 31,		
	2012	2011	2010	2012	2011	2010
Inside United States	$20,305	$18,004	$13,674	$ 8,573	$ 7,388	$ 6,427
Outside United States	45,570[2]	42,134	28,914	7,888	7,007	6,112[3]
Total	$65,875	$60,138	$42,588	$16,461	$14,395	$12,539

[1] Sales of machinery and power systems are based on dealer or customer location. Revenues from services provided are based on where service is rendered.

[2] The only country with greater than 10 percent of external sales and revenues for any of the periods presented, other than the United States, is Australia with $6,822 million as of December 31, 2012.

[3] The only country with greater than 10 percent of total property, plant and equipment—net for any of the periods presented, other than the United States, is Japan with $1,266 million as of December 31, 2010.

Accounting Changes and Error Corrections

PRESENTATION

1.36 FASB ASC 250 defines various types of accounting changes, including a change in accounting principle, and provides guidance on the manner of reporting each type of change.

1.37 FASB ASC 250-10-45-1 include the presumption that, once adopted, an entity should not change an accounting principle (policy) to account for events and transactions of a similar type. FASB ASC 250-10-45-2 permits an entity to change an accounting principle in certain circumstances, such as when required to do so by new authoritative accounting guidance that mandates the use of a new accounting principle, interprets an existing principle, expresses a preference for an accounting principle, or rejects a specific principle. This paragraph also permits an entity to change an accounting principle if it can justify the use of an allowable alternative accounting principle on the basis that it is preferable.

1.38 FASB ASC 250-10-45-1 does not consider the following to be changes in accounting principle:
- Initial adoption of an accounting principle for new events or transactions
- Initial adoption of an accounting principle for new events or transactions that previously were immaterial in their effect
- Adoption or modification of an accounting principle for substantively different transactions or events from those occurring previously

1.39 FASB ASC 250-10-45-5 requires an entity to apply a change in accounting principle retrospectively to all prior periods, unless it is impracticable to do so. Retrospective application requires cumulative adjustments to the carrying amounts of assets and liabilities at the beginning of the earliest period presented; an adjustment, if any, to the opening balance of retained earnings or other relevant equity account; and adjusted financial statements for each individual prior period presented to reflect the period-specific effects of applying the new accounting principle. FASB ASC 250-10-45-7 provides an impracticability exception for period-specific effects or all periods. However, FASB ASC 250-10-45-8 permits only direct effects of the change, including any related income tax effects, to be included in the retrospective adjustment and prohibits an entity from including indirect effects that would have been recognized if the newly adopted accounting principle had been followed in prior periods. If indirect effects are actually incurred and recognized, an entity should only report for those indirect effects in the period in which the accounting change is made.

1.40 FASB ASC 250-10-45-17 requires an entity to account for a change in accounting estimate prospectively in the period of change if the change affects that period only or in the period of change and future periods if the change affects both.

1.41 Paragraphs 18–19 of FASB ASC 250-10-45 recognize that it may be difficult to distinguish between a change in an accounting principle and a change in an accounting estimate. Additional guidance is provided for those circumstances when an entity's change in estimate is affected by a change in accounting principle, recognizing that the effect of a change in accounting principle or the method of applying it may be inseparable from the effect of the change in accounting estimate. An example of such change is a change in the method of depreciation, amortization, or depletion for long-lived nonfinancial assets. Although an entity is permitted to apply this change prospectively as a change in accounting estimate, an entity should only make a change in accounting estimate affected by a change in accounting principle if the entity can justify the new accounting principle on the basis that it is preferable.

1.42 Paragraphs 23–24 of FASB ASC 250-10-45 require an entity to correct any error in the financial statements of a prior period discovered after the financial statements are issued or available to be issued by restating the prior-period financial statements. Such errors are required to be reported as an error correction by restating the prior-period financial statements retrospectively with adjustments to the financial statements.

DISCLOSURE

1.43 As discussed in FASB ASC 250-10-50, among the required disclosures for a change in accounting principle, the reason should be disclosed, including an explanation about why the new method is preferable. Specific disclosures are also required for a change in accounting estimate, a change in reporting entity, correction of an error in previously-issued financial statements, and error corrections related to prior interim periods of the current fiscal year.

PRESENTATION AND DISCLOSURE EXCERPTS

CHANGE IN ACCOUNTING PRINCIPLE—DEPRECIATION

1.44 WEIS MARKETS, INC. (DEC)
NOTES TO THE CONSOLIDATED FINANCIAL STATEMENTS

Note 1 Summary of Significant Accounting Policies (in part)

(j) Property and Equipment (in part)

In the first quarter of 2012, the Company changed its accounting policy for property and equipment. Property and equipment continue to be recorded at cost. Prior to January 1, 2012, the Company provided for depreciation of buildings and improvements and equipment using accelerated methods. Effective January 1, 2012, the Company changed its method of depreciation for this group of assets from the accelerated methods to straight-line. Management deemed the change preferable because the straight-line method will more accurately reflect the pattern of usage and the expected benefits of such assets. Management also considered that the change will provide greater consistency with the depreciation methods used by other companies in the Company's industry. The change was accounted for as a change in accounting estimate effected by a change in accounting principle. The net book value of assets acquired prior to January 1, 2012 with useful lives remaining will be depreciated using the straight-line method prospectively. If the Company had continued using accelerated methods, depreciation expense would have been $11.5 million greater in 2012. Had accelerated methods continued to be used, after considering the impact of income taxes, the effect would decrease net income by $6.8 million or $.25 per share in 2012.

CHANGE IN ACCOUNTING PRINCIPLE—PENSION AND OTHER POSTRETIREMENT BENEFITS

1.45 EASTMAN CHEMICAL COMPANY (DEC)
NOTES TO THE AUDITED CONSOLIDATED FINANCIAL STATEMENTS

1. Significant Accounting Policies (in part)

Beginning January 1, 2012, the Company elected to change its method of accounting for actuarial gains and losses for its pension and other postretirement benefit ("OPEB") plans as described in Note 14, "Accounting Methodology Change for Pension and Other Postretirement Benefit Plans." Beginning January 1, 2012, the Company adopted amended accounting guidance related to the presentation of other comprehensive income which became effective for reporting periods beginning after December 15, 2011. These changes have been retrospectively applied to all periods presented.

Pension and Other Post-Employment Benefits

The Company maintains defined benefit pension plans that provide eligible employees with retirement benefits. Additionally, Eastman provides a subsidy toward life insurance, health care, and dental benefits for eligible retirees and a subsidy toward health care and dental benefits for retirees' eligible survivors. The costs and obligations related to these benefits reflect the Company's assumptions related to general economic conditions (particularly interest rates), expected return on plan assets, rate of compensation increase or decrease for employees, and health care cost trends. The cost of providing plan benefits depends on demographic assumptions including retirements, mortality, turnover, and plan participation.

During 2012, Eastman changed its method of accounting for actuarial gains and losses for its pension and OPEB plans. Historically, Eastman recognized pension and OPEB actuarial gains and losses annually in its Consolidated Statements of Financial Position as Accumulated Other Comprehensive Income and Loss as a component of Stockholders' Equity, and then amortized these gains and losses each quarter in its Statements of Earnings. The expected return on assets component of Eastman's pension expense had historically been calculated using a five-year smoothing of asset gains and losses, and the gain or loss component of pension and OPEB expense has historically been based on amortization of actuarial gains and losses that exceed 10 percent of the greater of plan assets or projected benefit obligations over the average future service period of active employees.

Under the current method of accounting, Eastman's pension and OPEB costs consist of two elements: 1) ongoing costs recognized quarterly, which are comprised of service and interest costs, expected returns on plan assets, and amortization of prior service credits; and 2) mark-to-market ("MTM") gains and losses recognized annually, in the fourth quarter of each year, resulting from changes in actuarial assumptions for discount rates and the differences between actual and expected returns on plan assets. Any interim remeasurements triggered by a curtailment, settlement, or significant plan changes are recognized as an MTM adjustment in the quarter in which such remeasurement event occurs. This change has been retrospectively applied to all periods presented.

In connection with the above change in accounting for pension and OPEB costs, management also elected to change its method of accounting for certain related costs included in inventory. Management elected, effective in first quarter 2012, to exclude the portion of pension and OPEB costs attributable to former employees (inactives) as a component of inventoriable costs and instead charge them directly to the cost of sales line item as a period cost. Applying this change in inventory retrospectively did not have a material impact on previously reported inventory, cost of sales, or financial results in any prior period and, as such, prior period results have not been retrospectively adjusted for this change in accounting for certain related costs included in inventory.

For additional information, see Note 13, "Retirement Plans" and Note 14, "Accounting Methodology Change for Pension and Other Postretirement Plans."

14. Accounting Methodology Change for Pension and Other Postretirement Benefit Plans

As previously reported on March 7, 2012, Eastman elected to change its method of accounting for actuarial gains and losses for its pension and OPEB plans to a more preferable method permitted under GAAP. The current method recognizes actuarial gains and losses in the Company's operating results in the year in which the gains and losses occur rather than amortizing them over future periods. Eastman management believes that this change in accounting improves transparency of reporting of its operating results by recognizing the effects of economic and interest rate trends on pension and OPEB plan investments and assumptions in the year these actuarial gains and losses are incurred. Historically, Eastman has recognized pension and OPEB actuarial gains and losses annually in its Consolidated Statements of Financial Position as Accumulated Other Comprehensive Income and Loss as a component of Stockholders' Equity, and then amortized these gains and losses each period in its Consolidated Statements of Earnings. The expected return on assets component of Eastman's pension expense has historically been calculated using a five-year smoothing of asset gains and losses, and the gain or loss component of pension and OPEB expense has historically been based on amortization of actuarial gains and losses that exceed 10 percent of the greater of plan assets or projected benefit obligations over the average future service period of active employees. Under the current method of accounting, these gains and losses are measured annually at the plan's December 31 measurement date and recorded as an MTM adjustment during the fourth quarter of each year, and any quarters in which an interim remeasurement is triggered. This methodology is preferable under GAAP since it aligns more closely with fair value principles and does not delay the recognition of gains and losses into future periods. The current method has been retrospectively applied to the financial results of all periods presented.

Under the current method of accounting, Eastman's pension and OPEB costs consist of two elements: 1) ongoing costs recognized quarterly, which are comprised of service and interest costs, expected returns on plan assets, and amortization of prior service credits; and 2) MTM gains and losses recognized annually, in the fourth quarter of each year, resulting from changes in actuarial assumptions for discount rates and the differences between actual and expected returns on plan assets. Any interim remeasurement triggered by a curtailment, settlement, or significant plan change is recognized as an MTM adjustment in the quarter in which such remeasurement event occurs.

Eastman's operating segment results follow internal management reporting, which is used for making operating decisions and assessing performance. Historically, total pension and OPEB costs have been allocated to each segment. In conjunction with the change in accounting principle, the service cost, which represents the benefits earned by active employees during the period, and amortization of prior service credits continue to be allocated to each segment. Interest costs, expected return on assets, and the MTM adjustment (including any interim remeasurement) for actuarial gains and losses are under the changed accounting method included in corporate expense and not allocated to segments. Management believes this change in expense allocation better reflects the operating results of each business.

Management also elected to change its method of accounting for certain costs included in inventory. Effective in first quarter 2012, the portion of pension and OPEB costs attributable to former employees (inactives) is not a component of inventoriable costs and instead is charged directly to the cost of sales line item as a period cost. Applying this change in inventory retrospectively did not have a material impact on previously reported inventory, cost of sales, or financial results in any prior period and prior period results have not been retrospectively adjusted for this change in accounting for certain related costs included in inventory.

The cumulative effect of the change in accounting for pension and OPEB plans was a decrease in Retained Earnings as of December 31, 2010 (the most recent measurement date prior to the change) of $626 million, and an equivalent increase in Accumulated Other Comprehensive Income, leaving total stockholders' equity unchanged. See Note 13, "Retirement Plans."

Following are the changes to financial statement line items as a result of the accounting methodology change for the periods presented in the accompanying consolidated financial statements:

Condensed Consolidated Statement of Earnings, Comprehensive Income and Retained Earnings

(Dollars in millions, except per share amounts)	For Year Ended December 31, 2012		
	Previous Accounting Method	Effect of Accounting Change	As Reported
Cost of sales[1]	$6,192	$ 148	$6,340
Gross profit	1,910	(148)	1,762
Selling, general and administrative expenses[1]	600	44	644
Research and development expenses[1]	190	8	198
Operating earnings	1,000	(200)	800
Other charges (income), net	6	2	8
Earnings from continuing operations before income taxes	851	(202)	649
Provision for income taxes from continuing operations	275	(69)	206
Earnings from continuing operations	576	(133)	443
Net earnings	577	(133)	444
Net earnings attributable to Eastman	570	(133)	437
Amounts attributable to Eastman stockholders			
Earnings from continuing operations, net of tax	569	(133)	436
Net earnings attributable to Eastman stockholders	570	(133)	437
Basic earnings per share attributable to Eastman			
Earnings from continuing operations	$ 3.91	$(0.92)	$ 2.99
Earnings from discontinued operations	0.01	—	0.01
Basic earnings per share attributable to Eastman	3.92	(0.92)	3.00
Diluted earnings per share attributable to Eastman			
Earnings from continuing operations	$ 3.81	$(0.89)	$ 2.92
Diluted earnings per share attributable to Eastman	3.82	(0.89)	2.93
Comprehensive Income			
Net earnings including noncontrolling interest	$ 577	$ (133)	$ 444
Amortization of unrecognized prior service credits included in net periodic costs[2]	(146)	133	(13)
Total other comprehensive loss, net of tax	(148)	133	(15)
Comprehensive income including noncontrolling interest	429	—	429
Comprehensive income attributable to Eastman	422	—	422
Retained Earnings			
Retained earnings at beginning of period	$3,436	$ (676)	$2,760
Net earnings attributable to Eastman	570	(133)	437
Retained earnings at end of period	3,847	(809)	3,038

[1] Includes MTM adjustment for pension and OPEB plans actuarial net losses of $276 million.
[2] Updated to reflect first quarter 2012 presentation of other comprehensive income.

Condensed Consolidated Statement of Earnings, Comprehensive Income and Retained Earnings

(Dollars in millions, except per share amounts)	For Year Ended December 31, 2011		
	Previous Accounting Method	Effect of Accounting Change	As Reported
Cost of sales[1]	$5,538	$ 71	$5,609
Gross profit	1,640	(71)	1,569
Selling, general and administrative expenses[1]	469	12	481
Research and development expenses[1]	158	1	159
Operating earnings	1,021	(84)	937
Earnings from continuing operations before income taxes	965	(84)	881
Provision for income taxes from continuing operations	307	(33)	274
Earnings from continuing operations	658	(51)	607
Earnings from discontinued operations, net of tax	8	1	9
Net earnings	697	(50)	647
Net earnings attributable to Eastman	696	(50)	646
Amounts attributable to Eastman stockholders			
Earnings from continuing operations, net of tax	657	(51)	606
Net earnings attributable to Eastman stockholders	696	(50)	646
Basic earnings per share attributable to Eastman			
Earnings from continuing operations	$ 4.70	$(0.36)	$ 4.34
Earnings from discontinued operations	0.28	0.01	0.29
Basic earnings per share attributable to Eastman	4.98	(0.35)	4.63
Diluted earnings per share attributable to Eastman			
Earnings from continuing operations	$ 4.59	$(0.35)	$ 4.24
Earnings from discontinued operations	0.27	0.01	0.28
Diluted earnings per share attributable to Eastman	4.86	(0.34)	4.52
Comprehensive Income			
Net earnings including noncontrolling interest	$ 697	$ (50)	$ 647
Amortization of unrecognized prior service credits included in net periodic costs[2]	(71)	50	(21)
Total other comprehensive loss, net of tax	(106)	50	(56)

(continued)

(Dollars in millions, except per share amounts)	For Year Ended December 31, 2011		
	Previous Accounting Method	Effect of Accounting Change	As Reported
Comprehensive income including noncontrolling interest	591	—	591
Comprehensive income attributable to Eastman	590	—	590
Retained Earnings			
Retained earnings at beginning of period	$2,879	$ (626)	$2,253
Net earnings attributable to Eastman	696	(50)	646
Retained earnings at end of period	3,436	(676)	2,760

[1] Includes MTM adjustment for pension and OPEB plans actuarial net losses of $144 million.
[2] Updated to reflect first quarter 2012 presentation of other comprehensive income.

Condensed Consolidated Statement of Earnings, Comprehensive Income and Retained Earnings

(Dollars in millions, except per share amounts)	For Year Ended December 31, 2010		
	Previous Accounting Method	Effect of Accounting Change	As Reported
Cost of sales[1]	$4,368	$ 15	$4,383
Gross profit	1,474	(15)	1,459
Selling, general and administrative expenses[1]	431	3	434
Operating earnings	862	(18)	844
Earnings from continuing operations before income taxes	638	(18)	620
Provision for income taxes from continuing operations	211	(9)	202
Earnings from continuing operations	427	(9)	418
Earnings from discontinued operations, net of tax	13	(4)	9
Net earnings	440	(13)	427
Net earnings attributable to Eastman	438	(13)	425
Amounts attributable to Eastman stockholders			
Earnings from continuing operations, net of tax	425	(9)	416
Earnings from discontinued operations, net of tax	13	(4)	9
Net earnings attributable to Eastman stockholders	438	(13)	425
Basic earnings per share attributable to Eastman			
Earnings from continuing operations	$ 2.95	$(0.07)	$ 2.88
Earnings from discontinued operations	0.09	(0.02)	0.07
Basic earnings per share attributable to Eastman	3.04	(0.09)	2.95
Diluted earnings per share attributable to Eastman			
Earnings from continuing operations	$ 2.88	$(0.07)	$ 2.81
Earnings from discontinued operations	0.08	(0.01)	0.07
Diluted earnings per share attributable to Eastman	2.96	(0.08)	2.88
Comprehensive Income			
Net earnings including noncontrolling interest	$ 440	$ (13)	$ 427
Amortization of unrecognized prior service credits included in net periodic costs[2]	(39)	13	(26)
Total other comprehensive loss, net of tax	(47)	13	(34)
Comprehensive income including noncontrolling interest	393	—	393
Comprehensive income attributable to Eastman	391	—	391
Retained Earnings			
Retained earnings at beginning of period	$2,570	$ (613)	$1,957
Net earnings attributable to Eastman	438	(13)	425
Retained earnings at end of period	2,879	(626)	2,253

[1] Includes MTM adjustment for pension and OPEB plans actuarial net losses of $53 million.
[2] Updated to reflect first quarter 2012 presentation of other comprehensive income.

Condensed Consolidated Statements of Financial Position

(Dollars in millions)	December 31, 2012		
	Previous Accounting Method	Effect of Accounting Change	As Reported
Retained earnings	$3,847	$ (809)	$3,038
Accumulated other comprehensive income (loss)	(686)	809	123

(Dollars in millions)	December 31, 2011		
	Previous Accounting Method	Effect of Accounting Change	As Reported
Retained earnings	$3,436	$ (676)	$2,760
Accumulated other comprehensive income (loss)	(538)	676	138

(Dollars in millions)	For Year Ended December 31, 2012		
	Previous Accounting Method	Effect of Accounting Change	As Reported
Net earnings (loss) including noncontrolling interest	$577	$(133)	$444
Provision (benefit) for deferred income taxes	117	(69)	48
Pension and other postretirement contributions (in excess of) less than expenses	17	133	150
Other items, net	(111)	69	(42)

(Dollars in millions)	For Year Ended December 31, 2011		
	Previous Accounting Method	Effect of Accounting Change	As Reported
Net earnings (loss) including noncontrolling interest	$697	$ (50)	$647
Provision (benefit) for deferred income taxes	11	(33)	(22)
Pension and other postretirement contributions (in excess of) less than expenses, net[1]	(65)	50	(15)
Other items, net[1]	44	33	77

[1] Updated to reflect first quarter 2012 presentation of cash flows from operating activities.

(Dollars in millions)	For Year Ended December 31, 2010		
	Previous Accounting Method	Effect of Accounting Change	As Reported
Net earnings (loss) including noncontrolling interest	$440	$ (13)	$427
Provision (benefit) for deferred income taxes	59	(12)	47
Pension and other postretirement contributions (in excess of) less than expenses, net[1]	(1)	13	12
Other items, net[1]	3	12	15

[1] Updated to reflect first quarter 2012 presentation of cash flows from operating activities.

CHANGE IN ACCOUNTING PRINCIPLE—INVENTORY

1.46 CVS CAREMARK CORPORATION (DEC)
NOTES TO CONSOLIDATED FINANCIAL STATEMENTS

2. Changes in Accounting Principle

Effective January 1, 2012, the Company changed its methods of accounting for prescription drug inventories in the Retail Pharmacy Segment. Prior to 2012, the Company valued prescription drug inventories at the lower of cost or market on a first-in, first-out ("FIFO") basis in retail pharmacies using the retail inventory method and in distribution centers using the FIFO cost method. Effective January 1, 2012, all prescription drug inventories in the Retail Pharmacy Segment have been valued at the lower of cost or market using the weighted average cost method. These changes affected approximately 51% of consolidated inventories.

These changes were made primarily to bring all of the pharmacy operations of the Company to a common inventory valuation methodology and to provide the Company with better information to manage its retail pharmacy operations. The Company believes the weighted average cost method is preferable to the retail inventory method and the FIFO cost method because it results in greater precision in the determination of cost of revenues and inventories by specific drug product and results in a consistent inventory valuation method for all of the Company's prescription drug inventories as the Pharmacy Services Segment's mail service and specialty pharmacies were already on the weighted average cost method. Most of these mail service and specialty pharmacies in the Pharmacy Services Segment were acquired in the Company's 2007 acquisition of Caremark Rx, Inc.

The Company recorded the cumulative effect of these changes in accounting principle as of January 1, 2012. The Company determined that retrospective application for periods prior to 2012 is impracticable, as the period-specific information necessary to value prescription drug inventories in the Retail Pharmacy Segment under the weighted average cost method is unavailable. The Company implemented a new pharmacy cost accounting system to value prescription drug inventory as of January 1, 2012 and calculated the cumulative impact. The effect of these changes in accounting principle as of January 1, 2012 was a decrease in inventories of $146 million, an increase in current deferred income tax assets of $57 million and a decrease in retained earnings of $89 million.

Had the Company not made these changes in accounting principle, for the year ended December 31, 2012, income from continuing operations and net income attributable to CVS Caremark would have been approximately $19 million lower. For the year ended December 31, 2012, basic and diluted earnings per common share for income from continuing operations attributable to CVS Caremark and net income attributable to CVS Caremark would have been reduced by $0.01.

1.47 NEWS CORPORATION (JUN)
NOTES TO THE CONSOLIDATED FINANCIAL STATEMENTS

Note 2. Summary of Significant Accounting Policies (in part)

Recently Adopted and Recently Issued Accounting Guidance (in part)

Adopted (in part)

In the fourth quarter of fiscal 2012, the Company adopted ASU 2011-09, "Compensation—Retirement Benefits—Multiemployer Plans (Subtopic 715-80): Disclosures about an Employer's Participation in a Multiemployer Plan" ("ASU 2011-09"). ASU 2011-09 requires enhanced qualitative and quantitative disclosures about an employer's participation in multiemployer pension plans, including additional information about the plans, the level of an employer's participation in the plans and the financial health of significant plans. ASU 2011-09 is retrospectively effective for the Company for the annual periods presented for the fiscal year ending June 30, 2012. The application of the amended accounting guidance resulted in additional financial statement disclosures.

Note 16. Pension and Other Postretirement Benefits (in part)

Multi-Employer Pension and Postretirements Plans

The Company contributes to various multiemployer defined benefit pension plans under the terms of collective-bargaining agreements that cover certain of its union-represented employees, primarily at the Filmed Entertainment segment. The risks of participating in these multiemployer pension plans are different from single-employer pension plans such that (i) contributions made by the Company to the multiemployer pension plans may be used to provide benefits to employees of other participating employers; (ii) if the Company chooses to stop participating in certain of these multiemployer pension plans, it may be required to pay those plans an amount based on the underfunded status of the plan, which is referred to as a withdrawal liability; and (iii) actions taken by a participating employer that lead to a deterioration of the financial health of a multiemployer pension plan may result in the unfunded obligations of the multiemployer pension plan to be borne by its remaining participating employers. While no multiemployer pension plan that the Company contributed to is individually significant to the Company, the Company was listed on four Form 5500s as providing more than 5% of total contributions based on the current information available. The financial health of a multiemployer plan is indicated by the zone status, as defined by the Pension Protection Act of 2006, which represents the funded status of the plan as certified by the plan's actuary. Plans in the red zone are less than 65% funded, the yellow zone are between 65% and 80% funded, and green zone are at least 80% funded. The most recent available funded status of the four plans in which the Company was listed as providing more than 5% of total contributions are all green. Total contributions made by the Company to multiemployer pension plans for the fiscal years ended June 30, 2012, 2011 and 2010 were $66 million, $55 million and $55 million, respectively.

The Company also contributes to various other multiemployer benefit plans that provide health and welfare benefits to active and retired participants, primarily at the Filmed Entertainment segment. Total contributions made by the Company to these other multiemployer benefit plans for the fiscal years ended June 30, 2012, 2011 and 2010 were $67 million, $62 million and $55 million, respectively.

CHANGE IN ACCOUNTING PRINCIPLE—COMPREHENSIVE INCOME

1.48 BRUNSWICK CORPORATION (DEC)
CONSOLIDATED STATEMENTS OF COMPREHENSIVE INCOME

	For the Years Ended December 31		
(In millions)	2012	2011	2010
Net earnings (loss)	$ 50.0	$ 71.9	$(110.6)
Other comprehensive income, net of tax:			
Foreign currency translation:			
Foreign currency translation adjustments arising during period	6.4	(4.2)	(7.2)
Less: reclassification of foreign currency translation included in Net earnings (loss)	—	(16.2)	(0.1)
Net foreign currency translation(A)	6.4	(20.4)	(7.3)
Defined benefit plans:			
Prior service credits arising during period	0.2	6.1	0.7
Net actuarial losses arising during period	(30.0)	(122.7)	(43.2)
Less: amortization of prior service credits included in Net earnings (loss)	(7.5)	(5.9)	(4.7)
Less: amortization of net actuarial losses included in Net earnings (loss)	22.9	22.4	22.2
Net defined benefit plans(B)	(14.4)	(100.1)	(25.0)
Investments:			
Unrealized holding gains (losses) arising during period	0.1	(1.0)	(1.9)
Less: reclassification adjustment included in Net earnings (loss)	—	0.2	—
Net unrealized investment gains (losses)(A)	0.1	(0.8)	(1.9)

(continued)

(In millions)		For the Years Ended December 31	
	2012	**2011**	**2010**
Derivatives:			
Losses on derivatives arising during period	(10.0)	(9.8)	(1.7)
Less: reclassification adjustment included in Net earnings (loss)	3.6	5.8	(4.8)
Net unrealized losses on derivatives[A]	(6.4)	(4.0)	(6.5)
Other comprehensive loss	(14.3)	(125.3)	(40.7)
Comprehensive income (loss)	$ 35.7	$ (53.4)	$(151.3)

[A] The tax effect for all periods presented was $0.0 million as a result of corresponding tax valuation allowance adjustments.

[B] The tax effect for the years ended December 31, 2012, 2011 and 2010 was to increase Other comprehensive loss by $0.9 million, $0.3 million and $0.9 million, respectively, primarily related to certain foreign defined benefit plans as all other defined benefit plans included corresponding tax valuation allowance adjustments.

The Notes to Consolidated Financial Statements are an integral part of these consolidated statements.

NOTES TO CONSOLIDATED FINANCIAL STATEMENTS

Note 1—Significant Accounting Policies (in part)

Comprehensive Income: In June 2011, the FASB amended the ASC to increase the prominence of the items reported in other comprehensive income. Specifically, the amendment to the ASC eliminates the option to present the components of other comprehensive income as part of the Consolidated Statements of Shareholders' Equity. The amendment must be applied retrospectively and is effective for fiscal years and the interim periods within those years, beginning after December 15, 2011. The Company disclosed comprehensive income on the Consolidated Statements of Comprehensive Income as a result of adopting this amendment.

In February 2013, the FASB amended the ASC to require entities to provide information about amounts reclassified out of other comprehensive income by component. The Company is required to present, either on the face of the financial statements or in the notes, the amounts reclassified from other comprehensive income to the respective line items in the Consolidated Statements of Operations. This amendment is effective for interim and annual periods beginning after December 15, 2012.

CHANGE IN ACCOUNTING PRINCIPLE—GOODWILL

1.49 CAREER EDUCATION CORPORATION (DEC)
NOTES TO CONSOLIDATED FINANCIAL STATEMENTS

2. Summary of Significant Accounting Policies (in part)

n. Goodwill and Intangible Assets (in part)

Goodwill represents the excess of cost over fair market value of identifiable net assets acquired through business purchases. In accordance with FASB ASC Topic 350—*Intangibles-Goodwill and Other,* we review goodwill for impairment on at least an annual basis by applying a fair-value-based test. In evaluating the recoverability of the carrying value of goodwill, we must make assumptions regarding the fair value of our reporting units, as defined under FASB ASC Topic 350. Goodwill is evaluated using a two-step impairment test at the reporting unit level. A reporting unit can be a strategic business unit or business within a strategic business unit. The first step compares the book value of a reporting unit, including goodwill, with its fair value, as determined by its discounted cash flows. If the book value of a reporting unit exceeds its fair value, we complete the second step to determine the amount of goodwill impairment loss that we should record. In the second step, we determine an implied fair value of the reporting unit's goodwill by allocating the fair value of the reporting unit to all of the assets and liabilities other than goodwill (including any unrecognized intangible assets). The amount of impairment loss is equal to the excess of the book value of the goodwill over the implied fair value of goodwill.

In performing our annual review of goodwill balances for impairment, we estimate the fair value of each of our reporting units based on projected future operating results and cash flows, market assumptions and comparative market multiple methods. Determining fair value requires significant estimates and assumptions based on an evaluation of a number of factors, such as marketplace participants, relative market share, new student interest, student retention, future expansion or contraction expectations, amount and timing of future cash flows and the discount rate applied to the cash flows. Projected future operating results and cash flows used for valuation purposes may reflect considerable improvements relative to recent historical periods with respect to, among other things, revenue growth and operating margins. Although we believe our projected future operating results and cash flows and related estimates regarding fair values are based on reasonable assumptions, historically projected operating results and cash flows have not always been achieved. The failure of one of our reporting units to achieve projected operating results and cash flows in the near term or long term may reduce the estimated fair value of the reporting unit below its carrying value and result in the recognition of a goodwill impairment charge. Significant management judgment is necessary to evaluate the impact of operating and macroeconomic changes and to estimate future cash flows. Assumptions used in our impairment evaluations, such as forecasted growth rates and our cost of capital, are based on the best available market information and are consistent with our internal forecasts and operating plans. In addition to cash flow estimates, our valuations are sensitive to the rate used to discount cash flows and future growth assumptions. These assumptions could be adversely impacted by certain of the risks discussed in "Risk Factors" in Item 1A on Form 10-K.

4. Recent Accounting Pronouncements (in part)

In July 2012, the Financial Accounting Standards Board ("FASB") issued Accounting Standards Update ("ASU") 2012-02, *Intangibles-Goodwill and Other (Topic 350): Testing Indefinite-Lived Intangible Assets for Impairment*. The amendments in this ASU give entities the option to first assess qualitative factors to determine whether the existence of events and circumstances indicates that it is more likely than not that an indefinite-lived intangible asset is impaired. If impairment is indicated, the fair value of the indefinite–lived intangible asset should be determined and the quantitative impairment test should be performed by comparing the fair value with the carrying amount in accordance with Subtopic 350-30; if impairment is not indicated, the entity is not required to take further action. ASU 2012-02 is effective for annual and interim impairment tests performed for fiscal years beginning after September 15, 2012. Early adoption is permitted, including for annual and interim impairment tests performed as of a date before July 27, 2012, if a public entity's financial statements for the most recent annual or interim period have not yet been issued. We have elected to early adopt this guidance, and the early adoption did not impact the presentation of our financial condition, results of operation and disclosures.

10. Goodwill and Other Intangible Assets (in part)

Changes in the carrying amount of goodwill for continuing operations during the years ended December 31, 2012 and 2011 are as follows by segment:

(Dollars in thousands)	CTU	AIU	Health Education	Culinary Arts	Design & Technology	International	Transitional	Total
Goodwill balance as of December 31, 2010[1]	$46,148	$41,418	$106,497	$73,748	$31,899	$44,037	$30,840	$374,587
Goodwill impairment	(210)	—	(64,626)	(73,748)	—	—	(30,113)	(168,697)
Business acquisition	—	—	—	—	8,853	—	—	8,853
Effect of foreign currency exchange rate changes	—	—	—	—	—	(2,117)	—	(2,117)
Goodwill balance as of December 31, 2011[1]	$45,938	$41,418	$ 41,871	$ —	$ 40,752	$41,920	$ 727	$ 212,626
Goodwill impairment	—	—	(41,871)	—	(40,752)	—	(727)	(83,350)
Business acquisition	—	—	—	—	—	2,896	—	2,896
Effect of foreign currency exchange rate changes	—	—	—	—	—	853	—	853
Goodwill balance as of December 31, 2012	$45,938	$41,418	$ —	$ —	$ —	$45,669	$ —	$ 133,025

[1] Goodwill balances were reclassified upon the reorganization of our reporting segments during the fourth quarter of 2012.

We performed our annual impairment testing of goodwill as of October 1, 2012 and determined that none of our reporting units were at risk of failing the first step of the goodwill impairment test as of October 1, 2012.

During the second quarter of 2012, in conjunction with the quarterly review process, we concluded that certain indicators existed to suggest the Health Education and Design & Technology reporting units were at risk of their respective carrying values exceeding fair values as of June 30, 2012. A significant amount of judgment is involved in determining if an indicator of impairment has occurred. These indicators included, but were not limited to, a decline in cash flows, a decline in actual revenue and earnings as compared to projected results and a marked decline in new student interest which negatively impacted our overall student population.

In calculating the fair value for both of these reporting units, we performed extensive valuation analyses, utilizing both income and market approaches, in our goodwill assessment process. The following describes the valuation methodologies used to derive the fair value of our reporting units:
- *Income Approach:* To determine the estimated fair value of each reporting unit, we discount the expected cash flows which are developed by management. We estimate our future cash flows after considering current economic conditions and trends, estimated future operating results, our views of growth rates and anticipated future economic and regulatory conditions. The discount rate used represents the estimated weighted average cost of capital, which reflects the overall level of inherent risk involved in our future expected cash flows and the rate of return an outside investor would expect to earn. To estimate cash flows beyond the final year of our models, we use a terminal value approach and incorporate the present value of the resulting terminal value into our estimate of fair value.
- *Market-Based Approach:* To corroborate the results of the income approach described above, we estimate the fair value of our reporting units using several market-based approaches, including the guideline company method, which focuses on comparing our risk profile and growth prospects to select reasonably similar publicly traded companies.

The determination of estimated fair value of each reporting unit requires significant estimates and assumptions, and as such, these fair value measurements are categorized as Level 3 per ASC Topic 820. These estimates and assumptions primarily include, but are not limited to, the discount rate, terminal growth rates, operating cash flow projections and capital expenditure forecasts. Due to the inherent uncertainty involved in deriving those estimates, actual results could differ from those estimates. We evaluate the merits of each significant assumption used, both individually and in the aggregate, to determine the fair value of each reporting unit for reasonableness.

As a result of the interim impairment test during the second quarter of 2012, we recorded goodwill impairment charges of $41.9 million and $41.5 million within Health Education and Design & Technology, respectively, during the second quarter of 2012; of which $0.7 million was reclassified to Transitional Schools as a result of the segment reorganization in the fourth quarter of 2012. Of the total charge, $9.8 million will be deductible for income tax purposes. In addition, in conjunction with the second step of the goodwill impairment test, fair values are assigned to all assets and liabilities for each reporting unit, including all other intangible assets, as if the reporting unit had been acquired in a business combination. The fair values for our indefinite-lived trade names within the Health Education segment declined below their respective carrying values, and as a result, we recorded a $1.0 million charge for our Sanford-Brown and Missouri College trade names during the second quarter of 2012.

In connection with the acquisition of Luxury Attitude during the second quarter of 2012, we recorded goodwill of approximately $2.9 million. During December 2012, we acquired ESC Chambéry. The preliminary allocation of purchase price resulted in a bargain purchase of $0.7 million, which was recorded as a gain on purchase within other income (expense) on our consolidated statement of income and comprehensive income for the year ended December 31, 2012. The preliminary purchase price allocation is subject to change upon finalization of the closing balance sheet.

CHANGE IN ACCOUNTING PRINCIPLE—INSURANCE CONTRACTS

1.50 AMERICAN INTERNATIONAL GROUP, INC. (DEC)
NOTES TO CONSOLIDATED FINANCIAL STATEMENTS

2. Summary of Significant Accounting Policies (in part)

Accounting Standards Adopted During 2012 (in part)

We adopted the following accounting standards on January 1, 2012

Accounting for Costs Associated with Acquiring or Renewing Insurance Contracts

In October 2010, the FASB issued an accounting standard update that amends the accounting for costs incurred by insurance companies that can be capitalized in connection with acquiring or renewing insurance contracts. The standard clarifies how to determine whether the costs incurred in connection with the acquisition of new or renewal insurance contracts qualify as DAC. We adopted the standard retrospectively on January 1, 2012.

Deferred policy acquisition costs represent those costs that are incremental and directly related to the successful acquisition of new or renewal insurance contracts. We defer incremental costs that result directly from, and are essential to, the acquisition or renewal of an insurance contract. Such costs generally include agent or broker commissions and bonuses, premium taxes, and medical and inspection fees that would not have been incurred if the insurance contract had not been acquired or renewed. Each cost is analyzed to assess whether it is fully deferrable. We partially defer costs, including certain commissions, when we do not believe the entire cost is directly related to the acquisition or renewal of insurance contracts.

We also defer a portion of employee total compensation and payroll-related fringe benefits directly related to time spent performing specific acquisition or renewal activities, including costs associated with the time spent on underwriting, policy issuance and processing, and sales force contract selling. The amounts deferred are those that resulted in successful policy acquisition or renewal for each distribution channel and/or cost center from which the cost originates.

Advertising costs related to the issuance of insurance contracts that meet the direct-advertising criteria are deferred and amortized as part of DAC.

The method we use to amortize DAC for either short- or long-duration insurance contracts did not change as a result of the adoption of the standard.

The adoption of the standard resulted in a reduction to beginning of period retained earnings for the earliest period presented and a decrease in the amount of capitalized costs in connection with the acquisition or renewal of insurance contracts. Accordingly, we revised our historical financial statements and accompanying notes to the consolidated financial statements for the changes in DAC and associated changes in acquisition expenses and income taxes for affected entities and segments, including divested entities presented in continuing and discontinued operations.

The following table presents amounts previously reported as of December 31, 2011, to reflect the effect of the change due to the retrospective adoption of the standard, and the adjusted amounts that are reflected in our Consolidated Balance Sheet.

December 31, 2011	As Previously Reported	Effect of Change	As Currently Reported
(In millions)			
Balance Sheet:			
Deferred income taxes	$ 17,897	$ 1,718	$ 19,615
Deferred policy acquisition costs	14,026	(5,089)	8,937
Other assets	11,705	(42)	11,663
Total assets	556,467	(3,413)	553,054
Retained earnings	14,332	(3,558)	10,774
Accumulated other comprehensive income	6,336	145	6,481
Total AIG shareholders' equity	104,951	(3,413)	101,538

The following tables present amounts previously reported for the years ended December 31, 2011 and 2010 to reflect the effect of the change due to the retrospective adoption of the standard, and the adjusted amounts that are reflected in our Consolidated Statement of Operations and Consolidated Statement of Cash Flows.

Year Ended December 31, 2011	As Previously Reported[a]	Effect of Change	As Currently Reported
(Dollars in millions, except per share data)			
Statement of Operations:			
Total net realized capital gains	$ 681	$ 20	$ 701
Total revenues	59,792	20	59,812
Interest credited to policyholder account balances	4,446	21	4,467
Amortization of deferred acquisition costs	8,019	(2,533)	5,486
Other acquisition and other insurance expenses	6,091	2,367	8,458
Net (gain) loss on sale of properties and divested businesses	74	—	74
Total benefits, claims and expenses	59,840	(144)	59,696
Income (loss) from continuing operations before income tax benefit	(48)	164	116
Income tax benefit[b]	(17,696)	(1,728)	(19,424)
Income from continuing operations	17,648	1,892	19,540
Income from discontinued operations, net of income tax expense[c]	858	932	1,790
Net income	18,506	2,824	21,330
Net income attributable to AIG	17,798	2,824	20,622
Net income attributable to AIG common shareholders	16,986	2,824	19,810
Income per share attributable to AIG common shareholders:			
Basic and diluted			
Income from continuing operations	$ 8.98	$ 1.05	$ 10.03
Income from discontinued operations	$ 0.46	$ 0.52	$ 0.98

[a] Includes $140 million in Total net realized capital gains attributable to the effect of the reclassification of certain derivative activity discussed in Note 1 herein. Also includes the effect of the reclassification of ILFC as discontinued operations.

[b] Includes an adjustment to the deferred tax valuation allowance of $1.8 billion in the fourth quarter of 2011.

[c] Represents the effect on the gain on sale of AIG Star and AIG Edison which were sold in first quarter of 2011.

Year Ended December 31, 2010	As Previously Reported[a]	Effect of Change	As Currently Reported
(Dollars in millions, except per share data)			
Statement of Operations:			
Total net realized capital losses	$ (727)	$ 11	$ (716)
Total revenues	72,818	11	72,829
Interest credited to policyholder account balances	4,480	7	4,487
Amortization of deferred acquisition costs	9,134	(3,313)	5,821
Other acquisition and other insurance expenses	6,775	3,388	10,163
Net (gain) loss on sale of properties and divested businesses[b]	(17,767)	(1,799)	(19,566)
Total benefits, claims and expenses	54,301	(1,719)	52,582
Income from continuing operations before income tax expense	18,517	1,730	20,247
Income tax expense[c]	6,116	877	6,993
Income from continuing operations	12,401	853	13,254
Income (loss) from discontinued operations, net of income tax expense[d]	(2,388)	1,419	(969)
Net income	10,013	2,272	12,285
Net income attributable to AIG	7,786	2,272	10,058
Net income attributable to AIG common shareholders	1,583	463	2,046
Income (loss) per share attributable to AIG common shareholders:			
Basic and diluted			
Income from continuing operations	$ 15.23	$ 1.27	$ 16.50
Loss from discontinued operations	$ (3.63)	$ 2.11	$ (1.52)

[a] Includes $783 million in Total net realized capital gains attributable to the effect of the reclassification of certain derivative activity discussed in Note 1 herein. Also includes the effect of the reclassification of ILFC as discontinued operations.

[b] Represents the effect on the gain on sale of AIA ordinary shares, which were sold in the fourth quarter of 2010.

[c] Includes the tax impact to the AIA gain adjustment of $1.0 billion in the fourth quarter of 2010.

[d] Includes an adjustment to the after-tax gain on the sale of ALICO of $1.6 billion in the fourth quarter of 2010.

Adoption of the standard did not affect the previously reported totals for net cash flows provided by (used in) operating, investing, or financing activities, but did affect the following components of net cash flows provided by (used in) operating activities.

Year Ended December 31, 2011	As Previously Reported[a]	Effect of Change	As Currently Reported
(In millions)			
Cash flows from operating activities:			
Net income	$ 18,506	$ 2,824	$ 21,330
(Income) loss from discontinued operations	(858)	(932)	(1,790)
Adjustments to reconcile net income to net cash provided by (used in) operating activities:			
Noncash revenues, expenses, gains and losses included in income (loss):			
Unrealized gains in earnings—net	(937)	(20)	(957)
Depreciation and other amortization	7,935	(2,511)	5,424
Changes in operating assets and liabilities:			
Capitalization of deferred policy acquisition costs	(7,796)	2,367	(5,429)
Current and deferred income taxes—net	(18,333)	(1,728)	(20,061)
Total adjustments	(23,904)	(1,892)	(25,796)

Year Ended December 31, 2010	As Previously Reported[a]	Effect of Change	As Currently Reported
(In millions)			
Cash flows from operating activities:			
Net income	$ 10,013	$ 2,272	$ 12,285
(Income) loss from discontinued operations	2,388	(1,419)	969
Adjustments to reconcile net income to net cash provided by (used in) operating activities:			
Noncash revenues, expenses, gains and losses included in income (loss):			
Net (gains) losses on sales of divested businesses	(17,767)	(1,799)	(19,566)
Unrealized gains in earnings—net	(1,509)	(20)	(1,529)
Depreciation and other amortization	8,488	(2,511)	5,977
Changes in operating assets and liabilities:			
Capitalization of deferred policy acquisition costs	(8,300)	2,367	(5,933)
Current and deferred income taxes—net	7,780	(1,728)	6,052
Total adjustments	$ (5,201)	$ (1,892)	$ (7,093)

[a] Includes the effect of the reclassification of ILFC as discontinued operations.

For short-duration insurance contracts, starting in 2012, we elected to include anticipated investment income in our determination of whether the deferred policy acquisition costs are recoverable. We believe the inclusion of anticipated investment income in the recoverability analysis is a preferable accounting policy because it includes in the recoverability analysis the fact that there is a timing difference between when premiums are collected and in turn invested and when losses and related expenses are paid. This is considered a change in accounting principle that required retrospective application to all periods presented. Because we historically have not recorded any premium deficiency on our short-duration insurance contracts even without the inclusion of anticipated investment income, there were no changes to the historical financial statements for the change in accounting principle.

CHANGE IN ACCOUNTING PRINCIPLE—FAIR VALUE MEASUREMENTS

1.51 BERKSHIRE HATHAWAY INC. (DEC)
NOTES TO CONSOLIDATED FINANCIAL STATEMENTS

(1) Significant Accounting Policies and Practices (in part)

(g) Fair Value Measurements

As defined under GAAP, fair value is the price that would be received to sell an asset or paid to transfer a liability between market participants in the principal market or in the most advantageous market when no principal market exists. Adjustments to transaction prices or quoted market prices may be required in illiquid or disorderly markets in order to estimate fair value. Alternative valuation techniques may be appropriate under the circumstances to determine the value that would be received to sell an asset or paid to transfer a liability in an orderly transaction. Market participants are assumed to be independent, knowledgeable, able and willing to transact an exchange and not acting under duress. Nonperformance or credit risk is considered in determining the fair value of liabilities. Considerable judgment may be required in interpreting market data used to develop the estimates of fair value. Accordingly, estimates of fair value presented herein are not necessarily indicative of the amounts that could be realized in a current or future market exchange.

(t) New Accounting Pronouncements (in part)

As of January 1, 2012, we also adopted ASU 2011-04, "Amendments to Achieve Common Fair Value Measurement and Disclosure Requirements in U.S. GAAP and IFRSs." As a result of adopting ASU 2011-04, we have expanded our fair value disclosures.

(17) Fair Value Measurements

Our financial assets and liabilities are summarized below according to the fair value hierarchy. The carrying values of cash and cash equivalents, accounts receivable and accounts payable, accruals and other liabilities are considered to be reasonable estimates of their fair values. As of December 31, 2012 and 2011, the carrying values and fair values of financial assets and liabilities were as follows (in millions).

	Carrying Value	Fair Value	Quoted Prices (Level 1)	Significant Other Observable Inputs (Level 2)	Significant Unobservable Inputs (Level 3)
December 31, 2012—Assets and liabilities carried at fair value:					
Investments in fixed maturity securities:					
U.S. Treasury, U.S. government corporations and agencies	$ 2,775	$ 2,775	$ 1,225	$ 1,549	$ 1
States, municipalities and political subdivisions	2,913	2,913	—	2,912	1
Foreign governments	11,355	11,355	4,571	6,784	—
Corporate bonds	12,661	12,661	—	12,011	650
Mortgage-backed securities	2,587	2,587	—	2,587	—
Investments in equity securities	87,662	87,662	87,563	64	35
Other investments	15,750	15,750	—	—	15,750
Derivative contract assets[1]	220	220	1	128	91
Derivative contract liabilities:					
Railroad, utilities and energy[2]	234	234	10	217	7
Finance and financial products:					
Equity index put options	7,502	7,502	—	—	7,502
Credit default	429	429	—	—	429
Other	2	2	—	2	—
December 31, 2012—Assets and liabilities not carried at fair value:					
Other investments	$ 5,259	$ 6,134	$ —	$ —	$ 6,134
Loans and finance receivables	12,809	11,991	—	304	11,687
Notes payable and other borrowings:					
Insurance and other	13,535	14,284	—	14,284	—
Railroad, utilities and energy	36,156	42,074	—	42,074	—
Finance and financial products	13,045	14,005	—	13,194	811

	Carrying Value	Fair Value	Quoted Prices (Level 1)	Significant Other Observable Inputs (Level 2)	Significant Unobservable Inputs (Level 3)
December 31, 2011—Assets and liabilities carried at fair value:					
Investments in fixed maturity securities:					
U.S. Treasury, U.S. government corporations and agencies	$ 2,935	$ 2,935	$ 843	$ 2,090	$ 2
States, municipalities and political subdivisions	3,070	3,070	—	3,069	1
Foreign governments	10,843	10,843	4,444	6,265	134
Corporate bonds	12,448	12,448	—	11,801	647
Mortgage-backed securities	2,892	2,892	—	2,892	—
Investments in equity securities	76,991	76,991	76,906	63	22
Other investments	11,669	11,669	—	—	11,669
Derivative contract assets[1]	327	327	—	205	122
Derivative contract liabilities:					
Railroad, utilities and energy[2]	336	336	12	320	4
Finance and financial products:					
Equity index put options	8,499	8,499	—	—	8,499
Credit default	1,527	1,527	—	—	1,527
Other	113	113	—	113	—

[1] Included in other assets.
[2] Included in accounts payable, accruals and other liabilities.

As of December 31, 2011, the carrying values and fair values of financial assets and liabilities that are not carried at fair value were as follows (in millions).

	Carrying Value	Fair Value
Other investments	$ 5,252	$ 6,258
Loans and finance receivables	13,934	13,126
Notes payable and other borrowings:		
Insurance and other	13,768	14,334
Railroad, utilities and energy	32,580	38,257
Finance and financial products	14,036	14,959

The fair values of substantially all of our financial instruments were measured using market or income approaches. Considerable judgment may be required in interpreting market data used to develop the estimates of fair value. Accordingly, the estimates presented are not necessarily indicative of the amounts that could be realized in an actual current market exchange. The use of alternative market assumptions and/or estimation methodologies may have a material effect on the estimated fair value.

The hierarchy for measuring fair value consists of Levels 1 through 3, which are described below.

Level 1—Inputs represent unadjusted quoted prices for identical assets or liabilities exchanged in active markets. Substantially all of our investments in equity securities are traded on an exchange in active markets and fair values are based on the closing prices as of the balance sheet date.

Level 2—Inputs include directly or indirectly observable inputs (other than Level 1 inputs) such as quoted prices for similar assets or liabilities exchanged in active or inactive markets; quoted prices for identical assets or liabilities exchanged in inactive markets; other inputs that may be considered in fair value determinations of the assets or liabilities, such as interest rates and yield curves, volatilities, prepayment speeds, loss severities, credit risks and default rates; and inputs that are derived principally from or corroborated by observable market data by correlation or other means. Fair values of investments in fixed maturity securities and notes payable and other borrowings are primarily based on price evaluations which incorporate market prices for identical instruments in inactive markets and market data available for instruments with similar characteristics. Pricing evaluations generally reflect discounted expected future cash flows, which incorporate yield curves for instruments with similar characteristics, such as credit rating, estimated duration and yields for other instruments of the issuer or entities in the same industry sector.

Level 3—Inputs include unobservable inputs used in the measurement of assets and liabilities. Management is required to use its own assumptions regarding unobservable inputs because there is little, if any, market activity in the assets or liabilities and we may be unable to corroborate the related observable inputs. Unobservable inputs require management to make certain projections and assumptions about the information that would be used by market participants in pricing assets or liabilities. Fair value measurements of non-exchange traded derivative contracts and certain other investments are based primarily on valuation models, discounted cash flow models or other valuation techniques that are believed to be used by market participants.

Reconciliations of assets and liabilities measured and carried at fair value on a recurring basis with the use of significant unobservable inputs (Level 3) for each of the three years ending December 31, 2012 follow (in millions).

	Investments in Fixed Maturity Securities	Investments in Equity Securities	Other Investments	Net Derivative Contract Liabilities
Balance at December 31, 2009	$918	$304	$20,614	$(9,196)
Gains (losses) included in:				
Earnings	—	—	1,305	471
Other comprehensive income	16	(8)	(358)	—
Regulatory assets and liabilities	—	—	—	(33)
Acquisitions, dispositions and settlements	9	(1)	(3,972)	533
Transfers into (out of) Level 3	(142)	(260)	—	3
Balance at December 31, 2010	801	35	17,589	(8,222)
Gains (losses) included in:				
Earnings	—	—	—	(2,035)
Other comprehensive income	5	(13)	(2,120)	(3)
Regulatory assets and liabilities	—	—	—	144
Acquisitions	17	—	5,000	(68)
Dispositions	(39)	—	—	—
Settlements, net	—	—	—	275
Transfers into (out of) Level 3	—	—	(8,800)	1
Balance at December 31, 2011	784	22	11,669	(9,908)
Gains (losses) included in:				
Earnings	—	—	—	1,873
Other comprehensive income	5	13	4,081	—
Regulatory assets and liabilities	—	—	—	(2)
Dispositions	(8)	—	—	—
Settlements, net	—	—	—	190
Transfers out of Level 3	(129)	—	—	—
Balance at December 31, 2012	$652	$35	$15,750	$(7,847)

During 2011, we transferred our investments in GS Preferred Stock and GE Preferred Stock from Level 3 to Level 2 given the then pending redemptions of the investments which occurred on April 18, 2011 and October 17, 2011, respectively. On September 1, 2011, we acquired preferred stock and common stock warrants of the Bank of America Corporation at an aggregate cost of $5 billion.

Gains and losses included in earnings are included as components of investment gains/losses, derivative gains/losses and other revenues, as appropriate and are related to changes in valuations of derivative contracts and settlement transactions. Gains and losses included in other comprehensive income are included as components of the net change in unrealized appreciation of investments and the reclassification of investment appreciation in earnings, as appropriate in the Consolidated Statements of Comprehensive Income.

Quantitative information as of December 31, 2012, with respect to assets and liabilities measured and carried at fair value on a recurring basis with the use of significant unobservable inputs (Level 3) follows (in millions).

	Fair Value	Principal Valuation Techniques	Unobservable Input	Weighted Average
Other investments:				
Preferred stocks	$11,860	Discounted cash flow	Expected duration	10 years
			Discount for transferability restrictions and subordination	97 basis points
Common stock warrants	3,890	Warrant pricing model	Discount for transferability and hedging restrictions	19%
Net derivative liabilities:				
Equity index put options	7,502	Option pricing model	Volatility	21%
Credit default-states/municipalities	421	Discounted cash flow	Credit spreads	85 basis points

For certain credit default and other derivative contracts where we could not corroborate that the fair values or the inputs were observable in the market, fair values were based on non-binding price indications obtained from third party sources. Management reviewed these values relative to the terms of the contracts, the current facts, circumstances and market conditions, and concluded they were reasonable. We did not adjust these prices and therefore, they have been excluded from the preceding table.

Our other investments that are carried at fair value consist of a few relatively large private placement transactions and include perpetual preferred stocks and common stock warrants. These investments are subject to contractual restrictions on transferability and/or provisions that prevent us from economically hedging our investments. In applying discounted estimated cash flow techniques in valuing the perpetual preferred stocks, we made assumptions regarding the expected durations of the investments, as the issuers may have the right to redeem or convert these investments. We also made estimates regarding the impact of subordination, as the preferred stocks have a lower priority in liquidation than the investment grade debt instruments of the issuers, which affected the discount rates. In valuing the common stock warrants, we used a warrant valuation model. While most of the inputs to the model are observable, we are subject to the aforementioned contractual restrictions. We have applied discounts with respect to the contractual restrictions. Increases or decreases to these inputs would result in decreases or increases to the fair values.

Our equity index put option and credit default contracts are not exchange traded and certain contract terms are not standard in derivatives markets. For example, we are not required to post collateral under most of our contracts and many contracts have long durations, and therefore are illiquid. For these and other reasons, we classified these contracts as Level 3. The methods we use to value these contracts are those that we believe market participants would use in determining exchange prices with respect to our contracts.

We value equity index put option contracts based on the Black-Scholes option valuation model. Inputs to this model include current index price, contract duration, dividend and interest rate inputs (which include a Berkshire non-performance input) which are observable. However, the valuation of long-duration options is inherently subjective, given the lack of observable transactions and prices, and acceptable values may be subject to wide ranges. Expected volatility inputs represent our expectations after considering the remaining duration of each contract and that the contracts will remain outstanding until the expiration dates without offsetting transactions occurring in the interim. Increases or decreases in the volatility inputs will produce increases or decreases in the fair values.

Our state and municipality credit default contract values reflect credit spreads, contract durations, interest rates, bond prices and other inputs believed to be used by market participants in estimating fair value. We utilize discounted cash flow valuation models, which incorporate the aforementioned inputs as well as our own estimates of credit spreads for states and municipalities where there is no observable input. Increases or decreases to the credit spreads will produce increases or decreases in the fair values.

CHANGE IN ACCOUNTING ESTIMATES

1.52 DIRECTV (DEC)
NOTES TO THE CONSOLIDATED FINANCIAL STATEMENTS

Note 3: Change in Accounting Estimate

Depreciable Lives of Leased Set-Top Receivers. We currently lease most set-top receivers provided to new and existing subscribers and therefore capitalize the cost of those set-top receivers. We depreciate capitalized set-top receivers over the estimated useful life of the equipment. As a result of the completion of an extensive evaluation of the estimated useful life of the set-top receivers in the third quarter of 2011, including consideration of historical write-offs, improved efficiencies in our refurbishment program, improved set-top receiver failure rates over time and management's judgment of the risk of technological obsolescence, we determined that the estimated useful life of HD set-top receivers used in our DIRECTV U.S. business has increased to four years, from three years as previously estimated. We continue to depreciate standard-definition, or SD, set-top receivers at DIRECTV U.S. over a three-year estimated useful life. We accounted for this change in the useful life of the HD set-top receivers at DIRECTV U.S. as a change in an accounting estimate beginning July 1, 2011. This change had the effect of reducing depreciation and amortization expense and increasing both net income attributable to DIRECTV and earnings per share in our consolidated results of operations as follows:

(Dollars in Millions, Except Per Share Amounts)	Years Ended December 31,	
	2012	2011
Depreciation and amortization expense	$(176)	$(141)
Net income attributable to DIRECTV	109	86
Basic earnings attributable to DIRECTV common stockholders per common share	$ 0.17	$ 0.12
Diluted earnings attributable to DIRECTV common stockholders per common share	$ 0.17	$ 0.11

1.53 CITIGROUP INC. (DEC)

MANAGEMENT'S DISCUSSION AND ANALYSIS OF FINANCIAL CONDITION AND RESULTS OF OPERATIONS (in part)

Managing Global Risk (in part)

Credit Risk (in part)

Citigroup Residential Mortgages—Representations and Warranties (in part)

Repurchase Reserve—Whole Loan Sales

To date, issues related to (i) misrepresentation of facts by either the borrower or a third party (e.g., income, employment, debts, etc.), (ii) appraisal issues (e.g., an error or misrepresentation of value), and (iii) program requirements (e.g., a loan that does not meet investor guidelines, such as contractual interest rate) have been the primary drivers of Citi's repurchases and make-whole payments to the GSEs. The type of defect that results in a repurchase or make-whole payment has varied and will likely continue to vary over time. There has not been a meaningful difference in Citi's incurred or estimated loss for any particular type of defect.

The repurchase reserve is based on various assumptions which, as referenced above, are primarily based on Citi's historical repurchase activity with the GSEs. As of December 31, 2012, the most significant assumptions used to calculate the reserve levels are the: (i) probability of a claim based on correlation between loan characteristics and repurchase claims; (ii) claims appeal success rates; and (iii) estimated loss per repurchase or make-whole payment. In addition, Citi considers reimbursements estimated to be received from third-party sellers, which are generally based on Citi's analysis of its most recent collection trends and the financial solvency or viability of the third-party sellers, in estimating its repurchase reserve.

During 2012, Citi recorded an additional reserve of $706 million (of which $164 million was in the fourth quarter of 2012) relating to its whole loan sales repurchase exposure. The change in estimate in fourth quarter and full year 2012 primarily resulted from (i) a continued heightened focus by the GSEs resulting in increasing estimates of repurchase claims, and (ii) increasing trends in repurchase claims, repurchases/make-whole payments, and default rates, especially for higher risk loans associated with servicing sold to a third party in the fourth quarter of 2010. These increases were partially offset by an improvement in expected recoveries from third-party sellers. Citi's claims appeal success rate remained stable during 2012, with approximately half of repurchase claims successfully appealed and thus resulting in no loss to Citi. Although the GSEs continued to exhibit elevated loan documentation requests during 2012, which could ultimately lead to higher claims and repurchases in future periods, Citi continues to believe the activity in and change in estimate relating to its repurchase reserve will remain volatile in the near term.

As referenced above, the repurchase reserve estimation process for potential whole loan representation and warranty claims relies on various assumptions that involve numerous estimates and judgments, including with respect to certain future events, and thus entails inherent uncertainty. Citi estimates that the range of reasonably possible loss for whole loan sale representation and warranty claims in excess of amounts accrued as of December 31, 2012 could be up to $0.6 billion. This estimate was derived by modifying the key assumptions discussed above to reflect management's judgment regarding reasonably possible adverse changes to those assumptions. Citi's estimate of reasonably possible loss is based on currently available information, significant judgment and numerous assumptions that are subject to change.

The table below sets forth the activity in the repurchase reserve for each of the quarterly periods below:

(In millions of dollars)	Three Months Ended				
	December 31, 2012	September 30, 2012	June 30, 2012	March 31, 2012	December 31, 2011
Balance, beginning of period	$1,516	$1,476	$1,376	$1,188	$1,076
Additions for new sales[1]	6	7	4	6	7
Change in estimate[2]	173	200	242	335	306
Utilizations	(130)	(167)	(146)	(153)	(201)
Balance, end of period	$1,565	$1,516	$1,476	$1,376	$1,188

[1] Reflects new whole loan sales, primarily to the GSEs.

[2] Change in estimate for the fourth quarter of 2012 includes $164 million related to whole loan sales to the GSEs and private investors and $9 million related to loans sold through private-label securitizations.

CORRECTION OF ERRORS

1.54 GENUINE PARTS COMPANY (DEC)
NOTES TO CONSOLIDATED FINANCIAL STATEMENTS

1. Summary of Significant Accounting Policies (in part)

Customer Sales Returns

Subsequent to September 30, 2012, the Company reconsidered its interpretation of the authoritative literature related to accounting for potential sales returns of automotive parts sold by the NAPA distribution businesses in its automotive segment. Upon review, the Company concluded that there was an error in the Company's method of accounting for such potential sales returns. The error is not material to any individual year, but material on a cumulative basis and, therefore, an adjustment to correct the cumulative effect of the error, as calculated at December 31, 2012, has been reflected on the Company's consolidated balance sheets and is summarized below as of December 31, 2011. The consolidated statements of income and comprehensive income for 2012, 2011, and 2010 presented herein have not been adjusted because the impact of the correction of the error is not material to these financial statements.

The effect of the understatement of inventory (included in merchandise inventories, net and other assets) and customer deposits (included in accrued expenses and other long-term liabilities) resulted in an adjustment to the consolidated balance sheet increasing both assets and liabilities with the net result being an immaterial impact on working capital. The impact on retained earnings, net of deferred taxes, is $39,228,000, or less than 2% of consolidated equity as of December 31, 2012 and 2011. Retained earnings as of January 1, 2010 has been adjusted by $39,228,000 on the consolidated statements of equity. The impact on net income was less than $3,000,000, or less than 1% of consolidated net income for each of the years ended December 31, 2012, 2011, and 2010; therefore, the Company recorded the errors arising in these three years as of January 1, 2010. The impact on the consolidated statements of cash flows was considered immaterial for each of the years ended December 31, 2012, 2011, and 2010.

	December 31, 2011		
(In thousands)	As Previously Reported	Adjustment	As Revised
Merchandise inventories, net	$2,261,997	$ 178,114	$2,440,111
Total current assets	4,576,596	178,114	4,754,710
Deferred tax asset	250,906	10,702	261,608
Other assets	272,110	134,367	406,477
Total assets	$5,879,591	$ 323,183	$6,202,774
Other accrued expenses	$ 116,921	$ 214,661	$ 331,582
Income taxes payable	35,267	(14,186)	21,081
Total current liabilities	1,812,073	200,475	2,012,548
Other long-term liabilities	280,978	161,936	442,914
Retained earnings	3,109,622	(39,228)	3,070,394
Total parent equity	2,783,235	(39,228)	2,744,007
Total equity	2,792,819	(39,228)	2,753,591
Total liabilities and equity	$5,879,591	$ 323,183	$6,202,774

1.55 GREIF, INC. (OCT)
NOTES TO CONSOLIDATED FINANCIAL STATEMENTS

Note 19—Correction of Errors and Restatement

As previously disclosed in its Quarterly Report on Form 10-Q for the fiscal quarter ended July 31, 2012 (the "preceding Form 10-Q"), the Company's internal audit process identified deficiencies in internal controls over financial reporting within its Rigid Industrial Packaging & Services business unit in Brazil and financial statement errors in that business unit were discovered in several prior periods. Consequently, the Company restated certain prior period amounts in the preceding Form 10-Q. During the fourth quarter of 2012, the Company concluded its review of internal controls in that business unit and in the other business units in Latin America. This further investigation identified additional prior period errors related to the Brazil business unit. The errors related to improperly stated reserves, inventory misstatements, and asset balances which the Company was unable to substantiate.

During the fourth quarter of 2012, the Company also identified several prior period errors related to accounting for non-routine and complex activities and transactions. The errors related primarily to the financing structures of two of the Company's joint ventures formed in 2010 and 2011, which resulted in reclassifications to the balance sheets and statements of cash flows. In addition, there were other errors that resulted in balance sheet reclassifications between noncontrolling interest and foreign currency translation.

The impact of these additional prior period errors, plus the prior period errors reported in the preceding Form 10-Q, were not material to the Company in any of those years. However, the aggregate amount of prior period errors, net of tax, of $25.6 million, including the $18.4 million reported in the preceding Form 10-Q, would have been material to the Company's current year consolidated statement of income. The Company has corrected these errors for all prior periods presented, including each of the quarters ended in 2012, by restating the consolidated financial statements and other financial information included herein. The adjustments were not material to the 2012 quarters which were also adjusted.

The following are the previously stated and corrected balances of certain consolidated statements of income, consolidated balance sheets and consolidated statements of cash flows. The "As Reported" amounts are the amounts reported in the Annual Report on Form 10-K for the fiscal year ended October 31, 2011 (Dollars in millions, except per share amounts):

	For the Year Ended October 31, 2011		
	As Reported	Adjustments	As Adjusted
Net Sales	$4,247.9	$ 0.3	$4,248.2
Cost of products sold	3,446.8	3.0	3,449.8
Gross profit	801.1	(2.7)	798.4
Selling, general and administrative expenses	448.4	4.9	453.3
(Gain) on disposal of properties, plants and equipment, net	(14.9)	(1.2)	(16.1)
Operating profit	337.1	(6.4)	330.7
Interest expense, net	79.6	(3.6)	76.0
Income before income tax expense and equity earnings of unconsolidated affilitates, net	243.4	(2.8)	240.6
Income tax expense	71.1	(6.1)	65.0
Net income	177.1	3.3	180.4
Net (income) loss attibutable to noncontrolling interests	(1.1)	(1.8)	(2.9)
Net income attributable to Greif, Inc.	176.0	1.5	177.5
Basic Earnings per Share Attributable to Greif, Inc. Common Shareholders:			
Class A Common Stock	$ 3.02	$0.03	$ 3.05
Class B Common Stock	$ 4.52	$0.04	$ 4.56
Diluted Earnings per Share Attributable to Greif, Inc. Common Shareholders:			
Class A Common Stock	$ 3.01	$0.03	$ 3.04
Class B Common Stock	$ 4.52	$0.04	$ 4.56

	October 31, 2011		
	As Reported	Adjustments	As Adjusted
Current Assets			
Trade accounts receivable, less allowance	$ 568.6	$ (7.2)	$ 561.4
Inventories	432.5	(3.5)	429.0
Net assets held for sale	11.4	(2.0)	9.4
Prepaid expenses and other current assets	140.0	(7.5)	132.5
Total current assets	1,305.3	(20.2)	1,285.1
Long-Term Assets			
Goodwill	1,004.9	(2.3)	1,002.6
Other intangible assets, net of amortization	229.8	(1.0)	228.8
Deferred tax assets	70.6	4.4	75.0
Other long-term assets	92.2	1.2	93.4
Total long-term assets	1,466.7	2.3	1,469.0
Properties, Plants and Equipment			
Machinery and equipment	1,389.0	(0.6)	1,388.4
Total properties, plants and equipment, net	1,435.3	(0.6)	1,434.7
Total assets	4,207.3	(18.5)	4,188.8
Current Liabilities			
Accounts payable	487.8	5.5	493.3
Other current liabilities	167.7	(3.3)	164.4
Total current liabilities	929.8	2.2	932.0
Long-Term Liabilities			
Long-term debt	1,345.1	26.3	1,371.4
Deferred tax liabilities	196.7	(0.1)	196.6
Other long-term liabilities	203.3	3.1	206.4
Total long-term liabilities	1,885.3	29.4	1,914.7
Shareholders' Equity			
Retained earnings	1,401.7	(25.7)	1,376.0
Foreign currency translation	(46.4)	4.5	(41.9)
Total Greif, Inc. shareholders' equity	1,235.4	(21.2)	1,214.2
Noncontrolling interests	156.8	(28.9)	127.9
Total shareholders' equity	1,392.2	(50.1)	1,342.1
Total liabilities and shareholders' equity	4,207.3	(18.5)	4,188.8

(continued)

	For the Year Ended October 31, 2010		
	As Reported	Adjustments	As Adjusted
Net sales	$3,461.5	$ 0.3	$3,461.8
Cost of products sold	2,757.9	2.5	2,760.4
Gross profit	703.6	(2.2)	701.4
Selling, general and administrative expenses	362.9	2.2	365.1
Operating profit	325.4	(4.4)	321.0
Interest expense, net	65.8	(0.3)	65.5
Income before income tax expense and equity earnings of unconsolidated affilitates, net	252.5	(4.1)	248.4
Income tax expense	40.6	2.9	43.5
Net income	215.5	(7.0)	208.5
Net income attributable to noncontrolling interests	(5.5)	(0.2)	(5.7)
Net income attributable to Greif, Inc.	210.0	(7.2)	202.8
Basic Earnings per Share Attributable to Greif, Inc. Common Shareholders:			
Class A Common Stock	$ 3.60	$(0.12)	$ 3.48
Class B Common Stock	$ 5.40	$(0.19)	$ 5.21
Diluted Earnings per Share Attributable to Greif, Inc. Common Shareholders:			
Class A Common Stock	$ 3.58	$(0.12)	$ 3.46
Class B Common Stock	$ 5.40	$(0.19)	$ 5.21

	October 31, 2010		
	As Reported	Adjustments	As Adjusted
Current Assets			
Trade accounts receivable, less allowance	$ 480.2	$ (5.3)	$ 474.9
Inventories	396.6	(1.5)	395.1
Prepaid expenses and other current assets	134.3	(6.6)	127.7
Total current assets	1,149.3	(13.4)	1,135.9
Long-Term Assets			
Goodwill	709.7	(2.3)	707.4
Other intangible assets, net of amortization	173.2	(0.7)	172.5
Deferred tax assets	30.0	1.3	31.3
Total long-term assets	1,057.4	(1.7)	1,055.7
Properties, Plants and Equipment			
Machinery and equipment	1,319.3	(1.8)	1,317.5
Total properties, plants and equipment, net	1,291.7	(1.8)	1,289.9
Total assets	3,498.4	(16.9)	3,481.5
Current Liabilities			
Accounts payable	467.9	5.3	473.2
Other current liabilities	123.8	(0.3)	123.5
Total current liabilities	781.3	5.0	786.3
Long-Term Liabilities			
Deferred tax liabilities	180.5	(0.1)	180.4
Other long-term liabilities	116.9	5.2	122.1
Total long-term liabilities	1,381.2	5.1	1,386.3
Shareholders' Equity			
Retained earnings	1,323.5	(27.2)	1,296.3
Foreign currency translation	0.4	(14.1)	(13.7)
Total Greif, Inc. shareholders' equity	1,234.5	(41.3)	1,193.2
Noncontrolling interests	101.4	14.3	115.7
Total shareholders' equity	1,335.9	(27.0)	1,308.9
Total liabilities and shareholders' equity	3,498.4	(16.9)	3,481.5

	For the Year Ended October 31, 2010		
	As Reported	Adjustments	As Adjusted
Cash Flows From Operating Activities:			
Net cash provided by operating activities	178.1	—	178.1
Cash Flows From Investing Activities:			
Acquisitions of companies, net of cash acquired	(179.4)	(98.2)	(277.6)
Net cash used in investing activities	(327.2)	(98.2)	(425.4)
Cash flows From Financing Activities:			
Proceeds from joint venture partner	—	98.2	98.2
Net cash provided by (used in) financing activities	145.9	98.2	244.1

(continued)

	October 31, 2009		
	As Reported	Adjustments	As Adjusted
Retained Earnings	$1,206.6	$(20.2)	$1,186.4
Noncontrolling interests	7.0	3.9	10.9
Accumulated Other Comprehensive Income (Loss)	(107.8)	(3.9)	(111.7)
Shareholders' Equity	1,087.0	(20.2)	1,066.8

1.56 THE L.S. STARRETT COMPANY (JUN)
NOTES TO CONSOLIDATED FINANCIAL STATEMENTS

17. Prior Period Adjustments

During the first quarter of fiscal 2012, the Company identified a prior period error in the method of calculating compensation expense imputed under the Employee Stock Purchase Plan (ESPP) which had accumulated over a period of years. This error, which was immaterial to previously issued financial statements, resulted in an understatement of compensation expense in the Consolidated Statement of Operations for prior periods. The recorded balance of additional paid-in capital was likewise understated in the consolidated balance sheets for prior periods. The Company evaluated the effects of this error on prior periods' consolidated financial statements, individually and in the aggregate, in accordance with the guidance in ASC Topic 250, Accounting Changes and Error Corrections, ASC Topic 250-10-S99-1, Assessing Materiality, and ASC Topic 250-10-S99-2, Considering the Effects of Prior Year Misstatements when Quantifying Misstatements in Current Year Financial Statements ("ASC 250"), and concluded that no prior period is materially misstated. In order to correct this immaterial error, the Company has revised the accompanying statements of stockholders' equity and comprehensive income (loss) as of the earliest period presented (June 27, 2009) to decrease retained earnings by $548,000 and to increase additional paid-in capital by the same amount. We made no adjustments to the accompanying fiscal 2011 and 2010 statements of operations and cash flows due to the deminimis impact of the errors to those statements.

During the fourth quarter of fiscal 2012, the Company identified a prior period error in the estimate of a potential income tax exposure arising in fiscal 2008. This error, which was immaterial to previously issued financial statements, resulted in an understatement of income tax expense in the consolidated statement of operations for such fiscal year. The recorded balance of other tax obligations was likewise understated in the consolidated balance sheets for since fiscal 2008. The Company evaluated the effects of this error on prior periods' consolidated financial statements, individually and in the aggregate, in accordance with the guidance in ASC 250 and concluded that no prior period financial statements are materially misstated. In order to correct this immaterial error, the Company has revised the accompanying statements of stockholders' equity and comprehensive income (loss) as of the earliest period presented (June 27, 2009) to decrease retained earnings by $677,000 and to increase other tax obligations by the same amount. No adjustments were required to be made to the accompanying fiscal 2011 and 2010 statements of operations and cash flows.

Consolidation

RECOGNITION AND MEASUREMENT

1.57 FASB ASC 810-10-10 states that the purpose of consolidated financial statements is to present, primarily for the benefit of the owners and creditors of the parent, the results of operations and the financial position of a parent and all its subsidiaries as if the consolidated group were a single economic entity. It is presumed that consolidated financial statements are more meaningful than separate financial statements and are usually necessary for a fair presentation when one of the entities in the consolidated group directly or indirectly has a controlling financial interest in the other entities.

1.58 As explained by FASB ASC 810-10-05-8, the "General" subsections of FASB ASC 810, *Consolidation*, apply to certain legal entities in which equity investors do not have sufficient equity at risk for the legal entity to finance its activities without additional subordinated financial support, or as a group, the holders of the equity investment at risk lack any of the following three characteristics:
- The power, through voting or similar rights, to direct the activities of a legal entity that most significantly affect the entity's economic performance
- The obligation to absorb the expected losses of the legal entity
- The right to receive the expected residual returns of the legal entity

Consolidated financial statements are usually necessary for a fair presentation if one of the entities in the consolidated group directly or indirectly has a controlling financial interest, typically a majority voting interest. Application of the majority voting interest requirement to certain types of entities may not identify the party with a controlling financial interest because that interest may be achieved through other arrangements. FASB ASC 810-10-25-38A explains that a reporting entity with a variable interest in a variable interest entity (VIE) should assess whether the reporting entity has a controlling financial interest in the VIE and, thus, is the VIE's primary beneficiary. The reporting enterprise with a variable interest(s) that provides the reporting entity with a controlling financial interest in a VIE will have both the following characteristics: (*a*) the power to direct the activities of a VIE that most significantly affect the VIE's performance and (*b*) the obligation to absorb losses of the VIE that could potentially be significant to the VIE or the right to receive benefits from the VIE that could potentially be significant to the VIE. Only one reporting entity, if any, is expected to be identified as the primary beneficiary of a VIE. Although more than one reporting entity could have the obligation to absorb losses previously mentioned, only one reporting entity (if any) will have the power to direct the activities of a VIE that most significantly affect the VIE's economic performance. Further, the concept of a qualifying special-purpose entity no longer exists in FASB ASC.

1.59 FASB ASC 810 also establishes accounting and reporting standards for the noncontrolling interest in a subsidiary and the deconsolidation of a subsidiary. A *noncontrolling interest* is the portion of equity (net assets) in a subsidiary not directly or indirectly attributable to a parent. FASB ASC 810-10-45-16 requires the entity to present any noncontrolling interest within the "Equity" or "Net Assets" section of the consolidated statement of financial position separately from the parent's equity or net assets.

1.60 It is preferable under FASB ASC that the subsidiary's financial statements have the same or nearly the same fiscal period as the parent. However, FASB ASC 810-10-45-12 states that for consolidation purposes, it is usually acceptable to use the subsidiary's financial statements if the difference in fiscal period is not more than approximately three months. In addition, when a difference in the fiscal periods exists, FASB ASC does not require adjustments to be made for the effects of significant transactions that occurred between the parents' and subsidiaries' fiscal year-ends. FASB ASC 810-10-45-12 does require recognition by disclosure or otherwise of the effect of intervening events that materially affect the financial position or results of operations.

1.61 FASB ASC 810-10-45-11 recognizes that an entity may need to prepare parent-entity (separate) financial statements in addition to consolidated financial statements. This paragraph provides guidance on how an entity may choose to present these statements. For example, consolidating financial statements, in which one column is used for the parent and other columns for particular subsidiaries or groups of subsidiaries, is an effective means of presenting the pertinent information.

PRESENTATION

1.62 FASB ASC 810-10-45-23 requires that a change in a parent's ownership interest while the parent retains its controlling financial interest in its subsidiary should be accounted for as equity transactions (investments by owners and distributions to owners acting in their capacity as owners). Therefore, no gain or loss shall be recognized in consolidated net income or comprehensive income. The carrying amount of the noncontrolling interest should be adjusted to reflect the change in its ownership interest in the subsidiary. Any difference between the fair value of the consideration received or paid and the amount by which the noncontrolling interest is adjusted should be recognized in equity attributable to the parent.

1.63 Paragraphs 4–5 of FASB ASC 810-10-40 state that a parent should deconsolidate a subsidiary or derecognize a group of assets specified in FASB ASC 810-10-40-3A as of the date the parent ceases to have a controlling financial interest in that subsidiary or group of assets. If a parent deconsolidates a subsidiary or derecognizes a group of assets through a nonreciprocal transfer to owners, such as a spinoff, the applicable guidance is in FASB ASC 845-10. Otherwise, a parent should account for the deconsolidation of a subsidiary or derecognition of a group of assets by recognizing a gain or loss in net income attributable to the parent. This gain or loss is measured as the difference between (*a*) the aggregate of the fair value of any consideration received; the fair value of any retained noncontrolling interest in the former subsidiary of the group of assets at the date the subsidiary is deconsolidated or the group of assets is derecognized, and the carrying amount of any noncontrolling interest in the former subsidiary, including any accumulated other comprehensive income attributable to the noncontrolling interest, at the date the subsidiary is deconsolidated and (*b*) the carrying amount of the former subsidiary's assets and liabilities or the carrying amount of the group of assets.

DISCLOSURE

1.64 FASB ASC 810-10-50-1 states in part that consolidated financial statements should disclose the consolidation policy that is being followed. In most cases, this can be made apparent by the headings or other information in the financial statements, but in other cases, a footnote is required.

1.65 FASB ASC 810-10-50-1A also requires disclosure on the face of the consolidated financial statements of the amounts of consolidated net income and consolidated comprehensive income attributable to the parent and noncontrolling interest. Disclosures in the consolidated financial statements should clearly identify and distinguish between the interests of the parent's owners and the interests of the noncontrolling owners of a subsidiary. Those disclosures include a reconciliation of the beginning and ending balances of the equity attributable to the parent and noncontrolling owners and a schedule showing the effects of changes in a parent's ownership interest in a subsidiary on the equity attributable to the parent.

CONSOLIDATION

1.66 FORD MOTOR COMPANY (DEC)
NOTES TO THE FINANCIAL STATEMENTS

Note 1. Presentation (in part)

For purposes of this report, "Ford," the "Company," "we," "our," "us" or similar references mean Ford Motor Company and our consolidated subsidiaries and our consolidated VIEs of which we are the primary beneficiary, unless the context requires otherwise.

We prepare our financial statements in accordance with generally accepted accounting principles in the United States ("GAAP"). We present the financial statements on a consolidated basis and on a sector basis for our Automotive and Financial Services sectors. The additional information provided in the sector statements enables the reader to better understand the operating performance, financial position, cash flows, and liquidity of our two very different businesses. We eliminate all intercompany items and transactions in the consolidated and sector balance sheets. In certain circumstances, presentation of these intercompany eliminations or consolidated adjustments differ between the consolidated and sector financial statements. These line items are reconciled below under "Reconciliations between Consolidated and Sector Financial Statements" or in related footnotes.

Reconciliations between Consolidated and Sector Financial Statements

Sector to Consolidated Deferred Tax Assets and Liabilities. The difference between the total assets and total liabilities as presented in our sector balance sheet and consolidated balance sheet is the result of netting deferred income tax assets and liabilities. The reconciliation between the totals for the sector and consolidated balance sheets was as follows (in millions):

	December 31, 2012	December 31, 2011
Sector Balance Sheet Presentation of Deferred Income Tax Assets		
Automotive sector current deferred income tax assets	$ 3,488	$ 1,791
Automotive sector non-current deferred income tax assets	13,325	13,932
Financial Services sector deferred income tax assets[a]	184	302
Total	16,997	16,025
Reclassification for netting of deferred income taxes	(1,812)	(900)
Consolidated balance sheet presentation of deferred income tax assets	$15,185	$15,125
Sector balance sheet presentation of deferred income tax liabilities		
Automotive sector current deferred income tax liabilities	$ 81	$ 40
Automotive sector non-current deferred income tax liabilities	514	255
Financial Services sector deferred income tax liabilities	1,687	1,301
Total	2,282	1,596
Reclassification for netting of deferred income taxes	(1,812)	(900)
Consolidated balance sheet presentation of deferred income tax liabilities	$ 470	$ 696

[a] Financial Services deferred income tax assets are included in *Financial Services other assets* on our sector balance sheet.

Sector to Consolidated Cash Flow. We present certain cash flows from wholesale receivables, finance receivables and the acquisition of intersector debt differently on our sector and consolidated statements of cash flows. The reconciliation between totals for the sector and consolidated cash flows for the years ended December 31 was as follows (in millions):

	2012	2011	2010
Automotive net cash provided by/(used in) operating activities	$ 6,266	$ 9,368	$ 6,363
Financial Services net cash provided by/(used in) operating activities	3,957	2,405	3,798
Total sector net cash provided by/(used in) operating activities (Note 27)	10,223	11,773	10,161
Reclassifications from investing to operating cash flows			
Wholesale receivables[a]	(1,235)	(2,010)	(46)
Finance receivables[b]	57	21	62
Reclassifications from operating to financing cash flows			
Payments on notes to the UAW VEBA Trust[c]	—	—	1,300
Consolidated net cash provided by/(used in) operating activities	$ 9,045	$ 9,784	$11,477
Automotive net cash provided by/(used in) investing activities	$ (8,024)	$(1,541)	$ 577
Financial Services net cash provided by/(used in) investing activities	(6,318)	(586)	9,256
Total sector net cash provided by/(used in) investing activities	(14,342)	(2,127)	9,833
Reclassifications from investing to operating cash flows			
Wholesale receivables[a]	1,235	2,010	46
Finance receivables[b]	(57)	(21)	(62)
Reclassifications from investing to financing cash flows			
Maturity of Financial Services sector debt held by Automotive sector[d]	(201)	—	(454)
Elimination of investing activity to/(from) Financial Services in consolidation	(925)	(2,903)	(2,455)

(continued)

	2012	2011	2010
Consolidated net cash provided by/(used in) investing activities	$(14,290)	$(3,041)	$ 6,908
Automotive net cash provided by/(used in) financing activities	$ 40	$(5,932)	$(10,476)
Financial Services net cash provided by/(used in) financing activities	2,539	(1,212)	(15,554)
Total sector net cash provided by/(used in) financing activities	2,579	(7,144)	(26,030)
Reclassifications from investing to financing cash flows			
Maturity of Financial Services sector debt held by Automotive sector[d]	201	—	454
Elimination of investing activity to/(from) Financial Services in consolidation	925	2,903	2,455
Reclassifications from operating to financing cash flows			
Payments on notes to the UAW VEBA Trust[c]	—	—	(1,300)
Consolidated net cash provided by/(used in) financing activities	$ 3,705	$(4,241)	$(24,421)

[a] In addition to the cash flow from vehicles sold by us, the cash flow from wholesale finance receivables (being reclassified from investing to operating) includes dealer financing by Ford Credit of used and non-Ford vehicles. One hundred percent of cash flows from these wholesale finance receivables have been reclassified for consolidated presentation as the portion of these cash flows from used and non-Ford vehicles is impracticable to separate.

[b] Includes cash flows of finance receivables purchased/collected by the Financial Services sector from certain divisions and subsidiaries of the Automotive sector.

[c] Cash outflows related to this transaction are reported as financing activities on the consolidated statement of cash flows and operating activities on the sector statement of cash flows.

[d] Cash inflows related to these transactions are reported as financing activities on the consolidated statement of cash flows and investing activities on the sector statement of cash flows.

Note 12. Variable Interest Entities

A VIE is an entity that either (i) has insufficient equity to permit the entity to finance its activities without additional subordinated financial support or (ii) has equity investors who lack the characteristics of a controlling financial interest. A VIE is consolidated by its primary beneficiary. The primary beneficiary has both the power to direct the activities that most significantly impact the entity's economic performance and the obligation to absorb losses or the right to receive benefits from the entity that could potentially be significant to the VIE.

We have the power to direct the activities of an entity when our management has the ability to make key operating decisions, such as decisions regarding capital or product investment or manufacturing production schedules. We have the power to direct the activities of our special purpose entities when we have the ability to exercise discretion in the servicing of financial assets, issue additional debt, exercise a unilateral call option, add assets to revolving structures, or control investment decisions.

Assets recognized as a result of consolidating these VIEs do not represent additional assets that could be used to satisfy claims against our general assets. Conversely, liabilities recognized as a result of consolidating these VIEs do not represent additional claims on our general assets; rather, they represent claims against the specific assets of the consolidated VIEs.

Automotive Sector

VIEs of Which We are Not the Primary Beneficiary

Getrag Ford Transmissions GmbH ("GFT") is a joint venture that constitutes a significant VIE of which we are not the primary beneficiary, and which was not consolidated as of December 31, 2012 or December 31, 2011. GFT is a 50/50 joint venture with Getrag Deutsche Venture GmbH and Co. KG. Ford and its related parties purchase substantially all of the joint venture's output. We do not, however, have the power to direct economically-significant activities of the joint venture.

We also have suppliers that are VIEs of which we are not the primary beneficiary. Although we have provided certain suppliers guarantees and other financial support, we do not have any key decision making power related to their businesses.

Our maximum exposure to loss from VIEs of which we are not the primary beneficiary was as follows (in millions):

	December 31, 2012	December 31, 2011	Change in Maximum Exposure
Investments	$242	$229	$13
Guarantees and other supplier arrangements	5	6	(1)
Total maximum exposure	$247	$235	$12

Financial Services Sector

VIEs of Which We are the Primary Beneficiary

Our Financial Services sector uses special purpose entities to issue asset-backed securities in transactions to public and private investors, bank conduits, and government-sponsored entities or others who obtain funding from government programs. We have deemed most of these special purpose entities to be VIEs. The asset-backed securities are secured by finance receivables and interests in net investments in operating leases. The assets continue to be consolidated by us.

We retain interests in our securitization VIEs, including subordinated securities issued by the VIEs, rights to cash held for the benefit of the securitization investors, and rights to the excess cash flows not needed to pay the debt and other obligations issued or arising in the securitization transactions.

The transactions create and pass along risks to the variable interest holders, depending on the assets securing the debt and the specific terms of the transactions. We aggregate and analyze the asset-backed securitization transactions based on the risk profile of the product and the type of funding structure, including:
- Retail—consumer credit risk and pre-payment risk
- Wholesale—dealer credit risk
- Net investments in operating lease—vehicle residual value risk, consumer credit risk, and pre-payment risk

As a residual interest holder, we are exposed to the underlying residual and credit risk of the collateral, and are exposed to interest rate risk in some transactions. The amount of risk absorbed by our residual interests generally is represented by and limited to the amount of overcollaterization of the assets securing the debt and any cash reserves.

We have no obligation to repurchase or replace any securitized asset that subsequently becomes delinquent in payment or otherwise is in default, except under standard representations and warranties such as good and marketable title to the assets, or when certain changes are made to the underlying asset contracts. Securitization investors have no recourse to us or our other assets and have no right to require us to repurchase the investments. We generally have no obligation to provide liquidity or contribute cash or additional assets to the VIEs and do not guarantee any asset-backed securities. We may be required to support the performance of certain securitization transactions, however, by increasing cash reserves.

Although not contractually required, we regularly support our wholesale securitization programs by repurchasing receivables of a dealer from a VIE when the dealer's performance is at risk, which transfers the corresponding risk of loss from the VIE to us. In order to continue to fund the wholesale receivables, we also may contribute additional cash or wholesale receivables if the collateral falls below required levels. The balances of cash related to these contributions were $0 at December 31, 2012 and 2011, respectively, and ranged from $0 to $373 million during 2012 and $0 to $490 million during 2011. In addition, while not contractually required, we may purchase the commercial paper issued by Ford Credit's FCAR Owner Trust asset-backed commercial paper program ("FCAR").

The following table includes assets to be used to settle the liabilities of the consolidated VIEs. We may retain debt issued by consolidated VIEs and this debt is excluded from the table below. We hold the right to the excess cash flows from the assets that are not needed to pay liabilities of the consolidated VIEs. The assets and debt reflected on our consolidated balance sheet were as follows (in billions):

| | December 31, 2012 | | |
	Cash and Cash Equivalents	Finance Receivables, Net and Net Investment in Operating Leases	Debt
Finance receivables			
Retail	$2.2	$27.0	$23.2
Wholesale	0.3	20.5	12.8
Total finance receivables	2.5	47.5	36.0
Net investment in operating leases	0.4	6.3	4.2
Total[a]	$2.9	$53.8	$40.2

[a] Certain notes issued by the VIEs to affiliated companies served as collateral for accessing the European Central Bank ("ECB") open market operations program. This external funding of $145 million at December 31, 2012 was not reflected as debt of the VIEs and is excluded from the table above, but was included in our consolidated debt. The finance receivables backing this external funding are included in the table above.

| | December 31, 2011 | | |
	Cash and Cash Equivalents	Finance Receivables, Net and Net Investment in Operating Leases	Debt
Finance receivables			
Retail	$2.5	$31.9	$26.0
Wholesale	0.5	17.9	11.2
Total finance receivables	3.0	49.8	37.2
Net investment in operating leases	0.4	6.4	4.2
Total[a]	$3.4	$56.2	$41.4

[a] Certain notes issued by the VIEs to affiliated companies served as collateral for accessing the ECB open market operations program. This external funding of $246 million at December 31, 2011 was not reflected as debt of the VIEs and is excluded from the table above, but was included in our consolidated debt. The finance receivables backing this external funding are included in the table above.

Interest expense on securitization debt related to consolidated VIEs was $760 million, $994 million, and $1,247 million in 2012, 2011, and 2010, respectively.

VIEs that are exposed to interest rate or currency risk have reduced their risks by entering into derivative transactions. In certain instances, we have entered into offsetting derivative transactions with the VIE to protect the VIE from the risks that are not mitigated through the derivative transactions between the VIE and its external counterparty. In other instances, we have entered into derivative transactions with the counterparty to protect the counterparty from risks absorbed through derivative transactions with the VIEs. See Note 18 for additional information regarding the accounting for derivatives.

Our exposures based on the fair value of derivative instruments with external counterparties related to consolidated VIEs that support our securitization transactions were as follows (in millions):

| | December 31, 2012 | | December 31, 2011 | |
	Derivative Asset	Derivative Liability	Derivative Asset	Derivative Liability
Derivatives of the VIEs	$ 4	$134	$157	$ 97
Derivatives related to the VIEs	74	63	81	63
Total exposures related to the VIEs	$78	$197	$238	$160

Derivative expense/(income) related to consolidated VIEs that support Ford Credit's securitization programs for the years ended December 31 was as follows (in millions):

	2012	2011	2010
VIEs	$227	$31	$225
Related to the VIEs	(5)	11	(73)
Total derivative expense/(income) related to the VIEs	$222	$42	$152

VIEs of Which We are Not the Primary Beneficiary

We have an investment in Forso Nordic AB, a joint venture determined to be a VIE of which we are not the primary beneficiary. The joint venture provides consumer and dealer financing in its local markets and is financed by external debt and additional subordinated debt provided by the joint venture partner. The operating agreement indicates that the power to direct economically significant activities is shared with the joint venture partner, and the obligation to absorb losses or right to receive benefits resides primarily with the joint venture partner. Our investment in the joint venture is accounted for as an equity method investment and is included in *Equity in net assets of affiliated companies*. Our maximum exposure to any potential losses associated with this VIE is limited to our equity investment, and amounted to $71 million at December 31, 2012 and 2011, respectively.

1.67 LENNAR CORPORATION (NOV)
CONSOLIDATED BALANCE SHEETS

(Dollars in thousands, except shares and per share amounts)	2012[1]	2011[1]
Assets		
Lennar Homebuilding:		
Cash and cash equivalents	$ 1,146,867	1,024,212
Restricted cash	8,096	8,590
Receivables, net	53,745	53,977
Inventories:		
Finished homes and construction in progress	1,625,048	1,334,703
Land and land under development	3,119,804	2,636,510
Consolidated inventory not owned	326,861	389,322
Total inventories	5,071,713	4,360,535
Investments in unconsolidated entities	565,360	545,760
Other assets	956,070	524,694
	7,801,851	6,517,768
Rialto Investments:		
Cash and cash equivalents	105,310	83,938
Defeasance cash to retire notes payable	223,813	219,386
Loans receivable, net	436,535	713,354
Real estate owned—held-for-sale	134,161	143,677
Real estate owned—held-and-used, net	601,022	582,111
Investments in unconsolidated entities	108,140	124,712
Other assets	38,379	29,970
	1,647,360	1,897,148
Lennar Financial Services	912,995	739,755
Total assets	$10,362,206	9,154,671

[1] Under certain provisions of Accounting Standards Codification ("ASC") Topic 810, Consolidations, ("ASC 810") the Company is required to separately disclose on its consolidated balance sheets the assets of consolidated variable interest entities ("VIEs") that are owned by the consolidated VIEs and liabilities of consolidated VIEs as to which there is no recourse against the Company.

As of November 30, 2012, total assets include $2,128.6 million related to consolidated VIEs of which $13.2 million is included in Lennar Homebuilding cash and cash equivalents, $6.0 million in Lennar Homebuilding receivables, net, $57.4 million in Lennar Homebuilding finished homes and construction in progress, $482.6 million in Lennar Homebuilding land and land under development, $65.2 million in Lennar Homebuilding consolidated inventory not owned, $43.7 million in Lennar Homebuilding investments in unconsolidated entities, $224.1 million in Lennar Homebuilding other assets, $104.8 million in Rialto Investments cash and cash equivalents, $223.8 million in Rialto Investments defeasance cash to retire notes payable, $350.2 million in Rialto Investments loans receivable, net, $94.2 million in Rialto Investments real estate owned held-for-sale, $454.9 million in Rialto Investments real estate owned held-and-used, net, $0.7 million in Rialto Investments in unconsolidated entities and $7.8 million in Rialto Investments other assets.

As of November 30, 2011, total assets include $2,317.4 million related to consolidated VIEs of which $19.6 million is included in Lennar Homebuilding cash and cash equivalents, $5.3 million in Lennar Homebuilding receivables, net, $0.1 million in Lennar Homebuilding finished homes and construction in progress, $538.2 million in Lennar Homebuilding land and land under development, $71.6 million in Lennar Homebuilding consolidated inventory not owned, $43.4 million in Lennar Homebuilding investments in unconsolidated entities, $219.6 million in Lennar Homebuilding other assets, $80.0 million in Rialto Investments cash and cash equivalents, $219.4 million in Rialto Investments defeasance cash to retire notes payable, $565.6 million in Rialto Investments loans receivable, net, $115.4 million in Rialto Investments real estate owned held-for-sale, $428.0 million in Rialto Investments real estate owned held-and-used, net, $0.6 million in Rialto Investments in unconsolidated entities and $10.6 million in Rialto Investments other assets.

(Dollars in thousands, except shares and per share amounts)	2012[2]	2011[2]
Liabilities and Equity		
Lennar Homebuilding:		
Accounts payable	$ 220,690	201,101
Liabilities related to consolidated inventory not owned	268,159	326,200
Senior notes and other debts payable	4,005,051	3,362,759
Other liabilities	635,524	602,231
	5,129,424	4,492,291
Rialto Investments:		
Notes payable and other liabilities	600,602	796,120
Lennar Financial Services	630,972	562,735
Total liabilities	6,360,998	5,851,146
Stockholders' equity:		
Preferred stock	—	—
Class A common stock of $0.10 par value per share; Authorized: 2012 and 2011—300,000,000 shares Issued: 2012—172,397,149 shares; 2011—169,099,760 shares	17,240	16,910
Class B common stock of $0.10 par value per share; Authorized: 2012 and 2010—90,000,000 shares Issued: 2012—32,982,815 shares; 2011—32,982,815 shares	3,298	3,298
Additional paid-in capital	2,421,941	2,341,079
Retained earnings	1,605,131	956,401
Treasury stock, at cost; 2012—12,152,816 Class A common shares and 1,679,620 Class B common shares; 2011—12,000,017 Class A common shares and 1,679,620 Class B common shares	(632,846)	(621,220)
Total stockholders' equity	3,414,764	2,696,468
Noncontrolling interests	586,444	607,057
Total equity	4,001,208	3,303,525
Total liabilities and equity	$10,362,206	9,154,671

[2] As of November 30, 2012, total liabilities include $737.2 million related to consolidated VIEs as to which there was no recourse against the Company, of which $10.6 million is included in Lennar Homebuilding accounts payable, $35.9 million in Lennar Homebuilding liabilities related to consolidated inventory not owned, $181.6 million in Lennar Homebuilding senior notes and other debts payable, $15.7 million in Lennar Homebuilding other liabilities and $493.4 million in Rialto Investments notes payable and other liabilities.

As of November 30, 2011, total liabilities include $902.3 million related to consolidated VIEs as to which there was no recourse against the Company, of which $12.7 million is included in Lennar Homebuilding accounts payable, $43.6 million in Lennar Homebuilding liabilities related to consolidated inventory not owned, $175.3 million in Lennar Homebuilding senior notes and other debts payable, $16.7 million in Lennar Homebuilding other liabilities and $654.0 million in Rialto Investments notes payable and other liabilities.

See accompanying notes to consolidated financial statements.

NOTES TO CONSOLIDATED FINANCIAL STATEMENTS

1. Summary of Significant Accounting Policies (in part)

Basis of Consolidation

The accompanying consolidated financial statements include the accounts of Lennar Corporation and all subsidiaries, partnerships and other entities in which Lennar Corporation has a controlling interest and VIEs (see Note 15) in which Lennar Corporation is deemed the primary beneficiary (the "Company"). The Company's investments in both unconsolidated entities in which a significant, but less than controlling, interest is held and in VIEs in which the Company is not deemed to be the primary beneficiary are accounted for by the equity method. All intercompany transactions and balances have been eliminated in consolidation.

Consolidation of Variable Interest Entities

GAAP requires the consolidation of VIEs in which an enterprise has a controlling financial interest. A controlling financial interest will have both of the following characteristics: (a) the power to direct the activities of a VIE that most significantly impact the VIE's economic performance and (b) the obligation to absorb losses of the VIE that could potentially be significant to the VIE or the right to receive benefits from the VIE that could potentially be significant to the VIE.

The Company's variable interest in VIEs may be in the form of (1) equity ownership, (2) contracts to purchase assets, (3) management services and development agreements between the Company and a VIE, (4) loans provided by the Company to a VIE or other partner and/or (5) guarantees provided by members to banks and other third parties. The Company examines specific criteria and uses its judgment when determining if it is the primary beneficiary of a VIE. Factors considered in determining whether the Company is the primary beneficiary include risk and reward sharing, experience and financial condition of other partner(s), voting rights, involvement in day-to-day capital and operating decisions, representation on a VIE's executive committee, existence of unilateral kick-out rights or voting rights, level of economic disproportionality between the Company and the other partner(s) and contracts to purchase assets from VIEs. The determination whether an entity is a VIE and, if so, whether the Company is primary beneficiary may require it to exercise significant judgment.

Generally, all major decision making in the Company's joint ventures is shared between all partners. In particular, business plans and budgets are generally required to be unanimously approved by all partners. Usually, management and other fees earned by the Company are nominal and believed to be at market and there is no significant economic disproportionality between the Company and other partners. Generally, the Company purchases less than a majority of the JV's assets and the purchase prices under its option contracts are believed to be at market.

Generally, Lennar Homebuilding unconsolidated entities become VIEs and consolidate when the other partner(s) lack the intent and financial wherewithal to remain in the entity. As a result, the Company continues to fund operations and debt paydowns through partner loans or substituted capital contributions.

Rialto Investments (in part)

Consolidations of Variable Interest Entities

In 2010, the Rialto segment acquired indirectly 40% managing member equity interests in two limited liability companies ("LLCs"), in partnership with the FDIC. The Company determined that each of the LLCs met the definition of a VIE and that the Company was the primary beneficiary. In accordance with ASC 810-10-65-2, *Consolidations*, ("ASC 810-10-65-2"), the Company identified the activities that most significantly impact the LLCs' economic performance and determined that it has the power to direct those activities. The economic performance of the LLCs is most significantly impacted by the performance of the LLCs' portfolios of assets, which consisted primarily of distressed residential and commercial mortgage loans. Thus, the activities that most significantly impact the LLCs' economic performance are the servicing and disposition of mortgage loans and real estate obtained through foreclosure of loans, restructuring of loans, or other planned activities associated with the monetizing of loans.

The FDIC does not have the unilateral power to terminate the Company's role in managing the LLCs and servicing the loan portfolio. While the FDIC has the right to prevent certain types of transactions (i.e., bulk sales, selling assets with recourse back to the selling entity, selling assets with representations and warranties and financing the sales of assets without the FDIC's approval), the FDIC does not have full voting or blocking rights over the LLCs' activities, making their voting rights protective in nature, not substantive participating voting rights. Other than as described in the preceding sentence, which are not the primary activities of the LLCs, the Company can cause the LLCs to enter into both the disposition and restructuring of loans without any involvement of the FDIC. Additionally, the FDIC has no voting rights with regard to the operation/management of the operating properties that are acquired upon foreclosure of loans (e.g. REO) and no voting rights over the business plans of the LLCs. The FDIC can make suggestions regarding the business plans, but the Company can decide not to follow the FDIC's suggestions and not to incorporate them in the business plans. Since the FDIC's voting rights are protective in nature and not substantive participating voting rights, the Company has the power to direct the activities that most significantly impact the LLCs' economic performance.

In accordance with ASC 810-10-65-2, the Company determined that it had an obligation to absorb losses of the LLCs that could potentially be significant to the LLCs or the right to receive benefits from the LLCs that could potentially be significant to the LLCs based on the following factors:

- Rialto/Lennar owns 40% of the equity of the LLCs. The LLCs have issued notes to the FDIC totaling $626.9 million. The notes issued by the LLCs must be repaid before any distributions can be made with regard to the equity. Accordingly, the equity of the LLCs has the obligation to absorb losses of the LLCs up to the amount of the notes issued.
- Rialto/Lennar has a management/servicer contract under which the Company earns a 0.5% servicing fee.
- Rialto/Lennar has guaranteed, as the servicer, its obligations under the servicing agreement up to $10 million.

The Company is aware that the FDIC, as the owner of 60% of the equity of each of the LLCs, may also have an obligation to absorb losses of the LLCs that could potentially be significant to the LLCs. However, in accordance with ASC Topic 810-10-25-38A, only one enterprise, if any, is expected to be identified as the primary beneficiary of a VIE.

Since both criteria for consolidation in ASC 810-10-65-2 are met, the Company consolidated the LLCs.

15. Consolidation of Variable Interest Entities

GAAP requires the consolidation of VIEs in which an enterprise has a controlling financial interest. A controlling financial interest will have both of the following characteristics: (a) the power to direct the activities of a VIE that most significantly impact the VIEs economic performance and (b) the obligation to absorb losses of the VIE that could potentially be significant to the VIE or the right to receive benefits from the VIE that could potentially be significant to the VIE.

The Company's variable interest in VIEs may be in the form of (1) equity ownership, (2) contracts to purchase assets, (3) management and development agreements between the Company and a VIE, (4) loans provided by the Company to a VIE or other partner and/or (5) guarantees provided by members to banks and other third parties. The Company examines specific criteria and uses its judgment when determining if the Company is the primary beneficiary of a VIE. Factors considered in determining whether the Company is the primary beneficiary include risk and reward sharing, experience and financial condition of other partner(s), voting rights, involvement in day-to-day capital and operating decisions, representation on a VIE's executive committee, existence of unilateral kick-out rights or voting rights, level of economic disproportionality, if any, between the Company and the other partner(s) and contracts to purchase assets from VIEs.

Generally, all major decision making in the Company's joint ventures is shared between all partners. In particular, business plans and budgets are generally required to be unanimously approved by all partners. Usually, management and other fees earned by the Company are nominal and believed to be at market and there is no significant economic disproportionality between the Company and other partners. Generally, the Company purchases less than a majority of the joint venture's assets and the purchase prices under the Company's option contracts are believed to be at market.

Generally, Lennar Homebuilding unconsolidated entities become VIEs and consolidate when the other partner(s) lack the intent and financial wherewithal to remain in the entity. As a result, the Company continues to fund operations and debt paydowns through partner loans or substituted capital contributions.

The Company evaluated the joint venture agreements of its joint ventures that had reconsideration events during the year ended November 30, 2012. Based on the Company's evaluation, it consolidated an entity within its Lennar Homebuilding segment that at November 30, 2012 had total assets of $7.3 million and an immaterial amount of liabilities. In addition, during the year ended November 30, 2012, there were no VIEs that deconsolidated.

At November 30, 2012 and 2011, the Company's recorded investments in Lennar Homebuilding unconsolidated entities were $565.4 million and $545.8 million, respectively, and the Rialto Investments segment's investments in unconsolidated entities as of November 30, 2012 and 2011 were $108.1 million and $124.7 million, respectively.

Consolidated VIEs

As of November 30, 2012, the carrying amount of the VIEs' assets and non-recourse liabilities that consolidated were $2.1 billion and $0.7 billion, respectively. As of November 30, 2011, the carrying amount of the VIEs' assets and non-recourse liabilities that consolidated were $2.3 billion and $0.9 billion, respectively. Those assets are owned by, and those liabilities are obligations of, the VIEs, not the Company.

A VIE's assets can only be used to settle obligations of that VIE. The VIEs are not guarantors of Company's senior notes and other debts payable. In addition, the assets held by a VIE usually are collateral for that VIE's debt. The Company and other partners do not generally have an obligation to make capital contributions to a VIE unless the Company and/or the other partner(s) have entered into debt guarantees with a VIE's banks. Other than debt guarantee agreements with a VIE's banks, there are no liquidity arrangements or agreements to fund capital or purchase assets that could require the Company to provide financial support to a VIE. While the Company has option contracts to purchase land from certain of its VIEs, the Company is not required to purchase the assets and could walk away from the contract.

Unconsolidated VIEs

At November 30, 2012 and November 30, 2011, the Company's recorded investments in VIEs that are unconsolidated and its estimated maximum exposure to loss were as follows:

(In thousands)	Investments in Unconsolidated VIEs	Lennar's Maximum Exposure to Loss
November 30, 2012		
Lennar Homebuilding[1]	$ 85,500	109,278
Rialto Investments[2]	23,587	23,587
	$109,087	132,865
November 30, 2011		
Lennar Homebuilding[1]	$ 94,517	123,038
Rialto Investments[2]	88,076	95,576
	$182,593	218,614

[1] At November 30, 2012, the maximum exposure to loss of Lennar Homebuilding's investments in unconsolidated VIEs is limited to its investment in the unconsolidated VIEs, except with regard to $18.7 million of recourse debt of one of the unconsolidated VIEs, which is included in the Company's maximum recourse exposure related to Lennar Homebuilding unconsolidated entities, and $4.8 million of letters of credit outstanding for certain of the unconsolidated VIEs that in the event of default under its debt agreement the letter of credit will be drawn upon. At November 30, 2011, the maximum exposure to loss of Lennar Homebuilding's investments in unconsolidated VIEs is limited to its investment in the unconsolidated VIEs, except with regard to $28.3 million of recourse debt of one of the unconsolidated VIEs, which is included in the Company's maximum recourse exposure related to Lennar Homebuilding unconsolidated entities.

[2] At November 30, 2012, the maximum recourse exposure to loss of Rialto's investment in unconsolidated VIEs was limited to its investments in the unconsolidated entities. During the year ended November 30, 2012, the AB PPIP fund finalized its operations and made liquidating distributions; therefore, the Company does not have any outstanding commitment to the AB PPIP fund as of November 30, 2012. As of November 30, 2011, the Company had contributed $67.5 million of the $75 million commitment to fund capital in the AB PPIP fund, and it could not walk away from its remaining commitment to fund capital. Therefore, as of November 30, 2011, the maximum exposure to loss for Rialto's unconsolidated VIEs was higher than the carrying amount of its investments. In addition, at November 30, 2012 and 2011, investments in unconsolidated VIEs and Lennar's maximum exposure to loss include $15.0 million and $14.1 million, respectively, related to Rialto's investments held-to-maturity.

While these entities are VIEs, the Company has determined that the power to direct the activities of the VIEs that most significantly impact the VIEs' economic performance is generally shared. While the Company generally manages the day-to-day operations of the VIEs, the VIEs have an executive committee made up of representatives from each partner. The members of the executive committee have equal votes and major decisions require unanimous consent and approval from all members. The Company does not have the unilateral ability to exercise participating voting rights without partner consent. Furthermore, the Company's economic interest is not significantly disproportionate to the point where it would indicate that the Company has the power to direct these activities.

The Company and other partners do not generally have an obligation to make capital contributions to the VIEs, except for $18.7 million of recourse debt of one of the Lennar Homebuilding unconsolidated VIEs and $4.8 million of letters of credit outstanding for certain of the Lennar Homebuilding unconsolidated VIEs that in the event of default under its debt agreement the letter of credit will be drawn upon. Except for Lennar Homebuilding unconsolidated VIEs discussed above, the Company and the other partners did not guarantee any debt of these unconsolidated VIEs. There are no liquidity arrangements or agreements to fund capital or purchase assets that could require the Company to provide financial support to the VIEs. While the Company has option contracts to purchase land from certain of its unconsolidated VIEs, the Company is not required to purchase the assets and could walk away from the contracts.

Option Contracts

The Company has access to land through option contracts, which generally enables it to control portions of properties owned by third parties (including land funds) and unconsolidated entities until the Company has determined whether to exercise the option.

A majority of the Company's option contracts require a non-refundable cash deposit or irrevocable letter of credit based on a percentage of the purchase price of the land. The Company's option contracts sometimes include price adjustment provisions, which adjust the purchase price of the land to its approximate fair value at the time of acquisition or are based on the fair value at the time of takedown.

The Company's investments in option contracts are recorded at cost unless those investments are determined to be impaired, in which case the Company's investments are written down to fair value. The Company reviews option contracts for indicators of impairment during each reporting period. The most significant indicator of impairment is a decline in the fair value of the optioned property such that the purchase and development of the optioned property would no longer meet the Company's targeted return on investment with appropriate consideration given to the length of time available to exercise the option. Such declines could be caused by a variety of factors including increased competition, decreases in demand or changes in local regulations that adversely impact the cost of development. Changes in any of these factors would cause the Company to re-evaluate the likelihood of exercising its land options.

Some option contracts contain a predetermined take-down schedule for the optioned land parcels. However, in almost all instances, the Company is not required to purchase land in accordance with those take-down schedules. In substantially all instances, the Company has the right and ability to not exercise its option and forfeit its deposit without further penalty, other than termination of the option and loss of any unapplied portion of its deposit and pre-acquisition costs. Therefore, in substantially all instances, the Company does not consider the take-down price to be a firm contractual obligation.

When the Company does not intend to exercise an option, it writes off any unapplied deposit and pre-acquisition costs associated with the option contract. For the years ended November 30, 2012, 2011 and 2010, the Company wrote-off $2.4 million, $1.8 million and $3.1 million, respectively, of option deposits and pre-acquisition costs related to land under option that it does not intend to purchase.

The Company evaluates all option contracts for land to determine whether they are VIEs and, if so, whether the Company is the primary beneficiary of certain of these option contracts. Although the Company does not have legal title to the optioned land, if the Company is deemed to be the primary beneficiary, it is required to consolidate the land under option at the purchase price of the optioned land. During the year ended November 30, 2012, the effect of consolidation of these option contracts was a net increase of $12.2 million to consolidated inventory not owned with a corresponding increase to liabilities related to consolidated inventory not owned in the accompanying consolidated balance sheet as of November 30, 2012. To reflect the purchase price of the inventory consolidated, the Company reclassified the related option deposits from land under development to consolidated inventory not owned in the accompanying consolidated balance sheet as of November 30, 2012. The liabilities related to consolidated inventory not owned primarily represent the difference between the option exercise prices for the optioned land and the Company's cash deposits. The increase to consolidated inventory not owned was offset by the Company exercising its options to acquire land under previously consolidated contracts, resulting in a net decrease in consolidated inventory not owned of $62.5 million for the year ended November 30, 2012.

The Company's exposure to loss related to its option contracts with third parties and unconsolidated entities consisted of its non-refundable option deposits and pre-acquisition costs totaling $176.7 million and $156.8 million, respectively, at November 30, 2012 and 2011. Additionally, the Company had posted $42.5 million and $44.1 million, respectively, of letters of credit in lieu of cash deposits under certain option contracts as of November 30, 2012 and 2011.

Business Combinations

RECOGNITION AND MEASUREMENT

1.68 FASB ASC 805, *Business Combinations*, requires that the acquisition method be used for all business combinations. An acquirer is required to recognize the identifiable acquired assets, the liabilities assumed, and any noncontrolling interest in the acquiree at the acquisition date, measured at their fair values as of that date. Additionally, FASB ASC 805-10-25-23 requires costs incurred to affect the acquisition to be recognized as expenses as incurred, rather than included in the cost allocated to the acquired assets and assumed liabilities. However, the costs to issue debt or equity securities should be recognized in accordance with other applicable GAAP. In a business combination achieved in stages, FASB ASC 805-10-25-10 also requires the acquirer to remeasure its previously-held equity interest in the acquiree at its acquisition date fair value and recognize the resulting gain or loss, if any, in earnings. For all business combinations, the guidance requires the acquirer to recognize goodwill as of the acquisition date, measured as the excess of (a) over (b):

a. The aggregate of the following:
   i. The transferred consideration measured in accordance with FASB ASC 805-30, which generally requires acquisition-date fair value
   ii. The fair value of any noncontrolling interest in the acquire
   iii. In a business combination achieved in stages, the acquisition-date fair value of the acquirer's previously-held equity interest in the acquiree
b. The net of the acquisition-date amounts of the identifiable acquired assets and the assumed liabilities, measured in accordance with FASB ASC 805

If the amounts in (b) are in excess of those in (a), a bargain purchase has occurred. Before recognizing a gain on a bargain purchase, FASB ASC 805-30-30-5 requires the acquirer to reassess whether it has correctly identified all the acquired assets and assumed liabilities and to recognize any additional assets or liabilities identified in that review. If an excess still remains, the acquirer should recognize the resulting gain in earnings on the acquisition date.

DISCLOSURE

1.69 FASB ASC 805-10-50 requires the acquirer to disclose information that enables financial statement users to evaluate the nature and financial statement effect of a business combination that occurs during the current reporting period or after the reporting date but before the financial statements are issued or available to be issued. To meet this objective, the following items should be disclosed:

- The name and a description of the acquiree
- The acquisition date
- The percentage of voting equity interests acquired
- The primary reasons for the business combination and a description of how control was obtained
- For public business entities
  — The amounts of revenue and earnings of the acquiree since the acquisition date included in the consolidated income statement for the reporting period
  — Pro forma information that differs depending upon whether the entity presents comparative financial statements. If an entity presents comparative financial statements, it should provide pro forma disclosures for the comparative prior period for revenue and earnings of the combined entity
  — Nature and amount of any material, nonrecurring pro forma adjustments directly attributable to the business combination, that are included in the reported pro forma revenue and earnings
- For a business combination achieved in stages:
  — Acquisition date fair value of the equity interest in the acquiree held by the acquirer immediately before the acquisition
  — Amount of any gain or loss recognized as a result of remeasuring to fair value the equity interest that the acquirer held immediately before the business combination
  — Valuation technique(s) used to measure the acquisition date fair value of the equity interest the acquirer held immediately before the business combination
  — Other information helpful to users in assessing the inputs used to develop the fair value measurement of the equity interest in the acquiree held by the acquirer immediately before the business combination.

If any of the preceding disclosures for public business entities are impracticable, the acquirer should disclose that fact and explain why. Additional disclosures are required for transactions that are recognized separately from the acquisition of assets and assumptions of liabilities in the business combination.

PRESENTATION AND DISCLOSURE EXCERPTS

BUSINESS COMBINATIONS

1.70 FLOWERS FOODS, INC. (DEC)
NOTES TO CONSOLIDATED FINANCIAL STATEMENTS

Note 7. Acquisitions (in part)

Lepage Acquisition

On July 21, 2012, we completed the acquisition of Lepage Bakeries, Inc. ("Lepage") in two separate but concurrent transactions. Pursuant to the Acquisition Agreement dated May 31, 2012 (the "Acquisition Agreement"), by and among Flowers, Lobsterco I, LLC, a Maine single-member limited liability company and direct wholly owned subsidiary of Flowers ("Lobsterco I"), Lepage, RAL, Inc., a Maine corporation ("RAL"), Bakeast Company, a Maine general partnership ("Bakeast Partnership"), Bakeast Holdings, Inc., a Delaware corporation ("Bakeast Holdings," and collectively with Lepage, RAL and Bakeast Partnership, the "Acquired Entities"), and the equityholders of the Acquired Entities named in the Acquisition Agreement (collectively, the "Equityholders"), Lobsterco I purchased from the Equityholders all of the issued and outstanding shares of the Acquired Entities in exchange for approximately $318.4 million in cash and $17.7 million in deferred obligations, which is the fair value of gross payments of $20.0 million.

Pursuant to the Agreement and Plan of Merger dated May 31, 2012 (the "Merger Agreement"), by and among Flowers, Lobsterco II, LLC, a Maine single-member limited liability company and direct wholly owned subsidiary of Flowers ("Lobsterco II"), Aarow Leasing, Inc., a Maine corporation ("Aarow"), The Everest Company, Incorporated, a Maine corporation ("Everest," and together with Aarow, the "Acquired Companies"), and certain equityholders of Lepage, the Acquired Companies merged with and into Lobsterco II (the "Merger") and all of the issued and outstanding shares of common stock of the Acquired Companies were exchanged for 2,178,648 shares of Flowers common stock.

Lepage operates three bakeries, two in Lewiston, Maine, and one in Brattleboro, Vermont. Lepage serves customers in the New England and New York markets making fresh bakery products under the *Country Kitchen* and *Barowsky's* brands. This acquisition provides a DSD platform to accelerate penetration of *Nature's Own* and *Tastykake* brands in the Northeast. The Lepage acquisition has been accounted for as a business combination. The results of Lepage's operations are included in the company's consolidated financial statements beginning on July 21, 2012 and are included in the company's DSD operating segment.

The preliminary aggregate purchase price was $381.9 million as described in the table below. We incurred $7.1 million in acquisition-related costs during 2012 for Lepage. These expenses are included in the selling, distribution and administrative line item in the company's consolidated statement of income for the fifty-two weeks ending on December 29, 2012.

The following table summarizes the consideration transferred to acquire Lepage and the amounts of identified assets acquired and liabilities assumed based on the estimated fair value at the acquisition date (amounts in thousands):

Fair Value of Consideration Transferred:	
Cash	$300,000
Cash paid for preliminary tax adjustment	18,426
Net working capital adjustment estimate	(55)
Deferred payment obligations	17,663
Flowers Foods, Inc. common stock	45,887
Total fair value of consideration transferred	$381,921
Recognized Amounts of Identifiable Assets Acquired and Liabilities Assumed:	
Financial assets	$ 11,658
Inventories	4,537
Property, plant, and equipment	59,970
Assets Held for sale—Distributor routes	16,161
Identifiable intangible assets estimate	256,400
Deferred income taxes, net	(1,137)
Financial liabilities	(15,617)
Net recognized amounts of identifiable assets acquired	$331,972
Goodwill	$ 49,949

The $18.4 million cash payment for the preliminary tax adjustment is the amount paid to the Lepage equityholders at the closing of the acquisition in connection with certain incremental tax liabilities that will be incurred by those equityholders if the parties jointly make an election under Section 338(h)(10) of the Internal Revenue Code. In the event the parties decide not to make such an election, the payment will be returned to the company. There is an additional $2.1 million preliminary tax adjustment (recorded in the financial liabilities figure in the table above) the company will pay for entity level state taxes.

The $17.7 million obligation for the deferred payments represents the fair value of the fixed payments of $1,250,000 beginning on the first business day of each of the sixteen calendar quarters following the fourth anniversary of the closing of the acquisition (total of $20.0 million in gross payments). The first payment will be made by Flowers on October 1, 2016 and the final payment will be made on July 1, 2020. The difference between the fair value and the gross payments of $2.3 million is recorded as a reduction to the liability and is being amortized to interest expense over eight years.

We issued 2,178,648 shares of Flowers common stock to certain equityholders of Lepage with a fair value of $45.9 million. The number of shares issued was calculated by dividing $50.0 million by the average closing price of Flowers Foods, Inc. common stock for the twenty consecutive trading day period ending five trading days prior to the closing. The shares issued to the equityholders were separated into five categories with each category having a different holding period requirement. As a result, each holding period had a fair value assignment based on an implied fair value which was determined using the Black-Scholes call option formula for an option expiring on each restriction lapse date. The estimated exercise price is equal to the stock price on the last trading day before the closing on July 21, 2012 of $20.48. The table below outlines the determination of fair value and provides the assumptions used in the calculation:

Restriction Lapse Year	2012	2013	2014	2015	2016	Total
Value of Flowers shares issued (thousands)	$25,000	$10,000	$5,000	$5,000	$5,000	$50,000
Implied Fair Value of Restricted shares (thousands)	$23,626	$ 9,154	$4,447	$4,363	$4,297	$45,887
Exercise price (per share)	$ 20.48	$ 20.48	$20.48	$20.48	$20.48	
Expected term (yrs)	0.37	1.00	2.00	3.00	4.00	
Volatility (%)	25.0%	25.0%	25.0%	25.0%	25.0%	
Risk-free rate (%)	0.1%	0.2%	0.2%	0.3%	0.4%	
Dividend Yield (%)	3.0%	3.0%	3.0%	3.0%	3.0%	

The following table presents the intangible assets subject to amortization (amounts in thousands, except amortization periods):

	Amount	Weighted Average Amortization Years
Customer relationships	$69,000	25.0
Non-compete agreements	2,400	4.0
	$71,400	24.3

The primary reasons for the acquisition are to expand the company's footprint into the northeastern United States, to distribute *Country Kitchen* and *Barowsky's* products throughout our distribution network and to distribute *Nature's Own* and *Tastykake* products throughout the Lepage markets. In addition to the amortizable intangible assets, there is an additional $185.0 million in indefinite-lived trademark intangible assets. Goodwill of $49.9 million is allocated to the DSD segment. Approximately $10.2 million of goodwill is deductible for income tax purposes.

The fair value of trade receivables is $7.4 million. The gross amount of the receivable is $7.5 million of which $0.1 million is determined to be uncollectible. We did not acquire any other class of receivables as a result of the acquisition.

Acquisition pro formas

Lepage contributed revenues of $80.7 million and income from operations of $12.4 million for fiscal 2012. The following unaudited pro forma consolidated results of operations have been prepared as if the acquisition of Tasty occurred at the beginning of fiscal 2010 and as if the acquisition of Lepage occurred at the beginning of fiscal 2011 (amounts in thousands, except per share data):

	For Fiscal		
	2012	2011	2010
Sales:			
As reported	$3,046,491	$2,773,356	$2,573,769
Pro forma	$3,146,011	$2,995,233	$2,783,120
Net income:			
As reported	$ 136,121	$ 123,428	$ 137,047
Pro forma	$ 136,714	$ 128,022	$ 137,113
Basic net income per common share:			
As reported	$ 1.00	$ 0.91	$ 1.00
Pro forma	$ 0.98	$ 0.93	$ 1.00
Diluted net Income per common share:			
As reported	$ 0.98	$ 0.90	$ 0.99
Pro forma	$ 0.97	$ 0.92	$ 0.99

These amounts have been calculated after applying the company's accounting policies and adjusting the results to reflect additional depreciation and amortization that would have been charged assuming the fair value adjustments to property, plant, and equipment, and amortizable intangible assets had been applied. In addition, pro forma adjustments have been made for the interest incurred for financing the acquisitions with either the credit facility or the senior notes and to conform Tasty's revenue recognition policies to ours. Lepage's revenue recognition policy was consistent with ours and adjustments are not required. Taxes have also been adjusted for the effect of the items discussed. These pro forma results of operations have been prepared for comparative purposes only, and they do not purport to be indicative of the results of operations that actually would have resulted had the acquisition occurred on the date indicated or that may result in the future.

1.71 LAM RESEARCH CORPORATION (JUN)
NOTES TO CONSOLIDATED FINANCIAL STATEMENTS

Note 16: Acquisitions

On June 4, 2012 ("the acquisition date"), the Company acquired all of the outstanding common shares of Novellus in an all-stock transaction valued at approximately $3.0 billion. The results of Novellus' operations have been included in the consolidated financial statements for the period from June 4, 2012 to June 24, 2012. Lam's primary reasons for this acquisition were to complement existing product offerings and to provide opportunities for revenue and cost synergies. Novellus' primary business focus is to develop, manufacture, sell and support equipment used in the fabrication of integrated circuits, commonly called chips or semiconductors. Customers for this equipment manufacture chips for sale or for incorporation in their own products, or provide chip-manufacturing services to third parties. Novellus also develops, manufactures, sells and supports grinding, lapping and polishing equipment for a broad spectrum of industrial applications.

As a result of the acquisition, Lam Research issued common stock and equity-based awards, subject to certain exceptions, as follows:

(i) each issued and outstanding share of common stock of Novellus was converted into 1.125 (the "exchange ratio") shares of Lam Research common stock, with cash paid in lieu of fractional shares;

(ii) each outstanding option for Novellus' common stock held by a then-current employee of Novellus, whether vested or unvested, was assumed by Lam Research and converted into an option (A) to acquire that number of shares of Lam Research common stock (rounded down to the nearest whole share) equal to the product of (x) the number of shares of Novellus common stock for which such option was exercisable immediately prior to the acquisition date multiplied by (y) the exchange ratio and (B) with an exercise price per share of Lam Research (rounded up to the nearest whole penny) equal to the quotient obtained by dividing (z) the exercise price per share of Novellus common stock subject to such option immediately prior to the acquisition date divided by (y) the exchange ratio. Each assumed stock option will be subject to, and exercisable and vested on, the same terms and conditions applicable to such assumed stock option (consistent with the terms of the applicable Novellus stock plan, the applicable stock option agreement and any other applicable Novellus plan) as of immediately prior to the acquisition date; and

(iii) each outstanding Novellus RSU and each outstanding Novellus performance-based RSU ("PSU") held by a then-current employee of Novellus, whether vested or unvested, was assumed by Lam Research and converted into a restricted stock unit to acquire the number of shares of Lam Research common stock (rounded down to the nearest whole share) equal to the product obtained by multiplying (x) the number of shares of Novellus common stock subject to such RSU or PSU, as applicable, immediately prior to the acquisition date by (y) 1.125. Novellus PSUs that vest in connection with the consummation of the acquisition will become fully vested with respect to the maximum number of shares of Novellus common stock payable pursuant to such Novellus PSU. Each assumed RSU or PSU, as applicable, will be subject to, and vested on, the same terms and conditions applicable to such assumed RSU or PSU.

Consideration Transferred

The table below details the consideration transferred to acquire Novellus:

(In thousands, except per share amounts)	Conversion Calculation	Estimated Fair Value
Lam common stock issued at merger	82,689	
Per share price of Lam common stock as of June 4, 2012	$ 35.99	$2,975,977
Estimated fair value of vested Lam equivalent restricted stock[1]		$ 9,599
Estimated fair value of vested Lam equivalent stock options[2]		41,412
Estimated purchase price consideration		$3,026,988

[1] The fair value of Lam Research equivalent restricted stock as of the acquisition date was estimated based upon the per share price of Lam Research common stock as of June 4, 2012, and giving effect to the exchange ratio of 1.125.

[2] The fair value of the Lam Research equivalent stock options as of the acquisition date was estimated using the Black-Scholes valuation model. Assumptions used are the same as those for acquired awards as disclosed in Note 11 of Notes to Condensed Consolidated Financial Statements.

Net Assets Acquired

The transaction has been accounted for using the acquisition method of accounting which requires that assets acquired and liabilities assumed be recognized at their fair values as of the acquisition date. The following table summarizes the assets acquired and liabilities assumed as of the acquisition date:

(In thousands)	June 4, 2012
Cash and investments	$1,059,859
Accounts receivable	241,924
Inventory	309,213
Other current assets	56,314
Property and equipment	289,126
Intangible assets	1,219,100
Goodwill	1,277,121
Other long-term assets	35,826
Total assets acquired	4,488,483
Accounts payable	(83,028)
Accrued expenses and other current liabilities	(196,677)
Deferred revenue	(20,388)
Debt	(509,805)
Other long-term liabilities	(323,471)
Convertible notes—equity component	(328,126)
Net assets acquired	$3,026,988

The following table is a summary of the fair value estimates of the identifiable intangible assets and their useful lives:

(In thousands, except years)	Useful Lives	Estimated Fair Value June 4, 2012
Existing technology	7	$580,000
Customer relationships	6–10	580,000
In-process research and design	Indefinite	30,000
Patents	6	10,000
Backlog	1	10,000
Additional development rights	Indefinite	9,100
Total		$1,219,100

The goodwill recognized is attributable primarily to expected synergies and other benefits that the Company believes will result from combining the operations of Novellus with the operations of Lam. The $1.3 billion goodwill that was acquired is not expected to be deductible for income tax purposes. As of June 24, 2012, there were no changes in the recognized amounts of goodwill resulting from the acquisition of Novellus.

Preliminary Pre-Acquisition Contingencies Assumed

We have evaluated and continue to evaluate pre-acquisition contingencies relating to Novellus that existed as of the acquisition date. We have determined that certain of these pre-acquisition contingencies are probable in nature and estimable as of the acquisition date and, accordingly, have preliminarily recorded our best estimates for these contingencies as a part of the purchase price allocation for Novellus. We continue to gather information for and evaluate these pre-acquisition contingencies, primarily related to tax positions that we have assumed from Novellus. If we make changes to the amounts recorded or identify additional pre-acquisition contingencies during the remainder of the measurement period, such amounts recorded will be included in the purchase price allocation during the measurement period and, subsequently, in our results of operations.

Acquisition Costs

The Company recognized $36 million of acquisition related costs that were expensed in the year ended June 24, 2012. These costs are included within selling, general, and administrative expense in the Consolidated Statement of Operations.

Actual and Pro-forma Results

The amounts of revenue and net income (loss) of Novellus included in the Company's consolidated Statement of Operations from the acquisition date to June 24, 2012 are as follows:

	(In thousands)
Revenue	$ 25,843
Net income (loss)	$(29,187)

The unaudited pro-forma results presented below include the effects of the Novellus acquisition as if it had been consummated as of June 28, 2010. The pro forma results below include adjustments related to conforming revenue accounting policies, depreciation and amortization to reflect the fair value of acquired property, plant and equipment and identifiable intangible assets, and the associated income tax impacts. The pro forma results for the years ended June 24, 2012 include $122 million of costs related to inventory fair value adjustments on products sold, share-based compensation associated with accelerated vesting and acquisition-related costs, which are not expected to occur in future quarters. The pro forma information does not necessarily reflect the actual results of operations had the acquisition been consummated at the beginning of the fiscal reporting period indicated nor is it indicative of future operating results. The pro forma information does not include any adjustment for (i) potential revenue enhancements, cost synergies or other operating efficiencies that could result from the acquisition or (ii) transaction or integration costs relating to the acquisition.

	Year Ended	
(In thousands, except per share amounts)	June 24, 2012	June 26, 2011
Pro forma revenue	$3,804,252	$4,743,797
Pro forma net income	$ 152,981	$ 894,864
Pro forma basic earnings per share	$ 0.76	$ 4.34
Pro forma diluted earnings per share	$ 0.74	$ 4.18

Commitments

DISCLOSURE

1.72 FASB ASC 440, *Commitments*, requires the disclosure of commitments such as those for unused letters of credit; long-term leases; assets pledged as security for loans; pension plans; cumulative preferred stock dividends in arrears; plant acquisition, obligations to reduce debts, maintain working capital, and restrict dividends; and unconditional purchase obligations.

1.73 SPRINT NEXTEL CORPORATION (DEC)
NOTES TO THE CONSOLIDATED FINANCIAL STATEMENTS

Note 8. Long-Term Debt, Financing and Capital Lease Obligations (in part)

	Interest Rates	Maturities	December 31, 2012	December 31, 2011
			(In millions)	
Notes				
Senior notes				
Sprint Nextel Corporation	6.00–11.50%	2016–2022	$ 9,280	$ 4,500
Sprint Capital Corporation	6.88–8.75%	2019–2032	6,204	6,204
Serial redeemable senior notes				
Nextel Communications, Inc.	5.95–7.38%	2013–2015	—	4,780
Guaranteed notes				
Sprint Nextel Corporation	7.00–9.00%	2018–2020	4,000	3,000
Secured notes				
iPCS, Inc.	2.44–3.56%	2013–2014	481	481
Convertible bonds				
Sprint Nextel Corporation	1.00%	2019	3,100	—
Credit facilities				
Bank credit facility	4.31%	2013	—	—
Export Development Canada	5.39%	2015	500	500
Secured equipment credit facility	2.03%	2017	296	—
Financing obligation	9.50%	2030	698	698
Capital lease obligations and other	4.11–15.49%	2014–2022	74	71
Net discount from beneficial conversion feature on convertible bond			(247)	—
Net (discounts) premiums			(45)	40
			24,341	20,274
Less current portion			(379)	(8)
Long-term debt, financing and capital lease obligations			$23,962	$20,266

As of December 31, 2012, Sprint Nextel Corporation, the parent corporation, had $16.9 billion in principal amount of debt outstanding, including amounts drawn under the credit facilities. In addition, as of December 31, 2012, $7.0 billion in principal amount of our long-term debt issued by 100% owned subsidiaries was fully and unconditionally guaranteed by the parent. The indentures and financing arrangements governing certain subsidiaries' debt contain provisions that limit cash dividend payments on subsidiary common stock. The transfer of cash in the form of advances from the subsidiaries to the parent corporation generally is not restricted.

As of December 31, 2012, about $1.5 billion of our outstanding debt, comprised of certain notes, financing and capital lease obligations and mortgages, is secured by $995 million of property, plant and equipment and other assets, net (gross book value of $1.4 billion). Cash interest payments, net of amounts capitalized of $278 million, $413 million, and $13 million, totaled $1.4 billion, $1.0 billion, and $1.5 billion during each of the years ended December 31, 2012, 2011 and 2010, respectively. Our weighted average effective interest rate related to our notes and credit facilities was 7.5% in 2012 and 7.0% in 2011.

Notes

Notes consist of senior notes, serial redeemable senior notes, guaranteed notes, and convertible bonds, all of which are unsecured, as well as secured notes of iPCS, Inc. (iPCS), which are secured solely with the underlying assets of iPCS. Cash interest on all of the notes is generally payable semi-annually in arrears. As of December 31, 2012, approximately $19.8 billion of the notes were redeemable at the Company's discretion at the then-applicable redemption prices plus accrued interest.

As of December 31, 2012, approximately $11.1 billion of our senior notes and guaranteed notes provide holders with the right to require us to repurchase the notes if a change of control triggering event (as defined in our indentures and supplemental indentures governing applicable notes) occurs, which includes both a change of control and a ratings decline of the applicable notes by each of Moody's Investor Services and Standard & Poor's Rating Services. If we are required to make a change of control offer, we will offer a cash payment equal to 101% of the aggregate principal amount of notes repurchased plus accrued and unpaid interest. A change in control resulting from the Softbank Merger has been excluded as a triggering event for the $11.1 billion of our senior and guaranteed notes subject to both a change in control and ratings decline.

Credit Facilities

In May 2012, certain of our subsidiaries entered into a $1.0 billion secured equipment credit facility to finance equipment-related purchases from Ericsson for Network Vision. The cost of funds under this facility includes a fixed interest rate of 2.03%, and export credit agency premiums and other fees that, in total, equate to an expected effective interest rate of approximately 6% based on assumptions such as timing and amounts of drawdowns. The facility is secured by a lien on the equipment purchased and is fully and unconditionally guaranteed by the parent. The facility is equally divided into two consecutive tranches of $500 million, with drawdown availability contingent upon Sprint's equipment-related purchases from Ericsson, up to the maximum of each tranche. The first tranche of $500 million may be drawn upon through May 31, 2013, while the second tranche of $500 million may be drawn upon beginning April 1, 2013 through May 31, 2014. Interest and fully-amortizing principal payments are payable semi-annually on March 30 and September 30, with a final maturity date of March 2017 for both tranches. As of December 31, 2012, we had drawn approximately $296 million on the first tranche of the facility. The covenants under the secured equipment credit facility are similar to those of our revolving bank credit facility, our EDC facility, and those of our guaranteed notes due 2018 and 2020.

As of December 31, 2012, approximately $925 million in letters of credit were outstanding under our $2.2 billion revolving bank credit facility, including the letter of credit required by the 2004 FCC Report and Order to reconfigure the 800 MHz band (the "Report and Order"). As a result, the Company had $1.3 billion of borrowing capacity available under the revolving bank credit facility as of December 31, 2012. Our revolving bank credit facility expires in October 2013, although we expect to enter into a new facility prior to expiration. The terms of the revolving bank credit facility provide for an interest rate equal to the London Interbank Offered Rate (LIBOR) plus a spread that varies depending on the Company's credit ratings. Certain of our domestic subsidiaries have guaranteed the revolving bank credit facility. The Company's unsecured loan agreement with EDC has terms similar to those of the revolving bank credit facility, except that under the terms of the EDC loan, repayments of outstanding amounts cannot be re-drawn. As of December 31, 2012, the EDC loan was fully drawn. In addition, as of December 31, 2012, up to $204 million was available through May 31, 2013 under the first tranche of our secured equipment credit facility, although the use of such funds is limited to equipment-related purchases from Ericsson.

Under the terms of Sprint's and its consolidated subsidiaries' existing credit facilities, if a change of control occurs, including the SoftBank Merger, we will be required to repay all outstanding balances in the amount of $796 million as of December 31, 2012, under the EDC facility, the secured equipment credit facility, and our revolving bank credit facility, as well as letters of credit issued of approximately $925 million under our revolving bank credit facility. Sprint intends to amend these facilities to, among other things, exclude the SoftBank Merger from the change of control provisions.

Covenants

As of December 31, 2012, the Company was in compliance with all restrictive and financial covenants associated with its borrowings. A default under any of our borrowings could trigger defaults under our other debt obligations, which in turn could result in the maturities being accelerated. Certain indentures that govern our outstanding notes require compliance with various covenants, including covenants that limit the Company's ability to sell all or substantially all of its assets, covenants that limit the ability of the Company and its subsidiaries to incur indebtedness, and covenants that limit the ability of the Company and its subsidiaries to incur liens, as defined by the terms of the indentures.

We are currently restricted from paying cash dividends because our ratio of total indebtedness to trailing four quarters earnings before interest, taxes, depreciation and amortization and certain other non-recurring items, as defined in the credit facilities (adjusted EBITDA), exceeds 2.5 to 1.0.

1.74 VALASSIS COMMUNICATIONS, INC. (DEC)
NOTES TO CONSOLIDATED FINANCIAL STATEMENTS

3. Long-Term Debt (in part)

Long-term debt included on the consolidated balance sheets consisted of:

	December 31,	
(In thousands of U.S. dollars)	2012	2011
Senior Secured Revolving Credit Facility	$ 50,000	$ 50,000
Senior Secured Term Loan A	277,500	292,500
Senior Secured Convertible Notes due 2033, net of discount	61	60
6 $\frac{5}{8}$ % Senior Notes due 2021	260,000	260,000
Total debt	587,561	602,560
Current portion long-term debt	22,500	15,000
Long-term debt	$565,061	$587,560

Maturities of long-term debt are $22.5 million, $37.5 million, $45.0 million, and $222.5 million and $0 for the years ended December 31, 2013, 2014, 2015, 2016 and 2017, respectively, and $260.1 million thereafter.

Senior Secured Credit Facility (in part)

General

On June 27, 2011, we entered into a senior secured credit facility with JPMorgan Chase Bank, N.A., as administrative agent, and a syndicate of lenders jointly arranged by J.P. Morgan Securities LLC, Merrill Lynch, Pierce, Fenner & Smith Incorporated and RBS Securities Inc. (the "Senior Secured Credit Facility"). The Senior Secured Credit Facility and related loan documents replaced and terminated our prior credit agreement, dated as of March 2, 2007, as amended (the "Prior Senior Secured Credit Facility"), by and among Valassis, Bear Stearns Corporate Lending Inc., as Administrative Agent, and a syndicate of lenders jointly arranged by Bear, Stearns & Co. Inc. and Banc of America Securities LLC. In connection with the termination of the Prior Senior Secured Credit Facility, all obligations and rights under the related guarantee, security and collateral agency agreement, dated as of March 2, 2007, as amended (the "Prior Security Agreement"), by Valassis and certain of its domestic subsidiaries signatory thereto, as grantors, in favor of Bear Stearns Corporate Lending Inc., in its capacity as collateral agent for the benefit of the Secured Parties (as defined in the Prior Security Agreement), were also simultaneously terminated.

The Senior Secured Credit Facility consists of:
- a five-year term loan A in an aggregate principal amount equal to $300.0 million, with principal repayable in quarterly installments at a rate of 5.0% during each of the first two years from issuance, 10.0% during the third year from issuance, 15.0% during the fourth year from issuance and 11.25% during the fifth year from issuance, with the remaining 53.75% due at maturity (the "Term Loan A");
- a five-year revolving credit facility in an aggregate principal amount of $100.0 million (the "Revolving Line of Credit"), including $15.0 million available in Euros, Pounds Sterling or Canadian Dollars, $50.0 million available for letters of credit and a $20.0 million swingline loan subfacility, of which $50.0 million was drawn at closing and remains outstanding as of December 31, 2012 (exclusive of outstanding letters of credit described below); and
- an incremental facility pursuant to which, prior to the maturity of the Senior Secured Credit Facility, we may incur additional indebtedness in an amount up to $150.0 million under the Revolving Line of Credit or the Term Loan A or a combination thereof, subject to certain conditions, including receipt of additional lending commitments for such additional indebtedness. The terms of the incremental facility will be substantially similar to the terms of the Senior Secured Credit Facility, except with respect to the pricing of the incremental facility, the interest rate for which could be higher than that for the Revolving Line of Credit and the Term Loan A.

We used the initial borrowing under the Revolving Line of Credit, the proceeds from the Term Loan A and existing cash of $120.0 million to repay the $462.2 million outstanding under our Prior Senior Secured Credit Facility (reflecting all outstanding borrowings thereunder), to pay accrued interest with respect to such loans and to pay the fees and expenses related to the Senior Secured Credit Facility. We recognized a pre-tax loss on extinguishment of debt of $3.0 million during the year ended December 31, 2011, which represents the write-off of related capitalized debt issuance costs. In addition, as further discussed in Note 9, *Derivative Financial Instruments and Fair Value Measurements*, we recorded in interest expense a pre-tax loss of $2.6 million related to the discontinuation of hedge accounting on the related interest rate swap. We capitalized related debt issuance costs of approximately $6.6 million, which will be amortized over the term of the Senior Secured Credit Facility.

All borrowings under our Senior Secured Credit Facility, including, without limitation, amounts drawn under the Revolving Line of Credit, are subject to the satisfaction of customary conditions, including absence of a default and accuracy of representations and warranties. As of December 31, 2012, we had approximately $42.6 million available under the Revolving Line of Credit portion of our Senior Secured Credit Facility (after giving effect to the reductions in availability pursuant to $7.4 million in standby letters of credit outstanding as of December 31, 2012).

Covenants

Subject to customary and otherwise agreed upon exceptions, our Senior Secured Credit Facility contains affirmative and negative covenants, including, but not limited to:
- the payment of other obligations;
- the maintenance of organizational existences, including, but not limited to, maintaining our property and insurance;
- compliance with all material contractual obligations and requirements of law;
- limitations on the incurrence of indebtedness;
- limitations on creation and existence of liens;
- limitations on certain fundamental changes to our corporate structure and nature of our business, including mergers;
- limitations on asset sales;
- limitations on restricted payments, including certain dividends and stock repurchases and redemptions;
- limitations on capital expenditures;
- limitations on any investments, provided that certain "permitted acquisitions" and strategic investments are allowed;
- limitations on optional prepayments and modifications of certain debt instruments;
- limitations on modifications to organizational documents;
- limitations on transactions with affiliates;
- limitations on entering into certain swap agreements;
- limitations on negative pledge clauses or clauses restricting subsidiary distributions;
- limitations on sale-leaseback and other lease transactions; and
- limitations on changes to our fiscal year.

Our Senior Secured Credit Facility also requires us to comply with:
- a maximum consolidated leverage ratio, as defined in our Senior Secured Credit Facility (generally, the ratio of our consolidated total debt to consolidated earnings before interest, taxes, depreciation and amortization, or EBITDA, for the most recent four quarters), of 3.50:1.00; and
- a minimum consolidated interest coverage ratio, as defined in our Senior Secured Credit Facility (generally, the ratio of our consolidated EBITDA to consolidated interest expense for the most recent four quarters), of 3.00:1.00.

The following table shows the required and actual financial ratios under our Senior Secured Credit Facility as of December 31, 2012 :

	Required Ratio	Actual Ratio
Maximum consolidated leverage ratio	No greater than 3.50:1.00	1.96:1.00
Minimum consolidated interest coverage ratio	No less than 3.00:1.00	10.97:1.00

In addition, we are required to give notice to the administrative agent and the lenders under our Senior Secured Credit Facility of defaults under the facility documentation and other material events, make any new wholly-owned domestic subsidiary (other than an immaterial subsidiary) a subsidiary guarantor and pledge substantially all after-acquired property as collateral to secure our and our subsidiary guarantors' obligations in respect of the facility.

1.75 ARMSTRONG WORLD INDUSTRIES, INC. (DEC)
NOTES TO CONSOLIDATED FINANCIAL STATEMENTS

(Dollar amounts in millions)

Note 18. Debt (in part)

	December 31, 2012	Average Year-End Interest Rate	December 31, 2011	Average Year-End Interest Rate
Term loan A due 2015	$ 237.5	3.47%	$250.0	3.30%
Term loan B due 2018	788.5	4.00%	545.9	4.25%
Tax exempt bonds due 2025–2041	45.0	1.00%	45.0	0.99%
Other	—	—	2.1	1.98%
Subtotal	1,071.0	3.76%	843.0	3.79%
Less current portion and short-term debt	33.0	3.60%	20.1	3.42%
Total long-term debt, less current portion	$1,038.0	3.76%	$822.9	3.80%

On November 23, 2010, we refinanced our $1.1 billion credit facility and executed a $1.05 billion senior credit facility. This facility consisted of a $250 million revolving credit facility (with a $150 million sublimit for letters of credit), a $250 million Term Loan A and a $550 million Term Loan B. This $1.05 billion senior credit facility was secured by U.S. personal property, the capital stock of material U.S. subsidiaries, and a pledge of 65% of the stock of our material first tier foreign subsidiaries. In 2010, in connection with the refinancing, we repaid amounts owed under the previous credit facility and wrote off $3.8 million of unamortized debt financing costs related to our previous credit facility to interest expense.

On March 10, 2011, we amended our $1.05 billion senior credit facility. The amended terms of Term Loan B resulted in a lower LIBOR floor (1.0% vs. 1.5%) and interest rate spread (3.0% vs. 3.5%). We also extended its maturity from May 2017 to March 2018. All other terms, conditions and covenants were unchanged from the November 23, 2010 agreement. In connection with the amendment to Term Loan B, we paid a $5.5 million prepayment premium (representing one percent of the principal amount of Term Loan B). The premium was capitalized and is being amortized into interest expense over the life of the loan. Additionally, we paid approximately $1.6 million of fees to third parties which was reflected in interest expense.

On March 22, 2012, we amended our $1.05 billion senior credit facility. We added $250 million to our existing Term Loan B facility. The amended $1.3 billion facility is made up of a $250 million revolving credit facility (with a $150 million sublimit for letters of credit), a $250 million Term Loan A and an $800 million Term Loan B. The facility is secured by U.S. personal property, the capital stock of material U.S. subsidiaries, and a pledge of 65% of the stock of our material first tier foreign subsidiaries. In connection with the additional $250 million Term Loan B borrowings, we paid $8.1 million for bank fees. This amount was capitalized and is being amortized into interest expense over the life of the loan.

The senior credit facility includes two financial covenants which require the ratio of consolidated earnings before interest, taxes, depreciation and amortization ("EBITDA") to consolidated cash interest expense minus cash consolidated interest income ("consolidated interest coverage ratio") to be greater than or equal to 3.0 to 1.0 and require the ratio of consolidated funded indebtedness minus AWI and domestic subsidiary unrestricted cash and cash equivalents up to $100 million to consolidated EBITDA ("consolidated leverage ratio") to be less than or equal to 4.5 to 1.0 through December 31, 2013, 4.0 to 1.0 through March 31, 2015, and 3.75 to 1.0 thereafter. Our debt agreements include other restrictions, including restrictions pertaining to the acquisition of additional debt, the redemption, repurchase or retirement of our capital stock, payment of dividends, and certain financial transactions as it relates to specified assets. We currently believe that default under these covenants is unlikely. Fully borrowing under our revolving credit facility would not violate these covenants. As of December 31, 2012 we were in compliance with all covenants of the credit agreement.

The Revolving Credit and Term Loan A portions are currently priced at a spread of 3.0% over LIBOR and the Term Loan B portion is priced at 3.0% over LIBOR with a 1.0% LIBOR floor for its entire term. The Term Loan A and Term Loan B were both fully drawn and are currently priced on a variable interest rate basis. The unpaid balances of Term Loan A ($237.5 million), Revolving Credit ($0 million) and Term Loan B ($788.5 million) of the credit facility may be prepaid without penalty at the maturity of their respective interest reset periods. Any amounts prepaid on the Term Loan A or Term Loan B may not be re-borrowed.

Under the senior credit facility beginning December 31, 2013, we are subject to year-end leverage tests that may trigger mandatory prepayments. If our consolidated leverage ratio is greater than 2.0 to 1.0 but less than 2.5 to 1.0 as of December 31, 2013, we would be required to make a prepayment of 25% of fiscal year Consolidated Excess Cash Flow as defined by the credit agreement. If our Consolidated Leverage Ratio is greater than 2.5 to 1.0, the prepayment amount would be 50% of fiscal year Consolidated Excess Cash Flow. These annual payments would be made beginning in the first quarter of 2014.

OPERATING LEASES & RELATED GUARANTEES

1.76 LAM RESEARCH CORPORATION (JUN)
NOTES TO CONSOLIDATED FINANCIAL STATEMENTS

Note 14: Commitments (in part)

Operating Leases and Related Guarantees

The Company leases the majority of its administrative, R&D and manufacturing facilities, regional sales/service offices and certain equipment under non-cancelable operating leases. Certain of the Company's facility leases for buildings located at its Fremont, California headquarters and certain other facility leases provide the Company with options to extend the leases for additional periods or to purchase the facilities. Certain of the Company's facility leases provide for periodic rent increases based on the general rate of inflation. The Company's rental expense for facilities occupied during fiscal years 2012, 2011, and 2010 was approximately $11 million, $9 million, and $6 million, respectively.

On December 18, 2007, the Company entered into two operating leases regarding certain improved properties in Livermore, California. These leases were amended on April 3, 2008 and July 9, 2008 (as so amended, the "Livermore Leases"). On December 21, 2007, the Company entered into a series of four amended and restated operating leases (the "New Fremont Leases," and collectively with the Livermore Leases, the "Operating Leases") with regard to certain improved properties at the Company's headquarters in Fremont, California.

The Operating Leases have a term of approximately seven years ending on the first business day in January 2015. The Company may, at its discretion and with 30 days' notice, elect to purchase the property that is the subject of the Operating Lease for an amount approximating the sum required to pay the amount of the lessor's investment in the property and any accrued but unpaid rent.

The Company is required, pursuant to the terms of the Operating Leases, to maintain collateral in an aggregate of approximately $164.9 million in separate interest-bearing accounts as security for the Company's obligations under the Operating Leases. This amount is recorded as restricted cash in the Company's Consolidated Balance Sheet as of as of June 24, 2012.

When the terms of the Operating Leases expire, the property subject to that Operating Lease may be remarketed. The Company has guaranteed to the lessor that each property will have a certain minimum residual value. The aggregate guarantee made by the Company under the Operating Leases is generally no more than approximately $141.7 million; however, under certain default circumstances, the guarantee with regard to an Operating Lease may be 100% of the lessor's aggregate investment in the applicable property, which in no case will exceed $164.9 million, in the aggregate.

The Company recognized at lease inception $0.6 million in estimated liabilities related to the Operating Leases, which represents the fair value guarantee premium that would be required had the guarantee been issued in a standalone transaction. These liabilities are recorded in other long-term liabilities with the offsetting entry recorded as prepaid rent in other assets. The balances in prepaid rent and the guarantee liability are amortized to the statement of operations on a straight line basis over the life of the leases. If it becomes probable that the Company will be required to make a payment under the residual guarantee, the Company will increase its liability with a corresponding increase to prepaid rent and amortize the increased prepaid rent over the remaining lease term with no corresponding reduction in the liability. As of June 24, 2012, the unamortized portion of the fair value of the residual value guarantees remaining in other long-term liabilities and prepaid rent was $0.2 million.

During fiscal years 2011 and 2010, the Company recognized restructuring charges of $13.7 million and $13.0 million, respectively, related to the reassessment of the residual value guarantee for such lease. Accordingly, an amount of $26.7 million has been recorded in other long-term liabilities as of June 24, 2012.

The Company's contractual cash obligations with respect to operating leases, excluding the residual value guarantees discussed above, as of June 24, 2012 were as follows:

(In thousands)	Operating Leases
Payments due by period:	
One year	$ 15,620
Two years	12,537
Three years	9,960
Four years	5,886
Five years	4,777
Over 5 years	1,423
Less: Sublease Income	(12,822)
Total	$ 37,381

ROYALTY AND LICENSING AGREEMENTS

1.77 THE JONES GROUP INC. (DEC)
NOTES TO CONSOLIDATED FINANCIAL STATEMENTS

Commitments and Contingencies (in part)

(b) ROYALTIES. We have an exclusive license to produce, market and distribute costume jewelry in the United States, Canada, Mexico and Japan under the *Givenchy* trademark pursuant to an agreement with Givenchy, which expires on December 31, 2013. The agreement requires us to pay a percentage of net sales against guaranteed minimum royalty and advertising payments as set forth in the agreement.

We have a sub-license agreement with VCJS LLC ("VCJS") to design, develop, produce and distribute in the United States, Mexico and Canada *Jessica Simpson* jeanswear and sportswear under the *Jessica Simpson* (signature) trademark which VCJS licenses from With You, Inc. ("WYI"). The agreement, which expires on December 31, 2014 (October 15, 2014 if the master license between WYI and VCJS is not renewed), requires us to pay a percentage of net sales against guaranteed minimum royalty and pooled marketing fee payments as set forth in the agreement.

We also have a distribution and retail license agreement with VCJS to distribute products bearing the trademarks *Vince Camuto*, *Vince Camuto Signature* and *Jessica Simpson* in various European territories. The agreement, which ends on December 31, 2018 (unless terminated earlier or renewed) requires us to pay a percentage of net sales against guaranteed minimum royalty and pooled marketing fee payments as set forth in the agreement. The agreement contains renewal options under certain conditions through December 31, 2024.

We have an exclusive licensing and distribution agreement with Rafe IP Holdings LLC, a company affiliated with one of our employees, to design, develop, produce and distribute women's footwear, handbags, small leather goods and jewelry in the United States, Australia, Canada, Japan, the Philippines, Singapore and Korea under the *Rafe* and *Rafe New York* trademarks. The agreement, which expires on December 31, 2016, requires us to pay a percentage of net sales as set forth in the agreement. The agreement contains renewal options under certain conditions through December 31, 2026.

We have an exclusive license to design, develop, produce and distribute footwear worldwide under the *Lipsy* trademark pursuant to an agreement with Lipsy Limited, which expires on March 18, 2015. The agreement requires us to pay a percentage of net sales against guaranteed minimum royalty payments as set forth in the agreement.

Minimum payments under these license agreements are as follows.

Year Ending December 31, (In millions)	2013	2014	2015	2016	2017	2018
Givenchy	$0.6	$—	$—	$—	$—	$—
Jessica Simpson/Vince Camuto	3.1	3.9	0.5	0.5	0.5	0.5
Lipsy	0.1	0.1	0.1	—	—	—
	$3.8	$4.0	$0.6	$0.5	$0.5	$0.5

SUPPLY AGREEMENTS

1.78 AIRGAS, INC. (MAR)
NOTES TO CONSOLIDATED FINANCIAL STATEMENTS

(17) Commitments and Contingencies (in part)

(c) Supply Agreements

The Company purchases bulk quantities of industrial gases under long-term take-or-pay supply agreements. The Company is a party to a long-term take-or-pay supply agreement, in effect through August 2017, under which Air Products will supply the Company with bulk nitrogen, oxygen, argon, hydrogen and helium. The Company is committed to purchase approximately $55 million annually in bulk gases under the Air Products supply agreement. The Company also has long-term take-or-pay supply agreements with Linde AG to purchase oxygen, nitrogen, argon and helium. The agreements expire at various dates through July 2019 and represent approximately $41 million in annual bulk gas purchases. Additionally, the Company has long-term take-or-pay supply agreements to purchase oxygen, nitrogen and argon from other major producers. Annual purchases under these contracts are approximately $20 million and they expire at various dates through June 2024. The annual purchase commitments above reflect estimates based on fiscal 2012 purchases.

The Company also purchases liquid carbon dioxide and ammonia under take-or-pay supply agreements. The Company is a party to long-term take-or-pay supply agreements for the purchase of liquid carbon dioxide with approximately 15 suppliers that expire at various dates through 2044 and represent annual purchases of approximately $22 million. The Company purchases ammonia from a variety of sources and is obligated to purchase approximately $2.6 million annually under these contracts. The annual purchase commitments reflect estimates based on fiscal 2012 purchases.

The supply agreements noted above contain periodic pricing adjustments based on certain economic indices and market analyses. The Company believes the minimum product purchases under the agreements are within the Company's normal product purchases. Actual purchases in future periods under the supply agreements could differ materially from those presented above due to fluctuations in demand requirements related to varying sales levels as well as changes in economic conditions. The Company believes that if a long-term supply agreement with a major supplier of gases or other raw materials was terminated, it would look to utilize excess internal production capacity and to locate alternative sources of supply to meet customer requirements. The Company purchases hardgoods from major manufacturers and suppliers. For certain products, the Company has negotiated national purchasing arrangements. The Company believes that if an arrangement with any supplier of hardgoods was terminated, it would be able to negotiate comparable alternative supply arrangements.

At March 31, 2012, future commitments under take-or-pay supply agreements were as follows:

(In thousands) Years Ending March 31,	
2013	$140,915
2014	157,425
2015	137,859
2016	123,067
2017	128,057
Thereafter	136,744
	$824,067

Contingencies

RECOGNITION AND MEASUREMENT

1.79 The FASB ASC glossary defines a *contingency* as an existing condition, situation, or set of circumstances involving uncertainty about possible gain (gain contingency) or loss (loss contingency) to an entity that will ultimately be resolved when one or more future events occur or fail to occur. FASB ASC 450-20 sets forth guidance for the recognition and disclosure of loss contingencies. An estimated loss from a loss contingency should be accrued by a charge to income if both of the following conditions are met:

- Information available before the financial statements are issued or available to be issued indicates that it is probable that an asset had been impaired or a liability had been incurred at the date of the financial statements. It is implicit in this condition that it must be probable that one or more future events will occur confirming the fact of the loss.
- The amount of loss can be reasonably estimated.

1.80 Disclosure is preferable to accrual when a reasonable estimate of loss cannot be made. Even losses that are reasonably estimable should not be accrued if it is not probable that an asset has been impaired or a liability has been incurred at the date of the entity's financial statements because those losses relate to a future period, rather than the current period. In accordance with FASB ASC 450-20-30-1, if some amount within a range of loss appears at the time to be a better estimate than any other amount within the range, that amount should be accrued. When no amount within the range is a better estimate than any other amount, however, the minimum amount in that range should be accrued. Select loss contingency disclosures do not apply to loss contingencies arising from an entity's recurring estimation of its allowance for credit losses. FASB ASC 450-30-25-1 usually does not permit recognition of gain contingencies because to do so might be to recognize revenue before its realization. When contingency disclosures exist, public companies generally present a balance sheet caption for contingencies, in accordance with Rule 5-02 of Regulation S-X.

1.81 FASB ASC 460-10-25-5 considers warranties to fall within the definition of a contingency. Therefore, an entity should meet the two conditions described in paragraph 1.79 before recognizing a loss and related liability. FASB ASC 460-10 contains additional guidance concerning the items that an entity should consider in order to meet the probability recognition criteria, including references to the entity's own and others' experience. FASB ASC also provides more specific guidance for extended warranties and product maintenance contracts.

PRESENTATION AND DISCLOSURE EXCERPTS

LEGAL MATTERS

1.82 THE GOLDMAN SACHS GROUP, INC. (DEC)
NOTES TO CONSOLIDATED FINANCIAL STATEMENTS

Note 27. Legal Proceedings

The firm is involved in a number of judicial, regulatory and arbitration proceedings (including those described below) concerning matters arising in connection with the conduct of the firm's businesses. Many of these proceedings are in early stages, and many of these cases seek an indeterminate amount of damages.

Under ASC 450, an event is "reasonably possible" if "the chance of the future event or events occurring is more than remote but less than likely" and an event is "remote" if "the chance of the future event or events occurring is slight." Thus, references to the upper end of the range of reasonably possible loss for cases in which the firm is able to estimate a range of reasonably possible loss mean the upper end of the range of loss for cases for which the firm believes the risk of loss is more than slight. The amounts reserved against such matters are not significant as compared to the upper end of the range of reasonably possible loss.

With respect to proceedings described below for which management has been able to estimate a range of reasonably possible loss where (i) plaintiffs have claimed an amount of money damages, (ii) the firm is being sued by purchasers in an underwriting and is not being indemnified by a party that the firm believes will pay any judgment, or (iii) the purchasers are demanding that the firm repurchase securities, management has estimated the upper end of the range of reasonably possible loss as being equal to (a) in the case of (i), the amount of money damages claimed, (b) in the case of (ii), the amount of securities that the firm sold in the underwritings and (c) in the case of (iii), the price that purchasers paid for the securities less the estimated value, if any, as of December 2012 of the relevant securities, in each of cases (i), (ii) and (iii), taking into account any factors believed to be relevant to the particular proceeding or proceedings of that type. As of the date hereof, the firm has estimated the upper end of the range of reasonably possible aggregate loss for such proceedings and for any other proceedings described below where management has been able to estimate a range of reasonably possible aggregate loss to be approximately $3.5 billion.

Management is generally unable to estimate a range of reasonably possible loss for proceedings other than those included in the estimate above, including where (i) plaintiffs have not claimed an amount of money damages, unless management can otherwise determine an appropriate amount, (ii) the proceedings are in early stages, (iii) there is uncertainty as to the likelihood of a class being certified or the ultimate size of the class, (iv) there is uncertainty as to the outcome of pending appeals or motions, (v) there are significant factual issues to be resolved, and/or (vi) there are novel legal issues presented. However, for these cases, management does not believe, based on currently available information, that the outcomes of such proceedings will have a material adverse effect on the firm's financial condition, though the outcomes could be material to the firm's operating results for any particular period, depending, in part, upon the operating results for such period.

IPO Process Matters. Group Inc. and GS&Co. are among the numerous financial services companies that have been named as defendants in a variety of lawsuits alleging improprieties in the process by which those companies participated in the underwriting of public offerings.

GS&Co. has been named as a defendant in an action commenced on May 15, 2002 in New York Supreme Court, New York County, by an official committee of unsecured creditors on behalf of eToys, Inc., alleging that the firm intentionally underpriced eToys, Inc.'s initial public offering. The action seeks, among other things, unspecified compensatory damages resulting from the alleged lower amount of offering proceeds. On appeal from rulings on GS&Co.'s motion to dismiss, the New York Court of Appeals dismissed claims for breach of contract, professional malpractice and unjust enrichment, but permitted claims for breach of fiduciary duty and fraud to continue. On remand, the lower court granted GS&Co.'s motion for summary judgment and, on December 8, 2011, the appellate court affirmed the lower court's decision. On September 6, 2012, the New York Court of Appeals granted the creditors' motion for leave to appeal.

Group Inc. and certain of its affiliates have, together with various underwriters in certain offerings, received subpoenas and requests for documents and information from various governmental agencies and self-regulatory organizations in connection with investigations relating to the public offering process. Goldman Sachs has cooperated with these investigations.

World Online Litigation. In March 2001, a Dutch shareholders' association initiated legal proceedings for an unspecified amount of damages against GSI and others in Amsterdam District Court in connection with the initial public offering of World Online in March 2000, alleging misstatements and omissions in the offering materials and that the market was artificially inflated by improper public statements and stabilization activities. Goldman Sachs and ABN AMRO Rothschild served as joint global coordinators of the approximately €2.9 billion offering. GSI underwrote 20,268,846 shares and GS&Co. underwrote 6,756,282 shares for a total offering price of approximately €1.16 billion.

The district court rejected the claims against GSI and ABN AMRO, but found World Online liable in an amount to be determined. On appeal, the Netherlands Court of Appeals affirmed in part and reversed in part the decision of the district court, holding that certain of the alleged disclosure deficiencies were actionable as to GSI and ABN AMRO. On further appeal, the Netherlands Supreme Court affirmed the rulings of the Court of Appeals, except that it found certain additional aspects of the offering materials actionable and held that individual investors could potentially hold GSI and ABN AMRO responsible for certain public statements and press releases by World Online and its former CEO. The parties entered into a definitive settlement agreement, dated July 15, 2011, and GSI has paid the full amount of its contribution. In the first quarter of 2012, GSI and ABN AMRO, on behalf of the underwriting syndicate, entered into a settlement agreement with respect to a claim filed by another shareholders' association, and has paid the settlement amount in full. Other shareholders have made demands for compensation of alleged damages, and GSI and other syndicate members are discussing the possibility of settlement with certain of these shareholders.

Adelphia Communications Fraudulent Conveyance Litigation. GS&Co. is named as a defendant in two proceedings commenced in the U.S. Bankruptcy Court for the Southern District of New York, one on July 6, 2003 by a creditors committee, and the second on or about July 31, 2003 by an equity committee of Adelphia Communications, Inc. Those proceedings were consolidated in a single amended complaint filed by the Adelphia Recovery Trust on October 31, 2007. The complaint seeks, among other things, to recover, as fraudulent conveyances, approximately $62.9 million allegedly paid to GS&Co. by Adelphia Communications, Inc. and its affiliates in respect of margin calls made in the ordinary course of business on accounts owned by members of the family that formerly controlled Adelphia Communications, Inc. The district court assumed jurisdiction over the action and, on April 8, 2011, granted GS&Co.'s motion for summary judgment. The plaintiff appealed on May 6, 2011.

Specialist Matters. Spear, Leeds & Kellogg Specialists LLC, Spear, Leeds & Kellogg, L.P. and Group Inc. are among numerous defendants named in purported class actions brought beginning in October 2003 on behalf of investors in the U.S. District Court for the Southern District of New York alleging violations of the federal securities laws and state common law in connection with NYSE floor specialist activities. On October 24, 2012, the parties entered into a definitive settlement agreement, subject to court approval. The firm has reserved the full amount of its proposed contribution to the settlement.

Fannie Mae Litigation. GS&Co. was added as a defendant in an amended complaint filed on August 14, 2006 in a purported class action pending in the U.S. District Court for the District of Columbia. The complaint asserts violations of the federal securities laws generally arising from allegations concerning Fannie Mae's accounting practices in connection with certain Fannie Mae-sponsored REMIC transactions that were allegedly arranged by GS&Co. The complaint does not specify a dollar amount of damages. The other defendants include Fannie Mae, certain of its past and present officers and directors, and accountants. By a decision dated May 8, 2007, the district court granted GS&Co.'s motion to dismiss the claim against it. The time for an appeal will not begin to run until disposition of the claims against other defendants. A motion to stay the action filed by the Federal Housing Finance Agency (FHFA), which took control of the foregoing action following Fannie Mae's conservatorship, was denied on November 14, 2011.

Compensation-Related Litigation. On January 17, 2008, Group Inc., its Board, executive officers and members of its management committee were named as defendants in a purported shareholder derivative action in the U.S. District Court for the Eastern District of New York predicting that the firm's 2008 Proxy Statement would violate the federal securities laws by undervaluing certain stock option awards and alleging that senior management received excessive compensation for 2007. The complaint seeks, among other things, an equitable accounting for the allegedly excessive compensation. Plaintiff's motion for a preliminary injunction to prevent the 2008 Proxy Statement from using options valuations that the plaintiff alleges are incorrect and to require the amendment of SEC Forms 4 filed by certain of the executive officers named in the complaint to reflect the stock option valuations alleged by the plaintiff was denied, and plaintiff's appeal from this denial was dismissed. On February 13, 2009, the plaintiff filed an amended complaint, which added purported direct (i.e., non-derivative) claims based on substantially the same theory. The plaintiff filed a further amended complaint on March 24, 2010, and the defendants' motion to dismiss this further amended complaint was granted on the ground that dismissal of the shareholder plaintiff's prior action relating to the firm's 2007 Proxy Statement based on the failure to make a demand to the Board precluded relitigation of demand futility. On December 19, 2011, the appellate court vacated the order of dismissal, holding only that preclusion principles did not mandate dismissal and remanding for consideration of the alternative grounds for dismissal. On April 18, 2012, plaintiff disclosed that he no longer is a Group Inc. shareholder and thus lacks standing to continue to prosecute the action. On January 7, 2013, the district court dismissed the claim due to the plaintiff's lack of standing and the lack of any intervening shareholder.

On March 24, 2009, the same plaintiff filed an action in New York Supreme Court, New York County, against Group Inc., its directors and certain senior executives alleging violation of Delaware statutory and common law in connection with substantively similar allegations regarding stock option awards. On January 4, 2013, another purported shareholder moved to intervene as plaintiff, which defendants have opposed. On January 15, 2013, the court dismissed the action only as to the original plaintiff with prejudice due to his lack of standing.

Mortgage-Related Matters. On April 16, 2010, the SEC brought an action (SEC Action) under the U.S. federal securities laws in the U.S. District Court for the Southern District of New York against GS&Co. and Fabrice Tourre, a former employee, in connection with a CDO offering made in early 2007 (ABACUS 2007-AC1 transaction), alleging that the defendants made materially false and misleading statements to investors and seeking, among other things, unspecified monetary penalties. Investigations of GS&Co. by FINRA and of GSI by the FSA were subsequently initiated, and Group Inc. and certain of its affiliates have received subpoenas and requests for information from other regulators, regarding CDO offerings, including the ABACUS 2007-AC1 transaction, and related matters.

On July 14, 2010, GS&Co. entered into a consent agreement with the SEC, settling all claims made against GS&Co. in the SEC Action, pursuant to which GS&Co. paid $550 million of disgorgement and civil penalties, and which was approved by the U.S. District Court for the Southern District of New York on July 20, 2010.

On January 6, 2011, ACA Financial Guaranty Corp. filed an action against GS&Co. in respect of the ABACUS 2007-AC1 transaction in New York Supreme Court, New York County. The complaint includes allegations of fraudulent inducement, fraudulent concealment and unjust enrichment and seeks at least $30 million in compensatory damages, at least $90 million in punitive damages and unspecified disgorgement. On April 25, 2011, the plaintiff filed an amended complaint and, on June 3, 2011, GS&Co. moved to dismiss the amended complaint. By a decision dated April 23, 2012, the court granted the motion to dismiss as to the unjust enrichment claim and denied the motion as to the other claims, and on May 29, 2012, GS&Co. appealed the decision to the extent that its motion was denied and filed counterclaims for breach of contract and fraudulent inducement, and third-party claims against ACA Management, LLC for breach of contract, unjust enrichment and indemnification. ACA Financial Guaranty Corp. and ACA Management, LLC moved to dismiss GS&Co.'s counterclaims and third-party claims on August 31, 2012. On January 30, 2013, the court granted ACA's motion for leave to file an amended complaint naming a third party to the ABACUS 2007-AC1 transaction as an additional defendant.

Since April 23, 2010, the Board has received letters from shareholders demanding that the Board take action to address alleged misconduct by GS&Co., the Board and certain officers and employees of Group Inc. and its affiliates. These demands, which the Board has rejected, generally alleged misconduct in connection with the firm's securitization practices, including the ABACUS 2007-AC1 transaction, the alleged failure by Group Inc. to adequately disclose the SEC investigation that led to the SEC Action, and Group Inc.'s 2009 compensation practices.

In addition, the Board has received books and records demands from several shareholders for materials relating to, among other subjects, the firm's mortgage servicing and foreclosure activities, participation in federal programs providing assistance to financial institutions and homeowners, loan sales to Fannie Mae and Freddie Mac, mortgage-related activities and conflicts management.

Beginning April 26, 2010, a number of purported securities law class actions have been filed in the U.S. District Court for the Southern District of New York challenging the adequacy of Group Inc.'s public disclosure of, among other things, the firm's activities in the CDO market and the SEC investigation that led to the SEC Action. The purported class action complaints, which name as defendants Group Inc. and certain officers and employees of Group Inc. and its affiliates, have been consolidated, generally allege violations of Sections 10(b) and 20(a) of the Exchange Act and seek unspecified damages. Plaintiffs filed a consolidated amended complaint on July 25, 2011. On October 6, 2011, the defendants moved to dismiss, and by a decision dated June 21, 2012, the district court dismissed the claims based on Group Inc.'s not disclosing that it had received a "Wells" notice from the staff of the SEC related to the ABACUS 2007-AC1 transaction, but permitted the plaintiffs' other claims to proceed.

On February 1, 2013, a putative shareholder derivative action was filed in the U.S. District Court for the Southern District of New York against Group Inc. and certain of its officers and directors in connection with mortgage-related activities during 2006 and 2007, including three CDO offerings. The derivative complaint, which is based on similar allegations to those at issue in the consolidated class action discussed above and purported shareholder derivative actions that were previously dismissed, includes allegations of breach of fiduciary duty, challenges the accuracy and adequacy of Group Inc.'s disclosure and seeks, among other things, declaratory relief, unspecified compensatory and punitive damages and restitution from the individual defendants and certain corporate governance reforms.

In June 2012, the Board received a demand from a shareholder that the Board investigate and take action relating to the firm's mortgage-related activities and to stock sales by certain directors and executives of the firm. On February 15, 2013, this shareholder filed a putative shareholder derivative action in the New York Supreme Court, New York County, against Group Inc. and certain current or former directors and employees, based on these activities and stock sales. The derivative complaint includes allegations of breach of fiduciary duty, unjust enrichment, abuse of control, gross mismanagement and corporate waste, and seeks, among other things, unspecified monetary damages, disgorgement of profits and certain corporate governance and disclosure reforms.

GS&Co., Goldman Sachs Mortgage Company (GSMC) and GS Mortgage Securities Corp. (GSMSC) and three current or former Goldman Sachs employees are defendants in a putative class action commenced on December 11, 2008 in the U.S. District Court for the Southern District of New York brought on behalf of purchasers of various mortgage pass-through certificates and asset-backed certificates issued by various securitization trusts established by the firm and underwritten by GS&Co. in 2007. The complaint generally alleges that the registration statement and prospectus supplements for the certificates violated the federal securities laws, and seeks unspecified compensatory damages and rescission or rescissionary damages. Following dismissals of certain of the plaintiff's claims under the initial and three amended complaints, on May 5, 2011, the court granted plaintiff's motion for entry of a final judgment dismissing all its claims, thereby allowing plaintiff to appeal. The plaintiff appealed from the dismissal with respect to all 17 of the offerings included in its original complaint. By a decision dated September 6, 2012, the U.S. Court of Appeals for the Second Circuit affirmed the district court's dismissal of plaintiff's claims with respect to 10 of the offerings included in plaintiff's original complaint but vacated the dismissal and remanded the case to the district court with instructions to reinstate the plaintiff's claims with respect to the other seven offerings. On October 26, 2012, the defendants filed a petition for certiorari with the U.S. Supreme Court seeking review of the Second Circuit decision. On October 31, 2012, the plaintiff served defendants with a fourth amended complaint relating to those seven offerings, plus seven additional offerings. On June 3, 2010, another investor (who had unsuccessfully sought to intervene in the action) filed a separate putative class action asserting substantively similar allegations relating to one of the offerings included in the initial plaintiff's complaint. The district court twice granted defendants' motions to dismiss this separate action, both times with leave to replead. On July 9, 2012, that separate plaintiff filed a second amended complaint, and the defendants moved to dismiss on September 21, 2012. On December 26, 2012, that separate plaintiff filed a motion to amend the second amended complaint to add claims with respect to two additional offerings included in the initial plaintiff's complaint. The securitization trusts issued, and GS&Co. underwrote, approximately $11 billion principal amount of certificates to all purchasers in the fourteen offerings at issue in the complaints.

Group Inc., GS&Co., GSMC and GSMSC are among the defendants in a separate putative class action commenced on February 6, 2009 in the U.S. District Court for the Southern District of New York brought on behalf of purchasers of various mortgage pass-through certificates and asset-backed certificates issued by various securitization trusts established by the firm and underwritten by GS&Co. in 2006. The other original defendants include three current or former Goldman Sachs employees and various rating agencies. The second amended complaint generally alleges that the registration statement and prospectus supplements for the certificates violated the federal securities laws, and seeks unspecified compensatory and rescissionary damages. Defendants moved to dismiss the second amended complaint. On January 12, 2011, the district court granted the motion to dismiss with respect to offerings in which plaintiff had not purchased securities as well as all claims against the rating agencies, but denied the motion to dismiss with respect to a single offering in which the plaintiff allegedly purchased securities. These trusts issued, and GS&Co. underwrote, approximately $698 million principal amount of certificates to all purchasers in the offerings at issue in the complaint (excluding those offerings for which the claims have been dismissed). On February 2, 2012, the district court granted the plaintiff's motion for class certification and on June 13, 2012, the U.S. Court of Appeals for the Second Circuit granted defendants' petition to review that ruling. On November 8, 2012, the court approved a settlement between the parties, and GS&Co. has paid the full amount of the settlement into an escrow account. The time for any appeal from the approval of the settlement has expired.

On September 30, 2010, a putative class action was filed in the U.S. District Court for the Southern District of New York against GS&Co., Group Inc. and two former GS&Co. employees on behalf of investors in $821 million of notes issued in 2006 and 2007 by two synthetic CDOs (Hudson Mezzanine 2006-1 and 2006-2). The complaint, which was amended on February 4, 2011, asserts federal securities law and common law claims, and seeks unspecified compensatory, punitive and other damages. The defendants moved to dismiss on April 5, 2011, and the motion was granted as to plaintiff's claim of market manipulation and denied as to the remainder of plaintiff's claims by a decision dated March 21, 2012. On May 21, 2012, the defendants counterclaimed for breach of contract and fraud. On December 17, 2012, the plaintiff moved for class certification.

GS&Co., GSMC and GSMSC are among the defendants in a lawsuit filed in August 2011 by CIFG Assurance of North America, Inc. (CIFG) in New York Supreme Court, New York County. The complaint alleges that CIFG was fraudulently induced to provide credit enhancement for a 2007 securitization sponsored by GSMC, and seeks, among other things, the repurchase of $24.7 million in aggregate principal amount of mortgages that CIFG had previously stated to be non-conforming, an accounting for any proceeds associated with mortgages discharged from the securitization and unspecified compensatory damages. On October 17, 2011, the Goldman Sachs defendants moved to dismiss. By a decision dated May 1, 2012, the court dismissed the fraud and accounting claims but denied the motion as to certain breach of contract claims that were also alleged. On June 6, 2012, the Goldman Sachs defendants filed counterclaims for breach of contract. In addition, the parties have each appealed the court's May 1, 2012 decision to the extent adverse. The parties have been ordered to mediate, and proceedings in the trial court have been stayed pending mediation.

In addition, on January 15, 2013, CIFG filed a complaint against GS&Co. in New York Supreme Court, New York County, alleging that GS&Co. falsely represented that a third party would independently select the collateral for a 2006 CDO. CIFG seeks unspecified compensatory and punitive damages, including approximately $10 million in connection with its purchase of notes and over $30 million for payments to discharge alleged liabilities arising from its issuance of a financial guaranty insurance policy guaranteeing payment on a credit default swap referencing the CDO.

Various alleged purchasers of, and counterparties involved in transactions relating to, mortgage pass-through certificates, CDOs and other mortgage-related products (including certain Allstate affiliates, Bank Hapoalim B.M., Basis Yield Alpha Fund (Master), Bayerische Landesbank, Cambridge Place Investment Management Inc., the Charles Schwab Corporation, Deutsche Zentral-Genossenschaftbank, the FDIC (as receiver for Guaranty Bank), the Federal Home Loan Banks of Boston, Chicago, Indianapolis and Seattle, the FHFA (as conservator for Fannie Mae and Freddie Mac), HSH Nordbank, IKB Deutsche Industriebank AG, Landesbank Baden-Württemberg, Joel I. Sher (Chapter 11 Trustee) on behalf of TMST, Inc. (TMST), f/k/a Thornburg Mortgage, Inc. and certain TMST affiliates, John Hancock and related parties, Massachusetts Mutual Life Insurance Company, MoneyGram Payment Systems, Inc., National Australia Bank, the National Credit Union Administration, Phoenix Light SF Limited and related parties, Prudential Insurance Company of America and related parties, Royal Park Investments SA/NV, Sealink Funding Limited, Stichting Pensioenfonds ABP, The Union Central Life Insurance Company, Ameritas Life Insurance Corp., Acacia Life Insurance Company, Watertown Savings Bank, and The Western and Southern Life Insurance Co.) have filed complaints or summonses with notice in state and federal court or initiated arbitration proceedings against firm affiliates, generally alleging that the offering documents for the securities that they purchased contained untrue statements of material fact and material omissions and generally seeking rescission and/or damages. Certain of these complaints allege fraud and seek punitive damages. Certain of these complaints also name other firms as defendants.

A number of other entities (including American International Group, Inc. (AIG), Deutsche Bank National Trust Company, John Hancock and related parties, M&T Bank, Norges Bank Investment Management and Selective Insurance Company) have threatened to assert claims of various types against the firm in connection with various mortgage-related transactions, and the firm has entered into agreements with a number of these entities to toll the relevant statute of limitations.

As of the date hereof, the aggregate notional amount of mortgage-related securities sold to plaintiffs in active cases brought against the firm where those plaintiffs are seeking rescission of such securities was approximately $20.7 billion (which does not reflect adjustment for any subsequent paydowns or distributions or any residual value of such securities, statutory interest or any other adjustments that may be claimed). This amount does not include the threatened claims noted above, potential claims by these or other purchasers in the same or other mortgage-related offerings that have not actually been brought against the firm, or claims that have been dismissed.

In June 2011, Heungkuk Life Insurance Co. Limited (Heungkuk) filed a criminal complaint against certain past and present employees of the firm in South Korea relating to its purchase of a CDO securitization from Goldman Sachs. Heungkuk had earlier initiated civil litigation against the firm relating to this matter. This civil litigation has now been settled and, on January 23, 2013, Heungkuk withdrew the criminal complaint in its entirety.

Group Inc. and GS Bank USA have entered into a Consent Order and a settlement in principle with the Federal Reserve Board relating to the servicing of residential mortgage loans and foreclosure practices. In addition, GS Bank USA has entered into an Agreement on Mortgage Servicing Practices with the New York State Department of Financial Services, Litton and Ocwen. See Note 18 for information about these settlements.

Group Inc., GS&Co. and GSMC are among the numerous financial services firms named as defendants in a *qui tam* action originally filed by a relator on April 7, 2010 purportedly on behalf of the City of Chicago and State of Illinois in Cook County, Illinois Circuit Court asserting claims under the Illinois Whistleblower Reward and Protection Act and Chicago False Claims Act, based on allegations that defendants had falsely certified compliance with various Illinois laws, which were purportedly violated in connection with mortgage origination and servicing activities. The complaint, which was originally filed under seal, seeks treble damages and civil penalties. Plaintiff filed an amended complaint on December 28, 2011, naming GS&Co. and GSMC, among others, as additional defendants and a second amended complaint on February 8, 2012. On March 12, 2012, the action was removed to the U.S. District Court for the Northern District of Illinois, and on September 17, 2012 the district court granted the plaintiff's motion to remand the action to state court. On November 16, 2012, the defendants moved to dismiss and to stay discovery.

Group Inc., Litton and Ocwen are defendants in a putative class action filed on January 23, 2013 in the U.S. District Court for the Southern District of New York generally challenging the procurement manner and scope of "force-placed" hazard insurance arranged by Litton when homeowners failed to arrange for insurance as required by their mortgages. The complaint asserts claims for breach of contract, breach of fiduciary duty, misappropriation, conversion, unjust enrichment and violation of Florida unfair practices law, and seeks unspecified compensatory and punitive damages as well as declaratory and injunctive relief.

The firm has also received, and continues to receive, requests for information and/or subpoenas from federal, state and local regulators and law enforcement authorities, relating to the mortgage-related securitization process, subprime mortgages, CDOs, synthetic mortgage-related products, particular transactions involving these products, and servicing and foreclosure activities, and is cooperating with these regulators and other authorities, including in some cases agreeing to the tolling of the relevant statute of limitations. See also "Financial Crisis-Related Matters" below.

The firm expects to be the subject of additional putative shareholder derivative actions, purported class actions, rescission and "put back" claims and other litigation, additional investor and shareholder demands, and additional regulatory and other investigations and actions with respect to mortgage-related offerings, loan sales, CDOs, and servicing and foreclosure activities. See Note 18 for further information regarding mortgage-related contingencies.

Private Equity-Sponsored Acquisitions Litigation. Group Inc. and "GS Capital Partners" are among numerous private equity firms and investment banks named as defendants in a federal antitrust action filed in the U.S. District Court for the District of Massachusetts in December 2007. As amended, the complaint generally alleges that the defendants have colluded to limit competition in bidding for private equity-sponsored acquisitions of public companies, thereby resulting in lower prevailing bids and, by extension, less consideration for shareholders of those companies in violation of Section 1 of the U.S. Sherman Antitrust Act and common law. The complaint seeks, among other things, treble damages in an unspecified amount. Defendants moved to dismiss on August 27, 2008. The district court dismissed claims relating to certain transactions that were the subject of releases as part of the settlement of shareholder actions challenging such transactions, and by an order dated December 15, 2008 otherwise denied the motion to dismiss. On April 26, 2010, the plaintiffs moved for leave to proceed with a second phase of discovery encompassing additional transactions. On August 18, 2010, the court permitted discovery on eight additional transactions, and the plaintiffs filed a fourth amended complaint on October 7, 2010. On January 13, 2011, the court granted defendants' motion to dismiss certain aspects of the fourth amended complaint. On March 1, 2011, the court granted the motion filed by certain defendants, including Group Inc., to dismiss another claim of the fourth amended complaint on the grounds that the transaction was the subject of a release as part of the settlement of a shareholder action challenging the transaction. On June 14, 2012, the plaintiffs filed a fifth amended complaint encompassing additional transactions. On July 18, 2012, the court granted defendants' motion to dismiss certain newly asserted claims on the grounds that certain transactions are subject to releases as part of settlements of shareholder actions challenging those transactions, and denied defendants' motion to dismiss certain additional claims as time-barred. On July 23, 2012, the defendants filed motions for summary judgment.

IndyMac Pass-Through Certificates Litigation. GS&Co. is among numerous underwriters named as defendants in a putative securities class action filed on May 14, 2009 in the U.S. District Court for the Southern District of New York. As to the underwriters, plaintiffs allege that the offering documents in connection with various securitizations of mortgage-related assets violated the disclosure requirements of the federal securities laws. The defendants include IndyMac-related entities formed in connection with the securitizations, the underwriters of the offerings, certain ratings agencies which evaluated the credit quality of the securities, and certain former officers and directors of IndyMac affiliates. On November 2, 2009, the underwriters moved to dismiss the complaint. The motion was granted in part on February 17, 2010 to the extent of dismissing claims based on offerings in which no plaintiff purchased, and the court reserved judgment as to the other aspects of the motion. By a decision dated June 21, 2010, the district court formally dismissed all claims relating to offerings in which no named plaintiff purchased certificates (including all offerings underwritten by GS&Co.), and both granted and denied the defendants' motions to dismiss in various other respects. On November 16, 2012 the district court denied the plaintiffs' motion seeking reinstatement of claims relating to 42 offerings previously dismissed for lack of standing (one of which was co-underwritten by GS&Co.) without prejudice to renewal depending on the outcome of the petition for a writ of certiorari to the U.S. Supreme Court with respect to the Second Circuit's decision described above. On May 17, 2010, four additional investors filed a motion seeking to intervene in order to assert claims based on additional offerings (including two underwritten by GS&Co.). The defendants opposed the motion on the ground that the putative intervenors' claims were time-barred and, on June 21, 2011, the court denied the motion to intervene with respect to, among others, the claims based on the offerings underwritten by GS&Co. Certain of the putative intervenors (including those seeking to assert claims based on two offerings underwritten by GS&Co.) have appealed. GS&Co. underwrote approximately $751 million principal amount of securities to all purchasers in the offerings at issue in the May 2010 motion to intervene.

On July 11, 2008, IndyMac Bank was placed under an FDIC receivership, and on July 31, 2008, IndyMac Bancorp, Inc. filed for Chapter 7 bankruptcy in the U.S. Bankruptcy Court in Los Angeles, California.

RALI Pass-Through Certificates Litigation. GS&Co. is among numerous underwriters named as defendants in a putative securities class action initially filed in September 2008 in New York Supreme Court, and subsequently removed to the U.S. District Court for the Southern District of New York. As to the underwriters, plaintiffs allege that the offering documents in connection with various offerings of mortgage-backed pass-through certificates violated the disclosure requirements of the federal securities laws. In addition to the underwriters, the defendants include Residential Capital, LLC (ResCap), Residential Accredit Loans, Inc. (RALI), Residential Funding Corporation (RFC), Residential Funding Securities Corporation (RFSC), and certain of their officers and directors. On March 31, 2010, the defendants' motion to dismiss was granted in part and denied in part by the district court, resulting in dismissal on the basis of standing of all claims relating to offerings in which no plaintiff purchased securities and, by an order dated January 3, 2013, the district court denied, without prejudice, plaintiffs' motion for reconsideration. In June and July 2010, the lead plaintiff and five additional investors moved to intervene in order to assert claims based on additional offerings (including two underwritten by GS&Co.). On April 28, 2011, the court granted defendants' motion to dismiss as to certain of these claims (including those relating to one offering underwritten by GS&Co. based on a release in an unrelated settlement), but otherwise permitted the intervenor case to proceed. By an order dated January 3, 2013, the district court denied the defendants' motions to dismiss certain of the intervenors' remaining claims as time barred. Class certification of the claims based on the pre-intervention offerings was initially denied by the district court, and that denial was upheld on appeal; however, following remand, on October 15, 2012, the district court certified a class in connection with the pre-intervention offerings. On November 5, 2012, the defendants filed a petition seeking leave from the U.S. Court of Appeals to appeal the certification order. By an order dated January 3, 2013, the district court granted the plaintiffs' application to modify the class definition to include initial purchasers who bought the securities directly from the underwriters or their agents no later than ten trading days after the offering date (rather than just on the offering date). On January 18, 2013, the defendants filed a supplemental petition seeking leave from the U.S. Court of Appeals to appeal the order modifying the class definition.

GS&Co. underwrote approximately $1.28 billion principal amount of securities to all purchasers in the offerings for which claims have not been dismissed. On May 14, 2012, ResCap, RALI and RFC filed for Chapter 11 bankruptcy in the U.S. Bankruptcy Court for the Southern District of New York and the action has been stayed with respect to them, RFSC and certain of their officers and directors.

MF Global Securities Litigation. GS&Co. is among numerous underwriters named as defendants in class action complaints filed in the U.S. District Court for the Southern District of New York commencing November 18, 2011. These complaints generally allege that the offering materials for two offerings of MF Global Holdings Ltd. convertible notes (aggregating approximately $575 million in principal amount) in February 2011 and July 2011, among other things, failed to describe adequately the nature, scope and risks of MF Global's exposure to European sovereign debt, in violation of the disclosure requirements of the federal securities laws. On August 20, 2012, the plaintiffs filed a consolidated amended complaint and on October 19, 2012, the defendants filed motions to dismiss the amended complaint. GS&Co. underwrote an aggregate principal amount of approximately $214 million of the notes. On October 31, 2011, MF Global Holdings Ltd. filed for Chapter 11 bankruptcy in the U.S. Bankruptcy Court in Manhattan, New York.

GS&Co. has also received inquiries from various governmental and regulatory bodies and self-regulatory organizations concerning certain transactions with MF Global prior to its bankruptcy filing. Goldman Sachs is cooperating with all such inquiries.

Employment-Related Matters. On September 15, 2010, a putative class action was filed in the U.S. District for the Southern District of New York by three former female employees alleging that Group Inc. and GS&Co. have systematically discriminated against female employees in respect of compensation, promotion, assignments, mentoring and performance evaluations. The complaint alleges a class consisting of all female employees employed at specified levels by Group Inc. and GS&Co. since July 2002, and asserts claims under federal and New York City discrimination laws. The complaint seeks class action status, injunctive relief and unspecified amounts of compensatory, punitive and other damages. Group Inc. and GS&Co. filed a motion to stay the claims of one of the named plaintiffs and to compel individual arbitration with that individual, based on an arbitration provision contained in an employment agreement between Group Inc. and the individual. On April 28, 2011, the magistrate judge to whom the district judge assigned the motion denied the motion, and the district court affirmed the magistrate judge's decision on November 15, 2011. Group Inc. and GS&Co. have appealed that decision to the U.S. Court of Appeals for the Second Circuit. On June 13, 2011, Group Inc. and GS&Co. moved to strike the class allegations of one of the three named plaintiffs based on her failure to exhaust administrative remedies. On September 29, 2011, the magistrate judge recommended denial of the motion to strike and, on January 10, 2012, the district court denied the motion to strike. On July 22, 2011, Group Inc. and GS&Co. moved to strike all of the plaintiffs' class allegations, and for partial summary judgment as to plaintiffs' disparate impact claims. By a decision dated January 19, 2012, the magistrate judge recommended that defendants' motion be denied as premature. The defendants filed objections to that recommendation with the district judge and on July 17, 2012, the district court issued a decision granting in part Group Inc.'s and GS&Co.'s motion to strike plaintiffs' class allegations on the ground that plaintiffs lacked standing to pursue certain equitable remedies and denying in part Group Inc.'s and GS&Co.'s motion to strike plaintiffs' class allegations in their entirety as premature.

Investment Management Services. Group Inc. and certain of its affiliates are parties to various civil litigation and arbitration proceedings and other disputes with clients relating to losses allegedly sustained as a result of the firm's investment management services. These claims generally seek, among other things, restitution or other compensatory damages and, in some cases, punitive damages. In addition, Group Inc. and its affiliates are subject from time to time to investigations and reviews by various governmental and regulatory bodies and self-regulatory organizations in connection with the firm's investment management services. Goldman Sachs is cooperating with all such investigations and reviews.

Goldman Sachs Asset Management International (GSAMI) is the defendant in an action filed on July 9, 2012 with the High Court of Justice in London by certain entities representing Vervoer, a Dutch pension fund, alleging that GSAMI was negligent in performing its duties as investment manager in connection with the allocation of the plaintiffs' funds among asset managers in accordance with asset allocations provided by plaintiffs and that GSAMI breached its contractual and common law duties to the plaintiffs. Specifically, plaintiffs allege that GSAMI caused their assets to be invested in unsuitable products for an extended period, thereby causing in excess of €67 million in losses, and caused them to be under-exposed for a period of time to certain other investments that performed well, thereby resulting in foregone potential gains. The plaintiffs are seeking unspecified monetary damages. On November 2, 2012, GSAMI served its defense to the allegations and on December 21, 2012, the plaintiffs served their reply to the defense.

Financial Advisory Services. Group Inc. and certain of its affiliates are parties to various civil litigation and arbitration proceedings and other disputes with clients and third parties relating to the firm's financial advisory activities. These claims generally seek, among other things, compensatory damages and, in some cases, punitive damages, and in certain cases allege that the firm did not appropriately disclose or deal with conflicts of interest. In addition, Group Inc. and its affiliates are subject from time to time to investigations and reviews by various governmental and regulatory bodies and self-regulatory organizations in connection with conflicts of interest. Goldman Sachs is cooperating with all such investigations and reviews.

Group Inc., GS&Co. and The Goldman, Sachs & Co. L.L.C. are defendants in an action brought by the founders and former majority shareholders of Dragon Systems, Inc. (Dragon) on November 18, 2008, alleging that the plaintiffs incurred losses due to GS&Co.'s financial advisory services provided in connection with the plaintiffs' exchange of their purported $300 million interest in Dragon for stock of Lernout & Hauspie Speech Products, N.V. (L&H) in 2000. L&H filed for Chapter 11 bankruptcy in the U.S. Bankruptcy Court in Wilmington, Delaware on November 29, 2000. The action is pending in the United States District Court for the District of Massachusetts. The complaint, which was amended in November 2011 following the 2009 dismissal of certain of the plaintiffs' initial claims, seeks unspecified compensatory, punitive and other damages, and alleges breach of fiduciary duty, violation of Massachusetts unfair trade practices laws, negligence, negligent and intentional misrepresentation, gross negligence, willful misconduct and bad faith. Former minority shareholders of Dragon have brought a similar action against GS&Co. with respect to their purported $49 million interest in Dragon, and this action has been consolidated with the action described above. All parties moved for summary judgment. By an order dated October 31, 2012, the court granted summary judgment with respect to certain counterclaims and an indemnification claim brought by the Goldman Sachs defendants against one of the shareholders, but denied summary judgment with respect to all other claims. On January 23, 2013, a jury found in favor of the Goldman Sachs defendants on the plaintiffs' claims for negligence, negligent and intentional misrepresentation, gross negligence, and breach of fiduciary duty. The plaintiffs' claims for violation of Massachusetts unfair trade practices laws will be addressed by the district court and have not yet been decided.

Sales, Trading and Clearance Practices. Group Inc. and certain of its affiliates are subject to a number of investigations and reviews, certain of which are industry-wide, by various governmental and regulatory bodies and self-regulatory organizations relating to the sales, trading and clearance of corporate and government securities and other financial products, including compliance with the SEC's short sale rule, algorithmic and quantitative trading, futures trading, transaction reporting, securities lending practices, trading and clearance of credit derivative instruments, commodities trading, private placement practices and compliance with the U.S. Foreign Corrupt Practices Act.

The European Commission announced in April 2011 that it was initiating proceedings to investigate further numerous financial services companies, including Group Inc., in connection with the supply of data related to credit default swaps and in connection with profit sharing and fee arrangements for clearing of credit default swaps, including potential anti-competitive practices. The proceedings in connection with the supply of data related to credit default swaps are ongoing. Group Inc.'s current understanding is that the proceedings related to profit sharing and fee arrangements for clearing of credit default swaps have been suspended indefinitely. The firm has received civil investigative demands from the U.S. Department of Justice (DOJ) for information on similar matters. Goldman Sachs is cooperating with the investigations and reviews.

Insider Trading Investigations. From time to time, the firm and its employees are the subject of or otherwise involved in regulatory investigations relating to insider trading, the potential misuse of material nonpublic information and the effectiveness of the firm's insider trading controls and information barriers. It is the firm's practice to cooperate fully with any such investigations.

Research Investigations. From time to time, the firm is the subject of or otherwise involved in regulatory investigations relating to research practices, including research independence and interactions between research analysts and other firm personnel, including investment banking personnel. It is the firm's practice to cooperate fully with any such investigations.

EU Price-Fixing Matter. On July 5, 2011, the European Commission issued a Statement of Objections to Group Inc. raising allegations of an industry-wide conspiracy to fix prices for power cables, including by an Italian cable company in which certain Goldman Sachs-affiliated investment funds held ownership interests from 2005 to 2009. The Statement of Objections proposes to hold Group Inc. jointly and severally liable for some or all of any fine levied against the cable company under the concept of parental liability under EU competition law.

Municipal Securities Matters. Group Inc. and certain of its affiliates are subject to a number of investigations and reviews by various governmental and regulatory bodies and self-regulatory organizations relating to transactions involving municipal securities, including wall-cross procedures and conflict of interest disclosure with respect to state and municipal clients, the trading and structuring of municipal derivative instruments in connection with municipal offerings, political contribution rules, underwriting of Build America Bonds and the possible impact of credit default swap transactions on municipal issuers. Goldman Sachs is cooperating with the investigations and reviews.

Group Inc., Goldman Sachs Mitsui Marine Derivative Products, L.P. (GSMMDP) and GS Bank USA are among numerous financial services firms that have been named as defendants in numerous substantially identical individual antitrust actions filed beginning on November 12, 2009 that have been coordinated with related antitrust class action litigation and individual actions, in which no Goldman Sachs affiliate is named, for pre-trial proceedings in the U.S. District Court for the Southern District of New York. The plaintiffs include individual California municipal entities and three New York non-profit entities. All of these complaints against Group Inc., GSMMDP and GS Bank USA generally allege that the Goldman Sachs defendants participated in a conspiracy to arrange bids, fix prices and divide up the market for derivatives used by municipalities in refinancing and hedging transactions from 1992 to 2008. The complaints assert claims under the federal antitrust laws and either California's Cartwright Act or New York's Donnelly Act, and seek, among other things, treble damages under the antitrust laws in an unspecified amount and injunctive relief. On April 26, 2010, the Goldman Sachs defendants' motion to dismiss complaints filed by several individual California municipal plaintiffs was denied. On August 19, 2011, Group Inc., GSMMDP and GS Bank USA were voluntarily dismissed without prejudice from all actions except one brought by a California municipal entity.

On August 21, 2008, GS&Co. entered into a settlement in principle with the Office of the Attorney General of the State of New York and the Illinois Securities Department (on behalf of the North American Securities Administrators Association) regarding auction rate securities. Under the agreement, Goldman Sachs agreed, among other things, (i) to offer to repurchase at par the outstanding auction rate securities that its private wealth management clients purchased through the firm prior to February 11, 2008, with the exception of those auction rate securities where auctions were clearing, (ii) to continue to work with issuers and other interested parties, including regulatory and governmental entities, to expeditiously provide liquidity solutions for institutional investors, and (iii) to pay a $22.5 million fine. The settlement is subject to approval by the various states. GS&Co. has entered into consent orders with New York, Illinois and most other states and is in the process of doing so with the remaining states.

On September 4, 2008, Group Inc. was named as a defendant, together with numerous other financial services firms, in two complaints filed in the U.S. District Court for the Southern District of New York alleging that the defendants engaged in a conspiracy to manipulate the auction securities market in violation of federal antitrust laws. The actions were filed, respectively, on behalf of putative classes of issuers of and investors in auction rate securities and seek, among other things, treble damages in an unspecified amount. Defendants' motion to dismiss was granted on January 26, 2010. On March 1, 2010, the plaintiffs appealed from the dismissal of their complaints.

Beginning in February 2012, GS&Co. was named as respondent in four FINRA arbitrations filed, respectively, by the cities of Houston, Texas and Reno, Nevada, a California school district and a North Carolina municipal power authority, based on GS&Co.'s role as underwriter and broker-dealer of the claimants' issuances of an aggregate of over $1.8 billion of auction rate securities from 2003 through 2007 (in the Houston arbitration, two other financial services firms were named as respondents, and in the North Carolina arbitration, one other financial services firm was named). Each claimant alleges that GS&Co. failed to disclose that it had a practice of placing cover bids on auctions, and failed to offer the claimant the option of a formulaic maximum rate (rather than a fixed maximum rate), and that, as a result, the claimant was forced to engage in a series of expensive refinancing and conversion transactions after the failure of the auction market (at an estimated cost, in the case of Houston, of approximately $90 million). Houston and Reno also allege that GS&Co. advised them to enter into interest rate swaps in connection with their auction rate securities issuances, causing them to incur additional losses (including, in the case of Reno, a swap termination obligation of over $8 million). The claimants assert claims for breach of fiduciary duty, fraudulent concealment, negligent misrepresentation, breach of contract, violations of the Exchange Act and state securities laws, and breach of duties under the rules of the Municipal Securities Rulemaking Board and the NASD, and seek unspecified damages. GS&Co. has moved in federal court to enjoin the Reno and California school district arbitrations pursuant to an exclusive forum selection clause in the transaction documents. On November 26, 2012, this motion was denied with regard to the Reno arbitration and, on February 8, 2013, this motion was granted with regard to the California school district arbitration.

Financial Crisis-Related Matters. Group Inc. and certain of its affiliates are subject to a number of investigations and reviews by various governmental and regulatory bodies and self-regulatory organizations and litigation relating to the 2008 financial crisis. Goldman Sachs is cooperating with the investigations and reviews.

TAX CONTINGENCIES

1.83 INSPERITY, INC. (DEC)
NOTES TO CONSOLIDATED FINANCIAL STATEMENTS

13. Commitments and Contingencies (in part)

Massachusetts Tax Assessment

During the fourth quarter of 2012, we received assessments of approximately $2.5 million, including interest and penalties, related to the alleged underpayment of corporate income taxes to the State of Massachusetts for tax years 2006 through 2008. In 2009, we received similar assessments of approximately $470,000, including interest and penalties, which covered tax years 2003 through 2005. We believe the assessments are without merit and intend to vigorously contest them. At this time, we are unable to determine the ultimate outcome of this matter. However, in the event the State of Massachusetts succeeds with enforcement of the assessments, we may be required to pay some or all of the assessments, which would reduce net income and could have a material adverse effect on net income in the reported period.

Pennsylvania Sales Taxes

Pennsylvania imposes a sales tax on "help" supply services. The Pennsylvania Department of Revenue ("department") had maintained that PEO services constitute help supply services and are subject to the tax. On February 21, 2012, the Pennsylvania Supreme Court affirmed the Appeals Court decision in the matter titled All Staffing vs. Commonwealth of Pennsylvania, which ruled that PEO services are not subject to the Pennsylvania sales tax.

For the period January 1, 2010, through September 30, 2011, we accrued approximately $2.5 million in Pennsylvania sales tax. As we believed our PEO services were not subject to the sales tax, we reduced our accrual for such amounts in the fourth quarter of 2011.

In 2010, we filed refund claims totaling $2.9 million with the Department for the sales taxes paid in error for the period April 1, 2007 through December 31, 2009. In the second quarter of 2012, the Pennsylvania Board of Finance and Revenue approved our refund claims, and we recognized a $2.9 million receivable and a corresponding reduction to payroll tax expense, a component of direct costs. During the third quarter of 2012, we received the $2.9 million refund.

As a result of a 2001 corporate restructuring, we filed for a transfer of our state unemployment tax reserve account with the Employment Development Department of the State of California ("EDD"). The EDD approved our request for transfer of the reserve account in May 2002 and also notified us of our new contribution rates based upon the approved transfer. In December 2003, we received a Notice of Duplicate Accounts and Notification of Assessment ("notice") from the EDD. The Notice stated that the EDD was collapsing the accounts of our subsidiaries into the account of the entity with the highest unemployment tax rate. The Notice also retroactively imposed the higher unemployment insurance rate on all of our California employees for 2003, resulting in an assessment of $5.6 million. In January 2004, we filed petitions with an administrative law judge of the California Unemployment Insurance Appeals Board ("ALJ") to protest the validity of the Notice, asserting several procedural and substantive defenses.

One procedural defense included in our appeal asserts that the EDD failed to meet the statutory requirement related to serving a proper notice within the stipulated time frame and that all of the statutes of limitations concerning the EDD's ability to reassess or modify unemployment tax rates for the periods addressed in the Notice had expired ("motification Defense"). During 2010, a California Circuit Court issued a ruling in favor of the EDD regarding a dispute involving a taxpayer who made arguments similar to our Notification Defense. The Supreme Court of California subsequently denied the taxpayer's petition for review. We subsequently received a statement of account from the EDD indicating taxes, penalties and interest due of approximately $8.1 million.

While still denying all liability, we entered into a written agreement with the EDD in September 2011 to fully and finally settle this dispute (the "settlement Agreement"). Pursuant to the terms of the Settlement Agreement, we agreed to pay $3.1 million (the "settlement Amount") to the EDD. The Settlement Amount of $3.1 million was paid and recorded in other income (expense) during the year ended December 31, 2011.

ENVIRONMENTAL MATTERS

1.84 LOUISIANA-PACIFIC CORPORATION (DEC)
CONSOLIDATED BALANCE SHEETS (in part)

Dollar amounts in millions, except per share

	December 31,	
	2012	2011
Liabilities and Stockholders' Equity		
Current liabilities:		
Current portion of long-term debt	$ 7.8	$ 5.3
Current portion of limited recourse notes payable	90.0	7.9
Accounts payable and accrued liabilities	139.5	122.3
Current portion of contingency reserves	2.0	4.0
Total current liabilities	239.3	139.5
Long-term debt, excluding current portion	782.7	715.9
Deferred income taxes	93.6	106.0
Contingency reserves, excluding current portion	12.8	17.2
Other long-term liabilities	168.8	160.4
Stockholders' equity:		
Preferred stock, $1 par value, 15,000,000 shares authorized, no shares issued	—	—
Common stock, $1 par value, 200,000,000 shares authorized, 150,423,999 and 149,818,301 shares issued	150.4	149.8
Additional paid-in capital	533.6	549.9
Retained earnings	710.6	681.8
Treasury stock, 11,889,468 shares and 12,678,360 shares, at cost	(252.9)	(274.4)
Accumulated comprehensive loss	(107.9)	(106.2)
Total stockholders' equity	1,033.8	1,000.9
Total liabilities and stockholders' equity	$2,331.0	$2,139.9

See Notes to the Financial Statements.

NOTES TO THE FINANCIAL STATEMENTS

18. Contingencies (in part)

LP maintains reserves for various contingent liabilities as follows:

	December 31,	
Dollar amounts in millions	2012	2011
Environmental reserves	$14.1	$15.0
Hardboard siding reserves	0.7	6.2
Total contingencies	14.8	21.2
Current portion	(2.0)	(4.0)
Long-term portion	$12.8	$17.2

LP's estimates of its loss contingencies are based on various assumptions and judgments. Due to the numerous uncertainties and variables associated with these assumptions and judgments, both the precision and reliability of the resulting estimates of the related contingencies are subject to substantial uncertainties. LP regularly monitors its estimated exposure to contingencies and, as additional information becomes known, may change its estimates significantly. While no estimate of the range of any such change can be made at this time, the amount that LP may ultimately pay in connection with these matters could materially exceed, in either the near term or the longer term, the amounts accrued to date. LP's estimates of its loss contingencies do not reflect potential future recoveries from insurance carriers except to the extent that recovery may from time to time be deemed probable as a result of an insurer's agreement to payment terms.

Environmental Proceedings

LP is involved in a number of environmental proceedings and activities, and may be wholly or partially responsible for known or unknown contamination existing at a number of other sites at which it has conducted operations or disposed of wastes. Based on the information currently available, management believes that any fines, penalties or other costs or losses resulting from these matters will not have a material effect on the financial position, results of operations, cash flows or liquidity of LP.

LP maintains a reserve for undiscounted estimated environmental loss contingencies. This reserve is primarily for estimated future costs of remediation of hazardous or toxic substances at numerous sites currently or previously owned by the Company. LP's estimates of its environmental loss contingencies are based on various assumptions and judgments, the specific nature of which varies in light of the particular facts and circumstances surrounding each environmental loss contingency. These estimates typically reflect assumptions and judgments as to the probable nature, magnitude and timing of required investigation, remediation and/or monitoring activities and the probable cost of these activities, and in some cases reflect assumptions and judgments as to the obligation or willingness and ability of third parties to bear a proportionate or allocated share of the cost of these activities. Due to the numerous uncertainties and variables associated with these assumptions and judgments, and the effects of changes in governmental regulation and environmental technologies, both the precision and reliability of the resulting estimates of the related contingencies are subject to substantial uncertainties. LP regularly monitors its estimated exposure to environmental loss contingencies and, as additional information becomes known, may change its estimates significantly. However, no estimate of the range of any such change can be made at this time.

In those instances in which LP's estimated exposure reflects actual or anticipated cost-sharing arrangements with third parties, LP does not believe that it will be exposed to additional material liability as a result of non-performance by such third parties. There are three forms of cost-sharing arrangements under which costs are apportioned to others and are therefore not reflected in LP's environmental reserves. The amounts involved, the number of sites and a description of each are as follows:
- Approximately $2.2 million of costs, relating to three sites, pursuant to formal cost-sharing arrangements between LP and one or more third parties.
- Approximately $2.7 million of costs, related to four transactions each covering multiple sites, pursuant to agreements contained in purchase and sale documents where LP has sold an asset to a third party and that third party has assumed responsibility for all or a portion of any remediation costs required for the sold asset.
- Approximately $0.2 million of costs, related to one site undergoing cleanup pursuant to federal or state environmental laws, where multiple parties are involved.

LP considers the financial condition of third parties subject to the cost-sharing arrangements discussed above in determining the amounts to be reflected in LP's environmental reserves. In addition, LP is a party to clean-up activities at two additional sites for which LP does not believe that the failure of a third party to discharge its allocated responsibility would significantly increase LP's financial responsibility based on the manner in which financial responsibility has been, or is expected to be, allocated.

LP's estimates of its environmental loss contingencies do not reflect potential future recoveries from insurance carriers except to the extent that recovery may from time to time be deemed probable as a result of a carrier's agreement to payment terms.

The activity in LP's reserve for estimated environmental loss contingency reserves for the last three years is summarized in the following table.

	Year Ended December 31,		
(Dollar amounts in millions)	2012	2011	2010
Beginning balance	$15.0	$14.3	$14.7
Adjusted to expense (income) during the year	0.7	1.5	0.3
Payments made	(1.6)	(0.8)	(0.7)
Ending balance	$14.1	$15.0	$14.3

During 2012, 2011 and 2010, LP adjusted its reserves at a number of sites to reflect current estimates of remediation costs.

ABT Hardboard Siding Matters

Between 1995 and 1999, ABT Building Products Corporation ("ABT"), ABTco, Inc., a wholly owned subsidiary of ABT ("ABTco" and, together with ABT, the "ABT Entities"), Abitibi-Price Corporation ("Abitibi"), a predecessor of ABT, and certain affiliates of Abitibi (the "Abitibi Affiliates" and, together with Abitibi, the "Abitibi Entities") were named as defendants in numerous class action and non-class action proceedings brought on behalf of various persons or purported classes of persons (including nationwide classes in the United States and Canada) who own or have purchased or installed hardboard siding manufactured or sold by the defendants. In general, the plaintiffs in these actions have claimed unfair business practices, breach of warranty, fraud, misrepresentation, negligence, and other theories related to alleged defects, deterioration, or other failure of such hardboard siding, and seek unspecified compensatory, punitive, and other damages (including consequential damage to the structures on which the siding was installed), attorneys' fees and other relief.

LP acquired ABT in February 1999 and ABT was merged into LP in January of 2001. On September 21, 2000, the Circuit Court of Choctaw County, Alabama, under the caption *Foster, et al. v. ABTco, Inc., ABT Building Products Corporation, Abitibi-Price, Inc. and Abitibi-Price Corporation* (No. CV95-151-M), approved a settlement agreement among the defendants and attorneys representing a nationwide class composed of all persons who own or formerly owned homes or, subject to limited exceptions, other buildings or structures on which hardboard siding manufactured by the defendants was installed between May 15, 1975 and May 15, 2000. Except for approximately 30 persons who timely opted out, the settlement includes and binds all members of the settlement class and resolves all claims asserted in the various proceedings described above. Under the settlement agreement, class members will have twenty-five years after their siding was installed to file a claim.

Under the settlement agreement, the defendants will be entitled to elect to make an offer of settlement to an eligible claimant based on the information set forth in the claim submitted by such claimant, and such claimant will be entitled to accept or reject the offer. If an eligible claimant declines the offer, or if no offer is made, such claimant will be entitled to a payment based on an independent inspection. Such payments will be based on a specified dollar amount (calculated on the basis of statewide averages and ranging from $2.65 to $6.21, depending upon the state) per square foot of covered siding that has experienced specified types of damage, subject to reduction based on the age of the damaged siding and any failure to paint the damaged siding within stated intervals (except in the case of damaged siding installed on mobile homes, as to which a uniform 50% reduction will apply in all circumstances). If applicable, payments under the settlement will also be subject to reduction to reflect any warranty payments or certain other payments previously recovered by a claimant on account of the damaged siding. Under the settlement agreement, LP (as a successor to ABT) will be required to pay the expenses of administering the settlement and certain other costs.

ABT and Abitibi were parties to an agreement of an allocation of liability with respect to claims related to siding sold prior to October 22, 1992. On June 13, 2001, In exchange for a cash payment from Abitibi of approximately $19.0 million which was received in July 2001, LPC, a wholly owned subsidiary of LP, agreed to accept a transfer of all of Abitibi's rights and obligations under the settlement agreement and the allocation agreement; and LP and LPC agreed to indemnify and hold harmless Abitibi from any cost or liability arising from its sale of hardboard siding in the United States. From the date of the agreement, Abitibi has no further rights, obligations or liabilities under either the class action settlement agreement or the allocation agreement. All such rights, obligations and liabilities have been assigned to and accepted and assumed by LPC.

During 2010, LP increased its reserves in connection with this class action settlement. The additional reserves reflect revised estimates of undiscounted future claim payments and related administrative costs. During 2011 and 2012, LP decreased its reserves in connection with this settlement due to reductions in claims activity. LP believes that the reserve balance at December 31, 2012 will be adequate to cover future payments to claimants and related administrative costs. However, it is possible that additional charges may be required in the future.

The activity in the portion of LP's loss contingency reserves relating to hardboard siding contingencies for the last three years is summarized in the following table. Included in this table for 2012 and 2011 are reimbursements received by LP from an insurance company for a portion of the claims payments and administrative costs covered under a court judgment related to production and sales of the specific products for specific years.

	Year Ended December 31,		
(Dollar amounts in millions)	2012	2011	2010
Beginning balance	$ 6.2	$ 17.8	$ 24.2
Accrued (reversed) to expense	(5.0)	(10.7)	(2.5)
Claims reimbursement	—	0.6	1.0
Payments made for claims	(0.4)	(1.1)	(3.6)
Payments made for administrative costs	(0.1)	(0.4)	(1.3)
Ending balance	$ 0.7	$ 6.2	$ 17.8

SELF-INSURANCE

1.85 THE MCCLATCHY COMPANY (DEC)
NOTES TO CONSOLIDATED FINANCIAL STATEMENTS

9. Commitments and Contingencies (in part)

Self-Insurance

We retain the risk for workers' compensation resulting from uninsured deductibles per accident or occurrence that are subject to annual aggregate limits. Losses up to the deductible amounts are accrued based upon known claims incurred and an estimate of claims incurred but not reported. For the year ended December 30, 2012, we compiled our historical data pertaining to the self-insurance experiences and actuarially developed the ultimate loss associated with our self-insurance programs for workers' compensation liability. We believe that the actuarial valuation provides the best estimate of the ultimate losses to be expected under these programs.

The undiscounted ultimate losses of all our self-insurance reserve related to our workers' compensation liabilities, net of insurance recoveries at December 30, 2012 and December 25, 2011, were $19.8 million and $20.5 million, respectively. Based on historical payment patterns, we expect payments of undiscounted ultimate losses, net of estimated insurance recoveries of approximately $9.1 million, to be as follows:

Year	Net Amount (In thousands)
2013	$ 4,827
2014	3,377
2015	2,478
2016	1,889
2017	1,481
Thereafter	5,717
Total	$19,769

We discount the net amount above to present value using an approximate risk-free rate over the average life of our insurance claims. For the years ended December 30, 2012 and December 25, 2011, the discount rate used was 1.1% and 1.4%, respectively. The present value of all self-insurance reserves, net of estimated insurance recoveries, for our workers' compensation liability recorded at December 30, 2012 and December 25, 2011, was $19.8 million and $20.4 million, respectively.

GOVERNMENT MATTERS

1.86 IRON MOUNTAIN INCORPORATED (DEC)
NOTES TO CONSOLIDATED FINANCIAL STATEMENTS

(In thousands, except share and per share data)

10. Commitments and Contingencies (in part)

e. Government Contract Billing Matter

Since October 2001, we have provided services to the U.S. Government under several General Services Administration ("GSA") multiple award schedule contracts (the "Schedules"). The earliest of the Schedules was renewed in October 2006 with certain modifications to its terms. The Schedules contain a price reductions clause ("Price Reductions Clause") that requires us to offer to reduce the prices billed to the Government under the Schedules to correspond to the prices billed to certain benchmark commercial customers. Through December 31, 2012, we billed approximately $54,000 under the Schedules. In 2011, we initiated an internal review covering the contract period commencing in October 2006, and we discovered potential non-compliance with the Price Reductions Clause. We voluntarily disclosed the potential non-compliance to the GSA and its Office of Inspector General ("OIG") in June 2011.

We continue to review this matter and provide the GSA and OIG with information regarding our pricing practices and the proposed pricing adjustment amount to be refunded. The GSA and OIG, however, may not agree with our determination of the refund amount and may request additional pricing adjustments, refunds, civil penalties, up to treble damages and/or interest related to our Schedules.

In April 2012, the U.S. Government sent us a subpoena seeking information that substantially overlaps with the subjects that are covered by the voluntary disclosure process that we initiated with the GSA and OIG in June 2011, except that the subpoena seeks information dating back to 2000 and seeks information about non-GSA federal and state and local customers. Despite the substantial overlap, we understand that the subpoena relates to a separate inquiry, under the civil False Claims Act, that has been initiated independent of the GSA and OIG voluntary disclosure matter. We cannot determine at this time whether this separate inquiry will result in liability in addition to the amount that may be paid in connection with the voluntary disclosure to the OIG and GSA described above.

Given the above, it is reasonably possible that an adjustment to our estimates may be required in the future as a result of updated facts and circumstances. To the extent that an adjustment to our estimates is necessary in a future period, we will assess, at that time, whether the adjustment is a result of a change in estimate or the correction of an error. A change in estimate would be reflected as an adjustment through the then-current period statement of operations. A correction of an error would require a quantitative and qualitative analysis to determine the approach to correcting the error. A correction of an error could be reflected in the then-current period statement of operations or as a restatement of prior period financial information, depending upon the underlying facts and circumstances and our quantitative and qualitative analysis.

f. State of Massachusetts Assessment

During the third quarter of 2012, we applied for abatement of assessments from the state of Massachusetts. The assessments related to a corporate excise audit of the 2004 through 2006 tax years in the aggregate amount of $8,191, including tax, interest and penalties through the assessment date. The applications for abatement were denied during the third quarter of 2012. On October 19, 2012 we filed petitions with the Massachusetts Appellate Tax Board challenging the assessments. The final outcome of this matter may require payment of additional corporate excise tax, which consists of two measures, an income tax, which is a component of the provision for income taxes, and a net worth tax, which is an operating charge. We intend to defend this matter vigorously at the Massachusetts Appellate Tax Board. In addition, we are currently under a corporate excise audit by the state of Massachusetts for the 2007 and 2008 tax years. The adjustments being proposed are for issues consistent with those assessed in the earlier years. The state has also informed us that an audit of the 2009-2011 years will begin shortly.

GUARANTEES

1.87 UNIVERSAL CORPORATION (MAR)
NOTES TO CONSOLIDATED FINANCIAL STATEMENTS

Note 10. Fair Value Measurements (in part)

Guarantees of Bank Loans to Tobacco Growers

The Company guarantees bank loans to tobacco growers in Brazil for crop financing and construction of curing barns or other tobacco producing assets. In the event that the farmers default on their payments to the banks, the Company would be required to perform under the guarantees. The Company regularly evaluates the likelihood of farmer defaults based on an expected loss analysis and records the fair value of its guarantees as an obligation in its consolidated financial statements. The fair value of the guarantees is determined using the expected loss data for all loans outstanding at each measurement date. The present value of the cash flows associated with the estimated losses is then calculated at a risk-adjusted interest rate (6.6% as of March 31, 2012 and 9.5% as of March 31, 2011) that is aligned with the expected duration of the liability and includes an adjustment for nonperformance risk. This approach is sometimes referred to as the "contingent claims valuation method." Although historical loss data is an observable input, significant judgment is required in applying this information to the portfolio of guaranteed loans outstanding at each measurement date and in selecting a risk-adjusted interest rate. Significant increases or decreases in the risk-adjusted interest rate may result in a significantly higher or lower fair value measurement. The guarantees of bank loans to tobacco growers are therefore classified within Level 3 of the fair value hierarchy.

A reconciliation of the change in the balance of the financial liability for guarantees of bank loans to tobacco growers (Level 3) for the fiscal years ended March 31, 2012 and 2011 is provided below. A significant number of the loans in the portfolio reached their maturity dates during fiscal year 2012. The Company satisfied its obligations under the related guarantees by remitting payment to the banks and taking title to the loans, thereby reducing the guarantee liability.

	Fiscal Year Ended March 31,	
	2012	2011
Balance at beginning of year	$ 20,699	$ 25,997
Transfer to allowance for loss on direct loans to farmers (removal of prior crop year and other loans from portfolio)	(18,305)	(14,724)
Transfer from allowance for loss on direct loans to farmers (addition of current crop year loans)	4,279	7,559
Transfer of guarantees to assignee of farmer contracts (see Note 14)	—	(1,110)
Change in discount rate and estimated collection period	780	1,389
Currency remeasurement	(1,521)	1,588
Balance at end of year	$ 5,932	$ 20,699

Universal has not elected to report at fair value any financial instruments or any other assets or liabilities that are not required to be reported at fair value under current accounting guidance.

Note 14. Commitments and Other Matters (in part)

Guarantees and Other Contingent Liabilities

Guarantees of bank loans to growers for crop financing and construction of curing barns or other tobacco producing assets are industry practice in Brazil and support the farmers' production of tobacco there. At March 31, 2012, the Company's total exposure under guarantees issued by its operating subsidiary in Brazil for banking facilities of farmers in that country was approximately $20 million ($26 million face amount including unpaid accrued interest, less $6 million recorded for the fair value of the guarantees). About 90% of these guarantees expire within one year, and all of the remainder expire within two years. As noted above, the subsidiary withholds payments due to the farmers on delivery of tobacco and forwards those payments to the third-party banks. Failure of farmers to deliver sufficient quantities of tobacco to the subsidiary to cover their obligations to the third-party banks could result in a liability for the subsidiary under the related guarantees; however, in that case, the subsidiary would have recourse against the farmers. The maximum potential amount of future payments that the Company's subsidiary could be required to make at March 31, 2012, was the face amount, $26 million including unpaid accrued interest ($73 million as of March

31, 2011). The fair value of the guarantees was a liability of approximately $6 million at March 31, 2012, and $21 million at March 31, 2011. In addition to these guarantees, the Company has other contingent liabilities totaling approximately $4 million.

1.88 CONOCOPHILLIPS (DEC)
NOTES TO CONSOLIDATED FINANCIAL STATEMENTS

Note 3—Variable Interest Entities (VIEs) (in part)

Australia Pacific LNG (APLNG)

APLNG is considered a VIE, as it has entered into certain contractual arrangements that provide it with additional forms of subordinated financial support. We are not the primary beneficiary of APLNG because we share with Origin Energy and China Petrochemical Corporation (Sinopec) the power to direct the key activities of APLNG that most significantly impact its economic performance, which involve activities related to the production and commercialization of coalbed methane, as well as LNG processing and export marketing. As a result, we do not consolidate APLNG, and it is accounted for as an equity method investment.

As of December 31, 2012, we have not provided, nor do we expect to provide in the future, any financial support to APLNG other than amounts previously contractually required. In addition, unless we elect otherwise, we have no requirement to provide liquidity or purchase the assets of APLNG. See Note 6—Investments, Loans and Long-Term Receivables, and Note 13—Guarantees, for additional information.

Note 13—Guarantees (in part)

At December 31, 2012, we were liable for certain contingent obligations under various contractual arrangements as described below. We recognize a liability at inception for the fair value of our obligation as a guarantor for newly issued or modified guarantees. Unless the carrying amount of the liability is noted below, we have not recognized a liability either because the guarantees were issued prior to December 31, 2002, or because the fair value of the obligation is immaterial. In addition, unless otherwise stated, we are not currently performing with any significance under the guarantee and expect future performance to be either immaterial or have only a remote chance of occurrence.

APLNG Guarantees

At December 31, 2012, we have outstanding multiple guarantees in connection with our 37.5 percent ownership interest in APLNG. The following is a description of the guarantees with values calculated utilizing December 2012 exchange rates:
- We have guaranteed APLNG's performance with regard to a construction contract executed in connection with APLNG's issuance of the Train 1 and Train 2 Notices to Proceed. We estimate the remaining term of this guarantee is 4 years. Our maximum potential amount of future payments related to this guarantee is approximately $180 million and would become payable if APLNG cancels the applicable construction contract and does not perform with respect to the amounts owed to the contractor.
- We have issued a construction completion guarantee related to the third-party project financing secured by APLNG. Our maximum potential amount of future payments under the guarantee is estimated to be $3.2 billion, which could be payable if the full debt financing capacity is utilized and completion of the project is not achieved. Our guarantee of the project financing will be released upon meeting certain completion milestones, which we estimate would occur beginning in 2016. Our maximum exposure at December 31, 2012, is $860 million based upon our pro-rata share of the facility used at that date. At December 31, 2012, the carrying value of this guarantee is approximately $114 million.
- In conjunction with our original purchase of an ownership interest in APLNG from Origin Energy in October 2008, we agreed to guarantee an existing obligation of APLNG to deliver natural gas under several sales agreements with remaining terms of 4 to 19 years. Our maximum potential amount of future payments, or cost of volume delivery, under these guarantees is estimated to be $1.0 billion ($2.4 billion in the event of intentional or reckless breach) and would become payable if APLNG fails to meet its obligations under these agreements and the obligations cannot otherwise be mitigated. Future payments are considered unlikely, as the payments, or cost of volume delivery, would only be triggered if APLNG does not have enough natural gas to meet these sales commitments and if the co-venturers do not make necessary equity contributions into APLNG.
- We have guaranteed the performance of APLNG with regard to certain other contracts executed in connection with the project's continued development. The guarantees have remaining terms of up to 33 years or the life of the venture. Our maximum potential amount of future payments related to these guarantees is approximately $150 million and would become payable if APLNG does not perform.

1.89 THE DOW CHEMICAL COMPANY (DEC)
NOTES TO THE CONSOLIDATED FINANCIAL STATEMENTS

Note 14—Commitments and Contingent Liabilities (in part)

Gain Contingency

Matters Involving the Formation of K-Dow Petrochemicals

Introduction

On December 13, 2007, the Company and Petrochemical Industries Company (K.S.C.) ("PIC") of Kuwait, a wholly owned subsidiary of Kuwait Petroleum Corporation, announced plans to form a 50:50 global petrochemicals joint venture. The proposed joint venture, K-Dow Petrochemicals ("K-Dow"), was expected to have revenues of more than $11 billion and employ more than 5,000 people worldwide.

On November 28, 2008, the Company entered into a Joint Venture Formation Agreement (the "JVFA") with PIC that provided for the establishment of K-Dow. To form the joint venture, the Company would transfer by way of contribution and sale to K-Dow, assets used in the research, development, manufacture, distribution, marketing and sale of polyethylene, polypropylene, polycarbonate, polycarbonate compounds and blends, ethyleneamines, ethanolamines, and related licensing and catalyst technologies; and K-Dow would assume certain related liabilities. PIC would receive a 50 percent equity interest in K-Dow in exchange for the payment by PIC of the initial purchase price, estimated to be $7.5 billion. The purchase price was subject to certain post-closing adjustments.

Failure to Close

On December 31, 2008, the Company received a written notice from PIC with respect to the JVFA advising the Company of PIC's position that certain conditions to closing were not satisfied and, therefore, PIC was not obligated to close the transaction. On January 2, 2009, PIC refused to close the K-Dow transaction in accordance with the JVFA. The Company disagreed with the characterizations and conclusions expressed by PIC in the written notice and the Company informed PIC that it breached the JVFA. On January 6, 2009, the Company announced that it would seek to fully enforce its rights under the terms of the JVFA and various related agreements.

Arbitration

The Company's claims against PIC were subject to an agreement between the parties to arbitrate under the Rules of Arbitration of the International Court of Arbitration of the International Chamber of Commerce ("ICC"). On February 18, 2009, the Company initiated arbitration proceedings against PIC alleging that PIC breached the JVFA by failing to close the transaction on January 2, 2009, and as a result, Dow suffered substantial damages.

On May 24, 2012, the ICC released to the parties a unanimous Partial Award in favor of the Company on both liability and damages. A three-member arbitration Tribunal found that PIC breached the JVFA by not closing K-Dow on January 2, 2009, and awarded the Company $2.16 billion in damages, not including pre- and post-award interest and arbitration costs.

On June 15, 2012, PIC filed an application for remand under the English Arbitration Act of 1996 ("Remand Application") in the High Court of Justice in London ("High Court"). In its Remand Application, PIC did not challenge the Tribunal's finding of liability but it requested that the High Court remand the case back to the Tribunal for further consideration of the Company's claim for consequential damages. On October 11, 2012, the High Court ruled in favor of the Company and dismissed PIC's Remand Application; and on October 19, 2012, the High Court denied PIC's request for leave to appeal its ruling, bringing an end to PIC's Remand Application.

The ICC is expected to issue a Final Award covering the Company's substantial claim for pre- and post-award interest and arbitration costs in early 2013.

The Company expects to record a gain related to this matter when the uncertainty regarding the timing of collection and the amount to be realized has been resolved.

1.90 PEABODY ENERGY CORPORATION (DEC)
NOTES TO CONSOLIDATED FINANCIAL STATEMENTS

(10) Income Taxes (in part)

The tax effects of temporary differences that give rise to significant portions of the deferred tax assets and liabilities consisted of the following:

	December 31,	
(Dollars in millions)	2012	2011
Deferred tax assets:		
Tax credits and loss carryforwards	$1,390.1	$ 432.8
Minerals resource rent tax	689.7	—
Postretirement benefit obligations	473.3	485.4
Intangible tax asset and purchased contract rights	7.9	13.4
Accrued reclamation and mine closing liabilities	137.9	112.9
Accrued long-term workers' compensation liabilities	15.7	15.6
Employee benefits	64.7	53.3
Financial guarantees	18.6	18.5
Other	56.5	57.8
Total gross deferred tax assets	2,854.4	1,189.7
Deferred tax liabilities:		
Property, plant, equipment and mine development, leased coal interests and advance royalties, principally due to differences in depreciation, depletion and asset writedowns	1,596.9	1,318.0
Unamortized discount on Convertible Junior Subordinated Debentures	132.8	132.5
Hedge activities	37.5	45.5
Investments and other assets	126.3	109.8
Total gross deferred tax liabilities	1,893.5	1,605.8
Valuation allowance, income tax	(714.9)	(79.8)
Valuation allowance, minerals resource rent tax	(766.9)	—
Net deferred tax liability	$ (520.9)	$ (495.9)
Deferred taxes are classified as follows:		
Current deferred income taxes	$ 56.4	$ 27.3
Noncurrent deferred income taxes	(577.3)	(523.2)
Net deferred tax liability	$ (520.9)	$ (495.9)

The Company's tax credits and tax effected loss carryforwards includes U.S. alternative minimum tax (AMT) credits of $232.6 million, general business credits of $52.6 million, U.S. capital losses of $113.2 million, state net operating loss (NOL) carryforwards of $36.1 million and foreign NOL carryforwards of $955.6 million as of December 31, 2012. The AMT credits and foreign NOLs have no expiration date. The U.S. capital loss and the general business credits begin to expire in 2017 and 2027, respectively. The state NOLs begin to expire in the year 2013. In assessing the near term use of NOLs and tax credits and corresponding valuation allowance adjustments, the Company evaluated the expected level of future taxable income, available tax planning strategies, reversals of existing taxable temporary differences and taxable income in carryback years. The $521.5 million change in the valuation allowance recorded directly to deferred income tax expense was primarily due to limitations on the U.S. capital losses, a loss utilization factor on certain Australian loss carryforwards which will limit recoverability and foreign deferred tax assets with limited recoverability. The income tax valuation allowance at December 31, 2012 of $714.9 million represents a reserve for U.S. capital losses, state NOLs, foreign NOLs and certain deferred tax assets.

During the year ended December 31, 2012, Australia passed legislation creating a minerals resource rent tax (the MRRT) effective from July 1, 2012. The MRRT is a profits-based tax on the Company's existing and future Australian coal projects at an effective tax rate of 22.5%. Under the MRRT, taxpayers are able to elect a market value asset starting base for existing projects which allows for the fair market value of the tenements to be deducted over the life of the mine as an allowance against MRRT. The realization of the market value allowance is subject to numerous uncertainties including utilization of other MRRT allowances provided under the law and estimates of long-term pricing and cost data. During 2012, the Company recorded a net deferred tax liability relating to MRRT of $77.2 million. As of December 31, 2012, the Company has recorded a gross deferred tax asset of $871.8 million from the market value allowance, royalty credit carryforwards and other adjustments. The gross deferred tax asset is offset by a deferred tax liability of $182.1 million primarily relating to excess book over tax basis in certain exploration properties. The Company separately recorded a valuation allowance of $766.9 million on the market value allowance due to limitations on recoverability.

During the year ended December 31, 2012, the Company realized a net tax benefit of $74.7 million due to restructuring of foreign operations associated with the acquisition of PEA-PCI. The net tax benefit included a U.S. federal and state capital loss benefit of $39.6 million and a foreign tax benefit of $35.1 million due to the tax basis reset required upon the PEA-PCI operations joining the Company's Australian consolidated tax group.

Financial Instruments

RECOGNITION AND MEASUREMENT

1.91 FASB ASC 815, *Derivatives and Hedging*, establishes accounting and reporting standards for derivative instruments, including certain derivative instruments embedded in other contracts (collectively referred to as derivatives), and hedging activities. FASB ASC 815 requires that an entity recognize all derivatives as either assets or liabilities in the statement of financial position and measure those instruments at fair value. In addition, paragraphs 4–6 of FASB ASC 815-15-25 simplify the accounting for certain hybrid financial instruments by permitting an entity to irrevocably elect to initially and subsequently measure that hybrid financial instrument in its entirety at fair value, with changes recognized in earnings. This election is also available when a previously-recognized financial instrument is subject to a remeasurement (new basis) event and the separate recognition of an embedded derivative.

1.92 FASB ASC 825, *Financial Instruments*, permits entities to choose to measure at fair value many financial instruments and certain other items that are not currently required to be measured at fair value. Further, under FASB ASC 825, a business entity should report unrealized gains and losses on eligible items for which the fair value option has been elected in earnings at each subsequent reporting date. The irrevocable election of the fair value option is made on an instrument-by-instrument basis, with certain exceptions, and applied to the entire instrument, not only to specified risks, specific cash flows, or portions of that instrument.

DISCLOSURE

1.93 The disclosures required by FASB ASC 815 for entities with derivative instruments or nonderivative instruments that are designated and qualify as hedging instruments are intended to enable users of financial statements to understand
- How and why an entity uses derivative or nonderivative instruments.
- How derivative instruments or such nonderivative instruments and related hedged items are accounted for under FASB ASC 815.
- How derivative instruments or such nonderivative instruments and related hedged items affect an entity's financial position, financial performance, and cash flows.

1.94 To meet those objectives, FASB ASC 815-10-50-1A requires qualitative disclosures about an entity's objectives and strategies for using derivatives and such nonderivative instruments. An entity that holds or issues derivative instruments or such nonderivative instruments should disclose all of the following for each interim and annual reporting period for which a statement of financial position and statement of financial performance are presented:
- Its objectives for holding or issuing those instruments.
- The context needed to understand those objectives. This should be disclosed in the context of each instrument's primary underlying risk exposure.
- Its strategies for achieving those objectives. This should be disclosed in the context of each instrument's primary underlying risk exposure.
- Information that would enable users of its financial statements to understand the volume of its activity in those instruments.

1.95 These instruments should be disclosed in the context of each instrument's primary underlying risk exposure and should be distinguished among those used for risk management purposes, those used as economic hedges and other purposes related to risk exposure, and those used for other purposes. Those used for risk management purposes should be distinguished between those designated as hedging instruments and, further, whether they are fair value hedges, cash flow hedges, or foreign currency hedges. An entity should select the format and specifics for this that are most relevant and practicable for its individual facts and circumstances. For any derivatives not designated as hedging instruments under FASB ASC 815-20, the description should include the purpose of the derivative activity.

1.96 Paragraphs .4A–.4E of FASB ASC 815-10-50 explains the quantitative disclosures about derivatives and such nonderivative instruments. For every annual and interim reporting period for which a statement of financial position and statement of financial performance are presented, an entity that holds or issues derivative instruments is required to disclose the location and fair value amounts of derivative instruments and such nonderivative instruments reported in the statement of financial position. The fair value of those instruments should be presented on a gross basis, even when those instruments are subject to master netting arrangements and qualify for net presentation in the statement of financial position. Cash collateral payables and receivables associated with these instruments should not be added to, or netted against, the fair value amounts.

1.97 Fair value amounts should be presented as separate asset and liability values segregated between derivatives that are designated and qualifying as hedging instruments presented separately by type of contract and those that are not. The disclosure should also identify the line item(s) in the statement of financial position in which the fair value amounts for these categories of derivative instruments are included. Also, disclosure of the location and amount of the gains and losses on derivative instruments and such nonderivative instruments and related hedged items in the statement of financial performance or statement of financial position (for example, in other comprehensive income) is required. These gain and loss disclosures should be presented separately by type of contract. These quantitative disclosures are required to be presented in tabular format, except for disclosures regarding hedged items that can be presented in either tabular or nontabular format.

1.98 For derivative instruments not designated or qualifying as hedging instruments under FASB ASC 815-20, if the entity's policy is to include them in its trading activities, the entity can elect not to separately disclose gains and losses, provided that the entity discloses certain other information. Additionally, FASB ASC 815 requires specific disclosures for derivative instruments that contain credit-risk-related features and credit derivatives.

1.99 FASB ASC 825 requires certain reporting entities to disclose the fair value of financial instruments and disclosure requirements of credit risk concentrations of all financial instruments, and it provides guidance on the fair value option. FASB ASC 825 also establishes presentation and disclosure requirements designed to facilitate comparison between entities that choose different measurement attributes for similar types of assets and liabilities.

PRESENTATION AND DISCLOSURE EXCERPTS

FINANCIAL GUARANTEES AND INDEMNIFICATIONS—LINE OF CREDIT

1.100 ABM INDUSTRIES INCORPORATED (OCT)
CONSOLIDATED BALANCE SHEETS (in part)

Liabilities and Stockholders' Equity (in part)

	October 31,	
	2012	**2011**
Current liabilities		
Trade accounts payable	$ 130,410	$ 130,464
Accrued liabilities		
Compensation	121,855	112,233
Taxes—other than income	19,437	19,144
Insurance claims	80,192	78,828
Other	113,566	102,220
Income taxes payable	8,450	307
Total current liabilities	473,910	443,196
Noncurrent income taxes payable	27,773	38,236
Line of credit	215,000	300,000
Retirement plans and other	38,558	39,707
Noncurrent insurance claims	263,612	262,573
Total liabilities	1,018,853	1,083,712

NOTES TO CONSOLIDATED FINANCIAL STATEMENTS

5. Fair Value of Financial Instruments (in part)

The following table presents the fair value hierarchy, carrying amounts, and fair values of the Company's financial instruments measured on a recurring basis and other select significant financial instruments as of October 31, 2012 and 2011:

(In thousands)	Fair Value Hierarchy	October 31, 2012		October 31, 2011	
		Carrying Amount	**Fair Value**	**Carrying Amount**	**Fair Value**
Financial Assets Measured at Fair Value on a Recurring Basis					
Assets held in funded deferred compensation plan	1	$ 5,029	$ 5,029	$ 4,717	$ 4,717
Investments in auction rate securities	3	17,780	17,780	15,670	15,670
		22,809	22,809	20,387	20,387
Other Select Financial Asset					
Cash and cash equivalents	1	43,459	43,459	26,467	26,467
Total		$ 66,268	$ 66,268	$ 46,854	$ 46,854
Financial Liability Measured at Fair Value on a Recurring Basis					
Interest rate swap	2	$ 214	$ 214	$ 253	$ 253
Other Select Financial Liability					
Line of credit	2	215,000	215,000	300,000	300,000
Total		$215,214	$215,214	$300,253	$300,253

Due to variable interest rates, the carrying value of outstanding borrowings under the Company's line of credit approximates its fair value. See Note 10, "Line of Credit."

10. Line of Credit (in part)

On November 30, 2010, the Company entered into a five-year syndicated credit agreement ("Credit Agreement") that replaced the Company's then-existing $450.0 million syndicated credit agreement dated November 14, 2007. The Credit Agreement provides for revolving loans, swingline loans and letters of credit up to an aggregate amount of $650.0 million (the "Facility"). The Company, at its option, may increase the size of the Facility to $850.0 million at any time prior to the expiration (subject to receipt of commitments for the increased amount from existing and new lenders). During the year ended October 31, 2011, the

Credit Agreement was amended to reduce the borrowing spread interest on loans, extend the maturity date to September 8, 2016 and revise certain defined terms.

Borrowings under the Facility bear interest at a rate equal to an applicable margin plus, at the Company's option, either a (a) eurodollar rate (generally LIBOR), or (b) base rate determined by reference to the highest of (1) the federal funds rate plus 0.50%, (2) the prime rate announced by Bank of America, N.A. from time to time and (3) the eurodollar rate plus 1.00%. The applicable margin is a percentage per annum varying from 0.00% to 0.75% for base rate loans and 1.00% to 1.75% for eurodollar loans, based upon the Company's leverage ratio. The Company also pays a commitment fee, based on the leverage ratio, payable quarterly in arrears, ranging from 0.225% to 0.300% on the average daily unused portion of the Facility. For purposes of this calculation, irrevocable standby letters of credit, issued primarily in conjunction with the Company's self-insurance program, and cash borrowings are included as outstanding under the Facility.

The Credit Agreement contains certain leverage and liquidity covenants that require us to maintain a maximum leverage ratio of 3.25× at the end of each fiscal quarter, a minimum fixed charge coverage ratio of 1.50× at any time, and a consolidated net worth in an amount of not less than the sum of (i) $570.0 million, (ii) 50% of our consolidated net income (with no deduction for net loss) and (iii) 100% of our aggregate increases in stockholder's equity, beginning on November 30, 2010, each as further described in the Credit Agreement, as amended. The Company was in compliance with all covenants as of October 31, 2012.

If an event of default occurs under the Credit Agreement, including certain cross-defaults, insolvency, change in control, and violation of specific covenants, among others, the lenders: can terminate or suspend the Company's access to the Facility; can declare all amounts outstanding under the Facility, including all accrued interest and unpaid fees, to be immediately due and payable; and may also require that the Company cash collateralize the outstanding standby letters of credit obligations.

The Facility is available for working capital, the issuance of up to $300.0 million for standby letters of credit, the issuance of up to $50.0 million in swing line advances, the financing of capital expenditures and for other general corporate purposes, including acquisitions. As of October 31, 2012, the total outstanding amounts under the Facility in the form of cash borrowings and standby letters of credit were $215.0 million and $105.0 million, respectively. As of October 31, 2011, the total outstanding amounts under the Facility in the form of cash borrowings and standby letters of credit were $300.0 million and $96.8 million, respectively. At October 31, 2012 and 2011, the Company had $330.0 million and $253.2 million borrowing capacity, respectively, available under the Facility, subject to compliance with the covenants described above.

DERIVATIVE FINANCIAL INSTRUMENTS—INTEREST RATE SWAP AGREEMENTS

1.101 AVON PRODUCTS, INC. (DEC)

CONSOLIDATED BALANCE SHEETS (in part)

	December 31	
(In millions, except per share data)	2012	2011
Assets		
Current Assets		
Cash, including cash equivalents of $762.9 and $623.7	$ 1,209.6	$ 1,245.1
Accounts receivable (less allowances of $161.4 and $174.5)	751.9	761.5
Inventories	1,135.4	1,161.3
Prepaid expenses and other	832.0	930.9
Total current assets	$ 3,928.9	$ 4,098.8
Property, plant and equipment, at cost		
Land	66.6	65.4
Buildings and improvements	1,165.9	1,150.4
Equipment	1,479.3	1,493.0
	2,711.8	2,708.8
Less accumulated depreciation	(1,161.6)	(1,137.3)
	1,550.2	1,571.5
Goodwill	374.9	473.1
Other intangible assets, net	120.3	279.9
Other assets	1,408.2	1,311.7
Total assets	$ 7,382.5	$ 7,735.0
Liabilities and Shareholders' Equity		
Current Liabilities		
Debt maturing within one year	$ 572.0	$ 849.3
Accounts payable	920.0	850.2
Accrued compensation	266.6	217.1
Other accrued liabilities	661.0	663.6
Sales and taxes other than income	211.4	212.4
Income taxes	73.6	98.4
Total current liabilities	2,704.6	2,891.0
Long-term debt	2,623.9	2,459.1
Employee benefit plans	637.6	603.0
Long-term income taxes	52.0	67.0
Other liabilities	131.1	129.7
Total liabilities	$ 6,149.2	$ 6,149.8

(In millions, except per share and share data)

Note 1. Description of the Business and Summary of Significant Accounting Policies (in part)

Financial Instruments

We use derivative financial instruments, including interest-rate swap agreements and forward foreign currency contracts to manage interest rate and foreign currency exposures. We record all derivative instruments at their fair values on the Consolidated Balance Sheets as either assets or liabilities. See Note 8, Financial Instruments and Risk Management.

Note 5. Debt and Other Financing (in part)

We held interest-rate swap contracts that effectively converted approximately 62% at December 31, 2012 and 74% at December 31, 2011, of our long-term fixed-rate borrowings to a variable interest rate based on LIBOR. In January 2013, we terminated eight of our interest-rate swap agreements designated as fair value hedges, with notional amounts totaling $1,000. See Note 8, Financial Instruments and Risk Management.

Note 8. Financial Instruments and Risk Management (in part)

We operate globally, with manufacturing and distribution facilities in various locations around the world. We may reduce our exposure to fluctuations in the fair value and cash flows associated with changes in interest rates and foreign exchange rates by creating offsetting positions through the use of derivative financial instruments. Since we use foreign currency-rate sensitive and interest-rate sensitive instruments to hedge a certain portion of our existing and forecasted transactions, we expect that any gain or loss in value of the hedge instruments generally would be offset by decreases or increases in the value of the underlying forecasted transactions.

We do not enter into derivative financial instruments for trading or speculative purposes, nor are we a party to leveraged derivatives. The master agreements governing our derivative contracts generally contain standard provisions that could trigger early termination of the contracts in certain circumstances, including if we were to merge with another entity and the creditworthiness of the surviving entity were to be "materially weaker" than that of Avon prior to the merger.

Derivatives are recognized on the balance sheet at their fair values. The following table presents the fair value of derivative instruments outstanding at December 31, 2012:

	Asset		Liability	
	Balance Sheet Classification	Fair Value	Balance Sheet Classification	Fair Value
Derivatives Designated as Hedges:				
Interest-rate swap agreements	Other assets/Prepaid expenses and other	$93.1	Other liabilities	$—
Total derivatives designated as hedges		$93.1		$—
Derivatives not Designated as Hedges:				
Interest-rate swap agreements	Prepaid expenses and other	$ 1.7	Accounts payable	$1.7
Foreign exchange forward contracts	Prepaid expenses and other	4.9	Accounts payable	1.5
Total derivatives not designated as hedges		$ 6.6		$3.2
Total derivatives		$99.7		$3.2

The following table presents the fair value of derivative instruments outstanding at December 31, 2011:

	Asset		Liability	
	Balance Sheet Classification	Fair Value	Balance Sheet Classification	Fair Value
Derivatives Designated as Hedges:				
Interest-rate swap agreements	Other assets	$147.6	Other liabilities	$ —
Foreign exchange forward contracts	Prepaid expenses and other	1.2	Accounts payable	—
Total derivatives designated as hedges		$148.8		$ —
Derivatives not Designated as Hedges:				
Interest-rate swap agreements	Other assets	$ 6.0	Other liabilities	$ 6.0
Foreign exchange forward contracts	Prepaid expenses and other	4.4	Accounts payable	10.5
Total derivatives not designated as hedges		$ 10.4		$16.5
Total derivatives		$159.2		$16.5

Accounting Policies

Derivatives are recognized on the balance sheet at their fair values. When we become a party to a derivative instrument and intend to apply hedge accounting, we designate the instrument, for financial reporting purposes, as a fair value hedge, a cash flow hedge, or a net investment hedge. The accounting for changes in fair value (gains or losses) of a derivative instrument depends on whether we had designated it and it qualified as part of a hedging relationship and further, on the type of hedging relationship. We apply the following accounting policies:

- Changes in the fair value of a derivative that is designated as a fair value hedge, along with the loss or gain on the hedged asset or liability that is attributable to the hedged risk are recorded in earnings.
- Changes in the fair value of a derivative that is designated as a cash flow hedge are recorded in AOCI to the extent effective and reclassified into earnings in the same period or periods during which the transaction hedged by that derivative also affects earnings.
- Changes in the fair value of a derivative that is designated as a hedge of a net investment in a foreign operation are recorded in foreign currency translation adjustments within AOCI to the extent effective as a hedge.
- Changes in the fair value of a derivative not designated as a hedging instrument are recognized in earnings in other expense, net on the Consolidated Statements of Income.

Realized gains and losses on a derivative are reported on the Consolidated Statements of Cash Flows consistent with the underlying hedged item.

For derivatives designated as hedges, we assess, both at the hedge's inception and on an ongoing basis, whether the derivatives that are used in hedging transactions are highly effective in offsetting changes in fair values or cash flows of hedged items.

Highly effective means that cumulative changes in the fair value of the derivative are between 85%–125% of the cumulative changes in the fair value of the hedged item. The ineffective portion of a derivative's gain or loss, if any, is recorded in earnings in other expense, net on the Consolidated Statements of Income. In addition, when we determine that a derivative is not highly effective as a hedge, hedge accounting is discontinued. When it is probable that a hedged forecasted transaction will not occur, we discontinue hedge accounting for the affected portion of the forecasted transaction, and reclassify gains or losses that were accumulated in AOCI to earnings in other expense, net on the Consolidated Statements of Income.

Interest Rate Risk

Our borrowings are subject to interest rate risk. We use interest-rate swap agreements, which effectively convert the fixed rate on long-term debt to a floating interest rate, to manage our interest rate exposure. The agreements are designated as fair value hedges. We held interest-rate swap agreements that effectively converted approximately 62% at December 31, 2012, and 74% at December 31, 2011, of our outstanding long-term, fixed-rate borrowings to a variable interest rate based on LIBOR. Our total exposure to floating interest rates was approximately 69% at December 31, 2012, and 82% at December 31, 2011; however, in January 2013, we terminated eight of our interest-rate swap agreements designated as fair value hedges, with notional amounts totaling $1,000.

In March 2012, we terminated two of our interest-rate swap agreements designated as fair value hedges, with notional amounts totaling $350. As of the interest-rate swap agreements' termination date, the aggregate favorable adjustment to the carrying value of our debt was $46.1, which is being amortized as a reduction to interest expense over the remaining term of the underlying debt obligations through March 2019. We incurred termination fees of $2.5 which were recorded in other expense, net. For the year ended December 31, 2012, the net impact of the gain amortization was $4.4. The interest-rate swap agreements were terminated in order to increase our ratio of fixed-rate debt.

At December 31, 2012, we had interest-rate swap agreements designated as fair value hedges of fixed-rate debt, with notional amounts totaling $1,375. Unrealized gains were $93.1 at December 31, 2012, of which $90.3 were included within long-term debt and $2.8 were included within debt maturing within one year. Unrealized gains were $147.6 at December 31, 2011, and were included within long-term debt. During 2012 and 2011, we recorded a net loss of $8.4 and a net gain of $53.2, respectively, in interest expense for these interest-rate swap agreements designated as fair value hedges. The impact on interest expense of these interest-rate swap agreements was offset by an equal and offsetting impact in interest expense on our fixed-rate debt.

At times, we may de-designate the hedging relationship of a receive-fixed/pay-variable interest-rate swap agreement. In these cases, we enter into receive-variable/pay-fixed interest-rate swap agreements that are designated to offset the gain or loss on the de-designated contract. At December 31, 2012, we had interest-rate swap agreements that are not designated as hedges with notional amounts totaling $250. Unrealized losses on these agreements were immaterial at December 31, 2012 and 2011. During 2012, we recorded an immaterial net gain in other expense, net associated with these undesignated interest-rate swap agreements.

There was no hedge ineffectiveness for the years ended December 31, 2012, 2011 and 2010, related to these interest-rate swaps.

During 2007, we entered into treasury lock agreements (the "2007 locks") with notional amounts totaling $500.0 that expired on July 31, 2008. The 2007 locks were designated as cash flow hedges of the anticipated interest payments on $250.0 principal amount of the 2013 Notes and $250.0 principal amount of the 2018 Notes. The losses on the 2007 locks of $38.0 were recorded in AOCI. $19.2 of the losses are being amortized to interest expense over five years and $18.8 are being amortized over ten years.

During 2005, we entered into treasury lock agreements (the "2005 locks") that we designated as cash flow hedges and used to hedge exposure to a possible rise in interest rates prior to the anticipated issuance of ten- and 30-year bonds. In December 2005, we decided that a more appropriate strategy was to issue five-year bonds given our strong cash flow and high level of cash and cash equivalents. As a result of the change in strategy, in December 2005, we de-designated the 2005 locks as hedges and reclassified the gain of $2.5 on the 2005 locks from AOCI to other expense, net. Upon the change in strategy in December 2005, we entered into a treasury lock agreement (the "additional 2005 locks") with a notional amount of $250.0 designated as a cash flow hedge of the $500.0 principal amount of five-year notes payable issued in January 2006. The loss on the additional 2005 locks of $1.9 was recorded in AOCI and has been amortized to interest expense over five years.

During 2003, we entered into treasury lock agreements (the "2003 locks") that we designated as cash flow hedges and used to hedge the exposure to the possible rise in interest rates prior to the issuance of the 4.625% Notes. The loss on the 2003 locks of $2.6 was recorded in AOCI and is being amortized to interest expense over ten years.

As of December 31, 2012, we expect to reclassify $1.7, net of taxes, of net losses on derivative instruments designated as cash flow hedges from AOCI to earnings during the next 12 months.

For the years ended December 31, 2012 and 2011, treasury lock agreements impacted AOCI as follows:

	2012	2011
Net unamortized losses at beginning of year, net of taxes of $5.8 and $7.9	$(10.7)	$(14.6)
Reclassification of net losses to earnings, net of taxes of $2.1 and $2.1	3.9	3.9
Net unamortized losses at end of year, net of taxes of $3.7 and $5.8	$ (6.8)	$(10.7)

Credit Risk of Financial Instruments

We attempt to minimize our credit exposure to counterparties by entering into derivative transactions and similar agreements with major international financial institutions with "A" or higher credit ratings as issued by Standard & Poor's Corporation. Our foreign currency and interest rate derivatives are comprised of over-the-counter forward contracts, swaps or options with major international financial institutions. Although our theoretical credit risk is the replacement cost at the then estimated fair value of these instruments, we believe that the risk of incurring credit risk losses is remote and that such losses, if any, would not be material.

Non-performance of the counterparties on the balance of all the foreign exchange and interest rate agreements would have resulted in a write-off of $99.7 at December 31, 2012. In addition, in the event of non-performance by such counterparties, we would be exposed to market risk on the underlying items being hedged as a result of changes in foreign exchange and interest rates; however, as mentioned above, in January 2013 we terminated eight of our interest-rate swap agreements designated as fair value hedges, with notional amounts totaling $1,000. As of the interest-rate swap agreements' termination date, the aggregate favorable adjustment to the carrying value of our debt was $90.4, which will be amortized as a reduction to interest expense over the remaining term of the underlying debt obligations.

Note 18. Supplemental Balance Sheet Information

At December 31, 2012 and 2011, prepaid expenses and other included the following:

Prepaid Expenses and Other	2012	2011
Deferred tax assets (Note 7)	$ 273.5	$ 319.0
Prepaid taxes and tax refunds receivable	141.4	192.0
Receivables other than trade	131.9	142.8
Prepaid brochure costs, paper and other literature	112.1	126.9
Healthcare trust assets (Note 12)	26.9	—
Interest-rate swap agreements, including interest (Notes 8 and 9)	19.5	18.8
Short-term investments	16.5	18.0
Other	110.2	113.4
Prepaid expenses and other	$ 832.0	$ 930.9

At December 31, 2012 and 2011, other assets included the following:

Other Assets	2012	2011
Deferred tax assets (Note 7)	$ 827.2	$ 759.5
Capitalized software (Note 1)	235.4	176.7
Long-term receivables	174.9	138.3
Interest-rate swap agreements (Notes 8 and 9)	94.8	153.6
Investments	44.5	44.4
Other	31.4	39.2
Other assets	$1,408.2	$1,311.7

1.102 INGREDION INCORPORATED (DEC)
NOTES TO THE CONSOLIDATED FINANCIAL STATEMENTS

Note 2—Summary of Significant Accounting Policies (in part)

Hedging instruments—The Company uses derivative financial instruments principally to offset exposure to market risks arising from changes in commodity prices, foreign currency exchange rates and interest rates. Derivative financial instruments used by the Company consist of commodity futures and option contracts, forward currency contracts and options, interest rate swap agreements and treasury lock agreements. The Company enters into futures and option contracts, which are designated as hedges of specific volumes of commodities (corn and natural gas) that will be purchased in a future month. These derivative financial instruments are recognized in the Consolidated Balance Sheets at fair value. The Company has also entered into interest rate swap agreements that effectively convert the interest rate on certain fixed rate debt to a variable interest rate and, on certain variable rate debt, to a fixed interest rate. The Company periodically enters into treasury lock agreements to lock the benchmark rate for an anticipated fixed rate borrowing. See also Note 5 and Note 6 of the notes to the consolidated financial statements for additional information.

On the date a derivative contract is entered into, the Company designates the derivative as either a hedge of variable cash flows to be paid related to interest on variable rate debt, as a hedge of market variation in the benchmark rate for a future fixed rate debt issue or as a hedge of certain forecasted purchases of corn or natural gas used in the manufacturing process ("a cash-flow hedge"), or as a hedge of the fair value of certain debt obligations (a fair-value hedge"). This process includes linking all derivatives that are designated as fair-value or cash-flow hedges to specific assets and liabilities on the Consolidated Balance Sheet, or to specific firm commitments or forecasted transactions. For all hedging relationships, the Company formally documents the hedging relationships and its risk-management objective and strategy for undertaking the hedge transactions, the hedging instrument, the hedged item, the nature of the risk being hedged, how the hedging instrument's effectiveness in offsetting the hedged risk will be assessed, and a description of the method of measuring ineffectiveness. The Company also formally assesses, both at the hedge's inception and on an ongoing basis, whether the derivatives that are used in hedging transactions are highly effective in offsetting changes in cash flows or fair values of hedged items. When it is determined that a derivative is not highly effective as a hedge or that it has ceased to be a highly effective hedge, the Company discontinues hedge accounting prospectively.

Changes in the fair value of floating-to-fixed interest rate swaps, treasury locks or commodity futures and option contracts that are highly effective and that are designated and qualify as cash-flow hedges are recorded in other comprehensive income, net of applicable income taxes. Realized gains and losses associated with changes in the fair value of interest rate swaps and treasury locks are reclassified from accumulated other comprehensive income (AOCI") to the Consolidated Statement of Income over the life of the underlying debt. Gains and losses on commodity hedging contracts are reclassified from AOCI to the Consolidated Statement of Income when the finished goods produced using the hedged item are sold. The maximum term over which the Company hedges exposures to the variability of cash flows for commodity price risk is 24 months. Changes in the fair value of a fixed-to-floating interest rate swap agreement that is highly effective and that is designated and qualifies as a fair-value hedge, along with the loss or gain on the hedged debt obligation, are recorded in earnings. The ineffective portion of the change in fair value of a derivative instrument that qualifies as either a cash-flow hedge or a fair-value hedge is reported in earnings.

The Company discontinues hedge accounting prospectively when it is determined that the derivative is no longer effective in offsetting changes in the cash flows or fair value of the hedged item, the derivative is de-designated as a hedging instrument because it is unlikely that a forecasted transaction will occur, or management determines that designation of the derivative as a hedging instrument is no longer appropriate. When hedge accounting is discontinued, the Company continues to carry the derivative on the Consolidated Balance Sheet at its fair value, and gains and losses that were included in AOCI are recognized in earnings.

Note 5—Financial Instruments, Derivatives and Hedging Activities (in part)

Foreign currency hedging: Due to the Company's global operations, it is exposed to fluctuations in foreign currency exchange rates. As a result, the Company has exposure to translational foreign exchange risk when its foreign operation results are translated to US dollars and to transactional foreign exchange risk when transactions not denominated in the functional currency of the operating unit are revalued. The Company primarily uses derivative financial instruments such as foreign currency forward contracts, swaps and options to manage its transactional foreign exchange risk. These derivative financial instruments are primarily accounted for as fair value hedges. At December 31, 2012, the Company had $268 million of foreign currency forward sales contracts and $167 million of foreign currency forward purchase contracts that hedged transactional exposures. At December 31, 2011, the Company had $287 million of foreign currency forward sales contracts and $163 million of foreign currency forward purchase contracts that hedged transactional exposures. The fair value of these derivative instruments was approximately $5 million and $1 million at December 31, 2012 and 2011, respectively.

By using derivative financial instruments to hedge exposures, the Company exposes itself to credit risk and market risk. Credit risk is the risk that the counterparty will fail to perform under the terms of the derivative contract. When the fair value of a derivative contract is positive, the counterparty owes the Company, which creates credit risk for the Company. When the fair value of a derivative contract is negative, the Company owes the counterparty and, therefore, it does not possess credit risk. The Company minimizes the credit risk in derivative instruments by entering into over-the-counter transactions only with investment grade counterparties or by utilizing exchange-traded derivatives. Market risk is the adverse effect on the value of a financial instrument that results from a change in commodity prices, interest rates or foreign exchange rates. The market risk associated with commodity-price, interest rate, or foreign exchange contracts is managed by establishing and monitoring parameters that limit the types and degree of market risk that may be undertaken.

The fair value and balance sheet location of the Company's derivative instruments accounted for as cash flow hedges are presented below:

		Fair Value of Derivative Instruments					
		Fair Value				Fair Value	
Derivatives designated as hedging instruments: (In millions)	Balance Sheet Location	At December 31, 2012	At December 31, 2011	Balance Sheet Location	At December 31, 2012	At December 31, 2011
Commodity and foreign currency contracts	Accounts receivable-net	$5	$14	Accounts payable and accrued liabilities	$34	$34
Commodity contracts				Non-current liabilities	6	11
Total		$5	$14		$40	$45

At December 31, 2012, the Company had outstanding futures and option contracts that hedged approximately 97 million bushels of forecasted corn purchases. Also at December 31, 2012, the Company had outstanding swap and option contracts that hedged approximately 18 million mmbtu's of forecasted natural gas purchases.

Additional information relating to the Company's derivative instruments is presented below (in millions):

	Amount of Gains (Losses) Recognized in OCI on Derivatives			Location of Gains (Losses)	Amount of Gains (Losses) Reclassified from AOCI into Income		
Derivatives in Cash Flow Hedging Relationships	Year Ended December 31, 2012	Year Ended December 31, 2011	Year Ended December 31, 2010	Reclassified from AOCI into Income	Year Ended December 31, 2012	Year Ended December 31, 2011	Year Ended December 31, 2010
Commodity and foreign currency contracts	$68	$48	$47	Cost of Sales	$43	$169	$(87)
Interest rate contracts	—	—	(15)	Financing costs, net	(3)	(3)	(1)
Total	$68	$48	$32		$40	$166	$(88)

Presented below are the fair values of the Company's financial instruments and derivatives for the periods presented:

	As of December 31, 2012				As of December 31, 2011			
(In millions)	Total	Level 1	Level 2	Level 3	Total	Level 1	Level 2	Level 3
Available for sale securities	$ 3	$ 3	$ —	$—	$ 2	$ 2	$ —	$—
Derivative assets	25	5	20	—	33	14	19	—
Derivative liabilities	45	24	21	—	46	16	30	—
Long-term debt	1,914	—	1,914	—	1,921	—	1,921	—

Level 1 inputs consist of quoted prices (unadjusted) in active markets for identical assets or liabilities. Level 2 inputs are inputs other than quoted prices included within Level 1 that are observable for the asset or liability, either directly or indirectly for substantially the full term of the financial instrument. Level 2 inputs are based on quoted prices for similar assets or liabilities in active markets, quoted prices for identical or similar assets or liabilities in markets that are not active, or inputs other than quoted prices that are observable for the asset or liability or can be derived principally from or corroborated by observable market data. Level 3 inputs are unobservable inputs for the asset or liability. Unobservable inputs shall be used to measure fair value to the extent that observable inputs are not available, thereby allowing for situations in which there is little, if any, market activity for the asset or liability at the measurement date.

CREDIT FACILITY

1.103 SEALED AIR CORPORATION (DEC)
CONSOLIDATED BALANCE SHEETS (in part)

Liabilities and Stockholders' Equity (in part)

Current Liabilities:		
Short-term borrowings	$ 39.2	$ 34.5
Current portion of long-term debt	1.8	1.9
Accounts payable	483.8	554.9
Deferred tax liabilities	10.3	16.0
Settlement agreement and related accrued interest	876.9	831.2
Accrued restructuring costs	72.4	36.3
Liabilities held for sale	—	216.7
Other current liabilities	849.2	814.7
Total current liabilities	2,333.6	2,506.2
Long-term debt, less current portion	4,540.8	4,966.7
Non-current deferred tax liabilities	472.5	439.7
Other liabilities	646.0	567.0
Total liabilities	7,992.9	8,479.6

Note 12 Debt and Credit Facilities (in part)

Our total debt outstanding consisted of the amounts set forth on the following table:

	December 31, 2012	December 31, 2011
Short-term borrowings	$ 39.2	$ 34.5
Current portion of long-term debt	1.8	1.9
Total current debt	41.0	36.4
5.625% Senior Notes due July 2013, less unamortized discount of $0.3 in 2011[1][2]	—	401.0
12% Senior Notes due February 2014[1]	153.4	156.3
Term Loan A Facility due October 2016, less unamortized lender fees of $15.4 in 2012 and $21.7 in 2011[3]	843.9	945.7
7.875% Senior Notes due June 2017, less unamortized discount of $5.5 in 2012 and $6.5 in 2011	394.5	393.5
Term Loan B Facility due October 2018, less unamortized lender fees of $10.7 in 2012 and $21.3 in 2011, and unamortized discount of $15.6 in 2012 and $26.5 in 2011[3]	771.6	1,118.8
8.125% Senior Notes due September 2019	750.0	750.0
6.50% Senior Notes due December 2020	425.0	—
8.375% Senior Notes due September 2021	750.0	750.0
6.875% Senior Notes due July 2033, less unamortized discount of $1.4 in 2012 and $1.4 in 2011	448.6	448.6
Other	3.8	2.8
Total long-term debt, less current portion	4,540.8	4,966.7
Total debt[4]	$4,581.8	$5,003.1

[1] Amount includes adjustments due to interest rate swaps. See "Interest Rate Swaps," of Note 13, "Derivatives and Hedging Activities," for further discussion.

[2] During 2012, we purchased all of our outstanding $400 million 5.625% Senior Notes due 2013. See below for further discussion.

[3] In 2012, we prepaid $95 million of euro and U.S. dollar denominated portions of the original Term Loan A. In addition, we prepaid $1.1 billion and refinanced the remaining principal amount of $801 million of the euro and U.S dollar denominated portions of the original Term Loan B at 99.75% of the face value. Also, in connection with the sale of Diversey Japan, we prepaid $90 million and refinanced the remaining principal amount of $80 million of the Japanese yen denominated balances owed under the original Term Loan A. See below for further discussion.

[4] The weighted average interest rate on our outstanding debt was 6.4% as of December 31, 2012 and 6.2% as of December 31, 2011.

Credit Facility

2012 Activity

Amended Credit Facility

In connection with the sale of Diversey Japan (see Note 3, "Divestiture"), and the repayment of existing indebtedness of the Company and to provide for ongoing liquidity requirements, on November 14, 2012, we entered into an amended senior secured credit facility (the "Amended Credit Facility"). The Amended Credit Facility consists of: (a) a multicurrency Term Loan A facility denominated in U.S. dollars, Canadian dollars, euros and Japanese yen, ("Amended Term Loan A Facility"), (b) a multicurrency Term Loan B facility denominated in U.S. dollars and euros ("Amended Term Loan B Facility") and (c) a $700 million revolving credit facility available in U.S. dollars, Canadian dollars, euros, and Australian dollars ("Amended Revolving Credit Facility"). Our obligations under the Amended Credit Facility have been guaranteed by certain of Sealed Air's subsidiaries and secured by pledges of certain assets and the capital stock of certain subsidiaries.

The Amended Term Loan A Facility and the Amended Revolving Credit Facility each have a five-year term and bear interest at either LIBOR or the base rate (or an equivalent rate in the relevant currency) plus 250 basis points (bps) per annum in the case of LIBOR loans and 150 bps per annum in the case of base rate loans, provided that the interest rates shall be decreased to 225 bps and 125 bps, respectively, upon achievement of a specified leverage ratio. The Amended Term Loan B Facility has a seven-year term. The U.S. dollar-denominated tranche bears interest at either LIBOR or the base rate plus 300 bps per annum in the case of LIBOR loans and 200 bps per annum in the case of base rate loans, and the euro-denominated tranche bears interest at either EURIBOR or the base rate plus 350 bps per annum in the case of EURIBOR loans and 250 bps per annum in the case of base rate loans. LIBOR and EURIBOR are subject to a 1.0% floor under the Amended Term Loan B Facility.

In connection with the sale of Diversey Japan, we prepaid $90 million and refinanced the remaining principal amount of $80 million of Japanese yen denominated balances owned of the original Term Loan A. As a result, we accelerated $1 million of original unamortized lender fees included as a reduction of the pre-tax gain on the sale of Diversey Japan. We also carried forward $1 million of unamortized lender fees in the carrying amount of the debt instrument. Incremental lender fees and non-lender fees related to the transactions mentioned above were insignificant. These non-lender fees are included in other assets on our consolidated balance sheet. We prepaid $95 million of euro and U.S. dollar denominated portions of the original Term Loan A for other Sealed Air companies.

We prepaid $1.1 billion and refinanced the remaining principal amount of $801 million of the euro and U.S. dollars denominated portions of the original Term Loan B at 99.75% of the face value for other Sealed Air companies. As a result, we accelerated unamortized original issuance discounts of $9 million and unamortized lender fees of $7 million, which are included in loss on debt redemption on our consolidated statements of operations. We also recorded new original issuance discount and non-lender fees for a total of $2 million, which are included in the carrying amount of the debt instruments. In addition, we recorded $7 million of non-lender fees related to the transactions mentioned above. Those fees are included in loss on debt redemption on our consolidated statements of operations.

The amortization expense of the original issuance discount and lender and non-lender fees is calculated using the effective interest rate method over the lives of the respective debt instruments. Total amortization expense in 2012 related to the debt instruments above was $23 million and is included in interest expense on our consolidated statements of operations.

The Amended Credit Facility provides for customary events of default, including failure to pay principal or interest when due, failure to comply with covenants, materially false representation or warranty made by the Company, certain insolvency or receivership events and a change in control. For certain events of default, the commitments of the lenders will be automatically terminated, and all outstanding obligations under the Amended Credit Facility may be declared immediately due and payable.

The Amended Revolving Credit Facility may be used for working capital needs and general corporate purposes, including the payment of the amounts required upon effectiveness of the Settlement agreement (defined below in Note 18, "Commitments and Contingencies"). We used our Amended Revolving Facility for a short time period in connection with the sale of Diversey Japan. Interest paid for the year ended December 31, 2012 under the Amended Revolving Credit Facility was insignificant. There were no amounts outstanding under the Amended Credit Facility at December 31, 2012.

2011 Activity

Original Credit Facility

In connection with the funding of the cash consideration for the acquisition and the repayment of existing indebtedness of Diversey and to provide for ongoing liquidity requirements, on October 3, 2011, we entered into a senior secured credit facility (the "Credit Facility"). The Credit Facility consists of: (a) a multicurrency Term Loan A facility denominated in U.S. dollars, Canadian dollars, euros and Japanese yen, ("Term Loan A Facility"), (b) a multicurrency Term Loan B Facility and (c) a $700 million revolving facility available in U.S. dollars, Canadian dollars, euros and Australian dollars ("Revolving Credit Facility"). Our obligations under the Credit Facility have been guaranteed by certain of Sealed Air's subsidiaries and secured by pledges of certain assets and the capital stock of certain of our subsidiaries. In connection with entering into the Credit Facility, we terminated our former global credit facility and European credit facility.

The U.S. dollar denominated tranche of the Term Loan B Facility was sold to investors at 98% of its principal amount, and the euro-denominated tranche of the Term Loan B Facility was sold to investors at 97% of its principal amount. As a result, we recorded $28 million of original issuance discounts, which were included in the carrying amount of the Term Loan B Facility prior to its refinancing in 2012. We also recorded $48 million of lender fees related to the transactions mentioned above. These fees are also included in the carrying amount of the respective debt instruments. In addition, we recorded $51 million of non-lender fees related to the transactions mentioned above. Those fees were included in other assets on our consolidated balance sheet.

The amortization expense of the original issuance discount and lender and non-lender fees is calculated using the effective interest rate method over the lives of the respective debt instruments. Total amortization expense in 2011 related to the debt instruments above was $7 million and is included in interest expense on our consolidated statements of operations.

Fair Value

RECOGNITION AND MEASUREMENT

1.104 FASB ASC 820 defines fair value, establishes a framework for measuring fair value, and requires certain disclosures about fair value measurements. *Fair value* is defined as an exit price (that is, a price that would be received to sell, versus acquire, an asset or transfer a liability). Further, fair value is a market-based measurement. It establishes a fair value hierarchy that distinguishes between assumptions developed based on market data obtained from independent external sources and the reporting entity's own assumptions. Further, fair value measurement should consider adjustment for risk, such as the risk inherent in a valuation technique or its inputs.

1.105 "Pending Content" in FASB ASC 820-10-35-10A provides that a fair value measurement of a nonfinancial asset takes into account a market participant's ability to generate economic benefit by using the asset in its highest and best use or by selling it to another market participant that would use the asset in its highest and best use. "Pending Content" in FASB ASC 820-10-35-10B states that the highest and best use for a nonfinancial asset takes into account the use of the asset that is physically possible, legally permissible, and financial feasible. "Pending Content" in FASB ASC 820-10-35-10E states that the highest and best use of a nonfinancial asset might provide maximum value to market participants through its use in combination with other assets as a group (as installed or otherwise configured for use) or in combination with other assets and liabilities The highest and best use is determined from the perspective of market participants, even if the reporting entity intends a different use. An asset's value in use should be based on the price that would be received in a current transaction to sell the asset, assuming that the asset would be used with other assets as a group and that those other assets would be available to market participants. An asset's value in exchange is determined based on the price that would be received in a current transaction to sell the asset on a stand-alone basis.

1.106 According to "Pending Content" in paragraphs 16–16AA of FASB ASC 820-10-35, a fair value measurement of a financial or nonfinancial liability or an instrument classified in a reporting entity's shareholders' equity is transferred to a market participant at the measurement date. Even when there is no observable market to provide pricing information about the transfer of a liability or an instrument classified in a reporting entity's shareholders' equity, there might be an observable market for such items if they are held by other parties as assets. In all cases, a reporting entity shall maximize the use of relevant observable inputs and minimize the use of unobservable inputs to meet the objective of a fair value measurement. A reporting entity is permitted, as a practical expedient, to estimate the fair value of an investment within the scope of paragraphs 4–5 of FASB ASC 820-10-15 using the net asset value per share (or its equivalent) of the investment if the net asset value per share or its equivalent is calculated in a manner consistent with the measurement principles of FASB ASC 946, *Financial Services—Investment Companies*, as of the reporting entity's measurement date.

DISCLOSURE

1.107 For assets and liabilities measured at fair value, whether on a recurring or nonrecurring basis, FASB ASC 820-10-50 specifies the required disclosures concerning the inputs used to measure fair value. "Pending Content" in FASB ASC 820-10-50-1 explains that the reporting entity should disclose information that enables users of its financial statements to assess the following: (*a*) for assets and liabilities measured at fair value on a recurring basis in periods subsequent to initial recognition or measured on a nonrecurring basis in periods subsequent to initial recognition, the valuation techniques and inputs used to develop those measurements and (*b*) for recurring fair value measurements using significant unobservable inputs (level 3), the effect of the measurements on earnings for the period.

PRESENTATION AND DISCLOSURE EXCERPT

FAIR VALUE MEASUREMENTS

1.108 MORGAN STANLEY (DEC)
NOTES TO CONSOLIDATED FINANCIAL STATEMENTS

2. Significant Accounting Policies (in part)

Financial Instruments and Fair Value.

A significant portion of the Company's financial instruments is carried at fair value with changes in fair value recognized in earnings each period. A description of the Company's policies regarding fair value measurement and its application to these financial instruments follows.

Financial Instruments Measured at Fair Value. All of the instruments within Financial instruments owned and Financial instruments sold, not yet purchased, are measured at fair value, either through the fair value option election (discussed below) or as required by other accounting guidance. These financial instruments primarily represent the Company's trading and investment positions and include both cash and derivative products. In addition, debt securities classified as Securities available for sale are measured at fair value in accordance with accounting guidance for certain investments in debt securities. Furthermore, Securities received as collateral and Obligation to return securities received as collateral are measured at fair value as required by other accounting guidance. Additionally, certain Deposits, certain Commercial paper and other short-term borrowings (structured notes), certain Other secured financings, certain Securities sold under agreements to repurchase and certain Long-term borrowings (primarily structured notes) are measured at fair value through the fair value option election.

Gains and losses on all of these instruments carried at fair value are reflected in Principal transactions—Trading revenues, Principal transactions—Investments revenues or Investment banking revenues in the consolidated statements of income, except for Securities available for sale (see "Securities Available for Sale" section herein and Note 5) and derivatives accounted for as hedges (see "Hedge Accounting" section herein and Note 12). Interest income and expense are recorded within the consolidated statements of income depending on the nature of the instrument and related market conventions. When interest is included as a component of the instruments' fair value, interest is included within Principal transactions—Trading revenues or Principal transactions—Investments revenues. Otherwise, it is included within Interest income or Interest expense. Dividend income is recorded in Principal transactions—Trading revenues or Principal transactions—Investments revenues depending on the business activity. The fair value of OTC financial instruments, including derivative contracts related to financial instruments and commodities, is presented in the accompanying consolidated statements of financial condition on a net-by-counterparty basis, when appropriate. Additionally, the Company nets the fair value of cash collateral paid or received against the fair value amounts recognized for net derivative positions executed with the same counterparty under the same master netting arrangement.

Fair Value Option. The fair value option permits the irrevocable fair value option election on an instrument-by-instrument basis at initial recognition of an asset or liability or upon an event that gives rise to a new basis of accounting for that instrument. The Company applies the fair value option for eligible instruments, including certain securities purchased under agreements to resell, certain loans and lending commitments, certain equity method investments, certain securities sold under agreements to repurchase, certain structured notes, certain time deposits and certain other secured financings.

Fair Value Measurement—Definition and Hierarchy. Fair value is defined as the price that would be received to sell an asset or paid to transfer a liability (*i.e.*, the "exit price") in an orderly transaction between market participants at the measurement date.

In determining fair value, the Company uses various valuation approaches and establishes a hierarchy for inputs used in measuring fair value that maximizes the use of relevant observable inputs and minimizes the use of unobservable inputs by requiring that the most observable inputs be used when available. Observable inputs are inputs that market participants would use in pricing the asset or liability developed based on market data obtained from sources independent of the Company. Unobservable inputs are inputs that reflect the Company's assumptions about the assumptions other market participants would use in pricing the asset or liability developed based on the best information available in the circumstances. The hierarchy is broken down into three levels based on the observability of inputs as follows:

- Level 1—Valuations based on quoted prices in active markets for identical assets or liabilities that the Company has the ability to access. Valuation adjustments and block discounts are not applied to Level 1 instruments. Since valuations are based on quoted prices that are readily and regularly available in an active market, valuation of these products does not entail a significant degree of judgment.
- Level 2—Valuations based on one or more quoted prices in markets that are not active or for which all significant inputs are observable, either directly or indirectly.
- Level 3—Valuations based on inputs that are unobservable and significant to the overall fair value measurement.

The availability of observable inputs can vary from product to product and is affected by a wide variety of factors, including, for example, the type of product, whether the product is new and not yet established in the marketplace, the liquidity of markets and other characteristics particular to the product. To the extent that valuation is based on models or inputs that are less observable or unobservable in the market, the determination of fair value requires more judgment. Accordingly, the degree of judgment exercised by the Company in determining fair value is greatest for instruments categorized in Level 3 of the fair value hierarchy.

The Company considers prices and inputs that are current as of the measurement date, including during periods of market dislocation. In periods of market dislocation, the observability of prices and inputs may be reduced for many instruments. This condition could cause an instrument to be reclassified from Level 1 to Level 2 or Level 2 to Level 3 of the fair value hierarchy (see Note 4). In addition, a downturn in market conditions could lead to declines in the valuation of many instruments.

In certain cases, the inputs used to measure fair value may fall into different levels of the fair value hierarchy. In such cases, for disclosure purposes, the level in the fair value hierarchy within which the fair value measurement falls in its entirety is determined based on the lowest level input that is significant to the fair value measurement in its entirety.

Valuation Techniques. Many cash instruments and OTC derivative contracts have bid and ask prices that can be observed in the marketplace. Bid prices reflect the highest price that a party is willing to pay for an asset. Ask prices represent the lowest price that a party is willing to accept for an asset. For financial instruments whose inputs are based on bid-ask prices, the Company does not require that the fair value estimate always be a predetermined point in the bid-ask range. The Company's policy is to allow for mid-market pricing and to adjust to the point within the bid-ask range that meets the Company's best estimate of fair value. For offsetting positions in the same financial instrument, the same price within the bid-ask spread is used to measure both the long and short positions.

Fair value for many cash instruments and OTC derivative contracts is derived using pricing models. Pricing models take into account the contract terms (including maturity) as well as multiple inputs, including, where applicable, commodity prices, equity prices, interest rate yield curves, credit curves, correlation, creditworthiness of the counterparty, creditworthiness of the Company, option volatility and currency rates. Where appropriate, valuation adjustments are made to account for various factors such as liquidity risk (bid-ask adjustments), credit quality, model uncertainty and concentration risk. Adjustments for liquidity risk adjust model-derived mid-market levels of Level 2 and Level 3 financial instruments for the bid-mid or mid-ask spread required to properly reflect the exit price of a risk position. Bid-mid and mid-ask spreads are marked to levels observed in trade activity, broker quotes or other external third-party data. Where these spreads are unobservable for the particular position in question, spreads are derived from observable levels of similar positions. The Company applies credit-related valuation adjustments to its short-term and long-term borrowings (primarily structured notes) for which the fair value option was elected and to OTC derivatives. The Company considers the impact of changes in its own credit spreads based upon observations of the Company's secondary bond market spreads when measuring the fair value for short-term and long-term borrowings. For OTC derivatives, the impact of changes in both the Company's and the counterparty's credit standing is considered when measuring fair value. In determining the expected exposure, the Company simulates the distribution of the future exposure to a counterparty, then applies market-based default probabilities to the future exposure, leveraging external third-party credit default swap ("CDS") spread data. Where CDS spread data are unavailable for a specific counterparty, bond market spreads, CDS spread data based on the counterparty's credit rating or CDS spread data that reference a comparable counterparty may be utilized. The Company also considers collateral held and legally enforceable master netting agreements that mitigate the Company's exposure to each counterparty. Adjustments for model uncertainty are taken for positions whose underlying models are reliant on significant inputs that are neither directly nor indirectly observable, hence requiring reliance on established theoretical concepts in their derivation. These adjustments are derived by making assessments of the possible degree of variability using statistical approaches and market-based information where possible. The Company generally subjects all valuations and models to a review process initially and on a periodic basis thereafter. The Company may apply a concentration adjustment to certain of its OTC derivatives portfolios to reflect the additional cost of closing out a particularly large risk exposure. Where possible, these adjustments are based on observable market information but in many instances significant judgment is required to estimate the costs of closing out concentrated risk exposures due to the lack of liquidity in the marketplace.

Fair value is a market-based measure considered from the perspective of a market participant rather than an entity-specific measure. Therefore, even when market assumptions are not readily available, the Company's own assumptions are set to reflect those that the Company believes market participants would use in pricing the asset or liability at the measurement date.

See Note 4 for a description of valuation techniques applied to the major categories of financial instruments measured at fair value.

Assets and Liabilities Measured at Fair Value on a Non-Recurring Basis. Certain of the Company's assets are measured at fair value on a non-recurring basis. The Company incurs losses or gains for any adjustments of these assets to fair value. A downturn in market conditions could result in impairment charges in future periods.

For assets and liabilities measured at fair value on a non-recurring basis, fair value is determined by using various valuation approaches. The same hierarchy for inputs as described above, which maximizes the use of observable inputs and minimizes the use of unobservable inputs by generally requiring that the observable inputs be used when available, is used in measuring fair value for these items.

Valuation Process. The Valuation Review Group ("VRG") within the Financial Control Group ("FCG") is responsible for the Company's fair value valuation policies, processes and procedures. VRG is independent of the business units and reports to the Chief Financial Officer ("CFO"), who has final authority over the valuation of the Company's financial instruments. VRG implements valuation control processes to validate the fair value of the Company's financial instruments measured at fair value including those derived from pricing models. These control processes are designed to assure that the values used for financial reporting are based on observable inputs wherever possible. In the event that observable inputs are not available, the control processes are designed to ensure that the valuation approach utilized is appropriate and consistently applied and that the assumptions are reasonable.

The Company's control processes apply to financial instruments categorized in Level 1, Level 2 or Level 3 of the fair value hierarchy, unless otherwise noted. These control processes include:

Model Review. VRG, in conjunction with the Market Risk Department ("MRD") and, where appropriate, the Credit Risk Management Department, both of which report to the Chief Risk Officer, independently review valuation models' theoretical soundness, the appropriateness of the valuation methodology and calibration techniques developed by the business units using observable inputs. Where inputs are not observable, VRG reviews the appropriateness of the proposed valuation methodology to ensure it is consistent with how a market participant would arrive at the unobservable input. The valuation methodologies utilized in the absence of observable inputs may include extrapolation techniques and the use of comparable observable inputs. As part of the review, VRG develops a methodology to independently verify the fair value generated by the business unit's valuation models. Before trades are executed using new valuation models, those models are required to be independently reviewed. All of the Company's valuation models are subject to an independent annual VRG review.

Independent Price Verification. The business units are responsible for determining the fair value of financial instruments using approved valuation models and valuation methodologies. Generally on a monthly basis, VRG independently validates the fair values of financial instruments determined using valuation models by determining the appropriateness of the inputs used by the business units and by testing compliance with the documented valuation methodologies approved in the model review process described above.

VRG uses recently executed transactions, other observable market data such as exchange data, broker/dealer quotes, third-party pricing vendors and aggregation services for validating the fair values of financial instruments generated using valuation models. VRG assesses the external sources and their valuation methodologies to determine if the external providers meet the minimum standards expected of a third-party pricing source. Pricing data provided by approved external sources are evaluated using a number of approaches; for example, by corroborating the external sources' prices to executed trades, by analyzing the methodology and assumptions used by the external source to generate a price and/or by evaluating how active the third-party pricing source (or originating sources used by the third-party pricing source) is in the market. Based on this analysis, VRG generates a ranking of the observable market data to ensure that the highest-ranked market data source is used to validate the business unit's fair value of financial instruments.

For financial instruments categorized within Level 3 of the fair value hierarchy, VRG reviews the business unit's valuation techniques to ensure these are consistent with market participant assumptions.

The results of this independent price verification and any adjustments made by VRG to the fair value generated by the business units are presented to management of the Company's three business segments (*i.e.*, Institutional Securities, Global Wealth Management Group and Asset Management), the CFO and the Chief Risk Officer on a regular basis.

Review of New Level 3 Transactions. VRG reviews the models and valuation methodology used to price all new material Level 3 transactions and both FCG and MRD management must approve the fair value of the trade that is initially recognized.

For further information on financial assets and liabilities that are measured at fair value on a recurring and non-recurring basis, see Note 4.

4. Fair Value Disclosures

Fair Value Measurements.

A description of the valuation techniques applied to the Company's major categories of assets and liabilities measured at fair value on a recurring basis follows.

Financial Instruments Owned and Financial Instruments Sold, Not Yet Purchased.

U.S. Government and Agency Securities.
- U.S. Treasury Securities. U.S. Treasury securities are valued using quoted market prices. Valuation adjustments are not applied. Accordingly, U.S. Treasury securities are generally categorized in Level 1 of the fair value hierarchy.
- U.S. Agency Securities. U.S. agency securities are composed of three main categories consisting of agency-issued debt, agency mortgage pass-through pool securities and collateralized mortgage obligations. Non-callable agency-issued debt securities are generally valued using quoted market prices. Callable agency-issued debt securities are valued by benchmarking model-derived prices to quoted market prices and trade data for identical or comparable securities. The fair value of agency mortgage pass-through pool securities is model-driven based on spreads of the comparable To-be-announced ("TBA") security. Collateralized mortgage obligations are valued using quoted market prices and trade data adjusted by subsequent changes in related indices for identical or comparable securities. Actively traded non-callable agency-issued debt securities are generally categorized in Level 1 of the fair value hierarchy. Callable agency-issued debt securities, agency mortgage pass-through pool securities and collateralized mortgage obligations are generally categorized in Level 2 of the fair value hierarchy.

Other Sovereign Government Obligations.
- Foreign sovereign government obligations are valued using quoted prices in active markets when available. These bonds are generally categorized in Level 1 of the fair value hierarchy. If the market is less active or prices are dispersed, these bonds are categorized in Level 2 of the fair value hierarchy.

Corporate and Other Debt.
- State and Municipal Securities. The fair value of state and municipal securities is determined using recently executed transactions, market price quotations and pricing models that factor in, where applicable, interest rates, bond or credit default swap spreads and volatility. These bonds are generally categorized in Level 2 of the fair value hierarchy.
- Residential Mortgage-Backed Securities ("RMBS"), Commercial Mortgage-Backed Securities ("CMBS") and other Asset-Backed Securities ("ABS"). RMBS, CMBS and other ABS may be valued based on price or spread data obtained from observed transactions or independent external parties such as vendors or brokers. When position-specific external price data are not observable, the fair value determination may require benchmarking to similar instruments and/or analyzing expected credit losses, default and recovery rates. In evaluating the fair value of each security, the Company considers security collateral-specific attributes, including payment priority, credit enhancement levels, type of collateral, delinquency rates and loss severity. In addition, for RMBS borrowers, Fair Isaac Corporation ("FICO") scores and the level of documentation for the loan are also considered. Market standard models, such as Intex, Trepp or others, may be deployed to model the specific collateral composition and cash flow structure of each transaction. Key inputs to these models are market spreads, forecasted credit losses, default and prepayment rates for each asset category. Valuation levels of RMBS and CMBS indices are also used as an additional data point for benchmarking purposes or to price outright index positions.

RMBS, CMBS and other ABS are generally categorized in Level 2 of the fair value hierarchy. If external prices or significant spread inputs are unobservable or if the comparability assessment involves significant subjectivity related to property type differences, cash flows, performance and other inputs, then RMBS, CMBS and other ABS are categorized in Level 3 of the fair value hierarchy.
- Corporate Bonds. The fair value of corporate bonds is determined using recently executed transactions, market price quotations (where observable), bond spreads or credit default swap spreads obtained from independent external parties such as vendors and brokers adjusted for any basis difference between cash and derivative instruments. The spread data used are for the same maturity as the bond. If the spread data do not reference the issuer, then data that reference a comparable issuer are used. When position-specific external price data are not observable, fair value is determined based on either benchmarking to similar instruments or cash flow models with yield curves, bond or single-name credit default swap spreads and recovery rates as

- significant inputs. Corporate bonds are generally categorized in Level 2 of the fair value hierarchy; in instances where prices, spreads or any of the other aforementioned key inputs are unobservable, they are categorized in Level 3 of the fair value hierarchy.
- <u>Collateralized Debt Obligations ("CDO")</u>. The Company holds cash CDOs that typically reference a tranche of an underlying synthetic portfolio of single name credit default swaps collateralized by corporate bonds ("credit-linked notes") or cash portfolio of asset-backed securities ("asset-backed CDOs"). Credit correlation, a primary input used to determine the fair value of credit-linked notes, is usually unobservable and derived using a benchmarking technique. The other credit-linked note model inputs such as credit spreads, including collateral spreads, and interest rates are typically observable. Asset-backed CDOs are valued based on an evaluation of the market and model input parameters sourced from similar positions as indicated by primary and secondary market activity. Each asset-backed CDO position is evaluated independently taking into consideration available comparable market levels, underlying collateral performance and pricing, and deal structures, as well as liquidity. Cash CDOs are categorized in Level 2 of the fair value hierarchy when either the credit correlation input is insignificant or comparable market transactions are observable. In instances where the credit correlation input is deemed to be significant or comparable market transactions are unobservable, cash CDOs are categorized in Level 3 of the fair value hierarchy.
- <u>Corporate Loans and Lending Commitments</u>. The fair value of corporate loans is determined using recently executed transactions, market price quotations (where observable), implied yields from comparable debt, and market observable credit default swap spread levels obtained from independent external parties such as vendors and brokers adjusted for any basis difference between cash and derivative instruments, along with proprietary valuation models and default recovery analysis where such transactions and quotations are unobservable. The fair value of contingent corporate lending commitments is determined by using executed transactions on comparable loans and the anticipated market price based on pricing indications from syndicate banks and customers. The valuation of loans and lending commitments also takes into account fee income that is considered an attribute of the contract. Corporate loans and lending commitments are categorized in Level 2 of the fair value hierarchy except in instances where prices or significant spread inputs are unobservable, in which case they are categorized in Level 3 of the fair value hierarchy.
- <u>Mortgage Loans</u>. Mortgage loans are valued using observable prices based on transactional data or third-party pricing for identical or comparable instruments, when available. Where position-specific external prices are not observable, the Company estimates fair value based on benchmarking to prices and rates observed in the primary market for similar loan or borrower types or based on the present value of expected future cash flows using its best estimates of the key assumptions, including forecasted credit losses, prepayment rates, forward yield curves and discount rates commensurate with the risks involved or a methodology that utilizes the capital structure and credit spreads of recent comparable securitization transactions. Mortgage loans valued based on observable market data for identical or comparable instruments are categorized in Level 2 of the fair value hierarchy. Where observable prices are not available, due to the subjectivity involved in the comparability assessment related to mortgage loan vintage, geographical concentration, prepayment speed and projected loss assumptions, mortgage loans are categorized in Level 3 of the fair value hierarchy. Mortgage loans are presented within Loans and lending commitments in the fair value hierarchy table.
- <u>Auction Rate Securities ("ARS")</u>. The Company primarily holds investments in Student Loan Auction Rate Securities ("SLARS") and Municipal Auction Rate Securities ("MARS") with interest rates that are reset through periodic auctions. SLARS are ABS backed by pools of student loans. MARS are municipal bonds often wrapped by municipal bond insurance. ARS were historically traded and valued as floating rate notes, priced at par due to the auction mechanism. Beginning in fiscal 2008, uncertainties in the credit markets have resulted in auctions failing for certain types of ARS. Once the auctions failed, ARS could no longer be valued using observations of auction market prices. Accordingly, the fair value of ARS is determined using independent external market data where available and an internally developed methodology to discount for the lack of liquidity and non-performance risk.

Inputs that impact the valuation of SLARS are independent external market data, the underlying collateral types, level of seniority in the capital structure, amount of leverage in each structure, credit rating and liquidity considerations. Inputs that impact the valuation of MARS are recently executed transactions, the maximum rate, quality of underlying issuers/insurers and evidence of issuer calls/prepayment. ARS are generally categorized in Level 2 of the fair value hierarchy as the valuation technique relies on observable external data. SLARS and MARS are presented within Asset-backed securities and State and municipal securities, respectively, in the fair value hierarchy table.

Corporate Equities.
- <u>Exchange-Traded Equity Securities</u>. Exchange-traded equity securities are generally valued based on quoted prices from the exchange. To the extent these securities are actively traded, valuation adjustments are not applied, and they are categorized in Level 1 of the fair value hierarchy; otherwise, they are categorized in Level 2 or Level 3 of the fair value hierarchy.
- <u>Unlisted Equity Securities</u>. Unlisted equity securities are valued based on an assessment of each underlying security, considering rounds of financing and third-party transactions, discounted cash flow analyses and market-based information, including comparable company transactions, trading multiples and changes in market outlook, among other factors. These securities are generally categorized in Level 3 of the fair value hierarchy.
- <u>Fund Units</u>. Listed fund units are generally marked to the exchange-traded price or net asset value ("NAV") and are categorized in Level 1 of the fair value hierarchy if actively traded on an exchange or in Level 2 of the fair value hierarchy if trading is not active. Unlisted fund units are generally marked to NAV and categorized as Level 2; however, positions which are not redeemable at the measurement date or in the near future are categorized in Level 3 of the fair value hierarchy.

Derivative and Other Contracts.
- <u>Listed Derivative Contracts</u>. Listed derivatives that are actively traded are valued based on quoted prices from the exchange and are categorized in Level 1 of the fair value hierarchy. Listed derivatives that are not actively traded are valued using the same approaches as those applied to OTC derivatives; they are generally categorized in Level 2 of the fair value hierarchy.
- <u>OTC Derivative Contracts</u>. OTC derivative contracts include forward, swap and option contracts related to interest rates, foreign currencies, credit standing of reference entities, equity prices or commodity prices.

Depending on the product and the terms of the transaction, the fair value of OTC derivative products can be either observed or modeled using a series of techniques and model inputs from comparable benchmarks, including closed-form analytic formulas, such as the Black-Scholes option-pricing model, and simulation models or a combination thereof. Many pricing models do not entail material subjectivity because the methodologies employed do not necessitate significant judgment, and the pricing inputs are observed from actively quoted markets, as is the case for generic interest rate swaps, certain option contracts and certain credit default swaps. In the case of more established derivative products, the pricing models used by the Company are widely accepted by the financial services industry. A substantial majority of OTC derivative products valued by the Company using pricing models fall into this category and are categorized in Level 2 of the fair value hierarchy.

Other derivative products, including complex products that have become illiquid, require more judgment in the implementation of the valuation technique applied due to the complexity of the valuation assumptions and the reduced observability of inputs. This includes certain types of interest rate derivatives with both volatility and correlation exposure and credit derivatives including credit default swaps on certain mortgage-backed or asset-backed securities, basket credit default swaps and CDO-squared positions (a CDO-squared position is a special purpose vehicle that issues interests, or tranches, that are backed by tranches issued by other CDOs) where direct trading activity or quotes are unobservable. These instruments involve significant unobservable inputs and are categorized in Level 3 of the fair value hierarchy.

Derivative interests in credit default swaps on certain mortgage-backed or asset-backed securities, for which observability of external price data is limited, are valued based on an evaluation of the market and model input parameters sourced from similar positions as indicated by primary and secondary market activity. Each position is evaluated independently taking into consideration available comparable market levels as well as cash-synthetic basis, or the underlying collateral performance and pricing, behavior of the tranche under various cumulative loss and prepayment scenarios, deal structures (*e.g.*, non-amortizing reference obligations, call features, etc.) and liquidity. While these factors may be supported by historical and actual external observations, the determination of their value as it relates to specific positions nevertheless requires significant judgment.

For basket credit default swaps and CDO-squared positions, the correlation input between reference credits is unobservable for each specific swap or position and is benchmarked to standardized proxy baskets for which correlation data are available. The other model inputs such as credit spread, interest rates and recovery rates are observable. In instances where the correlation input is deemed to be significant, these instruments are categorized in Level 3 of the fair value hierarchy; otherwise, these instruments are categorized in Level 2 of the fair value hierarchy.

The Company trades various derivative structures with commodity underlyings. Depending on the type of structure, the model inputs generally include interest rate yield curves, commodity underlier price curves, implied volatility of the underlying commodities and, in some cases, the implied correlation between these inputs. The fair value of these products is determined using executed trades and broker and consensus data to provide values for the aforementioned inputs. Where these inputs are unobservable, relationships to observable commodities and data points, based on historic and/or implied observations, are employed as a technique to estimate the model input values. Commodity derivatives are generally categorized in Level 2 of the fair value hierarchy; in instances where significant inputs are unobservable, they are categorized in Level 3 of the fair value hierarchy.

- Collateralized Derivative Contracts. In the fourth quarter of 2010, the Company began using the overnight indexed swap ("OIS") curve as an input to value its collateralized interest rate derivative contracts. During the fourth quarter of 2011, the Company recognized a pre-tax loss of approximately $108 million in Principal transactions—Trading upon application of the OIS curve to certain additional fixed income products within the Institutional Securities business segment. Previously, the Company discounted these contracts based on London Interbank Offered Rate ("LIBOR"). At December 31, 2012 and December 31, 2011, substantially all of the Company's collateralized derivative contracts were valued using the OIS curve.

For further information on derivative instruments and hedging activities, see Note 12.

Investments

- The Company's investments include direct investments in equity securities as well as investments in private equity funds, real estate funds and hedge funds, which include investments made in connection with certain employee deferred compensation plans. Direct investments are presented in the fair value hierarchy table as Principal investments and Other. Initially, the transaction price is generally considered by the Company as the exit price and is the Company's best estimate of fair value.

After initial recognition, in determining the fair value of non-exchange-traded internally and externally managed funds, the Company generally considers the NAV of the fund provided by the fund manager to be the best estimate of fair value. For non-exchange-traded investments either held directly or held within internally managed funds, fair value after initial recognition is based on an assessment of each underlying investment, considering rounds of financing and third-party transactions, discounted cash flow analyses and market-based information, including comparable company transactions, trading multiples and changes in market outlook, among other factors. Exchange-traded direct equity investments are generally valued based on quoted prices from the exchange.

Exchange-traded direct equity investments that are actively traded are categorized in Level 1 of the fair value hierarchy. Non-exchange-traded direct equity investments and investments in private equity and real estate funds are generally categorized in Level 3 of the fair value hierarchy. Investments in hedge funds that are redeemable at the measurement date or in the near future are categorized in Level 2 of the fair value hierarchy; otherwise, they are categorized in Level 3 of the fair value hierarchy.

Physical Commodities.
- The Company trades various physical commodities, including crude oil and refined products, natural gas, base and precious metals, and agricultural products. Fair value for physical commodities is determined using observable inputs, including broker quotations and published indices. Physical commodities are categorized in Level 2 of the fair value hierarchy; in instances where significant inputs are unobservable, they are categorized in Level 3 of the fair value hierarchy.

Securities Available for Sale.
- Securities available for sale are composed of U.S. government and agency securities (*e.g.*, U.S. Treasury securities, agency-issued debt, agency mortgage pass-through securities and collateralized mortgage obligations), CMBS, Federal Family Education Loan Program ("FFELP") student loan asset-backed securities, auto loan asset-backed securities, corporate bonds and equity securities. Actively traded U.S. Treasury securities, non-callable agency-issued debt securities and equity securities are generally categorized in Level 1 of the fair value hierarchy. Callable agency-issued debt securities, agency mortgage pass-through securities, collateralized mortgage obligations, CMBS, FFELP student loan asset-backed securities, auto loan asset-backed securities and corporate bonds are generally categorized in Level 2 of the fair value hierarchy. For further information on securities available for sale, see Note 5.

Deposits.
- Time Deposits. The fair value of certificates of deposit is determined using third-party quotations. These deposits are generally categorized in Level 2 of the fair value hierarchy.

Commercial Paper and Other Short-Term Borrowings/Long-Term Borrowings.
- Structured Notes. The Company issues structured notes that have coupon or repayment terms linked to the performance of debt or equity securities, indices, currencies or commodities. Fair value of structured notes is determined using valuation models for the derivative and debt portions of the notes. These models incorporate observable inputs referencing identical or comparable securities, including prices to which the notes are linked, interest rate yield curves, option volatility and currency, commodity or equity prices. Independent, external and traded prices for the notes are considered as well. The impact of the Company's own credit spreads is also included based on the Company's observed secondary bond market spreads. Most structured notes are categorized in Level 2 of the fair value hierarchy.

Securities Purchased under Agreements to Resell and Securities Sold under Agreements to Repurchase.
- The fair value of a reverse repurchase agreement or repurchase agreement is computed using a standard cash flow discounting methodology. The inputs to the valuation include contractual cash flows and collateral funding spreads, which are estimated using various benchmarks, interest rate yield curves and option volatilities. In instances where the unobservable inputs are deemed significant, reverse repurchase agreements and repurchase agreements are categorized in Level 3 of the fair value hierarchy; otherwise, they are categorized in Level 2 of the fair value hierarchy.

The following fair value hierarchy tables present information about the Company's assets and liabilities measured at fair value on a recurring basis at December 31, 2012 and December 31, 2011.

Assets and Liabilities Measured at Fair Value on a Recurring Basis at December 31, 2012.

(Dollars in millions)	Quoted Prices in Active Markets for Identical Assets (Level 1)	Significant Observable Inputs (Level 2)	Significant Unobservable Inputs (Level 3)	Counterparty and Cash Collateral Netting	Balance at December 31, 2012
Assets at Fair Value					
Financial instruments owned:					
U.S. government and agency securities:					
U.S. Treasury securities	$24,662	$ 14	$ —	$—	$24,676
U.S. agency securities	1,451	27,888	—	—	29,339
Total U.S. government and agency securities	26,113	27,902	—	—	54,015
Other sovereign government obligations	37,669	5,487	6	—	43,162
Corporate and other debt:					
State and municipal securities	—	1,558	—	—	1,558
Residential mortgage-backed securities	—	1,439	45	—	1,484
Commercial mortgage-backed securities	—	1,347	232	—	1,579
Asset-backed securities	—	915	109	—	1,024
Corporate bonds	—	18,403	660	—	19,063
Collateralized debt obligations	—	685	1,951	—	2,636
Loans and lending commitments	—	12,617	4,694	—	17,311
Other debt	—	4,457	45	—	4,502
Total corporate and other debt	—	41,421	7,736	—	49,157

(continued)

(Dollars in millions)	Quoted Prices in Active Markets for Identical Assets (Level 1)	Significant Observable Inputs (Level 2)	Significant Unobservable Inputs (Level 3)	Counterparty and Cash Collateral Netting	Balance at December 31, 2012
Corporate equities[1]	$ 68,072	$ 1,067	$ 288	$ —	$ 69,427
Derivative and other contracts:					
Interest rate contracts	446	819,581	3,774	—	823,801
Credit contracts	—	63,234	5,033	—	68,267
Foreign exchange contracts	34	52,729	31	—	52,794
Equity contracts	760	37,074	766	—	38,600
Commodity contracts	4,082	14,256	2,308	—	20,646
Other	—	143	—	—	143
Netting[2]	(4,740)	(883,733)	(6,947)	(72,634)	(968,054)
Total derivative and other contracts	582	103,284	4,965	(72,634)	36,197
Investments:					
Private equity funds	—	—	2,179	—	2,179
Real estate funds	—	6	1,370	—	1,376
Hedge funds	—	382	552	—	934
Principal investments	185	83	2,833	—	3,101
Other	199	71	486	—	756
Total investments	384	542	7,420	—	8,346
Physical commodities	—	7,299	—	—	7,299
Total financial instruments owned	132,820	187,002	20,415	(72,634)	267,603
Securities available for sale	14,466	25,403	—	—	39,869
Securities received as collateral	14,232	46	—	—	14,278
Federal funds sold and securities purchased under agreements to resell	—	621	—	—	621
Intangible assets[3]	—	—	7	—	7
Total assets measured at fair value	$161,518	$213,072	$20,422	$(72,634)	$322,378
Liabilities at Fair Value					
Deposits	$ —	$ 1,485	$ —	$ —	$ 1,485
Commercial paper and other short-term borrowings	—	706	19	—	725
Financial instruments sold, not yet purchased:					
U.S. government and agency securities:					
U.S. Treasury securities	20,098	21	—	—	20,119
U.S. agency securities	1,394	107	—	—	1,501
Total U.S. government and agency securities	21,492	128	—	—	21,620
Other sovereign government obligations	27,583	2,031	—	—	29,614
Corporate and other debt:					
State and municipal securities	—	47	—	—	47
Residential mortgage-backed securities	—	—	4	—	4
Corporate bonds	—	3,942	177	—	4,119
Collateralized debt obligations	—	328	—	—	328
Unfunded lending commitments	—	305	46	—	351
Other debt	—	156	49	—	205
Total corporate and other debt	—	4,778	276	—	5,054
Corporate equities[1]	25,216	1,655	5	—	26,876
Derivative and other contracts:					
Interest rate contracts	533	789,715	3,856	—	794,104
Credit contracts	—	61,283	3,211	—	64,494
Foreign exchange contracts	2	56,021	390	—	56,413
Equity contracts	748	39,212	1,910	—	41,870
Commodity contracts	4,530	15,702	1,599	—	21,831
Other	—	54	7	—	61
Netting[2]	(4,740)	(883,733)	(6,947)	(46,395)	(941,815)
Total derivative and other contracts	1,073	78,254	4,026	(46,395)	36,958
Total financial instruments sold, not yet purchased	75,364	86,846	4,307	(46,395)	120,122
Obligation to return securities received as collateral	18,179	47	—	—	18,226
Securities sold under agreements to repurchase	—	212	151	—	363
Other secured financings	—	9,060	406	—	9,466
Long-term borrowings	—	41,255	2,789	—	44,044
Total liabilities measured at fair value	$ 93,543	$139,611	$ 7,672	$(46,395)	$194,431

[1] The Company holds or sells short for trading purposes equity securities issued by entities in diverse industries and of varying size.

[2] For positions with the same counterparty that cross over the levels of the fair value hierarchy, both counterparty netting and cash collateral netting are included in the column titled "Counterparty and Cash Collateral Netting." For contracts with the same counterparty, counterparty netting among positions classified within the same level is included within that level. For further information on derivative instruments and hedging activities, see Note 12.

[3] Amount represents mortgage servicing rights ("MSR") accounted for at fair value. See Note 7 for further information on MSRs.

Transfers Between Level 1 and Level 2 During 2012.

For assets and liabilities that were transferred between Level 1 and Level 2 during the period, fair values are ascribed as if the assets or liabilities had been transferred as of the beginning of the period.

Financial instruments owned—Derivative and other contracts and Financial instruments sold, not yet purchased—Derivative and other contracts. During 2012, the Company reclassified approximately $3.2 billion of derivative assets and approximately $2.5 billion of derivative liabilities from Level 2 to Level 1 as these listed derivatives became actively traded and were valued based on quoted prices from the exchange. Also during 2012, the Company reclassified approximately $0.4 billion of derivative assets and approximately $0.3 billion of derivative liabilities from Level 1 to Level 2 as transactions in these contracts did not occur with sufficient frequency and volume to constitute an active market.

Assets and Liabilities Measured at Fair Value on a Recurring Basis at December 31, 2011.

(Dollars in millions)	Quoted Prices in Active Markets for Identical Assets (Level 1)	Significant Observable Inputs (Level 2)	Significant Unobservable Inputs (Level 3)	Counterparty and Cash Collateral Netting	Balance at December 31, 2011
Assets at Fair Value					
Financial instruments owned:					
U.S. government and agency securities:					
U.S. Treasury securities	$ 38,769	$ 1	$ —	$ —	$ 38,770
U.S. agency securities	4,332	20,339	8	—	24,679
Total U.S. government and agency securities	43,101	20,340	8	—	63,449
Other sovereign government obligations	22,650	6,290	119	—	29,059
Corporate and other debt:					
State and municipal securities	—	2,261	—	—	2,261
Residential mortgage-backed securities	—	1,304	494	—	1,798
Commercial mortgage-backed securities	—	1,686	134	—	1,820
Asset-backed securities	—	937	31	—	968
Corporate bonds	—	25,873	675	—	26,548
Collateralized debt obligations	—	1,711	980	—	2,691
Loans and lending commitments	—	14,854	9,590	—	24,444
Other debt	—	8,265	128	—	8,393
Total corporate and other debt	—	56,891	12,032	—	68,923
Corporate equities[1]	45,173	2,376	417	—	47,966
Derivative and other contracts:					
Interest rate contracts	1,493	906,082	5,301	—	912,876
Credit contracts	—	123,689	15,102	—	138,791
Foreign exchange contracts	—	61,770	573	—	62,343
Equity contracts	929	44,558	800	—	46,287
Commodity contracts	6,356	31,246	2,176	—	39,778
Other	—	292	306	—	598
Netting[2]	(7,596)	(1,045,912)	(11,837)	(87,264)	(1,152,609)
Total derivative and other contracts	1,182	121,725	12,421	(87,264)	48,064
Investments:					
Private equity funds	—	7	1,936	—	1,943
Real estate funds	—	5	1,213	—	1,218
Hedge funds	—	473	696	—	1,169
Principal investments	161	104	2,937	—	3,202
Other	141	21	501	—	663
Total investments	302	610	7,283	—	8,195
Physical commodities	—	9,651	46	—	9,697
Total financial instruments owned	112,408	217,883	32,326	(87,264)	275,353
Securities available for sale	13,437	17,058	—	—	30,495
Securities received as collateral	11,530	121	—	—	11,651
Federal funds sold and securities purchased under agreements to resell	—	112	—	—	112
Intangible assets[3]	—	—	133	—	133
Total assets measured at fair value	$137,375	$ 235,174	$32,459	$(87,264)	$ 317,744
Liabilities at Fair Value					
Deposits	$—	$ 2,101	$ —	$ —	$2,101
Commercial paper and other short-term borrowings	—	1,337	2	—	1,339
Financial instruments sold, not yet purchased:					
U.S. government and agency securities:					
U.S. Treasury securities	17,776	—	—	—	17,776
U.S. agency securities	1,748	106	—	—	1,854
Total U.S. government and agency securities	19,524	106	—	—	19,630
Other sovereign government obligations	14,981	2,152	8	—	17,141
Corporate and other debt:					
State and municipal securities	—	3	—	—	3
Residential mortgage-backed securities	—	—	355	—	355
Commercial mortgage-backed securities	—	14	—	—	14
Corporate bonds	—	6,217	219	—	6,436
Collateralized debt obligations	—	3	—	—	3

(continued)

(Dollars in millions)	Quoted Prices in Active Markets for Identical Assets (Level 1)	Significant Observable Inputs (Level 2)	Significant Unobservable Inputs (Level 3)	Counterparty and Cash Collateral Netting	Balance at December 31, 2011
Unfunded lending commitments	$ —	$ 1,284	$ 85	$ —	$ 1,369
Other debt	—	157	73	—	230
Total corporate and other debt	—	7,678	732	—	8,410
Corporate equities[1]	24,347	149	1	—	24,497
Derivative and other contracts:					
Interest rate contracts	1,680	873,466	4,881	—	880,027
Credit contracts	—	121,438	9,288	—	130,726
Foreign exchange contracts	—	64,218	530	—	64,748
Equity contracts	877	45,375	2,034	—	48,286
Commodity contracts	7,144	31,248	1,606	—	39,998
Other	—	879	1,396	—	2,275
Netting[2]	(7,596)	(1,045,912)	(11,837)	(54,262)	(1,119,607)
Total derivative and other contracts	2,105	90,712	7,898	(54,262)	46,453
Physical commodities	—	16	—	—	16
Total financial instruments sold, not yet purchased	60,957	100,813	8,639	(54,262)	116,147
Obligation to return securities received as collateral	15,267	127	—	—	15,394
Securities sold under agreements to repurchase	—	8	340	—	348
Other secured financings	—	14,024	570	—	14,594
Long-term borrowings	10	38,050	1,603	—	39,663
Total liabilities measured at fair value	$76,234	$ 156,460	$ 11,154	$(54,262)	$ 189,586

[1] The Company holds or sells short for trading purposes equity securities issued by entities in diverse industries and of varying size.

[2] For positions with the same counterparty that cross over the levels of the fair value hierarchy, both counterparty netting and cash collateral netting are included in the column titled "Counterparty and Cash Collateral Netting." For contracts with the same counterparty, counterparty netting among positions classified within the same level is included within that level. For further information on derivative instruments and hedging activities, see Note 12.

[3] Amount represents MSRs accounted for at fair value. See Note 7 for further information on MSRs.

Transfers Between Level 1 and Level 2 During 2011.

Financial instruments owned—Other sovereign government obligations and Financial instruments sold, not yet purchased—Other sovereign government obligations. During 2011, the Company reclassified approximately $0.9 billion of other sovereign government obligations assets and approximately $1.7 billion of other sovereign government obligations liabilities from Level 1 to Level 2. These reclassifications primarily related to certain European peripheral government bonds as these securities traded with a high degree of pricing volatility, dispersion and wider bid-ask spreads. The Company continues to mark these securities to observable market price quotations.

Financial instruments owned—Derivative and other contracts and Financial instruments sold, not yet purchased—Derivative and other contracts. During 2011, the Company reclassified approximately $0.7 billion of derivative assets and approximately $1.0 billion of derivative liabilities from Level 2 to Level 1 as these listed derivatives became actively traded and were valued based on quoted prices from the exchange. Also during 2011, the Company reclassified approximately $1.3 billion of derivative assets and approximately $1.4 billion of derivative liabilities from Level 1 to Level 2 as transactions in these contracts did not occur with sufficient frequency and volume to constitute an active market.

Level 3 Assets and Liabilities Measured at Fair Value on a Recurring Basis.

The following tables present additional information about Level 3 assets and liabilities measured at fair value on a recurring basis for 2012, 2011 and 2010, respectively. Level 3 instruments may be hedged with instruments classified in Level 1 and Level 2. As a result, the realized and unrealized gains (losses) for assets and liabilities within the Level 3 category presented in the tables below do not reflect the related realized and unrealized gains (losses) on hedging instruments that have been classified by the Company within the Level 1 and/or Level 2 categories.

Additionally, both observable and unobservable inputs may be used to determine the fair value of positions that the Company has classified within the Level 3 category. As a result, the unrealized gains (losses) during the period for assets and liabilities within the Level 3 category presented in the tables below may include changes in fair value during the period that were attributable to both observable (*e.g.*, changes in market interest rates) and unobservable (*e.g.*, changes in unobservable long-dated volatilities) inputs.

For assets and liabilities that were transferred into Level 3 during the period, gains (losses) are presented as if the assets or liabilities had been transferred into Level 3 at the beginning of the period; similarly, for assets and liabilities that were transferred out of Level 3 during the period, gains (losses) are presented as if the assets or liabilities had been transferred out at the beginning of the period.

(Dollars in millions)	Beginning Balance at December 31, 2011	Total Realized and Unrealized Gains (Losses)[1]	Purchases	Sales	Issuances	Settlements	Net Transfers	Ending Balance at December 31, 2012	Unrealized Gains (Losses) for Level 3 Assets/ Liabilities Outstanding at December 31, 2012[2]
Assets at Fair Value									
Financial instruments owned:									
U.S. agency securities	$ 8	$ —	$ —	$ (7)	$ —	$ —	$ (1)	$ —	$ —
Other sovereign government obligations	119	—	12	(125)	—	—	—	6	(9)
Corporate and other debt:									
Residential mortgage-backed securities	494	(9)	32	(285)	—	—	(187)	45	(26)
Commercial mortgage-backed securities	134	32	218	(49)	—	(100)	(3)	232	28
Asset-backed securities	31	1	109	(32)	—	—	—	109	(1)
Corporate bonds	675	22	447	(450)	—	—	(34)	660	(7)
Collateralized debt obligations	980	216	1,178	(384)	—	—	(39)	1,951	142
Loans and lending commitments	9,590	37	2,648	(2,095)	—	(4,316)	(1,170)	4,694	(91)
Other debt	128	2	—	(95)	—	—	10	45	(6)
Total corporate and other debt	12,032	301	4,632	(3,390)	—	(4,416)	(1,423)	7,736	39
Corporate equities	417	(59)	134	(172)	—	—	(32)	288	(83)
Net derivative and other contracts[3]:									
Interest rate contracts	420	(275)	28	—	(7)	(217)	(31)	(82)	297
Credit contracts	5,814	(2,799)	112	—	(502)	(961)	158	1,822	(3,216)
Foreign exchange contracts	43	(279)	—	—	—	19	(142)	(359)	(225)
Equity contracts	(1,234)	390	202	(9)	(112)	(210)	(171)	(1,144)	241
Commodity contracts	570	114	16	—	(41)	(20)	70	709	222
Other	(1,090)	57	—	—	—	236	790	(7)	53
Total net derivative and other contracts	4,523	(2,792)	358	(9)	(662)	(1,153)	674	939	(2,628)
Investments:									
Private equity funds	1,936	228	308	(294)	—	—	1	2,179	147
Real estate funds	1,213	149	143	(136)	—	—	1	1,370	229
Hedge funds	696	61	81	(151)	—	—	(135)	552	51
Principal investments	2,937	130	160	(419)	—	—	25	2,833	93
Other	501	(45)	158	(70)	—	—	(58)	486	(48)
Total investments	7,283	523	850	(1,070)	—	—	(166)	7,420	472
Physical commodities	46	—	—	—	—	(46)	—	—	—
Intangible assets	133	(39)	—	(83)	—	(4)	—	7	(7)
Liabilities at Fair Value									
Commercial paper and other short-term borrowings	$ 2	$ (5)	$ —	$ —	$ 3	$ (3)	$ 12	$ 19	$ (4)
Financial instruments sold, not yet purchased:									
Other sovereign government obligations	8	—	(8)	—	—	—	—	—	—
Corporate and other debt:									
Residential mortgage-backed securities	355	(4)	(355)	—	—	—	—	4	(4)
Corporate bonds	219	(15)	(129)	110	—	—	(38)	177	(23)
Unfunded lending commitments	85	39	—	—	—	—	—	46	39
Other debt	73	9	(1)	36	—	(55)	5	49	11
Total corporate and other debt	732	29	(485)	146	—	(55)	(33)	276	23
Corporate equities	1	(1)	(21)	22	—	—	2	5	(3)
Securities sold under agreements to repurchase	340	(14)	—	—	—	—	(203)	151	(14)
Other secured financings	570	(69)	—	—	21	(232)	(22)	406	(67)
Long-term borrowings	1,603	(651)	—	—	1,050	(279)	(236)	2,789	(652)

[1] Total realized and unrealized gains (losses) are primarily included in Principal transactions—Trading in the consolidated statements of income except for $523 million related to Financial instruments owned—Investments, which is included in Principal transactions—Investments.

[2] Amounts represent unrealized gains (losses) for 2012 related to assets and liabilities still outstanding at December 31, 2012.

[3] Net derivative and other contracts represent Financial instruments owned—Derivative and other contracts net of Financial instruments sold, not yet purchased—Derivative and other contracts. For further information on derivative instruments and hedging activities, see Note 12.

Financial instruments owned—Corporate and other debt. During 2012, the Company reclassified approximately $1.9 billion of certain Corporate and other debt, primarily loans, from Level 3 to Level 2. The Company reclassified the loans as external prices and/or spread inputs for these instruments became observable.

The Company also reclassified approximately $0.5 billion of certain Corporate and other debt from Level 2 to Level 3. The reclassifications were primarily related to corporate loans and were generally due to a reduction in market price quotations for these or comparable instruments, or a lack of available broker quotes, such that unobservable inputs had to be utilized for the fair value measurement of these instruments.

Financial instruments owned—Net derivative and other contracts. During 2012, the Company reclassified approximately $1.4 billion of certain credit derivative assets and approximately $1.2 billion of certain credit derivative liabilities from Level 3 to Level 2. These reclassifications were primarily related to single name credit default swaps and basket credit default swaps for which certain unobservable inputs became insignificant to the overall measurement.

The Company also reclassified approximately $0.6 billion of certain credit derivative assets and approximately $0.3 billion of certain credit derivative liabilities from Level 2 to Level 3. The reclassifications were primarily related to basket credit default swaps for which certain unobservable inputs became significant to the overall measurement.

The net losses in Net derivative and other contracts were primarily driven by tightening of credit spreads on underlying reference entities of basket credit default swaps where the Company was long protection.

Changes in Level 3 Assets and Liabilities Measured at Fair Value on a Recurring Basis for 2011.

(Dollars in millions)	Beginning Balance at December 31, 2010	Total Realized and Unrealized Gains (Losses)[1]	Purchases	Sales	Issuances	Settlements	Net Transfers	Ending Balance at December 31, 2011	Unrealized Gains (Losses) for Level 3 Assets/ Liabilities Outstanding at December 31, 2011[2]
Assets at Fair Value									
Financial instruments owned:									
U.S. agency securities	$ 13	$ —	$ 66	$ (68)	$ —	$ —	$ (3)	$ 8	$ —
Other sovereign government obligations	73	(4)	56	(2)	—	—	(4)	119	(2)
Corporate and other debt:									
State and municipal securities	110	(1)	—	(96)	—	—	(13)	—	—
Residential mortgage-backed securities	319	(61)	382	(221)	—	(1)	76	494	(59)
Commercial mortgage-backed securities	188	12	75	(90)	—	—	(51)	134	(18)
Asset-backed securities	13	4	13	(19)	—	—	20	31	2
Corporate bonds	1,368	(136)	467	(661)	—	—	(363)	675	(20)
Collateralized debt obligations	1,659	109	613	(1,296)	—	(55)	(50)	980	(84)
Loans and lending commitments	11,666	(251)	2,932	(1,241)	—	(2,900)	(616)	9,590	(431)
Other debt	193	42	14	(76)	—	(11)	(34)	128	—
Total corporate and other debt	15,516	(282)	4,496	(3,700)	—	(2,967)	(1,031)	12,032	(610)
Corporate equities	484	(46)	416	(360)	—	—	(77)	417	16
Net derivative and other contracts[3]:									
Interest rate contracts	424	628	45	—	(714)	(150)	187	420	522
Credit contracts	6,594	319	1,199	—	(277)	(2,165)	144	5,814	1,818
Foreign exchange contracts	46	(35)	2	—	—	28	2	43	(13)
Equity contracts	(762)	592	214	(133)	(1,329)	136	48	(1,234)	564
Commodity contracts	188	708	52	—	—	(433)	55	570	689
Other	(913)	(552)	1	—	(118)	405	87	(1,090)	(536)
Total net derivative and other contracts	5,577	1,660	1,513	(133)	(2,438)	(2,179)	523	4,523	3,044
Investments:									
Private equity funds	1,986	159	245	(513)	—	—	59	1,936	85
Real estate funds	1,176	21	196	(171)	—	—	(9)	1,213	251
Hedge funds	901	(20)	169	(380)	—	—	26	696	(31)
Principal investments	3,131	288	368	(819)	—	—	(31)	2,937	87
Other	560	38	8	(34)	—	—	(71)	501	23
Total investments	7,754	486	986	(1,917)	—	—	(26)	7,283	415
Physical commodities	—	(47)	771	—	—	(673)	(5)	46	1
Securities received as collateral	1	—	—	(1)	—	—	—	—	—
Intangible assets	157	(25)	6	(1)	—	(4)	—	133	(27)
Liabilities at Fair Value									
Deposits	$ 16	$ 2	$ —	$ —	$ —	$ (14)	$ —	$ —	$ —
Commercial paper and other short-term borrowings	2	—	—	—	—	—	—	2	—
Financial instruments sold, not yet purchased:									
Other sovereign government obligations	—	1	—	9	—	—	—	8	—
Corporate and other debt:									
Residential mortgage-backed securities	—	(8)	—	347	—	—	—	355	(8)
Corporate bonds	44	37	(407)	694	—	—	(75)	219	51
Unfunded lending commitments	263	178	—	—	—	—	—	85	178
Other debt	194	123	(12)	22	—	(2)	(6)	73	12
Total corporate and other debt	501	330	(419)	1,063	—	(2)	(81)	732	233
Corporate equities	15	(1)	(15)	5	—	—	(5)	1	—
Obligation to return securities received as collateral	1	—	(1)	—	—	—	—	—	—
Securities sold under agreements to repurchase	351	11	—	—	—	—	—	340	11
Other secured financings	1,016	27	—	—	154	(267)	(306)	570	13
Long-term borrowings	1,316	39	—	—	769	(377)	(66)	1,603	32

[1] Total realized and unrealized gains (losses) are primarily included in Principal transactions—Trading in the consolidated statements of income except for $486 million related to Financial instruments owned—Investments, which is included in Principal transactions—Investments.

[2] Amounts represent unrealized gains (losses) for 2011 related to assets and liabilities still outstanding at December 31, 2011.

[3] Net derivative and other contracts represent Financial instruments owned—Derivative and other contracts net of Financial instruments sold, not yet purchased—Derivative and other contracts. For further information on derivative instruments and hedging activities, see Note 12.

Financial instruments owned—Corporate and other debt. During 2011, the Company reclassified approximately $1.8 billion of certain Corporate and other debt, primarily corporate loans, from Level 3 to Level 2. The Company reclassified these corporate loans as external prices and/or spread inputs for these instruments became observable.

The Company also reclassified approximately $0.8 billion of certain Corporate and other debt from Level 2 to Level 3. The reclassifications were primarily related to corporate loans and were generally due to a reduction in market price quotations for these or comparable instruments, or a lack of available broker quotes, such that unobservable inputs had to be utilized for the fair value measurement of these instruments.

Financial instruments owned—Net derivative and other contracts. The net gains in Net derivative and other contracts were primarily driven by market movements and certain transactions during 2011 related to interest rate, equity and commodity contracts.

Changes in Level 3 Assets and Liabilities Measured at Fair Value on a Recurring Basis for 2010.

(Dollars in millions)	Beginning Balance at December 31, 2009	Total Realized and Unrealized Gains (Losses)[1]	Purchases, Sales, Other Settlements and Issuances, net	Net Transfers	Ending Balance at December 31, 2010	Unrealized Gains (Losses) for Level 3 Assets/ Liabilities Outstanding at December 31, 2010[2]
Assets at Fair Value						
Financial instruments owned:						
U.S. agency securities	$ 36	$ (1)	$ 13	$ (35)	$ 13	$ (1)
Other sovereign government obligations	3	5	66	(1)	73	5
Corporate and other debt:						
State and municipal securities	713	(11)	(533)	(59)	110	(12)
Residential mortgage-backed securities	818	12	(607)	96	319	(2)
Commercial mortgage-backed securities	1,573	35	(1,054)	(366)	188	(61)
Asset-backed securities	591	10	(436)	(152)	13	7
Corporate bonds	1,038	(84)	403	11	1,368	41
Collateralized debt obligations	1,553	368	(259)	(3)	1,659	189
Loans and lending commitments	12,506	203	(376)	(667)	11,666	214
Other debt	1,662	44	(92)	(1,421)	193	49
Total corporate and other debt	20,454	577	(2,954)	(2,561)	15,516	425
Corporate equities	536	118	(189)	19	484	59
Net derivative and other contracts[3]:						
Interest rate contracts	387	238	(178)	(23)	424	260
Credit contracts	8,824	(1,179)	128	(1,179)	6,594	58
Foreign exchange contracts	254	(77)	33	(164)	46	(109)
Equity contracts	(689)	(131)	(146)	204	(762)	(143)
Commodity contracts	7	121	60	—	188	268
Other	(437)	(266)	(220)	10	(913)	(284)
Total net derivative and other contracts	8,346	(1,294)	(323)	(1,152)	5,577	50
Investments:						
Private equity funds	1,296	496	202	(8)	1,986	462
Real estate funds	833	251	89	3	1,176	399
Hedge funds	1,708	(161)	(327)	(319)	901	(160)
Principal investments	3,195	470	229	(763)	3,131	412
Other	581	109	(129)	(1)	560	49
Total investments	7,613	1,165	64	(1,088)	7,754	1,162
Securities received as collateral	23	—	(22)	—	1	—
Intangible assets	137	43	(23)	—	157	23
Liabilities at Fair Value						
Deposits	$ 24	$ —	$ —	$ (8)	$ 16	$ —
Commercial paper and other short-term borrowings			2		2	
Financial instruments sold, not yet purchased:						
Corporate and other debt:						
Asset-backed securities	4	—	(4)	—	—	—
Corporate bonds	29	(15)	13	(13)	44	(9)
Collateralized debt obligations	3	—	(3)	—	—	—
Unfunded lending commitments	252	(4)	7	—	263	(2)
Other debt	431	65	(161)	(11)	194	62
Total corporate and other debt	719	46	(148)	(24)	501	51
Corporate equities	4	17	54	(26)	15	9
Obligation to return securities received as collateral	23	—	(22)	—	1	—
Securities sold under agreements to repurchase	—	(1)	350	—	351	(1)
Other secured financings	1,532	(44)	(612)	52	1,016	(44)
Long-term borrowings	6,865	66	(5,175)	(308)	1,316	(84)

[1] Total realized and unrealized gains (losses) are primarily included in Principal transactions—Trading in the consolidated statements of income except for $1,165 million related to Financial instruments owned—Investments, which is included in Principal transactions—Investments.

[2] Amounts represent unrealized gains (losses) for 2010 related to assets and liabilities still outstanding at December 31, 2010.

[3] Net derivative and other contracts represent Financial instruments owned—Derivative and other contracts net of Financial instruments sold, not yet purchased—Derivative and other contracts. For further information on derivative instruments and hedging activities, see Note 12.

Financial instruments owned—Corporate and other debt. During 2010, the Company reclassified approximately $3.5 billion of certain Corporate and other debt, primarily loans and hybrid contracts, from Level 3 to Level 2. The Company reclassified these loans and hybrid contracts as external prices and/or spread inputs for these instruments became observable and certain unobservable inputs were deemed insignificant to the overall measurement.

The Company also reclassified approximately $0.9 billion of certain Corporate and other debt from Level 2 to Level 3. The reclassifications were primarily related to certain corporate loans and were generally due to a reduction in market price quotations for these or comparable instruments, or a lack of available broker quotes, such that unobservable inputs had to be utilized for the fair value measurement of these instruments.

Financial instruments owned—Net derivative and other contracts. The net losses in Net derivative and other contracts were primarily driven by tightening of credit spreads on underlying reference entities of single name and basket credit default swaps.

During 2010, the Company reclassified approximately $1.2 billion of certain Net derivative contracts from Level 3 to Level 2. These reclassifications were related to certain tranched bespoke credit basket default swaps and single name credit default swaps for which certain unobservable inputs were deemed insignificant.

Financial instruments owned—Investments. During 2010, the Company reclassified approximately $1.0 billion from Level 3 to Level 2. These reclassifications were primarily related to principal investments for which external prices became unobservable.

Quantitative Information about and Sensitivity of Significant Unobservable Inputs Used in Recurring Level 3 Fair Value Measurements at December 31, 2012.

The disclosures below provide information on the valuation techniques, significant unobservable inputs and their ranges for each major category of assets and liabilities measured at fair value on a recurring basis with a significant Level 3 balance. The level of aggregation and breadth of products cause the range of inputs to be wide and not evenly distributed across the inventory. Further, the range of unobservable inputs may differ across firms in the financial services industry because of diversity in the types of products included in each firm's inventory.

The disclosures below also include qualitative information on the sensitivity of the fair value measurements to changes in the significant unobservable inputs.

	Balance at December 31, 2012 (Dollars in Millions)	Valuation Technique(s)	Significant Unobservable Input(s)/Sensitivity of the Fair Value to Changes in the Unobservable Inputs	Range[1]			Weighted Average
Assets							
Financial instruments owned:							
Corporate and other debt:							
Commercial mortgage-backed securities	$ 232	Comparable pricing	Comparable bond price/(A)	46	to	100 points	76 points
Asset-backed securities	109	Discounted cash flow	Internal rate of return/(C)			21%	21%
Corporate bonds	660	Comparable pricing	Comparable bond price/(A)	0	to	143 points	24 points
Collateralized debt obligations	1,951	Comparable pricing	Comparable bond price/(A)	15	to	88 points	59 points
		Correlation model	Credit correlation/(B)	15	to	45%	40%
Loans and lending commitments	4,694	Corporate loan model	Credit spread/(C)	17	to	1,004 Basis points	281 basis points
		Comparable pricing	Comparable bond price/(A)	80	to	120 points	104 points
		Comparable pricing	Comparable loan price/(A)	55	to	100 points	88 points
Corporate equities[2]	288	Net asset value	Discount to net asset value/(C)	0	to	37%	8%
		Comparable pricing	Discount to comparable equity price/(C)	0	to	27 points	14 points
		Market approach	Earnings before interest, taxes, depreciation and amortization ("EBITDA") multiple/(A)			6 times	6 times
Net derivative and other contracts:							
Interest rate contracts	(82)	Option model	Interest rate volatility concentration liquidity multiple/(C)(D)	0	to	8 times	See[3]
			Comparable bond price/(A)(D)	5	to	98 points	
			Interest rate—Foreign exchange correlation/(A)(D)	2	to	63%	
			Interest rate volatility skew/(A)(D)	9	to	95%	
			Interest rate quanto correlation/(A)(D)	−53	to	33%	
			Interest rate curve correlation/(A)(D)	48	to	99%	
			Inflation volatility/(A)(D)	49	to	100%	
		Discounted cash flow	Forward commercial paper rate-LIBOR basis/(A)	−18	to	95 Basis points	

(continued)

	Balance at December 31, 2012 (Dollars in Millions)	Valuation Technique(s)	Significant Unobservable Input(s)/Sensitivity of the Fair Value to Changes in the Unobservable Inputs	Range[1]			Weighted Average
Assets							
Credit contracts	1,822	Comparable pricing	Cash synthetic basis/(C)	2	to	14 points	See[4]
			Comparable bond price/(C)	0	to	80 points	
		Correlation model	Credit correlation/(B)	14	to	94%	
Foreign exchange contracts[5]	(359)	Option model	Comparable bond price/(A)(D)	5	to	98 points	See[6]
			Interest rate quanto correlation/(A)(D)	− 53	to	33%	
			Interest rate—Credit spread correlation/(A)(D)	− 59	to	65%	
			Interest rate—Foreign exchange correlation/(A)(D)	2	to	63%	
			Interest rate volatility skew/(A)(D)	9	to	95%	
Equity contracts[5]	(1,144)	Option model	At the money volatility/(C)(D)	7	to	24%	See[7]
			Volatility skew/(C)(D)	− 2	to	0%	
			Equity—Equity correlation/(C)(D)	40	to	96%	
			Equity—Foreign exchange correlation/(C)(D)	− 70	to	38%	
			Equity—Interest rate correlation/(C)(D)	18	to	65%	
Commodity contracts	709	Option model	Forward power price/(C)(D)	$28	to	$84 per	
			Commodity volatility/(A)(D)	17	to	29%	
			Cross commodity correlation/(C)(D)	43	to	97%	
Investments[2]:							
Principal investments	2,833	Discounted cash flow	Implied weighted average cost of capital/(C)(D)	8	to	15%	9%
			Exit multiple/(A)(D)	5	to	10 times	9 times
		Discounted cash flow	Capitalization rate/(C)(D)	6	to	10%	7%
			Equity discount rate/(C)(D)	15	to	35%	23%
		Market approach	EBITDA multiple/(A)	3	to	17 times	10 times
Other	486	Discounted cash flow	Implied weighted average cost of capital/(C)(D)			11%	11%
			Exit multiple/(A)(D)			6 times	6 times
		Market approach	EBITDA multiple/(A)	6	to	8 times	7 times
Liabilities							
Financial instruments sold, not yet purchased:							
Corporate and other debt:							
Corporate bonds	$ 177	Comparable pricing	Comparable bond price/(A)	0	to	150 points	50 points
Securities sold under agreements to repurchase	151	Discounted cash flow	Funding spread/(A)	110	to	184 basis points	166 basis points
Other secured financings	406	Comparable pricing	Comparable bond price/(A)	55	to	139 points	102 points
		Discounted cash flow	Funding spread/(A)	183	to	186 basis points	184 basis points
Long-term borrowings	2,789	Option model	At the money volatility/(A)(D)	20	to	24%	24%
			Volatility skew/(A)(D)	− 1	to	0%	0%
			Equity—Equity correlation/(C)(D)	50	to	90%	77%
			Equity—Foreign exchange correlation/(A)(D)	− 70	to	36%	− 15%

[1] The ranges of significant unobservable inputs are represented in points, percentages, basis points, times or megawatt hours. Points are a percentage of par; for example, 100 points would be 100% of par. A basis point equals 1/100th of 1%; for example, 1,004 basis points would equal 10.04%.

[2] Investments in funds measured using an unadjusted net asset value are excluded.

[3] See below for a qualitative discussion of the wide unobservable input ranges for comparable bond prices, interest rate volatility skew, interest rate quanto correlation and forward commercial paper rate—LIBOR basis.

[4] See below for a qualitative discussion of the wide unobservable input ranges for comparable bond prices and credit correlation.

[5] Includes derivative contracts with multiple risks (i.e., hybrid products).

[6] See below for a qualitative discussion of the wide unobservable input ranges for comparable bond prices, interest rate quanto correlation, interest rate-credit spread correlation and interest rate volatility skew.

[7] See below for a qualitative discussion of the wide unobservable input range for equity-foreign exchange correlation.

Sensitivity of the fair value to changes in the unobservable inputs:

(A) Significant increase (decrease) In the unobservable Input in isolation would result in a significantly higher (lower) fair value measurement.

(B) Significant changes in credit correlation may result in a significantly higher or lower fair value measurement Increasing (decreasing) correlation drives a redistribution of risk within the capital structure such that junior tranches become less (more) risky and senior tranches become more (less) risky.

(C) Significant increase (decrease) in the unobservable Input in isolation would result in a significantly lower (higher) fair value measurement.

(D) There are no predictable relationships between the significant unobservable inputs.

The following provides a description of significant unobservable inputs included in the table above for all major categories of assets and liabilities and a qualitative discussion of wide unobservable input ranges for derivative products:

- *Comparable bond price*—a pricing input used when prices for the identical instrument are not available. Significant subjectivity may be involved when fair value is determined using pricing data available for comparable instruments. Valuation using comparable instruments can be done by calculating an implied yield (or spread over a liquid benchmark) from the price of a comparable bond, then adjusting that yield (or spread) to derive a value for the bond. The adjustment to yield (or spread) should account for relevant differences in the bonds such as maturity or credit quality. Alternatively, a price-to-price basis can be assumed between the comparable instrument and bond being valued in order to establish the value of the bond. Additionally, as the probability of default increases for a given bond (*i.e.*, as the bond becomes more distressed), the valuation of that bond will increasingly reflect its expected recovery level assuming default. The decision to use price-to-price or yield/spread comparisons largely reflects trading market convention for the financial instruments in question. Price-to-price comparisons are primarily employed for CMBS, CDO, mortgage loans and distressed corporate bonds. Implied yield (or spread over a liquid benchmark) is utilized predominately for non-distressed corporate bonds, loans and credit contracts.
  - *Interest rate contracts, credit contracts and foreign exchange contracts*—For interest rate, credit and foreign exchange contracts, the wide range of the bond price inputs is largely driven by dispersion in the credit quality and ratings of the underlying assets and the maturity of the contracts.
- *Internal rate of return*—the discount factor required for the net present value of future cash flows to equal zero. The internal rate of return represents the minimum average annual return required for an investment.
- *Correlation*—a pricing input where the payoff is driven by more than one underlying risk. Correlation is a measure of the relationship between the movements of two variables (*i.e.*, how the change in one variable influences a change in the other variable). Credit correlation, for example, is the factor that describes the relationship between the probability of individual entities to default on obligations and the joint probability of multiple entities to default on obligations. The correlation ranges may be wide since any two underlying inputs may be highly correlated (either positively or negatively) or weakly correlated.
  - *Equity contracts*—For equity derivative contracts, the wide range of equity-foreign exchange correlation inputs is primarily due to the large number of correlation pairs, the diverse nature of the correlation pairs, and the maturity of the contracts.
  - *Interest rate contracts and foreign exchange contracts*—The interest rate quanto correlation and interest rate-credit spread correlation input ranges for interest rate and foreign exchange contracts reflect differences in economic terms for the underlying instruments. For example, a change in a currency pair can significantly impact the implied quanto correlation and a change in the reference entity can significantly impact the implied interest rate-credit spread correlation.
  - *Credit contracts*—The Company holds positions covering a wide range of maturities, capital structure subordinations, and credit quality of underlying reference entities, all of which affect the marking of the credit correlation input.
- *Credit spread*—the difference in yield between different securities due to differences in credit quality. The credit spread reflects the additional net yield an investor can earn from a security with more credit risk relative to one with less credit risk. The credit spread of a particular security is often quoted in relation to the yield on a credit risk-free benchmark security or reference rate, typically either U.S. Treasury or LIBOR.
- *EBITDA multiple/Exit multiple*—is the Enterprise Value to EBITDA ratio, where the Enterprise Value is the aggregate value of equity and debt minus cash and cash equivalents. The EBITDA multiple reflects the value of the company in terms of its full-year EBITDA, whereas the exit multiple reflects the value of the company in terms of its full year expected EBITDA at exit. Either multiple allows comparison between companies from an operational perspective as the effect of capital structure, taxation and depreciation/amortization is excluded.
- *Volatility*—the measure of the variability in possible returns for an instrument given how much that instrument changes in value over time. Volatility is a pricing input for options and, generally, the lower the volatility, the less risky the option. The level of volatility used in the valuation of a particular option depends on a number of factors, including the nature of the risk underlying that option (*e.g.*, the volatility of a particular underlying equity security may be significantly different from that of a particular underlying commodity index), the tenor and the strike price of the option.
- *Volatility skew*—the measure of the difference in implied volatility for options with identical underliers and expiry dates but with different strikes. The implied volatility for an option with a strike price that is above or below the current price of an underlying asset will typically deviate from the implied volatility for an option with a strike price equal to the current price of that same underlying asset.
  - *Interest rate contracts and foreign exchange contracts*—The volatility skew input range for interest rate and foreign exchange contracts reflects differences in economic terms for the underlying instruments as well as market factors specific to each underlier for which volatility is being estimated. For example, a change in the strike of an option can significantly impact the implied interest rate volatility skew.
- *Forward commercial paper rate–LIBOR basis*—the basis added to the LIBOR rate when the commercial paper yield is expressed as a spread over the LIBOR rate.
  - *Interest rate contracts*—There are multiple credit ratings of commercial paper, each of which will lead to a different basis to LIBOR. The basis to LIBOR is dependent on a number of factors, including, but not limited to, collateralization of the commercial paper, credit rating of the issuer, and the supply of commercial paper. For example, the higher the credit rating, the lower the basis. The basis may become negative, *i.e.*, the return for highly-rated commercial paper, such as asset-backed commercial paper, may be less than LIBOR.
- *Cash synthetic basis*—the measure of the price differential between cash financial instruments ("cash instruments") and their synthetic derivative-based equivalents ("synthetic instruments"). The range disclosed in the table above signifies the number of points by which the synthetic bond equivalent price is higher than the quoted price of the underlying cash bonds.
- *Implied WACC*—the weighted average cost of capital ("WACC") implied by the current value of equity in a discounted cash flow model. The model assumes that the cash flow assumptions, including projections, are fully reflected in the current equity value while the debt to equity ratio is held constant. The WACC theoretically represents the required rate of return to debt and equity investors, respectively.
- *Capitalization rate*—the ratio between net operating income produced by an asset and its market value at the projected disposition date.

- *Funding spread*—the difference between the general collateral rate (which refers to the rate applicable to a broad class of U.S. Treasury issuances) and the specific collateral rate (which refers to the rate applicable to a specific type of security pledged as collateral, such as a municipal bond). Repurchase agreements are discounted based on collateral curves. The curves are constructed as spreads over the corresponding OIS/LIBOR curves, with the short end of the curve representing spreads over the corresponding OIS curves and the long end of the curve representing spreads over LIBOR.

Fair Value of Investments that Calculate Net Asset Value.

The Company's Investments measured at fair value were $8,346 million and $8,195 million at December 31, 2012 and 2011, respectively. The following table presents information solely about the Company's investments in private equity funds, real estate funds and hedge funds measured at fair value based on net asset value at December 31, 2012 and 2011, respectively.

(Dollars in millions)	At December 31, 2012		At December 31, 2011	
	Fair Value	Unfunded Commitment	Fair Value	Unfunded Commitment
Private equity funds	$2,179	$644	$1,906	$ 938
Real estate funds	1,376	221	1,188	448
Hedge funds[1]:				
Long-short equity hedge funds	475	—	545	5
Fixed income/credit-related hedge funds	86	—	124	—
Event-driven hedge funds	52	—	163	—
Multi-strategy hedge funds	321	3	335	—
Total	$4,489	$868	$4,261	$1,391

[1] Fixed income/credit-related hedge funds, event-driven hedge funds, and multi-strategy hedge funds are redeemable at least on a six-month period basis primarily with a notice period of 90 days or less. At December 31, 2012, approximately 36% of the fair value amount of long-short equity hedge funds is redeemable at least quarterly, 38% is redeemable every six months and 26% of these funds have a redemption frequency of greater than six months. The notice period for long-short equity hedge funds at December 31, 2012 is primarily greater than six months. At December 31, 2011, approximately 38% of the fair value amount of long-short equity hedge funds is redeemable at least quarterly, 32% is redeemable every six months and 30% of these funds have a redemption frequency of greater than six months. The notice period for long-short equity hedge funds at December 31, 2011 is primarily greater than six months.

Private Equity Funds. Amount includes several private equity funds that pursue multiple strategies including leveraged buyouts, venture capital, infrastructure growth capital, distressed investments, and mezzanine capital. In addition, the funds may be structured with a focus on specific domestic or foreign geographic regions. These investments are generally not redeemable with the funds. Instead, the nature of the investments in this category is that distributions are received through the liquidation of the underlying assets of the fund. At December 31, 2012, it is estimated that 5% of the fair value of the funds will be liquidated in the next five years, another 27% of the fair value of the funds will be liquidated between five to 10 years and the remaining 68% of the fair value of the funds have a remaining life of greater than 10 years.

Real Estate Funds. Amount includes several real estate funds that invest in real estate assets such as commercial office buildings, retail properties, multi-family residential properties, developments or hotels. In addition, the funds may be structured with a focus on specific geographic domestic or foreign regions. These investments are generally not redeemable with the funds. Distributions from each fund will be received as the underlying investments of the funds are liquidated. At December 31, 2012, it is estimated that 4% of the fair value of the funds will be liquidated within the next five years, another 46% of the fair value of the funds will be liquidated between five to 10 years and the remaining 50% of the fair value of the funds have a remaining life of greater than 10 years.

Hedge Funds. Investments in hedge funds may be subject to initial period lock-up restrictions or gates. A hedge fund lock-up provision is a provision that provides that, during a certain initial period, an investor may not make a withdrawal from the fund. The purpose of a gate is to restrict the level of redemptions that an investor in a particular hedge fund can demand on any redemption date.

- *Long-short Equity Hedge Funds.* Amount includes investments in hedge funds that invest, long or short, in equities. Equity value and growth hedge funds purchase stocks perceived to be undervalued and sell stocks perceived to be overvalued. Investments representing approximately 7% of the fair value of the investments in this category cannot be redeemed currently because the investments include certain initial period lock-up restrictions. The remaining restriction period for these investments subject to lock-up restrictions was primarily two years or less at December 31, 2012. Investments representing approximately 7% of the fair value of the investments in long-short equity hedge funds cannot be redeemed currently because an exit restriction has been imposed by the hedge fund manager. The restriction period for these investments subject to an exit restriction was primarily one year or less at December 31, 2012.
- *Fixed Income/Credit-Related Hedge Funds.* Amount includes investments in hedge funds that employ long-short, distressed or relative value strategies in order to benefit from investments in undervalued or overvalued securities that are primarily debt or credit related. At December 31, 2012, investments representing approximately 5% of the fair value of the investments in fixed income/credit-related hedge funds cannot be redeemed currently because the investments include certain initial period lock-up restrictions. The remaining restriction period for these investments subject to lock-up restrictions was primarily one year or less at December 31, 2012.
- *Event-Driven Hedge Funds.* Amount includes investments in hedge funds that invest in event-driven situations such as mergers, hostile takeovers, reorganizations, or leveraged buyouts. This may involve the simultaneous purchase of stock in companies being acquired and the sale of stock in its acquirer, with the expectation to profit from the spread between the current market price and the ultimate purchase price of the target company. At December 31, 2012, there were no restrictions on redemptions.
- *Multi-strategy Hedge Funds.* Amount includes investments in hedge funds that pursue multiple strategies to realize short- and long-term gains. Management of the hedge funds has the ability to overweight or underweight different strategies to best capitalize on current investment opportunities. At December 31, 2012, investments representing approximately 66% of the fair value of the investments in this category cannot be redeemed currently because the investments include certain initial period lock-up restrictions. The remaining restriction period for these investments subject to lock-up

restrictions was primarily two years or less at December 31, 2012. Investments representing approximately 9% of the fair value of the investments in multi-strategy hedge funds cannot be redeemed currently because an exit restriction has been imposed by the hedge fund manager. The restriction period for these investments subject to an exit restriction was indefinite at December 31, 2012.

Fair Value Option.

The Company elected the fair value option for certain eligible instruments that are risk managed on a fair value basis to mitigate income statement volatility caused by measurement basis differences between the elected instruments and their associated risk management transactions or to eliminate complexities of applying certain accounting models. The following tables present net gains (losses) due to changes in fair value for items measured at fair value pursuant to the fair value option election for 2012, 2011 and 2010, respectively:

(Dollars in millions)	Principal Transactions- Trading	Interest Income (Expense)	Gains (Losses) Included in Net Revenues
Year Ended December 31, 2012			
Federal funds sold and securities purchased under agreements to resell	$ 8	$ 5	$ 13
Deposits	57	(86)	(29)
Commercial paper and other short-term borrowings[1]	(31)	—	(31)
Securities sold under agreements to repurchase	(15)	(4)	(19)
Long-term borrowings[1]	(5,687)	(1,321)	(7,008)
Year Ended December 31, 2011			
Federal funds sold and securities purchased under agreements to resell	$ 12	$ —	$ 12
Deposits	66	(117)	(51)
Commercial paper and other short-term borrowings[1]	567	—	567
Securities sold under agreements to repurchase	3	(7)	(4)
Long-term borrowings[1]	4,204	(1,075)	3,129
Year Ended December 31, 2010			
Deposits	$ 2	$ (173)	$ (171)
Commercial paper and other short-term borrowings[1]	(8)	—	(8)
Securities sold under agreements to repurchase	9	(1)	8
Long-term borrowings[1]	(872)	(849)	(1,721)

[1] Of the total gains (losses) recorded in Principal transactions—Trading for short-term and long-term borrowings for 2012, 2011 and 2010, $(4,402) million, $3,681 million and $(873) million, respectively, are attributable to changes in the credit quality of the Company, and the respective remainder is attributable to changes in foreign currency rates or interest rates or movements in the reference price or index for structured notes before the impact of related hedges.

In addition to the amounts in the above table, as discussed in Note 2, all of the instruments within Financial instruments owned or Financial instruments sold, not yet purchased are measured at fair value, either through the election of the fair value option or as required by other accounting guidance. The amounts in the above table are included within Net revenues and do not reflect gains or losses on related hedging instruments, if any.

The Company hedges the economics of market risk for short-term and long-term borrowings (*i.e.*, risks other than that related to the credit quality of the Company) as part of its overall trading strategy and manages the market risks embedded within the issuance by the related business unit as part of the business units' portfolio. The gains and losses on related economic hedges are recorded in Principal transactions—Trading and largely offset the gains and losses on short-term and long-term borrowings attributable to market risk.

At December 31, 2012 and 2011, a breakdown of the short-term and long-term borrowings by business unit responsible for risk-managing the borrowing is shown in the table below:

(Dollars in millions) Business Unit	Short-Term and Long-Term Borrowings	
	At December 31, 2012	At December 31, 2011
Interest rates	$23,330	$23,188
Equity	17,326	13,926
Credit and foreign exchange	3,337	3,012
Commodities	776	876
Total	$44,769	$41,002

The following tables present information on the Company's short-term and long-term borrowings (primarily structured notes), loans and unfunded lending commitments for which the fair value option was elected.

Gains (Losses) due to Changes in Instrument-Specific Credit Risk.

(Dollars in millions)	2012	2011	2010
Short-term and long-term borrowings[1]	$(4,402)	$3,681	$(873)
Loans[2]	340	(585)	448
Unfunded lending commitments[3]	1,026	(787)	(148)

[1] The change in the fair value of short-term and long-term borrowings (primarily structured notes) includes an adjustment to reflect the change in credit quality of the Company based upon observations of the Company's secondary bond market spreads.

[2] Instrument-specific credit gains (losses) were determined by excluding the non-credit components of gains and losses, such as those due to changes in interest rates.

[3] Gains (losses) were generally determined based on the differential between estimated expected client yields and contractual yields at each respective period end.

Net Difference between Contractual Principal Amount and Fair Value.

	Contractual Principal Amount Exceeds Fair Value	
(Dollars in billions)	At December 31, 2012	At December 31, 2011
Short-term and long-term borrowings[1]	$(0.4)	$ 2.5
Loans[2]	25.2	27.2
Loans 90 or more days past due and/or on non-accrual status[2][3]	20.5	22.1

[1] These amounts do not include structured notes where the repayment of the initial principal amount fluctuates based on changes in the reference price or index.

[2] The majority of this difference between principal and fair value amounts emanates from the Company's distressed debt trading business, which purchases distressed debt at amounts well below par.

[3] The aggregate fair value of loans that were in non-accrual status, which includes all loans 90 or more days past due, was $1.4 billion and $2.0 billion at December 31, 2012 and December 31, 2011, respectively. The aggregate fair value of loans that were 90 or more days past due was $0.8 billion and $1.5 billion at December 31, 2012 and December 31, 2011, respectively.

The tables above exclude non-recourse debt from consolidated VIEs, liabilities related to failed sales of financial assets, pledged commodities and other liabilities that have specified assets attributable to them.

Assets and Liabilities Measured at Fair Value on a Non-recurring Basis.

Certain assets were measured at fair value on a non-recurring basis and are not included in the tables above. These assets may include loans, other investments, premises, equipment and software costs, and intangible assets.

The following tables present, by caption on the consolidated statements of financial condition, the fair value hierarchy for those assets measured at fair value on a non-recurring basis for which the Company recognized a non-recurring fair value adjustment for 2012, 2011 and 2010, respectively.

2012

		Fair Value Measurements Using:			
(Dollars in millions)	Carrying Value At December 31, 2012	Quoted Prices in Active Markets for Identical Assets (Level 1)	Significant Observable Inputs (Level 2)	Significant Unobservable Inputs (Level 3)	Total Gains (Losses) for 2012[1]
Loans[2]	$1,821	$—	$277	$1,544	$ (60)
Other investments[3]	90	—	—	90	(37)
Premises, equipment and software costs[4]	33	—	—	33	(170)
Intangible assets[3]	—	—	—	—	(4)
Total	$1,944	$—	$277	$1,667	$(271)

[1] Losses are recorded within Other expenses in the consolidated statements of income except for fair value adjustments related to Loans and losses related to Other investments, which are included in Other revenues.

[2] Non-recurring changes in fair value for loans held for investment were calculated based upon the fair value of the underlying collateral. The fair value of the collateral was determined using internal expected recovery models. The non-recurring change in fair value for mortgage loans held for sale is based upon a valuation model incorporating market observable inputs.

[3] Losses recorded were determined primarily using discounted cash flow models.

[4] Losses were determined using discounted cash flow models and primarily represented the write-off of the carrying value of certain premises and software that were abandoned during 2012 in association with the Morgan Stanley Wealth Management integration.

In addition to the losses included in the table above, there was a pre-tax gain of approximately $51 million (related to Other assets) included in discontinued operations in 2012 in connection with the disposition of Saxon (see Notes 1 and 25). This pre-tax gain was primarily due to the subsequent increase in the fair value of Saxon, which had incurred impairment losses of $98 million in the quarter ended December 31, 2011. The fair value of Saxon was determined based on the revised purchase price agreed upon with the buyer.

There were no liabilities measured at fair value on a non-recurring basis during 2012.

2011

		Fair Value Measurements Using:			
(Dollars in millions)	Carrying Value At December 31, 2011	Quoted Prices in Active Markets for Identical Assets (Level 1)	Significant Observable Inputs (Level 2)	Significant Unobservable Inputs (Level 3)	Total Gains (Losses) for 2011[1]
Loans[2]	$ 70	$—	$—	$ 70	$ 5
Other investments[3]	71	—	—	71	(52)
Premises, equipment and software costs[3]	4	—	—	4	(7)
Intangible assets[4]	—	—	—	—	(7)
Total	$145	$—	$—	$145	$(61)

[1] Losses are recorded within Other expenses in the consolidated statements of income except for fair value adjustments related to Loans and losses related to Other investments, which are included in Other revenues.

[2] Non-recurring changes in fair value for loans held for investment were calculated based upon the fair value of the underlying collateral. The fair value of the collateral was determined using internal expected recovery models. The non-recurring change in fair value for mortgage loans held for sale is based upon a valuation model incorporating market observable inputs.

[3] Losses recorded were determined primarily using discounted cash flow models.

[4] Losses were determined primarily using discounted cash flow models or a valuation technique incorporating an observable market index.

In addition to the losses included in the table above, impairment losses of approximately $98 million (of which $83 million related to Other assets and $15 million related to Premises, equipment and software costs) were included in discontinued operations related to Saxon (see Notes 1 and 25). These losses were determined using the purchase price agreed upon with the buyer.

There were no liabilities measured at fair value on a non-recurring basis during 2011.

2010

| | | Fair Value Measurements Using: | | | |
(Dollars in millions)	Carrying Value At December 31, 2010	Quoted Prices in Active Markets for Identical Assets (Level 1)	Significant Observable Inputs (Level 2)	Significant Unobservable Inputs (Level 3)	Total Gains (Losses) for 2010[1]
Loans[2]	$680	$—	$151	$529	$ (12)
Other investments[3]	88	—	—	88	(19)
Goodwill[4]	—	—	—	—	(27)
Intangible assets[5]	3	—	—	3	(174)
Total	$771	$—	$151	$620	$(232)

[1] Losses related to Loans, impairments related to Other investments and losses related to Goodwill and certain Intangibles associated with the disposition of FrontPoint Partners LLC ("FrontPoint") are included in Other revenues in the consolidated statements of income (see Notes 19 and 24 for further information on FrontPoint). Remaining losses were included in Other expenses in the consolidated statements of income.

[2] Non-recurring changes in fair value for loans held for investment were calculated based upon the fair value of the underlying collateral. The fair value of the collateral was determined using internal expected recovery models. The non-recurring change in fair value for mortgage loans held for sale is based upon a valuation model incorporating market observable inputs.

[3] Losses recorded were determined primarily using discounted cash flow models.

[4] Loss relates to FrontPoint, determined primarily using discounted cash flow models (see Notes 19 and 24 for further information on FrontPoint).

[5] Losses primarily related to investment management contracts, including contracts associated with FrontPoint, and were determined primarily using discounted cash flow models.

In addition to the losses included in the table above, the Company incurred a loss of approximately $1.2 billion in connection with the disposition of Revel, which was included in discontinued operations. The loss primarily related to premises, equipment and software costs and was included in discontinued operations (see Notes 1 and 25). The fair value of Revel, net of estimated costs to sell, included in Premises, equipment and software costs was approximately $28 million at December 31, 2010 and was classified in Level 3. Fair value was determined using discounted cash flow models.

There were no liabilities measured at fair value on a non-recurring basis during 2010.

Financial Instruments Not Measured at Fair Value.

The table below presents the carrying value, fair value and fair value hierarchy category of certain financial instruments that are not measured at fair value in the consolidated statements of financial condition. The table below excludes certain financial instruments such as equity method investments and all non-financial assets and liabilities such as the value of the long-term relationships with our deposit customers.

The carrying value of cash and cash equivalents, including Interest bearing deposits with banks, and other short-term financial instruments such as Federal funds sold and securities purchased under agreements to resell, Securities borrowed, Securities sold under agreements to repurchase, Securities loaned, certain receivables and payables arising in the ordinary course of business, certain Deposits, Commercial paper and other short-term borrowings and Other secured financings approximate fair value because of the relatively short period of time between their origination and expected maturity.

The fair value of sweep facilities whereby cash balances are swept into separate money market savings deposits and transaction accounts included within Deposits is determined using a standard cash flow discounting methodology.

For longer-dated Federal funds sold and securities purchased under agreements to resell, Securities borrowed, Securities sold under agreements to repurchase, Securities loaned and Other secured financings, fair value is determined using a standard cash flow discounting methodology. The inputs to the valuation include contractual cash flows and collateral funding spreads, which are estimated using various benchmarks and interest rate yield curves.

For consumer and residential real estate loans where position-specific external price data is not observable, the fair value is based on the credit risks of the borrower using a probability of default and loss given default method, discounted at the estimated external cost of funding level. The fair value of corporate loans is determined using recently executed transactions, market price quotations (where observable), implied yields from comparable debt, and market observable credit default swap spread levels along with proprietary valuation models and default recovery analysis where such transactions and quotations are unobservable.

The fair value of long-term borrowings is generally determined based on transactional data or third party pricing for identical or comparable instruments, when available. Where position-specific external prices are not observable, fair value is determined based on current interest rates and credit spreads for debt instruments with similar terms and maturity.

Financial Instruments Not Measured at Fair Value at December 31, 2012.

(Dollars in millions)	At December 31, 2012 Carrying Value	Fair Value	Fair Value Measurements Using: Quoted Prices in Active Markets for Identical Assets (Level 1)	Significant Observable Inputs (Level 2)	Significant Unobservable Inputs (Level 3)
Financial Assets:					
Cash and due from banks	$ 20,878	$ 20,878	$ 20,878	$ —	$ —
Interest bearing deposits with banks	26,026	26,026	26,026	—	—
Cash deposited with clearing organizations or segregated under federal and other regulations or requirements	30,970	30,970	30,970	—	—
Federal funds sold and securities purchased under agreements to resell	133,791	133,792	—	133,035	757
Securities borrowed	121,701	121,705	—	121,691	14
Receivables[1]:					
Customers	46,197	46,197	—	46,197	—
Brokers, dealers and clearing organizations	7,335	7,335	—	7,335	—
Fees, interest and other	6,170	6,102	—	—	6,102
Loans[2]	29,046	27,263	—	5,307	21,956
Financial Liabilities:					
Deposits	$ 81,781	$ 81,781	$ —	$ 81,781	$ —
Commercial paper and other short-term borrowings	1,413	1,413	—	1,107	306
Securities sold under agreements to repurchase	122,311	122,389	—	111,722	10,667
Securities loaned	36,849	37,163	—	35,978	1,185
Other secured financings	6,261	6,276	—	3,649	2,627
Payables[1]:					
Customers	122,540	122,540	—	122,540	—
Brokers, dealers and clearing organizations	2,497	2,497	—	2,497	—
Long-term borrowings	125,527	126,683	—	116,511	10,172

[1] Accrued interest, fees and dividend receivables and payables where carrying value approximates fair value have been excluded.
[2] Includes all loans measured at fair value on a non-recurring basis.

The fair value of the Company's unfunded lending commitments, primarily related to corporate lending in the Institutional Securities business segment, that are not carried at fair value at December 31, 2012 was $755 million, of which $543 million and $212 million would be categorized in Level 2 and Level 3 of the fair value hierarchy, respectively. The carrying value of these commitments, if fully funded, would be $50.0 billion.

Subsequent Events

RECOGNITION AND MEASUREMENT

1.109 The FASB ASC glossary defines *subsequent events* as events or transactions that occur subsequent to the balance sheet date but before financial statements are issued or available to be issued. FASB ASC 855, *Subsequent Events*, includes general guidance applicable to all entities on accounting for, and disclosure of, events after the reporting period (subsequent events) that are not addressed specifically in other topics within FASB ASC. The following are the two types of subsequent events: the first type existed at the balance sheet date and includes the estimates inherent in the process of preparing financial statements (recognized subsequent events); the second type did not exist at the balance sheet date but arose subsequent to that date (nonrecognized subsequent events). The first type of subsequent event should be recognized in the entity's financial statements.

1.110 FASB ASC 855-10-25-1 requires an entity to recognize only the effects of events that provide evidence of conditions that existed at the balance sheet date, including accounting estimates. FASB ASC 855-10-25-1A indicates that an SEC filer or a conduit bond obligor for conduit debt securities that are traded in a public market (a domestic or foreign stock exchange or an over-the-counter market, including local or regional markets) should evaluate subsequent events through the date the financial statements are issued. In addition, FASB ASC 855-10-25-2 requires all other entities that do not meet the criteria outlined in FASB ASC 855-10-25-1A to evaluate such events through the date the financial statements are available to be issued. As defined in the FASB ASC glossary, *financial statements* are considered available to be issued when they are complete in a form and format that complies with GAAP and all approvals necessary for issuance have been obtained from, for example, management, the board of directors, or significant shareholders.

1.111 FASB ASC 855-10-25 3 prohibits an entity from recognizing subsequent events that provide evidence about conditions that did not exist at the date of the balance sheet but arose after that date and before the financial statements are issued or are available to be issued.

1.112 FASB ASC 855-10-25-4 also addresses the potential for reissue of the financial statements in reports filed with regulatory agencies. In this circumstance, an entity should not recognize events occurring between the time the financial statements were originally issued or were available to be issued and the time the financial statements were reissued, unless U.S. GAAP or regulatory requirements require the adjustment. Similarly, an entity should not recognize events or

DISCLOSURE

1.113 FASB ASC 855-10-50-3 requires an entity to consider supplementing the historical financial statements with pro forma financial data when an unrecognized subsequent event occurs. An entity should present pro forma financial data when an unrecognized subsequent event is sufficiently significant that pro forma information provides the best disclosure. In preparing pro forma data, an entity should include the event as if it had occurred on the balance sheet date. An entity should also consider presenting pro forma statements, usually a statement of financial position only, in columnar form on the face of the historical statements.

1.114 Paragraphs 1 and 4 of FASB ASC 855-10-50 state that an entity, except an SEC registrant, should disclose the date through which subsequent events have been evaluated, as well as whether that date is the date the financial statements were issued or the date the financial statements were available to be issued. An entity, except an SEC registrant, should also disclose in the revised financial statements the date through which subsequent events have been evaluated in both the originally issued financial statements and the reissued financial statements.

PRESENTATION AND DISCLOSURE EXCERPTS

NOTES

1.115 GENCORP INC. (NOV)
NOTES TO CONSOLIDATED FINANCIAL STATEMENTS

Note 15. Subsequent Events

7.125% Second-Priority Senior Secured Notes

On January 28, 2013, the Company issued $460.0 million in aggregate principal amount of its 7.125% Second-Priority Senior Secured Notes due 2021 (the "$7\frac{1}{8}$% Notes"). The $7\frac{1}{8}$% Notes were sold to qualified institutional buyers in accordance with Rule 144A under the Securities Act of 1933, as amended (the "Securities Act") and outside the U.S. in accordance with Regulation S under the Securities Act. The $7\frac{1}{8}$% Notes mature on March 15, 2021, subject to early redemption described below. The $7\frac{1}{8}$% Notes will pay interest semi-annually in cash in arrears on March 15, and September 15, of each year, beginning on March 15, 2013.

The gross proceeds from the sale of the $7\frac{1}{8}$% Notes (after deducting underwriting discounts), plus an amount sufficient to fund a Special Mandatory Redemption (as defined below) on February 28, 2013, including accrued interest on the $7\frac{1}{8}$% Notes, were deposited into escrow pending the consummation of the proposed acquisition of the Rocketdyne Business pursuant to an escrow agreement (the "Escrow Agreement") by and among the Company and U.S. Bank National Association, as trustee for the $7\frac{1}{8}$% Notes, as escrow agent and as bank and securities intermediary. Pursuant to the Escrow Agreement, the Company will continue to deposit accrued interest on the $7\frac{1}{8}$% Notes on a monthly basis until the satisfaction of the conditions to release the proceeds from escrow. If the conditions to the release of the escrow, including the consummation of the acquisition of the Rocketdyne Business, are not satisfied on or prior to July 21, 2013 (subject to a one-month extension upon satisfaction of certain conditions) or upon the occurrence of certain other events, the $7\frac{1}{8}$% Notes will be subject to a special mandatory redemption (the "Special Mandatory Redemption") at a price equal to 100% of the issue price of the $7\frac{1}{8}$% Notes, plus accrued and unpaid interest, if any, to, but not including the date of the Special Mandatory Redemption.

The $7\frac{1}{8}$% Notes will be redeemable at the Company's option, in whole or in part, at any time prior to March 15, 2016 at a price equal to 100% of the principal amount, plus any accrued and unpaid interest to the date of redemption, plus a "make-whole" premium. Thereafter, the Company may redeem the $7\frac{1}{8}$% Notes, at any time on or after March 15, 2016, at redemption prices (expressed as percentages of principal amount) set forth below plus accrued and unpaid interest and additional interest, if any, thereon, to the applicable redemption date, if redeemed during the twelve-month period beginning March 15 of the years indicated below:

Year	Redemption Price
2016	105.344%
2017	103.563%
2018	101.781%
2019 and thereafter	100.000%

In addition, before March 15, 2016, the Company may redeem up to 35% of the original aggregate principal amount of the $7\frac{1}{8}$% Notes at a redemption price equal to 107.125% of the aggregate principal amount of the $7\frac{1}{8}$% Notes, plus accrued interest, with the proceeds from certain types of public equity offerings.

The $7\frac{1}{8}$% Notes are guaranteed by Aerojet. Following the consummation of the proposed Acquisition, the $7\frac{1}{8}$% Notes will be fully and unconditionally guaranteed on a second-priority senior secured basis by each of the Company's existing and future subsidiaries that guarantee its obligations under the Company's existing Senior Credit Facility. Prior to the consummation of the Acquisition, the $7\frac{1}{8}$% Notes will be secured by a first priority security interest in the escrow account and all deposits and investment property therein. Following the consummation of the Acquisition, the $7\frac{1}{8}$% Notes will be secured on a second-priority basis by the assets (other than real property) that secure the Company's and its guarantors' obligations under the Senior Credit Facility, subject to certain exceptions and permitted liens.

Upon the occurrence of a change of control (as defined in the $7\frac{1}{8}$% Notes indenture), if the Company has not previously exercised its right to redeem all of the outstanding $7\frac{1}{8}$% Notes pursuant to the Special Mandatory Redemption or an optional redemption as described in the indenture, the Company must offer to repurchase the $7\frac{1}{8}$% Notes at 101% of the principal amount of the $7\frac{1}{8}$% Notes, plus accrued and unpaid interest to the date of repurchase.

The $7\frac{1}{8}$% Notes indenture contains certain covenants limiting the Company's ability and the ability of its restricted subsidiaries (as defined in the $7\frac{1}{8}$% Notes indenture) to, subject to certain exceptions and qualifications: (i) incur additional indebtedness; (ii) pay dividends or make other distributions on, redeem or repurchase, capital stock; (iii) make investments or other restricted payments; (iv) create or incur certain liens; (v) incur restrictions on the payment of dividends or other distributions from its restricted subsidiaries; (vi) enter into transactions with affiliates; (vii) sell assets; or (viii) effect a consolidation or merger.

The $7\frac{1}{8}$% Notes indenture also contains customary events of default, including, among other things, failure to pay interest, failure to comply with certain repurchase provisions, breach of certain covenants, failure to pay at maturity or acceleration of other indebtedness, failure to pay certain judgments, and certain events of insolvency or bankruptcy. Generally, if any event of default occurs, $7\frac{1}{8}$% Notes trustee or the holders of at least 25% in principal amount of the $7\frac{1}{8}$% Notes may declare the $7\frac{1}{8}$% Notes due and payable by providing notice to the Company. In case of default arising from certain events of bankruptcy or insolvency, the $7\frac{1}{8}$% Notes will become immediately due and payable.

In connection with the issuance of the $7\frac{1}{8}$% Notes, the Company entered into a registration rights agreement dated as of January 28, 2013 (the "Registration Rights Agreement"), by and among the Company, Aerojet, as guarantor, and Morgan Stanley & Co. LLC, Citigroup Global Markets Inc., Wells Fargo Securities, LLC and SunTrust Robinson Humphrey, Inc., as initial purchasers of the $7\frac{1}{8}$% Notes. Pursuant to the Registration Rights Agreement, the Company has agreed to: (i) file a registration statement within 180 days after January 28, 2013, with respect to an offer to exchange the $7\frac{1}{8}$% Notes for freely tradable notes that have substantially identical terms as the $7\frac{1}{8}$% Notes and are registered under the Securities Act; (ii) use reasonable best efforts to cause such registration statement to become effective within 270 days after January 28, 2013; (iii) use reasonable best efforts to consummate the exchange offer within 300 days after January 28, 2013; and (iv) file a shelf registration statement for the resale of the $7\frac{1}{8}$% Notes if the Company cannot effect an exchange offer within the time periods listed above and in certain other circumstances. If the Company does not comply with its registration obligations under the Registration Rights Agreement (each, a "Registration Default"), the annual interest rate on the $7\frac{1}{8}$% Notes will increase by 0.25% per annum and thereafter by an additional 0.25% per annum for any subsequent 90-day period during which a Registration Default continues, up to a maximum additional interest rate of 1.0% per annum. If the Company corrects the Registration Default, the interest rate on the $7\frac{1}{8}$% Notes will revert immediately to the original rate.

The Company intends to use the net proceeds of the $7\frac{1}{8}$% Notes offering to fund, in part, the proposed acquisition of the Rocketdyne Business, and to pay related fees and expenses.

Amendment to Senior Credit Facility

In January 2013, the Company, with its wholly-owned subsidiary Aerojet as guarantor, executed an amendment (the "Third Amendment") to the Senior Credit Facility with the lenders identified therein, and Wells Fargo Bank, National Association, as administrative agent. The Third Amendment, among other things, allowed for the $7\frac{1}{8}$% Notes to be secured by a first priority security interest in the escrow account into which the gross proceeds of the $7\frac{1}{8}$% Notes offering were deposited pending the consummation of the acquisition of the Rocketdyne Business.

LITIGATION

1.116 JPMORGAN CHASE & CO. (DEC)
NOTES TO CONSOLIDATED FINANCIAL STATEMENTS

Note 2—Business Changes and Developments (in part)

Subsequent Events

Mortgage foreclosure settlement agreement with the Office of the Comptroller of the Currency and the Board of Governors of the Federal Reserve System

On January 7, 2013, the Firm announced that it and a number of other financial institutions entered into a settlement agreement with the Office of the Comptroller of the Currency and the Board of Governors of the Federal Reserve System providing for the termination of the independent foreclosure review programs (the "Independent Foreclosure Review"). Under this settlement, the Firm will make a cash payment of $753 million into a settlement fund for distribution to qualified borrowers. The Firm has also committed an additional $1.2 billion to foreclosure prevention actions, which will be fulfilled through credits given to the Firm for modifications, short sales and other specified types of borrower relief. Foreclosure prevention actions that earn credit under the Independent Foreclosure Review settlement are in addition to actions taken by the Firm to earn credit under the global settlement entered into by the Firm with state and federal agencies. The estimated impact of the foreclosure prevention actions required under the Independent Foreclosure Review settlement have been considered in the Firm's allowance for loan losses. The Firm recognized a pretax charge of approximately $700 million in the fourth quarter of 2012 related to the Independent Foreclosure Review settlement.

MERGER AGREEMENT & DEBT FACILITIES

1.117 AXIALL CORPORATION (DEC)
NOTES TO CONSOLIDATED FINANCIAL STATEMENTS

2. Subsequent Events

Merger with the PPG Chemicals Business

On July 18, 2012, Georgia Gulf Corporation (now known as Axiall Corporation), PPG Industries, Inc. ("PPG"), Splitco, a wholly-owned subsidiary of PPG, and Grizzly Acquisition Sub, Inc., a wholly-owned subsidiary of the Company ("Merger Sub"), entered into an Agreement and Plan of Merger (as amended, the "Merger Agreement") pursuant to which we combined with the Merged Business (as defined below) in a Reverse Morris Trust transaction (the "Transactions"). On January 28, 2013 (the "Closing Date"), we completed the Transactions and changed our name to Axiall Corporation.

In connection with the Transactions, PPG and Splitco, among other things, entered into a Separation Agreement, dated as of July 18, 2012 (the "Separation Agreement"), pursuant to which PPG transferred to Splitco, substantially all of the assets and liabilities of PPG's business relating to the production of chlorine, caustic soda and related chemicals, including, among other things, PPG's 60 percent interest in Taiwan Chlorine Industries, Ltd., a joint venture between PPG and China Petrochemical Development Corporation (collectively, the "Merged Business"). In addition, PPG completed an exchange offer made to PPG shareholders, which resulted in (i) the exchange of each share of PPG common stock, par value $1.66 ²/₃ per share, accepted by PPG in the exchange offer for 3.2562 shares of Splitco common stock, par value $0.001 per share; and (ii) the separation of Splitco from PPG. Immediately after the expiration and consummation of the PPG exchange offer, Merger Sub merged with and into Splitco, whereby the separate corporate existence of Merger Sub ceased and Splitco continued as the surviving company and as our wholly-owned subsidiary (the "Merger"). In the Merger, each share of Splitco common stock was converted into the right to receive one share of our common stock which means that each share of PPG common stock accepted by PPG in the exchange offer was effectively converted into 3.2562 shares of our common stock.

Upon consummation of the Transactions, we issued 35,249,104 shares of our common stock to the former PPG shareholders, participating in the exchange offer, together with cash in lieu of any fractional shares. Immediately after the consummation of the Merger, approximately 50.5 percent of the outstanding shares of our common stock were held by pre-Merger holders of PPG common stock and approximately 49.5 percent of the outstanding shares of our common stock were held by our pre-Merger stockholders. In connection with the Merger and the related transactions, we entered into certain additional agreements with PPG and Splitco relating to, among other things, certain tax matters, certain employee matters, the provision of certain transition services during a transition period following the consummation of the Merger and the sharing of facilities, services and supplies.

As consideration for Splitco's acquisition of the Merged Business, Splitco distributed (the "Special Distribution") to PPG: (i) the cash proceeds of approximately $279.0 million in new bank debt incurred by Splitco under a senior secured term loan facility (the "Term Facility"), which included $67.0 million necessary to fund a net working capital adjustment under the Merger Agreement; and (ii) $688.0 million in aggregate principal amount of 4.625 percent senior notes due 2021 issued by Splitco (the "Splitco Notes"). Upon the consummation of the Merger, the Company and certain subsidiaries of the Company became guarantors of the Term Facility and the Splitco Notes.

The value of the Transactions of approximately $2.7 billion consists of $967 million of cash paid to PPG, shares of our common stock received by PPG shareholders valued at approximately $1.8 billion, based on the closing stock sale price of $50.24 on the last trade date prior to the Closing Date of the Transactions, plus the assumption of liabilities, including pension liabilities and other post-retirement obligations. The initial accounting for the Transactions (including the allocation of the purchase price to acquired assets and liabilities) is not complete given the limited amount of time since the Closing Date.

Splitco Senior Notes Offering

On the Closing Date, Splitco issued $688.0 million in aggregate principal amount of the Splitco Notes. The Splitco Notes were initially issued by Splitco to PPG in the Special Distribution as partial consideration for Splitco's acquisition of the Merged Business. PPG then transferred the Splitco Notes to certain financial institutions in satisfaction of existing debt obligations of PPG held by those financial institutions. Pursuant to a purchase agreement, dated January 17, 2013, among Splitco, the financial institutions and the initial purchasers thereunder, on January 30, 2013, the initial purchasers purchased the Splitco Notes held by the financial institutions and resold them to investors in the Splitco Notes offering. Splitco did not receive any net proceeds from the sale of the Splitco Notes.

The Splitco Notes bear interest at a rate of 4.625 percent per annum, payable semi-annually in arrears on February 15 and August 15, commencing on August 15, 2013. Interest will accrue from January 30, 2013. The Splitco Notes will mature on February 15, 2021.

Upon the consummation of the Merger, the Company and certain subsidiaries of the Company became guarantors of the Splitco Notes. The Splitco Notes are fully and unconditionally guaranteed, jointly and severally, on a senior unsecured basis by the Company and by each of the Company's and Splitco's existing and future domestic subsidiaries, other than certain excluded subsidiaries.

The indenture governing the Splitco Notes contains customary covenants, including certain restrictions on the Company and its subsidiaries to pay dividends. These covenants are subject to a number of important exceptions and qualifications. Further, certain of these covenants will cease to apply at all times after the date on which the Splitco Notes receive investment grade ratings from both Moody's Investors Service, Inc. ("Moody's") and Standard & Poor's Rating Service, a division of The McGraw Hill Companies, Inc. ("Standard & Poor's"), provided no default or event of default under the Indenture exists at that time. Such terminated covenants will not be reinstated if the Splitco Notes lose their investment grade ratings at any time thereafter.

In connection with the issuance of the Splitco Notes, Splitco and the Company entered into a registration rights agreement on January 30, 2013 relating to the Splitco Notes, pursuant to which Splitco, the Company and the guarantors agreed to use their commercially reasonable efforts to file an exchange offer registration statement registering exchange notes and to use commercially reasonable efforts to complete the exchange offer within 560 calendar days following the closing of the Splitco Notes offering.

Senior Secured Term Loan Facility

In connection with the Merger, on January 28, 2013, Splitco entered into a credit agreement with a syndicate of banks led by Barclays Bank PLC (the "Splitco Term Loan Agreement") in order to finance the cash portion of the Special Distribution and the net working capital adjustment as required by the Merger Agreement. Upon consummation of the Merger, the Company and each of its existing domestic subsidiaries that guarantee any other indebtedness of the Company joined as guarantors under the Splitco Term Loan Agreement. Splitco has the option to repay amounts outstanding under the Term Facility within 45 days after the Closing Date, or at any time thereafter prior to its maturity date. Borrowings under the Term Facility are expected to mature on the fourth anniversary of the Closing Date.

Upon consummation of the Merger, the Company and certain subsidiaries of the Company became guarantors of the Term Facility. Obligations under the Term Facility are fully and unconditionally guaranteed, on a senior secured basis, by the Company and by each of the Company's and Splitco's existing and future domestic subsidiaries, other than certain excluded subsidiaries. The obligations under the Term Facility are secured by all assets of Splitco, the Company and the subsidiary guarantors.

At the election of Splitco, the Term Facility bears interest at a rate equal to: (i) the Base Rate (as defined in the Splitco Term Loan Agreement) plus 1.75 percent per annum; or (ii) the reserve adjusted Eurodollar Rate (as defined in the Splitco Term Loan Agreement) plus 2.75 percent per annum; provided that at no time will the Base Rate be deemed to be less than 2.00 percent per annum or the reserve adjusted Eurodollar Rate be deemed to be less than 1.00 percent per annum. Outstanding borrowings under the Term Facility currently bear interest at an effective rate of 3.75 percent per annum.

The Splitco Term Loan Agreement contains customary covenants (subject to exceptions), including certain restrictions on the Company and its subsidiaries to pay dividends. In addition, the Company will be subject to a senior secured leverage ratio (as defined in the Splitco Term Loan Agreement) of 3.50 to 1.00.

New ABL Revolver

On the Closing Date, the Company refinanced its current asset-based revolving credit facility with a syndicate of banks led by General Electric Capital Corporation (the "New ABL Revolver"), pursuant to an amended and restated credit agreement (the "ABL Credit Agreement" and, together with the Splitco Term Loan Agreement, the "Credit Agreements") in order to fund working capital and operating activities, including future acquisitions and the repayment of certain outstanding indebtedness after the Closing Date. Among other things, the New ABL Revolver (i) increases revolver availability from $300.0 million to $500.0 million, subject to applicable borrowing base limitations and certain other conditions; and (ii) includes a $200.0 million sub-facility for borrowings by the Canadian subsidiaries of the Company, a $200.0 million sub-facility for letters of credit and, subject to lender commitments, a $200.0 million "accordion" feature that permits us to increase the size of the facility. Borrowings under the New ABL Revolver are expected to mature on the fifth anniversary of the Closing Date.

U.S. borrowing obligations under the New ABL Revolver are fully and unconditionally guaranteed, on a senior secured basis, by each of the Company's existing and subsequently acquired or organized direct or indirect domestic subsidiaries (other than certain excluded subsidiaries). On the Closing Date, Splitco and its subsidiaries became guarantors under the New ABL Revolver. Canadian borrowing obligations under the New ABL Revolver are unconditionally guaranteed by each of the Company's existing and subsequently acquired or organized direct or indirect domestic and Canadian subsidiaries (other than certain excluded subsidiaries). All obligations under the New ABL Revolver, and the guarantees of those obligations, are secured, subject to certain exceptions, by substantially all of the Company's assets and the assets of the guarantors.

At our election, with respect to U.S. borrowings under the New ABL Revolver, the New ABL Revolver will bear interest at a rate equal to either (i) the higher of certain U.S. index rates; or (ii) three-month London Interbank Offered Rate ("LIBOR"), in each case, plus an applicable margin based on the Company's utilization under the New ABL Revolver. At the election of the Company, with respect to Canadian borrowings under the New ABL Revolver, the New ABL Revolver will bear interest at a rate equal to either (i) the higher of certain Canadian index rates; or (ii) three-month LIBOR, in each case, plus an applicable margin based on the Company's utilization under the New ABL Revolver.

The ABL Credit Agreement contains customary covenants (subject to exceptions), including certain restrictions on the Company and its subsidiaries to pay dividends. In addition, the Company will be subject to a fixed charge coverage ratio (as defined in the ABL Credit Agreement) of 1.10 to 1.00 if excess availability is less than $62.5 million for three consecutive business days.

In connection with closing the Transactions, we borrowed $33.0 million under the New ABL Revolver. Outstanding borrowings under the New ABL Revolver currently bear interest at an effective rate of 3.75 percent per annum.

Senior Notes Offering

On February 1, 2013, we issued $450.0 million in aggregate principal amount of 4.875 percent senior notes due 2023 (the "Senior Notes"). The Senior Notes bear interest at a rate of 4.875 percent per annum, payable semi-annually in arrears on May 15 and November 15 of each year, commencing on May 15, 2013. Interest will accrue from February 1, 2013. The Senior Notes will mature on May 15, 2023. The Senior Notes are fully and unconditionally guaranteed, jointly and severally, on a senior unsecured basis by each of our existing and future domestic subsidiaries, other than certain excluded subsidiaries.

We used the net proceeds from the offering of the Senior Notes, together with cash on hand, to fund the repurchase of our 9.0 percent senior secured notes due 2017 (the "9 percent notes") that were validly tendered and not validly withdrawn in our previously announced tender offer and related consent solicitation for the 9 percent notes (the "Tender Offer").

The indenture governing the Senior Notes contains customary covenants, including certain restrictions on the Company and its subsidiaries to pay dividends. Each of these covenants is subject to a number of important exceptions and qualifications. Further, certain of these covenants will cease to apply at all times after the date on which the Senior Notes receive investment grade ratings from both Moody's and Standard & Poor's, provided no default or event of default under the indenture exists at that time. Such terminated covenants will not be reinstated if the Senior Notes lose their investment grade ratings at any time thereafter.

In connection with the issuance of the Senior Notes, we entered into a registration rights agreement on February 1, 2013 relating to the Senior Notes, pursuant to which we and the guarantors agreed to use our commercially reasonable efforts to file an exchange offer registration statement registering exchange notes and to use commercially reasonable efforts to complete the exchange offer within 560 calendar days following the closing of the Senior Notes offering.

9 Percent Notes Tender Offer and Redemption

On February 1, 2013 and February 15, 2013, we accepted $444.5 million and $2.3 million, respectively, in aggregate principal amount of 9 percent notes that were validly tendered and not validly withdrawn at, or prior to the applicable tender deadlines. The Company used the net proceeds from the sale of the Senior Notes, together with cash on hand, to repurchase the 9 percent notes that were tendered in the Tender Offer for an aggregate tender price of $502.3 million including a make whole payment of $55.4 million. Also, on February 1, 2013, the Company entered into a supplemental indenture to the indenture governing the 9 percent notes with the trustee thereunder following receipt of consents of the requisite holders of the 9 percent notes, which removed substantially all of the restrictive covenants and certain events of default and other provisions in the indenture governing the 9 percent notes. In addition, on February 1, 2013, the Company delivered an irrevocable notice of redemption with respect to all 9 percent notes that remain outstanding following the expiration of the Tender Offer and the purchase of all 9 percent notes validly tendered. Pursuant to the redemption notice and the terms of the indenture governing the 9 percent notes, the Company will redeem the 9 percent notes that remain outstanding on or before March 4, 2013. Following such redemption, the Company's payment obligations under the indenture governing the 9 percent notes, will be terminated.

Certificate of Amendment to Increase Authorized Shares

In connection with the Transactions and effective January 28, 2013, the Company also filed a Certificate of Amendment to the Company's certificate of incorporation to increase the number of authorized shares of Company common stock from 100,000,000 shares to 200,000,000 shares.

1.118 CAMPBELL SOUP COMPANY (JUL)

NOTES TO CONSOLIDATED FINANCIAL STATEMENTS

(currency in millions, except per share amounts)

19. Subsequent Events

On August 6, 2012, the company completed the acquisition of BF Bolthouse Holdco LLC (Bolthouse Farms) from a fund managed by Madison Dearborn Partners, LLC, a private equity firm, for $1,550 in cash, subject to customary purchase price adjustments related to the amount of Bolthouse Farms' cash, debt, working capital, transaction expenses and taxes. Bolthouse Farms is a vertically integrated food and beverage company focused on developing, manufacturing and marketing fresh carrots and proprietary, high value-added natural, healthy products. Bolthouse Farms has leading market positions in retail fresh carrots and super-premium beverages in the U.S. and Canada. The acquisition was funded through a combination of short- and long-term borrowings. Approximately $300 was funded through the issuance of commercial paper. The terms of long-term borrowings, which were issued on August 2, 2012 to fund the transaction, were as follows:

- $400 floating rate notes that mature on August 1, 2014. Interest on the notes is based on 3-month U.S. dollar LIBOR. plus 0.30% Interest is payable quarterly beginning November 1, 2012;
- $450 of 2.50% notes that mature on August 2, 2022. Interest is payable semi-annually beginning February 2, 2013. The company may redeem the notes in whole or in part at any time at a redemption price of 100% of the principal amount plus accrued interest or an amount designed to ensure that the note holders are not penalized by the early redemption; and
- $400 of 3.80% notes that mature on August 2, 2042. Interest is payable semi-annually beginning February 2, 2013. The company may redeem the notes in whole or in part at any time at a redemption price of 100% of the principal amount plus accrued interest or an amount designed to ensure that the note holders are not penalized by the early redemption.

In 2012, the company recorded pre-tax transaction costs of $5 ($3 after tax or $.01 per share) related to the acquisition of Bolthouse Farms. The company expects to incur an additional $11 in transaction costs in 2013. The company is currently working through the purchase price allocation process.

On September 27, 2012, the company announced several initiatives to improve its U.S. supply chain cost structure and increase asset utilization across its U.S. thermal plant network. The company expects to eliminate approximately 727 positions in connection with the initiatives, which include the following:

- The company will close its thermal plant In Sacramento, California, which produces soups, sauces and beverages. The closure will result in the elimination of approximately 700 full-time positions and will be completed in phases, with plans to cease operations in July 2013. The company plans to shift the majority of Sacramento's soup, sauce and beverage production to its thermal plants in Maxton, North Carolina; Napoleon, Ohio; and Paris, Texas.
- The company will also close its spice plant in South Plainfield, New Jersey, which will result in the elimination of 27 positions. The company will consolidate spice production at its Milwaukee, Wisconsin, plant in 2013.

As a result of these initiatives, the company expects to incur aggregate pre-tax costs of approximately $115, consisting of the following:

- approximately $25 in employee severance and benefits;
- approximately $75 in accelerated depreciation of property, plant and equipment; and
- approximately $15 in other costs

The company expects to incur the majority of these costs in 2013. Approximately $38 of the pre-tax costs are expected to be cash expenditures. In addition, the company expects to invest approximately $27 in capital expenditures, primarily to relocate and refurbish a beverage filling and packaging line.

Related Party Transactions

DISCLOSURE

1.119 FASB ASC 850, *Related Party Disclosures*, specifies the nature of information that should be disclosed in financial statements about related-party transactions and certain common control relationships. FASB ASC 850-10-50-1 requires an entity to disclose material related party transactions but exempts compensation arrangements, expense allowances, and other similar items in the ordinary course of business from disclosure requirements. However, Item 402, "Executive Compensation," of SEC Regulation S-K requires SEC registrants to provide compensation information outside the financial statements for specified members of management. The disclosures should include the nature of the relationship(s) involved, a description of the transactions, the dollar amounts of the transactions, and amounts due to or from related parties for each period for which the entity presents an income statement. FASB ASC 740-10-50-17 also includes guidance for entities with separately issued financial statements that are members of a consolidated tax return, additional disclosures are required. Further, if the reporting entity and one or more other companies are under common ownership or management control, and the existence of that control could result in operating results or a financial position of the reporting entity significantly different from those that would have been obtained if the companies were autonomous, FASB ASC 850-10-50-6 requires the nature of the control relationship to be disclosed even if there are no transactions between the entities.

PRESENTATION AND DISCLOSURE EXCERPTS

TRANSACTIONS WITH RELATED PARTIES

1.120 BARNES & NOBLE, INC. (APR)
NOTES TO CONSOLIDATED FINANCIAL STATEMENTS

19. Certain Relationships and Related Transactions

The Company believes that the transactions and agreements discussed below (including renewals of any existing agreements) between the Company and related third parties are at least as favorable to the Company as could have been obtained from unrelated parties at the time they were entered into. The Audit Committee of the Board of Directors utilizes procedures in evaluating the terms and provisions of proposed related party transactions or agreements in accordance with the fiduciary duties of directors under Delaware law. The Company's related party transaction procedures contemplate Audit Committee review and approval of all new agreements, transactions or courses of dealing with related parties, including any modifications, waivers or amendments to existing related party transactions. The Company tests to ensure that the terms of related party transactions are at least as favorable to the Company as could have been obtained from unrelated parties at the time of the transaction. The Audit Committee considers, at a minimum, the nature of the relationship between the Company and the related party, the history of the transaction (in the case of modifications, waivers or amendments), the terms of the proposed transaction, the Company's rationale for entering the transaction and the terms of comparable transactions with unrelated third parties. In addition, management and internal audit annually analyzes all existing related party agreements and transactions and reviews them with the Audit Committee.

The Company completed the Acquisition of B&N College from Leonard Riggio and Louise Riggio (Sellers) on September 30, 2009 (see Note 14). Mr. Riggio is the Chairman of the Company's Board of Directors and a significant stockholder. The Company is a party to a Stock Purchase Agreement dated as of August 7, 2009 among the Company and the Sellers. As part of the Acquisition, the Company acquired the Barnes & Noble trade name that had been owned by B&N College and licensed to the Company (described below). The purchase price paid to the Sellers was $596,000, consisting of $346,000 in cash and $250,000 in Seller Notes (described below). However, the cash paid to the Sellers was reduced by approximately $82,352 in cash bonuses paid by B&N College to 192 members of its management team and employees (Bonus Recipients), not including Leonard Riggio. Pursuant to the terms of the Purchase Agreement, prior to the closing of the Acquisition, B&N College distributed to the Sellers certain assets that are not related to B&N College's core business, including common stock in the Company. In connection with such distribution, 667,058 shares of the common stock in the Company previously held by B&N College were transferred to certain of the Bonus Recipients. The Company financed the Acquisition through $250,000 of Seller Notes, $150,000 from the 2009 Credit Facility and the remainder from both the Company's and B&N College's cash on hand.

In connection with the closing of the Acquisition, the Company issued the Sellers (i) a senior subordinated note in the principal amount of $100,000, payable in full on December 15, 2010, with interest of 8% per annum payable on the unpaid principal amount (the Senior Seller Note), and (ii) a junior subordinated note in the principal amount of $150,000 (the Junior Seller Note), payable in full on the fifth anniversary of the closing of the Acquisition, with interest of 10% per annum payable on the unpaid principal amount. The Senior Seller Note was paid on its scheduled due date, December 15, 2010. The Senior Seller Note was unsecured and subordinated to the obligations under the 2009 Credit Facility and certain other senior obligations. The Company had the right to prepay the Senior Seller Note at any time without premium or penalty to the extent not prohibited by senior debt documents, provided that the Company did not have the right to prepay the Junior Seller Note until the Senior Seller Note had been repaid in full. On December 22, 2009, the Company consented to the pledge and assignment of the Senior Seller Note by the Sellers as collateral security. The Junior Seller Note was and is unsecured and subordinated to the obligations under the 2009 Credit Facility, the 2011 Amended Credit Facility and the 2012 Amended Credit Facility, as applicable, as well as certain other senior obligations. The Company may prepay the Junior Seller Note at any time without premium or penalty to the extent not prohibited by the 2012 Amended Credit Facility and senior debt documents. Pursuant to a settlement agreed to on June 13, 2012 and described in Note 18, the Sellers have agreed to waive $22,750 of the purchase price by waiving a corresponding principal amount (and interest on) of the Junior Seller Note, subject to receipt of court approval.

Also in connection with the Acquisition, and as set forth in the Purchase Agreement, B&N College made a tax distribution payment of $54,997 to the Sellers related to taxes imposed on the Sellers' pro rata share of B&N College S corporation taxable earnings from January 1, 2009 through the date of Acquisition.

The Company paid COBRA benefits for certain former employees and family members that were on the B&N College health benefit plan (prior to the Acquisition). Leonard Riggio has reimbursed the Company $140 to cover such costs, based upon standard COBRA rates, for the period subsequent to Acquisition through fiscal 2010.

In connection with the Acquisition, B&N College and the Company amended and restated B&N College's existing long-term supply agreement (Supply Agreement) with MBS Textbook Exchange, Inc. (MBS), which is majority owned by Leonard Riggio, Stephen Riggio (formerly the Company's Vice Chairman and Chief Executive Officer) and other members of the Riggio family. MBS is a new and used textbook wholesaler, which also sells textbooks online and provides bookstore systems and distant learning distribution services. Pursuant to the Supply Agreement, which has a term of ten years, and subject to availability and competitive terms and conditions, B&N College will continue to purchase new and used printed textbooks for a given academic term from MBS prior to buying them from other suppliers, other than in connection with student buy-back programs. MBS pays B&N College commissions based on the volume of textbooks sold to MBS each year and with respect to the textbook requirements of certain distance learning programs that MBS fulfills on B&N College's behalf. MBS paid B&N College $10,941, $13,031 and $7,014 related to these commissions in fiscal 2012, fiscal 2011 and fiscal 2010 from the date of Acquisition, respectively. In addition, the Supply Agreement contains restrictive covenants that limit the ability of B&N College and the Company to become a used textbook wholesaler and that place certain limitations on MBS's business activities. B&N College and Barnes & Noble.com also entered into an agreement with MBS in fiscal 2011 pursuant to which MBS agrees to purchase at the end of a given semester certain agreed upon textbooks which B&N College and Barnes & Noble.com shall have rented to students during such semester. Total sales to MBS under this program were $13,339 and $506 for fiscal 2012 and fiscal 2011, respectively. In addition, B&N College entered into an agreement with MBS in fiscal 2011 pursuant to which MBS purchases books from B&N College, which have no resale value for a flat rate per box. Total sales to MBS under this program were $364 and $427 for fiscal 2012 and fiscal 2011, respectively.

The Company purchases new and used textbooks at market prices directly from MBS. Total purchases were $101,980, $102,573 and $24,186 for fiscal 2012, fiscal 2011 and fiscal 2010, respectively. MBS sells used books through the Barnes & Noble.com dealer network. Barnes & Noble.com earned a commission of $4,661, $5,474 and $3,115 on the MBS used book sales in fiscal 2012, fiscal 2011 and fiscal 2010, respectively. In addition, Barnes & Noble.com hosts pages on its website through which Barnes & Noble.com customers are able to sell used books directly to MBS. Barnes & Noble.com is paid a fixed commission on the price paid by MBS to the customer. Total commissions paid to Barnes & Noble.com were $160, $184 and $172 for fiscal 2012, fiscal 2011 and fiscal 2010, respectively.

In fiscal 2010, the Company's wholly owned subsidiary Barnes & Noble Bookquest LLC (Bookquest) entered into an agreement with TXTB.com LLC (TXTB), a subsidiary of MBS, pursuant to which the marketplace database of third party sellers on the Barnes & Noble.com website was made available on the TXTB website. In fiscal 2012, Bookquest was merged into Barnes & Noble.com. Barnes & Noble.com receives a fee from third party sellers for sales of marketplace items and, upon receipt of such fee, Barnes & Noble.com remits a separate fee to TXTB for any marketplace items sold on the TXTB website. Total commissions paid to TXTB were $559, $775 and $0 during fiscal 2012, fiscal 2011 and fiscal 2010, respectively. Outstanding amounts payable to TXTB were $6, $8 and $33 for fiscal 2012, fiscal 2011 and fiscal 2010, respectively.

In fiscal 2011, Barnes & Noble.com entered into an agreement with TXTB pursuant to which Barnes & Noble.com became the exclusive provider of trade books to TXTB customers through www.textbooks.com. TXTB receives a commission from Barnes & Noble.com on each purchase by a TXTB customer. Total commissions paid to TXTB were $148 and $0 during fiscal 2012 and fiscal 2011. Outstanding amounts payable to TXTB were $1 and $4 for fiscal 2012 and fiscal 2011.

Prior to the Acquisition, the Company licensed the "Barnes & Noble name under a royalty-free license agreement dated February 11, 1987, as amended, from B&N College. Barnes & Noble.com licensed the "Barnes & Noble" name under a royalty-free license agreement, dated October 31, 1998, as amended, between Barnes & Noble.com and B&N College (the License Agreement). Pursuant to the License Agreement, Barnes & Noble.com had been granted an exclusive license to use the "Barnes & Noble" name and trademark in perpetuity for the purpose of selling books over the Internet (excluding sales of college textbooks). Under a separate agreement dated as of January 31, 2001 (the Textbook License Agreement), between Barnes & Noble.com, B&N College and Textbooks.com, Barnes & Noble.com was granted the right to sell college textbooks over the Internet using the "Barnes & Noble" name. Pursuant to the Textbook License Agreement, Barnes & Noble.com paid Textbooks.com a royalty on revenues (net of product returns, applicable sales tax and excluding shipping and handling) realized by Barnes & Noble.com from the sale of books designated as textbooks. Royalty expense was $3,431 during fiscal 2010 prior to the Acquisition, under the terms of the Textbook License Agreement. During fiscal 2010, subsequent to the closing of the Acquisition, Textbooks.com paid $146 to B&N College for funds that were received by Textbooks.com and were earned by B&N College. In connection with the closing of the Acquisition, the Company terminated the Textbook License Agreement and as a result no longer pays a royalty with respect to online textbook sales.

In fiscal 2010, the Company entered into an Aircraft Time Sharing Agreement with LR Enterprises Management LLC (LR Enterprises), which is owned by Leonard Riggio and Louise Riggio, pursuant to which LR Enterprises granted the Company the right to use a jet aircraft owned by it on a time-sharing basis in accordance with, and subject to the reimbursement of certain operating costs and expenses as provided in, the Federal Aviation Regulations (FAR). Such operating costs were $1,015, $932 and $429 during fiscal 2012, fiscal 2011 and fiscal 2010, respectively. LR Enterprises is solely responsible for the physical and technical operation of the aircraft, aircraft maintenance and the cost of maintaining aircraft liability insurance, other than insurance obtained for the specific flight as requested by the Company, as provided in the FAR. Prior to the Acquisition, the Company used a jet aircraft owned by B&N College and paid for the costs and expenses of operating the aircraft based upon the Company's usage. Such costs which included fuel, insurance and other costs were $113 during fiscal 2010 prior to the Acquisition, and were included in the accompanying consolidated statements of operations.

The Company has leases for two locations for its corporate offices with related parties: the first location is leased from an entity in which Leonard Riggio has a majority interest and expires in 2013; the second location is leased from an entity in which Leonard Riggio has a minority interest and expires in 2016. The space was rented at an aggregate annual rent including real estate taxes of approximately $4,843, $4,868 and $4,889 during fiscal 2012, fiscal 2011 and fiscal 2010, respectively.

The Company leases one of its B&N College stores from a partnership owned by Leonard and Stephen Riggio, pursuant to a lease expiring in 2014. Rent of $862, $862 and $512 was paid during fiscal 2012, fiscal 2011 and fiscal 2010 from the date of the Acquisition, respectively.

The Company leases an office/warehouse from a partnership in which Leonard Riggio has a 50% interest, pursuant to a lease expiring in 2023. The space was rented at an annual rent of $759, $763 and $759 during fiscal 2012, fiscal 2011 and fiscal 2010, respectively. Net of subtenant income, the Company paid $376, $246 and $241 during fiscal 2012, fiscal 2011 and fiscal 2010, respectively.

Prior to the Acquisition, the Company leased retail space in a building in which B&N College subleased space from the Company, pursuant to a sublease expiring in 2020. Pursuant to such sublease, the Company charged B&N College $347 for such subleased space and other operating costs incurred on its behalf during fiscal year 2010 prior to the Acquisition. The amount paid by B&N College to the Company exceeded the cost per square foot paid by the Company to its unaffiliated third-party landlord.

Prior to the Acquisition, the Company reimbursed B&N College certain operating costs B&N College incurred on the Company's behalf. These charges were $71 during fiscal 2010 prior to the Acquisition. Prior to the Acquisition, B&N College purchased inventory, at cost plus an incremental fee, of $25,187 from the Company during fiscal 2010 prior to the Acquisition. Also prior to the Acquisition, B&N College reimbursed the Company $2,700 for fiscal year 2010 prior to the Acquisition for capital expenditures, business insurance and other operating costs incurred on its behalf.

GameStop Corp. (GameStop), a company in which Leonard Riggio was a member of the Board of Directors and is a minority shareholder, operates departments within some of the Company's bookstores. GameStop pays a license fee to the Company in an amount equal to 7% of the gross sales of such departments, which totaled $871, $989 and $1,061 during fiscal 2012, fiscal 2011 and fiscal 2010, respectively. GameStop sold new and used video games and consoles on the Barnes & Noble.com website up until May 1, 2011, when the agreement between GameStop and Barnes & Noble.com terminated. Barnes & Noble.com received a commission on sales made by GameStop. For fiscal 2012, fiscal 2011 and fiscal 2010, the commission earned by Barnes & Noble.com was $1 (from residual activity after the agreement terminated), $356 and $334, respectively. Until June 2005, GameStop participated in the Company's workers' compensation, property and general liability insurance programs. The costs incurred by the Company under these programs were allocated to GameStop based upon GameStop's total payroll expense, property and equipment, and insurance claim history. GameStop reimbursed the Company for these services $3, $51 and $128 during fiscal 2012, fiscal 2011 and fiscal 2010, respectively. Although GameStop secured its own insurance coverage, costs are continuing to be incurred by the Company on insurance claims which were made under its programs prior to June 2005 and any such costs applicable to insurance claims against GameStop will be charged to GameStop at the time incurred.

The Company is provided with national freight distribution, including trucking services by Argix Direct Inc. (Argix), a company in which a brother of Leonard and Stephen Riggio owns a 20% interest, pursuant to a transportation agreement expiring in 2014 (following an automatic renewal of the agreement by its terms in 2012 for an additional two-year term, although at all times the agreement requires a two-year notice to terminate). The Company paid Argix $14,414, $15,890 and $16,536 for such services during fiscal 2012, fiscal 2011 and fiscal 2010, respectively. At the time of the agreement, the cost of freight delivered to the stores by Argix was comparable to the prices charged by publishers and the Company's other third party freight distributors. However, due to higher contracted fuel surcharge and transportation costs, Argix's rates were higher than the Company's other third party freight distributors. As a result, the Company amended its existing agreement with Argix effective January 1, 2009. The amendment provides the Company with a $3,000 annual credit to its freight and transportation costs for the remaining life of the existing agreement. The $3,000 annual credit expired with the April 1, 2012 renewal of the agreement. Argix provides B&N College with transportation services under a separate agreement that expired and was renewed in 2011. The renewed agreement expires in 2013. The Company believes that the transportation costs that B&N College paid to Argix are comparable to the transportation costs charged by third party distributors. B&N College paid Argix $1,294, $1,477 and $658 for such services during fiscal 2012, fiscal 2011 and fiscal 2010 from the date of Acquisition, respectively. Argix also leased office and warehouse space from the Company in Jamesburg, New Jersey, pursuant to a lease expiring in 2011. This lease was renewed for additional space in 2011. However, the Company subsequently sold the warehouse on December 29, 2011 (see Note 16). The Company charged Argix $1,514, $2,719 and $2,646 for such leased space and other operating costs incurred on its behalf prior to the sale of the warehouse during fiscal 2012, fiscal 2011 and fiscal 2010, respectively.

The Company used Source Interlink Companies, Inc. (Source Interlink) as its primary supplier of music and DVD/video, as well as magazines and newspapers. Leonard Riggio is an investor in an investment company that formerly owned a minority interest in Source Interlink. Pursuant to the confirmation order of the United States Bankruptcy Court of the District of Delaware, as of June 19, 2009 (the Discharge Date) the equity interests held by the then owners of Source Interlink were discharged, cancelled, released and extinguished. The Company paid Source Interlink $33,979 for merchandise purchased at market prices during fiscal 2010 prior to the Discharge Date. In addition, Source Interlink purchases certain data related to magazine sales of the Company. Source Interlink paid the Company $20 during fiscal 2010 prior to the Discharge Date.

The Company uses Digital on Demand as its provider of music and video database equipment and services. Leonard Riggio owns a minority interest in Digital on Demand through the same investment company through which he owned a minority interest in Source Interlink. The Company paid Digital on Demand $185, $1,932 and $2,593 for music and video database equipment and services during fiscal 2012, fiscal 2011 and fiscal 2010, respectively. This agreement was terminated on May 31, 2011.

On August 18, 2011, the Company entered into an investment agreement between the Company and Liberty GIC, Inc. (Liberty), a subsidiary of Liberty Media Corporation (Liberty Media), pursuant to which the Company issued and sold to Liberty, and Liberty purchased, 204,000 shares of the Company's Series J

Preferred Stock, par value $0.001 per share, for an aggregate purchase price of $204,000 in a private placement exempt from the registration requirements of the 1933 Act (see Note 12).

In fiscal 2012, the Company entered into agreements with third parties who sell Barnes & Noble products through QVC and Home Shopping Network (HSN), affiliates of Liberty Media. The Liberty entity that indirectly holds the Barnes & Noble investment (Liberty Media) is a separate public company from the Liberty entity that owns QVC and HSN (Liberty Interactive). Liberty Media was split-off (the Split-Off) from Liberty Interactive on September 28, 2011. No products were sold to the third parties from August 18, 2011, the date of the investment through the date of the Split-Off. The Company purchases trade books, primarily craft/hobbies, from Leisure Arts, Inc. (Leisure Arts), a subsidiary of Liberty Interactive. Total purchases from Leisure Arts following the date of the Liberty investment and prior to the date of the Split-Off were $16. The Company also purchases Halloween costumes from BuySeasons Inc. (BuySeasons), a subsidiary of Liberty Interactive. Total purchases from BuySeasons following the date of the Liberty investment and prior to the date of the Split-Off were $33. On July 19, 2011, the Company renewed a one-year contract with Commerce Technologies, Inc. (Commerce Hub), a subsidiary of Liberty Interactive, who provides services to help facilitate and integrate sales with drop-ship vendors. Total fees paid to Commerce Hub following the date of the Liberty investment and prior to the date of the Split-Off were $22. The Company purchases textbooks from AI2, Inc. (AI2), a subsidiary of Liberty Interactive. There were no purchases from AI2 following the date of the Liberty investment and prior to the date of the Split-Off. The Company paid commissions to Liberty Interactive Advertising (LIA), a subsidiary of Liberty Interactive, who serves as the exclusive premium advertising sales agency for the Company. Total commissions paid to LIA following the date of the Liberty investment and prior to the date of the Split-Off were $5.

TRANSACTION BETWEEN REPORTING ENTITY AND OFFICER/DIRECTOR

1.121 CHESAPEAKE ENERGY CORPORATION (DEC)
NOTES TO CONSOLIDATED FINANCIAL STATEMENTS

6. Related Party Transactions (in part)

Chief Executive Officer

As of December 31, 2012 and 2011, we had accrued accounts receivable from our Chief Executive Officer, Aubrey K. McClendon, of $23 million and $45 million, respectively, representing joint interest billings from December 2012 and 2011 related to Mr. McClendon's participation in Company wells pursuant to the Founder Well Participation Program (FWPP). These amounts were invoiced and timely paid in the following month. Since Chesapeake was founded in 1989, Mr. McClendon has acquired working interests in virtually all of our natural gas and oil properties by participating in our drilling activities under the terms of his employment agreement and the FWPP and predecessor participation arrangements provided for in Mr. McClendon's employment agreements. On April 30, 2012, the Company's Board of Directors and Mr. McClendon agreed to the early termination of the FWPP on June 30, 2014, 18 months before the end of the 10-year term approved by our shareholders in June 2005. Under the FWPP, Mr. McClendon may elect to participate in all or none of the wells drilled by or on behalf of Chesapeake during a calendar year, but he is not allowed to participate only in selected wells. A participation election is required to be received by the Compensation Committee of Chesapeake's Board of Directors not less than 30 days prior to the start of each calendar year. His participation is permitted only under the terms outlined in the FWPP, which, among other things, limits his individual participation to a maximum working interest of 2.5% in a well and prohibits participation in situations where Chesapeake's working interest would be reduced below 12.5% as a result of his participation. In addition, the Company is reimbursed for costs associated with leasehold acquired by Mr. McClendon as a result of his well participation. In conjunction with certain sales of natural gas and oil properties by the Company, affiliates of Mr. McClendon have sold interests in the same properties and on the same terms as those that applied to the interests sold by the Company, and the proceeds were paid to the sellers based on their respective ownership.

On December 31, 2008, we entered into a new five-year employment agreement with Mr. McClendon that contained a one-time well cost incentive award to him. The total cost of the award to Chesapeake was $75 million plus employment taxes in the amount of approximately $1 million. The incentive award was subject to a clawback equal to any unvested portion of the award if during the initial five-year term of the employment agreement, Mr. McClendon resigned from the Company or was terminated for cause by the Company. We are recognizing the incentive award as general and administrative expense over the five-year vesting period for the clawback resulting in an expense of approximately $15 million per year beginning in 2009. The net incentive award, after deduction of applicable withholding and employment taxes, of approximately $44 million was fully applied against costs attributable to interests in Company wells acquired by Mr. McClendon or his affiliates under the FWPP. On January 29, 2013, the Company announced that Mr. McClendon had agreed to retire from the Company on the earlier to occur of April 1, 2013 or the time at which his successor is appointed. Mr. McClendon's participation rights under the FWPP will continue through the expiration of the FWPP on June 30, 2014, and the incentive award clawback applicable to 2013 will not apply. See Note 21 for additional information on the terms of his separation from the Company.

In 2011, Chesapeake entered into a license and naming rights agreement with The Professional Basketball Club, LLC (PBC) for the arena in downtown Oklahoma City. PBC is the owner of the Oklahoma City Thunder basketball team, a National Basketball Association franchise and the arena's primary tenant. Mr. McClendon has a 19.2% equity interest in PBC. Under the terms of the agreement, Chesapeake has committed to pay fees ranging from $3 million to $4 million per year through 2023 for the arena naming rights and other associated benefits. In addition, since 2008, Chesapeake has been a founding sponsor of the Oklahoma City Thunder, initially under successive one-year contracts. In 2011, it entered into a 12 -year sponsorship agreement, committing to pay an average annual fee of $3 million for advertising, use of an arena suite and other benefits. Chesapeake also has committed to purchase tickets to all 2012–2013 home games. In 2012 and 2011, the Company paid PBC approximately $7 million and $6 million, respectively, for naming rights fees, sponsorship fees and game tickets, and for 2013, the amount payable for such 2012–2013 season fees and tickets is approximately $3 million, not including any amounts for playoff tickets.

Pursuant to a court-approved litigation settlement with certain plaintiff shareholders described in Note 4, the sale of an antique map collection that occurred in December 2008 between Mr. McClendon and the Company will be rescinded. Mr. McClendon will pay the Company approximately $12 million plus interest, and the Company will reconvey the map collection to Mr. McClendon. The transaction is scheduled to be completed not later than 30 days after entry of a final non-appealable judgment.

21. Subsequent Events (in part)

On January 29, 2013, we announced that Aubrey K. McClendon, our President, Chief Executive Officer (CEO) and a director, agreed to retire from the Company. Mr. McClendon will continue to serve as President, CEO and a director until the earlier of April 1, 2013 or the time at which his successor is appointed. Mr. McClendon's departure from the Company will be treated as a termination without cause under his employment agreement.

LOANS & LONG-TERM RECEIVABLES

1.122 CONOCOPHILLIPS (DEC)
CONSOLIDATED BALANCE SHEET (in part)

	Millions of Dollars	
At December 31	2012	2011
Assets		
Cash and cash equivalents	$ 3,618	5,780
Short-term investments*	—	581
Restricted cash	748	—
Accounts and notes receivable (net of allowance of $10 million in 2012 and $30 million in 2011)	8,929	14,648
Accounts and notes receivable—related parties	253	1,878
Inventories	965	4,631
Prepaid expenses and other current assets	9,476	2,700
Total Current Assets	23,989	30,218
Investments and long-term receivables	23,489	32,108
Loans and advances—related parties	1,517	1,675
Net properties, plants and equipment (net of accumulated depreciation, depletion and amortization of $58,916 million in 2012 and $65,029 million in 2011)	67,263	84,180
Goodwill	—	3,332
Intangibles	4	745
Other assets	882	972
Total Assets	$117,144	153,230

NOTES TO CONSOLIDATED FINANCIAL STATEMENTS

Note 6—Investments, Loans and Long-Term Receivables (in part)

Loans and Long-term Receivables

As part of our normal ongoing business operations and consistent with industry practice, we enter into numerous agreements with other parties to pursue business opportunities. Included in such activity are loans and long-term receivables to certain affiliated and non-affiliated companies. Loans are recorded when cash is transferred or seller financing is provided to the affiliated or non-affiliated company pursuant to a loan agreement. The loan balance will increase as interest is earned on the outstanding loan balance and will decrease as interest and principal payments are received. Interest is earned at the loan agreement's stated interest rate. Loans and long-term receivables are assessed for impairment when events indicate the loan balance may not be fully recovered.

At December 31, 2012, significant loans to affiliated companies include the following:
- $565 million in loan financing to Freeport LNG Development, L.P. for the construction of an LNG receiving terminal that became operational in June 2008. Freeport began making repayments in 2008 and is required to continue making repayments through full repayment of the loan in 2026. Repayment by Freeport is supported by "process-or-pay" capacity service payments made by us to Freeport under our terminal use agreement.
- $1,092 million in project financing to QG3. We own a 30 percent interest in QG3, for which we use the equity method of accounting. The other participants in the project are affiliates of Qatar Petroleum and Mitsui. QG3 secured project financing of $4.0 billion in December 2005, consisting of $1.3 billion of loans from export credit agencies (ECA), $1.5 billion from commercial banks, and $1.2 billion from ConocoPhillips. The ConocoPhillips loan facilities have substantially the same terms as the ECA and commercial bank facilities. On December 15, 2011, QG3 achieved financial completion and all project loan facilities became nonrecourse to the project participants. Semi-annual repayments began in January 2011 and will extend through July 2022.

The long-term portion of these loans are included in the "Loans and advances—related parties" line on our consolidated balance sheet, while the short-term portion is in "Accounts and notes receivable—related parties."

Inflationary Accounting

DISCLOSURE

1.123 FASB ASC 255, *Changing Prices*, states that entities are encouraged to disclose supplementary information on the effects of changing prices (inflation). Entities are not discouraged from experimenting with other forms of disclosure.

1.124 However, the Item 303 of the SEC's Regulation S-K requires that registrants discuss in "Management's Discussion and Analysis of Financial Condition and Results of Operations" the effects of inflation and other changes in prices when considered material. The SEC also encourages experimentation with these disclosures in order to provide the most meaningful presentation of the impact of price changes on the registrant's financial statements. Accordingly, many of the survey entities include comments about inflation in MD&A.

PRESENTATION AND DISCLOSURE EXCERPT

INFLATIONARY ACCOUNTING

1.125 THE COCA-COLA COMPANY (DEC)
NOTES TO CONSOLIDATED FINANCIAL STATEMENTS

Note 1: Business and Summary of Significant Accounting Policies (in part)

Hyperinflationary Economies

A hyperinflationary economy is one that has cumulative inflation of approximately 100 percent or more over a three-year period. Effective January 1, 2010, Venezuela was determined to be a hyperinflationary economy, and the Venezuelan government devalued the bolivar by resetting the official rate of exchange ("official rate") from 2.15 bolivars per U.S. dollar to 2.6 bolivars per U.S. dollar for essential goods and 4.3 bolivars per U.S. dollar for nonessential goods. In accordance with hyperinflationary accounting under accounting principles generally accepted in the United States, our local subsidiary was required to use the U.S. dollar as its functional currency. As a result, we remeasured the net assets of our Venezuelan subsidiary using the official rate for nonessential goods of 4.3 bolivars per U.S. dollar, which resulted in a loss of $ 103 million during the first quarter of 2010. The loss was recorded in the line item other income (loss)—net in our consolidated statement of income. We classified the impact of the remeasurement loss in the line item effect of exchange rate changes on cash and cash equivalents in our consolidated statement of cash flows.

In June 2010, the Venezuelan government introduced a newly regulated foreign currency exchange system known as the Transaction System for Foreign Currency Denominated Securities ("SITME"). This system, which was subject to annual limits, enabled entities domiciled in Venezuela to exchange their bolivars to U.S. dollars through authorized financial institutions (commercial banks, savings and lending institutions, etc.).

In December 2010, the Venezuelan government announced that it was eliminating the official rate of 2.6 bolivars per U.S. dollar for essential goods. As a result, the only two exchange rates available for remeasuring bolivar-denominated transactions as of December 31, 2010, were the official rate of 4.3 bolivars per U.S. dollar and the SITME rate. As discussed above, the Company remeasured the net assets of our Venezuelan subsidiary using the official rate for nonessential goods of 4.3 bolivars per U.S. dollar starting on January 1, 2010. Therefore, the elimination of the official rate for essential goods had no impact on the remeasurement of the net assets of our Venezuelan subsidiary.

Subsequent to December 31, 2012, the Venezuelan government devalued its currency further to an official rate of 6.3 bolivars per U.S. dollar. The government also announced that it was discontinuing the SITME foreign exchange system. As a result, the Company will remeasure the net assets of our local subsidiary and recognize the related gains or losses from remeasurement in the line item other income (loss) — net in our consolidated statement of income. Based on the carrying value of our assets and liabilities denominated in Venezuelan bolivar as of December 31, 2012, we anticipate recognizing a remeasurement loss of $ 100 million to $ 125 million during the first quarter of 2013.

The Company will continue to use the official rate to remeasure the net assets of our Venezuelan subsidiary. If the official rate devalues further, it would result in our Company recognizing additional foreign currency exchange gains or losses in our consolidated financial statements. As of December 31, 2012, our Venezuelan subsidiary held monetary assets of approximately $ 450 million and monetary liabilities of approximately $ 85 million.

In addition to the foreign currency exchange exposure related to our Venezuelan subsidiary's net assets, we also sell concentrate to our bottling partner in Venezuela from outside the country. These sales are denominated in U.S. dollars. If we are unable to utilize a government-approved exchange rate mechanism for future concentrate sales to our bottling partner in Venezuela, the amount of receivables related to these sales will increase. In addition, we have certain intangible assets associated with products sold in Venezuela. If the bolivar further devalues, it could result in the impairment of these intangible assets. As of December 31, 2012, the carrying value of our accounts receivable from our bottling partner in Venezuela and intangible assets associated with products sold in Venezuela was $ 216 million.

General Balance Sheet Considerations

PRESENTATION

2.01 Financial Accounting Standards Board (FASB) *Accounting Standards Codification*™ (ASC) describes the benefits of presenting comparative financial statements instead of single-period financial statements and addresses the required disclosures and how the comparative information should be presented. Securities and Exchange Commission (SEC) Regulation S-X, together with Financial Reporting Releases and Staff Accounting Bulletins, prescribe the form and content of, and requirements for, financial statements filed with the SEC. However, those requirements are modified for smaller reporting companies, as defined by SEC Regulation S-K, in Article 8 of Regulation S-X.

2.02 FASB ASC 810, *Consolidation*, and Rule 3A-02 of Regulation S-X state that a presumption exists that consolidated financial statements are more meaningful than separate financial statements and that they are usually necessary for a fair presentation when one of the entities in the consolidated group directly or indirectly has a controlling financial interest in the other entities. Rule 3-01(a) of Regulation S-X requires an entity to present consolidated balance sheets as of the end of each of the two most recent fiscal years, unless the entity has been in existence for less than one year.

2.03 FASB ASC does not require an entity to present a classified balance sheet or mandate any particular ordering of balance sheet accounts. However, FASB ASC 210-10-05-4 states that entities usually present a classified balance sheet to facilitate calculation of working capital. FASB ASC 210-10-05-5 indicates that in the statements of manufacturing, trading, and service entities, assets and liabilities are generally classified and segregated. Financial institutions generally present unclassified balance sheets. The FASB ASC glossary includes definitions of *current assets* and *current liabilities* for when an entity presents a classified balance sheet. FASB ASC 210-10-45 provides additional guidance for determining these classifications.

DISCLOSURE

> **Author's Note**
> In December 2011, FASB issued Accounting Standards Update (ASU) No. 2011-11, *Balance Sheet (Topic 210): Disclosures about Offsetting Assets and Liabilities*, to enhance comparability of financial statements prepared in accordance with GAAP and IFRS. The amendments in this update will enhance disclosures by requiring improved information about financial instruments and derivative instruments that are either (*a*) offset in accordance with either FASB ASC 210-20-45 or 815-10-45 or (*b*) subject to an enforceable master netting arrangement or similar agreement, irrespective of whether they are offset in accordance with either of the aforementioned FASB ASC sections. The additional disclosures will enable financial statement users to better understand the effect of such arrangements on their financial position. Entities are required to apply the amendments in this Update for annual reporting periods beginning on or after January 1, 2013, and interim periods within those annual periods. Given the effective date of this Update, no survey entity will have adopted these requirements in its 2012 financial statements.

2.04 FASB ASC sets forth disclosure guidelines regarding capital structure and other balance sheet items. SEC regulations also contain additional requirements for disclosures that registrants should provide outside the financial statements.

2.05 FASB ASC 205-10-50 states that reclassifications or other changes in the manner of, or basis for, presenting corresponding items for two or more periods should be explained. This conforms with the well-recognized principle that any change that affects comparability of financial statements should be disclosed.

2.06 ENERGIZER HOLDINGS, INC. (SEP)
NOTES TO CONSOLIDATED FINANCIAL STATEMENTS

(Dollars in millions, except per share and percentage data)

(16) Supplemental Financial Statement Information

The components of certain balance sheet accounts at September 30 for the years indicated are as follows:

	2012	2011
Inventories		
Raw materials and supplies	$ 100.7	$ 95.5
Work in process	141.2	139.9
Finished products	430.5	418.0
Total inventories	$ 672.4	$ 653.4
Other Current Assets		
Miscellaneous receivables	$ 81.5	$ 58.6
Deferred income tax benefits	207.0	189.2
Prepaid expenses	90.0	84.3
Value added tax collectible from customers	53.5	51.9
Other	23.0	42.3
Total other current assets	$ 455.0	$ 426.3
Property, Plant and Equipment		
Land	$ 39.0	$ 39.4
Buildings	278.2	297.4
Machinery and equipment	1,775.7	1,719.8
Construction in progress	75.6	71.7
Total gross property	2,168.5	2,128.3
Accumulated depreciation	(1,320.0)	(1,242.9)
Total property, plant and equipment, net	$ 848.5	$ 885.4
Other Current Liabilities		
Accrued advertising, sales promotion and allowances	$ 70.1	$ 96.2
Accrued trade allowances	101.4	87.9
Accrued salaries, vacations and incentive compensation	115.9	110.4
Income taxes payable	25.2	—
Returns reserve	52.8	48.5
Other	223.0	232.8
Total other current liabilities	$ 588.4	$ 575.8
Other Liabilities		
Pensions and other retirement benefits	$ 506.0	$ 497.2
Deferred compensation	166.3	151.7
Deferred income tax liabilities	455.0	453.8
Other non-current liabilities	88.3	93.6
Total other liabilities	$ 1,215.6	$ 1,196.3

Allowance for Doubtful Accounts	2012	2011	2010
Balance at beginning of year	$ 15.9	$ 13.2	$ 11.3
Impact of acquisition	—	0.8	—
Provision charged to expense, net of reversals	2.2	4.6	4.6
Write-offs, less recoveries, translation, other	(2.2)	(2.7)	(2.7)
Balance at end of year	$ 15.9	$ 15.9	$ 13.2

Income Tax Valuation Allowance	2012	2011	2010
Balance at beginning of year	$ 12.6	$ 11.0	$ 10.3
Provision charged to expense	—	11.4	2.7
Reversal of provision charged to expense	(0.8)	(4.6)	(1.3)
Write-offs, translation, other	0.1	(5.2)	(0.7)
Balance at end of year	$ 11.9	$ 12.6	$ 11.0

Supplemental Disclosure of Cash Flow Information	2012	2011	2010
Interest paid, including cost of early debt retirement	$117.5	$141.8	$122.1
Income taxes paid	$113.0	$206.4	$131.5

The Company has made two reclassifications for financial reporting purposes that impact the September 30, 2011, balance sheet only. They are as follows:

- In many of the Company's foreign affiliates, a value-added tax (VAT) is included on the invoice to the customer. The VAT is not included as part of the Company's revenue because the Company is simply collecting required taxes related to the sale of its goods to a third party and passing that tax collection to the proper tax authorities. Historically, the Company has reported this VAT component as part of trade receivables. We have reclassified this outstanding VAT amount from trade receivables to other current assets. The amount of the reclassification at September 30, 2011 is $51.9.
- The Company engages in a variety of trade promotional activities with its customers to promote its brands. The cost of these programs have historically been accounted for as a reduction of net sales in accordance with GAAP, with an offsetting establishment of an accrued liability. A large portion of these liabilities are paid via a customer deduction from amounts owed to the Company for invoiced sales as the customer exercises a right of offset against trade receivables to recoup payment for trade promotion allowances. While practice may vary depending on the type and nature of the trade promotional activities, we believe reduction of trade receivables to reflect this estimated right of offset is common in the industry and appropriate to reflect on the reported balance sheet. The amount reclassified to reflect this presentation change was $131.9 at September 30, 2011.

Cash and Cash Equivalents

PRESENTATION

2.07 Cash is commonly considered to consist of currency and demand deposits. The FASB ASC glossary defines *cash equivalents* as short-term, highly liquid investments that are both readily convertible into known amounts of cash and so near their maturity that they present an insignificant risk of changes in value because of changes in interest rates. Generally, only investments with original maturities of three months or less qualify under that definition.

DISCLOSURE

2.08 Rule 5-02.1 of Regulation S-X states that separate disclosure should be made of the cash and cash items that are restricted regarding withdrawal or usage. The provisions of any restrictions should be described in a note to the financial statements. Restrictions may include legally restricted deposits held as compensating balances against short-term borrowing arrangements, contracts entered into with others, or company statements of intention with regard to particular deposits; however, time deposits and short-term certificates of deposit are not generally included in legally restricted deposits. Compensating balance arrangements that do not legally restrict the use of cash should be described in the notes to the financial statements; the amount involved, if determinable, for the most recent audited balance sheet and any subsequent unaudited balance sheet should be disclosed. Compensating balances maintained under an agreement to assure future credit availability should be disclosed, along with the amount and terms of such agreement.

Marketable Securities

RECOGNITION AND MEASUREMENT

2.09 FASB ASC 320, *Investments—Debt and Equity Securities*, provides guidance on accounting for and reporting investments in equity securities that have readily determinable fair values and all investments in debt securities.

2.10 FASB ASC 320-10-25-1 requires that at acquisition, entities classify certain debt and equity securities into one of three categories: held to maturity, trading, or available for sale. Investments in debt securities that the entity has the positive intent and ability to hold to maturity are classified as held to maturity and reported at amortized cost in the statement of financial position. Securities that are bought and held principally for the purpose of selling them in the near term (thus held for only a short period of time) are classified as trading securities and reported at fair value. Trading generally reflects active and frequent buying and selling, and trading securities are generally used to generate profit on short-term differences in price. Investments not classified as either held-to-maturity or trading securities are classified as available-for-sale securities and reported at fair value. FASB ASC 320-10-35-1 explains that unrealized holding gains and losses are included in earnings for trading securities and other comprehensive income for available-for-sale securities.

2.11 FASB ASC 320 indicates when certain investments are considered impaired, whether that impairment is other than temporary, and the measurement and recognition of an impairment loss. FASB ASC 320 also provides guidance on accounting considerations for debt securities subsequent to the recognition of an other-than-temporary impairment and requires certain disclosures about unrealized losses that have not been recognized as other-than-temporary impairments.

PRESENTATION

2.12 Under FASB ASC 320-10-45-2, an entity that presents a classified balance sheet should report individual held-to-maturity securities, individual available-for-sale securities, and individual trading securities as either current or noncurrent.

DISCLOSURE

2.13 FASB ASC 320-10-50 includes detailed disclosure requirements for various marketable securities, including matters such as the nature and risks of the securities; cost, fair value, and transaction information; contractual maturities; impairment of securities; and certain transaction information.

2.14 By definition, investments in debt and equity securities are financial instruments. FASB ASC 825, *Financial Instruments*, requires disclosure of the fair value of those investments for which it is practicable to estimate that value, the methods and assumptions used in estimating the fair value of marketable securities, and a description of any changes in the methods and assumptions during the period. Under FASB ASC 825-10-50-3, the fair value disclosures are optional for certain nonpublic entities with assets less than $100 million.

2.15 FASB ASC 820, *Fair Value Measurement*, defines *fair value*, sets out a framework for measuring fair value, and requires certain disclosures about fair value measurements. FASB ASC 820 clarifies the definition of fair value as an exit price (that is, a price that would be received to sell, versus acquire, an asset or paid to transfer a liability). FASB ASC 820 emphasizes that fair value is a market-based measurement. It establishes a fair value hierarchy that distinguishes between assumptions developed based on market data obtained from independent external sources and the reporting entity's own assumptions. Further, FASB ASC 820 specifies that fair value measurement should consider adjustment for risk, such as the risk inherent in a valuation technique or its inputs. For assets measured at fair value, whether on a recurring or nonrecurring basis, FASB ASC 820 specifies the required disclosures concerning the inputs used to measure fair value.

2.16 FASB ASC 820-10-50 requires robust disclosures about different classes of assets and liabilities measured at fair value; the valuation techniques and inputs used; the activity in level 3 fair value measurements; and the transfers between levels 1, 2, and 3. "Pending Content" in FASB ASC 820-10-50-1 states that the reporting entity should disclose information that helps users of its financial statements assess both of the following:
- **a.** For assets and liabilities that are measured at fair value on a recurring or nonrecurring basis in the statement of financial position after initial recognition, the valuation techniques and inputs used to develop those measurements
- **b.** For recurring fair value measurements using significant unobservable inputs (Level 3), the effect of the measurements on earnings (or changes in net assets) or other comprehensive income for the period.

2.17 "Pending Content" in FASB ASC 820-10-5-2 states that the reporting entity should disclose all of the following information for each interim and annual period separately for each class of assets and liabilities:
- **a.** the fair value measurement at the reporting date
- **b.** the level within the fair value hierarchy in which the fair value measurement in its entirety falls (quoted prices in active markets for identical assets or liabilities—Level 1, significant other observable inputs—Level 2; significant unobservable inputs—Level 3)
- **c.** the amounts of significant transfers between Level 1 and Level 2 and the reasons for the transfers
- **d.** for Level 3 measurements, a reconciliation of beginning and ending balances showing gains and losses for the period, purchases, sales, issuances, and settlements, and transfers in and/or out of Level 3 and reasons for those transfers.
- **e.** the amount of total gains or losses for the period that are attributable to the change in unrealized gains or losses relating to those assets and liabilities still held at the reporting date and a description of where those unrealized gains or losses are reported in the statement of income (or activities).
- **f.** for Level 2 and Level 3 measurements, a description of the valuation technique and the inputs used in determining the fair values of each class of assets or liabilities.

2.18 FASB ASC 825 permits entities to choose to measure many financial instruments and certain other items at fair value that are not currently required to be measured at fair value. Further, under FASB ASC 825, a business entity shall report unrealized gains and losses on eligible items for which the fair value option has been elected in earnings at each subsequent reporting date. The irrevocable election of the fair value option is made on an instrument-by-instrument basis and applied to the entire instrument, not just a portion of it. FASB ASC 825 also establishes presentation and disclosure requirements designed to facilitate comparison between entities that choose different measurement attributes for similar types of assets and liabilities. The required disclosures are optional for certain nonpublic entities.

PRESENTATION AND DISCLOSURE EXCERPTS

MARKETABLE SECURITIES—AVAILABLE-FOR-SALE SECURITIES

2.19 CITIGROUP INC. (DEC)

CONSOLIDATED BALANCE SHEET (in part)

	Citigroup Inc. and Subsidiaries	
	December 31,	
(In millions of dollars)	2012	2011
Assets		
Cash and due from banks (including segregated cash and other deposits)	$ 36,453	$ 28,701
Deposits with banks	102,134	155,784
Federal funds sold and securities borrowed or purchased under agreements to resell (including $160,589 and $142,862 as of December 31, 2012 and December 31, 2011, respectively, at fair value)	261,311	275,849
Brokerage receivables	22,490	27,777
Trading account assets (including $105,458 and $119,054 pledged to creditors at December 31, 2012 and December 31, 2011, respectively)	320,929	291,734
Investments (including $21,423 and $14,940 pledged to creditors at December 31, 2012 and December 31, 2011, respectively, and $294,463 and $274,040 as of December 31, 2012 and December 31, 2011, respectively, at fair value)	312,326	293,413
Loans, net of unearned income		
Consumer (including $1,231 and $1,326 as of December 31, 2012 and December 31, 2011, respectively, at fair value)	408,671	423,340
Corporate (including $4,056 and $3,939 as of December 31, 2012 and December 31, 2011, respectively, at fair value)	246,793	223,902
Loans, net of unearned income	$ 655,464	$ 647,242
Allowance for loan losses	(25,455)	(30,115)
Total loans, net	$ 630,009	$ 617,127
Goodwill	25,673	25,413
Intangible assets (other than MSRs)	5,697	6,600
Mortgage servicing rights (MSRs)	1,942	2,569
Other assets (including $13,299 and $13,360 as of December 31, 2012 and December 31, 2011, respectively, at fair value)	145,660	148,911
Assets of discontinued operations held for sale	36	—
Total assets	$1,864,660	$1,873,878

NOTES TO CONSOLIDATED FINANCIAL STATEMENTS

1. Summary of Significant Accounting Policies (in part)

Investment Securities (in part)

Investments include fixed income and equity securities. Fixed income instruments include bonds, notes and redeemable preferred stocks, as well as certain loan-backed and structured securities that are subject to prepayment risk. Equity securities include common and nonredeemable preferred stock.

Investment securities are classified and accounted for as follows:

- Fixed income securities and marketable equity securities classified as "available-for-sale" are carried at fair value with changes in fair value reported in Accumulated other comprehensive income (loss), a component of Stockholders' equity, net of applicable income taxes and hedges. As described in more detail in Note 15 to the Consolidated Financial Statements, declines in fair value that are determined to be other-than-temporary are recorded in earnings immediately. Realized gains and losses on sales are included in income primarily on a specific identification cost basis. Interest and dividend income on such securities is included in Interest revenue.

15. Investments (in part)

Overview

(In millions of dollars)	2012	2011
Securities available-for-sale	$288,695	$265,204
Debt securities held-to-maturity[1]	10,130	11,483
Non-marketable equity securities carried at fair value[2]	5,768	8,836
Non-marketable equity securities carried at cost[3]	7,733	7,890
Total investments	$312,326	$293,413

[1] Recorded at amortized cost less impairment for securities that have credit-related impairment.

[2] Unrealized gains and losses for non-marketable equity securities carried at fair value are recognized in earnings. During the third quarter of 2012, the Company sold EMI Music resulting in a total $1.5 billion decrease in non-marketable equity securities carried at fair value. During the second quarter of 2012, the Company sold EMI Music Publishing resulting in a total of $1.3 billion decrease in non-marketable equity securities carried at fair value.

[3] Non-marketable equity securities carried at cost primarily consist of shares issued by the Federal Reserve Bank, Federal Home Loan Banks, foreign central banks and various clearing houses of which Citigroup is a member.

Securities Available-for-Sale

The amortized cost and fair value of securities available-for-sale (AFS) at December 31, 2012 and 2011 were as follows:

(In millions of dollars)	2012 Amortized Cost	2012 Gross Unrealized Gains	2012 Gross Unrealized Losses	2012 Fair Value	2011 Amortized Cost	2011 Gross Unrealized Gains	2011 Gross Unrealized Losses	2011 Fair Value
Debt Securities AFS								
Mortgage-backed securities[1]								
U.S. government-sponsored agency guaranteed	$ 46,001	$1,507	$ 163	$ 47,345	$ 44,394	$1,438	$ 51	$ 45,781
Prime	85	1	—	86	118	1	6	113
Alt-A	1	—	—	1	1	—	—	1
Non-U.S. residential	7,442	148	—	7,590	4,671	9	22	4,658
Commercial	436	16	3	449	465	16	9	472
Total mortgage-backed securities	$ 53,965	$1,672	$ 166	$ 55,471	$ 49,649	$1,464	$ 88	$ 51,025
U.S. Treasury and federal agency securities								
U.S. Treasury	$ 64,456	$1,172	$ 34	$ 65,594	$ 48,790	$1,439	$ —	$ 50,229
Agency obligations	25,844	404	1	26,247	34,310	601	2	34,909
Total U.S. Treasury and federal agency securities	$ 90,300	$1,576	$ 35	$ 91,841	$ 83,100	$2,040	$ 2	$ 85,138
State and municipal[2]	$ 20,020	$ 132	$1,820	$ 18,332	$ 16,819	$ 134	$2,554	$ 14,399
Foreign government	93,259	918	130	94,047	84,360	558	404	84,514
Corporate	9,302	398	26	9,674	10,005	305	53	10,257
Asset-backed securities[1]	14,188	85	143	14,130	11,053	31	81	11,003
Other debt securities	256	2	—	258	670	13	—	683
Total debt securities AFS	$281,290	$4,783	$2,320	$283,753	$255,656	$4,545	$3,182	$257,019
Marketable equity securities AFS	$ 4,643	$ 444	$ 145	$ 4,942	$ 6,722	$1,658	$ 195	$ 8,185
Total securities AFS	$285,933	$5,227	$2,465	$288,695	$262,378	$6,203	$3,377	$265,204

[1] The Company invests in mortgage-backed and asset-backed securities. These securitizations are generally considered VIEs. The Company's maximum exposure to loss from these VIEs is equal to the carrying amount of the securities, which is reflected in the table above. For mortgage-backed and asset-backed securitizations in which the Company has other involvement, see Note 22 to the Consolidated Financial Statements.

[2] The unrealized losses on state and municipal debt securities are primarily attributable to the result of yields on taxable fixed income instruments decreasing relatively faster than the general tax-exempt municipal yields and the effects of fair value hedge accounting.

At December 31, 2012, the amortized cost of approximately 3,500 investments in equity and fixed-income securities exceeded their fair value by $2.465 billion. Of the $2.465 billion, the gross unrealized loss on equity securities was $145 million. Of the remainder, $238 million represents fixed-income investments that have been in a gross-unrealized-loss position for less than a year and, of these, 98% are rated investment grade; $2.082 billion represents fixed-income investments that have been in a gross-unrealized-loss position for a year or more and, of these, 92% are rated investment grade.

The AFS mortgage-backed securities portfolio fair value balance of $55.471 billion consists of $47.345 billion of government-sponsored agency securities, and $8.126 billion of privately sponsored securities, of which the majority are backed by mortgages that are not Alt-A or subprime.

As discussed in more detail below, the Company conducts and documents periodic reviews of all securities with unrealized losses to evaluate whether the impairment is other than temporary. Any credit-related impairment related to debt securities that the Company does not plan to sell and is not likely to be required to sell is recognized in the Consolidated Statement of Income, with the non-credit-related impairment recognized in accumulated other comprehensive income (AOCI). For other impaired debt securities, the entire impairment is recognized in the Consolidated Statement of Income.

The table below shows the fair value of AFS securities that have been in an unrealized loss position for less than 12 months or for 12 months or longer as of December 31, 2012 and 2011:

(In millions of dollars)	Less Than 12 Months Fair Value	Less Than 12 Months Gross Unrealized Losses	12 Months or Longer Fair Value	12 Months or Longer Gross Unrealized Losses	Total Fair Value	Total Gross Unrealized Losses
December 31, 2012						
Securities AFS						
Mortgage-backed securities						
U.S. government-sponsored agency guaranteed	$ 8,759	$138	$464	$ 25	$ 9,223	$163
Prime	15	—	5	—	20	—
Non-U.S. residential	5	—	7	—	12	—
Commercial	29	—	24	3	53	3
Total mortgage-backed securities	$ 8,808	$138	$500	$ 28	$ 9,308	$166
U.S. Treasury and federal agency securities						
U.S. Treasury	$10,558	$ 34	$—	$—	$10,558	$ 34
Agency obligations	496	1	—	—	496	1
Total U.S. Treasury and federal agency securities	$11,054	$ 35	$—	$—	$11,054	$ 35

(continued)

(In millions of dollars)	Less Than 12 Months		12 Months or Longer		Total	
	Fair Value	Gross Unrealized Losses	Fair Value	Gross Unrealized Losses	Fair Value	Gross Unrealized Losses
State and municipal	$ 10	$ —	$11,095	$1,820	$11,105	$1,820
Foreign government	22,806	54	3,910	76	26,716	130
Corporate	1,420	8	225	18	1,645	26
Asset-backed securities	1,942	4	2,888	139	4,830	143
Marketable equity securities AFS	15	1	764	144	779	145
Total securities AFS	$46,055	$240	$19,382	$2,225	$65,437	$2,465
December 31, 2011						
Securities AFS						
Mortgage-backed securities						
U.S. government-sponsored agency guaranteed	$ 5,398	$ 32	$ 51	$ 19	$ 5,449	$ 51
Prime	27	1	40	5	67	6
Non-U.S. residential	3,418	22	57	—	3,475	22
Commercial	35	1	31	8	66	9
Total mortgage-backed securities	$ 8,878	$ 56	$ 179	$ 32	$ 9,057	$ 88
U.S. Treasury and federal agency securities						
U.S. Treasury	$ 553	$ —	$ —	$ —	$ 553	$ —
Agency obligations	2,970	2	—	—	2,970	2
Total U.S. Treasury and federal agency securities	$ 3,523	$ 2	$ —	$ —	$ 3,523	$ 2
State and municipal	$ 59	$ 2	$11,591	$2,552	$11,650	$2,554
Foreign government	33,109	211	11,205	193	44,314	404
Corporate	2,104	24	203	29	2,307	53
Asset-backed securities	4,625	68	466	13	5,091	81
Other debt securities	164	—	—	—	164	—
Marketable equity securities AFS	47	5	1,457	190	1,504	195
Total securities AFS	$52,509	$368	$25,101	$3,009	$77,610	$3,377

The following table presents the amortized cost and fair value of AFS debt securities by contractual maturity dates as of December 31, 2012 and 2011:

(In millions of dollars)	2012		2011	
	Amortized Cost	Fair Value	Amortized Cost	Fair Value
Mortgage-backed securities[1]				
Due within 1 year	$ 10	$ 10	$ —	$ —
After 1 but within 5 years	365	374	422	423
After 5 but within 10 years	1,992	2,124	2,757	2,834
After 10 years[2]	51,598	52,963	46,470	47,768
Total	$ 53,965	$ 55,471	$ 49,649	$ 51,025
U.S. Treasury and federal agency securities				
Due within 1 year	$ 9,492	$ 9,499	$ 14,615	$ 14,637
After 1 but within 5 years	75,967	77,267	62,241	63,823
After 5 but within 10 years	2,171	2,408	5,862	6,239
After 10 years[2]	2,670	2,667	382	439
Total	$ 90,300	$ 91,841	$ 83,100	$ 85,138
State and municipal				
Due within 1 year	$ 208	$ 208	$ 142	$ 142
After 1 but within 5 years	3,221	3,223	455	457
After 5 but within 10 years	155	165	182	188
After 10 years[2]	16,436	14,736	16,040	13,612
Total	$ 20,020	$ 18,332	$ 16,819	$ 14,399
Foreign government				
Due within 1 year	$ 34,873	$ 34,869	$ 34,924	$ 34,864
After 1 but within 5 years	49,548	49,933	41,612	41,675
After 5 but within 10 years	7,239	7,380	6,993	6,998
After 10 years[2]	1,599	1,865	831	977
Total	$ 93,259	$ 94,047	$ 84,360	$ 84,514
All other[3]				
Due within 1 year	$ 1,001	$ 1,009	$ 4,055	$ 4,072
After 1 but within 5 years	11,285	11,351	9,843	9,928
After 5 but within 10 years	4,330	4,505	3,009	3,160
After 10 years[2]	7,130	7,197	4,821	4,783
Total	$ 23,746	$ 24,062	$ 21,728	$ 21,943
Total debt securities AFS	$281,290	$283,753	$255,656	$257,019

[1] Includes mortgage-backed securities of U.S. government-sponsored entities.

[2] Investments with no stated maturities are included as contractual maturities of greater than 10 years. Actual maturities may differ due to call or prepayment rights.

[3] Includes corporate, asset-backed and other debt securities.

The following table presents interest and dividends on investments:

(In millions of dollars)	2012	2011	2010
Taxable interest	$6,509	$7,257	$ 9,922
Interest exempt from U.S. federal income tax	683	746	760
Dividends	333	317	322
Total interest and dividends	$7,525	$8,320	$11,004

The following table presents realized gains and losses on all investments. The gross realized investment losses exclude losses from other-than-temporary impairment:

(In millions of dollars)	2012	2011	2010
Gross realized investment gains	$3,663	$2,498	$2,873
Gross realized investment losses	(412)	(501)	(462)
Net realized gains	$3,251	$1,997	$2,411

During 2012, 2011 and 2010, the Company sold various debt securities that were classified as held-to-maturity. These sales were in response to a significant deterioration in the creditworthiness of the issuers or securities. In addition, during 2012 certain securities were reclassified to AFS investments in response to significant credit deterioration. The Company intended to sell the securities at the time of reclassification to AFS investments and recorded other-than-temporary impairment reflected in the following table. The securities sold during 2012, 2011 and 2010 had carrying values of $2,110 million, $1,612 million and $413 million respectively, and the Company recorded realized losses of $187 million, $299 million and $49 million, respectively. The securities reclassified to AFS investments during 2012 totaled $244 million and the Company recorded other-than-temporary impairment of $59 million.

MARKETABLE SECURITIES—HELD-TO-MATURITY SECURITIES

2.20 UNITEDHEALTH GROUP INCORPORATED (DEC)

CONSOLIDATED BALANCE SHEETS (in part)

(In millions, except per share data)	December 31, 2012	December 31, 2011
Assets		
Current assets:		
Cash and cash equivalents	$ 8,406	$ 9,429
Short-term investments	3,031	2,577
Accounts receivable, net of allowances of $189 and $196	2,709	2,294
Other current receivables, net of allowances of $206 and $72	2,889	2,255
Assets under management	2,773	2,708
Deferred income taxes	463	472
Prepaid expenses and other current assets	781	615
Total current assets	21,052	20,350
Long-term investments	17,711	16,166
Property, equipment and capitalized software, net of accumulated depreciation and amortization of $2,564 and $2,440	3,939	2,515
Goodwill	31,286	23,975
Other intangible assets, net of accumulated amortization of $1,824 and $1,451	4,682	2,795
Other assets	2,215	2,088
Total assets	$80,885	$67,889

NOTES TO THE CONSOLIDATED FINANCIAL STATEMENTS

2. Basis of Presentation, Use of Estimates and Significant Accounting Policies (in part)

Cash, Cash Equivalents and Investments (in part)

Investments with maturities of less than one year are classified as short-term. Because of regulatory requirements, certain investments are included in long-term investments regardless of their maturity date. The Company classifies these investments as held-to-maturity and reports them at amortized cost. Substantially all other investments are classified as available-for-sale and reported at fair value based on quoted market prices, where available.

3. Investments (in part)

A summary of short-term and long-term investments by major security type is as follows:

(In millions)	Amortized Cost	Gross Unrealized Gains	Gross Unrealized Losses	Fair Value
December 31, 2012				
Debt securities—available-for-sale:				
U.S. government and agency obligations	$ 2,501	$ 38	$ (1)	$ 2,538
State and municipal obligations	6,282	388	(3)	6,667
Corporate obligations	6,930	283	(4)	7,209
U.S. agency mortgage-backed securities	2,168	70	—	2,238
Non-U.S. agency mortgage-backed securities	538	36	—	574
Total debt securities—available-for-sale	18,419	815	(8)	19,226
Equity securities—available-for-sale	668	10	(1)	677
Debt securities—held-to-maturity:				
U.S. government and agency obligations	168	6	—	174
State and municipal obligations	30	—	—	30
Corporate obligations	641	2	—	643
Total debt securities—held-to-maturity	839	8	—	847
Total investments	$19,926	$833	$ (9)	$20,750
December 31, 2011				
Debt securities—available-for-sale:				
U.S. government and agency obligations	$ 2,319	$ 54	$—	$ 2,373
State and municipal obligations	6,363	403	(1)	6,765
Corporate obligations	5,825	205	(23)	6,007
U.S. agency mortgage-backed securities	2,279	74	—	2,353
Non-U.S. agency mortgage-backed securities	476	28	—	504
Total debt securities—available-for-sale	17,262	764	(24)	18,002
Equity securities—available-for-sale	529	23	(8)	544
Debt securities—held-to-maturity:				
U.S. government and agency obligations	166	7	—	173
State and municipal obligations	13	—	—	13
Corporate obligations	18	—	—	18
Total debt securities—held-to-maturity	197	7	—	204
Total investments	$17,988	$794	$(32)	$18,750

The amortized cost and fair value of held-to-maturity debt securities as of December 31, 2012, by contractual maturity, were as follows:

(In millions)	Amortized Cost	Fair Value
Due in one year or less	$435	$436
Due after one year through five years	126	129
Due after five years through ten years	177	180
Due after ten years	101	102
Total debt securities—held-to-maturity	$839	$847

4. Fair Value (in part)

The following table presents a summary of fair value measurements by level and carrying values for certain financial instruments not measured at fair value on a recurring basis in the Consolidated Balance Sheets:

(In millions)	Quoted Prices in Active Markets (Level 1)	Other Observable Inputs (Level 2)	Unobservable Inputs (Level 3)	Total Fair Value	Total Carrying Value
December 31, 2012					
Debt securities—held-to-maturity:					
U.S. government and agency obligations	$174	$ —	$—	$ 174	$ 168
State and municipal obligations	—	1	29	30	30
Corporate obligations	10	346	287	643	641
Total debt securities—held-to-maturity	$184	$ 347	$316	$ 847	$ 839
Long-term debt	$ —	$17,034	$ —	$17,034	$15,167
December 31, 2011					
Debt securities—held-to-maturity:					
U.S. government and agency obligations	$173	$ —	$—	$ 173	$ 166
State and municipal obligations	—	1	12	13	13
Corporate obligations	9	9	—	18	18
Total debt securities—held-to-maturity	$182	$ 10	$ 12	$ 204	$ 197
Long-term debt	$ —	$13,149	$ —	$13,149	$11,638

2.21 THE PNC FINANCIAL SERVICES GROUP, INC. (DEC)

CONSOLIDATED BALANCE SHEET (in part)

(In millions, except par value)	December 31, 2012	December 31, 2011
Assets		
Cash and due from banks (includes $4 and $7 for VIEs)[a]	$ 5,220	$ 4,105
Federal funds sold and resale agreements (includes $256 and $732 measured at fair value)[b]	1,463	2,205
Trading securities	2,096	2,513
Interest-earning deposits with banks (includes $6 and $325 for VIEs)[a]	3,984	1,169
Loans held for sale (includes $2,868 and $2,258 measured at fair value)[b]	3,693	2,936
Investment securities (includes $9 and $109 for VIEs)[a]	61,406	60,634
Loans (includes $7,781 and $6,096 for VIEs) (includes $244 and $104 measured at fair value)[a][b]	185,856	159,014
Allowance for loan and lease losses (includes $(75) and $(91) for VIEs)[a]	(4,036)	(4,347)
Net loans	181,820	154,667
Goodwill	9,072	8,285
Other intangible assets	1,797	1,859
Equity investments (includes $1,429 and $1,643 for VIEs) (a)	10,877	10,134
Other (includes $1,281 and $1,205 for VIEs) (includes $319 and $210 measured at fair value)[a][b]	23,679	22,698
Total assets	$305,107	$271,205

NOTES TO CONSOLIDATED FINANCIAL STATEMENTS

Note 1 Accounting Policies (in part)

Debt Securities (in part)

Debt securities are recorded on a trade-date basis. We classify debt securities as held to maturity and carry them at amortized cost if we have the positive intent and ability to hold the securities to maturity. Debt securities that we purchase for short-term appreciation, trading purposes or those with non-bifurcated embedded derivatives are carried at fair value and classified as Trading securities on our Consolidated Balance Sheet. Realized and unrealized gains and losses on trading securities are included in Other noninterest income.

Equity Securities and Partnership Interests (in part)

We account for equity securities and equity investments other than BlackRock and private equity investments under one of the following methods:
- Marketable equity securities are recorded on a trade-date basis and are accounted for based on the securities' quoted market prices from a national securities exchange. Those purchased with the intention of recognizing short-term profits are classified as trading and included in trading securities on our Consolidated Balance Sheet. Both realized and unrealized gains and losses on trading securities are included in Noninterest income. Marketable equity securities not classified as trading are designated as securities available for sale with unrealized gains and losses, net of income taxes, reflected in Accumulated other comprehensive income (loss). Any unrealized losses that we have determined to be other-than-temporary on securities classified as available for sale are recognized in current period earnings.

Note 9 Fair Value (in part)

Financial Instruments Accounted for at Fair Value on a Recurring Basis (in part)

Securities Available for Sale and Trading Securities

Securities accounted for at fair value include both the available for sale and trading portfolios. We primarily use prices obtained from pricing services, dealer quotes, or recent trades to determine the fair value of securities. As of December 31, 2012, 84% of the positions in these portfolios were priced by using pricing services provided by third-party vendors. The third-party vendors use a variety of methods when pricing securities that incorporate relevant market data to arrive at an estimate of what a buyer in the marketplace would pay for a security under current market conditions. One of the vendor's prices are set with reference to market activity for highly liquid assets such as U.S. Treasury and agency securities and agency residential mortgage-backed securities, and matrix pricing for other asset classes, such as commercial mortgage and other asset-backed securities. Another vendor primarily uses discounted cash flow pricing models considering adjustments for spreads and prepayments for the instruments we value using this service, such as non-agency residential mortgage-backed securities, agency adjustable rate mortgage securities, agency collateralized mortgage obligations (CMOs), commercial mortgage-backed securities and municipal bonds. The vendors we use provide pricing services on a global basis and have quality management processes in place to monitor the integrity of the valuation inputs and the prices provided to users, including procedures to consider and incorporate information received from pricing service users who may challenge a price. We monitor and validate the reliability of vendor pricing on an ongoing basis through pricing methodology reviews, by performing detailed reviews of the assumptions and inputs used by the vendor to price individual securities, and through price validation testing. Price validation testing is performed independent of the risk-taking function and involves corroborating the prices received from third-party vendors with prices from another third-party source, by reviewing valuations of comparable instruments, by comparison to internal valuations, or by reference to recent sales of similar securities. Securities not priced by one of our pricing vendors may be valued using a dealer quote. Dealer quotes received are typically non-binding. Securities priced using a dealer quote are subject to corroboration either with another dealer quote, by comparison to similar securities priced by either a third-party vendor or another dealer, or through internal valuation in order to validate that the quote is representative of the market. Security prices are also validated through actual cash settlement upon sale of a security.

A cross-functional team comprised of representatives from Asset & Liability Management, Finance, and Market Risk Management oversees the governance of the processes and methodologies used to estimate the fair value of securities and the price validation testing that is performed. This management team reviews pricing sources and trends and the results of validation testing.

Securities are classified within the fair value hierarchy after giving consideration to the activity level in the market for the security type and the observability of the inputs used to determine the fair value. When a quoted price in an active market exists for the identical security, this price is used to determine fair value and the security is classified within Level 1 of the hierarchy. Level 1 securities include certain U.S. Treasury securities and exchange traded equities. When a quoted price in an active market for the identical security is not available, fair value is estimated using either an alternative market approach, such as a recent trade or matrix pricing, or an income approach, such as a discounted cash flow pricing model. If the inputs to the valuation are based primarily on market observable information, then the security is classified within Level 2 of the hierarchy. Level 2 securities include agency debt securities, agency residential mortgage-backed securities, agency and non-agency commercial mortgage-backed securities, asset-backed securities collateralized by non-mortgage-related consumer loans, municipal securities, and other debt securities. Level 2 securities are predominantly priced by third parties, either a pricing vendor or dealer.

In certain cases where there is limited activity or less transparency around the inputs to the valuation, securities are classified within Level 3 of the hierarchy. Securities classified as Level 3 consist primarily of non-agency residential mortgage-backed and asset-backed securities collateralized by first- and second-lien residential mortgage loans. Fair value for these securities is primarily estimated using pricing obtained from third-party vendors. In some cases, fair value is estimated using a dealer quote, by reference to prices of securities of a similar vintage and collateral type or by reference to recent sales of similar securities. Market activity for these security types is limited with little price transparency. As a result, these securities are generally valued by the third-party vendor using a discounted cash flow approach that incorporates observable market activity where available. Significant inputs to the valuation include prepayment projections and credit loss assumptions (default rate and loss severity) and discount rates that are deemed representative of current market conditions. The discount rates used incorporate a spread over the benchmark curve that takes into consideration liquidity risk and potential credit risk not already included in the credit loss assumptions. Significant increases (decreases) in any of those assumptions in isolation would result in a significantly lower (higher) fair value measurement. Prepayment estimates generally increase when market interest rates decline and decrease when market interest rates rise. Credit loss estimates are driven by the ability of borrowers to pay their loans and housing market prices and are impacted by changes in overall macroeconomic conditions, typically increasing when economic conditions worsen and decreasing when conditions improve. An increase in the estimated prepayment rate typically results in a decrease in estimated credit losses and vice versa. Discount rates typically Increase when market interest rates increase and/or credit and liquidity risks increase and decrease when market interest rates decline and/or credit and liquidity conditions improve. Price validation procedures are performed and the results are reviewed for these Level 3 securities by a cross-functional Asset & Liability Management, Finance, and Market Risk Management team. Specific price validation procedures performed for these securities include comparing current prices to historical pricing trends by collateral type and vintage, comparing prices by product type to indicative pricing grids published by market makers, and by obtaining corroborating prices from another third-party source.

Certain infrequently traded debt securities within the State and municipal and Other debt securities available-for-sale and Trading securities categories are also classified in Level 3. The significant unobservable inputs used to estimate the fair value of these securities include an estimate of expected credit losses and a discount for liquidity risk. These inputs are incorporated into the fair value measurement by either increasing the spread over the benchmark curve or by applying a credit and liquidity discount to the par value of the security. Significant increases (decreases) in credit and/or liquidity risk could result in a significantly lower (higher) fair value estimate.

Table 93: Fair Value Measurements—Summary

(In millions)	December 31, 2012 Level 1	Level 2	Level 3	Total Fair Value	December 31, 2011 Level 1	Level 2	Level 3	Total Fair Value
Assets								
Securities available for sale								
US Treasury and government agencies	$2,269	$ 844		$ 3,113	$1,659	$ 2,058		$ 3,717
Residential mortgage-backed								
Agency		26,784		26,784		26,792		26,792
Non-agency			$ 6,107	6,107			$ 5,557	5,557
Commercial mortgage-backed								
Agency		633		633		1,140		1,140
Non-agency		3,264		3,264		2,756		2,756
Asset-backed		4,945	708	5,653		2,882	787	3,669
State and municipal		1,948	339	2,287		1,471	336	1,807
Other debt		2,796	48	2,844		2,713	49	2,762
Total debt securities	2,269	41,214	7,202	50,685	1,659	39,812	6,729	48,200
Corporate stocks and other	351	16		367	368			368
Total securities available for sale	2,620	41,230	7,202	51,052	2,027	39,812	6,729	48,568
Financial derivatives[(a)][(b)]								
Interest rate contracts	5	8,326	101	8,432		9,150	60	9,210
Other contracts		131	5	136		246	7	253
Total financial derivatives	5	8,457	106	8,568		9,396	67	9,463
Residential mortgage loans held for sale[(c)]		2,069	27	2,096		1,415		1,415
Trading securities[(d)]								
Debt[(e)(f)]	1,062	951	32	2,045	1,058	1,371	39	2,468
Equity	42	9		51	42	3		45
Total trading securities	1,104	960	32	2,096	1,100	1,374	39	2,513
Trading loans		76		76				
Residential mortgage servicing rights[(g)]			650	650			647	647
Commercial mortgage loans held for sale[(c)]			772	772			843	843
Equity investments								
Direct investments			1,171	1,171			856	856
Indirect investments[(h)]			642	642			648	648
Total equity investments			1,813	1,813			1,504	1,504
Customer resale agreements[(i)]		256		256		732		732
Loans[(j)]		110	134	244		99	5	104
Other assets								
BlackRock Series C Preferred Stock[(k)]			243	243			210	210
Other	283	194	9	486	280	140	9	429
Total other assets	283	194	252	729	280	140	219	639
Total assets	$4,012	$53,352	$10,988	$68,352	$3,407	$52,968	$10,053	$66,428
Liabilities								
Financial derivatives[(b)(l)]								
Interest rate contracts	$ 1	$ 6,105	$ 12	$ 6,118		$ 7,065	$ 6	$ 7,071
BlackRock LTIP			243	243			210	210
Other contracts		128	121	249		233	92	325
Total financial derivatives	1	6,233	376	6,610		7,298	308	7,606
Trading securities sold short[(m)]								
Debt	731	10		741	$ 997	19		1,016
Total trading securities sold short	731	10		741	997	19		1,016
Other liabilities		5		5		3		3
Total liabilities	$ 732	$ 6,248	$ 376	$ 7,356	$ 997	$ 7,320	$ 308	$ 8,625

(a) Included in Other assets on our Consolidated Balance Sheet.

(b) Amounts at December 31, 2012 and December 31, 2011 are presented gross and are not reduced by the impact of legally enforceable master netting agreements that allow PNC to net positive and negative positions and cash collateral held or placed with the same counterparty. At December 31, 2012 and December 31, 2011, respectively, the net asset amounts were $2.4 billion and $2.4 billion and the net liability amounts were $.6 billion and $.7 billion.

(c) Included in Loans held for sale on our Consolidated Balance Sheet. PNC has elected the fair value option for certain commercial and residential mortgage loans held for sale.

(d) Fair value includes net unrealized gains of $59 million at December 31, 2012 compared with net unrealized gains of $102 million at December 31, 2011.

(e) Approximately 25% of these securities are residential mortgage-backed securities and 52% are US Treasury and government agencies securities at December 31, 2012. Comparable amounts at December 31, 2011 were 57% and 34%, respectively.

(f) At December 31, 2011, $1.1 billion of residential mortgage-backed agency securities with embedded derivatives were carried in Trading securities. At December 31, 2012, the balance was zero.

(g) Included in Other intangible assets on our Consolidated Balance Sheet.

(h) The indirect equity funds are not redeemable, but PNC receives distributions over the life of the partnership from liquidation of the underlying investments by the investee, which we expect to occur over the next twelve years. The amount of unfunded contractual commitments related to indirect equity investments was $145 million and related to direct equity investments was $37 million as of December 31, 2012, respectively.

(i) Included in Federal funds sold and resale agreements on our Consolidated Balance Sheet. PNC has elected the fair value option for these items.

(j) Included in Loans on our Consolidated Balance Sheet.

(k) PNC has elected the fair value option for these shares.

(l) Included in Other liabilities on our Consolidated Balance Sheet.

(m) Included in Other borrowed funds on our Consolidated Balance Sheet.

Reconciliations of assets and liabilities measured at fair value on a recurring basis using Level 3 inputs for 2012 and 2011 follow.

Table 94: Reconciliation of Level 3 Assets and Liabilities

Year Ended December 31, 2012

Level 3 Instruments Only (In millions)	Fair Value Dec. 31, 2011	Total Realized/ Unrealized Gains or Losses for the Period[a] — Included in Earnings	Included in Other Comprehensive Income	Purchases	Sales	Issuances	Settlements	Transfers into Level 3[b]	Transfers Out of Level 3[b]	Fair Value Dec. 31, 2012	Unrealized Gains (Losses) on Assets and Liabilities Held on Consolidated Balance Sheet at Dec. 31, 2012[c]
Assets											
Securities available for sale											
Residential mortgage-backed non-agency	$ 5,557	$ 76	$1,178	$ 49	$(164)		$(1,047)	$458		$ 6,107	$ (99)
Commercial mortgage-backed non-agency		1					(1)				
Asset-backed	787	(7)	142		(87)		(127)			708	(11)
State and municipal	336		21	6			(4)	20	$(40)	339	
Other debt	49	(1)	1	16	(17)					48	(1)
Total securities available for sale	6,729	69	1,342	71	(268)		(1,179)	478	(40)	7,202	(111)
Financial derivatives	67	433		5			(400)	3	(2)	106	364
Residential mortgage loans held for sale								27		27	
Trading securities—Debt	39	7					(14)			32	3
Residential mortgage servicing rights	647	(138)		191		$117	(167)			650	(123)
Commercial mortgage loans held for sale	843	(5)			(26)		(40)			772	(8)
Equity investments											
Direct investments	856	91		399	(175)					1,171	71
Indirect investments	648	102		63	(171)					642	94
Total equity investments	1,504	193		462	(346)					1,813	165
Loans	5			3			(1)	127		134	
Other assets											
BlackRock Series C Preferred Stock	210	33								243	33
Other	9									9	
Total other assets	219	33								252	33
Total assets	$10,053	$592[e]	$1,342	$732	$(640)	$117	$(1,801)	$635	$(42)	$10,988	$ 323[f]
Total liabilities[d]	$ 308	$134[e]		$ 3			$ (68)	$ 1	$ (2)	$ 376	$ 69[f]

Year Ended December 31, 2011

Level 3 Instruments Only (In millions)	Fair Value Dec. 31, 2010	Total Realized/ Unrealized Gains or Losses for the Period[a] — Included in Earnings	Included in Other Comprehensive Income	Purchases	Sales	Issuances	Settlements	Transfers Out of Level 3[b]	Fair Value Dec. 31, 2011	Unrealized Gains (Losses) on Assets and Liabilities Held on Consolidated Balance Sheet at Dec. 31, 2011[c]
Assets										
Securities available for sale										
Residential mortgage-backed non-agency	$ 7,233	$ (80)	$(157)	$ 45	$(280)		$(1,204)		$ 5,557	$(130)
Asset-backed	1,045	(11)	21	48			(316)		787	(21)
State and municipal	228		10	121			(23)		336	
Other debt	73	(2)	3	3	(3)		1	$(26)	49	(1)
Corporate stocks and other	4						(4)			
Total securities available for sale	8,583	(93)	(123)	217	(283)		(1,546)	(26)	6,729	(152)

(continued)

Level 3 Instruments Only (In millions)	Fair Value Dec. 31, 2010	Total Realized/ Unrealized Gains or Losses for the Period[a]		Purchases	Sales	Issuances	Settlements	Transfers Out of Level 3[b]	Fair Value Dec. 31, 2011	Unrealized Gains (Losses) on Assets and Liabilities Held on Consolidated Balance Sheet at Dec. 31, 2011[c]
		Included in Earnings	Included in Other Comprehensive Income							
Financial derivatives	77	263		5			(278)		67	188
Trading securities—Debt	69	4					(29)	(5)	39	(5)
Residential mortgage servicing rights	1,033	(406)		65		$118	(163)		647	(383)
Commercial mortgage loans held for sale	877	3			(13)		(24)		843	(4)
Equity investments										
Direct investments	749	87		176	(156)				856	58
Indirect investments	635	89		66	(142)				648	91
Total equity investments	1,384	176		242	(298)				1,504	149
Loans	2			4			(1)		5	
Other assets										
BlackRock Series C										
Preferred Stock	396	(14)					(172)		210	(14)
Other	11		1	(2)			(1)		9	
Total other assets	407	(14)		1	(2)		(173)		219	(14)
Total assets	$12,432	$ (67)[e]	$(123)	$534	$(596)	$118	$(2,214)	$(31)	$10,053	$(221)[f]
Total liabilities[d]	$ 460	$ 7[e]			$ 10		$ (169)		$ 308	$ (17)[f]

[a] Losses for assets are bracketed while losses for liabilities are not.

[b] PNC's policy is to recognize transfers in and transfers out as of the end of the reporting period.

[c] The amount of the total gains or losses for the period included in earnings that is attributable to the change in unrealized gains or losses related to those assets and liabilities held at the end of the reporting period.

[d] Financial derivatives, which includes $43 million related to swaps entered into in connection with sales of certain Visa Class B common shares which were included in earnings in 2012.

[e] Net gains (realized and unrealized) included in earnings relating to Level 3 assets and liabilities were $458 million for 2012 compared with net losses (realized and unrealized) of $74 million for 2011. These amounts also included amortization and accretion of $189 million for 2012 compared with $109 million for 2011. The amortization and accretion amounts were included in Interest income on the Consolidated Income Statement, and the remaining net gains/(losses) (realized and unrealized) were included in Noninterest income on the Consolidated Income Statement.

[f] Net unrealized gains relating to those assets and liabilities held at the end of the reporting period were $254 million for 2012, compared with net unrealized losses of $204 million for 2011. These amounts were included in Noninterest income on the Consolidated Income Statement.

An instrument's categorization within the hierarchy is based on the lowest level of input that is significant to the fair value measurement. PNC reviews and updates fair value hierarchy classifications quarterly. Changes from one quarter to the next related to the observability of inputs to a fair value measurement may result in a reclassification (transfer) of assets or liabilities between hierarchy levels. PNC's policy is to recognize transfers in and transfers out as of the end of the reporting period. During 2012, there were transfers of securities available for sale from Level 2 to Level 3 of $478 million consisting of mortgage-backed securities as a result of a ratings downgrade which reduced the observability of valuation inputs and certain state and municipal securities with valuation inputs that were determined to be unobservable. Level 2 to Level 3 transfers also included $127 million and $27 million for loans and residential mortgage loans held for sale, respectively, as a result of reduced market activity in the nonperforming residential mortgage sales market which reduced the observability of valuation inputs. Also during 2012, there was a transfer out of Level 3 securities available for sale of $40 million due to an instrument being reclassified to a loan and no longer being carried at fair value. During 2011, there were no material transfers of assets or liabilities between the hierarchy levels.

Quantitative information about the significant unobservable inputs within Level 3 recurring assets and liabilities follows.

Table 95: Fair Value Measurement—Recurring Quantitative Information

Level 3 Instruments Only (Dollars in millions)	Fair Value Dec. 31, 2012	Valuation Techniques	Unobservable Inputs	Range (Weighted Average)
Residential mortgage-backed non-agency	$ 6,107	Priced by a third-party vendor using a discounted cash flow pricing model[a]	Constant prepayment rate (CPR)	1.0%–30.0% (5.0%)[a]
			Constant default rate (CDR)	0.0%–24.0% (7.0%)[a]
			Loss Severity	10.0%–95.0% (52.0%)[a]
			Spread over the benchmark curve[b]	315bps weighted average[a]
Asset-backed	708	Priced by a third-party vendor using a discounted cash flow pricing model[a]	Constant prepayment rate (CPR)	1.0%–11.0% (3.0%)[a]
			Constant default rate (CDR)	1.0%–25.0% (9.0%)[a]
			Loss Severity	10.0%–100.0% (70.0%)[a]
			Spread over the benchmark curve[b]	511bps weighted average[a]
State and municipal	130	Discounted cash flow	Spread over the benchmark curve[b]	100bps–280bps (119bps)
	209	Consensus pricing[c]	Credit and Liquidity discount	0.0%–30.0% (8.0%)
Other debt	48	Consensus pricing[c]	Credit and Liquidity discount	7.0%–95.0% (86.0%)
Residential mortgage loan commitments	85	Discounted cash flow	Probability of funding	8.5%–99.0% (71.1%)
			Embedded servicing value	.5%–1.2% (.9%)

(continued)

Level 3 Instruments Only (Dollars in millions)	Fair Value Dec. 31, 2012	Valuation Techniques	Unobservable Inputs	Range (Weighted Average)
Trading securities—Debt	32	Consensus pricing[c]	Credit and Liquidity discount	8.0%–20.0% (12.0%)
Residential mortgage loans held for sale	27	Consensus pricing[c]	Cumulative default rate	2.6%–100.0% (76.1%)
			Loss Severity	0.0%–92.7% (55.8%)
			Gross discount rate	14.0%–15.3% (14.9%)
Residential mortgage servicing rights	650	Discounted cash flow	Constant prepayment rate (CPR)	3.9%–57.3% (18.8%)
			Spread over the benchmark curve[b]	939bps–1,929bps (1,115bps)
Commercial mortgage loans held for sale	772	Discounted cash flow	Spread over the benchmark curve[b]	485bps–4,155bps (999bps)
Equity investments—Direct investments	1,171	Multiple of adjusted earnings	Multiple of earnings	4.5–10.0 (7.1)
Equity investments—Indirect[d]	642	Net asset value	Net asset value	
Loans	127	Consensus pricing[c]	Cumulative default rate	2.6%–100.0% (76.3%)
			Loss Severity	0.0%–99.4% (61.1%)
			Gross discount rate	12.0%–12.5% (12.2%)
BlackRock Series C Preferred Stock	243	Consensus pricing[c]	Liquidity discount	22.5%
BlackRock LTIP	(243)	Consensus pricing[c]	Liquidity discount	22.5%
Other derivative contracts	(72)	Discounted cash flow	Credit and Liquidity discount	37.0%–99.0% (46.0%)
			Spread over the benchmark curve[b]	79bps
Swaps related to sales of certain Visa Class B common shares	(43)	Discounted cash flow	Estimated conversion factor of Class B shares into Class A shares	41.5%
			Estimated growth rate of Visa Class A share price	12.6%
Insignificant Level 3 assets, net of liabilities[e]	19			
Total Level 3 assets, net of liabilities[f]	$10,612			

(a) Level 3 residential mortgage-backed non-agency and asset-backed securities with fair values as of December 31, 2012 totaling $5,363 million and $677 million, respectively, were priced by a third-party vendor using a discounted cash flow pricing model, that incorporates consensus pricing, where available. The significant unobservable inputs for these securities were provided by the third-party vendor and are disclosed in the table. Our procedures to validate the prices provided by the third-party vendor related to these securities are discussed further in the Fair Value Measurement section of this Note 9. Certain Level 3 residential mortgage-backed non-agency and asset-backed securities with fair value as of December 31, 2012 of $744 million and $31 million, respectively, were valued using a pricing source, such as a dealer quote or comparable security price, for which the significant unobservable inputs used to determine the price were not reasonably available.

(b) The assumed yield spread over the benchmark curve for each instrument is generally intended to incorporate non-interest-rate risks such as credit and liquidity risks.

(c) Consensus pricing refers to fair value estimates that are generally internally developed using information such as dealer quotes or other third-party provided valuations or comparable asset prices.

(d) The range on these indirect equity investments has not been disclosed since these investments are recorded at their net asset redemption values.

(e) Represents the aggregate amount of Level 3 assets and liabilities measured at fair value on a recurring basis that are individually and in the aggregate insignificant. The amount includes loans and certain financial derivative assets and liabilities and other assets.

(f) Consists of total Level 3 assets of $10,988 million and total Level 3 liabilities of $376 million.

Table 100: Additional Fair Value Information Related to Financial Instruments

(In millions)	December 31, 2012					December 31, 2011	
	Carrying Amount	Fair Value				Carrying Amount	Fair Value
		Total	Level 1	Level 2	Level 3		
Assets							
Cash and due from banks	$ 5,220	$ 5,220	$5,220			$ 4,105	$ 4,105
Short-term assets	6,495	6,495		$ 6,495		4,462	4,462
Trading securities	2,096	2,096	1,104	960	$ 32	2,513	2,513
Investment securities	61,406	61,912	2,897	51,789	7,226	60,634	61,018
Trading loans	76	76		76			
Loans held for sale	3,693	3,697		2,069	1,628	2,936	2,939
Net loans (excludes leases)	174,575	177,215		110	177,105	148,254	151,167
Other assets	4,265	4,265	283	1,917	2,065	4,019	4,019
Mortgage servicing rights	1,070	1,077			1,077	1,115	1,118
Financial derivatives							
Designated as hedging instruments under GAAP	1,872	1,872		1,872		1,888	1,888
Not designated as hedging instruments under GAAP	6,696	6,696	5	6,585	106	7,575	7,575
Total assets	$267,464	$270,621	$9,509	$ 71,873	$189,239	$237,501	$240,804
Liabilities							
Demand, savings and money market deposits	$187,051	$187,051		$187,051		$156,335	$156,335
Time deposits	26,091	26,347		26,347		31,632	31,882
Borrowed funds	40,907	42,329	$ 731	40,505	$ 1,093	36,966	39,064
Financial derivatives							
Designated as hedging instruments under GAAP	152	152		152		116	116
Not designated as hedging instruments under GAAP	6,458	6,458	1	6,081	376	7,490	7,490
Unfunded loan commitments and letters of credit	231	231			231	223	223
Total liabilities	$260,890	$262,568	$ 732	$260,136	$ 1,700	$232,762	$235,110

Current Receivables

PRESENTATION

2.22 FASB ASC 310, *Receivables*, indicates that loans or trade receivables may be presented on the balance sheet as aggregate amounts. However, major categories of loans or trade receivables should be presented separately either in the balance sheet or notes to the financial statements. Also, any such receivables held for sale should be a separate balance sheet category. Receivables from officers, employees, or affiliated companies should be shown separately and not included under a general heading, such as "Accounts Receivable." Valuation allowance for credit losses or doubtful accounts and any unearned income included in the face amount of receivables should be shown as a deduction from the related receivables.

DISCLOSURE

2.23 FASB ASC 310 states that allowances for doubtful accounts should be deducted from the related receivables and appropriately disclosed. FASB ASC 310-10-50-4 requires, as applicable, any unearned income, unamortized premiums and discounts, and net unamortized deferred fees and costs be disclosed in the financial statements. Under FASB ASC 825, fair value disclosure is not required for trade receivables when the carrying amount of the trade receivable approximates its fair value.

PRESENTATION AND DISCLOSURE EXCERPTS

TAX SETTLEMENT

2.24 ANADARKO PETROLEUM CORPORATION (DEC)
CONSOLIDATED BALANCE SHEETS (in part)

	December 31,	
(Millions)	2012	2011
Assets		
Current assets		
Cash and cash equivalents	$2,471	$2,697
Accounts receivable (net of allowance of $7 million and $6 million)		
Customers	1,473	1,269
Others	1,274	1,990
Algeria exceptional profits tax settlement	730	—
Other current assets	847	975
Total	6,795	6,931

NOTES TO CONSOLIDATED FINANCIAL STATEMENTS

17. Contingencies (in part)

Algeria Exceptional Profits Tax Settlement. In 2006, the Algerian parliament approved legislation establishing an exceptional profits tax on foreign companies' Algerian oil production and issued regulations implementing this legislation. The Company disagreed with Sonatrach's collection of the exceptional profits tax and initiated arbitration against Sonatrach in 2009. In March 2012, the Company and Sonatrach resolved this dispute. The resolution provided for delivery to the Company of crude oil valued at approximately $1.7 billion and the elimination of $62 million of the Company's previously recorded and unpaid transportation charges. The crude oil is to be delivered to the Company over a 12-month period that began in June 2012. At December 31, 2012, a receivable of $730 million was included on the Company's Consolidated Balance Sheet and is in the oil and gas exploration and production reporting segment. The Company recognized a $1.8 billion credit in the Costs and Expenses section of the Consolidated Statement of Income for the year ended December 31, 2012, to reflect the effect of this agreement for previously recorded expenses. Additionally, the parties amended the existing Production Sharing Agreement (PSA) to increase the Company's sales volumes and to lower the effective exceptional profits tax rate. The amendment confirmed the length of each exploitation license to be 25 years from the date the license was granted under the PSA with expiration dates ranging from December 2022 to December 2036.

RECEIVABLES FROM RELATED PARTIES

2.25 STEEL DYNAMICS, INC. (DEC)
CONSOLIDATED BALANCE SHEETS (in part)

(In thousands, except share data)

	December 31,	
	2012	2011
Assets		
Current assets		
Cash and equivalents	$ 375,917	$ 390,761
Investments in short-term commercial paper	31,520	84,830
Accounts receivable, net of related allowances of $11,571 and $18,303 as of December 31, 2012 and 2011, respectively	599,499	679,898
Accounts receivable-related parties	42,864	42,893
Inventories	1,202,507	1,199,584
Deferred income taxes	23,449	25,341
Income taxes receivable	893	16,722
Other current assets	19,576	15,229
Total current assets	2,296,225	2,455,258
Property, plant and equipment, net	2,231,198	2,193,745
Restricted cash	27,749	26,528
Intangible assets, net of accumulated amortization of $215,485 and $181,227 as of December 31, 2012 and 2011, respectively	416,635	450,893
Goodwill	738,542	745,066
Other assets	105,067	107,736
Total assets	$5,815,416	$5,979,226

NOTES TO CONSOLIDATED FINANCIAL STATEMENTS

Note 9. Transactions with Affiliated Companies

The company sells flat rolled products and occasionally purchases ferrous materials from Heidtman. The president and chief executive officer of Heidtman is a member of the company's board of directors and a stockholder of the company. Transactions with Heidtman for the years ended December 31, are as follows (in thousands):

	2012	2011	2010
Sales	$244,531	$242,300	$202,897
Percentage of consolidated net sales	3%	3%	3%
Accounts receivable	38,093	35,646	31,544
Purchases	11,372	18,998	18,275
Accounts payable	800	882	969

On September 15, 2009, the company purchased from Heidtman a 32 acre tract of land adjacent to the company's Flat Roll Division in Butler, Indiana, together with a 387,000 square foot building for a purchase price of $9.3 million. Contemporaneously the company purchased from Heidtman equipment located at this site for a purchase price of $18.6 million. Immediately following the acquisition of this property, the company leased the real estate and equipment to Heidtman for a term of five years commencing on September 15, 2009, and terminating on August 31, 2014, at which time Heidtman has the option to repurchase the real estate and equipment for $27.9 million. Heidtman pays the company monthly rental of approximately $289,000 for the real estate and for the equipment. The real estate and equipment have been used, and will continue to be used, by Heidtman in its steel processing operations.

The company also purchases and sells recycled and scrap metal with other smaller affiliated companies. These transactions are as follows (in thousands):

	2012	2011	2010
Sales	$ 38,286	$ 36,486	$ 37,057
Accounts receivable	4,771	7,247	6,577
Purchases	238,114	239,395	177,166
Accounts payable	14,344	5,702	12,601

2.26 L-3 COMMUNICATIONS HOLDINGS, INC. (DEC)

CONSOLIDATED BALANCE SHEETS (in part)

(In millions, except share data)

	December 31,	
	2012	**2011**
Assets		
Current assets:		
Cash and cash equivalents	$ 349	$ 764
Billed receivables, net of allowances of $33 in 2012 and $25 in 2011	968	1,093
Contracts in process	2,652	2,386
Inventories	363	317
Deferred income taxes	95	132
Other current assets	144	177
Assets of discontinued operations	—	1,729
Total current assets	4,571	6,598
Property, plant and equipment, net	1,017	921
Goodwill	7,744	7,472
Identifiable intangible assets	314	308
Deferred debt issue costs	29	33
Other assets	151	176
Total assets	$13,826	$15,508

NOTES TO CONSOLIDATED FINANCIAL STATEMENTS

2. Summary of Significant Accounting Policies (in part)

Revenue Recognition: Substantially all of the Company's sales are generated from written contractual (revenue) arrangements. The sales price for the Company's revenue arrangements are either fixed-price, cost-plus or time-and-material type. Depending on the contractual scope of work, the Company utilizes either contract accounting standards or accounting standards for revenue arrangements with commercial customers to account for these contracts. Approximately 48% of the Company's 2012 sales were accounted for under contract accounting standards, of which approximately 39% were fixed-price type contracts and approximately 9% were cost-plus type contracts. For contracts that are accounted for under contract accounting standards, sales and profits are recognized based on: (1) a Percentage-of-Completion (POC) method of accounting (fixed-price contracts), (2) allowable costs incurred plus the estimated profit on those costs (cost-plus contracts), or (3) direct labor hours expended multiplied by the contractual fixed rate per hour plus incurred costs for material (time-and-material contracts). Aggregate net changes in contract estimates increased operating income by $78 million, or 6%, for the year ended December 31, 2012, $73 million, or 5%, for the year ended December 31, 2011, and $45 million, or 3%, for the year ended December 31, 2010.

Sales and profits on fixed-price type contracts covered by contract accounting standards are substantially recognized using POC methods of accounting. Sales and profits on fixed-price production contracts under which units are produced and delivered in a continuous or sequential process are recorded as units are delivered based on their contractual selling prices (the "units-of-delivery" method). Sales and profits on each fixed-price production contract under which units are not produced and delivered in a continuous or sequential process, or under which a relatively few number of units are produced, are recorded based on the ratio of actual cumulative costs incurred to the total estimated costs at completion of the contract, multiplied by the total estimated contract revenue, less cumulative sales recognized in prior periods (the "cost-to-cost" method). Under both POC methods of accounting, a single estimated total profit margin is used to recognize profit for each contract over its entire period of performance, which can exceed one year. Losses on contracts are recognized in the period in which they become evident. The impact of revisions of contract estimates, which may result from contract modifications, performance or other reasons, are recognized on a cumulative catch-up basis in the period in which the revisions are made.

Sales and profits on cost-plus type contracts covered by contract accounting standards are recognized as allowable costs are incurred on the contract, at an amount equal to the allowable costs plus the estimated profit on those costs. The estimated profit on a cost-plus type contract is fixed or variable based on the contractual fee arrangement. Incentive and award fees are the primary variable fee contractual arrangements. Incentive and award fees on cost-plus type contracts are included as an element of total estimated contract revenues and are recorded as sales when a basis exists for the reasonable prediction of performance in relation to established contractual targets and the Company is able to make reasonably dependable estimates for them.

Sales and profits on time-and-material type contracts are recognized on the basis of direct labor hours expended multiplied by the contractual fixed rate per hour, plus the actual costs of materials and other direct non-labor costs.

Sales on arrangements for (1) fixed-price type contracts that require us to perform services that are not related to the production of tangible assets (Fixed-Price Service Contracts) and (2) certain commercial customers are recognized in accordance with accounting standards for revenue arrangements with commercial customers. Sales for the Company's businesses whose customers are primarily commercial business enterprises are substantially all generated from single element revenue arrangements. Sales are recognized when there is persuasive evidence of an arrangement, delivery has occurred or services have been performed, the selling price to the buyer is fixed or determinable and collectability is reasonably assured. Sales for Fixed-Price Service Contracts that do not contain measurable units of work performed are generally recognized on a straight-line basis over the contractual service period, unless evidence suggests that the revenue is earned, or obligations fulfilled, in a different manner. Sales for Fixed-Price Service Contracts that contain measurable units of work performed are generally recognized when the units of work are completed. Sales and profit on cost-plus and time-and-material type contracts to perform services are recognized in the same manner as those within the scope of contract accounting standards, except for incentive and award fees. Cost-based incentive fees are recognized when they are realizable in the amount that would be due under the contractual termination provisions as if the contract was terminated. Performance based incentive fees and award fees are recorded as sales when awarded by the customer.

For contracts with multiple deliverables, the Company applies the separation and allocation guidance under the accounting standard for revenue arrangements with multiple deliverables, unless all the deliverables are covered by contract accounting standards, in which case the Company applies the separation and allocation guidance under contract accounting standards. Revenue arrangements with multiple deliverables are evaluated to determine if the deliverables should be separated into more than one unit of accounting. The Company recognizes revenue for each unit of accounting based on the revenue recognition policies discussed above.

Sales and profit in connection with contracts to provide services to the U.S. Government that contain collection risk because the contracts are incrementally funded and subject to the availability of funds appropriated, are deferred until a contract modification is obtained, indicating that adequate funds are available to the contract or task order.

Contracts in Process: Contracts in process include unbilled contract receivables and inventoried contract costs for which sales and profits are recognized using a POC method of accounting. Unbilled Contract Receivables represent accumulated incurred costs and earned profits or losses on contracts in process that have been recorded as sales, primarily using the cost-to-cost method, which have not yet been billed to customers. Inventoried Contract Costs represent incurred costs on contracts in process that have not yet been recognized as costs and expenses because the related sales, which are primarily recorded using the units-of-delivery method, have not been recognized. Contract costs include direct costs and indirect costs, including overhead costs. As discussed in Note 5, the Company's inventoried contract costs for U.S. Government contracts, and contracts with prime contractors or subcontractors of the U.S. Government include allocated general and administrative costs (G&A), IRAD costs and B&P costs. Contracts in Process contain amounts relating to contracts and programs with long performance cycles, a portion of which may not be realized within one year. For contracts in a loss position, the unrecoverable costs expected to be incurred in future periods are recorded in Estimated Costs in Excess of Estimated Contract Value to Complete Contracts in Process in a Loss Position, which is a component of Other Current Liabilities. Under the terms of certain revenue arrangements (contracts) with the U.S. Government, the Company may receive progress payments as costs are incurred or milestone payments as work is performed. The U.S. Government has a security interest in the Unbilled Contract Receivables and Inventoried Contract Costs to which progress payments have been applied, and such progress payments are reflected as a reduction of the related amounts. Milestone payments that have been received in excess of contract costs incurred and related estimated profits are reported on the Company's balance sheet as Advance Payments and Billings in Excess of Costs Incurred.

The Company values its acquired contracts in process in connection with business acquisitions on the date of acquisition at contract value less the Company's estimated costs to complete the contract and a reasonable profit allowance on the Company's completion effort commensurate with the profit margin that the Company earns on similar contracts.

5. Contracts in Process

The components of contracts in process are presented in the table below. The unbilled contract receivables, inventoried contract costs and unliquidated progress payments principally relate to contracts with the U.S. Government and prime contractors or subcontractors of the U.S. Government. In connection with contracts in process assumed by the Company in its business acquisitions, the underlying contractual customer relationships are separately recognized as identifiable intangible assets at the date of acquisition, and are discussed and presented in Note 7.

	December 31,	
(In millions)	2012	2011
Unbilled contract receivables, gross	$ 2,874	$ 2,677
Unliquidated progress payments	(1,265)	(1,146)
Unbilled contract receivables, net	1,609	1,531
Inventoried contract costs, gross	1,111	934
Unliquidated progress payments	(68)	(79)
Inventoried contract costs, net	1,043	855
Total contracts in process	$ 2,652	$ 2,386

Unbilled Contract Receivables. Unbilled contract receivables represent accumulated incurred costs and earned profits on contracts (revenue arrangements), which have been recorded as sales, but have not yet been billed to customers. Unbilled contract receivables arise from the cost-to-cost method of revenue recognition that is used to record sales on certain fixed-price contracts. Unbilled contract receivables from fixed-price type contracts are converted to billed receivables when amounts are invoiced to customers according to contractual billing terms, which generally occur when deliveries or other performance milestones are completed. Unbilled contract receivables also arise from cost-plus type contracts and time-and-material type contracts, for revenue amounts that have not been billed by the end of the accounting period due to the timing of preparation of invoices to customers. The Company believes that approximately 97% of the unbilled contract receivables at December 31, 2012 will be billed and collected within one year.

Unliquidated Progress Payments. Unliquidated progress payments arise from fixed-price type contracts with the U.S. Government that contain progress payment clauses, and represent progress payments on invoices that have been collected in cash, but have not yet been liquidated. Progress payment invoices are billed to the customer as contract costs are incurred at an amount generally equal to 75% to 80% of incurred costs. Unliquidated progress payments are liquidated as deliveries or other contract performance milestones are completed, at an amount equal to a percentage of the contract sales price for the items delivered or work performed, based on a contractual liquidation rate. Therefore, unliquidated progress payments are a contra asset account, and are classified against unbilled contract receivables if revenue for the underlying contract is recorded using the cost-to-cost method, and against inventoried contract costs if revenue is recorded using the units-of-delivery method.

Inventoried Contract Costs. In accordance with contract accounting standards, the Company's U.S. Government contractor businesses account for the portion of their G&A, IRAD and B&P costs that are allowable and reimbursable indirect contract costs under U.S. Government procurement regulations on their U.S. Government contracts (revenue arrangements) as inventoried contract costs. G&A, IRAD and B&P costs are allocated to contracts for which the U.S. Government is the end customer and are charged to costs of sales when sales on the related contracts are recognized. The Company's U.S. Government contractor businesses record the unallowable portion of their G&A, IRAD and B&P costs to expense as incurred, and do not include them in inventoried contract costs.

The table below presents a summary of G&A, IRAD and B&P costs included in inventoried contract costs and the changes to them, including amounts charged to cost of sales by the Company's U.S. Government contractor businesses for the periods presented.

(In millions)	Year Ended December 31,		
	2012	2011	2010
Amounts included in inventoried contract costs at beginning of the year	$ 91	$ 97	$ 72
Add: IRAD and B&P costs incurred	336	314	306
Other G&A costs incurred	896	824	836
Total contract costs incurred	1,232	1,138	1,142
Less: Amounts charged to cost of sales	(1,213)	(1,144)	(1,117)
Amounts included in inventoried contract costs at end of the year	$ 110	$ 91	$ 97

The table below presents a summary of selling, general and administrative expenses and research and development expenses for the Company's commercial businesses, which are expensed as incurred and included in cost of sales on the Consolidated Statements of Operations.

(In millions)	Year Ended December 31,		
	2012	2011	2010
Selling, general and administrative expenses	$303	$319	$301
Research and development expenses	88	85	80
Total	$391	$404	$381

FINANCE RECEIVABLES

2.27 FORD MOTOR COMPANY (DEC)
CONSOLIDATED BALANCE SHEET (in part)

(In millions)

	December 31, 2012	December 31, 2011
Assets		
Cash and cash equivalents	$ 15,659	$ 17,148
Marketable securities (Note 6)	20,284	18,618
Finance receivables, net (Note 7)	71,510	69,976
Other receivables, net	10,828	8,565
Net investment in operating leases (Note 8)	16,451	12,838
Inventories (Note 10)	7,362	5,901
Equity in net assets of affiliated companies (Note 11)	3,246	2,936
Net property (Note 13)	24,942	22,371
Deferred income taxes (Note 24)	15,185	15,125
Net intangible assets (Note 14)	87	100
Other assets	5,000	4,770
Total assets	$190,554	$178,348

Note 4. Fair Value Measurements (in part)

Finance Receivables. We measure finance receivables at fair value for purposes of disclosure (see Note 7) using internal valuation models. These models project future cash flows of financing contracts based on scheduled contract payments (including principal and interest). The projected cash flows are discounted to present value based on assumptions regarding credit losses, pre-payment speed, and applicable spreads to approximate current rates. Our assumptions regarding pre-payment speed and credit losses are based on historical performance. The fair value of finance receivables is categorized within Level 3 of the hierarchy.

On a nonrecurring basis, when retail contracts are greater than 120 days past due or deemed to be uncollectible, or if individual dealer loans are probable of foreclosure, we use the fair value of collateral, adjusted for estimated costs to sell, to determine the fair value adjustment to our receivables. The collateral for retail receivables is the vehicle financed, and for dealer loans is real estate or other property.

The fair value measurements for retail receivables are based on the number of contracts multiplied by the loss severity and the probability of default ("POD") percentage, or the outstanding receivable balances multiplied by the average recovery value ("ARV") percentage to determine the fair value adjustment.

The fair value measurements for dealer loans are based on an assessment of the estimated fair value of collateral. The assessment is performed by reviewing various appraisals, which include total adjusted appraised value of land and improvements, alternate use appraised value, broker's opinion of value, and purchase offers. The fair value adjustment is determined by comparing the net carrying value of the dealer loan and the estimated fair value of collateral.

Note 7. Finance Receivables (in part)

Finance receivable balances were as follows (in millions):

	December 31, 2012	December 31, 2011
Automotive sector[a]	$ 519	$ 355
Financial Services sector	75,770	73,330
Reclassification of receivables purchased by Financial Services sector from Automotive sector to *Other receivables, net*	(4,779)	(3,709)
Finance receivables, net	$71,510	$69,976

[a] Finance receivables are reported on our sector balance sheet in *Receivables, less allowances* and *Other assets.*

Automotive Sector

Our Automotive sector notes receivable consist primarily of amounts loaned to our unconsolidated affiliates. Performance of this group of receivables is evaluated based on payment activity and the financial stability of the debtor. Notes receivable initially are recorded at fair value and subsequently measured at amortized cost.

Notes receivable, net were as follows (in millions):

	December 31, 2012	December 31, 2011
Notes receivable	$542	$384
Less: Allowance for credit losses	(23)	(29)
Notes receivable, net	$519	$355

Financial Services Sector

Our Financial Services sector finance receivables primarily relate to Ford Credit, but also include the Other Financial Services segment and certain intersector eliminations.

Our Financial Services sector segments the North America and International portfolio of finance receivables into "consumer" and "non-consumer" receivables. The receivables are secured by the vehicles, inventory, or other property being financed.

Consumer Segment. Receivables in this portfolio segment include products offered to individuals and businesses that finance the acquisition of Ford and Lincoln vehicles from dealers for personal or commercial use. Retail financing includes retail installment contracts for new and used vehicles and direct financing leases with retail customers, government entities, daily rental companies, and fleet customers.

Non-Consumer Segment. Receivables in this portfolio segment include products offered to automotive dealers. The products include:

- *Dealer financing*—wholesale loans to dealers to finance the purchase of vehicle inventory, also known as floorplan financing, and loans to dealers to finance working capital and improvements to dealership facilities, finance the purchase of dealership real estate, and other dealer vehicle program financing. Wholesale is approximately 95% of our dealer financing
- *Other financing*—purchased receivables primarily related to the sale of parts and accessories to dealers

Finance receivables are recorded at the time of origination or purchase for the principal amount financed and are subsequently reported at amortized cost, net of any allowance for credit losses. Amortized cost is the outstanding principal adjusted for any charge-offs, unamortized deferred fees or costs, and unearned interest supplements.

Finance receivables, net were as follows (in millions):

	December 31, 2012			December 31, 2011		
	North America	International	Total Finance Receivables	North America	International	Total Finance Receivables
Consumer						
Retail financing, gross	$39,504	$10,460	$49,964	$38,410	$11,083	$49,493
Less: Unearned interest supplements	(1,264)	(287)	(1,551)	(1,407)	(335)	(1,742)
Consumer finance receivables	$38,240	$10,173	$48,413	$37,003	$10,748	$47,751
Non-Consumer						
Dealer financing	$19,429	$ 7,242	$26,671	$16,501	$ 8,479	$24,980
Other	689	386	1,075	723	377	1,100
Non-Consumer finance receivables	20,118	7,628	27,746	17,224	8,856	26,080
Total recorded investment	$58,358	$17,801	$76,159	$54,227	$19,604	$73,831
Recorded investment in finance receivables	$58,358	$17,801	$76,159	$54,227	$19,604	$73,831
Less: Allowance for credit losses	(309)	(80)	(389)	(388)	(113)	(501)
Finance receivables, net	$58,049	$17,721	$75,770	$53,839	$19,491	$73,330
Net finance receivables subject to fair value[(a)]			$73,618			$70,754
Fair value			75,618			72,294

[(a)] At December 31, 2012 and 2011, excludes $2.2 billion and $2.6 billion, respectively, of certain receivables (primarily direct financing leases) that are not subject to fair value disclosure requirements. All finance receivables are categorized within Level 3 of the fair value hierarchy. See Note 4 for additional information.

Excluded from Financial Services sector finance receivables at December 31, 2012 and 2011, was $183 million and $180 million, respectively, of accrued uncollected interest receivable, which we report in *Other assets* on the balance sheet.

Included in the recorded investment in finance receivables at December 31, 2012 and 2011 were North America consumer receivables of $23 billion and $29.4 billion and non-consumer receivables of $17.1 billion and $14.2 billion, respectively, and International consumer receivables of $6.6 billion and $7.1 billion and non-consumer receivables of $4.5 billion and $5.6 billion, respectively, that secure certain debt obligations. The receivables are available only for payment of the debt and other obligations issued or arising in securitization transactions; they are not available to pay the other obligations of our Financial Services sector or the claims of our other creditors. We hold the right to receive the excess cash flows not needed to pay the debt and other obligations issued or arising in securitization transactions (see Notes 12 and 17).

Contractual maturities of total finance receivables, excluding unearned interest supplements, outstanding at December 31, 2012 reflect contractual repayments due from customers or borrowers as follows (in millions):

	Due in Year Ending December 31,				
	2013	2014	2015	Thereafter	Total
North America					
Consumer					
Retail financing, gross	$11,599	$ 9,992	$8,096	$ 9,817	$39,504
Non-Consumer					
Dealer financing	17,966	546	72	845	19,429
Other	685	2	1	1	689
Total North America	$30,250	$10,540	$8,169	$10,663	$59,622
International					
Consumer					
Retail financing, gross	$ 4,381	$ 3,096	$1,826	$ 1,157	$10,460
Non-Consumer					
Dealer financing	6,464	717	58	3	7,242
Other	386	—	—	—	386
Total International	$11,231	$ 3,813	$1,884	$ 1,160	$18,088

Our finance receivables are pre-payable without penalty, so prepayments may cause actual maturities to differ from contractual maturities. The above table, therefore, is not to be regarded as a forecast of future cash collections. For wholesale receivables, which are included in dealer financing, maturities stated above are estimated based on historical trends, as maturities on outstanding amounts are scheduled upon the sale of the underlying vehicle by the dealer.

Investment in direct financing leases, which are included in consumer receivables, were as follows (in millions):

	December 31, 2012			December 31, 2011		
	North America	International	Total Direct Financing Leases	North America	International	Total Direct Financing Leases
Total minimum lease rentals to be received	$ 58	$1,466	$1,524	$ 4	$1,897	$1,901
Initial direct costs	1	16	17	—	18	18
Estimated residual values	—	851	851	1	971	972
Less: Unearned income	(7)	(152)	(159)	(1)	(203)	(204)
Less: Unearned interest supplements	—	(82)	(82)	—	(116)	(116)
Recorded investment in direct financing leases	52	2,099	2,151	4	2,567	2,571
Less: Allowance for credit losses	(1)	(8)	(9)	—	(12)	(12)
Net investment in direct financing leases	$ 51	$2,091	$2,142	$ 4	$2,555	$2,559

Future minimum rental payments due from direct financing leases at December 31, 2012 were as follows (in millions):

	2013	2014	2015	2016	Thereafter
North America	$ 21	$ 12	$ 13	$ 9	$ 3
International	571	430	317	136	12

Aging. For all classes of finance receivables, we define "past due" as any payment, including principal and interest, that has not been collected and is at least 31 days past the contractual due date. Recorded investment of consumer accounts greater than 90 days past due and still accruing interest was $13 million and $14 million at December 31, 2012 and 2011, respectively. The recorded investment of non-consumer accounts greater than 90 days past due and still accruing interest was $5 million and de minimis at December 31, 2012 and 2011, respectively.

The aging analysis of our Financial Services sector finance receivables balances at December 31 were as follows (in millions):

	2012			2011		
	North America	International	Total	North America	International	Total
Consumer						
31–60 days past due	$ 783	$ 50	$ 833	$ 732	$ 64	$ 796
61–90 days past due	97	18	115	68	28	96
91–120 days past due	21	9	30	22	12	34
Greater than 120 days past due	52	29	81	70	43	113
Total past due	953	106	1,059	892	147	1,039
Current	37,287	10,067	47,354	36,111	10,601	46,712
Consumer finance receivables	$38,240	$10,173	$48,413	$37,003	$10,748	$47,751
Non-Consumer						
Total past due	$ 29	$ 11	$ 40	$ 30	$ 9	$ 39
Current	20,089	7,617	27,706	17,194	8,847	26,041
Non-Consumer finance receivables	20,118	7,628	27,746	17,224	8,856	26,080
Total recorded investment	$58,358	$17,801	$76,159	$54,227	$19,604	$73,831

Consumer Credit Quality. When originating all classes of consumer receivables, we use a proprietary scoring system that measures the credit quality of the receivables using several factors, such as credit bureau information, consumer credit risk scores (e.g., FICO score), and contract characteristics. In addition to our proprietary scoring system, we consider other individual consumer factors, such as employment history, financial stability, and capacity to pay.

Subsequent to origination, we review the credit quality of retail and direct financing lease receivables based on customer payment activity. As each customer develops a payment history, we use an internally-developed behavioral scoring model to assist in determining the best collection strategies. Based on data from this scoring model, contracts are categorized by collection risk. Our collection models evaluate several factors, including origination characteristics, updated credit bureau data, and payment patterns. These models allow for more focused collection activity on higher-risk accounts and are used to refine our risk-based staffing model to ensure collection resources are aligned with portfolio risk.

Credit quality ratings for our consumer receivables are based on aging (as described in the aging table above). Consumer receivables credit quality ratings are as follows:
- *Pass*—current to 60 days past due
- *Special Mention*—61 to 120 days past due and in intensified collection status
- *Substandard*—greater than 120 days past due and for which the uncollectible portion of the receivables has already been charged-off, as measured using the fair value of collateral

Non-Consumer Credit Quality. We extend credit to dealers primarily in the form of lines of credit to purchase new Ford and Lincoln vehicles as well as used vehicles. Each non-consumer lending request is evaluated by taking into consideration the borrower's financial condition and the underlying collateral securing the loan. We use a proprietary model to assign each dealer a risk rating. This model uses historical performance data to identify key factors about a dealer that we consider significant in predicting a dealer's ability to meet its financial obligations. We also consider numerous other financial and qualitative factors including capitalization and leverage, liquidity and cash flow, profitability, and credit history with ourselves and other creditors. A dealer's risk rating does not reflect any guarantees or a dealer owner's net worth.

Dealers are assigned to one of four groups according to their risk rating as follows:

- *Group I*—strong to superior financial metrics
- *Group II*—fair to favorable financial metrics
- *Group III*—marginal to weak financial metrics
- *Group IV*—poor financial metrics, including dealers classified as uncollectible

We suspend credit lines and extend no further funding to dealers classified in Group IV.

We regularly review our model to confirm the continued business significance and statistical predictability of the factors and update the model to incorporate new factors or other information that improves its statistical predictability. In addition, we verify the existence of the assets collateralizing the receivables by physical audits of vehicle inventories, which are performed with increased frequency for higher-risk (i.e., Group III and Group IV) dealers. We perform a credit review of each dealer at least annually and adjust the dealer's risk rating, if necessary.

Performance of non-consumer receivables is evaluated based on our internal dealer risk rating analysis, as payment for wholesale receivables generally is not required until the dealer has sold the vehicle. A dealer has the same risk rating for all of its dealer financing regardless of the type of financing.

The credit quality analysis of our dealer financing receivables at December 31 were as follows (in millions):

	2012			2011		
	North America	International	Total	North America	International	Total
Dealer Financing						
Group I	$16,526	$4,551	$21,077	$13,506	$5,157	$18,663
Group II	2,608	1,405	4,013	2,654	1,975	4,629
Group III	277	1,279	1,556	331	1,337	1,668
Group IV	18	7	25	10	10	20
Total recorded investment	$19,429	$7,242	$26,671	$16,501	$8,479	$24,980

Impaired Receivables. Impaired consumer receivables include accounts that have been re-written or modified in reorganization proceedings pursuant to the U.S. Bankruptcy Code that are considered to be Troubled Debt Restructurings ("TDRs"), as well as all accounts greater than 120 days past due. Impaired non-consumer receivables represent accounts with dealers that have weak or poor financial metrics or dealer financing that have been modified in TDRs. The recorded investment of consumer receivables that were impaired at December 31, 2012 and 2011 was $422 million or 0.9% of consumer receivables, and $382 million or 0.8% of consumer receivables, respectively. The recorded investment of non-consumer receivables that were impaired at December 31, 2012 and 2011 was $47 million or 0.2% of non-consumer receivables, and $64 million or 0.2% of the non-consumer receivables, respectively. Impaired finance receivables are evaluated both collectively and specifically. See Note 9 for additional information related to the development of our allowance for credit losses.

Non-Accrual Receivables. The accrual of revenue is discontinued at the earlier of the time a receivable is determined to be uncollectible, at bankruptcy status notification, or greater than 120 days past due. Accounts may be restored to accrual status only when a customer settles all past-due deficiency balances and future payments are reasonably assured. For receivables in non-accrual status, subsequent financing revenue is recognized only to the extent a payment is received. Payments generally are applied first to outstanding interest and then to the unpaid principal balance.

The recorded investment of consumer receivables in non-accrual status was $304 million or 0.6% of our consumer receivables, at December 31, 2012, and $402 million or 0.9% of our consumer receivables, at December 31, 2011. The recorded investment of non-consumer receivables in non-accrual status was $29 million or 0.1% of our non-consumer receivables, at December 31, 2012, and $27 million or 0.1% of our non-consumer receivables, at December 31, 2011.

Troubled Debt Restructurings. A restructuring of debt constitutes a TDR if we grant a concession to a customer or borrower for economic or legal reasons related to the debtor's financial difficulties that we otherwise would not consider. Consumer contracts that have a modified interest rate that is below the market rate and those modified in reorganization proceedings pursuant to the U.S. Bankruptcy Code are considered to be TDRs. Non-consumer receivables subject to forbearance, moratoriums, extension agreements, or other actions intended to minimize economic loss and to avoid foreclosure or repossession of collateral are classified as TDRs. We do not grant concessions on the principal balance of our loans. If a contract is modified in reorganization proceeding, all payment requirements of the reorganization plan need to be met before remaining balances are forgiven. The outstanding recorded investment at time of modification for consumer receivables that are considered to be TDRs were $249 million or 0.5% and $370 million or 0.8% of our consumer receivables during the period ended December 31, 2012 and 2011, respectively. The subsequent default rate of TDRs that were previously modified in TDRs within the last twelve months and resulted in repossession for consumer contracts was 5.8% and 3.7% of TDRs at December 31, 2012 and 2011, respectively. The outstanding recorded investment of non-consumer loans involved in TDRs was de minimis during the years ended December 31, 2012 and 2011.

Finance receivables involved in TDRs are specifically assessed for impairment. An impairment charge is recorded as part of the provision to the allowance for credit losses for the amount that the recorded investment of the receivable exceeds its estimated fair value. Estimated fair value is based on either the present value of the expected future cash flows of the receivable discounted at the loan's original effective interest rate, or for loans where foreclosure is probable the fair value of the collateral adjusted for estimated costs to sell. The allowance for credit losses related to consumer TDRs was $19 million and $16 million at

December 31, 2012 and 2011, respectively. The allowance for credit losses related to non-consumer TDRs was de minimis during the years ended December 31, 2012 and 2011.

INSURANCE CLAIMS

2.28 CRANE CO. (DEC)
CONSOLIDATED BALANCE SHEETS (in part)

	Balance at December 31,	
(In thousands, except shares and per share data)	2012	2011
Assets		
Current assets:		
Cash and cash equivalents	$ 423,947	$ 245,089
Current insurance receivable—asbestos	33,722	16,345
Accounts receivable, net	333,330	349,250
Inventories	352,725	360,689
Current deferred tax assets	21,618	46,664
Other current assets	15,179	14,195
Total current assets	1,180,521	1,032,232
Property, plant and equipment, net	268,283	284,146
Insurance receivable—asbestos	171,752	208,952
Long-term deferred tax assets	245,843	265,849
Other assets	83,774	85,301
Intangible assets, net	125,913	146,227
Goodwill	813,792	820,824
Total assets	$2,889,878	$2,843,531

NOTES TO CONSOLIDATED FINANCIAL STATEMENTS

Note 11—Commitments and Contingencies (in part)

Insurance Coverage and Receivables. Prior to 2005, a significant portion of the Company's settlement and defense costs were paid by its primary insurers. With the exhaustion of that primary coverage, the Company began negotiations with its excess insurers to reimburse the Company for a portion of its settlement and/or defense costs as incurred. To date, the Company has entered into agreements providing for such reimbursements, known as "coverage-in-place," with eleven of its excess insurer groups. Under such coverage-in-place agreements, an insurer's policies remain in force and the insurer undertakes to provide coverage for the Company's present and future asbestos claims on specified terms and conditions that address, among other things, the share of asbestos claims costs to be paid by the insurer, payment terms, claims handling procedures and the expiration of the insurer's obligations. Similarly, under a variant of coverage-in-place, the Company has entered into an agreement with a group of insurers confirming the aggregate amount of available coverage under the subject policies and setting forth a schedule for future reimbursement payments to the Company based on aggregate indemnity and defense payments made. In addition, with eight of its excess insurer groups, the Company entered into policy buyout agreements, settling all asbestos and other coverage obligations for an agreed sum, totaling $81.1 million in aggregate. Reimbursements from insurers for past and ongoing settlement and defense costs allocable to their policies have been made in accordance with these coverage-in-place and other agreements. All of these agreements include provisions for mutual releases, indemnification of the insurer and, for coverage-in-place, claims handling procedures. With the agreements referenced above, the Company has concluded settlements with all but one of its solvent excess insurers whose policies are expected to respond to the aggregate costs included in the updated liability estimate. That insurer, which issued a single applicable policy, has been paying the shares of defense and indemnity costs the Company has allocated to it, subject to a reservation of rights. There are no pending legal proceedings between the Company and any insurer contesting the Company's asbestos claims under its insurance policies.

In conjunction with developing the aggregate liability estimate referenced above, the Company also developed an estimate of probable insurance recoveries for its asbestos liabilities. In developing this estimate, the Company considered its coverage-in-place and other settlement agreements described above, as well as a number of additional factors. These additional factors include the financial viability of the insurance companies, the method by which losses will be allocated to the various insurance policies and the years covered by those policies, how settlement and defense costs will be covered by the insurance policies and interpretation of the effect on coverage of various policy terms and limits and their interrelationships. In addition, the timing and amount of reimbursements will vary because the Company's insurance coverage for asbestos claims involves multiple insurers, with different policy terms and certain gaps in coverage. In addition to consulting with legal counsel on these insurance matters, the Company retained insurance consultants to assist management in the estimation of probable insurance recoveries based upon the aggregate liability estimate described above and assuming the continued viability of all solvent insurance carriers. Based upon the analysis of policy terms and other factors noted above by the Company's legal counsel, and incorporating risk mitigation judgments by the Company where policy terms or other factors were not certain, the Company's insurance consultants compiled a model indicating how the Company's historical insurance policies would respond to varying levels of asbestos settlement and defense costs and the allocation of such costs between such insurers and the Company. Using the estimated liability as of December 31, 2011 (for claims filed or expected to be filed through 2021), the insurance consultant's model forecasted that approximately 25% of the liability would be reimbursed by the Company's insurers. While there are overall limits on the aggregate amount of insurance available to the Company with respect to asbestos claims, those overall limits were not reached by the total estimated liability currently recorded by the Company, and such overall limits did not influence the Company in its determination of the asset amount to record. The proportion of the asbestos liability that is allocated to certain insurance coverage years, however, exceeds the limits of available insurance in those years. The Company allocates to itself the amount of the asbestos liability (for claims filed or expected to be filed through 2021) that is in excess of available insurance coverage allocated to such years. An asset of $225 million was recorded as of December 31, 2011 representing the probable insurance reimbursement for such claims expected through 2021. The asset is reduced as reimbursements and other payments from insurers are received. The asset was $205 million as of December 31, 2012.

The Company reviews the aforementioned estimated reimbursement rate with its insurance consultants on a periodic basis in order to confirm its overall consistency with the Company's established reserves. The reviews encompass consideration of the performance of the insurers under coverage-in-place agreements and the effect of any additional lump-sum payments under policy buyout agreements. Since December 2011, there have been no developments that have caused the Company to change the estimated 25% rate, although actual insurance reimbursements vary from period to period, and will decline over time, for the reasons cited above.

Uncertainties. Estimation of the Company's ultimate exposure for asbestos-related claims is subject to significant uncertainties, as there are multiple variables that can affect the timing, severity and quantity of claims and the manner of their resolution. The Company cautions that its estimated liability is based on assumptions with respect to future claims, settlement and defense costs based on past experience that may not prove reliable as predictors. A significant upward or downward trend in the number of claims filed, depending on the nature of the alleged injury, the jurisdiction where filed and the quality of the product identification, or a significant upward or downward trend in the costs of defending claims, could change the estimated liability, as would substantial adverse verdicts at trial that withstand appeal. A legislative solution, structured settlement transaction, or significant change in relevant case law could also change the estimated liability.

The same factors that affect developing estimates of probable settlement and defense costs for asbestos-related liabilities also affect estimates of the probable insurance reimbursements, as do a number of additional factors. These additional factors include the financial viability of the insurance companies, the method by which losses will be allocated to the various insurance policies and the years covered by those policies, how settlement and defense costs will be covered by the insurance policies and interpretation of the effect on coverage of various policy terms and limits and their interrelationships. In addition, due to the uncertainties inherent in litigation matters, no assurances can be given regarding the outcome of any litigation, if necessary, to enforce the Company's rights under its insurance policies or settlement agreements.

Many uncertainties exist surrounding asbestos litigation, and the Company will continue to evaluate its estimated asbestos-related liability and corresponding estimated insurance reimbursement as well as the underlying assumptions and process used to derive these amounts. These uncertainties may result in the Company incurring future charges or increases to income to adjust the carrying value of recorded liabilities and assets, particularly if the number of claims and settlement and defense costs change significantly, or if there are significant developments in the trend of case law or court procedures, or if legislation or another alternative solution is implemented; however, the Company is currently unable to estimate such future changes and, accordingly, while it is probable that the Company will incur additional charges for asbestos liabilities and defense costs in excess of the amounts currently provided, the Company does not believe that any such amount can be reasonably determined beyond 2021. Although the resolution of these claims may take many years, the effect on the results of operations, financial position and cash flow in any given period from a revision to these estimates could be material.

Receivables Sold or Collateralized

RECOGNITION AND MEASUREMENT

2.29 FASB ASC 860, *Transfers and Servicing*, establishes criteria for determining whether a transfer of financial assets in exchange for cash or other consideration should be accounted for as a sale or pledge of collateral in a secured borrowing. FASB ASC 860 also establishes the criteria for accounting for securitizations and other transfers of financial assets and collateral and requires certain disclosures.

2.30 FASB ASC 860 requires that all separately recognized servicing assets and liabilities be initially measured at fair value. Further, FASB ASC 860 permits, but does not require, the subsequent measurement of servicing assets and liabilities at fair value.

2.31 ASU No. 2009-16, *Transfers and Servicing (Topic 860): Accounting for Transfers of Financial Assets*, eliminated the exceptions for qualifying special-purpose entities from the consolidation guidance. Further, ASU No. 2009-16 provides clarifications of the requirements for isolation and limitations on portions of financial assets that are eligible for sale accounting. ASU No. 2009-16 was effective for fiscal years beginning after November 15, 2009.

DISCLOSURE

2.32 FASB ASC 860 requires additional disclosures and separate balance sheet presentation of the carrying amounts of servicing assets and liabilities that are subsequently measured at fair value. FASB ASC 860-50-50-2 requires disclosures including (*a*) a description of the risks inherent in servicing assets and servicing liabilities, (*b*) the amount of contractually specified servicing fees, late fees, and ancillary fees earned for each period, including a description of where each amount is reported in the statement of income, and (*c*) quantitative and qualitative information about the assumptions used to estimate fair value.

PRESENTATION AND DISCLOSURE EXCERPTS

RECEIVABLES SOLD OR COLLATERALIZED

2.33 MONSANTO COMPANY (AUG)
STATEMENTS OF CONSOLIDATED FINANCIAL POSITION (in part)

	As of Aug. 31,	
(Dollars in millions, except share amounts)	2012	2011
Assets		
Current assets:		
Cash and cash equivalents (variable interest entities restricted—2012: $120 and 2011: $96)	$ 3,283	$ 2,572
Short-term investments	302	302
Trade receivables, net (variable interest entities restricted—2012: $52 and 2011: $51)	1,897	2,117
Miscellaneous receivables	620	629
Deferred tax assets	534	446
Inventory, net	2,839	2,591
Other current assets	183	152
Total current assets	9,658	8,809
Total property, plant and equipment	8,835	8,697
Less: Accumulated depreciation	4,470	4,303
Property, plant and equipment, net	4,365	4,394
Goodwill	3,435	3,365
Other intangible assets, net	1,237	1,309
Noncurrent deferred tax Assets	551	873
Long-Term receivables, net	376	475
Other assets	602	619
Total assets	$20,224	$19,844

NOTES TO THE CONSOLIDATED FINANCIAL STATEMENTS

Note 7. Customer Financing Programs

Monsanto participates in customer financing programs as follows:

	As of Aug. 31,	
(Dollars in millions)	2012	2011
Transactions that Qualify for Sales Treatment		
U.S. agreement to sell customer receivables[1]		
Outstanding balance	$291	$ 3
Maximum future payout under recourse provisions	17	—
Other U.S. and European agreements to sell accounts receivables[2]		
Outstanding balance	$ 34	$ 55
Maximum future payout under recourse provisions	21	46
Agreements with Lenders [3]		
Outstanding balance	$ 85	$ 82
Maximum future payout under the guarantee	56	76

The gross amount of receivables sold under transactions that qualify for sales treatment were:

	Gross Amount of Receivables Sold		
	Year Ended Aug. 31,		
(Dollars in millions)	2012	2011	2010
Transactions that Qualify for Sales Treatment			
U.S. agreement to sell customer receivables[1]	$506	$ 3	$221
Other U.S. and European agreement to sell accounts receivables[2]	62	61	107

[1] Monsanto has an agreement in the United States to sell customer receivables up to a maximum outstanding balance of $500 million and to service such accounts. These receivables qualify for sales treatment under the Transfers and Servicing topic of the ASC and, accordingly, the proceeds are included in net cash provided by operating activities in the Statements of Consolidated Cash Flows. The agreement includes recourse provisions and thus a liability is established at the time of sale that approximates fair value based upon the company's historical collection experience and a current assessment of credit exposure.

[2] Monsanto also sells accounts receivables in the United States and European regions, both with and without recourse. The sales within these programs qualify for sales treatment under the Transfers and Servicing topic of the ASC and, accordingly, the proceeds are included in net cash provided by operating activities in the Statements of Consolidated Cash Flows. The liability for the guarantees for sales with recourse is recorded at an amount that approximates fair value, based on the company's historical collection experience for the customers associated with the sale of the receivables and a current assessment of credit exposure.

[3] Monsanto has additional agreements with lenders to establish programs that provide financing for select customers in the United States, Brazil, Latin America and Europe. Monsanto provides various levels of recourse through guarantees of the accounts in the event of customer default. The term of the guarantee is equivalent to the term of the customer loans. The liability for the guarantees is recorded at an amount that approximates fair value, based on the company's historical collection experience with customers that participate in the program and a current assessment of credit exposure. If performance is required under the guarantee, Monsanto may retain amounts that are subsequently collected from customers.

In addition to the arrangements in the above table, Monsanto also participates in a financing program in Brazil that allowed Monsanto to transfer up to 1 billion Brazilian reais (approximately $490 million) for select customers in Brazil to a special purpose entity (SPE), formerly a qualified special purpose entity (QSPE). Under the arrangement, a recourse provision requires Monsanto to cover the first 12 percent of credit losses within the program. The company has evaluated its relationship with the entity under the updated guidance within the Consolidation topic of the ASC and, as a result, the entity has been consolidated on a prospective basis effective Sept. 1, 2010. For further information on this topic, see Note 8—Variable Interest Entities. Proceeds from customer receivables sold through the financing program and derecognized from the Statements of Consolidated Financial Position totaled $115 million for fiscal year 2010.

There were no significant GAAP recourse or non-recourse liabilities for all programs as of Aug. 31, 2012, and 2011. There were no significant delinquent loans for all programs as of Aug. 31, 2012, and 2011.

2.34 THE DOW CHEMICAL COMPANY (DEC)

CONSOLIDATED BALANCE SHEETS (in part)

	At December 31	
(In millions, except share amounts)	2012	2011
Assets		
Current assets		
Cash and cash equivalents (variable interest entities restricted—2012: $146; 2011: $170)	$ 4,318	$ 5,444
Marketable securities and interest-bearing deposits	—	2
Accounts and notes receivable:		
Trade (net of allowance for doubtful receivables—2012: $121; 2011: $121)	5,074	4,900
Other	4,605	4,726
Inventories	8,476	7,577
Deferred income tax assets—current	877	471
Other current assets	334	302
Total current assets	23,684	23,422
Investments		
Investment in nonconsolidated affiliates	4,121	3,405
Other investments (investments carried at fair value—2012: $2,061; 2011: $2,008)	2,565	2,508
Noncurrent receivables	313	1,144
Total investments	6,999	7,057
Property		
Property	54,366	52,216
Less accumulated depreciation	36,846	34,917
Net property (variable interest entities restricted—2012: $2,554; 2011: $2,169)	17,520	17,299
Other assets		
Goodwill	12,739	12,930
Other intangible assets (net of accumulated amortization—2012: $2,785; 2011: $2,349)	4,711	5,061
Deferred income tax assets—noncurrent	3,333	2,559
Asbestos-related insurance receivables—noncurrent	155	172
Deferred charges and other assets	464	724
Total other assets	21,402	21,446
Total assets	$69,605	$69,224

NOTES TO THE CONSOLIDATED FINANCIAL STATEMENTS

Note 15—Transfers of Financial Assets

Sale of Trade Accounts Receivable in North America and Europe

The Company sells trade accounts receivable of select North America entities and qualifying trade accounts receivable of select European entities on a revolving basis to certain multi-seller commercial paper conduit entities ("conduits"). The Company maintains servicing responsibilities and the related costs are insignificant. The proceeds received are comprised of cash and interests in specified assets of the conduits (the receivables sold by the Company) that entitle the Company to the residual cash flows of such specified assets in the conduits after the commercial paper has been repaid. Neither the conduits nor the investors in those entities have recourse to other assets of the Company in the event of nonpayment by the debtors.

During the year ended December 31, 2012, the Company recognized a loss of $17 million on the sale of these receivables ($24 million loss for the year ended December 31, 2011, and $26 million loss for the year ended December 31, 2010), which is included in "Interest expense and amortization of debt discount" in the consolidated statements of income. The Company's interests in the conduits are carried at fair value and included in "Accounts and notes receivable—Other" in the consolidated balance sheets. Fair value of the interests is determined by calculating the expected amount of cash to be received and is based on unobservable inputs (a Level 3 measurement). The key input in the valuation is the percentage of anticipated credit losses in the portfolio of receivables sold that have not yet been collected. Given the short-term nature of the underlying receivables, discount rates and prepayments are not factors in determining the fair value of the interests.

The following table summarizes the carrying value of interests held, which represents the Company's maximum exposure to loss related to the receivables sold, and the percentage of anticipated credit losses related to the trade accounts receivable sold. Also provided is the sensitivity of the fair value of the interests held to hypothetical adverse changes in the anticipated credit losses; amounts shown below are the corresponding hypothetical decreases in the carrying value of interests.

(In millions)	Interests Held at December 31	
	2012	2011
Carrying value of interests held	$1,057	$1,141
Percentage of anticipated credit losses	0.73%	1.22%
Impact to carrying value—10% adverse change	$ 1	$ 2
Impact to carrying value—20% adverse change	$ 2	$ 4

Credit losses, net of any recoveries, were $1 million for the year ended December 31, 2012 ($8 million for the year ended December 31, 2011, and $2 million for the year ended December 31, 2010).

Following is an analysis of certain cash flows between the Company and the conduits:

(In millions)	Cash Proceeds		
	2012	2011	2010
Sale of receivables	$ 57	$ 16	$ 818
Collections reinvested in revolving receivables	$25,828	$28,609	$22,866
Interests in conduits[1]	$ 2,650	$ 1,737	$ 1,038

[1] Presented in "Operating Activities" in the consolidated statements of cash flows.

Following is additional information related to the sale of receivables under these facilities:

(In millions)	Trade Accounts Receivable Sold at December 31	
	2012	2011
Delinquencies on sold receivables still outstanding	$ 164	$ 155
Trade accounts receivable outstanding and derecognized	$2,294	$2,385

In September 2011, the Company repurchased $71 million of previously sold receivables related to a divestiture.

Sale of Trade Accounts Receivable in Asia Pacific

The Company sells participating interests in trade accounts receivable of select Asia Pacific entities. The Company maintains servicing responsibilities and the related costs are insignificant. The third-party holders of the participating interests do not have recourse to the Company's assets in the event of nonpayment by the debtors.

During the years ended December 31, 2012, 2011 and 2010, the Company recognized insignificant losses on the sale of the participating interests in the receivables, which is included in "Interest expense and amortization of debt discount" in the consolidated statements of income. The Company receives cash upon the sale of the participating interests in the receivables.

Following is an analysis of certain cash flows between the Company and the third-party holders of the participating interests:

(In millions)	Cash Proceeds		
	2012	2011	2010
Sale of participating interests	$64	$143	$218
Collections reinvested in revolving receivables	$58	$120	$195

Following is additional information related to the sale of participating interests in the receivables under this facility:

(In millions)	Trade Accounts Receivable at December 31	
	2012	2011
Derecognized from the consolidated balance sheets	$ 13	$ 13
Outstanding in the consolidated balance sheets	283	303
Total accounts receivable in select Asia Pacific entities	$296	$316

There were no credit losses on receivables relating to the participating interests sold during the years ended December 31, 2012, 2011 and 2010. There were no delinquencies on the outstanding receivables related to the participating interests sold at December 31, 2012 or December 31, 2011.

CONSOLIDATED BALANCE SHEETS (in part)

(Thousands, except share amounts)	June 30, 2012	July 2, 2011
Assets		
Current assets:		
Cash and cash equivalents	$ 1,006,864	$ 675,334
Receivables, less allowances of $106,319 and $107,739, respectively (Note 3)	4,607,324	4,764,293
Inventories	2,388,642	2,596,470
Prepaid and other current assets	251,609	191,110
Total current assets	8,254,439	8,227,207
Property, plant and equipment, net (Note 5)	461,230	419,173
Goodwill (Notes 2 and 6)	1,100,621	885,072
Other assets	351,576	374,117
Total assets	$10,167,866	$9,905,569
Liabilities and Shareholders' Equity		
Current liabilities:		
Borrowings due within one year (Note 3 and 7)	$ 872,404	$ 243,079
Accounts payable	3,230,765	3,561,633
Accrued expenses and other (Note 8)	695,483	673,016
Total current liabilities	4,798,652	4,477,728
Long-term debt (Note 7)	1,271,985	1,273,509
Other long-term liabilities (Notes 9 and 10)	191,497	98,262
Total liabilities	6,262,134	5,849,499

NOTES TO CONSOLIDATED FINANCIAL STATEMENTS

1. Summary of Significant Accounting Policies (in part)

Accounts receivable securitization—The Company has an accounts receivable securitization program whereby the Company may sell receivables in securitization transactions and retain a subordinated interest and servicing rights to those receivables. The securitization program is accounted for as an on-balance sheet financing through the securitization of accounts receivable (see Note 3).

3. Accounts Receivable Securitization

In August 2011, the Company amended its accounts receivable securitization program (the "Program") with a group of financial institutions to allow the Company to sell, on a revolving basis, an undivided interest of up to $750,000,000 (600,000,000 prior to the amendment) in eligible U.S. receivables while retaining a subordinated interest in a portion of the receivables. The eligible receivables are sold through a wholly-owned bankruptcy-remote special purpose entity that is consolidated for financial reporting purposes. Such eligible receivables are not directly available to satisfy claims of the Company's creditors. Financing under the Program does not qualify as off-balance sheet financing, as a result, the receivables and related debt obligation remain on the Company's consolidated balance sheet as amounts are drawn on the Program. The Program has a one year term that expires at the end of August 2012, which is expected to be renewed for another year on comparable terms. The Program contains certain covenants, all of which the Company was in compliance with as of June 30, 2012. There were $670,000,000 in borrowings outstanding under the Program at June 30, 2012 and $160,000,000 as of July 2, 2011. (See Note 7 for discussion of other short-term and long-term debt outstanding). Interest on borrowings is calculated using a base rate or a commercial paper rate plus a spread of 0.35%. The facility fee is 0.35%. Expenses associated with the Program, which were not material in the past three fiscal years, consisted of program, facility and professional fees recorded in selling, general and administrative expenses in the accompanying consolidated statements of operations.

7. External Financing (in part)

Short-term debt consists of the following:

(Thousands)	June 30, 2012	July 2, 2011
Bank credit facilities	$201,390	$ 81,951
Borrowings under the accounts receivable securitization program (see Note 3)	670,000	160,000
Other debt due within one year	1,014	1,128
Short-term debt	$872,404	$243,079

Bank credit facilities consist of various committed and uncommitted lines of credit with financial institutions utilized primarily to support the working capital requirements of foreign operations. The weighted average interest rate on the bank credit facilities was 6.1% and 7.8% at the end of fiscal 2012 and 2011, respectively.

See Note 3 for the discussion of the accounts receivable securitization program and associated borrowings outstanding.

Inventory

RECOGNITION AND MEASUREMENT

2.36 FASB ASC 330, *Inventory*, states that the primary basis of accounting for inventories is cost, but a departure from the cost basis of pricing the inventory is required when the utility of the goods is no longer as great as their cost. FASB ASC 330-10-35-1 requires an entity to measure inventories at the lower of cost or market. *Market*, as defined in the FASB ASC glossary, means current replacement cost, with the constraint that market should not exceed net realizable value and should not be lower than net realizable value less an allowance for an approximately normal profit margin.

2.37 FASB ASC 330-10-35-14 states that if inventories are written down below cost at the close of a fiscal year, such reduced amount is to be considered the cost for subsequent accounting purposes. Similarly, the Topic 5(BB), "Inventory Valuation Allowances," of the SEC's *Codification of Staff Accounting Bulletins* indicates that a write-down of inventory creates a new cost basis that subsequently cannot be marked up.

PRESENTATION

2.38 Rule 5-02.6 of Regulation S-X requires separate presentation in the balance sheet or notes of the amounts of major classes of inventory, such as finished goods, work in process, raw materials, and supplies. Additional disclosures are required for amounts related to long-term contracts or programs.

DISCLOSURE

2.39 FASB ASC 330 requires disclosure of the basis for stating inventories. Rule 5-02.6 of Regulation S-X requires disclosure of the method by which amounts are removed from inventory (for example, average cost; first in, first out (FIFO); last in, first out (LIFO); estimated average cost per unit).

2.40 Rule 5-02.6c of Regulation S-X requires that registrants using LIFO disclose the excess of replacement or current cost over stated LIFO value, if material.

PRESENTATION AND DISCLOSURE EXCERPTS

FIRST-IN FIRST-OUT

2.41 SNAP-ON INCORPORATED (DEC)
CONSOLIDATED BALANCE SHEETS (in part)

	Fiscal Year End	
(Amounts in millions, except share data)	2012	2011
Assets		
Current assets:		
Cash and cash equivalents	$ 214.5	$ 185.6
Trade and other accounts receivable—net	497.9	463.5
Finance receivables—net	323.1	277.2
Contract receivables—net	62.7	49.7
Inventories—net	404.2	386.4
Deferred income tax assets	81.8	92.6
Prepaid expenses and other assets	84.8	75.7
Total current assets	1,669.0	1,530.7

NOTES TO CONSOLIDATED FINANCIAL STATEMENTS

Note 1: Summary of Accounting Policies (in part)

Inventories: Snap-on values its inventory at the lower of cost or market and adjusts for the value of inventory that is estimated to be excess, obsolete or otherwise unmarketable. Snap-on records allowances for excess and obsolete inventory based on historical and estimated future demand and market conditions. Allowances for raw materials are largely based on an analysis of raw material age and actual physical inspection of raw material for fitness for use. As part of evaluating the adequacy of allowances for work-in-progress and finished goods, management reviews individual product stock-keeping units (SKUs) by product category and product life cycle. Cost adjustments for each product category/product life-cycle state are generally established and maintained based on a combination of historical experience, forecasted sales and promotions, technological obsolescence, inventory age and other actual known conditions and circumstances. Should actual product marketability and raw material fitness for use be affected by conditions that are different from management estimates, further adjustments to inventory allowances may be required.

Snap-on adopted the "last-in, first-out" ("LIFO") inventory valuation method in 1973 for its U.S. locations. Snap-on's U.S. inventories accounted for on a LIFO basis consist of purchased product and inventory manufactured at the company's heritage U.S. manufacturing facilities (primarily hand tools and tool storage). As Snap-on began acquiring businesses in the 1990's, the company retained the "first-in, first-out" ("FIFO") inventory valuation methodology used by the predecessor businesses prior to their acquisition by Snap-on; the company does not adopt the LIFO inventory valuation methodology for new acquisitions. See Note 4 for further information on inventories.

Note 4: Inventories

Inventories by major classification as of 2012 and 2011 year end are as follows:

(Amounts in millions)	2012	2011
Finished goods	$353.6	$343.8
Work in progress	38.6	32.2
Raw materials	83.8	80.5
Total FIFO value	476.0	456.5
Excess of current cost over LIFO cost	(71.8)	(70.1)
Total inventories—net	$404.2	$386.4

Inventories accounted for using the FIFO method as of 2012 and 2011 year end approximated 60% and 62%, respectively, of total inventories. The company accounts for its non-U.S. inventory on the FIFO method. As of 2012 year end, approximately 26% of the company's U.S. inventory was accounted for using the FIFO method and 74% was accounted for using the LIFO method. There were no LIFO inventory liquidations in 2012, 2011 or 2010.

LAST-IN FIRST-OUT

2.42 McKESSON CORPORATION (MAR)

CONSOLIDATED BALANCE SHEETS (in part)

(In millions, except per share amounts)

	March 31,	
	2012	2011
Assets		
Current assets		
Cash and cash equivalents	$ 3,149	$ 3,612
Receivables, net	9,977	9,187
Inventories, net	10,073	9,225
Prepaid expenses and other	404	333
Total current assets	23,603	22,357

FINANCIAL NOTES

1. Significant Accounting Policies (n part)

Inventories: We report inventories at the lower of cost or market ("LCM"). Inventories for our Distribution Solutions segment consist of merchandise held for resale. For our Distribution Solutions segment, the majority of the cost of domestic inventories is determined using the last-in, first-out ("LIFO") method and the cost of Canadian inventories is determined using the first-in, first-out ("FIFO") method. Technology Solutions segment inventories consist of computer hardware with cost generally determined by the standard cost method, which approximates average cost. Rebates, fees, cash discounts, allowances, chargebacks and other incentives received from vendors are generally accounted for as a reduction in the cost of inventory and are recognized when the inventory is sold.

The LIFO method was used to value approximately 88% and 87% of our inventories at March 31, 2012 and 2011. At March 31, 2012 and 2011, our LIFO reserves, net of LCM adjustments, were $107 million and $96 million. LIFO reserves include both pharmaceutical and non-pharmaceutical products. In 2012, 2011 and 2010, we recognized net LIFO expense of $11 million, $3 million and $8 million within our consolidated statements of operations, which related to our non-pharmaceutical products. A LIFO expense is recognized when the net effect of price increases on branded pharmaceuticals and non-pharmaceutical products held in inventory exceeds the impact of price declines and shifts towards generic pharmaceuticals, including the effect of branded pharmaceutical products that have lost market exclusivity. A LIFO credit is recognized when the net effect of price declines and shifts towards generic pharmaceuticals exceeds the impact of price increases on branded pharmaceuticals and non-pharmaceutical products held in inventory.

We believe that the average cost or FIFO inventory costing method provides a reasonable estimation of the current cost of replacing inventory (*i.e.*, "market"). As such, our LIFO inventory is valued at the lower of LIFO or market. Primarily due to continued net deflation in generic pharmaceutical inventories, pharmaceutical inventories at LIFO were $76 million and $156 million higher than market as of March 31, 2012 and 2011. As a result, we recorded a LCM credit of $80 million in 2012 and a LCM charge of $44 million in 2011 within our consolidated statements of operations to adjust our LIFO inventories to market.

AVERAGE COST

2.43 TEREX CORPORATION (DEC)
CONSOLIDATED BALANCE SHEET (in part)

(In millions, except par value)

	December 31,	
	2012	2011
Assets		
Current assets		
Cash and cash equivalents	$ 678.0	$ 774.1
Trade receivables (net of allowance of $38.8 and $42.5 at December 31, 2012 and 2011, respectively)	1,077.7	1,178.1
Inventories	1,715.6	1,758.1
Other current assets	326.1	342.9
Total current assets	3,797.4	4,053.2

NOTES TO CONSOLIDATED FINANCIAL STATEMENTS

(Dollar amounts in millions, unless otherwise noted, except per share amounts)

Note A—Basis of Presentation (in part)

Inventories. Inventories are stated at the lower of cost or market ("LCM") value. Cost is determined principally by the average cost method and the first-in, first-out ("FIFO") (approximately 57% and 43%, respectively). In valuing inventory, the Company is required to make assumptions regarding the level of reserves required to value potentially obsolete or over-valued items at the lower of cost or market. These assumptions require the Company to analyze the aging of and forecasted demand for its inventory, forecast future products sales prices, pricing trends and margins, and to make judgments and estimates regarding obsolete or excess inventory. Future product sales prices, pricing trends and margins are based on the best available information at that time including actual orders received, negotiations with the Company's customers for future orders, including their plans for expenditures, and market trends for similar products. The Company's judgments and estimates for excess or obsolete inventory are based on analysis of actual and forecasted usage. The valuation of used equipment taken in trade from customers requires the Company to use the best information available to determine the value of the equipment to potential customers. This value is subject to change based on numerous conditions. Inventory reserves are established taking into account age, frequency of use, or sale, and in the case of repair parts, the installed base of machines. While calculations are made involving these factors, significant management judgment regarding expectations for future events is involved. Future events that could significantly influence the Company's judgment and related estimates include general economic conditions in markets where the Company's products are sold, new equipment price fluctuations, actions of the Company's competitors, including the introduction of new products and technological advances, as well as new products and design changes the Company introduces. The Company makes adjustments to its inventory reserve based on the identification of specific situations and increases its inventory reserves accordingly. As further changes in future economic or industry conditions occur, the Company will revise the estimates that were used to calculate its inventory reserves. At December 31, 2012 and 2011, reserves for LCM, excess and obsolete inventory totaled $135.6 million and $120.1 million, respectively.

If actual conditions are less favorable than those the Company has projected, the Company will increase its reserves for LCM, excess and obsolete inventory accordingly. Any increase in the Company's reserves will adversely impact its results of operations. The establishment of a reserve for LCM, excess and obsolete inventory establishes a new cost basis in the inventory. Such reserves are not reduced until the product is sold.

Note F—Inventories

Inventories consist of the following (in millions):

	December 31,	
	2012	2011
Finished equipment	$ 485.4	$ 465.2
Replacement parts	201.4	217.7
Work-in-process	507.4	508.7
Raw materials and supplies	521.4	566.5
Inventories	$1,715.6	$1,758.1

Reserves for lower of cost or market value, excess and obsolete inventory were $135.6 million and $120.1 million at December 31, 2012 and 2011, respectively.

2.44 PVH CORP. (JAN)

CONSOLIDATED BALANCE SHEETS (in part)

(In thousands, except share and per share data)

Assets	January 29, 2012	January 30, 2011
Current assets:		
Cash and cash equivalents	$ 233,197	$ 498,718
Trade receivables, net of allowances for doubtful accounts of $15,744 and $11,105	467,628	433,900
Other receivables	13,337	13,261
Inventories, net	809,009	710,868
Prepaid expenses	111,228	80,974
Other, including deferred taxes of $53,645 and $68,307	104,836	97,568
Total current assets	1,739,235	1,835,289

NOTES TO CONSOLIDATED FINANCIAL STATEMENTS

(Currency and share amounts in thousands, except per share data)

1. Summary of Significant Accounting Policies (in part)

Inventories—Inventories related to the Company's wholesale operations and international retail operations, comprised principally of finished goods, are stated at the lower of cost or market. Inventories related to the Company's North American retail operations, comprised entirely of finished goods, are stated at the lower of cost or market.

In the first quarter of 2011, the Company voluntarily changed its method of accounting for its United States retail apparel inventories that were previously on the last-in, first-out ("LIFO") method to the weighted average cost method and for its United States wholesale inventories that were previously on the LIFO method to the first-in, first-out ("FIFO") method. As a result, the Company no longer has any inventory valued based on LIFO.

The Company believes the change is preferable because (i) the FIFO and weighted average cost methods provide more consistency across the Company and its segments, as only two inventory valuation methods will be applied as compared to three; (ii) the Company had experienced decreasing costs over the past several years, eliminating the reporting impact of LIFO; and (iii) the change results in a more meaningful presentation of financial position, as the FIFO and weighted average cost methods reflect more recent costs in the Consolidated Balance Sheet and improve comparability with the Company's peers.

The accounting change had no impact on the Company's consolidated financial statements because the inventory valued under LIFO, including lower of cost or market adjustments, was at current cost for the past several years. As a result, retrospective application of the accounting change resulted in no adjustments to amounts previously reported in the Company's consolidated financial statements.

Inventory held on consignment by third parties totaled $9,959 at January 29, 2012 and $5,949 at January 30, 2011.

RETAIL METHOD

2.45 WAL-MART STORES, INC. (JAN)

CONSOLIDATED BALANCE SHEETS (in part)

	As of January 31,	
(Amounts in millions except per share data)	2012	2011
Assets		
Current assets:		
Cash and cash equivalents	$ 6,550	$ 7,395
Receivables, net	5,937	5,089
Inventories	40,714	36,437
Prepaid expenses and other	1,685	2,960
Current assets of discontinued operations	89	131
Total current assets	54,975	52,012

Note 1. Summary of Significant Accounting Policies (in part)

Inventories

The Company values inventories at the lower of cost or market as determined primarily by the retail method of accounting, using the last-in, first-out ("LIFO") method for substantially all of the Walmart U.S. segment's merchandise inventories. The retail method of accounting results in inventory being valued at the lower of cost or market since permanent markdowns are currently taken as a reduction of the retail value of inventory. The Sam's Club segment's merchandise is valued based on the weighted-average cost using the LIFO method. Inventories for the Walmart International operations are primarily valued by the retail method of accounting and are stated using the first-in, first-out ("FIFO") method. At January 31, 2012 and 2011, the Company's inventories valued at LIFO approximate those inventories as if they were valued at FIFO.

Other Current Assets

PRESENTATION

2.46 Rule 5-02.8 of Regulation S-X requires that any amounts in excess of 5 percent of total current assets be stated separately on the balance sheet or disclosed in the notes.

PRESENTATION AND DISCLOSURE EXCERPTS

DEFERRED TAXES

2.47 TENNECO INC. (DEC)
CONSOLIDATED BALANCE SHEETS (in part)

	December 31,	
(Millions)	2012	2011
Assets		
Current assets:		
Cash and cash equivalents	$ 223	$ 214
Receivables—		
Customer notes and accounts, net	966	936
Other	20	44
Inventories	667	592
Deferred income taxes	72	40
Prepayments and other	176	153
Total current assets	2,124	1,979

1. Summary of Accounting Policies (in part)

Income Taxes

We reported income tax expenses of $19 million, $88 million and $69 million in the years ended 2012, 2011 and 2010, respectively. The tax expense recorded in 2012 differs from the expense that would be recorded using a U.S. Federal statutory rate of 35 percent due primarily to the impact of the U.S. 2012 valuation allowance release described below and income generated in lower tax rate jurisdictions, partially offset by the impact of recording a valuation allowance against the tax benefit for tax credits and losses in certain foreign jurisdictions.

We evaluate our deferred income taxes quarterly to determine if valuation allowances are required or should be adjusted. U.S. GAAP requires that companies assess whether valuation allowances should be established against their deferred tax assets based on consideration of all available evidence, both positive and negative, using a "more likely than not" standard. This assessment considers, among other matters, the nature, frequency and amount of recent losses, the duration of statutory carryforward periods, and tax planning strategies. In making such judgments, significant weight is given to evidence that can be objectively verified.

In 2008, given our historical losses in the U.S., we concluded that our ability to fully utilize our federal and state net operating loss carryforward ("NOL") was limited. As a result, we recorded a valuation allowance against all of our U.S. deferred tax assets except for our tax planning strategies which had not yet been implemented and which did not depend upon generating future taxable income. Prior to the reversal of the valuation allowance in the third quarter of 2012, we carried a deferred tax asset in the U.S. of $90 million relating to the expected utilization of the federal and state NOL. The recording of a valuation allowance did not impact the amount of the NOL that would be available for federal and state income tax purposes in future periods.

In 2012, we reversed the tax valuation allowance against our net deferred tax assets in the U.S. based on operating improvements we had made, the outlook for light and commercial vehicle production in the U.S. and the positive impact this should have on our U.S. operations. The net income impact of the tax valuation allowance release in the U.S. was a tax benefit of approximately $81 million. We now have a federal NOL at December 31, 2012 of $190 million, which expires beginning in tax years ending in 2022 through 2030. The state NOLs expire in various tax years through 2032.

Valuation allowances have been established in certain foreign jurisdictions for deferred tax assets based on a "more likely than not" threshold. The ability to realize deferred tax assets depends on our ability to generate sufficient taxable income within the carryforward periods provided for in the tax law for each tax jurisdiction. We have considered the following possible sources of taxable income when assessing the realization of our deferred tax assets:
- Future reversals of existing taxable temporary differences;
- Taxable income or loss, based on recent results, exclusive of reversing temporary differences and carryforwards;
- Tax-planning strategies; and
- Taxable income in prior carryback years if carryback is permitted under the relevant tax law.

In 2012, after considering all available evidence and all possible sources of taxable income, we recorded a $19 million tax valuation allowance in Spain for tax credits that may not be utilized due to tax losses in Spain.

The valuation allowances recorded against deferred tax assets generated by taxable losses in Spain and certain other foreign jurisdictions will impact our provision for income taxes until the valuation allowances are released. Our provision for income taxes will include no tax benefit for losses incurred and no tax expense with respect to income generated in these jurisdictions until the respective valuation allowance is eliminated.

7. Income Taxes

The domestic and foreign components of our income before income taxes and noncontrolling interests are as follows:

(Millions)	Year Ended December 31,		
	2012	2011	2010
U.S. income (loss) before income taxes	$166	$ 55	$ (45)
Foreign income before income taxes	157	216	177
Income before income taxes and noncontrolling interests	$323	$271	$132

Following is a comparative analysis of the components of income tax expense:

(Millions)	Year Ended December 31,		
	2012	2011	2010
Current—			
U.S. federal	$ —	$ —	$ —
State and local	4	2	1
Foreign	89	91	64
	93	93	65
Deferred—			
U.S. federal	(25)	—	—
State and local	(20)	—	—
Foreign	(29)	(5)	4
	(74)	(5)	4
Income tax expense	$ 19	$ 88	$ 69

Following is a reconciliation of income taxes computed at the statutory U.S. federal income tax rate (35 percent for all years presented) to the income tax expense reflected in the statements of income:

(Millions)	2012	2011	2010
		Year Ended December 31,	
Income tax expense computed at the statutory U.S. federal income tax rate	$113	$ 95	$ 46
Increases (reductions) in income tax expense resulting from:			
Foreign income taxed at different rates	(21)	(14)	(16)
Taxes on repatriation of dividends	8	6	4
State and local taxes on income, net of U.S. federal income tax benefit	4	2	2
Changes in valuation allowance for tax loss carryforwards and credits	(91)	(11)	16
Foreign tax holidays	(5)	(4)	(5)
Investment and R&D tax credits	(1)	(4)	(2)
Foreign earnings subject to U.S. federal income tax	23	6	5
Adjustment of prior years taxes	(5)	—	4
Impact of foreign tax law changes	(1)	—	(1)
Tax contingencies	(6)	3	12
Goodwill impairment	—	3	—
Other	1	6	4
Income tax expense	$ 19	$ 88	$ 69

The components of our net deferred tax assets were as follows:

(Millions)	2012	2011
	Year Ended December 31,	
Deferred tax assets—		
Tax loss carryforwards:		
U.S. federal	$ —	$ 41
State	23	45
Foreign	63	57
Investment tax credit benefits	51	45
Postretirement benefits other than pensions	50	54
Pensions	87	79
Bad debts	1	3
Sales allowances	6	6
Payroll and other accruals	119	98
Valuation allowance	(118)	(225)
Total deferred tax assets	282	203
Deferred tax liabilities—		
Tax over book depreciation	57	65
Other	70	62
Total deferred tax liabilities	127	127
Net deferred tax assets	$ 155	$ 76

U.S. and state tax loss carryforwards have been presented net of uncertain tax positions that if realized, would reduce tax loss carryforwards in 2012 and 2011 by $47 million and $53 million, respectively.

Following is a reconciliation of deferred taxes to the deferred taxes shown in the balance sheet:

(Millions)	2012	2011
	Year Ended December 31,	
Balance sheet:		
Current portion—deferred tax asset	$ 72	$ 40
Non-current portion—deferred tax asset	116	92
Current portion—deferred tax liability shown in other current liabilities	(6)	(5)
Non-current portion—deferred tax liability	(27)	(51)
Net deferred tax assets	$155	$ 76

As a result of the valuation allowances recorded for $118 million and $225 million at December 31, 2012 and 2011, respectively, we have potential tax assets that were not recognized on our balance sheet. These unrecognized tax assets resulted primarily from foreign tax loss carryforwards, foreign investment tax credits and U.S. state net operating losses that are available to reduce future tax liabilities.

We reported income tax expense of $19 million, $88 million and $69 million in the years ended 2012, 2011 and 2010, respectively. The tax expense recorded in 2012 differs from the expense that would be recorded using a U.S. Federal statutory rate of 35 percent due primarily to the impact of the U.S. 2012 valuation allowance release described below and income generated in lower tax rate jurisdictions, partially offset by the impact of recording a valuation allowance against the tax benefit for tax credits and losses in certain foreign jurisdictions.

We evaluate our deferred income taxes quarterly to determine if valuation allowances are required or should be adjusted. U.S. GAAP requires that companies assess whether valuation allowances should be established against their deferred tax assets based on consideration of all available evidence, both positive and negative, using a "more likely than not" standard. This assessment considers, among other matters, the nature, frequency and amount of recent losses, the duration of statutory carryforward periods, and tax planning strategies. In making such judgments, significant weight is given to evidence that can be objectively verified.

In 2008, given our historical losses in the U.S., we concluded that our ability to fully utilize our federal and state net operating loss carryforward ("NOL") was limited. As a result, we recorded a valuation allowance against all of our U.S. deferred tax assets except for our tax planning strategies which had not yet been implemented and which did not depend upon generating future taxable income. Prior to the reversal of the valuation allowance in the third quarter of 2012, we carried a deferred tax asset in the U.S. of $90 million relating to the expected utilization of the federal and state NOL. The recording of a valuation allowance did not impact the amount of the NOL that would be available for federal and state income tax purposes in future periods.

In 2012, we reversed the tax valuation allowance against our net deferred tax assets in the U.S. based on operating improvements we had made, the outlook for light and commercial vehicle production in the U.S. and the positive impact this should have on our U.S. operations. The net income impact of the tax valuation allowance release in the U.S was a tax benefit of approximately $81 million. We now have a federal NOL at December 31, 2012 of $190 million, which expires beginning in tax years ending in 2022 through 2030. The state NOLs expire in various tax years through 2032.

Valuation allowances have been established in certain foreign jurisdictions for deferred tax assets based on a "more likely than not" threshold. The ability to realize deferred tax assets depends on our ability to generate sufficient taxable income within the carryforward periods provided for in the tax law for each tax jurisdiction. We have considered the following possible sources of taxable income when assessing the realization of our deferred tax assets:
- Future reversals of existing taxable temporary differences;
- Taxable income or loss, based on recent results, exclusive of reversing temporary differences and carryforwards;
- Tax-planning strategies; and
- Taxable income in prior carryback years if carryback is permitted under the relevant tax law.

In 2012, after considering all available evidence and all possible sources of taxable income, we recorded a $19 million tax valuation allowance in Spain for tax credits that may not be utilized due to tax losses in Spain.

The valuation allowances recorded against deferred tax assets generated by taxable losses in Spain and certain other foreign jurisdictions will impact our provision for income taxes until the valuation allowances are released. Our provision for income taxes will include no tax benefit for losses incurred and no tax expense with respect to income generated in these jurisdictions until the respective valuation allowance is eliminated.

We do not provide for U.S. income taxes on unremitted earnings of foreign subsidiaries, except for the earnings of certain of our China operations, as our present intention is to reinvest the unremitted earnings in our foreign operations. Unremitted earnings of foreign subsidiaries were approximately $728 million at December 31, 2012. We estimated that the amount of U.S. and foreign income taxes that would be accrued or paid upon remittance of the assets that represent those unremitted earnings was $239 million. The estimated U.S. and foreign income taxes on unremitted earnings may be impacted in the future if we are able to claim a U.S. foreign tax credit.

We have tax sharing agreements with our former affiliates that allocate tax liabilities for periods prior to year 2000 and establish indemnity rights on certain tax issues.

U.S. GAAP provides that a tax benefit from an uncertain tax position may be recognized when it is "more likely than not" that the position will be sustained upon examination, including resolutions of any related appeals or litigation processes, based on the technical merits.

A reconciliation of our uncertain tax positions is as follows:

(Millions)	2012	2011	2010
Uncertain tax positions—			
Balance January 1	$119	$111	$ 96
Gross increases in tax positions in current period	13	19	23
Gross increases in tax positions in prior period	1	3	4
Gross decreases in tax positions in prior period	(12)	(10)	(6)
Gross decreases—settlements	(5)	—	(2)
Gross decreases—statute of limitations expired	(9)	(4)	(4)
Balance December 31	$107	$119	$111

Included in the balance of uncertain tax positions were $101 million in 2012 and $36 million at both December 31, 2011 and 2010, of tax benefits, that if recognized, would affect the effective tax rate. We recognize accrued interest and penalties related to unrecognized tax benefits as income tax expense. Penalties of less than $1 million were accrued in 2012, 2011 and 2010. Additionally, we accrued interest related to uncertain tax positions of less than $1 million in 2012, $2 million in 2011, and less than $1 million in 2010. Our liability for penalties was $3 million at 2012, $2 million at December 31, 2011 and $3 million at December 31, 2010, respectively, and our liability for interest was $5 million, $7 million, and $5 million at December 31, 2012, 2011 and 2010, respectively.

Our uncertain tax position at December 31, 2012 and 2011 included exposures relating to the disallowance of deductions, global transfer pricing and various other issues. We believe it is reasonably possible that a decrease of up to $27 million in unrecognized tax benefits related to the expiration of foreign statute of limitations and the conclusion of income tax examinations may occur within the coming year.

We are subject to taxation in the U.S. and various state and foreign jurisdictions. As of December 31, 2012, our tax years open to examination in primary jurisdictions are as follows:

	Open To Tax Year
United States—due to NOL	1998
China	2002
Spain	2003
Brazil	2007
Canada	2007
Mexico	2007
Belgium	2010
Germany	2010
United Kingdom	2011

ADVANCES

2.48 UNIVERSAL CORPORATION (MAR)
CONSOLIDATED BALANCE SHEETS (in part)

	March 31,	
(in thousands of dollars)	2012	2011
Assets		
Current assets		
Cash and cash equivalents	$ 261,699	$ 141,007
Accounts receivable, net	390,790	335,575
Advances to suppliers, net	135,317	160,616
Accounts receivable—unconsolidated affiliates	7,370	10,433
Inventories—at lower of cost or market:		
Tobacco	682,095	742,422
Other	53,197	48,647
Prepaid income taxes	20,819	18,661
Deferred income taxes	51,025	47,009
Other current assets	88,317	73,864
Total current assets	1,690,629	1,578,234

NOTES TO CONSOLIDATED FINANCIAL STATEMENTS

(All dollar amounts are in thousands, except per share amounts or as otherwise noted.)

Note 1. Nature of Operations and Significant Accounting Policies (in part)

Advances to Suppliers

In some regions where the Company operates, it provides agronomy services and seasonal advances of seed, fertilizer, and other supplies to tobacco farmers for crop production, or makes seasonal cash advances to farmers for the procurement of those inputs. These advances are short term, are repaid upon delivery of tobacco to the Company, and are reported in advances to suppliers in the consolidated balance sheets. Primarily in Brazil, the Company has made long-term advances to tobacco farmers to finance curing barns and other farm infrastructure. In addition, due to low crop yields and other factors, in some years individual farmers may not deliver sufficient volumes of tobacco to fully repay their seasonal advances, and the Company may extend repayment of those advances into the following crop year. The long-term portion of advances is included in other noncurrent assets in the consolidated balance sheets. Both the current and the long-term portions of advances to suppliers are reported net of allowances recorded when the Company determines that amounts outstanding are not likely to be collected. Short-term and long-term advances to suppliers totaled $225.0 million at March 31, 2012 and $271.4 million at March 31, 2011. The related valuation allowances totaled $74.4 million at March 31, 2012, and $74.9 million at March 31, 2011, and were estimated based on the Company's historical loss information and crop projections. The allowances were increased by provisions for estimated uncollectible amounts of approximately $11.9 million in fiscal year 2012, $18.7 million in fiscal year 2011, and $18.5 million in fiscal year 2010. These provisions are included in selling, general, and administrative expenses in the consolidated statements of income. Interest on advances is recognized in earnings upon the farmers' delivery of tobacco in payment of principal and interest. Accrual of interest is discontinued when an advance is not expected to be fully collected. Advances on which interest accrual had been discontinued totaled approximately $59.9 million at March 31, 2012, and $76.0 million at March 31, 2011.

ASSETS HELD FOR SALE

2.49 STANLEY BLACK & DECKER, INC. (DEC)
CONSOLIDATED BALANCE SHEETS (in part)

(Millions of Dollars)

	2012	2011
Assets		
Current assets		
Cash and cash equivalents	$ 716.0	$ 906.9
Accounts and notes receivable, net	1,538.2	1,445.0
Inventories, net	1,316.6	1,270.9
Prepaid expenses	199.6	201.9
Assets held for sale	133.4	1,050.2
Other current assets	194.5	214.6
Total current assets	4,098.3	5,089.5
Property, plant and equipment, net	1,333.7	1,142.6
Goodwill	7,021.1	6,438.2
Customer relationships, net	1,079.8	1,139.2
Trade names, net	1,681.7	1,697.1
Other intangible assets, net	173.1	107.6
Other assets	456.3	334.8
Total assets	$15,844.0	$15,949.0

NOTES TO CONSOLIDATED FINANCIAL STATEMENTS

T. Discontinued Operations

In October 2012, the Company entered into a definitive agreement to sell its Hardware & Home Improvement business ("HHI") to Spectrum Brands Holdings, Inc. ("Spectrum") for approximately $1.4 billion in cash, with the price subject to revision for the level of working capital at the date of sale. The purchase and sale agreement stipulates that the sale occur in a First and Second Closing, for approximately $1.3 billion and $100 million, respectively. HHI is a provider of residential locksets, residential builders hardware and plumbing products marketed under the Kwikset, Weiser, Baldwin, Stanley, National and Pfister brands. The majority of the HHI business was part of the Company's Security segment, with the remainder being part of the Company's CDIY segment. The divestiture of the HHI business is part of the continued diversification of the Company's revenue streams and geographic footprint. The HHI sale also includes the residential portion of the Tong Lung hardware business, which the Company acquired in the third quarter of 2012. The First Closing occurred on December 17, 2012 in which HHI, excluding the residential portion of the Tong Lung business, was sold for $1.261 billion in cash. The First Closing of the HHI sale resulted in an after-tax gain of $358.9 million. The Second Closing to sell the residential Tong Lung business for approximately $100 million is expected to occur no later than April 2013. The $100 million payment relating to the Second Closing has been held in escrow at December 29, 2012.

As part of the purchase and sale agreement, the Company will perform transition services relating to certain administrative functions for Spectrum primarily for a period of one year or less, pending Spectrum's integration of these functions into their pre-existing business processes. Spectrum will pay a transition service fee to the Company as reimbursement for transition service costs incurred. As discussed above, the divestiture of the residential Tong Long portion of the HHI business for $100 million is expected to occur no later than April 2013 and accordingly, there will be continuing cash flows associated with Tong Long. The Company evaluated the transition services and other continuing involvement and concluded that the expected continuing cash flows are not a significant portion of the disposed business.

During 2011, the Company sold three small businesses for total cash proceeds of $27.1 million and a cumulative after-tax loss of $18.8 million. These businesses were sold as the related product lines provided limited growth opportunity or were not considered part of the Company's core offerings.

As a result of these actions, the operating results of the businesses above, including the related gain and loss, are reported as discontinued operations. Amounts previously reported have been reclassified to conform to this presentation in accordance with ASC 205 to allow for meaningful comparison of continuing operations. The Consolidated Balance Sheets as of December 29, 2012 and December 31, 2011 aggregate amounts associated with discontinued operations as described above. Summarized operating results of discontinued operations are presented in the following table:

(Millions of dollars)	2012	2011	2010
Net sales	$930.6	$1,001.9	$913.0
Earnings from discontinued operations before income taxes (including pretax gain on HHI sale of $384.7 million in 2012)	$503.5	$ 114.9	$ 68.4
Income taxes on discontinued operations (including income taxes for gain on HHI sale of $25.8 million in 2012)	69.2	38.7	20.8
Net earnings from discontinued operations	$434.3	$ 76.2	$ 47.6

As of December 29, 2012, assets and liabilities held for sale relating to the residential portion of the Tong Lung business totaled $133.4 million and $30.3 million, respectively. The carrying amounts of the assets and liabilities that were aggregated in assets held for sale and liabilities held for sale as of December 31, 2011 are presented in the following table:

(Millions of dollars)	2011
Accounts and notes receivable, net	108.2
Inventories, net	167.7
Property, Plant and Equipment, net	108.3
Goodwill and other intangibles, net	655.0
Other Assets	11.0
Total assets	1,050.2
Accounts payable and accrued expenses	152.5
Other liabilities	61.4
Total liabilities	213.9

CURRENT ASSETS OF DISCONTINUED OPERATIONS

2.50 DEAN FOODS COMPANY (DEC)
CONSOLIDATED BALANCE SHEETS (in part)

	December 31	
(Dollars in thousands, except share data)	2012	2011
Assets		
Current assets:		
Cash and cash equivalents	$ 78,975	$ 115,650
Receivables, net of allowance of $13,693 and $10,391	881,410	872,958
Income tax receivable	—	24,960
Inventories	407,912	384,991
Deferred income taxes	103,207	109,475
Prepaid expenses and other current assets	58,285	62,001
Assets of discontinued operations	672,989	668,673
Total current assets	2,202,778	2,238,708

NOTES TO CONSOLIDATED FINANCIAL STATEMENTS

3. Discontinued Operations and Divestitures (in part)

Discontinued Operations—Morningstar (in part)

On December 2, 2012, we entered into an agreement to sell our Morningstar division to a third party. Morningstar is a leading manufacturer of dairy and non-dairy extended shelf-life and cultured products, including creams and creamers, ice cream mixes, whipping cream, aerosol whipped toppings, iced coffee, half and half, value-added milks, sour cream and cottage cheese. The sale closed on January 3, 2013 and we received net proceeds of approximately $1.45 billion, a portion of which was used to retire outstanding debt under our senior secured credit facility. We expect to record a net pre-tax gain of approximately $850 million on the sale of our Morningstar division, excluding $22.9 million of transaction costs recognized in discontinued operations during 2012. The operating results of our Morningstar division, previously reported within the Morningstar segment, have been reclassified as discontinued operations in our Consolidated Financial Statements for the years ended December 31, 2012, 2011 and 2010 and as of December 31, 2012 and 2011.

The following is a summary of Morningstar's assets and liabilities classified as discontinued operations as of December 31, 2012 and 2011:

	December 31	
	2012	2011
Assets		
Current assets	$154,211	$147,091
Property, plant and equipment, net	176,582	178,145
Goodwill	306,095	306,095
Identifiable intangibles and other assets, net	36,101	37,342
Assets of discontinued operations	$672,989	$668,673
Liabilities		
Accounts payable and accrued expenses	$ 94,188	$105,252
Debt	97	22,001
Other long-term liabilities	7,047	5,949
Liabilities of discontinued operations	$101,332	$133,202

COSTS AND ESTIMATED EARNINGS IN EXCESS OF BILLINGS

2.51 TUTOR PERINI CORPORATION (DEC)

CONSOLIDATED BALANCE SHEETS (in part)

(In thousands, except share data)

	At December 31, 2012	At December 31, 2011
Assets		
Current assets:		
Cash, including cash equivalents of $23,140 and $19,197	$ 168,056	$ 204,240
Restricted cash	38,717	35,437
Accounts receivable, including retainage of $354,269 and $358,511	1,224,613	1,275,031
Costs and estimated earnings in excess of billings	465,002	358,398
Deferred income taxes	10,071	—
Other current assets	75,388	76,928
Total current assets	1,981,847	1,950,034

NOTES TO CONSOLIDATED FINANCIAL STATEMENTS

[1] Description of Business and Summary of Significant Accounting Policies (in part)

(e) Method of Accounting for Contracts

Revenues and profits from the Company's contracts and construction joint venture contracts are recognized by applying percentages of completion for the period to the total estimated revenues for the respective contracts. Percentage of completion is determined by relating the actual cost of the work performed to date to the current estimated total cost of the respective contracts. However, on construction management contracts, profit is generally recognized in accordance with the contract terms, usually on the as-billed method, which is generally consistent with the level of effort incurred over the contract period. When the estimate on a contract indicates a loss, the Company's policy is to record the entire loss during the accounting period in which it is estimable. In the ordinary course of business, at a minimum on a quarterly basis, the Company updates estimates projected total contract revenue, cost and profit or loss for each contract based on changes in facts, such as an approved scope change, and changes in estimates. The cumulative effect of revisions in estimates of the total forecasted revenue and costs, including unapproved change orders and claims, during the course of the work is reflected in the accounting period in which the facts that caused the revision become known. The financial impact of these revisions to any one contract is a function of both the amount of the revision and the percentage of completion of the contract. Amounts up to the costs incurred which are attributable to unapproved change orders and claims are included in the total estimated revenue when realization is probable. Profit from unapproved change orders and claims is recorded in the period such amounts are resolved.

In accordance with normal practice in the construction industry, the Company includes in current assets and current liabilities amounts related to construction contracts realizable and payable over a period in excess of one year. Billings in excess of costs and estimated earnings represents the excess of contract billings to date over the amount of contract costs and profits (or contract revenue) recognized to date on the percentage of completion accounting method on certain contracts. Costs and estimated earnings in excess of billings represents the excess of contract costs and profits (or contract revenue) recognized to date on the percentage of completion accounting method over the amount of contract billings to date on the remaining contracts. Costs and estimated earnings in excess of billings results when (1) the appropriate contract revenue amount has been recognized in accordance with the percentage of completion accounting method, but a portion of the revenue recorded cannot be billed currently due to the billing terms defined in the contract and/or (2) costs, recorded at estimated realizable value, related to unapproved change orders or claims are incurred.

For unapproved change orders or claims that cannot be resolved in accordance with the normal change order process as defined in the contract, the Company employs other dispute resolution methods, including mediation, binding and non-binding arbitration, or litigation.

Costs and estimated earnings in excess of billings related to the Company's contracts and joint venture contracts consisted of the following:

(In thousands)	At December 31, 2012	At December 31, 2011
Unbilled costs and profits incurred to date*	$157,119	$107,645
Unapproved change orders	141,596	136,704
Claims	166,287	114,049
	$465,002	$358,398

* Represents the excess of contract costs and profits recognized to date on the percentage of completion accounting method over the amount of contract billings to date on certain contracts.

Of the balance of "Unapproved change orders" and "Claims" included above in costs and estimated earnings in excess of billings at December 31, 2012 and December 31, 2011, approximately $62.0 million and $85.2 million, respectively, are amounts subject to pending litigation or dispute resolution proceedings as described in Note 9—*Contingencies and Commitments*. These amounts are management's estimate of the probable cost recovery from the disputed claims considering such factors as evaluation of entitlement, settlements reached to date and experience with the customer. In the event that future facts and circumstances, including the resolution of disputed claims, cause a reduction in the aggregate amount of the estimated probable cost recovery from the disputed claims, the amount of such reduction will be recorded against earnings in the relevant future period.

The prerequisite for billing "Unbilled costs and profits incurred to date" is provided in the defined billing terms of each of the applicable contracts. The prerequisite for billing "Unapproved change orders" or "Claims" is the final resolution and agreement between the parties. The amount of costs and estimated earnings in excess of billings at December 31, 2012 estimated by management to be collected beyond one year is approximately $181.3 million.

DERIVATIVES

2.52 UNITED CONTINENTAL HOLDINGS, INC. (DEC)
CONSOLIDATED BALANCE SHEETS (in part)

(In millions, except shares)

	At December 31,	
Assets	2012	2011
Current assets:		
Cash and cash equivalents	$4,770	$6,246
Short-term investments	1,773	1,516
Total unrestricted cash, cash equivalents and short-term investments	6,543	7,762
Restricted cash	65	40
Receivables, less allowance for doubtful accounts (2012—$13; 2011—$7)	1,338	1,358
Aircraft fuel, spare parts and supplies, less obsolescence allowance (2012—$125; 2011—$89)	695	615
Deferred income taxes	543	615
Prepaid expenses and other	865	607
	10,049	10,997

COMBINED NOTES TO CONSOLIDATED FINANCIAL STATEMENTS

Note 13—Hedging Activities (in part)

Fuel Derivatives (in part)

Aircraft fuel has been the Company's single largest and most volatile operating expense for the last several years. The availability and price of aircraft fuel significantly affects the Company's operations, results of operations, financial position and liquidity. Aircraft fuel prices can fluctuate based on a multitude of factors including market expectations of supply and demand balance, inventory levels, geopolitical events, economic growth expectations, fiscal/monetary policies and financial investment flows. To protect against increases in the prices of aircraft fuel, the Company routinely hedges a portion of its future fuel requirements. As of December 31, 2012, the Company had hedged approximately 31% and 2% of its projected fuel requirements (1.2 billion and 63 million gallons, respectively) for 2013 and 2014, respectively, with commonly used financial hedge instruments based on aircraft fuel or closely related commodities, such as heating oil, diesel fuel and crude oil. The Company does not enter into derivative instruments for non-risk management purposes.

Accounting pronouncements pertaining to derivative instruments and hedging are complex with stringent requirements, including documentation of hedging strategy, statistical analysis to qualify a commodity for hedge accounting both on a historical and a prospective basis, and strict contemporaneous documentation that is required at the time each hedge is designated as a cash flow hedge. As required, the Company assesses the effectiveness of each of its individual hedges on a quarterly basis. The Company also examines the effectiveness of its entire hedging program on a quarterly basis utilizing statistical analysis. This analysis involves utilizing regression and other statistical analyses that compare changes in the price of aircraft fuel to changes in the prices of the commodities used for hedging purposes.

Upon proper qualification, the Company accounts for certain fuel derivative instruments as cash flow hedges. All derivatives designated as hedges that meet certain requirements are granted special hedge accounting treatment. The types of instruments the Company utilizes that qualify for special hedge accounting treatment typically include swaps, call options and collars (which consist of a purchased call option and a sold put option). Generally, utilizing the special hedge accounting, all periodic changes in fair value of the derivatives designated as hedges that are considered to be effective are recorded in AOCI until the underlying fuel is consumed and recorded in fuel expense. The Company is exposed to the risk that its hedges may not be effective in offsetting changes in the cost of fuel and that its hedges may not continue to qualify for special hedge accounting. Hedge ineffectiveness results when the change in the fair value of the derivative instrument exceeds the change in the value of the Company's expected future cash outlay to purchase and consume fuel. To the extent that the periodic changes in the fair value of the derivatives are not effective, that ineffectiveness is classified as Nonoperating income (expense): Miscellaneous, net.

The Company also utilizes certain derivative instruments that are economic hedges but do not qualify for hedge accounting under U.S. GAAP. As with derivatives that qualify for hedge accounting, the purpose of these economic hedges is to mitigate the adverse financial impact of potential increases in the price of fuel.

Currently, the only such economic hedges in the Company's hedging portfolio are three-way collars (which consist of a collar with a cap on maximum price protection available). The Company records changes in the fair value of three-way collars to Nonoperating income (expense): Miscellaneous, net.

If the Company terminates a derivative prior to its contractual settlement date, then the cumulative gain or loss recognized in AOCI at the termination date remains in AOCI until the forecasted transaction occurs. In a situation where it becomes probable that a hedged forecasted transaction will not occur, any gains and/or losses that have been recorded to AOCI would be required to be immediately reclassified into earnings. All cash flows associated with purchasing and settling derivatives are classified as operating cash flows in the statements of cash flows.

The Company records each derivative instrument as a derivative asset or liability (on a gross basis) in its consolidated balance sheets, and, accordingly, records any related collateral on a gross basis. The table below presents the fair value amounts of fuel derivative assets and liabilities and the location of amounts recognized in the Company's financial statements.

At December 31, the Company's derivatives were reported in its consolidated balance sheets as follows (in millions):

Classification	Balance Sheet Location	2012			2011		
		UAL	United	Continental	UAL	United	Continental
Derivatives Designated as Cash Flow Hedges							
Assets:							
Fuel contracts due within one year	Receivables	$ 7	$ 5	$ 2	$ 77	$ 48	$ 29
Liabilities:							
Fuel contracts due within one year	Current liabilities: Other	$ 2	$ 1	$ 1	$ 4	$ 4	$—
Derivatives Not Designated as Hedges							
Assets:							
Fuel contracts due within one year	Receivables	$44	$26	$ 18	$—	$—	$—
Liabilities:							
Fuel contracts due within one year	Current liabilities: Other	$ 2	$ 1	$ 1	$—	$—	$—
Fuel contracts with maturities greater than one year	Other liabilities and deferred credits: Other	1	1	—	—	—	—
Total liabilities		$ 3	$ 2	$ 1	$—	$—	$—
Total Derivatives							
Assets:							
Fuel contracts due within one year	Receivables	$51	$31	$ 20	$ 77	$ 48	$ 29
Liabilities:							
Fuel contracts due within one year	Current liabilities: Other	$ 4	$ 2	$ 2	$ 4	$ 4	$—
Fuel contracts with maturities greater than one year	Other liabilities and deferred credits: Other	1	1	—	—	—	—
Total liabilities		$ 5	$ 3	$ 2	$ 4	$ 4	$—

RESTRICTED CASH

2.53 MASTERCARD INCORPORATED (DEC)
CONSOLIDATED BALANCE SHEET (in part)

	December 31,	
(In millions, except share data)	2012	2011
Assets		
Cash and cash equivalents	$2,052	$3,734
Restricted cash for litigation settlement	726	—
Investment securities available-for-sale, at fair value	2,951	1,215
Accounts receivable	925	808
Settlement due from customers	1,117	601
Restricted security deposits held for customers	777	636
Prepaid expenses and other current assets	681	404
Deferred income taxes	128	343
Total current assets	9,357	7,741

NOTES TO CONSOLIDATED FINANCIAL STATEMENTS

Note 1. Summary of Significant Accounting Policies (in part)

Significant Accounting Policies (in part)

Restricted cash—The Company classifies cash as restricted when the cash is unavailable for withdrawal or usage. Restrictions may include legally restricted deposits, contracts entered into with others, or the Company's statements of intention with regard to particular deposits. In December 2012, the Company made a $726 million payment into a qualified settlement fund related to the U.S. merchant class litigation. The Company has presented these funds as restricted cash since the use of the funds under the qualified settlement fund is restricted for payment under the preliminary settlement agreement. Subject to court approval, all or a portion of the funds would be returned to the Company in the event that the settlement is not finalized or certain merchants opt out of the settlement agreement. See Note 5 (Fair Value and Investment Securities), Note 10 (Accrued Expenses) and Note 18 (Legal and Regulatory Proceedings) for further detail.

Note 18. Legal and Regulatory Proceedings (in part)

Interchange Litigation and Regulatory Proceedings (in part)

On July 13, 2012, MasterCard entered into a Memorandum of Understanding ("MOU") to settle the merchant class litigation, and separately agreed in principle to settle all claims brought by the individual merchant plaintiffs. The MOU sets out a binding obligation to enter into a settlement agreement, and is subject to: (1) the successful completion of certain appendices, (2) the successful negotiation of a settlement agreement with the individual merchant plaintiffs, (3) final court approval of the class settlement, and (4) any necessary internal approvals for the parties. MasterCard's financial portion of the settlements is estimated to total $790 million on a pre-tax basis. Of that total, MasterCard recorded a pre-tax charge of $770 million in the fourth quarter of 2011 and an additional $20 million pre-tax charge in the second quarter of 2012. In addition to the financial portion of the settlement, U.S. merchant class members would also receive a 10 basis point reduction in default credit interchange fees for a period of eight months, funded by a corresponding reduction in the default credit interchange fees paid by acquirers to issuers. MasterCard would also be required to modify its No Surcharge Rule to permit U.S. merchants to surcharge MasterCard credit cards, subject to certain limitations set forth in the class settlement agreement. On October 19, 2012, the parties entered into a definitive settlement agreement with respect to the merchant class litigation (consistent with the terms of the MOU), and separately also entered into a settlement agreement with the individual merchant plaintiffs. The merchant class litigation settlement agreement is subject to court approval. The parties to the merchant class litigation filed a motion seeking preliminary approval of the settlement on October 19, 2012, and the court granted preliminary approval of the settlement on November 27, 2012 and scheduled a final approval hearing for September 2013. In 2012, the Company paid $790 million with respect to the settlements, of which $726 million was paid into a qualified settlement fund related to the merchant class litigations. Rule practice changes required by the settlement were implemented in late January 2013. In the event that the merchant class litigation settlement agreement is not approved by the court, or if the class settlement agreement is otherwise terminated by the defendants pursuant to the conditions in the settlement agreement and the litigations are not settled, a negative outcome in the litigation could have a material adverse effect on MasterCard's results of operations, financial position and cash flows.

PREPAID EXPENSES

2.54 WILLIAMS-SONOMA, INC. (JAN)
CONSOLIDATED BALANCE SHEETS (in part)

(Dollars and shares in thousands, except per share amounts)	Jan. 29, 2012	Jan. 30, 2011
Assets		
Current assets		
Cash and cash equivalents	$ 502,757	$ 628,403
Restricted cash	14,732	12,512
Accounts receivable, net	45,961	41,565
Merchandise inventories, net	553,461	513,381
Prepaid catalog expenses	34,294	36,825
Prepaid expenses	24,188	21,120
Deferred income taxes, net	91,744	85,612
Other assets	9,229	8,176
Total current assets	1,276,366	1,347,594

NOTES TO CONSOLIDATED FINANCIAL STATEMENTS

Note A: Summary of Significant Accounting Policies (in part)

Advertising and Prepaid Catalog Expenses (in part)

Advertising expenses consist of media and production costs related to catalog mailings, e-commerce advertising and other direct marketing activities. All advertising costs are expensed as incurred, or upon the release of the initial advertisement, with the exception of prepaid catalog expenses. Prepaid catalog expenses consist primarily of third party incremental direct costs, including creative design, paper, printing, postage and mailing costs for all of our direct response catalogs. Such costs are capitalized as prepaid catalog expenses and are amortized over their expected period of future benefit. Such amortization is based upon the ratio of actual direct-to-customer revenues to the total of actual and estimated future direct-to-customer revenues on an individual catalog basis. Estimated future direct-to-customer revenues are based upon various factors such as the total number of catalogs and pages circulated, the probability and magnitude of consumer response and the assortment of merchandise offered. Each catalog is generally fully amortized over a six to nine month period, with the majority of the amortization occurring within the first four to five months. Prepaid catalog expenses are evaluated for realizability on a monthly basis by comparing the carrying amount associated with each catalog to the estimated probable remaining future profitability (remaining direct-to-customer net revenues less merchandise cost of goods sold, selling expenses and catalog-related costs) associated with that catalog. If the catalog is not expected to be profitable, the carrying amount of the catalog is impaired accordingly.

CONTRACTS

2.55 RAYTHEON COMPANY (DEC)

CONSOLIDATED BALANCE SHEETS (in part)

| (In millions, except per share amount) | December 31: | |
	2012	2011
Assets		
Current assets		
Cash and cash equivalents	$3,188	$4,000
Short-term investments	856	—
Contracts in process, net	4,543	4,526
Inventories	381	336
Deferred taxes	96	221
Prepaid expenses and other current assets	182	226
Total current assets	9,246	9,309

NOTES TO CONSOLIDATED FINANCIAL STATEMENTS

Note 1: Summary of Significant Accounting Policies (in part)

Contracts in Process, Net—Contracts in process, net are stated at cost plus estimated profit, but not in excess of estimated realizable value. Included in contracts in process are accounts receivable, which include amounts billed and due from customers. We maintain an allowance for doubtful accounts to provide for the estimated amount of accounts receivable that will not be collected. The allowance is based upon an assessment of customer creditworthiness, historical payment experience, the age of outstanding receivables and collateral to the extent applicable.

Note 5: Contracts in Process, Net

Contracts in process, net consisted of the following at December 31:

| (In millions) | Cost-Type | | Fixed-Price | | Total | |
	2012	2011	2012	2011	2012	2011
U.S. Government contracts (including foreign military sales):						
Billed	$ 363	$ 397	$ 212	$ 218	$ 575	$ 615
Unbilled	956	865	8,890	10,185	9,846	11,050
Progress payments	—	—	(6,870)	(8,392)	(6,870)	(8,392)
	1,319	1,262	2,232	2,011	3,551	3,273
Other customers:						
Billed	11	17	545	551	556	568
Unbilled	27	31	1,072	1,327	1,099	1,358
Progress payments	—	—	(659)	(666)	(659)	(666)
	38	48	958	1,212	996	1,260
Allowance for doubtful accounts	—	—	(4)	(7)	(4)	(7)
Total contracts in process, net	$1,357	$1,310	$3,186	$ 3,216	$ 4,543	$ 4,526

The U.S. Government has title to the assets related to unbilled amounts on contracts that provide progress payments. Unbilled amounts are recorded under the percentage-of-completion method and are recoverable from the customer upon shipment of the product, presentation of billings or completion of the contract. Included in unbilled at December 31, 2012 was $120 million which is expected to be collected outside of one year.

Billed and unbilled contracts in process include retentions arising from contractual provisions. At December 31, 2012, retentions were $38 million. We anticipate collecting $22 million of these retentions in 2013 and the balance thereafter.

Property, Plant, and Equipment

RECOGNITION AND MEASUREMENT

> **Author's Note**
>
> In December 2011, FASB issued ASU No. 2011-10, *Property, Plant, and Equipment (Topic 360): Derecognition of in Substance Real Estate—a Scope Clarification (a consensus of the FASB Emerging Issues Task Force)*. FASB ASU 2011-10 addresses the accounting for situations in which a parent company ceases to have a controlling financial interest (as described in FASB ASC 810-10) in a subsidiary that is in-substance real estate as a result of default on the subsidiary's nonrecourse debt. The amendments in this update state that the parent company should apply the guidance in FASB ASC 360-20 to determine whether it should derecognize the in-substance real estate. This guidance is effective for public entities for fiscal years, and interim periods within those years, beginning on or after June 15, 2012, and after December 15, 2013, for nonpublic entities. Early adoption is permitted. Given the effective dates of FASB ASU 2011-10, no survey entity will have adopted these requirements in its 2012 financial statements.

2.56 *Property, plant, and equipment* are the long-lived, physical assets of the entity acquired for use in the entity's normal business operations and not intended for resale by the entity. FASB ASC 360, *Property, Plant, and Equipment*, states that these assets are initially recorded at historical cost, which includes the costs necessarily incurred to bring them to the condition and location necessary for their intended use. FASB ASC 835-20 establishes standards for capitalizing interest cost as part of the historical cost of acquiring assets constructed by an entity for its own use or produced for the entity by others for which deposits or progress payments have been made.

2.57 An entity may acquire or develop computer software either for internal use or for sale or lease to others. If for internal use, FASB ASC 350-40 provides guidance on accounting for the costs of computer software and for determining whether the software is for internal use. Under FASB ASC 350-40, internal and external costs incurred to develop internal use software during the application development stage should be capitalized and amortized over the software's estimated useful life. Accounting for software acquired or developed for sale or lease is addressed by FASB ASC 985-20. Whether for internal use or sale or lease, FASB ASC refers to capitalized software costs as amortizable intangible assets.

PRESENTATION

2.58 FASB ASC 210 10 45 4 indicates that property, plant, and equipment should be classified as noncurrent when a classified balance sheet is presented. Under FASB ASC 805-20-55-37, some use rights acquired in a business combination may have characteristics of tangible, rather than intangible, assets. An example is mineral rights.

2.59 Under FASB ASC 985-20-45-2, capitalized costs related to software for sale or lease having a life of more than one year or one operating cycle should be presented as an other asset. Under FASB ASC 985-20, amortization expense should be on a product-by-product basis and charged to cost of sales or a similar expense category because it relates to a software product that is marketed to others. Presentations of capitalized computer software costs by survey entities vary.

DISCLOSURE

2.60 FASB ASC 360-10-50-1 requires the following disclosures in the financial statements or notes thereto:
  a. Depreciation expense for the period
  b. Balance of major classes of depreciable assets, by nature or function, at the balance sheet date
  c. Accumulated depreciation, either by major classes of depreciable assets or in total, at the balance sheet date
  d. A general description of the method(s) used in computing depreciation with respect to major classes of depreciable assets.

FASB ASC 360 also provides accounting and disclosure guidance for the long-lived assets that are impaired or held for disposal. Rule 5-02 of Regulation S-X requires that registrants state the basis of determining the amounts of property, plant, and equipment.

PROPERTY, PLANT, AND EQUIPMENT

2.61 MURPHY OIL CORPORATION (DEC)

CONSOLIDATED BALANCE SHEETS (in part)

	December 31	
(Thousands of dollars)	2012	2011
Assets		
Current assets		
Cash and cash equivalents	$ 947,316	513,873
Canadian government securities with maturities greater than 90 days at the date of acquisition	115,603	532,093
Accounts receivable, less allowance for doubtful accounts of $6,697 in 2012 and $7,892 in 2011	1,853,364	1,554,184
Inventories, at lower of cost or market		
Crude oil and blend stocks	226,541	189,320
Finished products	266,307	254,880
Materials and supplies	259,462	222,438
Prepaid expenses	335,831	93,397
Deferred income taxes	89,040	87,486
Assets held for sale	15,119	0
Total current assets	4,108,583	3,447,671
Property, plant and equipment, at cost less accumulated depreciation, depletion and amortization of $8,138,587 in 2012 and $6,861,494 in 2011	13,011,606	10,475,149
Goodwill	43,103	41,863
Deferred charges and other assets	151,183	173,455
Assets held for sale	208,168	0
Total assets	$17,522,643	14,138,138

NOTES TO CONSOLIDATED FINANCIAL STATEMENTS

Note A—Significant Accounting Policies (in part)

Property, Plant and Equipment—The Company uses the successful efforts method to account for exploration and development expenditures. Leasehold acquisition costs are capitalized. If proved reserves are found on an undeveloped property, leasehold cost is transferred to proved properties. Costs of undeveloped leases are generally expensed over the life of the leases. Exploratory well costs are capitalized pending determination about whether proved reserves have been found. In certain cases, a determination of whether a drilled exploratory well has found proved reserves cannot be made immediately. This is generally due to the need for a major capital expenditure to produce and/or evacuate the hydrocarbon(s) found. The determination of whether to make such a capital expenditure is usually dependent on whether further exploratory wells find a sufficient quantity of additional reserves. The Company continues to capitalize exploratory well costs in Property, Plant and Equipment when the well has found a sufficient quantity of reserves to justify its completion as a producing well and the Company is making sufficient progress assessing the reserves and the economic and operating viability of the project. The Company reevaluates its capitalized drilling costs at least annually to ascertain whether drilling costs continue to qualify for ongoing capitalization. Other exploratory costs, including geological and geophysical costs, are charged to expense as incurred. Development costs, including unsuccessful development wells, are capitalized. Interest is capitalized on development projects that are expected to take one year or more to complete.

Oil and gas properties are evaluated by field for potential impairment. Other properties are evaluated for impairment on a specific asset basis or in groups of similar assets as applicable. An impairment is recognized when the estimated undiscounted future net cash flows of an asset are less than its carrying value. If an impairment occurs, the carrying value of the impaired asset is reduced to fair value.

The Company records a liability for asset retirement obligations (ARO) equal to the fair value of the estimated cost to retire an asset. The ARO liability is initially recorded in the period in which the obligation meets the definition of a liability, which is generally when a well is drilled or the asset is placed in service. The ARO liability is estimated by the Company's engineers using existing regulatory requirements and anticipated future inflation rates. When the liability is initially recorded, the Company increases the carrying amount of the related long-lived asset by an amount equal to the original liability. The liability is increased over time to reflect the change in its present value, and the capitalized cost is depreciated over the useful life of the related long-lived asset. The Company reevaluates the adequacy of its recorded ARO liability at least annually. Actual costs of asset retirements such as dismantling oil and gas production facilities and site restoration are charged against the related liability. Any difference between costs incurred upon settlement of an asset retirement obligation and the recorded liability is recognized as a gain or loss in the Company's earnings.

Depreciation and depletion of producing oil and gas properties is recorded based on units of production. Unit rates are computed for unamortized exploration drilling and development costs using proved developed reserves; unit rates for unamortized leasehold costs and asset retirement costs are amortized over proved reserves. Proved reserves are estimated by the Company's engineers and are subject to future revisions based on availability of additional information. Refineries, certain marketing facilities and certain natural gas processing facilities are depreciated primarily using the composite straight-line method with depreciable lives ranging from 14 to 25 years. Gasoline stations and other properties are depreciated over 3 to 20 years by individual unit on the straight-line method. Gains and losses on asset disposals or retirements are included in income as a separate component of revenues.

Turnarounds for major processing units at the Milford Haven, Wales refinery are scheduled at four to five year intervals. Turnarounds for coking units at Syncrude Canada Ltd. are scheduled at intervals of two to three years. Turnaround work associated with various other less significant units at Milford Haven and Syncrude varies depending on operating requirements and events. Murphy defers turnaround costs incurred and amortizes such costs through Operating Expenses over the period until the next scheduled turnaround. All other maintenance and repairs are expensed as incurred. Renewals and betterments are capitalized. Major turnarounds occurred in 2010 at both the Meraux, Louisiana, and Milford Haven, Wales, refineries.

Note D—Property, Plant and Equipment

	December 31, 2012		December 31, 2011	
(Thousands of dollars)	Cost	Net	Cost	Net
Exploration and production[1]	$18,408,904	11,294,933[2]	14,766,637	8,730,124[2]
Refining and marketing	2,619,844	1,661,081	2,456,822	1,688,709
Corporate and other	121,445	55,592	113,184	56,316
	$21,150,193	13,011,606	17,336,643	10,475,149
[1] Includes mineral rights as follows:	$ 1,051,153	556,399	1,078,770	619,950

[2] Includes $26,611 in 2012 and $21,154 in 2011 related to administrative assets and support equipment.

Under FASB guidance exploratory well costs should continue to be capitalized when the well has found a sufficient quantity of reserves to justify its completion as a producing well and the company is making sufficient progress assessing the reserves and the economic and operating viability of the project.

At December 31, 2012, 2011 and 2010, the Company had total capitalized drilling costs pending the determination of proved reserves of $445,697,000, $556,412,000 and $497,765,000, respectively. The following table reflects the net changes in capitalized exploratory well costs during the three-year period ended December 31, 2012.

(Thousands of dollars)	2012	2011	2010
Beginning balance at January 1	$ 556,412	497,765	369,862
Additions to capitalized exploratory well costs pending the determination of proved reserves	135,849	86,035	137,403
Reclassifications to proved properties based on the determination of proved reserves	(165,377)	0	0
Capitalized exploratory well costs charged to expense or sold	(81,187)	(27,388)	(9,500)
Ending balance at December 31	$445,697	556,412	497,765

The following table provides an aging of capitalized exploratory well costs based on the date the drilling was completed and the number of projects for which exploratory well costs has been capitalized since the completion of drilling.

	2012			2011			2010		
(Thousands of dollars)	Amount	No. of Wells	No. of Projects	Amount	No. of Wells	No. of Projects	Amount	No. of Wells	No. of Projects
Aging of capitalized well costs:									
Zero to one year	$ 59,833	7	2	$ 69,757	11	5	$135,494	15	4
One to two years	18,335	2	3	143,611	15	3	115,418	10	4
Two to three years	83,314	9	4	101,696	9	2	42,571	3	3
Three years or more	284,215	26	6	241,348	33	6	204,282	31	4
	$ 445,697	44	15	$556,412	68	16	$497,765	59	15

Of the $385,864,000 of exploratory well costs capitalized more than one year at December 31, 2012, $270,093,000 is in Malaysia and $115,771,000 is in the U.S. In Malaysia either further appraisal or development drilling is planned and/or development studies/plans are in various stages of completion. In the U.S. further drilling is anticipated and development plans are being formulated. The capitalized well costs charged to expense in 2012 included a suspended well in the northern block of the Republic of the Congo that was written off following unsuccessful wildcat drilling in 2012 at a nearby prospect, two suspended wells offshore Sarawak Malaysia that were written off following a government denial of a request to delay the timing of an oil development project, and a well drilled in the Gulf of Mexico in 2010 that the owners decided not to develop. The capitalized well costs expensed in 2011 related to exploration costs offshore Republic of the Congo and Brunei. The costs in Republic of the Congo were written off following an impairment charge at the nearby Azurite field, and the Brunei costs were written off based on unsuccessful wells drilled in the area in late 2011.

At year-end 2012, Murphy determined that the Azurite field, offshore Republic of the Congo, was impaired due to removal of all proved oil reserves after an unsuccessful redrill of a key well in the field. The impairment charge in 2012 totaled $200,000,000 and included a write-off of the remaining book value of the Azurite field plus other anticipated losses related to operations of the field. At year-end 2011, an impairment charge of $368,600,000 was recorded to reduce the carrying value of the Azurite field to fair value. The Company determined that a downward revision of proved oil reserves for Azurite was necessary at year-end 2011. The determination was made after an extensive study of the declining well production at the field. It was determined that the remaining reserves, including risked estimated probable and possible reserves, would not allow for recovery of the Company's net investment in the Azurite field. Fair value was determined each year at Azurite using a discounted cash flow model based on certain key assumptions, including future estimated net production levels, future estimated oil prices for the field based on year-end futures prices, and future estimated operating and capital expenditures. The carrying value of the net property, plant and equipment for the Azurite field was reduced at December 31, 2011 to the present value of the net cash inflows for the field based on the results of the discounted cash flow calculation.

At year-end 2012, the Company also wrote down its net investment in the ethanol production facility in Hereford, Texas, taking an impairment charge of $60,988,000. The write down was required based on expected weak ethanol production margins at the plant in future periods. Fair value was determined using a discounted cash flow model for three years, plus an estimated terminal value based on a multiple of the last year's cash flow. Certain key assumptions used in the cash flow model included use of available futures prices for corn and ethanol products. Additional key assumptions included estimated future ethanol and distillers grain production levels, estimated future operating expenses, and estimated sales prices for distillers grain.

In 2012, the Company announced that its Board of Directors had approved a plan to separate its U.S. downstream subsidiary into a separate publicly owned company. In 2010, the Company announced that its Board of Directors had approved plans to exit the U.K. refining and marketing business. These operations are presented as the U.S. and U.K. refining and marketing segments in Note T. The separation of the U.S. downstream subsidiary is expected to be completed during 2013. The sale process for the U.K. downstream assets continues in 2013. Based on current market conditions, it is possible that the Company could incur a loss when the U.K. downstream assets are sold. If the separation of the U.S. downstream subsidiary and the sale of the U.K. downstream assets continue to progress, the results of these operations are likely to be presented as discontinued operations in future periods when the operations no longer qualify as continuing operations under U.S. generally accepted accounting principles.

2.62 LAS VEGAS SANDS CORP. (DEC)
CONSOLIDATED BALANCE SHEETS (in part)

	December 31,	
(In thousands, except share data)	2012	2011
Assets		
Current assets:		
Cash and cash equivalents	$ 2,512,766	$ 3,902,718
Restricted cash and cash equivalents	4,521	4,828
Accounts receivable, net	1,819,260	1,336,817
Inventories	43,875	34,990
Deferred income taxes, net	2,299	72,192
Prepaid expenses and other	94,793	45,607
Total current assets	4,477,514	5,397,152
Property and equipment, net	15,766,748	15,030,979
Deferred financing costs, net	214,465	173,636
Restricted cash and cash equivalents	1,938	2,315
Deferred income taxes, net	43,280	153
Leasehold interests in land, net	1,458,741	1,390,468
Intangible assets, net	70,618	80,068
Other assets, net	130,348	169,352
Total assets	$22,163,652	$22,244,123

NOTES TO CONSOLIDATED FINANCIAL STATEMENTS

Note 2—Summary of Significant Accounting Policies (in part)

Property and Equipment

Property and equipment are stated at the lower of cost or fair value. Depreciation and amortization are provided on a straight-line basis over the estimated useful lives of the assets, which do not exceed the lease term for leasehold improvements, as follows:

Land improvements, building and building improvements	15 to 40 years
Furniture, fixtures and equipment	3 to 15 years
Leasehold improvements	5 to 10 years
Transportation	5 to 20 years

The estimated useful lives are based on the nature of the assets as well as current operating strategy and legal considerations such as contractual life. Future events, such as property expansions, property developments, new competition or new regulations, could result in a change in the manner in which the Company uses certain assets requiring a change in the estimated useful lives of such assets.

Maintenance and repairs that neither materially add to the value of the asset nor appreciably prolong its life are charged to expense as incurred. Gains or losses on disposition of property and equipment are included in the consolidated statements of operations.

The Company evaluates its property and equipment and other long-lived assets for impairment in accordance with related accounting standards. For assets to be disposed of, the Company recognizes the asset to be sold at the lower of carrying value or fair value less costs of disposal. Fair value for assets to be disposed of is estimated based on comparable asset sales, solicited offers or a discounted cash flow model.

For assets to be held and used (including projects under development), fixed assets are reviewed for impairment whenever indicators of impairment exist. If an indicator of impairment exists, the Company first groups its assets with other assets and liabilities at the lowest level for which identifiable cash flows are largely independent of the cash flows of other assets and liabilities (the "asset group"). Secondly, the Company estimates the undiscounted future cash flows that are directly associated with and expected to arise from the completion, use and eventual disposition of such asset group. The Company estimates the undiscounted cash flows over the remaining useful life of the primary asset within the asset group. If the undiscounted cash flows exceed the carrying value, no impairment is indicated. If the undiscounted cash flows do not exceed the carrying value, then an impairment is measured based on fair value compared to carrying value, with fair value typically based on a discounted cash flow model. If an asset is still under development, future cash flows include remaining construction costs.

To estimate the undiscounted cash flows of the Company's asset groups, the Company considers all potential cash flow scenarios, which are probability weighted based on management's estimates given current conditions. Determining the recoverability of the Company's asset groups is judgmental in nature and requires the use of significant estimates and assumptions, including estimated cash flows, probability weighting of potential scenarios, costs to complete construction for assets under development, growth rates and future market conditions, among others. Future changes to the Company's estimates and assumptions based upon changes in macro-economic factors, regulatory environments, operating results or management's intentions may result in future changes to the recoverability of these asset groups.

For assets to be held for sale, the fixed assets (the "disposal group") are measured at the lower of their carrying amount or fair value less cost to sell. Losses are recognized for any initial or subsequent write-down to fair value less cost to sell, while gains are recognized for any subsequent increase in fair value less cost to sell, but not in excess of the cumulative loss previously recognized. Any gains or losses not previously recognized that result from the sale of the disposal group shall be recognized at the date of sale. Fixed assets are not depreciated while classified as held for sale.

During the year ended December 31, 2012, the Company recognized an impairment loss of $143.7 million primarily related to $100.7 million of capitalized construction costs related to the Company's former Cotai Strip development (referred to as parcels 7 and 8) and a $42.9 million impairment due to the termination of ZAiA at The Venetian Macao. No assets were impaired during the year ended December 31, 2011. During the year ended December 31, 2010, the Company recognized an impairment loss of $16.1 million related to equipment disposed of in Macao.

Note 4—Property and Equipment, Net

Property and equipment consists of the following (in thousands):

	December 31,	
	2012	2011
Land and improvements	$ 515,538	$ 436,768
Building and improvements	14,414,026	11,456,407
Furniture, fixtures, equipment and leasehold improvements	2,557,071	2,147,326
Transportation	411,671	405,156
Construction in progress	1,824,531	3,677,479
	19,722,837	18,123,136
Less—accumulated depreciation and amortization	(3,956,089)	(3,092,157)
	$15,766,748	$15,030,979

Construction in progress consists of the following (in thousands):

	December 31,	
	2012	2011
Sands Cotai Central	$ 913,432	$2,902,743
Four Seasons Macao (principally the Four Seasons Apartments)	415,367	404,650
The Parisian Macao	59,510	34,492
Other	436,222	335,594
	$1,824,531	$3,677,479

The $436.2 million in other construction in progress consists primarily of construction of the Las Vegas Condo Tower and The Venetian Macao.

The final purchase price for The Shoppes at The Palazzo was to be determined in accordance with the April 2004 purchase and sale agreement, as amended, between Venetian Casino Resort, LLC ("VCR") and GGP (the "Amended Agreement") based on net operating income ("NOI") of The Shoppes at The Palazzo calculated 30 months after the closing date of the sale, as defined under the Amended Agreement (the "Final Purchase Price") and subject to certain later audit adjustments (see "—Note 12—Mall Sales—The Shoppes at The Palazzo"). The Company and GGP had entered into several amendments to the Amended Agreement to defer the time to reach agreement on the Final Purchase Price and on June 24, 2011, the Company reached a settlement with GGP regarding the Final Purchase Price. Under the terms of the settlement, the Company retained the $295.4 million of proceeds previously received and participates in certain future revenues earned by GGP. Under generally accepted accounting principles, the transaction has not been accounted for as a sale because the Company's participation in certain future revenues constitutes continuing involvement in The Shoppes at The Palazzo. Therefore, $266.2 million of the proceeds allocated to the mall sale transaction has been recorded as deferred proceeds (a long-term financing obligation), which will accrue interest at an imputed rate and will be offset by (i) imputed rental income and (ii) rent payments made to GGP related to spaces leased back from GGP by the Company. The property and equipment legally sold to GGP totaling $250.8 million (net of $60.6 million of accumulated depreciation) as of December 31, 2012, will continue to be recorded on the Company's consolidated balance sheet and will continue to be depreciated in the Company's consolidated statement of operations.

The cost and accumulated depreciation of property and equipment that the Company is leasing to third parties, primarily as part of its mall operations, was $1.01 billion and $154.2 million, respectively, as of December 31, 2012. The cost and accumulated depreciation of property and equipment that the Company is leasing to these third parties was $807.3 million and $112.2 million, respectively, as of December 31, 2011.

The cost and accumulated depreciation of property and equipment that the Company is leasing under capital lease arrangements is $38.8 million and $8.8 million, respectively, as of December 31, 2012. The cost and accumulated depreciation of property and equipment that the Company is leasing under capital lease arrangements was $29.5 million and $6.0 million, respectively, as of December 31, 2011.

The Company had commenced pre-construction activities on its former Cotai Strip development on parcels 7 and 8. During December 2010, the Company received notice from the Macao government that its application for a land concession for parcels 7 and 8 was not approved and the Company applied to the Chief Executive of Macao for an executive review of the decision. In January 2011, the Company filed a judicial appeal with the Court of Second Instance in Macao. In May 2012, the Company withdrew its appeal and recorded an impairment loss of $100.7 million during the year ended December 31, 2012, related to the capitalized construction costs of its development on parcels 7 and 8.

The Company also recorded a one-time impairment loss of $42.9 million related to the termination of the ZAiA show at The Venetian Macao during the year ended December 31, 2012.

The Company suspended portions of its development projects. As described in "—Note 1—Organization and Business of Company—Development Projects," the Company may be required to record an impairment charge related to these developments in the future.

Equity Method and Joint Ventures

RECOGNITION AND MEASUREMENT

2.63 FASB ASC 323, *Investments—Equity Method and Joint Ventures*, stipulates that the equity method should be used to account for investments in corporate joint ventures and certain other noncontrolled entities when an investor has the ability to exercise significant influence over operating and financial policies of an investee, even though the investor holds 50 percent or less of the common stock. FASB ASC 323 considers an investor to have the ability to exercise significant influence when it owns 20 percent or more of the voting stock of an investee. FASB ASC 323 specifies the criteria for applying the equity method of accounting to 50 percent or less owned entities and lists circumstances under which, despite 20 percent ownership, an investor may not be able to exercise significant influence.

PRESENTATION

2.64 Under the equity method, FASB ASC 323-10-45-1 requires that an investment in common stock be shown in the balance sheet of an investor as a single amount.

DISCLOSURE

2.65 Under FASB ASC 323-10-50-2, the significance of an equity method investment to the investor's financial position and results of operations should be considered in evaluating the extent of disclosures of the financial position and results of operations of an investee. If the investor has more than one investment in common stock, disclosures wholly or partly on a combined basis may be appropriate. FASB ASC 323-10-50-3 details disclosures required for equity method investments, including name and percentage of ownership of the investee, investor accounting policies, any difference between the amount at which an investment is carried and the amount of underlying equity in net assets, and the accounting treatment of the difference.

EQUITY METHOD

2.66 DISCOVERY COMMUNICATIONS, INC. (DEC)
CONSOLIDATED BALANCE SHEETS (in part)

(In millions, except par value)

| | December 31, | |
	2012	2011
Assets		
Current assets:		
Cash and cash equivalents	$ 1,201	$ 1,048
Receivables, net	1,130	1,042
Content rights, net	122	93
Deferred income taxes	74	73
Prepaid expenses and other current assets	203	175
Total current assets	2,730	2,431
Noncurrent content rights, net	1,555	1,302
Property and equipment, net	388	379
Goodwill	6,399	6,291
Intangible assets, net	611	571
Equity method investments	1,095	807
Other noncurrent assets	152	132
Total assets	$12,930	$11,913

NOTES TO CONSOLIDATED FINANCIAL STATEMENTS

Note 2. Summary of Significant Accounting Policies (in part)

Investments

The Company holds investments in equity method investees and other marketable securities. Investments in equity method investees are those for which the Company has the ability to exercise significant influence but does not control and is not the primary beneficiary. Significant influence typically exists if the Company has a 20% to 50% ownership interest in the venture unless predominant evidence to the contrary exists. Under this method of accounting, the Company records its proportionate share of the net earnings or losses of equity method investees and a corresponding increase or decrease to the investment balances. Cash payments to equity method investees such as additional investments, loans and advances and expenses incurred on behalf of investees, as well as payments from equity method investees such as dividends, distributions and repayments of loans and advances are recorded as adjustments to investment balances. The Company evaluates its equity method investments for impairment whenever events or changes in circumstances indicate that the carrying amounts of such investments may not be recoverable. (See Asset Impairment Analysis below.)

Investments in entities over which the Company has no control or significant influence and is not the primary beneficiary, and investments in other securities, are accounted for at fair value or cost. Investments in equity securities with readily determinable fair values are accounted for at fair value, based on quoted market prices, and classified as either trading securities or available-for-sale securities. For investments classified as trading securities, which include securities held in a separate trust in connection with the Company's deferred compensation plan, unrealized and realized gains and losses related to the investment and corresponding liability are recorded in earnings. For investments classified as available-for-sale securities, which include investments in mutual funds, unrealized gains and losses are recorded net of income taxes in other comprehensive income (loss) until the security is sold or considered impaired. If declines in the value of available-for-sale securities are determined to be other than temporary, a loss is recorded in earnings in the current period. Impairments are determined based on, among other factors, the length of time the fair value of the investment has been less than the carrying value, future business prospects for the investee, and information regarding market and industry trends for the investee's business, if available. For purposes of computing realized gains and losses, the Company determines cost on a specific identification basis.

Asset Impairment Analysis (in part)

Equity Method Investments

Equity method investments are reviewed for impairment on a quarterly basis. An equity method investment is written down to fair value if there is evidence of a loss in value which is other than temporary. The Company may estimate the fair value of its equity method investments by considering recent investee equity transactions, discounted cash flow analysis, recent operating results, comparable public company operating cash flow multiples and in certain situations, balance sheet liquidation values. If the fair value of the investment has dropped below the carrying amount, management considers several factors when determining whether an other-than temporary decline has occurred, such as: the length of the time and the extent to which the estimated fair value or market value has been below the carrying value, the financial condition and the near-term prospects of the investee, the intent and ability of the Company to retain its investment in the investee for a period of time sufficient to allow for any anticipated recovery in market value and general market conditions. The estimation of fair value and whether an other-than temporary impairment has occurred requires the application of significant judgment and future results may vary from current assumptions. (See Note 4.)

Note 4. Variable Interest Entities

In the normal course of business, the Company makes investments that support its underlying business strategy and provide it the ability to enter new markets for its brands, develop programming, and distribute its existing content. In certain instances, an investment may qualify as a VIE. (See Note 2.) As of December 31, 2012 and 2011, the Company's VIEs primarily consisted of Hub Television Networks LLC and OWN LLC, which operate pay-television networks.

The Company accounted for its interests in VIEs using the equity method. The aggregate carrying values of these equity method investments were $825 million and $807 million as of December 31, 2012 and 2011, respectively. The Company recognized equity losses in other expense, net on the consolidated statements of operations of $92 million, $33 million, and $55 million for 2012, 2011 and 2010, respectively, for its portion of net losses generated by VIEs.

As of December 31, 2012, the Company's estimated risk of loss for investment carrying values, unfunded contractual commitments and guarantees made on behalf of equity method investees was approximately $851 million. The estimated risk of loss excludes the Company's non-contractual expected future funding of OWN and its operating performance guarantee for Hub Television Networks LLC, which is discussed below.

Hub Television Networks LLC

Hub Television Networks LLC operates The Hub, which is a pay-television network that provides children's and family entertainment and educational programming. The Company is obligated to provide The Hub with funding up to $15 million; the Company has not provided funding as of December 31, 2012. The Company also provides services such as distribution, sales and administrative support for a fee. (See Note 19.)

Based upon the level of equity investment at risk, The Hub is a VIE. Discovery and its partner, Hasbro Inc. ("Hasbro"), share equally in voting control and jointly consent to decisions about programming and marketing strategy and thereby direct the activities of The Hub that most significantly impact its economic performance. Neither has special governance rights, and both are equally represented on the board of The Hub. The partners also share equally in the profits, losses and funding of The Hub. The Company has determined that it is not the primary beneficiary of The Hub. Accordingly, the Company accounts for its investment in The Hub using the equity method.

Through December 31, 2015, the Company has guaranteed the performance of The Hub and is required to compensate Hasbro to the extent that distribution metrics decline versus levels historically achieved by the Discovery Kids channel. This guarantee extends on a declining basis through the period of guarantee. Upon inception of The Hub on May 22, 2009, the maximum amount potentially due under this guarantee was $300 million. As of December 31, 2012, the maximum amount potentially due under this guarantee was less than $110 million. The maximum exposure to loss is expected to decline to zero during 2014. As The Hub's distribution is generally provided under long-term contracts with stable subscriber levels, the Company believes the likelihood is remote that the guaranteed performance levels will not be achieved and, therefore, believes the performance guarantee is unlikely to have an adverse impact on the Company.

The carrying values of the Company's investment in The Hub were $322 million and $334 million as of December 31, 2012 and 2011, respectively. During the fourth quarter of 2012, The Hub completed its annual impairment review of goodwill. In addition, the Company monitors the valuation of its investment and may record an impairment charge if there is an other-than-temporary decline in the investment's value. No impairments have been recorded.

OWN LLC

OWN LLC operates OWN, which is a pay-television network and website that provides adult lifestyle content focused on self-discovery and self-improvement. Based on insufficient equity to finance its activities, OWN is a VIE. While the Company and Harpo, Inc. ("Harpo") are partners who share in voting control, power is not shared because certain activities that significantly impact OWN's economic performance are directed by Harpo. Harpo holds operational rights related to programming and marketing, as well as selection and retention of key management personnel. Accordingly, the Company has determined that it is not the primary beneficiary of OWN and accounts for its investment in OWN using the equity method.

In connection with the launch of OWN on January 1, 2011, the Company contributed the domestic Discovery Health network to the venture. The contribution did not impact the Company's ownership interest, voting control or governance rights related to OWN. Subsequent to the contribution, the Company no longer consolidates the domestic Discovery Health network, which was a component of its U.S. Networks segment. However, the Company provides OWN funding, content licenses and services such as distribution, sales and administrative support for a fee. (See Note 19.)

The Company recorded the contribution at fair value, which resulted in a pretax gain of $129 million and tax expense of $27 million. The fair value of the Company's retained equity interest in OWN was estimated to be $273 million. The gain represents the fair value of the equity investment retained less the carrying values of contributed assets, which included goodwill and other identifiable assets with carrying values of $136 million and $8 million, respectively.

The fair value of the contribution of the Discovery Health network to OWN was determined utilizing customary valuation methodologies including discounted cash flow valuation models. The underlying assumptions, such as future cash flows, weighted average costs of capital and long-term growth rates were generally not observable in the marketplace and therefore involved significant judgment.

The Company reviewed the carrying value of its equity and note receivable investment in OWN as of December 31, 2012. Using the current long-term projections, the fair value of the network was assessed using a DCF valuation model. The underlying assumptions, such as future cash flows, weighted average cost of capital and long-term growth rates were generally not observable in the marketplace, and therefore, involved significant judgment. The fair value of the investment in OWN exceeded the Company's carrying value as of December 31, 2012. No impairment of the investment balance was recorded. The Company will continue to monitor the financial results of OWN along with other relevant business information to determine if an impairment has occurred regarding the recoverability of the OWN loan and valuation of the Company's investment in OWN.

The Company's combined advances to and note receivable from OWN were $482 million and $317 million as of December 31, 2012 and 2011, respectively. During 2012, the Company provided OWN with funding of $136 million and accrued interest earned on the note receivable of $29 million. The note receivable is secured by the net assets of OWN. While the Company has no further funding commitments, the Company expects to provide additional funding to OWN and to recoup amounts funded. The funding to OWN accrues interest at 7.5% compounded annually. There can be no event of default on the borrowing until 2023. However, borrowings are scheduled for repayment four years after the borrowing date to the extent that OWN has excess cash to repay the borrowings then due; following such repayment, OWN's subsequent cash distributions will be shared equally between the Company and Harpo.

In accordance with the venture agreement, losses generated by OWN are generally allocated to investors based on their proportionate ownership interests. However, the Company has recorded its portion of OWN's losses based upon accounting policies for equity method investments. Prior to the contribution of the Discovery Health network to OWN at its launch, the Company recognized $104 million or 100% of OWN's net losses. During the three months ended March 31, 2012, accumulated operating losses at OWN exceeded the equity contributed to OWN, and Discovery resumed recording 100% of OWN's net losses. The Company will continue to record 100% of OWN's operating losses as long as Discovery provides all funding to OWN and OWN's accumulated losses continue to exceed the equity contributed. Future net income generated by OWN will initially be recorded 100% by the Company until Discovery recovers losses absorbed in excess of Discovery's equity ownership interest.

The carrying value of the Company's investment in OWN, including its equity method investment and note receivable balance, was $469 million and $420 million as of December 31, 2012 and 2011, respectively.

Harpo has the right to require the Company to purchase all or part of Harpo's interest in OWN at fair market value up to a maximum put amount every two and one half years commencing January 1, 2016. The maximum put amount ranges from $100 million on the first put exercise date up to $400 million on the fourth put exercise date. The Company has recorded no amounts for the put right.

Note 5. Investments

The Company's investments consisted of the following (in millions).

	Balance Sheet Location	December 31,	
		2012	2011
Trading securities:			
Mutual funds	Prepaid expenses and other current assets	$ 96	$ 76
Available-for-sale securities:			
Money market mutual funds	Cash and cash equivalents	475	635
Equity method investments	Equity method investments	1,095	807
Cost method investments	Other noncurrent assets	34	—
Total investments		$1,700	$1,518

Trading Securities

Trading securities include investments in mutual funds held in a separate trust, which are owned as part of the Company's supplemental retirement plan. (See Note 14.)

Equity Method Investments

On December 21, 2012, the Company acquired 20% equity ownership interests in Eurosport, a European sports satellite and cable network, and a portfolio of pay television networks from a French media company, TF1, for $264 million, including transaction costs. The Company has a call right that enables it to purchase a controlling interest in Eurosport starting December 2014 and for one year thereafter. If Discovery exercises its call right, TF1 will have the right to put its remaining interest to the Company for one year thereafter. The arrangement is intended to increase the growth of Eurosport, which focuses on niche but regionally popular sports such as tennis, skiing, cycling and skating, and enhance the Company's pay television offerings in France.

Other equity method investments include ownership interests in unconsolidated ventures, principally VIEs. All equity method investees are privately owned. The carrying values of the Company's equity-method investments are consistent with its ownership in the underlying net assets of the investees, except for OWN because the Company has recorded losses in excess of its ownership interest. (See Note 4.) The carrying values of equity method investments increased as a result of additional funding provided and interest earnings recorded on the note receivable from OWN and the investment in Eurosport network. These increases were partially offset by losses and dividends from equity method investments.

2.67 THE COCA-COLA COMPANY (DEC)
CONSOLIDATED BALANCE SHEETS (in part)

	December 31,	
(In millions except par value)	2012	2011 As Adjusted
Assets		
Current assets		
Cash and cash equivalents	$ 8,442	$ 12,803
Short-term investments	5,017	1,088
Total cash, cash equivalents and short-term investments	13,459	13,891
Marketable securities	3,092	144
Trade accounts receivable, less allowances of $53 and $83, respectively	4,759	4,920
Inventories	3,264	3,092
Prepaid expenses and other assets	2,781	3,450
Assets held for sale	2,973	—
Total current assets	30,328	25,497
Equity method investments	9,216	7,233
Other investments, principally bottling companies	1,232	1,141
Other assets	3,585	3,495
Property, plant and equipment—net	14,476	14,939
Trademarks with indefinite lives	6,527	6,430
Bottlers' franchise rights with indefinite lives	7,405	7,770
Goodwill	12,255	12,219
Other intangible assets	1,150	1,250
Total assets	$86,174	$79,974

NOTES TO CONSOLIDATED FINANCIAL STATEMENTS

Note 1: Business and Summary of Significant Accounting Policies (in part)

Summary of Significant Accounting Policies (in part)

Basis of Presentation (in part)

Our consolidated financial statements are prepared in accordance with accounting principles generally accepted in the United States. The preparation of our consolidated financial statements requires us to make estimates and assumptions that affect the reported amounts of assets, liabilities, revenues and expenses and the disclosure of contingent assets and liabilities in our consolidated financial statements and accompanying notes. Although these estimates are based on our knowledge of current events and actions we may undertake in the future, actual results may ultimately differ from these estimates and assumptions. Furthermore, when testing assets for impairment in future periods, if management uses different assumptions or if different conditions occur, impairment charges may result.

We use the equity method to account for investments in companies, if our investment provides us with the ability to exercise significant influence over operating and financial policies of the investee. Our consolidated net income includes our Company's proportionate share of the net income or loss of these companies. Our judgment regarding the level of influence over each equity method investment includes considering key factors such as our ownership interest, representation on the board of directors, participation in policy-making decisions and material intercompany transactions.

Note 6: Equity Method Investments

Our consolidated net income includes our Company's proportionate share of the net income or loss of our equity method investees. When we record our proportionate share of net income, it increases equity income (loss)—net in our consolidated statements of income and our carrying value in that investment. Conversely, when we record our proportionate share of a net loss, it decreases equity income (loss)—net in our consolidated statements of income and our carrying value in that investment. The Company's proportionate share of the net income or loss of our equity method investees includes significant operating and nonoperating items recorded by our equity method investees. These items can have a significant impact on the amount of equity income (loss)—net in our consolidated statements of income and our carrying value in those investments. Refer to Note 17 for additional information related to significant operating and nonoperating items recorded by our equity method investees. The carrying values of our equity method investments are also impacted by our proportionate share of items impacting the equity investee's AOCI.

We eliminate from our financial results all significant intercompany transactions, including the intercompany portion of transactions with equity method investees.

Coca-Cola Enterprises Inc.

On October 2, 2010, we completed our acquisition of CCE's former North America business and relinquished our indirect ownership interest in CCE's European operations. As a result of this transaction, the Company does not own any interest in New CCE. Refer to Note 2 for additional information related to this transaction.

We accounted for our investment in CCE under the equity method of accounting until our acquisition of CCE's former North America business was completed on October 2, 2010. Therefore, our consolidated net income for the year ended December 31, 2010, included equity income from CCE during the first nine months of 2010. The Company owned 33 percent of the outstanding common stock of CCE immediately prior to the acquisition. The following table provides summarized financial information for CCE for the nine months ended October 1, 2010 (in millions):

	Nine Months Ended October 1, 2010
Net operating revenues	$16,464
Cost of goods sold	10,028
Gross profit	$ 6,436
Operating income (loss)	$ 1,369
Net income (loss)	$ 677

The following table provides a summary of our significant transactions with CCE for the nine months ended October 1, 2010 (in millions):

	Nine Months Ended October 1, 2010
Concentrate, syrup and finished product sales to CCE	$4,737
Syrup and finished product purchases from CCE	263
CCE purchases of sweeteners through our Company	251
Marketing payments made by us directly to CCE	314
Marketing payments made to third parties on behalf of CCE	106
Local media and marketing program reimbursements from CCE	268
Payments made to CCE for dispensing equipment repair services	64
Other payments—net	19

Syrup and finished product purchases from CCE represent purchases of fountain syrup in certain territories that have been resold by our Company to major customers and purchases of bottle and can products. Marketing payments made by us directly to CCE represent support of certain marketing activities and our participation with CCE in cooperative advertising and other marketing activities to promote the sale of Company trademark products within CCE territories. These programs were agreed to on an annual basis. Marketing payments made to third parties on behalf of CCE represent support of certain marketing activities and programs to promote the sale of Company trademark products within CCE's territories in conjunction with certain of CCE's customers. Pursuant to cooperative advertising and trade agreements with CCE, we received funds from CCE for local media and marketing program reimbursements. Payments made to CCE for dispensing equipment repair services represent reimbursement to CCE for its costs of parts and labor for repairs on cooler, dispensing or post-mix equipment owned by us or our customers. The other payments—net line in the table above represents payments made to and received from CCE that are individually insignificant.

Our Company had previously entered into programs with CCE designed to help develop cold-drink infrastructure. Under these programs, we paid CCE for a portion of the cost of developing the infrastructure necessary to support accelerated placements of cold-drink equipment. These payments supported a common objective of increased sales of Company Trademark Beverages from increased availability and consumption in the cold-drink channel.

Preexisting Relationships

The Company evaluated all of our preexisting relationships with CCE prior to the close of the transaction. Based on these evaluations, the Company recognized charges of $265 million in 2010 related to preexisting relationships with CCE. These charges were primarily related to the write-off of our investment in cold-drink infrastructure programs with CCE as our investment in these programs did not meet the criteria to be recognized as an asset subsequent to the acquisition. These charges were included in the line item other income (loss)—net in our consolidated statements of income and impacted the Corporate operating segment. Refer to Note 17.

Other Equity Method Investments

The Company's other equity method investments include our ownership interests in Coca-Cola Hellenic, Coca-Cola FEMSA and Coca-Cola Amatil. As of December 31, 2012, we owned approximately 23 percent, 29 percent and 29 percent, respectively, of these companies' common shares. As of December 31, 2012, our investment in our equity method investees in the aggregate exceeded our proportionate share of the net assets of these equity method investees by $2,241 million. This difference is not amortized.

A summary of financial information for our equity method investees in the aggregate, other than CCE, is as follows (in millions):

	Year Ended December 31,		
	2012	2011	2010
Net operating revenues	$47,087	$42,472	$38,663
Cost of goods sold	28,821	26,271	23,053
Gross profit	$18,266	$16,201	$15,610
Operating income	$ 4,605	$ 4,181	$ 4,134
Consolidated net income	$ 2,993	$ 2,237	$ 2,659
Less: Net income attributable to noncontrolling interests	89	99	89
Net income attributable to common shareowners	$ 2,904	$ 2,138	$ 2,570

	December 31,	
	2012	2011
Current assets	$16,054	$13,960
Noncurrent assets	32,687	27,152
Total assets	$48,741	$41,112
Current liabilities	$12,004	$10,545
Noncurrent liabilities	12,272	11,646
Total liabilities	$24,276	$22,191
Equity attributable to shareowners of investees	$23,827	$18,392
Equity attributable to noncontrolling interests	638	529
Total equity	$24,465	$18,921
Company equity investment	$ 9,216	$ 7,233

Net sales to equity method investees other than CCE, the majority of which are located outside the United States, were $7.1 billion, $6.9 billion and $6.2 billion in 2012, 2011 and 2010, respectively. Total payments, primarily marketing, made to equity method investees other than CCE were $1,587 million, $1,147 million and $1,034 million in 2012, 2011 and 2010, respectively. In addition, purchases of finished products from equity method investees other than CCE were $392 million, $430 million and $205 million in 2012, 2011 and 2010, respectively.

If valued at the December 31, 2012, quoted closing prices of shares actively traded on stock markets, the value of our equity method investments in publicly traded bottlers would have exceeded our carrying value by $10.4 billion.

Net Receivables and Dividends from Equity Method Investees

Total net receivables due from equity method investees were $1,162 million and $1,042 million as of December 31, 2012 and 2011, respectively. The total amount of dividends received from equity method investees was $393 million, $421 million and $354 million for the years ended December 31, 2012, 2011 and 2010, respectively. Dividends received included a $35 million and $60 million special dividend from Coca-Cola Hellenic during 2012 and 2011, respectively. We classified the receipt of these cash dividends in cash flows from operating activities because our cumulative equity in earnings from Coca-Cola Hellenic exceeded the cumulative distributions received; therefore, the dividends were deemed to be a return on our investment and not a return of our investment.

COST METHOD

2.68 IAC/INTERACTIVECORP (DEC)
CONSOLIDATED BALANCE SHEET (in part)

	December 31,	
(In thousands, except share data)	2012	2011
Assets		
Cash and cash equivalents	$ 749,977	$ 704,153
Marketable securities	20,604	165,695
Accounts receivable, net of allowance of $11,088 and $7,309, respectively	229,830	177,030
Other current assets	156,339	112,255
Total current assets	1,156,750	1,159,133
Property and equipment, net	270,512	259,588
Goodwill	1,616,154	1,358,524
Intangible assets, net	482,904	378,107
Long-term investments	161,278	173,752
Other non-current assets	118,230	80,761
Total assets	$3,805,828	$3,409,865

Note 2—Summary of Significant Accounting Policies (in part)

Basis of Consolidation and Accounting for Investments

The consolidated financial statements include the accounts of the Company, all entities that are wholly-owned by the Company and all entities in which the Company has a controlling financial interest. Intercompany transactions and accounts have been eliminated.

Investments in entities in which the Company has the ability to exercise significant influence over the operating and financial matters of the investee, but does not have a controlling financial interest, are accounted for using the equity method. Investments in entities in which the Company does not have the ability to exercise significant influence over the operating and financial matters of the investee are accounted for using the cost method. The Company evaluates each cost and equity method investment for impairment on a quarterly basis and recognizes an impairment loss if a decline in value is determined to be other-than-temporary. Such impairment evaluations include, but are not limited to: the current business environment, including competition; going concern considerations such as financial condition and the rate at which the investee company utilizes cash and the investee company's ability to obtain additional financing to achieve its business plan; the need for changes to the investee company's existing business model due to changing business environments and its ability to successfully implement necessary changes; and comparable valuations. If the Company has not identified events or changes in circumstances that may have a significant adverse effect on the fair value of a cost method investment, then the fair value of such cost method investment is not estimated, as it is impracticable to do so.

Note 8—Long-Term Investments (in part)

The balance of long-term investments is comprised of:

	December 31,	
(In thousands)	2012	2011
Cost method investments	$113,830	$ 82,318
Long-term marketable equity securities	31,244	74,691
Equity method investments	8,104	10,873
Auction rate security	8,100	5,870
Total long-term investments	$161,278	$173,752

Cost Method Investments

In the third quarter of 2011, the Company acquired a 20% interest in Zhenai Inc. ("Zhenai"), a leading provider of online matchmaking services in China. Our voting power is limited by a shareholders agreement. In light of this limitation and the significance of our interest relative to other shareholders, we do not have the ability to exercise significant influence over the operating and financial matters of Zhenai and this investment is accounted for as a cost method investment.

In the fourth quarter of 2010, the Company recorded a $7.8 million impairment charge related to the write-down of a cost method investment to fair value. The impairment charge was determined to be other-than-temporary due to the investee's inability to achieve its 2010 cash flow forecast during its seasonally strongest fourth quarter and the Company's assessment that the investee would be unable to continue to operate without new outside financing. The impairment charge is included in "Other (expense) income, net" in the accompanying consolidated statement of operations.

FAIR VALUE

2.69 TEXAS INSTRUMENTS INCORPORATED (DEC)
CONSOLIDATED BALANCE SHEETS (in part)

	December 31,	
(Millions of dollars, except share amounts)	2012	2011
Assets		
Current assets:		
Cash and cash equivalents	$1,416	$ 992
Short-term investments	2,549	1,943
Accounts receivable, net of allowances of ($31) and ($19)	1,230	1,545
Raw materials	116	115
Work in process	935	1,004
Finished goods	706	669
Inventories	1,757	1,788

(continued)

(Millions of dollars, except share amounts)	December 31,	
	2012	2011
Deferred income taxes	$ 1,044	$ 1,174
Prepaid expenses and other current assets	234	386
Total current assets	8,230	7,828
Property, plant and equipment at cost	6,891	7,133
Less accumulated depreciation	(2,979)	(2,705)
Property, plant and equipment, net	3,912	4,428
Long-term investments	215	265
Goodwill	4,362	4,452
Acquisition-related intangibles, net	2,558	2,900
Deferred income taxes	280	321
Capitalized software licenses, net	142	206
Overfunded retirement plans	68	40
Other assets	254	57
Total assets	$20,021	$20,497

NOTES TO FINANCIAL STATEMENTS

1. Description of Business and Significant Accounting Policies and Practices (in part)

Investments

We present investments on our balance sheets as cash equivalents, short-term investments or long-term investments. Specific details are as follows:

- *Cash equivalents and short-term investments:* We consider investments in debt securities with maturities of 90 days or less from the date of our investment to be cash equivalents. We consider investments in debt securities with maturities beyond 90 days from the date of our investment as being available for use in current operations and include these investments in short-term investments. The primary objectives of our cash equivalent and short-term investment activities are to preserve capital and maintain liquidity while generating appropriate returns.
- *Long-term investments:* Long-term investments consist of mutual funds, venture capital funds and non-marketable equity securities. Prior to the fourth quarter of 2012, this also included auction-rate securities.
- *Classification of investments:* Depending on our reasons for holding the investment and our ownership percentage, we classify investments in securities as available for sale, trading, or equity- or cost-method investments, which are more fully described in Note 9. We determine cost or amortized cost, as appropriate, on a specific identification basis.

8. Financial Instruments and Risk Concentration (in part)

Financial Instruments (in part)

Our investments in cash equivalents, short-term investments and certain long-term investments, as well as our postretirement plan assets and deferred compensation liabilities are carried at fair value, which is described in Note 9. The carrying values for other current financial assets and liabilities, such as accounts receivable and accounts payable, approximate fair value due to the short maturity of such instruments. The carrying value of our long-term debt approximates the fair value as measured using broker-dealer quotes, which are Level 2 inputs. See Note 9 for the definition of Level 2 inputs.

9. Valuation of Debt and Equity Investments and Certain Liabilities (in part)

Debt and Equity Investments (in part)

We classify our investments as available for sale, trading, equity method or cost method. Most of our investments are classified as available for sale.

Available-for-sale and trading securities are stated at fair value, which is generally based on market prices, broker quotes or, when necessary, financial models (see fair-value discussion below). Unrealized gains and losses on available-for-sale securities are recorded as an increase or decrease, net of taxes, in AOCI on our Consolidated balance sheets. We record other-than-temporary impairments on available-for-sale securities in OI&E in our Consolidated statements of income.

We classify certain mutual funds as trading securities. These mutual funds hold a variety of debt and equity investments intended to generate returns that offset changes in certain deferred compensation liabilities. We record changes in the fair value of these mutual funds and the related deferred compensation liabilities in SG&A. Changes in the fair value of debt securities classified as trading securities are recorded in OI&E.

Our other investments are not measured at fair value but are accounted for using either the equity method or cost method. These investments consist of interests in venture capital funds and other non-marketable equity securities. Gains and losses from equity-method investments are reflected in OI&E based on our ownership share of the investee's financial results. Gains and losses on cost-method investments are recorded in OI&E when realized or when an impairment of the investment's value is warranted based on our assessment of the recoverability of each investment.

Details of our investments and related unrealized gains and losses included in AOCI are as follows:

| | December 31, 2012 | | | December 31, 2011 | | |
	Cash and Cash Equivalents	Short-Term Investments	Long-Term Investments	Cash and Cash Equivalents	Short-Term Investments	Long-Term Investments
Measured at fair value:						
Available-for-sale securities						
Money market funds	$ 211	$ —	$ —	$ 55	$ —	$ —
Corporate obligations	188	325	—	135	159	—
U.S. Government agency and Treasury securities	795	2,224	—	430	1,691	—
Auction-rate securities	—	—	—	—	—	41
Trading securities						
Auction-rate securities	—	—	—	—	93	—
Mutual funds	—	—	159	—	—	169
Total	1,194	2,549	159	620	1,943	210
Other measurement basis:						
Equity-method investments	—	—	34	—	—	32
Cost-method investments	—	—	22	—	—	23
Cash on hand	222	—	—	372	—	—
Total	$1,416	$2,549	$215	$992	$1,943	$265

Fair-Value Considerations (in part)

We measure and report certain financial assets and liabilities at fair value on a recurring basis. Fair value is defined as the price that would be received to sell an asset or paid to transfer a liability (an exit price) in the principal or most advantageous market for the asset or liability in an orderly transaction between market participants on the measurement date.

The three-level hierarchy discussed below indicates the extent and level of judgment used to estimate fair-value measurements.
- Level 1—Uses unadjusted quoted prices that are available in active markets for identical assets or liabilities as of the reporting date.
- Level 2—Uses inputs other than Level 1 that are either directly or indirectly observable as of the reporting date through correlation with market data, including quoted prices for similar assets and liabilities in active markets and quoted prices in markets that are not active. Level 2 also includes assets and liabilities that are valued using models or other pricing methodologies that do not require significant judgment since the input assumptions used in the models, such as interest rates and volatility factors, are corroborated by readily observable data. Our Level 2 assets consist of corporate obligations and some U.S. government agency and Treasury securities. We utilize a third-party data service to provide Level 2 valuations, verifying these valuations for reasonableness relative to unadjusted quotes obtained from brokers or dealers based on observable prices for similar assets in active markets.
- Level 3—Uses inputs that are unobservable, supported by little or no market activity and reflect the use of significant management judgment. These values are generally determined using pricing models that utilize management estimates of market participant assumptions.

The following are our assets and liabilities that were accounted for at fair value on a recurring basis as of December 31, 2012 and 2011. These tables do not include cash on hand, assets held by our postretirement plans, or assets and liabilities that are measured at historical cost or any basis other than fair value.

	Fair Value December 31, 2012	Level 1	Level 2	Level 3
Assets				
Money market funds	$ 211	$ 211	$ —	$ —
Corporate obligations	513	—	513	—
U.S. Government agency and Treasury securities	3,019	1,145	1,874	—
Mutual funds	159	159	—	—
Total assets	$3,902	$1,515	$2,387	$ —
Liabilities				
Deferred compensation	$ 174	$ 174	$ —	$ —
Total liabilities	$ 174	$ 174	$ —	$ —

	Fair Value December 31, 2011	Level 1	Level 2	Level 3
Assets				
Money market funds	$ 55	$ 55	$ —	$ —
Corporate obligations	294	—	294	—
U.S. Government agency and Treasury securities	2,121	606	1,515	—
Auction-rate securities	134	—	—	134
Mutual funds	169	169	—	—
Total assets	$2,773	$830	$1,809	$134
Liabilities				
Deferred compensation	$ 191	$191	$ —	$ —
Total liabilities	$ 191	$191	$ —	$ —

Noncurrent Receivables

PRESENTATION

2.70 FASB ASC 210, *Balance Sheet*, states that the concept of current assets excludes receivables arising from unusual transactions that are not expected to be collected within 12 months, such as the sale of capital assets or loans or advances to affiliates, officers, or employees.

2.71 FASB ASC 825 includes noncurrent receivables as financial instruments. FASB ASC 820 requires disclosure of both the fair value and bases for estimating the fair value of noncurrent receivables, unless it is not practicable to estimate that value. However, FASB ASC 825-10-50-14 indicates that for trade receivables and payables, fair value disclosure is not required if the carrying amount approximates fair value.

PRESENTATION AND DISCLOSURE EXCERPTS

LONG-TERM RECEIVABLES

2.72 CABOT CORPORATION (SEP)
CONSOLIDATED BALANCE SHEETS (in part)

Assets

	September 30	
(In millions, except share and per share amounts)	2012	2011
Current assets:		
Cash and cash equivalents	$ 120	$ 286
Accounts and notes receivable, net of reserve for doubtful accounts of $5 and $4	687	659
Inventories	533	393
Prepaid expenses and other current assets	71	76
Deferred income taxes	32	35
Current assets held for sale	—	106
Total current assets	1,443	1,555
Property, plant and equipment	3,511	2,967
Accumulated depreciation and amortization	(1,959)	(1,931)
Net property, plant and equipment	1,552	1,036
Goodwill	480	40
Equity affiliates	115	60
Intangible assets, net	330	3
Assets held for rent	46	46
Notes receivable from sale of business	242	—
Deferred income taxes	94	261
Other assets	97	101
Noncurrent assets held for sale	—	39
Total assets	$ 4,399	$ 3,141

NOTES TO CONSOLIDATED FINANCIAL STATEMENTS

Note D. Discontinued Operations (in part)

In January 2012, the Company completed the sale of its Supermetals Business to Global Advanced Metals Pty Ltd., an Australian company ("GAM"), pursuant to a Sale and Purchase Agreement entered into between the Company and GAM in August 2011. The total minimum consideration for the sale was approximately $450 million, including cash consideration of $175 million received on the closing date. In addition, the Company (i) received two-year promissory notes, which may be prepaid by GAM at any time prior to maturity, for total aggregate payments of $215 million (consisting of principal, imputed interest and a prepayment penalty, if applicable), secured by liens on the property and assets of the acquired business and guaranteed by the GAM corporate group and (ii) will receive quarterly cash payments in each calendar quarter that the promissory notes are outstanding in an amount equal to 50% of cumulative year to date adjusted earnings before interest, taxes, depreciation and amortization ("Adjusted EBITDA") of the acquired business for the relevant calendar quarter. Regardless of the Adjusted EBITDA generated, a minimum payment of $11.5 million is guaranteed in the first year following the closing of the transaction. Together, these notes are referred to as the "GAM Promissory Notes".

Included in the $450 million minimum consideration the Company will receive for the sale of the business is approximately $50 million for the excess Supermetals inventory the Company sold to GAM in connection with the transaction. Payment for the excess inventory was made with a two-year promissory note ("Inventory Note"), which is also secured by liens on the property and assets of the acquired business and guaranteed by the GAM corporate group. The

Inventory Note may be repaid at any time, and is subject to prepayment if excess cash flows, as defined in the agreement, are generated by the business. The Inventory Note bears interest of 10% per annum beginning January 2013. If the GAM Promissory Notes are prepaid in full, the Inventory Note must also be prepaid. Other than the $11.5 million guaranteed to be paid within the first year, the remaining balance of the GAM Promissory Notes and Inventory Note will mature in the second quarter of fiscal 2014.

The GAM Promissory Notes and Inventory Note (referred to collectively as the "GAM Notes") were recorded at their fair value of $273 million at the closing date. The fair value of the GAM Notes was based on the timing of expected cash flows and appropriate discount rates. The difference between the carrying value of the GAM Notes and the contractual payment obligation (the discount) is being accreted into interest income over the term of the GAM Notes. Payments made while the GAM Promissory Notes are outstanding that are contingent upon the finalization of the annual Adjusted EBITDA calculation will be recognized into interest income when such amounts have been finalized. The carrying value of the GAM Notes at September 30, 2012 is $252 million, of which $10 million is included in Prepaid expenses and other current assets on the Consolidated Balance Sheet as of September 30, 2012 and $242 million is presented as Notes receivable from sale of business. As of September 30, 2012, the Company received $23 million payable under the GAM Notes.

2.73 SNAP-ON INCORPORATED (DEC)
CONSOLIDATED BALANCE SHEETS (in part)

(Amounts in millions, except share data)	Fiscal Year End	
	2012	2011
Assets		
Current assets:		
Cash and cash equivalents	$ 214.5	$ 185.6
Trade and other accounts receivable—net	497.9	463.5
Finance receivables—net	323.1	277.2
Contract receivables—net	62.7	49.7
Inventories—net	404.2	386.4
Deferred income tax assets	81.8	92.6
Prepaid expenses and other assets	84.8	75.7
Total current assets	1,669.0	1,530.7
Property and equipment—net	375.2	352.9
Deferred income tax assets	110.4	125.2
Long-term finance receivables—net	494.6	431.8
Long-term contract receivables—net	194.4	165.1
Goodwill	807.4	795.8
Other intangibles—net	187.2	188.3
Other assets	64.1	83.1
Total assets	$3,902.3	$3,672.9

NOTES TO CONSOLIDATED FINANCIAL STATEMENTS

Note 1: Summary of Accounting Policies (in part)

Receivables and allowances for doubtful accounts: All trade, finance and contract receivables are reported on the Consolidated Balance Sheets at their outstanding principal balance adjusted for any charge-offs and net of allowances for doubtful accounts. Finance and contract receivables also include accrued interest and loan acquisition costs, net of loan acquisition fees.

Snap-on maintains allowances for doubtful accounts to absorb probable losses inherent in its portfolio of receivables. The allowances for doubtful accounts represent management's estimate of the losses inherent in the company's receivables portfolio based on ongoing assessments and evaluations of collectability and historical loss experience. In estimating losses inherent in each of its receivable portfolios (trade, finance and contract receivables), Snap-on uses historical loss experience rates by portfolio and applies them to a related aging analysis. Determination of the proper level of allowances by portfolio requires management to exercise significant judgment about the timing, frequency and severity of credit losses that could materially affect the provision for credit losses and, therefore, net income. The allowances for doubtful accounts takes into consideration numerous quantitative and qualitative factors, by loan type, including historical loss experience, portfolio duration, collection experience, delinquency trends, economic conditions and credit risk quality as follows:

- Snap-on evaluates the collectability of receivables based on a combination of various financial and qualitative factors that may affect the customers' ability to pay. These factors may include customers' financial condition, collateral, debt-servicing ability, past payment experience and credit bureau information.
- For finance and contract receivables, Snap-on assesses quantitative and qualitative factors through the use of credit quality indicators consisting primarily of customer credit risk scores combined with internal credit risk grades, collection experience and other internal metrics as follows:
  — Credit risk—Customer credit risk is monitored regularly on an account by account basis through customer credit scores obtained from major credit bureaus as well as through the use of internal proprietary, custom scoring models used to evaluate each transaction at the time of the application for credit and by periodically updating those credit scores for ongoing monitoring purposes. In addition, Snap-on evaluates credit quality through the use of a loan risk grading measurement system that provides a framework to analyze the finance and contract receivables on the basis of risk factors of the individual obligor as well as transaction specific risk.

— Collection experience—Snap-on conducts monthly reviews of credit and collection performance for each of its finance and contract receivable portfolios focusing on data such as delinquency trends, non-performing assets, charge-off and recovery activity. These reviews allow for the formulation of collection strategies and potential collection policy modifications in response to changing risk profiles in the finance and contract receivable portfolios.

— Other internal metrics—Snap-on maintains a system that aggregates credit exposure by customer, industry, risk classification and geographical area, among other factors, to further monitor changing risk profiles.

Management performs detailed reviews of its receivables on a monthly and/or quarterly basis to assess the adequacy of the allowances based on historical and current trends and other factors affecting credit losses and to determine if any impairment has occurred. A receivable is impaired when it is probable that all amounts related to the receivable will not be collected according to the contractual terms of the agreement. In circumstances where the company is aware of a specific customer's inability to meet its financial obligations, a specific reserve is recorded against amounts due to reduce the net recognized receivable to the amount reasonably expected to be collected. Additions to the allowances for doubtful accounts are maintained through adjustments to the provision for credit losses, which are charged to current period earnings; amounts determined to be uncollectable are charged directly against the allowances, while amounts recovered on previously charged-off accounts increase the allowances. Net charge-offs include the principal amount of losses charged off as well as charged-off interest and fees. Recovered interest and fees previously charged-off are recorded through the allowances for doubtful accounts and increase the allowances. Finance receivables are assessed for charge-off when an account becomes 120 days past due and are charged-off typically within 60 days of asset repossession. Contract receivables related to equipment leases are generally charged-off when an account becomes 150 days past due, while contract receivables related to franchise finance and van leases are generally charged off up to 180 days past the asset return. For finance and contract receivables, customer bankruptcies are generally charged-off upon notification that the associated debt is not being reaffirmed or, in any event, no later than 180 days past due.

Snap-on does not believe that its trade accounts, finance or contract receivables represent significant concentrations of credit risk because of the diversified portfolio of individual customers and geographical areas. See Note 3 for further information on receivables and allowances for doubtful accounts.

Note 3: Receivables

Trade and Other Accounts Receivable

Snap-on's trade and other accounts receivable primarily arise from the sale of tools, diagnostics and equipment to a broad range of industrial and commercial customers and to Snap-on's independent franchise van channel on a non-extended-term basis with payment terms generally ranging from 30 to 120 days.

The components of Snap-on's trade and other accounts receivable as of 2012 and 2011 year end are as follows:

(Amounts in millions)	2012	2011
Trade and other accounts receivable	$516.9	$485.5
Allowances for doubtful accounts	(19.0)	(22.0)
Total trade and other accounts receivable—net	$497.9	$463.5

Finance and Contract Receivables

SOC originates extended-term finance and contract receivables on sales of Snap-on product sold through the U.S. franchisee and customer network and to Snap-on's industrial and other customers; Snap-on's foreign finance subsidiaries provide similar financing internationally. Interest income on finance and contract receivables is included in "Financial services revenue" on the accompanying Consolidated Statements of Earnings.

Snap-on's finance receivables are comprised of extended-term installment loans to both technicians and independent shop owners (i.e., franchisees' customers) to enable them to purchase tools, diagnostics and equipment on an extended-term payment plan, generally with average payment terms of 32 months. Contract receivables, with payment terms of up to 10 years, are comprised of extended-term installment loans to a broad base of industrial and other customers worldwide, including shop owners, both independents and national chains, for their purchase of tools, diagnostics and equipment. Contract receivables also include extended-term installment loans to franchisees to meet a number of financing needs including van and truck leases, working capital loans, and loans to enable new franchisees to fund the purchase of the franchise. Finance and contract receivables are generally secured by the underlying tools, diagnostics or equipment financed and, for installment loans to franchisees, other franchisee assets.

Snap-on did not purchase or sell any finance or contract receivables during 2012, 2011 or 2010.

The components of Snap-on's current finance and contract receivables as of 2012 and 2011 year end are as follows:

(Amounts in millions)	2012	2011
Finance receivables, net of unearned finance charges of $8.4 million and $7.6 million, respectively	$331.7	$285.3
Contract receivables, net of unearned finance charges of $9.3 million and $9.1 million, respectively	63.7	51.2
Total	395.4	336.5
Allowances for doubtful accounts:		
Finance receivables	(8.6)	(8.1)
Contract receivables	(1.0)	(1.5)
Total	(9.6)	(9.6)
Total current finance and contract receivables—net	$385.8	$326.9
Finance receivables—net	$323.1	$277.2
Contract receivables—net	62.7	49.7
Total current finance and contract receivables—net	$385.8	$326.9

The components of Snap-on's finance and contract receivables with payment terms beyond one year as of 2012 and 2011 year end are as follows:

(Amounts in millions)	2012	2011
Finance receivables, net of unearned finance charges of $11.8 million and $9.4 million, respectively	$512.5	$447.9
Contract receivables, net of unearned finance charges of $18.1 million and $12.1 million, respectively	196.6	167.7
Total	709.1	615.6
Allowances for doubtful accounts:		
Finance receivables	(17.9)	(16.1)
Contract receivables	(2.2)	(2.6)
Total	(20.1)	(18.7)
Total long-term finance and contract receivables—net	$689.0	$596.9
Finance receivables—net	$494.6	$431.8
Contract receivables—net	194.4	165.1
Total long-term finance and contract receivables—net	$689.0	$596.9

Long-term finance and contract receivables Installments, net of unearned finance charges, as of 2012 and 2011 year end are scheduled as follows:

(Amounts in millions)	2012		2011	
	Finance Receivables	Contract Receivables	Finance Receivables	Contract Receivables
Due in Months:				
13—24	$261.1	$ 54.6	$223.8	$ 44.9
25—36	160.1	45.4	141.9	37.0
37—48	65.1	32.4	59.2	28.6
49—60	25.5	21.4	22.4	18.6
Thereafter	0.7	42.8	0.6	38.6
Total	$512.5	$196.6	$447.9	$167.7

Delinquency is the primary indicator of credit quality for finance and contract receivables. Receivable balances are considered delinquent when contractual payments on the loans become 30 days past due.

Finance receivables are generally placed on nonaccrual status (nonaccrual of interest and other fees) (i) when a customer is placed on repossession status; (ii) upon receipt of notification of bankruptcy; (iii) upon notification of the death of a customer; or (iv) in other instances in which management concludes collectability is not reasonably assured. Finance receivables that are considered nonperforming include receivables that are on nonaccrual status and receivables that are generally more than 90 days past due.

Contract receivables are generally placed on nonaccrual status (i) when a receivable is more than 90 days past due or at the point a customer's account is placed on terminated status regardless of its delinquency status; (ii) upon notification of the death of a customer; or (iii) in other instances in which management concludes collectability is not reasonably assured. Contract receivables that are considered nonperforming include receivables that are on nonaccrual status and receivables that are generally more than 90 days past due.

The accrual of interest and other fees is resumed when the finance or contract receivable becomes contractually current and collection of all remaining contractual amounts due is reasonably assured. Finance and contract receivables are evaluated for impairment on a collective basis; however, in circumstances where the company is aware of a specific customer's inability to meet its financial obligations, a specific reserve is recorded against amounts due to reduce the net recognized receivable to the amount reasonably expected to be collected. A receivable is impaired when it is probable that all amounts related to the receivable will not be collected according to the contractual terms of the loan agreement. Impaired receivables are covered by the company's finance and contract allowances for doubtful accounts reserves and are charged-off against the reserves when appropriate. As of 2012 and 2011 year end, there were $13.4 million and $11.5 million, respectively, of impaired finance receivables, and there were $0.9 million and $0.7 million, respectively, of impaired contract receivables.

The aging of finance and contract receivables as of 2012 and 2011 year end is as follows:

(Amounts in millions)	30–59 Days Past Due	60–90 Days Past Due	Greater Than 90 Days Past Due	Total Past Due	Total Not Past Due	Total	Greater Than 90 Days Past Due and Accruing
2012 Year End:							
Finance receivables	$9.2	$5.5	$8.4	$23.1	$821.1	$844.2	$6.2
Contract receivables	1.3	0.6	1.0	2.9	257.4	260.3	0.3
2011 Year End:							
Finance receivables	$8.0	$3.0	$6.6	$17.6	$715.6	$733.2	$4.8
Contract receivables	0.9	0.4	0.6	1.9	217.0	218.9	0.2

The amount of performing and nonperforming finance and contract receivables based on payment activity as of 2012 and 2011 year end is as follows:

(Amounts in millions)	2012		2011	
	Finance Receivables	Contract Receivables	Finance Receivables	Contract Receivables
Performing	$830.8	$259.4	$721.7	$218.2
Nonperforming	13.4	0.9	11.5	0.7
Total	$844.2	$260.3	$733.2	$218.9

The amount of finance and contract receivables on nonaccrual status as of 2012 and 2011 year end is as follows:

(Amounts in millions)	2012	2011
Finance receivables	$7.2	$6.8
Contract receivables	0.9	0.7

The following is a rollforward of the allowances for credit losses for finance and contract receivables for 2012 and 2011:

(Amounts in millions)	2012		2011	
	Finance Receivables	Contract Receivables	Finance Receivables	Contract Receivables
Allowances for doubtful accounts:				
Beginning of year	$ 24.2	$ 4.1	$ 21.5	$ 4.0
Provision for bad debt expense	18.7	0.5	13.3	0.8
Charge-offs	(20.6)	(1.7)	(14.3)	(1.5)
Recoveries	4.2	0.3	3.8	0.8
Currency translation	—	—	(0.1)	—
End of year	$ 26.5	$ 3.2	$ 24.2	$ 4.1

The following is a rollforward of the combined allowances for doubtful accounts related to trade and other accounts receivable, as well as finance and contract receivables for 2012, 2011 and 2010:

(Amounts in millions)	Balance at Beginning of Year	Expenses	Deductions[1]	Balance at End of Year
Allowances for doubtful accounts:				
2012	$50.3	$31.3	$(32.9)	$48.7
2011	52.5	26.2	(28.4)	50.3
2010	40.6	34.4	(22.5)	52.5

[1] Represents write-offs of bad debts, net of recoveries, and the net impact of currency translation.

The increase in the allowances for doubtful accounts over beginning-of-year 2010 levels primarily reflects the building of allowances as a result of the growth of the on-book finance portfolio at SOC following the July 2009 termination of the company's financial services joint venture with CIT.

Prior to the termination of the financial services joint venture with CIT, SOC sold substantially all new finance and contract loan originations to CIT on a limited recourse basis and SOC retained the right to service such loans for a contractual servicing fee. As of 2012 year end, the remaining portfolio of receivables owned by CIT that is being serviced by SOC was $53.8 million. Contractual servicing fees were $1.4 million in 2012, $2.3 million in 2011 and $4.9 million in 2010.

Intangible Assets

RECOGNITION AND MEASUREMENT

2.74 FASB ASC 350, *Intangibles—Goodwill and Other*, specifies that goodwill and intangible assets that have indefinite lives are not subject to amortization but, rather, should be tested at least annually for impairment. In addition, FASB ASC 350 provides specific guidance on how to determine and measure impairment of goodwill and intangible assets not subject to amortization. Intangible assets that have finite useful lives should be amortized over their useful lives.

2.75 FASB ASC 350-20-35 delineates a comprehensive two-step approach to impairment testing of a reporting unit that includes goodwill. If an entity chooses, it may assess qualitative factors to determine whether it is more likely than not that the fair value of a reporting unit is less than its carrying amount; the entity may use this determination as a basis for deciding whether it is necessary to perform the two-step goodwill impairment test. The *more-likely-than-not threshold* is defined as having a likelihood of more than 50 percent. An entity has an unconditional option to bypass the qualitative assessment described in the preceding paragraph for any reporting unit in any period and proceed directly to performing the first step of the goodwill impairment test. An entity may resume performing the qualitative assessment in any subsequent period.

2.76 If the entity decides that the quantitative impairment test is required, then the first step is to compare the fair value of a reporting unit with its carrying amount, including goodwill. When the carrying amount is greater than zero and its fair value exceeds its carrying amount, the entity should not consider the goodwill impaired and the second step is unnecessary. When the carrying amount of the reporting unit exceeds its fair value, an entity should proceed to step two to measure the loss by comparing the implied fair value of the goodwill with its carrying value. When the carrying amount of the reporting unit is zero or negative, an entity should proceed to step two to measure an impairment loss, if any, when it is more likely than not that a goodwill impairment exists. An entity should evaluate whether there are adverse qualitative factors in making that "more likely than not" assessment. FASB ASC 350-20-35-30 (a)–(g) provide examples of such qualitative factors.

2.77 FASB ASC 350 also provides guidance on accounting for the cost of computer software developed or obtained for internal use and website development costs.

PRESENTATION

2.78 FASB ASC 350-20-45-1 requires that the aggregate amount of goodwill be presented as a separate line item in the balance sheet. Under FASB ASC 350-30-45-1, at minimum, all intangible assets should be aggregated and presented as a separate line item in the balance sheet. However, that requirement does not preclude the presentation of individual intangible assets or classes of intangible assets as separate line items. Rule 5-02 of Regulation S-X also calls for separately stating each class of intangible assets in excess of 5 percent of total assets and for separate presentation of the amount of accumulated amortization of intangible assets.

DISCLOSURE

2.79 FASB ASC 350 requires additional disclosures for each period for which a balance sheet is presented, including information about gross carrying amounts and changes therein of goodwill and other intangible assets, accumulated amortization for amortizable assets, and estimates about intangible asset amortization expense for each of the five succeeding fiscal years. For intangibles, the balance sheet disclosures should be in total and by major intangible asset class.

2.80 HEWLETT-PACKARD COMPANY (OCT)
CONSOLIDATED BALANCE SHEETS (in part)

	October 31	
(In millions, except par value)	2012	2011
Assets		
Current assets:		
Cash and cash equivalents	$ 11,301	$ 8,043
Accounts receivable	16,407	18,224
Financing receivables	3,252	3,162
Inventory	6,317	7,490
Other current assets	13,360	14,102
Total current assets	50,637	51,021
Property, plant and equipment	11,954	12,292
Long-term financing receivables and other assets	10,593	10,755
Goodwill	31,069	44,551
Purchased intangible assets	4,515	10,898
Total assets	$108,768	$129,517

NOTES TO CONSOLIDATED FINANCIAL STATEMENTS

Note 1: Summary of Significant Accounting Policies (in part)

Goodwill and Purchased Intangible Assets (in part)

Goodwill and purchased intangible assets with indefinite useful lives are not amortized but are tested for impairment at least annually. HP reviews goodwill and purchased intangible assets with indefinite lives for impairment annually at the beginning of its fourth fiscal quarter and whenever events or changes in circumstances indicate the carrying value of an asset may not be recoverable. For goodwill, HP performs a two-step impairment test. In the first step, HP compares the fair value of each reporting unit to its carrying value. HP determines the fair values of its reporting units using a weighting of fair values derived most significantly from the income approach and to a lesser extent the market approach. Under the income approach, HP calculates the fair value of a reporting unit based on the present value of estimated future cash flows. Cash flow projections are based on management's estimates of revenue growth rates and operating margins, taking into consideration industry and market conditions. The discount rate used is based on the weighted-average cost of capital adjusted for the relevant risk associated with business-specific characteristics and the uncertainty related to the business's ability to execute on the projected cash flows. Under the market approach, HP estimates the fair value based on market multiples of revenue and earnings derived from comparable publicly-traded companies with similar operating and investment characteristics as the reporting unit. The weighting of the fair value derived from the market approach ranges from 0% to 50% depending on the level of comparability of these publicly-traded companies to the reporting unit. When market comparables are not meaningful or not available, HP may estimate the fair value of a reporting unit using only the income approach. In order to assess the reasonableness of the calculated fair values of its reporting units, HP also compares the sum of the reporting units' fair values to HP's market capitalization and calculates an implied control premium (the excess of the sum of the reporting units' fair values over the market capitalization). HP evaluates the control premium by comparing it to control premiums of recent comparable transactions. If the implied control premium is not reasonable in light of these recent transactions, HP will reevaluate its fair value estimates of the reporting units by adjusting the discount rates and/or other assumptions. As a result, when there is a significant decline in HP's stock price, as occurred during fiscal 2012, this reevaluation could correlate to lower estimated fair values for certain or all of HP's reporting units. If the fair value of the reporting unit exceeds the carrying value of the net assets assigned to that unit, goodwill is not impaired, and no further testing is required. If the fair value of the reporting unit is less than the carrying value, HP must perform the second step of the impairment test to measure the amount of impairment loss, if any. In the second step, the reporting unit's fair value is allocated to all of the assets and liabilities of the reporting unit, including any unrecognized intangible assets, in a hypothetical analysis that calculates the implied fair value of goodwill in the same manner as if the reporting unit was being acquired in a business combination. If the implied fair value of the reporting unit's goodwill is less than the carrying value, the difference is recorded as an impairment loss.

Accounting Pronouncements

In September 2011, the Financial Accounting Standards Board issued new guidance on testing goodwill for impairment. The new guidance will allow an entity to first assess qualitative factors to determine whether it is necessary to perform the two-step quantitative goodwill impairment test. An entity no longer will be required to calculate the fair value of a reporting unit unless the entity determines, based on a qualitative assessment, that it is more likely than not that its fair value is less than its carrying amount. HP adopted this accounting standard in the fourth fiscal quarter of 2012. For HP's annual goodwill impairment test in the fourth quarter of fiscal 2012, HP performed a quantitative test for all of its reporting units. Due to the recent trading values of HP's stock price, HP believed it was appropriate to have recent fair values for each of its reporting units in order to assess the reasonableness of the sum of these fair values as compared to HP's market capitalization.

Note 7: Goodwill and Purchased Intangible Assets (in part)

Goodwill

Goodwill allocated to HP's reportable segments as of October 31, 2012 and 2011 and changes in the carrying amount of goodwill during the fiscal years ended October 31, 2012 and 2011 are as follows:

(In millions)	Personal Systems	Printing	Services	Enterprise Servers, Storage and Networking	Software	HP Financial Services	Corporate Investments	Total
Net balance at October 31, 2010	$2,500	$2,456	$16,967	$6,610	$ 7,545	$144	$ 2,261	$ 38,483
Goodwill acquired during the period	—	16	66	—	6,786	—	—	6,868
Goodwill adjustments/reclassifications	(2)	(1)	247	1,460	(268)	—	(1,423)	13
Impairment loss	—	—	—	—	—	—	(813)	(813)
Net balance at October 31, 2011	$2,498	$2,471	$17,280	$8,070	$14,063	$144	$ 25	$ 44,551
Goodwill acquired during the period	—	16	—	—	—	—	—	16
Goodwill adjustments/reclassifications	—	—	(40)	(308)	580	—	(25)	207
Impairment loss	—	—	(7,961)	—	(5,744)	—	—	(13,705)
Net balance at October 31, 2012	$2,498	$2,487	$ 9,279	$7,762	$ 8,899	$144	$ —	$ 31,069

During fiscal 2012, the decrease in goodwill is related to the impairment loss within the Services and Software segments as discussed further below. In connection with certain fiscal 2012 organizational realignments, HP reclassified $280 million of goodwill related to the TippingPoint network security solutions business from the Enterprise Servers, Storage and Networking ("ESSN") segment to the Software segment. Additionally, HP recorded an increase to goodwill of $244 million in the Software segment due to a change in the estimated fair values of purchased intangible assets and net tangible assets associated with the acquisition of Autonomy in conjunction with completing the purchase accounting in the first quarter.

Goodwill at October 31, 2011 is net of accumulated impairment losses of $813 million related to the Corporate Investments segment. Goodwill at October 31, 2012 is net of accumulated impairment losses of $14,518 million. Of that amount, $7,961 million relates to Services, $5,744 million relates to Software, and the remaining $813 million relates to the fiscal 2011 charge related to Corporate Investments mentioned above.

HP reviews goodwill for impairment annually as of the first day of its fourth fiscal quarter and whenever events or changes in circumstances indicate the carrying value of goodwill may not be recoverable. HP's goodwill impairment test involves a two-step process. In the first step, HP compares the fair value of each reporting unit to its carrying value. If the fair value of the reporting unit exceeds its carrying value, goodwill is not impaired and no further testing is required. If the fair value of the reporting unit is less than the carrying value, HP must perform the second step of the impairment test to measure the amount of impairment loss, if any. In the second step, the reporting unit's fair value is allocated to all of the assets and liabilities of the reporting unit, including any unrecognized intangible assets, in a hypothetical analysis that calculates the implied fair value of goodwill in the same manner as if the reporting unit was being acquired in a business combination. If the implied fair value of the reporting unit's goodwill is less than the carrying value, the difference is recorded as an impairment loss.

Except for Services, Software and Corporate Investments, HP's reporting units are consistent with the reportable segments identified in Note 19. The ES and TS businesses are the reporting units within the Services segment. ES includes the ITO and ABS business units. The Software segment includes two reporting units, which are Autonomy and the legacy HP software business. The webOS business is also a separate reporting unit within the Corporate Investments segment.

HP estimated the fair value of its reporting units using a weighting of fair values derived most significantly from the income approach and, to a lesser extent, the market approach. Under the income approach, HP calculates the fair value of a reporting unit based on the present value of estimated future cash flows. Cash flow projections are based on management's estimates of revenue growth rates and operating margins, taking into consideration industry and market conditions. The discount rate used is based on the weighted-average cost of capital adjusted for the relevant risk associated with business-specific characteristics and the uncertainty related to the business's ability to execute on the projected cash flows. The market approach estimates fair value based on market multiples of revenue and earnings derived from comparable publicly-traded companies with similar operating and investment characteristics as the reporting unit. The weighting of the fair value derived from the market approach ranges from 0% to 50% depending on the level of comparability of these publicly-traded companies to the reporting unit. When market comparables are not meaningful or not available, HP may estimate the fair value of a reporting unit using only the income approach.

In order to assess the reasonableness of the calculated fair values of its reporting units, HP also compares the sum of the reporting units' fair values to HP's market capitalization and calculates an implied control premium (the excess of the sum of the reporting units' fair values over the market capitalization). HP evaluates the control premium by comparing it to control premiums of recent comparable market transactions. If the implied control premium is not reasonable in light of these recent transactions, HP will reevaluate its fair value estimates of the reporting units by adjusting the discount rates and/or other assumptions. As a result, when there is a significant decline in HP's stock price, as occurred during fiscal 2012, this reevaluation could correlate to lower estimated fair values for certain or all of HP's reporting units.

During fiscal 2012, HP determined that sufficient indicators of potential impairment existed to require an interim goodwill impairment analysis for the ES reporting unit. These indicators included the recent trading values of HP's stock, coupled with market conditions and business trends within ES. The fair value of the ES reporting unit was based on the income approach. The decline in the fair value of the ES reporting unit resulted from lower projected revenue growth rates and profitability levels as well as an increase in the risk factor that is included in the discount rate used to calculate the discounted cash flows. The increase in the discount rate was due to the implied control premium resulting from recent trading values of HP stock. The resulting adjustments to discount rates caused a significant reduction in the fair value for the ES reporting unit. Based on the step one and step two analyses, HP recorded an $8.0 billion goodwill impairment charge in fiscal 2012, and there is no remaining goodwill in the ES reporting unit as of October 31, 2012. Prior to completing the goodwill impairment test, HP tested the recoverability of the ES long-lived assets (other than goodwill) and concluded that such assets were not impaired.

HP initiated its annual goodwill impairment analysis in the fourth quarter of fiscal 2012 and concluded that fair value was below carrying value for the Autonomy reporting unit. The fair value of the Autonomy reporting unit was based on the income approach.

The decline in the estimated fair value of the Autonomy reporting unit results from lower projected revenue growth rates and profitability levels as well as an increase in the risk factor that is included in the discount rate used to calculate the discounted cash flows. The increase in the discount rate was due to the implied control premium resulting from recent trading values of HP stock. The lower projected operating results reflect changes in assumptions related to organic revenue growth rates, market trends, business mix, cost structure, expected deal synergies and other expectations about the anticipated short-term and long-term operating results of the Autonomy business. These assumptions incorporate HP's analysis of what it believes were accounting improprieties, incomplete disclosures and misrepresentations at Autonomy that occurred prior to the Autonomy acquisition with respect to Autonomy's pre-acquisition business and related operating results. In addition, as noted above, when estimating the fair value of a reporting unit HP may need to adjust discount rates and/or other assumptions in order to derive a reasonable implied control premium when comparing the sum of the fair values of HP's reporting units to HP's market capitalization. Due to the recent trading values of HP stock, the resulting adjustments to the discount rate to arrive at an appropriate control premium caused a significant reduction in the fair value for the Autonomy reporting unit as well as the fair values for HP's other reporting units.

Prior to conducting the step one of the goodwill impairment test for the Autonomy reporting unit, HP first evaluated the recoverability of the long-lived assets, including purchased intangible assets. When indicators of impairment are present, HP tests long-lived assets (other than goodwill) for recoverability by comparing the carrying value of an asset group to its undiscounted cash flows. HP considered the lower than expected revenue and profitability levels over a sustained period of time, the trading values of HP stock and downward revisions to management's short-term and long-term forecast for the Autonomy business to be indicators of impairment for the Autonomy long-lived assets. Based on the results of the recoverability test, HP determined that the carrying value of the Autonomy asset group exceeded its undiscounted cash flows and was therefore not recoverable. HP then compared the fair value of the asset group to its carrying value and determined the impairment loss. The impairment loss was allocated to the carrying values of the long-lived assets but not below their individual fair values. HP estimated the fair value of the purchased intangible assets, primarily technology assets, under an income approach as described above. Based on the analysis, HP recorded an impairment charge of $3.1 billion on purchased intangible assets, which resulted in a remaining carrying value of approximately $0.8 billion as of October 31, 2012. The decline in the fair value of the Autonomy intangible assets is attributable to the same factors as discussed above for the fair value of the Autonomy reporting unit.

The decline in the fair value of the Autonomy reporting unit and Autonomy intangibles, as well as fair value changes for other assets and liabilities in the step two goodwill impairment test, resulted in an implied fair value of goodwill substantially below the carrying value of the goodwill for the Autonomy reporting unit. As a result, HP recorded a goodwill impairment charge of $5.7 billion, which resulted in a $1.2 billion remaining carrying value of Autonomy goodwill as of October 31, 2012. Both the goodwill impairment charge and the purchased intangible assets impairment charge, totaling $8.8 billion, were included in the Impairment of Goodwill and Purchased Intangible Assets line item in the Consolidated Statements of Earnings.

Subsequent to the Autonomy purchase price allocation period, which concluded in the first quarter of fiscal 2012, and in conjunction with HP's annual goodwill impairment testing, HP identified certain indicators of impairment. The indicators of impairment included lower than expected revenue and profitability levels over a sustained period of time, the trading values of HP stock and downward revisions to management's short-term and long-term forecast for the Autonomy business. HP revised its multi-year forecast for the Autonomy business, and the timing of this forecast revision coincided with the timing of HP's overall forecasting process for all reporting units, which is completed each year in the fourth fiscal quarter in conjunction with the annual goodwill impairment analysis. The change in assumptions used in the revised forecast and the fair value estimates utilized in the impairment testing of the Autonomy goodwill and long-lived assets incorporated insights gained from having owned the Autonomy business for the preceding year. The revised forecast reflected changes related to organic revenue growth rates, current market trends, business mix, cost structure, expected deal synergies and other expectations about the anticipated short-term and long-term operating results of the Autonomy business, driven by HP's analysis regarding certain accounting improprieties, incomplete disclosures and misrepresentations at Autonomy that occurred prior to the Autonomy acquisition with respect to Autonomy's pre-acquisition business and related operating results. Accordingly, the change in fair values represented a change in accounting estimate that occurred outside the purchase price allocation period, resulting in the recorded impairment charge.

Based on the results of the annual impairment test for all other reporting units, HP concluded that no other goodwill impairment existed as of August 1, 2012, apart from the impairment charges discussed above. The excess of fair value over carrying value for each of HP's reporting units as of August 1, 2012, the annual testing date, ranged from approximately 9% to approximately 330% of carrying value. The Autonomy and legacy HP software reporting units have the lowest excess of fair value over carrying value at 10% and 9%, respectively. HP will continue to evaluate goodwill, on an annual basis as of the beginning of its fourth fiscal quarter, and whenever events or changes in circumstances, such as significant adverse changes in business climate or operating results, changes in management's business strategy or further significant declines in HP's stock price, indicate that there may be a potential indicator of impairment.

During fiscal 2011, HP recorded approximately $6.9 billion of goodwill related to acquisitions based on its preliminary estimated fair values of the assets acquired and liabilities assumed. In connection with organizational realignments implemented in the first quarter of fiscal 2011, HP also reclassified goodwill related to the Networking business from Corporate Investments to ESSN and goodwill related to the communications and media solutions business from Software to Services. In the fourth quarter of fiscal 2011, HP determined that it would wind down the manufacture and sale of webOS devices resulting from the Palm acquisition, including webOS smartphones and the HP TouchPad. HP also announced that it would continue to explore alternatives to optimize the value of the webOS technology, including, among others, licensing the webOS software or the related intellectual property or selling all or a portion of the webOS assets. The decision triggered an impairment review of the related goodwill and purchased intangible assets recorded in connection with the Palm acquisition. HP first performed an impairment review of the purchased intangible assets, which represents the value for the webOS technology, carrier relationships and the trade name. Based on the information available at the time of the review, HP determined that there was no future value for the carrier relationships and the trade name but that the carrying value of the webOS technology approximated its fair value. HP estimated the fair value of the webOS technology based on several methods, including the market approach using recent comparable transactions and the discounted cash flow approach using estimated cash flows from potential licensing agreements. Based on that analysis, HP recognized an impairment loss of $72 million primarily related to the carrier relationships and the trade name. HP then performed a goodwill impairment test by comparing the carrying value of the relevant reporting unit to the fair value of that reporting unit. The fair value of the reporting unit was significantly below the carrying value due to HP's decision to wind down the sale of all webOS devices. As a result, HP recorded a goodwill impairment charge of $813 million. Both the goodwill impairment charge and the intangible asset impairment charge were included in the Impairment of Goodwill and Purchased Intangible Assets line item in the Consolidated Statement of Earnings.

TRADE NAMES

2.81 FURNITURE BRANDS INTERNATIONAL, INC. (DEC)

CONSOLIDATED BALANCE SHEETS (in part)

(Dollars in thousands except per share data)

	December 29, 2012	December 31, 2011
Assets		
Current assets:		
Cash and cash equivalents	$ 11,869	$ 25,387
Receivables, less allowances of $11,615 ($10,413 at December 31, 2011)	125,739	107,974
Inventories	244,333	228,155
Prepaid expenses and other current assets	11,287	9,490
Total current assets	393,228	371,006
Property, plant, and equipment, net	103,403	115,803
Trade names	76,105	77,508
Other assets	45,705	50,179
Total assets	$618,441	$614,496

NOTES TO CONSOLIDATED FINANCIAL STATEMENTS

(In thousands except per share data)

5. Trade Names

Trade names activity is as follows:

	Fiscal Year Ended	
	2012	2011
Beginning balance of trade names	$77,508	$86,508
Impairment	(1,403)	(9,000)
Ending balance of trade names	$76,105	$77,508

Our trade names are tested for impairment annually, in the fourth fiscal quarter. Trade names, and long-lived assets, are also tested for impairment whenever events or changes in circumstances indicate that the asset may be impaired. Each quarter, we assess whether events or changes in circumstances indicate a potential impairment of these assets considering many factors, including significant changes in market capitalization, cash flow or projected cash flow, the condition of assets, and the manner in which assets are used.

Trade names are tested by comparing the carrying value and fair value of each trade name to determine the amount, if any, of impairment. The fair value of trade names is calculated using a "relief from royalty payments" methodology. This approach involves two steps: (i) estimating royalty rates for each trademark and (ii) applying these royalty rates to a projected net sales stream and discounting the resulting cash flows to determine fair value.

Accordingly, we tested our trade names for impairment in the fourth quarter of 2012. As a result, we recorded an impairment charge of $1,403 caused by the carrying value being greater than the fair value of certain of our trade names. The decrease in the fair value of these trade names in 2012 was primarily caused by a decrease in projected sales.

We tested our trade names for impairment in the third quarter of 2011 primarily due to deterioration in sales in certain brands. As a result, we recorded an impairment charge of $9,000 caused by the carrying value being greater than the fair value of certain of our trade names. The decrease in the fair value of these trade names in the third quarter of 2011 was primarily caused by a decrease in projected sales and an increase in the discount rate used in our valuation calculations.

A future decrease in the fair value of our trade names could result in a corresponding impairment charge. The estimated fair value of our trade names is highly contingent upon sales trends and assumptions including royalty rates, projected net sales streams, and a discount rate. Decreases in projected sales, decreases in royalty rates, or increases in the discount rate would cause additional impairment charges and a corresponding reduction in our earnings.

We determine royalty rates for each trademark considering contracted rates and industry benchmarks. Royalty rates generally are not volatile and do not fluctuate significantly with short term changes in economic conditions.

Weighted average net sales streams are calculated for each trademark based on a probability weighting assigned to each reasonably possible future net sales stream. The probability weightings are determined considering historical performance, management forecasts and other factors such as economic conditions and trends. Projected net sales streams could fluctuate significantly based on changes in the economy, actual sales, or forecasted sales.

The discount rate is a calculated weighted average cost of capital determined by observing typical rates and proportions of interest-bearing debt, preferred equity, and common equity of publicly traded companies engaged in lines of business similar to our company. The fair value was calculated using a discount rate of 15.5% in the fourth quarter of 2012, 17.0% in the third quarter of 2011 and 16.5% in the fourth quarter of 2010; and we recorded impairment charges of $1,403 in the fourth quarter of 2012, $9,000 in the third quarter of 2011 and $1,100 in the fourth quarter of 2010, which are included in Impairment of assets, net of recoveries on the Consolidated Statement of Operations. The discount rate could fluctuate significantly with changes in the risk profile of our industry or in the general economy.

CUSTOMER CONTRACTS AND RELATIONSHIPS

2.82 NASH-FINCH COMPANY (DEC)
CONSOLIDATED BALANCE SHEETS (in part)

(In thousands, except per share amounts)

	December 29, 2012	December 31, 2011
Assets		
Current assets:		
Cash	$ 1,291	$ 773
Accounts and notes receivable, net	239,925	243,763
Inventories	362,526	308,621
Prepaid expenses and other	18,569	17,329
Deferred tax assets, net	3,724	6,896
Total current assets	626,035	577,382
Notes receivable, net	21,360	23,221
Property, plant and equipment:		
Property, plant and equipment	738,857	686,794
Less accumulated depreciation and amortization	(436,572)	(413,695)
Net property, plant and equipment	302,285	273,099
Goodwill	22,877	170,941
Customer contracts & relationships, net	6,649	15,399
Investment in direct financing leases	1,923	2,677
Deferred tax assets, net	2,780	—
Other assets	19,708	11,049
Total assets	$1,003,617	$1,073,768

(1) Summary of Significant Accounting Policies (in part)

Goodwill and Intangible Assets (in part)

Intangible assets, consisting primarily of goodwill and customer contracts resulting from business acquisitions, are carried at cost unless a determination has been made that their value is impaired.

During the fourth quarter of fiscal 2012, we tested the customer relationships associated with the purchase of our Westville and Lima Food Distribution facilities in 2005 for impairment. In the first step of our analysis, the undiscounted cash flows generated by the related asset groups (the Westville and Lima distribution centers, individually, inclusive of the value of the customer relationships allocated to each distribution center) were compared to the book value of the asset groups. In the case of the Westville asset group, the cash flows did not exceed the book value, necessitating the second step of the recoverability test.

In the second step of the recoverability test, the discounted cash flows attributable to the asset group were compared to the fair value of the other assets in the Westville asset group in order to determine the implied fair value of the intangible assets in the group. We utilized a recent appraisal of the value of the Westville distribution center's land and building to determine the fair value of the other assets in the asset group. The discounted cash flow analysis determined that there was not enough value in the asset group to recognize any value in the customer relationships related to the Westville facility. This resulted in a $6.5 million impairment charge in the fourth quarter of fiscal 2012 related to the customer relationships associated with the Westville facility. This impairment charge is included in the Consolidated Statements of Income (Loss) under selling, general and administrative expenses.

Customer contracts and relationships intangibles were as follows (in thousands):

| | December 29, 2012 | | | |
	Gross Carrying Value	Accum. Amort.	Net Carrying Amount	Estimated Life (Years)
Customer contracts and relationships	$28,569	$(21,920)	$6,649	10–20

| | December 31, 2011 | | | |
	Gross Carrying Value	Accum. Amort.	Net Carrying Amount	Estimated Life (Years)
Customer contracts and relationships	$42,218	$(26,819)	$15,399	10–20

TECHNOLOGY

2.83 INTERNATIONAL BUSINESS MACHINES CORPORATION (DEC)
CONSOLIDATED STATEMENT OF FINANCIAL POSITION (in part)

($ in millions except per share amounts)

		At December 31,	
	Notes	2012	2011
Assets			
Current assets			
Cash and cash equivalents		$ 10,412	$ 11,922
Marketable securities	D	717	0
Notes and accounts receivable—trade (net of allowances of $255 in 2012 and $256 in 2011)		10,667	11,179
Short-term financing receivables (net of allowances of $288 in 2012 and $311 in 2011)	F	18,038	16,901
Other accounts receivable (net of allowances of $17 in 2012 and $11 in 2011)		1,873	1,481
Inventories	E	2,287	2,595
Deferred taxes	N	1,415	1,601
Prepaid expenses and other current assets		4,024	5,249
Total current assets		49,433	50,928
Property, plant and equipment	G	40,501	40,124
Less: Accumulated depreciation	G	26,505	26,241
Property, plant and equipment—net	G	13,996	13,883
Long-term financing receivables (net of allowances of $66 in 2012 and $38 in 2011)	F	12,812	10,776
Prepaid pension assets	S	945	2,843
Deferred taxes	N	3,973	3,503
Goodwill	I	29,247	26,213
Intangible assets—net	I	3,787	3,392
Investments and sundry assets	H	5,021	4,895
Total assets		$119,213	$116,433

NOTES TO CONSOLIDATED FINANCIAL STATEMENTS

Note C. Acquisitions/Divestitures (in part)

Acquisitions (in part)

Purchase price consideration for all acquisitions, as reflected in the tables in this note, is paid primarily in cash. All acquisitions are reported in the Consolidated Statement of Cash Flows net of acquired cash and cash equivalents.

In 2012, the company completed 11 acquisitions at an aggregate cost of $3,964 million.

Kenexa Corporation (Kenexa)—On December 3, 2012, the company completed the acquisition of 100 percent of Kenexa, a publicly held company, for cash consideration of $1,351 million. Kenexa, a leading provider of recruiting and talent management solutions, brings a unique combination of cloud-based technology and consulting services that integrates both people and processes, providing solutions to engage a smarter, more effective workforce across their most critical businesses functions. Goodwill of $1,014 million has been assigned to the Software ($771 million) and Global Technology Services (GTS) ($243 million) segments. As of the acquisition date, it is expected that approximately 10 percent of the goodwill will be deductible for tax purposes. The overall weighted average useful life of the identified intangible assets acquired is 6.5 years.

Other Acquisitions—The Software segment also completed eight other acquisitions: in the first quarter, Green Hat Software Limited (Green Hat), Emptoris Inc. (Emptoris) and Worklight, Inc. (Worklight), all privately held companies, and DemandTec, Inc. (DemandTec), a publicly held company; in the second quarter, Varicent Software Inc. (Varicent), Vivisimo Inc. (Vivisimo) and Tealeaf Technology Inc. (Tealeaf), all privately held companies; and in the third quarter, Butterfly Software, Ltd. (Butterfly), a privately held company. Systems and Technology (STG) completed two acquisitions: in the first quarter, Platform Computing Corporation (Platform Computing), a privately held company; and in the third quarter, Texas Memory Systems (TMS), a privately held company. All acquisitions were for 100 percent of the acquired companies.

The table below reflects the purchase price related to these acquisitions and the resulting purchase price allocations as of December 31, 2012.

2012 Acquisitions

($ in millions)

	Amortization Life (in Years)	Kenexa	Other Acquisitions
Current assets		$ 133	$ 278
Fixed assets/noncurrent assets		98	217
Intangible assets			
Goodwill	N/A	1,014	1,880
Completed technology	3 to 7	169	403
Client relationships	4 to 7	179	194
In-process R&D	N/A	—	11
Patents/trademarks	1 to 7	39	37
Total assets acquired		1,632	3,020
Current liabilities		(93)	(143)
Noncurrent liabilities		(188)	(264)
Total liabilities assumed		(281)	(407)
Total purchase price		$1,351	$2,613

N/A—Not applicable

Each acquisition further complemented and enhanced the company's portfolio of product and services offerings. Green Hat helps customers improve the quality of software applications by enabling developers to use cloud computing technologies to conduct testing of a software application prior to its delivery. Emptoris expands the company's cloud-based analytics offerings that provide supply chain intelligence leading to better inventory management and cost efficiencies. Worklight delivers mobile application management capabilities to clients across a wide range of industries. The acquisition enhances the company's comprehensive mobile portfolio, which is designed to help global corporations leverage the proliferation of all mobile devices—from laptops and smartphones to tablets. DemandTec delivers cloud-based analytics software to help organizations improve their price, promotion and product mix within the broad context of enterprise commerce. Varicent's software automates and analyzes data across sales, finance, human resources and IT departments to uncover trends and optimize sales performance and operations. Vivisimo software automates the discovery of big data, regardless of its format or where it resides, providing decision makers with a view of key business information necessary to drive new initiatives. Tealeaf provides a full suite of customer experience management software, which analyzes interactions on websites and mobile devices. Butterfly offers storage planning software and storage migration tools, helping companies save storage space, operational time, IT budget and power consumption. Platform Computing's focused technical and distributed computing management software helps clients create, integrate and manage shared computing environments that are used in compute-and-data intensive applications such as simulations, computer modeling and analytics. TMS designs and sells high-performance solid state storage solutions.

For the "Other Acquisitions," the overall weighted-average life of the identified amortizable intangible assets acquired is 6.6 years. These identified intangible assets will be amortized on a straight-line basis over their useful lives. Goodwill of $1,880 million has been assigned to the Software ($1,412 million), Global Business Services (GBS) ($5 million), GTS ($21 million) and STG ($443 million) segments. As of the acquisition dates, it is expected that approximately 15 percent of the goodwill will be deductible for tax purposes.

On February 1, 2013, the company announced that it had entered into a definitive agreement to acquire the software portfolio of Star Analytics Inc., a privately held business analytics company based in Redwood City, California. The combination of the company's and Star Analytics software will advance the company's business analytics initiatives. The acquisition is subject to customary closing conditions and is expected to be completed in the first quarter of 2013.

On February 7, 2013, the company completed the acquisition of StoredIQ Inc. (StoredIQ), a privately held company based in Austin, Texas. StoredIQ will advance the company's efforts to help clients derive value from big data and respond more efficiently to litigation and regulations, dispose of information that has outlived its purpose and lower data storage costs. At the date of issuance of the financial statements, the initial purchase accounting was not complete for this acquisition.

Note I. Intangible Assets Including Goodwill (in part)

Intangible Assets

The following table details the company's intangible asset balances by major asset class.

($ in millions)

At December 31, 2012:	Gross Carrying Amount	Accumulated Amortization	Net Carrying Amount
Intangible asset class			
Capitalized software	$1,527	$ (665)	$ 861
Client relationships	2,103	(961)	1,142
Completed technology	2,709	(1,112)	1,597
In-process R&D	28	—	28
Patents/trademarks	281	(127)	154
Other*	31	(27)	3
Total	$6,679	$(2,892)	$3,787

($ in millions)

At December 31, 2011:	Gross Carrying Amount	Accumulated Amortization	Net Carrying Amount
Intangible asset class			
Capitalized software	$1,478	$ (678)	$ 799
Client relationships	1,751	(715)	1,035
Completed technology	2,160	(746)	1,414
In-process R&D	18	—	18
Patents/trademarks	207	(88)	119
Other*	29	(22)	7
Total	$5,642	$(2,250)	$3,392

* Other intangibles are primarily acquired proprietary and nonproprietary business processes, methodologies and systems.

The net carrying amount of intangible assets increased $395 million during the year ended December 31, 2012, primarily due to intangible asset additions resulting from acquisitions, partially offset by amortization. There was no impairment of intangible assets recorded in 2012 and 2011.

Total amortization was $1,284 million and $1,226 million for the years ended December 31, 2012 and 2011, respectively. The aggregate amortization expense for acquired intangibles assets (excluding capitalized software) was $709 million and $634 million for the years ended December 31, 2012 and 2011, respectively. In addition, in 2012 the company retired $641 million of fully amortized intangible assets, impacting both the gross carrying amount and accumulated amortization by this amount.

The amortization expense for each of the five succeeding years relating to intangible assets currently recorded in the Consolidated Statement of Financial Position is estimated to be the following at December 31, 2012:

($ in millions)

	Capitalized Software	Acquired Intangibles	Total
2013	$501	$729	$1,230
2014	277	626	903
2015	83	498	581
2016	—	458	458
2017	—	340	340

2.84 THE WESTERN UNION COMPANY (DEC)

CONSOLIDATED BALANCE SHEETS (in part)

(In millions, except per share amounts)

	December 31,	
	2012	2011
Assets		
Cash and cash equivalents	$1,776.5	$1,370.9
Settlement assets	3,114.6	3,091.2
Property and equipment, net of accumulated depreciation of $384.5 and $429.7, respectively	196.1	198.1
Goodwill	3,179.7	3,198.9
Other intangible assets, net of accumulated amortization of $519.7 and $462.5, respectively	878.9	847.4
Other assets	319.9	363.4
Total assets	$9,465.7	$9,069.9

NOTES TO CONSOLIDATED FINANCIAL STATEMENTS

2. Summary of Significant Accounting Policies (in part)

Other Intangible Assets (in part)

Other intangible assets primarily consist of acquired contracts, contract costs (primarily amounts paid to agents in connection with establishing and renewing long-term contracts) and software. Other intangible assets are amortized on a straight-line basis over the length of the contract or benefit periods. Included in the Consolidated Statements of Income is amortization expense of $184.4 million, $131.6 million and $114.4 million for the years ended December 31, 2012, 2011 and 2010, respectively.

The Company develops software that is used in providing services. Software development costs are capitalized once technological feasibility of the software has been established. Costs incurred prior to establishing technological feasibility are expensed as incurred. Technological feasibility is established when the Company has completed all planning and designing activities that are necessary to determine that a product can be produced to meet its design specifications, including functions, features and technical performance requirements. Capitalization of costs ceases when the product is available for general use. Software development costs and purchased software are generally amortized over a term of three to five years.

The following table provides the components of other intangible assets (in millions):

	December 31, 2012			December 31, 2011	
	Weighted-Average Period (In Years)	**Initial Cost**	**Net of Accumulated Amortization**	**Initial Cost**	**Net of Accumulated Amortization**
Acquired contracts	11.3	$ 627.2	$466.2	$ 629.5	$526.5
Capitalized contract costs	6.1	457.2	303.7	399.1	213.8
Internal use software	3.2	221.0	54.7	197.4	61.0
Acquired trademarks	22.7	43.4	28.4	41.5	31.0
Projects in process	3.0	15.4	15.4	0.8	0.8
Other intangibles	2.7	34.4	10.5	41.6	14.3
Total other intangible assets	8.4	$1,398.6	$878.9	$1,309.9	$847.4

The estimated future aggregate amortization expense for existing other intangible assets as of December 31, 2012 is expected to be $188.4 million in 2013, $161.0 million in 2014, $117.4 million in 2015, $89.7 million in 2016, $75.0 million in 2017 and $ 247.4 million thereafter.

LICENSES

2.85 VERIZON COMMUNICATIONS INC. (DEC)

CONSOLIDATED BALANCE SHEETS (in part)

	At December 31,	
(Dollars in millions, except per share amounts)	2012	2011
Assets		
Current assets		
Cash and cash equivalents	$ 3,093	$ 13,362
Short-term investments	470	592
Accounts receivable, net of allowances of $641 and $802	12,576	11,776
Inventories	1,075	940
Prepaid expenses and other	4,021	4,269
Total current assets	21,235	30,939
Plant, property and equipment	209,575	215,626
Less accumulated depreciation	120,933	127,192
	88,642	88,434
Investments in unconsolidated businesses	3,401	3,448
Wireless licenses	77,744	73,250
Goodwill	24,139	23,357
Other intangible assets, net	5,933	5,878
Other assets	4,128	5,155
Total assets	$225,222	$230,461

NOTES TO CONSOLIDATED FINANCIAL STATEMENTS

Note 1—Description of Business and Summary of Significant Accounting Policies (in part)

Goodwill and Other Intangible Assets (in part)

Intangible Assets Not Subject to Amortization

A significant portion of our intangible assets are wireless licenses that provide our wireless operations with the exclusive right to utilize designated radio frequency spectrum to provide wireless communication services. While licenses are issued for only a fixed time, generally ten years, such licenses are subject to renewal by the Federal Communications Commission (FCC). Renewals of licenses have occurred routinely and at nominal cost. Moreover, we have determined that there are currently no legal, regulatory, contractual, competitive, economic or other factors that limit the useful life of our wireless licenses. As a result, we treat the wireless licenses as an indefinite-lived intangible asset. We reevaluate the useful life determination for wireless licenses each year to determine whether events and circumstances continue to support an indefinite useful life.

We test our wireless licenses for potential impairment annually. We evaluate our licenses on an aggregate basis using a direct value approach. The direct value approach estimates fair value using a discounted cash flow analysis to estimate what a marketplace participant would be willing to pay to purchase the aggregated wireless licenses as of the valuation date. If the fair value of the aggregated wireless licenses is less than the aggregated carrying amount of the licenses, an impairment is recognized.

Interest expense incurred while qualifying activities are performed to ready wireless licenses for their intended use is capitalized as part of wireless licenses. The capitalization period ends when the development is discontinued or substantially complete and the license is ready for its intended use.

Note 3—Wireless Licenses, Goodwill and Other Intangible Assets (in part)

Wireless Licenses

Changes in the carrying amount of Wireless licenses are as follows:

	(Dollars in millions)
Balance at January 1, 2011	$72,996
Acquisitions (Note 2)	58
Capitalized interest on wireless licenses	196
Balance at December 31, 2011	$73,250
Acquisitions (Note 2)	4,544
Capitalized interest on wireless licenses	205
Reclassifications, adjustments and other	(255)
Balance at December 31, 2012	$77,744

Reclassifications, adjustments, and other includes the exchanges of wireless licenses in 2012. See Note 2 ("Acquisitions and Divestitures") for additional details.

At December 31, 2012 and 2011, approximately $7.3 billion and $2.2 billion, respectively, of wireless licenses were under development for commercial service for which we were capitalizing interest costs.

The average remaining renewal period of our wireless license portfolio was 6.1 years as of December 31, 2012 (see Note 1, Goodwill and Other Intangible Assets—*Intangible Assets Not Subject to Amortization*).

PURCHASED INTANGIBLE ASSETS

2.86 JUNIPER NETWORKS, INC. (DEC)
CONSOLIDATED BALANCE SHEETS (in part)

(In millions, except par values)

	December 31, 2012	December 31, 2011
Assets		
Current assets:		
Cash and cash equivalents	$2,407.8	$2,910.4
Short-term investments	441.5	641.3
Accounts receivable, net of allowance for doubtful accounts of $9.5 for 2012 and 2011, respectively	438.4	577.4
Deferred tax assets, net	172.6	154.3
Prepaid expenses and other current assets	140.4	156.3
Total current assets	3,600.7	4,439.7
Property and equipment, net	811.9	598.6
Long-term investments	988.1	740.7
Restricted cash and investments	106.4	78.3
Purchased intangible assets, net	128.9	123.1
Goodwill	4,057.8	3,928.1
Other long-term assets	138.3	75.3
Total assets	9,832.1	9,983.8

NOTES TO CONSOLIDATED FINANCIAL STATEMENTS

Note 2. Significant Accounting Policies (in part)

Goodwill and Other Long-Lived Assets (in part)

Goodwill represents the future economic benefits arising from other assets acquired in a business combination or an acquisition that are not individually identified and separately recorded. The excess of the purchase price over the estimated fair value of net assets of businesses acquired in a business combination is recognized as goodwill. Goodwill and other intangible assets acquired in a business combination and determined to have an indefinite useful life are not amortized, but instead tested for impairment at least annually during the fourth quarter. Such goodwill and other intangible assets may also be tested for impairment between annual tests in the presence of impairment indicators such as, but not limited to: (a) a significant adverse change in legal factors or in the business climate; (b) a substantial decline in our market capitalization, (c) an adverse action or assessment by a regulator; (d) unanticipated competition; (e) loss of key personnel; (f) a more likely-than-not expectation of sale or disposal of a reporting unit or a significant portion thereof; (g) a realignment of our resources or restructuring of our existing businesses in response to changes to industry and market conditions; (h) testing for recoverability of a significant asset group within a reporting unit; or (i) higher discount rate used in the impairment analysis as impacted by an increase in interest rates.

The Company performs its annual goodwill impairment analysis at its reporting unit level, which is one level below its operating segment level during the fourth quarter of each year. The fair value of the Company's reporting units is determined using both the income and market valuation approaches. Under the income approach, the fair value of the reporting unit is based on the present value of estimated future cash flows that the reporting unit is expected to generate over its remaining life. Under the market approach, the value of the reporting unit is based on an analysis that compares the value of the reporting unit to values of publicly traded companies in similar lines of business. In the application of the income and market valuation approaches, the Company is required to make estimates of future operating trends and judgments on discount rates and other variables. Actual future results related to assumed variables could differ from these estimates.

Long-lived assets, such as property, plant, and equipment, and purchased intangible assets subject to amortization, are reviewed for impairment whenever events or changes in circumstances indicate that the carrying amount of an asset may not be recoverable. Such events or circumstances include, but are not limited to, a significant decrease in the fair value of the underlying business, a significant decrease in the benefits realized from an acquired business, difficulties or delays in integrating the business or a significant change in the operations of an acquired business. Recoverability of assets to be held and used is measured by a comparison of the carrying amount of an asset, or asset group, to estimated undiscounted future cash flows expected to be generated by the asset, or asset group. An impairment charge is recognized by the amount by which the carrying amount of the asset, or asset group, exceeds its fair value.

The Company amortizes intangible assets with estimable useful lives on a straight-line basis over their useful lives.

Note 3. Business Combinations

The Company's Consolidated Financial Statements include the operating results of acquired businesses from the date of each acquisition. Pro forma results of operations for these acquisitions have not been presented as the financial impact to the Company's consolidated results of operations, both individually and in aggregate, is not material. Additional information existing as of the acquisition dates but unknown to the Company may become known during the remainder of the measurement period, not to exceed 12 months from the acquisition date, which may result in changes to the amounts and allocations recorded.

The Company completed three business combinations in 2012, two business combinations in 2011, and four business combinations in 2010 for either cash consideration and/or stock related to the fair value of vested share-based awards assumed of approximately $187.3 million, $30.5 million, and $394.5 million, respectively. The following table presents the purchase consideration allocations for these acquisitions based upon their acquisition-date fair values, including cash and cash equivalents acquired (in millions):

	2012 Acquisitions	2011 Acquisitions	2010 Acquisitions
Net tangible assets acquired	$ 3.5	$ 1.7	$ 8.8
Intangible assets acquired	54.1	28.4	116.5
Goodwill	129.7	0.4	269.2
Total	$187.3	$30.5	$394.5

The Company recognized $2.0 million, $9.6 million, and $6.3 million of acquisition-related costs during the years ended December 31, 2012, 2011, and 2010, respectively. These acquisition-related charges were expensed in the period incurred and reported in the Company's Consolidated Statements of Operations within cost of revenues and operating expense.

The goodwill recognized for the 2012 and 2011 acquisitions was primarily attributable to expected synergies and was not deductible for U.S. federal income tax purposes. Approximately $88.9 million of the acquired goodwill from a 2010 acquisition was deductible for income tax purposes.

Fiscal 2012 Acquisitions

Contrail Systems Inc.

On December 14, 2012, the Company acquired the remaining ownership interest in Contrail Systems, Inc. ("Contrail"), increasing its ownership from 12% to 100%, in a cash and stock transaction for approximately $91.7 million. Contrail, a privately-held software networking company, provides software-defined networking solutions technology that augments Juniper's portfolio of products and services.

The aggregate consideration of $91.7 million was allocated as follows: net tangible assets acquired of $3.6 million, including cash and cash equivalents of $8.6 million; intangible assets of $17.4 million; and recognized goodwill of $70.7 million, which was assigned to the Company's PSD segment.

The Company previously accounted for its investment in Contrail at cost, which was $3.0 million prior to the acquisition. As of the acquisition date, the fair value of the Company's previous equity interest in Contrail was remeasured to its fair value of $17.7 million, which was based upon adjustments market participants would consider when estimating the fair value of the previously held interest in Contrail. This resulted in a $14.7 million gain, which was reported within other (expense) income, net in the Consolidated Statements of Operations.

Mykonos Software, Inc.

On February 13, 2012, the Company acquired 100% of the equity securities of Mykonos Software, Inc. ("Mykonos") for $82.6 million in cash. The acquisition of Mykonos extended Juniper Networks' security portfolio with an intrusion deception system capable of detecting an attacker before an attack is in process. In connection with this acquisition, the Company acquired net tangible liabilities of $0.2 million, intangible assets of $24.3 million, and recognized goodwill of $58.5 million, which was assigned to the Company's SSD segment.

BitGravity, Inc.

On March 8, 2012, the Company acquired a source code license, patent joint-ownership, and employees related to the service management layer of BitGravity, Inc.'s ("BitGravity") Content Delivery Network ("CDN") technology for $13.0 million in cash. In connection with this acquisition, the Company acquired net tangible assets of $0.1 million, intangible assets of $12.4 million, and recognized goodwill of $0.5 million, which was assigned to the Company's SSD segment.

The following table presents details of the intangible assets acquired for the business combinations completed during 2012 as of their respective acquisition dates (in millions, except years):

	Contrail		Mykonos		BitGravity	
	Weighted Average Estimated Useful Life (In Years)	Amount	Weighted Average Estimated Useful Life (In Years)	Amount	Weighted Average Estimated Useful Life (In Years)	Amount
Existing technology	—	$ —	6	$19.3	3	$12.4
Trade name and trademarks	—	—	7	1.0	—	—
In-process research and development	N/A	17.4	N/A	4.0	—	—
Total		$17.4		$24.3		$12.4

Acquired in-process research and development ("IPR&D") consists of existing research and development projects at the time of the acquisition. Projects that qualify as IPR&D assets represent those that have not yet reached technological feasibility and have no alternative future use. After initial recognition, acquired IPR&D assets are accounted for as indefinite-lived intangible assets. Development costs incurred after acquisition on acquired development projects are expensed as incurred. Upon completion of development, acquired IPR&D assets are considered amortizable intangible assets. If the IPR&D project is abandoned, the Company writes off the related purchased intangible asset in the period it is abandoned.

Fiscal 2011 Acquisitions

OpNext

On February 9, 2011, the Company acquired certain IP assets of OpNext for $26.0 million in cash, which was accounted for as a business combination. The acquisition of OpNext's ASIC technology furthers Juniper's next-generation development of converged packet optical solutions for the Company's service provider customers. In connection with this acquisition, the Company acquired the fair value of intangible assets of $25.7 million and recognized goodwill of $0.3 million.

Brilliant

On February 18, 2011, the Company acquired certain assets, including all the intellectual property ("IP"), of Brilliant, a supplier of next-generation packet-based, network synchronization equipment and monitoring solutions, for $4.5 million in cash. This IP assists the Company in extending its market position by delivering solutions that offer greater flexibility for service providers as they continue to deploy 3G and 4G networks. In connection with this acquisition, the Company acquired net tangible assets of $1.7 million, intangible assets of $2.7 million, and recognized goodwill of $0.1 million.

Intangible Assets Acquired

The following table presents details of the intangible assets acquired for the business combinations completed during 2011 as of their respective acquisition dates (in millions, except years):

	OpNext		Brilliant	
	Weighted Average Estimated Useful Life (In Years)	Amount	Weighted Average Estimated Useful Life (In Years)	Amount
Existing or core technology	10	$20.6	5	$1.3
Support agreements and related relationships	4	5.1	—	—
Patents	—	—	5	1.4
Total		$25.7		$2.7

Fiscal 2010 Acquisitions

Ankeena Networks, Inc.

On April 19, 2010, the Company acquired the remaining ownership interest in Ankeena Networks, Inc. ("Ankeena"), increasing its ownership from 7.7% to 100%, in a cash and stock transaction for $68.9 million. The acquisition of Ankeena, a privately-held provider of new media infrastructure technology, provides the Company with strong video delivery capabilities, as Ankeena's products optimize web-based video delivery, provides key components of a content delivery network architecture/solution, improves consumers' online video experience, and reduces service provider and carrier service provider infrastructure costs for providing web-based video.

The aggregate consideration of $68.9 million was allocated as follows: net tangible assets acquired of $3.6 million, including cash and cash equivalents of $2.3 million; intangible assets of $12.2 million; and recognized goodwill of $53.1 million.

The Company previously accounted for its investment in Ankeena at cost, which was $2.0 million prior to the acquisition. As of the acquisition-date, the fair value of the Company's previous equity interest in Ankeena was remeasured to its fair value of $5.2 million, which was based upon adjustments market participants would consider when estimating the fair value of the previously held equity interest in Ankeena. This resulted in a gain of $3.2 million, which was reported within other (expense) income, net in the Consolidated Statements of Operations.

SMobile Systems, Inc.

On July 30, 2010, the Company acquired 100% of the equity securities of SMobile Systems, Inc. ("SMobile"), a privately-held software company focused solely on smartphone and tablet security solutions for the enterprise, service provider, and consumer markets for $69.5 million in cash. The acquisition of SMobile allows the Company to extend its security focus through integration of SMobile's product portfolio with Junos®Pulse. In connection with the acquisition of SMobile, the Company acquired net tangible liabilities of $5.2 million, including cash and cash equivalents of $0.4 million, intangible assets of $26.6 million, and recognized goodwill of $48.1 million.

Altor

On December 6, 2010, the Company acquired the remaining ownership interest in Altor, increasing its ownership from 5.0% to 100%, in a cash transaction for $104.0 million. The acquisition of Altor, a privately-held provider of virtualization security, provides the Company with data center and cloud security solutions, including products that optimize web-based video delivery, provides key components of a content delivery network architecture/solution, improves consumers' online video experience, and reduces service provider and carrier service provider infrastructure costs for providing web-based video.

The aggregate consideration of $104.0 million was allocated as follows: net tangible assets acquired of $4.5 million, including cash and cash equivalents of $6.4 million; intangible assets of $21.3 million; and recognized goodwill of $78.2 million.

The Company previously accounted for its investment in Altor at cost, which was $2.0 million prior to the acquisition. As of the acquisition-date, the fair value of the Company's previous equity interest in Altor was remeasured to its fair value of $4.1 million, which was based upon adjustments market participants would consider when estimating the fair value of the previously held equity interest in Altor. This resulted in a gain of $2.1 million, which was reported within other (expense) income, net in the Consolidated Statements of Operations.

Trapeze Networks

On December 16, 2010, the Company acquired 100% of the equity securities of Trapeze Networks ("Trapeze"), a subsidiary of Belden Inc. and a provider of enterprise wireless local area network ("WLAN") solutions for $152.1 million in cash. The acquisition made WLAN infrastructure a key part of Juniper's portfolio and accelerates our growth in the enterprise market. In connection with the acquisition of Trapeze, the Company acquired net tangible assets of $5.9 million, including cash and cash equivalents of $0.8 million, intangible assets of $56.4 million, and recognized goodwill of $89.8 million.

Intangible Assets Acquired

The following table presents details of the intangible assets acquired for the business combinations completed during 2010 as of their respective acquisition dates (in millions, except years):

	Ankeena		SMobile		Altor		Trapeze	
	Weighted Average Estimated Useful Life (In Years)	Amount	Weighted Average Estimated Useful Life (In Years)	Amount	Weighted Average Estimated Useful Life (In Years)	Amount	Weighted Average Estimated Useful Life (In Years)	Amount
Existing technology	4	$ 9.0	5	$24.3	6	$13.9	5	$45.0
In-process research and development	—	—	—	—	N/A	2.8	—	—
Core technology	4	3.2	—	—	6	4.6	—	—
Customer contracts and related relationships	—	—	6	2.1	—	—	7	8.6
Support agreements and related relationships	—	—	6	0.1	—	—	7	2.6
Non-compete agreements	—	—	2	0.1	—	—	—	—
OEM customer contracts	—	—	—	—	—	—	2	0.2
Total		$12.2		$26.6		$21.3		$56.4

Purchased Intangible Assets

The Company's purchased intangible assets were as follows (in millions):

	Gross	Accumulated Amortization	Accumulated Impairment and Other Charges	Net
As of December 31, 2012				
Intangible assets with finite lives:				
Technologies and patents	$554.1	$(425.0)	$(30.5)	$ 98.6
Customer contracts, support agreements, and related relationships	74.3	(59.2)	(2.2)	12.9
Other	18.8	(18.8)	—	—
Total intangible assets with finite lives	647.2	(503.0)	(32.7)	111.5
IPR&D with indefinite lives	17.4	—	—	17.4
Total purchased intangible assets	$664.6	$(503.0)	$(32.7)	$128.9
As of December 31, 2011				
Intangible assets with finite lives:				
Technologies and patents	$515.5	$(396.4)	$(14.4)	$104.7
Customer contracts, support agreements, and related relationships	73.3	(55.6)	(2.2)	15.5
Other	18.8	(18.7)	—	0.1
Total intangible assets with finite lives	607.6	(470.7)	(16.6)	120.3
IPR&D with indefinite lives	2.8	—	—	2.8
Total purchased intangible assets	$610.4	$(470.7)	$(16.6)	$123.1

During the years ended December 31, 2012, 2011, and 2010, the Company added $54.1 million, $28.4 million, $116.5 million of purchased intangible assets as a result of acquisitions completed during 2012, 2011, and 2010, respectively. Refer to Note 3, *Business Combinations*, for further details.

During the year ended December 31, 2012, $6.8 million of acquired IPR&D accounted for as indefinite lived assets reached technological feasibility and were reclassified as amortizable finite-lived assets. Amortization of purchased intangible assets included in operating expenses and cost of product revenues totaled $32.3 million, $27.1 million, and $8.6 million for the years ended December 31, 2012, 2011, and 2010, respectively.

In connection with the restructuring plan in 2012 discussed in Note 9, *Restructuring and Other Charges*, the Company assessed the impairment and remaining useful life of certain intangible assets and determined intangible assets of $5.4 million were impaired and written-down to their fair value of zero and other intangible assets of $10.7 million will no longer be utilized. As a result, the Company recorded $16.1 million in charges related to these items during the year ended December 31, 2012, which are included in cost of revenues in the Consolidated Statements of Operations and recorded in the Company's SSD segment.

As of December 31, 2012, the estimated future amortization expense of purchased intangible assets with finite lives is as follows (in millions):

Years Ending December 31	Amount
2013	$ 28.6
2014	28.5
2015	24.9
2016	12.2
2017	8.5
Thereafter	8.8
Total	$111.5

Other Noncurrent Assets

RECOGNITION AND MEASUREMENT

2.87 FASB ASC 210 indicates that the concept of current assets excludes resources such as the following:
- Cash restricted regarding withdrawal or use for other than current operations, designated for expenditure in the acquisition or construction of noncurrent assets, or segregated for the liquidation of long-term debts
- Investments or advances for the purposes of control, affiliation, or other continuing business advantage
- Certain receivables (see the "Noncurrent Receivables" section)
- Cash surrender value of life insurance
- Land and other natural resources
- Long-term prepayments chargeable to operations over several years

DISCLOSURE

2.88 Rule 5-02 of Regulation S-X requires that any item not classed in another Regulation S-X caption and in excess of 5 percent of total assets be stated separately on the balance sheet or disclosed in the notes.

PRESENTATION AND DISCLOSURE EXCERPTS

ASSETS HELD FOR SALE

2.89 MURPHY OIL CORPORATION (DEC)
CONSOLIDATED BALANCE SHEETS (in part)

	December 31	
(Thousands of dollars)	2012	2011
Assets		
Current assets		
Cash and cash equivalents	$ 947,316	513,873
Canadian government securities with maturities greater than 90 days at the date of acquisition	115,603	532,093
Accounts receivable, less allowance for doubtful accounts of $6,697 in 2012 and $7,892 in 2011	1,853,364	1,554,184
Inventories, at lower of cost or market		
Crude oil and blend stocks	226,541	189,320
Finished products	266,307	254,880
Materials and supplies	259,462	222,438
Prepaid expenses	335,831	93,397
Deferred income taxes	89,040	87,486
Assets held for sale	15,119	0
Total current assets	4,108,583	3,447,671
Property, plant and equipment, at cost less accumulated depreciation, depletion and amortization of $8,138,587 in 2012 and $6,861,494 in 2011	13,011,606	10,475,149
Goodwill	43,103	41,863
Deferred charges and other assets	151,183	173,455
Assets held for sale	208,168	0
Total assets	$17,522,643	14,138,138

NOTES TO CONSOLIDATED FINANCIAL STATEMENTS

Note C—Discontinued Operations

During the third quarter 2012, Murphy's Board of Directors authorized management to sell the Company's exploration and production (upstream) operations in the United Kingdom. Beginning in 2012, the Company has accounted for U.K. upstream operations as discontinued operations for all periods presented, including a reclassification of all prior years' results for these operations to discontinued operations. The U.K. upstream operations were formerly reported as a separate segment within the Company's exploration and production business. The Company currently expects to complete the sale of these U.K. operations in early 2013.

Assets and liabilities presented in the December 31, 2012 Consolidated Balance Sheet as held for sale related to the U.K. exploration and production operations were as follows:

(Thousands of dollars)	
Current assets:	
Accounts receivable	$ 10,143
Inventories and other	4,976
	$ 15,119
Noncurrent assets:	
Property, plant and equipment—net	$205,746
Other	2,422
	$208,168
Current liabilities:	
Accounts payable	$ 27,578
Income taxes payable	19,893
	$ 47,471
Noncurrent liabilities:	
Deferred income taxes payable	$ 87,893
Asset retirement obligation	53,284
	$141,177

In July 2010, the Company announced that it planned to exit the U.S. refining business. On September 30, 2011, the Company sold the Superior, Wisconsin refinery and related assets for $214,000,000, plus certain capital expenditures between July 25, 2011, and the date of closing and the fair value of all associated hydrocarbon inventories at these locations. On October 1, 2011, the Company sold its Meraux, Louisiana refinery and related assets for $325,000,000, plus the fair value of associated hydrocarbon inventories. The Company has accounted for the results of the Superior, Wisconsin and Meraux, Louisiana refineries and associated marketing assets as discontinued operations. The after-tax gain in 2011 from disposal of the two refineries netted to $18,724,000, made up of a gain on the Superior refinery (including associated inventories) of $77,585,000 and a loss on the Meraux refinery (including associated inventories) of $58,861,000. The gain on disposal was based on refinery selling prices, plus the sales of all associated inventories at fair value, which was significantly above the last-in, first-out carrying value of the inventories sold. The net gain on sale of the refineries included an after-tax benefit of $179,152,000 from liquidation of inventories formerly carried primarily under the last-in, first-out cost method. The U.S. refineries sold were formerly reported in the U.S. manufacturing segment.

RETIREMENT SAVINGS PLAN ASSETS

2.90 CACI INTERNATIONAL INC (JUN)
CONSOLIDATED BALANCE SHEETS (in part)

(Amounts in thousands, except per share data)

	June 30,	
	2012	2011
Assets		
Current assets:		
Cash and cash equivalents	$ 15,740	$ 164,817
Accounts receivable, net	628,842	573,042
Deferred income taxes	16,747	16,080
Prepaid expenses and other current assets	24,463	28,139
Total current assets	685,792	782,078
Goodwill	1,406,953	1,266,285
Intangible assets, net	114,816	108,102
Property and equipment, net	67,449	62,755
Supplemental retirement savings plan assets	77,371	66,880
Accounts receivable, long-term	9,942	8,657
Other long-term assets	30,553	25,374
Total assets	$2,392,876	$2,320,131

NOTES TO CONSOLIDATED FINANCIAL STATEMENTS

Note 2. Summary of Significant Accounting Policies (in part)

Supplemental Retirement Savings Plan

The Company maintains the CACI International Inc Group Executive Retirement Plan (the Supplemental Savings Plan) and maintains the underlying assets in a Rabbi Trust. The Supplemental Savings Plan is a non-qualified defined contribution supplemental retirement savings plan for certain key employees whereby participants may elect to defer and contribute a portion of their compensation, as permitted by the plan. Each participant directs his or her investments in the Supplemental Savings Plan (see Note 20).

A Rabbi Trust is a grantor trust established to fund compensation for a select group of management. The assets of this trust are available to satisfy the claims of general creditors in the event of bankruptcy of the Company. The assets held by the Rabbi Trust are invested in both corporate owned life insurance (COLI) products and in non-COLI products. The COLI products are recorded at cash surrender value in the consolidated financial statements as supplemental retirement savings plan assets and the non-COLI products are recorded at fair value in the consolidated financial statements as supplemental retirement savings plan assets. The amounts due to participants are based on contributions, participant investment elections, and other participant activity and are recorded as supplemental retirement savings plan obligations.

Note 20. Retirement Savings Plans (in part)

Supplemental Savings Plan (in part)

The Company maintains the Supplemental Savings Plan through which, on a calendar year basis, officers at the director level and above can elect to defer for contribution to the Supplemental Savings Plan up to 50 percent of their base compensation and up to 100 percent of their bonuses and commissions. Prior to January 1, 2011, officers at the vice president level and above were eligible to participate. During the year ended June 30, 2011, the Supplemental Savings Plan was amended to allow employees at the director level to participate. The Company provides a contribution of 5 percent of compensation for each participant's compensation that exceeds the limit as set forth in IRC 401(a)(17) (currently $250,000 per year). The Company also has the option to make annual discretionary contributions. Company contributions vest over a 5-year period, and vesting is accelerated in the event of a change of control of the Company. Participant deferrals and Company contributions will be credited with the rate of return based on the investment options and asset allocations selected by the Participant. Participants may change their asset allocation as often as daily, if they so choose. A Rabbi Trust has been established to hold and provide a measure of security for the investments that finance benefit payments. Distributions from the Supplemental Savings Plan are made upon retirement, termination, death, or total disability. The Supplemental Savings Plan also allows for in-service distributions.

Supplemental Savings Plan obligations due to participants totaled $76.6 million at June 30, 2012, of which $3.4 million is included in accrued compensation and benefits in the accompanying consolidated balance sheet. Supplemental Savings Plan obligations increased by $9.3 million during the year ended June 30, 2012, consisting of $1.4 million of investment gains, $12.2 million of participant compensation deferrals, and $1.4 million of Company contributions, offset by $5.7 million of distributions.

The Company maintains investment assets in a Rabbi Trust to offset the obligations under the Supplemental Savings Plan. The value of the investments in the Rabbi Trust was $77.4 million at June 30, 2012. Investment gains were $1.2 million for the year ended June 30, 2012.

DEFERRED INCOME TAXES

2.91 ALLIANCE ONE INTERNATIONAL, INC. (MAR)

CONSOLIDATED BALANCE SHEETS (in part)

(In thousands)	March 31, 2012	March 31, 2011
Assets		
Current assets		
Cash and cash equivalents	$ 119,743	$ 43,506
Trade and other receivables, net	303,090	279,904
Accounts receivable, related parties	32,316	61,981
Inventories	839,902	800,365
Advances to tobacco suppliers	89,378	74,556
Recoverable income taxes	9,592	7,191
Current deferred taxes	23,855	3,955
Prepaid expenses	45,097	42,319
Assets held for sale	—	413
Current derivative asset	312	2,543
Other current assets	14,562	542
Total current assets	1,477,847	1,317,275
Other assets		
Investments in unconsolidated affiliates	24,530	25,665
Goodwill and other intangible assets	35,865	41,205
Deferred income taxes	73,378	82,707
Other deferred charges	12,467	21,019
Other noncurrent assets	66,079	83,371
	212,319	253,967
Property, plant and equipment, net	259,679	237,088
	$1,949,845	$1,808,330

NOTES TO CONSOLIDATED FINANCIAL STATEMENTS

(In thousands)

Note 1—Significant Accounting Policies (in part)

Income Taxes

The Company uses the asset and liability method to account for income taxes. The objective of the asset and liability method is to establish deferred tax assets and liabilities for the temporary differences between the financial reporting basis and the income tax basis of the Company's assets and liabilities at enacted tax rates expected to be in effect when such amounts are realized or settled.

The Company's annual tax rate is based on its income, statutory tax rates and tax planning opportunities available to it in the various jurisdictions in which it operates. Tax laws are complex and subject to different interpretations by the taxpayer and respective governmental taxing authorities. Significant judgment is required in determining tax expense and in evaluating tax positions, including evaluating uncertainties. The Company reviews its tax positions quarterly and adjusts the balances as new information becomes available.

Deferred income tax assets represent amounts available to reduce income taxes payable on taxable income in future years. Such assets arise because of temporary differences between the financial reporting and tax bases of assets and liabilities, as well as from net operating loss and tax credit carryforwards. The Company evaluates the recoverability of these future tax deductions by assessing the adequacy of future expected taxable income from all sources, including reversal of taxable temporary differences, forecasted operating earnings and available tax planning strategies. These sources of income inherently rely on estimates. The Company uses historical experience and short and long-range business forecasts to provide insight. The Company believes it is more likely than not that a portion of the deferred income tax assets may expire unused and has established a valuation allowance against them. Although realization is not assured for the remaining deferred income tax assets, the Company believes it is more likely than not the deferred tax assets will be fully recoverable within the applicable statutory expiration periods. However, deferred tax assets could be reduced in the near term if estimates of taxable income are significantly reduced or available tax planning strategies are no longer viable. See Note 12 "Income Taxes" and Note 16 "Contingencies and Other Information" to the "Notes to Consolidated Financial Statements" for further information.

Note 12—Income Taxes

Accounting for Uncertainty in Income Taxes

As of March 31, 2012, 2011 and 2010, the Company's unrecognized tax benefits totaled $11,804, $9,019 and $9,004, respectively, all of which would impact the Company's effective tax rate if recognized. The following table presents the changes to unrecognized tax benefits during the years ended March 31, 2012, 2011 and 2010:

	2012	2011	2010
Balance at April 1	$ 9,019	$ 9,004	$ 20,129
Increase for current year tax positions	58	3,500	2,292
Increases (reductions) for prior year tax positions	3,030	5,539	(1,698)
Impact of changes in exchange rates	(303)	(63)	3,664
Reduction for settlements	—	(8,961)	(15,383)
Balance at March 31	$11,804	$ 9,019	$ 9,004

The Company recognizes interest and penalties related to unrecognized tax benefits in income tax expense. During the years ended March 31, 2012 and 2011, the Company accrued an additional $1,176 and $2,446, respectively, of interest, penalties and related exchange losses related to unrecognized tax benefits. As of March 31, 2012, accrued interest and penalties totaled $8,690 and $1,190, respectively. During the year ending March 31, 2012, the Company reduced its accrued interest and penalties for $307 related to settlements and for $203 related to the expiration of statute of limitations. As of March 31, 2011, accrued interest and penalties totaled $7,780 and $1,434, respectively.

During the fiscal year ending March 31, 2012, the Company's total liability for unrecognized tax benefits, including the related interest and penalties, increased from $18,233 0 to $21,683. The increase relates to settlements of approximately $307, expiration of statute of limitations of approximately $355, and increases related to current period activity of approximately $4,112.

The Company expects to continue accruing interest expenses related to the remaining unrecognized tax benefits. Additionally, the Company may be subject to fluctuations in the unrecognized tax liability due to currency exchange rate movements.

Other than the expiration of an assessment period under local guidance and administrative practice pertaining to an international unrecognized tax benefit for the amount of $1,359, interest of $7,789 and penalties $343, the Company does not foresee any reasonably possible changes in the unrecognized tax benefits in the next twelve months but must acknowledge circumstances can change due to unexpected developments in the law. In certain jurisdictions, tax authorities have challenged positions that the Company has taken that resulted in recognizing benefits that are material to its financial statements. The Company believes it is more likely than not that it will prevail in these situations and accordingly have not recorded liabilities for these positions. The Company expects the challenged positions to be settled at a time greater than twelve months from its balance sheet date.

The Company and its subsidiaries file a U.S. federal consolidated income tax return as well as returns in several U.S. states and a number of foreign jurisdictions. As of March 31, 2012, the Company's earliest open tax year for U.S. federal income tax purposes was its fiscal year ended March 31, 2009. Open tax years in state and foreign jurisdictions generally range from three to six years.

Income Tax Provision

The components of income before income taxes, equity in net income of investee companies and minority interests consisted of the following:

	Years Ended March 31,		
	2012	2011	2010
U.S.	$(21,923)	$(51,092)	$(43,645)
Non-U.S.	76,081	83,941	117,837
Total	$ 54,158	$ 32,849	$ 74,192

The details of the amount shown for income taxes in the Statements of Consolidated Operations and Comprehensive Income (Loss) follow:

	Years Ended March 31,		
	2012	2011	2010
Current			
Federal	$ —	$ 472	$ —
State	—	—	(7,509)
Non-U.S.	31,798	7,346	6,173
	$31,798	$ 7,818	$(1,336)
Deferred			
Federal	$ —	$ 97,311	$(9,271)
State	—	631	(631)
Non-U.S.	(6,759)	1,700	7,447
	$ (6,759)	$ 99,642	$(2,455)
Total	$25,039	$107,460	$(3,791)

The reasons for the difference between income tax expense based on income before income taxes, equity in net income of investee companies and minority interests and the amount computed by applying the U.S. statutory federal income tax rate to such income are as follows:

	Years Ended March 31,		
	2012	2011	2010
Tax expense at U.S. statutory rate	$18,955	$ 11,497	$ 25,967
Effect of non-U.S. income taxes	(4,712)	(7,322)	(16,309)
Goodwill amortization	—	(4,640)	(8,374)
Change in valuation allowance	1,617	111,679	(3,345)
Increase (decrease) in reserves for uncertain tax positions	3,452	4,489	(8,060)
Exchange effects and currency translation	3,958	(7,120)	5,680
Permanent items	1,769	(1,123)	650
Actual tax expense (benefit)	$25,039	$107,460	$ (3,791)

The deferred tax liabilities (assets) are comprised of the following:

	March 31, 2012	March 31, 2011
Deferred tax liabilities:		
Intangible assets	$ 8,404	$ 9,044
Fixed assets	10,662	9,135
Total deferred tax liabilities	$ 19,066	$ 18,179
Deferred tax assets:		
Reserves and accruals	$ (58,786)	$ (77,746)
Tax credits	(48,897)	(48,659)
Tax loss carryforwards	(64,624)	(63,228)
Derivative transactions	(10,775)	(12,760)
Postretirement and other benefits	(32,361)	(29,786)
Unrealized exchange loss	(14,530)	—
Other	(14,713)	(752)
Gross deferred tax assets	(244,686)	(232,931)
Valuation allowance	143,345	138,787
Total deferred tax assets	$(101,341)	$ (94,144)
Net deferred tax asset	$ (82,275)	$ (75,965)

The following table presents the breakdown between current and non-current (assets) liabilities:

	March 31, 2012	March 31, 2011
Current asset	$(23,855)	$ (3,955)
Current liability	5,464	6,881
Non-current asset	(73,378)	(82,707)
Non-current liability	9,494	3,816
Net deferred tax asset	$(82,275)	$(75,965)

The current portion of deferred tax liability is included in income taxes.

During the year ended March 31, 2012, the net deferred tax asset balance decreased by $449 for certain adjustments not included in the deferred tax expense (benefit), primarily for deferred tax assets related to pension accruals recorded in equity as part of Other Comprehensive Income (Loss) and currency translation adjustments.

For the year ended March 31, 2012, the valuation allowance increased by $4,558. The valuation allowance increased primarily due to U.S. federal, U.S state and non-U.S. tax losses. The valuation allowance is based on the Company's assessment that it is more likely than not that certain deferred tax assets, primarily foreign tax credits and net operating loss carryovers, will not be realized in the foreseeable future. Recent years' cumulative losses incurred in the United States as of March 31, 2012, combined with the effects of certain changes in the market, provide significant objective negative evidence in the evaluation of whether the U.S. entity will generate sufficient taxable income to realize the tax benefits of the deferred tax assets. This negative evidence carries greater weight than the more subjective positive evidence of favorable future projected income in the assessment of whether realization of the tax benefits of the deferred tax assets is more likely than not. Therefore, based on the weight of presently objectively verifiable positive and negative evidence, it is management's judgment that realization of the tax benefits of the deferred tax assets is less than more likely than not.

At March 31, 2012, the Company has U.S federal tax loss carryovers of $105,186, non-U.S. tax loss carryovers of $66,662, and U.S. state tax loss carryovers of $250,381. Of the non-U.S. tax loss carryovers, $35,267 will expire within the next five years, $18,994 will expire in later years, and $12,401 can be carried forward indefinitely. Of the U.S. state tax loss carryovers, $41,336 will expire within the next five years and $209,045 will expire thereafter. At March 31, 2012, the Company has foreign tax credit carryovers in the United States of $45,085 that will substantially expire in 2016.

Realization of deferred tax assets is dependent on generating sufficient taxable income prior to expiration of the loss carryovers. Although realization is not assured, management believes it is more likely than not that all of the deferred tax assets, net of applicable valuation allowances, will be realized. The amount of the deferred tax assets considered realizable could be reduced or increased if estimates of future taxable income change during the carryover period.

No provision has been made for U.S. or foreign taxes that may result from future remittances of approximately $316,046 at March 31, 2012 and $226,971 at March 31, 2011 of undistributed earnings of foreign subsidiaries because management expects that such earnings will be reinvested overseas indefinitely. Determination of the amount of any unrecognized deferred income tax liability on these unremitted earnings is not practicable.

CASH SURRENDER VALUE OF LIFE INSURANCE

2.92 STEELCASE INC. (FEB)
CONSOLIDATED BALANCE SHEETS (in part)

(In millions, except share data)

Assets	February 24, 2012	February 25, 2011
Current assets:		
Cash and cash equivalents	$ 112.1	$ 142.2
Short-term investments	79.1	350.8
Accounts receivable, net of allowances of $19.6 and $23.1	271.4	271.0
Inventories	139.5	127.1
Deferred income taxes	42.4	58.0
Prepaid expenses	17.5	17.6
Other current assets	40.1	45.6
Total current assets	702.1	1,012.3
Property, plant and equipment, net of accumulated depreciation of $1,215.3 and $1,228.1	346.9	345.8
Company-owned life insurance	227.6	223.1
Deferred income taxes	132.5	132.2
Goodwill	176.6	174.8
Other intangible assets, net of accumulated amortization of $60.2 and $58.7	18.8	21.7
Investments in unconsolidated affiliates	47.7	45.2
Other assets	48.8	41.4
Total assets	$1,701.0	$1,996.5

NOTES TO THE CONSOLIDATED FINANCIAL STATEMENTS

9. Company-Owned Life Insurance

Our investments in company-owned life insurance ("COLI") policies are recorded at their net cash surrender value.

Our investments in whole life COLI policies are intended to be utilized as a long-term funding source for post-retirement medical benefits, deferred compensation and supplemental retirement plan obligations, which as of February 24, 2012 aggregated approximately $159, with a related deferred tax asset of approximately $59. See Note 13 for additional information. We believe the investments in whole life COLI policies represent a stable source for these long-term benefit obligations. Consequently, we allocate COLI income related to our investments in whole life COLI policies between *Cost of sales* and *Operating expenses* on the Consolidated Statements of Operations consistent with the costs associated with the long-term employee benefit obligations that the investments in whole life policies are intended to fund. This designation does not result in our investments in whole life COLI policies representing a committed funding source for employee benefit obligations. They are subject to claims from creditors, and we can designate them to another purpose at any time.

To more efficiently manage our balance sheet and liquidity position, in Q1 2011, we began considering our investments in variable life COLI policies to be primarily a source of corporate liquidity. As a result of this change, we adjusted the target asset allocation of the investments in variable life COLI policies to more heavily weight the portfolio to fixed income securities; and beginning in Q1 2011, net returns in cash surrender value, normal insurance expenses and any death benefit gains ("COLI income") related to our investments in variable life COLI policies have been recorded in *Investment income* on the Consolidated Statements of Operations. In Q4 2012, we further revised the allocation of our investments in variable life COLI policies to include only fixed income securities.

Type	Ability to Choose Investments	Net Return	Target Asset Allocation as of February 24, 2012	Net Cash Surrender Value	
				February 24, 2012	February 25, 2011
Whole life COLI policies	No ability	A rate of return set periodically by the insurance companies	Not Applicable	$114.5	$112.8
Variable life COLI policies	Can allocate across a set of choices provided by the insurance companies	Fluctuates depending on performance of underlying investments	100% Fixed Income[(1)]	113.1	110.3
				$227.6	$223.1

(1) For the majority of 2012 the target asset allocation was set at 80% fixed income and 20% equity. In Q4, this allocation was adjusted to 100% fixed income.

Following is a summary of the allocation of COLI income for 2010, 2011 and 2012:

COLI Income	Whole Life Policies	Variable Life Policies	Total
2012			
Cost of sales	$1.0	$ —	$ 1.0
Operating expenses	4.1	—	4.1
Operating income	5.1	—	5.1
Investment income	—	3.2	3.2
Income before income tax expense	$5.1	$ 3.2	$ 8.3
2011			
Cost of sales	$1.2	$ —	$ 1.2
Operating expenses	4.6	—	4.6
Operating income	5.8	—	5.8
Investment income	—	10.6	10.6
Income before income tax expense	$5.8	$10.6	$16.4
2010			
Cost of sales	$1.2	$19.3	$20.5
Operating expenses	4.4	13.8	18.2
Operating income	5.6	33.1	38.7
Investment income	—	—	—
Income before income tax expense	$5.6	$33.1	$38.7

DERIVATIVES

2.93 UNITED PARCEL SERVICE, INC. (DEC)
CONSOLIDATED BALANCE SHEETS (in part)

(In millions)

	December 31,	
	2012	2011
Assets		
Current assets:		
Cash and cash equivalents	$ 7,327	$ 3,034
Marketable securities	597	1,241
Accounts receivable, net	6,111	6,246
Deferred income tax assets	583	611
Other current assets	973	1,152
Total current assets	15,591	12,284
Property, plant and equipment, net	17,894	17,621
Goodwill	2,173	2,101
Intangible assets, net	603	585
Investments and restricted cash	307	303
Derivative assets	535	483
Deferred Income tax assets	684	118
Other non-current assets	1,076	1,206
Total assets	$38,863	$34,701

NOTES TO CONSOLIDATED FINANCIAL STATEMENTS

Note 1. Summary of Accounting Policies (in part)

Derivative Instruments

All financial derivative instruments are recorded on our consolidated balance sheets at fair value. Derivatives not designated as hedges must be adjusted to fair value through income. If a derivative is designated as a hedge, depending on the nature of the hedge, changes in its fair value that are considered to be effective, as defined, either offset the change in fair value of the hedged assets, liabilities or firm commitments through income, or are recorded in AOCI until the hedged item is recorded in income. Any portion of a change in a hedge's fair value that is considered to be ineffective, or is excluded from the measurement of effectiveness, is recorded immediately in income.

Note 14. Derivative Instruments and Risk Management (in part)

Accounting Policy for Derivative Instruments

We recognize all derivative instruments as assets or liabilities in the consolidated balance sheets at fair value. The accounting for changes in the fair value of a derivative instrument depends on whether it has been designated and qualifies as part of a hedging relationship and, further, on the type of hedging relationship. For those derivative instruments that are designated and qualify as hedging instruments, a company must designate the derivative, based upon the exposure being hedged, as a cash flow hedge, a fair value hedge or a hedge of a net investment in a foreign operation.

A cash flow hedge refers to hedging the exposure to variability in expected future cash flows that is attributable to a particular risk. For derivative instruments that are designated and qualify as a cash flow hedge, the effective portion of the gain or loss on the derivative instrument is reported as a component of AOCI, and reclassified into earnings in the same period during which the hedged transaction affects earnings. The remaining gain or loss on the derivative instrument in excess of the cumulative change in the present value of future cash flows of the hedged item, or hedge components excluded from the assessment of effectiveness, are recognized in the statements of consolidated income during the current period.

A fair value hedge refers to hedging the exposure to changes in the fair value of an existing asset or liability on the consolidated balance sheets that is attributable to a particular risk. For derivative instruments that are designated and qualify as a fair value hedge, the gain or loss on the derivative instrument is recognized in the statements of consolidated income during the current period, as well as the offsetting gain or loss on the hedged item.

A net investment hedge refers to the use of cross currency swaps, forward contracts or foreign currency denominated debt to hedge portions of our net investments in foreign operations. For hedges that meet the effectiveness requirements, the net gains or losses attributable to changes in spot exchange rates are recorded in the cumulative translation adjustment within AOCI. The remainder of the change in value of such instruments is recorded in earnings.

Types of Hedges

Commodity Risk Management

Currently, the fuel surcharges that we apply to our domestic and international package and LTL services are the primary means of reducing the risk of adverse fuel price changes on our business. We periodically enter into option contracts on energy commodity products to manage the price risk associated with forecasted transactions involving refined fuels, principally jet-A, diesel and unleaded gasoline. The objective of the hedges is to reduce the variability of cash flows, due to changing fuel prices, associated with the forecasted transactions involving those products. We designate and account for these contracts as cash flow hedges of the underlying forecasted transactions involving these fuel products and, therefore, the resulting gains and losses from these hedges are recognized as a component of fuel expense or revenue when the underlying transactions occur.

Foreign Currency Risk Management

To protect against the reduction in value of forecasted foreign currency cash flows from our international package business, we maintain a foreign currency cash flow hedging program. Our most significant foreign currency exposures relate to the Euro, the British Pound Sterling, Canadian Dollar, Chinese Renminbi and Hong Kong Dollar. We hedge portions of our forecasted revenue denominated in foreign currencies with option contracts. We have designated and account for these contracts as cash flow hedges of anticipated foreign currency denominated revenue and, therefore, the resulting gains and losses from these hedges are recognized as a component of international package revenue when the underlying sales transactions occur.

We also hedge portions of our anticipated cash settlements of intercompany transactions subject to foreign currency remeasurement using foreign currency forward contracts. We have designated and account for these contracts as cash flow hedges of forecasted foreign currency denominated transactions, and therefore the resulting gains and losses from these hedges are recognized as a component of other operating expense when the underlying transactions are subject to currency remeasurement.

We have foreign currency denominated debt obligations and capital lease obligations associated with our aircraft. For some of these debt obligations and leases, we hedge the foreign currency denominated contractual payments using cross-currency interest rate swaps, which effectively convert the foreign currency denominated contractual payments into U.S. Dollar denominated payments. We have designated and account for these swaps as cash flow hedges of the forecasted contractual payments and, therefore, the resulting gains and losses from these hedges are recognized in the statements of consolidated income when the currency remeasurement gains and losses on the underlying debt obligations and leases are incurred.

Interest Rate Risk Management

Our indebtedness under our various financing arrangements creates interest rate risk. We use a combination of derivative instruments, including interest rate swaps and cross-currency interest rate swaps, as part of our program to manage the fixed and floating interest rate mix of our total debt portfolio and related overall cost of borrowing. The notional amount, interest payment and maturity dates of the swaps match the terms of the associated debt being hedged. Interest rate swaps allow us to maintain a target range of floating rate debt within our capital structure.

We have designated and account for interest rate swaps that convert fixed rate interest payments into floating rate interest payments as hedges of the fair value of the associated debt instruments. Therefore, the gains and losses resulting from fair value adjustments to the interest rate swaps and fair value adjustments to the associated debt instruments are recorded to interest expense in the period in which the gains and losses occur. We have designated and account for interest rate swaps that convert floating rate interest payments into fixed rate interest payments as cash flow hedges of the forecasted payment obligations. The gains and losses resulting from fair value adjustments to the interest rate swap are recorded to AOCI.

We periodically hedge the forecasted fixed-coupon interest payments associated with anticipated debt offerings, using forward starting interest rate swaps, interest rate locks or similar derivatives. These agreements effectively lock a portion of our interest rate exposure between the time the agreement is entered into and the date when the debt offering is completed, thereby mitigating the impact of interest rate changes on future interest expense. These derivatives are settled commensurate with the issuance of the debt, and any gain or loss upon settlement is amortized as an adjustment to the effective interest yield on the debt.

Outstanding Positions

The notional amounts of our outstanding derivative positions were as follows as of December 31, 2012 and 2011 (in millions):

		2012	2011
Currency Hedges:			
Euro	EUR	1,783	1,685
British Pound Sterling	GBP	797	870
Canadian Dollar	CAD	341	318
United Arab Emirates Dirham	AED	551	—
Malaysian Ringgit	MYR	500	—
Interest Rate Hedges:			
Fixed to Floating Interest Rate Swaps	USD	7,274	6,424
Floating to Fixed Interest Rate Swaps	USD	781	791
Interest Rate Basis Swaps	USD	2,500	—

As of December 31, 2012, we had no outstanding commodity hedge positions. The maximum term over which we are hedging exposures to the variability of cash flow is 37 years.

Balance Sheet Recognition

The following table indicates the location on the balance sheet in which our derivative assets and liabilities have been recognized, and the related fair values of those derivatives as of December 31, 2012 and 2011 (in millions). The table is segregated between those derivative instruments that qualify and are designated as hedging instruments and those that are not, as well as by type of contract and whether the derivative is in an asset or liability position.

Asset Derivatives	Balance Sheet Location	Fair Value Hierarchy Level	2012	2011
Derivatives Designated as Hedges:				
Foreign exchange contracts	Other current assets	Level 2	$ 27	$164
Interest rate contracts	Other current assets	Level 2	1	—
Foreign exchange contracts	Other non-current assets	Level 2	14	—
Interest rate contracts	Other non-current assets	Level 2	420	401
Derivatives Not Designated as Hedges:				
Foreign exchange contracts	Other current assets	Level 2	3	2
Interest rate contracts	Other non-current assets	Level 2	101	82
Total asset derivatives			$566	$649

Liability Derivatives	Balance Sheet Location	Fair Value Hierarchy Level	2012	2011
Derivatives Designated as Hedges:				
Foreign exchange contracts	Other non-current liabilities	Level 2	103	185
Interest rate contracts	Other non-current liabilities	Level 2	14	13
Derivatives Not Designated as Hedges:				
Foreign exchange contracts	Other current liabilities	Level 2	1	—
Interest rate contracts	Other non-current liabilities	Level 2	41	10
Total liability derivatives			$159	$208

2.94 URS CORPORATION (DEC)

CONSOLIDATED BALANCE SHEETS (in part)

(In millions, except per share data)

	December 28, 2012	December 30, 2011
Assets		
Current assets:		
Cash and cash equivalents	$ 314.5	$ 436.0
Accounts receivable, including retentions of $114.4 and $67.5, respectively	1,554.8	1,114.7
Costs and accrued earnings in excess of billings on contracts	1,384.3	1,132.0
Less receivable allowances	(69.7)	(43.1)
Net accounts receivable	2,869.4	2,203.6
Deferred tax assets	67.6	63.0
Inventory	61.5	19.5
Other current assets	204.2	181.8
Total current assets	3,517.2	2,903.9
Investments in and advances to unconsolidated joint ventures	278.3	107.7
Property and equipment at cost, net	687.5	269.4
Intangible assets, net	692.2	522.0
Goodwill	3,247.1	2,773.0
Other long-term assets	364.2	286.6
Total assets	$8,786.5	$6,862.6

NOTES TO CONSOLIDATED FINANCIAL STATEMENTS

Note 1. Business, Basis of Presentation, and Accounting Policies (in part)

Internal-Use Computer Software

We expense or capitalize costs associated with the development of internal-use software as follows:

Preliminary Project Stage: Both internal and external costs incurred during this stage are expensed as incurred.

Application Development Stage: Both internal and external costs incurred to purchase and develop computer software are capitalized after the preliminary project stage is completed and management authorizes the computer software project. However, training costs and the process of data conversion from the old system to the new system, which includes purging or cleansing of existing data, reconciliation or balancing of old data to the converted data in the new system, are expensed as incurred.

Post-Implementation/Operation Stage: All training costs and maintenance costs incurred during this stage are expensed as incurred.

Costs of upgrades and enhancements are capitalized if the expenditures will result in adding functionality to the software. Capitalized software costs are depreciated using the straight-line method over the estimated useful life of the related software, which may be up to ten years.

Note 7. Property and Equipment (in part)

Our property and equipment consisted of the following:

(In millions)	December 28, 2012	December 30, 2011
Construction and mining equipment	$ 266.4	$ 95.3
Computer software	219.5	186.3
Computer hardware	198.2	186.8
Vehicles and automotive equipment	172.2	7.7
Leasehold improvements	130.1	109.0
Land and buildings	114.1	9.2
Furniture and fixtures	97.7	91.5
Other equipment	72.4	70.8
Construction in progress	15.6	0.2
	1,286.2	756.8
Accumulated depreciation and amortization	(598.7)	(487.4)
Property and equipment at cost, net[1]	$ 687.5	$ 269.4

[1] The unamortized computer software costs were $71.1 million and $60.8 million, respectively, as of December 28, 2012 and December 30, 2011. The increase in property and equipment from December 30, 2011 to December 28, 2012 was due primarily to the assets acquired as part of the Flint acquisition on May 14, 2012.

Property and equipment was depreciated by using the following estimated useful lives:

	Estimated Useful Lives
Computer software and hardware and other equipment	3–10 years
Vehicles and automotive equipment	3–12 years
Construction and mining equipment	3–15 years
Furniture and fixtures	3–10 years
Leasehold improvements[1]	1–20 years
Buildings	10–45 years

[1] Leasehold improvements are amortized over the length of the lease or estimated useful life, whichever is less.

DEBT ISSUANCE COSTS

2.95 SEALY CORPORATION (DEC)
CONSOLIDATED BALANCE SHEETS (in part)

(In thousands, except per share amounts)

	December 2, 2012	November 27, 2011
Assets		
Current assets:		
Cash and equivalents	$ 128,154	$ 107,975
Accounts receivable (net of allowance for doubtful accounts, discounts and returns, 2012— $29,959; 2011—$30,104)	152,619	126,494
Inventories	72,364	57,002
Prepaid expenses	31,358	29,275
Deferred income taxes	21,579	21,349
Total current assets	406,074	342,095
Property, plant and equipment—at cost:		
Land	6,761	7,351
Buildings and improvements	128,039	128,700
Machinery and equipment	281,345	261,650
Construction in progress	7,861	8,414
	424,006	406,115
Less accumulated depreciation	(259,983)	(239,370)
	164,023	166,745
Other assets:		
Goodwill	363,229	361,026
Other intangibles—net of accumulated amortization (2012—$5,005; 2011—$3,496)	14,710	1,116
Deferred income taxes	3,945	1,772
Debt issuance costs, net, and other assets	53,364	46,440
	435,248	410,354
Total assets	$1,005,345	$ 919,194

NOTES TO CONSOLIDATED FINANCIAL STATEMENTS

Note 1: Basis of Presentation and Significant Accounting Policies (in part)

Supply Agreements

The Company from time to time enters into long term supply agreements with its customers to sell its branded products to customers in exchange for minimum sales volume or a minimum percentage of the customer's sales or space on the retail floor. Such agreements generally cover a period of two to five years. In these long term agreements, the Company reserves the right to pass on its cost increases to its customers. Other costs such as transportation and warranty costs are factored into the wholesale price of the Company's products and passed on to the customer. Initial cash outlays by the Company for such agreements are capitalized and amortized generally as a reduction of sales over the life of the contract. The majority of these cash outlays are ratably recoverable upon contract termination. Such capitalized amounts are included in "Prepaid expenses" and "Debt issuance costs, net, and other assets" in the Company's Consolidated Balance Sheets.

Debt Issuance Costs

The Company capitalizes costs associated with the issuance of debt and amortizes them as additional interest expense over the lives of the debt on a straight-line basis which approximates the effective interest method. Upon the prepayment of the related debt, the Company accelerates the recognition of an appropriate amount of the costs as refinancing and extinguishment of debt and interest rate derivatives. Additional expense arising from such prepayments during fiscal 2012, 2011 and 2010 was $2.0 million, $0.6 million and $2.7 million, respectively.

On May 9, 2012, the Company amended and restated its existing senior secured asset-based revolving credit facility to extend the stated maturity of this facility until May 2017 and amend certain other provisions. In connection with this amendment, the Company recorded fees of $1.2 million which were deferred and will be amortized over the life of the amended agreement. As of December 2, 2012, $0.3 million of these fees had not yet been paid and were recorded as a component of other accrued liabilities in the accompanying Condensed Consolidated Balance Sheets. In addition, the remaining unamortized debt issuance costs associated with the existing senior revolving credit facility will continue to be amortized over the life of the agreement, as amended, in accordance with the authoritative accounting guidance surrounding debtor's accounting for changes in line-of-credit or revolving-debt arrangements.

Short-Term Debt

PRESENTATION

2.96 FASB ASC 470, *Debt*, addresses classification determination for specific debt obligations, such as the following:
- Short-term obligations expected to be refinanced on a long-term basis
- Due-on-demand loan arrangements
- Callable debt
- Sales of future revenue
- Increasing-rate debt
- Debt that includes covenants
- Revolving credit agreements subject to lock-box arrangements and subjective acceleration clauses

DISCLOSURE

2.97 Rule 5-02 of Regulation S-X calls for disclosure of the amount and terms of unused lines of credit for short-term financing, if significant. The weighted average interest rate on short-term borrowings outstanding as of the date of each balance sheet presented should be furnished. Further, the amount of these lines of credit that support commercial paper or similar borrowing arrangements should be separately identified.

2.98 By definition, *short-term notes payable*, *loans payable*, and *commercial paper* are financial instruments. FASB ASC 825 requires disclosure of both the fair value and bases for estimating the fair value of short-term notes payable, loans payable, and commercial paper, unless it is not practicable to estimate that value.

PRESENTATION AND DISCLOSURE EXCERPTS

SHORT-TERM DEBT

2.99 MEDTRONIC, INC. (APR)
CONSOLIDATED BALANCE SHEETS (in part)

(In millions, except per share data)	April 27, 2012	April 29, 2011
Liabilities and Shareholders' Equity		
Current liabilities:		
Short-term borrowings	$3,274	$1,723
Accounts payable	565	495
Accrued compensation	912	874
Accrued income taxes	65	50
Deferred tax liabilities, net	33	7
Other accrued expenses	1,008	1,489
Liabilities held for sale	—	88
Total current liabilities	5,857	4,726

9. Financing Arrangements

Debt consisted of the following:

(In millions, except interest rates)	Maturity by Fiscal Year	April 27, 2012			April 29, 2011		
		Payable	Average Interest Rate	Effective Interest Rate	Payable	Average Interest Rate	Effective Interest Rate
Short-Term Borrowings:							
Commercial paper	2012–2013	$ 950	0.14%	—	$1,500	0.22%	—
Capital lease obligations	2012–2013	14	3.38%	—	2	7.47%	—
Bank borrowings	2012–2013	200	0.93%	—	222	1.25%	—
Seven-year senior convertible notes	2013	2,200	1.63%	6.03%	—	—	—
Debt discount	2012–2013	(90)	—	—	(1)	—	—
Total short-term borrowings		$3,274			$1,723		
Long-Term Debt:							
Contingent convertible debentures	2012	$ —	—	—	$15	1.25%	—
Seven-year senior convertible notes	2013	—	—	—	2,200	1.63%	6.03%
Five-year 2009 senior notes	2014	550	4.50%	4.50%	550	4.50%	4.50%
Five-year 2010 senior notes	2015	1,250	3.00%	3.00%	1,250	3.00%	3.00%
Ten-year 2005 senior notes	2016	600	4.75%	4.76%	600	4.75%	4.76%
Five-year 2011 senior notes	2016	500	2.63%	2.72%	500	2.63%	2.72%
Ten-year 2009 senior notes	2019	400	5.60%	5.61%	400	5.60%	5.61%
Ten-year 2010 senior notes	2020	1,250	4.45%	4.47%	1,250	4.45%	4.47%
Ten-year 2011 senior notes	2021	500	4.13%	4.19%	500	4.13%	4.19%
Ten-year 2012 senior notes	2022	675	3.13%	3.16%	—	—	—
Thirty-year 2009 senior notes	2039	300	6.50%	6.52%	300	6.50%	6.52%
Thirty-year 2010 senior notes	2040	500	5.55%	5.56%	500	5.55%	5.56%
Thirty-year 2012 senior notes	2042	400	4.50%	4.51%	—	—	—
Interest rate swaps	2013–2022	167	—	—	110	—	—
Gains from interest rate swap terminations	2012–2016	102	—	—	68	—	—
Capital lease obligations	2013–2025	165	3.57%	—	32	6.28%	—
Bank borrowings	2013	—	—	—	14	5.60%	—
Debt discount	2012–2013	—	—	—	(177)	—	—
Total long-term debt		$7,359			$8,112		

Senior Convertible Notes. In April 2006, the Company issued $2.200 billion of 1.500 percent Senior Convertible Notes due 2011 (2011 Senior Convertible Notes) and $2.200 billion of 1.625 percent Senior Convertible Notes due 2013 (2013 Senior Convertible Notes) (collectively, the Senior Convertible Notes). The Senior Convertible Notes were issued at par and pay interest in cash semi-annually in arrears on April 15 and October 15 of each year. The 2011 Senior Convertible Notes were repaid in April 2011. The 2013 Senior Convertible Notes are unsecured unsubordinated obligations and rank equally with all other unsecured and unsubordinated indebtedness. The Senior Convertible Notes had an initial conversion price of $56.14 per share. As of April 27, 2012, pursuant to provisions in the indentures relating to the Company's increase of its quarterly dividend to shareholders, the conversion rate for the Senior Convertible Notes is now 18.8218, which correspondingly changed the conversion price per share for the Senior Convertible Notes to $53.13.

Concurrent with the issuance of the Senior Convertible Notes, the Company purchased call options on its common stock in private transactions. The call options allow the Company to receive shares of the Company's common stock and/or cash from counterparties equal to the amounts of common stock and/or cash related to the excess conversion value that it would pay to the holders of the 2013 Senior Convertible Notes upon conversion. These call options will terminate upon the earlier of the maturity dates of the related Senior Convertible Notes or the first day all of the related Senior Convertible Notes are no longer outstanding due to conversion or otherwise. The call options, which cost an aggregate $1.075 billion ($699 million net of tax benefit), were recorded as a reduction of shareholders' equity.

In separate transactions, the Company sold warrants to issue shares of the Company's common stock at an exercise price of $76.56 per share in private transactions. Pursuant to these transactions, warrants for 41 million shares of the Company's common stock may be settled over a specified period that began in July 2011 and warrants for 41 million shares of the Company's common stock may be settled over a specified period beginning in July 2013 (the settlement dates). If the average price of the Company's common stock during a defined period ending on or about the respective settlement dates exceeds the exercise price of the warrants, the warrants will be settled in shares of the Company's common stock. Proceeds received from the issuance of the warrants totaled approximately $517 million and were recorded as an addition to shareholders' equity. As of April 27, 2012, warrants for 41 million shares of the Company's common stock had expired.

Under authoritative guidance, the Company concluded that the purchased call options and sold warrants were indexed to its own stock and should continue to be classified in shareholders' equity and not be separated as a derivative.

Authoritative guidance provides that contracts are initially classified as equity if (1) the contract requires physical settlement or net-share settlement, or (2) the contract gives the Company a choice of net-cash settlement or settlement in its own shares (physical settlement or net-share settlement). The settlement terms of the Company's purchased call options and sold warrant contracts provide for net-cash settlement for the particular contract or net-share settlement, depending on the method of settlement, as discussed above, which is at the option of the Company. Based on existing guidance, the purchased call option contracts were recorded as a reduction of equity and the warrants were recorded as an addition to equity as of the trade date. Existing guidance states that a reporting entity shall not consider contracts to be derivative instruments if the contract issued or held by the reporting entity is both indexed to its own stock and classified in shareholders' equity in its statement of financial position. The Company concluded that the purchased call option contracts and the sold warrant contracts should be accounted for in shareholders' equity.

The Company accounted for the Senior Convertible Notes in accordance with the authoritative guidance for convertible debt, which requires the proceeds from the issuance of the Senior Convertible Notes to be allocated between a liability component (issued at a discount) and an equity component. The resulting debt discount is amortized over the period the 2013 Senior Convertible Notes are expected to be outstanding as additional non-cash interest expense.

The following table provides equity and debt information for the 2013 Senior Convertible Notes under the convertible debt guidance:

(In millions)	2013 Senior Convertible Notes	
	April 27, 2012	April 29, 2011
Carrying amount of the equity component	$ 547	$ 547
Principal amount of the Senior Convertible Notes	$2,200	$2,200
Unamortized discount	(90)	(177)
Net carrying amount of the debt component	$2,110	$2,023

As of April 27, 2012, the unamortized balance of the debt discount will be amortized over the remaining life of the 2013 Senior Convertible Notes, which is approximately one year. The following table provides interest expense amounts related to the Senior Convertible Notes.

(In millions)	2013 Senior Convertible Notes		2011 Senior Convertible Notes	
	2012	2011	2012	2011
Interest cost related to contractual interest coupon	$36	$36	$—	$32
Interest cost related to amortization of the discount	87	82	—	90

Senior Notes. Senior Notes are unsecured, senior obligations of the Company and rank equally with all other secured and unsubordinated indebtedness of the Company. The indentures under which the Senior Notes were issued contain customary covenants, all of which the Company remains in compliance with as of April 27, 2012. The Company used the net proceeds from the sale of the Senior Notes primarily for working capital and general corporate purposes, which include the repayment of other indebtedness of the Company.

In March 2012, the Company issued two tranches of Senior Notes (collectively, the 2012 Senior Notes) with an aggregate face value of $1.075 billion. The first tranche consisted of $675 million of 3.125 percent Senior Notes due 2022. The second tranche consisted of $400 million of 4.500 percent Senior Notes due 2042. Interest on each series of 2012 Senior Notes is payable semi-annually, on March 15 and September 15 of each year, commencing September 15, 2012. The Company used the net proceeds from the sale of the 2012 Senior Notes for working capital and general corporate purposes.

As of April 27, 2012 and April 29, 2011, the Company had interest rate swap agreements designated as fair value hedges of underlying fixed-rate obligations including the Company's $1.250 billion 3.000 percent 2010 Senior Notes due 2015, the $600 million 4.750 percent 2005 Senior Notes due 2015, the Company's $500 million 2.625 percent 2011 Senior Notes due 2016, and the Company's $500 million 4.125 percent 2011 Senior Notes due 2021. Additionally, as of April 27, 2012, the Company had interest rate swap agreements designated as fair value hedges of underlying fixed-rate obligations including the Company's $675 million 3.125 percent 2012 Senior Notes due 2022. As of April 29, 2011, the Company had interest rate swap agreements designated as fair value hedges of underlying fixed-rate obligations including the $2.200 billion 1.625 percent Senior Convertible Notes due 2013, and the $550 million 4.500 percent 2009 Senior Notes due 2014. For additional information regarding the interest rate swap agreements, refer to Note 10.

Contingent Convertible Debentures. As of April 29, 2011, the Company had $15 million remaining in aggregate principal amount of 1.250 percent Contingent Convertible Debentures, Series B due 2021 (the Debentures) outstanding. Each Debenture was convertible into shares of common stock at an initial conversion price of $61.81 per share. In July 2011, the Company gave notice to the holders of the Debentures of its intent to redeem the Debentures for cash at a price equal to 100% of the principal amount, plus any accrued and unpaid interest, on September 15, 2011 (the Redemption Date). All of the outstanding Debentures were settled for cash on the Redemption Date and no holders converted Debentures into shares of the Company's common stock.

Commercial Paper. The Company maintains a commercial paper program that allows the Company to have a maximum of $2.250 billion in commercial paper outstanding, with maturities up to 364 days from the date of issuance. As of April 27, 2012 and April 29, 2011, outstanding commercial paper totaled $950 million and $1.500 billion, respectively. During fiscal years 2012 and 2011, the weighted average original maturity of the commercial paper outstanding was approximately 102 and 73 days, respectively, and the weighted average interest rate was 0.15 percent and 0.25 percent, respectively. The issuance of commercial paper reduces the amount of credit available under the Company's existing lines of credit.

Bank Borrowings. Bank borrowings consist primarily of borrowings from non-U.S. banks at interest rates considered favorable by management and where natural hedges can be gained for foreign exchange purposes and borrowings from U.S. banks. Approximately $184 million of the $200 million outstanding bank borrowings as of April 27, 2012 were short-term advances to certain subsidiaries under credit agreements with various banks. These advances are guaranteed by the Company.

Lines of Credit. The Company has committed and uncommitted lines of credit with various banks. The committed lines of credit include a four-year $2.250 billion syndicated credit facility dated December 9, 2010 that will expire on December 9, 2014 (Credit Facility). The Credit Facility provides the Company with the ability to increase its capacity by an additional $500 million at any time during the life of the four-year term of the agreement. The Company can also request the extension of the Credit Facility maturity date for one additional year, at the first and second anniversary of the date of the Credit Facility. The Credit Facility provides backup funding for the commercial paper program, and therefore, the issuance of commercial paper reduces the amount of credit available under the committed lines of credit. As of April 27, 2012 and April 29, 2011, no amounts were outstanding on the committed lines of credit.

Interest rates on these borrowings are determined by a pricing matrix, based on the Company's long-term debt ratings assigned by Standard and Poor's Ratings Services and Moody's Investors Service. Facility fees are payable on the credit facilities and are determined in the same manner as the interest rates. The agreements also contain customary covenants, all of which the Company remains in compliance with as of April 27, 2012.

Contractual maturities of long-term debt for the next five fiscal years and thereafter, including current portions, capital leases, and $13 million of bank borrowings related to the term loan discussed in Note 16, and excluding the debt discount, the fair value impact of outstanding interest rate swap agreements, and the remaining gains from terminated interest rate swap agreements are as follows:

Fiscal Year	Obligation (In millions)
2013	$2,227
2014	563
2015	1,263
2016	1,113
2017	30
Thereafter	4,121
Total long-term debt	9,317
Less: Current portion of long-term debt	2,227
Long-term portion of long-term debt	$7,090

2.100 ALCOA INC. (DEC)
CONSOLIDATED BALANCE SHEET (in part)

(In millions)

	December 31,	
	2012	2011
Liabilities		
Current liabilities:		
Short-term borrowings (K & X)	$ 53	$ 62
Commercial paper (K & X)	—	224
Accounts payable, trade	2,702	2,692
Accrued compensation and retirement costs	1,058	985
Taxes, including income taxes	366	438
Other current liabilities	1,298	1,167
Long-term debt due within one year (K & X)	465	445
Total current liabilities	5,942	6,013

NOTES TO THE CONSOLIDATED FINANCIAL STATEMENTS

(Dollars in millions, except per-share amounts)

K. Debt (in part)

Long-Term Debt (in part)

	December 31,	
	2012	2011
6% Notes, due 2012	$ —	$ 322
6% Notes, due 2013	422	422
5.25% Convertible Notes, due 2014	575	575

(continued)

	December 31,	
	2012	**2011**
5.55% Notes, due 2017	750	750
6.5% Bonds, due 2018	250	250
6.75% Notes, due 2018	750	750
5.72% Notes, due 2019	750	750
6.15% Notes, due 2020	1,000	1,000
5.40% Notes, due 2021	1,250	1,250
5.87% Notes, due 2022	627	627
5.9% Notes, due 2027	625	625
6.75% Bonds, due 2028	300	300
5.95% Notes due 2037	625	625
BNDES Loans, due 2013–2029 (see below for weighted average rates)	397	627
Iowa Finance Authority Loan, due 2042 (4.75%)	250	—
Other*	205	212
	8,776	9,085
Less: amount due within one year	465	445
	$8,311	$8,640

* Other includes various financing arrangements related to subsidiaries, unamortized debt discounts related to the outstanding notes and bonds listed in the table above, a beneficial conversion feature related to the convertible notes, and adjustments to the carrying value of long-term debt related to interest swap contracts accounted for as fair value hedges (see the Derivatives section of Note X).

Short-Term Borrowings. At December 31, 2012 and 2011, Short-term borrowings were $53 and $62, respectively. These amounts included $48 and $53 at December 31, 2012 and 2011, respectively, related to accounts payable settlement arrangements with certain vendors and third-party intermediaries. These arrangements provide that, at the vendor's request, the third-party intermediary advances the amount of the scheduled payment to the vendor, less an appropriate discount, before the scheduled payment date and Alcoa makes payment to the third-party intermediary on the date stipulated in accordance with the commercial terms negotiated with its vendors. Alcoa records imputed interest related to these arrangements as interest expense in the Statement of Consolidated Operations.

In January 2012, Alcoa entered into two term loan agreements, totaling $350, with two separate financial institutions. Additionally, throughout 2012, Alcoa entered into six revolving credit agreements, providing a combined $640 in credit facilities, with six different financial institutions. The purpose of any borrowings under all eight arrangements will be to provide working capital and for other general corporate purposes, including contributions to Alcoa's pension plans ($561 was contributed in 2012).

The two term loans were fully drawn on the same dates as the agreements and were subject to an interest rate equivalent to the 1-month LIBOR (changed from the 3-month LIBOR in April 2012) plus a 1.5% margin. A $150 term loan was repaid between October and November 2012 and a $200 term loan was repaid in December 2012, effectively terminating both agreements. In February 2012, Alcoa fully borrowed $100 under one of the credit facilities, which was repaid in August 2012. This borrowing was subject to an interest rate equivalent to the 6-month LIBOR plus a 1.25% margin. In July 2012, Alcoa fully borrowed $150 under one of the credit facilities, which was repaid in December 2012. This borrowing was subject to an interest rate equivalent to the 3-month LIBOR plus a 1.375% margin.

The six revolving credit facilities expire as follows: $150 in March 2013; $100 in September 2013 (originally December 2012, extended in September 2012); $100 in September 2013; $140 in October 2013; $100 in December 2013 (originally December 2012, extended in December 2012); and $50 in December 2015. The covenants contained in all eight arrangements are the same as the Credit Agreement (see the Commercial Paper section above).

During 2012, Alcoa's subsidiary, Alumínio, borrowed and repaid a total of $280 in new loans with a weighted-average interest rate of 2.32% and a weighted-average maturity of 172 days from two financial institutions. The purpose of these borrowings was to support Alumínio's export operations.

X. Derivatives and Other Financial Instruments (in part)

Other Financial Instruments. The carrying values and fair values of Alcoa's other financial instruments were as follows:

	December 31, 2012		December 31, 2011	
	Carrying Value	**Fair Value**	**Carrying Value**	**Fair Value**
Cash and cash equivalents	$1,861	$1,861	$1,939	$1,939
Restricted cash	189	189	25	25
Noncurrent receivables	20	20	30	30
Available-for-sale securities	67	67	92	92
Short-term borrowings	53	53	62	62
Commercial paper	—	—	224	224
Long-term debt due within one year	465	465	445	445
Long-term debt, less amount due within one year	8,311	9,028	8,640	9,274

The following methods were used to estimate the fair values of other financial instruments:

Cash and cash equivalents, Restricted cash, Short-term borrowings, Commercial paper, and Long-term debt due within one year. The carrying amounts approximate fair value because of the short maturity of the instruments. The fair value amounts for Cash and cash equivalents, Restricted cash, and Commercial paper were classified in Level 1; Short-term borrowings were classified in Level 2; and Long-term debt due within one year was classified in Level 1 of the fair value hierarchy for public debt ($422) and Level 2 of the fair value hierarchy for non-public debt ($43).

Long-term debt, less amount due within one year. The fair value was based on quoted market prices for public debt and on interest rates that are currently available to Alcoa for issuance of debt with similar terms and maturities for non-public debt. At December 31, 2012 and 2011, $8,456 and $8,576, respectively, was classified in Level 1 of the fair value hierarchy for public debt and $572 and $698, respectively, was classified in Level 2 of the fair value hierarchy for non-public debt.

Trade Accounts Payable

RECOGNITION AND MEASUREMENT

2.101 FASB ASC 210 states that current liabilities generally include obligations for items that have entered into the operating cycle, such as payables incurred in the acquisition of materials and supplies to be used in the production of goods or in providing services to be offered for sale.

PRESENTATION

2.102 Rule 5.02 of Regulation S-X requires that amounts payable to trade creditors be separately stated.

DISCLOSURE

2.103 Under FASB ASC 825, fair value disclosure is not required for trade payables when the carrying amount of the trade payable approximates its fair value.

Employee-Related Liabilities

PRESENTATION

2.104 FASB ASC 715, *Compensation—Retirement Benefits*, requires that an entity recognize the overfunded or underfunded status of a single-employer defined benefit postretirement plan as an asset or a liability in its statement of financial position. FASB ASC 715 also requires that an employer that presents a classified balance sheet should classify the liability for an underfunded plan as a current liability, a noncurrent liability, or a combination of both. The current portion (determined on a plan-by-plan basis) is the amount by which the actuarial present value of benefits included in the benefit obligation that is payable in the next 12 months, or operating cycle if longer, exceeds the fair value of plan assets. The asset for an overfunded plan shall be classified as a noncurrent asset in a classified balance sheet. The amount classified as a current liability is limited to the amount of the plan's unfunded status recognized in the employer's balance sheet.

DISCLOSURE

2.105 FASB ASC 715 requires that employers recognize changes in that funded status in comprehensive income and disclose in the notes to financial statements additional information about plan assets, the benefit obligation, reconciliations of beginning and ending balances of both plan assets and obligations, and net periodic benefit cost.

2.106 FASB ASC 715-80 requires additional discloses related to multiemployer plans. An entity should include details in these disclosures including plan names and identifying numbers for significant multiemployer plans, the level of employers' participation in the plans, the financial health of the plans, and the nature of the employer commitments to the plans.

EMPLOYEE-RELATED LIABILITIES

2.107 PEABODY ENERGY CORPORATION (DEC)

CONSOLIDATED BALANCE SHEETS (in part)

	December 31,	
(Amounts in millions, except per share data)	2012	2011
Liabilities and Stockholders' Equity		
Current liabilities		
Current maturities of long-term debt	$ 47.8	$ 101.1
Liabilities from coal trading activities, net	19.4	10.3
Accounts payable and accrued expenses	1,606.9	1,712.3
Total current liabilities	1,674.1	1,823.7
Long-term debt, less current maturities	6,205.1	6,556.4
Deferred income taxes	577.3	523.2
Asset retirement obligations	687.5	615.2
Accrued postretirement benefit costs	960.7	1,053.1
Other noncurrent liabilities	765.5	645.6
Total liabilities	10,870.2	11,217.2

NOTES TO CONSOLIDATED FINANCIAL STATEMENTS

(1) Summary of Significant Accounting Policies (in part)

Postretirement Health Care and Life Insurance Benefits

The Company accounts for postretirement benefits other than pensions by accruing the costs of benefits to be provided over the employees' period of active service. These costs are determined on an actuarial basis. The Company's consolidated balance sheets reflect the accumulated postretirement benefit obligations of its postretirement benefit plans. See Note 15. "Postretirement Health Care and Life Insurance Benefits" for information related to postretirement benefits.

(15) Postretirement Health Care and Life Insurance Benefits

The Company currently provides health care and life insurance benefits to qualifying salaried and hourly retirees and their dependents from benefit plans established by the Company. Plan coverage for health benefits is provided to future hourly and salaried retirees in accordance with the applicable plan document. Life insurance benefits are provided to future hourly retirees in accordance with the applicable labor agreement.

Net periodic postretirement benefit cost included the following components:

	Year Ended December 31,		
(Dollars in millions)	2012	2011	2010
Service cost for benefits earned	$ 14.9	$ 13.9	$12.9
Interest cost on accumulated postretirement benefit obligation	54.9	57.9	58.2
Amortization of prior service cost	2.5	2.8	2.6
Amortization of actuarial loss	32.8	26.9	24.9
Net periodic postretirement benefit cost	$105.1	$101.5	$98.6

The following includes pre-tax amounts recorded in "Accumulated other comprehensive income (loss)":

	Year Ended December 31,		
(Dollars in millions)	2012	2011	2010
Net actuarial (gain) loss arising during year	$ (68.3)	$ 86.0	$ 45.3
Prior service (credit) cost arising during year	(31.9)	(1.4)	7.9
Amortization:			
Actuarial loss	(32.8)	(26.9)	(24.9)
Prior service cost	(2.5)	(2.8)	(2.6)
Total recorded in other comprehensive (income) loss	(135.5)	54.9	25.7
Net periodic postretirement benefit cost	105.1	101.5	98.6
Net periodic postretirement benefit cost, net of amounts recorded in other comprehensive (income) loss	$ (30.4)	$156.4	$124.3

The Company amortizes actuarial gain and loss using a 0% corridor with an amortization period that covers the average future working lifetime of active employees (11.75 years and 11.70 years at January 1, 2013 and 2012, respectively). The estimated net actuarial loss and prior service cost that will be amortized from accumulated other comprehensive income (loss) into net periodic postretirement benefit cost during the year ending December 31, 2013 are $24.1 million and $1.7 million, respectively.

The following table sets forth the plans' funded status reconciled with the amounts shown in the consolidated balance sheets:

(Dollars in millions)	December 31, 2012	December 31, 2011
Change in benefit obligation:		
Accumulated postretirement benefit obligation at beginning of period	$ 1,121.5	$ 1,031.2
Service cost	14.9	13.9
Interest cost	54.9	57.9
Participant contributions	2.3	1.9
Plan changes[1]	(31.9)	(1.4)
Benefits paid	(67.3)	(68.0)
Actuarial (gain) loss	(68.3)	86.0
Accumulated postretirement benefit obligation at end of period	1,026.1	1,121.5
Change in plan assets:		
Fair value of plan assets at beginning of period	—	—
Employer contributions	65.0	66.1
Participant contributions	2.3	1.9
Benefits paid and administrative fees (net of Medicare Part D reimbursements)	(67.3)	(68.0)
Fair value of plan assets at end of period	—	—
Funded status at end of year	(1,026.1)	(1,121.5)
Less current portion (included in "Accounts payable and accrued expenses")	65.4	68.4
Noncurrent obligation (included in "Accrued postretirement benefit costs")	$ (960.7)	$(1,053.1)

[1] Effective January 1, 2013, certain participants for whom the Company pays retiree healthcare liabilities began participation in a Medicare Advantage Program.

The weighted-average assumptions used to determine the benefit obligations as of the end of each year were as follows:

	December 31, 2012	December 31, 2011
Discount rate	4.21%	5.05%
Rate of compensation increase	N/A	N/A
Measurement date	December 31, 2012	December 31, 2011

The weighted-average assumptions used to determine net periodic benefit cost during each year were as follows:

	Year Ended December 31, 2012	Year Ended December 31, 2011	Year Ended December 31, 2010
Discount rate	5.05%	5.81%	6.14%
Rate of compensation increase	N/A	3.50%	3.50%
Measurement date	December 31, 2011	December 31, 2010	December 31, 2009

The following presents information about the assumed health care cost trend rate:

	Year Ended December 31, 2012	Year Ended December 31, 2011
Health care cost trend rate assumed for next year	6.43%	9.00%
Rate to which the cost trend is assumed to decline (the ultimate trend rate)	4.67%	5.00%
Year that the rate reaches the ultimate trend rate	2023	2018

Assumed health care cost trend rates have a significant effect on the expense and liability amounts reported for health care plans. A one-percentage-point change in the assumed health care cost trend would have the following effects:

(Dollars in millions)	One Percentage-Point Increase	One Percentage-Point Decrease
Effect on total service and interest cost components[1]	$ 18.1	$(15.6)
Effect on total postretirement benefit obligation[1]	$107.5	$(93.0)

[1] In addition to the effect on total service and interest cost components of expense, changes in trend rates would also increase or decrease the actuarial gain or loss amortization expense component. The impact on actuarial gain or loss amortization would approximate the increase or decrease in the obligation divided by 11.75 years at January 1, 2013.

Plan Assets

The Company's postretirement benefit plans are unfunded.

Estimated Future Benefit Payments

The following benefit payments (net of retiree contributions), which reflect expected future service, as appropriate, are expected to be paid by the Company:

(Dollars in millions)	Postretirement Benefits
2013	$ 65.4
2014	66.5
2015	67.6
2016	68.8
2017	69.5
Years 2018–2022	355.7

2.108 THE BOEING COMPANY (DEC)

CONSOLIDATED STATEMENTS OF FINANCIAL POSITION (in part)

	December 31,	
(Dollars in millions, except per share data)	2012	2011
Liabilities and Equity		
Accounts payable	$ 9,394	$ 8,406
Accrued liabilities	12,995	12,239
Advances and billings in excess of related costs	16,672	15,496
Deferred income taxes and income taxes payable	4,485	2,780
Short-term debt and current portion of long-term debt	1,436	2,353
Total current liabilities	44,982	41,274
Accrued retiree health care	7,528	7,520
Accrued pension plan liability, net	19,651	16,537
Non-current income taxes payable	366	122
Other long-term liabilities	1,429	907
Long-term debt	8,973	10,018

NOTES TO THE CONSOLIDATED FINANCIAL STATEMENTS

(Dollars in millions, except per share data)

Note 1—Summary of Significant Accounting Policies (in part)

Postretirement Plans

The majority of our employees are covered by defined benefit pension plans. All nonunion and some union employees hired after December 31, 2008 are not covered by defined benefit plans. We also provide postretirement benefit plans other than pensions, consisting principally of health care coverage to eligible retirees and qualifying dependents. Benefits under the pension and other postretirement benefit plans are generally based on age at retirement and years of service and, for some pension plans, benefits are also based on the employee's annual earnings. The net periodic cost of our pension and other postretirement plans is determined using the projected unit credit method and several actuarial assumptions, the most significant of which are the discount rate, the long-term rate of asset return, and medical trend (rate of growth for medical costs). A portion of net periodic pension and other postretirement income or expense is not recognized in net earnings in the year incurred because it is allocated to production as product costs, and reflected in inventory at the end of a reporting period. Actuarial gains and losses, which occur when actual experience differs from actuarial assumptions, are reflected in Shareholders' equity (net of taxes). If actuarial gains and losses exceed ten percent of the greater of plan assets or plan liabilities we amortize them over the average future service period of employees. The funded status of our pension and postretirement plans is reflected on the Consolidated Statements of Financial Position.

Note 15—Postretirement Plans (in part)

The majority of our employees are covered by defined benefit pension plans. All nonunion and some union employees hired after December 31, 2008 are not covered by defined benefit plans. We fund our major pension plans through trusts. Pension assets are placed in trust solely for the benefit of the plans' participants, and are structured to maintain liquidity that is sufficient to pay benefit obligations as well as to keep pace over the long-term with the growth of obligations for future benefit payments.

We also have other postretirement benefits (OPB) other than pensions which consist principally of health care coverage for eligible retirees and qualifying dependents, and to a lesser extent, life insurance to certain groups of retirees. Retiree health care is provided principally until age 65 for approximately half those retirees who are eligible for health care coverage. Certain employee groups, including employees covered by most United Auto Workers bargaining agreements, are provided lifetime health care coverage.

The funded status of the plans is measured as the difference between the plan assets at fair value and the projected benefit obligation (PBO). We have recognized the aggregate of all overfunded plans in Pension plan assets, net, and the aggregate of all underfunded plans in either Accrued retiree health care or Accrued pension plan liability, net. The portion of the amount by which the actuarial present value of benefits included in the PBO exceeds the fair value of plan assets, payable in the next 12 months, is reflected in Accrued liabilities. The components of net periodic benefit cost were as follows:

	Pension			Other Postretirement Plans		
Years Ended December 31,	**2012**	**2011**	**2010**	**2012**	**2011**	**2010**
Service cost	$ 1,649	$ 1,406	$ 1,176	$ 146	$221	$121
Interest cost	3,005	3,116	3,002	313	484	404
Expected return on plan assets	(3,831)	(3,741)	(3,850)	(7)	(6)	(6)
Amortization of prior service costs	225	244	248	(197)	(96)	(78)
Recognized net actuarial loss	1,937	1,254	777	119	178	56
Settlement and curtailment loss	25	64	14	(1)	3	
Net periodic benefit cost	$ 3,010	$ 2,343	$ 1,367	$ 373	$784	$497
Net periodic benefit cost included in Earnings from operations	$ 2,407	$ 1,648	$ 1,101	$ 543	$692	$480

During the quarter ended September 30, 2011, we determined the accumulated benefit obligation (ABO) for certain other postretirement benefit plans was understated. As a result, we recognized an additional $294 of postretirement benefit obligations at September 30, 2011. This increased net periodic benefit cost during 2011 by $184, which includes service cost of $73, interest cost of $68 and recognized net actuarial loss of $43. Had the understatement been recorded at December 31, 2010, the postretirement benefit obligation would have increased by $274 from $8,546 to $8,820. Management believes that these understatements were not material.

Under our accounting policy, a portion of net periodic benefit cost is allocated to production as inventoried costs. Of the $184 increase in net periodic benefit cost described above, the associated cost included in Earnings from operations was $161 for the quarter ended September 30, 2011, with the remaining cost of $23 classified as inventory.

The following tables show changes in the benefit obligation, plan assets and funded status of both pensions and OPB for the years ended December 31, 2012 and 2011. Benefit obligation balances presented below reflect the PBO for our pension plans, and accumulated postretirement benefit obligations (APBO) for our OPB plans.

	Pension		Other Postretirement Benefits	
	2012	**2011**	**2012**	**2011**
Change in benefit obligation				
Beginning balance	$67,651	$59,106	$7,997	$8,546
Service cost	1,649	1,406	146	221
Interest cost	3,005	3,116	313	484
Plan participants' contributions	9	9		
Amendments	13	186	12	(719)
Actuarial loss/(gain)	6,378	6,586	(53)	(63)
Settlement/curtailment/acquisitions/dispositions, net	(76)	(104)	(1)	3
Gross benefits paid	(2,744)	(2,644)	(474)	(503)
Medicare Part D and other subsidies			37	31
Exchange rate adjustment	10	(10)	4	(3)
Ending balance	$75,895	$67,651	$7,981	$7,997
Change in plan assets				
Beginning balance at fair value	$51,051	$49,252	$ 102	$ 98
Actual return on plan assets	6,300	3,953	1	4
Company contribution	1,550	531	15	17
Plan participants' contributions	9	9	3	3
Settlement/curtailment/acquisitions/dispositions, net	(71)	(104)	10	
Benefits paid	(2,669)	(2,581)	(21)	(20)
Exchange rate adjustment	8	(9)		
Ending balance at fair value	$56,178	$51,051	$ 110	$ 102
Amounts recognized in statement of financial position at December 31 consist of:				
Pension plan assets, net	5	1		
Other accrued liabilities	(71)	(64)	(343)	(375)
Accrued retiree health care			(7,528)	(7,520)
Accrued pension plan liability, net	(19,651)	(16,537)		
Net amount recognized	($19,717)	($16,600)	($7,871)	($7,895)

Dollar amounts in millions, except per share

	December 31,	
	2012	**2011**
Liabilities and Stockholders' Equity		
Current liabilities:		
Current portion of long-term debt	$ 7.8	$ 5.3
Current portion of limited recourse notes payable	90.0	7.9
Accounts payable and accrued liabilities	139.5	122.3
Current portion of contingency reserves	2.0	4.0
Total current liabilities	239.3	139.5
Long-term debt, excluding current portion	782.7	715.9
Deferred income taxes	93.6	106.0
Contingency reserves, excluding current portion	12.8	17.2
Other long-term liabilities	168.8	160.4

NOTES TO THE FINANCIAL STATEMENTS

1. Summary of Significant Accounting Policies (in part)

Retirement Benefits

LP is required to use actuarial methods and assumptions in the valuation of defined benefit obligations and the determination of expense. Difference between actual and expected results or changes in the values of the obligations and plan assets are not recognized in earnings as they occur but, rather, systematically and gradually over subsequent periods. Prior to January 1, 2010, the cost of retiree benefits was recognized over the employees' service period. As of January 1, 2010, LP froze the U.S. defined benefit plan and accordingly changed the method of accounting for such amounts to be amortized over the period until retirement as opposed to the estimated service period. The change in this method lengthened the amortization period for U.S. plans. See Note 13 for further information.

13. Retirement Plans and Postretirement Benefits (in part)

LP sponsors various defined benefit and defined contribution retirement plans that provide retirement benefits to substantially all of its employees. Most regularly scheduled employees are eligible to participate in these plans except those covered by a collective bargaining agreement, unless the collective bargaining agreement specifically allows for participation in LP's plans. LP contributes to a multiemployer plan for certain employees covered by collective bargaining agreements. LP also provides other post retirement benefits consisting primarily of healthcare benefits to certain retirees who meet age and service requirements.

Defined Benefit Plans (in part)

Pension benefits are earned generally based upon years of service and compensation during active employment. Contributions to the qualified defined benefit pension plans are based on actuarial calculations of amounts to cover current service costs and amortization of prior service costs over periods ranging up to 20 years. LP contributes additional funds as necessary to maintain desired funding levels.

Benefit accruals under our most significant plans, which account for approximately 80% of the assets and 82% of the benefit obligations in the tables below, had been credited at the rate of 4% of eligible compensation with an interest credit based upon the 30-year U.S. Treasury rate. The Company discontinued providing contribution credits effective January 1, 2010 to these plans. The remaining defined benefit pension plans (primarily in Canada) use a variety of benefit formulas.

LP also maintains a Supplemental Executive Retirement Plan (SERP), an unfunded, non-qualified defined benefit plan intended to provide supplemental retirement benefits to key executives. Benefits are generally based on compensation in the years immediately preceding normal retirement. LP has established a grantor trust that provides funds for the benefits payable under the SERP. The assets of the grantor trust are invested in corporate-owned life insurance policies. At December 31, 2012 and 2011, the trust assets were valued at $8.8 million and $16.7 million and are included in "Other assets" on the Consolidated Balance Sheets. LP did not contribute to this trust in 2012 or 2011. During the year ended December 31, 2012, LP paid its retiring CEO his accumulated SERP liability of $10.4 million through the use of the assets included in the grantor trust. In connection with this distribution, LP recorded a plan settlement charge of $2.2 million.

The components of LP's net periodic pension costs and the assumptions related to those costs consisted of the following:

(Dollar amounts in millions)	Year Ended December 31,		
	2012	2011	2010
Service cost	$ 3.7	$ 2.9	$ 2.8
Interest cost	14.6	15.9	16.5
Expected return on plan assets	(16.8)	(18.2)	(18.2)
Amortization of prior service cost and net transition asset	0.3	0.3	0.3
Amortization of net actuarial loss	6.6	4.6	2.7
Net periodic pension cost	$ 8.4	$ 5.5	$ 4.1
Loss (gain) due to settlement	$ 2.2	$ —	$ 0.2
Discount rate	4.41%	5.12%	5.95%
Rate of compensation increase	0.7%	0.6%	0.6%
Expected return on plan assets	6.87%	7.04%	7.17%

Other changes in plan assets and benefit obligations recognized in other comprehensive income:

(Dollar amounts in millions)	Year Ended December 31,		
	2012	2011	2010
Net actuarial (gain) loss	$11.3	$43.2	$13.1
Amortization of net actuarial loss	(6.6)	(4.6)	(2.7)
Amortization of prior service cost	(0.3)	(0.3)	(0.4)
Settlement	(2.2)	—	—
Foreign exchange rate changes	—	(0.1)	0.2
Total recognized in OCI	$ 2.2	$38.2	$10.2

LP calculates the net periodic pension cost for a given fiscal year based upon assumptions developed at the end of the previous fiscal year. LP made the decision in the fourth quarter of 2008 to freeze future contribution credits as of January 1, 2010 to its qualified U.S. defined benefit pension plans. The decrease in net periodic pension cost from 2009 to 2010 was attributable to the decrease in service cost and a decrease in the amount of net actuarial loss amortized due to the lengthening of the amortization period based upon the frozen U.S. plans. LP recognized settlement charges of $2.2 million related to the LP SERP pension plan associated with the retirement of LP's previous CEO.

The expected long-term rate of return on plan assets reflects the weighted-average expected long-term rates of return for the broad categories of investments currently held in the plans (adjusted for expected changes), based on historical rates of return for each broad category, as well as factors that may constrain or enhance returns in the broad categories in the future. The expected long-term rate of return on plan assets is adjusted when there are fundamental changes in expected returns in one or more broad asset categories and when the weighted-average mix of assets in the plans changes significantly.

The projected benefit obligation is the actuarial present value of benefits attributable to employee service rendered to date, including the effects of estimated salary increases. The benefit plan obligation, funded status and the assumptions related to the obligations as of the measurement date for each year presented as of December 31 follow:

Dollar amounts in millions	December 31,	
	2012	2011
Change in benefit obligation:		
Beginning of year balance	$339.3	$316.2
Service cost	3.7	2.9
Interest cost	14.6	15.9
Actuarial (gain)/loss	23.1	23.4
Curtailments/settlements	(2.2)	—
Foreign exchange rate changes	1.3	(1.5)
Benefits paid	(27.8)	(17.6)
End of year balance	$352.0	$339.3
Change in assets (fair value):		
Beginning of year balance	$247.1	$255.2
Actual return on plan assets	26.4	(1.7)
Employer contribution	12.6	11.9
Foreign exchange rate changes	1.0	(0.7)
Benefits paid	(27.8)	(17.6)
End of year balance	$259.3	$247.1
Funded status	$ (92.7)	$ (92.2)
Weighted average assumptions for obligations as of measurement date		
Discount rate for obligations	3.78%	4.41%
Rate of compensation increase	0.64%	0.61%

The table above reflects contribution for the year ended December 31, 2012 which include the $10.4 million of assets used from the guarantor fund in payment of the SERP liability related to the retirement of LP's former CEO as noted above.

The amounts recognized in LP's Consolidated Balance Sheets as of December 31 consist of the following:

(Dollar amounts in millions)	2012	2011
Noncurrent pension assets, included in "Other assets"	$ 0.4	$ 1.0
Current pension liabilities, included in "Accounts payable and accrued liabilities"	(0.2)	(0.2)
Noncurrent pension liabilities, included in "Other long-term liabilities"	(92.9)	(93.0)
Total	$(92.7)	$(92.2)
Amounts recognized in other comprehensive income—pre-tax		
Net actuarial loss	$156.0	$153.2
Prior service cost	0.4	0.7
Total	$156.4	$153.9

The total accumulated benefit obligation for all pension plans as of December 31, 2012 and 2011 was $346.0 million and $334.0 million.

The accumulated benefit obligation and fair value of plan assets for pension plans with accumulated benefit obligations in excess of plan assets were $331.7 million and $244.6 million at December 31, 2012 and $320.8 million and $232.9 million at December 31, 2011. The projected benefit obligations and fair value of plan assets of plans with projected benefit obligations in excess of plan assets were $337.7 million and $244.6 million at December 31, 2012 and $326.1 million and $232.9 million at December 31, 2011.

The amounts of accumulated other comprehensive income that is expected to be amortized as expense during 2013 is:

(Dollar amounts in millions)	
Net actuarial loss	$7.2
Prior service cost	0.3
Total	$7.5

LP expects to contribute approximately $1.9 million to its pension plans in 2013.

The benefits expected to be paid from the benefit plans, which reflect expected future service, are as follows:

(Dollar amounts in millions) Year	
2013	$ 18.1
2014	25.5
2015	20.0
2016	20.5
2017	23.6
2018–2022	112.5

These estimated benefit payments are based upon assumptions about future events. Actual benefit payments may vary significantly from these estimates.

Other Benefit Plans

LP has several plans that provide postretirement benefits other than pensions, primarily for salaried employees in the U.S. and certain groups of Canadian employees. The funded status at December 31, 2012 and 2011 was $9.7 million and $8.5 million. Net expense related to these plans was not significant in 2012 or 2011.

Effective August 16, 2004, LP adopted the Louisiana-Pacific Corporation 2004 Executive Deferred Compensation Plan (the Plan). Pursuant to the Plan, certain management employees are eligible to defer up to 90% of their regular salary and annual cash incentives that exceed the limitation as set forth by the Internal Revenue Service. Each plan participant is fully vested in all employee deferred compensation and earnings credited associated with employee contributions. Employer contributions and associated earnings vest over periods not exceeding five years. The liability under this plan amounted to $1.5 million and $2.1 million at December 31, 2012 and December 31, 2011 and is included in "Other long-term liabilities" on LP's Consolidated Balance Sheets.

Income Tax Liability

PRESENTATION

2.110 FASB ASC 210 provides general guidance for classification of accounts in balance sheets. FASB 740-10-45 addresses classification matters applicable to income tax accounts and is incremental to the general guidance.

DISCLOSURE

2.111 FASB 740-10-50 provides detailed disclosures for income taxes, including the components of the net deferred tax liability or asset recognized in an entity's balance sheet.

PRESENTATION AND DISCLOSURE EXCERPT

INCOME TAXES PAYABLE

2.112 TOLL BROTHERS, INC. (OCT)
CONSOLIDATED BALANCE SHEETS (in part)

(Amounts in thousands)

	October 31,	
	2012	**2011**
Liabilities and Equity		
Liabilities		
Loans payable	$ 99,817	$ 106,556
Senior notes	2,080,463	1,490,972
Mortgage company warehouse loan	72,664	57,409
Customer deposits	142,977	83,824
Accounts payable	99,911	96,817
Accrued expenses	476,350	521,051
Income taxes payable	80,991	106,066
Total liabilities	3,053,173	2,462,695

NOTES TO CONSOLIDATED FINANCIAL STATEMENTS

1. Significant Accounting Policies (in part)

Income Taxes

The Company accounts for income taxes in accordance with ASC 740, "Income Taxes" ("ASC 740"). Deferred tax assets and liabilities are recorded based on temporary differences between the amounts reported for financial reporting purposes and the amounts reported for income tax purposes. In accordance with the provisions of ASC 740, the Company assesses the realizability of its deferred tax assets. A valuation allowance must be established when, based upon available evidence, it is more likely than not that all or a portion of the deferred tax assets will not be realized. See "Income Taxes—Valuation Allowance" below.

Federal and state income taxes are calculated on reported pre-tax earnings (losses) based on current tax law and also include, in the applicable period, the cumulative effect of any changes in tax rates from those used previously in determining deferred tax assets and liabilities. Such provisions (benefits) differ from the amounts currently receivable or payable because certain items of income and expense are recognized for financial reporting purposes in different periods than for income tax purposes. Significant judgment is required in determining income tax provisions (benefits) and evaluating tax positions. The Company establishes reserves for income taxes when, despite the belief that its tax positions are fully supportable, it believes that its positions may be challenged and disallowed by various tax authorities. The consolidated tax provisions (benefits) and related accruals include the impact of such reasonably estimable disallowances as deemed appropriate. To the extent that the probable tax outcome of these matters changes, such changes in estimates will impact the income tax provision (benefit) in the period in which such determination is made.

ASC 740 clarifies the accounting for uncertainty in income taxes recognized and prescribes a recognition threshold and measurement attributes for the financial statement recognition and measurement of a tax position taken or expected to be taken in a tax return. ASC 740 also provides guidance on de-recognition, classification, interest and penalties, accounting in interim periods, disclosure and transition. ASC 740 requires a company to recognize the financial statement effect of a tax position when it is "more-likely-than-not" (defined as a substantiated likelihood of more than 50%), based on the technical merits of the position, that the position will be sustained upon examination. A tax position that meets the "more-likely-than-not" recognition threshold is measured to determine the amount of benefit to be recognized in the financial statements based upon the largest amount of benefit that is greater than 50% likely of being realized upon ultimate settlement with a taxing authority that has full knowledge of all relevant information. The inability of the Company to determine that a tax position meets the "more-likely-than-not" recognition threshold does not mean that the Internal Revenue Service ("IRS") or any other taxing authority will disagree with the position that the Company has taken.

If a tax position does not meet the "more-likely-than-not" recognition threshold, despite the Company's belief that its filing position is supportable, the benefit of that tax position is not recognized in the Consolidated Statements of Operations and the Company is required to accrue potential interest and penalties until the uncertainty is resolved. Potential interest and penalties are recognized as a component of the provision for income taxes which is consistent with the Company's historical accounting policy. Differences between amounts taken in a tax return and amounts recognized in the financial statements are considered unrecognized tax benefits. The Company believes that it has a reasonable basis for each of its filing positions and intends to defend those positions if challenged by the IRS or other taxing jurisdiction. If the IRS or other taxing authorities do not disagree with the Company's position, and after the statute of limitations expires, the Company will recognize the unrecognized tax benefit in the period that the uncertainty of the tax position is eliminated.

Income Taxes—Valuation Allowance

Significant judgment is applied in assessing the realizability of deferred tax assets. In accordance with GAAP, a valuation allowance is established against a deferred tax asset if, based on the available evidence, it is more-likely-than-not that such asset will not be realized. The realization of a deferred tax asset ultimately depends on the existence of sufficient taxable income in either the carryback or carryforward periods under tax law. The Company assesses the need for valuation allowances for deferred tax assets based on GAAP's "more-likely-than-not" realization threshold criteria. In the Company's assessment, appropriate consideration is given to all positive and negative evidence related to the realization of the deferred tax assets. Forming a conclusion that a valuation allowance is not needed is difficult when there is negative evidence such as cumulative losses in recent years. This assessment considers, among other matters, the nature, consistency and magnitude of current and cumulative income and losses, forecasts of future profitability, the duration of statutory carryback or carryforward periods, the Company's experience with operating loss and tax credit carryforwards being used before expiration, and tax planning alternatives.

The Company's assessment of the need for a valuation allowance on its deferred tax assets includes assessing the likely future tax consequences of events that have been recognized in its consolidated financial statements or tax returns. Changes in existing tax laws or rates could affect the Company's actual tax results and its future business results may affect the amount of its deferred tax liabilities or the valuation of its deferred tax assets over time. The Company's accounting for deferred tax assets represents its best estimate of future events.

Due to uncertainties in the estimation process, particularly with respect to changes in facts and circumstances in future reporting periods (carryforward period assumptions), actual results could differ from the estimates used in the Company's analysis. The Company's assumptions require significant judgment because the residential home building industry is cyclical and is highly sensitive to changes in economic conditions. If the Company's results of operations are less than projected and there is insufficient objectively verifiable positive evidence to support the "more-likely-than-not" realization of its deferred tax assets, a valuation allowance would be required to reduce or eliminate its deferred tax assets.

8. Income Taxes (in part)

The following table provides a reconciliation of the Company's effective tax rate from the federal statutory tax rate for the fiscal years ended October 31, 2012, 2011 and 2010 ($ amounts in thousands).

	2012		2011		2010	
	$	%*	$	%*	$	%*
Federal tax benefit at statutory rate	39,530	35.0	(10,278)	35.0	(41,015)	35.0
State taxes, net of federal benefit	4,711	4.2	(954)	3.2	(3,809)	3.3
Reversal of accrual for uncertain tax positions	(34,167)	(30.3)	(52,306)	178.1	(39,485)	33.7
Accrued interest on anticipated tax assessments	5,000	4.4	3,055	(10.4)	9,263	(7.9)
Increase in unrecognized tax benefits	5,489	4.9			35,575	(30.4)
Increase in deferred tax assets, net			(25,948)	88.4		
Valuation allowance—recognized			43,876	(149.4)	55,492	(47.4)
Valuation allowance—reversed	(394,718)	(349.5)	(25,689)	87.5	(128,640)	109.8
Other	(49)	—	(917)	3.1	(1,194)	1.0
Tax benefit	(374,204)	(331.3)	(69,161)	235.5	(113,813)	97.1

* Due to rounding, amounts may not add.

The Company currently operates in 19 states and is subject to various state tax jurisdictions. The Company estimates its state tax liability based upon the individual taxing authorities' regulations, estimates of income by taxing jurisdiction and the Company's ability to utilize certain tax-saving strategies. Due primarily to a change in the Company's estimate of the allocation of income or loss, as the case may be, among the various taxing jurisdictions and changes in tax regulations and their impact on the Company's tax strategies, the Company's estimated rate for state income taxes was 6.4% in fiscal 2012 and 5.0% for each of fiscal 2011 and 2010.

The following table provides information regarding the (benefit) provision for income taxes for each of the fiscal years ended October 31, 2012, 2011 and 2010 (amounts in thousands).

	2012	2011	2010
Federal	$(329,277)	$(21,517)	$ (67,318)
State	(44,927)	(47,644)	(46,495)
	$(374,204)	$(69,161)	$(113,813)
Current	$ (21,296)	$(43,212)	$(156,985)
Deferred	(352,908)	(25,949)	43,172
	$(374,204)	$(69,161)	$(113,813)

In November 2009, the Worker, Homeownership, and Business Assistance Act of 2009 was enacted into law which allowed the Company to carry back its fiscal 2010 taxable loss against taxable income reported in fiscal 2006 and receive a federal tax refund in its second quarter of fiscal 2011 of $154.3 million. The tax losses generated in fiscal 2010 were primarily from the recognition for tax purposes of previously recognized book impairments and the recognition of stock option expenses recognized for book purposes in prior years.

The following table provides a reconciliation of the change in the unrecognized tax benefits for the years ended October 31, 2012, 2011 and 2010 (amounts in thousands).

	2012	2011	2010
Balance, beginning of year	$104,669	$160,446	$171,366
Increase in benefit as a result of tax positions taken in prior years	5,000	8,168	14,251
Increase in benefit as a result of tax positions taken in current year	5,489		15,675
Decrease in benefit as a result of settlements	—	(17,954)	
Decrease in benefit as a result of completion of audits	(1,782)	(33,370)	
Decrease in benefit as a result of lapse of statute of limitation	(32,385)	(12,621)	(40,846)
Balance, end of year	$ 80,991	$104,669	$160,446

The Company has reached final settlement of its federal tax returns for fiscal years through 2009. The federal settlements resulted in a reduction in the Company's unrecognized tax benefits. The state impact of any amended federal return remains subject to examination by various states for a period of up to one year after formal notification of such amendments is made to the states.

The Company's unrecognized tax benefits are included in "Income taxes payable" on the Company's consolidated balance sheets. If these unrecognized tax benefits reverse in the future, they would have a beneficial impact on the Company's effective tax rate at that time. During the next twelve months, it is reasonably possible that the amount of unrecognized tax benefits will change but we are not able to provide a range of such change. The anticipated changes will be principally due to the expiration of tax statutes, settlements with taxing jurisdictions, increases due to new tax positions taken and the accrual of estimated interest and penalties.

The Company recognizes in its tax benefit, potential interest and penalties. The following table provides information as to the amounts recognized in its tax provision, before reduction for applicable taxes and reversal of previously accrued interest and penalties, of potential interest and penalties in the twelve-month periods ended October 31, 2012, 2011 and 2010, and the amounts accrued for potential interest and penalties at October 31, 2012 and 2011 (amounts in thousands).

Expense Recognized in Statements of Operations	
Fiscal year	
2012	$ 5,000
2011	$ 4,700
2010	$14,300
Accrued at:	
October 31, 2012	$24,906
October 31, 2011	$29,200

The amounts accrued for interest and penalties are included in "Income taxes payable" on the Company's consolidated balance sheets.

Current Amount of Long-Term Debt

PRESENTATION

2.113 FASB ASC 470 addresses classification determination for specific debt obligations, such as the following:
- Short-term obligations expected to be refinanced on a long-term basis
- 'Due-on-demand loan arrangements
- Callable debt
- Sales of future revenue
- Increasing rate debt
- Debt that includes covenants
- Revolving credit agreements subject to lock-box arrangements and subjective acceleration clauses

DISCLOSURE

2.114 FASB ASC 470 includes disclosures required for long-term debt (see the "Long-Term Debt" section). FASB ASC 825 requires disclosure of both the fair value and bases for estimating the fair value of the current amount of long-term debt, unless it is not practicable to estimate that value.

PRESENTATION AND DISCLOSURE EXCERPT

CURRENT AMOUNT OF LONG-TERM DEBT

2.115 CONSTELLATION BRANDS, INC. (FEB)
CONSOLIDATED BALANCE SHEETS (in part)

(In millions, except share and per share data)

	February 29, 2012	February 28, 2011
Liabilities and Stockholders' Equity		
Current liabilities:		
Notes payable to banks	$ 377.9	$ 83.7
Current maturities of long-term debt	330.2	15.9
Accounts payable	130.5	129.2
Accrued excise taxes	24.8	14.2
Other accrued expenses and liabilities	336.2	419.9
Total current liabilities	1,199.6	662.9

NOTES TO CONSOLIDATED FINANCIAL STATEMENTS

11. Borrowings (in part)

Borrowings consist of the following:

(In millions)	February 29, 2012			February 28, 2011
	Current	Long-Term	Total	Total
Notes Payable to Banks:				
Senior Credit Facility—Revolving Credit Loans	$298.0	$ —	$ 298.0	$ 74.9
Other	79.9	—	79.9	8.8
	$377.9	$ —	$ 377.9	$ 83.7
Long-term Debt:				
Senior Credit Facility—Term Loans	$314.1	$ 512.5	$ 826.6	$1,228.0
Senior Notes	—	1,894.8	1,894.8	1,893.6
Other Long-term Debt	16.1	14.1	30.2	31.0
	$330.2	$2,421.4	$2,751.6	$3,152.6

Senior Credit Facility—

The Company and certain of its U.S. subsidiaries, JPMorgan Chase Bank, N.A. as a lender and administrative agent, and certain other agents, lenders, and financial institutions are parties to a credit agreement, as amended (the "2006 Credit Agreement"). The 2006 Credit Agreement provides for aggregate credit facilities of $3,842.0 million, consisting of (i) a $1,200.0 million tranche A term loan facility with an original final maturity in June 2011, fully repaid as of

February 28, 2011, (ii) a $1,800.0 million tranche B term loan facility, of which $1,500.0 million has a final maturity in June 2013 (the "2013 Tranche B Term Loans") and $300.0 million has a final maturity in June 2015 (the "2015 Tranche B Term Loans"), and (iii) an $842.0 million revolving credit facility (including a sub-facility for letters of credit of up to $200.0 million), of which $192.0 million terminated in June 2011 and $650.0 million terminates in June 2013 (the "2013 Revolving Facility"). The Company uses its revolving credit facility under the 2006 Credit Agreement for general corporate purposes.

The rate of interest on borrowings under the 2006 Credit Agreement is a function of LIBOR plus a margin, the federal funds rate plus a margin, or the prime rate plus a margin. The margin is adjustable based upon the Company's debt ratio (as defined in the 2006 Credit Agreement) with respect to the 2013 Revolving Facility, and is fixed with respect to the 2013 Tranche B Term Loans and the 2015 Tranche B Term Loans. As of February 29, 2012, the LIBOR margin for the 2013 Revolving Facility is 2.50%; the LIBOR margin for the 2013 Tranche B Term Loans is 1.50%; and the LIBOR margin on the 2015 Tranche B Term Loans is 2.75%.

The Company's obligations are guaranteed by certain of its U.S. subsidiaries. These obligations are also secured by a pledge of (i) 100% of the ownership interests in certain of the Company's U.S. subsidiaries and (ii) 65% of the voting capital stock of certain of the Company's foreign subsidiaries.

The Company and its subsidiaries are also subject to covenants that are contained in the 2006 Credit Agreement, including those restricting the incurrence of additional indebtedness (including guarantees of indebtedness), additional liens, mergers and consolidations, the disposition or acquisition of property, the payment of dividends, transactions with affiliates and the making of certain investments, in each case subject to numerous conditions, exceptions and thresholds. The financial covenants are limited to maintaining a maximum total debt coverage ratio and minimum interest coverage ratio.

As of February 29, 2012, following the prepayment of $400.0 million of the tranche B term loan facility during the first quarter of fiscal 2012, under the 2006 Credit Agreement, the Company had outstanding 2013 Tranche B Term Loans of $624.7 million bearing an interest rate of 2.0%, 2015 Tranche B Term Loans of $201.9 million bearing an interest rate of 3.1%, 2013 Revolving Facility of $298.0 million bearing an interest rate of 2.7%, outstanding letters of credit of $12.2 million, and $339.8 million in revolving loans available to be drawn.

As of February 29, 2012, the required principal repayments of the tranche B term loan facility for each of the four succeeding fiscal years are as follows:

(In millions)	Tranche B Term Loan Facility
2013	$314.1
2014	314.1
2015	99.7
2016	98.7
	$826.6

In April 2009, the Company transitioned its interest rate swap agreements to a one-month LIBOR base rate versus the then existing three-month LIBOR base rate. Accordingly, the Company entered into new interest rate swap agreements which were designated as cash flow hedges of $1,200.0 million of the Company's floating LIBOR rate debt. In addition, the then existing interest rate swap agreements were dedesignated by the Company and the Company entered into additional undesignated interest rate swap agreements for $1,200.0 million to offset the prospective impact of the newly undesignated interest rate swap agreements. As a result, the Company fixed its interest rates on $1,200.0 million of the Company's floating LIBOR rate debt at an average rate of 4.0% through February 28, 2010. On March 1, 2010, the Company paid $11.9 million in connection with the maturity of these outstanding interest rate swap agreements, which is reported in other, net in cash flows from operating activities in the Company's Consolidated Statements of Cash Flows. In June 2010, the Company entered into a new five year delayed start interest rate swap agreement effective September 1, 2011, which was designated as a cash flow hedge for $500.0 million of the Company's floating LIBOR rate debt. Accordingly, the Company fixed its interest rates on $500.0 million of the Company's floating LIBOR rate debt at an average rate of 2.9% (exclusive of borrowing margins) through September 1, 2016. For the year ended February 29, 2012, the Company reclassified net losses of $3.8 million, net of income tax effect, from AOCI to interest expense, net on the Company's Consolidated Statements of Operations. For the year ended February 28, 2011, the Company did not reclassify any amount from AOCI to interest expense, net on its Consolidated Statements of Operations. For the year ended February 28, 2010, the Company reclassified net losses of $27.7 million, net of income tax effect, respectively, from AOCI to interest expense, net on the Company's Consolidated Statements of Operations.

Subsidiary Credit Facilities—

The Company has additional credit arrangements totaling $253.8 million and $154.2 million as of February 29, 2012, and February 28, 2011, respectively. These arrangements primarily support the financing needs of the Company's domestic and foreign subsidiary operations. Interest rates and other terms of these borrowings vary from country to country, depending on local market conditions. As of February 29, 2012, and February 28, 2011, amounts outstanding under these arrangements were $110.1 million and $39.8 million, respectively, the majority of which is classified as current as of the respective date.

Other Current Liabilities

PRESENTATION

2.116 Rule 5-02 of Regulation S-X requires that any items in excess of 5 percent of total current liabilities be stated separately on the balance sheet or disclosed in the notes. In addition, registrants should state separately amounts payable to the following:

- Banks for borrowings
- Factors or other financial institutions for borrowings
- Holders of commercial paper
- Trade creditors
- Related parties
- Underwriters, promoters, and employees (other than related parties)
- Others

Amounts applicable to the first three categories may be stated separately in the balance sheet or in a note thereto.

PRESENTATION AND DISCLOSURE EXCERPTS

DIVIDENDS

2.117 ST. JUDE MEDICAL, INC. (DEC)
CONSOLIDATED BALANCE SHEETS (in part)

(In millions, except par value and share amounts)

	December 29, 2012	December 31, 2011
Liabilities and Shareholders' Equity		
Current liabilities		
Current debt obligations	$ 530	$ 83
Accounts payable	254	202
Dividends payable	68	67
Income taxes payable	142	1
Employee compensation and related benefits	299	305
Other current liabilities	482	403
Total current liabilities	1,775	1,061

NOTES TO THE CONDENSED CONSOLIDATED FINANCIAL STATEMENTS

Note 6—Shareholders' Equity (in part)

Dividends: During 2012, the Company's Board of Directors authorized four quarterly cash dividend payments of $0.23 per share paid on April 30, 2012, July 31, 2012, October 31, 2012 and January 31, 2013. During 2011, the Company's Board of Directors authorized four quarterly cash dividend payments of $0.21 per share paid on April 29, 2011, July 29, 2011, October 31, 2011 and January 31, 2012. No cash dividends were paid in 2010.

On February 23, 2013, the Company's Board of Directors authorized a cash dividend of $0.25 per share payable on April 30, 2013 to share holders of record as of March 29, 2013.

Note 15—Quarterly Financial Data (Unaudited)

(In millions, except per share amounts)	First Quarter	Second Quarter	Third Quarter	Fourth Quarter
Fiscal Year 2012:				
Net sales	$1,395	$1,410	$1,326	$1,372
Gross profit	1,014	1,027	971	953
Net earnings[a]	212[b]	244	176[c]	120[d]
Basic net earnings per share	$ 0.67	$ 0.78	$ 0.56	$ 0.39
Diluted net earnings per share	$ 0.67	$ 0.78	$ 0.56	$ 0.39
Cash dividends declared per share	$ 0.23	$ 0.23	$ 0.23	$ 0.23

(continued)

(In millions, except per share amounts)	First Quarter	Second Quarter	Third Quarter	Fourth Quarter
Fiscal Year 2011:				
Net sales	$1,376	$1,446	$1,383	$1,407
Gross profit	1,011	1,051	1,013	1,004
Net earnings[e]	233	241	227	125[f]
Basic net earnings per share	$ 0.72	$ 0.73	$ 0.70	$ 0.39
Diluted net earnings per share	$ 0.71	$ 0.72	$ 0.69	$ 0.39
Cash dividends declared per share	$ 0.21	$ 0.21	$ 0.21	$ 0.21

[a] Restructuring activities resulted in after-tax special charges of $29 million for the first quarter, $27 million for the second quarter, $66 million for the third quarter and $75 million for the fourth quarter.

[b] Includes after-tax special charges of $25 million related to a license dispute settlement charge.

[c] Includes after-tax special charges of $15 million for intangible asset impairment charges.

[d] Includes after-tax special charges of $27 million related to IESD litigation and field action costs and after-tax charges of $11 million for intangible asset impairment charges and CATD inventory write-offs associated with discontinued product lines. Additionally, the Company recognized $46 million of additional income tax expense related to adjustments to uncertain tax positions associated with the effective settlement of certain income tax audits.

[e] Restructuring activities resulted in after-tax special charges of $29 million for the second quarter, $21 million for the third quarter and $71 million for the fourth quarter.

[f] Includes after-tax special charges of $31 million for intangible asset impairment charges and $38 million of after-tax accounts receivable allowance charges for collection risk in Europe.

ADVANCE PAYMENTS FROM CUSTOMERS

2.118 LOCKHEED MARTIN CORPORATION (DEC)

CONSOLIDATED BALANCE SHEETS (in part)

(In millions, except par value)

	December 31,	
	2012	2011
Liabilities and Stockholders' Equity		
Current liabilities		
Accounts payable	$ 2,038	$ 2,269
Customer advances and amounts in excess of costs incurred	6,503	6,399
Salaries, benefits, and payroll taxes	1,649	1,664
Current portion of long-term debt	150	—
Other current liabilities	1,815	1,798
Total current liabilities	12,155	12,130

NOTES TO CONSOLIDATED FINANCIAL STATEMENTS

Note 1—Significant Accounting Policies (in part)

Customer advances and amounts in excess of cost incurred—We receive advances, performance-based payments, and progress payments from customers that may exceed costs incurred on certain contracts, including contracts with agencies of the U.S. Government. We classify such advances, other than those reflected as a reduction of receivables or inventories as discussed above, as current liabilities.

Note 3—Information on Business Segments (in part)

Total assets, goodwill, and customer advances and amounts in excess of costs incurred for each of our business segments were as follows (in millions):

	2012	2011
Assets[a]		
Aeronautics	$ 6,525	$ 5,752
Information Systems & Global Solutions	5,664	5,838
Missiles and Fire Control	4,186	4,096
Mission Systems and Training	6,589	6,159
Space Systems	3,478	3,346
Total business segment assets	26,442	25,191
Corporate assets[b]	12,215	12,717
Total assets	$38,657	$37,908
Goodwill		
Aeronautics	$ 146	$ 146
Information Systems & Global Solutions	3,767	3,749
Missiles and Fire Control	2,485	2,481
Mission Systems and Training	3,264	3,065
Space Systems	708	707
Total goodwill[c]	$10,370	$10,148

(continued)

	2012	2011
Customer Advances and Amounts in Excess of Costs Incurred		
Aeronautics	$ 2,382	$ 2,443
Information Systems & Global Solutions	323	350
Missiles and Fire Control	1,988	1,888
Mission Systems and Training	1,335	1,326
Space Systems	475	392
Total customer advances and amounts in excess of costs incurred	$ 6,503	$ 6,399

(a) We have no significant long-lived assets located in foreign countries.

(b) Corporate assets primarily include cash and cash equivalents, deferred income taxes, environmental receivables, and investments held in a separate trust.

(c) During 2012, the increase in goodwill primarily was due to the acquisitions of Chandler/May, CDL, and Procerus at our MST business segment (Note 14). During 2011, goodwill increased $543 million primarily due to the acquisitions of QTC at our IS&GS business segment and Sim-Industries at our MST business segment (Note 14). As a result of the previously discussed reorganization, the goodwill related to the former Electronic Systems business segment was reassigned on a relative fair value basis to the MFC, MST, and Space Systems business segments.

DEFERRED INCOME TAXES

2.119 McKESSON CORPORATION (MAR)
CONSOLIDATED BALANCE SHEETS (in part)

(In millions, except per share amounts)

	March 31,	
	2012	2011
Liabilities and Stockholders' Equity		
Current liabilities		
Drafts and accounts payable	$16,114	$14,090
Short-term borrowings	400	—
Deferred revenue	1,423	1,321
Deferred tax liabilities	1,092	1,037
Current portion of long-term debt	508	417
Other accrued liabilities	2,149	1,861
Total current liabilities	21,686	18,726

FINANCIAL NOTES

1. Significant Accounting Policies (in part)

Income Taxes: We account for income taxes under the asset and liability method, which requires the recognition of deferred tax assets and liabilities for the expected future tax consequences of events that have been included in the financial statements. Under this method, deferred tax assets and liabilities are determined based on the difference between the financial statements and the tax basis of assets and liabilities using enacted tax rates in effect for the year in which the differences are expected to reverse. Tax benefits from uncertain tax positions are recognized when it is more likely than not that the position will be sustained upon examination, including resolutions of any related appeals or litigation processes, based on the technical merits. The amount recognized is measured as the largest amount of tax benefit that is greater than 50 percent likely of being realized upon effective settlements. Deferred taxes are not provided on undistributed earnings of our foreign operations that are considered to be permanently reinvested.

6. Income Taxes (in part)

Deferred tax balances consisted of the following:

	March 31,	
(In millions)	2012	2011
Assets		
Receivable allowances	$ 44	$ 48
Deferred revenue	114	107
Compensation and benefit related accruals	447	409
AWP litigation accrual	175	97
Loss and credit carryforwards	400	494
Other	256	241
Subtotal	1,436	1,396
Less: valuation allowance	(101)	(99)
Total assets	1,335	1,297

(continued)

(In millions)	March 31,	
	2012	**2011**
Liabilities		
Inventory valuation and other assets	$(1,635)	$(1,450)
Fixed assets and systems development costs	(263)	(221)
Intangibles	(544)	(532)
Other	(53)	(58)
Total liabilities	(2,495)	(2,261)
Net deferred tax liability	$(1,160)	$ (964)
Current net deferred tax liability	$(1,092)	$(1,036)
Long-term deferred tax asset	20	72
Long-term deferred tax liability	(88)	—
Net deferred tax liability	$(1,160)	$ (964)

WARRANTIES

2.120 APPLE INC. (SEP)

CONSOLIDATED BALANCE SHEETS (in part)

(In millions, except number of shares which are reflected in thousands)

	September 29, 2012	September 24, 2011
Liabilities and Shareholders' Equity:		
Current liabilities:		
Accounts payable	$21,175	$14,632
Accrued expenses	11,414	9,247
Deferred revenue	5,953	4,091
Total current liabilities	38,542	27,970

NOTES TO CONSOLIDATED FINANCIAL STATFMENTS

Note 1—Summary of Significant Accounting Policies (in part)

Warranty Expense

The Company generally provides for the estimated cost of hardware and software warranties at the time the related revenue is recognized. The Company assesses the adequacy of its pre-existing warranty liabilities and adjusts the amounts as necessary based on actual experience and changes in future estimates.

Note 3—Consolidated Financial Statement Details (in part)

The following tables show the Company's consolidated financial statement details as of September 29, 2012 and September 24, 2011 (in millions):

Accrued Expenses

	2012	2011
Accrued warranty and related costs	$ 1,638	$1,240
Accrued taxes	1,535	1,140
Deferred margin on component sales	1,492	2,038
Accrued marketing and selling expenses	910	598
Accrued compensation and employee benefits	735	590
Other current liabilities	5,104	3,641
Total accrued expenses	$11,414	$9,247

Note 7—Commitments and Contingencies (in part)

Accrued Warranty and Indemnification

The Company offers a basic limited parts and labor warranty on its hardware products. The basic warranty period for hardware products is typically one year from the date of purchase by the end-user. The Company also offers a 90-day basic warranty for its service parts used to repair the Company's hardware products. The Company provides currently for the estimated cost that may be incurred under its basic limited product warranties at the time related revenue is recognized. Factors considered in determining appropriate accruals for product warranty obligations include the size of the installed base of products subject to warranty protection, historical and projected warranty claim rates, historical and projected cost-per-claim, and knowledge of specific product failures that are outside of the Company's typical experience. The Company assesses the adequacy of its pre-existing warranty liabilities and adjusts the amounts as necessary based on actual experience and changes in future estimates.

The following table shows changes in the Company's accrued warranties and related costs for 2012, 2011, and 2010 (in millions):

	2012	2011	2010
Beginning accrued warranty and related costs	$ 1,240	$ 761	$ 577
Cost of warranty claims	(1,786)	(1,147)	(713)
Accruals for product warranty	2,184	1,626	897
Ending accrued warranty and related costs	$ 1,638	$ 1,240	$ 761

The Company generally does not indemnify end-users of its operating system and application software against legal claims that the software infringes third-party intellectual property rights. Other agreements entered into by the Company sometimes include indemnification provisions under which the Company could be subject to costs and/or damages in the event of an infringement claim against the Company or an indemnified third-party. However, the Company has not been required to make any significant payments resulting from such an infringement claim asserted against it or an indemnified third-party and, in the opinion of management, does not have a potential liability related to unresolved infringement claims subject to indemnification that would materially adversely affect its financial condition or operating results. Therefore, the Company did not record a liability for infringement costs related to indemnification as of either September 29, 2012 or September 24, 2011.

The Company has entered into indemnification agreements with its directors and executive officers. Under these agreements, the Company has agreed to indemnify such individuals to the fullest extent permitted by law against liabilities that arise by reason of their status as directors or officers and to advance expenses incurred by such individuals in connection with related legal proceedings. It is not possible to determine the maximum potential amount of payments the Company could be required to make under these agreements due to the limited history of prior indemnification claims and the unique facts and circumstances involved in each claim. However, the Company maintains directors and officers liability insurance coverage to reduce its exposure to such obligations, and payments made under these agreements historically have not been material.

BILLINGS IN EXCESS OF COSTS AND ESTIMATED EARNINGS

2.121 EMCOR GROUP, INC. (DEC)
CONSOLIDATED BALANCE SHEETS (in part)

(In thousands, except share and share data)

	December 31, 2012	December 31, 2011
Liabilities and Equity		
Current liabilities:		
Borrowings under revolving credit facility	$ —	$ —
Current maturities of long-term debt and capital lease obligations	1,787	1,522
Accounts payable	490,621	477,801
Billings in excess of costs and estimated earnings on uncompleted contracts	383,527	441,695
Accrued payroll and benefits	224,555	204,785
Other accrued expenses and liabilities	194,029	205,110
Total current liabilities	1,294,519	1,330,913

NOTES TO CONSOLIDATED FINANCIAL STATEMENTS

Note 2—Summary of Significant Accounting Policies (in part)

Costs and Estimated Earnings on Uncompleted Contracts

Costs and estimated earnings in excess of billings on uncompleted contracts arise in the consolidated balance sheets when revenues have been recognized but the amounts cannot be billed under the terms of the contracts. Such amounts are recoverable from customers upon various measures of performance, including achievement of certain milestones, completion of specified units, or completion of a contract. Also included in costs and estimated earnings on uncompleted contracts are amounts we seek or will seek to collect from customers or others for errors or changes in contract specifications or design, contract change orders in dispute or unapproved as to both scope and/or price or other customer-related causes of unanticipated additional contract costs (claims and unapproved change orders). Such amounts are recorded at estimated net realizable value when realization is probable and can be reasonably estimated. No profit is recognized on construction costs incurred in connection with claim amounts. Claims and unapproved change orders made by us involve negotiation and, in certain cases, litigation. In the event litigation costs are incurred by us in connection with claims or unapproved change orders, such litigation costs are expensed as incurred, although we may seek to recover these costs. We believe that we have established legal bases for pursuing recovery of our recorded unapproved change orders and claims, and it is management's intention to pursue and litigate such claims, if necessary, until a decision or settlement is reached. Unapproved change orders and claims also involve the use of estimates, and it is reasonably possible that revisions to the estimated recoverable amounts of recorded claims and unapproved change orders may be made in the near term. If we do not successfully resolve these matters, a net expense (recorded as a reduction in revenues) may be required, in addition to amounts that may have been previously provided for. We record the profit associated with the settlement of claims upon receipt of final payment. Claims against us are recognized when a loss is considered probable and amounts are reasonably determinable.

Costs and estimated earnings on uncompleted contracts and related amounts billed as of December 31, 2012 and 2011 were as follows (in thousands):

	2012	2011
Costs incurred on uncompleted contracts	$7,675,049	$7,598,325
Estimated earnings, thereon	876,496	830,622
	8,551,545	8,428,947
Less: billings to date	8,842,011	8,755,806
	$ (290,466)	$ (326,859)

Such amounts were included in the accompanying Consolidated Balance Sheets at December 31, 2012 and 2011 under the following captions (in thousands):

	2012	2011
Costs and estimated earnings in excess of billings on uncompleted contracts	$ 93,061	$ 114,836
Billings in excess of costs and estimated earnings on uncompleted contracts	(383,527)	(441,695)
	$ (290,466)	$ (326,859)

As of December 31, 2012 and 2011, costs and estimated earnings in excess of billings on uncompleted contracts included unbilled revenues for unapproved change orders of approximately $13.8 million and $14.5 million, respectively, and claims of approximately $0.7 million and $1.6 million, respectively. In addition, accounts receivable as of December 31, 2012 and 2011 included claims of approximately $0.8 million and $0.2 million, respectively. Additionally, there are contractually billed amounts and retention related to such contracts of $41.0 million and $40.4 million as of December 31, 2012 and 2011, respectively. Generally, contractually billed amounts will not be paid by the customer to us until final resolution of related claims.

LIABILITIES OF FACILITIES HELD FOR SALE

2.122 UNIVERSAL HEALTH SERVICES, INC. (DEC)
CONSOLIDATED BALANCE SHEETS (in part)

	December 31,	
(Dollar amounts in thousands)	2012	2011
Liabilities and Stockholders' Equity		
Current liabilities:		
Current maturities of long-term debt	$ 2,589	$ 2,479
Accounts payable	247,033	228,043
Liabilities of facilities held for sale	850	2,329
Accrued liabilities		
Compensation and related benefits	259,646	233,583
Interest	10,774	10,622
Taxes other than income	49,829	45,359
Other	322,275	314,518
Current federal and state income taxes	1,062	0
Total current liabilities	894,058	836,933

NOTES TO CONSOLIDATED FINANCIAL STATEMENTS

2) Acquisitions and Divestitures (in part)

Year Ended December 31, 2012 (in part)

2012 Divestiture of Assets and Businesses:

During 2012, we received $149 million from the divestiture of assets and businesses, including the following:
- received $93 million for the sale of Auburn Regional Medical Center ("Auburn"), a 159-bed acute care hospital located in Auburn, Washington (sold in October);
- received $50 million for the sale of the Hospital San Juan Capestrano, a 108-bed acute care hospital located in Rio Piedras, Puerto Rico (sold in January pursuant to our below-mentioned agreement with the FTC in connection with our acquisition of PSI in November, 2010), and;
- received an aggregate of $6 million for the sale of the real property of two non-operating behavioral health facilities and our majority ownership interest in an outpatient surgery center located in Puerto Rico.

In connection with the receipt of antitrust clearance from the Federal Trade Commission ("FTC") in connection with our acquisition of Ascend Health Corporation in October of 2012, we agreed to certain conditions, including the divestiture, within approximately six months, of Peak Behavioral Health Services ("Peak"), a 104-bed behavioral health care facility located in Santa Teresa, New Mexico. The revenues of Peak were approximately $18 million and $14 million during 2012 and 2011, respectively.

In connection with the receipt of antitrust clearance from the FTC in connection with our acquisition of PSI in November, 2010, we agreed to divest three former PSI facilities as well as one of our legacy behavioral health facilities in Puerto Rico. Pursuant to the terms of our agreement with the FTC, we divested:

- in July, 2011, the MeadowWood Behavioral Health System, a 58-bed facility located in New Castle, Delaware;
- in December, 2011, the Montevista Hospital (101-bed) and Red Rock Hospital (21-bed), both of which are located in Las Vegas, Nevada, and;
- in January, 2012, the Hospital San Juan Capestrano, a 108-bed facility located in Rio Piedras, Puerto Rico.

The operating results for Auburn, Peak and the three former PSI facilities located in Delaware and Nevada are reflected as discontinued operations during our period of ownership during each of the years presented herein. Since the aggregate income from discontinued operations before income tax expense for these facilities is not material to our consolidated financial statements, it is included as a reduction to other operating expenses. As reflected on the table below, the aggregate pre-tax gain on the divestiture of Auburn, was approximately $26 million. The aggregate pre-tax net gain on the divestiture of San Juan Capestrano in January, 2012 did not have a material impact on our consolidated results of operations during 2012. Assets and liabilities for Peak are reflected as "held for sale" on our Consolidated Balance Sheet as of December 31, 2012, and the assets and liabilities for the Hospital San Juan Capestrano were reflected as "held for sale" on our Consolidated Balance Sheet as of December 31, 2011.

INSURANCE

2.123 WASTE MANAGEMENT, INC. (DEC)
CONSOLIDATED BALANCE SHEETS (in part)

(In millions, except share and par value amounts)

	December 31,	
	2012	2011
Liabilities and Equity		
Current liabilities:		
Accounts payable	$ 842	$ 838
Accrued liabilities	986	1,129
Deferred revenues	465	470
Current portion of long-term debt	743	631
Total current liabilities	3,036	3,068

NOTES TO CONSOLIDATED FINANCIAL STATEMENTS

3. Summary of Significant Accounting Policies (in part)

Insured and Self-Insured Claims

We have retained a significant portion of the risks related to our health and welfare, automobile, general liability and workers' compensation claims programs. The exposure for unpaid claims and associated expenses, including incurred but not reported losses, generally is estimated with the assistance of external actuaries and by factoring in pending claims and historical trends and data. The gross estimated liability associated with settling unpaid claims is included in "Accrued liabilities" in our Consolidated Balance Sheets if expected to be settled within one year, or otherwise is included in long-term "Other liabilities." Estimated insurance recoveries related to recorded liabilities are reflected as current "Other receivables" or long-term "Other assets" in our Consolidated Balance Sheets when we believe that the receipt of such amounts is probable.

11. Commitments and Contingencies (in part)

Financial Instruments (in part)—We have obtained letters of credit, performance bonds and insurance policies and have established trust funds and issued financial guarantees to support tax-exempt bonds, contracts, performance of landfill final capping, closure and post-closure requirements, environmental remediation, and other obligations. Letters of credit generally are supported by our revolving credit facility and other credit facilities established for that purpose. These facilities are discussed further in Note 7. We obtain surety bonds and insurance policies from an entity in which we have a noncontrolling financial interest. We also obtain insurance from a wholly-owned insurance company, the sole business of which is to issue policies for us. In those instances where our use of financial assurance from entities we own or have financial interests in is not allowed, we have available alternative financial assurance mechanisms.

Insurance—We carry insurance coverage for protection of our assets and operations from certain risks including automobile liability, general liability, real and personal property, workers' compensation, directors' and officers' liability, pollution legal liability and other coverages we believe are customary to the industry. Our exposure to loss for insurance claims is generally limited to the per incident deductible under the related insurance policy. Our exposure, however, could increase if our insurers are unable to meet their commitments on a timely basis.

We have retained a significant portion of the risks related to our automobile, general liability and workers' compensation claims programs. "General liability" refers to the self-insured portion of specific third party claims made against us that may be covered under our commercial General Liability Insurance Policy. For our self-insured retentions, the exposure for unpaid claims and associated expenses, including incurred but not reported losses, is based on an actuarial valuation and internal estimates. The accruals for these liabilities could be revised if future occurrences or loss development significantly differ from our assumptions used. As of December 31, 2012, our commercial General Liability Insurance Policy carried self-insurance exposures of up to $2.5 million per incident and our workers' compensation insurance program carried self-insurance exposures of up to $5 million per incident. As of December 31, 2012, our auto liability insurance program included a per-incident base deductible of $5 million, subject to additional deductibles of $4.8 million in the $5 million to $10 million layer. Self-insurance claims reserves acquired as part of our acquisition of WM Holdings in July 1998 were discounted at 1.75% at December 31, 2012, 2.0% at December 31, 2011 and 3.50% at December 31, 2010. The changes to our net insurance liabilities for the three years ended December 31, 2012 are summarized below (in millions):

	Gross Claims Liability	Receivables Associated with Insured Claims[a]	Net Claims Liability
Balance, December 31, 2009	$ 541	$(194)	$ 347
Self-insurance expense (benefit)	179	(38)	141
Cash (paid) received	(197)	62	(135)
Balance, December 31, 2010	523	(170)	353
Self-insurance expense (benefit)	176	(14)	162
Cash (paid) received	(188)	23	(165)
Balance, December 31, 2011	511	(161)	350
Self-insurance expense (benefit)	222	(59)	163
Cash (paid) received	(164)	18	(146)
Balance, December 31, 2012[b]	$ 569	$(202)	$ 367
Current portion at December 31, 2012	$ 109	$ (19)	$ 90
Long-term portion at December 31, 2012	$ 460	$(183)	$ 277

[a] Amounts reported as receivables associated with insured claims are related to both paid and unpaid claims liabilities.
[b] We currently expect substantially all of our net claims liability to be settled in cash over the next five years.

The Directors' and Officers' Liability Insurance policy we choose to maintain covers only individual executive liability, often referred to as "Broad Form Side A," and does not provide corporate reimbursement coverage, often referred to as "Side B." The Side A policy covers directors and officers directly for loss, including defense costs, when corporate indemnification is unavailable. Side A-only coverage cannot be exhausted by payments to the Company, as the Company is not insured for any money it advances for defense costs or pays as indemnity to the insured directors and officers.

We do not expect the impact of any known casualty, property, environmental or other contingency to have a material impact on our financial condition, results of operations or cash flows.

MARKETING

2.124 H. J. HEINZ COMPANY (APR)
CONSOLIDATED BALANCE SHEETS (in part)

(In thousands)	April 29, 2012	April 27, 2011
Liabilities and Equity		
Current liabilities:		
Short-term debt	$ 46,460	$ 87,800
Portion of long-term debt due within one year	200,248	1,447,132
Trade payables	1,202,398	1,337,620
Other payables	146,414	162,047
Accrued marketing	303,132	313,389
Other accrued liabilities	647,769	715,147
Income taxes	101,540	98,325
Total current liabilities	2,647,961	4,161,460

NOTES TO CONSOLIDATED FINANCIAL STATEMENTS

1. Significant Accounting Policies (in part)

Marketing Costs

The Company promotes its products with advertising, consumer incentives and trade promotions. Such programs include, but are not limited to, discounts, coupons, rebates, in-store display incentives and volume-based incentives. Advertising costs are expensed as incurred. Consumer incentive and trade promotion activities are recorded as a reduction of revenue or as a component of cost of products sold based on amounts estimated as being due to customers and consumers at the end of a period, based principally on historical utilization and redemption rates. Advertising costs are recognized as an expense within selling, general and administrative expenses if the Company determines that it will receive an identifiable, separable benefit in return for the consideration paid and it can reasonably estimate the fair value of the benefit identified. Accruals for trade promotions are initially recorded at the time of sale of product to the customer based on an estimate of the expected levels of performance of the trade promotion, which is dependent upon factors such as historical trends with similar promotions, expectations regarding customer participation, and sales and payment trends with similar previously offered programs. The Company performs monthly evaluations of its outstanding trade promotions, making adjustments where appropriate to reflect changes in estimates. Settlement of these liabilities typically occurs in subsequent periods primarily through an authorization process for deductions taken by a customer from amounts otherwise due to the Company. Coupon redemption costs are accrued in the period in which the coupons are offered. The initial estimates made for each coupon offering are based upon historical redemption experience rates for similar products or coupon amounts. The Company performs monthly evaluations of outstanding coupon accruals that compare actual redemption rates to the original estimates. For interim reporting purposes, advertising, consumer incentive and product placement expenses are charged to operations as a percentage of volume, based on estimated volume and related expense for the full year.

DEFERRED REVENUE

2.125 EQUIFAX INC. (DEC)
CONSOLIDATED BALANCE SHEETS (in part)

	December 31,	
(In millions, except par values)	**2012**	**2011**
Liabilities and Equity		
Current liabilities:		
Short-term debt and current maturities	$283.3	$ 47.2
Accounts payable	25.1	27.5
Accrued expenses	84.9	56.3
Accrued salaries and bonuses	104.7	79.2
Deferred revenue	57.9	55.8
Other current liabilities	90.6	98.9
Total current liabilities	646.5	364.9

NOTES TO CONSOLIDATED FINANCIAL STATEMENTS

1. Summary of Significant Accounting Policies (in part)

Revenue Recognition and Deferred Revenue. Revenue is recognized when persuasive evidence of an arrangement exists, collectibility of arrangement consideration is reasonably assured, the arrangement fees are fixed or determinable and delivery of the product or service has been completed. A significant portion of our revenue is derived from the provision of information services to our customers on a transaction basis, in which case revenue is recognized, assuming all other revenue recognition criteria are met, when the services are provided. A smaller portion of our revenues relates to subscription-based contracts under which a customer pays a preset fee for a predetermined or unlimited number of transactions or services provided during the subscription period, generally one year. Revenue related to subscription-based contracts having a preset number of transactions is recognized as the services are provided, using an effective transaction rate as the actual transactions are completed. Any remaining revenue related to unfulfilled units is not recognized until the end of the related contract's subscription period. Revenue related to subscription-based contracts having an unlimited volume is recognized ratably during the contract term. Revenue is recorded net of sales taxes.

If at the outset of an arrangement, we determine that collectibility is not reasonably assured, revenue is deferred until the earlier of when collectibility becomes probable or the receipt of payment. If there is uncertainty as to the customer's acceptance of our deliverables, revenue is not recognized until the earlier of receipt of customer acceptance or expiration of the acceptance period. If at the outset of an arrangement, we determine that the arrangement fee is not fixed or determinable, revenue is deferred until the arrangement fee becomes fixed or determinable, assuming all other revenue recognition criteria have been met.

The determination of certain of our tax management services revenue requires the use of estimates, principally related to transaction volumes in instances where these volumes are reported to us by our clients on a monthly basis in arrears. In these instances, we estimate transaction volumes based on average actual volumes reported in the past. Differences between our estimates and actual final volumes reported are recorded in the period in which actual volumes are reported. We have not experienced significant variances between our estimates and actual reported volumes in the past. We monitor actual volumes to ensure that we will continue to make reasonable estimates in the future. If we determine that we are unable to make reasonable future estimates, revenue may be deferred until actual customer data is obtained. Also within our Workforce Solutions operating segment, the fees for certain of our tax credits and incentives revenue are based on a portion of the credit delivered to our clients. Revenue for these arrangements is recognized based on the achievement of milestones, upon calculation of the credit, or when the credit is utilized by our client, depending on the provisions of the client contract.

We have certain offerings that are sold as multiple element arrangements. The multiple elements may include consumer or commercial information, file updates for certain solutions, services provided by our decisioning technologies personnel, training services, statistical models and other services. To account for each of these elements separately, the delivered elements must have stand-alone value to our customer. For certain customer contracts, the total arrangement fee is allocated to the undelivered elements. If we are unable to unbundle the arrangement into separate units of accounting, we apply one of the accounting policies described above. This may lead to the arrangement consideration being recognized as the final contract element is delivered to our customer or ratably over the contract.

Many of our multiple element arrangements involve the delivery of services generated by a combination of services provided by one or more of our operating segments. No individual information service impacts the value or usage of other information services included in an arrangement and each service can be sold alone or, in most cases, purchased from another vendor without affecting the quality of use or value to the customer of the other information services included in the arrangement. Some of our products require the development of interfaces or platforms by our decisioning technologies personnel that allow our customers to interact with our proprietary information databases. These development services do not meet the requirement for having stand-alone value, thus any related development fees are deferred when billed and are recognized over the expected period that the customer will benefit from the related decisioning technologies service. Revenue from the provision of statistical models is recognized as the service is provided and accepted, assuming all other revenue recognition criteria are met. The direct costs of set up of a customer are capitalized and amortized as a cost of service during the term of the related customer contract.

We have some multiple element arrangements that include software. We recognize the elements for which we have established vendor specific objective evidence at fair value upon delivery, in accordance with the applicable guidance.

We record revenue on a net basis for those sales in which we have in substance acted as an agent or broker in the transaction.

Deferred revenue consists of amounts billed in excess of revenue recognized on sales of our information services relating generally to the deferral of subscription fees and arrangement consideration from elements not meeting the criteria for having stand-alone value discussed above. Deferred revenues are subsequently recognized as revenue in accordance with our revenue recognition policies.

ENVIRONMENT

2.126 REPUBLIC SERVICES, INC. (DEC)
CONSOLIDATED BALANCE SHEETS (in part)

(In millions, except per share data)

	December 31, 2012	December 31, 2011
Liabilities and Stockholders' Equity		
Current liabilities:		
Accounts payable	$ 474.5	$ 563.6
Notes payable and current maturities of long-term debt	19.4	34.8
Deferred revenue	313.2	290.2
Accrued landfill and environmental costs, current portion	195.5	184.2
Accrued interest	68.8	72.2
Other accrued liabilities	623.6	752.5
Total current liabilities	1,695.0	1,897.5

NOTES TO CONSOLIDATED FINANCIAL STATEMENTS

2. Summary of Significant Accounting Policies (in part)

Management's Estimates and Assumptions

In preparing our financial statements, we make numerous estimates and assumptions that affect the amounts reported in these financial statements and accompanying notes. We must make these estimates and assumptions because certain information that we use is dependent on future events, cannot be calculated with a high degree of precision from data available or simply cannot be readily calculated based on generally accepted methodologies. In preparing our financial statements, the more critical and subjective areas that deal with the greatest amount of uncertainty relate to our accounting for our long-lived assets, including recoverability, landfill development costs, and final capping, closure and post-closure costs, our valuation allowances for accounts receivable and deferred tax assets, our liabilities for potential litigation, claims and assessments, our liabilities for environmental remediation, employee benefit plans, deferred taxes, uncertain tax positions, self-insurance reserves, and our estimates of the fair values of assets acquired and liabilities assumed in any acquisition. Each of these items is discussed in more detail elsewhere in these Notes to the Consolidated Financial Statements. Our actual results may differ significantly from our estimates.

Landfill and Environmental Costs (in part)

Environmental Liabilities

We are subject to an array of laws and regulations relating to the protection of the environment, and we remediate sites in the ordinary course of our business. Under current laws and regulations, we may be responsible for environmental remediation at sites that we either own or operate, including sites that we have acquired, or sites where we have (or a company that we have acquired has) delivered waste. Our environmental remediation liabilities primarily include costs associated with remediating groundwater, surface water and soil contamination, as well as controlling and containing methane gas migration and the related legal costs. To estimate our ultimate liability at these sites, we evaluate several factors, including the nature and extent of contamination at each identified site, the required remediation methods, the apportionment of responsibility among the potentially responsible parties and the financial viability of those parties. We accrue for costs associated with environmental remediation obligations when such costs are probable and reasonably estimable in accordance with accounting for loss contingencies. We periodically review the status of all environmental matters and update our estimates of the likelihood of and future expenditures for remediation as necessary. Changes in the liabilities resulting from these reviews are recognized currently in earnings in the period in which the adjustment is known. Adjustments to estimates are reasonably possible in the near term and may result in changes to recorded amounts. With the exception of those obligations assumed in the acquisition of Allied that were recorded at estimated fair values, environmental obligations are recorded on an undiscounted basis. We have not reduced the liabilities we have recorded for recoveries from other potentially responsible parties or insurance companies.

8. Landfill and Environmental Costs

As of December 31, 2012, we owned or operated 191 active solid waste landfills with total available disposal capacity of approximately 4.8 billion in-place cubic yards. Additionally, we currently have post-closure responsibility for 128 closed landfills.

Accrued Landfill and Environmental Costs

A summary of our landfill and environmental liabilities as of December 31 is as follows:

	2012	2011
Landfill final capping, closure and post-closure liabilities	$1,052.4	$1,037.0
Remediation	563.7	543.7
Total accrued landfill and environmental costs	1,616.1	1,580.7
Less: Current portion	(195.5)	(184.2)
Long-term portion	$1,420.6	$1,396.5

Final Capping, Closure and Post-Closure Costs

The following table summarizes the activity in our asset retirement obligation liabilities, which include liabilities for final capping, closure and post-closure, for the years ended December 31:

	2012	2011	2010
Asset retirement obligation liabilities, beginning of year	$1,037.0	$1,046.5	$1,074.5
Non-cash additions	33.8	33.9	31.4
Acquisitions and other adjustments	(14.6)	15.8	(3.0)
Asset retirement obligation adjustments	(4.6)	(31.5)	(27.9)
Payments	(77.6)	(105.7)	(111.3)
Accretion expense	78.4	78.0	80.5
Adjustments to liabilities related to assets held for sale	—	—	2.3
Asset retirement obligation liabilities, end of period	1,052.4	1,037.0	1,046.5
Less: Current portion	(110.4)	(85.2)	(93.9)
Long-term portion	$ 942.0	$ 951.8	$ 952.6

The initial liabilities recorded as part of the Allied acquisition were developed using provisional amounts based upon information available at that time. During 2009, we gathered and assessed new information about the facts and circumstances surrounding our sites, and, as a result, increased the fair value of our closure and post-closure reserves by $72.3 million. The amounts we have recorded for these obligations are not comparable to the amounts Allied recorded. As part of the initial application of purchase accounting, we have recorded these obligations at their estimated fair values, inflated them to the expected payment date and then discounted the obligations using our credit-adjusted, risk-free rate at the time of the acquisition of 9.75%. Any further adjustments to our final capping, closure and post-closure liabilities will be reflected prospectively in our consolidated statement of income in the periods in which such adjustments become known.

We review our landfill asset retirement obligations annually. As a result, we recorded a net increase in amortization expense of of $4.9 million for 2012 and a net decrease in amortization expense of $9.6 million and $10.2 million for 2011 and 2010, respectively, primarily related to changes in estimates and assumptions concerning the anticipated waste flow, cost and timing of future final capping, closure and post-closure activities.

The fair value of assets that are legally restricted for purposes of settling final capping, closure and post-closure obligations was approximately $54.8 million at December 31, 2012 and is included in restricted cash and marketable securities in our consolidated balance sheet.

The expected future payments for final capping, closure and post-closure as of December 31, 2012 are as follows:

2013	$ 110.4
2014	110.1
2015	109.4
2016	77.0
2017	76.4
Thereafter	4,829.6
	$5,312.9

The estimated remaining final capping, closure and post-closure expenditures presented above are not inflated and not discounted and reflect the estimated future payments for liabilities incurred and recorded as of December 31, 2012.

Environmental Remediation Liabilities

We accrue for remediation costs when they become probable and can be reasonably estimated. There can sometimes be a range of reasonable estimates of the costs associated with remediation of a site. In these cases, we use the amount within the range that constitutes our best estimate. If no amount within the range appears to be a better estimate than any other, we use the amount that is at the low end of such range. It is reasonably possible that we will need to adjust the liabilities recorded for remediation to reflect the effects of new or additional information, to the extent such information impacts the costs, timing or duration of the required actions. If we used the reasonably possible high ends of our ranges, our aggregate potential remediation liability at December 31, 2012 would be approximately $374 million higher than the amounts recorded. Future changes in our estimates of the cost, timing or duration of the required actions could have a material adverse effect on our consolidated financial position, results of operations or cash flows.

The following table summarizes the activity in our environmental remediation liabilities for the years ended December 31:

	2012	2011	2010
Remediation liabilities, beginning of year	$543.7	$552.1	$554.1
Acquisitions and other adjustments	—	—	1.5
Additions charged to expense	62.4	3.6	17.9
Payments	(73.1)	(45.0)	(50.5)
Accretion expense (non-cash interest expense)	30.7	33.0	29.1
Remediation liabilities, end of period	563.7	543.7	552.1
Less: Current portion	(85.1)	(99.0)	(88.1)
Long-term portion	$478.6	$444.7	$464.0

The expected undiscounted future payments for remediation costs as of December 31, 2012 are as follows:

2013	$ 85.1
2014	60.7
2015	38.4
2016	29.6
2017	29.3
Thereafter	356.4
	$599.5

The following is a discussion of certain of our significant remediation matters:

Missouri Closed Landfill. During 2012, we encountered certain environmental issues at a closed landfill in Missouri. During 2012, we recorded a charge of $74.1 million to manage the remediation area as well as future monitoring of the site. The remediation liability for this site is $ 64.2 million as of December 31, 2012, of which $ 14.5 million is expected to be paid during 2013. We believe the reasonably possible range of loss for remediation costs is $ 50 million to $ 240 million.

Countywide Landfill. In September 2009, Republic Services of Ohio II, LLC entered into Final Findings and Orders with the Ohio Environmental Protection Agency that require us to implement a comprehensive operation and maintenance program to manage the remediation area at the Countywide Recycling and Disposal Facility (Countywide). The remediation liability for Countywide recorded as of December 31, 2012 is $52.4 million, of which $4.4 million is expected to be paid during 2013. We believe the reasonably possible range of loss for remediation costs is $50 million to $71 million.

Congress Landfill. In August 2010, Congress Development Company agreed with the State of Illinois to have a Final Consent Order (Final Order) entered by the Circuit Court of Illinois, Cook County. Pursuant to the Final Order, we have agreed to continue to implement certain remedial activities at the Congress Landfill. The remediation liability recorded as of December 31, 2012 is $83.4 million, of which $7.5 million is expected to be paid during 2013. We believe the reasonably possible range of loss for remediation costs is $53 million to $153 million.

It is reasonably possible that we will need to adjust the liabilities noted above to reflect the effects of new or additional information, to the extent that such information impacts the costs, timing or duration of the required actions. Future changes in our estimates of the costs, timing or duration of the required actions could have a material adverse effect on our consolidated financial position, results of operations or cash flows.

2.127 TELEFLEX INCORPORATED (DEC)

CONSOLIDATED BALANCE SHEETS (in part)

(Dollars and shares in thousands)	December 31, 2012	2011
Liabilities and Equity		
Current liabilities		
Notes payable	$ 4,700	$ 4,986
Accounts payable	75,165	67,092
Accrued expenses	65,064	74,207
Current portion of contingent consideration	23,693	3,953
Payroll and benefit-related liabilities	74,586	64,386
Derivative liabilities	598	633
Accrued interest	9,418	10,960
Income taxes payable	15,573	21,084
Current liability for uncertain tax positions	4,684	22,656
Deferred tax liabilities	924	1,050
Total current liabilities	274,405	271,007

NOTES TO CONSOLIDATED FINANCIAL STATEMENTS

(Dollars in millions, except per share)

Note 1—Summary of Significant Accounting Policies (in part)

Use of estimates: The preparation of financial statements in conformity with accounting principles generally accepted in the United States of America requires management to make estimates and assumptions that affect the reported amounts of assets and liabilities and disclosure of contingent assets and liabilities at the date of the financial statements and the reported amounts of net revenues and expenses during the reporting period. Actual results could differ from those estimates.

Note 3—Acquisitions

The Company made the following acquisitions during 2012, all of which were accounted for as business combinations:

- On October 23, 2012, the Company acquired substantially all of the assets of LMA International N.V. ("LMA"), a global provider of laryngeal masks whose products are used in anesthesia and emergency care. The Company paid $292.2 million in cash as initial consideration for the business. On October 23, 2012, in a separate transaction, the Company also acquired the LMA branded laryngeal mask supraglottic airway business and certain other products in the United Kingdom, Ireland and Channel Islands from the shareholders of Intravent Direct Limited and affiliates for $19.9 million in cash. In February 2013, the Company received $1.5 million in cash from the sellers of the LMA business related to a working capital adjustment provided for under the terms of the purchase agreement. These acquisitions complement the anesthesia product portfolio in the Company's Critical Care division.
- On June 22, 2012, the Company acquired Hotspur Technologies, a developer of catheter-based technologies designed to restore blood flow in patients with obstructed vessels. The acquisition of this business complements the dialysis access product line in the Company's Cardiac Care division. The Company paid $15.0 million in cash as initial consideration for the business.
- On May 22, 2012, the Company acquired Semprus BioSciences, a biomedical company that developed a long-lasting, covalently bonded, non-leaching polymer designed to reduce infections and thrombus related complications. While the Company will explore opportunities to apply this technology to a broad array of its product offerings, the initial focus for the technology will be with respect to vascular devices within the Company's Critical Care division. The Company paid $30.0 million in cash as initial consideration for the business.
- On May 3, 2012, the Company acquired substantially all of the assets of Axiom Technology Partners, LLC, constituting its EFx laparoscopic fascial closure system, which is designed for the closure of abdominal trocar defects through which access ports and instruments were used during laparoscopic surgeries. The acquisition of this business complements the surgical closure product line in the Company's Surgical Care division. The Company paid $7.5 million in cash as initial consideration for the business.
- On April 5, 2012, the Company acquired the EZ-Blocker product line, a single-use catheter used to perform lung isolation and one-lung ventilation. The acquisition of this product line complements the Anesthesia product portfolio in the Company's Critical Care division. The Company paid $3.3 million in cash as initial consideration for the business.

In connection with the acquisitions, the Company agreed to pay contingent consideration based on the achievement of specified objectives, including regulatory approvals and sales targets. The range of undiscounted amounts the Company could be required to pay under these contingent consideration arrangements is between $2.0 million to $90.0 million.

The total fair value of consideration for the acquisitions is estimated at $422.2 million, which includes the initial payments of $367.9 million in cash and the estimated fair value of the contingent consideration to be paid to the sellers of $55.8 million, partially offset by a $1.5 million favorable working capital adjustment related to the LMA acquisition. The fair value of each component of contingent consideration was estimated based on the probability of achieving the specified objective using a probability-weighted discounted cash flow model. This fair value measurement is based on significant inputs not observed in the market and thus represents a Level 3 measurement as defined in connection with the fair value hierarchy (see Note 11, "Fair value measurements"). Any future change in the estimated fair value of the contingent consideration will be recognized in selling, general and administrative expenses in the statement of income for the period in which the estimated fair value changes. A change in fair value of the contingent consideration could have a material effect on the Company's results of operations and financial position for the period in which the change in estimate occurs.

Transaction expenses associated with the acquisitions, which are included in selling, general and administrative expenses on the consolidated statements of income (loss) were $7.2 million for the year ended December 31, 2012. The Company has recorded an aggregate segment operating loss of approximately $8.1 million in connection with the businesses acquired in 2012. The loss is primarily related to operating losses associated with the late-stage technology acquisitions (approximately $12.7 million). The results of operations of the acquired businesses and assets are included in the consolidated statements of income (loss) from their respective acquisition date. Pro forma information is not presented as the operations of the acquired businesses are not significant compared to the overall operations of the Company.

The following table presents the purchase price allocation among the assets acquired and liabilities assumed in the acquisitions that occurred during the year ended December 31, 2012:

(Dollars in millions)	
Assets	
Current assets	$ 62.8
Property, plant and equipment	22.0
Intangible assets:	
Intellectual property	70.7
Tradenames	65.3
In-process research and development ("IPR&D")	46.9
Customer lists	44.6
Goodwill	164.0
Total assets acquired	476.3
Less:	
Current liabilities	21.4
Deferred tax liabilities	24.3
Other long term liabilities	8.4
Liabilities assumed	54.1
Net assets acquired	$422.2

In the third quarter of 2012, the Company refined the purchase price allocation, principally with respect to contingent consideration, due to changes in probabilities of achieving specified objectives and changes in discount rates. These changes also impacted the fair values of the acquired intangibles and deferred taxes. The Company is continuing to evaluate the initial purchase price allocation of all 2012 acquisitions. Further adjustments may be necessary as a result of the Company's assessment of additional information related to the fair values of assets acquired and liabilities assumed.

Certain assets acquired in the acquisitions constitute intangible assets, apart from goodwill. The estimated fair values of intangible assets acquired include intellectual property of $70.7 million, tradenames of $65.3 million, in-process research and development (IPR&D) of $46.9 million and customer lists of $44.6 million. Intellectual property has useful lives ranging from 10 to 20 years, customer lists have a useful life of 15 years and finite tradenames have a useful life of 10 years. Tradenames of approximately $63.3 million have an indefinite useful life. IPR&D has an indefinite life and is not amortized until completion and development of the related project, at which time the IPR&D becomes an amortizable asset. If the related project is not completed in a timely manner, the Company may incur an impairment charge related to the IPR&D, calculated as the excess of the asset's carrying value over its fair value. The goodwill resulting from the acquisitions primarily reflects the expected revenue growth attributable to anticipated increased market penetration from future products and customers. Goodwill and the step-up in basis of the intangible assets in connection with the acquisitions are not deductible for tax purposes.

Note 11—Fair Value Measurement (in part)

The following tables provide the financial assets and liabilities carried at fair value measured on a recurring basis as of December 31, 2012 and December 31, 2011:

(Dollars in thousands)	Total Carrying Value at December 31, 2012	Quoted Prices in Active Markets (Level 1)	Significant Other Observable Inputs (Level 2)	Significant Unobservable Inputs (Level 3)
Investments in marketable securities	$ 4,785	$ 4,785	$ —	$ —
Derivative assets	1,279	—	1,279	—
Derivative liabilities	598	—	598	—
Contingent consideration liabilities	51,196	—	—	51,196

(Dollars in thousands)	Total Carrying Value at December 31, 2011	Quoted Prices in Active Markets (Level 1)	Significant Other Observable Inputs (Level 2)	Significant Unobservable Inputs (Level 3)
Cash and cash equivalents	$40,005	$40,005	$ —	$ —
Bonds—foreign government	880	880	—	—
Investments in marketable securities	4,189	4,189	—	—
Derivative assets	204	—	204	—
Derivative liabilities	633	—	633	—
Contingent consideration liabilities	9,676	—	—	9,676

The following table provides a reconciliation of changes in Level 3 financial liabilities measured at fair value on a recurring basis for the years ended December 31, 2012 and December 31, 2011:

	Contingent Consideration	
(Dollars in thousands)	2012	2011
Beginning balance	$ 9,676	$ —
Initial estimate upon acquisition	58,895	15,400
Payment	(18,426)	(6,000)
Revaluations	1,055	276
Translation adjustment	(4)	—
Ending balance	$ 51,196	$ 9,676

Valuation Techniques Used to Determine Fair Value (in part)

The Company's financial liabilities valued based upon Level 3 inputs are comprised of contingent consideration arrangements pertaining to the Company's acquisitions. The Company accounts for contingent consideration in accordance with applicable accounting guidance pertaining to business combinations. The Company is contractually obligated to pay contingent consideration upon the achievement of specified objectives, including regulatory approvals, sales targets and, in some instances, the passage of time, referred to as milestone payments, and therefore recorded contingent consideration liabilities at the time of the acquisitions. The Company updates its assumptions each reporting period based on new developments and records such amounts at fair value based on the revised assumptions, until such consideration is satisfied through payment upon the achievement of the specified objectives or eliminated upon failure to achieve the specified objectives.

It is estimated that milestone payments will occur in 2013 and may extend until 2018 or later. As of December 31, 2012, the range of undiscounted amounts the Company could be required to pay for contingent consideration arrangements is between $7.0 million and $94.4 million. The Company has determined the fair value of the liabilities for the contingent consideration based on a probability-weighted discounted cash flow analysis. This fair value measurement is based on significant inputs not observable in the market and thus represents a Level 3 measurement within the fair value hierarchy. The fair value of the contingent consideration liability associated with future milestone payments was based on several factors including:

- estimated cash flows projected from the success of market launches;
- the estimated time and resources needed to complete the development of the acquired technologies;
- the uncertainty of obtaining regulatory approvals within the required time periods; and
- the risk adjusted discount rate for fair value measurement.

The following table provides information regarding the valuation techniques and inputs used in determining the fair value of assets or liabilities categorized as Level 3 measurements:

	Valuation Technique	Unobservable Input	Range (Weighted Average)
Contingent consideration	Discounted cash flow	Discount rate	2.8%–10%(6%)
		Probability of payment	0–100%(60%)

As of December 31, 2012, of the $51.2 million of total contingent consideration, the Company has recorded approximately $23.7 million in Current portion of contingent consideration and the remaining $27.5 million in Other liabilities.

LITIGATION

2.128 DEAN FOODS COMPANY (DEC)

CONSOLIDATED BALANCE SHEETS (in part)

	December 31	
(Dollars in thousands, except share data)	2012	2011
Liabilities and Stockholders' Equity (Deficit)		
Current liabilities:		
Accounts payable and accrued expenses	$1,192,940	$1,127,717
Income tax payable	1,186	—
Current portion of debt	25,535	202,292
Current portion of litigation settlements	20,000	60,838
Liabilities of discontinued operations	101,332	133,202
Total current liabilities	1,340,993	1,524,049

NOTES TO CONSOLIDATED FINANCIAL STATEMENTS

19. Commitments and Contingencies (in part)

Litigation, Investigations and Audits—We are not party to, nor are our properties the subject of, any material pending legal proceedings, other than as set forth below:

Tennessee Dairy Farmer Actions

On June 15, 2012, we received final approval of a settlement agreement with respect to a group of six antitrust class actions alleging that we and others in the milk industry worked together to limit the price Southeastern dairy farmers are paid for their raw milk and to deny these farmers access to fluid Grade A milk processing facilities. Under the settlement agreement, we agreed to pay a total of up to $140 million over a period of four to five years into a fund for distribution to dairy farmer class members in a number of Southeastern states. In the second quarter of 2011, we recorded a $131.3 million charge and a corresponding liability for the present value of our obligations under the original settlement agreement, based on imputed interest computed at a rate of 4.77%, which approximates our like-term incremental fixed rate borrowing cost.

Per the terms of the settlement agreement, on February 21, 2012, we made a payment of $60 million into an escrow account to be distributed following the Court's final approval, and issued a standby letter of credit in the amount of $80 million to support subsequent payments due under the agreement. The settlement agreement requires us to make a payment of up to $20 million on each of the following four anniversaries of the settlement agreement's final approval date. We expect to make the first installment payment in June 2013.

DERIVATIVES

2.129 THE SHAW GROUP INC. (AUG)

CONSOLIDATED BALANCE SHEETS (in part)

(In thousands, except share amounts)

	At August 31,	
	2012	2011
Liabilities and Shareholders' Equity		
Current liabilities:		
Accounts payable	$ 683,645	$ 822,476
Accrued salaries, wages and benefits	127,960	132,857
Other accrued liabilities	205,279	199,947
Advanced billings and billings in excess of costs and estimated earnings on uncompleted contracts	1,223,991	1,535,037
Japanese Yen-denominated bonds secured by Investment in Westinghouse	1,640,497	1,679,836
Interest rate swap contract on Japanese Yen-denominated bonds	13,370	27,059
Short-term debt and current maturities of long-term debt	10,416	349
Total current liabilities	3,905,158	4,397,561

Note 1—Description of Business and Summary of Significant Accounting Policies (in part)

Derivative Instruments and Hedging Activities

We account for derivative instruments and hedging activities in accordance with ASC 815, Derivatives and Hedging, which requires entities to recognize all derivative instruments as either assets or liabilities on the balance sheet at their respective fair values. If the derivative instrument is designated as a hedge, depending on the nature of the hedge, changes in the fair value of the derivative instrument are either offset against the change in fair value of the hedged assets, liabilities, or firm commitments through earnings or recognized in other comprehensive income until the hedged item is recognized in earnings. Recognized gains or losses on derivative instruments entered into to manage foreign exchange risk are included in foreign currency transaction gains (losses) on Japanese Yen-denominated bonds, net or in other foreign currency transaction gains (losses), net, in the consolidated statements of operations.

We do not enter into derivative instruments for speculative or trading purposes. We utilize forward foreign exchange contracts to reduce our risk from foreign currency price fluctuations related to firm or anticipated sales transactions, commitments to purchase or sell equipment, materials and/or services and interest payments denominated in a foreign currency. The net gain (loss) recognized in earnings from our hedges was approximately $(2.0) million, $4.7 million and $2.8 million at August 31, 2012, 2011 and 2010, respectively.

Note 4—Fair Value Measurements (in part)

We follow the authoritative guidance set forth in ASC 820, Fair Value Measurements and Disclosures, for fair value measurements relating to financial and nonfinancial assets and liabilities, including presentation of required disclosures in our consolidated financial statements. This guidance defines fair value as the price that would be received to sell an asset or paid to transfer a liability (an exit price) in an orderly transaction between market participants at the measurement date. The guidance also establishes a fair value hierarchy, which requires maximizing the use of observable inputs when measuring fair value.

The three levels of inputs that may be used are:
- Level 1: Quoted market prices in active markets for identical assets or liabilities.
- Level 2: Observable market based inputs or unobservable inputs that are corroborated by market data.
- Level 3: Significant unobservable inputs that are not corroborated by market data.

Assets and Liabilities Measured at Fair Value on a Recurring Basis

At August 31, 2012, our financial assets and liabilities measured at fair value on a recurring basis were as follows (in thousands):

| | Fair Value | Fair Value Measurements Using | | |
		(Level 1)	(Level 2)	(Level 3)
Assets:				
Short-term and restricted short-term investments				
Certificates of deposit	$253,493	$ —	$253,493	$—
Stock and bond mutual funds[a]	30,171	30,171	—	—
U.S. government and agency securities	603	—	603	—
Corporate bonds	36,626	—	36,626	—
Total	$320,893	$30,171	$290,722	$—
Liabilities:				
Interest rate swap contract	$ 13,370	$ —	$ 13,370	$—
Derivatives not designated as hedging instruments:				
Other current assets				
Foreign currency forward assets	$ 1,482	$ —	$ 1,482	$—
Other accrued liabilities				
Foreign currency forward liabilities	$ 158	$ —	$ 158	$—

[a] This class includes investments in a mutual fund that invests at least 80% of its assets in short-term bonds issued or guaranteed by U.S. government agencies and instrumentalities.

At August 31, 2011, our financial assets and liabilities measured at fair value on a recurring basis were as follows (in thousands):

		Fair Value Measurements Using		
	Fair Value	(Level 1)	(Level 2)	(Level 3)
Assets:				
Short-term and restricted short-term investments				
Certificates of deposit	$461,786	$ —	$461,786	$—
Stock and bond mutual funds[a]	6,473	6,473	—	—
U.S. government and agency securities	1,806	—	1,806	—
Corporate bonds	34,187	—	34,187	—
Total	$504,252	$ 6,473	$497,779	$—
Liabilities:				
Interest rate swap contract	$ 27,059	$ —	$ 27,059	$—
Derivatives not designated as hedging instruments:				
Other current assets				
Foreign currency forward assets	$ 1,955	$ —	$ 1,955	$—
Other accrued liabilities				
Foreign currency forward liabilities	$ 16	$ —	$ 16	$—

(a) This class includes investments in a mutual fund that invests at least 80% of its assets in short-term bonds issued or guaranteed by U.S. government agencies and instrumentalities.

The following are the primary valuation methodologies used for valuing our short-term and restricted short-term investments:
- Corporate bonds and U.S. government and agency securities: Valued at quoted prices in markets that are not active, broker dealer quotations or other methods by which all significant inputs are observable, either directly or indirectly.
- Stock and bond mutual funds: Valued at the net asset value of shares held at period end as quoted in the active market. These mutual funds contain no unusual terms or trade restrictions.
- Equity investments: Valued at the closing price of the shares held at period end as quoted in active markets.

We value the interest rate swap liability utilizing a discounted cash flow model that takes into consideration forward interest rates observable in the market and the counterparty's credit risk. Our counterparty to this instrument is a major U.S. bank. As discussed in Note 10—Debt and Revolving Lines of Credit, we designated the swap as a hedge against changes in cash flows attributable to changes in the benchmark interest rate related to our Westinghouse Bonds.

Note 10—Debt and Revolving Lines of Credit (in part)

Westinghouse Bonds

On October 13, 2006, NEH, our wholly owned, special purpose subsidiary, issued JPY 128.98 billion (equivalent to approximately $1.1 billion at the time of issuance) principal amount limited recourse bonds, maturing March 15, 2013, at a discount receiving approximately $1.0 billion in proceeds, excluding offering costs. NEH used the proceeds of these bonds to purchase the Westinghouse Equity for approximately $1.1 billion. The Westinghouse Bonds are limited recourse to us (except to NEH), are governed by the Bond Trust Deed and are collateralized primarily by the Westinghouse Equity, the JPY-denominated Put Options between NEH and Toshiba and the Principal Letter of credit, which cover interest owed to bond holders and the possible 3.3% principal exposure.

The holders of the Westinghouse Bond may have the ability to cause us to put our Westinghouse Equity back to Toshiba as a result of the occurrence of a "Toshiba Event" (as defined under the Bond Trust Deed) that occurred in May 2009. A Toshiba Event is not an event of default or other violation of the Bond Trust Deed or the Put Option Agreements, but due to the Toshiba Event, the Westinghouse Bond holders had an opportunity to direct us to exercise the Put Options, through which we would have received the pre-determined JPY-denominated put price whose proceeds must be used to pay off the JPY-denominated Westinghouse Bond debt. To do so, a "supermajority" of the Westinghouse bond holders representing a majority of not less than an aggregate 75% of the principal amount outstanding must have passed a resolution instructing the bond trustee to direct us to exercise the Put Options.

Because the holders of the bonds had the ability to require us to exercise the Put Options to retire the bonds, we reclassified the Westinghouse Bonds from long-term debt to short-term debt and our Investment in Westinghouse to current assets in May 2009.

The Put Options, executed as part of the Investment in Westinghouse transaction, provide NEH the option to sell all or part of the Westinghouse Equity to Toshiba for a pre-determined JPY-denominated put price. On October 6, 2012, NEH exercised its Put Options to sell the Westinghouse Equity to Toshiba. Under the terms of the put option agreements, the Put Options will be cash settled on or before January 4, 2013 with the proceeds deposited in trust to fund retirement of the Westinghouse Bonds on March 15, 2013.

The Put Options require Toshiba to purchase the Westinghouse Equity at a price equivalent to not less than 96.7 percent of the principal amount of the bonds, which was approximately $1,586.4 million (JPY 124.7 billion at August 31, 2012). NEH will fund up to the 3.3 percent shortfall of the principal amount of the bonds, which was approximately $54.1 million (JPY 4.3 billion) at August 31, 2012. We may recognize a non-operating gain once the Put Options are settled, resulting principally from foreign exchange movements. If the bonds would have been repaid at August 31, 2012, from an early exercise of the Put Options, the gain would have been approximately $504.1 million pre-tax. The actual gain or loss will be determined at settlement.

Because any proceeds from the repurchase of the Westinghouse Equity (including funds received in connection with settlement of the Put Options) must be used to repay the Westinghouse Bonds, ultimate settlement of the Westinghouse Bonds may be significantly influenced by Toshiba's financial condition as well as conditions in the general credit markets.

The exchange rate of the JPY to the USD at August 31, 2012, and August 31, 2011, was 78.6 and 76.8, respectively.

The Westinghouse Bonds consisted of the following (in thousands):

	August 31, 2012	August 31, 2011
Westinghouse Bonds, face value 50.98 billion JPY due March 15, 2013; interest only payments; coupon rate of 2.20%;	$ 426,875	$ 426,875
Westinghouse Bonds, face value 78 billion JPY due March 15, 2013; interest only payments; coupon rate of 0.70% above the six-month JPY LIBOR rate (0.33% at August 31, 2012)	653,125	653,125
Increase in debt due to foreign currency transaction adjustments since date of issuance	560,497	599,836
Total Westinghouse debt	$1,640,497	$1,679,836

On October 16, 2006, we entered into an interest rate swap agreement through March 15, 2013, in the aggregate notional amount of JPY 78 billion. We designated the swap as a hedge against changes in cash flows attributable to changes in the benchmark interest rate. Under the agreement, we make fixed interest payments at a rate of 2.398%, and we receive a variable interest payment equal to the six-month JPY London Interbank Offered Rate (LIBOR) plus a fixed margin of 0.70%, effectively fixing our interest rate on the floating rate portion of the JPY 78 billion Westinghouse Bonds at 2.398%. At August 31, 2012, and August 31, 2011, the fair value of the swap totaled approximately $13.4 million and $27.1 million, respectively, and is included as a current liability and in accumulated other comprehensive loss, net of deferred taxes, in the accompanying consolidated balance sheets. There was no material ineffectiveness of our interest rate swap for the three and nine months ended August 31, 2012.

RETURNS, REBATES AND INCENTIVES

2.130 ROCKWELL AUTOMATION, INC. (SEP)
CONSOLIDATED BALANCE SHEET (in part)

(In millions)

	September 30,	
	2012	2011
Liabilities and Shareowners' Equity		
Current liabilities:		
Short-term debt	$ 157.0	$ —
Accounts payable	547.6	455.1
Compensation and benefits	246.4	319.6
Advance payments from customers and deferred revenue	204.1	189.0
Customer returns, rebates and incentives	168.7	154.0
Other current liabilities	207.8	212.2
Total current liabilities	1,531.6	1,329.9

NOTES TO CONSOLIDATED FINANCIAL STATEMENTS

1. Basis of Presentation and Accounting Policies (in part)

Use of Estimates

The consolidated financial statements have been prepared in accordance with accounting principles generally accepted in the United States (U.S. GAAP), which require us to make estimates and assumptions that affect the reported amounts of assets and liabilities at the date of the consolidated financial statements and revenues and expenses during the periods reported. Actual results could differ from those estimates. We use estimates in accounting for, among other items, customer returns, rebates and incentives; allowance for doubtful accounts; excess and obsolete inventory; share-based compensation; acquisitions; product warranty obligations; retirement benefits; litigation, claims and contingencies, including environmental matters, conditional asset retirement obligations and contractual indemnifications; and income taxes. We account for changes to estimates and assumptions prospectively when warranted by factually based experience.

Returns, Rebates and Incentives

Our primary incentive program provides distributors with cash rebates or account credits based on agreed amounts that vary depending on the customer to whom our distributor ultimately sells the product. We also offer various other incentive programs that provide distributors and direct sale customers with cash rebates, account credits or additional products and services based on meeting specified program criteria. Certain distributors are offered a right to return product, subject to contractual limitations.

We record accruals for customer returns, rebates and incentives at the time of sale based primarily on historical experience. Returns, rebates and incentives are recognized as a reduction of sales if distributed in cash or customer account credits. Rebates and incentives are recognized in cost of sales for additional products and services to be provided. Accruals are reported as a current liability in our balance sheet or, where a right of offset exists, as a reduction of accounts receivable.

ASSET RETIREMENT OBLIGATION

2.131 THE MOSAIC COMPANY (MAY)
CONSOLIDATED BALANCE SHEETS (in part)

In millions, except per share amounts

	May 31,	
	2012	2011
Liabilities and Equity		
Current liabilities:		
Short-term debt	$ 42.5	$ 23.6
Current maturities of long-term debt	0.5	48.0
Accounts payable	912.4	941.1
Accrued liabilities	899.9	843.6
Deferred income taxes	62.4	72.2
Total current liabilities	1,917.7	1,928.5

NOTES TO CONSOLIDATED FINANCIAL STATEMENTS

Tables in millions, except per share amounts

3. Summary of Significant Accounting Policies (in part)

Accounting Estimates

Preparation of the Consolidated Financial Statements in conformity with U.S. GAAP requires management to make estimates and assumptions that affect the reported amounts of assets and liabilities and disclosure of contingent assets and liabilities at the date of the financial statements and the reported amounts of revenues and expenses during the reporting periods. The more significant estimates made by management relate to the recoverability of non-current assets including goodwill, the useful lives and net realizable values of long-lived assets, environmental and reclamation liabilities including asset retirement obligations ("AROs"), the costs of our employee benefit obligations for pension plans and postretirement benefits, income tax related accounts including the valuation allowance against deferred income tax assets, Canadian resource tax and royalties, inventory valuation and accruals for pending legal and environmental matters. Actual results could differ from these estimates.

Asset Retirement Obligations

We recognize AROs in the period in which we have an existing legal obligation associated with the retirement of a tangible long-lived asset, and the amount of the liability can be reasonably estimated. The ARO is recognized at fair value when the liability is incurred. Upon initial recognition of a liability, that cost is capitalized as part of the related long-lived asset and depreciated on a straight-line basis over the remaining estimated useful life of the related asset. The liability is adjusted in subsequent periods through accretion expense which represents the increase in the present value of the liability due to the passage of time. Such depreciation and accretion expenses are included in cost of goods sold for operating facilities and other operating expense for indefinitely closed facilities.

4. Other Financial Statement Data (in part)

The following provides additional information concerning selected balance sheet accounts:

	May 31,	
(In millions)	2012	2011
Accrued Liabilities		
Non-income taxes	$ 78.5	$132.6
Payroll and employee benefits	119.6	116.3
Asset retirement obligations	87.0	90.6
Customer prepayments	323.0	243.2
Other	291.8	260.9
	$899.9	$843.6

15. Accounting for Asset Retirement Obligations

We recognize AROs in the period in which we have an existing legal obligation associated with the retirement of a tangible long-lived asset, and the amount of the liability can be reasonably estimated. The ARO is recognized at fair value when the liability is incurred with a corresponding increase in the carrying amount of the related long lived asset. We depreciate the tangible asset over its estimated useful life. Our legal obligations related to asset retirement require us to: (i) reclaim lands disturbed by mining as a condition to receive permits to mine phosphate ore reserves; (ii) treat low pH process water in phosphogypsum management systems (the "*Gypstacks*") to neutralize acidity; (iii) close and monitor Gypstacks at our Florida and Louisiana facilities at the end of their useful lives; (iv) remediate certain other conditional obligations; and (v) remove all surface structures and equipment, plug and abandon mine shafts, contour and revegetate, as necessary, and monitor for five years after closing our Carlsbad, New Mexico facility. The estimated liability for these legal obligations is based on the estimated cost to satisfy the above obligations which is discounted using a credit-adjusted risk-free rate.

A reconciliation of our AROs is as follows:

| (In millions) | May 31, | |
	2012	2011
AROs, beginning of year	$573.1	$525.9
Liabilities incurred	27.8	35.0
Liabilities settled	(98.4)	(73.1)
Accretion expense	32.4	31.6
Revisions in estimated cash flows	65.4	53.7
AROs, end of year	600.3	573.1
Less current portion	87.0	90.6
	$513.3	$482.5

Long-Term Debt

PRESENTATION

2.132 FASB ASC 470 addresses classification determination for specific debt obligations. FASB ASC 470-10-45-11 states that the current liability classification is intended to include long-term obligations that are or will be callable by the creditor either because the debtors' violation of a provision of the debt agreement at the balance sheet date makes the obligation callable, or the violation, if not cured within a specified grace period, will make the obligation callable. Accordingly, such callable obligations should be classified as current liabilities, unless one of the following conditions is met:

- The creditor has waived or subsequently lost the right to demand payment for more than one year, or operating cycle if longer, from the balance sheet date. For example, the debtor may have cured the violation after the balance sheet date, and the obligation is not callable at the time the financial statements are issued or available to be issued.
- For long-term obligations containing a grace period within which the debtor may cure the violation, it is probable that the violation will be cured within that period, thus preventing the obligation from becoming callable.

DISCLOSURE

2.133 FASB ASC 470 requires, for each of the five years following the date of the latest balance sheet presented, disclosure of the combined aggregate amount of maturities and sinking fund requirements for all long-term borrowings. In addition, FASB ASC 440, *Commitments*, requires disclosure of terms and conditions provided in loan agreements, such as assets pledged as collateral and covenants to limit additional debt, maintain working capital, and restrict dividends. Regulation S-X has similar or expanded requirements for matters such as debt details, assets subject to lien, defaults, dividend restrictions, and changes in long-term debt.

2.134 FASB ASC 825 requires disclosure of both the fair value and bases for estimating the fair value of long-term debt, unless it is not practicable to estimate the value.

UNSECURED

2.135 LEAR CORPORATION (DEC)
CONSOLIDATED BALANCE SHEETS (in part)

(In millions, except share data)

	December 31,	
	2012	2011
Liabilities and Equity		
Current liabilities:		
Accounts payable and drafts	$2,233.0	$2,014.3
Accrued liabilities	983.9	1,049.2
Total current liabilities	3,216.9	3,063.5
Long-term liabilities:		
Long-term debt	626.3	695.4
Other	738.7	690.9
Total long-term liabilities	1,365.0	1,386.3

NOTES TO CONSOLIDATED FINANCIAL STATEMENTS

(7) Long-Term Debt (in part)

A summary of long-term debt and the related weighted average interest rates is shown below (in millions):

Debt Instrument	December 31, 2012		December 31, 2011	
	Long-Term Debt	Weighted Average Interest Rate	Long-Term Debt	Weighted Average Interest Rate
7.875% Senior Notes due 2018	$313.4	8.00%	$347.9	8.00%
8.125% Senior Notes due 2020	312.9	8.25%	347.5	8.25%
Long-term debt	$626.3		$695.4	

Senior Notes

As of December 31, 2012, the Company's long-term debt consisted of $315 million in aggregate principal amount of senior unsecured notes due 2018 at a stated coupon rate of 7.875% (the "2018 Notes") and $315 million in aggregate principal amount of senior unsecured notes due 2020 at a stated coupon rate of 8.125% (the "2020 Notes" and together with the 2018 Notes, the "Notes"). The 2018 Notes were priced at 99.276% of par, resulting in a yield to maturity of 8.00%, and the 2020 Notes were priced at 99.164% of par, resulting in a yield to maturity of 8.25%. These Notes were issued on March 26, 2010, and the net proceeds from issuance, together with existing cash on hand, were used to repay in full an aggregate amount of $925.0 million of term loans provided under the Company's first and second lien credit agreements (described below).

On August 24, 2012, the Company redeemed 10% of the original aggregate principal amount of each of the 2018 Notes and the 2020 Notes at a redemption price equal to 103% of the aggregate principal amount redeemed, plus accrued and unpaid interest. In connection with this transaction, the Company paid $72.1 million and recognized a loss of $3.7 million on the partial extinguishment of debt.

Interest is payable on the Notes on March 15 and September 15 of each year. The 2018 Notes mature on March 15, 2018, and the 2020 Notes mature on March 15, 2020.

The Company may redeem all or part of the Notes, at its option, at any time on or after March 15, 2014, in the case of the 2018 Notes, and March 15, 2015, in the case of the 2020 Notes, at the redemption prices set forth below, plus accrued and unpaid interest to the redemption date.

Twelve-Month Period Commencing March 15,	2018 Notes	2020 Notes
2014	103.938%	N/A
2015	101.969%	104.063%
2016	100.0%	102.708%
2017	100.0%	101.354%
2018 and thereafter	100.0%	100.0%

Prior to March 15, 2013, the Company may redeem up to 35% of the original aggregate principal amount of the 2018 Notes and the 2020 Notes at a price equal to 107.875% and 108.125%, respectively, of the principal amount thereof, plus accrued and unpaid interest to the redemption date, with the net cash proceeds of one or more equity offerings, provided that at least 65% of the original aggregate principal amount of each series of Notes remains outstanding after the redemption. The Company may also redeem all or part of the Notes at any time prior to March 15, 2014, in the case of the 2018 Notes, and March 15, 2015, in the case of the 2020 Notes, at a price equal to 100% of the principal amount thereof, plus accrued and unpaid interest to the redemption date and a "make-whole" premium. In addition, the Company may redeem up to 10% of the original aggregate principal amount of each series of Notes during any 12-month period prior to March 15, 2014, in the case of the 2018 Notes, and March 15, 2015, in the case of the 2020 Notes, at a price equal to 103% of the principal amount thereof, plus accrued and unpaid interest to the redemption date.

Subject to certain limitations, in the event of a change of control of the Company, the Company will be required to make an offer to purchase the Notes at a purchase price equal to 101% of the principal amount of the Notes, plus accrued and unpaid interest to the date of purchase.

The Notes are senior unsecured obligations. The Company's obligations under the Notes are fully and unconditionally guaranteed, jointly and severally, on a senior unsecured basis by certain domestic subsidiaries, which are directly or indirectly 100% owned by Lear. See Note 17, "Supplemental Guarantor Condensed Consolidating Financial Statements."

The indenture governing the Notes contains restrictive covenants that, among other things, limit the ability of the Company and its subsidiaries to: (i) incur additional debt, (ii) pay dividends and make other restricted payments, (iii) create or permit certain liens, (iv) issue or sell capital stock of the Company's restricted subsidiaries, (v) use the proceeds from sales of assets and subsidiary stock, (vi) create or permit restrictions on the ability of the Company's restricted subsidiaries to pay dividends or make other distributions to the Company, (vii) enter into transactions with affiliates, (viii) enter into sale and leaseback transactions and (ix) consolidate or merge or sell all or substantially all of the Company's assets. The foregoing limitations are subject to exceptions as set forth in the Notes. In addition, if in the future the Notes have an investment grade credit rating from both Moody's Investors Service and Standard & Poor's Ratings Services and no default has occurred and is continuing, certain of these covenants will, thereafter, no longer apply to the Notes for so long as the Notes have an investment grade credit rating by both rating agencies. The indenture governing the Notes also contains customary events of default.

As of December 31, 2012, the Company was in compliance with all covenants under the indenture governing the Notes.

For further information, see "—Subsequent Events" below.

Subsequent Events (in part)

2023 Notes

On January 17, 2013, the Company issued $500 million in aggregate principal amount of senior unsecured notes due 2023 at a stated coupon rate of 4.75% (the "2023 Notes"). The 2023 Notes were offered and sold in a private transaction to qualified institutional buyers under Rule 144A and outside of the United States pursuant to Regulation S of the Securities Act of 1933, as amended (the "Securities Act"), have not been registered under the Securities Act and may not be offered or sold in the United States absent registration or an exemption from the registration requirements of the Securities Act. The net proceeds from the offering of $493.4 million, together with the Company's existing sources of liquidity, will be used for general corporate purposes, including, without limitation, the redemption of $70 million in aggregate principal amount of the 2018 Notes and the 2020 Notes during 2013 (see "—2018 Notes and 2020 Notes" below), investments in additional component capabilities and emerging markets and share repurchases under the Company's common stock share repurchase program (see Note 10, "Capital Stock and Equity).

The 2023 Notes are senior unsecured obligations of the Company, are fully and unconditionally guaranteed, jointly and severally, on a senior unsecured basis by certain domestic subsidiaries, which are directly or indirectly 100% owned by Lear and will mature on January 15, 2023. Interest is payable on January 15 and July 15 of each year, beginning on July 15, 2013.

The Company may redeem the 2023 Notes, in whole or in part, on or after January 15, 2018, at the redemption prices set forth below, plus accrued and unpaid interest to the redemption date.

Twelve-Month Period Commencing January 15,	2023 Notes
2018	102.375%
2019	101.583%
2020	100.792%
2021 and thereafter	100.0%

Prior to January 15, 2016, the Company may redeem up to 35% of the aggregate principal amount of the 2023 Notes, in an amount not to exceed the amount of net cash proceeds of one or more equity offerings, at a redemption price equal to 104.75% of the aggregate principal amount thereof, plus accrued and unpaid interest to the redemption date, provided that at least 65% of the original aggregate principal amount of the 2023 Notes remains outstanding after the redemption and any such redemption is made within 90 days after the closing of such equity offering. Prior to January 15, 2018, the Company may redeem the 2023 Notes, in whole or in part, at a redemption price equal to 100% of the aggregate principal amount thereof, plus a "make-whole" premium as of, and accrued and unpaid interest to, the redemption date.

Subject to certain exceptions, the indenture governing the 2023 Notes contains restrictive covenants that, among other things, limit the ability of the Company to: (i) create or permit liens, (ii) enter into sale and leaseback transactions and (iii) consolidate or merge or sell all or substantially all of the Company's assets. The indenture governing the 2023 Notes also provides for customary events of default.

COLLATERALIZED

2.136 FURNITURE BRANDS INTERNATIONAL, INC. (DEC)
CONSOLIDATED BALANCE SHEETS (in part)

(Dollars in thousands except per share data)

	December 29, 2012	December 31, 2011
Liabilities and Shareholders' Equity		
Current liabilities:		
Accounts payable	$113,590	$ 85,603
Accrued employee compensation	18,431	15,161
Other accrued expenses	40,310	38,390
Total current liabilities	172,331	139,154
Long-term debt	105,000	77,000
Deferred income taxes	18,002	19,330
Pension liability	213,295	185,991
Other long-term liabilities	55,015	60,740

NOTES TO CONSOLIDATED FINANCIAL STATEMENTS

(In thousands except per share data)

6. Long-Term Debt (in part)

Long-term debt consists of the following:

	December 29, 2012	December 31, 2011
Term loan	$ 50,000	$ —
Asset-based loan	55,000	77,000
Less: current maturities	—	—
Long-term debt	$105,000	$77,000

On September 25, 2012 (the "effective date"), the Company refinanced its existing asset-based credit facility (the "Prior Credit Agreement") by entering into a new five -year asset based credit facility (the "ABL") with a group of financial institutions and a new five -year Term Loan Agreement (the "Term Loan") in order to provide financial flexibility and increase the Company's borrowing availability. The new ABL is an asset-based revolving facility with a commitment of $200,000 subject to a borrowing base of eligible accounts receivable and inventory. The ABL also includes an accordion feature that will allow the Company to increase the ABL by up to $50,000 subject to securing additional commitments from the lenders. The Term Loan is a $50,000 secured facility. Capitalized fees incurred in the third quarter of 2012 for both of these facilities totaled $8,498.

On September 26, 2012, the Company borrowed funds under the ABL and Term Loan to pay in full the existing indebtedness in the amount of $77,000 owed by the Company pursuant to the terms of the Prior Credit Agreement. The Prior Credit Agreement was an asset-based revolving facility provided by a syndicate of financial institutions with a commitment of $250,000, subject to a borrowing base of eligible accounts receivable and inventory. Capitalized fees of $927 related to the Prior Credit Agreement were written off and are reflected in interest expense in the current period.

Asset-Based Revolving Credit Facility

The ABL provides for the issuance of letters of credit and cash borrowings, and is secured by a first priority lien on the Company's accounts receivable, inventory, cash deposit and securities accounts and certain related assets (the "ABL Collateral"), and a second priority lien on the Term Loan priority collateral described below. The issuance of letters of credit and cash borrowings are limited by the level of a borrowing base consisting of eligible accounts receivable and inventory, less a $25,000 availability block and certain reserves set forth in the ABL agreement (the "Borrowing Base"). The amount of the Borrowing Base above the current level of letters of credit and cash borrowings outstanding represents the total borrowing availability ("Total Availability"). Certain covenants and restrictions, including cash dominion and weekly borrowing base reporting would become effective if Total Availability falls below various thresholds. Weekly borrowing base reporting is triggered if Total Availability is less than the greater of (i) $25,000 and (ii) 12.50% of the aggregate loan commitments. Cash Dominion is triggered if Total Availability is less than the greater of (i) 5.00% of the aggregate loan commitments and (ii) $10,000. We intend to manage our availability to remain above these thresholds, as we choose not to be subject to the cash dominion and weekly reporting covenants. The ABL contains certain negative covenants which limit or restrict the Company's ability to among other things, incur indebtedness and contingent obligations, make investments, intercompany loans and capital contributions, and dispose of property or assets. The ABL also includes customary representations and warranties of the Company, imposes on the Company certain affirmative covenants, and includes other typical provisions. The ABL does not contain any financial covenant tests.

The borrowing base is reported on the 25th day of each fiscal month based on the Company's financial position at the end of the previous month for the first six months following the effective date of the ABL, and on the 20th day of each fiscal month based on our financial position at the end of the previous month thereafter. As of December 29, 2012, based on the Company's November 24, 2012 financial position, the Company had $75,392 of Total Availability to borrow under the ABL. The Company's borrowing base calculations are subject to periodic examinations by the financial institutions, which can result in adjustments to the borrowing base and the Company's availability under the ABL.

The interest rate on cash borrowings outstanding under the ABL is either (i) a base rate (the greater of the prime rate, the Federal Funds Rate plus 0.50% and LIBOR plus 1.00%) or (ii) LIBOR; plus a margin. The applicable margin ranges from 1.25% to 2.00% for base rate borrowings and 2.25% to 3.00% for LIBOR borrowings. The initial applicable margin for the first six months following the effective date for base rate borrowings is 1.75% and for LIBOR borrowings is 2.75%. These margins fluctuate with average availability, and will be reduced by 0.25% if certain EBITDA performance measures are met by the Company. As of December 29, 2012, loans outstanding were $55,000 with a weighted average interest rate of 3.02%.

CONVERTIBLE

2.137 ELECTRONIC ARTS INC. (MAR)

CONSOLIDATED BALANCE SHEETS (in part)

(In millions, except par value data)	March 31, 2012	March 31, 2011
Liabilities and Stockholders' Equity		
Current liabilities:		
Accounts payable	$ 215	$ 228
Accrued and other current liabilities	857	768
Deferred net revenue (packaged goods and digital content)	1,048	1,005
Total current liabilities	2,120	2,001
0.75% convertible senior notes due 2016, net	539	—
Income tax obligations	189	192
Deferred income taxes, net	8	37
Other liabilities	177	134
Total liabilities	3,033	2,364
Commitments and contingencies (See Note 12)		
Stockholders' equity:		
Preferred stock, $0.01 par value. 10 shares authorized	—	—
Common stock, $0.01 par value. 1,000 shares authorized; 320 and 333 shares issued and outstanding, respectively	3	3
Paid-in capital	2,359	2,495
Accumulated deficit	(77)	(153)
Accumulated other comprehensive income	173	219
Total stockholders' equity	2,458	2,564
Total liabilities and stockholders' equity	$5,491	$4,928

NOTES TO CONSOLIDATED FINANCIAL STATEMENTS

(3) Financial Instruments (in part)

0.75% Convertible Senior Notes Due 2016

The following table summarizes the carrying value and fair value of our 0.75% Convertible Senior Notes due 2016 as of March 31, 2012 (in millions):

	As of March 31, 2012	
	Carrying Value	Fair Value
0.75% Convertible Senior Notes due 2016	$539	$584

The carrying value of the 0.75% Convertible Senior Notes due 2016 excludes the fair value of the equity conversion feature, which was classified as equity upon issuance, while the fair value is based on quoted market prices for the 0.75% Convertible Senior Notes due 2016, which includes the equity conversion feature. The fair value of the 0.75% Convertible Senior Notes due 2016 is classified as level 2 within the fair value hierarchy. See Note 11 for additional information related to our 0.75% Convertible Senior Notes due 2016.

(11) Financing Arrangement

0.75% Convertible Senior Notes Due 2016

In July 2011, we issued $632.5 million aggregate principal amount of 0.75% Convertible Senior Notes due 2016 (the "Notes"). The Notes are senior unsecured obligations which pay interest semi-annually in arrears at a rate of 0.75 percent per annum on January 15 and July 15 of each year, beginning on January 15, 2012 and will mature on July 15, 2016, unless earlier purchased or converted in accordance with their terms prior to such date. The Notes are senior in right of payment to any unsecured indebtedness that is expressly subordinated in right of payment to the Notes.

The Notes are convertible into cash and shares of our common stock based on an initial conversion value of 31.5075 shares of our common stock per $1,000 principal amount of Notes (equivalent to an initial conversion price of approximately $31.74 per share). Upon conversion of the Notes, holders will receive cash up to the principal amount of each Note, and any excess conversion value will be delivered in shares of our common stock. Prior to April 15, 2016, the Notes are convertible only if (1) the last reported sale price of the common stock for at least 20 trading days (whether or not consecutive) during the period of 30 consecutive trading days ending on the last trading day of the immediately preceding fiscal quarter is greater than or equal to 130 percent of the conversion price ($41.26 per share) on each applicable trading day; (2) during the five business day period after any ten consecutive trading day period in which the trading price per $1,000 principal amount of notes falls below 98 percent of the last reported sale price of our common stock multiplied by the conversion rate on each trading day; or (3) specified corporate transactions, including a change in control, occur. On or after April 15, 2016 a holder may convert any of its Notes at any time prior to the close of business on the second scheduled trading day immediately preceding the maturity date. The conversion rate is subject to customary anti-dilution adjustments (for example, certain dividend distributions or tender or exchange offer of our common stock), but will not be adjusted for any accrued and unpaid interest. The Notes are not redeemable prior to maturity except for specified corporate transactions and events of default, and no sinking fund is provided for the Notes. The Notes do not contain any financial covenants.

We separately account for the liability and equity components of the Notes. The carrying amount of the equity component representing the conversion option is equal to the fair value of the Convertible Note Hedge, as described below, which is a substantially identical instrument and was purchased on the same day as the Notes. The carrying amount of the liability component was determined by deducting the fair value of the equity component from the par value of the Notes as a whole, and represents the fair value of a similar liability that does not have an associated convertible feature. A liability of $525 million as of the date of issuance was recognized for the principal amount of the Notes representing the present value of the Notes' cash flows using a discount rate of 4.54 percent. The excess of the principal amount of the liability component over its carrying amount is amortized to interest expense over the term of the Notes using the effective interest method. The equity component is not remeasured as long as it continues to meet the conditions for equity classification.

In accounting for $15 million of issuance costs related to the Notes issuance, we allocated $13 million to the liability component and $2 million to the equity component. Debt issuance costs attributable to the liability component are being amortized to expense over the term of the Notes, and issuance costs attributable to the equity component were netted with the equity component in additional paid-in capital.

The carrying values of the liability and equity components of the Notes are reflected in our Consolidated Balance Sheets as follows (in millions):

	As of March 31, 2012
Principal amount of Notes	$633
Unamortized discount of the liability component	(94)
Net carrying amount of Notes	$539
Equity component, net	$105

Interest expense recognized related to the Notes are as follows (in millions):

	Year Ended March 31, 2012
Amortization of debt discount	$14
Amortization of debt issuance costs	2
Coupon interest expense	3
Total interest expense related to Notes	$19

As of March 31, 2012, the remaining life of the Notes is 4.3 years.

Convertible Note Hedge and Warrants Issuance

In addition, in July 2011, we entered into privately-negotiated convertible note hedge transactions (the "Convertible Note Hedge") with certain counterparties to reduce the potential dilution with respect to our common stock upon conversion of the Notes. The Convertible Note Hedge, subject to customary anti-dilution adjustments, provide us with the option to acquire, on a net settlement basis, approximately 19.9 million shares of our common stock at a strike price of $31.74, which corresponds to the conversion price of the Notes and is equal to the number of shares of our common stock that notionally underlie the Notes. As of March 31, 2012, we have not purchased any shares under the Convertible Note Hedge. We paid $107 million for the Convertible Note Hedge, which was recorded as an equity transaction.

Separately, we have also entered into privately-negotiated warrant transactions with the certain counterparties whereby we sold to independent third parties warrants (the "Warrants") to acquire, subject to customary anti-dilution adjustments that are substantially the same as the anti-dilution provisions contained in the Notes, up to 19.9 million shares of our common stock (which is also equal to the number of shares of our common stock that notionally underlie the Notes), with a strike price of $41.14. The Warrants could have a dilutive effect with respect to our common stock to the extent that the market price per share of its common stock exceeds $41.14 on or prior to the expiration date of the Warrants. We received proceeds of $65 million from the sale of the Warrants.

Credit Agreements

DISCLOSURE

2.138 Regulation S-X requires disclosure of the amounts and terms, including commitment fees and conditions for draw-downs, of unused commitments for short-term and long-term financing.

PRESENTATION AND DISCLOSURE EXCERPTS

CREDIT AGREEMENTS

2.139 CABLEVISION SYSTEMS CORPORATION (DEC)
CONSOLIDATED BALANCE SHEETS (continued)

(Dollars in thousands, except share and per share amounts)

	2012	2011
Liabilities and Stockholders' Deficiency		
Current liabilities:		
Accounts payable	$ 489,631	$ 455,654
Accrued liabilities:		
Interest	118,928	146,885
Employee related costs	194,957	246,756
Other accrued expenses	212,611	210,599
Amounts due to affiliates	34,838	32,682
Deferred revenue	64,030	61,599
Liabilities under derivative contracts	134,524	75,223
Credit facility debt	172,984	103,245
Collateralized indebtedness	248,760	148,175
Capital lease obligations	11,009	9,174
Notes payable	10,676	17,614
Senior notes	—	87,822
Total current liabilities	1,692,948	1,595,428
Defined benefit plan and other postretirement plan obligations	99,307	50,297
Deferred revenue	9,736	10,896
Liabilities under derivative contracts	13,739	3,141
Other liabilities	202,394	170,568
Deferred tax liability	275,905	80,546
Credit facility debt	4,485,122	5,080,949
Collateralized indebtedness	307,392	307,763
Capital lease obligations	45,560	33,589
Notes payable	1,909	11,613
Senior notes and debentures	5,738,219	5,358,838
Total liabilities	12,872,231	12,703,628

COMBINED NOTES TO CONSOLIDATED FINANCIAL STATEMENTS

(Dollars in thousands, except per share amounts)

Note 10. Debt (in part)

Credit Facility Debt

The following table provides details of the Company's outstanding credit facility debt:

	Maturity Date	Interest Rate at December 31, 2012[d]	Amounts Payable on or Prior to December 31, 2013	Carrying Value at December 31, 2012	2011
Restricted Group:					
Revolving loan facility[a]	February 24, 2012	—	$ —	$ —	$ —
Extended revolving loan facility[b]	March 31, 2015	—			
Term A-3 extended loan facility	March 31, 2015	2.46%	91,067	333,908	400,690
Term A-4 extended loan facility	December 31, 2016	2.46%	30,000	600,000	600,000
Term B-2 extended loan facility	March 29, 2016	3.46%	7,483	697,807	1,133,699
Term B-3 extended loan facility	March 29, 2016	3.21%	16,784	1,632,286	1,649,071
Restricted Group credit facility debt			145,334	3,264,001	3,783,460
Bresnan Cable:					
Term loan facility	December 14, 2017	4.50%	7,650	744,105	750,734
Revolving loan facility[c]	December 14, 2015	—	—	—	—
Bresnan Cable credit facility debt			7,650	744,105	750,734
Newsday:					
Fixed rate term loan facility	August 1, 2013	—	—	—	525,000
Floating rate term loan facility	August 1, 2013	—	—	—	125,000
Floating rate term loan facility	October 12, 2016	3.71%	20,000	650,000	—
Newsday credit facility debt			20,000	650,000	650,000
Total credit facility debt			$172,984	$4,658,106	$5,184,194

(a) On February 24, 2012, this $158,500 undrawn revolving loan facility matured.

(b) At December 31, 2012, $68,025 of the extended revolving loan facility was restricted for certain letters of credit issued on behalf of CSC Holdings and $1,185,928 of the extended revolving loan facility was undrawn and available, subject to covenant limitations, to be drawn to meet the net funding and investment requirements of the Restricted Group.

(c) At December 31, 2012, $300 of the revolving loan facility was restricted for certain letters of credit issued on behalf of Bresnan Cable and $74,700 of the revolving loan facility was undrawn and available, subject to covenant limitations, to be drawn to meet the net funding and investment requirements of Bresnan Cable.

(d) Includes extension fees, where applicable.

See Note 11 for details relating to interest rate swap contracts outstanding at December 31, 2011.

Restricted Group Credit Facility

Credit Agreement

On April 13, 2010, CSC Holdings and certain of its subsidiaries, the "Restricted Subsidiaries", entered into an amended credit agreement (the "Credit Agreement"), providing for (i) an amendment and restatement of the credit agreement, dated as of February 24, 2006, as first amended and restated in its entirety as of May 27, 2009 and further amended and restated in its entirety as of April 13, 2010, and (ii) an amendment to the incremental term supplement, dated as of March 29, 2006 and amended as of May 27, 2009.

Among other things, the Credit Agreement provides for the specific mechanics of extending, from time to time, the revolving credit commitments, term A loans, incremental term loans and any additional facility commitments or additional facility loans, as applicable, with the terms of such extended facility to be documented at the time of such extension in an extended facility agreement. Under the terms of the Credit Agreement, CSC Holdings entered into three extended facilities as of April 13, 2010, as follows:

- an extended revolving loan facility agreement (the "Extended Revolving Loan Facility") that provided for the extension of the availability period for lenders holding approximately $820,000 of revolving credit commitments under CSC Holdings' $1,000,000 Revolving Credit Facility to March 31, 2015. Lenders under the Extended Revolving Loan Facility are entitled to an extension fee payment of between 2.00% and 2.50% per annum of the outstanding loans under the Extended Revolving Loan Facility, based upon the cash flow ratio applicable from time to time. In addition, revolving credit lenders with revolving credit commitments in the aggregate amount of $412,000 executed joinders to the Credit Agreement agreeing to provide increased revolving credit commitments with an availability period expiring on March 31, 2015.
- an extended term A facility agreement (the "Term A-3 extended loan facility") that provided for the extension of the maturity date for lenders holding approximately $480,000 of loans under CSC Holdings' existing $650,000 Term A loan facility, at the time of the launch of the transaction, to March 31, 2015. Lenders under the Term A-3 extended loan facility are entitled to an extension fee payment of between 2.00% and 2.50% per annum of the outstanding loans under the Term A-3 extended facility, based upon the cash flow ratio applicable from time to time.
- an extended incremental term facility agreement (the "Term B-3 extended loan facility") that provided for the extension of the maturity date for lenders holding approximately $1,678,000 under CSC Holdings' existing $2,200,000 incremental term facility, at the time of the launch of the transaction, to March 29, 2016. Lenders under the Term B-3 extended loan facility are entitled to an extension fee payment of 3.00% per annum of the outstanding loans under the Term B-3 extended loan facility.

In April 2010, the Company utilized $200,000 of its increased revolver commitments to make a $200,000 prepayment on the unextended term B loan facility. In addition, in December 2010, the Company utilized $395,000 of its revolver commitments to make a $395,000 equity contribution in Bresnan Cable.

On June 30, 2010, the availability period for $20,000 of revolving credit commitments under CSC Holdings' Revolving Loan Facility was extended to March 31, 2015 and the maturity date of $4,786 of loans under CSC Holdings' existing term A facility was extended to March 31, 2015.

On November 14, 2011, CSC Holdings entered into an extended term A facility agreement (the "Term A-4 extended loan facility") pursuant to the terms of the Credit Agreement. The Term A-4 extended loan facility agreement increases the commitments of certain existing term A lenders and includes commitments of certain new term A lenders, with the effect being to create the Term A-4 extended loan facility, providing for $600,000 of extended term A loans with a final maturity date of December 31, 2016. Lenders under the Term A-4 extended loan facility are entitled to an extension fee payment of between 1.50% and 2.50% per annum of the outstanding extended facility loans under the Term A-4 extended loan facility, based upon the Cash Flow Ratio applicable from time to time; provided that until June 2012 the extension fee shall remain at 2.00% per annum. In connection with the Term A-4 extended loan facility, the Company incurred deferred financing costs of $4,490, which are being amortized to interest expense over the term of the facility. A portion of the proceeds from the Term A-4 extended loan facility was used to repay the outstanding balances of the Term A-1 loan facility and Term B loan facility. In connection with the repayments, the Company recorded a write-off of the remaining unamortized deferred financing costs associated with the Term A-1 loan facility and Term B loan facility of approximately $470.

The Restricted Group credit facility requires the Restricted Group to pay a commitment fee of 0.50% in respect of the average daily unused commitments under the revolving loan facilities.

Loans under the Restricted Group credit facility are direct obligations of CSC Holdings, guaranteed by most Restricted Group subsidiaries and secured by the pledge of the stock of most Restricted Group subsidiaries.

Credit Facility Repayments

The extended revolving loan facility has no required interim repayments. The Term A-3 extended loan facility is subject to quarterly repayments of approximately $18,213 through March 2013, approximately $24,284 beginning in June 2013 through March 2014 and approximately $54,640 beginning in June 2014 through its maturity date in March 2015. The principal amount of the Term A-4 extended loan facility will be repaid beginning in March 2013 in quarterly installments of $7,500 through December 2013, $15,000 through December 2015, $30,000 through September 2016, and a final principal repayment of $360,000 in December 2016. The Term B-2 extended loan facility is subject to quarterly repayments of approximately $1,871 through December 2015 and a final payment of approximately $675,357 upon maturity in March 2016. The Term B-3 extended loan facility is subject to quarterly repayments of approximately $4,196 through December 2015 and a final payment of approximately $1,581,933 upon maturity in March 2016. The borrowings under the Restricted Group credit facility may be repaid without penalty at any time.

AMC Networks Distribution

In connection with the AMC Networks Distribution, AMC Networks issued senior notes and senior secured term loans under its new senior secured credit facility to the Company as partial consideration for the transfer of certain businesses to AMC Networks. The Company exchanged the AMC Networks senior notes and senior secured term loans in satisfaction and discharge of $1,250,000 outstanding indebtedness under its Restricted Group revolving loan and extended revolving loan facilities.

Financial Covenants for the Restricted Group Credit Facility

The principal financial covenants for the Restricted Group credit facility are summarized below:

	Maximum Ratio of Total Indebtedness to Cash Flow[a]	Maximum Ratio of Senior Secured Indebtedness to Cash Flow[a]	Minimum Ratio of Cash Flow to Interest Expense[a]	Minimum Ratio of Cash Flow Less Cash Taxes to Total Debt[a]
Revolving loan facility	4.5 to 1	3.0 to 1	2.0 to 1	1.5 to 1
Extended revolving loan facility	4.5 to 1	3.0 to 1	2.0 to 1	1.5 to 1
Term A-3 extended loan facility	4.5 to 1	3.0 to 1	2.0 to 1	1.5 to 1
Term A-4 extended loan facility	4.5 to 1	3.0 to 1	2.0 to 1	1.5 to 1
Term B-2 extended loan facility[b]	5.0 to 1	4.5 to 1	n/a	n/a
Term B-3 extended loan facility[b]	5.0 to 1	4.5 to 1	n/a	n/a

[a] As defined in each respective loan facility.
[b] Incurrence based only.

These covenants and restrictions on the permitted use of borrowed funds in the revolving loan facility may limit CSC Holdings' ability to utilize all of the undrawn revolver funds. Additional covenants include limitations on liens and the issuance of additional debt.

Under the Restricted Group credit facility there are generally no restrictions on investments that the Restricted Group may make, provided it is not in default; however, CSC Holdings must also remain in compliance with the maximum ratio of total indebtedness to cash flow and the maximum ratio of senior secured indebtedness to cash flow. CSC Holdings' ability to make restricted payments is also limited by provisions in the Term B-2 extended loan facility, Term B-3 extended loan facility, and the indentures covering CSC Holdings' notes and debentures.

The Restricted Group was in compliance with all of its financial covenants under the Restricted Group credit facility as of December 31, 2012.

Bresnan Cable Credit Facility

Bresnan Cable has an $840,000 senior secured credit facility which is comprised of two components : a $765,000 term loan facility (of which $749,700 was outstanding at December 31, 2012) and a $75,000 revolving loan facility (collectively, the "Bresnan Credit Agreement"). In connection with the financing of the Bresnan acquisition in December 2010, the full $765,000 amount of the term loan facility was drawn, net of an original issue discount of approximately $7,700. The revolving loan facility, which includes a $25,000 sublimit for the issuance of standby letters of credit and a $5,000 sublimit for swingline loans, was not drawn in connection with the transaction. Such revolving loan facility is expected to be available to provide for ongoing working capital requirements and for other general corporate purposes of the Company and its subsidiaries.

Borrowings under the Bresnan Credit Agreement bear interest at a floating rate, which at the option of Bresnan Cable may be either 2.0% over a floating base rate or 3.0% over an adjusted LIBOR rate, subject to a LIBOR floor of 1.50%. The Bresnan Credit Agreement requires Bresnan Cable to pay a commitment fee of 0.75% in respect of the average daily unused commitments under the revolving loan facility. Bresnan Cable is also required to pay customary letter of credit fees, as well as fronting fees, to banks that issue letters of credit pursuant to the Bresnan Credit Agreement.

All obligations under the Bresnan Credit Agreement are guaranteed by BBHI Holdings LLC (the direct parent of Bresnan Cable) and each of Bresnan Cable's existing and future direct and indirect domestic subsidiaries that are not designated as unrestricted subsidiaries in accordance with the Bresnan Credit Agreement (the "Guarantors"). All obligations under the Bresnan Credit Agreement, including the guarantees of those obligations, will be secured by certain assets of the Bresnan Cable and the Guarantors, including a pledge of the equity interests of Bresnan Cable.

Bresnan Cable may voluntarily prepay outstanding loans under the Bresnan Credit Agreement at any time, in whole or in part, without premium or penalty (except for customary breakage costs with respect to Eurodollar loans, if applicable). If Bresnan Cable makes a prepayment of term loans in connection with certain refinancing transactions, Bresnan Cable must pay a prepayment premium of 1.00% of the amount of term loans prepaid.

With certain exceptions, Bresnan Cable is required to make mandatory prepayments in certain circumstances, including (i) a specified percentage of excess cash flow depending on its cash flow ratio, (ii) from the net cash proceeds of certain sales of assets (subject to reinvestment rights), (iii) from casualty insurance and/or condemnation proceeds, and (iv) upon the incurrence of certain indebtedness.

The term loan facility requires remaining quarterly repayments of $1,913 through September 2017, and a final payment of approximately $713,363 upon maturity in December 2017. Any amounts outstanding under the revolving loan facility are due at maturity in December 2015.

The Bresnan Credit Agreement contains customary affirmative and negative covenants and also requires Bresnan Cable to comply with the following financial covenants: (i) a maximum ratio of total indebtedness to operating cash flow (as defined) of 6.75:1 decreasing periodically to 5.00:1 on March 31, 2014; (ii) a minimum ratio of operating cash flow to interest expense of 2.25:1 increasing periodically to 2.75:1 on March 31, 2014, and (iii) minimum liquidity (as defined) of $25,000. In connection with the Bresnan Credit Agreement, the Company incurred deferred financing costs of $20,754 in 2010, which are being amortized to interest expense over the term of the credit agreement.

Bresnan Cable was in compliance with all of its financial covenants under its credit agreement as of December 31, 2012.

Newsday LLC Credit Facility

On October 12, 2012, Newsday LLC entered into a new senior secured credit agreement (the "New Credit Agreement"), the proceeds of which were used to repay all amounts outstanding under its existing credit agreement dated as of July 29, 2008. The New Credit Agreement consists of a $650,000 floating rate term loan which matures on October 12, 2016. Interest under the New Credit Agreement is calculated, at the election of Newsday LLC, at either the base rate or the eurodollar rate, plus 2.50% or 3.50%, respectively, as specified in the New Credit Agreement. Borrowings by Newsday LLC under the New Credit Agreement are guaranteed by CSC Holdings on a senior unsecured basis and certain of its subsidiaries that own interests in Newsday LLC on a senior secured basis. The New Credit Agreement is secured by a lien on the assets of Newsday LLC and Cablevision senior notes with an aggregate principal amount of $753,717 owned by Newsday Holdings. In connection with the New Credit Agreement, the Company incurred deferred financing costs of approximately $4,558, which are being amortized to interest expense over the term of the New Credit Agreement.

The principal financial covenant for the New Credit Agreement is a minimum liquidity test of $25,000 which is tested bi-annually on June 30 and December 31. The New Credit Agreement also contains customary affirmative and negative covenants, subject to certain exceptions, including limitations on indebtedness, investments and restricted payments. Certain of the covenants applicable to CSC Holdings under the New Credit Agreement are similar to the covenants applicable to CSC Holdings under its outstanding senior notes.

Prior to the New Credit Agreement, Newsday LLC's had a $650,000 senior secured loan facility comprised of two components: a $525,000 10.50% fixed rate term loan facility and a $125,000 floating rate term loan facility. The senior secured loan facility was to mature on August 1, 2013 and, subject to certain exceptions, required mandatory prepayments out of the proceeds of certain sales of property or assets, insurance proceeds and debt and equity issuances. No mandatory prepayments were required prior to July 29, 2011, and the amount of prepayments thereafter were limited to $105,000 in the aggregate prior to July 29, 2012 and $140,000 in the aggregate prior to the maturity date. Optional prepayments were also permitted, subject to specified prepayment premiums. Unamortized deferred financing costs related to this senior secured loan facility aggregating approximately $5,083 were written-off in 2012.

Newsday LLC was in compliance with all of its financial covenants under its credit agreement as of December 31, 2012.

2.140 REGAL ENTERTAINMENT GROUP (DEC)

CONSOLIDATED BALANCE SHEETS (in part)

(In millions, except share data)

	December 27, 2012	December 29, 2011
Liabilities and Deficit		
Current liabilities:		
Current portion of debt obligations	$ 22.0	$ 20.6
Accounts payable	157.0	174.5
Accrued expenses	67.6	69.0
Deferred revenue	102.2	89.6
Interest payable	38.7	47.0
Total current liabilities	387.5	400.7
Long-term debt, less current portion	1,912.4	1,925.0
Lease financing arrangements, less current portion	52.2	59.6
Capital lease obligations, less current portion	8.6	11.1
Deferred income tax liability	7.7	—
Non-Current deferred revenue	341.4	348.0
Other non-current liabilities	198.3	169.4
Total liabilities	2,908.1	2,913.8

NOTES TO CONSOLIDATED FINANCIAL STATEMENTS

5. Debt Obligations (in part)

Debt obligations at December 27, 2012 and December 29, 2011 consist of the following (in millions):

	December 27, 2012	December 29, 2011
Regal Cinemas Amended Senior Credit Facility, net of debt discount	$ 988.4	$ 998.5
Regal 9⅛% Senior Notes, including premium	533.4	534.8
Regal Cinemas 8⅝% Senior Notes, net of debt discount	393.7	392.7
Lease financing arrangements, weighted average interest rate of 11.31% maturing in various installments through January 2021	59.6	66.0
Capital lease obligations, 8.5% to 10.3%, maturing in various installments through December 2017	11.1	13.3
Other	9.0	11.0
Total debt obligations	1,995.2	2,016.3
Less current portion	22.0	20.6
Total debt obligations, less current portion	$1,973.2	$1,995.7

Regal Cinemas Sixth Amended and Restated Credit Agreement—On May 19, 2010, Regal Cinemas entered into a sixth amended and restated credit agreement (the "Amended Senior Credit Facility"), with Credit Suisse AG, Cayman Islands Branch, as Administrative Agent ("Credit Suisse") and the lenders party thereto (the "Lenders") which amended, restated and refinanced the fifth amended and restated credit agreement (the "Prior Senior Credit Facility") among Regal Cinemas, Credit Suisse, Cayman Islands Branch, and the lenders party thereto. The Amended Senior Credit Facility consisted of a term loan facility (the "Term Facility") in an aggregate principal amount of $1,250.0 million with a final maturity date in November 2016 and a revolving credit facility (the "Revolving Facility") in an aggregate principal amount of $85.0 million with a final maturity date in May 2015. Proceeds of the Term Facility (approximately $1,237.5 million, net of a $12.5 million debt discount) were applied to refinance the term loan under the Prior Senior Credit Facility, which had an aggregate principal balance of approximately $1,262.1 million. Upon the execution of the Amended Senior Credit Facility, Regal recognized a loss on debt extinguishment of approximately $18.4 million during the year ended December 30, 2010.

On February 23, 2011, Regal Cinemas entered into a permitted secured refinancing agreement (the "Refinancing Agreement") with Regal, the Guarantors, Credit Suisse, and the Lenders, which amended and refinanced the Term Facility under the Amended Senior Credit Facility. Pursuant to the Refinancing Agreement, Regal Cinemas consummated a permitted secured refinancing of the Term Facility in the amount of $1,006.0 million, and in accordance therewith, the Lenders advanced term loans in an aggregate principal amount of $1,006.0 million with a final maturity date in August 2017 (the "New Term Loans"). Together with other amounts provided by Regal Cinemas, proceeds of the New Term Loans were applied to repay all of the outstanding principal and accrued and unpaid interest on the Term Facility under the Amended Senior Credit Facility in effect immediately prior to the making of the New Term Loans.

In addition to extending the maturity date of the New Term Loans, the Refinancing Agreement also amended the Amended Senior Credit Facility by reducing the interest rate on the New Term Loans, by providing, at Regal Cinemas' option, either a base rate or an adjusted LIBOR rate plus, in each case, an applicable margin that is determined according to the consolidated leverage ratio of Regal Cinemas and its subsidiaries. Such applicable margin will be either 2.00% or 2.25% in the case of base rate loans and either 3.00% or 3.25% in the case of LIBOR rate loans. Interest is payable (a) in the case of base rate loans, quarterly in arrears, and (b) in the case of LIBOR rate loans, at the end of each interest period, but in no event less often than every 3 months. The Refinancing Agreement also amended the Second Amended and Restated Guaranty and Collateral Agreement, dated May 19, 2010, to exclude Margin Stock (as such term is defined therein) from the grant of the security interest in the Collateral (as such term is defined therein) used to secure the obligations under the Amended Senior Credit Facility.

As described below, in connection with the additional offerings of the Company's 9⅛% Senior Notes (defined below) during the year ended December 29, 2011, the Company used a portion of the net proceeds to repay approximately $234.6 million of the Amended Senior Credit Facility. As a result of this repayment, coupled with the execution of the Refinancing Agreement, the Company recorded an aggregate loss on extinguishment of debt of approximately $21.9 million during the year ended December 29, 2011.

The obligations of Regal Cinemas are secured by, among other things, a lien on substantially all of its tangible and intangible personal property (including but not limited to accounts receivable, inventory, equipment, general intangibles, investment property, deposit and securities accounts, and intellectual property) and certain owned real property. The obligations under the Amended Senior Credit Facility are also guaranteed by certain subsidiaries of Regal Cinemas and secured by a lien on all or substantially all of such subsidiaries' personal property and certain real property pursuant to that certain second amended and restated guaranty and collateral agreement, dated as of May 19, 2010, among Regal Cinemas, certain subsidiaries of Regal Cinemas party thereto and Credit Suisse AG, Cayman Islands Branch, as Administrative Agent (the "Amended Guaranty Agreement"). The obligations are further guaranteed by REH, on a limited recourse basis, with such guaranty being secured by a lien on the capital stock of Regal Cinemas, and by Regal on an unsecured basis.

Regal Cinemas may prepay borrowings under the Amended Senior Credit Facility, in whole or in part, in minimum amounts and subject to other conditions set forth in the Amended Senior Credit Facility. Regal Cinemas is required to make mandatory prepayments with:
- 50% of excess cash flow in any fiscal year (as reduced by voluntary repayments of the Amended Senior Credit Facility), with elimination based upon achievement and maintenance of a leverage ratio of 3.75 : 1.00 or less;
- 100% of the net cash proceeds of all asset sales or other dispositions of property by Regal Cinemas and its subsidiaries, subject to certain exceptions (including reinvestment rights);
- 100% of the net cash proceeds of issuances of funded debt of Regal Cinemas and its subsidiaries, subject to exceptions; and
- 50% of the net cash proceeds of issuances of equity securities by Regal Cinemas, including the net cash proceeds of capital contributions to Regal Cinemas, with elimination based upon achievement and maintenance of a leverage ratio of 3.75 : 1.00 or less.

The above-described mandatory prepayments are required to be applied pro rata to the remaining amortization payments under the Amended Senior Credit Facility. When there are no longer outstanding loans under the Amended Senior Credit Facility, mandatory prepayments are to be applied to prepay outstanding loans under the Revolving Facility with no corresponding permanent reduction of commitments under the Revolving Facility.

The Amended Senior Credit Facility includes several financial covenants including:
- maximum ratio of (i) the sum of funded debt (net of unencumbered cash) plus the product of eight (8) times lease expense to (ii) consolidated EBITDAR (as defined in the Amended Senior Credit Facility) of 6.00 to 1.0 throughout the term of the Amended Senior Credit Facility;
- maximum ratio of funded debt (net of unencumbered cash) to consolidated EBITDA of 4.00 to 1.0 throughout the term of the Amended Senior Credit Facility;
- minimum ratio of (i) consolidated EBITDAR to (ii) the sum of interest expense plus lease expense of 1.50 to 1.0 throughout the term of the Amended Senior Credit Facility; and
- maximum capital expenditures not to exceed 35% of consolidated EBITDA for the prior fiscal year plus a 1 year carryforward for unused amounts from the prior fiscal year.

The Amended Senior Credit Facility requires that Regal Cinemas and its subsidiaries comply with certain customary covenants, including with respect to incurring indebtedness and liens, making investments and acquisitions, effecting mergers and asset sales, prepaying indebtedness, and paying dividends. Among other things, such limitations will restrict the ability of Regal Cinemas to fund the operations of Regal or any subsidiary of Regal that is not a subsidiary of Regal Cinemas, which guaranties the Amended Senior Credit Facility.

The Amended Senior Credit Facility includes events of default relating to customary matters, including, among other things, nonpayment of principal, interest or other amounts; violation of covenants; any material inaccuracy of representations and warranties; cross default and cross acceleration with respect to indebtedness in an aggregate principal amount of $25.0 million or more; bankruptcy; judgments involving liability of $25.0 million or more that are not paid; ERISA events; actual or asserted invalidity of guarantees or security documents; and change of control.

No amounts have been drawn on the Revolving Facility. The Amended Senior Credit Facility also permits Regal Cinemas to borrow additional term loans thereunder, subject to lenders providing additional commitments of up to $200.0 million and satisfaction of other conditions, as well as other term loans for acquisitions and certain capital expenditures subject to lenders providing additional commitments and satisfaction of other conditions.

As of December 27, 2012 and December 29, 2011, borrowings of $988.4 million and $998.5 million (net of debt discount), respectively, were outstanding under the New Term Loans at an effective interest rate of 3.53% (as of December 27, 2012) and 4.96% (as of December 29, 2011), after the impact of the interest rate swaps described below is taken into account.

Long-Term Leases

RECOGNITION AND MEASUREMENT

2.141 FASB ASC 840 establishes standards of financial accounting and reporting for leases on the financial statements of lessees and lessors. FASB ASC 840 classifies leases as capital or operating. Capital leases are accounted for as the acquisition of an asset and the incurrence of an obligation by the lessee and as a sale or financing by the lessor. All other leases are accounted for as operating leases.

PRESENTATION

2.142 Under FASB ASC 840-30-45-1, lessees should separately identify on the balance sheet or notes thereto assets recorded under capital leases, the accumulated amortization thereon, and obligations. Capital lease obligations are subject to the same considerations as other obligations in classifying them with current and noncurrent liabilities in classified balance sheets. Similarly, a lessor's net investment in a sales-type or direct financing lease is also subject to the same considerations as other assets in classification as current or noncurrent assets.

2.143 FASB ASC 840-20-45-2 requires that lessors include property subject to operating leases with or near property, plant, and equipment in the balance sheet. Accumulated depreciation should be deducted by lessors from the investments in the leased property, as explained in FASB ASC 840-20-45-3.

DISCLOSURE

2.144 FASB ASC 840-20-50 and 840-30-50 contain detailed disclosure requirements for lessors and lessees under operating and capital leases, respectively.

PRESENTATION AND DISCLOSURE EXCERPTS

LESSEE LEASES

2.145 GUESS?, INC. (JAN)
CONSOLIDATED BALANCE SHEETS (in part)

(In thousands, except share data)

	January 28, 2012	January 29, 2011
Liabilities and Stockholders' Equity		
Current liabilities:		
Current portion of capital lease obligations and borrowings	$ 2,030	$ 2,177
Accounts payable	224,859	233,846
Accrued expenses	193,147	194,993
Total current liabilities	420,036	431,016
Capital lease obligations	10,206	12,218
Deferred rent and lease incentives	87,795	76,455
Other long-term liabilities	123,880	85,210
	641,917	604,899

NOTES TO CONSOLIDATED FINANCIAL STATEMENTS

(1) Summary of Significant Accounting Policies and Practices (in part)

Depreciation and Amortization

Depreciation and amortization of property and equipment, which includes depreciation of the property under the capital lease, and purchased intangibles are provided using the straight-line method over the following useful lives:

Building and building improvements including properties under capital lease	10 to 33 years
Land improvements	5 years
Furniture, fixtures and equipment	2 to 10 years
Purchased intangibles	4 to 20 years

Leasehold improvements are amortized over the lesser of the estimated useful life of the asset or the term of the lease, unless the renewal is reasonably assured. Construction in progress is not depreciated until the related asset is completed and placed in service.

(8) Borrowings and Capital Lease Obligations (in part)

Borrowings and capital lease obligations are summarized as follows (in thousands):

	Jan. 28, 2012	Jan. 29, 2011
European capital lease, maturing quarterly through 2016	$11,925	$13,871
Other	311	524
	12,236	14,395
Less current installments	2,030	2,177
Long-term capital lease obligations	$10,206	$12,218

The Company entered into a capital lease in December 2005 for a new building in Florence, Italy. At January 28, 2012, the capital lease obligation was $11.9 million. The Company entered into a separate interest rate swap agreement designated as a non-hedging instrument that resulted in a swap fixed rate of 3.55%. This interest rate swap agreement matures in 2016 and converts the nature of the capital lease obligation from Euribor floating rate debt to fixed rate debt. The fair value of the interest rate swap liability at January 28, 2012 was approximately $1.0 million.

(12) Commitments and Contingencies (in part)

Leases

The Company leases its showrooms and retail store locations under operating lease agreements expiring on various dates through September 2031. Some of these leases require the Company to make periodic payments for property taxes, utilities and common area operating expenses. Certain retail store leases provide for rents based upon the minimum annual rental amount and a percentage of annual sales volume, generally ranging from 3% to 11%, when specific sales volumes are exceeded. Some leases include lease incentives, rent abatements and fixed rent escalations, which are amortized and recorded over the initial lease term on a straight-line basis. The Company also leases some of its equipment under operating lease agreements expiring at various dates through January 2017. As discussed in further detail in Note 8, the Company leases a building in Florence, Italy under a capital lease.

Future minimum property and equipment lease payments under the capital lease and non-cancelable operating leases at January 28, 2012 are as follows (in thousands):

		Operating Leases		
	Capital Lease	Non-Related Parties	Related Parties	Total
Fiscal 2013	$ 2,197	$ 175,537	$ 5,021	$ 182,755
Fiscal 2014	2,118	163,762	4,969	170,849
Fiscal 2015	2,096	152,149	4,965	159,210
Fiscal 2016	2,073	132,383	4,918	139,374
Fiscal 2017	4,943	113,660	4,397	123,000
Thereafter	—	321,994	15,182	337,176
Total minimum lease payments	$13,427	$1,059,485	$39,452	$1,112,364
Less interest	(1,502)			
Capital lease obligations	$11,925			
Less current portion	(1,719)			
Long-term capital lease obligations	$10,206			

Rental expense for all property and equipment operating leases during fiscal 2012, fiscal 2011 and fiscal 2010 aggregated $252.4 million, $217.8 million and $180.5 million, respectively, including percentage rent of $71.7 million, $57.6 million and $33.8 million, respectively.

2.146 CAREER EDUCATION CORPORATION (DEC)
CONSOLIDATED BALANCE SHEETS (in part)

(In thousands, except share and per share amounts)

	As of December 31,	
	2012	2011
Liabilities and Stockholders' Equity		
Current liabilities:		
Short-term borrowings and current maturities of capital lease obligations	$ 80,211	$ 844
Accounts payable	38,440	48,362
Accrued expenses:		
Payroll and related benefits	46,586	41,853
Advertising and production costs	20,963	17,717
Other	44,651	67,077
Deferred tuition revenue	112,038	144,696
Liabilities of discontinued operations	9,826	8,894
Total current liabilities	352,715	329,443

(continued)

	2012	2011
Non-current liabilities:		
Capital lease obligations, net of current maturities	—	207
Deferred rent obligations	95,164	102,034
Other liabilities	29,931	40,365
Liabilities of discontinued operations	33,103	37,980
Total non-current liabilities	158,198	180,586

NOTES TO CONSOLIDATED FINANCIAL STATEMENTS

9. Leases

We lease most of our administrative and educational facilities and certain equipment under non-cancelable operating leases expiring at various dates through 2028. Lease terms generally range from five to ten years with one to two renewal options for extended terms. In most cases, we are required to make additional payments under facility operating leases for taxes, insurance and other operating expenses incurred during the operating lease period.

Certain of our leases contain rent escalation clauses or lease incentives, including rent abatements and tenant improvement allowances. Rent escalation clauses and lease incentives are taken into account in determining total rent expense to be recognized during the term of the lease, which begins on the date we take control of the leased space. Renewal options are considered when determining the overall lease term. In accordance with FASB ASC Topic 840— *Leases*, differences between periodic rent expense and periodic cash rental payments, caused primarily by the recognition of rent expense on a straight-line basis and tenant improvement allowances due or received from lessors, are recorded as deferred rent obligations on our consolidated balance sheets.

In addition, we have financed the acquisition of certain property and equipment through capital lease arrangements and have assumed capital lease obligations in connection with certain acquisitions. The current portion of our capital lease obligations for continuing operations is included within short-term borrowings and current maturities of capital lease obligations on our consolidated balance sheets, and the non-current portion of our capital lease obligations is included within capital lease obligations, net of current maturities on our consolidated balance sheets. The cost basis and accumulated depreciation of assets recorded under capital leases from continuing operating activities, which are included in property and equipment, are as follows as of December 31, 2012 and 2011:

	December 31,	
(Dollars in thousands)	2012	2011
Cost	$ 9,224	$ 9,143
Accumulated depreciation	(6,993)	(6,691)
Net book value	$ 2,231	$ 2,452

Depreciation expense for continuing operations recorded in connection with assets recorded under capital leases was $0.3 million, $0.9 million, and $0.6 million for the years ended December 31, 2012, 2011 and 2010, respectively.

Rent expense, exclusive of related taxes, insurance, and maintenance costs, for continuing operations totaled approximately $103.2 million, $106.3 million and $110.0 million for the years ended December 31, 2012, 2011 and 2010, respectively, and is reflected in educational services and facilities expense in our consolidated statements of income and comprehensive income. Rent expense for discontinued operations, which is included in (loss) income from discontinued operations, was approximately $7.1 million, $13.6 million and $14.5 million for the years ended December 31, 2012, 2011 and 2010, respectively.

Remaining Lease Obligations

We have recorded lease exit costs over the past three years associated with the exit of real estate space for certain campuses related to our continuing operations. These costs are recorded within educational services and facilities expense on our consolidated statements of income and comprehensive income. The current portion of the liability for these charges is reflected within other accrued expenses under current liabilities and the long-term portion of these charges are included in other liabilities under the non-current liabilities section of our consolidated balance sheets. Changes in our future minimum lease obligations for the years ended December 31, 2012, 2011 and 2010 were as follows:

(Dollars in thousands)	Balance, Beginning of Period	Charges Incurred[1]	Net Cash Payments	Other[2]	Balance, End of Period
For the year ended December 31, 2012	$12,831	$4,249	$(3,818)	$—	$13,262
For the year ended December 31, 2011	$17,770	$1,313	$(6,544)	$292	$12,831
For the year ended December 31, 2010	$19,609	$4,364	$(6,115)	$(88)	$17,770

[1] Includes charges for newly vacated spaces and subsequent adjustments for accretion, revised estimates and variances between estimated and actual charges, net of any reversals for terminated lease obligations.
[2] Includes existing prepaid rent and deferred rent liability balances for newly vacated spaces that offset the losses incurred in the period recorded.

As of December 31, 2012, future minimum lease payments under capital leases and operating leases for continuing and discontinued operations are as follows:

(Dollars in thousands)	Capital Leases	Operating Leases Continuing Operations	Discontinued Operations	Total
2013	$214	$103,010	$13,253	$116,477
2014	—	97,597	13,613	$111,210
2015	—	86,132	12,728	$ 98,860
2016	—	71,801	10,213	$ 82,014
2017	—	59,038	10,012	$ 69,050
2018 and thereafter	—	157,349	4,669	$162,018
Total	$214	$574,927	$64,488	$639,629
Less—Portion representing interest at annual rates of 6.25%	(3)			
Principal	$211			

As of December 31, 2012, future minimum sublease rental income under operating leases for continuing and discontinued operations is as follows:

(Dollars in thousands)	Continuing Operations	Discontinued Operations
2013	$52	$ 2,478
2014	—	2,509
2015	—	2,555
2016	—	2,569
2017	—	2,590
2018 and thereafter	—	—
Total	$52	$12,701

LESSOR LEASES

2.147 VERIZON COMMUNICATIONS INC. (DEC)
NOTES TO CONSOLIDATED FINANCIAL STATEMENTS

Note 7—Leasing Arrangements (in part)

As Lessor

We are the lessor in leveraged and direct financing lease agreements for commercial aircraft and power generating facilities, which comprise the majority of our leasing portfolio along with telecommunications equipment, commercial real estate property and other equipment. These leases have remaining terms of up to 38 years as of December 31, 2012. In addition, we lease space on certain of our cell towers to other wireless carriers. Minimum lease payments receivable represent unpaid rentals, less principal and interest on third-party nonrecourse debt relating to leveraged lease transactions. Since we have no general liability for this debt, which is secured by a senior security interest in the leased equipment and rentals, the related principal and interest have been offset against the minimum lease payments receivable in accordance with GAAP. All recourse debt is reflected in our consolidated balance sheets.

At each reporting period, we monitor the credit quality of the various lessees in our portfolios. Regarding the leveraged lease portfolio, external credit reports are used where available and where not available we use internally developed indicators. These indicators or internal credit risk grades factor historic loss experience, the value of the underlying collateral, delinquency trends, and industry and general economic conditions. The credit quality of our lessees primarily varies from AAA to CCC+. For each reporting period the leveraged leases within the portfolio are reviewed for indicators of impairment where it is probable the rent due according to the contractual terms of the lease will not be collected. All significant accounts, individually or in the aggregate, are current and none are classified as impaired.

Finance lease receivables, which are included in Prepaid expenses and other and Other assets in our consolidated balance sheets, are comprised of the following:

	At December 31,					
	2012			2011		
(Dollars in millions)	Leveraged Leases	Direct Finance Leases	Total	Leveraged Leases	Direct Finance Leases	Total
Minimum lease payments receivable	$1,253	$ 58	$1,311	$1,610	$119	$1,729
Estimated residual value	923	6	929	1,202	9	1,211
Unearned income	(654)	(10)	(664)	(874)	(19)	(893)
Total	$1,522	$ 54	$1,576	$1,938	$109	$2,047
Allowance for doubtful accounts			(99)			(137)
Finance lease receivables, net			$1,477			$1,910
Prepaid expenses and other			$22			$ 46
Other assets			1,455			1,864
			$1,477			$1,910

Accumulated deferred taxes arising from leveraged leases, which are included in Deferred income taxes, amounted to $1.2 billion at December 31, 2012 and $1.6 billion at December 31, 2011.

The following table is a summary of the components of income from leveraged leases:

(Dollars in millions)	Years Ended December 31,		
	2012	2011	2010
Pretax income	$30	$61	$74
Income tax expense	12	24	32

The future minimum lease payments to be received from noncancelable capital leases (direct financing and leveraged leases), net of nonrecourse loan payments related to leveraged leases and allowances for doubtful accounts, along with expected receipts relating to operating leases for the periods shown at December 31, 2012, are as follows:

Years	(Dollars in millions)	
	Capital Leases	Operating Leases
2013	$ 123	$184
2014	45	162
2015	52	139
2016	122	114
2017	38	89
Thereafter	931	90
Total	$1,311	$778

Other Noncurrent Liabilities

PRESENTATION

2.148 FASB ASC 210 indicates that liabilities classified as noncurrent (that is, beyond the operating cycle) include long-term deferments of the delivery of goods or services, such as the issuance of a long-term warranty or the advance receipt by a lessor of rental for the final period of a 10-year lease. Similarly, a loan on a life insurance policy with the intent that it will not be paid but will be liquidated by deduction from the proceeds of the policy upon maturity or cancellation should be excluded from current liabilities.

2.149 FASB ASC 480, *Distinguishing Liabilities from Equity*, requires that an issuer classify certain financial instruments with characteristics of both liabilities and equity as liabilities. Some issuances of stock, such as mandatorily redeemable preferred stock, impose unconditional obligations requiring the issuer to transfer assets or issue its equity shares. FASB ASC 480 requires an issuer to classify such financial instruments as liabilities, not present them between the "Liabilities" and "Equity" sections of the balance sheet. Rule 5-02 of Regulation S-X includes matters related to redeemable preferred stocks to be stated on the face of the balance sheet or included in the notes.

2.150 Rule 5-02 of Regulation S-X requires that any item not classed in another Regulation S-X liability caption and in excess of 5 percent of total liabilities be stated separately on the balance sheet or disclosed in the notes. Regulation S-X also requires that deferred income taxes, deferred tax credits, and deferred income be stated separately in the balance sheet.

2.151 Rule 5-02 of Regulation S-X includes a balance sheet caption for commitments and contingent liabilities. When commitments or contingent liabilities exist and are disclosed in footnotes, registrants customarily include a caption on the balance sheet without an amount but with a reference to the related footnote.

DEFERRED INCOME TAXES

2.152 BRUNSWICK CORPORATION (DEC)

CONSOLIDATED BALANCE SHEETS (in part)

	As of December 31	
(In millions)	2012	2011
Liabilities and Shareholders' Equity		
Current liabilities		
Short-term debt, including $6.5 and $1.5 of current maturities of long-term debt	$ 8.2	$ 2.4
Accounts payable	334.4	276.6
Accrued expenses	576.2	607.3
Current liabilities held for sale	18.4	21.8
Current liabilities	937.2	908.1
Long-term liabilities		
Debt	563.6	690.4
Deferred income taxes	92.7	82.0
Postretirement benefits	552.6	592.6
Other	197.5	187.8
Long-term liabilities held for sale	2.9	2.4
Long-term liabilities	1,409.3	1,555.2

NOTES TO CONSOLIDATED FINANCIAL STATEMENTS

Note 11—Income Taxes (in part)

Temporary differences and carryforwards giving rise to deferred tax assets and liabilities at December 31, 2012 and 2011, were as follows:

(In millions)	2012	2011
Current deferred tax assets:		
Product warranties	$ 48.1	$ 48.5
Sales incentives and discounts	26.8	23.6
Other	81.5	86.7
Gross current deferred tax assets	156.4	158.8
Valuation allowance	(130.1)	(135.8)
Total net current deferred tax assets	26.3	23.0
Current deferred tax liabilities:		
Other	(7.5)	(8.0)
Total current deferred tax liabilities	(7.5)	(8.0)
Total net current deferred taxes	$ 18.8	$ 15.0
Non-current deferred tax assets:		
Pension	$ 183.3	$ 196.0
Loss carryforwards	107.3	147.9
Tax credit carryforwards	156.2	158.2
Postretirement and postemployment benefits	28.8	34.1
Equity compensation	25.7	23.4
Other	68.6	48.5
Gross non-current deferred tax assets	569.9	608.1
Valuation allowance	(587.4)	(592.6)
Total net non-current deferred tax assets	(17.5)	15.5
Non-current deferred tax liabilities:		
Unremitted foreign earnings and withholding	(29.9)	(33.3)
State and local income taxes	(35.0)	(34.9)
Other	(10.3)	(29.3)
Total non-current deferred tax liabilities	(75.2)	(97.5)
Total net non-current deferred taxes	$ (92.7)	$ (82.0)

At December 31, 2012, the Company had a total valuation allowance of $717.5 million, of which $130.1 million was current and $587.4 million was non-current. This valuation allowance is primarily due to uncertainty concerning the realization of certain net deferred tax assets. For the year ended December 31, 2012, the valuation allowance decreased $10.9 million, mainly as a result of loss carryforwards being utilized. The remaining realizable value of net deferred tax assets at December 31, 2012 was determined by evaluating the potential to recover the value of these assets through the utilization of tax loss and credit carrybacks and certain tax planning strategies.

At December 31, 2012, in certain jurisdictions, the Company remained in a cumulative loss position over the last three years for book purposes; however, it is possible the Company will be out of this position by the end of 2013 in certain significant jurisdictions. Accordingly, the Company will be evaluating the need to maintain its valuation allowances against the corresponding deferred tax assets. It is possible that a significant portion of the Company's December 31, 2012 valuation allowance balances could be reversed by the end of 2013.

At December 31, 2012, the tax benefit of loss carryovers totaling $107.9 million were available to reduce future tax liabilities. This deferred tax asset was comprised of $69.6 million for the tax benefit of state net operating loss (NOL) carryforwards, $20.1 million for the tax benefit of foreign NOL carryforwards and $18.2 million for the tax benefit of unused capital losses. NOL carryforwards of $72.5 million expire at various intervals between the years 2013 and 2032, while $17.2 million have an unlimited life.

At December 31, 2012, tax credit carryforwards totaling $156.2 million were available to reduce future tax liabilities. This deferred tax asset was comprised of $60.3 million related to foreign tax credits, $66.6 million related to general business credits and other miscellaneous federal credits, and $29.3 million of various state tax credits related to research and development, capital investment and job incentives. The above credits expire at various intervals between the years 2013 and 2032.

The Company has historically provided deferred taxes for the presumed ultimate repatriation to the United States of earnings from all non-U.S. subsidiaries and unconsolidated affiliates. The indefinite reversal criterion has been applied to certain entities and allows the Company to overcome that presumption to the extent the earnings are indefinitely reinvested outside the United States.

The Company had undistributed earnings of foreign subsidiaries of $21.5 million and $34.8 million at December 31, 2012 and 2011, respectively, for which deferred taxes have not been provided as such earnings are presumed to be indefinitely reinvested in the foreign subsidiaries. If such earnings were repatriated, additional tax provisions may result. The Company continues to provide deferred taxes, as required, on the undistributed net earnings of foreign subsidiaries and unconsolidated affiliates that are not deemed to be indefinitely reinvested in operations outside the United States.

As of December 31, 2012, 2011 and 2010 the Company had $27.8 million, $26.9 million and $36.9 million of gross unrecognized tax benefits, including interest, respectively. Of these amounts, $26.8 million, $25.3 million, and $35.0 million, respectively, represent the portion that, if recognized, would impact the Company's tax provision and the effective tax rate.

The Company recognizes interest and penalties related to unrecognized tax benefits in income tax expense. As of December 31, 2012, 2011 and 2010 the Company had $3.1 million, $2.5 million and $4.9 million accrued for the payments of interest, respectively, and no amounts accrued for penalties.

TAXES PAYABLE

2.153 WINNEBAGO INDUSTRIES, INC. (AUG)
CONSOLIDATED BALANCE SHEETS (in part)

(In thousands, except per share data)	August 25, 2012	August 27, 2011
Liabilities and Stockholders' Equity		
Current liabilities:		
Accounts payable	$24,920	$21,610
Income taxes payable	348	104
Accrued expenses:		
Accrued compensation	16,038	10,841
Product warranties	6,990	7,335
Self-insurance	4,137	3,203
Accrued loss on repurchases	627	1,174
Promotional	2,661	2,177
Other	5,297	4,874
Total current liabilities	61,018	51,318
Total long-term liabilities:		
Unrecognized tax benefits	5,228	5,387
Postretirement health care and deferred compensations benefits	75,135	74,492
Total long-term liabilities	80,363	79,879

NOTES TO CONSOLIDATED FINANCIAL STATEMENTS

Note 1: Summary of Significant Accounting Policies (in part)

Income Taxes

We account for income taxes in accordance with ASC 740, *Income Taxes*. As part of the process of preparing our financial statements, we are required to estimate our income taxes in each of the jurisdictions in which we operate. This process involves estimating our current tax exposure together with assessing temporary differences resulting from differing treatment of items for tax and accounting purposes. These temporary differences result in deferred tax assets and liabilities, which are included within our balance sheet. We then assess the likelihood that our deferred tax assets will be realized based on future taxable income and, to the extent we believe that recovery is not likely, we establish a valuation allowance. To the extent we establish a valuation allowance or change this allowance in a period, we include an expense or a benefit within the tax provision in our Statements of Operations.

Note 12: Income Taxes (in part)

Significant items comprising our net deferred tax assets are as follows:

(In thousands)	August 25, 2012 Total	August 27, 2011 Total
Current		
Warranty reserves	$ 2,759	$ 2,588
Self-insurance reserve	1,556	1,204
Accrued vacation	1,595	1,625
Inventory	186	669
Deferred compensation	1,215	1,022
Miscellaneous reserves	1,142	1,349
Total current	8,453	8,457
Noncurrent		
Postretirement health care benefits	16,508	15,087
Deferred compensation	12,416	13,493
Tax credits and NOL carryforwards	2,750	2,755
Unrecognized tax benefit	1,416	1,625
Depreciation	(2,037)	(2,426)
Other	1,036	908
Total noncurrent	32,089	31,442
Total gross deferred tax assets	40,542	39,899
Valuation allowance	(1,569)	(39,250)
Total deferred tax assets	$38,973	$ 649

Deferred income taxes reflect the net tax effects of temporary differences between the carrying amounts of assets and liabilities for financial reporting purposes and the amounts used for income tax purposes. ASC 740 requires that companies assess whether valuation allowances should be established against their deferred tax assets based on the consideration of all available evidence, using a "more likely than not" standard. In making such assessments, significant weight is to be given to evidence that can be objectively verified. A company's current or previous losses are given more weight than its future outlook.

- In Fiscal 2009, we established a full valuation allowance on all deferred tax assets due to our three -year historical cumulative losses incurred combined with the uncertain market and economic conditions that reduced our ability to rely on our projections of any future taxable income.
- In Fiscal 2011, we re-established deferred tax assets of $649,000, primarily due to taxable earnings achieved in Fiscal 2011 which increased the likelihood of realizing a portion of gross deferred tax assets in the future.
- During the fourth quarter of Fiscal 2012, we evaluated the sustainability of our deferred tax assets which included the assessment of cumulative income or losses over recent prior periods. We determined that $39.0 million of our deferred tax assets were sustainable due to the fact that we are now in a three-year historical cumulative income position as opposed to a three-year historical loss position and have a positive future outlook. This resulted in a tax benefit through the reduction of our valuation allowance. At August 25, 2012, our deferred tax assets included $1.4 million of unused tax credits, which will expire in Fiscal 2014, and $1.4 million of state NOLs that will begin to expire in Fiscal 2013, if not otherwise used by us. A valuation allowance of $1.6 million has been maintained for these assets as it is unlikely that the $1.4 million of tax credits will be utilized before they expire and $200,000 of state NOLs are currently not available to be utilized due to a suspension put in place by that state. Based on ASC 740 guidelines, we determined a valuation allowance of $1.6 million was appropriate as of August 25, 2012.

Unrecognized Tax Benefits

Changes in the unrecognized tax benefits are as follows:

(In thousands)	Fiscal 2012	Fiscal 2011	Fiscal 2010
Unrecognized tax benefits—beginning balance	$(5,387)	$(5,877)	$(9,012)
Gross increases—tax positions in a prior period	—	—	(254)
Gross decreases—tax positions in a prior period	599	490	2,900[1]
Gross increases—current period tax positions	(440)	—	(57)
Settlements	—	—	546[2]
Unrecognized tax benefits—ending balance	$(5,228)	$(5,387)	$(5,877)
Accrued interest and penalties (included in unrecognized tax benefits)	$(2,180)	$(2,398)	$(2,509)

[1] The $2.9 million decrease in unrecognized benefit reserves is primarily a reduction of reserves associated with positive settlements of uncertain tax positions related to the finalization of the IRS examination of our federal income tax returns for Fiscal 2006 through Fiscal 2008.

[2] The $546,000 reduction in reserves is actual cash payments as a result of settlements of uncertain tax positions in various taxing jurisdictions.

If the remaining uncertain positions are ultimately favorably resolved, $3.3 million of unrecognized benefits could have a positive impact on our effective tax rate, as the Company has recorded deferred tax assets associated with these positions, and the valuation allowance associated with this liability has been eliminated. It is our policy to recognize interest and penalties accrued relative to unrecognized tax benefits into tax expense.

U.S. GAAP Financial Statements—Best Practices in Presentation and Disclosure | 2. Balance Sheet and Related Disclosures | 2.153

295

We file tax returns in the US federal jurisdiction, as well as various international and state jurisdictions. Our federal income tax return for Fiscal 2009, with source years 2004 and 2005 as a result of carryback claims, were under examination by the IRS and finalized during Fiscal 2011. This examination was concluded during the fourth quarter of Fiscal 2011, resulting with no changes being recommended by the IRS. Although certain years are no longer subject to examinations by the IRS and various state taxing authorities, NOL carryforwards generated in those years may still be adjusted upon examination by the IRS or state taxing authorities if they either have been or will be used in a future period. A number of years may elapse before an uncertain tax position is audited and finally resolved, and it is often very difficult to predict the outcome of such audits. Periodically, various state and local jurisdictions conduct audits, therefore, a variety of years are subject to state and local jurisdiction review.

We do not believe within the next twelve months there will be a significant change in the total amount of unrecognized tax benefits as of August 25, 2012.

INSURANCE

2.154 UNIVERSAL HEALTH SERVICES, INC. (DEC)

CONSOLIDATED BALANCE SHEETS (in part)

	December 31,	
(Dollar amounts in thousands)	2012	2011
Liabilities and Stockholders' Equity		
Current liabilities:		
Current maturities of long-term debt	$ 2,589	$ 2,479
Accounts payable	247,033	228,043
Liabilities of facilities held for sale	850	2,329
Accrued liabilities		
Compensation and related benefits	259,646	233,583
Interest	10,774	10,622
Taxes other than income	49,829	45,359
Other	322,275	314,518
Current federal and state income taxes	1,062	0
Total current liabilities	894,058	836,933
Other noncurrent liabilities	395,355	401,908
Long-term debt	3,727,431	3,651,428
Deferred income taxes	183,747	209,592
Commitments and contingencies (Note 8)		
Redeemable noncontrolling interest	234,303	218,266

NOTES TO CONSOLIDATED FINANCIAL STATEMENTS

1) Business and Summary of Significant Accounting Policies (in part)

M) Self-Insured Risks: We provide for self-insured risks, primarily general and professional liability claims and workers' compensation claims. Our estimated liability for self-insured professional and general liability claims is based on a number of factors including, among other things, the number of asserted claims and reported incidents, estimates of losses for these claims based on recent and historical settlement amounts, estimate of incurred but not reported claims based on historical experience, and estimates of amounts recoverable under our commercial insurance policies. All relevant information, including our own historical experience is used in estimating the expected amount of claims. While we continuously monitor these factors, our ultimate liability for professional and general liability claims could change materially from our current estimates due to inherent uncertainties involved in making this estimate. Our estimated self-insured reserves are reviewed and changed, if necessary, at each reporting date and changes are recognized currently as additional expense or as a reduction of expense. See Note 8 for discussion of adjustments to our prior year reserves for claims related to our self-insured general and professional liability and workers' compensation liability.

In addition, we also maintain self-insured employee benefits programs for employee healthcare and dental claims. The ultimate costs related to these programs include expenses for claims incurred and paid in addition to an accrual for the estimated expenses incurred in connection with claims incurred but not yet reported.

8) Commitments and Contingencies (in part)

Professional and General Liability, Workers' Compensation Liability and Property Insurance

Professional and General Liability and Workers Compensation Liability:

Effective January 1, 2008, most of our subsidiaries became self-insured for professional and general liability exposure up to $10 million per occurrence. Prior to our acquisition of Psychiatric Solutions, Inc. ("PSI") in November, 2010, our subsidiaries purchased several excess policies through commercial insurance carriers which provide for coverage in excess of $10 million up to $200 million per occurrence and in the aggregate. However, we are liable for 10% of the claims paid pursuant to the commercially insured coverage in excess of $10 million up to $60 million per occurrence and in the aggregate.

Prior to our acquisition in November, 2010, the PSI subsidiaries were commercially insured for professional and general liability insurance claims in excess of a $3 million self-insured retention to a limit of $75 million. PSI utilized its captive insurance company and that captive insurance company remains in place after our acquisition of PSI to manage the self-insured retention for all former PSI subsidiaries for claims incurred prior to January 1, 2011. The captive insurance company also continues to insure all professional and general liability claims, regardless of date incurred, for the former PSI subsidiaries located in Florida and Puerto Rico.

Since our acquisition of PSI on November 15, 2010, the former PSI subsidiaries are self-insured for professional and general liability exposure up to $3 million per occurrence and our legacy subsidiaries (which are not former PSI subsidiaries) are self-insured for professional and general liability exposure up to $10 million per occurrence. Effective November, 2010, our subsidiaries (including the former PSI subsidiaries) were provided with several excess policies through commercial insurance carriers which provide for coverage in excess of the applicable per occurrence self-insured retention (either $3 million or $10 million) up to $200 million per occurrence and in the aggregate. We remain liable for 10% of the claims paid pursuant to the commercially insured coverage in excess of $10 million up to $60 million per occurrence and in the aggregate. The 9 behavioral health facilities acquired from Ascend Health Corporation in October, 2012 have general and professional liability policies through commercial insurance carriers which provide for up to $20 million of aggregate coverage, subject to a $10,000 per occurrence deductible. These facilities, like our other facilities, are also provided excess coverage through commercial insurance carriers for coverage in excess of the underlying commercial policy limitations up to $200 million per occurrence and in the aggregate.

Our estimated liability for self-insured professional and general liability claims is based on a number of factors including, among other things, the number of asserted claims and reported incidents, estimates of losses for these claims based on recent and historical settlement amounts, estimates of incurred but not reported claims based on historical experience, and estimates of amounts recoverable under our commercial insurance policies. While we continuously monitor these factors, our ultimate liability for professional and general liability claims could change materially from our current estimates due to inherent uncertainties involved in making this estimate. Given our significant self-insured exposure for professional and general liability claims, there can be no assurance that a sharp increase in the number and/or severity of claims asserted against us will not have a material adverse effect on our future results of operations.

As of December 31, 2012, the total accrual for our professional and general liability claims, including the estimated claims related to the facilities acquired from PSI, was $279 million, of which $48 million is included in current liabilities. As of December 31, 2011, the total accrual for our professional and general liability claims, including the estimated claims related to the facilities acquired from PSI, was $292 million, of which $60 million is included in current liabilities.

We recorded reductions to our professional and general liability self-insurance reserves (relating to prior years) amounting to $27 million during 2012, $11 million during 2011 and $49 million during 2010. The favorable change recorded during 2012 resulted from favorable changes in our estimated future claims payments pursuant to a reserve analysis. The favorable change recorded during 2011 consisted primarily of third-party recoveries and reserve reductions in connection with PHICO–related claims which we became liable for upon PHICO's (a former commercial insurance carrier) liquidation in 2002. The favorable changes in our estimated future claims payments recorded during 2010 were due to: (i) an increased weighting given to company-specific metrics (to 75% from 50%), and decreased general industry metrics (to 25% from 50%), related to projected incidents per exposure, historical claims experience and loss development factors; (ii) historical data which measured the realized favorable impact of medical malpractice tort reform experienced in several states in which we operate, and; (iii) a decrease in claims related to certain higher risk specialties (such as obstetrical) due to a continuation of the company-wide patient safety initiative undertaken during the last several years. As the number of our facilities and our patient volumes have increased, thereby providing for a statistically significant data group, and taking into consideration our long-history of company-specific risk management programs and claims experience, our reserve analyses have included a greater emphasis on our historical professional and general liability experience which has developed favorably as compared to general industry trends.

As of December 31, 2012, the total accrual for our workers' compensation liability claims was $66 million, of which $35 million is included in current liabilities. As of December 31, 2011, the total accrual for our workers' compensation liability claims was $65 million, of which $34 million is included in current liabilities.

There were no material adjustments to our prior year reserves for workers' compensation claims recorded during 2012 or 2011. Based upon the results of workers' compensation reserves analyses, during 2010, we recorded a reduction to our prior year reserves for workers' compensation claims amounting to $4 million.

Property Insurance:

We have commercial property insurance policies covering catastrophic losses, including windstorm damage, up to a $1 billion policy limit per occurrence, subject to a $250,000 deductible for the majority of our properties (the properties acquired from Psychiatric Solutions, Inc. are subject to a $50,000 deductible). Losses resulting from named windstorms are subject to deductibles between 3% and 5% of the declared total insurable value of the property. In addition, we have commercial property insurance policies covering catastrophic losses resulting from earthquake and flood damage, each subject to aggregated loss limits (as opposed to per occurrence losses). Our earthquake limit is $250 million, subject to a deductible of $250,000, except for facilities located within documented

U.S. GAAP Financial Statements—Best Practices in Presentation and Disclosure | 2. Balance Sheet and Related Disclosures | 2.154

297

fault zones. Earthquake losses that affect facilities located in fault zones within the United States are subject to a $100 million limit and will have applied deductibles ranging from 1% to 5% of the declared total insurable value of the property. The earthquake limit in Puerto Rico is $25 million. Flood losses have either a $250,000 or $500,000 deductible, based upon the location of the facility. The 9 behavioral health facilities acquired from Ascend Health Corporation in October, 2012 have commercial property insurance policies which provide for full replacement cost coverage, subject to a $10,000 deductible.

DISCONTINUED OPERATIONS

2.155 EXPRESS SCRIPTS HOLDING COMPANY (DEC)
CONSOLIDATED BALANCE SHEET (in part)

(In millions)	December 31,	
	2012	2011
Liabilities and Stockholders' Equity		
Current liabilities:		
Claims and rebates payable	$ 7,440.0	$ 2,874.1
Accounts payable	2,909.1	928.1
Accrued expenses	1,630.0	656.0
Current maturities of long-term debt	934.9	999.9
Current liabilities of discontinued operations	143.4	—
Total current liabilities	13,057.4	5,458.1
Long-term debt	14,980.1	7,076.4
Deferred taxes	5,948.8	546.5
Other liabilities	692.9	50.7
Noncurrent liabilities of discontinued operations	36.3	—
Total liabilities	34,715.5	13,131.7

NOTES TO CONSOLIDATED FINANCIAL STATEMENTS

4. Dispositions (in part)

Held for sale classification of UBC and Europe. During the fourth quarter of 2012, we determined that portions of the business within UBC, which is located in Chevy Chase, Maryland and our operations in Europe, which were included within our Other Business Operations segment, were not core to our future operations and committed to a plan to dispose of these businesses. As a result, these businesses have been classified as discontinued as of December 31, 2012. It is expected that these businesses will be sold in the first half of 2013. UBC is a global medical and scientific affairs organization that partners with life science companies to develop and commercialize their products. The portions of the business held for sale include specialty services for pre-market trials; providing health economics, outcome research, data analytics and market access services; and providing technology solutions and publications to biopharmaceutical companies.

The results of operations for portions of UBC and our European operations are reported as discontinued operations for all periods presented in the accompanying consolidated statement of operations in accordance with applicable accounting guidance (see select statement of operations information below). For all periods presented, cash flows of our discontinued operations are segregated in our accompanying consolidated statement of cash flows. Finally, assets and liabilities of these businesses held as of December 31, 2012 were segregated in our accompanying consolidated balance sheet. As these businesses were acquired through the Merger, no assets or liabilities of these businesses were held as of December 31, 2011. As of December 31, 2012, the major components of assets and liabilities of these discontinued operations are as follows:

(In millions)	December 31, 2012
Current assets	$198.0
Goodwill	88.5
Other intangible assets, net	157.4
Other assets	19.8
Total assets	$463.7
Current liabilities	$143.4
Deferred taxes	32.6
Other liabilities	3.7
Total liabilities	$179.7

WARRANTY

2.156 FIRST SOLAR, INC. (DEC)

CONSOLIDATED BALANCE SHEETS (in part)

(In thousands, except share data)

	December 31, 2012	December 31, 2011
Liabilities and Stockholders' Equity		
Current liabilities:		
Accounts payable	$ 350,230	$ 176,448
Income taxes payable	5,474	9,541
Accrued expenses	554,433	406,659
Current portion of long-term debt	62,349	44,505
Deferred revenue	2,056	41,925
Other current liabilities	126,832	294,646
Total current liabilities	1,101,374	973,724
Accrued solar module collection and recycling liability	212,835	167,378
Long-term debt	500,223	619,143
Payments and billings for deferred project costs	636,518	167,374
Other liabilities	292,216	206,132
Total liabilities	2,743,166	2,133,751

NOTES TO CONSOLIDATED FINANCIAL STATEMENTS

Note 2. Summary of Significant Accounting Policies (in part)

Product Warranties. We provide a limited warranty against defects in materials and workmanship under normal use and service conditions for 10 years following delivery to the owners of our solar modules.

We also typically warrant to the owners of our solar modules that solar modules installed in accordance with agreed-upon specifications will produce at least 90% of their labeled power output rating during the first 10 years following their installation and at least 80% of their labeled power output rating during the following 15 years. In resolving claims under both the defects and power output warranties, we have the option of either repairing or replacing the covered solar modules or, under the power output warranty, providing additional solar modules to remedy the power shortfall. We also have the option to make a payment for the then current market price for solar modules to resolve claims. Our warranties are automatically transferred from the original purchasers of our solar modules to subsequent purchasers upon resale.

As an alternative to our module power output warranty, we have offered a system level module performance warranty for a limited number of our recent system sales. This system level module performance warranty is designed for utility scale systems and provides 25-year plant-level energy degradation protection. The system level module performance warranty is typically calculated as a percentage of a system's expected energy production, adjusted for certain actual site conditions including weather, with the warranted level of performance declining each year in a linear fashion, but never falling below 80% during the term of the warranty. In resolving claims under the system level module performance warranty to restore the system to warranted performance levels, we first must validate that the root cause is due to module performance, then we typically have the option of either repairing or replacing modules, providing supplemental modules or making a cash payment. Consistent with our module power output warranty, when we elect to satisfy a valid warranty claim by providing replacement or supplement modules under the system level module performance warranty, we do not have any obligation to pay for the labor to remove or install modules.

In addition to our solar module warranty described above, for solar power plants built by our systems business, we typically provide a limited warranty on the balance of the system against defects in engineering design, installation, and workmanship for a period of one to two years following the substantial completion of a phase or the entire solar power plant. In resolving claims under the engineering design, installation, and workmanship warranties, we have the option of remedying the defect through repair, or replacement.

When we recognize revenue for module or systems project sales, we accrue a liability for the estimated future costs of meeting our limited warranty obligations. We make and revise these estimates based primarily on the number of our solar modules under warranty installed at customer locations, our historical experience with warranty claims, our monitoring of field installation sites, our internal testing of and the expected future performance of our solar modules and BoS components, and our estimated per-module replacement cost.

From time to time we have taken remediation actions in respect of affected modules beyond our limited warranty, and we may elect to do so in the future, in which case we would incur additional expenses that are beyond our limited warranty, which may be material to our consolidated statement of operations.

Note 9. Consolidated Balance Sheet Details (in part)

Other Liabilities

Other liabilities consisted of the following at December 31, 2012 and December 31, 2011 (in thousands):

	December 31, 2012	December 31, 2011
Product warranty liability	$101,015	$ 79,105
Other taxes payable	102,599	73,054
Billings in excess of costs and estimated earnings	47,623	—
Other liabilities—noncurrent	40,979	53,973
Other liabilities	$292,216	$206,132

Note 17. Commitments and Contingencies (in part)

Product Warranties

When we recognize revenue for module or systems project sales, we accrue a liability for the estimated future costs of meeting our limited warranty obligations. We make and revise this estimate based primarily on the number of our solar modules under warranty installed at customer locations, our historical experience with warranty claims, our monitoring of field installation sites, our internal testing of and the expected future performance of our solar modules and BoS components, and our estimated per-module replacement cost.

From time to time, we have taken remediation actions in respect of affected modules beyond our limited warranty obligation, and we may elect to do so in the future, in which case we would incur additional expenses. Such potential voluntary future remediation actions beyond our limited warranty obligation could have a material adverse effect on our results of operations if we commit to any such remediation actions.

Product warranty activities during the years ended December 31, 2012, December 31, 2011, and December 31, 2010 were as follows (in thousands):

	December 31, 2012	December 31, 2011	December 31, 2010
Product warranty liability, beginning of period	$157,742	$ 27,894	$ 22,583
Accruals for new warranties issued	40,863	22,411	18,309
Settlements	(60,644)	(24,425)	(24,616)
Change in estimate of product warranty liability[(1)]	53,635	131,862	11,618
Product warranty liability, end of period	$191,596	$157,742	$ 27,894
Current portion of warranty liability	$ 90,581	$ 78,637	$ 11,226
Noncurrent portion of warranty liability	$101,015	$ 79,105	$ 16,668

[(1)] Changes in estimate of product warranty liability during 2012 includes a net increase to our best estimate of $22.6 million in the first quarter of 2012 partially related to a net increase in the expected number of replacement modules required for certain remediation efforts related to the manufacturing excursion that occurred between June 2008 and June 2009. Such estimated increase was primarily due to the completion of the analysis on certain outstanding claims as of December 31, 2011. The remaining portion of this increase was primarily related to a change in estimate in the first quarter of 2012 for the market value of the modules that we estimate will be returned to us under the voluntary remediation efforts that meet the required performance standards to be re-sold as refurbished modules. If the actual market value for such refurbished modules is less than the estimated market value for such modules, we may be required to incur additional expense for further write-downs.

Changes in estimate of product warranty liability during 2011 includes increases to our best estimate during the fourth quarter of 2011 of $114.5 million primarily related to: (i) $70.1 million due to a net increase in the expected number of replacement modules required for certain remediation efforts related to the manufacturing excursion that occurred between June 2008 and June 2009. Such estimated increase was primarily due to additional information received during the quarter from completed remediation efforts at certain sites and from the evaluation of information available after completion of the analysis on certain outstanding claims. Such additional information provided a further understanding of, and additional data regarding, the number of replacement modules expected to be required in connection with our remediation efforts; and (ii) $37.8 million for an increase in the expected number of warranty claims primarily due to increases related to future claims expected due to modules installed in certain climates.

At December 31, 2012, our accrued liability for product warranty was $191.6 million. We have historically estimated our product warranty liability for power output and defects in materials and workmanship under normal use and service conditions to have an estimated warranty return rate of approximately 3% of modules covered under warranty. A 1 percentage point change in the estimated warranty return rate would change estimated product warranty liability by approximately $46 million.

2.157 FMC CORPORATION (DEC)

CONSOLIDATED BALANCE SHEETS (in part)

	December 31,	
(In millions, except share and par value data)	2012	2011
Liabilities and Equity		
Current liabilities		
Short-term debt	$ 50.6	$ 27.0
Current portion of long-term debt	5.7	19.5
Accounts payable, trade and other	443.2	382.1
Advance payments from customers	140.3	76.2
Accrued and other liabilities	192.0	186.2
Accrued payroll	75.1	70.6
Accrued customer rebates	142.9	115.1
Guarantees of vendor financing	31.4	18.5
Accrued pension and other postretirement benefits, current	21.3	9.2
Income taxes	32.9	15.5
Total current liabilities	1,135.4	919.9
Long-term debt, less current portion	908.8	779.1
Accrued pension and other postretirement benefits, long-term	375.8	368.7
Environmental liabilities, continuing and discontinued	200.2	213.3
Reserve for discontinued operations	44.4	41.6
Other long-term liabilities	154.5	116.8

NOTES TO CONSOLIDATED FINANCIAL STATEMENTS

Note 1: Principal Accounting Policies and Related Financial Information (in part)

Environmental obligations. We provide for environmental-related obligations when they are probable and amounts can be reasonably estimated. Where the available information is sufficient to estimate the amount of liability, that estimate has been used. Where the information is only sufficient to establish a range of probable liability and no point within the range is more likely than any other, the lower end of the range has been used.

Estimated obligations to remediate sites that involve oversight by the United States Environmental Protection Agency ("EPA"), or similar government agencies, are generally accrued no later than when a Record of Decision ("ROD"), or equivalent, is issued, or upon completion of a Remedial Investigation/Feasibility Study ("RI/FS"), or equivalent, that is submitted by us and the appropriate government agency or agencies. Estimates are reviewed quarterly and, if necessary, adjusted as additional information becomes available. The estimates can change substantially as additional information becomes available regarding the nature or extent of site contamination, required remediation methods, and other actions by or against governmental agencies or private parties.

Our environmental liabilities for continuing and discontinued operations are principally for costs associated with the remediation and/or study of sites at which we are alleged to have released hazardous substances into the environment. Such costs principally include, among other items, RI/FS, site remediation, costs of operation and maintenance of the remediation plan, management costs, fees to outside law firms and consultants for work related to the environmental effort, and future monitoring costs. Estimated site liabilities are determined based upon existing remediation laws and technologies, specific site consultants' engineering studies or by extrapolating experience with environmental issues at comparable sites.

Included in our environmental liabilities are costs for the operation, maintenance and monitoring of site remediation plans (OM&M). Such reserves are based on our best estimates for these OM&M plans. Over time we may incur OM&M costs in excess of these reserves. However, we are unable to reasonably estimate an amount in excess of our recorded reserves because we cannot reasonably estimate the period for which such OM&M plans will need to be in place or the future annual cost of such remediation, as conditions at these environmental sites change over time. Such additional OM&M costs could be significant in total but would be incurred over an extended period of years.

Included in the environmental reserve balance, other assets balance and disclosure of reasonably possible loss contingencies are amounts from third party insurance policies which we believe are probable of recovery.

Provisions for environmental costs are reflected in income, net of probable and estimable recoveries from named Potentially Responsible Parties ("PRPs") or other third parties. Such provisions incorporate inflation and are not discounted to their present values.

In calculating and evaluating the adequacy of our environmental reserves, we have taken into account the joint and several liability imposed by Comprehensive Environmental Remediation, Compensation and Liability Act ("CERCLA") and the analogous state laws on all PRPs and have considered the identity and financial condition of the other PRPs at each site to the extent possible. We have also considered the identity and financial condition of other third parties from whom recovery is anticipated, as well as the status of our claims against such parties. Although we are unable to forecast the ultimate contributions of PRPs and other third parties with absolute certainty, the degree of uncertainty with respect to each party is taken into account when determining the environmental reserve on a site-by-site basis. Our liability includes our best estimate of the costs expected to be paid before the consideration of any potential recoveries from third parties. We believe that any recorded recoveries related to PRPs are realizable in all material respects. Recoveries are recorded as either an offset in "Environmental liabilities, continuing and discontinued" or as "Other Assets" in our consolidated balance sheets in accordance with U.S. accounting literature.

Note 10: Environmental Obligations (in part)

We are subject to various federal, state, local and foreign environmental laws and regulations that govern emissions of air pollutants, discharges of water pollutants, and the manufacture, storage, handling and disposal of hazardous substances, hazardous wastes and other toxic materials and remediation of contaminated sites. We are also subject to liabilities arising under the Comprehensive Environmental Response, Compensation and Liability Act ("CERCLA") and similar state laws that impose responsibility on persons who arranged for the disposal of hazardous substances, and on current and previous owners and operators of a facility for the clean-up of hazardous substances released from the facility into the environment. We are also subject to liabilities under the Resource Conservation and Recovery Act ("RCRA") and analogous state laws that require owners and operators of facilities that have treated, stored or disposed of hazardous waste pursuant to a RCRA permit to follow certain waste management practices and to clean up releases of hazardous substances into the environment associated with past or present practices. In addition, when deemed appropriate, we enter certain sites with potential liability into voluntary remediation compliance programs, which are also subject to guidelines that require owners and operators, current and previous, to clean up releases of hazardous substances into the environment associated with past or present practices.

We have been named a Potentially Responsible Party ("PRP") at 29 sites on the federal government's National Priorities List ("NPL"), at which our potential liability has not yet been settled. In addition, we received notice from the EPA or other regulatory agencies that we may be a PRP, or PRP equivalent, at other sites, including 38 sites at which we have determined that it is reasonably possible that we have an environmental liability. In cooperation with appropriate government agencies, we are currently participating in, or have participated in, a Remedial Investigation/Feasibility Study ("RI/FS"), or equivalent, at most of the identified sites, with the status of each investigation varying from site to site. At certain sites, a RI/FS has only recently begun, providing limited information, if any, relating to cost estimates, timing, or the involvement of other PRPs; whereas, at other sites, the studies are complete, remedial action plans have been chosen, or a Record of Decision ("ROD") has been issued.

Environmental liabilities consist of obligations relating to waste handling and the remediation and/or study of sites at which we are alleged to have released or disposed of hazardous substances. These sites include current operations, previously operated sites, and sites associated with discontinued operations. We have provided reserves for potential environmental obligations that we consider probable and for which a reasonable estimate of the obligation can be made. Accordingly, total reserves of $236.5 million and $251.2 million, respectively, before recoveries, existed at December 31, 2012 and 2011.

The estimated reasonably possible environmental loss contingencies, net of expected recoveries, exceed amounts accrued by approximately $160 million at December 31, 2012. This reasonably possible estimate is based upon information available as of the date of the filing and the actual future losses may be higher given the uncertainties regarding the status of laws, regulations, enforcement policies, the impact of potentially responsible parties, technology and information related to individual sites.

Additionally, although potential environmental remediation expenditures in excess of the reserves and estimated loss contingencies could be significant, the impact on our future consolidated financial results is not subject to reasonable estimation due to numerous uncertainties concerning the nature and scope of possible contamination at many sites, identification of remediation alternatives under constantly changing requirements, selection of new and diverse clean-up technologies to meet compliance standards, the timing of potential expenditures and the allocation of costs among PRPs as well as other third parties. The liabilities arising from potential environmental obligations that have not been reserved for at this time may be material to any one quarter's or year's results of operations in the future. However, we believe any liability arising from such potential environmental obligations is not likely to have a material adverse effect on our liquidity or financial condition as it may be satisfied over many years.

The table below is a roll forward of our total environmental reserves, continuing and discontinued, from December 31, 2009 to December 31, 2012.

(In millions)	Operating and Discontinued Sites Total
Total environmental reserves, net of recoveries at December 31, 2009	$184.1
2010	
Provision	76.1
Spending, net of recoveries	(35.3)
Net Change	40.8
Total environmental reserves, net of recoveries at December 31, 2010	$224.9
2011	
Provision	45.2
Spending, net of recoveries	(43.2)
Net Change	2.0
Total environmental reserves, net of recoveries at December 31, 2011	$226.9
2012	
Provision	31.2
Spending, net of recoveries	(42.1)
Net Change	(10.9)
Total environmental reserves, net of recoveries at December 31, 2012	$216.0

To ensure we are held responsible only for our equitable share of site remediation costs, we have initiated, and will continue to initiate, legal proceedings for contributions from other PRPs. At December 31, 2012 and 2011, we have recorded recoveries representing probable realization of claims against U.S. government agencies, insurance carriers and other third parties. Recoveries are recorded as either an offset to the "Environmental liabilities, continuing and discontinued" or as "Other assets" in the consolidated balance sheets. The table below is a roll forward of our total recorded recoveries from December 31, 2011 to December 31, 2012 :

(In millions)	12/31/2011	Increase in Recoveries	Cash Received	12/31/2012
Environmental liabilities, continuing and discontinued	$24.3	$2.2	$ 6.0	$20.5
Other assets	58.3	5.0	11.7	51.6
Total	$82.6	$7.2	$17.7	$72.1

The table below provides detail of current and long-term environmental reserves, continuing and discontinued.

	December 31,	
(In millions)	2012	2011
Environmental reserves, current, net of recoveries[1]	$ 15.8	$ 13.6
Environmental reserves, long-term continuing and discontinued, net of recoveries[2]	200.2	213.3
Total environmental reserves, net of recoveries	$216.0	$226.9

[1] "Current" includes only those reserves related to continuing operations. These amounts are included within "Accrued and other liabilities" on the consolidated balance sheets.
[2] These amounts are included in "Environmental liabilities, continuing and discontinued" on the consolidated balance sheets.

Our net environmental provisions relate to costs for the continued cleanup of both operating sites and for certain discontinued manufacturing operations from previous years. The net provisions are comprised as follows:

	Year Ended December 31,		
(In millions)	2012	2011	2010
Continuing operations[1]	$ 5.8	$ 3.1	$14.2
Discontinued operations[2]	20.4	25.4	38.1
Net environmental provision	$26.2	$28.5	$52.3

[1] Recorded as a component of "Restructuring and other charges (income)" on our consolidated statements of income. See Note 7.
[2] Recorded as a component of "Discontinued operations, net" on our consolidated statements of income. See Note 9.

On our consolidated balance sheets, the net environmental provisions affect assets and liabilities as follows:

	Year Ended December 31,		
(In millions)	2012	2011	2010
Environmental reserves[1]	$31.2	$ 45.2	$ 76.1
Other assets[2]	(5.0)	(16.7)	(23.8)
Net environmental provision	$26.2	$ 28.5	$ 52.3

[1] See above roll forward of our total environmental reserves as presented on our consolidated balance sheets.
[2] Represents certain environmental recoveries. See Note 20 for details of Other assets as presented on our consolidated balance sheets.

ASSET RETIREMENT OBLIGATIONS

2.158 FREEPORT-MCMORAN COPPER & GOLD INC. (DEC)
NOTES TO CONSOLIDATED FINANCIAL STATEMENTS

Note 1. Summary of Significant Accounting Policies (in part)

Asset Retirement Obligations. FCX records the fair value of estimated asset retirement obligations (AROs) associated with tangible long-lived assets in the period incurred. Retirement obligations associated with long-lived assets are those for which there is a legal obligation to settle under existing or enacted law, statute, written or oral contract or by legal construction. These obligations, which are initially estimated based on discounted cash flow estimates, are accreted to full value over time through charges to cost of sales. In addition, asset retirement costs (ARCs) are capitalized as part of the related asset's carrying value and are depreciated (primarily on a unit-of-production basis) over the asset's respective useful life. Reclamation costs for disturbances are recognized as an ARO and as a related ARC in the period of the disturbance. FCX's AROs consist primarily of costs associated with mine reclamation and closure activities. These activities, which are site specific, generally include costs for earthwork, revegetation, water treatment and demolition (refer to Note 13 for further discussion). At least annually, FCX reviews its ARO estimates for changes in the projected timing of certain reclamation costs, changes in cost estimates and additional AROs incurred during the period.

Note 13. Contingencies (in part)

Asset Retirement Obligations (AROs). FCX's ARO cost estimates are reflected on a third-party cost basis and comply with FCX's legal obligation to retire tangible, long-lived assets.

A summary of changes in FCX's AROs for the years ended December 31 follows:

	2012	2011	2010
Balance at beginning of year	$ 921	$856	$731
Liabilities incurred	6	9	5
Revisions to cash flow estimates[a]	211	48	105
Accretion expense	55	58	54
Spending	(47)	(49)	(38)
Foreign currency translation adjustment	—	(1)	(1)
Balance at end of year	1,146	921	856
Less current portion	(55)	(31)	(69)
Long-term portion	$1,091	$890	$787

[a] Revisions to cash flow estimates were primarily related to updated closure plans that included revised cost estimates and accelerated timing of certain closure activities.

ARO costs may increase or decrease significantly in the future as a result of changes in regulations, changes in engineering designs and technology, permit modifications or updates, changes in mine plans, inflation or other factors and as actual reclamation spending occurs. ARO activities and expenditures generally are made over an extended period of time commencing near the end of the mine life; however, certain reclamation activities may be accelerated if legally required or if determined to be economically beneficial.

Legal requirements in New Mexico, Arizona, Colorado and other states require financial assurance to be provided for the estimated costs of reclamation and closure, including groundwater quality protection programs. FCX has satisfied financial assurance requirements by using a variety of mechanisms, such as performance guarantees, financial capability demonstrations, trust funds, surety bonds, letters of credit and collateral. The applicable regulations specify financial strength tests that are designed to confirm a company's or guarantor's financial capability to fund estimated reclamation and closure costs. The amount of financial assurance FCX is required to provide will vary with changes in laws, regulations and reclamation and closure requirements, and cost estimates. At December 31, 2012, FCX's financial assurance obligations associated with these closure and reclamation costs totaled $970 million, of which $601 million was in the form of guarantees issued by FCX and financial capability demonstrations. At December 31, 2012, FCX had trust assets totaling $161 million (included in other assets), which are legally restricted to fund a portion of its AROs for properties in New Mexico as required by New Mexico regulatory authorities.

New Mexico Environmental and Reclamation Programs. FCX's New Mexico operations are regulated under the New Mexico Water Quality Act and regulations adopted under that act by the Water Quality Control Commission (WQCC). The New Mexico Environment Department (NMED) has required each of these operations to submit closure plans for NMED's approval. The closure plans must include measures to assure meeting groundwater quality standards following the closure of discharging facilities and to abate any groundwater or surface water contamination. In March 2009, the Tyrone operation appealed the WQCC Final Order, dated February 4, 2009, regarding location of the "places of withdrawal of water," a legal criterion used to determine where groundwater quality standards must be met at FCX's New Mexico mining sites. In December 2010, FCX's Tyrone mine entered into a settlement agreement with NMED that calls for a stay of the appeal while NMED and the WQCC complete several administrative actions, including renewal of Tyrone's closure permit consistent with the terms of the settlement, review and approval of a groundwater abatement plan and adoption of alternative abatement standards, and adoption of new groundwater discharge permit rules for copper mines. If the administrative actions are concluded consistent with the terms of the settlement agreement within the period of the stay, then Tyrone will move to dismiss the appeal. In December 2012, Tyrone and NMED agreed to extend the period to conclude the administrative actions through December 31, 2013. The Court of Appeals also extended the stay for another year. Finalized closure plan requirements, including those resulting from the actions to be taken under the settlement agreement, could result in increases in closure costs for FCX's New Mexico operations.

FCX's New Mexico operations also are subject to regulation under the 1993 New Mexico Mining Act (the Mining Act) and the related rules that are administered by the Mining and Minerals Division (MMD) of the New Mexico Energy, Minerals and Natural Resources Department. Under the Mining Act, mines are required to obtain approval of plans describing the reclamation to be performed following cessation of mining operations. At December 31, 2012, FCX had accrued reclamation and closure costs of $476 million for its New Mexico operations. As stated above, additional accruals may be required based on the state's review of FCX's updated closure plans and any resulting permit conditions, and the amount of those accruals could be material.

Arizona Environmental and Reclamation Programs. FCX's Arizona properties are subject to regulatory oversight in several areas. ADEQ has adopted regulations for its aquifer protection permit (APP) program that require permits for, among other things, certain facilities, activities and structures used for mining, concentrating and smelting and require compliance with aquifer water quality standards at an applicable point of compliance well or location. The APP program also may require mitigation and discharge reduction or elimination of some discharges.

An application for an APP requires a description of a closure strategy that will meet applicable groundwater protection requirements following cessation of operations and an estimate of the cost to implement the closure strategy. An APP may specify closure requirements, which may include post-closure monitoring and maintenance. A more detailed closure plan must be submitted within 90 days after a permitted entity notifies ADEQ of its intent to cease operations. A permit applicant must demonstrate its financial ability to meet the closure costs estimated in the APP.

Portions of Arizona mining facilities that operated after January 1, 1986, also are subject to the Arizona Mined Land Reclamation Act (AMLRA). AMLRA requires reclamation to achieve stability and safety consistent with post-mining land use objectives specified in a reclamation plan. Reclamation plans must be approved by the State Mine Inspector and must include an estimate of the cost to perform the reclamation measures specified in the plan.

FCX will continue to evaluate options for future reclamation and closure activities at its operating and non-operating sites, which are likely to result in adjustments to FCX's ARO liabilities. At December 31, 2012, FCX had accrued reclamation and closure costs of $240 million for its Arizona operations.

Colorado Reclamation Programs. FCX's Colorado operations are regulated by the Colorado Mined Land Reclamation Act (Reclamation Act) and regulations promulgated thereunder. Under the Reclamation Act, mines are required to obtain approval of reclamation plans describing the reclamation of lands affected by mining operations to be performed during mining or upon cessation of mining operations. As of December 31, 2012, FCX had accrued reclamation and closure costs of $47 million for its Colorado operations.

Chilean Reclamation and Closure Programs. In July 2011, the Chilean senate passed legislation regulating mine closure, which establishes new requirements for closure plans and became effective in November 2012. FCX's Chilean operations will be required to update closure plans and provide financial assurance for these obligations. FCX cannot predict at this time the cost of these closure plans or the levels or forms of financial assurance that may be required. Revised closure plans for the Chilean mine sites are due in November 2014. At December 31, 2012, FCX had accrued reclamation and closure costs of $54 million for its Chilean operations.

Peruvian Reclamation and Closure Programs. Cerro Verde is subject to regulation under the Mine Closure Law administered by the Peruvian Ministry of Energy and Mines. Under the closure regulations, mines must submit a closure plan that includes the reclamation methods, closure cost estimates, methods of control and verification, closure and post-closure plans and financial assurance. The updated closure plan for the Cerro Verde mine expansion must be submitted to the Peruvian regulatory authorities in December 2013. At December 31, 2012, Cerro Verde had accrued reclamation and closure costs of $89 million and had financial assurance obligations associated with these reclamation and closure costs totaling $9 million in the form of letters of credit.

Indonesian Reclamation and Closure Programs. The ultimate amount of reclamation and closure costs to be incurred at PT Freeport Indonesia's operations will be determined based on applicable laws and regulations and PT Freeport Indonesia's assessment of appropriate remedial activities in the circumstances, after consultation with governmental authorities, affected local residents and other affected parties and cannot currently be projected with precision. Estimates of the ultimate reclamation and closure costs PT Freeport Indonesia will incur in the future involve complex issues requiring integrated assessments over a period of many years and are subject to revision over time as more complete studies are performed. Some reclamation costs will be incurred during mining activities, while most closure costs and the remaining reclamation costs will be incurred at the end of mining activities, which are currently estimated to continue for nearly 30 years. At December 31, 2012, PT Freeport Indonesia had accrued reclamation and closure costs of $195 million and a long-term receivable for Rio Tinto's share of the obligation of $18 million (included in long-term receivables).

In 1996, PT Freeport Indonesia began contributing to a cash fund ($16 million balance at December 31, 2012) designed to accumulate at least $100 million (including interest) by the end of its Indonesia mining activities. PT Freeport Indonesia plans to use this fund, including accrued interest, to pay mine closure and reclamation costs. Any costs in excess of the $100 million fund would be funded by operational cash flow or other sources.

In December 2009, PT Freeport Indonesia submitted its revised mine closure plan to the Department of Energy and Mineral Resources for review and has addressed comments received during the course of this review process. In December 2010, the President of Indonesia issued a regulation regarding mine reclamation and closure, which requires a company to provide a mine closure guarantee in the form of a time deposit placed in a state-owned bank in Indonesia. In accordance with its Contract of Work, PT Freeport Indonesia is working with the Department of Energy and Mineral Resources to review these requirements, including discussion of other options for the mine closure guarantee.

LITIGATION

2.159 OWENS-ILLINOIS, INC. (DEC)
CONSOLIDATED BALANCE SHEETS (in part)

Dollars in millions, except per share amounts

	December 31,	
	2012	2011
Liabilities and Share Owners' Equity		
Current liabilities:		
Short-term loans	$ 296	$ 330
Accounts payable	1,032	1,038
Salaries and wages	172	149
U.S. and foreign income taxes	43	38
Current portion of asbestos-related liabilities	155	165
Other accrued liabilities	441	449
Long-term debt due within one year	23	76
Total current liabilities	2,162	2,245

(continued)

	December 31,		
	2012		**2011**
Long-term debt	$3,454		$3,627
Deferred taxes	182		212
Pension benefits	846		871
Nonpension postretirement benefits	264		269
Other liabilities	329		404
Asbestos-related liabilities	306		306
Commitments and contingencies			

NOTES TO CONSOLIDATED FINANCIAL STATEMENTS

Tabular data dollars in millions, except per share amounts

12. Contingencies

The Company is a defendant in numerous lawsuits alleging bodily injury and death as a result of exposure to asbestos dust. From 1948 to 1958, one of the Company's former business units commercially produced and sold approximately $40 million of a high-temperature, calcium-silicate based pipe and block insulation material containing asbestos. The Company exited the pipe and block insulation business in April 1958. The typical asbestos personal injury lawsuit alleges various theories of liability, including negligence, gross negligence and strict liability and seeks compensatory and in some cases, punitive damages in various amounts (herein referred to as "asbestos claims").

The following table shows the approximate number of plaintiffs and claimants who had asbestos claims pending against the Company at the beginning of each listed year, the number of claims disposed of during that year, the year's filings and the claims pending at the end of each listed year (eliminating duplicate filings):

	2012	**2011**	**2010**
Pending at beginning of year	4,600	5,900	6,900
Disposed	4,400	4,500	4,200
Filed	2,400	3,200	3,200
Pending at end of year	2,600	4,600	5,900

Based on an analysis of the lawsuits pending as of December 31, 2012, approximately 66% of plaintiffs either do not specify the monetary damages sought, or in the case of court filings, claim an amount sufficient to invoke the jurisdictional minimum of the trial court. Approximately 30% of plaintiffs specifically plead damages of $15 million or less, and 4% of plaintiffs specifically plead damages greater than $15 million but less than $100 million. Fewer than 1% of plaintiffs specifically plead damages equal to or greater than $100 million.

As indicated by the foregoing summary, current pleading practice permits considerable variation in the assertion of monetary damages. The Company's experience resolving hundreds of thousands of asbestos claims and lawsuits over an extended period demonstrates that the monetary relief that may be alleged in a complaint bears little relevance to a claim's merits or disposition value. Rather, the amount potentially recoverable is determined by such factors as the severity of the plaintiff's asbestos disease, the product identification evidence against the Company and other defendants, the defenses available to the Company and other defendants, the specific jurisdiction in which the claim is made, and the plaintiff's medical history and exposure to other disease-causing agents.

In addition to the pending claims set forth above, the Company has claims-handling agreements in place with many plaintiffs' counsel throughout the country. These agreements require evaluation and negotiation regarding whether particular claimants qualify under the criteria established by such agreements. The criteria for such claims include verification of a compensable illness and a reasonable probability of exposure to a product manufactured by the Company's former business unit during its manufacturing period ending in 1958.

The Company has also been a defendant in other asbestos-related lawsuits or claims involving maritime workers, medical monitoring claimants, co-defendants and property damage claimants. Based upon its past experience, the Company believes that these categories of lawsuits and claims will not involve any material liability and they are not included in the above description of pending matters or in the following description of disposed matters.

Since receiving its first asbestos claim, the Company as of December 31, 2012, has disposed of the asbestos claims of approximately 391,000 plaintiffs and claimants at an average indemnity payment per claim of approximately $8,400. Certain of these dispositions have included deferred amounts payable over a number of years. Deferred amounts payable totaled approximately $24 million at December 31, 2012 ($18 million at December 31, 2011) and are included in the foregoing average indemnity payment per claim. The Company's asbestos indemnity payments have varied on a per claim basis, and are expected to continue to vary considerably over time. As discussed above, a part of the Company's objective is to achieve, where possible, resolution of asbestos claims pursuant to claims-handling agreements. Failure of claimants to meet certain medical and product exposure criteria in the Company's administrative claims handling agreements has generally reduced the number of marginal or suspect claims that would otherwise have been received. In addition, certain courts and legislatures have reduced or eliminated the number of marginal or suspect claims that the Company otherwise would have received. These developments generally have had the effect of increasing the Company's per-claim average indemnity payment over time.

The Company believes that its ultimate asbestos-related liability (i.e., its indemnity payments or other claim disposition costs plus related legal fees) cannot reasonably be estimated. Beginning with the initial liability of $975 million established in 1993, the Company has accrued a total of approximately $4.3 billion through 2012, before insurance recoveries, for its asbestos-related liability. The Company's ability to reasonably estimate its liability has been significantly affected by, among other factors, the volatility of asbestos-related litigation in the United States, the significant number of co-defendants that have filed for bankruptcy, the magnitude and timing of co-defendant bankruptcy trust payments, the inherent uncertainty of future disease incidence and claiming patterns, the expanding list of non-traditional defendants that have been sued in this litigation, and the use of mass litigation screenings to generate large numbers of claims by parties who allege exposure to asbestos dust but have no present physical asbestos impairment.

The Company has continued to monitor trends that may affect its ultimate liability and has continued to analyze the developments and variables affecting or likely to affect the resolution of pending and future asbestos claims against the Company. The material components of the Company's accrued liability are based on amounts determined by the Company in connection with its annual comprehensive review and consist of the following estimates, to the extent it is probable that such liabilities have been incurred and can be reasonably estimated: (i) the liability for asbestos claims already asserted against the Company; (ii) the liability for preexisting but unasserted asbestos claims for prior periods arising under its administrative claims-handling agreements with various plaintiffs' counsel; (iii) the liability for asbestos claims not yet asserted against the Company, but which the Company believes will be asserted in the next several years; and (iv) the legal defense costs likely to be incurred in connection with the foregoing types of claims.

The significant assumptions underlying the material components of the Company's accrual are:
(a) the extent to which settlements are limited to claimants who were exposed to the Company's asbestos-containing insulation prior to its exit from that business in 1958;
(b) the extent to which claims are resolved under the Company's administrative claims agreements or on terms comparable to those set forth in those agreements;
(c) the extent of decrease or increase in the incidence of serious disease cases and claiming patterns for such cases;
(d) the extent to which the Company is able to defend itself successfully at trial;
(e) the extent to which courts and legislatures eliminate, reduce or permit the diversion of financial resources for unimpaired claimants;
(f) the number and timing of additional co-defendant bankruptcies;
(g) the extent to which bankruptcy trusts direct resources to resolve claims that are also presented to the Company and the timing of the payments made by the bankruptcy trusts; and
(h) the extent to which co-defendants with substantial resources and assets continue to participate significantly in the resolution of future asbestos lawsuits and claims.

As noted above, the Company conducts a comprehensive review of its asbestos-related liabilities and costs annually in connection with finalizing and reporting its annual results of operations, unless significant changes in trends or new developments warrant an earlier review. If the results of an annual comprehensive review indicate that the existing amount of the accrued liability is insufficient to cover its estimated future asbestos-related costs, then the Company will record an appropriate charge to increase the accrued liability. The Company believes that a reasonable estimation of the probable amount of the liability for claims not yet asserted against the Company is not possible beyond a period of several years. Therefore, while the results of future annual comprehensive reviews cannot be determined, the Company expects the addition of one year to the estimation period will result in an annual charge.

On March 11, 2011, the Company received a verdict in an asbestos case in which conspiracy claims had been asserted against the Company. Of the total nearly $90 million awarded by the jury against the four defendants in the case, almost $10 million in compensatory damages were assessed against all four defendants, and $40 million in punitive damages were assessed against the Company. On August 31, 2012, the trial judge who presided over the original trial vacated all of the damages awarded against the Company in the trial and entered judgment in the Company's favor. The plaintiff has appealed the trial judge's ruling to an intermediate appellate court, and while the Company cannot predict the ultimate outcome of this appeal, the Company believes that the trial judge ruled appropriately based upon applicable appellate precedent.

A prominent Baltimore plaintiffs' firm recently filed a motion in Maryland to consolidate for trial more than 13,000 non mesothelioma claims (the "Motion"). The plaintiffs' proposal is to consolidate these cases for trial on "common issues" and then have "mini trials" on damages. Most of these cases are currently on an inactive docket. The initial hearing on the Motion to consolidate was in December 2012 but no ruling was issued at that time. The Company cannot predict whether or not the Motion will be granted and, if so, the number, timing or format of any trial or the costs that might be required to litigate or resolve cases subject to the Motion. If the Motion is granted, then a substantial number of these previously inactive cases may be activated against the Company.

The Company's reported results of operations for 2012 were materially affected by the $155 million fourth quarter charge for asbestos-related costs and asbestos-related payments continue to be substantial. Any future additional charge would likewise materially affect the Company's results of operations for the period in which it is recorded. Also, the continued use of significant amounts of cash for asbestos-related costs has affected and may continue to affect the Company's cost of borrowing and its ability to pursue global or domestic acquisitions. However, the Company believes that its operating cash flows and other sources of liquidity will be sufficient to pay its obligations for asbestos-related costs and to fund its working capital and capital expenditure requirements on a short-term and long-term basis.

The Company is conducting an internal investigation into conduct in certain of its overseas operations that may have violated the anti-bribery provisions of the United States Foreign Corrupt Practices Act (the "FCPA"), the FCPA's books and records and internal controls provisions, the Company's own internal policies, and various local laws. In October 2012, the Company voluntarily disclosed these matters to the U.S. Department of Justice (the "DOJ") and the Securities and Exchange Commission (the "SEC"). The Company intends to cooperate with any investigation by the DOJ and the SEC.

The Company is presently unable to predict the duration, scope or result of its internal investigation, of any investigations by the DOJ or the SEC or whether either agency will commence any legal action. The DOJ and the SEC have a broad range of civil and criminal sanctions under the FCPA and other laws and regulations including, but not limited to, injunctive relief, disgorgement, fines, penalties, and modifications to business practices. The Company also could be subject to investigation and sanctions outside the United States. While the Company is currently unable to quantify the impact of any potential sanctions or remedial measures, it does not expect such actions will have a material adverse effect on the Company's liquidity, results of operations or financial condition.

In 2012, the Company reached a settlement with the U.S. Environmental Protection Agency to resolve alleged Clean Air Act violations at certain of its glass manufacturing facilities. As part of the settlement, the Company agreed to pay a penalty of $1 million and install pollution control equipment at these facilities. The pollution control equipment is estimated to cost approximately $38 million, of which the Company has already spent approximately $17 million. The remaining equipment will be purchased and installed during 2013.

Other litigation is pending against the Company, in many cases involving ordinary and routine claims incidental to the business of the Company and in others presenting allegations that are non-routine and involve compensatory, punitive or treble damage claims as well as other types of relief. The Company records a liability for such matters when it is both probable that the liability has been incurred and the amount of the liability can be reasonably estimated. Recorded amounts are reviewed and adjusted to reflect changes in the factors upon which the estimates are based, including additional information, negotiations, settlements and other events.

DERIVATIVES

2.160 MOLSON COORS BREWING COMPANY (DEC)
CONSOLIDATED BALANCE SHEETS (in part)

(In millions, except par value)

	As of	
	December 29, 2012	December 31, 2011
Liabilities and equity		
Current liabilities:		
Accounts payable:		
Trade	$ 392.9	$ 268.5
Affiliates	34.1	32.7
Accrued expenses and other liabilities	759.9	646.8
Derivative hedging instruments	6.0	107.6
Deferred tax liabilities	152.3	161.3
Current portion of long-term debt and short-term borrowings	1,245.6	46.9
Discontinued operations	7.9	13.4
Total current liabilities	2,598.7	1,277.2
Long-term debt	3,422.5	1,914.9
Pension and postretirement benefits	833.0	697.5
Derivative hedging instruments	222.2	212.5
Deferred tax liabilities	948.5	455.6
Unrecognized tax benefits	81.8	76.4
Other liabilities	93.9	77.5
Discontinued operations	20.0	22.0
Total liabilities	8,220.6	4,733.6
Commitments and contingencies (Note 20)		

NOTES TO CONSOLIDATED FINANCIAL STATEMENTS

1. Basis of Presentation and Summary of Significant Accounting Policies (in part)

Derivative Hedging Instruments

We use derivatives as part of our normal business operations to manage our exposure to fluctuations in interest, foreign currency exchange, commodity, production and packaging material costs and for other strategic purposes related to our core business. We enter into derivatives for risk management purposes only, including derivatives designated in hedge accounting relationships as well as those derivatives utilized as economic hedges. We do not enter into derivatives for trading or speculative purposes. We recognize our derivatives on the consolidated balance sheets as assets or liabilities at fair value and are classified in either current or non-current assets or liabilities based on each contract's respective unrealized gain or loss position and each contract's respective maturity. Our policy is to present all derivative balances on a gross basis, without regard to counterparty master netting agreements or similar arrangements.

Changes in fair values (to the extent of hedge effectiveness) of outstanding cash flow and net investment hedges are recorded in other comprehensive income ("OCI"), until earnings are affected by the variability of cash flows of the underlying hedged item or the sale of the underlying net investment, respectively. Effective cash flow hedges offset the gains or losses recognized on the underlying exposure in the consolidated statements of operations, or for net investment hedges the foreign exchange translation gain or loss recognized in accumulated other comprehensive income ("AOCI"). Any ineffectiveness is recorded directly into earnings.

We record realized gains and losses from derivative instruments in the same financial statement line item as the hedged item/forecasted transaction. Changes in unrealized gains and losses for derivatives not designated in a hedge accounting relationship are recorded directly in earnings each period and are recorded in the same financial statement line item as the associated realized (cash settled) gains and losses. Cash flows from the settlement of derivatives appear in the consolidated statements of cash flows in the same categories as the cash flows of the hedged item.

In accordance with authoritative accounting guidance, we do not record the fair value of derivatives for which we have elected the Normal Purchase Normal Sale ("NPNS") exemption. We account for these contracts on an accrual basis, recording realized settlements related to these contracts in the same financial statement line items as the corresponding transaction.

Fair Value Measurements (in part)

The carrying amounts of our cash and cash equivalents, accounts receivable, accounts payable and accrued liabilities approximate fair value as recorded due to the short-term maturity of these instruments. In addition, the carrying amounts of our trade loan receivables, net of allowances, approximate fair value. The fair value of derivatives is estimated by discounting the estimated future cash flows utilizing observable market interest, foreign exchange and commodity rates adjusted for non-performance credit risk associated with our counterparties (assets) or with MCBC (liabilities). See Note 18, "Derivative Instruments and Hedging Activities." Based on current market rates for similar instruments, the fair value of long-term debt is presented in Note 14, "Debt."

18. Derivative Instruments and Hedging Activities (in part)

Derivative Accounting Policies

Overview

The majority of our derivative contracts qualify and are designated in a hedge accounting relationship. Our cross currency swaps, historically designated as a cash flow hedge, were designated as a net investment hedge in 2011. Our other foreign currency and commodity derivative instruments that are designated in hedge accounting relationships are designated as cash flow hedges. In certain situations, we may execute derivatives that do not qualify for hedge accounting but are determined to be important for managing risk. Economic hedges are measured at fair value on our consolidated balance sheets with changes in fair value recorded in earnings. We have historically elected to apply the NPNS exemption to certain contracts, as applicable. These contracts are typically transacted with our suppliers and include risk management features that allow us to fix the price on specific volumes of purchases for specified delivery periods. We also consider whether any provisions in our contracts represent embedded derivative instruments as defined in authoritative accounting guidance. As of December 29, 2012, we have identified the equity conversion feature of our €500 million Convertible Note as the only embedded derivative instrument required to be bifurcated and separately accounted for at fair value with changes in fair value recorded in earnings. Refer to *"Derivative Activity Related to the Acquisition"* below for further discussion.

Hedge Accounting Policies

We formally document all relationships receiving hedge accounting treatment between hedging instruments and hedged items, as well as the risk-management objective and strategy for undertaking hedge transactions pursuant to prescribed guidance. We also formally assess effectiveness both at the hedge's inception and on an ongoing basis, specifically whether the derivatives that are used in hedging transactions have been highly effective in mitigating the risk designated as being hedged and whether those hedges may be expected to remain highly effective in future periods.

We discontinue hedge accounting prospectively when (1) the derivative is no longer highly effective in offsetting changes in the cash flows of a forecasted future transaction; (2) the derivative expires or is sold, terminated, or exercised; (3) it is no longer probable that the forecasted transaction will occur; (4) management determines that designating the derivative as a hedging instrument is no longer appropriate; or (5) management decides to cease hedge accounting.

When we discontinue hedge accounting prospectively, but it continues to be probable that the forecasted transaction will occur in the originally expected period, the existing gain or loss on the derivative remains in AOCI and is reclassified into earnings when the forecasted transaction affects earnings. However, if it is no longer probable that a forecasted transaction will occur by the end of the originally specified time period or within an additional two-month period of time thereafter, the gains and losses in AOCI are recognized immediately in earnings. In all situations in which hedge accounting is discontinued and the derivative remains outstanding, we carry the derivative at its fair value on the consolidated balance sheets until maturity, recognizing future changes in the fair value in current period earnings.

Significant Derivative/Hedge Positions

Derivative Activity Related to the Acquisition

In May 2012, in connection with the Acquisition, we issued $1.9 billion of senior notes with portions maturing in 2017, 2022 and 2042. Prior to the issuance of the notes, we systematically removed a portion of our interest rate market risk by entering into Treasury Locks. This resulted in an increase in the certainty of our yield to maturity when issuing the notes. Subsequent to entering into the hedges, market interest rates decreased, resulting in more favorable interest rates for the issued notes. Consequently, we recognized a cash loss of $39.2 million on settlement of the Treasury Locks recorded in interest expense. See Note 14, "Debt" for further discussion.

Additionally, in June 2012, we issued a Convertible Note to the Seller simultaneous with the closing of the Acquisition. The Seller may exercise a put right with respect to put the Convertible Note to us during the conversion period for the greater of the principal amount of the Convertible Note or the aggregate cash value of 12,894,044 shares of our Class B common stock, as adjusted for certain corporate events. The Convertible Note's embedded conversion feature was determined to meet the definition of a derivative required to be bifurcated and separately accounted for at fair value with changes in fair value recorded in earnings. At issuance, we recorded a liability of $15.2 million related to the conversion feature. See Note 14, "Debt" for further discussion.

On April 3, 2012, we entered into a term loan agreement that provides for a 4-year Euro-denominated term loan facility equal to $150 million (or €120 million at issuance), which was funded upon close of the Acquisition on June 15, 2012. In the third quarter of 2012, we designated the term loan as a net investment hedge of our Central European operations. As a result, all foreign exchange gains and losses due to fluctuations in the Euro-denominated borrowing have been prospectively recognized as currency translation adjustments in AOCI. See Note 14, "Debt" for further discussion of the term loan.

In the first quarter of 2013, we began executing a series of financial foreign exchange contracts to hedge our risk associated with payments of Euro-denominated debt. These contracts are not designated in hedge accounting relationships. As of the date of this filing, the outstanding notional amount of this hedging program is approximately €160 million.

Cross Currency Swaps

We historically designated the cross currency swap contracts as cash flow hedges of the variability of cash flows related to GBP denominated principal and interest payments on intercompany notes of GBP 530 million. In September 2011, we cash settled approximately 25% of our GBP 530 million/$774 million and CAD 1.2 billion/GBP 530 million cross currency swaps. As a result of the settlement, we extinguished $98.7 million of the outstanding liability. Cash flow hedge accounting was discontinued on the settled swaps and losses of $0.9 million were reclassified from AOCI to other income (expense), net related to the hedge termination. Simultaneously with the settlement of the swaps, we paid down an equal portion of the outstanding principal of the intercompany notes in the amount of GBP 132 million.

In October 2011, we simultaneously extended both the terms of approximately half of the original intercompany notes and cross currency swaps, such that the new maturities are March 2014. The remaining approximate 25% was left unadjusted and continued to be due in May 2012. Following this extension, in November 2011, we dedesignated all of the remaining swaps as cash flow hedges and designated the aggregate swaps as a net investment hedge of our Canadian business. Following the dedesignation of the cash flow hedges, a $6.7 million loss was reclassified from AOCI to earnings and recorded as other income (expense).

In March 2012, we cash settled the remaining approximate 25% of our original cross currency swaps that was not refinanced in October 2011 as discussed above. As a result of the settlement, we extinguished $110.6 million of the outstanding liability. Our outstanding cross currency swaps were in a net liability position of $220.4 million classified as non-current derivative hedging instruments at December 29, 2012.

Foreign Currency Forwards

As of year-end, we have financial foreign exchange forward contracts in place to manage our exposure to foreign currency fluctuations. We hedge foreign currency exposure related to certain royalty agreements, exposure associated with the purchase of production inputs and imports that are denominated in currencies other than the functional entity's local currency, and other foreign exchanges exposures. These contracts have been designated as cash flow hedges of forecasted foreign currency transactions. We use foreign currency forward contracts to hedge these future forecasted transactions up to a 36 month horizon.

Commodity Swaps

As of year-end, we had financial commodity swap contracts in place to hedge certain future expected purchases of natural gas. Essentially, these contracts allow us to swap our floating exposure to natural gas prices for a fixed rate. These contracts have been designated as cash flow hedges of forecasted natural gas purchases. The fair value of these swaps depends upon current market rates in relation to our fixed rate under the swap agreements at period end. MCBC uses these swaps to hedge forecasted purchases up to 24 months in advance.

Additionally, in 2011, we entered into financial commodity swap contracts to hedge our exposure to changes in the prices of aluminum and diesel. These contracts allow us to swap our floating exposure to changes in aluminum or diesel prices for a fixed rate. These contracts are not designated in hedge accounting relationships. As such, changes in fair value of these swaps are recorded in cost of goods sold in the consolidated statements of operations. We hedge forecasted purchases of aluminum up to 36 months and diesel up to 24 months out in the future for use in our supply chain. For purposes of measuring segment operating performance, the unrealized changes in fair value of the swaps not designated in hedge accounting relationships are reported in Corporate outside of segment specific operating results until such time that the exposure we are managing is realized. At that time we reclassify the gain or loss from Corporate to the operating segment, allowing our operating segments to realize the economic effects of the derivative without the resulting unrealized mark-to-market volatility.

Total Return Swaps

In 2008, we entered into a series of cash settled total return swap contracts. We transacted these swaps for the purpose of gaining exposure to Foster's, a major global brewer. These swaps were marked-to-market each period as these swaps did not qualify for hedge accounting. As such, all unrealized gains and losses related to these swaps were recorded directly to the income statement and were classified as other income (expense) in Corporate. During the third quarter of 2010, we accelerated the maturity dates of our total return swaps related to Foster's stock, and the majority of these swaps were settled prior to year end. Simultaneously, we entered into a series of option contracts to limit our exposure to future changes in Foster's stock price, effectively fixing a range of settlement values for our remaining open swap positions. The remaining total return swaps and related options matured in January of 2011.

Forward Starting Interest Rate Swaps

In order to manage our exposure to the volatility of the interest rates associated with the future interest payments on a forecasted debt issuance, we transacted forward starting interest rate swap contracts on our CAD 900 million and CAD 500 million private placements in Canada. These swaps had effective dates mirroring the terms of the forecasted debt issuances. Under these agreements we were required to early terminate these swaps at the approximate time we issued the previously forecasted debt. See Note 14, "Debt" for further discussion of our CAD 900 million and CAD 500 million fixed rate senior notes, and the impact of the forward starting interest rates swaps on the effective interest rate of each issuance. We had designated these contracts as cash flow hedges of a portion of the interest payments on a future forecasted debt issuance.

Results of Period Derivative Activity (in part)

The following tables include the year-to-date results of our derivative activity in our consolidated balance sheets as of December 29, 2012, and December 31, 2011, and our consolidated statements of operations for the year ended December 29, 2012, December 31, 2011, and December 25, 2010, respectively.

Fair Value of Derivative Instruments in the Consolidated Balance Sheets (in millions, except for certain commodity swaps with notional amounts measured in Metric Tonnes, as noted)

			As of December 29, 2012			
			Asset Derivatives		Liability Derivatives	
	Notional Amount		Balance Sheet Location	Fair Value	Balance Sheet Location	Fair Value
Derivatives Designated as Hedging Instruments:						
Cross currency swaps	CAD	601.3	Other current assets	$—	Current derivative hedging instruments	$ —
			Other non-current assets	—	Non-current derivative hedging instruments	(220.4)
Foreign currency forwards	USD	507.3	Other current assets	2.0	Current derivative hedging instruments	(3.4)
			Other non-current assets	1.4	Non-current derivative hedging instruments	(1.7)
Commodity swaps	kWh	486.1	Other current assets	—	Current derivative hedging instruments	(1.0)
			Other non-current assets	0.2	Non-current derivative hedging instruments	(0.1)
Total derivatives designated as hedging instruments				$3.6		$(226.6)

(continued)

	Notional Amount		Asset Derivatives		Liability Derivatives	
			Balance Sheet Location	Fair Value	Balance Sheet Location	Fair Value
As of December 29, 2012						
Derivatives Not Designated as Hedging Instruments:						
Equity conversion feature of debt	EUR	500.0			Current portion of long-term debt and short-term borrowings	$ (7.9)
Aluminum swaps	Metric tonnes (actual)	2,850	Other current assets	—	Current derivative hedging instruments	(1.4)
Diesel swaps	Metric tonnes (actual)	5,493	Other current assets	—	Current derivative hedging instruments	(0.2)
Total derivatives not designated as hedging instruments				$—		$ (9.5)
Non-Derivative Financial Instruments in Net Investment Hedge Relationships:						
€120 million term loan due 2016	EUR	93.7			Long-term debt	$(123.9)
Total non-derivative financial instruments in net investment hedge relationships						$(123.9)

	Notional Amount		Asset Derivatives		Liability Derivatives	
			Balance Sheet Location	Fair Value	Balance Sheet Location	Fair Value
As of December 31, 2011						
Derivatives Designated as Hedging Instruments:						
Cross currency swaps	CAD	901.3	Other current assets	$—	Current derivative hedging instruments	$(103.2)
			Other non-current assets	—	Non-current derivative hedging instruments	(208.7)
Foreign currency forwards	USD	464.6	Other current assets	—	Current derivative hedging instruments	(1.3)
			Other non-current assets	3.4	Non-current derivative hedging instruments	—
Commodity swaps	kWh	611.1	Other current assets	—	Current derivative hedging instruments	(1.8)
			Other non-current assets	—	Non-current derivative hedging instruments	(0.5)
Total derivatives designated as hedging instruments				$3.4		$(315.5)
Derivatives Not Designated as Hedging Instruments:						
Aluminum swaps	Metric tonnes (actual)	8,825	Other current assets	$—	Current derivative hedging instruments	$ (1.3)
			Other non-current assets	—	Non-current derivative hedging instruments	(3.3)
Diesel swaps	Metric tonnes (actual)	9,668	Other current assets	0.1	Current derivative hedging instruments	—
Total derivatives not designated as hedging instruments				$0.1		$ (4.6)

DEFERRED PROCEEDS & GAINS

2.161 LAS VEGAS SANDS CORP. (DEC)

CONSOLIDATED BALANCE SHEETS (in part)

	December 31,	
(In thousands, except share data)	2012	2011
Liabilities and Equity		
Current liabilities:		
Accounts payable	$ 106,498	$ 104,113
Construction payables	343,372	359,909
Accrued interest payable	15,542	31,668
Other accrued liabilities	1,895,483	1,439,110
Income taxes payable	164,126	108,060
Current maturities of long-term debt	97,802	455,846
Total current liabilities	2,622,823	2,498,706
Other long-term liabilities	133,936	89,445
Deferred income taxes	185,945	205,438
Deferred proceeds from sale of The Shoppes at The Palazzo	267,956	266,992
Deferred gain on sale of The Grand Canal Shoppes	43,880	47,344
Deferred rent from mall transactions	118,435	119,915
Long-term debt	10,132,265	9,577,131
Total liabilities	13,505,240	12,804,971

Note 12—Mall Sales

The Grand Canal Shoppes at The Venetian Las Vegas

In April 2004, the Company entered into an agreement to sell The Grand Canal Shoppes and lease certain restaurant and other retail space at the casino level of The Venetian Las Vegas (the "Master Lease") to GGP for approximately $766.0 million (the "Mall Sale"). The Mall Sale closed in May 2004, and the Company realized a gain of $417.6 million in connection with the Mall Sale. Under the Master Lease agreement, The Venetian Las Vegas leased nineteen retail and restaurant spaces on its casino level to GGP for 89 years with annual rent of one dollar and GGP assumed the various leases. In accordance with related accounting standards, the Master Lease agreement does not qualify as a sale of the real property assets, which real property was not separately legally demised. Accordingly, $109.2 million of the transaction has been deferred as prepaid operating lease payments to The Venetian Las Vegas, which will amortize into income on a straight-line basis over the 89-year lease term. During each of the years ended December 31, 2012, 2011 and 2010, $1.2 million of this deferred item was amortized and included in convention, retail and other revenue. In addition, the Company agreed with GGP to: (i) continue to be obligated to fulfill certain lease termination and asset purchase agreements as further described in "—Note 13—Commitments and Contingencies—Other Ventures and Commitments"; (ii) lease theater space located within The Grand Canal Shoppes from GGP for a period of 25 years with fixed minimum rent of $3.3 million per year with cost of living adjustments; (iii) operate the Gondola ride under an operating agreement for a period of 25 years for an annual fee of $3.5 million; and (iv) lease certain office space from GGP for a period of 10 years, subject to extension options for a period of up to 65 years, with annual rent of approximately $0.9 million. The lease payments under clauses (ii) through (iv) above are subject to automatic increases beginning on the sixth lease year. The net present value of the lease payments under clauses (ii) through (iv) on the closing date of the sale was $77.2 million. In accordance with related accounting standards, a portion of the transaction must be deferred in an amount equal to the present value of the minimum lease payments set forth in the lease back agreements. This deferred gain will be amortized to reduce lease expense on a straight-line basis over the life of the leases. During each of the years ended December 31, 2012, 2011 and 2010, $3.5 million of this deferred item was amortized as an offset to convention, retail and other expense.

As of December 31, 2012, the Company was obligated under (ii), (iii), and (iv) above to make future payments as follows (in thousands):

2013	$ 8,043
2014	7,725
2015	7,497
2016	7,497
2017	7,497
Thereafter	91,307
	$129,566

The Shoppes at The Palazzo

The Shoppes at The Palazzo opened on January 18, 2008, with some tenants not yet open and with construction of certain portions of the mall not yet completed. Pursuant to the Amended Agreement, the Company contracted to sell The Shoppes at The Palazzo to GGP. The Final Purchase Price for The Shoppes at The Palazzo was to be determined by taking The Shoppes at The Palazzo's NOI, as defined in the Amended Agreement, for months 19 through 30 of its operations (assuming that the fixed rent and other fixed periodic payments due from all tenants in month 30 were actually due in each of months 19 through 30, provided that this 12-month period could have been delayed if certain conditions were satisfied) divided by a capitalization rate. The capitalization rate was 0.06 for every dollar of NOI up to $38.0 million and 0.08 for every dollar of NOI above $38.0 million. On the closing date of the sale, February 29, 2008, GGP made its initial purchase price payment of $290.8 million based on projected net operating income for the first 12 months of operations (only taking into account tenants open for business or paying rent as of February 29, 2008). Pursuant to the Amended Agreement, periodic adjustments to the purchase price (up or down, but never to less than $250.0 million) were to be made based on projected NOI for the then upcoming 12 months. Pursuant to the Amended Agreement, the Company received an additional $4.6 million in June 2008, representing the adjustment payment at the fourth month after closing. Subject to adjustments for certain audit and other issues, the final adjustment to the purchase price was to be made on the 30-month anniversary of the closing date (or later if certain conditions are satisfied) based on the previously described formula. For all purchase price and purchase price adjustment calculations, NOI was to be calculated using the "accrual" method of accounting. The Company and GGP had entered into several amendments to the Amended Agreement to defer the time to reach agreement on the Final Purchase Price as both parties continued to work on various matters related to the calculation of NOI. On June 24, 2011, the Company reached a settlement with GGP regarding the Final Purchase Price. Under the terms of the settlement, the Company retained the $295.4 million of proceeds previously received and participates in certain future revenues earned by GGP. In addition, the Company agreed with GGP to lease certain spaces located within The Shoppes at The Palazzo for a period of 10 years with total fixed minimum rents of $0.7 million per year, subject to extension options for a period of up to 10 years and automatic increases beginning on the second lease year. As of December 31, 2012, the Company was obligated to make future payments of approximately $0.8 million annually for the two years ended December 31, 2014, approximately $0.9 million annually for the three years ended December 31, 2017, and $0.5 million thereafter. In accordance with related accounting standards, the transaction has not been accounted for as a sale because the Company's participation in certain future revenues constitutes continuing involvement in The Shoppes at The Palazzo. Therefore, $268.0 million of the mall sale transaction has been recorded as deferred proceeds from the sale as of December 31, 2012, which accrues interest at an imputed interest rate offset by (i) imputed rental income and (ii) rent payments made to GGP related to those spaces leased back from GGP.

In the Amended Agreement, the Company agreed to lease certain restaurant and retail space on the casino level of The Palazzo to GGP pursuant to a master lease agreement ("The Palazzo Master Lease"). Under The Palazzo Master Lease, which was executed concurrently with, and as a part of, the closing on the sale of The Shoppes at The Palazzo to GGP on February 29, 2008, The Palazzo leased nine restaurant and retail spaces on its casino level to GGP for 89 years with annual rent of one dollar and GGP assumed the various tenant operating leases for those spaces. In accordance with related accounting standards, The Palazzo Master Lease does not qualify as a sale of the real property, which real property was not separately legally demised. Accordingly, $22.5 million of the mall sale transaction has been deferred as prepaid operating lease payments to The Palazzo, which is amortized into income on a straight-line basis over the 89-year lease term, while $4.1 million of the total proceeds from the mall sale transaction (which represented the portion of the proceeds in excess of the guaranteed purchase price that was allocated to The Palazzo Master Lease) has been recognized as contingent rent revenue and included in convention, retail and other revenue during the year ended December 31, 2011.

DEFERRED REVENUE

2.162 LOWE'S COMPANIES, INC. (FEB)

CONSOLIDATED BALANCE SHEETS (in part)

(In millions, except par value and percentage data)	February 3, 2012	% Total	January 28, 2011	% Total
Liabilities and Shareholders' Equity				
Current liabilities:				
Current maturities of long-term debt	$ 592	1.8%	$ 36	0.1%
Accounts payable	4,352	13.0	4,351	12.9
Accrued compensation and employee benefits	613	1.8	667	2.0
Deferred revenue	801	2.4	707	2.1
Other current liabilities	1,533	4.5	1,358	4.0
Total current liabilities	7,891	23.5	7,119	21.1
Long-term debt, excluding current maturities	7,035	21.0	6,537	19.4
Deferred income taxes—net	531	1.6	467	1.4
Deferred revenue—extended protection plans	704	2.1	631	1.9
Other liabilities	865	2.5	833	2.5
Total liabilities	17,026	50.7	15,587	46.3

NOTES TO CONSOLIDATED FINANCIAL STATEMENTS

NOTE 1: Summary of Significant Accounting Policies (in part)

Revenue Recognition—The Company recognizes revenues, net of sales tax, when sales transactions occur and customers take possession of the merchandise. A provision for anticipated merchandise returns is provided through a reduction of sales and cost of sales in the period that the related sales are recorded. Revenues from product installation services are recognized when the installation is completed. Deferred revenues associated with amounts received for which customers have not yet taken possession of merchandise or for which installation has not yet been completed were $430 million and $371 million at February 3, 2012, and January 28, 2011, respectively.

Revenues from stored-value cards, which include gift cards and returned merchandise credits, are deferred and recognized when the cards are redeemed. The liability associated with outstanding stored-value cards was $371 million and $336 million at February 3, 2012, and January 28, 2011, respectively, and these amounts are included in deferred revenue on the consolidated balance sheets. The Company recognizes income from unredeemed stored-value cards at the point at which redemption becomes remote. The Company's stored-value cards have no expiration date or dormancy fees. Therefore, to determine when redemption is remote, the Company analyzes an aging of the unredeemed cards based on the date of last stored-value card use.

Extended Protection Plans—The Company sells separately-priced extended protection plan contracts under a Lowe's-branded program for which the Company is ultimately self-insured. The Company recognizes revenue from extended protection plan sales on a straight-line basis over the respective contract term. Extended protection plan contract terms primarily range from one to four years from the date of purchase or the end of the manufacturer's warranty, as applicable. Changes in deferred revenue for extended protection plan contracts are summarized as follows:

(In millions)	2011	2010
Deferred revenue—extended protection plans, beginning of year	$ 631	$ 549
Additions to deferred revenue	264	253
Deferred revenue recognized	(191)	(171)
Deferred revenue—extended protection plans, end of year	$ 704	$ 631

Incremental direct acquisition costs associated with the sale of extended protection plans are also deferred and recognized as expense on a straight-line basis over the respective contract term. Deferred costs associated with extended protection plan contracts were $145 million and $166 million at February 3, 2012 and January 28, 2011, respectively. The Company's extended protection plan deferred costs are included in other assets (noncurrent) on the consolidated balance sheets. All other costs, such as costs of services performed under the contract, general and administrative expenses and advertising expenses are expensed as incurred.

Accumulated Other Comprehensive Income

PRESENTATION

2.163 FASB ASC 220, *Comprehensive Income*, requires that a separate caption for accumulated other comprehensive income be presented in the "Equity" section of a balance sheet. An entity should disclose accumulated balances for each classification in that separate component of equity on the face of a balance sheet or in notes to the financial statements.

PRESENTATION AND DISCLOSURE EXCERPTS

ACCUMULATED OTHER COMPREHENSIVE INCOME—EQUITY SECTION OF BALANCE SHEET

2.164 WALTER ENERGY, INC. (DEC)
CONSOLIDATED BALANCE SHEETS (in part)

(In thousands, except share and per share amounts)

	December 31,	
	2012	Recast 2011[(1)]
Liabilities and Stockholders' Equity		
Stockholders' equity:		
Common stock, $0.01 par value per share:		
Authorized—200,000,000 shares; issued—62,521,300 and 62,444,905 shares, respectively	625	624
Preferred stock, $0.01 par value per share:		
Authorized—20,000,000 shares; issued—0 shares	—	—
Capital in excess of par value	1,628,244	1,620,430
Retained earnings (accumulated deficit)	(347,448)	744,939
Accumulated other comprehensive income (loss):		
Pension and other post-retirement benefit plans, net of tax	(266,042)	(225,541)
Foreign currency translation adjustment	(1,502)	(3,276)
Unrealized loss on hedges, net of tax	(4,203)	(787)
Unrealized investment gain, net of tax	897	128
Total stockholders' equity	1,010,571	2,136,517
	$5,768,420	$6,856,508

[(1)] Certain previously reported December 31, 2011 balances have been recast to reflect the effects of finalizing the allocation of the Western Coal purchase price during the 2012 first quarter. See Note 3 for further information.

ACCUMULATED OTHER COMPREHENSIVE INCOME—STATEMENT OF CHANGES IN EQUITY

2.165 WEYERHAEUSER COMPANY (DEC)
CONSOLIDATED STATEMENT OF CHANGES IN EQUITY

(Dollar amounts in millions)	2012	2011	2010
Common shares:			
Balance at beginning of year	$ 671	$ 670	$ 264
Issued for exercise of stock options	7	4	1
Share repurchases	—	(3)	—
Special dividend (Note 16)	—	—	405
Balance at end of year	$ 678	$ 671	$ 670
Other capital:			
Balance at beginning of year	$ 4,595	$ 4,552	$ 1,786
Exercise of stock options	105	35	2
Special Dividend (Note 16)	—	—	2,745
Repurchase of common shares	—	(34)	—
Share-based compensation	34	27	21
Other transactions, net	(3)	15	(2)
Balance at end of year	$ 4,731	$ 4,595	$ 4,552
Retained earnings:			
Balance at beginning of year	$ 176	$ 181	$ 2,658
Net earnings attributable to Weyerhaeuser common shareholders	385	331	1,281
Dividends on common shares (Note 16)	(342)	(336)	(3,758)
Balance at end of year	$ 219	$ 176	$ 181

(continued)

(Dollar amounts in millions)	2012	2011	2010
Cumulative other comprehensive loss:			
Balance at beginning of year	$(1,179)	$ (791)	$ (664)
Annual changes—net of tax:			
Foreign currency translation adjustments	2	(8)	30
Changes in unamortized net pension and other postretirement benefit loss (Note 8)	(258)	(463)	(166)
Changes in unamortized prior service credit (cost) (Note 8)	(123)	82	9
Unrealized gains on available-for-sale securities	—	1	—
Balance at end of year	$(1,558)	$(1,179)	$ (791)
Total Weyerhaeuser shareholders' interest:			
Balance at end of year	$ 4,070	$ 4,263	$ 4,612
Noncontrolling interests:			
Balance at beginning of year	$ 4	$ 2	$ 10
Net earnings (loss) attributable to noncontrolling interests	(1)	—	2
Contributions	—	2	—
New consolidations, de-consolidations and other transactions	40	—	(10)
Balance at end of year	$ 43	$ 4	$ 2
Total equity:			
Balance at end of year	$ 4,113	$ 4,267	$ 4,614

ACCUMULATED OTHER COMPREHENSIVE INCOME—NOTES TO CONSOLIDATED FINANCIAL STATEMENTS

2.166 OWENS-ILLINOIS, INC. (DEC)
NOTES TO CONSOLIDATED FINANCIAL STATEMENTS

Tabular data dollars in millions, except per share amounts

13. Accumulated Other Comprehensive Income (Loss)

The components of comprehensive income are: (a) net earnings; (b) change in fair value of certain derivative instruments; (c) pension and other postretirement benefit adjustments; and (d) foreign currency translation adjustments. The net effect of exchange rate fluctuations generally reflects changes in the relative strength of the U.S. dollar against major foreign currencies between the beginning and end of the year.

The following table lists the beginning balance, annual activity and ending balance of each component of accumulated other comprehensive income (loss):

	Net Effect of Exchange Rate Fluctuations	Deferred Tax Effect for Translation	Change in Certain Derivative Instruments	Employee Benefit Plans	Total Accumulated Other Comprehensive Income (Loss)
Balance on January 1, 2010	$ 290	$13	$(14)	$(1,607)	$(1,318)
2010 Change	382		(2)	60	440
Translation effect				(1)	(1)
Tax effect				(4)	(4)
Intraperiod tax allocation				(14)	(14)
Balance on December 31, 2010	672	13	(16)	(1,566)	(897)
2011 Change	(187)		(3)	(218)	(408)
Translation effect				1	1
Tax effect				(8)	(8)
Acquisition of noncontrolling interest	(9)				(9)
Balance on December 31, 2011	476	13	(19)	(1,791)	(1,321)
2012 Change	(34)		5	(200)	(229)
Translation effect				(9)	(9)
Tax effect				53	53
Balance on December 31,2012	$ 442	$13	$(14)	$(1,947)	$(1,506)

Exchange rate fluctuations in 2010 included the write-off of cumulative currency translation losses related to the disposal of the Venezuelan operations. See Note 21 to the Consolidated Financial Statements for further information.

The intraperiod tax allocation in 2010 related to a non-cash tax benefit transferred to continuing operations. See Note 10 to the Consolidated Financial Statements for further information.

Income Statement Format

PRESENTATION

3.01 Either a single-step or multistep form is acceptable for preparing a statement of income. In a single-step format, income tax is shown as a separate last item. In a multistep format, either costs are deducted from sales to show the gross margin, or costs and expenses are deducted from sales to show operating income. Further, net income should reflect all items of profit and loss recognized during the period, except for certain entities (investment companies, insurance entities, and certain not-for-profit entities) and with the sole exception of error corrections, as discussed in Financial Accounting Standards Board (FASB) *Accounting Standards Codification* (ASC) 250, *Accounting Changes and Error Corrections*.

3.02 FASB ASC 220, *Comprehensive Income*, requires that comprehensive income and its components be reported in a financial statement. Comprehensive income and its components can be reported in an income statement or a separate statement of comprehensive income.

PRESENTATION AND DISCLOSURE EXCERPT

RECLASSIFICATIONS

3.03 PEABODY ENERGY CORPORATION (DEC)
NOTES TO CONSOLIDATED FINANCIAL STATEMENTS

(7) Derivatives and Fair Value Measurements (in part)

Risk Management—Non Coal Trading Activities (in part)

Hedge Ineffectiveness. The Company assesses, both at inception and at least quarterly thereafter, whether the derivatives used in hedging activities are highly effective at offsetting the changes in the anticipated cash flows of the hedged item. The effective portion of the change in the fair value is recorded in "Accumulated other comprehensive income (loss)" until the hedged transaction impacts reported earnings, at which time any gain or loss is reclassified to earnings. To the extent that periodic changes in the fair value of derivatives deemed highly effective exceeds such changes in the hedged item, the ineffective portion of the periodic non-cash changes are recorded in earnings in the period of the change. If the hedge ceases to qualify for hedge accounting, the Company prospectively recognizes changes in the fair value of the instrument in earnings in the period of the change.

A measure of ineffectiveness is inherent in hedging future diesel fuel purchases with derivative positions based on refined petroleum products as a result of location and product differences.

The Company's derivative positions for the hedging of future explosives purchases are based on natural gas, which is the primary price component of explosives. However, a small measure of ineffectiveness exists as the contractual purchase price includes manufacturing fees that are subject to periodic adjustments. In addition, other fees, such as transportation surcharges, can result in ineffectiveness, but have historically changed infrequently and comprise a small portion of the total explosives cost.

The Company's derivative positions for the hedging of forecasted foreign currency expenditures contain a small measure of ineffectiveness due to timing differences between the hedge settlement and the purchase transaction, which could differ by less than a day and up to a maximum of 30 days.

The tables below show the classification and amounts of pre-tax gains and losses related to the Company's non-trading hedges during the years ended December 31, 2012, 2011 and 2010:

Financial Instrument	Statement of Operations Classification Gains (Losses)—Realized	Gain Recognized in Income on Non-Designated Derivatives	Gain Recognized in Other Comprehensive Income on Derivative (Effective Portion)	Gain Reclassified from Other Comprehensive Income Into Income (Effective Portion)	Loss Reclassified From Other Comprehensive Income Into Income (Ineffective Portion)
				Year Ended December 31, 2012	
			(Dollars in millions)		
Commodity swaps and options	Operating costs and expenses	$—	$ 14.5	$ 48.3	$(4.7)
Foreign currency cash flow hedge contracts	Operating costs and expenses	—	148.0	351.7	—
Total		$—	$162.5	$400.0	$(4.7)

Financial Instrument	Statement of Operations Classification Gains (Losses)—Realized	Loss Recognized in Income on Non-Designated Derivatives[1]	Gain (Loss) Recognized in Other Comprehensive Income on Derivative (Effective Portion)	Gain Reclassified From Other Comprehensive Income Into Income (Effective Portion)	Gain Reclassified From Other Comprehensive Income Into Income (Ineffective Portion)
				Year Ended December 31, 2011	
			(Dollars in millions)		
Commodity swaps and options	Operating costs and expenses	$ —	$ 30.7	$ 42.7	$4.8
Foreign currency cash flow hedge contracts					
—Operating costs	Operating costs and expenses	—	193.4	342.2	—
—Capital expenditures	Depreciation, depletion and amortization	—	(0.5)	—	—
Foreign currency economic hedge contracts	Acquisition costs related to PEA-PCI	(32.8)	—	—	—
Total		$(32.8)	$223.6	$384.9	$4.8

[1] Relates to foreign currency contracts associated with the acquisition of PEA-PCI shares under the takeover process.

Revenues and Gains

RECOGNITION AND MEASUREMENT

3.04 As explained by FASB ASC 605-10-25-1, the recognition of revenue and gains of an entity during a period involves consideration of the following two factors, with sometimes one and sometimes the other being the more important consideration:

- *Being realized or realizable.* Revenue and gains generally are not recognized until realized or realizable. Paragraph 83(a) of FASB Concepts Statement No. 5, *Recognition and Measurement in Financial Statements of Business Enterprises*, states that revenue and gains are realized when products (goods or services), merchandise, or other assets are exchanged for cash or claims to cash. That paragraph states that revenue and gains are realizable when related assets received or held are readily convertible to known amounts of cash or claims to cash.
- *Being earned.* Paragraph 83(b) of FASB Concepts Statement No. 5 states that revenue is not recognized until earned. That paragraph states that an entity's revenue-earning activities involve delivering or producing goods, rendering services, or other activities that constitute its ongoing major or central operations, and revenues are considered to have been earned when the entity has substantially accomplished what it must do to be entitled to the benefits represented by the revenues. That paragraph states that gains commonly result from transactions and other events that involve no earning process, and for recognizing gains, being earned is generally less significant than being realized or realizable.

3.05 FASB ASC 605-25 contains guidance on segmenting of transactions, referred to as *multiple element arrangements*, for both recognition and measurement. FASB ASC 605-25-25-2 requires that an entity should divide revenue arrangements with multiple deliverables into separate units of accounting if both the delivered item(s) have value to the customer on a standalone basis and, if the arrangement includes a general right of return, delivery and performance of the undelivered item(s) is probable and substantially in the vendor's control. FASB ASC 605-25-30-2 requires an entity to allocate the arrangement consideration at the inception of the arrangement to all deliverables based on their relative selling price (relative selling price method), except when another Topic in the FASB ASC requires a unit of accounting in the arrangement to be recorded at fair value or the amount that can be allocated to a unit of accounting is limited to an amount that is not contingent on delivery of additional deliverables or specified performance conditions. When a vendor applies the relative selling price method, an entity should determine the selling price using vendor-specific objective evidence of selling price, if it exists. Otherwise, the vendor should use its best estimate of selling price for that deliverable. Vendors should not ignore information that is reasonably available without undue cost or effort.

3.06 FASB ASC 605-25-50-1 requires an entity to provide specific disclosures regarding multiple element arrangements, including the accounting policy for such arrangements (for example, whether deliverables are separable into units of accounting) and the nature of such arrangements (for example, provisions for performance, termination, or cancellation of the arrangement). FASB ASC 605-25-50-1 explains that the objective of the disclosure guidance is to provide both qualitative and quantitative information about a vendor's revenue arrangements and the significant judgments made about the application of FASB ASC 605-25, changes in those judgments, or the application of FASB ASC 605-25 that may significantly affect the timing or amount of revenue recognition. Therefore, in addition to the required disclosures, a vendor shall also disclose other qualitative and quantitative information as necessary to comply with this objective. FASB ASC 605-25-50-2 requires a vendor to disclose specific information by similar arrangements including the nature of multiple deliverable arrangements; significant deliverables and the general timing of delivery or performance of service; contract provisions including performance, termination, and refund-type; discussion of significant factors, inputs, assumptions, and methods used to determine selling price; information about whether significant deliverables qualify as separate units of accounting; general timing of revenue recognition for significant deliverables; and effects of changes in selling price or methods for determining selling price.

PRESENTATION AND DISCLOSURE EXCERPTS

REVENUES

3.07 DELL INC. (FEB)
CONSOLIDATED STATEMENTS OF INCOME (in part)

(In millions, except per share amounts)

	Fiscal Year Ended		
	February 3, 2012	January 28, 2011	January 29, 2010
Net Revenue:			
Products	$49,906	$50,002	$43,697
Services, including software related	12,165	11,492	9,205
Total net revenue	62,071	61,494	52,902

NOTES TO CONSOLIDATED FINANCIAL STATEMENTS

Note 1—Description of Business and Summary of Significant Accounting Policies (in part)

Revenue Recognition—Net revenues include sales of hardware, software and peripherals, and services. Dell recognizes revenue for these products and services when it is realized or realizable and earned. Revenue is considered realized and earned when persuasive evidence of an arrangement exists; delivery has occurred or services have been rendered; Dell's fee to its customer is fixed and determinable; and collection of the resulting receivable is reasonably assured.

Dell classifies revenue and cost of revenue related to stand-alone software sold with Post Contract Support ("PCS") in the same line item as services on the Consolidated Statements of Income. Services revenue and cost of services revenue captions on the Consolidated Statements of Income include Dell's services and software from Dell's software and peripherals product category. This software revenue and related costs include software license fees and related PCS that is sold separately from computer systems through Dell's software and peripherals product category.

Products

Revenue from the sale of products is recognized when title and risk of loss passes to the customer. Delivery is considered complete when products have been shipped to Dell's customer, title and risk of loss has transferred to the customer, and customer acceptance has been satisfied. Customer acceptance is satisfied if acceptance is obtained from the customer, if all acceptance provisions lapse, or if Dell has evidence that all acceptance provisions have been satisfied.

Dell records reductions to revenue for estimated customer sales returns, rebates, and certain other customer incentive programs. These reductions to revenue are made based upon reasonable and reliable estimates that are determined by historical experience, contractual terms, and current conditions. The primary factors affecting Dell's accrual for estimated customer returns include estimated return rates as well as the number of units shipped that have a right of return that has not expired as of the balance sheet date. If returns cannot be reliably estimated, revenue is not recognized until a reliable estimate can be made or the return right lapses.

Dell sells its products directly to customers as well as through other distribution channels, such as retailers, distributors, and resellers. Dell recognizes revenue on these sales when the reseller has economic substance apart from Dell; any credit risk has been identified and quantified; title and risk of loss has passed to the sales channel; the fee paid to Dell is not contingent upon resale or payment by the end user; and Dell has no further obligations related to bringing about resale or delivery.

Sales through Dell's distribution channels are primarily made under agreements allowing for limited rights of return, price protection, rebates, and marketing development funds. Dell has generally limited return rights through contractual caps or has an established selling history for these arrangements. Therefore, there is sufficient data to establish reasonable and reliable estimates of returns for the majority of these sales. To the extent price protection or return rights are not limited and a reliable estimate cannot be made, all of the revenue and related costs are deferred until the product has been sold to the end-user or the rights expire. Dell records estimated reductions to revenue or an expense for distribution channel programs at the later of the offer or the time revenue is recognized.

Dell defers the cost of shipped products awaiting revenue recognition until revenue is recognized.

Services

Services include transactional, outsourcing and project-based offerings. Revenue is recognized for services contracts as earned, which is generally on a straight-line basis over the term of the contract or on a proportional performance basis as the services are rendered and Dell's obligations are fulfilled. Revenue from time and materials or cost-plus contracts is recognized as the services are performed. Revenue from fixed price contracts is recognized on a straight line basis, unless revenue is earned and obligations are fulfilled in a different pattern. These service contracts may include provisions for cancellation, termination, refunds, or service level adjustments. These contract provisions would not have a significant impact on recognized revenue as Dell generally recognizes revenue for these contracts as the services are performed.

For sales of extended warranties with a separate contract price, Dell defers revenue equal to the separately stated price. Revenue associated with undelivered elements is deferred and recorded when delivery occurs or services are provided. Revenue from extended warranty and service contracts, for which Dell is obligated to perform, is recorded as deferred revenue and subsequently recognized over the term of the contract on a straight-line basis.

Revenue from sales of third-party extended warranty and service contracts or software PCS, for which Dell is not obligated to perform, and for which Dell does not meet the criteria for gross revenue recognition under the guidance of the Financial Accounting Standards Board (the "FASB"), is recognized on a net basis. All other revenue is recognized on a gross basis.

Software

Dell recognizes revenue in accordance with industry specific software accounting guidance for all software and PCS that are not essential to the functionality of the hardware. Accounting for software that is essential to the functionality of the hardware is accounted for as specified below under "Multiple Deliverables." Dell has established vendor specific objective evidence ("VSOE") on a limited basis for certain software offerings. When Dell has not established VSOE to support a separation of the software license and PCS elements, the revenue and related costs are generally recognized over the term of the agreement.

In September 2009, the FASB issued revised guidance, which excluded sales of tangible products that contain essential software elements from the scope of software revenue recognition guidance. Accordingly, beginning in the first quarter of Fiscal 2011, certain Dell storage products were removed from the scope of software revenue recognition guidance. Prior to the new guidance, Dell established fair value for PCS for these products based on VSOE and used the residual method to allocate revenue to the delivered elements. Under the revised guidance, the revenue for what was previously deemed PCS is now considered part of a multiple deliverable arrangement. As such, any discount is allocated to all elements based on the relative selling price of both delivered and undelivered elements. The impact of applying this new guidance was not material to Dell's Consolidated Financial Statements for Fiscal 2011 or 2010.

Multiple Deliverables

Dell's multiple deliverable arrangements generally include hardware products that are sold with essential software or services such as extended warranty, installation, maintenance, and other services contracts. Dell's service contracts may include a combination of services arrangements, including deployment, asset recovery, recycling, IT outsourcing, consulting, applications development, applications maintenance, and business process services. The nature and terms of these multiple deliverable arrangements will vary based on the customized needs of Dell's customers. Each of these deliverables in an arrangement typically represents a separate unit of accounting.

In the first quarter of Fiscal 2011, based on new guidance, Dell began allocating revenue to all deliverables in a multiple-element arrangement based on the relative selling price of that deliverable. The hierarchy to be used to determine the selling price of a deliverable is: (1) VSOE, (2) third-party evidence of selling price ("TPE"), and (3) best estimate of the selling price ("ESP"). A majority of Dell product and service offerings are sold on a stand-alone basis. Because selling price is generally available based on stand-alone sales, Dell has limited application of TPE, as determined by comparison of pricing for products and services to the pricing of similar products and services as offered by Dell or its competitors in stand-alone sales to similarly situated customers. As new products are introduced in future periods, Dell may be required to use TPE or ESP, depending on the specific facts at the time.

For Fiscal 2010, pursuant to the previous guidance for *Revenue Arrangements with Multiple Deliverables*, Dell allocated revenue from multiple element arrangements to the elements based on the relative fair value of each element, which was generally based on the relative sales price of each element when sold separately. The adoption of the new guidance in the first quarter of Fiscal 2011 did not change the manner in which Dell accounts for its multiple deliverable arrangements as Dell did not use the residual method for the majority of its offerings and its services offerings are generally sold on a stand-alone basis where evidence of selling price is available.

Other

Dell records revenue from the sale of equipment under sales-type leases as product revenue in an amount equal to the present value of minimum lease payments at the inception of the lease. Sales-type leases also produce financing income, which is included in net revenue in the Consolidated Statements of Income and is recognized at consistent rates of return over the lease term. Dell also offers qualified customers revolving credit lines for the purchase of products and services offered by Dell. Financing income attributable to these revolving loans is recognized in net revenue on an accrual basis.

Dell reports revenue net of any revenue-based taxes assessed by governmental authorities that are imposed on and concurrent with specific revenue-producing transactions.

INTEREST

3.08 GENERAL ELECTRIC COMPANY (DEC)

STATEMENT OF EARNINGS (in part)

	General Electric Company and Consolidated Affiliates		
For the Years Ended December 31	2012	2011	2010
(In millions; per-share amounts in dollars)			
Revenues and Other Income			
Sales of goods	$ 72,991	$ 66,875	$ 60,811
Sales of services	27,158	27,648	39,625
Other income (Note 17)	2,563	5,064	1,151
GECC earnings from continuing operations	—	—	—
GECC revenues from services (Note 18)	44,647	47,701	47,980
Total revenues and other income	147,359	147,288	149,567

STATEMENT OF EARNINGS (in part)

	GE(a)			GECC		
For the Years Ended December 31	2012	2011	2010	2012	2011	2010
(In millions; per-share amounts in dollars)						
Revenues and Other Income						
Sales of goods	$ 73,304	$ 67,012	$ 60,344	$ 119	$ 148	$ 533
Sales of services	27,571	28,024	39,875	—	—	—
Other income (Note 17)	2,657	5,270	1,285	—	—	—
GECC earnings from continuing operations	7,401	6,584	3,120	—	—	—
GECC revenues from services (Note 18)	—	—	—	45,920	48,920	49,323
Total revenues and other income	110,933	106,890	104,624	46,039	49,068	49,856

NOTES TO CONSOLIDATED FINANCIAL STATEMENTS

Note 1. Basis of Presentation and Summary of Significant Accounting Policies (in part)

GECC Revenues From Services (Earned Income)

We use the interest method to recognize income on loans. Interest on loans includes origination, commitment and other non-refundable fees related to funding (recorded in earned income on the interest method). We stop accruing interest at the earlier of the time at which collection of an account becomes doubtful or the account becomes 90 days past due, and at that time, previously recognized interest income that was accrued but not collected from the borrower is reversed, unless the terms of the loan agreement permit capitalization of accrued interest to the principal balance. Although we stop accruing interest in advance of payments, we recognize interest income as cash is collected when appropriate, provided the amount does not exceed that which would have been earned at the historical effective interest rate; otherwise, payments received are applied to reduce the principal balance of the loan.

We resume accruing interest on nonaccrual, non-restructured commercial loans only when (a) payments are brought current according to the loan's original terms and (b) future payments are reasonably assured. When we agree to restructured terms with the borrower, we resume accruing interest only when it is reasonably assured that we will recover full contractual payments, and such loans pass underwriting reviews equivalent to those applied to new loans. We resume accruing interest on nonaccrual consumer loans when the customer's account is less than 90 days past due and collection of such amounts is probable. Interest accruals on modified consumer loans that are not considered to be troubled debt restructurings (TDRs) may return to current status (re-aged) only after receipt of at least three consecutive minimum monthly payments or the equivalent cumulative amount, subject to a re-aging limitation of once a year, or twice in a five-year period.

We recognize financing lease income on the interest method to produce a level yield on funds not yet recovered. Estimated unguaranteed residual values are based upon management's best estimates of the value of the leased asset at the end of the lease term. We use various sources of data in determining this estimate, including information obtained from third parties, which is adjusted for the attributes of the specific asset under lease. Guarantees of residual values by unrelated third parties are considered part of minimum lease payments. Significant assumptions we use in estimating residual values include estimated net cash flows over the remaining lease term, anticipated results of future remarketing, and estimated future component part and scrap metal prices, discounted at an appropriate rate.

We recognize operating lease income on a straight-line basis over the terms of underlying leases.

Fees include commitment fees related to loans that we do not expect to fund and line-of-credit fees. We record these fees in earned income on a straight-line basis over the period to which they relate. We record syndication fees in earned income at the time related services are performed, unless significant contingencies exist.

Note 18. GECC Revenues From Services

(In millions)	2012	2011	2010
Interest on loans	$19,074	$20,056	$20,810
Equipment leased to others	10,855	11,343	11,116
Fees	4,732	4,698	4,734
Investment income[a]	2,630	2,500	2,185
Financing leases	1,888	2,378	2,749
Associated companies[b]	1,538	2,337	2,035
Premiums earned by insurance activities	1,714	1,905	2,014
Real estate investments	1,709	1,625	1,240
Other items	1,780	2,078	2,440
	45,920	48,920	49,323
Eliminations	(1,273)	(1,219)	(1,343)
Total	$44,647	$47,701	$47,980

[a] Included net other-than-temporary impairments on investment securities of $140 million, $387 million and $253 million in 2012, 2011 and 2010, respectively. See Note 3.

[b] During 2011, we sold an 18.6% equity interest in Garanti Bank and recorded a pre-tax gain of $690 million. During 2012, we sold our remaining equity interest in Garanti Bank, which was classified as an available-for-sale security.

DIVIDENDS

3.09 THE WENDY'S COMPANY (DEC)
CONSOLIDATED STATEMENTS OF OPERATIONS (in part)

(In Thousands Except Per Share Amounts)

	Year Ended		
	December 30, 2012	January 1, 2012	January 2, 2011
Revenues:			
Sales	$2,198,323	$2,126,544	$2,079,081
Franchise revenues	306,919	304,814	296,358
	2,505,242	2,431,358	2,375,439
Costs and expenses:			
Cost of sales	1,881,248	1,816,109	1,756,954
General and administrative	287,808	292,390	311,511
Depreciation and amortization	146,976	122,992	126,846
Impairment of long-lived assets	21,097	12,883	26,326
Facilities relocation costs and other transactions	41,031	45,711	—
Other operating expense, net	4,335	4,152	3,357
	2,382,495	2,294,237	2,224,994
Operating profit	122,747	137,121	150,445
Interest expense	(98,604)	(114,110)	(118,385)
Loss on early extinguishment of debt	(75,076)	—	(26,197)
Investment income, net	36,243	484	5,259
Other income, net	1,565	945	2,434
(Loss) income from continuing operations before income taxes and noncontrolling interests	(13,125)	24,440	13,556
Benefit from (provision for) income taxes	21,083	(6,528)	4,555
Income from continuing operations	7,958	17,912	18,111

(In Thousands Except Per Share Amounts)

(8) Investments (in part)

Indirect Investment in Arby's

In connection with the sale of Arby's, Wendy's Restaurants obtained an 18.5% equity interest in Buyer Parent (through which Wendy's Restaurants indirectly retained an 18.5% interest in Arby's) with a fair value of $19,000. See Note 2 for more information on the sale of Arby's. We account for our interest in Arby's as a cost method investment. During 2012, we received a $4,625 dividend from our investment in Arby's which was included in "Investment income, net."

(14) Income Taxes (in part)

The reconciliation of income tax computed at the U.S. Federal statutory rate to reported income tax is set forth below:

	Year Ended		
	2012	2011	2010
Income tax benefit (provision) at the U.S. Federal statutory rate	$ 4,594	$(8,554)	$(4,745)
State income tax benefit (provision), net of U.S. Federal income tax effect	7,709	(2,251)	(1,122)
Corrections related to prior years' tax matters[a]	7,620	—	—
Foreign and U.S. tax effects of foreign operations[b]	347	1,147	7,693
Dividends received deduction[c]	1,133	—	—
Jobs tax credits, net	970	1,914	2,044
Non-deductible expenses	(1,263)	(622)	(439)
Adjustments related to prior year tax matters	(359)	1,881	983
Other, net[d]	332	(43)	141
	$21,083	$(6,528)	$ 4,555

[a] Corrections in 2012 related to tax matters in prior years for the effects of tax depreciation in states that do not follow federal law of $3,300 the effects of a one-time federal employment tax credit in 2011 of $2,220 and a correction to certain deferred tax assets and liabilities of $2,100.

[b] Includes previously unrecognized benefit in 2010 of foreign tax credits, net of foreign income and withholding taxes on the repatriation of foreign earnings.

[c] During 2012, we received a dividend of $4,625 from our investment in Arby's (see Note 8 for further information).

[d] Includes U.S. Federal uncertain tax positions in 2012.

ROYALTY REVENUE

3.10 SEALY CORPORATION (DEC)
CONSOLIDATED STATEMENTS OF OPERATIONS (in part)

(In thousands, except per share amounts)

	Twelve Months Ended		
	December 2, 2012	November 27, 2011	November 28, 2010
Net sales	$1,347,870	$1,230,151	$1,219,471
Cost of goods sold	808,363	751,449	709,971
Gross profit	539,507	478,702	509,500
Selling, general and administrative expenses	455,045	414,235	398,053
Asset impairment loss	827	—	—
Amortization expense	678	289	289
Restructuring expenses	2,421	—	—
Royalty income, net of royalty expense	(20,070)	(19,413)	(17,529)
Income from operations	100,606	83,591	128,687

Note 1: Basis of Presentation and Significant Accounting Policies (in part)

Business

Sealy Corporation and its subsidiaries (the "Company") are engaged in the consumer products business and manufacture, distribute and sell conventional bedding products including mattresses and box springs, as well as specialty bedding products which include latex and visco-elastic mattresses. The Company's products are manufactured in a number of countries in North and South America. Substantially all of the Company's trade accounts receivable are from retail customers. The Company also licenses its brands in domestic and international markets and receives royalty income from these arrangements. Further, the Company participates in joint ventures which manufacture and distribute products under its brand names in various Asian markets.

Royalty Income and Expense

The Company recognizes royalty income based on sales of *Sealy* and *Stearns & Foster* branded product by various licensees. The Company recognized gross royalty income of $20.1 million, $19.4 million and $17.6 million in fiscal 2012, 2011 and 2010, respectively. The increase in royalty income has been driven by increased royalties recognized related to our international licensees, including the new Brazil license agreements. The Company also pays royalties to other entities for the use of their names on product produced by the Company. The Company recognized royalty expense of an insignificant amount in fiscal 2012, an insignificant amount in fiscal 2011 and $0.1 million in fiscal 2010.

EQUITY IN EARNINGS OF AFFILIATES

3.11 MERCK & CO., INC. (DEC)
CONSOLIDATED STATEMENT OF INCOME (in part)

($ in millions except per share amounts)

	2012	2011	2010
Sales	$47,267	$48,047	$45,987
Costs, Expenses and Other			
Materials and production	16,446	16,871	18,396
Marketing and administrative	12,776	13,733	13,125
Research and development	8,168	8,467	11,111
Restructuring costs	664	1,306	985
Equity income from affiliates	(642)	(610)	(587)
Other (income) expense, net	1,116	946	1,304
	38,528	40,713	44,334

NOTES TO CONSOLIDATED FINANCIAL STATEMENTS

($ in millions except per share amounts)

9. Joint Ventures and Other Equity Method Affiliates

Equity income from affiliates reflects the performance of the Company's joint ventures and other equity method affiliates and was comprised of the following:

Years Ended December 31	2012	2011	2010
AstraZeneca LP	$621	$574	$546
Other[1]	21	36	41
	$642	$610	$587

[1] Primarily reflects results from Sanofi Pasteur MSD and Johnson & Johnson°Merck Consumer Pharmaceuticals Company (which was disposed of on September 29, 2011).

AstraZeneca LP

In 1982, Merck entered into an agreement with Astra AB ("Astra") to develop and market Astra products under a royalty-bearing license. In 1993, Merck's total sales of Astra products reached a level that triggered the first step in the establishment of a joint venture business carried on by Astra Merck Inc. ("AMI"), in which Merck and Astra each owned a 50% share. This joint venture, formed in 1994, developed and marketed most of Astra's new prescription medicines in the United States including Prilosec, the first of a class of medications known as proton pump inhibitors, which slows the production of acid from the cells of the stomach lining.

In 1998, Merck and Astra completed the restructuring of the ownership and operations of the joint venture whereby Merck acquired Astra's interest in AMI, renamed KBI Inc. ("KBI"), and contributed KBI's operating assets to a new U.S. limited partnership, Astra Pharmaceuticals L.P. (the "Partnership"), in exchange for a 1% limited partner interest. Astra contributed the net assets of its wholly owned subsidiary, Astra USA, Inc., to the Partnership in exchange for a 99% general partner interest. The Partnership, renamed AstraZeneca LP ("AZLP") upon Astra's 1999 merger with Zeneca Group Plc, became the exclusive distributor of the products for which KBI retained rights.

While maintaining a 1% limited partner interest in AZLP, Merck has consent and protective rights intended to preserve its business and economic interests, including restrictions on the power of the general partner to make certain distributions or dispositions. Furthermore, in limited events of default, additional rights will be granted to the Company, including powers to direct the actions of, or remove and replace, the Partnership's chief executive officer and chief financial officer. Merck earns ongoing revenue based on sales of KBI products and such revenue was $915 million, $1.2 billion and $1.3 billion in 2012, 2011 and 2010, respectively, primarily relating to sales of Nexium, as well as Prilosec. In addition, Merck earns certain Partnership returns, which are recorded in *Equity income from affiliates*, as reflected in the table above. Such returns include a priority return provided for in the Partnership Agreement, a preferential return representing Merck's share of undistributed AZLP GAAP earnings, and a variable return related to the Company's 1% limited partner interest.

In conjunction with the 1998 restructuring discussed above, Astra purchased an option (the "Asset Option") for a payment of $443 million, which was recorded as deferred income, to buy Merck's interest in the KBI products, excluding the gastrointestinal medicines Nexium and Prilosec (the "Non-PPI Products"). In April 2010, AstraZeneca exercised the Asset Option. Merck received $647 million from AstraZeneca representing the net present value as of March 31, 2008 of projected future pretax revenue to be received by Merck from the Non-PPI Products, which was recorded as a reduction to the Company's investment in AZLP. The Company recognized the $443 million of deferred income in 2010 as a component of *Other (income) expense, net*.

In addition, in 1998, Merck granted Astra an option to buy Merck's common stock interest in KBI and, through it, Merck's interest in Nexium and Prilosec as well as AZLP, exercisable in 2012. In June 2012, Merck and AstraZeneca amended the 1998 option agreement. The updated agreement eliminated AstraZeneca's option to acquire Merck's interest in KBI in 2012 and provides AstraZeneca a new option to acquire Merck's interest in KBI in June 2014. As a result of the amended agreement, Merck continues to record supply sales and equity income from the partnership. In 2014, AstraZeneca has the option to purchase Merck's interest in KBI based in part on the value of Merck's interest in Nexium and Prilosec. AstraZeneca's option is exercisable between March 1, 2014 and April 30, 2014. If AstraZeneca chooses to exercise this option, the closing date is expected to be June 30, 2014. Under the amended agreement, AstraZeneca will make a payment to Merck upon closing of $327 million, reflecting an estimate of the fair value of Merck's interest in Nexium and Prilosec. This portion of the exercise price is subject to a true-up in 2018 based on actual sales from closing in 2014 to June 2018. The exercise price will also include an additional amount equal to a multiple of ten times Merck's average 1% annual profit allocation in the partnership for the three years prior to exercise. The Company believes that it is likely that AstraZeneca will exercise its option in 2014.

Summarized financial information for AZLP is as follows:

Years Ended December 31	2012	2011	2010
Sales	$4,694	$4,659	$4,991
Materials and production costs	2,177	2,023	2,568
Other expense, net	1,312	1,392	886
Income before taxes [1]	1,205	1,244	1,537

December 31	2012	2011
Current assets	$3,662	$4,251
Noncurrent assets	206	250
Current liabilities	3,145	3,915

[1] Merck's partnership returns from AZLP are generally contractually determined as noted above and are not based on a percentage of income from AZLP, other than with respect to Merck's 1% limited partnership interest.

Sanofi Pasteur MSD

In 1994, Merck and Pasteur Mérieux Connaught (now Sanofi Pasteur S.A.) established an equally-owned joint venture to market vaccines in Europe and to collaborate in the development of combination vaccines for distribution in Europe. Joint venture vaccine sales were $1.1 billion for 2012, $1.1 billion for 2011 and $1.2 billion for 2010.

Johnson & Johnson° Merck Consumer Pharmaceuticals Company

In September 2011, Merck sold its 50% interest in the Johnson & Johnson° Merck Consumer Pharmaceuticals Company ("JJMCP") joint venture to J&J. The venture between Merck and J&J was formed in 1989 to develop, manufacture, market and distribute certain over-the-counter consumer products in the United States and Canada. Merck received a one-time payment of $175 million and recognized a pretax gain of $136 million in 2011 reflected in *Other (income) expense, net*. The partnership assets also included a manufacturing facility. Sales of products marketed by the joint venture were $62 million for the period from January 1, 2011 until the September 29, 2011 divestiture date and $129 million for 2010.

Investments in affiliates accounted for using the equity method, including the above joint ventures, totaled $1.3 billion at December 31, 2012 and $886 million at December 31, 2011. These amounts are reported in *Other assets*. Amounts due from the above joint ventures included in *Deferred income taxes and other current assets* were $302 million at December 31, 2012 and $276 million at December 31, 2011.

Summarized information for those affiliates (excluding AZLP disclosed separately above) is as follows:

Years Ended December 31	2012	2011[1]	2010
Sales	$1,295	$1,331	$1,486
Materials and production costs	573	584	598
Other expense, net	705	642	776
Income before taxes	17	105	112

(continued)

December 31	2012	2011
Current assets	$971	$614
Noncurrent assets	112	75
Current liabilities	480	478
Noncurrent liabilities	97	140

(1) Includes information for the JJMCP joint venture until its divestiture on September 29, 2011.

GAIN ON ASSET DISPOSALS

3.12 SEALED AIR CORPORATION (DEC)
CONSOLIDATED STATEMENTS OF OPERATIONS (in part)

(In millions, except per share amounts)	Year Ended December 31,		
	2012	2011	2010
Net sales	$ 7,648.1	$5,550.9	$4,490.1
Cost of sales	5,103.8	3,950.6	3,237.3
Gross profit	2,544.3	1,600.3	1,252.8
Marketing, administrative and development expenses	1,785.2	1,014.4	699.0
Amortization expense of intangible assets acquired	134.0	39.5	11.2
Impairment of goodwill and other intangible assets	1,892.3	—	—
Costs related to the acquisition and integration of Diversey	7.4	64.8	—
Restructuring and other charges	142.5	52.2	7.6
Operating (loss) profit	(1,417.1)	429.4	535.0
Interest expense	(384.7)	(216.6)	(161.6)
Loss on debt redemption	(36.9)	—	(38.5)
Impairment of equity method investment	(23.5)	—	—
Foreign currency exchange (losses) gains related to Venezuelan subsidiaries	(0.4)	(0.3)	5.5
Net gains on sale (other-than-temporary impairment) of available-for-sale securities	—	—	5.9
Other expense, net	(9.4)	(14.5)	(2.9)
(Loss) earnings from continuing operations before income tax provision	(1,872.0)	198.0	343.4
Income tax (benefit) provision	(261.9)	59.5	87.5
Net (loss) earnings from continuing operations	(1,610.1)	138.5	255.9
Net earnings from discontinued operations	20.9	10.6	—
Net gain on sale of discontinued operations	178.9	—	—
Net (loss) earnings available to common stockholders	$(1,410.3)	$ 149.1	$ 255.9

NOTES TO CONSOLIDATED FINANCIAL STATEMENTS

Note 2 Summary of Significant Accounting Policies and Recently Issued Accounting Standards (in part)

Summary of Significant Accounting Policies (in part)

On November 14, 2012, we completed the sale of Diversey G.K. ("Diversey Japan") (an indirect subsidiary of Diversey, Inc.). The operating results for Diversey Japan were reclassified to discontinued operations, net of tax, on the consolidated statements of operations for the years ended December 31, 2011 and 2012, and the assets and liabilities of the Diversey Japan operations were reclassified to assets and liabilities held for sale as of December 31, 2011. Prior year disclosures in the Consolidated Statement of Cash Flows and the Notes to Consolidated Financial Statements have been revised accordingly. See Note 3, "Divestiture," for further information about the sale.

Note 3 Divestiture (in part)

On November 14, 2012, we completed the sale of Diversey G.K. ("Diversey Japan") (an indirect subsidiary of Diversey, Inc.) to an investment vehicle of The Carlyle Group ("Carlyle") for gross proceeds of $323 million, including certain purchase price adjustments. After transaction costs of $10 million, we used substantially of all the net proceeds of $313 million to prepay a portion of our term loans outstanding under our senior secured credit facilities (see Note 12, "Debt and Credit Facilities"). We recorded a pre-tax gain on the sale of $211 million ($179 million net of tax) which is included in net earnings in the consolidated statement of operations for the year ended December 31, 2012.

Diversey Japan was acquired as part of the acquisition of Diversey on October 3, 2011. See Note 4, "Acquisition of Diversey Holdings, Inc." The Diversey Japan business was part of the Company's Diversey reportable segment. In accordance with the applicable accounting guidance for the disposal of long-lived assets, the results of the Diversey Japan business are presented as discontinued operations, net of tax, in the consolidated statements of operations for the years ended December 31, 2012 and 2011 and Cash Flows and related disclosures and, as such, have been excluded from both continuing operations and segment results for all years presented. Assets and liabilities of the Diversey Japan business have been segregated as assets and liabilities held for sale in the consolidated balance sheet as of December 31, 2011.

Following is selected financial information included in net earnings from discontinued operations:

	Year Ended December 31,	
	2012	2011
Net sales	$273.5	$90.0
Operating profit	$ 34.1	$17.9
Earnings from discontinued operations before income tax provision	$ 33.0	$18.1
Income tax provision	12.1	7.5
Net earnings from discontinued operations	$ 20.9	$10.6
Gain on sale of discontinued operations before income tax provision	$210.8	$ —
Income tax provision on sale	31.9	—
Net gain on sale of discontinued operations	$178.9	$ —

BARGAIN PURCHASE GAIN

3.13 AVNET, INC. (JUN)
CONSOLIDATED STATEMENTS OF OPERATIONS (in part)

	Years Ended		
(Thousands, except share amounts)	June 30, 2012	July 2, 2011	July 3, 2010
Sales	$25,707,522	$26,534,413	$19,160,172
Cost of sales	22,656,965	23,426,608	16,879,955
Gross profit	3,050,557	3,107,805	2,280,217
Selling, general and administrative expenses	2,092,807	2,100,650	1,619,198
Restructuring, integration and other charges (Note 17)	73,585	77,176	25,419
Operating income	884,165	929,979	635,600
Other income (expense), net	(5,442)	10,724	2,480
Interest expense	(90,859)	(92,452)	(61,748)
Gain on bargain purchase and other (Note 2)	2,918	22,715	—
Gain on sale of assets (Note 2)	—	—	8,751
Income before income taxes	790,782	870,966	585,083

NOTES TO CONSOLIDATED FINANCIAL STATEMENTS

2. Acquisitions and Divestitures (in part)

Acquisitions (in part)

Gain on Bargain Purchase and Other

In January 2012, the Company acquired Unidux Electronic Limited ("UEL"), a Singapore publicly traded company, through a tender offer. After assessing the assets acquired and liabilities assumed, the consideration paid was below book value even though the price paid per share represented a premium to the trading levels at that time. Accordingly, the Company recognized a gain on bargain purchase of $4,317,000 pre- and after tax and $0.03 per share on a diluted basis. In addition, during fiscal 2012, the Company recognized a loss of $1,399,000 pre-tax, $854,000 after tax and $0.01 per diluted share included in "Gain on bargain purchase and other" on the consolidated statements of operations related to a write-down of an investment in a small technology company and the write-off of certain deferred financing costs associated with the early termination of a credit facility (see Note 7 for further discussion of the credit facility).

During fiscal 2011, the Company acquired Unidux, Inc. ("Unidux"), an electronics component distributor in Japan, which is reported as part of the EM Asia region. Unidux was a publicly traded company which shares were trading below its book value for a period of time. In a tender offer, Avnet offered a purchase price per share for Unidux that was above the prevailing trading price at that time. Even though the purchase price was below book value, the Unidux shareholders tendered their shares. As a result, the Company recognized a gain on bargain purchase of $30,990,000 pre- and after tax and $0.20 per share on a diluted basis. Prior to recognizing the gain, the Company reassessed the assets acquired and liabilities assumed in the acquisition. Also during fiscal 2011, the Company recognized a loss of $6,308,000 pre-tax, $3,857,000 after tax and $0.02 per share on a diluted basis included in "Gain on bargain purchase and other" related to the write-down of prior investments in smaller technology start-up companies (see Note 5 for other amounts included in "Gain on bargain purchase and other").

3.14 MUELLER INDUSTRIES, INC. (DEC)

CONSOLIDATED STATEMENTS OF INCOME (in part)

(In thousands, except per share data)	2012	2011	2010
Net sales	$2,189,938	$2,417,797	$2,059,797
Cost of goods sold	1,904,463	2,115,677	1,774,811
Depreciation and amortization	31,495	36,865	40,364
Selling, general, and administrative expense	129,456	135,953	131,211
Litigation settlements	(4,050)	(10,500)	—
Insurance settlements	(1,500)	—	(22,736)
Severance	3,369	—	—
Operating income	126,705	139,802	136,147

NOTES TO CONSOLIDATED FINANCIAL STATEMENTS

Note 10—Commitments and Contingencies (in part)

Supplier Litigation

On May 6, 2011, the Company and two of its subsidiaries, Mueller Streamline Co. and B&K Industries, Inc. (B&K)(Plaintiffs), filed a civil lawsuit in federal district court in Los Angeles, California against a former supplier, Xiamen Lota International Co., Ltd (Xiamen Lota), its U.S. sales representative (Lota USA), and certain other persons (Defendants). The lawsuit alleged, among other things, that the Defendants gave Peter D. Berkman, a former executive of the Company and B&K, an undisclosed interest in Lota USA, and made payments and promises of payments to him, in return for Peter Berkman maintaining the Company as a customer, increasing purchasing levels, and acquiescing to non-competitive and excessive pricing for Xiamen Lota products. The lawsuit alleged violations of federal statutes 18 U.S.C. Sections 1962(c) and (d) (RICO claims) and California state law unfair competition. The lawsuit sought compensatory, treble and punitive damages, and other appropriate relief including an award of reasonable attorneys' fees and costs of suit. In October 2012, the lawsuit, together with certain related proceedings in Illinois and Tennessee, were settled on mutually agreeable terms and, in connection therewith, the Company received a $5.8 million cash payment. The amount recorded in the Consolidated Statement of Income is net of legal costs.

Litigation Settlement

The Company negotiated a settlement with Peter D. Berkman and Jeffrey A. Berkman, former executives of the Company and B&K Industries, Inc. (B&K), a wholly owned subsidiary of the Company, that required the payment of $10.5 million in cash by Peter Berkman, Jeffrey Berkman, and Homewerks Worldwide LLC to the Company. During 2011, the Company recorded a gain of $10.5 million upon receipt of the settlement proceeds.

DERIVATIVES

3.15 NOBLE ENERGY, INC. (DEC)

CONSOLIDATED STATEMENTS OF OPERATIONS (in part)

(Millions, except per share amounts)

	Year Ended December 31,		
	2012	2011	2010
Revenues			
Oil, Gas and NGL Sales	$4,037	$3,179	$2,523
Income from Equity Method Investees	186	193	118
Other revenues	—	32	72
Total revenues	4,223	3,404	2,713
Costs and Expenses			
Production expense	673	558	515
Exploration expense	409	277	242
Depreciation, depletion and amortization	1,370	878	819
General and administrative	384	339	273
Gain on divestitures	(154)	(25)	(113)
Asset impairments	104	757	144
Other operating (income) expense, net	25	86	64
Total operating expenses	2,811	2,870	1,944
Operating Income	1,412	534	769

(continued)

	Year Ended December 31,		
	2012	**2011**	**2010**
Other (Income) Expense			
Gain on commodity derivative instruments	(75)	(42)	(157)
Interest, net of amount capitalized	125	65	72
Other non-operating (Income) expense, net	6	9	6
Total Other (Income) Expense	56	32	(79)
Income from continuing operations before income taxes	1,356	502	848

NOTES TO CONSOLIDATED FINANCIAL STATEMENTS

Note 1. Summary of Significant Accounting Policies (in part)

Derivative Instruments and Hedging Activities. All derivative instruments (including certain derivative instruments embedded in other contracts) are recorded in our consolidated balance sheets as either an asset or liability and measured at fair value. Changes in the derivative instrument's fair value are recognized currently in earnings, unless the derivative instrument has been designated as a cash flow hedge and specific cash flow hedge accounting criteria are met. Under cash flow hedge accounting, unrealized gains and losses are reflected in shareholders' equity as accumulated other comprehensive loss (AOCL) until the forecasted transaction occurs. The derivative's gains or losses are then offset against related results on the hedged transaction in the statements of operations.

A company must formally document, designate and assess the effectiveness of transactions that receive hedge accounting. Only derivative instruments that are expected to be highly effective in offsetting anticipated gains or losses on the hedged cash flows and that are subsequently documented to have been highly effective can qualify for hedge accounting. Effectiveness must be assessed both at inception of the hedge and on an ongoing basis. Any ineffectiveness in hedging instruments whereby gains or losses do not exactly offset anticipated gains or losses of hedged cash flows is measured and recognized in earnings in the period in which it occurs. When using hedge accounting, we assess hedge effectiveness quarterly based on total changes in the derivative instrument's fair value by performing regression analysis. A hedge is considered effective if certain statistical tests are met. We record hedge ineffectiveness in (gain) loss on commodity derivative instruments.

Accounting for Commodity Derivative Instruments. We account for our commodity derivative instruments using mark-to-market accounting and recognize all gains and losses in earnings during the period in which they occur.

We offset the fair value amounts recognized for derivative instruments and the fair value amounts recognized for the right to reclaim cash collateral or the obligation to return cash collateral. The cash collateral (commonly referred to as a "margin") must arise from derivative instruments recognized at fair value that are executed with the same counterparty under a master arrangement with netting clauses.

Accounting for Interest Rate Derivative Instruments. We designate interest rate derivative instruments as cash flow hedges. Changes in fair value of interest rate swaps or interest rate "locks" used as cash flow hedges are reported in AOCL, to the extent the hedge is effective, until the forecasted transaction occurs, at which time they are recorded as adjustments to interest expense over the term of the related notes.

See Note 10. Derivative Instruments and Hedging Activities.

Note 10. Derivative Instruments and Hedging Activities

Objective and Strategies for Using Derivative Instruments. In order to mitigate the effect of commodity price volatility and enhance the predictability of cash flows relating to the marketing of our crude oil and natural gas, we enter into crude oil and natural gas price hedging arrangements with respect to a portion of our expected production. The derivative instruments we use include variable to fixed price commodity swaps, two-way and three-way collars and basis swaps.

The fixed price swap, two-way collar, and basis swap contracts entitle us (floating price payor) to receive settlement from the counterparty (fixed price payor) for each calculation period in amounts, if any, by which the settlement price for the scheduled trading days applicable for each calculation period is less than the fixed strike price or floor price. We would pay the counterparty if the settlement price for the scheduled trading days applicable for each calculation period is more than the fixed strike price or ceiling price. The amount payable by us, if the floating price is above the fixed or ceiling price, is the product of the notional quantity per calculation period and the excess of the floating price over the fixed or ceiling price in respect of each calculation period. The amount payable by the counterparty, if the floating price is below the fixed or floor price, is the product of the notional quantity per calculation period and the excess of the fixed or floor price over the floating price in respect of each calculation period.

A three-way collar consists of a two-way collar contract combined with a put option contract sold by us with a strike price below the floor price of the two-way collar. We receive price protection at the purchased put option floor price of the two-way collar if commodity prices are above the sold put option strike price. If commodity prices fall below the sold put option strike price, we receive the cash market price plus the delta between the two put option strike prices. This type of instrument allows us to capture more value in a rising commodity price environment, but limits our benefits in a downward commodity price environment.

We also may enter into forward contracts to hedge anticipated exposure to interest rate risk associated with public debt financing.

While these instruments mitigate the cash flow risk of future reductions in commodity prices or increases in interest rates, they may also curtail benefits from future increases in commodity prices or decreases in interest rates.

See Note 15. Fair Value Measurements and Disclosures for a discussion of methods and assumptions used to estimate the fair values of our derivative instruments.

Counterparty Credit Risk. Derivative instruments expose us to counterparty credit risk. Our commodity derivative instruments are currently with a diversified group of major banks or market participants, and we monitor and manage our level of financial exposure. Our commodity derivative contracts are executed under master agreements which allow us, in the event of default, to elect early termination of all contracts with the defaulting counterparty. If we choose to elect early termination, all asset and liability positions with the defaulting counterparty would be net settled at the time of election.

We monitor the creditworthiness of our commodity derivatives counterparties. However, we are not able to predict sudden changes in counterparties' creditworthiness. In addition, even if such changes are not sudden, we may be limited in our ability to mitigate an increase in counterparty credit risk.

Possible actions would be to transfer our position to another counterparty or request a voluntary termination of the derivative contracts resulting in a cash settlement. Should one of these financial counterparties not perform, we may not realize the benefit of some of our derivative instruments under lower commodity prices or higher interest rates, and could incur a loss.

Interest Rate Derivative Instrument. In January 2010, we entered into an interest rate forward starting swap to effectively fix the cash flows related to interest payments on our anticipated March 2011 debt issuance. During first quarter 2011, the net liability position on the swap was reduced in our mark to market calculation, and we recognized a corresponding gain of $23 million, net of tax, in AOCL. On February 15, 2011 we settled the interest rate swap, which had a net liability position of $40 million at the time of settlement. Approximately $26 million, net of tax, was recorded in accumulated other comprehensive loss (AOCL) and is being reclassified to interest expense over the term of the notes. The ineffective portion of the interest rate swap was de minimis.

Unsettled Derivative Instruments. As of December 31, 2012, we had entered into the following crude oil derivative instruments:

Settlement Period	Type of Contract	Index	Bbls Per Day	Swaps Weighted Average Fixed Price	Collars Weighted Average Short Put Price	Collars Weighted Average Floor Price	Collars Weighted Average Ceiling Price
Instruments Entered Into as of December 31, 2012							
2013	Swaps	NYMEX WTI	8,000	$ 89.63	$ —	$ —	$ —
2013	Swaps	Dated Brent	3,000	98.03	—	—	—
2013	Two-Way Collars	NYMEX WTI	5,000	—	—	95.00	115.00
2013	Three-Way Collars	NYMEX WTI	7,000	—	63.57	83.57	109.04
2013	Three-Way Collars	Dated Brent	26,000	—	82.50	100.93	126.63
2014	Swaps	NYMEX WTI	11,000	90.26	—	—	—
2014	Swaps	Dated Brent	10,000	105.14	—	—	—
2014	Three-Way Collars	NYMEX WTI	4,000	—	77.00	92.00	106.13
2014	Three-Way Collars	Dated Brent	11,000	—	85.45	99.09	128.40

As of December 31, 2012, we had entered into the following natural gas derivative instruments:

Settlement Period	Type of Contract	Index	MMBtu Per Day	Swaps Weighted Average Fixed Price	Collars Weighted Average Short Put Price	Collars Weighted Average Floor Price	Collars Weighted Average Ceiling Price
Instruments Entered Into as of December 31, 2012							
2013	Swaps	NYMEX HH	60,000	$4.58	$ —	$ —	$ —
2013	Two-Way Collars	NYMEX HH	40,000	—	—	3.25	5.14
2013	Three-Way Collars	NYMEX HH	100,000	—	3.88	4.75	5.63
2014	Swaps	NYMEX HH	60,000	4.24	—	—	—
2014	Three-Way Collars	NYMEX HH	130,000	—	2.56	3.56	5.21

Fair Value Amounts and Gains and Losses on Derivative Instruments. The fair values of derivative instruments in our consolidated balance sheets were as follows:

Fair Value of Derivative Instruments

| | Asset Derivative Instruments | | | | Liability Derivative Instruments | | | |
| | December 31, 2012 | | December 31, 2011 | | December 31, 2012 | | December 31, 2011 | |
(Millions)	Balance Sheet Location	Fair Value	Balance Sheet Location	Fair Value	Balance Sheet Location	Fair Value	Balance Sheet Location	Fair Value
Commodity Derivative Instruments	Current Assets	$63	Current Assets	$10	Current Liabilities	$ 7	Current Liabilities	$76
	Noncurrent Assets	21	Noncurrent Assets	37	Noncurrent Liabilities	3	Noncurrent Liabilities	7
Total		$84		$47		$10		$83

The effect of derivative instruments on our consolidated statements of operations was as follows:

| | Year Ended December 31, | | |
(Millions)	2012	2011	2010
Realized Mark-to-Market (Gain) loss	$ 34	$(64)	$ (87)
Unrealized Mark-to-Market (Gain) loss	(109)	22	(70)
Total (Gain) loss on commodity derivative instruments	$ (75)	$(42)	$(157)

| | Derivative Instruments in Cash Flow Hedge Relationships | | | | | |
| | Amount of (Gain) Loss on Derivative Instruments Recognized in Other Comprehensive (Income) Loss | | | Amount of (Gain) Loss on Derivative Instruments Reclassified from Accumulated Other Comprehensive (Income) Loss | | |
(Millions)	2012	2011	2010	2012	2011	2010
Commodity Derivative Instruments in Previously Designated Cash Flow Hedging Relationships[1]						
Crude Oil	$—	$—	$—	$—	$—	$19
Natural Gas	—	—	—	—	—	1
Interest Rate Derivative Instruments in Cash Flow Hedging Relationships	—	(23)	63	1	1	1
Total	$—	$(23)	$ 63	$ 1	$ 1	$21

[1] Includes effect of commodity derivative instruments previously accounted for as cash flow hedges. All net derivative gains and losses that were deferred in AOCL as a result of previous cash flow hedge accounting, had been reclassified to earnings by December 31, 2010.

AOCL at December 31, 2012 included deferred losses of $25 million, net of tax, related to interest rate derivative instruments. This amount will be reclassified to earnings as an adjustment to interest expense over the terms of our senior notes due April 2014 and March 2041. Approximately $2 million of deferred losses (net of tax) will be reclassified to earnings during the next 12 months and will be recorded as an increase in interest expense.

CHANGE IN VALUE OF INVESTMENTS

3.16 WELLPOINT, INC. (DEC)
CONSOLIDATED STATEMENTS OF INCOME (in part)

| | Years Ended December 31 | | |
(In millions, except per share data)	2012	2011	2010
Revenues			
Premiums	$56,496.7	$55,969.6	$53,973.6
Administrative fees	3,934.1	3,854.6	3,730.4
Other revenue	297.7	41.0	36.5
Total operating revenue	60,728.5	59,865.2	57,740.5
Net investment income	686.1	703.7	803.3
Net realized gains on investments	334.9	235.1	194.1
Other-than-temporary impairment losses on investments:			
Total other-than-temporary impairment losses on investments	(41.2)	(114.7)	(70.8)
Portion of other-than-temporary impairment losses recognized in other comprehensive income	3.4	21.4	31.4
Other-than-temporary impairment losses recognized in income	(37.8)	(93.3)	(39.4)
Total revenues	61,711.7	60,710.7	58,698.5

2. Basis of Presentation and Significant Accounting Policies (in part)

Investments: Certain Financial Accounting Standards Board, or FASB, other-than-temporary impairment, or FASB OTTI, guidance applies to fixed maturity securities and provides guidance on the recognition and presentation of other-than-temporary impairments. In addition, this FASB OTTI guidance requires disclosures related to other-than-temporary impairments. If a fixed maturity security is in an unrealized loss position and we have the intent to sell the fixed maturity security, or it is more likely than not that we will have to sell the fixed maturity security before recovery of its amortized cost basis, the decline in value is deemed to be other-than-temporary and is recorded to other-than-temporary impairment losses recognized in income in our consolidated income statements. For impaired fixed maturity securities that we do not intend to sell or it is more likely than not that we will not have to sell such securities, but we expect that we will not fully recover the amortized cost basis, the credit component of the other-than-temporary impairment is recognized in other-than-temporary impairment losses recognized in income in our consolidated income statements and the non-credit component of the other-than-temporary impairment is recognized in other comprehensive income. Furthermore, unrealized losses entirely caused by non-credit related factors related to fixed maturity securities for which we expect to fully recover the amortized cost basis continue to be recognized in accumulated other comprehensive income, or AOCI.

The credit component of an other-than-temporary impairment is determined by comparing the net present value of projected future cash flows with the amortized cost basis of the fixed maturity security. The net present value is calculated by discounting our best estimate of projected future cash flows at the effective interest rate implicit in the fixed maturity security at the date of acquisition. For mortgage-backed and asset-backed securities, cash flow estimates are based on assumptions regarding the underlying collateral including prepayment speeds, vintage, type of underlying asset, geographic concentrations, default rates, recoveries and changes in value. For all other debt securities, cash flow estimates are driven by assumptions regarding probability of default, including changes in credit ratings, and estimates regarding timing and amount of recoveries associated with a default.

The unrealized gains or losses on our current and long-term equity securities classified as available-for-sale are included in accumulated other comprehensive income as a separate component of shareholders' equity, unless the decline in value is deemed to be other-than-temporary and we do not have the intent and ability to hold such equity securities until their full cost can be recovered, in which case such equity securities are written down to fair value and the loss is charged to other-than-temporary impairment losses recognized in income.

We maintain various rabbi trusts to account for the assets and liabilities under certain deferred compensation plans. Under these plans, the participants can defer certain types of compensation and elect to receive a return on the deferred amounts based on the changes in fair value of various investment options, primarily a variety of mutual funds. Rabbi trust assets are classified as trading, which are reported in other invested assets, current, in the consolidated balance sheets.

We use the equity method of accounting for investments in companies in which our ownership interest enables us to influence the operating or financial decisions of the investee company. Our proportionate share of equity in net income of these unconsolidated affiliates is reported with net investment income.

For asset-backed securities included in fixed maturity securities, we recognize income using an effective yield based on anticipated prepayments and the estimated economic life of the securities. When estimates of prepayments change, the effective yield is recalculated to reflect actual payments to date and anticipated future payments. The net investment in the securities is adjusted to the amount that would have existed had the new effective yield been applied since the acquisition of the securities. Such adjustments are reported with net investment income.

Investment income is recorded when earned. All securities sold resulting in investment gains and losses are recorded on the trade date. Realized gains and losses are determined on the basis of the cost or amortized cost of the specific securities sold.

We participate in securities lending programs whereby marketable securities in our investment portfolio are transferred to independent brokers or dealers based on, among other things, their creditworthiness in exchange for cash collateral initially equal to at least 102% of the value of the securities on loan and is thereafter maintained at a minimum of 100% of the market value of the securities loaned (calculated as the ratio of initial market value of cash collateral to current market value of the securities on loan). Accordingly, the market value of the securities on loan to each borrower is monitored daily and the borrower is required to deliver additional cash collateral if the market value of the securities on loan exceeds the initial market value of cash collateral delivered. The fair value of the collateral received at the time of the transaction amounted to $564.7 and $872.5 at December 31, 2012 and 2011, respectively. The value of the cash collateral delivered represented 102% of the market value of the securities on loan at December 31, 2012 and 2011. Under the FASB guidance related to accounting for transfers and servicing of financial assets and extinguishments of liabilities, we recognize the cash collateral as an asset, which is reported as "securities lending collateral" on our consolidated balance sheets and we record a corresponding liability for the obligation to return the cash collateral to the borrower, which is reported as "securities lending payable." The securities on loan are reported in the applicable investment category on the consolidated balance sheets. Unrealized gains or losses on securities lending collateral are included in accumulated other comprehensive income as a separate component of shareholders' equity.

5. Investments (in part)

The major categories of net investment income for the years ended December 31 are as follows:

	2012	2011	2010
Fixed maturity securities	$652.8	$692.4	$740.7
Equity securities	38.4	34.0	29.6
Cash and cash equivalents	2.5	3.7	8.3
Other	34.6	2.4	61.9
Investment income	728.3	732.5	840.5
Investment expense	(42.2)	(28.8)	(37.2)
Net investment income	$686.1	$703.7	$803.3

Net realized investment gains/losses and net change in unrealized appreciation/depreciation in investments for the years ended December 31 are as follows:

	2012	2011	2010
Net realized gains/losses on investments:			
Fixed maturity securities:			
Gross realized gains from sales	$ 401.0	$289.2	$ 268.1
Gross realized losses from sales	(54.8)	(65.1)	(39.1)
Net realized gains/losses from sales of fixed maturity securities	346.2	224.1	229.0
Equity securities:			
Gross realized gains from sales	82.0	75.4	57.7
Gross realized losses from sales	(93.8)	(68.0)	(81.4)
Net realized gains/losses from sales of equity securities	(11.8)	7.4	(23.7)
Other realized gains/losses on investments	0.5	3.6	(11.2)
Net realized gains on investments	334.9	235.1	194.1
Other-than-temporary impairment losses recognized in income:			
Fixed maturity securities	(11.8)	(24.2)	(24.4)
Equity securities	(26.0)	(69.1)	(15.0)
Other-than-temporary Impairment losses recognized in income:	(37.8)	(93.3)	(39.4)
Change in net unrealized gains/losses on investments:			
Fixed maturity securities	199.8	155.9	29.7
Equity securities	94.7	(124.6)	164.7
Total change in net unrealized gains/losses on investments	294.5	31.3	194.4
Deferred income tax expense	(100.1)	(11.4)	(54.6)
Net change in net unrealized gains/losses on investments	194.4	19.9	139.8
Net realized gains/losses on investments, other-than-temporary impairment losses recognized in income and net change in net unrealized gains/losses on investments	$ 491.5	$161.7	$ 294.5

A primary objective in the management of our fixed maturity and equity portfolios is to maximize total return relative to underlying liabilities and respective liquidity needs. In achieving this goal, assets may be sold to take advantage of market conditions or other investment opportunities as well as tax considerations. Sales will generally produce realized gains and losses. In the ordinary course of business, we may sell securities at a loss for a number of reasons, including, but not limited to: (i) changes in the investment environment; (ii) expectations that the fair value could deteriorate further; (iii) desire to reduce exposure to an issuer or an industry; (iv) changes in credit quality; or (v) changes in expected cash flow. During the year ended December 31, 2012, we sold $14,098.6 of investments which resulted in gross realized gains of $483.0 and gross realized losses of $148.6.

A significant judgment in the valuation of investments is the determination of when an other-than-temporary decline in value has occurred. We follow a consistent and systematic process for recognizing impairments on securities that sustain other-than-temporary declines in value. We have established a committee responsible for the impairment review process. The decision to impair a security incorporates both quantitative criteria and qualitative information. The impairment review process considers a number of factors including, but not limited to: (i) the length of time and the extent to which the fair value has been less than book value, (ii) the financial condition and near term prospects of the issuer, (iii) our intent and ability to retain impaired equity security investments for a period of time sufficient to allow for any anticipated recovery in fair value, (iv) our intent to sell or the likelihood that we will need to sell a fixed maturity security before recovery of its amortized cost basis, (v) whether the debtor is current on interest and principal payments, (vi) the reasons for the decline in value (i.e., credit event compared to liquidity, general credit spread widening, currency exchange rate or interest rate factors) and (vii) general market conditions and industry or sector specific factors. For securities that are deemed to be other-than-temporarily impaired, the security is adjusted to fair value and the resulting losses are recognized in realized gains or losses in the consolidated statements of income. The new cost basis of the impaired securities is not increased for future recoveries in fair value.

Other-than-temporary impairments recorded in 2012, 2011 and 2010 were primarily the result of the continued credit deterioration on specific issuers in the bond markets and certain equity securities' fair values remaining below cost for an extended period of time. There were no individually significant other-than-temporary impairment losses on investments by issuer during 2012, 2011 or 2010.

3.17 FREEPORT-MCMORAN COPPER & GOLD INC. (DEC)

CONSOLIDATED STATEMENTS OF INCOME (in part)

	Years Ended December 31,		
(In millions, except per share amounts)	**2012**	**2011**	**2010**
Revenues	$18,010	$20,880	$18,982
Cost of sales:			
Production and delivery	10,382	9,898	8,335
Depreciation, depletion and amortization	1,179	1,022	1,036
Total cost of sales	11,561	10,920	9,371
Selling, general and administrative expenses	431	415	381
Exploration and research expenses	285	271	143
Environmental obligations and shutdown costs	(22)	134	19
Gain on insurance settlement	(59)	—	—
Total costs and expenses	12,196	11,740	9,914
Operating income	5,814	9,140	9,068

NOTES TO CONSOLIDATED FINANCIAL STATEMENTS

Note 13. Contingencies (in part)

Insurance. FCX purchases a variety of insurance products to mitigate potential losses. The various insurance products typically have specified deductible amounts or self-insured retentions and policy limits. FCX generally is self-insured for U.S. workers' compensation, but purchases excess insurance up to statutory limits. An actuarial analysis is performed twice a year for various FCX casualty programs, including workers' compensation, to estimate required insurance reserves. Insurance reserves totaled $52 million at December 31, 2012, which consisted of a current portion of $8 million (included in accounts payable and accrued liabilities) and a long-term portion of $44 million (included in other liabilities).

FCX maintains property damage and business interruption insurance related to its operations. FCX and its insurers entered into an insurance settlement agreement in December 2012. The insurers agreed to pay an aggregate of $63 million, including PT Freeport Indonesia's joint venture partner's share, for the settlement of the insurance claim for business interruption and property damage relating to the 2011 incidents affecting PT Freeport Indonesia's concentrate pipelines. As a result of the settlement, FCX recorded a gain of $59 million ($31 million to net income attributable to FCX common stockholders) in 2012.

GAINS ON EXTINGUISHMENT OF DEBT

3.18 THE BON-TON STORES, INC. (JAN)

MANAGEMENT'S DISCUSSION AND ANALYSIS OF FINANCIAL CONDITION AND RESULTS OF OPERATIONS (in part)

2011 Performance and Accomplishments (in part)

In 2011, as part of our financing strategy, we continued our focus on opportunities to improve our credit profile and deliver value to shareholders. In furtherance of our strategy, on January 31, 2011, we voluntarily prepaid our outstanding indebtedness under our Second Lien Loan and Security Agreement that provided for $75.0 million of term loans expiring November 18, 2013 (the "Term Loan Facility"). As a result of such prepayment, the Term Loan Facility was terminated.

On March 21, 2011, we entered into a $625.0 million senior secured Second Amended and Restated Loan and Security Agreement (the "Second Amended Revolving Credit Facility") that expires on the earlier of (a) March 21, 2016 and (b) the date that is 60 days prior to the earlier of the maturity date of our 10 ¼% Senior Notes (the "Senior Notes") and the mortgage loan facility. The Second Amended Revolving Credit Facility replaced our prior $675.0 million revolving credit facility, which was scheduled to mature on June 4, 2013 (the "2009 Revolving Credit Facility").

In the fourth quarter of 2011, we repurchased at a discount, in open market transactions, a total of $46.0 million principal amount of the $510.0 million aggregate principal outstanding of our Senior Notes.

As a result of the aforementioned financing activity, we reduced our interest expense in 2011 and realized a net gain on the extinguishment of debt. Our interest expense decreased $22.8 million, largely the result of reduced borrowing levels and lower interest rates due to our prepayment of the Term Loan Facility and entry into the Second Amended Revolving Credit Facility. The repurchase of our Senior Notes resulted in a gain of $18.2 million. This gain was partially offset by a $9.5 million loss primarily for an early termination fee associated with the prepayment of the Term Loan Facility and accelerated deferred financing fees associated with the Term Loan Facility and the 2009 Revolving Credit Facility, resulting in a net gain on extinguishment of debt of $8.7 million. See "Results of Operations—2011 Compared with 2010" for further discussion of our interest expense and Note 9 of the Notes to Consolidated Financial Statements for further discussion of our long-term debt.

2011 Compared With 2010 (in part)

Gain on extinguishment of debt: In the first quarter of 2011, we recorded a $9.5 million loss on the extinguishment of debt, which primarily consisted of an early termination fee of $3.8 million and accelerated deferred financing fees of $4.4 million associated with the prepayment of the Term Loan Facility and accelerated deferred financing fees of $1.3 million associated with the 2009 Revolving Credit Facility. In the fourth quarter of 2011, we repurchased at a discount, in open market transactions, $46.0 million (principal amount) of our Senior Notes. The repurchase resulted in a gain of $18.2 million. Together, the transactions resulted in a net gain on extinguishment of debt of $8.7 million.

CONSOLIDATED STATEMENTS OF OPERATIONS (in part)

	Fiscal Year Ended		
(In thousands except per share data)	January 28, 2012	January 29, 2011	January 30, 2010
Net sales	$2,884,661	$2,980,479	$2,959,824
Other income	68,869	66,006	75,113
	2,953,530	3,046,485	3,034,937
Costs and expenses:			
Costs of merchandise sold	1,847,369	1,860,182	1,862,192
Selling, general and administrative	936,060	942,660	963,639
Depreciation and amortization	95,033	102,202	111,635
Amortization of lease-related interests	4,747	4,555	4,866
Impairment charges	3,690	1,738	5,883
Income from operations	66,631	135,148	86,722
Interest expense, net	89,507	112,301	98,130
(Gain) loss on extinguishment of debt	(8,729)	—	678
(Loss) income before income taxes	(14,147)	22,847	(12,086)

Expenses and Losses

PRESENTATION

3.19 Paragraphs 80 and 83 of FASB Concepts Statement No. 6, *Elements of Financial Statements—a replacement of FASB Concepts Statement No. 3 (incorporating an amendment of FASB Concepts Statement No. 2)*, define expenses and losses as follows:

80. Expenses are outflows or other using up of assets or incurrences of liabilities (or a combination of both) from delivering or producing goods, rendering services, or carrying out other activities that constitute the entity's ongoing major or central operations.

83. Losses are decreases in equity (net assets) from peripheral or incidental transactions of an entity and from all other transactions and other events and circumstances affecting the entity except those that result from expenses or distributions to owners.

PRESENTATION AND DISCLOSURE EXCERPTS

SELLING, GENERAL, AND ADMINISTRATIVE

3.20 ANN INC. (JAN)
CONSOLIDATED STATEMENTS OF OPERATIONS (in part)

	Fiscal Year Ended		
(In thousands, except per share amounts)	January 28, 2012	January 29, 2011	January 30, 2010
Net sales	$2,212,493	$1,980,195	$1,828,523
Cost of sales	1,004,350	876,201	834,188
Gross margin	1,208,143	1,103,994	994,335
Selling, general and administrative expenses	1,062,644	978,580	966,603
Restructuring charges	—	5,624	36,368
Asset impairment charges	—	—	15,318
Operating income/(loss)	145,499	119,790	(23,954)

1. Summary of Significant Accounting Policies (in part)

Cost of Sales and Selling, General and Administrative Expenses

The following table illustrates the primary costs classified in each major expense category:

Cost of Sales	Selling, General and Administrative Expenses
• Cost of merchandise sold;	• Payroll, bonus and benefit costs for retail and corporate associates;
• Costs associated with the Company's sourcing operations;	• Design and merchandising costs;
• Freight costs associated with moving merchandise from suppliers to the Company's distribution center;	• Occupancy costs for retail and corporate facilities;
• Costs associated with the movement of merchandise through customs;	• Depreciation related to retail and corporate assets;
• Costs associated with the fulfillment and shipment of client orders from the Company's online stores;	• Advertising and marketing costs;
• Depreciation related to merchandise management systems;	• Occupancy and other costs associated with operating the Company's distribution center;
• Sample development costs;	• Freight expenses associated with moving merchandise from the Company's distribution center to its retail stores or from store to store; and
• Direct costs of the credit card client loyalty program;	• Legal, finance, information systems and other corporate overhead costs.
• Merchandise shortage; and	
• Client shipping costs for store merchandise shipments.	

RESEARCH AND DEVELOPMENT

3.21 JOHNSON & JOHNSON (DEC)
CONSOLIDATED STATEMENTS OF EARNINGS (in part)

(Dollars and Shares in Millions Except Per Share Amounts) (Note 1)

	2012	2011	2010
Sales to Customers	$67,224	65,030	61,587
Cost of products sold	21,658	20,360	18,792
Gross profit	45,566	44,670	42,795
Selling, marketing and administrative expenses	20,869	20,969	19,424
Research and development expense	7,665	7,548	6,844
In-process research and development (Note 5)	1,163	—	—
Interest income	(64)	(91)	(107)
Interest expense, net of portion capitalized (Note 4)	532	571	455
Other (income) expense, net	1,626	2,743	(768)
Restructuring (Note 22)	—	569	—
Earnings before provision for taxes on income	13,775	12,361	16,947

1. Summary of Significant Accounting Policies (in part)

Research and Development

Research and development expenses are expensed as incurred. Upfront and milestone payments made to third parties in connection with research and development collaborations are expensed as incurred up to the point of regulatory approval. Payments made to third parties subsequent to regulatory approval are capitalized and amortized over the remaining useful life of the related product. Amounts capitalized for such payments are included in other intangibles, net of accumulated amortization.

The Company enters into collaborative arrangements, typically with other pharmaceutical or biotechnology companies, to develop and commercialize drug candidates or intellectual property. These arrangements typically involve two (or more) parties who are active participants in the collaboration and are exposed to significant risks and rewards dependent on the commercial success of the activities. These collaborations usually involve various activities by one or more parties, including research and development, marketing and selling and distribution. Often, these collaborations require upfront, milestone and royalty or profit share payments, contingent upon the occurrence of certain future events linked to the success of the asset in development. Amounts due from collaborative partners related to development activities are generally reflected as a reduction of research and development expense because the performance of contract development services is not central to the Company's operations. In general, the income statement presentation for these collaborations is as follows:

Nature/Type of Collaboration	Statement of Earnings Presentation
Third-party sale of product	Sales to customers
Royalties/milestones paid to collaborative partner (post-regulatory approval)*	Cost of goods sold
Royalties received from collaborative partner	Other income (expense), net
Upfront payments & milestones paid to collaborative partner (pre-regulatory approval)	Research and development expense
Research and development payments to collaborative partner	Research and development expense
Research and development payments received from collaborative partner	Reduction of Research and development expense

* Milestones are capitalized as intangible assets and amortized to cost of goods sold over the useful life.

For all years presented, there was no individual project that represented greater than 5% of the total annual consolidated research and development expense.

EXPLORATION

3.22 ANADARKO PETROLEUM CORPORATION (DEC)
CONSOLIDATED STATEMENTS OF INCOME (in part)

(Millions except per-share amounts)	Years Ended December 31,		
	2012	2011	2010
Revenues and Other			
Natural-gas sales	$ 2,444	$ 3,300	$ 3,420
Oil and condensate sales	8,728	8,072	5,592
Natural-gas liquids sales	1,224	1,462	997
Gathering, processing, and marketing sales	911	1,048	833
Gains (losses) on divestitures and other, net	104	85	142
Total	13,411	13,967	10,984
Costs and Expenses			
Oil and gas operating	976	993	830
Oil and gas transportation and other	955	891	816
Exploration	1,946	1,076	974
Gathering, processing, and marketing	763	791	615
General and administrative	1,246	1,060	967
Depreciation, depletion, and amortization	3,964	3,830	3,714
Other taxes	1,224	1,492	1,068
Impairments	389	1,774	216
Algeria exceptional profits tax settlement	(1,797)	—	—
Deepwater Horizon settlement and related costs	18	3,930	15
Total	9,684	15,837	9,215
Operating income (Loss)	3,727	(1,870)	1,769

NOTES TO CONSOLIDATED FINANCIAL STATEMENTS

1. Summary of Significant Accounting Policies (in part)

Oil and Gas Properties. The Company applies the successful efforts method of accounting for oil and gas properties. Exploration costs such as exploratory geological and geophysical costs, delay rentals, and exploration overhead are charged against earnings as incurred. If an exploratory well provides evidence to justify potential completion as a producing well, drilling costs associated with the well are initially capitalized, or suspended, pending a determination as to whether a commercially sufficient quantity of proved reserves can be attributed to the area as a result of drilling. This determination may take longer than one year in certain areas (generally in deepwater and international locations) depending on, among other things, the amount of hydrocarbons discovered, the outcome of planned geological and engineering studies, the need for additional appraisal drilling activities to determine whether the discovery is sufficient to support an economic development plan, and government sanctioning of development activities in certain international locations. At the end of each quarter, management reviews the status of all suspended exploratory well costs in light of ongoing exploration activities—in particular, whether the Company is making sufficient progress in its ongoing exploration and appraisal efforts or, in the case of discoveries requiring government sanctioning, whether development negotiations are underway and proceeding as planned. If management determines that future appraisal drilling or development activities are unlikely to occur, associated suspended exploratory well costs are expensed.

Acquisition costs of unproved properties are periodically assessed for impairment and are transferred to proved oil and gas properties to the extent the costs are associated with successful exploration activities. Significant undeveloped leases are assessed individually for impairment, based on the Company's current exploration plans, and a valuation allowance is provided if impairment is indicated. Unproved oil and gas properties with individually insignificant lease acquisition costs are amortized on a group basis (thereby establishing a valuation allowance) over the average lease terms, at rates that provide for full amortization of unsuccessful leases upon lease expiration or abandonment. Costs of expired or abandoned leases are charged against the valuation allowance, while costs of productive leases are transferred to proved oil and gas properties. Costs of maintaining and retaining unproved properties, as well as amortization of individually insignificant leases and impairment of unsuccessful leases, are included in exploration expense in the Consolidated Statements of Income.

3.23 RALPH LAUREN CORPORATION (MAR)
CONSOLIDATED STATEMENTS OF OPERATIONS (in part)

	Fiscal Years Ended		
(Millions, except per share data)	March 31, 2012	April 2, 2011	April 3, 2010
Net sales	$ 6,678.8	$ 5,481.8	$ 4,795.5
Licensing revenue	180.7	178.5	183.4
Net revenues	6,859.5	5,660.3	4,978.9
Cost of goods sold[(a)]	(2,861.4)	(2,342.0)	(2,079.8)
Gross profit	3,998.1	3,318.3	2,899.1
Other Costs and Expenses:			
Selling, general and administrative expenses [(a)]	(2,915.2)	(2,442.7)	(2,157.0)
Amortization of intangible assets	(28.9)	(25.4)	(21.7)
Impairments of assets	(2.2)	(2.5)	(6.6)
Restructuring charges	(12.4)	(2.6)	(6.9)
Total other costs and expenses	(2,958.7)	(2,473.2)	(2,192.2)
Operating income	1,039.4	845.1	706.9

NOTES TO CONSOLIDATED FINANCIAL STATEMENTS

3. Summary of Significant Accounting Policies (in part)

Advertising, Marketing and Promotional Costs

Advertising costs, including the costs to produce advertising, are expensed when the advertisement is first exhibited. Costs of out-of-store advertising paid to wholesale customers under cooperative advertising programs are expensed as an advertising cost within SG&A expenses if both the identified advertising benefit is sufficiently separable from the purchase of the Company's products by customers and the fair value of such benefit is measurable. Otherwise, such costs are reflected as a reduction of revenue. Costs of in-store advertising paid to wholesale customers under cooperative advertising programs are not included in advertising costs, but are reflected as a reduction of revenues since the benefits are not sufficiently separable from the purchases of the Company's products by customers.

Costs associated with the marketing and promotion of the Company's products are expensed as incurred and included within SG&A expenses.

Advertising, marketing and promotional expenses amounted to approximately $213 million for Fiscal 2012, $192 million for Fiscal 2011 and $157 million for Fiscal 2010. Deferred advertising, marketing and promotional costs, which principally relate to advertisements that have not yet been exhibited or services that have not yet been received, were approximately $5 million and $9 million at the end of Fiscal 2012 and Fiscal 2011, respectively.

TAXES OTHER THAN INCOME TAXES

3.24 CHEVRON CORPORATION (DEC)
CONSOLIDATED STATEMENT OF INCOME (in part)

Millions of dollars, except per-share amounts

	Year Ended December 31		
Revenues and Other Income	2012	2011	2010
Sales and other operating revenues*	$230,590	$244,371	$198,198
Income from equity affiliates	6,889	7,363	5,637
Other income	4,430	1,972	1,093
Total revenues and other income	241,909	253,706	204,928
Costs and Other Deductions			
Purchased crude oil and products	140,766	149,923	116,467
Operating expenses	22,570	21,649	19,188
Selling, general and administrative expenses	4,724	4,745	4,767
Exploration expenses	1,728	1,216	1,147
Depreciation, depletion and amortization	13,413	12,911	13,063
Taxes other than on income*	12,376	15,628	18,191
Interest and debt expense	—	—	50
Total costs and other deductions	195,577	206,072	172,873
Income before income tax expense	46,332	47,634	32,055
Income tax expense	19,996	20,626	12,919
Net income	26,336	27,008	19,136
* Includes excise, value-added and similar taxes.	$ 8,010	$ 8,085	$ 8,591

Millions of dollars, except per-share amounts

Note 1—Summary of Significant Accounting Policies (in part)

Revenue Recognition. Revenues associated with sales of crude oil, natural gas, coal, petroleum and chemicals products, and all other sources are recorded when title passes to the customer, net of royalties, discounts and allowances, as applicable. Revenues from natural gas production from properties in which Chevron has an interest with other producers are generally recognized using the entitlement method. Excise, value-added and similar taxes assessed by a governmental authority on a revenue-producing transaction between a seller and a customer are presented on a gross basis. The associated amounts are shown as a footnote to the Consolidated Statement of Income, on page FS-23. Purchases and sales of inventory with the same counterparty that are entered into in contemplation of one another (including buy/sell arrangements) are combined and recorded on a net basis and reported in "Purchased crude oil and products" on the Consolidated Statement of Income.

Note 14—Taxes (in part)

Taxes Other Than on Income

	Year Ended December 31		
	2012	2011	2010
United States			
Excise and similar taxes on products and merchandise	$ 4,665	$ 4,199	$ 4,484
Import duties and other levies	1	4	—
Property and other miscellaneous taxes	782	726	567
Payroll taxes	240	236	219
Taxes on production	328	308	271
Total United States	6,016	5,473	5,541
International			
Excise and similar taxes on products and merchandise	3,345	3,886	4,107
Import duties and other levies	106	3,511	6,183
Property and other miscellaneous taxes	2,501	2,354	2,000
Payroll taxes	160	148	133
Taxes on production	248	256	227
Total International	6,360	10,155	12,650
Total taxes other than on income	$12,376	$15,628	$18,191

PROVISION FOR LOSSES

3.25 UNIVERSAL HEALTH SERVICES, INC. (DEC)
CONSOLIDATED STATEMENTS OF INCOME (in part)

	Year Ended December 31,		
(In thousands, except per share data)	2012	2011	2010
Net revenues before provision for doubtful accounts	$7,688,071	$7,356,798	$5,429,233
Less: Provision for doubtful accounts	726,671	596,576	529,086
Net revenues	6,961,400	6,760,222	4,900,147

NOTES TO CONSOLIDATED FINANCIAL STATEMENTS

1) Business and Summary of Significant Accounting Policies (in part)

C) Provision for Doubtful Accounts: Collection of receivables from third-party payers and patients is our primary source of cash and is critical to our operating performance. Our primary collection risks relate to uninsured patients and the portion of the bill which is the patient's responsibility, primarily co-payments and deductibles. We estimate our provisions for doubtful accounts based on general factors such as payer mix, the agings of the receivables and historical collection experience. We routinely review accounts receivable balances in conjunction with these factors and other economic conditions which might ultimately affect the collectability of the patient accounts and make adjustments to our allowances as warranted. At our acute care hospitals, third party liability accounts are pursued until all payment and adjustments are posted to the patient account. For those accounts with a patient balance after third party liability is finalized or accounts for uninsured patients, the patient receives statements and collection letters. Patients that express an inability to pay are reviewed for potential sources of financial assistance including our charity care policy. If the patient is deemed unwilling to pay, the account is written-off as bad debt and transferred to an outside collection agency for additional collection effort.

Uninsured patients that do not qualify as charity patients are extended an uninsured discount of a minimum of 30% of total charges. Our hospitals establish a partial reserve for self-pay accounts in the allowance for doubtful accounts for both unbilled balances and those that have been billed and are under 90 days old. All self-pay accounts are fully reserved at 90 days from the date of discharge. Third party liability accounts are fully reserved in the allowance for doubtful accounts when the balance ages past 180 days from the date of discharge. Potential charity accounts are fully reserved when it is determined the patient may be unable to pay.

As of December 31, 2012, our accounts receivable includes $70 million due from Illinois ($54 million as of December 31, 2011), the collection of which has been delayed due to budgetary and funding pressures experienced by the state. Although as of December 31, 2012 approximately $51 million of the receivables due from Illinois have been outstanding in excess of 60 days ($41 million as of December 31, 2011), and a large portion will likely remain outstanding for the foreseeable future, we expect to eventually collect all amounts due to us and therefore no related reserves have been established in our consolidated financial statements. However, we can provide no assurance that we will eventually collect all amounts due to us from Illinois. Failure to ultimately collect all outstanding amounts due from Illinois would have an adverse impact on our future consolidated results of operations and cash flows.

On a consolidated basis, we monitor our total self-pay receivables to ensure that the total allowance for doubtful accounts provides adequate coverage based on historical collection experience. Our accounts receivable are recorded net of allowance for doubtful accounts of $311 million and $253 million at December 31, 2012 and 2011, respectively.

X) Accounting Standards: (in part)

Presentation and Disclosure of Patient Service Revenue, Provision for Bad Debts, and the Allowance for Doubtful Accounts for Certain Health Care Entities: During the first quarter of 2012, we adopted the Financial Accounting Standards Board's Accounting Standards Update ("ASU") No. 2011-07, "Health Care Entities (Topic 954): Presentation and Disclosure of Patient Service Revenue, Provision for Bad Debts, and the Allowance for Doubtful Accounts for Certain Health Care Entities," which required certain health care entities to change the presentation in their statement of operations by reclassifying the provision for bad debts associated with patient service revenue from an operating expense to a deduction from patient service revenue (net of contractual allowances and discounts). As a result, the provision for doubtful accounts for our acute care and behavioral health care facilities is reflected as a deduction from net revenues in the accompanying consolidated statements of income for 2012, 2011 and 2010. The adoption of this standard had no impact on our financial position or overall results of operations.

WARRANTY

3.26 HARRIS CORPORATION (JUN)
CONSOLIDATED STATEMENT OF INCOME (in part)

	Fiscal Years Ended		
(In millions, except per share amounts)	2012	2011	2010
Revenue from product sales and services			
Revenue from product sales	$3,364.7	$3,691.5	$3,502.3
Revenue from services	2,086.6	1,726.9	1,222.7
	5,451.3	5,418.4	4,725.0
Cost of product sales and services			
Cost of product sales	(1,945.2)	(2,141.2)	(2,082.8)
Cost of services	(1,624.1)	(1,391.3)	(970.1)
	(3,569.3)	(3,532.5)	(3,052.9)
Engineering, selling and administrative expenses	(940.9)	(890.9)	(723.2)
Non-operating income (loss)	11.5	(1.9)	(1.9)
Interest income	2.5	2.8	1.5
Interest expense	(113.2)	(90.4)	(72.1)
Income from continuing operations before income taxes	841.9	905.5	876.4

NOTES TO CONSOLIDATED FINANCIAL STATEMENTS

Note 1: Significant Accounting Policies (in part)

Warranties—On development and production contract sales in our Government Communications Systems segment and in our Integrated Network Solutions segment, the value or price of our warranty is generally included in the contract and funded by the customer. A provision for warranties is built into the estimated program costs when determining the profit rate to accrue when applying the cost-to-cost percentage-of-completion revenue recognition method. Warranty costs, as incurred, are charged to the specific program's cost, and both revenue and cost are recognized at that time. Factors that affect the estimated program cost for warranties include terms of the contract, complexity of the delivered product or service, number of installed units, historical experience and management's judgment regarding anticipated rates of warranty claims and cost per claim.

On product sales in all our segments, we provide for future warranty costs upon product delivery. The specific terms and conditions of those warranties vary depending upon the product sold, customer and country in which we do business. In the case of products sold by us, our warranties start from the shipment, delivery or customer acceptance date and continue as follows:

Segment	Warranty Periods
RF Communications	One to twelve years
Integrated Network Solutions	Less than one year to five years
Government Communications Systems	One to two years

Because our products are manufactured, in many cases, to customer specifications and their acceptance is based on meeting those specifications, we historically have experienced minimal warranty costs. Factors that affect our warranty liability include the number of installed units, historical experience and management's judgment regarding anticipated rates of warranty claims and cost per claim. We assess the adequacy of our recorded warranty liabilities every quarter and make adjustments to the liability as necessary. See *Note 10: Accrued Warranties* for additional information regarding warranties.

Note 10: Accrued Warranties

Changes in our warranty liability, which is included as a component of the "Other accrued items" and "Other long-term liabilities" line items in our Consolidated Balance Sheet, during fiscal 2012 and 2011, were as follows:

(In millions)	2012	2011
Balance at beginning of the fiscal year	$ 52.8	$ 73.1
Balance reclassified to discontinued operations	(9.3)	—
Warranty provision for sales made during the fiscal year	14.0	19.6
Settlements made during the fiscal year	(16.2)	(38.7)
Other adjustments to the warranty liability, including those for acquisitions and foreign currency translation, during the fiscal year	(0.9)	(1.2)
Balance at end of the fiscal year	$ 40.4	$ 52.8

INTEREST

3.27 VERISIGN, INC. (DEC)
CONSOLIDATED STATEMENTS OF OPERATIONS AND COMPREHENSIVE INCOME (in part)

(In thousands, except per share data)

	Year Ended December 31,		
	2012	2011	2010
Revenues	$873,592	$ 771,978	$ 680,578
Costs and expenses:			
Cost of revenues	167,600	165,246	156,676
Sales and marketing	97,809	97,432	83,390
Research and development	61,694	53,277	53,664
General and administrative	89,927	111,122	137,704
Restructuring charges	(765)	15,512	16,861
Total costs and expenses	416,265	442,589	448,295
Operating income	457,327	329,389	232,283
Interest expense	(50,196)	(147,332)	(157,667)
Non-operating income, net	5,564	11,530	20,738
Income from continuing operations before income taxes	412,695	193,587	95,354

NOTES TO CONSOLIDATED FINANCIAL STATEMENTS

Note 7. Debt and Interest Expense

2011 Credit Facility

On November 22, 2011, Verisign entered into a credit agreement with a syndicate of lenders led by JPMorgan Chase Bank, N.A., as the administrative agent. The credit agreement provides for a $200.0 million committed senior unsecured revolving credit facility (the "2011 Facility"), under which Verisign and certain designated subsidiaries may be borrowers. Loans under the 2011 Facility may be denominated in U.S. dollars and certain other currencies. The Company has the option under the 2011 Facility to invite lenders to make competitive bid loans at negotiated interest rates. The facility expires on November 22, 2016 at which time any outstanding borrowings are due.

Borrowings under the 2011 Facility bear interest at one of the following rates as selected by the Company at the time of borrowing: the lender's base rate which is the higher of the Prime Rate or the sum of 0.5% plus the Federal Funds Rate, plus in each case a margin of 0.5% to 1.0% determined based on the Company's leverage ratio, or a LIBOR or EURIBOR based rate plus market-rate spreads of 1.5% to 2.0% that are determined based on the Company's leverage ratio.

On November 28, 2011, the Company borrowed $100.0 million as a LIBOR revolving loan denominated in US dollars to be used in connection with the purchase of Verisign's headquarters facility in Reston, Virginia and for general corporate purposes. As of December 31, 2012, this balance remains outstanding and the Company does not intend to repay the outstanding borrowing within the next year and, as such, has classified the debt as a long-term liability.

The Company is required to pay a commitment fee between 0.2% and 0.3% per year of the amount committed under the facility, depending on the Company's leverage ratio. The credit agreement contains customary representations and warranties, as well as covenants limiting the Company's ability to, among other things, incur additional indebtedness, merge or consolidate with others, change its business, sell or dispose of assets. The covenants also include limitations on investments, limitations on dividends, share redemptions and other restricted payments, limitations on entering into certain types of restrictive agreements, limitations on entering into hedging agreements, limitations on amendments, waivers or prepayments of the Convertible Debentures, limitations on transactions with affiliates and limitations on the use of proceeds from the facility.

The facility includes financial covenants requiring that the Company's interest coverage ratio not be less than 3.0 to 1.0 for any period of four consecutive quarters and the Company's leverage ratio not exceed 2.0 to 1.0. As of December 31, 2012, the Company was in compliance with the financial covenants of the 2011 Facility.

Verisign may from time to time request lenders to agree on a discretionary basis to increase the commitment amount by up to an aggregate of $150.0 million during the term of the 2011 Credit Facility.

Convertible Debentures

In August 2007, Verisign issued $1.25 billion principal amount of 3.25% convertible debentures due August 15, 2037, in a private offering. The Convertible Debentures are subordinated in right of payment to the Company's existing and future senior debt and to the other liabilities of the Company's subsidiaries. The Convertible Debentures are initially convertible, subject to certain conditions, into shares of the Company's common stock at a conversion rate of 29.0968 shares of common stock per $1,000 principal amount of Convertible Debentures, representing an initial effective conversion price of approximately $34.37 per share of common stock. The conversion rate will be subject to adjustment for certain events as outlined in the Indenture governing the Convertible Debentures but will not be adjusted for accrued interest. As of December 31, 2012, approximately 36.4 million shares of common stock were reserved for issuance upon conversion or repurchase of the Convertible Debentures.

On or after August 15, 2017, the Company may redeem all or part of the Convertible Debentures for the principal amount plus any accrued and unpaid interest if the closing price of the Company's common stock has been at least 150% of the conversion price then in effect for at least 20 trading days during any 30 consecutive trading-day period prior to the date on which the Company provides notice of redemption.

Holders of the debentures may convert their Convertible Debentures at the applicable conversion rate, in multiples of $1,000 principal amount, only under the following circumstances:
- during any fiscal quarter beginning after December 31, 2007, if the last reported sale price of the Company's common stock for at least 20 trading days during the period of 30 consecutive trading days ending on the last trading day of the immediately preceding fiscal quarter is greater than or equal to 130% of the applicable conversion price in effect on the last trading day of such preceding fiscal quarter (the "Conversion Price Threshold Trigger");
- during the five business-day period after any 10 consecutive trading-day period in which the trading price per $1,000 principal amount of Convertible Debentures for each day of that 10 consecutive trading-day period was less than 98% of the product of the last reported sale price of the Company's common stock and the conversion rate on such day;
- if the Company calls any or all of the Convertible Debentures for redemption pursuant to the terms of the Indenture, at any time prior to the close of business on the trading day immediately preceding the redemption date;
- upon the occurrence of any of several specified corporate transactions as specified in the Indenture governing the Convertible Debentures; or
- at any time on or after May 15, 2037, and prior to the maturity date.

If the conversion value exceeds $1,000, the Company may deliver, at its option, cash or common stock or a combination of cash and common stock for the conversion value in excess of $1,000 ("conversion spread").

The Company's common stock price exceeded the Conversion Price Threshold Trigger during the third quarter of 2012. Accordingly, the Convertible Debentures were convertible at the option of each holder during the fourth quarter of 2012. Further, in the event of conversion, the Company intends, and has the ability, to settle the principal amount of the Convertible Debentures in cash, and therefore, classified the debt component of the Convertible Debentures, the embedded contingent interest derivative and the related deferred tax liability as current liabilities, and also classified the related debt issuance costs as a current asset as of September 30, 2012. None of the Convertible Debentures were converted during the fourth quarter of 2012 and as of December 31, 2012, none of the conditions allowing holders of the Convertible Debentures to convert were met. Therefore, the Convertible Debentures are not convertible into common stock beginning January 1, 2013 unless and until one of the conversion criteria mentioned above is met. As such, the various Convertible Debentures related liabilities and assets were reclassified back to long-term as of December 31, 2012. The determination of whether or not the Convertible Debentures are convertible, and accordingly, the classification of the related liabilities and assets as long-term or current, must continue to be performed quarterly. The Company intends and has the ability to settle the principal amount of the Convertible Debentures in cash. As of December 31, 2012, the if-converted value of the Convertible

Debentures exceeded its principal amount. Based on the if-converted value of the Convertible Debentures as of December 31, 2012, the conversion spread could have required the Company to issue up to an additional 4.2 million shares of common stock.

In addition, holders of the Convertible Debentures who convert their Convertible Debentures in connection with a fundamental change may be entitled to a make-whole premium in the form of an increase in the conversion rate. Additionally, in the event of a fundamental change, the holders of the Convertible Debentures may require Verisign to purchase all or a portion of their Convertible Debentures at a purchase price equal to 100% of the principal amount of Convertible Debentures, plus accrued and unpaid interest, if any.

The Company calculated the carrying value of the liability component at issuance as the present value of its cash flows using a discount rate of 8.5% (borrowing rate for similar non-convertible debt with no contingent payment options), adjusted for the fair value of the contingent interest feature, yielding an effective interest rate of 8.39%. The excess of the principal amount of the debt over the carrying value of the liability component is also referred to as the "debt discount" or "equity component" of the Convertible Debentures. The debt discount is being amortized using the Company's effective interest rate of 8.39% over the term of the Convertible Debentures as a non-cash charge included in Interest expense. As of December 31, 2012, the remaining term of the Convertible Debentures is 24.6 years. Interest is payable semiannually in arrears on August 15 and February 15.

Proceeds upon issuance of the Convertible Debentures were as follows (in thousands):

Principal value of Convertible Debentures	$1,250,000
Less: Issuance costs	(25,777)
Net proceeds, Convertible Debentures	$1,224,223
Amounts recognized at issuance:	
Convertible debentures, including contingent interest derivative	$ 558,243
Additional paid-in capital	418,996
Long-term deferred tax liabilities	267,225
Other long-term assets	(11,328)
Non-operating loss	(8,913)
Net proceeds, Convertible Debentures	$1,224,223

The table below presents the carrying amounts of the liability and equity components:

	As of December 31,	
(In thousands)	2012	2011
Carrying amount of equity component (net of issuance costs of $14,449)	$ 418,996	$ 418,996
Principal amount of Convertible Debentures	$1,250,000	$1,250,000
Unamortized discount of liability component	(663,588)	(671,539)
Carrying amount of liability component	586,412	578,461
Contingent interest derivative	11,202	11,625
Convertible debentures, including contingent interest derivative	$ 597,614	$ 590,086

The following table presents the components of the Company's interest expense:

	Year Ended December 31,		
(In thousands)	2012	2011	2010
Contractual interest on Convertible Debentures	$40,625	$ 40,625	$ 40,625
Amortization of debt discount on the Convertible Debentures	7,986	7,355	6,775
Contingent interest to holders of Convertible Debentures	—	100,020	109,113
Interest capitalized to property and equipment, net	(934)	(980)	(676)
Credit facility and other interest expense	2,519	312	1,830
Total interest expense	$50,196	$147,332	$157,667

The Indenture governing the Convertible Debentures requires the payment of contingent interest to the holders of the Convertible Debentures if the Board of Directors (the "Board") declares a dividend to its stockholders that is designated by the Board as an extraordinary dividend. The contingent interest is calculated as the amount derived by multiplying the per share declared dividend with the if-converted number of shares applicable to the Convertible Debentures. The Board declared extraordinary dividends in April 2011 and December 2010, and consequently, the Company paid contingent interest of $100.0 million in 2011 and $109.1 million in 2010 to holders of the Convertible Debentures.

3.28 IRON MOUNTAIN INCORPORATED (DEC)

CONSOLIDATED STATEMENTS OF OPERATIONS (in part)

(In thousands, except per share data)

	Year Ended December 31,		
	2010	2011	2012
Revenues:			
Storage rental	$1,598,718	$1,682,990	$1,733,138
Service	1,293,631	1,331,713	1,272,117
Total revenues	2,892,349	3,014,703	3,005,255
Operating Expenses:			
Cost of sales (excluding depreciation and amortization)	1,192,862	1,245,200	1,277,113
Selling, general and administrative	772,811	834,591	850,371
Depreciation and amortization	304,205	319,499	316,344
Intangible impairments	85,909	46,500	—
(Gain) Loss on disposal/write-down of property, plant and equipment, net	(10,987)	(2,286)	4,400
Total operating expenses	2,344,800	2,443,504	2,448,228
Operating income (Loss)	547,549	571,199	557,027
Interest expense, net (includes Interest Income of $1,785, $2,313 and $2,418 in 2010, 2011 and 2012, respectively)	204,559	205,256	242,599
Other expense (Income), net	8,768	13,043	16,062
Income (Loss) from continuing operations before provision (Benefit) for income taxes	334,222	352,900	298,366
Provision (Benefit) for income taxes	167,483	106,488	114,873
Income (Loss) from continuing operations	166,739	246,412	183,493

NOTES TO CONSOLIDATED FINANCIAL STATEMENTS

(In thousands, except share and per share data)

2. Summary of Significant Accounting Policies (in part)

o. Income Taxes

Accounting for income taxes requires the recognition of deferred tax assets and liabilities for the expected future tax consequences of temporary differences between the tax and financial reporting basis of assets and liabilities and for loss and credit carryforwards. Valuation allowances are provided when recovery of deferred tax assets is not considered more likely than not. We have elected to recognize interest and penalties associated with uncertain tax positions as a component of the provision (benefit) for income taxes in the accompanying consolidated statements of operations.

7. Income Taxes (in part)

The evaluation of an uncertain tax position is a two-step process. The first step is a recognition process whereby we determine whether it is more likely than not that a tax position will be sustained upon examination, including resolution of any related appeals or litigation processes, based on the technical merits of the position. The second step is a measurement process whereby a tax position that meets the more likely than not recognition threshold is calculated to determine the amount of benefit to recognize in the financial statements. The tax position is measured at the largest amount of benefit that is greater than 50% likely of being realized upon ultimate settlement.

We have elected to recognize interest and penalties associated with uncertain tax positions as a component of the provision (benefit) for income taxes in the accompanying consolidated statements of operations. We recorded $(1,607), $(8,477) and $1,257 for gross interest and penalties for the years ended December 31, 2010, 2011 and 2012, respectively.

We had 2,819 and $3,554 accrued for the payment of interest and penalties as of December 31, 2011 and 2012, respectively.

ACCRETION ON ASSET RETIREMENT OBLIGATION

3.29 APACHE CORPORATION (DEC)

STATEMENT OF CONSOLIDATED OPERATIONS (in part)

(In millions, except per common share data)	For the Year Ended December 31,		
	2012	2011	2010
Revenues and Other:			
Oil and gas production revenues	$16,947	$16,810	$12,183
Other	131	78	(91)
	17,078	16,888	12,092
Operating Expenses:			
Depreciation, depletion, and amortization:			
Recurring	5,183	4,095	3,083
Additional	1,926	109	—
Asset retirement obligation accretion	232	154	111
Lease operating expenses	2,968	2,605	2,032
Gathering and transportation	303	296	178
Taxes other than income	862	899	690
General and administrative	531	459	380
Merger, acquisitions & transition	31	20	183
Financing costs, net	165	158	229
	12,201	8,795	6,886
Income before income taxes	4,877	8,093	5,206

NOTES TO CONSOLIDATED FINANCIAL STATEMENTS

1. Summary of Significant Accounting Policies (in part)

Use of Estimates

Preparation of financial statements in conformity with GAAP and disclosure of contingent assets and liabilities requires management to make estimates and assumptions that affect reported amounts of assets and liabilities at the date of the financial statements and the reported amounts of revenues and expenses during the reporting period. The Company bases its estimates on historical experience and various other assumptions that are believed to be reasonable under the circumstances, the results of which form the basis for making judgments about carrying values of assets and liabilities that are not readily apparent from other sources. Apache evaluates its estimates and assumptions on a regular basis. Actual results may differ from these estimates and assumptions used in preparation of its financial statements and changes in these estimates are recorded when known. Significant estimates made in preparing these financial statements include the fair value determination of acquired assets and liabilities (see Note 2—Acquisitions and Divestitures), the estimate of proved oil and gas reserves and related present value estimates of future net cash flows therefrom (see Note 14—Supplemental Oil and Gas Disclosures), the assessment of asset retirement obligations (see Note 5—Asset Retirement Obligation), and the valuation of income taxes (see Note 7—Income Taxes).

Property and Equipment (in part)

Asset Retirement Costs and Obligations

The initial estimated asset retirement obligation related to property and equipment is recorded as a liability at its fair value, with an offsetting asset retirement cost recorded as an increase to the associated property and equipment on the consolidated balance sheet. If the fair value of the recorded asset retirement obligation changes, a revision is recorded to both the asset retirement obligation and the asset retirement cost. Revisions in estimated liabilities can result from changes in estimated inflation rates, changes in service and equipment costs and changes in the estimated timing of an asset's retirement. Asset retirement costs are depreciated using a systematic and rational method similar to that used for the associated property and equipment. Accretion expense on the liability is recognized over the estimated productive life of the related assets.

5. Asset Retirement Obligation

The following table describes changes to the Company's asset retirement obligation (ARO) liability for the years ended December 31, 2012 and 2011:

(In millions)	2012	2011
Asset retirement obligation at beginning of year	$3,887	$2,872
Liabilities incurred	592	419
Liabilities acquired	72	592
Liabilities settled	(550)	(549)
Accretion expense	232	154
Revisions in estimated liabilities	345	399
Asset retirement obligation at end of year	4,578	3,887
Less current portion	(478)	(447)
Asset retirement obligation, long-term	$4,100	$3,440

The ARO liability reflects the estimated present value of the amount of dismantlement, removal, site reclamation, and similar activities associated with Apache's oil and gas properties. The Company utilizes current retirement costs to estimate the expected cash outflows for retirement obligations. The Company estimates the ultimate productive life of the properties, a risk-adjusted discount rate, and an inflation factor in order to determine the current present value of this obligation. To the extent future revisions to these assumptions impact the present value of the existing ARO liability, a corresponding adjustment is made to the oil and gas property balance.

During 2012, the company recorded $592 million in abandonment liabilities resulting from Apache's active exploration and development capital program. An additional $72 million of abandonment obligations were recognized on properties acquired during the year. An additional $345 million of abandonment costs were recognized for upward revisions to prior-year estimates of timing and costs, particularly in Australia and Canada.

Liabilities settled primarily relate to individual properties, platforms, and facilities plugged and abandoned during the period. Apache continues to have an active abandonment program that is focused in the U.S. Gulf of Mexico and Canada. The Company's level of abandonment activity is expected to continue, and $478 million has been recorded as a current liability to reflect our estimated expenditures over the next 12 months.

WRITE-DOWN OF ASSETS

3.30 SEALED AIR CORPORATION (DEC)
CONSOLIDATED STATEMENTS OF OPERATIONS (in part)

	Year Ended December 31,		
(In millions, except per share amounts)	2012	2011	2010
Net sales	$ 7,648.1	$5,550.9	$4,490.1
Cost of sales	5,103.8	3,950.6	3,237.3
Gross profit	2,544.3	1,600.3	1,252.8
Marketing, administrative and development expenses	1,785.2	1,014.4	699.0
Amortization expense of intangible assets acquired	134.0	39.5	11.2
Impairment of goodwill and other intangible assets	1,892.3	—	—
Costs related to the acquisition and integration of Diversey	7.4	64.8	—
Restructuring and other charges	142.5	52.2	7.6
Operating (loss) profit	(1,417.1)	429.4	535.0
Interest expense	(384.7)	(216.6)	(161.6)
Loss on debt redemption	(36.9)	—	(38.5)
Impairment of equity method investment	(23.5)	—	—
Foreign currency exchange (losses) gains related to Venezuelan subsidiaries	(0.4)	(0.3)	5.5
Net gains on sale (other-than-temporary impairment) of available-for-sale securities	—	—	5.9
Other expense, net	(9.4)	(14.5)	(2.9)
(Loss) earnings from continuing operations before income tax provision	(1,872.0)	198.0	343.4

NOTES TO CONSOLIDATED FINANCIAL STATEMENTS

Note 20 Other Expense, Net (in part)

Impairment of Equity Method Investment

In September 2007, we established a joint venture that supports our Food & Beverage segment. We account for the joint venture under the equity method of accounting with our proportionate share of net income or losses included in other expense, net, on the consolidated statements of operations.

During the first half of 2012, the joint venture performed below expectations, resulting in reduced cash flow and increasing debt obligations. Due to these events, we evaluated our equity method investment for impairment. During the three months ended June 30, 2012, based on reviewing undiscounted cash flow information, we determined that the fair value of our investment was less than its carrying value and that this impairment was other-than-temporary.

In connection with the establishment of the joint venture in 2007, we issued a guarantee in support of an uncommitted credit facility agreement that was entered into by the joint venture. Under the terms of the guarantee, if the joint venture were to default under the terms of the credit facility, the lender would be entitled to seek payment of the amounts due under the credit facility from us. However, as a result of the impairment, we have included the guarantee liability in other current liabilities on the consolidated balance sheet as of December 31, 2012 as we believe it is probable that we will need to perform under this guarantee. As of December 31, 2012, the joint venture has performed its obligations under the terms of the credit facility and the debt holders have not requested that we perform under the terms of the guarantee.

As a result, in the second quarter of 2012 we recognized other-than-temporary impairment of $26 million ($18 million, net of taxes, or $0.09 per diluted share). This impairment consisted of the recognition of a current liability for the guarantee of the uncommitted credit facility mentioned above of $20 million and a $4 million write-down of the carrying value of the investment to zero at June 30, 2012. We also recorded provisions for bad debt on receivables due from the joint venture to the Company of $2 million, which is included in marketing, administrative and development expenses and impacted our Food & Beverage segment. We have no additional obligations to support the operations of the joint venture in the future.

RESTRUCTURING

3.31 DEAN FOODS COMPANY (DEC)
CONSOLIDATED STATEMENTS OF OPERATIONS (in part)

	Year Ended December 31		
(Dollars in thousands, except share data)	**2012**	**2011**	**2010**
Net sales	$11,462,277	$11,641,191	$10,820,237
Cost of sales	8,562,279	8,861,574	8,063,932
Gross profit	2,899,998	2,779,617	2,756,305
Operating costs and expenses:			
Selling and distribution	1,912,588	1,878,372	1,816,958
General and administrative	555,012	585,288	601,177
Amortization of intangibles	6,283	7,616	8,342
Facility closing and reorganization costs	55,787	45,688	30,761
Litigation settlements	—	131,300	30,000
Goodwill impairment	—	2,075,836	—
Other operating (income) loss	(57,459)	6,561	—
Total operating costs and expenses	2,472,211	4,730,661	2,487,238
Operating income (loss)	427,787	(1,951,044)	269,067

NOTES TO CONSOLIDATED FINANCIAL STATEMENTS

17. Facility Closing and Reorganization Costs

Approved plans within our multi-year initiatives and related charges are summarized as follows:

	Year Ended December 31		
(In thousands)	**2012**	**2011**	**2010**
Fresh Dairy Direct:			
Closure of facilities[1]	$18,536	$18,751	$21,350
Broad-based reduction of facility and distribution personnel[2]	—	(282)	3,404
Organization Optimization Initiative[3]	(197)	4,269	—
Management Realignment[5]	—	(194)	3,100
Functional Realignment[6]	26,419	—	—
Field and Functional Reorganization[7]	6,000	—	—
Total Fresh Dairy Direct	50,758	22,544	27,854
Corporate:			
Department Realignment[4]	(96)	2,535	2,907
Organization Optimization Initiative[3]	(675)	20,609	—
Functional Realignment[6]	5,800	—	—
Total Corporate	5,029	23,144	2,907
Total	$55,787	$45,688	$30,761

[1] These charges in 2012, 2011 and 2010 primarily relate to facility closures in Evart, Michigan; Bangor, Maine; Newport, Kentucky; Baxley, Georgia; and Florence, South Carolina, as well as other approved closures. We have incurred $73.1 million of charges related to these initiatives to date. We expect to incur additional charges related to these facility closures of $1.2 million, related to shutdown and other costs. As we continue the evaluation of our supply chain described more fully below it is likely that we will close additional facilities in the future.

[2] These charges relate to a plan to reduce the workforce within our Fresh Dairy Direct segment impacting approximately 230 positions. Implementation began during the second quarter of 2010 and was carried out over the balance of the year. The reduction in workforce affected employees across the country and was a result of operational changes from supply chain initiatives. The workforce reduction costs related to this plan were part of an existing benefit arrangement; therefore, the full amount of expected severance benefits was accrued during the second quarter of 2010. We incurred total charges of $3.1 million related to this initiative and do not expect to incur any additional charges in the future.

[3] In the first quarter of 2011 we initiated a significant cost reduction program that is incremental to our other ongoing cost-savings initiatives. This initiative is focused on permanently removing costs out of our business through organizational and corporate departmental redesigns, driven by process simplification and standardization, centralization of activities and reorganization to drive growth in our core customers and categories. As part of this program, we eliminated approximately 300 corporate and field positions during 2011. The charges recorded during 2011 relate to workforce reduction costs and include costs associated with eliminating the position filled by our then President and Chief Operating Officer. We incurred $24.0 million of charges related to this initiative to date, and we do not expect to incur any material additional charges under this program going forward.

(continued)

(footnote continued)

(4) Charges relate to workforce reduction costs associated with a multi-year cost reduction plan aimed at centralization and process improvement, as well as business unit and functional organization redesigns. The plan was implemented during the fourth quarter of 2010 and resulted in the elimination of approximately 75 positions as each function reorganized its processes in line with peer comparisons and internally developed functional blueprints as approved by an executive operating team. We incurred total charges of $5.4 million related to this initiative and do not expect to incur any additional charges in the future.

(5) In 2010, we realigned management positions within our Fresh Dairy Direct segment to facilitate supply-chain and commercial focused functions across the segment. This resulted in the elimination of the position filled by the then President of Fresh Dairy Direct and we incurred $2.9 million of workforce reduction costs. We do not expect additional costs related to this initiative.

(6) During the first quarter of 2012, our management team reassessed our company-wide strategy, resulting in a shift in focus to deploying our capital and strategically investing in the value-added segments of our business. With this new strategy, our goal is to invest our strategic capital primarily in those initiatives that yield higher returns over shorter time frames. In connection with this change, our management team approved a cost reduction plan that is incremental to any other prior cost savings initiative. This initiative is focused on aligning key functions within the Fresh Dairy Direct organization under a single leadership team and permanently removing costs from the Fresh Dairy Direct organization as well as certain functions that support this segment of our business. During the first half of 2012, we eliminated approximately 120 positions at our corporate headquarters that directly supported our Fresh Dairy Direct business. Charges recorded during the year ended December 31, 2012 are related to workforce reduction costs, the write-down of certain information technology assets and leasehold improvements, lease termination costs and costs associated with exiting other commitments deemed not necessary to execute our new strategy. We have incurred total charges of approximately $32.2 million under this initiative to date and we may incur additional charges in the future under this plan, primarily related to lease termination costs at our corporate headquarters in Dallas, Texas.

(7) During the fourth quarter of 2012, our executive management team approved a plan to reorganize Fresh Dairy Direct's field organization and certain functional areas that support our regional business teams, including finance, distribution, operations and human resources. We believe this streamlined leadership structure will enable faster decision-making and create enhanced opportunities to build our Fresh Dairy Direct business. During 2012, we recorded charges of $6.0 million under this initiative, related to severance costs associated with the first tranche of this program. As future tranches have not been approved by our executive management team, future costs to be incurred are not yet estimable.

Activity for 2012 and 2011 with respect to facility closing and reorganization costs is summarized below and includes items expensed as incurred:

(In thousands)	Accrued Charges at December 31, 2010	Charges	Payments	Accrued Charges at December 31, 2011	Charges	Payments	Accrued Charges at December 31, 2012
Cash charges:							
Workforce reduction costs	$3,860	$25,171	$(23,846)	$5,185	$26,260	$(19,866)	$11,579
Shutdown costs	16	2,648	(2,705)	(41)	1,579	(1,538)	—
Lease obligations after shutdown	—	240	(240)	—	2,798	(812)	1,986
Other	5	852	(854)	3	2,158	(1,934)	227
Subtotal	$3,881	28,911	$(27,645)	$5,147	32,795	$(24,150)	$13,792
Non-cash charges:							
Write-down of assets[(1)]		16,535			23,411		
(Gain)/Loss on sale of related assets		(54)			(580)		
Other		296			161		
Total charges		$45,688			$55,787		

(1) The write-down of assets relates primarily to owned buildings, land and equipment of those facilities identified for closure. The assets were tested for recoverability at the time the decision to close the facilities was more likely than not to occur. Estimates of future cash flows used to test the recoverability of the assets included the net cash flows directly associated with and that are expected to arise as a direct result of the use and eventual disposition of the assets. The inputs for the fair value calculation were based on assessment of an individual asset's alternative use within other production facilities, evaluation of recent market data and historical liquidation sales values for similar assets. As the inputs into these calculations are largely based on management's judgments and are not generally observable in active markets, we consider such measurements to be Level 3 measurements in the fair value hierarchy. See Note 11.

INTANGIBLE ASSET AMORTIZATION

3.32 ALLERGAN, INC. (DEC)
CONSOLIDATED STATEMENTS OF EARNINGS (in part)

(In millions, except per share amounts)

	Year Ended December 31,		
	2012	2011	2010
Revenues:			
Product net sales	$5,708.8	$5,347.1	$4,819.6
Other revenues	97.3	72.0	99.8
Total revenues	5,806.1	5,419.1	4,919.4
Operating Costs and Expenses:			
Cost of sales (excludes amortization of intangible assets)	775.5	748.7	722.0
Selling, general and administrative	2,268.4	2,246.6	2,017.6
Research and development	989.6	902.8	804.6
Amortization of intangible assets	131.3	127.6	138.0
Legal settlement	—	—	609.2
Impairment of intangible assets and related costs	22.3	23.7	369.1
Restructuring charges	5.7	4.6	0.3
Operating income	1,613.3	1,365.1	258.6

Note 1: Summary of Significant Accounting Policies (in part)

Goodwill and Intangible Assets (in part)

Intangible assets include developed technology, customer relationships, licensing agreements, trademarks, core technology and other rights, which are being amortized over their estimated useful lives ranging from two years to 21 years, and in-process research and development assets with indefinite useful lives that are not amortized, but instead tested for impairment until the successful completion and commercialization or abandonment of the associated research and development efforts, at which point the in-process research and development assets are either amortized over their estimated useful lives or written-off immediately.

Note 5: Intangibles and Goodwill (in part)

Intangibles

At December 31, 2012 and 2011, the components of intangibles and certain other related information were as follows:

	December 31, 2012			December 31, 2011		
	Gross Amount (In millions)	Accumulated Amortization (In millions)	Weighted Average Amortization Period (In years)	Gross Amount (In millions)	Accumulated Amortization (In millions)	Weighted Average Amortization Period (In years)
Amortizable Intangible Assets:						
Developed technology	$1,202.8	$(525.1)	13.3	$1,111.0	$(435.1)	13.5
Customer relationships	54.5	(1.2)	2.7	42.3	(42.3)	3.1
Licensing	185.9	(157.8)	9.3	185.8	(137.2)	9.3
Trademarks	87.9	(25.3)	12.3	26.7	(25.0)	6.2
Core technology	182.0	(83.7)	15.2	181.3	(71.4)	15.2
Other	43.9	(14.1)	6.4	38.5	(5.4)	6.9
	1,757.0	(807.2)	12.5	1,585.6	(716.4)	12.6
Unamortizable Intangible Assets:						
In-process research and development	279.3	—		296.0	—	
	$2,036.3	$(807.2)		$1,881.6	$(716.4)	

Developed technology consists primarily of current product offerings, primarily breast aesthetics products, obesity intervention products, dermal fillers, skin care products and eye care products acquired in connection with business combinations, asset acquisitions and initial licensing transactions for products previously approved for marketing. Customer relationship assets consist of the estimated value of relationships with customers acquired in connection with business combinations. Licensing assets consist primarily of capitalized payments to third party licensors related to the achievement of regulatory approvals to commercialize products in specified markets and up-front payments associated with royalty obligations for products that have achieved regulatory approval for marketing. Core technology consists of proprietary technology associated with silicone gel breast implants, gastric bands and intragastric balloon systems acquired in connection with the Company's 2006 acquisition of Inamed Corporation, dermal filler technology acquired in connection with the Company's 2007 acquisition of Groupe Cornéal Laboratoires and a drug delivery technology acquired in connection with the Company's 2003 acquisition of Oculex Pharmaceuticals, Inc. Other intangible assets consist primarily of acquired product registration rights, distributor relationships, distribution rights, government permits and non-compete agreements. The in-process research and development assets consist primarily of a novel compound to treat erythema associated with rosacea acquired in connection with the Company's acquisition of Vicept in July 2011 that is currently under development and an intangible asset associated with technology acquired in connection with the Company's acquisition of Alacer in June 2011 that is not yet commercialized.

In the fourth quarter of 2012, the Company recorded a pre-tax charge of $17.0 million related to the partial impairment of the in-process research and development asset acquired in connection with the Company's 2011 acquisition of Vicept. The impairment charge was recognized because the carrying amount of the asset was determined to be in excess of its estimated fair value.

In March 2011, the Company discontinued development of *EasyBand* ™, a technology that the Company acquired in connection with its 2007 acquisition of EndoArt. As a result, in the first quarter of 2011 the Company recorded a pre-tax impairment charge of $16.1 million for the developed technology and core technology associated with the *EasyBand* ™ technology.

In the third quarter of 2011, the Company recorded a pre-tax charge of $4.3 million related to the impairment of an in-process research and development asset associated with a tissue reinforcement technology that has not yet achieved regulatory approval acquired in connection with the Company's 2010 acquisition of Serica Technologies, Inc. The impairment charge was recognized because estimates of the anticipated future undiscounted cash flows of the asset were not sufficient to recover its carrying amount.

In the third quarter of 2010, the Company concluded that the intangible assets and a related prepaid royalty asset associated with the Sanctura® franchise (the Sanctura® Assets), which the Company acquired in connection with its 2007 acquisition of Esprit Pharma Holding Company, Inc. and certain subsequent licensing and commercialization transactions, had become impaired. The Company determined that an impairment charge was required with respect to the Sanctura® Assets because the estimated undiscounted future cash flows over their remaining useful life were not sufficient to recover the carrying amount of the Sanctura® Assets and the carrying amount exceeded the estimated fair value of those assets due to a reduction in expected future financial performance for the Sanctura® franchise resulting from lower than anticipated acceptance by patients, physicians and payors. As a result, in the third quarter of 2010, the Company recorded an aggregate charge of $369.1 million ($228.6 million after-tax) related to the impairment of the Sanctura® Assets and related costs, which includes a pre-tax charge of $343.2 million for the impairment of the Sanctura® intangible assets. In the second quarter of 2011, the Company recorded additional related costs of $3.3 million. In the fourth quarter of 2012, the Company recorded an additional impairment charge of $5.3 million related to the prepaid royalty asset associated with the Sanctura® franchise due to the launch of a competitive generic version of Sanctura XR®.

The following table provides amortization expense by major categories of intangible assets for the years ended December 31, 2012, 2011 and 2010, respectively:

(In millions)	2012	2011	2010
Developed technology	$ 89.0	$ 89.6	$ 97.4
Customer relationships	1.1	—	0.3
Licensing	20.4	20.4	22.1
Trademarks	0.4	1.4	4.4
Core technology	12.0	12.3	12.4
Other	8.4	3.9	1.4
	$131.3	$127.6	$138.0

Amortization expense related to intangible assets generally benefits multiple business functions within the Company, such as the Company's ability to sell, manufacture, research, market and distribute products, compounds and intellectual property. The amount of amortization expense excluded from cost of sales consists primarily of amounts amortized with respect to developed technology and licensing intangible assets.

Estimated amortization expense is $145.6 million for 2013, $138.5 million for 2014, $124.9 million for 2015, $103.0 million for 2016 and $82.3 million for 2017.

FOREIGN CURRENCY

3.33 IRON MOUNTAIN INCORPORATED (DEC)
CONSOLIDATED STATEMENTS OF OPERATIONS (in part)

(In thousands, except per share data)

	Year Ended December 31,		
	2010	2011	2012
Revenues:			
Storage rental	$1,598,718	$1,682,990	$1,733,138
Service	1,293,631	1,331,713	1,272,117
Total revenues	2,892,349	3,014,703	3,005,255
Operating Expenses:			
Cost of sales (excluding depreciation and amortization)	1,192,862	1,245,200	1,277,113
Selling, general and administrative	772,811	834,591	850,371
Depreciation and amortization	304,205	319,499	316,344
Intangible impairments	85,909	46,500	—
(Gain) Loss on disposal/write-down of property, plant and equipment, net	(10,987)	(2,286)	4,400
Total operating expenses	2,344,800	2,443,504	2,448,228
Operating income (Loss)	547,549	571,199	557,027
Interest expense, net (includes Interest Income of $1,785, $2,313 and $2,418 in 2010, 2011 and 2012, respectively)	204,559	205,256	242,599
Other expense (Income), net	8,768	13,043	16,062
Income (Loss) from continuing operations before provision (Benefit) for income taxes	334,222	352,900	298,366

(In thousands, except share and per share data)

2. Summary of Significant Accounting Policies (in part)

d. Foreign Currency

Local currencies are the functional currencies for our operations outside the U.S., with the exception of certain foreign holding companies and our financing center in Switzerland, whose functional currencies are the U.S. dollar. In those instances where the local currency is the functional currency, assets and liabilities are translated at period-end exchange rates, and revenues and expenses are translated at average exchange rates for the applicable period. Resulting translation adjustments are reflected in the accumulated other comprehensive items, net component of Iron Mountain Incorporated Stockholders' Equity and Noncontrolling Interests. The gain or loss on foreign currency transactions, calculated as the difference between the historical exchange rate and the exchange rate at the applicable measurement date, including those related to (1) our 7 $\frac{1}{4}$% GBP Senior Subordinated Notes due 2014, (2) our 6 $\frac{3}{4}$% Euro Senior Subordinated Notes due 2018, (3) the borrowings in certain foreign currencies under our revolving credit agreement and (4) certain foreign currency denominated intercompany obligations of our foreign subsidiaries to us and between our foreign subsidiaries, which are not considered permanently invested, are included in other expense (income), net, on our consolidated statements of operations. The total gain or loss on foreign currency transactions amounted to a net loss of $5,664, $17,352 and $10,223 for the years ended December 31, 2010, 2011 and 2012, respectively.

x. Other Expense (Income), Net

Other expense (income), net consists of the following:

	Year Ended December 31,		
	2010	2011	2012
Foreign currency transaction losses (gains), net	$5,664	$17,352	$10,223
Debt extinguishment expense, net	1,792	993	10,628
Other, net	1,312	(5,302)	(4,789)
	$8,768	$13,043	$16,062

SOFTWARE AMORTIZATION

3.34 FLOWERS FOODS, INC. (DEC)

CONSOLIDATED STATEMENTS OF INCOME (in part)

	For the 52 Weeks Ended		
(Amounts in thousands, except per share data)	December 29, 2012	December 31, 2011	January 1, 2011
Sales	$3,046,491	$2,773,356	$2,573,769
Materials, supplies, labor and other production costs (exclusive of depreciation and amortization shown separately below)	1,617,810	1,473,201	1,346,790
Selling, distribution and administrative expenses	1,107,480	1,016,491	935,999
Depreciation and amortization	102,690	94,638	85,118
Income from operations	218,511	189,026	205,862
Interest expense	23,411	10,172	8,164
Interest income	(13,672)	(13,112)	(12,682)
Income before income taxes	208,772	191,966	210,380
Income tax expense	72,651	68,538	73,333
Net income	$ 136,121	$ 123,428	$ 137,047

Note 2. Summary of Significant Accounting Policies (in part)

Software Development Costs. The company expenses internal and external software development costs incurred in the preliminary project stage, and, thereafter, capitalizes costs incurred in developing or obtaining internally used software. Certain costs, such as maintenance and training, are expensed as incurred. Capitalized costs are amortized over a period of three to eight years and are subject to impairment evaluation. The net balance of capitalized software development costs included in plant, property and equipment was $7.5 million and $6.4 million at December 29, 2012 and December 31, 2011, respectively. Amortization expense of capitalized software development costs, which is included in depreciation expense in the consolidated statements of income, was $1.6 million, $1.4 million and $1.7 million in fiscal years 2012, 2011 and 2010, respectively.

3.35 CORNING INCORPORATED (DEC)

CONSOLIDATED STATEMENTS OF INCOME (in part)

	Years Ended December 31,		
(In millions, except per share amounts)	**2012**	**2011**	**2010**
Net sales	$8,012	$7,890	$6,632
Cost of sales	4,615	4,324	3,583
Gross margin	3,397	3,566	3,049
Operating expenses:			
Selling, general and administrative expenses	1,165	1,033	1,015
Research, development and engineering expenses	745	671	603
Amortization of purchased intangibles	19	15	8
Restructuring, impairment and other charges (credits) (Note 2)	133	129	(329)
Asbestos litigation charge (credit) (Note 7)	14	24	(49)
Operating income	1,321	1,694	1,801

NOTES TO CONSOLIDATED FINANCIAL STATEMENTS

7. Investments (in part)

Pittsburgh Corning Corporation (PCC)

Corning and PPG Industries, Inc. (PPG) each own 50% of the capital stock of Pittsburgh Corning Corporation (PCC). Over a period of more than two decades, PCC and several other defendants have been named in numerous lawsuits involving claims alleging personal injury from exposure to asbestos. On April 16, 2000, PCC filed for Chapter 11 reorganization in the U.S. Bankruptcy Court for the Western District of Pennsylvania. At the time PCC filed for bankruptcy protection, there were approximately 11,800 claims pending against Corning in state court lawsuits alleging various theories of liability based on exposure to PCC's asbestos products and typically requesting monetary damages in excess of one million dollars per claim. Corning has defended those claims on the basis of the separate corporate status of PCC and the absence of any facts supporting claims of direct liability arising from PCC's asbestos products. Corning is also currently involved in approximately 9,800 other cases (approximately 37,500 claims) alleging injuries from asbestos and similar amounts of monetary damages per case. Those cases have been covered by insurance without material impact to Corning to date. As of December 31, 2012, Corning had received for these cases approximately $18.6 million in insurance payments related to those claims. As described below, several of Corning's insurance carriers have filed a legal proceeding concerning the extent of any insurance coverage for past and future defense and indemnity costs for these claims. Asbestos litigation is inherently difficult, and past trends in resolving these claims may not be indicators of future outcomes.

Corning, with other relevant parties, has been involved in ongoing efforts to develop a Plan of Reorganization that would resolve the concerns and objections of the relevant courts and parties. In 2003, a plan was agreed to by various parties (the 2003 Plan), but, on December 21, 2006, the Bankruptcy Court issued an order denying the confirmation of that 2003 Plan. On January 29, 2009, an amended plan of reorganization (the Amended PCC Plan)—which addressed the issues raised by the Court when it denied confirmation of the 2003 Plan—was filed with the Bankruptcy Court.

The proposed resolution of PCC asbestos claims under the Amended PCC Plan would have required Corning to contribute its equity interests in PCC and Pittsburgh Corning Europe N.V. (PCE), a Belgian corporation, and to contribute a fixed series of payments, recorded at present value. Corning would have had the option to use its shares rather than cash to make these payments, but the liability would have been fixed by dollar value and not the number of shares. The Amended PCC Plan would, originally, have required Corning to make (1) one payment of $100 million one year from the date the Amended PCC Plan becomes effective and certain conditions are met and (2) five additional payments of $50 million, on each of the five subsequent anniversaries of the first payment, the final payment of which is subject to reduction based on the application of credits under certain circumstances. Documents were filed with the Bankruptcy Court further modifying the Amended PCC Plan by reducing Corning's initial payment by $30 million and reducing its second and fourth payments by $15 million each. In return, Corning would relinquish its claim for reimbursement of its payments and contributions under the Amended PCC Plan from the insurance carriers involved in the bankruptcy proceeding with certain exceptions.

On June 16, 2011, the Court entered an Order denying confirmation of the Amended PCC Plan. The Court's memorandum opinion accompanying the order rejected some objections to the Amended PCC Plan and made suggestions regarding modifications to the Amended PCC Plan that would allow the Plan to be confirmed. Corning and other parties have filed a motion for reconsideration, objecting to certain points of this Order. Certain parties to the proceeding filed specific Plan modifications in response to the Court's opinion and Corning supported these filings. Certain parties objected to the proposed Plan modifications and, to resolve some of those objections, further revisions to the Plan and other documents were filed. A modified Amended PCC Plan was then submitted by PCC, and objections to that Plan were filed by two parties. Those objections and the Plan are pending before the Court.

The Amended PCC Plan does not include certain non-PCC asbestos claims that may be or have been raised against Corning. Corning has recorded in its estimated asbestos litigation liability an additional $150 million for the approximately 9,800 current non-PCC cases alleging injuries from asbestos, and for any future non-PCC cases. The liability for non-PCC claims was estimated based upon industry data for asbestos claims since Corning does not have recent claim history due to the injunction issued by the Bankruptcy Court. The estimated liability represents the undiscounted projection of claims and related legal fees over the next 20 years. The amount may need to be adjusted in future periods as more data becomes available.

The liability for the Amended PCC Plan and the non-PCC asbestos claims was estimated to be $671 million at December 31, 2012, compared with an estimate of liability of $657 million at December 31, 2011. For the years ended December 31, 2012 and 2011, Corning recorded asbestos litigation expense of $14 million and $24 million, respectively. In the first quarter of 2010, Corning recorded a credit of $54 million to reflect the change in terms of Corning's proposed payments under the Amended Plan. The entire obligation is classified as a non-current liability as installment payments for the cash portion of the obligation are not planned to commence until more than 12 months after the Amended PCC Plan becomes effective and the PCE portion of the obligation will be fulfilled through the direct contribution of Corning's investment in PCE (currently recorded as a non-current other equity method investment).

The Amended PCC Plan with the modifications addressing issues raised by the Court's June 16, 2011 opinion remains subject to a number of contingencies. Payment of the amounts required to fund the Amended PCC Plan from insurance and other sources are subject to a number of conditions that may not be achieved. The approval of the (further modified) Amended PCC Plan by the Bankruptcy Court is not certain and faces objections by some parties. If the modified Amended PCC Plan is approved by the Bankruptcy Court, that approval will be subject to appeal. For these and other reasons, Corning's liability for these asbestos matters may be subject to changes in subsequent quarters. The estimate of the cost of resolving the non-PCC asbestos claims may also be subject to change as developments occur. Management continues to believe that the likelihood of the uncertainties surrounding these proceedings causing a material adverse impact to Corning's financial statements is remote.

Several of Corning's insurers have commenced litigation in state courts for a declaration of the rights and obligations of the parties under insurance policies, including rights that may be affected by the potential resolutions described above. Corning is vigorously contesting these cases. Management is unable to predict the outcome of this insurance litigation and therefore cannot estimate the range of any possible loss.

At December 31, 2012 and 2011, the fair value of PCE significantly exceeded its carrying value of $149 million and $138 million, respectively. There have been no impairment indicators for our investment in PCE and we continue to recognize equity earnings of this affiliate. PCC filed for Chapter 11 reorganization in the U.S. Bankruptcy Court on April 16, 2000. At that time, Corning determined it lacked the ability to recover the carrying amount of its investment in PCC and its investment was other than temporarily impaired. As a result, we reduced our investment in PCC to zero.

EQUITY IN LOSSES OF INVESTEES

3.36 PEABODY ENERGY CORPORATION (DEC)
CONSOLIDATED STATEMENTS OF OPERATIONS (in part)

| (Dollars in millions, except per share data) | Year Ended December 31, | | |
	2012	2011	2010
Revenues			
Sales	$7,041.7	$7,013.0	$6,139.6
Other revenues	1,035.8	882.9	528.6
Total revenues	8,077.5	7,895.9	6,668.2
Costs and Expenses			
Operating costs and expenses	5,932.7	5,477.6	4,637.7
Depreciation, depletion and amortization	663.4	474.3	429.5
Asset retirement obligation expenses	67.0	52.6	45.9
Selling and administrative expenses	268.8	268.2	232.2
Acquisition costs related to Macarthur Coal Limited	—	85.2	—
Other operating (income) loss:			
Net gain on disposal or exchange of assets	(17.1)	(76.9)	(29.9)
Asset impairment and mine closure costs	929.0	—	—
Loss from equity affiliates	61.2	19.2	1.7
Operating profit	172.5	1,595.7	1,351.1

NOTES TO CONSOLIDATED FINANCIAL STATEMENTS

(1) Summary of Significant Accounting Policies (in part)

Equity and Cost Method Investments

The Company accounts for its investments in less than majority owned corporate joint ventures under either the equity or cost method. The Company applies the equity method to investments in joint ventures when it has the ability to exercise significant influence over the operating and financial policies of the joint venture. Investments accounted for under the equity method are initially recorded at cost and any difference between the cost of the Company's investment and the underlying equity in the net assets of the joint venture at the investment date is amortized over the lives of the related assets that gave rise to the difference. The Company's pro-rata share of the operating results of joint ventures and basis difference amortization is reported in the consolidated statements of operations in "Loss from equity affiliates." Similarly, the Company's pro-rata share of the cumulative foreign currency translation adjustment of its equity method investments whose functional currency is not the U.S. dollar is reported in the consolidated balances sheet as a component of "Accumulated other comprehensive income (loss)," with periodic changes thereto reflected in the consolidated statements of comprehensive income.

The Company monitors its equity and cost method investments for indicators that a decrease in investment value has occurred that is other than temporary. Examples of such indicators include a sustained history of operating losses and adverse changes in earnings and cash flow outlook. In the absence of quoted market prices for an investment, discounted cash flow projections are used to assess fair value. If the fair value of an investment is determined to be below its carrying value and that loss in fair value is deemed other than temporary, an impairment loss is recognized. There were no impairment losses recorded during the years ended December 31, 2012, 2011 or 2010 associated with the Company's equity method investments. Refer to Note 3. "Asset Impairment and Mine Closure Costs" for details regarding impairment charges recognized during the year ended December 31, 2012 related to certain of the Company's cost method investments.

Included in the Company's equity method investments is its joint venture interest in the Middlemount Mine in Australia, which was acquired in connection with the 2011 acquisition of PEA-PCI (see Note 2. "Acquisition of Macarthur Coal Limited" for additional details). In addition to that equity interest, the Company also periodically makes loans to the Middlemount Mine joint venture pursuant to the related shareholders' agreement, which is discussed further in Note 9. "Financing Receivables." The Company's other equity method investments include an interest in Carbones del Guasare S.A., which owns and operates the Paso Diablo Mine in Venezuela. The Company fully impaired the carrying value of that investment in 2009.

The table below summarizes the book value of the Company's equity method investments, which is reported in "Investments and other assets" in the consolidated balance sheets, and the loss from its equity affiliates:

(Dollars in millions)	Book Value at December 31,		Loss from Equity Affiliates for the Year Ended December 31,		
	2012	2011	2012	2011	2010
Equity interest in Middlemount Coal Pty Ltd	$295.9	$449.7	$52.1	$ 7.3	$—
Other equity method investments	2.7	76.9	9.1	11.9	1.7
Total equity method investments	$298.6	$526.6	$61.2	$19.2	$1.7

The Company's equity interest in Middlemount Coal Pty Ltd reflected in the table above includes a remaining unamortized difference between the book value of that investment and the underlying equity in the net assets of the joint venture of $143.1 million as of December 31, 2012.

In addition to impact of the loss from its equity method affiliates and changes to its pro-rata portion of the cumulative foreign currency translation adjustment of those affiliates, the book value of the Company's equity method investments was affected during the year ended December 31, 2012 by provisional fair value adjustments recorded during that period related to the purchase price allocation for the 2011 acquisition of PEA-PCI.

ENVIRONMENTAL

3.37 WASTE MANAGEMENT, INC. (DEC)
NOTES TO CONSOLIDATED FINANCIAL STATEMENTS

3. Summary of Significant Accounting Policies (in part)

Estimates and Assumptions

In preparing our financial statements, we make numerous estimates and assumptions that affect the accounting for and recognition and disclosure of assets, liabilities, equity, revenues and expenses. We must make these estimates and assumptions because certain information that we use is dependent on future events, cannot be calculated with a high degree of precision from data available or simply cannot be readily calculated. In some cases, these estimates are particularly difficult to determine and we must exercise significant judgment. In preparing our financial statements, the most difficult, subjective and complex estimates and the assumptions that present the greatest amount of uncertainty relate to our accounting for landfills, environmental remediation liabilities, asset impairments, deferred income taxes and reserves associated with our insured and self-insured claims. Each of these items is discussed in additional detail below. Actual results could differ materially from the estimates and assumptions that we use in the preparation of our financial statements.

Environmental Remediation Liabilities

We are subject to an array of laws and regulations relating to the protection of the environment. Under current laws and regulations, we may have liabilities for environmental damage caused by operations, or for damage caused by conditions that existed before we acquired a site. These liabilities include potentially responsible party ("PRP") investigations, settlements, and certain legal and consultant fees, as well as costs directly associated with site investigation and clean up, such as materials, external contractor costs and incremental internal costs directly related to the remedy. We provide for expenses associated with environmental remediation obligations when such amounts are probable and can be reasonably estimated. We routinely review and evaluate sites that require remediation and determine our estimated cost for the likely remedy based on a number of estimates and assumptions.

Where it is probable that a liability has been incurred, we estimate costs required to remediate sites based on site-specific facts and circumstances. We routinely review and evaluate sites that require remediation, considering whether we were an owner, operator, transporter, or generator at the site, the amount and type of waste hauled to the site and the number of years we were associated with the site. Next, we review the same type of information with respect to other named and unnamed PRPs. Estimates of the costs for the likely remedy are then either developed using our internal resources or by third-party environmental engineers or other service providers. Internally developed estimates are based on:

- Management's judgment and experience in remediating our own and unrelated parties' sites;
- Information available from regulatory agencies as to costs of remediation;
- The number, financial resources and relative degree of responsibility of other PRPs who may be liable for remediation of a specific site; and
- The typical allocation of costs among PRPs, unless the actual allocation has been determined.

Estimating our degree of responsibility for remediation is inherently difficult. We recognize and accrue for an estimated remediation liability when we determine that such liability is both probable and reasonably estimable. Determining the method and ultimate cost of remediation requires that a number of assumptions be made. There can sometimes be a range of reasonable estimates of the costs associated with the likely site remediation alternatives identified in the investigation of the extent of environmental impact. In these cases, we use the amount within the range that constitutes our best estimate. If no amount within a range appears to be a better estimate than any other, we use the amount that is the low end of such range. If we used the high ends of such ranges, our aggregate potential liability would be approximately $140 million higher than the $253 million recorded in the Consolidated Financial Statements as of December 31, 2012. Our ultimate responsibility may differ materially from current estimates. It is possible that technological, regulatory or enforcement developments, the results of environmental studies, the inability to identify other PRPs, the inability of other PRPs to contribute to the settlements of such liabilities, or other factors could require us to record additional liabilities. Our ongoing review of our remediation liabilities, in light of relevant internal and external facts and circumstances, could result in revisions to our accruals that could cause upward or downward adjustments to income from operations. These adjustments could be material in any given period.

Where we believe that both the amount of a particular environmental remediation liability and the timing of the payments are reliably determinable, we inflate the cost in current dollars (by 2.5% at December 31, 2012 and 2011) until the expected time of payment and discount the cost to present value using a risk-free discount rate, which is based on the rate for United States Treasury bonds with a term approximating the weighted average period until settlement of the underlying obligation. We determine the risk-free discount rate and the inflation rate on an annual basis unless interim changes would significantly impact our results of operations. For remedial liabilities that have been discounted, we include interest accretion, based on the effective interest method, in "Operating" costs and expenses in our Consolidated Statements of Operations. The following table summarizes the impacts of revisions in the risk-free discount rate applied to our environmental remediation liabilities and recovery assets during the reported periods (in millions) and the risk-free discount rate applied as of each reporting date:

	Years Ended December 31,		
	2012	2011	2010
Charge to Operating expenses	$ 3	$ 17	$ 2
Risk-free discount rate applied to environmental remediation liabilities and recovery assets	1.75%	2.00%	3.50%

The portion of our recorded environmental remediation liabilities that has never been subject to inflation or discounting, as the amounts and timing of payments are not readily determinable, was $32 million at December 31, 2012 and $48 million at December 31, 2011. Had we not inflated and discounted any portion of our environmental remediation liability, the amount recorded would have decreased by $11 million at December 31, 2012 and decreased by $8 million at December 31, 2011.

SALE OF RECEIVABLES

3.38 ARCHER DANIELS MIDLAND COMPANY (JUN)
CONSOLIDATED STATEMENTS OF EARNINGS (in part)

	Year Ended June 30		
(In millions, except per share amounts)	2012	2011	2010
Net sales and other operating income	$89,038	$80,676	$61,682
Cost of products sold	85,370	76,376	57,839
Gross profit	3,668	4,300	3,843
Selling, general and administrative expenses	1,626	1,611	1,398
Asset impairment, exit, and restructuring costs	437	—	—
Interest expense	441	482	422
Equity in earnings of unconsolidated affiliates	(472)	(542)	(561)
Interest income	(112)	(136)	(126)
Other (income) expense—net	(17)	(130)	125
Earnings before income taxes	1,765	3,015	2,585

Note 20. Sale of Accounts Receivable

On March 27, 2012, the Company entered into an amendment of its accounts receivable securitization program (as amended, the "Program") with certain commercial paper conduit purchasers and committed purchasers (collectively, the "Purchasers"). Under the Program, certain U.S.-originated trade accounts receivable are sold to a wholly-owned bankruptcy-remote entity, ADM Receivables, LLC ("ADM Receivables"). ADM Receivables in turn transfers such purchased accounts receivable in their entirety to the Purchasers pursuant to a receivables purchase agreement. In exchange for the transfer of the accounts receivable, ADM Receivables receives a cash payment of up to $1.0 billion and an additional amount upon the collection of the accounts receivable (deferred consideration). ADM Receivables uses the cash proceeds from the transfer of receivables to the Purchasers and other consideration to finance the purchase of receivables from the Company and the ADM subsidiaries originating the receivables. The Company accounts for these transfers as sales. The Company has no retained interests in the transferred receivables, other than collection and administrative responsibilities and its right to the deferred consideration. At June 30, 2012, the Company did not record a servicing asset or liability related to its retained responsibility, based on its assessment of the servicing fee, market values for similar transactions and its cost of servicing the receivables sold. The Program terminates on June 28, 2013.

As of June 30, 2012, the fair value of trade receivables transferred to the Purchasers under the Program and derecognized from the Company's consolidated balance sheet was $1.6 billion. In exchange for the transfer, the Company received cash of $1.0 billion and recorded a receivable for deferred consideration included in other current assets. Cash collections from customers on receivables sold were $8.9 billion for the four months ended June 30, 2012. Of this amount, $8.9 billion pertains to cash collections on the deferred consideration. Deferred consideration is paid to the Company in cash on behalf of the Purchasers as receivables are collected; however, as this is a revolving facility, cash collected from the Company's customers is reinvested by the Purchasers daily in new receivable purchases under the Program.

The Company's risk of loss following the transfer of accounts receivable under the Program is limited to the deferred consideration outstanding, which is classified as other current assets and was $0.6 billion at June 30, 2012. The Company carries the deferred consideration at fair value determined by calculating the expected amount of cash to be received and is principally based on observable inputs (a Level 2 measurement under ASC 820) consisting mainly of the face amount of the receivables adjusted for anticipated credit losses and discounted at the appropriate market rate. Payment of deferred consideration is not subject to significant risks other than delinquencies and credit losses on accounts receivable transferred under the program which have historically been insignificant.

Transfers of receivables under the Program during the year ended June 30, 2012 resulted in an expense for the loss on sale of $4 million which is classified as selling, general, and administrative expenses in the consolidated statements of earnings.

The Company reflects all cash flows related to the Program as operating activities in its consolidated statement of cash flows for the year ended June 30, 2012 because the cash received from the Purchasers upon both the sale and collection of the receivables is not subject to significant interest rate risk given the short-term nature of the Company's trade receivables.

MERGERS AND ACQUISITIONS

3.39 PEPSICO, INC. (DEC)
NOTES TO CONSOLIDATED FINANCIAL STATEMENTS

Note 3—Restructuring, Impairment and Integration Charges (in part)

In 2012, we incurred merger and integration charges of $16 million ($12 million after-tax or $0.01 per share) related to our acquisition of WBD, including $11 million recorded in the Europe segment and $5 million recorded in interest expense. All of these net charges, other than the interest expense portion, were recorded in selling, general and administrative expenses. The majority of cash payments related to these charges were paid by the end of 2012.

In 2011, we incurred merger and integration charges of $329 million ($271 million after-tax or $0.17 per share) related to our acquisitions of PBG, PAS and WBD, including $112 million recorded in the PAB segment, $123 million recorded in the Europe segment, $78 million recorded in corporate unallocated expenses and $16 million recorded in interest expense. All of these net charges, other than the interest expense portion, were recorded in selling, general and administrative expenses. These charges also include closing costs and advisory fees related to our acquisition of WBD. Substantially all cash payments related to the above charges were made by the end of 2011.

In 2010, we incurred merger and integration charges of $799 million related to our acquisitions of PBG and PAS, as well as advisory fees in connection with our acquisition of WBD. $467 million of these charges were recorded in the PAB segment, $111 million recorded in the Europe segment, $191 million recorded in corporate unallocated expenses and $30 million recorded in interest expense. All of these charges, other than the interest expense portion, were recorded in selling, general and administrative expenses. The merger and integration charges related to our acquisitions of PBG and PAS were incurred to help create a more fully integrated supply chain and go-to-market business model, to improve the effectiveness and efficiency of the distribution of our brands and to enhance our revenue growth. These charges also include closing costs, one-time financing costs and advisory fees related to our acquisitions of PBG and PAS. In addition, we recorded $9 million of merger-related charges, representing our share of the respective merger costs of PBG and PAS, in bottling equity income. Substantially all cash payments related to the above charges were made by the end of 2011. In total, these charges had an after-tax impact of $648 million or $0.40 per share.

A summary of our merger and integration activity was as follows:

	Severance and Other Employee Costs	Asset Impairments	Other Costs	Total
2010 merger and integration charges	$ 396	$ 132	$ 280	$ 808
Cash payments	(114)	—	(271)	(385)
Non-cash charges	(103)	(132)	16	(219)
Liability as of December 25, 2010	179	—	25	204
2011 merger and integration charges	146	34	149	329
Cash payments	(191)	—	(186)	(377)
Non-cash charges	(36)	(34)	19	(51)
Liability as of December 31, 2011	98	—	7	105
2012 merger and integration charges	(3)	1	18	16
Cash payments	(65)	—	(18)	(83)
Non-cash charges	(12)	(1)	(1)	(14)
Liability as of December 29, 2012	$ 18	$ —	$ 6	$ 24

CHANGE IN FAIR VALUE OF DERIVATIVES

3.40 PRICELINE.COM INCORPORATED (DEC)
MANAGEMENT'S DISCUSSION AND ANALYSIS OF FINANCIAL CONDITION AND RESULTS OF OPERATIONS (in part)

Other Income (Expense) (in part)

	Year Ended December 31, ($000)		
	2012	2011	Change
Interest income	$ 3,860	$ 8,119	(52.5)%
Interest expense	(62,064)	(31,721)	95.7%
Foreign currency transactions and other	(9,720)	(7,526)	29.2%
Total	$(67,924)	$(31,128)	118.2%

Derivative contracts that hedge our exposure to the impact of currency fluctuations on the translation of our international operating results into U.S. Dollars upon consolidation resulted in foreign exchange gains of $0.7 million and $4.0 million for the years ended December 31, 2012 and 2011, respectively, and are recorded in "Foreign currency transactions and other" on the Consolidated Statements of Operations.

Foreign exchange transaction losses, including costs related to foreign exchange transactions, resulted in losses of $10.5 million and $11.3 million for the years ended December 31, 2012 and 2011, respectively, and are recorded in "Foreign currency transactions and other" on the Consolidated Statements of Operations. During the fourth quarter of 2011, we began classifying certain foreign currency processing fees as an offset to revenue earned from the third party that processes the payments for merchant hotel transactions. Such processing fees recorded to "Foreign currency transactions and other" for the nine months ended September 30, 2011 amounted to approximately $5.0 million.

CONSOLIDATED STATEMENTS OF OPERATIONS (in part)

(In thousands, except per share data)

	Year Ended December 31,		
	2012	2011	2010
Agency revenues	$3,142,815	$2,339,253	$1,380,603
Merchant revenues	2,104,752	2,004,432	1,691,640
Other revenues	13,389	11,925	12,662
Total revenues	5,260,956	4,355,610	3,084,905
Cost of revenues	1,177,275	1,275,730	1,175,934
Gross profit	4,083,681	3,079,880	1,908,971

(continued)

	Year Ended December 31,		
	2012	2011	2010
Operating expenses:			
Advertising—Online	$1,273,637	$ 919,214	$ 552,140
Advertising—Offline	35,492	35,470	35,714
Sales and marketing	195,934	162,690	116,303
Personnel, including stock-based compensation of $71,565, $65,724 and $68,200, respectively	466,828	352,295	270,071
General and administrative	173,171	123,652	81,185
Information technology	43,685	33,813	20,998
Depreciation and amortization	65,141	53,824	45,763
Total operating expenses	2,253,888	1,680,958	1,122,174
Operating income	1,829,793	1,398,922	786,797
Other income (expense):			
Interest income	3,860	8,119	3,857
Interest expense	(62,064)	(31,721)	(29,944)
Foreign currency transactions and other	(9,720)	(7,526)	(14,427)
Total other income (expense)	(67,924)	(31,128)	(40,514)
Earnings before income taxes	1,761,869	1,367,794	746,283

NOTES TO CONSOLIDATED FINANCIAL STATEMENTS

2. Summary of Significant Accounting Policies (in part)

Foreign Currency Translation—The functional currency of the Company's foreign subsidiaries is generally their respective local currency. Assets and liabilities are translated into U.S. dollars at the rate of exchange existing at the balance sheet date. Income statement amounts are translated at average monthly exchange rates applicable for the period. Translation gains and losses are included as a component of "Accumulated other comprehensive loss" on the Company's Consolidated Balance Sheets. Foreign currency transaction gains and losses are included in "Foreign currency transactions and other" in the Company's Consolidated Statements of Operations.

Derivative Financial Instruments—As a result of the Company's international operations, it is exposed to various market risks that may affect its consolidated results of operations, cash flow and financial position. These market risks include, but are not limited to, fluctuations in currency exchange rates. The Company's primary foreign currency exposures are in Euros and British Pound Sterling, in which it conducts a significant portion of its business activities. As a result, the Company faces exposure to adverse movements in currency exchange rates as the financial results of its international operations are translated from local currency into U.S. Dollars upon consolidation. Additionally, foreign exchange rate fluctuations on transactions denominated in currencies other than the functional currency result in gains and losses that are reflected in income.

The Company may enter into derivative instruments to hedge certain net exposures of nonfunctional currency denominated assets and liabilities and the volatility associated with translating foreign earnings into U.S. Dollars, even though it does not elect to apply hedge accounting or hedge accounting does not apply. Gains and losses resulting from a change in fair value for these derivatives are reflected in income in the period in which the change occurs and are recognized on the Consolidated Statements of Operations in "Foreign currency transactions and other." Cash flows related to these contracts are classified within "Net cash provided by operating activities" on the cash flow statement.

CHANGE IN FAIR VALUE

3.41 METLIFE, INC. (DEC)
CONSOLIDATED STATEMENTS OF OPERATIONS (in part)

(In millions, except per share data)

	2012	2011	2010
Revenues			
Premiums	$37,975	$36,361	$27,071
Universal life and investment-type product policy fees	8,556	7,806	6,028
Net investment income	21,984	19,585	17,493
Other revenues	1,906	2,532	2,328
Net investment gains (losses):			
Other-than-temporary impairments on fixed maturity securities	(346)	(924)	(682)
Other-than-temporary impairments on fixed maturity securities transferred to other comprehensive income (loss)	29	(31)	212
Other net investment gains (losses)	(35)	88	62
Total net investment gains (losses)	(352)	(867)	(408)
Net derivative gains (losses)	(1,919)	4,824	(265)
Total revenues	68,150	70,241	52,247

1. Business, Basis of Presentation and Summary of Significant Accounting Policies (in part)

Summary of Significant Accounting Policies (in part)

Investments (in part)

Fixed Maturity and Equity Securities

The majority of the Company's fixed maturity and equity securities are classified as available-for-sale ("AFS") and are reported at their estimated fair value. Unrealized investment gains and losses on these securities are recorded as a separate component of other comprehensive income (loss) ("OCI"), net of policyholder-related amounts and deferred income taxes. All security transactions are recorded on a trade date basis. Investment gains and losses on sales are determined on a specific identification basis.

Interest income on fixed maturity securities is recognized when earned using an effective yield method giving effect to amortization of premiums and accretion of discounts. Prepayment fees are recognized when earned. Dividends on equity securities are recognized when declared.

The Company periodically evaluates fixed maturity and equity securities for impairment. The assessment of whether impairments have occurred is based on management's case-by-case evaluation of the underlying reasons for the decline in estimated fair value and an analysis of the gross unrealized losses by severity and/or age. The analysis of gross unrealized losses is described further in Note 8 "—Evaluation of AFS Securities for OTTI and Evaluating Temporarily Impaired AFS Securities."

For fixed maturity securities in an unrealized loss position, an other-than-temporary impairment ("OTTI") is recognized in earnings when it is anticipated that the amortized cost will not be recovered. When either: (i) the Company has the intent to sell the security; or (ii) it is more likely than not that the Company will be required to sell the security before recovery, the OTTI recognized in earnings is the entire difference between the security's amortized cost and estimated fair value. If neither of these conditions exist, the difference between the amortized cost of the security and the present value of projected future cash flows expected to be collected is recognized as an OTTI in earnings ("credit loss"). If the estimated fair value is less than the present value of projected future cash flows expected to be collected, this portion of OTTI related to other-than-credit factors ("noncredit loss") is recorded in OCI. Adjustments are not made for subsequent recoveries in value.

With respect to equity securities, the Company considers in its OTTI analysis its intent and ability to hold a particular equity security for a period of time sufficient to allow for the recovery of its estimated fair value to an amount equal to or greater than cost. If a sale decision is made for an equity security and recovery to an amount at least equal to cost prior to the sale is not expected, the security will be deemed to be other-than-temporarily impaired in the period that the sale decision was made and an OTTI loss will be recorded in earnings. The OTTI loss recognized is the entire difference between the security's cost and its estimated fair value with a corresponding charge to earnings.

Fair Value Option and Trading Securities

FVO and trading securities are stated at estimated fair value and include investments for which the FVO has been elected ("FVO Securities") and investments that are actively purchased and sold ("Actively Traded Securities"). FVO Securities include:
- fixed maturity and equity securities held-for-investment by the general account to support asset and liability matching strategies for certain insurance products;
- contractholder-directed investments supporting unit-linked variable annuity type liabilities which do not qualify for presentation and reporting as separate account summary total assets and liabilities. These investments are primarily mutual funds and, to a lesser extent, fixed maturity and equity securities, short-term investments and cash and cash equivalents. The investment returns on these investments inure to contractholders and are offset by a corresponding change in PABs through interest credited to policyholder account balances; and
- securities held by consolidated securitization entities ("CSEs") (former qualifying special purpose entities), with changes in estimated fair value subsequent to consolidation included in net investment gains (losses).

Actively Traded Securities principally include fixed maturity securities and short sale agreement liabilities, which are included in other liabilities.

Changes in estimated fair value of these securities subsequent to purchase are included in net investment income, except for certain securities included in FVO Securities where changes are included in net investment gains (losses).

Mortgage Loans

The Company disaggregates its mortgage loan investments into three portfolio segments: commercial, agricultural, and residential. The accounting and valuation allowance policies that are applicable to all portfolio segments are presented below and policies related to each of the portfolio segments are included in Note 8.

Mortgage Loans Held-For-Investment

Mortgage loans held-for-investment are stated at unpaid principal balance, adjusted for any unamortized premium or discount, deferred fees or expenses, and are net of valuation allowances. Interest income and prepayment fees are recognized when earned. Interest is accrued on the principal amount of the loan based on the loan's contractual interest rate, while amortization of premiums and discounts is recognized using the effective yield method. Gains and losses from sales of loans and increases or decreases to valuation allowances are recorded in net investment gains (losses).

Also included in mortgage loans held-for-investment are commercial mortgage loans held by CSEs for which the FVO was elected. These loans are stated at estimated fair value with changes in estimated fair value subsequent to consolidation recognized in net investment gains (losses).

Mortgage Loans Held-For-Sale

Mortgage loans held-for-sale includes three categories of mortgage loans:
- *Residential mortgage loans—held-for-sale—FVO.* Forward and reverse residential mortgage loans originated with the intent to sell, for which the FVO was elected, are carried at estimated fair value. Subsequent changes in estimated fair value are recognized in other revenues.
- *Mortgage loans—held-for-sale—lower of amortized cost or estimated fair value.* Mortgage loans originated with the intent to sell for which FVO was not elected, certain repurchased mortgage loans, and mortgage loans that were previously designated as held-for-investment, but now are designated as held-for-sale, are stated at the lower of amortized cost or estimated fair value.
- *Securitized reverse residential mortgage loans.* Reverse residential mortgage loans originated with the intent to sell which have been transferred into Government National Mortgage Association securitizations, for which the FVO was elected, are stated at estimated fair value. The FVO was elected for certain loans and the corresponding secured borrowing, which is included within other liabilities. Subsequent changes in estimated fair value of both the asset and liability are recognized in other revenues.

Real Estate

Real estate held-for-investment is stated at cost less accumulated depreciation. Depreciation is provided on a straight-line basis over the estimated useful life of the asset (typically 20 to 55 years). Rental income associated with such real estate is recognized on a straight-line basis over the term of the respective leases. The Company periodically reviews its real estate held-for-investment for impairment and tests for recoverability whenever events or changes in circumstances indicate the carrying value may not be recoverable and exceeds its estimated fair value. Properties whose carrying values are greater than their undiscounted cash flows are written down to their estimated fair value, which is generally computed using the present value of expected future cash flows discounted at a rate commensurate with the underlying risks.

Real estate for which the Company commits to a plan to sell within one year and actively markets in its current condition for a reasonable price in comparison to its estimated fair value is classified as held for sale. Real estate held-for-sale is stated at the lower of depreciated cost or estimated fair value less expected disposition costs and is not depreciated.

Real estate acquired upon foreclosure is recorded at the lower of estimated fair value or the carrying value of the mortgage loan at the date of foreclosure.

Real Estate Joint Ventures and Other Limited Partnership Interests

The Company uses the equity method of accounting for investments in real estate joint ventures and other limited partnership interests in which it has more than a minor ownership interest or more than a minor influence over the joint venture's or partnership's operations, but does not have a controlling financial interest. Equity method investment income is recognized as earned by the investee. The Company records its share of earnings using a three-month lag methodology for instances where the timely financial information is not available and the contractual agreements provide for the delivery of the investees' financial information after the end of the Company's reporting period.

The Company uses the cost method of accounting for investments in which it has virtually no influence over the joint venture's or the partnership's operations. Based on the nature and structure of these investments, they do not meet the characteristics of an equity security in accordance with applicable accounting standards. The Company recognizes distributions on cost method investments as earned or received.

In addition to the investees performing regular evaluations for the impairment of underlying investments, the Company routinely evaluates these investments for impairments. For equity method investees, the Company considers financial and other information provided by the investee, other known information and inherent risks in the underlying investments, as well as future capital commitments, in determining whether an impairment has occurred. The Company considers its cost method investments for OTTI when the carrying value of such investments exceeds the net asset value ("NAV"). The Company takes into consideration the severity and duration of this excess when determining whether the cost method investment is other-than-temporarily impaired. When an OTTI has occurred, the impairment loss is recorded within net investment gains (losses).

Short-Term Investments

Short-term investments include securities and other investments with remaining maturities of one year or less, but greater than three months, at the time of purchase and are stated at estimated fair value or amortized cost, which approximates estimated fair value.

Other Invested Assets

Other invested assets consist principally of the following:
- Freestanding derivatives with positive estimated fair values are described in "—Derivatives" below.
- Tax credit partnerships derive their primary source of investment return in the form of income tax credits. Where tax credits are guaranteed by a creditworthy third party, the investment is accounted for under the effective yield method. Otherwise, the investment is accounted for under the equity method.
- Leveraged leases are recorded net of non-recourse debt. The Company recognizes income on the leveraged leases by applying the leveraged lease's estimated rate of return to the net investment in the lease. The Company regularly reviews residual values and impairs them to expected values.
- Funds withheld represent a receivable for amounts contractually withheld by ceding companies in accordance with reinsurance agreements. The Company recognizes interest on funds withheld at rates defined by the terms of the agreement which may be contractually specified or directly related to the underlying investments.
- Joint venture investments that engage in insurance underwriting activities are accounted for under the equity method.
- Mortgage Servicing Rights ("MSRs") are measured at estimated fair value with changes in fair value reported in other revenues in the period in which the change occurs.

Securities Lending Program

Securities lending transactions, whereby blocks of securities, which are included in fixed maturity securities, equity securities, and short-term investments, are loaned to third parties, primarily brokerage firms and commercial banks, and are treated as financing arrangements and the associated liability is recorded at the amount of cash received. The Company obtains collateral at the inception of the loan, usually cash, in an amount generally equal to 102% of the estimated fair value of the securities loaned, and maintains it at a level greater than or equal to 100% for the duration of the loan. The Company is liable to return to the counterparties the cash collateral received. Security collateral on deposit from counterparties in connection with the securities lending transactions may not be sold or repledged, unless the counterparty is in default, and is not reflected in the consolidated financial statements. The Company monitors the estimated fair value of the securities loaned on a daily basis with additional collateral obtained as necessary. Income and expenses associated with securities lending transactions are reported as investment income and investment expense, respectively, within net investment income.

8. Investments (in part)

Net Investment Income

The components of net investment income were as follows:

(In millions)	Years Ended December 31,		
	2012	2011	2010
Investment income:			
Fixed maturity securities	$15,218	$15,037	$12,407
Equity securities	133	141	128
FVO and trading securities—Actively Traded Securities and FVO general account securities[1]	88	31	73
Mortgage loans	3,191	3,164	2,824
Policy loans	626	641	649
Real estate and real estate joint ventures	834	688	372
Other limited partnership interests	845	681	879
Cash, cash equivalents and short-term investments	163	167	101
International joint ventures	19	(12)	(92)
Other	131	178	236
Subtotal	21,248	20,716	17,577
Less: Investment expenses	1,090	1,019	882
Subtotal, net	20,158	19,697	16,695

(continued)

(In millions)	Years Ended December 31,		
	2012	**2011**	**2010**
FVO and trading securities—FVO contractholder-directed unit-linked investments[1]	$ 1,473	$ (453)	$ 372
Securitized reverse residential mortgage loans	177	—	—
FVO CSEs—interest income:			
Commercial mortgage loans	172	332	411
Securities	4	9	15
Subtotal	1,826	(112)	798
Net investment income	$21,984	$19,585	$17,493

[1] Changes in estimated fair value subsequent to purchase for securities still held as of the end of the respective years included in net investment income were:

(In millions)	Years Ended December 31,		
	2012	**2011**	**2010**
Actively Traded Securities and FVO general account securities	$ 51	$ (3)	$ 30
FVO contractholder-directed unit-linked investments	$1,170	$(647)	$322

See "—Variable Interest Entities" for discussion of CSEs included in the table above.

Net Investment Gains (Losses)

Components of Net Investment Gains (Losses)

The components of net investment gains (losses) were as follows:

(In millions)	Years Ended December 31,		
	2012	**2011**	**2010**
Total gains (losses) on fixed maturity securities:			
Total OTTI losses recognized—by sector and industry:			
U.S. and foreign corporate securities—by industry:			
Utility	$ (61)	$ (10)	$ (3)
Finance	(32)	(56)	(126)
Consumer	(19)	(50)	(36)
Communications	(19)	(41)	(16)
Transportation	(17)	—	—
Technology	(6)	(1)	—
Industrial	(5)	(11)	(2)
Total U.S. and foreign corporate securities	(159)	(169)	(183)
RMBS	(97)	(214)	(117)
CMBS	(51)	(32)	(86)
ABS	(9)	(54)	(84)
State and political subdivision	(1)	—	—
Foreign government	—	(486)	—
OTTI losses on fixed maturity securities recognized in earnings	(317)	(955)	(470)
Fixed maturity securities—net gains (losses) on sales and disposals	253	25	215
Total gains (losses) on fixed maturity securities[1]	(64)	(930)	(255)
Total gains (losses) on equity securities:			
Total OTTI losses recognized—by sector:			
Common	(34)	(22)	(7)
Non-redeemable preferred	—	(38)	(7)
OTTI losses on equity securities recognized in earnings	(34)	(60)	(14)
Equity securities—net gains (losses) on sales and disposals	38	37	118
Total gains (losses) on equity securities	4	(23)	104
FVO and trading securities—FVO general account securities—changes in estimated fair value subsequent to consolidation	17	(2)	—
Mortgage loans[1]	57	175	22
Real estate and real estate joint ventures	(36)	134	(54)
Other limited partnership interests	(36)	4	(18)
Other investment portfolio gains (losses)	(151)	(7)	(6)
Subtotal—investment portfolio gains (losses)[1]	(209)	(649)	(207)

(continued)

(In millions)	Years Ended December 31,		
	2012	**2011**	**2010**
FVO CSEs—changes in estimated fair value subsequent to consolidation:			
Commercial mortgage loans	$ 7	$ (84)	$ 758
Securities	—	—	(78)
Long-term debt—related to commercial mortgage loans	25	97	(722)
Long-term debt—related to securities	(7)	(8)	48
Non-investment portfolio gains (losses)[2]	(168)	(223)	(207)
Subtotal FVO CSEs and non-investment portfolio gains (losses)	(143)	(218)	(201)
Total net investment gains (losses)	$(352)	$(867)	$(408)

[1] Investment portfolio gains (losses) for the years ended December 31, 2012 and 2011 includes a net gain (loss) of $37 million and ($153) million, respectively, as a result of the MetLife Bank Divestiture, which is comprised of gains (losses) on investments sold of $78 million and $1 million, and impairments of ($41) million and ($154) million, respectively. See Note 3.

[2] Non-investment portfolio gains (losses) for the year ended December 31, 2012 includes a gain of $33 million related to certain dispositions as more fully described in Note 3. Non-investment portfolio gains (losses) for the year ended December 31, 2011 includes a loss of $106 million related to certain dispositions and a goodwill impairment loss of $65 million. See Notes 3 and 11. Non-investment portfolio gains (losses) for the year ended December 31, 2010 includes a loss of $209 million related to a disposition. See Note 3.

See "—Variable Interest Entities" for discussion of CSEs included in the table above.

Gains (losses) from foreign currency transactions included within net investment gains (losses) were ($112) million, $37 million and $230 million for the years ended December 31, 2012, 2011 and 2010, respectively.

IMPAIRMENT OF GOODWILL AND INTANGIBLE ASSETS

3.42 TUPPERWARE BRANDS CORPORATION (DEC)

CONSOLIDATED STATEMENTS OF INCOME (in part)

(In millions, except per share amounts)	Year Ended		
	December 29, 2012	**December 31, 2011**	**December 25, 2010**
Net sales	$2,583.8	$2,585.0	$2,300.4
Cost of products sold	856.4	862.5	766.2
Gross margin	1,727.4	1,722.5	1,534.2
Delivery, sales and administrative expense	1,329.5	1,340.0	1,193.1
Re-engineering and impairment charges	22.4	7.9	7.6
Impairment of goodwill and intangible assets	76.9	36.1	4.3
Gains on disposal of assets	7.9	3.8	0.2
Operating income	306.5	342.3	329.4

NOTES TO THE CONSOLIDATED FINANCIAL STATEMENTS

Note 1: Summary of Significant Accounting Policies (in part)

Goodwill. The Company's recorded goodwill relates primarily to that generated by its acquisition of the Sara Lee direct-to-consumer businesses in December 2005 and BeautiControl in October 2000. The Company conducts an annual impairment assessment of its recorded goodwill in each of its eight reporting units during the third quarter of each year, except for goodwill associated with BeautiControl, which is completed in the second quarter. Additionally, in the event of a change in circumstances that leads the Company to determine that a triggering event for impairment testing has occurred, a test is completed at that time. The annual process for evaluating goodwill begins with an assessment for each entity of qualitative factors to determine whether the two-step goodwill impairment test is necessary. Further testing is only performed if the Company determines that it is more likely than not that the reporting unit's fair value is less than its carrying value. The qualitative factors evaluated by the Company include: macro-economic conditions of the local business environment, overall financial performance, sensitivity analysis from the most recent step one fair value test, and other entity specific factors as deemed appropriate. When the Company determines the two-step goodwill impairment test is necessary, the first step involves comparing the fair value of a reporting unit to its carrying amount, including goodwill, after any long-lived asset impairment charges. If the carrying amount of the reporting unit exceeds its fair value, a second step is performed to determine whether there is a goodwill impairment, and if so, the amount of the loss. This step revalues all assets and liabilities of the reporting unit to their current fair value and then compares the implied fair value of the reporting unit's goodwill to the carrying amount of that goodwill. If the carrying amount of the reporting unit's goodwill exceeds the implied fair value of the goodwill, an impairment loss is recognized in an amount equal to the excess. Prior to 2012, the Company's annual assessment began with the two-step impairment test.

When a determination of fair value of the Company's reporting units is necessary, it is determined by using either the income approach or a combination of the income and market approaches, with a greater weighting on the income approach (75 percent). The income approach, or discounted cash flow approach, requires significant assumptions to determine the fair value of each reporting unit. These include estimates regarding future operations and the ability to generate cash flows including projections of revenue, costs, utilization of assets and capital requirements, along with an estimate as to the appropriate discount rates to be used. Goodwill is further discussed in Note 6 to the Consolidated Financial Statements.

Intangible Assets. Intangible assets are recorded at their fair market values at the date of acquisition and definite lived intangibles are amortized over their estimated useful lives. The intangible assets included in the Company's Consolidated Financial Statements at December 29, 2012 and December 31, 2011 were related to the acquisition of the Sara Lee direct-to-consumer businesses in December 2005. The weighted average estimated useful lives of the Company's intangible assets were as follows:

	Weighted Average Estimated Useful Life
Trademarks and tradenames	Indefinite
Sales force relationships—single level	6–8 years
Sales force relationships—tiered	10–12 years
Acquired proprietary product formulations	3 years

The Company's indefinite lived intangible assets are evaluated for impairment annually similarly to goodwill. When necessary, the fair value of these assets is determined using the relief from royalty method, which is a form of the income approach. In this method, the value of the asset is calculated by selecting royalty rates, which estimate the amount a company would be willing to pay for the use of the asset. These rates are applied to the Company's projected revenue, tax affected and discounted to present value using an appropriate rate.

The Company's definite lived intangible assets consist of the value of the acquired independent sales force and product formulations. The Company amortizes project formulas over a straight line basis and as of December 29, 2012, the amount from the acquisition of the Sara Lee direct-to-consumer units had been fully amortized. The sales force relationships are amortized to reflect the estimated turnover rates of the sales force acquired and included in Delivery, Sales and Administration expense (DS&A) on the Consolidated Statements of Income.

Intangible assets are further discussed in Note 6 to the Consolidated Financial Statements.

Note 6: Goodwill and Intangible Assets

The Company's goodwill and intangible assets relate primarily to the December 2005 acquisition of the direct-to-consumer businesses of Sara Lee Corporation and the October 2000 acquisition of BeautiControl. The Company does not amortize its goodwill or tradename intangible assets. Instead, the Company performs an assessment to test these assets for impairment annually, or more frequently if events or changes in circumstances indicate they may be impaired. Certain tradenames are allocated between multiple reporting units.

The annual process for evaluating goodwill begins with an assessment for each entity of qualitative factors to determine whether the two-step goodwill impairment test is necessary. Further testing is only performed if the Company determines that it is more likely than not that the reporting unit's fair value is less than its carrying value. The qualitative factors evaluated by the Company include: macro-economic conditions of the local business environment, overall financial performance, sensitivity analysis from the most recent step one fair value test, and other entity specific factors as deemed appropriate. When the Company determines the two-step goodwill impairment test is necessary, the first step involves comparing the fair value of a reporting unit to its carrying amount, including goodwill, after any long-lived asset impairment charges. If the carrying amount of the reporting unit exceeds its fair value, a second step is performed to determine whether there is a goodwill impairment, and if so, the amount of the loss. This step revalues all assets and liabilities of the reporting unit to their current fair value and then compares the implied fair value of the reporting unit's goodwill to the carrying amount of that goodwill. If the carrying amount of the reporting unit's goodwill exceeds the implied fair value of the goodwill, an impairment loss is recognized in an amount equal to the excess. Prior to 2012, the Company's annual assessment began with the two-step impairment test.

The Company early adopted Accounting Standards Update 2012-02, "Testing Indefinite-Lived Intangibles for Impairment" ("the ASU") in connection with the performance of its 2012 annual impairment testing of its tradenames. Under the ASU, entities are provided the option of first performing a qualitative assessment that is similar to the assessment performed for goodwill. When the Company determines it is necessary, the quantitative impairment test for the Company's tradenames involves comparing the estimated fair value of the assets to the carrying amounts, to determine if fair value is lower and a write-down required. If the carrying amount of a tradename exceeds its estimated fair value, an impairment charge is recognized in an amount equal to the excess.

During the second quarter of 2012, the Company completed its annual impairment test of the BeautiControl reporting units, resulting in an impairment charge of $38.9 million related to the goodwill in the BeautiControl United States and Canada business. This was a result of the rates of growth of sales, profit and cash flow and expectations for future performance that were below the Company's previous projections. Also in the second quarter, the financial performance of the Nutrimetics reporting units fell below their previous trend line and it became apparent that they would fall significantly short of previous expectations for the year. Additionally, reductions in the forecasted operating trends of NaturCare relating to declines in the rates of growth of sales, profit and cash flows in the Japanese market led to interim impairment testing in both these businesses, as of the end of May and June 2012, respectively. The result of these tests was to record tradename impairments of $13.8 million for Nutrimetics and $9.0 million for NaturCare, primarily due to the use of lower estimated royalty rates in light of lower sales and profit forecasts for these units, as well as macroeconomic factors that increased the discount rates used in the valuations versus those used previously. In addition, the Company wrote off the $7.2 million and $7.7 million carrying value of the goodwill of the Nutrimetics Asia Pacific and Nutrimetics Europe reporting units, respectively, in light of then current operating trends and expected future results, as well as the macroeconomic factors that increased the discount rates used in the valuations. In the third quarter of 2012, the Company completed the annual impairment assessments for all of the reporting units and tradename intangibles, except for BeautiControl which was completed in the second quarter, determining there was no impairment.

In the third quarter of 2011, the Company completed the annual impairment tests for all of the reporting units and tradenames, other than BeautiControl, which was completed in the second quarter. During the third quarter of 2011, the financial results of Nutrimetics were below expectations. The Company also made at that time, the decision to cease operating its Nutrimetics business in Malaysia. As a result, the Company lowered its forecast of future sales and profit. The result of the impairment tests was to record a $31.1 million impairment to the Nutrimetics goodwill in the Asia Pacific reporting unit and a $5.0 million impairment to its tradename.

During 2010, the Company completed the annual impairment tests for all of the reporting units and tradenames, determining there was no impairment. The Company subsequently decided it would cease operating its Swissgarde unit in Southern Africa as a separate business. As a result of this decision, the Company concluded that its intangible assets and goodwill were impaired and recorded a $2.1 million impairment to the Swissgarde tradename, a $0.1 million impairment related to the sales force intangible and a $2.1 million impairment to goodwill relating to the South African beauty reporting unit. During 2011, the Company sold its interest in Swissgarde for $0.7 million that resulted in a gain of $0.1 million.

Fair value of the BeautiControl United States and Canada, Nutrimetics and NaturCare reporting units was determined by the Company in the second quarter of 2012, using a combination of the income and market approaches with generally a greater weighting on the income approach (75 percent). When the characteristics of the reporting unit were more similar to the guideline public companies in terms of size, markets and economy, then a more equal weighting was used between the income and market approaches. The income approach, or discounted cash flow approach, requires significant assumptions to determine the fair value of each reporting unit. These include estimates regarding future operations and the ability to generate cash flows, including projections of revenue, costs, utilization of assets and capital requirements, along with an estimate as to the appropriate discount rate to be used. The most sensitive estimate in this valuation is the projection of operating cash flows, as these provide the basis for the fair market valuation. The Company's cash flow model uses forecasts for periods of about 10 years and a terminal value. The significant assumptions for these forecasts in 2012 included annual revenue growth rates ranging from negative 7.0 percent to positive 10.0 percent with an average growth rate of positive 3.0 percent. The growth rates were determined by reviewing historical results of these units and the historical results of the Company's other business units that are similar to those of the reporting units, along with the expected contribution from growth strategies implemented in the units. Terminal values for all reporting units were calculated using a long-term growth rate of 3.0 percent. In estimating the fair value of these reporting units in 2012, the Company applied discount rates to the projected cash flows ranging from 12.5 to 14.0 percent. The discount rate at the high end of this range was for the Nutrimetics Asia Pacific reporting unit due to higher country-specific risks. The market approach relies on an analysis of publicly-traded companies similar to Tupperware and deriving a range of revenue and profit multiples. The publicly-traded companies used in the market approach were selected based on their having similar product lines of consumer goods, beauty products and/or companies using a direct-to-consumer distribution method. The resulting multiples were then applied to the reporting unit to determine fair value.

The fair value of the Nutrimetics and NaturCare tradenames were determined in the second quarter of 2012, using the relief from royalty method that is a form of the income approach. In this method, the value of the asset is calculated by selecting royalty rates, which estimate the amount a company would be willing to pay for the use of the asset. These rates were applied to the Company's projected revenue, tax affected and discounted to present value. Royalty rates used were selected by reviewing comparable trademark licensing agreements in the market and the forecasted performance of the business. As a result, the royalty rates were reduced to 1.5 percent from 3.0 percent for Nutrimetics and 3.75 percent from 4.75 percent for NaturCare. In estimating the fair value of the tradenames, the Company applied discount rates of 15.2 and 13.5 percent, respectively, and annual revenue growth ranging from negative 7.0 percent to positive 7.0 percent, with an average growth rate of positive 2.0 percent, and a long-term terminal growth rate of 3.0 percent.

With the tradename impairment recorded in the current year for Nutrimetics and NaturCare, these assets are at a higher risk of additional impairments in future periods if changes in certain assumptions occur. There is no longer a goodwill balance recorded related to Nutrimetics or BeautiControl United States and Canada. The estimated fair value of the NaturCare reporting unit exceeded the carrying value by 29 percent as of June 2012, when a step 1 impairment analysis was last performed. Given the sensitivity of the valuations to changes in cash flow or market multiples, the Company may be required to recognize an impairment of goodwill or intangible assets in the future due to changes in market conditions or other factors related to the Company's performance. Actual results below forecasted results or a decrease in the forecasted future results of the Company's business plans or changes in discount rates could also result in an impairment charge, as could changes in market characteristics including declines in valuation multiples of comparable publicly-traded companies. Further impairment charges would have an adverse impact on the Company's net income and shareholders' equity.

The following table reflects gross goodwill and accumulated impairments allocated to each reporting segment at December 29, 2012, December 31, 2011 and December 25, 2010:

(In millions)	Europe	Asia Pacific	TW North America	Beauty North America	South America	Total
Gross goodwill balance at December 25, 2010	$34.0	$86.1	$16.3	$160.5	$7.0	$303.9
Effect of changes in exchange rates	(0.9)	2.6	—	(12.9)	(0.4)	(11.6)
Gross goodwill balance at December 31, 2011	33.1	88.7	16.3	147.6	6.6	292.3
Effect of changes in exchange rates	(0.8)	(2.3)	—	8.6	(0.2)	5.3
Gross goodwill balance at December 29, 2012	$32.3	$86.4	$16.3	$156.2	$6.4	$297.6

(continued)

(In millions)	Europe	Asia Pacific	TW North America	Beauty North America	South America	Total
Accumulated impairment balance at December 25, 2010	$16.8	$ 3.0	$—	$ —	$—	$ 19.8
Goodwill impairment	—	31.1	—	—	—	31.1
Accumulated impairment balance at December 31, 2011	16.8	34.1	—	—	—	50.9
Goodwill impairment	7.7	7.2	—	38.9	—	53.8
Accumulated impairment balance at December 29, 2012	$24.5	$41.3	$—	$38.9	$—	$104.7

The gross carrying amount and accumulated amortization of the Company's intangible assets, other than goodwill, were as follows:

	December 29, 2012		
(In millions)	Gross Carrying Value	Accumulated Amortization	Net
Trademarks and tradenames	$138.4	$ —	$138.4
Sales force relationships—single level	29.0	26.6	2.4
Sales force relationships—tiered	31.9	29.3	2.6
Acquired proprietary product formulations	3.5	3.5	—
Total intangible assets	$202.8	$59.4	$143.4

	December 31, 2011		
(In millions)	Gross Carrying Value	Accumulated Amortization	Net
Trademarks and tradenames	$157.1	$ —	$157.1
Sales force relationships—single level	26.9	23.9	3.0
Sales force relationships—tiered	35.9	31.7	4.2
Acquired proprietary product formulations	3.6	3.6	—
Total intangible assets	$223.5	$59.2	$164.3

A summary of the identifiable intangible asset account activity is as follows:

	Year Ending	
(In millions)	December 29, 2012	December 31, 2011
Beginning balance	$223.5	$239.2
Impairment of intangible assets	(22.8)	(5.0)
Effect of changes in exchange rates	2.1	(10.7)
Ending balance	$202.8	$223.5

Amortization expense was $2.0 million, $2.9 million and $3.9 million in 2012, 2011 and 2010, respectively. The estimated annual amortization expense associated with the above intangibles for each of the five succeeding years is $1.4 million, $1.0 million, $0.7 million, $0.6 million and $0.4 million, respectively.

LOSS ON EXTINGUISHMENT OF DEBT

3.43 SERVICE CORPORATION INTERNATIONAL (DEC)
CONSOLIDATED STATEMENT OF OPERATIONS (in part)

	Years Ended December 31,		
(In thousands, except per share amounts)	2012	2011	2010
Revenues	$2,410,481	$2,316,040	$2,190,552
Costs and expenses	(1,885,254)	(1,837,504)	(1,741,329)
Gross profits	525,227	478,536	449,223
General and administrative expenses	(123,905)	(103,860)	(103,689)
(Losses) gains on divestitures and impairment charges, net	(1,533)	(10,977)	8,512
Operating income	399,789	363,699	354,046
Interest expense	(135,068)	(133,782)	(128,196)
Losses on early extinguishment of debt, net	(22,706)	(3,509)	(9,400)
Other income (expense), net	3,668	(772)	3,009
Income from continuing operations before income taxes	245,683	225,636	219,459

10. Debt (in part)

Debt Extinguishments and Reductions

During 2012, we paid an aggregate of $206.6 million, to redeem our 7.375% Senior Notes due October 2014 with a principal amount of $180.7 million and to retire $25.8 million in capital lease obligations. Subsequent to December 31, 2012, we paid $4.8 million to extinguish our 7.875% Debentures due February 2013.

Certain of the above transactions resulted in the recognition of a loss of $22.7 million recorded in *(Losses) gains on early extinguishment of debt, net* in our consolidated statement of operations, which represents the write-off of unamortized deferred loan costs of $1.3 million and $21.4 million in a make-whole provision paid in cash upon retiring our 7.375% Senior Notes due October 2014. This refinancing allowed the company to replace 7.375% debt due in 2014 with 4.5% debt due in 2020.

During 2011, we made debt payments of $46.0 million, which included the following purchases on the open market:
- $3.8 million aggregate principal amount of our 7.875% Debentures due February 2013;
- $20.8 million aggregate principal amount of our 6.75% Senior Notes due April 2015; and
- $15.6 million aggregate principal amount of our 6.75% Senior Notes due April 2016.

Certain of the above transactions resulted in the recognition of a loss of $3.5 million recorded in *(Losses) gains on early extinguishment of debt, net* during the year ended December 31, 2011, which represents the write-off of unamortized deferred loan costs of $0.4 million and $3.1 million in premium on the purchase of these notes.

Pensions and Other Postretirement Benefits

RECOGNITION AND MEASUREMENT

3.44 FASB ASC 715, *Compensation—Retirement Benefits*, requires that an entity recognize the overfunded or underfunded status of a single-employer defined benefit postretirement plan as an asset or a liability in its statement of financial position, recognize changes in that funded status in comprehensive income, and disclose in the notes to the financial statements additional information about net periodic benefit cost. FASB ASC 715 requires an entity to recognize as components of other comprehensive income the gains or losses and prior service costs or credits that arise during a period but are not recognized in the income statement as components of net periodic benefit cost of a period. Those amounts recognized in accumulated other comprehensive income are adjusted as they are subsequently recognized in the income statement as components of net periodic benefit cost. Additionally, FASB ASC 715 requires that an entity measure plan assets and benefit obligations as of the date of its fiscal year-end statement of financial position. An employer whose equity securities are publicly traded is required to initially recognize the funded status of a defined benefit postretirement plan.

DISCLOSURE

3.45 FASB ASC 715 states the disclosure requirements for pensions and other postretirement benefits, including disclosures about the assets, obligations, cash flows, investment strategy, and net periodic benefit cost of defined pension and postretirement plans. FASB ASC 715 also includes disclosures related to multiemployer plans. FASB ASC 715-20 calls for different disclosures about defined benefit plans for public and nonpublic entities.

3.46 The disclosure requirements of FASB ASC 715 include, but are not limited to, the actuarial gains and losses, the assumed health care cost trend rate for other postretirement benefits, the allocation by major category of plan assets, the inputs and valuation techniques used to measure the fair value of plan assets, the effect of fair value measurements using significant unobservable inputs (level 3) on changes in plan assets for the period, and significant concentrations of risk within plan assets.

3.47 FASB ASC 715-80 explains the additional disclosures required for multiemployer plans. An entity should include details in these disclosures, including plan names and identifying numbers for significant multiemployer plans, the level of employers' participation in the plans, the financial health of the plans, and the nature of the employer commitments to the plans.

3.48 CLIFFS NATURAL RESOURCES INC. (DEC)
STATEMENTS OF CONSOLIDATED FINANCIAL POSITION (in part)

(In millions)	December 31, 2012	December 31, 2011
Liabilities		
Current liabilities		
Accounts payable	$ 555.5	$ 364.7
Accrued employment costs	135.6	144.1
Income taxes payable	28.3	265.4
Current portion of debt	94.1	74.8
Accrued expenses	258.9	165.0
Accrued royalties	48.1	75.7
Deferred revenue	35.9	126.6
Liabilities held for sale	—	25.9
Other current liabilities	225.1	259.9
Total current liabilities	1,381.5	1,502.1
Postemployment benefit liabilities		
Pensions	403.8	394.7
Other postretirement benefits	214.5	271.1
Total postemployment benefit liabilities	618.3	665.8
Environmental and mine closure obligations	252.8	213.2
Deferred income taxes	1,108.1	1,062.4
Long-term debt	3,960.7	3,608.7
Other liabilities	492.6	449.8
Total liabilities	7,814.0	7,502.0

NOTES TO CONSOLIDATED FINANCIAL STATEMENTS

Note 1—Business Summary and Significant Accounting Policies (in part)

Pensions and Other Postretirement Benefits

We offer defined benefit pension plans, defined contribution pension plans and other postretirement benefit plans, primarily consisting of retiree healthcare benefits, to most employees in North America as part of a total compensation and benefits program. Upon the acquisition of the remaining 73.2 percent interest in Wabush in February 2010, we fully consolidated the related Canadian plans into our pension and OPEB obligations. We do not have employee pension or post-retirement benefit obligations at our Asia Pacific Iron Ore operations.

We recognize the funded or unfunded status of our postretirement benefit obligations on our December 31, 2012 and 2011 Statements of Consolidated Financial Position based on the difference between the market value of plan assets and the actuarial present value of our retirement obligations on that date, on a plan-by-plan basis. If the plan assets exceed the retirement obligations, the amount of the surplus is recorded as an asset; if the retirement obligations exceed the plan assets, the amount of the underfunded obligations are recorded as a liability. Year-end balance sheet adjustments to postretirement assets and obligations are recorded as *Accumulated other comprehensive loss*.

The market value of plan assets is measured at the year-end balance sheet date. The PBO is determined based upon an actuarial estimate of the present value of pension benefits to be paid to current employees and retirees. The APBO represents an actuarial estimate of the present value of OPEB benefits to be paid to current employees and retirees.

The actuarial estimates of the PBO and APBO retirement obligations incorporate various assumptions including the discount rates, the rates of increases in compensation, healthcare cost trend rates, mortality, retirement timing and employee turnover. For the U.S. and Canadian plans, the discount rate is determined based on the prevailing year-end rates for high-grade corporate bonds with a duration matching the expected cash flow timing of the benefit payments from the various plans. The remaining assumptions are based on our estimates of future events by incorporating historical trends and future expectations. The amount of net periodic cost that is recorded in the Statements of Consolidated Operations consists of several components including service cost, interest cost, expected return on plan assets, and amortization of previously unrecognized amounts. Service cost represents the value of the benefits earned in the current year by the participants. Interest cost represents the cost associated with the passage of time. Certain items, such as plan amendments, gains and/or losses resulting from differences between actual and assumed results for demographic and economic factors affecting the obligations and assets of the plans, and changes in other assumptions are subject to deferred recognition for income and expense purposes. The expected return on plan assets is determined utilizing the weighted average of expected returns for plan asset investments in various asset categories based on historical performance, adjusted for current trends. See NOTE 13—PENSIONS AND OTHER POSTRETIREMENT BENEFITS for further information.

Note 13—Pensions and Other Postretirement Benefits

We offer defined benefit pension plans, defined contribution pension plans and other postretirement benefit plans, primarily consisting of retiree healthcare benefits, to most employees in North America as part of a total compensation and benefits program. This includes employees of CLCC who became employees of the Company through the July 2010 acquisition. Upon the acquisition of the remaining 73.2 percent interest in Wabush in February 2010, we fully consolidated the related Canadian plans into our pension and OPEB obligations. We do not have employee retirement benefit obligations at our Asia Pacific Iron Ore operations. The defined benefit pension plans largely are noncontributory and benefits generally are based on employees' years of service and average earnings for a defined period prior to retirement or a minimum formula.

On November 9, 2012, the USW ratified 37 month labor contracts, which replaced the labor agreements that expired on September 1, 2012. The agreements cover approximately 2,400 USW-represented employees at our Empire and Tilden mines in Michigan and our United Taconite and Hibbing mines in Minnesota, or 32 percent of our total workforce. The new agreement set temporary monthly post-retirement medical premium maximums for participants who retire prior to January 1, 2015. These premium maximums will expire at the end of the contract period and revert to increasing premiums based on the terms of the 2004 bargaining agreement. Also agreed to, was an OPEB cap that will limit the amount of contributions that we have to make toward medical insurance coverage for each retiree and spouse of a retiree per calendar year after it goes into effect. The amount of the annual OPEB cap will be based upon the costs we incur in 2014. The OPEB cap will apply to employees who retire on or after January 1, 2015 and will not apply to surviving spouses. In addition, the bargaining agreement renewed the lump sum special payments for certain employees retiring in the near future. The changes also included renewal of and an increase in payments to surviving spouses of certain retirees, as well as, an increase in the temporary supplemental benefit amount paid to certain retirees. The agreements also provide that we and our partners fund an estimated $65.7 million into the bargaining unit VEBA plans during the term of the agreements. These agreements are effective through September 30, 2015.

In addition, we currently provide various levels of retirement health care and OPEB to most full-time employees who meet certain length of service and age requirements (a portion of which is pursuant to collective bargaining agreements). Most plans require retiree contributions and have deductibles, co-pay requirements and benefit limits. Most bargaining unit plans require retiree contributions and co-pays for major medical and prescription drug coverage. There is an annual limit on our cost for medical coverage under the U.S. salaried plans. The annual limit applies to each covered participant and equals $7,000 for coverage prior to age 65 and $3,000 for coverage after age 65, with the retiree's participation adjusted based on the age at which the retiree's benefits commence. For participants at our Northshore operation, the annual limit ranges from $4,020 to $4,500 for coverage prior to age 65, and equals $2,000 for coverage after age 65. Covered participants pay an amount for coverage equal to the excess of (i) the average cost of coverage for all covered participants, over (ii) the participant's individual limit, but in no event will the participant's cost be less than 15 percent of the average cost of coverage for all covered participants. For Northshore participants, the minimum participant cost is a fixed dollar amount. We do not provide OPEB for most U.S. salaried employees hired after January 1, 1993. OPEB are provided through programs administered by insurance companies whose charges are based on benefits paid.

Our North American Coal segment is required under an agreement with the UMWA to pay amounts into the UMWA pension trusts based principally on hours worked by UMWA-represented employees. This agreement covers approximately 800 UMWA-represented employees at our Pinnacle Complex in West Virginia and our Oak Grove mine in Alabama, or 11 percent of our total workforce. These multi-employer pension trusts provide benefits to eligible retirees through a defined benefit plan. The UMWA 1993 Benefit Plan is a defined contribution plan that was created as the result of negotiations for the NBCWA of 1993. The plan provides healthcare insurance to orphan UMWA retirees who are not eligible to participate in the UMWA Combined Benefit Fund or the 1992 Benefit Fund or whose last employer signed the 1993 or later NBCWA and who subsequently goes out of business. Contributions to the trust were at rates of $8.10, $6.50 and $6.42 per hour worked in 2012, 2011 and 2010, respectively. These amounted to $14.9 million, $9.5 million and $10.3 million in 2012, 2011 and 2010, respectively.

In December 2003, The Medicare Prescription Drug, Improvement, and Modernization Act of 2003 was enacted. This act introduced a prescription drug benefit under Medicare Part D as well as a federal subsidy to sponsors of retiree healthcare benefit plans that provide a benefit that at least actuarially is equivalent to Medicare Part D. Our measures of the accumulated postretirement benefit obligation and net periodic postretirement benefit cost as of December 31, 2004 and for periods thereafter reflect amounts associated with the subsidy. We elected to adopt the retroactive transition method for recognizing the OPEB cost reduction in 2004. The following table summarizes the annual costs related to the retirement plans for 2012, 2011 and 2010:

(In millions)	2012	2011	2010
Defined benefit pension plans	$55.2	$37.8	$45.6
Defined contribution pension plans	6.7	5.7	4.2
Other postretirement benefits	28.1	26.8	24.2
Total	$90.0	$70.3	$74.0

The following tables and information provide additional disclosures for our consolidated plans.

The following tables and information provide additional disclosures for the years ended December 31, 2012 and 2011:

(In millions)	Pension Benefits		Other Benefits	
	2012	2011	2012	2011
Change in Benefit Obligations:				
Benefit obligations—beginning of year	$ 1,141.4	$ 1,022.3	$ 488.4	$ 440.2
Service cost (excluding expenses)	32.0	23.6	14.7	11.1
Interest cost	48.4	51.4	20.6	22.3
Plan amendments	2.8	—	(58.3)	—
Actuarial loss	84.3	117.3	11.3	36.5
Benefits paid	(71.0)	(67.3)	(26.9)	(25.5)
Participant contributions	—	—	4.6	4.6
Federal subsidy on benefits paid	—	—	0.8	0.9
Exchange rate gain	6.4	(5.9)	4.6	(1.7)
Benefit obligations—end of year	$ 1,244.3	$ 1,141.4	$ 459.8	$ 488.4
Change in Plan Assets:				
Fair value of plan assets—beginning of year	$ 744.1	$ 734.3	$ 193.5	$ 174.2
Actual return on plan assets	92.5	10.8	26.1	1.9
Participant contributions	—	—	1.7	1.6
Employer contributions	67.7	70.1	23.3	23.2
Benefits paid	(71.0)	(67.3)	(7.6)	(7.4)
Exchange rate gain	5.4	(3.8)	—	—
Fair value of plan assets—end of year	$ 838.7	$ 744.1	$ 237.0	$ 193.5
Funded Status at December 31:				
Fair value of plan assets	$ 838.7	$ 744.1	$ 237.0	$ 193.5
Benefit obligations	(1,244.3)	(1,141.4)	(459.8)	(488.4)
Funded status (plan assets less benefit obligations)	$ (405.6)	$ (397.3)	$(222.8)	$(294.9)
Amount recognized at December 31	$ (405.6)	$ (397.3)	$(222.8)	$(294.9)
Amounts Recognized in Statements of Financial Position:				
Current liabilities	$ (1.8)	$ (2.6)	$ (8.3)	$ (23.8)
Noncurrent liabilities	(403.8)	(394.7)	(214.5)	(271.1)
Net amount recognized	$ (405.6)	$ (397.3)	$(222.8)	$(294.9)
Amounts Recognized in Accumulated Other Comprehensive Income:				
Net actuarial loss	$ 429.2	$ 409.1	$ 176.8	$ 182.9
Prior service cost	17.2	18.8	(48.8)	8.1
Transition asset	—	—	—	(3.0)
Net amount recognized	$ 446.4	$ 427.9	$ 128.0	$ 188.0
The Estimated Amounts that will be Amortized From Accumulated Other Comprehensive Income Into Net Periodic Benefit Cost in 2013:				
Net actuarial loss	$ 30.3		$ 11.1	
Prior service cost	3.0		(3.6)	
Net amount recognized	$ 33.3		$ 7.5	

	2012							
	Pension Plans					Other Benefits		
(In millions)	Salaried	Hourly	Mining	SERP	Total	Salaried	Hourly	Total
Fair value of plan assets	$ 328.2	$ 506.4	$ 4.1	$ —	$ 838.7	$ —	$ 237.0	$ 237.0
Benefit obligation	(464.4)	(764.8)	(6.4)	(8.7)	(1,244.3)	(72.6)	(387.2)	(459.8)
Funded status	$(136.2)	$(258.4)	$(2.3)	$(8.7)	$ (405.6)	$(72.6)	$(150.2)	$(222.8)

	2011							
	Pension Plans					Other Benefits		
	Salaried	Hourly	Mining	SERP	Total	Salaried	Hourly	Total
Fair value of plan assets	$ 289.1	$ 451.8	$ 3.2	$ —	$ 744.1	$ —	$ 193.5	$ 193.5
Benefit obligation	(419.3)	(708.0)	(5.3)	(8.8)	(1,141.4)	(70.7)	(417.7)	(488.4)
Funded status	$(130.2)	$(256.2)	$(2.1)	$(8.8)	$ (397.3)	$(70.7)	$(224.2)	$(294.9)

The accumulated benefit obligation for all defined benefit pension plans was $1,204.7 million and $1,114.7 million at December 31, 2012 and 2011, respectively. The increase in the accumulated benefit obligation primarily is a result of a decrease in the discount rates and actual asset returns lower than the previously assumed rate.

Components of Net Periodic Benefit Cost

(In millions)	Pension Benefits			Other Benefits		
	2012	2011	2010	2012	2011	2010
Service cost	$ 32.0	$ 23.6	$ 18.5	$ 14.7	$ 11.1	$ 7.5
Interest cost	48.4	51.4	52.9	20.6	22.3	22.0
Expected return on plan assets	(59.5)	(61.2)	(53.3)	(17.7)	(16.1)	(12.9)
Amortization:						
Net asset	—	—	—	(3.0)	(3.0)	(3.0)
Prior service costs (credits)	3.9	4.4	4.4	1.9	3.7	1.7
Net actuarial loss	30.4	19.6	23.1	11.6	8.8	8.9
Net periodic benefit cost	$ 55.2	$ 37.8	$ 45.6	$ 28.1	$ 26.8	$24.2
Acquired through business combinations	—	—	17.7	—	—	2.4
Current year actuarial (gain)/loss	53.1	165.3	(3.1)	3.2	46.8	34.6
Amortization of net loss	(30.4)	(19.6)	(23.1)	(11.6)	(8.8)	(8.9)
Current year prior service cost	2.8	—	3.7	(58.3)	—	—
Amortization of prior service (cost) credit	(3.9)	(4.4)	(4.4)	(1.9)	(3.7)	(1.7)
Amortization of transition asset	—	—	—	3.0	3.0	3.0
Total recognized in other comprehensive income	$ 21.6	$141.3	$ (9.2)	$(65.6)	$ 37.3	$29.4
Total recognized in net periodic cost and other comprehensive income	$ 76.8	$179.1	$ 36.4	$(37.5)	$ 64.1	$53.6

Additional Information

(In millions)	Pension Benefits			Other Benefits		
	2012	2011	2010	2012	2011	2010
Effect of change in mine ownership & noncontrolling interest	$54.8	$53.3	$49.9	$ 8.6	$12.5	$10.7
Actual return on plan assets	92.5	10.8	87.1	26.1	1.9	20.1

Assumptions

For our U.S. pension and other postretirement benefit plans, we used a discount rate as of December 31, 2012 of 3.70 percent, compared with a discount rate of 4.28 percent as of December 31, 2011. The U.S. discount rates are determined by matching the projected cash flows used to determine the PBO and APBO to a projected yield curve of 506 Aa graded bonds in the 10th to 90th percentiles. These bonds are either noncallable or callable with make-whole provisions. The duration matching produced rates ranging from 3.54 percent to 3.80 percent for our plans. Based upon these results, we selected a December 31, 2012 discount rate of 3.70 percent for our plans.

For our Canadian plans, we used a discount rate as of December 31, 2012 of 3.75 percent for the pension plans and 4.00 percent for the other postretirement benefit plans. Similar to the U.S. plans, the Canadian discount rates are determined by matching the projected cash flows used to determine the PBO and APBO to a projected yield curve of 240 corporate bonds in the 10th to 90th percentiles. The corporate bonds are either Aa graded, or (for maturities of 10 or more years) A or Aaa graded with an appropriate credit spread adjustment. These bonds are either noncallable or callable with make whole provisions.

Weighted-average assumptions used to determine benefit obligations at December 31 were:

	Pension Benefits		Other Benefits	
	2012	2011	2012	2011
U.S. plan discount rate	3.70%	4.28%	3.70%	4.28%
Canadian plan discount rate	3.75	4.00	4.00	4.25
Rate of compensation increase	4.00	4.00	4.00	4.00
U.S. expected return on plan assets	8.25	8.25	8.25	8.25
Canadian expected return on plan assets	7.25	7.25	N/A	7.25

Weighted-average assumptions used to determine net benefit cost for the years 2012, 2011 and 2010 were:

	Pension Benefits			Other Benefits		
	2012	2011	2010	2012	2011	2010
U.S. plan discount rate	4.28%	5.11%	5.66%	4.28/3.51%[1]	5.11%	5.66%
Canadian plan discount rate	4.00	5.00	5.75/5.50[2]	4.25	5.00	6.00/5.75[3]
U.S. expected return on plan assets	8.25	8.50	8.50	8.25	8.50	8.50
Canadian expected return on plan assets	7.25	7.50	7.50	N/A	7.50	7.50
Rate of compensation increase	4.00	4.00	4.00	4.00	4.00	4.00

[1] 4.28 percent for the Salaried Plan. For the Hourly Plan, 4.28 percent from January 1, 2012 through October 31, 2012, and 3.51 percent from November 1, 2012 through December 31, 2012.
[2] 5.75 percent from January 1, 2010 through January 31, 2010, and 5.50 percent from February 1, 2010 through December 31, 2010.
[3] 6.00 percent from January 1, 2010 through January 31, 2010, and 5.75 percent from February 1, 2010 through December 31, 2010.

Assumed health care cost trend rates at December 31 were:

	2012	2011
U.S. plan health care cost trend rate assumed for next year	7.50%	7.50%
Canadian plan health care cost trend rate assumed for next year	7.50	8.00
Ultimate health care cost trend rate	5.00	5.00
U.S. plan year that the ultimate rate is reached	2023	2017
Canadian plan year that the ultimate rate is reached	2018	2018

Assumed health care cost trend rates have a significant effect on the amounts reported for the health care plans. A change of one percentage point in assumed health care cost trend rates would have the following effects:

(In millions)	Increase	Decrease
Effect on total of service and interest cost	$7.0	$ (5.4)
Effect on postretirement benefit obligation	53.7	(43.4)

Plan Assets

Our financial objectives with respect to our pension and VEBA plan assets are to fully fund the actuarial accrued liability for each of the plans, to maximize investment returns within reasonable and prudent levels of risk, and to maintain sufficient liquidity to meet benefit obligations on a timely basis.

Our investment objective is to outperform the expected Return on Asset ("ROA") assumption used in the plans' actuarial reports over a full market cycle, which is considered a period during which the U.S. economy experiences the effects of both an upturn and a downturn in the level of economic activity. In general, these periods tend to last between three and five years. The expected ROA takes into account historical returns and estimated future long-term returns based on capital market assumptions applied to the asset allocation strategy.

The asset allocation strategy is determined through a detailed analysis of assets and liabilities by plan, which defines the overall risk that is acceptable with regard to the expected level and variability of portfolio returns, surplus (assets compared to liabilities), contributions and pension expense.

The asset allocation review process involves simulating the effect of financial market performance for various asset allocation scenarios and factoring in the current funded status and likely future funded status levels by taking into account expected growth or decline in the contributions over time. The modeling is then adjusted by simulating unexpected changes in inflation and interest rates. The process also includes quantifying the effect of investment performance and simulated changes to future levels of contributions, determining the appropriate asset mix with the highest likelihood of meeting financial objectives and regularly reviewing our asset allocation strategy.

The asset allocation strategy varies by plan. The following table reflects the actual asset allocations for pension and VEBA plan assets as of December 31, 2012 and 2011, as well as the 2013 weighted average target asset allocations as of December 31, 2012. Equity investments include securities in large-cap, mid-cap and small-cap companies located in the U.S. and worldwide. Fixed income investments primarily include corporate bonds and government debt securities. Alternative investments include hedge funds, private equity, structured credit and real estate.

	Pension Assets			VEBA Assets		
	2013 Target Allocation	Percentage of Plan Assets at December 31,		2013 Target Allocation	Percentage of Plan Assets at December 31,	
Asset Category		2012	2011		2012	2011
Equity securities	44.4%	45.9%	41.7%	39.9%	42.6%	42.0%
Fixed income	28.6%	29.5%	31.1%	32.0%	32.9%	33.5%
Hedge funds	10.0%	10.2%	13.5%	10.0%	9.8%	14.6%
Private equity	5.4%	3.5%	5.2%	6.1%	2.6%	4.5%
Structured credit	5.8%	6.7%	6.0%	5.0%	5.3%	—%
Real estate	5.8%	3.5%	2.2%	7.0%	6.7%	5.3%
Cash	—%	0.7%	0.3%	—%	0.1%	0.1%
Total	100.0%	100.0%	100.0%	100.0%	100.0%	100.0%

Pension

The fair values of our pension plan assets at December 31, 2012 and 2011 by asset category are as follows:

| (In millions) **Asset Category** | **December 31, 2012** | | | |
	Quoted Prices in Active Markets for Identical Assets/Liabilities (Level 1)	Significant Other Observable Inputs (Level 2)	Significant Unobservable Inputs (Level 3)	Total
Equity securities:				
U.S. large-cap	$231.1	$ —	$ —	$231.1
U.S. small/mid-cap	39.2	—	—	39.2
International	114.5	—	—	114.5
Fixed income	209.1	38.4	—	247.5
Hedge funds	—	—	85.6	85.6
Private equity	—	—	29.3	29.3
Structured credit	—	—	56.2	56.2
Real estate	—	—	29.4	29.4
Cash	5.9	—	—	5.9
Total	$599.8	$38.4	$200.5	$838.7

| (In millions) **Asset Category** | **December 31, 2011** | | | |
	Quoted Prices in Active Markets for Identical Assets/Liabilities (Level 1)	Significant Other Observable Inputs (Level 2)	Significant Unobservable Inputs (Level 3)	Total
Equity securities:				
U.S. large-cap	$191.1	$—	$ —	$191.1
U.S. small/mid-cap	29.2	—	—	29.2
International	90.0	—	—	90.0
Fixed income	231.1	—	—	231.1
Hedge funds	—	—	100.7	100.7
Private equity	8.6	—	30.1	38.7
Structured credit	—	—	44.9	44.9
Real estate	—	—	16.5	16.5
Cash	1.9	—	—	1.9
Total	$551.9	$—	$192.2	$744.1

Following is a description of the inputs and valuation methodologies used to measure the fair value of our plan assets.

Equity Securities

Equity securities classified as Level 1 investments include U.S. large, small and mid-cap investments and international equity. These investments are comprised of securities listed on an exchange, market or automated quotation system for which quotations are readily available. The valuation of these securities is determined using a market approach, and is based upon unadjusted quoted prices for identical assets in active markets.

Fixed Income

Fixed income securities classified as Level 1 investments include bonds and government debt securities. These investments are comprised of securities listed on an exchange, market or automated quotation system for which quotations are readily available. The valuation of these securities is determined using a market approach, and is based upon unadjusted quoted prices for identical assets in active markets. Also included in Fixed Income is a portfolio of U.S. Treasury STRIPS, which are zero-coupon bearing fixed income securities backed by the full faith and credit of the United States government. The securities sell at a discount to par because there are no incremental coupon payments. STRIPS are not issued directly by the Treasury, but rather are created by a financial institution, government securities broker, or government securities dealer. Liquidity on the issue varies depending on various market conditions; however, in general the STRIPS market is slightly less liquid than that of the U.S. Treasury Bond market. The STRIPS are priced daily through a bond pricing vendor and are classified as Level 2.

Hedge Funds

Hedge funds are alternative investments comprised of direct or indirect investment in offshore hedge funds of funds with an investment objective to achieve an attractive risk-adjusted return with moderate volatility and moderate directional market exposure over a full market cycle. The valuation techniques used to measure fair value attempt to maximize the use of observable inputs and minimize the use of unobservable inputs. Considerable judgment is required to interpret the factors used to develop estimates of fair value. Valuations of the underlying investment funds are obtained and reviewed. The securities that are valued by the funds are interests in the investment funds and not the underlying holdings of such investment funds. Thus, the inputs used to value the investments in each of the underlying funds may differ from the inputs used to value the underlying holdings of such funds.

In determining the fair value of a security, the fund managers may consider any information that is deemed relevant, which may include one or more of the following factors regarding the portfolio security, if appropriate: type of security or asset; cost at the date of purchase; size of holding; last trade price; most recent valuation; fundamental analytical data relating to the investment in the security; nature and duration of any restriction on the disposition of the security; evaluation of the factors that influence the market in which the security is purchased or sold; financial statements of the issuer; discount from market value of unrestricted securities of the same class at the time of purchase; special reports prepared by analysts; information as to any transactions or offers with respect to the security; existence of merger proposals or tender offers affecting the security; price and extent of public trading in similar securities of the issuer or compatible companies and other relevant matters; changes in interest rates; observations from financial institutions; domestic or foreign government actions or pronouncements; other recent events; existence of shelf registration for restricted securities; existence of any undertaking to register the security; and other acceptable methods of valuing portfolio securities.

Hedge fund investments in the SEI Opportunity Collective Fund are valued monthly and recorded on a one-month lag; investments in the SEI Special Situations Fund are valued quarterly. For alternative investment values reported on a lag, current market information is reviewed for any material changes in values at the reporting date. Share repurchases for the SEI Opportunity Collective Fund are available quarterly with notice of 65 business days. For the SEI Special Situations Fund, redemption requests are considered semi-annually subject to notice of 95 days.

Private Equity Funds

Private equity funds are alternative investments that represent direct or indirect investments in partnerships, venture funds or a diversified pool of private investment vehicles (fund of funds).

Investment commitments are made in private equity funds of funds based on an asset allocation strategy, and capital calls are made over the life of the funds to fund the commitments. As of December 31, 2012, remaining commitments total of which $10.7 million for both our pension and other benefits. Committed amounts are funded from plan assets when capital calls are made. Investment commitments are not pre-funded in reserve accounts. Refer to the valuation methodologies for equity securities above for further information.

The valuation of investments in private equity funds of funds initially is performed by the underlying fund managers. In determining the fair value, the fund managers may consider any information that is deemed relevant, which may include: type of security or asset; cost at the date of purchase; size of holding; last trade price; most recent valuation; fundamental analytical data relating to the investment in the security; nature and duration of any restriction on the disposition of the security; evaluation of the factors that influence the market in which the security is purchased or sold; financial statements of the issuer; discount from market value of unrestricted securities of the same class at the time of purchase; special reports prepared by analysts; information as to any transactions or offers with respect to the security; existence of merger proposals or tender offers affecting the security; price and extent of public trading in similar securities of the issuer or compatible companies and other relevant matters; changes in interest rates; observations from financial institutions; domestic or foreign government actions or pronouncements; other recent events; existence of shelf registration for restricted securities; existence of any undertaking to register the security; and other acceptable methods of valuing portfolio securities.

The valuations are obtained from the underlying fund managers, and the valuation methodology and process is reviewed for consistent application and adherence to policies. Considerable judgment is required to interpret the factors used to develop estimates of fair value.

Private equity investments are valued quarterly and recorded on a one-quarter lag. For alternative investment values reported on a lag, current market information is reviewed for any material changes in values at the reporting date. Capital distributions for the funds do not occur on a regular frequency. Liquidation of these investments would require sale of the partnership interest.

Structured Credit

Structured credit investments are alternative investments comprised of collateralized debt obligations and other structured credit investments that are priced based on valuations provided by independent, third-party pricing agents, if available. Such values generally reflect the last reported sales price if the security is actively traded. The third-party pricing agents may also value structured credit investments at an evaluated bid price by employing methodologies that utilize actual market transactions, broker-supplied valuations, or other methodologies designed to identify the market value of such securities. Such methodologies generally consider such factors as security prices, yields, maturities, call features, ratings and developments relating to specific securities in arriving at valuations. Securities listed on a securities exchange, market or automated quotation system for which quotations are readily available are valued at the last quoted sale price on the primary exchange or market on which they are traded. Debt obligations with remaining maturities of 60 days or less may be valued at amortized cost, which approximates fair value.

Structured credit investments are valued monthly and recorded on a one-month lag. For alternative investment values reported on a lag, current market information is reviewed for any material changes in values at the reporting date. Redemption requests are considered quarterly subject to notice of 90 days.

Real Estate

The real estate portfolio for the pension plans is an alternative investment comprised of three funds with strategic categories of real estate investments. All real estate holdings are appraised externally at least annually, and appraisals are conducted by reputable, independent appraisal firms that are members of the Appraisal Institute. All external appraisals are performed in accordance with the Uniform Standards of Professional Appraisal Practices. The property valuations and assumptions of each property are reviewed quarterly by the investment advisor and values are adjusted if there has been a significant change in circumstances relating to the property since the last external appraisal. The valuation methodology utilized in determining the fair value is consistent with the best practices prevailing within the real estate appraisal and real estate investment management industries, including the Real Estate Information Standards, and standards promulgated by the National Council of Real Estate Investment Fiduciaries, the National Association of Real Estate Investment Fiduciaries, and the National Association of Real Estate Managers. In addition, the investment advisor may cause additional appraisals to be performed. Two of the funds' fair values are updated monthly, and there is no lag in reported values. Redemption requests for these two funds are considered on a quarterly basis, subject to notice of 45 days.

Effective October 1, 2009, one of the real estate funds began an orderly wind-down over a three to four year period. The decision to wind down the fund primarily was driven by real estate market factors that adversely affected the availability of new investor capital. Third-party appraisals of this fund's assets were eliminated; however, internal valuation updates for all assets and liabilities of the fund are prepared quarterly. The fund's asset values are recorded on a one-quarter lag, and current market information is reviewed for any material changes in values at the reporting date. Distributions from sales of properties will be made on a pro-rata basis. Repurchase requests will not be honored during the wind-down period.

During 2011, a new real estate fund of funds investment was added for the Empire, Tilden, Hibbing and United Taconite VEBA plans as a result of the asset allocation review process. This fund invests in pooled investment vehicles that in turn invest in commercial real estate properties. Valuations are performed quarterly and financial statements are prepared on a semi-annual basis, with annual audited statements. Asset values for this fund are reported with a one-quarter lag and current market information is reviewed for any material changes in values at the reporting date. In most cases, values are based on valuations reported by underlying fund managers or other independent third-party sources, but the fund has discretion to use other valuation methods, subject to compliance with ERISA. Valuations are typically estimates only and subject to upward or downward revision based on each underlying fund's annual audit. Withdrawals are permitted on the last business day of each quarter subject to a 65-day prior written notice.

The following represents the effect of fair value measurements using significant unobservable inputs (Level 3) on changes in plan assets for the years ended December 31, 2012 and 2011:

(In millions)	Year Ended December 31, 2012				
	Hedge Funds	Private Equity Funds	Structured Credit Fund	Real Estate	Total
Beginning balance—January 1, 2012	$100.7	$30.1	$44.9	$16.5	$192.2
Actual return on plan assets:					
Relating to assets still held at the reporting date	4.2	1.4	11.3	4.9	21.8
Relating to assets sold during the period	(0.3)	—	—	(0.5)	(0.8)
Purchases	—	2.2	—	12.2	14.4
Sales	(19.0)	(4.4)	—	(3.7)	(27.1)
Ending balance—December 31, 2012	$ 85.6	$29.3	$56.2	$29.4	$200.5

(In millions)	Year Ended December 31, 2011				
	Hedge Funds	Private Equity Funds	Structured Credit Fund	Real Estate	Total
Beginning balance—January 1, 2011	$105.8	$25.0	$39.7	$15.5	$186.0
Actual return on plan assets:					
Relating to assets still held at the reporting date	(2.4)	2.6	5.2	1.6	7.0
Relating to assets sold during the period	0.5	3.0	—	0.5	4.0
Purchases	35.8	4.4	—	—	40.2
Sales	(39.0)	(4.9)	—	(1.1)	(45.0)
Ending balance—December 31, 2011	$100.7	$30.1	$44.9	$16.5	$192.2

The expected return on plan assets takes into account historical returns and the weighted average of estimated future long-term returns based on capital market assumptions for each asset category. The expected return is net of investment expenses paid by the plans.

Assets for other benefits include VEBA trusts pursuant to bargaining agreements that are available to fund retired employees' life insurance obligations and medical benefits. The fair values of our other benefit plan assets at December 31, 2012 and 2011 by asset category are as follows:

(In millions) Asset Category	December 31, 2012 Quoted Prices in Active Markets for Identical Assets/Liabilities (Level 1)	Significant Other Observable Inputs (Level 2)	Significant Unobservable Inputs (Level 3)	Total
Equity securities:				
U.S. large-cap	$ 58.2	$—	$ —	$ 58.2
U.S. small/mid-cap	10.3	—	—	10.3
International	32.3	—	—	32.3
Fixed income	78.1	—	—	78.1
Hedge funds	—	—	23.2	23.2
Private equity	—	—	6.2	6.2
Structured credit	—	—	12.5	12.5
Real estate	—	—	15.9	15.9
Cash	0.3	—	—	0.3
Total	$179.2	$—	$57.8	$237.0

(In millions) Asset Category	December 31, 2011 Quoted Prices in Active Markets for Identical Assets/Liabilities (Level 1)	Significant Other Observable Inputs (Level 2)	Significant Unobservable Inputs (Level 3)	Total
Equity securities:				
U.S. large-cap	$ 46.5	$—	$ —	$ 46.5
U.S. small/mid-cap	7.9	—	—	7.9
International	26.8	—	—	26.8
Fixed income	64.9	—	—	64.9
Hedge funds	—	—	28.3	28.3
Private equity	1.9	—	6.8	8.7
Real estate	—	—	10.2	10.2
Cash	0.2	—	—	0.2
Total	$148.2	$—	$45.3	$193.5

Refer to the pension asset discussion above for further information regarding the inputs and valuation methodologies used to measure the fair value of each respective category of plan assets.

The following represents the effect of fair value measurements using significant unobservable inputs (Level 3) on changes in plan assets for the year ended December 31, 2012 and 2011:

(In millions)	Year Ended December 31, 2012 Hedge Funds	Private Equity Funds	Structured Credit Fund	Real Estate	Total
Beginning balance—January 1	$28.3	$ 6.8	$ —	$10.2	$45.3
Actual return on plan assets:					
Relating to assets still held at the reporting date	0.9	0.3	1.5	1.3	4.0
Purchases	—	0.2	11.0	4.4	15.6
Sales	(6.0)	(1.1)	—	—	(7.1)
Ending balance—December 31	$23.2	$ 6.2	$12.5	$15.9	$57.8

(In millions)	Year Ended December 31, 2011 Hedge Funds	Private Equity Funds	Real Estate	Total
Beginning balance—January 1	$24.0	$ 4.9	$ —	$28.9
Actual return on plan assets:				
Relating to assets still held at the reporting date	(0.4)	1.4	0.4	1.4
Purchases	7.7	0.9	9.8	18.4
Sales	(3.0)	(0.4)	—	(3.4)
Ending balance—December 31	$28.3	$ 6.8	$10.2	$45.3

The expected return on plan assets takes into account historical returns and the weighted average of estimated future long-term returns based on capital market assumptions for each asset category. The expected return is net of investment expenses paid by the plans.

Contributions

Annual contributions to the pension plans are made within income tax deductibility restrictions in accordance with statutory regulations. In the event of plan termination, the plan sponsors could be required to fund additional shutdown and early retirement obligations that are not included in the pension obligations. The Company currently has no intention to shutdown, terminate or withdraw from any of its employee benefit plans.

(In millions)		Other Benefits		
Company Contributions	Pension Benefits	VEBA	Direct Payments	Payments
2011	70.1	17.4	20.0	37.4
2012	67.7	17.4	21.6	39.0
2013 (Expected)*	51.8	14.1	8.3	22.4

* Pursuant to the bargaining agreement, benefits can be paid from VEBA trusts that are at least 70 percent funded (all VEBA trusts are 70 percent funded at December 31, 2012). Funding obligations are suspended when Hibbing's, UTAC's, Tilden's and Empire's share of the value of their respective trust assets reaches 90 percent of their obligation.

VEBA plans are not subject to minimum regulatory funding requirements. Amounts contributed are pursuant to bargaining agreements.

Contributions by participants to the other benefit plans were $4.6 million for each of the years ended December 31, 2012 and 2011.

Estimated Cost for 2013

For 2013, we estimate net periodic benefit cost as follows:

	(In millions)
Defined benefit pension plans	$52.7
Other postretirement benefits	17.1
Total	$69.8

Estimated Future Benefit Payments

(In millions)	Pension Benefits	Other Benefits		
		Gross Company Benefits	Less Medicare Subsidy	Net Company Payments
2013	$ 74.8	$ 24.5	$1.0	$ 23.5
2014	80.8	26.1	1.1	25.0
2015	79.1	27.2	1.2	26.0
2016	79.4	27.3	1.3	26.0
2017	80.1	27.4	1.4	26.0
2018–2022	417.0	131.5	9.0	122.5

Other Potential Benefit Obligations

While the foregoing reflects our obligation, our total exposure in the event of non-performance is potentially greater. Following is a summary comparison of the total obligation:

(In millions)	December 31, 2012	
	Defined Benefit Pensions	Other Benefits
Fair value of plan assets	$ 838.7	$ 237.0
Benefit obligation	1,244.3	459.8
Underfunded status of plan	$ (405.6)	$(222.8)
Additional shutdown and early retirement benefits	$ 32.5	$ 31.5

DEFINED CONTRIBUTION PLANS

3.49 CONOCOPHILLIPS (DEC)
NOTES TO CONSOLIDATED FINANCIAL STATEMENTS

Note 19—Employee Benefit Plans (in part)

Defined Contribution Plans

Most U.S. employees are eligible to participate in the ConocoPhillips Savings Plan (CPSP). Employees can deposit up to 75 percent of their eligible pay up to the statutory limit ($17,000 in 2012) in the thrift feature of the CPSP to a choice of approximately 38 investment funds. Through 2012, ConocoPhillips matched contribution deposits, up to 1.25 percent of eligible pay. Company contributions charged to expense related to continuing and discontinued operations for the CPSP and predecessor plans, excluding the stock savings feature (discussed below), were $16 million in 2012, $25 million in 2011, and $24 million in 2010.

The stock savings feature of the CPSP is a leveraged employee stock ownership plan. Through 2012, employees could elect to participate in the stock savings feature by contributing 1 percent of eligible pay and receiving an allocation of shares of common stock proportionate to the amount of contribution.

In 1990, the Long-Term Stock Savings Plan of Phillips Petroleum Company (now the stock savings feature of the CPSP) borrowed funds that were used to purchase previously unissued shares of company common stock. Since the Company guarantees the CPSP's borrowings, the unpaid balance is reported as a liability of the Company and unearned compensation is shown as a reduction of common stockholders' equity. Dividends on all shares are charged against retained earnings. The debt is serviced by the CPSP from company contributions and dividends received on certain shares of common stock held by the plan, including all unallocated shares. The shares held by the stock savings feature of the CPSP are released for allocation to participant accounts based on debt service payments on CPSP borrowings. In 2012, the final debt service payment was made and all remaining unallocated shares were released for allocation to participant accounts.

We recognize interest expense as incurred and compensation expense based on the fair value of the stock contributed or on the cost of the unallocated shares released, using the shares-allocated method. We recognized total CPSP expense related to continuing and discontinued operations to the stock savings feature of $104 million, $77 million and $92 million in 2012, 2011 and 2010, respectively, all of which was compensation expense. In 2012 and 2011, we made cash contributions to the CPSP of $5 million and $4 million, respectively. No cash contributions were made in 2010. In 2011 and 2010, we contributed 660,755 shares and 1,776,873 shares, respectively, of company common stock from the Compensation and Benefits Trust. The shares had a fair value of $84 million and $103 million, respectively. In 2012 and 2011, we contributed 1,554,355 and 475,696 shares, respectively, of company common stock from treasury stock. Dividends used to service debt were $10 million, $45 million and $41 million in 2012, 2011 and 2010, respectively. These dividends reduced the amount of compensation expense recognized each period. Interest incurred on the CPSP debt in 2012, 2011 and 2010 was $0.1 million, $1 million and $2 million, respectively.

The total CPSP stock savings feature shares as of December 31 were:

	2012	2011
Unallocated shares	—	811,963
Allocated shares	11,246,660	19,315,372
Total shares	11,246,660	20,127,335

The fair value of unallocated shares at December 31, 2011 was $59 million.

Starting in 2013, employees who participate in the CPSP and contribute 1 percent of their eligible pay will receive a 9 percent company cash match. CPSP will no longer have a stock savings feature.

We have several defined contribution plans for our international employees, each with its own terms and eligibility depending on location. Total compensation expense related to continuing and discontinued operations recognized for these international plans was approximately $56 million in 2012 and 2011 and $52 million in 2010.

SUPPLEMENTAL RETIREMENT PLANS (SERP)

3.50 GUESS?, INC. (JAN)
NOTES TO CONSOLIDATED FINANCIAL STATEMENTS

(1) Summary of Significant Accounting Policies and Practices (in part)

Supplemental Executive Retirement Plan

In accordance with authoritative accounting guidance for defined benefit pension and other postretirement plans, an asset for a plan's overfunded status or a liability for a plan's underfunded status is recognized in the consolidated balance sheets; plan assets and obligations that determine the plan's funded status are measured as of the end of the Company's fiscal year; and changes in the funded status of defined benefit postretirement plans are recognized in the year in which they occur. Such changes are reported in other comprehensive income and as a separate component of stockholders' equity.

(10) Supplemental Executive Retirement Plan

On August 23, 2005, the Board of Directors of the Company adopted a Supplemental Executive Retirement Plan which became effective January 1, 2006. The SERP provides select employees who satisfy certain eligibility requirements with certain benefits upon retirement, termination of employment, death, disability or a change in control of the Company, in certain prescribed circumstances. Paul Marciano, Chief Executive Officer and Vice Chairman of the Board, is the only active participant in the SERP. Maurice Marciano, non-executive Chairman of the Board of Directors, was an active participant in the SERP until his retirement effective on January 28, 2012. Carlos Alberini, the Company's former President and Chief Operating Officer, was an active participant in the SERP until his departure from the Company on June 1, 2010. Mr. Maurice Marciano and Mr. Alberini will be eligible to receive vested SERP benefits in the future in accordance with the terms of the SERP.

During the year ended January 28, 2012, the Company recorded a SERP curtailment expense of $1.2 million before taxes related to the accelerated amortization of prior service cost resulting from the retirement of Mr. Maurice Marciano as an employee and executive officer, effective upon the expiration of his employment agreement on January 28, 2012. Mr. Maurice Marciano did not receive or earn any additional SERP-related benefits in connection with his retirement and, as of the date of his retirement, ceased vesting or accruing any additional benefits under the terms of the SERP. During the year ended January 29, 2011, the Company recorded a SERP curtailment expense of $5.8 million before taxes related to the accelerated amortization of prior service cost resulting from the departure of Mr. Alberini from the Company. Mr. Alberini did not receive any termination payments in connection with his departure and, as of the date of his departure, he ceased vesting or accruing any additional benefits under the terms of the SERP. Mr. Maurice Marciano's retirement and Mr. Alberini's departure each resulted in a significant reduction in the total expected remaining years of future service of all SERP participants combined, resulting in the pension curtailment during each of the separate periods.

As a non-qualified pension plan, no dedicated funding of the SERP is required; however, the Company has and expects to continue to make periodic payments into insurance policies held in a rabbi trust to fund the expected obligations arising under the non-qualified SERP. The amount of future payments may vary, depending on the future years of service, future annual compensation of the active participant and investment performance of the trust. The cash surrender values of the insurance policies were $38.4 million and $32.9 million as of January 28, 2012 and January 29, 2011, respectively, and were included in other assets in the Company's consolidated balance sheets. As a result of a change in value of the insurance policy investments, the Company recorded (losses) gains of $(0.2) million, $2.7 million and $3.1 million in other income during fiscal 2012, fiscal 2011 and fiscal 2010, respectively.

In accordance with authoritative accounting guidance for defined benefit pension and other postretirement plans, an asset for a plan's overfunded status or a liability for a plan's underfunded status is recognized in the consolidated balance sheet; plan assets and obligations that determine the plan's funded status are measured as of the end of the Company's fiscal year; and changes in the funded status of defined benefit postretirement plans are recognized in the year in which they occur. Such changes are reported in other comprehensive income and as a separate component of stockholders' equity.

The components of net periodic pension cost to comprehensive income for fiscal 2012, fiscal 2011 and fiscal 2010, are (in thousands):

	Year Ended Jan. 28, 2012	Year Ended Jan. 29, 2011	Year Ended Jan. 30, 2010
Service cost	$ —	$ 69	$ 213
Interest cost	2,641	2,177	2,053
Net amortization of unrecognized prior service cost	940	1,195	1,743
Net amortization of actuarial losses	2,048	619	—
Curtailment expense	1,242	5,819	—
Net periodic defined benefit pension cost	$ 6,871	$ 9,879	$ 4,009
Unrecognized prior service cost charged to comprehensive income	$ 940	$ 1,195	$ 1,743
Unrecognized net actuarial loss charged to comprehensive income	2,048	619	—
Actuarial losses	(9,342)	(8,361)	(5,569)
Curtailment expense	1,242	5,819	—
Related tax impact	2,057	251	1,435
Total periodic costs and other charges to comprehensive income	$(3,055)	$ (477)	$(2,391)

Included in accumulated other comprehensive income, before tax, as of January 28, 2012 and January 29, 2011 were the following amounts that have not yet been recognized in net periodic benefit cost (in thousands):

	Jan. 28, 2012	Jan. 29, 2011
Unrecognized prior service cost	$ 3,363	$ 5,545
Unrecognized net actuarial loss	22,681	15,387
Net balance sheet impact	$26,044	$20,932

The following chart summarizes the SERP's funded status and the amounts recognized in the Company's consolidated balance sheets (in thousands):

	Jan. 28, 2012	Jan. 29, 2011
Projected benefit obligation	$(59,755)	$(47,772)
Plan assets at fair value[(1)]	—	—
Net liability (included in other long-term liabilities)	$(59,755)	$(47,772)

[(1)] The SERP is a non-qualified pension plan and hence the insurance policies are not considered to be plan assets. Accordingly, the table above does not include the insurance policies with cash surrender values of $38.4 million and $32.9 million at January 28, 2012 and January 29, 2011, respectively.

A reconciliation of the changes in the projected benefit obligation for fiscal 2012 and fiscal 2011 is as follows (in thousands):

	Projected Benefit Obligation
Balance at January 30, 2010	$37,165
Service cost	69
Interest cost	2,177
Actuarial losses	8,361
Balance at January 29, 2011	$47,772
Interest cost	2,641
Actuarial losses	9,342
Balance at January 28, 2012	$59,755

The Company assumed a discount rate of 4.0% at January 28, 2012 compared to 5.5% at January 29, 2011, as part of the actuarial valuation performed to calculate the projected benefit obligation disclosed above, based on the timing of cash flows expected to be made in the future to the participants, applied to high quality yield curves. Compensation levels utilized in calculating the projected benefit obligation were derived from expected future compensation as outlined in employment contracts in effect at the time. At January 28, 2012, amounts included in comprehensive income that are expected to be recognized as components of net periodic defined benefit pension cost in fiscal 2013 consist of amortization of prior service costs of $0.6 million and actuarial losses of $3.3 million. Benefits projected to be paid in the next five fiscal years amount to $5.1 million with one-third of such payments to be paid in each of the third, fourth and fifth years. Aggregate benefits projected to be paid in the following five fiscal years amount to $25.2 million.

MULTI-EMPLOYER PLANS

3.51 THE KROGER CO. (JAN)
NOTES TO CONSOLIDATED FINANCIAL STATEMENTS

All dollar amounts are in millions except share and per share amounts.

Certain prior-year amounts have been reclassified to conform to current year presentation.

14. Multi-Employer Pension Plans

The Company contributes to various multi-employer pension plans based on obligations arising from collective bargaining agreements. These plans provide retirement benefits to participants based on their service to contributing employers. The benefits are paid from assets held in trust for that purpose. Trustees are appointed in equal number by employers and unions. The trustees typically are responsible for determining the level of benefits to be provided to participants as well as for such matters as the investment of the assets and the administration of the plans.

In the fourth quarter of 2011, the Company entered into a memorandum of understanding ("MOU") with 14 locals of the United Food and Commercial Workers International Union ("UFCW") that participated in four multi-employer pension funds. The MOU established a process that amended each of the collective bargaining agreements between the Company and the UFCW locals under which the Company made contributions to these funds and consolidated the four multi-employer pension funds into one multi-employer pension fund.

Under the terms of the MOU, the locals of the UFCW agreed to a future pension benefit formula through 2021. The Company was designated as the named fiduciary of the new consolidated pension plan with sole investment authority over the assets. The Company committed to contribute sufficient funds to cover the actuarial cost of current accruals and to fund the pre-consolidation Unfunded Actuarial Accrued Liability ("UAAL") that existed as of December 31, 2011, in a series of installments on or before March 31, 2018. At January 1, 2012, the UAAL was estimated to be $911 (pre-tax). In accordance with GAAP, the Company expensed $911 in 2011 related to the UAAL. The expense was based on a preliminary estimate of the contractual commitment. As the estimate is updated, we may incur additional expense. We do not expect any adjustments to be material. In the fourth quarter of 2011, the Company contributed $650 to the consolidated multi-employer pension plan of which $600 was allocated to the UAAL and $50 was allocated to service and interest costs and expensed in 2011. Future contributions will be dependent, among other things, on the investment performance of assets in the plan. The funding commitments under the MOU replace the prior commitments under the four existing funds to pay an agreed upon amount per hour worked by eligible employees.

The Company recognizes expense in connection with these plans as contributions are funded, or in the case of the UFCW consolidated pension plan, when commitments are made. The Company made contributions to these funds of $946 in 2011, $262 in 2010 and $233 in 2009. The cash contributions for 2011 include the Company's $650 contribution to the UFCW consolidated pension plan in the fourth quarter of 2011.

The risks of participating in multi-employer pension plans are different from the risks of participating in single-employer pension plans in the following respects:
   a) Assets contributed to the multi-employer plan by one employer may be used to provide benefits to employees of other participating employers.
   b) If a participating employer stops contributing to the plan, the unfunded obligations of the plan allocable to such withdrawing employer may be borne by the remaining participating employers.
   c) If the Company stops participating in some of its multi-employer pension plans, the Company may be required to pay those plans an amount based on its allocable share of the underfunded status of the plan, referred to as a withdrawal liability.

The Company's participation in these plans is outlined in the following tables. The EIN / Pension Plan Number column provides the Employer Identification Number ("EIN") and the three-digit pension plan number. The most recent Pension Protection Act Zone Status available in 2011 and 2010 is for the plan's year-end at December 31, 2010 and December 31, 2009, respectively. Among other factors, generally, plans in the red zone are less than 65 percent funded, plans in yellow zone are less than 80 percent funded, and plans in the green zone are at least 80 percent funded. The FIP/RP Status Pending / Implemented Column indicates plans for which a funding improvement plan ("FIP") or a rehabilitation plan ("RP") is either pending or has been implemented. Unless otherwise noted, the information for these tables was obtained from the Forms 5500 filed for each plan's year-end at December 31, 2010 and December 31, 2009. The multi-employer contributions listed in the table below are the Company's multi-employer contributions made in fiscal years 2011, 2010, and 2009.

The following table contains information about the Company's multi-employer pension plans:

Pension Fund	EIN/Pension Plan Number	Pension Protection Act Zone Status		FIP/RP Status Pending/ Implemented	Multi-Employer Contributions			Surcharge Imposed[8]
		2011	2010		2011	2010	2009	
SO CA UFCW Unions & Food Employers Joint Pension Trust Fund[1][2]	95-1939092-001	Red	Red	Implemented	$ 40	$ 41	$ 42	No
BD of Trustees of UNTD Food and Commercial[1][6]	58-6101602-001	Red	Red	Implemented	59	47	35	No
Desert States Employers & UFCW Unions Pension Plan[1]	84-6277982-001	Yellow	Red	Implemented	20	17	15	No
UFCW Unions and Food Employers Pension Plan of Central Ohio[1][6]	31-6089168-001	Red	Red	Implemented	23	21	20	No
Sound Retirement Trust (formerly Retail Clerks Pension Plan)[1][3]	91-6069306-001	Green	Yellow	Implemented	10	9	9	No
Rocky Mountain UFCW Unions and Employers Pension Plan[1]	84-6045986-001	Red	Red	Implemented	16	16	10	No
Indiana UFCW Unions and Retail Food Employers Pension Plan[1][6]	35-6244695-001	Red	Red	Pending	5	5	4	No
Oregon Retail Employees Pension Plan[1]	93-6074377-001	Red	Red	Implemented	6	6	5	No
Bakery and Confectionary Union & Industry International Pension Fund	52-6118572-001	Green	Yellow	No	9	6	5	No
Washington Meat Industry Pension Trust[1][4]	91-6134141-001	Red	Green	Implemented	2	2	2	Yes
Retail Food Employers & UFCW Local 711 Pension[1]	51-6031512-001	Red	Red	Implemented	7	7	7	No
Denver Area Meat Cutters and Employers Pension Plan[1]	84-6097461-001	Red	Red	Implemented	8	8	4	No
United Food & Commercial Workers Intl Union—Industry Pension Fund[1][5]	51-6055922-001	Green	Green	No	33	30	27	No
Northwest Ohio UFCW Union and Employers Joint Pension Fund[1][6]	34-0947187-001	Red	Red	Implemented	2	2	2	No
Western Conference of Teamsters Pension Plan	91-6145047-001	Green	Green	No	31	30	30	No
Central States, Southeast & Southwest Areas Pension Plan	36-6044243-001	Red	Red	Implemented	14	8	7	No
UFCW Consolidated Pension Plan[1][7]	58-6101602-001	N/A	N/A	N/A	650	—	—	No
Other					11	7	9	
Total Contributions					$946	$262	$233	

[1] The Company's multi-employer contributions to these respective funds represent more than 5% of the total contributions received by the pension funds.

[2] The information for this fund was obtained from the Form 5500 filed for the plan's year-end at March 31, 2011 and March 31, 2010.

[3] The information for this fund was obtained from the Form 5500 filed for the plan's year-end at September 30, 2010 and September 30, 2009.

[4] The information for this fund was obtained from the Form 5500 filed for the plan's year-end at June 30, 2010 and June 30, 2009.

[5] The information for this fund was obtained from the Form 5500 filed for the plan's year-end at June 30, 2010 and June 30, 2009.

[6] As of December 31, 2011, these four pension funds were consolidated into the UFCW consolidated pension plan. See the above information regarding this multi-employer pension fund consolidation.

[7] The UFCW consolidated pension plan was formed on January 1, 2012, as the result of the merger of four existing multi-employer pension plans. See the above information regarding this multi-employer pension fund consolidation.

[8] Under the Pension Protection Act, a surcharge may be imposed when employers make contributions under a collective bargaining agreement that is not in compliance with a rehabilitation plan. As of January 28, 2012, the collective bargaining agreements under which the Company was making contributions were in compliance with rehabilitation plans adopted by the applicable pension fund, except for the pension fund noted above with an imposed surcharge.

The following table describes (a) the expiration date of the Company's collective bargaining agreements and (b) the expiration date of the Company's most significant collective bargaining agreements for each of the material multi-employer funds in which the Company participates.

Pension Fund	Expiration Date of Collective Bargaining Agreement	Most Significant Collective Bargaining Agreements[1] (Not in Millions)	
		Count	Expiration
SO CA UFCW Unions & Food Employers Joint Pension Trust Fund	March 2014 to June 2014	2	March 2014 to June 2014
UFCW Consolidated Pension Fund[3]	October 2011[2] to October 2014	8	October 2011[2] to March 2014
Desert States Employers & UFCW Unions Pension Plan	October 2012 to June 2014	1	October 2012
Sound Retirement Trust (formerly Retail Clerks Pension Plan)	May 2013 to December 2013	2	May 2013 to August 2013
Rocky Mountain UFCW Unions and Employers Pension Plan	September 2013 to October 2013	1	September 2013
Oregon Retail Employees Pension Plan	February 2011[2] to April 2015	3	July 2012 to June 2013
Bakery and Confectionary Union & Industry International Pension Fund	May 2011[2] to April 2015	4	August 2012 to June 2014
Washington Meat Industry Pension Trust	January 2012[2] to July 2013	1	May 2013
Retail Food Employers & UFCW Local 711 Pension	February 2012 to November 2013	2	February 2012
Denver Area Meat Cutters and Employers Pension Plan	September 2013 to October 2013	1	September 2013
United Food & Commercial Workers Intl Union—Industry Pension Fund	September 2008[2] to October 2014	2	March 2012 to June 2013
Western Conference of Teamsters Pension Plan	April 2012 to September 2015	5	August 2014 to September 2015
Central States, Southeast & Southwest Areas Pension Plan	September 2014	2	September 2014

[1] This column represents the number of significant collective bargaining agreements and their expiration date range for each the Company's pension funds listed above. For purposes of this table, the "significant collective bargaining agreements" are the largest based on covered employees that, when aggregated, cover the majority of the employees for which we make multi-employer contributions for the referenced pension fund.

[2] Certain collective bargaining agreements for each of these pension funds are operating under an extension.

[3] As of January 1, 2012, four multi-employer pension funds were consolidated into the UFCW consolidated pension plan. See the above information regarding this multi-employer pension fund consolidation.

Based on the most recent information available to it, the Company believes that the present value of actuarial accrued liabilities in most of these multi-employer plans substantially exceeds the value of the assets held in trust to pay benefits. Moreover, if the Company were to exit certain markets or otherwise cease making contributions to these funds, the Company could trigger a substantial withdrawal liability. Any adjustment for withdrawal liability will be recorded when it is probable that a liability exists and can be reasonably estimated.

The Company also contributes to various other multi-employer benefit plans that provide health and welfare benefits to active and retired participants. Total contributions made by the Company to these other multi-employer benefit plans were approximately $1,000 in 2011 and $900 in 2010 and 2009.

PLAN AMENDMENT AND TERMINATION

3.52 SYSCO CORPORATION (JUN)
NOTES TO CONSOLIDATED FINANCIAL STATEMENTS

14. Multiemployer Employee Benefit Plans (in part)

Defined Benefit Pension Plans (in part)

Sysco contributes to several multiemployer defined benefit pension plans in the United States and Canada based on obligations arising under collective bargaining agreements covering union-represented employees. Sysco does not directly manage these multiemployer plans, which are generally managed by boards of trustees, half of whom are appointed by the unions and the other half by other employers contributing to the plan. Approximately 10 % of Sysco's current employees are participants in such multiemployer plans as of June 30, 2012.

The risks of participating in these multiemployer plans are different from single-employer plans in the following aspects:
* Assets contributed to the multiemployer plan by one employer may be used to provide benefits to employees of other participating employers.
* If a participating employer stops contributing to the plan, the unfunded obligations of the plan may be borne by the remaining participating employers.
* If Sysco chooses to stop participating in some of its multiemployer plans, Sysco may be required to pay those plans an amount based on the underfunded status of the plan, referred to as a withdrawal liability.

Based upon the information available from plan administrators, management believes that several of these multiemployer plans are underfunded. In addition, pension-related legislation in the United States requires underfunded pension plans to improve their funding ratios within prescribed intervals based on the level of their underfunding. As a result, Sysco expects its contributions to these plans to increase in the future. In addition, if a United States multiemployer defined benefit plan fails to satisfy certain minimum funding requirements, the IRS may impose a nondeductible excise tax of 5% on the amount of the accumulated funding deficiency for those employers contributing to the fund.

Withdrawal Activity

Sysco has voluntarily withdrawn from various multiemployer pension plans. Total withdrawal liability provisions recorded include $ 21.9 million in fiscal 2012, $41.5 million in fiscal 2011 and $2.9 million in fiscal 2010. As of June 30, 2012 and July 2, 2011, Sysco had approximately $ 30.7 million and $42.4 million, respectively, in liabilities recorded related to certain multiemployer defined benefit plans for which Sysco's voluntary withdrawal had already occurred. Recorded withdrawal liabilities are estimated at the time of withdrawal based on the most recently available valuation and participant data for the respective plans; amounts are subsequently adjusted to the period of payment to reflect any changes to these estimates. If any of these plans were to undergo a mass withdrawal, as defined by the Pension Benefit Guaranty Corporation, within a two year time frame from the point of our withdrawal, Sysco could have additional liability. The company does not currently believe any mass withdrawals are probable to occur in the applicable two year time frame relating to the plans from which Sysco has voluntarily withdrawn.

Potential Withdrawal Liability

Under current law regarding multiemployer defined benefit plans, a plan's termination, Sysco's voluntary withdrawal, or the mass withdrawal of all contributing employers from any underfunded multiemployer defined benefit plan would require Sysco to make payments to the plan for Sysco's proportionate share of the multiemployer plan's unfunded vested liabilities. Generally, Sysco does not have the greatest share of liability among the participants in any of the plans in which it participates. Sysco believes that one of the above-mentioned events is reasonably possible with certain plans in which it participates and estimates its share of withdrawal liability for these plans could have been as much as $ 100.0 million as of June 30, 2012. This estimate excludes plans for which Sysco has recorded withdrawal liabilities or where the likelihood of the above-mentioned events is deemed remote. This estimate is based on the information available from plan administrators, which has valuation dates ranging fro m December 31, 2009 to December 31, 2010. The majority of these plans have a valuation date of calendar year-end and therefore the estimate results from plans for which the valuation date was December 31, 2010; therefore, the company's estimate reflects the con dition of the financial markets as of that date. Due to the lack of current information, management believes Sysco's current share of the withdrawal liability could materially differ from this estimate.

Plan Contributions

Sysco's contributions to multiemployer defined benefit pension plans were as follows for each fiscal year:

(In thousands)	2012	2011	2010 (53 Weeks)
Individually significant plans	$63,718	$30,180	$47,483
All other plans	4,390	3,835	4,216
Total contributions	$68,108	$34,015	$51,699

Payments for voluntary withdrawals included in contributions were $ 33.6 million, zero and $17.4 million in fiscal 2012, 2011 and 2010, respectively.

Postemployment Benefits

RECOGNITION AND MEASUREMENT

3.53 FASB ASC 712, *Compensation—Nonretirement Post-employment Benefits*, requires that entities providing postemployment benefits to their employees accrue the cost of such benefits. FASB ASC 712 does not require that the amount of other postemployment benefits be disclosed.

PRESENTATION AND DISCLOSURE EXCERPT

POSTEMPLOYMENT BENEFITS

3.54 TRW AUTOMOTIVE HOLDINGS CORP. (DEC)
CONSOLIDATED BALANCE SHEETS (in part)

	As of December 31,	
(Dollars in millions)	2012	2011
Liabilities and Equity		
Current liabilities:		
Short-term debt	$ 67	$ 65
Current portion of long-term debt	26	39
Trade accounts payable	2,423	2,306
Accrued compensation	254	283
Income taxes	36	69
Other current liabilities	1,075	1,078
Total current liabilities	3,881	3,840
Long-term debt	1,369	1,428
Postretirement benefits other than pensions	396	421
Pension benefits	898	831
Deferred income taxes	123	173
Long-term liabilities	421	430
Total liabilities	7,088	7,123

9. Retirement Benefits (in part)

Postretirement Benefits Other Than Pensions ("OPEB")

The Company provides health care and life insurance benefits for a substantial number of its retired employees in the United States and Canada, and for certain future retirees. The health care plans provide for the sharing of costs, in the form of retiree contributions, deductibles and coinsurance. Life insurance benefits are generally noncontributory. The Company's policy is to fund the cost of postretirement health care and life insurance benefits as those benefits become payable.

The following table provides a reconciliation of the changes in the plans' benefit obligation and fair value of assets during the years ended December 31, 2012 and December 31, 2011, and a statement of the funded status of the programs as of December 31, 2012 and 2011:

(Dollars in millions)	2012 U.S.	2012 Rest of World	2011 U.S.	2011 Rest of World
Change in Benefit Obligation:				
Benefit obligations at beginning of period	$ 357	$ 105	$ 396	$ 99
Service cost	1	1	1	1
Interest cost	16	5	20	5
Actuarial (gain) loss	(6)	(7)	67	13
Foreign currency exchange rate changes	—	3	—	(3)
Plan amendments	—	3	(91)	—
Curtailment/settlement gain	(1)	—	—	(3)
Plan participant contributions	1	—	3	—
Benefits paid	(38)	(7)	(39)	(7)
Benefit obligations at December 31,	330	103	357	105
Change in Plan Assets:				
Fair value of plan assets at beginning of period	—	—	—	—
Company contributions	37	7	36	8
Plan participant contributions	1	—	3	—
Settlements	—	—	—	(1)
Benefits paid	(38)	(7)	(39)	(7)
Fair value of plan assets at December 31,	—	—	—	—
Funded status at December 31,	$(330)	$(103)	$(357)	$(105)

The following table provides the amounts recognized in the consolidated balance sheets:

	As of December 31,			
	2012		2011	
(Dollars in millions)	U.S.	Rest of World	U.S.	Rest of World
Current liabilities	$ (30)	$ (7)	$ (35)	$ (6)
Long-term liabilities	(300)	(96)	(322)	(99)
Total amount recognized	$(330)	$(103)	$(357)	$(105)

The pre-tax amounts recognized in accumulated other comprehensive earnings (losses) consist of:

	As of December 31,			
	2012		2011	
(Dollars in millions)	U.S.	Rest of World	U.S.	Rest of World
Prior service benefit (cost)	$146	$26	$198	$35
Net gain (loss)	(33)	(9)	(34)	(17)
Accumulated other comprehensive earnings (loss)	$113	$17	$164	$18

The following table provides the components of net postretirement benefit (income) cost and other amounts recognized in other comprehensive (earnings) loss for the plans.

	Years Ended December 31,					
	2012		2011		2010	
(Dollars in millions)	U.S.	Rest of World	U.S.	Rest of World	U.S.	Rest of World
Net Postretirement Benefit (Income) Cost:						
Service cost	$ 1	$ 1	$ 1	$ 1	$ 1	$ 1
Interest cost	16	5	20	5	23	6
Curtailment/Settlement (gain) loss	(36)	—	—	(2)	(3)	(5)
Amortization of prior service (benefit) cost	(22)	(7)	(15)	(6)	(15)	(6)
Amortization of net (gain) loss	—	1	(4)	—	(5)	—
Net postretirement benefit (income) cost	(41)	—	2	(2)	1	(4)

(continued)

| (Dollars in millions) | Years Ended December 31, | | | | | |
| | 2012 | | 2011 | | 2010 | |
	U.S.	Rest of World	U.S.	Rest of World	U.S.	Rest of World
Other Changes in Plan Assets and Benefit Obligations Recognized in Other Comprehensive (Earnings) Loss:						
Prior service (benefit) cost	$—	$ 3	$(89)	$ 1	$ (6)	$ (2)
Net (gain) loss	(6)	(8)	65	12	8	(5)
Amortization or curtailment recognition of prior service benefit (cost)	51	6	15	6	15	6
Amortization or settlement recognition of net gain (loss)	6	(1)	4	—	5	—
Total recognized in other comprehensive (earnings) loss	51	—	(5)	19	22	(1)
Total recognized net postretirement benefit (income) cost and other comprehensive (earnings) loss	$ 10	$—	$ (3)	$ 17	$23	$ (5)

Curtailments and Settlements. The Company recorded settlement gains during the year ended December 31, 2012 of approximately $36 million related to the termination of retiree medical benefits for certain salaried and hourly employees. During the years ended December 31, 2011 and 2010, the Company recorded settlement gains of approximately $2 million and $8 million, respectively, related to retiree medical buyouts.

The estimated amounts that will be amortized from accumulated other comprehensive earnings over the next fiscal year are as follows:

| (Dollars in millions) | Year Ending December 31, 2013 | |
	U.S.	Rest of World
Prior service (benefit) cost	$(17)	$(6)
Net actuarial (gain) loss	1	1
Total	$(16)	$(5)

Plan Assumptions. The weighted-average assumptions used to determine net postretirement benefit (income) cost were:

| | Years Ended December 31, | | | | | |
| | 2012 | | 2011 | | 2010 | |
	U.S.	Rest of World	U.S.	Rest of World	U.S.	Rest of World
Discount rate	4.75%	4.50%	5.50%	5.50%	6.00%	5.75%

The discount rate and assumed health care cost trend rates used in the measurement of the benefit obligation as of the applicable measurement dates were:

| | As of December 31, | | | |
| | 2012 | | 2011 | |
	U.S.	Rest of World	U.S.	Rest of World
Discount rate	4.00%	4.00%	4.75%	4.50%
Initial health care cost trend rate at end of year	7.00%	4.00%	7.00%	7.00%
Ultimate health care cost trend rate	5.00%	5.00%	5.00%	5.00%
Year in which ultimate rate is reached	2017	2017	2018	2015

A one-percentage-point change in the assumed health care cost trend rate would have had the following effects:

| | One-Percentage-Point | | | |
| | Increase | | Decrease | |
(Dollars in millions)	U.S.	Rest of World	U.S.	Rest of World
Effect on total of service and interest cost components for the year ended December 31, 2012	$1	$1	$ (1)	$(1)
Effect on postretirement benefit obligation as of measurement date	$20	$9	$(18)	$(8)

Contributions. The Company funds its OPEB obligations on a pay-as-you-go basis. In 2013, the Company expects to contribute approximately $38 million to its OPEB plans.

Expected Future Postretirement Benefit Payments. The following postretirement benefit payments, which reflect expected future service, as appropriate, are expected to be paid:

| Years Ending December 31, | U.S. | Rest of World |
	(Dollars in millions)	
2013	$ 31	$ 7
2014	30	6
2015	29	6
2016	28	6
2017	26	6
2018–2021	112	32

Employee Compensatory Plans

RECOGNITION AND MEASUREMENT

3.55 FASB ASC 718, *Compensation—Stock Compensation*, establishes accounting and reporting standards for share-based payment transactions with employees, including awards classified as equity, awards classified as liabilities, employee stock ownership plans, and employee stock purchase plans. FASB ASC 718 requires that share-based payment transactions be accounted for using a fair-value-based method. Thus, entities are required to recognize the cost of employee services received in exchange for award of equity instruments based on the grant-date fair value of those awards or the fair value of the liabilities incurred. FASB ASC 718 provides clarification and expanded guidance in several areas, including measuring fair value, classifying an award as equity or a liability, and attributing compensation cost to reporting periods.

PRESENTATION AND DISCLOSURE EXCERPTS

STOCK OPTION PLANS

3.56 ZIMMER HOLDINGS, INC. (DEC)
NOTES TO CONSOLIDATED FINANCIAL STATEMENTS

3. Share-Based Compensation (in part)

Our share-based payments primarily consist of stock options, restricted stock, restricted stock units (RSUs), and an employee stock purchase plan. Share-based compensation expense is as follows (in millions):

For the Years Ended December 31,	2012	2011	2010
Stock options	$ 32.4	$ 41.7	$ 47.6
RSUs and other	22.6	18.8	14.4
Total expense, pre-tax	55.0	60.5	62.0
Tax benefit related to awards	(16.6)	(17.8)	(16.2)
Total expense, net of tax	$ 38.4	$ 42.7	$ 45.8

Share-based compensation cost capitalized as part of inventory for the years ended December 31, 2012, 2011 and 2010 was $6.1 million, $8.8 million, and $12.2 million, respectively. As of December 31, 2012 and 2011, approximately $3.3 million and $4.8 million of capitalized costs remained in finished goods inventory.

Stock Options

We had two equity compensation plans in effect at December 31, 2012: the 2009 Stock Incentive Plan (2009 Plan) and the Stock Plan for Non-Employee Directors. The 2009 Plan succeeds the 2006 Stock Incentive Plan (2006 Plan) and the TeamShare Stock Option Plan (TeamShare Plan). No further awards have been granted under the 2006 Plan or under the TeamShare Plan since May 2009, and shares remaining available for grant under those plans have been merged into the 2009 Plan. Vested and unvested stock options and unvested restricted stock and RSUs previously granted under the 2006 Plan, the TeamShare Plan and another prior plan, the 2001 Stock Incentive Plan, remained outstanding as of December 31, 2012. We have reserved the maximum number of shares of common stock available for award under the terms of each of these plans. We have registered 57.9 million shares of common stock under these plans. The 2009 Plan provides for the grant of nonqualified stock options and incentive stock options, long-term performance awards in the form of performance shares or units, restricted stock, RSUs and stock appreciation rights. The Compensation and Management Development Committee of the Board of Directors determines the grant date for annual grants under our equity compensation plans. The date for annual grants under the 2009 Plan to our executive officers is expected to occur in the first quarter of each year following the earnings announcements for the previous quarter and full year. The Stock Plan for Non-Employee Directors provides for awards of stock options, restricted stock and RSUs to non-employee directors. It has been our practice to issue shares of common stock upon exercise of stock options from previously unissued shares, except in limited circumstances where they are issued from treasury stock. The total number of awards which may be granted in a given year and/or over the life of the plan under each of our equity compensation plans is limited. At December 31, 2012, an aggregate of 8.7 million shares were available for future grants and awards under these plans.

Stock options granted to date under our plans generally vest over four years and generally have a maximum contractual life of 10 years. As established under our equity compensation plans, vesting may accelerate upon retirement after the first anniversary date of the award if certain criteria are met. We recognize expense related to stock options on a straight-line basis over the requisite service period, less awards expected to be forfeited using estimated forfeiture rates. Due to the accelerated retirement provisions, the requisite service period of our stock options range from one to four years. Stock options are granted with an exercise price equal to the market price of our common stock on the date of grant, except in limited circumstances where local law may dictate otherwise.

A summary of stock option activity for the year ended December 31, 2012 is as follows (options in thousands):

	Stock Options	Weighted Average Exercise	Weighted Average Remaining Contractual Life	Intrinsic Value (In Millions)
Outstanding at January 1, 2012	16,748	$68.04		
Options granted	1,720	64.26		
Options exercised	(933)	46.05		
Options cancelled	(239)	60.21		
Options expired	(658)	75.43		
Outstanding at December 31, 2012	16,638	$68.74	4.8	$64.2
Vested or expected to vest as of December 31, 2012	16,169	$68.94	4.7	$61.9
Exercisable at December 31, 2012	12,977	$71.34	3.9	$38.0

We use a Black-Scholes option-pricing model to determine the fair value of our stock options. Expected volatility was derived from the implied volatility of traded options on our stock that were actively traded around the grant date of the stock options with exercise prices similar to the stock options and maturities of over one year. The expected term of the stock options has been derived from historical employee exercise behavior. The risk-free interest rate was determined using the implied yield currently available for zero-coupon U.S. government issues with a remaining term approximating the expected life of the options. We began paying dividends in 2012. Accordingly, prior to 2012 we assumed no dividend yield. Starting in 2012, the dividend yield was determined by using an estimated annual dividend and dividing it by the market price of our stock on the grant date.

The following table presents information regarding the weighted average fair value for stock options granted, the assumptions used to determine fair value, and the intrinsic value of options exercised in the indicated year:

For the Years Ended December 31,	2012	2011	2010
Dividend yield	1.1%	—%	—%
Volatility	25.6%	26.1%	26.3%
Risk-free interest rate	1.5%	2.2%	2.8%
Expected life (years)	6.1	6.1	5.9
Weighted average fair value of options granted	$15.40	$18.33	$18.17
Intrinsic value of options exercised (in millions)	$17.1	$27.5	$ 8.5

As of December 31, 2012, there was $38.4 million of unrecognized share-based payment expense related to nonvested stock options granted under our plans. That expense is expected to be recognized over a weighted average period of 2.5 years.

STOCK AWARD PLANS

3.57 TUTOR PERINI CORPORATION (DEC)
NOTES TO CONSOLIDATED FINANCIAL STATEMENTS

[1] Description of Business and Summary of Significant Accounting Policies (in part)

(m) Stock-Based Compensation

The Company's long-term incentive plan allows it to grant stock-based compensation awards in a variety of forms including restricted stock and stock options. The terms and conditions of the awards granted are established by the Compensation Committee of the Company's Board of Directors.

Restricted stock awards and stock option awards generally vest subject to the satisfaction of service requirements or the satisfaction of both service requirements and achievement of certain performance targets. For stock awards that vest subject to the satisfaction of service requirements, compensation expense is measured based on the fair value of the award on the date of grant and is recognized as expense on a straight-line basis (net of estimated forfeitures) over the requisite service period. For stock awards which have a performance component, compensation cost is measured based on the fair value on the grant date (the date performance targets are established) and is recognized on a straight-line basis (net of estimated forfeitures) over the applicable requisite service period as achievement of the performance objective becomes probable.

[11] Stock-Based Compensation (in part)

(a) Tutor Perini Corporation Long-Term Incentive Plan (in part)

The Company is authorized to grant up to 6,900,000 stock-based compensation awards to key executives, employees and directors of the Company under the Tutor Perini Corporation Long-Term Incentive Plan (the "Plan"). The Plan allows stock-based compensation awards to be granted in a variety of forms, including stock options, stock appreciation rights, restricted stock awards, unrestricted stock awards, deferred stock awards and dividend equivalent rights. The terms and conditions of the awards granted are established by the Compensation Committee of the Company's Board of Directors who also administers the Plan.

A total of 434,399 shares of common stock are available for future grant under the Plan at December 31, 2012.

Restricted Stock Awards

Restricted stock awards generally vest subject to the satisfaction of service requirements or the satisfaction of both service requirements and achievement of certain performance targets. Upon vesting, each award is exchanged for one share of the Company's common stock. The grant date fair values of these awards are determined based on the closing price of the Company's common stock on either the award date (if subject only to service conditions), or the date that the Compensation Committee establishes the applicable performance target (if subject to performance conditions). The related compensation expense is amortized over the applicable requisite service period. As of December 31, 2012, the Compensation Committee has approved the grant of an aggregate of 4,875,833 restricted stock awards to eligible participants.

The restricted stock awards granted in 2012, 2011 and 2010 had weighted-average grant date fair values of $14.39, $19.03 and $20.44, respectively. The grant date fair value is determined based on the closing price of the Company's common stock on the date of grant.

The following table presents the compensation expense recognized related to the restricted stock awards which is included in general and administrative expenses in the Consolidated Statements of Operations:

	Year Ended December 31,		
(In millions)	2012	2011	2010
Restricted Stock Compensation Expense	$7.1	$5.7	$9.5
Related Income Tax Benefit	$1.5	$2.5	$3.6

As of December 31, 2012, there was $4.8 million of unrecognized compensation expense related to the unvested restricted stock awards which, absent significant forfeitures in the future, is expected to be recognized over a weighted-average period of approximately 2.5 years.

During 2012, the Compensation Committee established the 2012 performance targets for 220,000 restricted stock units awarded in 2009 and 2010, and for 73,333 restricted stock units awarded in 2012. During 2012, the Compensation Committee approved the award of 783,333 new restricted stock units.

A summary of restricted stock awards activity during the year ended December 31, 2012 is as follows:

	Number of Shares	Weighted Average Grant Date Fair Value	Aggregate Intrinsic Value (In Thousands)
Total Granted and Unvested—January 1, 2012	1,185,832	$19.65	$14,633
Vested	(208,332)	$24.36	$ 2,627
Granted	293,333	$14.39	$ 4,019
Forfeited	(129,167)	$13.60	—
Total Granted and Unvested	1,141,666	$18.12	$15,641
Approved for grant	888,335	(a)	$12,170
Total Awarded and Unvested—December 31, 2012	2,030,001	n.a.	$27,811

(a) Grant date fair value cannot be determined currently because the related performance targets for future years have not yet been established by the Compensation Committee.

The outstanding unvested restricted stock awards at December 31, 2012 are scheduled to vest as follows, subject where applicable to the achievement of performance targets. As described above, certain performance targets have not yet been established.

Vesting Date	Number of Awards
2013	896,666
2014	408,335
2015	150,000
2016	165,000
2017	410,000
Total	2,030,001

Approximately 245,000 of the unvested restricted stock awards will vest based on the satisfaction of service requirements and 1,785,001 will vest based on the satisfaction of both service requirements and the achievement of pre-tax income performance targets.

SAVINGS AND INVESTMENT PLANS

3.58 MORGAN STANLEY (DEC)
NOTES TO CONSOLIDATED FINANCIAL STATEMENTS

21. Employee Benefit Plans (in part)

Morgan Stanley 401(k) Plan, Morgan Stanley 401(k) Savings Plan and Profit Sharing Awards. U.S. employees meeting certain eligibility requirements may participate in the Morgan Stanley 401(k) Plan or the Morgan Stanley 401(k) Savings Plan. Eligible U.S. employees receive 401(k) matching cash or stock contributions. Matching contributions for 2012 were funded with cash and allocated according to participants' current investment direction. Matching contributions for 2011 were funded in stock and invested in the Morgan Stanley Stock Fund.

Effective January 1, 2011, the Morgan Stanley 401(k) Plan was amended to conform with the Morgan Stanley 401(k) Savings Plan to provide a $1 for $1 Company match up to 4% of eligible pay up to the Internal Revenue Service ("IRS") limit. In addition, the fixed contribution was amended to apply to eligible employees in both the Morgan Stanley 401(k) Plan and Morgan Stanley 401(k) Savings Plan with eligible pay less than or equal to $100,000 who are not Financial Advisors or Senior Advisors. The fixed contribution is equal to 2% of eligible pay. Also effective January 1, 2011, an MS Transition Contribution was added for participants who received a 2010 accrual in the U.S. Qualified Plan or a 2010 retirement contribution in the 401(k) Plan and who met certain age and service requirements as of December 31, 2010.

Effective July 1, 2009, the Company introduced the Morgan Stanley 401(k) Savings Plan for legacy Smith Barney U.S. employees who were contributed to MSSB and certain other groups. In 2010, legacy Smith Barney U.S. employees with eligible pay less than or equal to $100,000 received a fixed contribution under the 401(k) Savings Plan. The amount of fixed contribution was included in the Company's 401(k) expense and equaled between 1% and 2% of eligible pay based on years of service at December 31. Additionally, certain eligible legacy Smith Barney employees were granted a transition contribution and, for their year of transfer, a one-time make-up Company match based on certain transition percentages of eligible pay and a comparison of the Company match under the Citi 401(k) Plan and Morgan Stanley 401(k) Savings Plan. The retirement contribution granted in lieu of a defined benefit pension plan and the fixed contribution, transition contribution and make-up Company match granted to legacy Smith Barney employees are included in the Company's 401(k) expense. Effective May 1, 2011, the Saxon 401(k) Plan was merged with the Morgan Stanley 401(k) Savings Plan. Effective December 31, 2012, the Morgan Stanley 401(k) Savings Plan was merged with the Morgan Stanley 401(k) Plan.

EMPLOYEE STOCK PURCHASE PLANS (ESPP)

3.59 APPLIED MATERIALS, INC. (OCT)
NOTES TO CONSOLIDATED FINANCIAL STATEMENTS

Note 12 Stockholders' Equity, Comprehensive Income and Share-Based Compensation (in part)

Share-Based Compensation

Applied has adopted stock plans that permit grants to employees of share-based awards, including stock options, restricted stock, restricted stock units, performance shares and performance units. In addition, the Employee Stock Incentive Plan provides for the automatic grant of restricted stock units to non-employee directors and permits the grant of share-based awards to non-employee directors and consultants. Applied also has two Employee Stock Purchase Plans, one generally for United States employees and a second for employees of international subsidiaries (collectively, ESPP), which enable eligible employees to purchase Applied common stock.

During fiscal 2012, 2011, and 2010, Applied recognized share-based compensation expense related to stock options, ESPP shares, restricted stock, restricted stock units, performance shares and performance units. Total share-based compensation and related tax benefits were as follows:

(In millions)	2012	2011	2010
Share-based compensation	$182	$146	$126
Tax benefit recognized	$ 52	$ 42	$ 38

The effect of share-based compensation on the results of operations for fiscal 2012, 2011, and 2010 was as follows:

(In millions)	2012	2011	2010
Cost of products sold	$ 54	$ 48	$ 32
Research, development, and engineering	54	46	43
Selling, general and administrative	74	52	51
Total	$182	$146	$126

The cost associated with share-based awards that are subject solely to time-based vesting requirements, less expected forfeitures, is recognized over the awards' service period for the entire award on a straight-line basis. The cost associated with performance-based equity awards is recognized for each tranche over the service period, based on an assessment of the likelihood that the applicable performance goals will be achieved.

At October 28, 2012, Applied had $259 million in total unrecognized compensation expense, net of estimated forfeitures, related to grants of stock options, restricted stock units, restricted stock, performance units, performance shares and shares issued under Applied's ESPP, which will be recognized over a weighted average period of 2.5 years. On March 6, 2012, Applied's stockholders approved the amended and restated Employee Stock Incentive Plan, which included an increase of 125 million shares of Applied common stock available for issuance under the plan and other amendments to the plan. Also, upon approval of the amended and restated plan, the 2000 Global Equity Incentive Plan, which had approximately 76 million shares available for issuance, became unavailable for any future grants. At October 28, 2012, there were 195 million shares available for grants of stock options, restricted stock units, restricted stock, performance units, performance shares and other share-based awards under the Employee Stock Incentive Plan, and an additional 47 million shares available for issuance under the ESPP.

Employee Stock Purchase Plans

Under the ESPP, substantially all employees may purchase Applied common stock through payroll deductions at a price equal to 85 percent of the lower of the fair market value of Applied common stock at the beginning or end of each 6-month purchase period, subject to certain limits. Based on the Black-Scholes option pricing model, the weighted average estimated fair value of purchase rights under the ESPP was $2.73 per share for the year ended October 28, 2012, $3.03 per share for the year ended October 30, 2011 and $2.76 per share for the year ended October 31, 2010. The number of shares issued under the ESPP during fiscal 2012, 2011 and 2010 was 7 million, 6 million and 5 million, respectively. At October 28, 2012, there were 47 million available for future issuance under the ESPP. Compensation expense is calculated using the fair value of the employees' purchase rights under the Black-Scholes model. Underlying assumptions used in the model for fiscal 2012, 2011 and 2010 are outlined in the following table:

ESPP:	2012	2011	2010
Dividend yield	3.01%	2.53%	2.44%
Expected volatility	29.6%	31.1%	33.3%
Risk-free interest rate	0.13%	0.09%	0.19%
Expected life (in years)	0.5	0.5	0.5

DEFERRED COMPENSATION PLANS

3.60 PRECISION CASTPARTS CORP. (APR)
NOTES TO CONSOLIDATED STATEMENTS

(In millions, except option share and per share data)

15. Stock-Based Compensation Plans (in part)

Deferred Compensation Plan

We have a deferred compensation plan whereby eligible executives may elect to defer up to 100% of their regular cash compensation and cash incentive awards, and non-employee Board members may elect to defer up to 100% of their cash compensation for Board service. The compensation deferred under this plan is credited with earnings and losses as determined by the rate of return on investments selected by the plan participants. Each participant is fully vested in all deferred compensation and those earnings that have been credited to their individual accounts. Our promise to pay amounts deferred under this plan is an unsecured obligation. Balances at April 1, 2012 and April 3, 2011 of approximately $66.5 million and $67.4 million, respectively, are reflected in pension and other postretirement benefit obligations in the Consolidated Balance Sheets.

One investment election of the deferred compensation plan is Phantom Stock Units, an investment that tracks the value of PCC common stock. Investments in Phantom Stock Units are permanent for the remaining period of employment at PCC. Effective March 20, 2009, the deferred compensation plan was amended such that payment of investments in Phantom Stock Units following retirement or termination of employment is made only in shares of PCC common stock. Under the amended plan, Phantom Stock Units are accounted for as equity awards. The stock based compensation expense is calculated at the date of purchase of Phantom Stock Units and recorded as additional paid in capital. At April 1, 2012 and April 3, 2011, there was $9.0 million and $8.3 million, respectively, of deferred compensation related to Phantom Stock Units included in additional paid-in capital. Phantom Stock Units for retirees receiving payments under the deferred compensation plan prior to March 20, 2009 continue to be accounted for as liability awards as they were grandfathered under the former plan. The change in market value of Phantom Stock Units accounted for as liability awards are recognized in the consolidated statement of income. We recognized expense of approximately $0.2 million, $0.3 million, and $0.8 million in fiscal 2012, 2011 and 2010, respectively.

The total amount of cash received from the exercise of stock options was $96.8 million, $93.3 million, and $67.4 million in fiscal 2012, 2011 and 2010, respectively. The related tax benefit was $38.1 million, $38.5 million, and $30.0 million in fiscal 2012, 2011 and 2010, respectively.

The outstanding options for stock incentive plan shares have expiration dates ranging from fiscal 2013 to fiscal 2022. At April 1, 2012, approximately 3,915,000 stock incentive plan shares were available for future grants.

There were approximately 215,000 shares issued under the 2008 ESPP during the year ended April 1, 2012. At April 1, 2012, there were approximately 1,735,000 shares available for issuance under the 2008 Employee Stock Purchase Plan.

The following table sets forth total stock-based compensation expense and related tax benefit recognized in the Consolidated Statements of Income:

Fiscal	2012	2011	2010
Cost of goods sold	$ 16.6	$ 16.9	$ 12.7
Selling and administrative expenses	31.8	30.4	28.4
Stock-based compensation expense before income taxes	48.4	47.3	41.1
Income tax benefit	(15.0)	(13.6)	(12.4)
Total stock-based compensation expense after income taxes	$ 33.4	$ 33.7	$ 28.7

No stock-based compensation expense was capitalized in fiscal 2012, 2011 or 2010 as it was not material. As of April 1, 2012, we had $89.3 million of total unrecognized stock-based compensation expense, net of estimated forfeitures, to be recognized over a weighted average period of 2.9 years.

The fair value of the stock-based awards, as determined under the Black-Scholes valuation model, was estimated using the weighted-average assumptions outlined below:

Fiscal	2012	2011	2010
Stock option plans:			
Risk-free interest rate	0.7%	1.0%	1.9%
Expected dividend yield	0.1%	0.1%	0.1%
Expected volatility	42.7%	44.0%	43.8%
Expected life (in years)	3.0–4.4	3.0–4.4	2.7–4.4
Employee Stock Purchase Plan:			
Risk-free interest rate	0.3%	0.4%	0.4%
Expected dividend yield	0.1%	0.1%	0.2%
Expected volatility	29.9%	38.4%	40.4%
Expected life (in years)	1.0	1.0	1.0

We use the U.S. Treasury (constant maturity) interest rate as the risk-free interest rate, and we use 4-year historical volatility for stock option plans and 1-year historical volatility for the Employee Stock Purchase Plan as the expected volatility. Our determination of expected terms and estimated pre-vesting forfeitures is based on an analysis of historical and expected patterns.

The weighted-average fair value of stock-based compensation awards granted and the intrinsic value of options exercised during the period were:

Fiscal	2012	2011	2010
Stock option plans:			
Grant date fair value per share	$ 55.81	$ 48.81	$37.25
Total fair value of awards granted	$ 56.4	$ 49.1	$51.8
Total intrinsic value of options exercised	$120.4	$119.4	$93.4
Employee Stock Purchase Plan:			
Grant date fair value per share	$ 36.95	$ 33.33	$21.68
Total fair value	$ 7.6	$ 8.2	$ 7.3

Additional information with respect to stock option activity is as follows:

	Option Shares	Weighted Average Exercise Price	Weighted Average Remaining Contractual Term (Years)	Aggregate Intrinsic Value (In Millions)
Outstanding at March 29, 2009	6,551,000	$ 62.67	7.29	$ 89.1
Granted	1,384,000	101.89		
Exercised	(1,618,000)	41.64		
Forfeited or expired	(266,000)	90.68		
Outstanding at March 28, 2010	6,051,000	76.21	7.42	303.0
Granted	1,005,000	137.27		
Exercised	(1,567,000)	59.51		
Forfeited or expired	(315,000)	97.45		
Outstanding at April 3, 2011	5,174,000	91.88	7.06	298.7
Granted	1,010,000	160.99		
Exercised	(1,323,000)	73.17		
Forfeited or expired	(126,000)	113.21		
Outstanding at April 1, 2012	4,735,000	111.29	7.29	291.7
Vested or expected to vest at April 3, 2011[1]	2,570,000	104.14	8.52	116.9
Vested or expected to vest at April 1, 2012[1]	2,382,000	126.45	8.47	110.7
Exercisable at April 3, 2011	2,346,000	76.39	5.28	171.8
Exercisable at April 1, 2012	2,113,000	90.97	5.77	173.1

[1] Represents outstanding options reduced by expected forfeitures.

INCENTIVE COMPENSATION PLANS

3.61 DOVER CORPORATION (DEC)
NOTES TO CONSOLIDATED FINANCIAL STATEMENTS

(Amounts in thousands except share data and where otherwise indicated)

12. Equity and Cash Incentive Program

2005 Equity and Cash Incentive Plan

The Company's share-based awards are typically granted annually at its regularly scheduled first quarter Compensation Committee meeting. For the years presented herein, employee awards were made pursuant to the terms of the Company's shareholder-approved 2005 Equity and Cash Incentive Plan (the "2005

Plan"). Under the 2005 Plan, a maximum aggregate of 20,000,000 shares was reserved for grants (non-qualified and incentive stock options, stock-settled stock appreciation rights ("SARs"), restricted stock, and performance share awards) to key personnel between February 1, 2005 and January 31, 2015, provided that no incentive stock options could be granted under the plan after February 11, 2014 and a maximum of 2,000,000 shares could be granted as restricted stock or performance share awards.

On May 3, 2012, the shareholders approved the Dover Corporation 2012 Equity and Cash Incentive Plan (the "2012 Plan"), to replace the 2005 Equity and Cash Incentive Plan, which otherwise would have terminated according to its terms on January 31, 2015, and the 1996 Non-Employee Directors Stock Compensation Plan (the "Directors Plan"), which would have otherwise terminated according to its terms on December 31, 2012. Upon approval of the 2012 Plan, no additional awards may be granted under the 2005 Plan. Officers and other key employees, as well as non-employee directors, are eligible to participate in the 2012 Plan, which has a ten year term and will terminate on May 3, 2022. The 2012 Plan provides for stock options and SARs grants, restricted stock awards, restricted stock unit awards, performance share awards, cash performance awards, directors' shares, and deferred stock units. Under the 2012 Plan, a total of 17,000,000 shares of common stock are reserved for issuance, subject to adjustments resulting from stock dividends, stock splits, recapitalizations, reorganizations, and other similar changes.

The exercise price per share for stock options and SARs is equal to the closing price of the Company's stock on the New York Stock Exchange on the date of grant. New common shares are issued when options or SARs are exercised. The period during which options and SARs are exercisable is fixed by the Company's Compensation Committee at the time of grant. Generally, the stock options or SARs vest after three years of service and expire at the end of ten years.

Stock-based compensation costs are reported within selling and administrative expenses. The following table summarizes the Company's compensation expense relating to all stock-based incentive plans:

	Years Ended December 31,		
	2012	2011	2010
Pre-tax compensation expense	$ 30,884	$ 25,130	$ 20,407
Tax benefit	(10,904)	(8,795)	(7,142)
Total stock-based compensation expense, net of tax	$ 19,980	$ 16,335	$ 13,265

SARs and Stock Options

In 2012, 2011, and 2010, the Company issued SARs covering 1,719,943, 1,524,329, and 2,304,574 shares, respectively, under the 2005 Plan. Since 2006, the Company has only issued SARs under the 2005 Plan and does not anticipate issuing stock options in the future. The fair value of each SAR grant was estimated on the date of grant using a Black-Scholes option-pricing model with the following assumptions:

	2012	2011	2010
Risk-free interest rate	1.05%	2.68%	2.77%
Dividend yield	2.03%	1.70%	2.33%
Expected life (years)	5.7	5.8	6.0
Volatility	36.41%	33.56%	31.93%
Grant price	$65.38	$66.59	$42.88
Fair value at date of grant	$18.51	$20.13	$11.66

Expected volatilities are based on Dover's stock price history, including implied volatilities from traded options on Dover stock. The Company uses historical data to estimate SAR exercise and employee termination patterns within the valuation model. The expected life of SARs granted is derived from the output of the option valuation model and represents the average period of time that SARs granted are expected to be outstanding. The interest rate for periods within the contractual life of the options is based on the U.S. Treasury yield curve in effect at the time of grant.

A summary of activity relating to SARs and stock options granted under the 2005 Plan and the predecessor plan for the year ended December 31, 2012 is as follows:

	SARs				Stock Options			
	Number of Shares	Weighted Average Exercise Price	Aggregate Intrinsic Value	Weighted Average Remaining Contractual Term (Years)	Number of Shares	Weighted Average Exercise Price	Aggregate Intrinsic Value	Weighted Average Remaining Contractual Term (Years)
Outstanding at 1/1/2012	9,393,634	$44.14			1,943,094	$36.96		
Granted	1,719,943	65.38			—	—		
Forfeited/expired	(194,943)	55.25			(14,122)	37.93		
Exercised	(2,367,026)	36.84			(1,204,566)	36.21		
Outstanding at 12/31/2012	8,551,608	50.17	$134,097	6.4	724,406	38.18	$19,941	1.5
Exercisable at 12/31/2012	3,431,600	$40.29	$ 87,227	4.3	724,406	$38.18	$19,941	1.5

The following table summarizes information about SAR and option awards outstanding that are vested and exercisable at December 31, 2012:

Range of Exercise Prices	SARs Outstanding			SARs Exercisable		
	Number of Shares	Weighted Average Exercise Price	Weighted Average Remaining Life In Years	Number of Shares	Weighted Average Exercise Price	Weighted Average Remaining Life In Years
$29.45–$35.50	1,229,923	$29.60	5.7	1,229,923	$29.60	5.7
$42.30–$46.00	3,468,269	43.32	5.5	1,439,583	43.95	3.7
$50.60–$66.59	3,853,416	62.91	7.5	762,094	50.64	3.2

Range of Exercise Prices	Stock Options Outstanding			Stock Options Exercisable		
	Number of Shares	Weighted Average Exercise Price	Weighted Average Remaining Life In Years	Number of Shares	Weighted Average Exercise Price	Weighted Average Remaining Life In Years
$24.50–$38.00	476,683	$36.60	1.8	476,683	$36.60	1.8
$38.50–$41.25	247,723	41.23	1.1	247,723	41.23	1.1

Unrecognized compensation expense related to SARs not yet exercisable was $27,722 at December 31, 2012. This cost is expected to be recognized over a weighted average period of 1.7 years.

The fair value of SARs which became exercisable during 2012, 2011, and 2010 was $16,484, $21,202, and $23,593, respectively. The aggregate intrinsic value of SARs exercised during 2012, 2011, and 2010 was $61,531, $24,322, and $1,083, respectively.

The aggregate intrinsic value of options exercised during 2012, 2011, and 2010 was $29,866, $24,726, and $28,699, respectively. Cash received by the Company for the exercise of options during 2012, 2011, and 2010 totaled $38,029, $26,519, and $66,962, respectively.

The company recognized tax benefits of $22,771, $8,752, and $6,466 during 2012, 2011, and 2010, respectively, for the exercise of SARs and stock options. These benefits have been recorded as an increase to additional paid-in capital and are reflected as financing cash inflows in the Consolidated Statements of Cash Flows.

Performance Share Awards

Performance share awards granted under the 2005 Plan, as amended in May of 2009, are being expensed over the three year period that is the requisite performance and service period. Awards shall become vested if (1) the Company achieves certain specified stock performance targets compared to a defined group of peer companies and (2) the employee remains continuously employed by the company during the performance period. Partial vesting may occur after separation from service in the case of certain terminations not for cause and for retirements.

In 2012, 2011, and 2010, the Company issued performance shares covering 50,416, 44,751, and 68,446 shares, respectively. The performance share awards are market condition awards and have been fair valued on the date of grant using the Monte Carlo simulation model (a binomial lattice-based valuation model) with the following assumptions:

	2012	2011	2010
Risk-free interest rate	0.37%	1.34%	1.37%
Dividend yield	2.03%	1.61%	2.38%
Expected life (years)	2.9	2.9	2.9
Volatility	34.10%	40.48%	39.98%
Fair value of performance award	$71.98	$91.41	$57.49

Expected volatilities are based on historical volatilities of each of the defined peer companies. The interest rate is based on the U.S. Treasury yield curve in effect at the time of grant.

A summary of activity for performance share awards for the year ended December 31, 2012 is as follows:

	Number of Shares	Weighted-Average Grant-Date Fair Value
Unvested at December 31, 2011	113,197	$57.23
Granted	50,416	71.98
Vested*	(68,446)	57.49
Unvested at December 31, 2012	95,167	$81.12

* Under the terms of the performance share award, the actual number of shares awarded can range from zero to 200% of the original target grant, depending on Dover's three-year performance relative to the peer group for the relevant performance period. Awards vesting at the end of 2012, as shown above, are expected to be paid out at approximately 158% of their original target.

Unrecognized compensation expense related to unvested performance shares as of December 31, 2012 was $3,525, which will be recognized over a weighted average period of 1.6 years.

The Company also has restricted stock authorized for grant (as part of the 2005 Plan), under which common stock of the Company may be granted at no cost to certain officers and key employees. In general, restrictions limit the sale or transfer of these shares during a two or three year period, and restrictions lapse proportionately over the two or three year period. The Company granted 55,200 and 15,500 restricted shares in 2011 and 2010, respectively. No restricted shares were granted in 2012.

The Company issued the following shares to its non-employee directors during 2012 under the 2012 Plan and during 2011 and 2010 under the Directors' Plan as partial compensation for serving as directors of the Company:

| | Years Ended December 31, | | |
	2012	2011	2010
Aggregate shares granted	20,344	20,929	20,853
Shares withheld to satisfy tax obligations	(544)	(562)	(574)
Net shares granted	19,800	20,367	20,279

EMPLOYEE STOCK OWNERSHIP PLANS (ESOP)

3.62 THE SHERWIN-WILLIAMS COMPANY (DEC)
NOTES TO CONSOLIDATED FINANCIAL STATEMENTS

(Thousands of dollars unless otherwise indicated)

Note 1—Significant Accounting Policies (in part)

Employee Stock Purchase and Savings Plan and preferred stock. The Company accounts for the Employee Stock Purchase and Savings Plan (ESOP) in accordance with the Employee Stock Ownership Plans Subtopic of the Compensation—Stock Ownership Topic of the ASC. The Company recognized compensation expense for amounts contributed to the ESOP, and the ESOP used dividends on unallocated preferred shares to service debt. Unallocated preferred shares held by the ESOP were not considered outstanding in calculating earnings per share of the Company. See Note 11.

Note 9—Litigation (in part)

2012 Subsequent Event—DOL Settlement. On February 20, 2013, the Company reached a settlement with the DOL of the previously disclosed investigation of transactions related to the ESOP that were implemented on August 1, 2006 and August 27, 2003. The DOL had notified the Company, certain current and former directors of the Company and the ESOP trustee of potential enforcement claims asserting breaches of fiduciary obligations. The DOL sought compensatory and equitable remedies, including monetary damages to the ESOP for alleged losses to the ESOP relating to third-party valuation of the Company's convertible serial preferred stock. The Company believes that the DOL's claims are subject to meritorious defenses, however, the Company's management and Board of Directors have decided that it would be in the best interest of the Company and its shareholders to avoid potentially costly litigation and enter into this settlement to resolve these claims.

The Company agreed to resolve all ESOP related claims with the DOL by making a one-time payment of $80,000 to the ESOP and has recorded a $49,163 after tax charge to earnings. In accordance with U.S. generally accepted accounting principles, the Company is required to recognize this subsequent event in its 2012 fiscal year results since this subsequent event is related to conditions that existed at the balance sheet date of December 31, 2012. The Company's financial results for the quarter and year ended December 31, 2012, which were set forth in the Company's earnings release issued on January 31, 2013 and furnished on the Company's Current Report on Form 8-K dated January 31, 2013, have been revised and furnished on the Company's Current Report on Form 8-K dated February 20, 2013 to reflect this subsequent event. As a result of recording this accrual in the Administrative segment, Cost of goods sold increased $16,000 and Selling, general and administrative expense increased $64,000 while income tax expense decreased $30,837 and diluted net income per common share decreased $.47 per share for both the quarter and year ended December 31, 2012.

Note 11—Stock Purchase Plan and Preferred Stock

As of December 31, 2012, 28,256 employees contributed to the Company's ESOP, a voluntary defined contribution plan available to all eligible salaried employees. Participants are allowed to contribute, on a pretax or after-tax basis, up to the lesser of twenty percent of their annual compensation or the maximum dollar amount allowed under the Internal Revenue Code. Prior to July 1, 2009, the Company matched one hundred percent of all contributions up to six percent of eligible employee contributions. Effective July 1, 2009, the ESOP was amended to change the Company match to one hundred percent on the first three percent of eligible employee contributions and fifty percent on the next two percent of eligible contributions. Effective July 1, 2011, the ESOP was amended to reinstate the Company match up to six percent of eligible employee contributions. Such participant contributions may be invested in a variety of investment funds or a Company common stock fund and may be exchanged between investments as directed by the participant. Participants are permitted to diversify both future and prior Company matching contributions previously allocated to the Company common stock fund into a variety of investment funds.

The Company made contributions to the ESOP on behalf of participating employees, representing amounts authorized by employees to be withheld from their earnings, of $88,363, $79,266 and $70,601 in 2012, 2011 and 2010, respectively. The Company's matching contributions to the ESOP charged to operations were $142,791, $48,816 and $37,894 for 2012, 2011 and 2010, respectively. The 2012 Company contributions include $80,000 related to the DOL Settlement. See Note 9 for additional information on the DOL Settlement.

At December 31, 2012, there were 14,616,378 shares of the Company's common stock being held by the ESOP, representing 14.2 percent of the total number of voting shares outstanding. Shares of Company common stock credited to each member's account under the ESOP are voted by the trustee under instructions from each individual plan member. Shares for which no instructions are received are voted by the trustee in the same proportion as those for which instructions are received.

On August 1, 2006, the Company issued 500,000 shares of convertible serial preferred stock, no par value (Series 2 Preferred stock) with cumulative quarterly dividends of $11.25 per share, for $500,000 to the ESOP. The ESOP financed the acquisition of the Series 2 Preferred stock by borrowing $500,000 from the Company at the rate of 5.5 percent per annum. This borrowing is payable over ten years in equal quarterly installments. Each share of Series 2 Preferred stock is entitled to one vote upon all matters presented to the Company's shareholders and generally votes with the common stock together as one class. The Series 2 Preferred stock is held by the ESOP in an unallocated account. As the value of compensation expense related to contributions to the ESOP is earned, the Company has the option of funding the ESOP by redeeming a portion of the preferred stock or with cash. Contributions are credited to the members' accounts at the time of funding. The Series 2 Preferred stock is redeemable for cash or convertible into common stock or any combination thereof at the option of the ESOP based on the relative fair value of the Series 2 Preferred and common stock at the time of conversion. At December 31, 2012, 2011 and 2010, there were no allocated or committed-to-be released shares of Series 2 Preferred stock outstanding. In 2012, the Company redeemed 59,187 shares of the Series 2 Preferred stock for cash. In 2011, the Company redeemed 56,480 shares of the Series 2 Preferred stock for cash. In 2010, the Company elected to fund the ESOP with cash. The fair value of the Series 2 Preferred stock is based on a conversion/redemption formula outlined in the preferred stock terms and was $210,773, $328,495 and $411,655 at December 31, 2012, 2011, and 2010 respectively.

PROFIT SHARING PLANS

3.63 CITIGROUP INC. (DEC)
NOTES TO CONSOLIDATED FINANCIAL STATEMENTS

8. Incentive Plans (in part)

Profit Sharing Plan

In October 2010, the Committee approved awards under the 2010 Key Employee Profit Sharing Plan (KEPSP), which may entitle participants to profit-sharing payments based on an initial performance measurement period of January 1, 2010 through December 31, 2012. Generally, if a participant remains employed and all other conditions to vesting and payment are satisfied, the participant will be entitled to an initial payment in 2013, as well as a holdback payment in 2014 that may be reduced based on performance during the subsequent holdback period (generally, January 1, 2013 through December 31, 2013). If the vesting and performance conditions are satisfied, a participant's initial payment will equal two-thirds of the product of the cumulative pretax income of Citicorp (as defined in the KEPSP) for the initial performance period and the participant's applicable percentage. The initial payment will be paid after January 20, 2013 but no later than March 15, 2013.

The participant's holdback payment, if any, will equal the product of (i) the lesser of cumulative pretax income of Citicorp for the initial performance period and cumulative pretax income of Citicorp for the initial performance period and the holdback period combined (generally, January 1, 2010 through December 31, 2013), and (ii) the participant's applicable percentage, less the initial payment; provided that the holdback payment may not be less than zero. The holdback payment, if any, will be paid after January 20, 2014 but no later than March 15, 2014. The holdback payment, if any, will be credited with notional interest during the holdback period. It is intended that the initial payment and holdback payment will be paid in cash; however, awards may be paid in Citigroup common stock if required by regulatory authority. Regulators have required that U.K. participants receive at least 50% of their initial payment and at least 50% of their holdback payment, if any, in shares of Citigroup common stock that will be subject to a six-month sales restriction. Clawbacks apply to the award.

Independent risk function employees were not eligible to participate in the KEPSP, as the independent risk function participates in the determination of whether payouts will be made under the KEPSP. Instead, key employees in the independent risk function were eligible to receive deferred cash retention awards, which vest two-thirds on January 20, 2013 and one-third on January 20, 2014. The deferred cash awards incentivize key risk employees to contribute to the Company's long-term profitability by ensuring that the Company's risk profile is properly aligned with its long-term strategies, objectives and risk appetite, thereby, aligning the employees' interests with those of Company shareholders.

On February 14, 2011, the Committee approved grants of awards under the 2011 KEPSP to certain executive officers, and on May 17, 2011 to the then-CEO Vikram Pandit. These awards have a performance period of January 1, 2011 to December 31, 2012 and other terms of the awards are similar to the 2010 KEPSP. The KEPSP award granted to Mr. Pandit was cancelled upon his resignation in October 2012.

Expense recognized in 2012 in respect of the KEPSP was $246 million.

Depreciation Expense

RECOGNITION AND MEASUREMENT

3.64 FASB ASC 360, *Property, Plant, and Equipment,* defines *depreciation accounting* (the process of allocating the cost of productive facilities over the expected useful lives of the facilities) as a system of accounting that aims to distribute the cost or other basic value of tangible capital assets, less salvage (if any), over the estimated useful life of the unit, which may be a group of assets, in a systematic and rational manner. It is a process of allocation, not valuation.

3.65 FASB ASC 250 requires that a change in depreciation, amortization, or depletion method for long-lived, nonfinancial assets be accounted for as a change in accounting estimate effected by a change in accounting principle. Changes in accounting estimate are accounted for prospectively, not retrospectively as is required for changes in accounting principle.

DISCLOSURE

3.66 FASB ASC 360 stipulates that both the amount of depreciation expense and method(s) of depreciation should be disclosed in the financial statements or notes thereto.

PRESENTATION AND DISCLOSURE EXCERPTS

STRAIGHT-LINE AND ACCELERATED METHOD

3.67 BALL CORPORATION (DEC)
CONSOLIDATED STATEMENTS OF EARNINGS (in part)

	Years Ended December 31,		
($ in millions, except per share amounts)	**2012**	**2011**	**2010**
Net sales	$ 8,735.7	$ 8,630.9	$ 7,630.0
Costs and expenses			
Cost of sales (excluding depreciation and amortization)	(7,174.0)	(7,081.2)	(6,254.1)
Depreciation and amortization	(282.9)	(301.1)	(265.5)
Selling, general and administrative	(385.5)	(381.4)	(356.8)
Business consolidation and other activities	(102.8)	(30.3)	11.0
	(7,945.2)	(7,794.0)	(6,865.4)
Earnings before interest and taxes	790.5	836.9	764.6

NOTES TO THE CONSOLIDATED FINANCIAL STATEMENTS

1. Critical and Significant Accounting Policies (in part)

Depreciation and Amortization (in part)

Property, plant and equipment are carried at the cost of acquisition or construction and depleted over the estimated useful lives of the assets. Assets are depreciated and amortized using the straight-line method over their estimated useful lives, generally 5 to 40 years for buildings and improvements and 2 to 20 years for machinery and equipment. Finite-lived intangible assets, including capitalized software costs, are generally amortized over their estimated useful lives of 3 to 23 years.

During 2012, the company utilized a third party appraiser to assist in the evaluation of the estimated useful lives of its drawn and ironed container and related end production equipment used to make beverage containers and ends and two-piece food containers. This evaluation was performed as a result of the global alignment of the company's use and maintenance practices for this equipment and the company's experience with the duration over which this equipment can be utilized. As a result, the company has revised the estimated useful lives of this type of equipment utilized throughout the company, which resulted in a net reduction in depreciation expense and cost of sales of $34.9 million ($22.3 million after tax, or $0.14 per diluted share) for the year ended December 31, 2012, as compared to the amount of depreciation expense and cost of sales that would have been recognized by utilizing the prior depreciable lives. The company has also evaluated its estimates of the accounting for tooling, spare parts and dunnage, as well as the related obsolescence, and aligned its practices for all operations, resulting in a one-time increase in cost of sales and depreciation expense of $11.0 million ($6.7 million after tax, or $0.04 per diluted share) for the year ended December 31, 2012, primarily attributable to the immediate recognition of expense as items are placed in service.

Effective January 1, 2012, the company changed the presentation of capitalized software in its consolidated statements of earnings to classify such assets as intangible assets rather than property, plant and equipment. As a result, the amounts included in the consolidated balance sheet in intangibles and other assets, net of accumulated amortization, were $50.4 million and $45.2 million as of December 31, 2012 and December 31, 2011, respectively. Capitalized software amounts that were previously reported as depreciation have been reclassified to amortization for all years presented in the statements of earnings and cash flows, as well as in the notes to the consolidated statements of earnings.

3.68 THE BOEING COMPANY (DEC)
NOTES TO THE CONSOLIDATED FINANCIAL STATEMENTS

(Dollars in millions, except per share data)

Note 1—Summary of Significant Accounting Policies (in part)

Property, Plant and Equipment (in part)

Property, plant and equipment are recorded at cost, including applicable construction-period interest, less accumulated depreciation and are depreciated principally over the following estimated useful lives: new buildings and land improvements, from 10 to 40 years; and new machinery and equipment, from 3 to 20 years. The principal methods of depreciation are as follows: buildings and land improvements, 150% declining balance; and machinery and equipment, sum-of-the-years' digits. Capitalized internal use software is included in Other assets and amortized using the straight line method over 5 years. We periodically evaluate the appropriateness of remaining depreciable lives assigned to long-lived assets, including assets that may be subject to a management plan for disposition.

Long-lived assets held for sale are stated at the lower of cost or fair value less cost to sell. Long-lived assets held for use are subject to an impairment assessment whenever events or changes in circumstances indicate that the carrying amount may not be recoverable. If the carrying value is no longer recoverable based upon the undiscounted future cash flows of the asset, the amount of the impairment is the difference between the carrying amount and the fair value of the asset.

Note 9—Property, Plant and Equipment (in part)

Property, plant and equipment at December 31 consisted of the following:

	2012	2011
Land	$ 531	$ 526
Buildings and land improvements	10,696	10,285
Machinery and equipment	11,847	11,353
Construction in progress	1,231	1,142
Gross property, plant and equipment	24,305	23,306
Less accumulated depreciation	(14,645)	(13,993)
Total	$ 9,660	$ 9,313

Depreciation expense was $1,248, $1,119 and $1,096 for the years ended December 31, 2012, 2011 and 2010, respectively. Interest capitalized during the years ended December 31, 2012, 2011 and 2010 totaled $74, $57 and $48, respectively.

UNITS-OF-PRODUCTION METHOD

3.69 ANADARKO PETROLEUM CORPORATION (DEC)
CONSOLIDATED STATEMENTS OF INCOME (in part)

	Years Ended December 31,		
(Millions except per-share amounts)	2012	2011	2010
Revenues and Other			
Natural-gas sales	$ 2,444	$ 3,300	$ 3,420
Oil and condensate sales	8,728	8,072	5,592
Natural-gas liquids sales	1,224	1,462	997
Gathering, processing, and marketing sales	911	1,048	833
Gains (losses) on divestitures and other, net	104	85	142
Total	13,411	13,967	10,984

(continued)

(Millions except per-share amounts)	Years Ended December 31,		
	2012	2011	2010
Costs and Expenses			
Oil and gas operating	$ 976	$ 993	$ 830
Oil and gas transportation and other	955	891	816
Exploration	1,946	1,076	974
Gathering, processing, and marketing	763	791	615
General and administrative	1,246	1,060	967
Depreciation, depletion, and amortization	3,964	3,830	3,714
Other taxes	1,224	1,492	1,068
Impairments	389	1,774	216
Algeria exceptional profits tax settlement	(1,797)	—	—
Deepwater Horizon settlement and related costs	18	3,930	15
Total	9,684	15,837	9,215
Operating income (Loss)	3,727	(1,870)	1,769

NOTES TO CONSOLIDATED FINANCIAL STATEMENTS

1. Summary of Significant Accounting Policies (in part)

Properties and Equipment. Properties and equipment are stated at cost less accumulated depreciation, depletion, and amortization expense (DD&A). Costs of improvements that appreciably improve the efficiency or productive capacity of existing properties or extend their lives are capitalized. Maintenance and repairs are expensed as incurred. Upon retirement or sale, the cost of properties and equipment, net of the related accumulated DD&A, is removed and, if appropriate, gain or loss is recognized in gains (losses) on divestitures and other, net.

Depreciation, Depletion, and Amortization. Costs of drilling and equipping successful wells, costs to construct or acquire facilities other than offshore platforms, associated asset retirement costs, and capital lease assets used in oil and gas activities are depreciated using the unit-of-production (UOP) method based on total estimated proved developed oil and gas reserves. Costs of acquiring proved properties, including leasehold acquisition costs transferred from unproved properties and costs to construct or acquire offshore platforms and associated asset retirement costs, are depleted using the UOP method based on total estimated proved developed and undeveloped reserves. Mineral properties are also depleted using the UOP method. All other properties are stated at historical acquisition cost, net of impairments, and are depreciated using the straight-line method over the useful lives of the assets, which range from 3 to 15 years for furniture and equipment, up to 40 years for buildings, and up to 47 years for gathering facilities.

COMPOSITE METHOD OF DEPRECIATION

3.70 VALERO ENERGY CORPORATION (DEC)
CONSOLIDATED STATEMENTS OF INCOME (in part)

(Millions of Dollars, Except per Share Amounts)

	Year Ended December 31,		
	2012	2011	2010
Operating revenues[a]	$139,250	$125,987	$82,233
Costs and expenses:			
Cost of sales	127,268	115,719	74,458
Operating expenses:			
Refining	3,668	3,406	2,944
Retail	686	678	654
Ethanol	332	399	363
General and administrative expenses	698	571	531
Depreciation and amortization expense	1,574	1,534	1,405
Asset impairment losses	1,014	—	2
Total costs and expenses	135,240	122,307	80,357
Operating income	4,010	3,680	1,876

NOTES TO CONSOLIDATED FINANCIAL STATEMENTS

1. Basis of Presentation and Summary of Significant Accounting Policies (in part)

Significant Accounting Policies (in part)

Property, Plant and Equipment

The cost of property, plant and equipment (property assets) purchased or constructed, including betterments of property assets, is capitalized. However, the cost of repairs to and normal maintenance of property assets is expensed as incurred. Betterments of property assets are those which extend the useful life, increase the capacity or improve the operating efficiency of the asset, or improve the safety of our operations. The cost of property assets constructed includes interest and certain overhead costs allocable to the construction activities.

Our operations, especially those of our refining segment, are highly capital intensive. Each of our refineries comprises a large base of property assets, consisting of a series of interconnected, highly integrated and interdependent crude oil processing facilities and supporting logistical infrastructure (Units), and these Units are continuously improved. Improvements consist of the addition of new Units and betterments of existing Units. We plan for these improvements by developing a multi-year capital program that is updated and revised based on changing internal and external factors.

Depreciation of property assets used in our refining segment is recorded on a straight-line basis over the estimated useful lives of these assets primarily using the composite method of depreciation. We maintain a separate composite group of property assets for each of our refineries. We estimate the useful life of each group based on an evaluation of the property assets comprising the group, and such evaluations consist of, but are not limited to, the physical inspection of the assets to determine their condition, consideration of the manner in which the assets are maintained, assessment of the need to replace assets, and evaluation of the manner in which improvements impact the useful life of the group. The estimated useful lives of our composite groups range primarily from 25 to 30 years.

Under the composite method of depreciation, the cost of an improvement is added to the composite group to which it relates and is depreciated over that group's estimated useful life. We design improvements to our refineries in accordance with engineering specifications, design standards and practices accepted in our industry, and these improvements have design lives consistent with our estimated useful lives. Therefore, we believe the use of the group life to depreciate the cost of improvements made to the group is reasonable because the estimated useful life of each improvement is consistent with that of the group. It should be noted, however, that factors such as competition, regulation, or environmental matters could cause us to change our estimates, thus impacting depreciation expense in the future.

Also under the composite method of depreciation, the historical cost of a minor property asset (net of salvage value) that is retired or replaced is charged to accumulated depreciation and no gain or loss is recognized in income. However, a gain or loss is recognized in income for a major property asset that is retired, replaced or sold and for an abnormal disposition of a property asset (primarily involuntary conversions). Gains and losses are reflected in depreciation and amortization expense, unless such amounts are reported separately due to materiality.

Depreciation of property assets used in our retail and ethanol segments is recorded on a straight-line basis over the estimated useful lives of the related assets. Leasehold improvements and assets acquired under capital leases are amortized using the straight-line method over the shorter of the lease term or the estimated useful life of the related asset.

7. Property, Plant and Equipment

Major classes of property, plant and equipment, which include capital lease assets, consisted of the following (in millions):

	December 31,	
	2012	2011
Land	$ 802	$ 722
Crude oil processing facilities	24,865	23,322
Pipeline and terminal facilities	1,471	856
Grain processing equipment	694	673
Retail facilities	1,480	1,346
Administrative buildings	734	712
Other	1,457	1,290
Construction in progress	2,629	3,332
Property, plant and equipment, at cost	34,132	32,253
Accumulated depreciation	(7,832)	(7,076)
Property, plant and equipment, net	$26,300	$25,177

We have miscellaneous assets under capital leases that primarily support our refining operations totaling $83 million and $77 million as of December 31, 2012 and 2011, respectively. Accumulated amortization on assets under capital leases was $35 million and $26 million, respectively, as of December 31, 2012 and 2011.

Depreciation expense for the years ended December 31, 2012, 2011, and 2010 was $1.1 billion, $1.1 billion, and $985 million, respectively.

Income Taxes

RECOGNITION AND MEASUREMENT

3.71 FASB ASC 740, *Income Taxes*, clarifies the accounting for tax positions in an entity's financial statements. FASB ASC 740 prescribes a more-likely-than-not recognition threshold and measurement attribute for the financial statement recognition and measurement of a tax position taken or expected to be taken. Under FASB ASC 740, tax positions will be evaluated for recognition, derecognition, and measurement using consistent criteria. In addition, FASB ASC 740 provides guidance on classification and disclosure. FASB ASC 740 requires, except in certain specified situations, that undistributed earnings of a subsidiary included in consolidated income be accounted for as a temporary difference. Finally, the provisions of FASB ASC 740 provide more information about the uncertainty in income tax assets and liabilities.

DISCLOSURE

3.72 FASB ASC 740 sets forth standards for financial presentation and disclosure of income tax liabilities or assets and expense. These requirements vary for public and nonpublic entities. FASB ASC 740 states that amounts and expiration dates of operating loss and tax credit carryforwards for tax purposes should be disclosed. Any portion of the valuation allowance for deferred tax assets for which subsequently recognized tax benefits will be credited directly to contributed capital should also be disclosed. An entity's temporary difference and carryforward information requires additional disclosure, which differs for public and nonpublic entities.

PRESENTATION AND DISCLOSURE EXCERPTS

EXPENSE PROVISION

3.73 YAHOO! INC. (DEC)

CONSOLIDATED STATEMENTS OF INCOME (in part)

	Years Ended December 31,		
(In thousands, except per share amounts)	2010	2011	2012
Revenue	$6,324,651	$4,984,199	$ 4,986,566
Operating expenses:			
Cost of revenue—Traffic acquisition costs	1,736,423	603,371	518,906
Cost of revenue—Other	945,651	983,626	1,101,660
Sales and marketing	1,263,992	1,122,193	1,101,572
Product development	1,028,716	919,368	885,824
General and administrative	487,762	497,288	540,247
Amortization of intangibles	31,626	33,592	35,819
Restructuring charges, net	57,957	24,420	236,170
Total operating expenses	5,552,127	4,183,858	4,420,198
Income from operations	772,524	800,341	566,368
Other income, net	297,869	27,175	4,647,839
Income before income taxes and earnings in equity interests	1,070,393	827,516	5,214,207
Provision for income taxes	(221,523)	(241,767)	(1,940,043)
Earnings in equity interests	395,758	476,920	676,438
Net income	1,244,628	1,062,669	3,950,602

NOTES TO CONSOLIDATED FINANCIAL STATEMENTS

Note 1 The Company and Summary of Significant Accounting Policies (in part)

Income Taxes. Deferred income taxes are determined based on the differences between the financial reporting and tax bases of assets and liabilities and are measured using the currently enacted tax rates and laws. The Company records a valuation allowance against particular deferred income tax assets if it is more likely than not that those assets will not be realized. The provision for income taxes comprises the Company's current tax liability and change in deferred income tax assets and liabilities.

Significant judgment is required in evaluating the Company's uncertain tax positions and determining its provision for income taxes. The Company establishes reserves for tax-related uncertainties based on estimates of whether, and the extent to which, additional taxes will be due. These reserves are established when the Company believes that certain positions might be challenged despite its belief that its tax return positions are in accordance with applicable tax laws. The Company adjusts these reserves in light of changing facts and circumstances, such as the closing of a tax audit, new tax legislation, or the change of an estimate. To the extent that the final tax outcome of these matters is different than the amounts recorded, such differences will affect the provision for income taxes in the period in which such determination is made. The provision for income taxes includes the effect of reserve provisions and changes to reserves that are considered appropriate, as well as the related net interest and penalties. Income taxes paid were $232 million, $96 million, and $2.3 billion in the years ended December 31, 2010, 2011, and 2012, respectively. Interest paid was not material in any of the years presented. See Note 15—"Income Taxes" for additional information.

Note 15 Income Taxes (in part)

The components of income before income taxes and earnings in equity interests are as follows (in thousands):

| | Years Ended December 31, | | |
	2010	2011	2012
United States	$ 872,042	$533,262	$5,056,643
Foreign	198,351	294,254	157,564
Income before income taxes and earnings in equity interests	$1,070,393	$827,516	$5,214,207

The provision for income taxes is composed of the following (in thousands):

| | Years Ended December 31, | | |
	2010	2011	2012
Current:			
United States federal	$ 26,342	$141,922	$2,278,759
State	39,258	(11,037)	361,788
Foreign	43,341	40,490	68,816
Total current provision for income taxes	108,941	171,375	2,709,363
Deferred:			
United States federal	67,621	77,012	(741,628)
State	37,438	(4,437)	(29,470)
Foreign	7,523	(2,183)	1,778
Total deferred provision (benefit) for income taxes	112,582	70,392	(769,320)
Provision for income taxes	$221,523	$241,767	$1,940,043

The provision for income taxes differs from the amount computed by applying the federal statutory income tax rate to income before income taxes and earnings in equity interests as follows (in thousands):

| | Years Ended December 31, | | |
	2010	2011	2012
Income tax at the U.S. federal statutory rate of 35 percent	$ 374,638	$289,630	$1,824,973
State income taxes, net of federal benefit	54,268	4,627	237,637
Change in valuation allowance	(1,315)	(5,975)	(82)
Stock-based compensation expense	4,404	18,213	17,703
Research tax credits	(10,345)	(10,499)	—
Effect of non-U.S. operations	(17,344)	(42,806)	(135,753)
Resolution with tax authorities	(159,168)	(14,685)	(4,711)
Tax gain in excess of book gain from sales of Zimbra, Inc. and HotJobs due to basis differences	23,184	—	—
Tax restructuring	(43,361)	—	—
Other	(3,438)	3,262	276
Provision for income taxes	$ 221,523	$241,767	$1,940,043

Significant variances year over year as shown above are further explained as follows:
- In 2012, the Company made a one-time distribution of foreign earnings resulting in an overall net benefit of approximately $117 million. The benefit is primarily due to excess foreign tax credits. Of the $117 million, $102 million is included above within "effect of non-U.S. operations."
- State taxes were higher in 2010 due to a reduction of deferred tax assets associated with an effective tax rate reduction in California that started in 2011.
- In 2010, the Company had a favorable resolution of certain issues in an IRS examination of its 2005 and 2006 U.S. federal income tax returns resulting in a reduction of reserves for tax uncertainties and the availability of capital loss carryforwards to offset the tax on the gain from the sales of Zimbra, Inc. and HotJobs.
- During 2010, in connection with tax restructuring activities, the Company reached a formal agreement with the IRS through a pre-filing agreement to treat certain intercompany bad debts as deductible business expenses on the 2009 federal income tax return.

3.74 PERKINELMER, INC. (DEC)

CONSOLIDATED STATEMENTS OF OPERATIONS (in part)

For the Fiscal Years Ended

(In thousands, except per share data)	December 30, 2012	January 1, 2012 (As adjusted)	January 2, 2011
Revenue			
Product revenue	$1,474,674	$1,319,510	$1,161,742
Service revenue	640,531	598,998	540,025
Total revenue	2,115,205	1,918,508	1,701,767
Cost of product revenue	762,989	686,812	609,217
Cost of service revenue	389,010	383,896	333,895
Selling, general and administrative expenses	632,734	624,393	487,313
Research and development expenses	132,639	115,821	94,811
Restructuring and contract termination charges, net	25,137	13,452	18,963
Impairment of assets	74,153	3,006	—
Operating income from continuing operations	98,543	91,128	157,568
Interest and other expense (income), net	47,956	26,774	(8,383)
Income from continuing operations before income taxes	50,587	64,354	165,951
(Benefit from) provision for income taxes	(17,854)	63,182	27,043
Income from continuing operations	68,441	1,172	138,908
Income from discontinued operations before income taxes	—	—	30,772
Gain on disposition of discontinued operations before income taxes	2,405	1,999	317,896
Provision for (benefit from) income taxes on discontinued operations and dispositions	906	(4,484)	96,593
Income from discontinued operations and dispositions	1,499	6,483	252,075
Net income	$ 69,940	$ 7,655	$ 390,983

NOTES TO CONSOLIDATED FINANCIAL STATEMENTS

Note 1: Nature of Operations and Accounting Policies (in part)

Income Taxes: The Company uses the asset and liability method of accounting for income taxes. Under the asset and liability method, deferred tax assets and liabilities are recognized for the estimated future tax consequences attributable to differences between the financial statement carrying amounts of assets and liabilities and their respective tax bases. This method also requires the recognition of future tax benefits such as net operating loss carryforwards, to the extent that realization of such benefits is more likely than not. Deferred tax assets and liabilities are measured using enacted tax rates expected to apply to taxable income in the fiscal years in which those temporary differences are expected to be recovered or settled. A valuation allowance is established for any deferred tax asset for which realization is not more likely than not. With respect to earnings expected to be indefinitely reinvested offshore, the Company does not accrue tax for the repatriation of such foreign earnings.

The Company provides reserves for potential payments of tax to various tax authorities related to uncertain tax positions and other issues. These reserves are based on a determination of whether and how much of a tax benefit taken by the Company in its tax filings or positions is more likely than not to be realized following resolution of any potential contingencies present related to the tax benefit. Potential interest and penalties associated with such uncertain tax positions is recorded as a component of income tax expense. See Note 6, below, for additional details.

Note 6: Income Taxes (in part)

The Company regularly reviews its tax positions in each significant taxing jurisdiction in the process of evaluating its unrecognized tax benefits. The Company makes adjustments to its unrecognized tax benefits when: (i) facts and circumstances regarding a tax position change, causing a change in management's judgment regarding that tax position; (ii) a tax position is effectively settled with a tax authority at a differing amount; and/or (iii) the statute of limitations expires regarding a tax position.

The tabular reconciliation of the total amounts of unrecognized tax benefits is as follows for the fiscal years ended:

(In thousands)	December 30, 2012	January 1, 2012	January 2, 2011
Unrecognized tax benefits, beginning of period	$51,740	$39,226	$ 39,431
Gross increases—tax positions in prior period	10,653	2,753	13,314
Gross decreases—tax positions in prior period	(4,665)	(4,729)	(11,190)
Gross increases—current-period tax positions	3,343	2,451	2,503
Gross increases—related to acquisitions	—	14,412	80
Settlements	(2,822)	(430)	(2,035)
Lapse of statute of limitations	(595)	(2,224)	(2,054)
Foreign currency translation adjustments	456	281	(823)
Unrecognized tax benefits, end of period	$58,110	$51,740	$ 39,226

The Company classifies interest and penalties as a component of income tax expense. At December 30, 2012, the Company had accrued interest and penalties of approximately $7.9 million and $4.0 million, respectively. During fiscal year 2012, the Company recognized a charge of approximately $1.1 million for interest and a benefit of $2.2 million for penalties in its total tax provision. During fiscal year 2011, the Company recognized interest and penalties of approximately $0.5 million and zero, respectively, in its total tax provision. During fiscal year 2010, the Company recognized interest and penalties of approximately $0.8 million and $0.9 million, respectively, in its total tax provision. At December 30, 2012, the Company had gross tax effected unrecognized tax benefits of $58.1 million, of which $51.1 million, if recognized, would affect the continuing operations effective tax rate. The remaining amount, if recognized, would affect discontinued operations.

The Company believes that it is reasonably possible that $13.2 million of its uncertain tax positions at December 30, 2012, including accrued interest and penalties, and net of tax benefits, may be recognized within the next year as a result of an aggregate $8.4 million lapse in the statute of limitations and settlements of $4.8 million. Tax years after 2005 remain open to examination by various tax jurisdictions in which the Company has significant business operations, such as Singapore, China, Finland, Germany, Netherlands, the United Kingdom, Italy and the United States. The tax years under examination vary by jurisdiction.

The components of (loss) income from continuing operations before income taxes were as follows for the fiscal years ended:

(In thousands)	December 30, 2012	January 1, 2012	January 2, 2011
U.S.	$(118,546)	$(145,298)	$ (22,014)
Non-U.S.	169,133	209,652	187,965
Total	$ 50,587	$ 64,354	$165,951

On a U. S. income tax basis, the Company has reported significant taxable income over the three year period ended December 30, 2012. The Company has utilized tax attributes to minimize cash taxes paid on that taxable income.

The components of the provision for (benefit from) income taxes for continuing operations were as follows:

(In thousands)	Current	Deferred Expense (Benefit)	Total
Fiscal year ended December 30, 2012			
Federal	$ (5,234)	$(34,920)	$(40,154)
State	2,617	(2,794)	(177)
Non-U.S.	50,314	(27,837)	22,477
Total	$47,697	$(65,551)	$(17,854)
Fiscal year ended January 1, 2012			
Federal	$18,309	$ 8,615	$ 26,924
State	3,397	(4,583)	(1,186)
Non-U.S.	41,765	(4,321)	37,444
Total	$63,471	$ (289)	$ 63,182
Fiscal year ended January 2, 2011			
Federal	$ 6,499	$(15,916)	$ (9,417)
State	6,772	(2,988)	3,784
Non-U.S.	38,267	(5,591)	32,676
Total	$51,538	$(24,495)	$ 27,043

The total provision for income taxes included in the consolidated financial statements is as follows for the fiscal years ended:

(In thousands)	December 30, 2012	January 1, 2012	January 2, 2011
Continuing operations	$(17,854)	$63,182	$ 27,043
Discontinued operations	906	(4,484)	96,593
Total	$(16,948)	$58,698	$123,636

A reconciliation of income tax expense at the U.S. federal statutory income tax rate to the recorded tax provision (benefit) is as follows for the fiscal years ended:

(In thousands)	December 30, 2012	January 1, 2012	January 2, 2011
Tax at statutory rate	$ 17,708	$ 22,526	$ 58,086
Non-U.S. rate differential, net	(26,652)	(37,797)	(23,873)
U.S. taxation of multinational operations	1,727	1,487	4,032
State income taxes, net	3,265	(5,536)	4,745
Prior year tax matters	3,389	(9,079)	(11,891)
Estimated taxes on repatriation	—	79,662	—
Federal tax credits	(1,657)	(1,509)	(3,867)
Change in valuation allowance	(14,446)	11,364	(3,529)
Other, net	(1,188)	2,064	3,340
Total	$(17,854)	$ 63,182	$ 27,043

3.75 MOTOROLA SOLUTIONS, INC. (DEC)
NOTES TO CONSOLIDATED FINANCIAL STATEMENTS

(Dollars in millions, except as noted)

1. Summary of Significant Accounting Policies (in part)

Income Taxes: Deferred tax assets and liabilities are recognized for the future tax consequences attributable to differences between the financial statement carrying amounts of existing assets and liabilities and their respective tax bases and operating loss and tax credit carryforwards. Deferred tax assets and liabilities are measured using enacted tax rates expected to apply to taxable income in the years in which those temporary differences are expected to be recovered or settled. The effect on deferred tax assets and liabilities from a change in tax rates is recognized in the period that includes the enactment date.

Deferred tax assets are reduced by valuation allowances if, based on the consideration of all available evidence, it is more-likely-than-not that some portion of the deferred tax asset will not be realized. Significant weight is given to evidence that can be objectively verified. The Company evaluates deferred tax assets on a quarterly basis to determine if valuation allowances are required by considering available evidence. Deferred tax assets are realized by having sufficient future taxable income to allow the related tax benefits to reduce taxes otherwise payable. The sources of taxable income that may be available to realize the benefit of deferred tax assets are future reversals of existing taxable temporary differences, future taxable income, exclusive of reversing temporary differences and carryforwards, taxable income in carry-back years and tax planning strategies that are both prudent and feasible.

The Company recognizes the effect of income tax positions only if sustaining those positions is more-likely-than-not. Changes in recognition or measurement are reflected in the period in which a change in judgment occurs. The Company records interest related to unrecognized tax benefits in Interest expense and penalties in Selling, general and administrative expenses in the Company's consolidated statements of operations.

6. Income Taxes (in part)

Significant components of deferred tax assets (liabilities) are as follows:

December 31	2012	2011
Inventory	$ 1	$ 38
Accrued liabilities and allowances	134	254
Employee benefits	1,544	1,279
Capitalized items	254	290
Tax basis differences on investments	28	44
Depreciation tax basis differences on fixed assets	19	13
Undistributed non-U.S. earnings	(150)	(275)
Tax carryforwards	1,155	1,438
Business reorganization	12	13
Warranty and customer reserves	45	44
Deferred revenue and costs	310	218
Valuation allowances	(308)	(366)
Deferred charges	36	39
Other	(63)	(46)
	$3,017	$2,983

At December 31, 2012 and 2011, the Company had valuation allowances of $308 million and $366 million, respectively, against its deferred tax assets, including $272 million and $336 million, respectively, relating to deferred tax assets for non-U.S. subsidiaries. The Company's valuation allowances for its non-U.S. subsidiaries had a net decrease of $64 million during 2012. The decrease in the valuation allowance relating to deferred tax assets of non-U.S. subsidiaries includes a $60 million reduction for loss carryforwards the Company now expects to utilize, decreases related to current year activity and exchange rate variances, offset by an increase related to foreign subsidiaries acquired during 2012.

In the first quarter of 2011, the Company reassessed its valuation allowance requirements taking into consideration the distribution of Motorola Mobility. The Company evaluated all available evidence in its analysis, including the historical and projected pre-tax profits generated by the Company's U.S. operations. The Company also considered tax planning strategies that are prudent and can be reasonably implemented. During 2011, the Company recorded $274 million of tax benefits related to the reversal of a significant portion of the valuation allowance established on U.S. deferred tax assets. The U.S. valuation allowance as of December 31, 2012 relates to state tax carryforwards and deferred tax assets of a U.S. subsidiary the Company expects to expire unutilized. The Company believes that the remaining deferred tax assets are more-likely-than-not to be realizable based on estimates of future taxable income and the implementation of tax planning strategies.

Tax carryforwards are as follows:

December 31, 2012	Gross Tax Loss	Tax Effected	Expiration Period
United States:			
U.S. tax losses	$ 94	$ 33	2018–2032
Foreign tax credits	n/a	400	2017–2019
General business credits	n/a	214	2024–2032
Minimum tax credits	n/a	104	Unlimited
State tax losses	2,245	54	2013–2031
State tax credits	n/a	27	2013–2026
Non-U.S. Subsidiaries:			
Canada tax losses	35	9	Unlimited
China tax losses	429	107	2013–2017
Japan tax losses	128	47	2017–2021
United Kingdom tax losses	93	21	Unlimited
Germany tax losses	177	53	Unlimited
Singapore tax losses	80	14	Unlimited
Other subsidiaries tax losses	62	15	Various
Canada tax credits	n/a	23	2024–2032
Spain tax credits	n/a	29	2017–2021
Other subsidiaries tax credits	n/a	5	Various
		$1,155	

3.76 NEWS CORPORATION (JUN)
NOTES TO THE CONSOLIDATED FINANCIAL STATEMENTS

Note 2. Summary of Significant Accounting Policies (in part)

Income Taxes

The Company accounts for income taxes in accordance with ASC 740, "Income Taxes" ("ASC 740"). ASC 740 requires an asset and liability approach for financial accounting and reporting for income taxes. Under the asset and liability approach, deferred taxes are provided for the net tax effects of temporary differences between the carrying amounts of assets and liabilities for financial reporting purposes and the amounts used for income tax purposes. Valuation allowances are established where management determines that it is more likely than not that some portion or all of a deferred tax asset will not be realized. Deferred taxes have not been provided on the cumulative undistributed earnings of foreign subsidiaries to the extent amounts are expected to be reinvested indefinitely.

Note 17. Income Taxes (in part)

The following is a summary of the components of the deferred tax accounts:

(In millions)	As of June 30,	
	2012	2011
Deferred tax assets:		
Net operating loss carryforwards	$ 230	$ 154
Capital loss carryforwards	1,433	1,421
Prior year tax credit carryforwards	657	695
Accrued liabilities	1,119	837
Other	28	141
Total deferred tax assets	3,467	3,248
Deferred tax liabilities:		
Basis difference and amortization	(2,560)	(3,127)
Revenue recognition	(412)	(311)
Sports rights contracts	(160)	(156)
Total deferred tax liabilities	(3,132)	(3,594)
Net deferred tax asset (liability) before valuation allowance	335	(346)
Less: valuation allowance	(2,700)	(2,645)
Net deferred tax liabilities	$(2,365)	$(2,991)

The Company had net current deferred tax assets of $1 million and $8 million at June 30, 2012 and 2011, respectively, and noncurrent deferred tax assets of $22 million and $150 million at June 30, 2012 and 2011, respectively. The Company also had non-current deferred tax liabilities of $2,388 million and $3,149 million at June 30, 2012 and 2011, respectively.

At June 30, 2012, the Company had approximately $752 million of net operating loss carryforwards available to offset future taxable income. The majority of these net operating loss carryforwards have an unlimited carryforward period. In accordance with the Company's accounting policy, valuation allowances of

$171 million and $144 million have been established to reflect the expected realization of these net operating loss carryforwards as of June 30, 2012 and 2011, respectively.

At June 30, 2012, the Company had approximately $5 billion of capital loss carryforwards available to offset future taxable income having no expiration. In accordance with the Company's accounting policy, valuation allowances of $1.1 billion and $1.2 billion have been established to reflect the expected realization of these capital loss carryforwards as of June 30, 2012 and 2011, respectively.

At June 30, 2012, the Company has approximately $657 million of tax credit carryovers available to offset future income tax expense. This amount resulted from the Company's election to credit certain prior year taxes instead of claiming deductions. If these credits are not utilized to offset future U.S. income tax expense, the credits will expire starting in the June 30, 2013 fiscal year through the fiscal year June 30, 2020. In accordance with the Company's accounting policy, valuation allowances of $657 million and $695 million have been established to reflect the expected realization of these tax credit carryovers as of June 30, 2012 and 2011, respectively.

TAXES ON UNDISTRIBUTED EARNINGS

3.77 SPECTRUM BRANDS HOLDINGS, INC. (SEP)
NOTES TO CONSOLIDATED FINANCIAL STATEMENTS

(In thousands, except per share amounts)

(9) Income Taxes (in part)

Effective October 1, 2012, the Company began recording residual U.S. and foreign taxes on current foreign earnings as a result of its change in position regarding future repatriation and the requirements of ASC 740. To the extent necessary, the Company intends to utilize earnings of foreign subsidiaries generated after September 30, 2011, to support management's plans to voluntarily accelerate pay down of U.S. debt, fund distributions to shareholders, fund U.S. acquisitions, and satisfy ongoing U.S. operational cash flow requirements. As a result, earnings of the Company's non-U.S. subsidiaries after September 30, 2011 are not considered to be permanently reinvested, except in jurisdiction where repatriation is either precluded or restricted by law. Accordingly, the Company is providing residual U.S. and foreign deferred taxes to these earnings to the extent they cannot be repatriated in a tax-free manner. Accordingly during Fiscal 2012, the Company has provided residual taxes on approximately $97,638 of foreign earnings resulting in an increase in tax expense, net of a corresponding adjustment to the Company's domestic valuation allowance, of approximately $3,278, including $2,465 of expected tax on $76,475 of earnings not yet taxed in the U.S. During Fiscal 2011, the Company recorded residual U.S. and foreign taxes on approximately $39,391 of distributions of foreign earnings resulting in an increase in tax expense, net of a corresponding adjustment to the Company's domestic valuation allowance, of approximately $771. The Fiscal 2011 distributions were primarily non-cash deemed distributions under U.S. tax law. During Fiscal 2010, the Company recorded residual U.S. and foreign taxes on approximately $26,600 of actual and deemed distributions of foreign earnings resulting in an increase in tax expense, net of a corresponding adjustment to the Company's domestic valuation allowance, of approximately $0. The Fiscal 2010 distributions were primarily non-cash deemed distributions under U.S. tax law.

Remaining undistributed earnings of the Company's foreign operations are approximately $415,713 at September 30, 2012, and are intended to remain permanently invested. Accordingly, no residual income taxes have been provided on those earnings at September 30, 2012. If at some future date these earnings cease to be permanently invested, the Company may be subject to U.S. income taxes and foreign withholding and other taxes on such amounts, which cannot be reasonably estimated at this time.

Construction-Type and Production-Type Contracts

RECOGNITION AND MEASUREMENT

3.78 Accounting and disclosure requirements for construction-type and production-type contracts are discussed in FASB ASC 605-35. In accounting for contracts, the basic accounting policy decision is the choice between the percentage-of-completion method and the completed-contract method. The determination of which is preferable is based on an evaluation of the circumstances.

CONSTRUCTION AND PRODUCTION TYPE CONTRACTS

3.79 CACI INTERNATIONAL INC (JUN)
CONSOLIDATED STATEMENTS OF OPERATIONS (in part)

(Amounts in thousands, except per share data)

	Fiscal Year Ended June 30,		
	2012	**2011**	**2010**
Revenue	$3,774,473	$3,577,780	$3,149,131
Costs of revenue:			
Direct costs	2,598,890	2,528,660	2,207,574
Indirect costs and selling expenses	819,772	741,652	693,736
Depreciation and amortization	55,962	56,067	53,039
Total costs of revenue	3,474,624	3,326,379	2,954,349
Income from operations	299,849	251,401	194,782

NOTES TO CONSOLIDATED FINANCIAL STATEMENTS

Note 2. Summary of Significant Accounting Policies (in part)

Revenue Recognition

The Company generates almost all of its revenue from three different types of contractual arrangements: cost-plus-fee contracts, time and materials contracts, and fixed price contracts. Revenue on cost-plus-fee contracts is recognized to the extent of costs incurred plus an estimate of the applicable fees earned. The Company considers fixed fees under cost-plus-fee contracts to be earned in proportion to the allowable costs incurred in performance of the contract. For cost-plus-fee contracts that include performance based fee incentives, and that are subject to the provisions of Accounting Standards Codification (ASC) 605-35, *Revenue Recognition—Construction-Type and Production-Type Contracts* (ASC 605-35), the Company recognizes the relevant portion of the expected fee to be awarded by the customer at the time such fee can be reasonably estimated, based on factors such as the Company's prior award experience and communications with the customer regarding performance. For such cost-plus-fee contracts subject to the provisions of ASC 605-10-S99, *Revenue Recognition—SEC Materials* (ASC 605-10-S99), the Company recognizes the relevant portion of the fee upon customer approval. Revenue on time and material contracts is recognized to the extent of billable rates times hours delivered for services provided, to the extent of material cost for products delivered to customers, and to the extent of expenses incurred on behalf of the customers. Shipping and handling fees charged to the customers are recognized as revenue at the time products are delivered to the customers.

The Company has four basic categories of fixed price contracts: fixed unit price, fixed price-level of effort, fixed price-completion, and fixed price-license. Revenue on fixed unit price contracts, where specified units of output under service arrangements are delivered, is recognized as units are delivered based on the specified price per unit. Revenue on fixed unit price maintenance contracts is recognized ratably over the length of the service period. Revenue for fixed price-level of effort contracts is recognized based upon the number of units of labor actually delivered multiplied by the agreed rate for each unit of labor.

A significant portion of the Company's fixed price-completion contracts involve the design and development of complex client systems. For these contracts that are within the scope of ASC 605-35, revenue is recognized on the percentage-of-completion method using costs incurred in relation to total estimated costs. For fixed price-completion contracts that are not within the scope of ASC 605-35, revenue is generally recognized ratably over the service period. The Company's fixed price-license agreements and related services contracts are primarily executed in its international operations. As the agreements to deliver software require significant production, modification or customization of software, revenue is recognized using the contract accounting guidance of ASC 605-35. For agreements to deliver data under license and related services, revenue is recognized as the data is delivered and services are performed. Except for losses on contracts accounted for under ASC 605-10-S99, provisions for estimated losses on uncompleted contracts are recorded in the period such losses are determined. Losses on contracts accounted for under ASC 605-10-S99 are recognized as the services and materials are provided.

The Company's contracts may include the provision of more than one of its services. In these situations, and for applicable arrangements, revenue recognition includes the proper identification of separate units of accounting and the allocation of revenue across all elements based on relative fair values, with proper consideration given to the guidance provided by other authoritative literature.

Contract accounting requires judgment relative to assessing risks, estimating contract revenue and costs, and making assumptions for schedule and technical issues. Due to the size and nature of many of the Company's contracts, the estimation of total revenue and cost at completion is complicated and subject to many variables. Contract costs include material, labor, subcontracting costs, and other direct costs, as well as an allocation of allowable indirect costs. Assumptions have to be made regarding the length of time to complete the contract because costs also include expected increases in wages and prices for materials. For contract change orders, claims or similar items, the Company applies judgment in estimating the amounts and assessing the potential for realization. These amounts are only included in contract value when they can be reliably estimated and realization is considered probable. Incentives or penalties related to performance on contracts are considered in estimating sales and profit rates, and are recorded when there is sufficient information for the

Company to assess anticipated performance. Estimates of award fees for certain contracts are also a factor in estimating revenue and profit rates based on actual and anticipated awards.

Long-term development and production contracts make up a large portion of the Company's business, and therefore the amounts recorded in the Company's financial statements using contract accounting methods are material. For federal government contracts, the Company follows U.S. government procurement and accounting standards in assessing the allowability and the allocability of costs to contracts. Due to the significance of the judgments and estimation processes, it is likely that materially different amounts could be recorded if the Company used different assumptions or if the underlying circumstances were to change. The Company closely monitors compliance with, and the consistent application of, its critical accounting policies related to contract accounting. Business operations personnel conduct thorough periodic contract status and performance reviews. When adjustments in estimated contract revenue or costs are required, any changes from prior estimates are generally included in earnings in the current period. Also, regular and recurring evaluations of contract cost, scheduling and technical matters are performed by management personnel who are independent from the business operations personnel performing work under the contract. Costs incurred and allocated to contracts with the U.S. government are scrutinized for compliance with regulatory standards by Company personnel, and are subject to audit by the Defense Contract Audit Agency (DCAA).

From time to time, the Company may proceed with work based on client direction prior to the completion and signing of formal contract documents. The Company has a formal review process for approving any such work. Revenue associated with such work is recognized only when it can be reliably estimated and realization is probable. The Company bases its estimates on previous experiences with the client, communications with the client regarding funding status, and its knowledge of available funding for the contract or program.

The Company's U.S. government contracts (94.5 percent of total revenue in the year ended June 30, 2012) are subject to subsequent government audit of direct and indirect costs. Incurred cost audits have been completed through June 30, 2005. Management does not anticipate any material adjustment to the consolidated financial statements in subsequent periods for audits not yet started or completed.

3.80 LOCKHEED MARTIN CORPORATION (DEC)
CONSOLIDATED STATEMENTS OF EARNINGS (in part)

(In millions, except per share data)

| | Years Ended December 31, | | |
	2012	2011	2010
Net Sales			
Products	$37,817	$36,925	$36,380
Services	9,365	9,574	9,291
Total net sales	47,182	46,499	45,671

NOTES TO CONSOLIDATED FINANCIAL STATEMENTS

Note 1—Significant Accounting Policies (in part)

Sales and earnings—We record net sales and estimated profits for substantially all of our contracts using the POC method for cost-reimbursable and fixed-price contracts for products and services with the U.S. Government. Sales are recorded on all time-and-materials contracts as the work is performed based on agreed-upon hourly rates and allowable costs. We account for our services contracts with non-U.S. Government customers using the services method of accounting. We classify net sales as products or services on our Statements of Earnings based on the attributes of the underlying contracts.

POC Method of Accounting—The POC method for product contracts depends on the nature of the products provided under the contract. For example, for contracts that require us to perform a significant level of development effort in comparison to the total value of the contract and/or to deliver minimal quantities, sales are recorded using the cost-to-cost method to measure progress toward completion. Under the cost-to-cost method of accounting, we recognize sales and an estimated profit as costs are incurred based on the proportion that the incurred costs bear to total estimated costs. For contracts that require us to provide a substantial number of similar items without a significant level of development, we record sales and an estimated profit on a POC basis using units-of-delivery as the basis to measure progress toward completing the contract. For contracts to provide services to the U.S. Government, sales are generally recorded using the cost-to-cost method.

Award and incentive fees, as well as penalties related to contract performance, are considered in estimating sales and profit rates on contracts accounted for under the POC method. Estimates of award fees are based on past experience and anticipated performance. We record incentives or penalties when there is sufficient information to assess anticipated contract performance. Incentive provisions that increase or decrease earnings based solely on a single significant event are not recognized until the event occurs.

Accounting for contracts using the POC method requires judgment relative to assessing risks, estimating contract sales and costs (including estimating award and incentive fees and penalties related to performance), and making assumptions for schedule and technical issues. Due to the scope and nature of the work required to be performed on many of our contracts, the estimation of total sales and cost at completion is complicated and subject to many variables and, accordingly, is subject to change. When adjustments in estimated contract sales or estimated costs at completion are required, any changes from prior estimates are recognized in the current period for the inception-to-date effect of such changes. When estimates of total costs to be incurred on a contract exceed total estimates of sales to be earned, a provision for the entire loss on the contract is recorded in the period in which the loss is determined.

Many of our contracts span several years and include highly complex technical requirements. At the outset of a contract, we identify and monitor risks to the achievement of the technical, schedule, and costs aspects of the contract, and assess the effects of those risks on our estimates of total costs to complete the contract. The estimates consider the technical requirements (for example, a newly-developed product versus a mature product), the schedule and associated tasks (for example, the number and type of milestone events), and costs (for example, material, labor, subcontractor and overhead). The initial profit booking rate of each contract considers risks surrounding the ability to achieve the technical requirements, schedule, and costs in the initial estimated costs at completion. Profit booking rates may increase during the performance of the contract if we successfully retire risks surrounding the technical, schedule and costs aspects of the contract. Alternatively, our profit booking rates may decrease if the estimated costs to complete the contract increase. All of the estimates are subject to change during the performance of the contract and may affect the profit booking rate.

In addition, comparability of our segment operating profit may be impacted by changes in estimated profit booking rates on our contracts accounted for using the POC method of accounting. Increases in the estimated profit booking rates, typically referred to as risk retirements, usually relate to revisions in the total estimated costs at completion that reflect improved conditions on a particular contract. Conversely, conditions on a particular contract may deteriorate resulting in an increase in the total estimated costs at completion and a reduction of the estimated profit booking rate. Increases or decreases in estimated profit booking rates are recognized in the current period and reflect the inception-to-date effect of such changes. Segment operating profit may also be impacted, favorably or unfavorably, by other matters such as the resolution of contractual matters, reserves for disputes, asset impairments and insurance recoveries, among others. Segment operating profit and items such as risk retirements, reductions of profit booking rates, or other matters are presented net of state income taxes.

Our consolidated net adjustments not related to volume, including net profit rate adjustments and other matters, increased segment operating profit, net of state income taxes, by approximately $1.9 billion in 2012, $1.6 billion in 2011, and $1.4 billion in 2010. These adjustments increased net earnings by approximately $1.2 billion ($3.70 per share) in 2012, $1.0 billion ($3.00 per share) in 2011, and $890 million ($2.40 per share) in 2010.

3.81 THE SHAW GROUP INC. (AUG)
CONSOLIDATED STATEMENTS OF OPERATIONS (In part)

(In thousands, except per share amounts)

| | Year Ended August 31, | | |
	2012	2011	2010
Revenues	$6,008,435	$5,937,734	$6,984,042
Cost of revenues	5,580,471	5,741,392	6,414,826
Gross profit	427,964	196,342	569,216
Selling, general and administrative expenses	276,338	273,512	288,014
Gain on disposal of E&C assets	83,315	—	—
Impairment of note receivable	—	48,133	—
Operating income (loss)	234,941	(125,303)	281,202

NOTES TO CONSOLIDATED FINANCIAL STATEMENTS

Note 1—Description of Business and Summary of Significant Accounting Policies (in part)

Nature of Operations and Types of Contracts

Our work is performed under two general types of contracts: cost-reimbursable plus a fee or mark-up contracts and fixed-price contracts, both of which may be modified by cost escalation provisions or other risk sharing mechanisms and incentive and penalty provisions. Each of our contracts may contain components of more than one of the contract types discussed below. During the term of a project, the contract or components of the contract may be renegotiated to include characteristics of a different contract type. We focus our EPC activities on a cost-reimbursable basis plus a fee or mark-up and negotiated fixed-price work, each as defined below. When we negotiate any type of contract, we frequently are required to accomplish the scope of work and meet certain performance criteria within a specified timeframe; otherwise, we could be assessed damages, which in some cases are agreed-upon liquidated damages.

Our cost-reimbursable contracts include the following:
- *Cost-plus and Time and Material contracts*—A contract under which we are reimbursed for allowable or otherwise defined costs incurred plus a fee or mark-up. The contracts may also include incentives for various performance criteria, including quality, timeliness, ingenuity, safety and cost-effectiveness. In addition, our costs are generally subject to review by our clients and regulatory audit agencies, and such reviews could result in costs being disputed as non-reimbursable under the terms of the contract.
- *Target-price contract*—A contract under which we are reimbursed for costs plus a fee consisting of two parts: (1) a fixed amount, which does not vary with performance, but may be at risk when a target price is exceeded; and (2) an award amount based on the performance and cost-effectiveness of the project. As a result, we are generally able to recover cost overruns on these contracts from actual damages for late delivery or the failure to meet certain performance criteria. Target-price contracts also generally provide for sharing of costs in excess of or savings for costs less than the target. In some contracts, we may agree to share cost overruns in excess of our fee, which could result in a loss on the project.

Our fixed-price contracts include the following:

- *Firm fixed-price contract*—May include contracts in which the price is not subject to any cost or performance adjustments and contracts where certain risks are shared with clients such as labor costs or commodity pricing changes. As a result, we may benefit or be penalized for cost variations from our original estimates. However, these contract prices may be adjusted for changes in scope of work, new or changing laws and regulations and other events negotiated.
- *Maximum price contract*—A contract that provides at the outset for an initial target cost, an initial target profit and a price ceiling. The price is subject to cost adjustments incurred, but the adjustment would generally not exceed the price ceiling established in the contract. In addition, these contracts usually include provisions whereby we share cost savings with our clients.
- *Unit-price contract*—A contract under which we are paid a specified amount for every unit of work performed. A unit-price contract is essentially a firm fixed-price contract with the only variable being the number of units of work performed. Variations in unit-price contracts include the same type of variations as firm fixed-price contracts. We are normally awarded these contracts on the basis of a total price that is the sum of the product of the specified units and the unit prices.

Discontinued Operations

RECOGNITION AND MEASUREMENT

3.82 FASB ASC 205-20 sets forth the financial accounting and reporting requirements for discontinued operations of a component of an entity. A *component of an entity* comprises operations and cash flows that can be clearly distinguished, operationally and for financial reporting purposes, from the rest of the entity. A component of an entity may be a reportable or an operating segment, a reporting unit, a subsidiary, or an asset group.

3.83 FASB ASC 205-20 uses a single accounting model to account for all long-lived assets to be disposed of (by sale, abandonment, or distribution to owners). This includes asset disposal groups meeting the criteria for presentation as a discontinued operation, as specified in FASB ASC 205-20. A long-lived asset group classified as held for sale should be measured at the lower of its carrying amount or fair value less cost to sell. Additionally, in accordance with FASB ASC 360, a loss shall be recognized for any write-down to fair value less cost to sell. A gain shall be recognized for any subsequent recovery of cost. Lastly, a gain or loss not previously recognized that results from the sale of the asset disposal group should be recognized at the date of sale.

PRESENTATION

3.84 The conditions for determining whether discontinued operations treatment is appropriate and the required income statement presentation are stated in FASB ASC 205-20-45-1, as follows:

The results of operations of a component of an entity that either has been disposed of or is classified as held for sale . . . [should] be reported in discontinued operations . . . if both of the following conditions are met:

a. The operations and cash flow of the component have been (or will be) eliminated from the ongoing operations of the entity as a result of the disposal transaction.
b. The entity will not have any significant continuing involvement in the operations of the component after the disposal transaction.

3.85 In a period in which a component of an entity either has been disposed of or is classified as held for sale, the income statement of a business entity or statement of activities of a not-for-profit entity for current and prior periods should report the results of operations of the component, including any gain or loss recognized from the sale or write-down, in discontinued operations. The results of operations of a component classified as held for sale should be reported in discontinued operations in the period(s) in which they occur. The results of discontinued operations, less applicable income taxes (benefit), should be reported as a separate component of income before extraordinary items (if applicable). For example, the results of discontinued operations may be reported in the income statement of a business entity as follows:

Income from continuing operations before income taxes	$XXXX	
Income taxes	XXX	
Income from continuing operations		$XXXX
Discontinued operations (Note X):		
Loss from operations of discontinued component X (including loss on disposal of $XXX)		$XXXX
Income tax benefit		XXXX
Loss on discontinued operations		XXXX
Net income		$XXXX

A gain or loss recognized on the disposal should be disclosed either on the face of the income statement or in the notes to the financial statements.

3.86 Illustrations of transactions that should and should not be accounted for as business segment disposals are presented in the implementation guidance and illustrations of FASB ASC 205-20-55.

BUSINESS COMPONENT DISPOSALS

3.87 HARRIS CORPORATION (JUN)
CONSOLIDATED STATEMENT OF INCOME

	Fiscal Years Ended		
(In millions, except per share amounts)	2012	2011	2010
Revenue from product sales and services			
Revenue from product sales	$ 3,364.7	$ 3,691.5	$ 3,502.3
Revenue from services	2,086.6	1,726.9	1,222.7
	5,451.3	5,418.4	4,725.0
Cost of product sales and services			
Cost of product sales	(1,945.2)	(2,141.2)	(2,082.8)
Cost of services	(1,624.1)	(1,391.3)	(970.1)
	(3,569.3)	(3,532.5)	(3,052.9)
Engineering, selling and administrative expenses	(940.9)	(890.9)	(723.2)
Non-operating income (loss)	11.5	(1.9)	(1.9)
Interest income	2.5	2.8	1.5
Interest expense	(113.2)	(90.4)	(72.1)
Income from continuing operations before income taxes	841.9	905.5	876.4
Income taxes	(286.0)	(306.8)	(295.4)
Income from continuing operations	555.9	598.7	581.0
Discontinued operations, net of income taxes	(528.1)	(11.6)	(19.4)
Net income	27.8	587.1	561.6
Noncontrolling interests, net of income taxes	2.8	0.9	—
Net income attributable to Harris Corporation	$ 30.6	$ 588.0	$ 561.6
Amounts attributable to Harris Corporation common shareholders			
Income from continuing operations	$ 558.7	$ 599.6	$ 581.0
Discontinued operations, net of income taxes	(528.1)	(11.6)	(19.4)
Net income	$ 30.6	$ 588.0	$ 561.6
Net income per common share attributable to Harris Corporation common shareholders			
Basic net income per common share attributable to Harris Corporation common shareholders			
Continuing operations	$ 4.83	$ 4.73	$ 4.46
Discontinued operations	(4.57)	(0.10)	(0.15)
	$ 0.26	$ 4.63	$ 4.31
Diluted net income per common share attributable to Harris Corporation common shareholders			
Continuing operations	$ 4.80	$ 4.69	$ 4.42
Discontinued operations	(4.54)	(0.09)	(0.14)
	$ 0.26	$ 4.60	$ 4.28

NOTES TO CONSOLIDATED FINANCIAL STATEMENTS

Note 1: Significant Accounting Policies (in part)

Principles of Consolidation

In the third quarter of fiscal 2012, our Board of Directors approved a plan to exit our cyber integrated solutions operation ("CIS"), which provided remote cloud hosting, and to dispose of the related assets, and we reported CIS as discontinued operations beginning with our financial results presented in our Quarterly Report on Form 10-Q for the third quarter of fiscal 2012. In the fourth quarter of fiscal 2012, our Board of Directors approved a plan to divest Broadcast Communications, which provides digital media management solutions in support of broadcast customers, and we are reporting Broadcast Communications as discontinued operations beginning with our financial results presented in our Annual Report on Form 10-K for fiscal 2012 and in our Consolidated Financial Statements and these Notes. Both CIS and Broadcast Communications were formerly part of our Integrated Network Solutions segment. Our results of operations for fiscal 2012 and our financial position as of the end of fiscal 2012 presented in our Consolidated Financial Statements and these Notes reflect both CIS and Broadcast Communications as discontinued operations. Our results of operations for all periods prior to fiscal 2012 presented in our Consolidated Financial Statements and these Notes have been restated to account for CIS and Broadcast Communications as discontinued operations. For additional information regarding discontinued operations, see *Note 3: Discontinued Operations*. Except for disclosures related to our financial position as of the end of periods prior to fiscal 2012 or to our cash flows, or unless otherwise specified, disclosures in this Report relate solely to our continuing operations.

Note 3: Discontinued Operations

On February 24, 2012, our Board of Directors approved a plan to exit CIS, which provided remote cloud hosting, and to dispose of the related assets, including the cyber integration center facility in Harrisonburg, Virginia and remote cloud hosting equipment. We concluded that although we believed demand would continue for cyber security and cloud-enabled solutions, our government and commercial customers would continue to prefer hosting mission-critical information on their own premises rather than remotely. We expect to complete the disposition of the assets of CIS during fiscal 2013.

On April 27, 2012, our Board of Directors approved a plan to divest Broadcast Communications. After a thorough review of our business portfolio and evaluation of strategic alternatives for Broadcast Communications, we no longer believed Broadcast Communications was aligned with our long-term strategy. As a result, we have initiated a sales process for Broadcast Communications. We expect to complete the divestiture of Broadcast Communications during fiscal 2013.

CIS and Broadcast Communications were part of our Integrated Network Solutions segment. Our results of operations for fiscal 2012 and our financial position as of the end of fiscal 2012 presented in our Consolidated Financial Statements and these Notes reflect CIS and Broadcast Communications as discontinued operations. Our results of operations for all periods prior to fiscal 2012 presented in our Consolidated Financial Statements and these Notes have been restated to account for CIS and Broadcast Communications as discontinued operations.

During fiscal 2012, in connection with our approved plan to exit CIS, we recorded pre-tax charges of $142.6 million ($90.2 million after-tax or $.78 per diluted share). These charges were comprised of $138.0 million for impairment of goodwill and other long-lived assets; $2.1 million for one-time employee termination costs, including severance and other benefits; and $2.5 million for other associated exit or disposal costs. See *Note 23: Fair Value Measurements* for additional information regarding such impairment charges.

We tested our goodwill related to Broadcast Communications for impairment as of the end of the third quarter of fiscal 2012 because indications of potential impairment were present at the end of the third quarter of fiscal 2012. Indications of potential impairment resulted from the following circumstances and other factors: (i) an unanticipated revenue decline and operating loss for Broadcast Communications for the third quarter of fiscal 2012 (as a result of weaker demand in North America and longer lead times for international sales), which also resulted in a decrease in the fiscal 2012 outlook for Broadcast Communications and (ii) depressed indicators of value resulting from analyses undertaken in the third quarter of fiscal 2012 in connection with the review of our business portfolio, including the evaluation of strategic alternatives for Broadcast Communications that included a potential divestiture of Broadcast Communications and the principal markets then available.

To test for potential impairment of goodwill related to Broadcast Communications, we preliminarily estimated the fair value of the reporting unit based on a combination of discounted projected cash flows and principal market-based multiples applied to sales and earnings. The carrying value of the Broadcast Communications reporting unit exceeded its estimated fair value, and accordingly, we preliminarily allocated the fair value to the assets and liabilities of the Broadcast Communications reporting unit to determine the implied fair value of goodwill.

In conjunction with the above-described impairment review, we also conducted a review for impairment of other long-lived assets related to Broadcast Communications, including amortizable intangible assets, fixed assets and capitalized software, and impairment of these assets was considered prior to the conclusion of the goodwill impairment review. The estimated fair value of other long-lived assets related to Broadcast Communications was determined based primarily on an analysis of discounted projected cash flows considering historical and future revenue and operating costs and other relevant factors for amortizable intangible assets and capitalized software; and replacement costs, market indications, asset ages, asset utilization and other relevant asset information for fixed assets.

As a result of these impairment reviews, we concluded that goodwill and other long-lived assets related to Broadcast Communications were impaired as of the end of the third quarter of fiscal 2012, and we recorded an estimated non-cash impairment charge of $424.0 million ($406.5 million after-tax) in the third quarter of fiscal 2012. Due to the length of time necessary to measure the impairment of goodwill and other long-lived assets, our impairment analysis was not complete as of the end of the third quarter of fiscal 2012. In the fourth quarter of fiscal 2012, we completed our impairment analysis and, as a result, recorded a $23.6 million ($10.5 million after-tax) increase to our initial estimated impairment charge. The portion of the total $447.6 million impairment charge related to goodwill was $395.6 million, a minor amount of which was deductible for tax purposes. We do not expect to make any current or future cash expenditures as a result of the impairment. The impairment does not impact covenant compliance under our credit arrangements, and we do not expect the impairment to impact our ongoing financial performance, although no assurance can be given.

Summarized financial information for our discontinued operations related to CIS and Broadcast Communications is as follows:

(In millions)	2012	2011	2010
Revenue from product sales and services	$ 512.7	$506.2	$481.1
Loss before income taxes	$(627.2)	$ (24.8)	$ (36.1)
Income taxes	99.1	13.2	16.7
Discontinued operations, net of income taxes	$(528.1)	$ (11.6)	$ (19.4)
Receivables	$ 103.6		
Inventories	128.0		
Other current assets	9.4		
Total current assets	241.0		
Property, plant and equipment	89.0		
Goodwill	267.7		
Other non-current assets	35.0		
Total assets	632.7		
Accounts payable	26.9		
Accrued and other liabilities	109.3		
Total liabilities	136.2		
Net assets of discontinued operations	$ 496.5		

3.88 CONOCOPHILLIPS (DEC)
NOTES TO CONSOLIDATED FINANCIAL STATEMENTS

Note 2—Discontinued Operations (in part)

Separation of Downstream Business

On April 30, 2012, the separation of our Downstream business was completed, creating two independent energy companies: ConocoPhillips and Phillips 66. After the close of the New York Stock Exchange on April 30, 2012, the shareholders of record as of 5:00 p.m. Eastern time on April 16, 2012 (the Record Date), received one share of Phillips 66 common stock for every two ConocoPhillips common shares held as of the Record Date.

In connection with the separation, Phillips 66 distributed approximately $7.8 billion to us in a special cash distribution, primarily using the proceeds from the $5.8 billion in Senior Notes issued by Phillips 66 in March 2012, as well as a portion of the approximately $3.6 billion in cash transferred to Phillips 66 at separation, comprised of funds received from the $2.0 billion term loan entered into by Phillips 66 immediately prior to the separation, and approximately $1.6 billion of cash held by Phillips 66 subsidiaries. Pursuant to the private letter ruling from the Internal Revenue Service, the principal funds from the special cash distribution will be used solely to pay dividends, repurchase common stock, repay debt, or a combination of the foregoing, within twelve months following the distribution. At December 31, 2012, the remaining balance of the cash distribution was $748 million and was included in the "Restricted cash" line on our consolidated balance sheet.

In order to effect the separation and govern our relationship with Phillips 66 after the separation, we entered into a Separation and Distribution Agreement, an Indemnification and Release Agreement, an Intellectual Property Assignment and License Agreement, a Tax Sharing Agreement, an Employee Matters Agreement and a Transition Services Agreement. The Separation and Distribution Agreement governs the separation of the Downstream business, the transfer of assets and other matters related to our relationship with Phillips 66. The Indemnification and Release Agreement provides for cross-indemnities between Phillips 66 and us and established procedures for handling claims subject to indemnification and related matters. The Intellectual Property Assignment and License Agreement governs the allocation of intellectual property rights and assets between Phillips 66 and us.

The Tax Sharing Agreement governs the respective rights, responsibilities and obligations of Phillips 66 and ConocoPhillips with respect to taxes, tax attributes, tax returns, tax proceedings and certain other tax matters. In addition, the Tax Sharing Agreement imposed certain restrictions on Phillips 66 and its subsidiaries (including restrictions on share issuances, business combinations, sales of assets and similar transactions) that are designed to preserve the tax-free status of the distribution and certain related transactions. The Tax Sharing Agreement sets forth the obligations of Phillips 66 and us as to the filing of tax returns, the administration of tax proceedings and assistance and cooperation on tax matters.

The Employee Matters Agreement governs the compensation and employee benefit obligations with respect to the current and former employees and non-employee directors of Phillips 66 and ConocoPhillips, and generally allocates liabilities and responsibilities relating to employee compensation, benefit plans and programs. The Employee Matters Agreement provides that employees of Phillips 66 will no longer participate in benefit plans sponsored or maintained by ConocoPhillips. In addition, the Employee Matters Agreement provides that each of the parties will be responsible for their respective current employees and compensation plans for such current employees, and we will be responsible for liabilities relating to former employees who left prior to the separation (other than in certain instances where a plan or program was sponsored by a company that became part of the Phillips 66 group of companies at the separation). The Employee Matters Agreement sets forth the general principles relating to employee matters and also addresses any special circumstances during the transition period. The Employee Matters Agreement also provides that (i) the distribution does not constitute a change in control under existing plans, programs, agreements or arrangements, and (ii) the distribution and the assignment, transfer or continuation of the employment of employees with another entity will not constitute a severance event under the applicable plans, programs, agreements or arrangements.

The Transition Services Agreement sets forth the terms on which we will provide Phillips 66, and Phillips 66 will provide to us, certain services or functions Phillips 66 and ConocoPhillips historically have shared. Transition services include administrative, payroll, human resources, data processing, environmental health and safety, financial audit support, financial transaction support, and other support services, information technology systems and various other corporate services. The agreement provides for the provision of specified transition services, generally for a period of up to 12 months, with a possible extension of 6 months (an aggregate of 18 months), on a cost or a cost-plus basis.

The following table presents the carrying value of the major categories of assets and liabilities of Phillips 66, reflected on our consolidated balance sheet at December 31, 2011:

	(Millions of dollars)
Assets	
Accounts and notes receivable	$ 8,353
Accounts and notes receivable—related parties	1,671
Inventories	3,403
Prepaid expenses and other current assets	443
Total current assets of discontinued operations	13,870
Investments and long-term receivables	10,304
Loans and advances—related parties	1
Net properties, plants and equipment	15,047
Goodwill	3,332
Intangibles	732
Other assets	121
Total assets of discontinued operations	$43,407
Liabilities	
Accounts payable	$10,007
Accounts payable—related parties	785
Short-term debt	30
Accrued income and other taxes	967
Employee benefit obligations	76
Other accruals	411
Total current liabilities of discontinued operations	12,276
Long-term debt	361
Asset retirement obligations and accrued environmental costs	787
Deferred income taxes	5,533
Employee benefit obligations	1,057
Other liabilities and deferred credits	417
Total liabilities of discontinued operations	$20,431

Sales and other operating revenues and income from discontinued operations related to Phillips 66 were as follows:

(Millions of dollars)	2012	2011	2010
Sales and other operating revenues from discontinued operations	$62,109	196,068	146,542
Income from discontinued operations before-tax	$ 1,768	6,776	1,438
Income tax expense	534	1,729	470
Income from discontinued operations	$ 1,234	5,047	968

Income from discontinued operations after-tax includes transaction, information systems and other costs incurred to effect the separation of $70 million and $17 million for the years ended December 31, 2012 and 2011. No separation costs were incurred in 2010.

Prior to the separation, commodity sales to Phillips 66 were $4,973 million for the year ended December 31, 2012; $15,822 million for the year ended December 31, 2011; and $13,412 million for the year ended December 31, 2010. Commodity purchases from Phillips 66 prior to the separation were $166 million for the year ended December 31, 2012; $516 million for the year ended December 31, 2011; and $479 million for the year ended December 31, 2010. Prior to May 1, 2012, commodity sales and related costs were eliminated in consolidation between ConocoPhillips and Phillips 66. Beginning May 1, 2012, these revenues and costs represent third-party transactions with Phillips 66. Although we expect certain transactions related to the sale and purchase of crude oil, natural gas and products to continue in the future with Phillips 66, the expected continuing cash flows are not considered significant; thus, the operations and cash flows of our former Downstream business are considered to be eliminated from our ongoing operations.

Extraordinary Items

RECOGNITION AND MEASUREMENT

3.89 FASB ASC 225-20 defines *extraordinary items* as events and transactions that are distinguished by their unusual nature and the infrequency of their occurrence. Both of the following criteria should be met to classify an event or a transaction as an extraordinary item:

- *Unusual nature.* The underlying event or transaction should possess a high degree of abnormality and be of a type clearly unrelated to or only incidentally related to the ordinary and typical activities of the entity, taking into account the environment in which the entity operates.
- *Infrequency of occurrence.* The underlying event or transaction should be of a type that would not reasonably be expected to recur in the foreseeable future, taking into account the environment in which the entity operates.

PRESENTATION

3.90 FASB ASC 225-20 also addresses the presentation and disclosure of unusual and infrequently occurring items that do not meet the extraordinary criteria. Such items are reported as a separate component of continuing operations either on the face of the income statement or in the notes. FASB ASC 225-20-55 illustrates events and transactions that should and should not be classified as extraordinary items.

EXTRAORDINARY ITEMS

3.91 HUNTSMAN CORPORATION (DEC)
CONSOLIDATED STATEMENTS OF OPERATIONS

(In Millions, Except Per Share Amounts)

	Year Ended December 31,		
	2012	**2011**	**2010**
Revenues:			
Trade sales, services and fees, net	$10,964	$11,041	$9,049
Related party sales	223	180	201
Total revenues	11,187	11,221	9,250
Cost of goods sold	9,153	9,381	7,789
Gross profit	2,034	1,840	1,461
Operating Expenses:			
Selling, general and administrative	951	921	861
Research and development	152	166	151
Other operating (income) expense	(6)	(20)	10
Restructuring, impairment and plant closing costs	92	167	29
Total expenses	1,189	1,234	1,051
Operating income	845	606	410
Interest expense, net	(226)	(249)	(229)
Equity in income of investment in unconsolidated affiliates	7	8	24
Loss on early extinguishment of debt	(80)	(7)	(183)
Expenses associated with the Terminated Merger and related litigation	—	—	(4)
Other income	1	2	2
Income from continuing operations before income taxes	547	360	20
Income tax expense	(169)	(109)	(29)
Income (loss) from continuing operations	378	251	(9)
(Loss) income from discontinued operations	(7)	(1)	42
Income before extraordinary gain (loss)	371	250	33
Extraordinary gain (loss) on the acquisition of a business, net of tax of nil	2	4	(1)
Net income	373	254	32
Net income attributable to noncontrolling interests	(10)	(7)	(5)
Net income attributable to Huntsman Corporation	$ 363	$ 247	$ 27

NOTES TO CONSOLIDATED FINANCIAL STATEMENTS

3. Business Combinations and Dispositions (in part)

Textile Effects Acquisition

On June 30, 2006, we acquired Ciba's textile effects business and accounted for the Textile Effects Acquisition using the purchase method. As such, we analyzed the fair value of tangible and intangible assets acquired and liabilities assumed and determined the excess of fair value of net assets over cost. Because the fair value of the acquired assets and liabilities assumed exceeded the purchase price, the value of the long-lived assets acquired was reduced to zero. Accordingly, no basis was assigned to property, plant and equipment or any other non-current nonfinancial assets and the remaining excess was recorded as an extraordinary gain. During 2012, 2011 and 2010, we recorded an additional extraordinary gain (loss) on the acquisition of $2 million, $4 million and $(1) million, respectively, related to settlement of contingent purchase price consideration, the reversal of accruals for certain restructuring and employee termination costs recorded in connection with the Textile Effects Acquisition and a reimbursement by Ciba of certain costs pursuant to the acquisition agreements.

UNUSUAL ITEMS

3.92 GENCORP INC. (NOV)
NOTES TO CONSOLIDATED FINANCIAL STATEMENTS

Note 10. Operating Segments and Related Disclosures

The Company's operations are organized into two operating segments based on different products and customer bases: Aerospace and Defense, and Real Estate. The accounting policies of the operating segments are the same as those described in the summary of significant accounting policies (see Note 1).

The Company evaluates its operating segments based on several factors, of which the primary financial measure is segment performance. Segment performance represents net sales from continuing operations less applicable costs, expenses and provisions for unusual items relating to the segment operations. Segment performance excludes corporate income and expenses, legacy income or expenses, provisions for unusual items not related to the segment operations, interest expense, interest income, and income taxes.

Selected financial information for each reportable segment was as follows:

(In millions)	Year Ended 2012	2011	2010
Net Sales:			
Aerospace and Defense	$986.1	$909.7	$850.7
Real Estate	8.8	8.4	7.2
Total	$994.9	$918.1	$857.9
Segment Performance:			
Aerospace and Defense	$115.5	$108.6	$ 99.6
Environmental remediation provision adjustments	(11.4)	(8.9)	(0.2)
Retirement benefit plan expense	(18.9)	(21.0)	(29.3)
Unusual items (see Note 14)	(0.7)	(4.1)	(2.8)
Aerospace and Defense Total	84.5	74.6	67.3
Real Estate	3.7	5.6	5.3
Total	$ 88.2	$ 80.2	$ 72.6
Reconciliation of Segment Performance to Income From Continuing Operations Before Income Taxes:			
Segment Performance	$ 88.2	$ 80.2	$ 72.6
Interest expense	(22.3)	(30.8)	(37.0)
Interest income	0.6	1.0	1.6
Stock-based compensation	(6.5)	(3.7)	(0.4)
Corporate retirement benefit plan expense	(22.1)	(25.4)	(12.6)
Corporate and other expenses	(12.7)	(10.8)	(21.5)
Corporate unusual items (see Note 14)	(12.0)	(1.5)	(0.6)
Income from continuing operations before income taxes	$ 13.2	$ 9.0	$ 2.1
Aerospace and Defense	$ 37.2	$ 21.1	$ 18.2
Real Estate	—	—	—
Corporate	—	—	4.4
Capital Expenditures, cash and non-cash	$ 37.2	$ 21.1	$ 22.6
Aerospace and Defense	$ 21.7	$ 24.3	$ 27.6
Real Estate	0.6	0.3	0.3
Corporate	—	—	—
Depreciation and Amortization	$ 22.3	$ 24.6	$ 27.9

(In millions)	As of November 30, 2012	2011
Aerospace and Defense[(1)]	$637.6	$622.8
Real Estate	82.3	79.1
Identifiable assets	719.9	701.9
Corporate	199.4	237.6
Assets	$919.3	$939.5

(1) The Aerospace and Defense operating segment had $94.9 million of goodwill as of November 30, 2012 and 2011. In addition, as of November 30, 2012 and 2011 intangible assets balances were $13.9 million and $15.4 million, respectively, for the Aerospace and Defense operating segment.

The Company's continuing operations are located in the United States. Inter-area sales are not significant to the total sales of any geographic area. Unusual items included in segment performance pertained only to the United States.

Note 14. Unusual Items

Total unusual items expense, a component of other expense, net in the consolidated statements of operations was as follows:

(In millions)	Year Ended 2012	2011	2010
Aerospace and Defense:			
Loss on legal matters and settlements	$ 0.7	$4.1	$ 2.8
Aerospace and defense unusual items	0.7	4.1	2.8
Corporate:			
Rocketdyne Business acquisition related costs	11.6	—	—
Executive severance agreements	—	—	1.4
Loss on debt repurchased	0.4	0.2	1.2
Loss on bank amendment	—	1.3	0.7
Gain on legal settlement	—	—	(2.7)
Corporate unusual items	12.0	1.5	0.6
Total unusual items	$12.7	$5.6	$ 3.4

Fiscal 2012 Activity:

The Company recorded $0.7 million for realized losses and interest associated with the failure to register with the SEC the issuance of certain of the Company's common shares under the defined contribution 401(k) employee benefit plan.

The Company incurred expenses of $11.6 million, including internal labor costs of $2.0 million, related to the proposed Rocketdyne Business acquisition announced in July 2012.

The Company redeemed $75.0 million of its 9 ½% Notes at a redemption price of 100% of the principal amount. The redemption resulted in a charge of $0.4 million associated with the write-off of the 9 ½% Notes deferred financing costs.

Fiscal 2011 Activity:

The Company recorded a charge of $3.3 million related to a legal settlement and $0.8 million for realized losses and interest associated with the failure to register with the SEC the issuance of certain of its common shares under the defined contribution 401(k) employee benefit plan.

During fiscal 2011, the Company repurchased $22.0 million principal amount of its 2 ¼% Debentures at various prices ranging from 99.0% of par to 99.6% of par resulting in a loss of $0.2 million.

In addition, during fiscal 2011, the Company recorded $1.3 million of losses related to an amendment to the Senior Credit Facility.

Fiscal 2010 Activity:

In fiscal 2010, the Company recorded $1.4 million associated with executive severance. In addition, the Company recorded a charge of $1.9 million related to the estimated unrecoverable costs of legal matters and $0.9 million for realized losses and interest associated with the failure to register with the SEC the issuance of certain of its common shares under the defined contribution 401(k) employee benefit plan. Further, the Company recorded a $2.7 million gain related to a legal settlement.

In addition, during fiscal 2010, the Company recorded $0.7 million of losses related to an amendment to the Senior Credit Facility.

A summary of the Company's losses on the 2 ¼% Debentures repurchased during fiscal 2010 is as follows (in millions):

Principal amount repurchased	$ 77.8
Cash repurchase price	(74.3)
	3.5
Write-off of the associated debt discount	(6.3)
Portion of the 2 ¼% Debentures repurchased attributed to the equity component	2.9
Write-off of the deferred financing costs	(0.4)
Loss on 2 ¼% Debentures repurchased	$ (0.3)

A summary of the Company's losses on the 9 ½% Notes repurchased during fiscal 2010 is as follows (in millions):

Principal amount repurchased	$ 22.5
Cash repurchase price	(23.0)
Write-off of the deferred financing costs	(0.4)
Loss on 9 ½% Notes repurchased	$ (0.9)

3.93 BEAM INC. (DEC)
NOTES TO CONSOLIDATED FINANCIAL STATEMENTS

22. Quarterly Financial Data (Unaudited)

Selected quarterly financial data for the years ended December 31, 2012 and 2011 are as follows (in millions, except per share data):

	2012			
	First Quarter	Second Quarter[a]	Third Quarter[b]	Fourth Quarter[c]
Net sales	$533.8	$595.5	$627.5	$709.1
Gross profit	314.7	346.9	371.5	405.3
Income from continuing operations	78.4	101.3	91.7	126.8
Income (loss) from discontinued operations	0.7	(0.8)	(15.2)	(0.5)
Net income	79.1	100.5	76.5	126.3
Basic earnings (loss) per Beam Inc. common share				
Continuing operations	$ 0.50	$ 0.64	$ 0.58	$ 0.79
Discontinued operations	—	(0.01)	(0.10)	—
Net income	$ 0.50	$ 0.63	$ 0.48	$ 0.79
Diluted earnings (loss) per Beam Inc. common share				
Continuing operations	$ 0.49	$ 0.63	$ 0.57	$ 0.79
Discontinued operations	—	(0.01)	(0.10)	—
Net income	$ 0.49	$ 0.62	$ 0.47	$ 0.79

	2011			
	First Quarter[d]	Second Quarter[e]	Third Quarter[f]	Fourth Quarter[g]
Net sales	$524.0	$570.4	$579.2	$637.5
Gross profit	294.4	328.7	335.8	364.4
Income (loss) from continuing operations	61.7	62.4	(82.0)	91.2
Income (loss) from discontinued operations	21.5	267.6	495.8	(2.7)
Net income	83.2	330.0	413.8	88.5
Net income attributable to Beam Inc.	81.2	328.6	413.1	88.5
Basic earnings (loss) per Beam Inc. common share				
Continuing operations	$ 0.40	$ 0.40	$ (0.53)	$ 0.59
Discontinued operations	0.13	1.73	3.20	(0.02)
Net income	$ 0.53	$ 2.13	$ 2.67	$ 0.57
Diluted earnings (loss) per Beam Inc. common share				
Continuing operations	$ 0.39	$ 0.40	$ (0.53)	$ 0.58
Discontinued operations	0.13	1.69	3.20	(0.02)
Net income	$ 0.52	$ 2.09	$ 2.67	$ 0.56

[a] Unusual items impacting the quarter ended June 30, 2012 include (on a pre-tax basis): $13.8 million for business separation costs, $12.1 million for acquisition and integration-related charges incurred in connection with the May 2012 acquisition of the Pinnacle assets, and $18.0 million tax indemnification income related to the resolution of routine foreign tax audits.

[b] Unusual items impacting the quarter ended September 30, 2012 include: an unfavorable income tax adjustment of $7 million related to the correction of prior year items, which were determined to be immaterial to all periods impacted.

[c] Unusual items impacting the quarter ended December 31, 2012 include: $15.6 million (pre-tax) for impairment of the Larios tradename, $22 million of excess net foreign tax credits related to U.S. taxes applicable to repatriation of current year foreign earnings, and $9 million net tax benefit related to the resolution of certain foreign and U.S. federal tax audits. In the fourth quarter of 2012, we discovered certain income tax errors related to our discontinued Golf operations (primarily relating to the 2011 tax return filing process). These income tax errors resulted in third quarter 2012 loss from discontinued operations being overstated and net income being understated by approximately $11 million. In addition, both income from discontinued operations and net income in 2011 were understated by $5 million related to these errors. The correction of these errors in the fourth quarter of 2012 understated loss from discontinued operations and overstated net income by $16 million. We consider these errors to be immaterial to all quarterly and annual periods impacted, based on several factors including the fact that the errors impact businesses previously discontinued and do not impact our continuing operations.

[d] Unusual items impacting the quarter ended March 31, 2011 include (on a pre-tax basis): $46.3 million favorable one-time sales impact and $23.6 million favorable one-time operating income impact associated with our transition to a new long-term manufacturing and distribution agreement in Australia and $9.2 million related to business separation costs.

[e] Unusual items impacting the quarter ended June 30, 2011 include (on a pre-tax basis): $8.0 million for business separation costs.

[f] Unusual items impacting the quarter ended September 30, 2011 include (on a pre-tax basis): $134.0 million loss on early extinguishment of debt, $68.6 million of business separation costs, $25.0 million of acquisition-related contingent consideration, and $7.6 million gain related to a distribution from our Maxxium investment.

[g] Unusual items impacting the quarter ended December 31, 2011 include: $31.3 million (pre-tax) for impairment of the DYC and Larios tradenames, $19 million tax benefit related to the resolution of routine foreign tax audits, and $15.2 million (pre-tax) loss on early extinguishment of debt.

Earnings Per Share

PRESENTATION

3.94 The computation, presentation, and disclosure requirements for earnings per share (EPS) for entities with publicly held common stock or potential common stock are stated in FASB ASC 260, *Earnings Per Share*. The objective of basic EPS is to measure the performance of an entity over the reporting period. The objective of diluted EPS is to measure the performance of an entity over the reporting period while giving effect to all dilutive potential common shares that were outstanding during the period. FASB ASC 260 also discusses the application of EPS guidance to master limited partnerships.

EARNINGS PER SHARE

3.95 VISHAY INTERTECHNOLOGY, INC. (DEC)
NOTES TO THE CONSOLIDATED FINANCIAL STATEMENTS

(Dollars in thousands, except per share amounts)

Note 16—Earnings Per Share

Basic earnings per share is computed using the weighted average number of common shares outstanding during the periods presented. Diluted earnings per share is computed using the weighted average number of common shares outstanding adjusted to include the potentially dilutive effect of stock options and restricted stock units (see Note 12), warrants (see Note 7), convertible debt instruments (see Note 6), and other potentially dilutive securities.

The following table sets forth the computation of basic and diluted earnings per share attributable to Vishay stockholders *(shares in thousands)*:

	Years Ended December 31,		
	2012	2011	2010
Numerator:			
Numerator for basic earnings per share:			
Net earnings	$122,738	$238,821	$359,106
Adjustment to the numerator for continuing operations and net earnings:			
Interest savings assuming conversion of dilutive convertible and exchangeable notes, net of tax	293	189	257
Numerator for diluted earnings per share:			
Net earnings	$123,031	$239,010	$359,363
Denominator:			
Denominator for basic earnings per share:			
Weighted average shares	149,020	160,094	183,618
Effect of dilutive securities:			
Convertible and exchangeable debt instruments	6,176	7,820	6,313
Restricted stock units	549	212	133
Other	99	388	163
Dilutive potential common shares	6,824	8,420	6,609
Denominator for diluted earnings per share:			
Adjusted weighted average shares	155,844	168,514	190,227
Basic earnings per share attributable to Vishay stockholders	$ 0.82	$ 1.49	$ 1.96
Diluted earnings per share attributable to Vishay stockholders	$ 0.79	$ 1.42	$ 1.89

Diluted earnings per share for the years presented do not reflect the following weighted average potential common shares, as the effect would be antidilutive *(in thousands)*:

	Years Ended December 31,		
	2012	2011	2010
Convertible and exchangeable notes:			
Convertible Senior Debentures, due 2040	19,809	9,905	—
Convertible Senior Debentures, due 2041	7,885	5,026	—
Convertible Senior Debentures, due 2042	7,434	—	—
Convertible Subordinated Notes, due 2023	—	—	51
Weighted average employee stock options	177	182	2,243
Weighted average warrants	8,390	8,824	8,824
Weighted average other	282	123	35

In periods in which they are dilutive, if the potential common shares related to the exchangeable notes are included in the computation, the related interest savings, net of tax, assuming conversion/exchange is added to the net earnings used to compute earnings per share.

The Company's convertible debt instruments are only convertible upon the occurrence of certain events. While none of these events has occurred as of December 31, 2012, certain conditions which could trigger conversion have been deemed to be non-substantive, and accordingly, the Company has always assumed the conversion of these instruments in its diluted earnings per share computation during periods in which they are dilutive.

At the direction of its Board of Directors, the Company intends, upon conversion, to repay the principal amount of the convertible senior debentures, due 2040, due 2041, and due 2042, in cash and settle any additional amounts in shares of Vishay common stock. Accordingly, the debentures are included in the diluted earnings per share computation using the "treasury stock method" (similar to options and warrants) rather than the "if converted method" otherwise required for convertible debt. Under the "treasury stock method," Vishay calculates the number of shares issuable under the terms of the notes based on the average market price of Vishay common stock during the period, and that number is included in the total diluted shares figure for the period. If the average market price is less than $13.88, no shares are included in the diluted earnings per share computation for the convertible senior debentures due 2040, if the average market price is less than $19.02, no shares are included in the diluted earnings per share computation for the convertible senior debentures due 2041, and if the average market price is less than $11.81, no shares are included in the diluted earnings per share computation for the convertible senior debentures due 2042.

As described in Note 6, the Company purchased 99.6% of the outstanding convertible subordinated notes due 2023 pursuant to the option of the holders to require the Company to repurchase their notes on August 1, 2008. The remaining notes, with an aggregate principal amount of $1,870, were redeemed at Vishay's option on August 1, 2010.

Comprehensive Income in Annual Filings

RECOGNITION AND MEASUREMENT

4.01 Financial Accounting Standards Board (FASB) *Accounting Standards Codification* (ASC) 220, *Comprehensive Income*, requires that items included in other comprehensive income should be classified based on their nature. Other comprehensive income includes the following: foreign currency items, changes in the fair value of certain derivatives, unrealized gains and losses on certain securities, and certain pension or other postretirement benefit items.

PRESENTATION

4.02 FASB ASC 220 requires entities that provide a full set of general-purpose financial statements (that is, financial position, results of operations, and cash flows) report comprehensive income and its components either in a single continuous financial statement or in two separate but consecutive financial statements. The FASB ASC glossary defines *comprehensive income* as the change in equity (net assets) of a business entity during a period from transactions and other events and circumstances from nonowner sources. It includes all changes in equity during a period, except those resulting from investments by owners and distributions to owners. *Other comprehensive income* is defined as revenues, expenses, gains, and losses that under generally accepted accounting principles are included in comprehensive income but excluded from net income. If an entity has only net income, it is not required to report comprehensive income. All items that meet the definition of *components of comprehensive income* must be reported in a financial statement for the period in which they are recognized. Further, a total amount for comprehensive income should be displayed in the financial statement when the components of other comprehensive income are reported.

4.03 FASB ASC 220-10-45-5 states that if an entity has an outstanding noncontrolling interest, amounts for both net income and comprehensive income attributable to the parent and net income and comprehensive income attributable to the noncontrolling interest in a less-than-wholly-owned subsidiary shall be reported on the face of the financial statement(s) in which net income and comprehensive income are presented in addition to presenting consolidated net income and comprehensive income.

4.04 FASB ASC 220-10-45-12 also states that an entity should disclose the amount of income tax expense or benefit allocated to each component of other comprehensive income, including reclassification adjustments, either on the face of the statement in which those components are displayed or in the notes thereto. Also, FASB ASC 810, *Consolidation*, states that if an entity has an outstanding noncontrolling interest (minority interest), the components of both net income and other comprehensive income attributable to the parent and noncontrolling interest in a less-than-wholly-owned subsidiary are required to be reported on the face of the financial statement in which net income and comprehensive income are presented, in addition to presenting consolidated comprehensive income.

4.05 FASB ASC 220-10-45-15 also requires that adjustments should be made to avoid double counting in comprehensive income items that are displayed as part of net income for a period that also had been displayed as part of other comprehensive income in that period or earlier periods. For example, gains on investment securities that were realized and included in net income of the current period that also had been included in other comprehensive income as unrealized holding gains in the period in which they arose must be deducted through other comprehensive income of the period in which they are included in net income to avoid including them in comprehensive income twice. These adjustments are called *reclassification adjustments*. An entity may display reclassification adjustments on the face of the financial statement in which comprehensive income is reported, or it may disclose them in the notes to the financial statements (that is, either a gross display on the face of the financial statement or a net display on the face of the financial statement and disclosure of the gross change in the notes to the financial statements).

COMBINED STATEMENT OF INCOME AND COMPREHENSIVE INCOME

4.06 ENERGIZER HOLDINGS, INC. (SEP)
CONSOLIDATED STATEMENTS OF EARNINGS AND COMPREHENSIVE INCOME

(Dollars in millions, except per share data)

	For The Years Ended September 30,		
	2012	2011	2010
Statement of Earnings			
Net sales	$4,567.2	$4,645.7	$4,248.3
Cost of products sold	2,429.3	2,500.0	2,229.0
Gross profit	2,137.9	2,145.7	2,019.3
Selling, general and administrative expense	895.1	856.1	765.7
Advertising and sales promotion expense	449.5	524.0	461.3
Research and development expense	112.5	108.3	97.1
Household Products restructuring	(6.8)	79.0	—
Interest expense	127.3	121.4	125.4
Cost of early debt retirements	—	19.9	—
Other financing (income)/expense, net	(5.1)	31.0	26.4
Earnings before income taxes	565.4	406.0	543.4
Income taxes	156.5	144.8	140.4
Net earnings	$ 408.9	$ 261.2	$ 403.0
Earnings Per Share			
Basic net earnings per share	$ 6.30	$ 3.75	$ 5.76
Diluted net earnings per share	$ 6.22	$ 3.72	$ 5.72
Statement of Comprehensive Income			
Net earnings	$ 408.9	$ 261.2	$ 403.0
Other comprehensive (loss)/income, net of tax			
Foreign currency translation adjustments	(11.9)	(8.7)	(43.2)
Pension/postretirement activity, net of tax of $(14.4) in 2012, $(25.6) in 2011 and $(19.8) in 2010	(24.8)	(26.4)	(47.5)
Deferred (loss)/gain on hedging activity, net of tax of $1.6 in 2012 $5.3 in 2011 and $(6.9) in 2010	(0.4)	11.7	(11.7)
Comprehensive income	$ 371.8	$ 237.8	$ 300.6

The above financial statements should be read in conjunction with the Notes To Consolidated Financial Statements.

SEPARATE STATEMENT OF COMPREHENSIVE INCOME

4.07 NEWMARKET CORPORATION (DEC)
CONSOLIDATED STATEMENTS OF COMPREHENSIVE INCOME

	Years Ended December 31,		
(In thousands)	2012	2011	2010
Net income	$239,593	$206,907	$177,125
Other comprehensive (loss) income:			
Pension plans and other postretirement benefits:			
Prior service cost arising during the period, net of income tax benefit of $471 in 2012 and $462 in 2010	(1,570)	0	(780)
Amortization of prior service cost included in net periodic benefit cost, net of income tax expense of $48 in 2012, $138 in 2011, and $130 in 2010	27	260	257
Actuarial net (loss) gain arising during the period, net of income tax (benefit) expense of $(13,290) in 2012, $(17,052) in 2011, and $3,624 in 2010	(22,721)	(27,577)	6,268
Amortization of actuarial net loss included in net periodic benefit cost, net of income tax expense of $2,331 in 2012, $1,322 in 2011, and $1,487 in 2010	4,066	2,423	2,738
Settlement gain, net of income tax expense of $145 in 2012	436	0	0
Amortization of transition obligation included in net periodic benefit cost, net of income tax expense of $14 in 2012, $13 in 2011, and $5 in 2010	39	40	10
Total pension plans and other postretirement benefits	(19,723)	(24,854)	8,493
Derivative instruments:			
Unrealized loss on derivative instruments, net of income tax benefit of $210 in 2012, $1,022 in 2011, and $1,561 in 2010	(330)	(1,605)	(2,451)
Reclassification adjustments for losses on derivative instruments included in net income, net of income tax expense of $569 in 2012, $649 in 2011, and $614 in 2010	893	1,020	964
Total derivative instruments	563	(585)	(1,487)
Foreign currency translation adjustments, net of income tax (benefit) expense of $(1,007) in 2012, $(558) in 2011, and $87 in 2010	7,567	163	(6,042)
Marketable securities:			
Unrealized gain on marketable securities, net of income tax expense of $419 in 2012 and $226 in 2011	676	364	0
Reclassification adjustment for gain on marketable securities included in net income, net of income tax benefit of $645 in 2012	(1,040)	0	0
Total marketable securities	(364)	364	0
Other comprehensive (loss) income	(11,957)	(24,912)	964
Comprehensive income	$227,636	$181,995	$178,089

See accompanying Notes to Consolidated Financial Statements

TAX EFFECT DISCLOSURE IN THE NOTES

4.08 CISCO SYSTEMS, INC. (JUL)
NOTES TO CONSOLIDATED FINANCIAL STATEMENTS

13. Shareholders' Equity (in part)

(e) Comprehensive Income

The components of comprehensive income, net of tax, are as follows (in millions):

Years Ended	July 28, 2012	July 30, 2011	July 31, 2010
Net income	$8,041	$6,490	$7,767
Net change in unrealized gains/losses on available-for-sale investments:			
Change in net unrealized (losses) gains, net of tax benefit (expense) of $6, $(151), and $(199) for fiscal 2012, 2011, and 2010, respectively	(31)	281	334
Net (gains) losses reclassified into earnings, net of tax effects of $36, $68, and $17 for fiscal 2012, 2011, and 2010, respectively	(65)	(112)	(151)
	(96)	169	183
Net change in unrealized gains/losses on derivative instruments:			
Change in derivative instruments, net of tax benefit (expense) of $0, $0 and $(9) for fiscal 2012, 2011, and 2010, respectively	(131)	87	46
Net losses (gains) reclassified into earnings	72	(108)	2
	(59)	(21)	48
Net change in cumulative translation adjustment and other, net of tax benefit (expense) of $36, $(34), and $(9) for fiscal 2012, 2011, and 2010, respectively	(496)	538	(55)
Comprehensive income	7,390	7,176	7,943
Comprehensive loss (income) attributable to noncontrolling interests	18	(15)	12
Comprehensive income attributable to Cisco Systems, Inc.	$7,408	$7,161	$7,955

The components of AOCI, net of tax, are summarized as follows (in millions):

	July 28, 2012	July 30, 2011	July 31, 2010
Net unrealized gains on investments	$409	$ 487	$333
Net unrealized (losses) gains on derivative instruments	(53)	6	27
Cumulative translation adjustment and other	305	801	263
Total	$661	$1,294	$623

TAX EFFECT DISCLOSURE ON THE FACE OF THE FINANCIAL STATEMENTS

4.09 BROWN-FORMAN CORPORATION (APR)
CONSOLIDATED STATEMENTS OF COMPREHENSIVE INCOME

(Dollars in millions)

	Year Ended April 30,		
	2010	2011	2012
Net income	$449	$572	$513
Other comprehensive (loss) income:			
Foreign currency translation adjustment, net of tax of $(5), $(9), and $7 in 2010, 2011, and 2012, respectively	21	37	(55)
Amounts related to postretirement benefit plans:			
Net actuarial (loss) gain and prior service cost, net of tax of $46, $(9), and $42 in 2010, 2011, and 2012, respectively	(66)	13	(67)
Reclassification to earnings, net of tax of $(2), $(8), and $(8) in 2010, 2011, and 2012, respectively	3	12	12
Amounts related to cash flow hedges:			
Net (loss) gain on hedging instruments, net of tax of $7, $10, and $(3) in 2010, 2011, and 2012, respectively	(11)	(17)	6
Reclassification to earnings, net of tax of $(6) in 2010 and $(3) in 2012	10	—	5
Net other comprehensive (loss) income	(43)	45	(99)
Total comprehensive income	$406	$617	$414

The accompanying notes are an integral part of the consolidated financial statements.

4.10 AXIALL CORPORATION (DEC)

CONSOLIDATED STATEMENTS OF COMPREHENSIVE INCOME

(In thousands)	Years Ended December 31,		
	2012	2011	2010
Net income	$120,561	$ 57,757	$42,678
Other comprehensive income (loss):			
Pension liability adjustment	(13,361)	(20,629)	(5,807)
Foreign currency translation gain (loss)	7,999	(8,125)	17,036
Unrealized gain (loss) on derivatives	727	(1,146)	168
Other comprehensive income (loss), before income taxes	(4,635)	(29,900)	11,397
Provision for (benefit from) income taxes related to other comprehensive income items	(916)	(11,959)	7,293
Other comprehensive income (loss)	(3,719)	(17,941)	4,104
Comprehensive income	$116,842	$ 39,816	$46,782

See accompanying notes to consolidated financial statements.

FOREIGN CURRENCY TRANSLATION

4.11 THE ESTÉE LAUDER COMPANIES INC. (JUN)

CONSOLIDATED STATEMENTS OF COMPREHENSIVE INCOME (LOSS)

(In millions)	Year Ended June 30		
	2012	2011	2010
Net earnings	$860.5	$703.8	$ 482.4
Other comprehensive income (loss):			
Net unrealized investment gain (loss), net of tax	—	0.3	0.4
Net derivative instrument gain (loss), net of tax	18.1	(15.0)	12.8
Net actuarial gain (loss), net of tax	(101.0)	25.9	(32.4)
Net prior service credit (cost), net of tax	6.5	(7.3)	5.5
Translation adjustments, net of tax	(156.8)	213.7	(69.3)
	(233.2)	217.6	(83.0)
Comprehensive income (loss)	627.3	921.4	399.4
Comprehensive (income) loss attributable to noncontrolling interests:			
Net earnings	(3.6)	(3.0)	(4.1)
Translation adjustments, net of tax	2.6	(3.2)	3.4
	(1.0)	(6.2)	(0.7)
Comprehensive income (loss) attributable to The Estée Lauder Companies Inc.	$626.3	$915.2	$398.7

NOTES TO CONSOLIDATED FINANCIAL STATEMENTS

Note 2—Summary of Significant Accounting Policies (in part)

Currency Translation and Transactions

All assets and liabilities of foreign subsidiaries and affiliates are translated at year-end rates of exchange, while revenue and expenses are translated at weighted-average rates of exchange for the period. Unrealized translation gains or losses are reported as cumulative translation adjustments through other comprehensive income (loss) ("OCI"). Such adjustments, attributable to The Estée Lauder Companies Inc., amounted to $(154.2) million, $210.5 million and $65.9 million of unrealized translation gains (losses), net of tax, in fiscal 2012, 2011 and 2010, respectively. For the Company's Venezuelan subsidiary operating in a highly inflationary economy, the U.S. dollar is the functional currency. Remeasurement adjustments in financial statements in a highly inflationary economy and other transactional gains and losses are reflected in earnings.

The Company enters into foreign currency forward contracts and may enter into option contracts to hedge foreign currency transactions for periods consistent with its identified exposures. Accordingly, the Company categorizes these instruments as entered into for purposes other than trading.

The accompanying consolidated statements of earnings include net exchange losses on foreign currency transactions of $0.5 million, $18.6 million and $33.3 million in fiscal 2012, 2011 and 2010, respectively.

Note 18—Accumulated Other Comprehensive Income (Loss)

The components of Accumulated OCI ("AOCI") included in the accompanying consolidated balance sheets consist of the following:

	Year Ended June 30		
(In millions)	2012	2011	2010
Net unrealized investment gains (losses), beginning of year	$ 0.5	$ 0.2	$ (0.2)
Unrealized investment gains (losses)	0.1	0.4	0.6
Benefit (provision) for deferred income taxes	(0.1)	(0.1)	(0.2)
Net unrealized investment gains, end of year	0.5	0.5	0.2
Net derivative instruments, beginning of year	(0.7)	14.3	1.5
Gain (loss) on derivative instruments	40.2	(38.0)	(0.2)
Benefit (provision) for deferred income taxes on derivative instruments	(14.3)	13.4	(0.1)
Reclassification to earnings during the year:			
Foreign currency forward contracts	(11.7)	15.1	20.3
Settled interest rate-related derivatives	(0.3)	(0.3)	(0.2)
Benefit (provision) for deferred income taxes on reclassification	4.2	(5.2)	(7.0)
Net derivative instruments, end of year	17.4	(0.7)	14.3
Net pension and post-retirement adjustments, beginning of year	(199.0)	(217.6)	(190.7)
Changes in plan assets and benefit obligations:			
Net actuarial gains (losses) recognized	(176.9)	30.7	(65.6)
Net prior service credit (cost) recognized	2.0	(10.6)	2.6
Translation adjustments	7.6	(16.4)	6.5
Amortization of amounts included in net periodic benefit cost:			
Net actuarial (gains) losses	14.7	26.3	9.3
Net prior service cost (credit)	4.3	3.1	3.1
Net transition asset (obligation)	—	—	—
Benefit (provision) for deferred income taxes	53.8	(14.5)	17.2
Net pension and post-retirement adjustments, end of year	(293.5)	(199.0)	(217.6)
Cumulative translation adjustments, beginning of year	216.9	6.4	72.3
Translation adjustments	(156.6)	213.2	(65.5)
Benefit (provision) for deferred income taxes	2.4	(2.7)	(0.4)
Cumulative translation adjustments, end of year	62.7	216.9	6.4
Accumulated other comprehensive income (loss)	$ 212.9	$ 17.7	$(196.7)

Of the $17.4 million, net of tax, derivative instrument gain recorded in AOCI at June 30, 2012, $9.8 million in gains, net of tax, related to foreign currency forward contracts, which the Company will reclassify to earnings through March 2014. Also included in the net derivative instrument gain recorded in AOCI was $8.2 million, net of tax, related to the October 2003 gain from the settlement of the treasury lock agreements upon the issuance of the Company's 2033 Senior Notes, which is being reclassified to earnings as an offset to interest expense over the life of the debt. These gains were partially offset by $0.6 million, net of tax, related to a loss from the settlement of a series of forward-starting interest rate swap agreements upon the issuance of the Company's 2037 Senior Notes, which is being reclassified to earnings as an addition to interest expense over the life of the debt.

Refer to Note 13—Pension, Deferred Compensation and Post-retirement Benefit Plans for the discussion regarding the net pension and post-retirement adjustments.

PENSION AND POSTRETIREMENT PLANS

4.12 THE WASHINGTON POST COMPANY (DEC)
CONSOLIDATED STATEMENTS OF COMPREHENSIVE INCOME

	Fiscal Year Ended		
(In thousands)	December 31, 2012	December 31, 2011	January 2, 2011
Net Income	$132,187	$117,157	$278,020
Other Comprehensive Income (Loss), Before Tax			
Foreign currency translation adjustments:			
Translation adjustments arising during the period	5,622	(21,375)	10,994
Adjustment for sales of businesses with foreign operations	(888)	—	—
	4,734	(21,375)	10,994
Unrealized gains (losses) on available-for-sale securities:			
Unrealized gains (losses) for the period	33,098	(37,708)	(12,974)
Reclassification adjustment for write-down on available-for-sale securities, net of gain, included in net income	17,226	53,793	—
	50,324	16,085	(12,974)

(continued)

(In thousands)	Fiscal Year Ended		
	December 31, 2012	December 31, 2011	January 2, 2011
Pension and other postretirement plans:			
Actuarial gain (loss)	$ 82,470	$ (16,048)	$126,987
Prior service credit	—	—	6,336
Amortization of net actuarial loss (gain) included in net income	9,368	(510)	(1,155)
Amortization of net prior service (credit) cost included in net income	(1,859)	(3,925)	1,952
Amortization of transition asset	—	—	(29)
Curtailments and other adjustments	(745)	—	(4,953)
Foreign affiliate pension adjustments	—	2,088	(2,667)
	89,234	(18,395)	126,471
Cash flow hedge (loss) gain	(1,581)	14	—
Other comprehensive income (loss), before tax	142,711	(23,671)	124,491
Income tax (expense) benefit related to items of other comprehensive income (loss)	(55,186)	6,861	(46,864)
Other comprehensive income (loss), net of tax	87,525	(16,810)	77,627
Comprehensive income	219,712	100,347	355,647
Comprehensive income attributable to noncontrolling interests	(103)	(126)	(13)
Total comprehensive income attributable to the Washington post company	$219,609	$100,221	$355,634

See accompanying Notes to Consolidated Financial Statements.

NOTES TO CONSOLIDATED FINANCIAL STATEMENTS

2. Summary of Significant Accounting Policies (in part)

Pensions and Other Postretirement Benefits. The Company maintains various pension and incentive savings plans and contributes to multiemployer plans on behalf of certain union-represented employee groups. Substantially all of the Company's employees are covered by these plans. The Company also provides health care and life insurance benefits to certain retired employees. These employees become eligible for benefits after meeting age and service requirements.

The Company recognizes the overfunded or underfunded status of a defined benefit postretirement plan (other than a multiemployer plan) as an asset or liability in its statement of financial position and recognizes changes in that funded status in the fiscal year in which the changes occur through comprehensive income. The Company measures changes in the funded status of its plans using the projected unit credit method and several actuarial assumptions, the most significant of which are the discount rate, the long-term rate of asset return and rate of compensation increase. The Company uses a measurement date of December 31 for its pension and other postretirement benefit plans.

13. Pensions and Other Postretirement Plans (in part)

The Company maintains various pension and incentive savings plans and contributes to multiemployer plans on behalf of certain union-represented employee groups. Most of the Company's employees are covered by these plans.

The Company also provides health care and life insurance benefits to certain retired employees. These employees become eligible for benefits after meeting age and service requirements.

The Company uses a measurement date of December 31 for its pension and other postretirement benefit plans.

Defined Benefit Plans. The Company's defined benefit pension plans consist of various pension plans and a Supplemental Executive Retirement Plan (SERP) offered to certain executives of the Company.

The following table sets forth obligation, asset and funding information for the Company's defined benefit pension plans at December 31, 2012 and 2011:

(In thousands)	Pension Plans	
	2012	2011
Change in benefit obligation		
Benefit obligation at beginning of year	$1,279,315	$1,113,205
Service cost	40,344	27,619
Interest cost	59,124	60,033
Amendments	8,508	2,776
Actuarial loss	144,286	140,126
Benefits paid and other	(65,255)	(64,444)
Benefit obligation at end of year	$1,466,322	$1,279,315
Change in plan assets		
Fair value of assets at beginning of year	$1,816,577	$1,651,958
Actual return on plan assets	319,823	229,063
Benefits paid and other	(65,255)	(64,444)
Fair value of assets at end of year	$2,071,145	$1,816,577
Funded status	$ 604,823	$ 537,262

(continued)

(in thousands)	SERP 2012	2011
Change in benefit obligation		
Benefit obligation at beginning of year	$ 92,863	$ 79,403
Service cost	1,467	1,655
Interest cost	4,241	4,342
Amendments	—	369
Actuarial loss	8,428	9,059
Benefits paid and other	(2,937)	(1,965)
Benefit obligation at end of year	$ 104,062	$ 92,863
Change in plan assets		
Fair value of assets at beginning of year	$ —	$ —
Employer contributions and other	3,681	3,114
Benefits paid	(3,681)	(3,114)
Fair value of assets at end of year	$ —	$ —
Funded status	$(104,062)	$(92,863)

The accumulated benefit obligation for the Company's pension plans at December 31, 2012 and 2011, was $1,349.2 million and $1,191.9 million, respectively. The accumulated benefit obligation for the Company's SERP at December 31, 2012 and 2011, was $97.6 million and $86.6 million, respectively.

Key assumptions utilized for determining the benefit obligation at December 31, 2012 and 2011, are as follows:

	Pension Plans		SERP	
	2012	2011	2012	2011
Discount rate	4.0%	4.7%	4.0%	4.7%
Rate of compensation increase	4.0%	4.0%	4.0%	4.0%

The Company made no contributions to its pension plans in 2012, 2011 and 2010, and the Company does not expect to make any contributions in 2013. The Company made contributions to its SERP of $3.7 million and $3.1 million for the years ended December 31, 2012 and 2011, respectively. As the plan is unfunded, the Company makes contributions to the SERP based on actual benefit payments.

The total cost (benefit) arising from the Company's defined benefit pension plans for the years ended December 31, 2012 and 2011, and January 2, 2011, including a portion included in discontinued operations, consists of the following components:

	Pension Plans		
(In thousands)	2012	2011	2010
Service cost	$ 40,344	$ 27,619	$ 26,976
Interest cost	59,124	60,033	60,329
Expected return on assets	(96,132)	(95,983)	(95,340)
Amortization of transition asset	—	—	(29)
Amortization of prior service cost	3,695	3,605	4,201
Recognized actuarial loss	9,013	—	—
Net periodic cost (benefit) for the year	16,044	(4,726)	(3,863)
Early retirement programs expense	8,508	634	
Special termination benefits	—	—	5,295
Recognition of prior service cost	—	—	2,369
Total cost (benefit) for the year	$ 24,552	$ (4,092)	$ 3,801
Other changes in plan assets and benefit obligations			
Recognized in other comprehensive income			
Current year actuarial (gain) loss	$(79,405)	$ 7,046	$(126,568)
Amortization of transition asset	—	—	29
Amortization of prior service cost	(3,695)	(1,463)	(6,570)
Recognized net actuarial loss	(9,013)	—	—
Total recognized in other comprehensive income (before tax effects)	$(92,113)	$ 5,583	$(133,109)
Total recognized in total cost (benefit) and other			
Comprehensive income (before tax effects)	$(67,561)	$ 1,491	$(129,308)

(continued)

| | | SERP | |
(In thousands)	2012	2011	2010
Service cost	$ 1,467	$ 1,655	$1,381
Interest cost	4,241	4,342	4,244
Plan amendment	—	369	—
Amortization of prior service cost	54	260	406
Recognized actuarial loss	1,833	1,411	1,068
Total cost for the year	$ 7,595	$ 8,037	$7,099
Other changes in benefit obligations recognized in other comprehensive income			
Current year actuarial loss	$ 8,428	$ 9,059	$2,656
Amortization of prior service cost	(54)	(260)	(406)
Recognized net actuarial loss	(1,833)	(1,411)	(877)
Other adjustments	745	—	—
Total recognized in other comprehensive income (before tax effects)	$ 7,286	$ 7,388	$1,373
Total recognized in total cost and other comprehensive income (before tax effects)	$14,881	$15,425	$8,472

The costs for the Company's defined benefit pension plans are actuarially determined. Below are the key assumptions utilized to determine periodic cost for the years ended December 31, 2012 and 2011, and January 2, 2011:

| | Pension Plans | | | SERP | | |
	2012	2011	2010	2012	2011	2010
Discount rate	4.7%	5.6%	6.0%	4.7%	5.6%	6.0%
Expected return on plan assets	6.5%	6.5%	6.5%	—	—	—
Rate of compensation increase	4.0%	4.0%	4.0%	4.0%	4.0%	4.0%

At December 31, 2012 and 2011, accumulated other comprehensive income (AOCI) includes the following components of unrecognized net periodic cost for the defined benefit plans:

| | Pension Plans | | SERP | |
(In thousands)	2012	2011	2012	2011
Unrecognized actuarial (gain) loss	$(193,469)	$(105,051)	$ 33,725	$ 26,385
Unrecognized prior service cost	15,931	19,626	191	245
Gross amount	(177,538)	(85,425)	33,916	26,630
Deferred tax liability (asset)	71,015	34,170	(13,566)	(10,652)
Net amount	$(106,523)	$ (51,255)	$ 20,350	$ 15,978

Other Postretirement Plans. The following table sets forth obligation, asset and funding information for the Company's other postretirement plans at December 31, 2012 and 2011:

| | Postretirement Plans | |
(In thousands)	2012	2011
Change in benefit obligation		
Benefit obligation at beginning of year	$ 72,412	$ 68,818
Service cost	3,113	2,872
Interest cost	2,735	3,063
Actuarial gain	(11,493)	(55)
Curtailment loss	438	—
Benefits paid, net of Medicare subsidy	(3,337)	(2,286)
Benefit obligation at end of year	$ 63,868	$ 72,412
Change in plan assets		
Fair value of assets at beginning of year	$ —	$ —
Employer contributions	3,337	2,286
Benefits paid, net of Medicare subsidy	(3,337)	(2,286)
Fair value of assets at end of year	$ —	$ —
Funded status	$(63,868)	$(72,412)

The discount rates utilized for determining the benefit obligation at December 31, 2012 and 2011, for the postretirement plans were 3.30% and 3.90%, respectively. The assumed health care cost trend rate used in measuring the postretirement benefit obligation at December 31, 2012, was 8.0% for pre-age 65, decreasing to 5.0% in the year 2025 and thereafter. The assumed health care cost trend rate used in measuring the postretirement benefit obligation at December 31, 2012, was 21.8% for the post-age 65 Medicare Advantage Prescription Drug (MA-PD) plan, decreasing to 5.0% in the year 2023 and thereafter, and was 7.0% for the post-age 65 non MA-PD plan, decreasing to 5.0% in the year 2021 and thereafter.

The total (benefit) cost arising from the Company's other postretirement plans for the years ended December 31, 2012 and 2011, and January 2, 2011, including a portion included in discontinued operations, consists of the following components:

| (in thousands) | Postretirement Plans | | |
	2012	2011	2010
Service cost	$ 3,113	$ 2,872	$ 3,275
Interest cost	2,735	3,063	3,934
Amortization of prior service credit	(5,608)	(5,650)	(5,026)
Recognized actuarial gain	(1,478)	(1,921)	(2,032)
Net periodic (benefit) cost	(1,238)	(1,636)	151
Curtailment loss (gain)	438	—	(8,583)
Total Benefit for the Year	$ (800)	$(1,636)	$(8,432)
Other changes in benefit obligations recognized in other comprehensive income			
Current year actuarial gain	$(11,493)	$ (55)	$(3,073)
Current year prior service credit	—	—	(6,336)
Amortization of prior service credit	5,608	5,650	5,026
Recognized actuarial gain	1,478	1,921	2,032
Curtailment loss	—	—	4,953
Total recognized in other comprehensive income (before tax effects)	$ (4,407)	$ 7,516	$ 2,602
Total recognized in (benefit) cost and other comprehensive income (before tax effect)	$ (5,207)	$ 5,880	$(5,830)

The costs for the Company's postretirement plans are actuarially determined. The discount rates utilized to determine periodic cost for the years ended December 31, 2012 and 2011, and January 2, 2011 were 3.90%, 4.60% and 5.25%, respectively.

At December 31, 2012 and 2011, AOCI included the following components of unrecognized net periodic benefit for the postretirement plans:

(In thousands)	2012	2011
Unrecognized actuarial gain	$(25,525)	$(15,510)
Unrecognized prior service credit	(26,128)	(31,736)
Gross amount	(51,653)	(47,246)
Deferred tax liability	20,661	18,898
Net amount	$(30,992)	$(28,348)

4.13 COOPER TIRE & RUBBER COMPANY (DEC)
CONSOLIDATED STATEMENTS OF COMPREHENSIVE INCOME

Years Ended December 31

(Dollar amounts in thousands except per share amounts)

	2010	2011	2012
Net income	$163,887	$269,603	$252,426
Other comprehensive income (loss)			
Cumulative currency translation adjustments			
Foreign currency translation adjustments	7,190	7,487	13,720
Currency loss recognized as part of acquisition of noncontrolling shareholder interest	—	4,893	—
Cumulative currency translation adjustments	7,190	12,380	13,720
Financial instruments			
Change in the fair value of derivatives and marketable securities	(1,026)	9,189	(7,469)
Income tax benefit (expense) on derivative instruments	206	(899)	2,555
Financial instruments, net of tax	(820)	8,290	(4,914)
Postretirement benefit plans			
Amortization of actuarial loss	33,665	37,333	46,712
Amortization of prior service credit	(1,142)	(1,435)	(873)
Pension curtailment gain	—	—	(7,460)
Actuarial loss	(38,729)	(162,065)	(97,972)
Income tax (expense) benefit on postretirement benefit plans	(2,003)	45,283	22,083
Foreign currency translation effect	5,260	169	199
Postretirement benefit plans, net of tax	(2,949)	(80,715)	(37,311)
Other comprehensive income (loss)	3,421	(60,045)	(28,505)
Comprehensive income	167,308	209,558	223,921
Less comprehensive income attributable to noncontrolling shareholders' interests	24,650	16,525	34,198
Comprehensive income attributable to Cooper Tire & Rubber Company	$142,658	$193,033	$189,723

See Notes to Consolidated Financial Statements.

(Dollar amounts in thousands except per share amounts)

Note 11—Pensions and Postretirement Benefits Other than Pensions (in part)

The Company and its subsidiaries have a number of plans providing pension, retirement or profit-sharing benefits. These plans include defined benefit and defined contribution plans. The plans cover substantially all U.S. domestic employees. There are also plans that cover a significant number of employees in the U.K. and Germany. The Company has an unfunded, nonqualified supplemental retirement benefit plan in the U.S. covering certain employees whose participation in the qualified plan is limited by provisions of the Internal Revenue Code.

For defined benefit plans, benefits are generally based on compensation and length of service for salaried employees and length of service for hourly employees. In the U.S., the Company froze the pension benefits in its Spectrum (salaried employees) Plan in 2009. In 2012, the Company closed the U.S. pension plans for the bargaining units to new participants. Certain grandfathered participants in the bargaining unit plans continue to accrue pension benefits. Employees of certain of the Company's foreign operations are covered by either contributory or non-contributory trusteed pension plans. In 2012, the Company froze the benefits in the U.K. pension plan.

Participation in the Company's defined contribution plans is voluntary. The Company matches certain plan participants' contributions up to various limits. Participants' contributions are limited based on their compensation and, for certain supplemental contributions which are not eligible for company matching, based on their age. Expense for those plans was $12,827, $14,311 and $12,003 for 2010, 2011 and 2012, respectively.

The Company currently provides retiree health care and life insurance benefits to a significant percentage of its U.S. salaried and hourly employees. U.S. salaried and non-bargained hourly employees hired on or after January 1, 2003 are not eligible for retiree health care or life insurance coverage. The Company has reserved the right to modify or terminate certain of these salaried benefits at any time.

The Company has implemented household caps on the amounts of retiree medical benefits it will provide to certain retirees. The caps do not apply to individuals who retired prior to certain specified dates. Costs in excess of these caps will be paid by plan participants. The Company implemented increased cost sharing in 2004 in the retiree medical coverage provided to certain eligible current and future retirees. Since then cost sharing has expanded such that nearly all covered retirees pay a charge to be enrolled.

In accordance with U.S. GAAP, the Company recognizes the funded status (i.e., the difference between the fair value of plan assets and the projected benefit obligation) of its pension and other postretirement benefit ("OPEB") plans and the net unrecognized actuarial losses and unrecognized prior service costs in the Consolidated Balance Sheets. The unrecognized actuarial losses and unrecognized prior service costs (components of cumulative other comprehensive loss in the stockholders' equity section of the balance sheet) will be subsequently recognized as net periodic pension cost pursuant to the Company's historical accounting policy for amortizing such amounts. Further, actuarial gains and losses that arise in subsequent periods and are not recognized as net periodic benefit costs in the same periods will be recognized as a component of other comprehensive income.

The following table reflects changes in the projected obligations and fair market values of assets in all defined benefit pension and other postretirement benefit plans of the Company:

	2011 Pension Benefits			2012 Pension Benefits			Other Postretirement Benefits	
	Domestic	International	Total	Domestic	International	Total	2011	2012
Change in benefit obligation:								
Projected benefit obligation at January 1	$ 865,982	$ 320,618	$1,186,600	$ 924,544	$ 343,219	$1,267,763	$ 275,348	$ 311,069
Service cost—employer	7,700	2,497	10,197	9,415	725	10,140	3,103	4,161
Service cost—employee	—	2,308	2,308	—	533	533	—	—
Interest cost	45,260	18,009	63,269	43,005	17,106	60,111	13,846	12,532
Plan curtailment	—	—	—	—	(9,933)	(9,933)	—	—
Actuarial (gain)/loss	54,022	13,846	67,868	137,141	20,331	157,472	27,928	(10,945)
Benefits paid	(48,420)	(12,506)	(60,926)	(50,035)	(12,700)	(62,735)	(9,156)	(8,591)
Foreign currency translation effect	—	(1,553)	(1,553)	—	15,644	15,644	—	—
Projected benefit obligation at December 31	$ 924,544	$ 343,219	$1,267,763	$1,064,070	$ 374,925	$1,438,995	$ 311,069	$ 308,226
Change in plans' assets:								
Fair value of plans' assets at January 1	$ 698,827	$ 229,496	$ 928,323	$ 680,217	$ 226,914	$ 907,131	$ —	$ —
Actual return on plans' assets	3,375	30	3,405	80,339	25,960	106,299	—	—
Employer contribution	26,435	8,420	34,855	35,350	8,215	43,565	—	—
Employee contribution	—	2,308	2,308	—	533	533	—	—
Benefits paid	(48,420)	(12,506)	(60,926)	(50,035)	(12,700)	(62,735)	—	—
Foreign currency translation effect	—	(834)	(834)	—	10,781	10,781	—	—
Fair value of plans' assets at December 31	$ 680,217	$ 226,914	$ 907,131	$ 745,871	$ 259,703	$1,005,574	$ —	$ —
Funded status	$(244,327)	$(116,305)	$ (360,632)	$ (318,199)	$(115,222)	$ (433,421)	$(311,069)	$(308,226)
Amounts recognized in the balance sheets:								
Other assets	$ —	$ —	$ —	$ —	$ —	$ —	$ —	$ —
Accrued liabilities	—	—	—	(500)	—	(500)	(17,802)	(16,680)
Postretirement benefits other than pensions	—	—	—	—	—	—	(293,267)	(291,546)
Pension benefits	(244,327)	(116,305)	(360,632)	(317,699)	(115,222)	(432,921)		

Included in cumulative other comprehensive loss at December 31, 2011 are the following amounts that have not yet been recognized in net periodic benefit cost: unrecognized prior service credits of ($12,002) (($8,501) net of tax) and unrecognized actuarial losses of $684,717 ($567,278 net of tax).

Included in cumulative other comprehensive loss at December 31, 2012 are the following amounts that have not yet been recognized in net periodic benefit cost: unrecognized prior service credits of ($3,867) (($2,777) net of tax) and unrecognized actuarial losses of $735,976 ($598,865 net of tax). The prior service credit and actuarial loss included in cumulative other comprehensive loss that are expected to be recognized in net periodic benefit cost during the fiscal year-ended December 31, 2013 are ($566) and $50,112, respectively.

The accumulated benefit obligation for all defined benefit pension plans was $1,264,377 and $1,435,193 at December 31, 2011 and 2012, respectively.

Weighted average assumptions used to determine benefit obligations at December 31:

	Pension Benefits		Other Postretirement Benefits	
	2011	2012	2011	2012
All plans				
Discount rate	4.81%	3.92%	4.15%	3.60%
Rate of compensation increase	0.81%	0.75%	—	—
Domestic plans				
Discount rate	4.80%	3.75%	4.15%	3.60%
Foreign plans				
Discount rate	4.85%	4.39%	—	—
Rate of compensation increase	2.99%	2.89%	—	—

At December 31, 2012, the weighted average assumed annual rate of increase in the cost of medical benefits was 7.80 percent for 2013 trending linearly to 5.00 percent per annum in 2020.

	Pension Benefits—Domestic			Pension Benefits—International		
	2010	2011	2012	2010	2011	2012
Components of net periodic benefit cost:						
Service cost	$ 4,316	$ 7,700	$ 9,415	$ 2,327	$ 2,497	$ 725
Interest cost	45,653	45,260	43,005	16,923	18,009	17,106
Expected return on plan assets	(50,457)	(50,206)	(43,269)	(15,249)	(16,646)	(15,323)
Amortization of prior service cost	—	—	—	(600)	(747)	(185)
Amortization of actuarial loss	27,741	30,300	36,818	5,924	5,772	6,818
Cooper Avon curtailment gain	—	—	—	—	—	(7,460)
Recognized actuarial loss (gain)	4,323	—	—	(673)	—	—
Net periodic benefit cost	$ 31,576	$ 33,054	$ 45,969	$ 8,652	$ 8,885	$ 1,681

	Other Post Retirement Benefits		
	2010	2011	2012
Components of net periodic benefit cost:			
Service cost	$ 3,160	$ 3,103	$ 4,161
Interest cost	14,115	13,846	12,532
Amortization of prior service cost	(542)	(688)	(688)
Amortization of actuarial loss	—	1,261	3,076
Net periodic benefit cost	$16,733	$17,522	$19,081

Effective April 6, 2012, the Company amended the Cooper Avon Pension Plan to freeze all future pension benefits. As a result of this amendment, the Company recognized a pre-tax pension curtailment gain of $7,460 which was credited to cost of goods sold in the second quarter of 2012. This curtailment gain represents the prior service credit from a previous plan amendment.

Weighted-average assumptions used to determine net periodic benefit cost for the years ended December 31:

	Pension Benefits			Other Postretirement Benefits		
	2010	2011	2012	2010	2011	2012
All plans						
Discount rate	5.74%	5.39%	4.83%	5.75%	5.20%	4.15%
Expected return on plan assets	8.24%	7.58%	6.86%	—	—	—
Rate of compensation increase	1.03%	0.92%	0.86%	—	—	—
Domestic plans						
Discount rate	5.75%	5.35%	4.80%	5.75%	5.20%	4.15%
Expected return on plan assets	8.50%	7.75%	7.00%	—	—	—
Foreign plans						
Discount rate	5.70%	5.50%	4.92%	—	—	—
Expected return on plan assets	7.44%	7.05%	6.43%	—	—	—
Rate of compensation increase	3.74%	3.39%	3.17%	—	—	—

The weighted-average assumptions for foreign plans includes the U.K. and German plans. The U.K. plan assumptions are blended rates including one rate from January 1, 2012 through April 6, 2012 when the plan was re-measured due to the plan freeze and one rate from April 7, 2012 through December 31, 2012. The 2012 Discount rate for foreign plans includes a rate of 5.10% for the German plan and a blended rate of 4.92% for the U.K. plan. The 2012 Expected return on plan assets for foreign plans consists of a return on German plan assets of 2.00% and a blended return on U.K. plans assets of 6.48%. The 2012 Rate of compensation increase consists of a rate for the German plan of 2.00% and a blended U.K. plan rate of 3.18%.

The following table lists the projected benefit obligation, accumulated benefit obligation and fair value of plan assets for the pension plans with projected benefit obligations and accumulated benefit obligations in excess of plan assets at December 31, 2011 and 2012:

| | 2011 | | 2012 | |
	Projected Benefit Obligation Exceeds Plan Assets	Accumulated Benefit Obligation Exceeds Plan Assets	Projected Benefit Obligation Exceeds Plan Assets	Accumulated Benefit Obligation Exceeds Plan Assets
Projected benefit obligation	$1,267,763	$1,267,763	$1,438,995	$1,438,995
Accumulated benefit obligation	1,264,377	1,264,377	1,435,193	1,435,193
Fair value of plan assets	907,131	907,131	1,005,574	1,005,574

Note 14—Cumulative Other Comprehensive Loss

The balances of each component of cumulative other comprehensive loss in the accompanying Consolidated Statements of Equity were as follows:

	2011	2012
Cumulative currency translation adjustment	$ 32,558	$ 44,135
Changes in the fair value of derivatives and unrealized gains/(losses) on marketable securities	6,009	(1,460)
Tax effect	(668)	1,887
Net	5,341	427
Unrecognized postretirement benefit plans	(672,715)	(732,109)
Tax effect, net of valuation allowance	113,938	136,021
Net	(558,777)	(596,088)
	$(520,878)	$(551,526)

NET CHANGE IN UNREALIZED GAINS AND LOSSES ON AVAILABLE-FOR-SALE SECURITIES

4.14 GOOGLE INC. (DEC)
CONSOLIDATED STATEMENTS OF COMPREHENSIVE INCOME

(In millions)

| | Year Ended December 31, | | |
	2010	2011	2012
Net income	$8,505	$9,737	$10,737
Other comprehensive income:			
Change in foreign currency translation adjustment	(124)	(107)	75
Available-for-sale investments:			
Change in net unrealized gains	232	348	493
Less: reclassification adjustment for net gains included in net income	(151)	(115)	(216)
Net change (net of tax effect of $52, $54, $68)	81	233	277
Cash flow hedges:			
Change in unrealized gains	196	39	47
Less: reclassification adjustment for gains included in net income	(120)	(27)	(137)
Net change (net of tax effect of $52, $2, $53)	76	12	(90)
Other comprehensive income	33	138	262
Comprehensive income	$8,538	$9,875	$10,999

See accompanying notes.

NOTES TO CONSOLIDATED FINANCIAL STATEMENTS

Note 1. Google Inc. and Summary of Significant Accounting Policies (in part)

Cash, Cash Equivalents, and Marketable Securities (in part)

We classify all highly liquid investments with stated maturities of three months or less from date of purchase as cash equivalents and all highly liquid investments with stated maturities of greater than three months as marketable securities.

We determine the appropriate classification of our investments in marketable securities at the time of purchase and reevaluate such designation at each balance sheet date. We have classified and accounted for our marketable securities as available-for-sale. We may or may not hold securities with stated maturities greater than 12 months until maturity. After consideration of our risk versus reward objectives, as well as our liquidity requirements, we may sell these securities prior to their stated maturities. As we view these securities as available to support current operations, we classify securities with maturities beyond 12 months as current assets under the caption marketable securities in the accompanying Consolidated Balance Sheets. We carry these securities at fair value, and report the unrealized gains and losses, net of taxes, as a component of stockholders' equity, except for unrealized losses determined to be other-than-temporary, which we record as interest and other income, net. We determine any realized gains or losses on the sale of marketable securities on a specific identification method, and we record such gains and losses as a component of interest and other income, net.

Impairment of Marketable and Non-Marketable Securities

We periodically review our marketable and non-marketable securities for impairment. If we conclude that any of these investments are impaired, we determine whether such impairment is other-than-temporary. Factors we consider to make such determination include the duration and severity of the impairment, the reason for the decline in value and the potential recovery period and our intent to sell. For marketable debt securities, we also consider whether (1) it is more likely than not that we will be required to sell the security before recovery of its amortized cost basis, and (2) the amortized cost basis cannot be recovered as a result of credit losses. If any impairment is considered other-than-temporary, we will write down the asset to its fair value and record the corresponding charge as interest and other income, net.

Note 3. Financial Instruments (in part)

Cash, Cash Equivalents and Marketable Securities

The following tables summarize our cash, cash equivalents and marketable securities measured at adjusted cost, gross unrealized gains, gross unrealized losses and fair value by significant investment categories as of December 31, 2011 and December 31, 2012 (in millions):

| | As of December 31, 2011 | | | | | |
	Adjusted Cost	Gross Unrealized Gains	Gross Unrealized Losses	Fair Value	Cash and Cash Equivalents	Marketable Securities
Cash	$ 4,712	$ 0	$ 0	$ 4,712	$4,712	$ 0
Level 1:						
Money market and other funds	3,202	0	0	3,202	3,202	0
U.S. government notes	11,475	104	0	11,579	0	11,579
Marketable equity securities	228	79	0	307	0	307
	14,905	183	0	15,088	3,202	11,886
Level 2:						
Time deposits	1,029	0	0	1,029	534	495
Money market and other funds[(1)]	1,260	0	0	1,260	1,260	0
U.S. government agencies	6,486	15	0	6,501	275	6,226
Foreign government bonds	1,608	32	(11)	1,629	0	1,629
Municipal securities	1,775	19	0	1,794	0	1,794
Corporate debt securities	6,023	187	(98)	6,112	0	6,112
Agency residential mortgage-backed securities	6,359	147	(5)	6,501	0	6,501
	24,540	400	(114)	24,826	2,069	22,757
Total	$44,157	$583	$(114)	$44,626	$9,983	$34,643

| | As of December 31, 2012 | | | | | |
	Adjusted Cost	Gross Unrealized Gains	Gross Unrealized Losses	Fair Value	Cash and Cash Equivalents	Marketable Securities
Cash	$ 8,066	$ 0	$ 0	$ 8,066	$ 8,066	$ 0
Level 1:						
Money market and other funds	5,221	0	0	5,221	5,221	0
U.S. government notes	10,853	77	(1)	10,929	0	10,929
Marketable equity securities	12	88	0	100	0	100
	16,086	165	(1)	16,250	5,221	11,029
Level 2:						
Time deposits	984	0	0	984	562	422
Money market and other funds[(1)]	929	0	0	929	929	0
U.S. government agencies	1,882	20	0	1,902	0	1,902
Foreign government bonds	1,996	81	(3)	2,074	0	2,074
Municipal securities	2,249	23	(6)	2,266	0	2,266
Corporate debt securities	7,200	414	(14)	7,600	0	7,600
Agency residential mortgage-backed securities	7,039	136	(6)	7,169	0	7,169
Asset-backed securities	847	1	0	848	0	848
	23,126	675	(29)	23,772	1,491	22,281
Total	$47,278	$840	$(30)	$48,088	$14,778	$33,310

(1) The balances at December 31, 2011 and December 31, 2012 were cash collateral received in connection with our securities lending program, which was invested in reverse repurchase agreements maturing within three months. See below for further discussion on this program.

We determine realized gains or losses on the sale of marketable securities on a specific identification method. We recognized gross realized gains of $381 million and $383 million for the years ended December 31, 2011 and December 31, 2012. We recognized gross realized losses of $127 million and $101 million for the years ended December 31, 2011 and December 31, 2012. In 2011, we also recorded an other-than-temporary impairment charge of $88 million related to our investment in Clearwire Corporation. We reflect these gains and losses as a component of interest and other income, net, in our accompanying Consolidated Statements of Income.

The following table summarizes the estimated fair value of our investments in marketable securities, excluding marketable equity securities, designated as available-for-sale and classified by the contractual maturity date of the securities (in millions):

	As of December 31, 2012
Due in 1 year	$ 4,708
Due in 1 year through 5 years	12,310
Due in 5 years through 10 years	7,296
Due after 10 years	8,896
Total	$33,210

The following tables present gross unrealized losses and fair values for those investments that were in an unrealized loss position as of December 31, 2011 and December 31, 2012, aggregated by investment category and the length of time that individual securities have been in a continuous loss position (in millions):

	As of December 31, 2011					
	Less Than 12 Months		12 Months or Greater		Total	
	Fair Value	Unrealized Loss	Fair Value	Unrealized Loss	Fair Value	Unrealized Loss
Foreign government bonds	$ 302	$ (11)	$ 6	$ 0	$ 308	$ (11)
Corporate debt securities	2,160	(97)	17	(1)	2,177	(98)
Agency residential mortgage-backed securities	716	(3)	19	(2)	735	(5)
Total	$3,178	$(111)	$42	$(3)	$3,220	$(114)

	As of December 31, 2012					
	Less Than 12 Months		12 Months or Greater		Total	
	Fair Value	Unrealized Loss	Fair Value	Unrealized Loss	Fair Value	Unrealized Loss
U.S. government notes	$ 842	$ (1)	$ 0	$ 0	$ 842	$ (1)
Foreign government bonds	509	(2)	12	(1)	521	(3)
Municipal securities	686	(6)	9	0	695	(6)
Corporate debt securities	820	(10)	81	(4)	901	(14)
Agency residential mortgage-backed securities	1,300	(6)	0	0	1,300	(6)
Total	$4,157	$(25)	$102	$(5)	$4,259	$(30)

Note 5. Balance Sheet Components (in part)

Accumulated Other Comprehensive Income

The components of accumulated other comprehensive income were as follows (in millions):

	As of December 31, 2011	As of December 31, 2012
Foreign currency translation adjustment	$(148)	$ (73)
Net unrealized gains on available-for-sale investments, net of taxes	327	604
Unrealized gains on cash flow hedges, net of taxes	97	7
Accumulated other comprehensive income	$ 276	$ 538

GAINS AND LOSSES ON DERIVATIVES HELD AS CASH FLOW HEDGES

4.15 ANALOG DEVICES, INC. (OCT)
CONSOLIDATED STATEMENTS OF COMPREHENSIVE INCOME

Years ended November 3, 2012, October 29, 2011 and October 30, 2010

(Thousands)	2012	2011	2010
Income from continuing operations, net of tax	$651,236	$860,894	$711,225
Foreign currency translation adjustment	3,020	(647)	6,085
Net unrealized (losses) gains on securities:			
Net unrealized holding gains (losses) (net of taxes of $115 in 2012, $67 in 2011 and $6 in 2010) on available-for-sale securities classified as short-term investments	525	(459)	(50)
Net unrealized holding (losses) gains (net of taxes of $301 in 2012, $64 in 2011 and $175 in 2010) on securities classified as other investments	(558)	(118)	325
Net unrealized (losses) gains on securities	(33)	(577)	275

(continued)

(Thousands)	2012	2011	2010
Derivative instruments designated as cash flow hedges:			
Changes in fair value of derivatives (net of taxes of $1,233 in 2012, $539 in 2011 and $449 in 2010)	$ (7,923)	$ 3,347	$ (1,339)
Realized loss (gain) reclassification (net of taxes of $1,160 in 2012, $1,171 in 2011 and $458 in 2010)	7,401	(7,793)	1,863
Net change in derivative instruments designated as cash flow hedges	(522)	(4,446)	524
Accumulated other comprehensive (loss) income—pension plans:			
Transition asset (obligation) (net of taxes of $1 in 2012, $1 in 2011 and $34 in 2010)	15	12	(80)
Net actuarial (loss) gain (net of taxes of $7,243 in 2012, $1,770 in 2011 and $4,594 in 2010)	(44,784)	13,084	(30,151)
Net prior service income (net of taxes of $584 in 2012, $0 in 2011 and $0 in 2010)	4,079	—	—
Net change in accumulated other comprehensive (loss) income—pension plans (net of taxes of $6,658 in 2012, $1,771 in 2011 and $4,560 in 2010)	(40,690)	13,096	(30,231)
Other comprehensive (loss) income	(38,225)	7,426	(23,347)
Comprehensive income from continuing operations	613,011	868,320	687,878
Gain on sale of discontinued operations, net of tax	—	6,500	859
Comprehensive income	$613,011	$874,820	$688,737

See accompanying Notes.

NOTES TO CONSOLIDATED FINANCIAL STATEMENTS

Years ended November 3, 2012, October 29, 2011 and October 30, 2010

(all tabular amounts in thousands except per share amounts)

2. Summary of Significant Accounting Policies (in part)

i. Derivative Instruments and Hedging Agreements

Foreign Exchange Exposure Management—The Company enters into forward foreign currency exchange contracts to offset certain operational and balance sheet exposures from the impact of changes in foreign currency exchange rates. Such exposures result from the portion of the Company's operations, assets and liabilities that are denominated in currencies other than the U.S. dollar, primarily the Euro; other significant exposures include the Philippine Peso and the British Pound. These foreign currency exchange contracts are entered into to support transactions made in the normal course of business, and accordingly, are not speculative in nature. The contracts are for periods consistent with the terms of the underlying transactions, generally one year or less. Hedges related to anticipated transactions are designated and documented at the inception of the respective hedges as cash flow hedges and are evaluated for effectiveness monthly. Derivative instruments are employed to eliminate or minimize certain foreign currency exposures that can be confidently identified and quantified. As the terms of the contract and the underlying transaction are matched at inception, forward contract effectiveness is calculated by comparing the change in fair value of the contract to the change in the forward value of the anticipated transaction, with the effective portion of the gain or loss on the derivative instrument reported as a component of accumulated other comprehensive (loss) income (OCI) in shareholders' equity and reclassified into earnings in the same period during which the hedged transaction effects earnings. Any residual change in fair value of the instruments, or ineffectiveness, is recognized immediately in other (income) expense. Additionally, the Company enters into forward foreign currency contracts that economically hedge the gains and losses generated by the re-measurement of certain recorded assets and liabilities in a non-functional currency. Changes in the fair value of these undesignated hedges are recognized in other (income) expense immediately as an offset to the changes in the fair value of the asset or liability being hedged. As of November 3, 2012 and October 29, 2011, the total notional amount of these undesignated hedges was $31.5 million and $41.2 million, respectively. The fair value of these hedging instruments in the Company's consolidated balance sheets as of November 3, 2012 and October 29, 2011 was immaterial.

Interest Rate Exposure Management—On June 30, 2009, the Company entered into interest rate swap transactions related to its outstanding 5.0% senior unsecured notes where the Company swapped the notional amount of its $375.0 million of fixed rate debt at 5.0% into floating interest rate debt through July 1, 2014. Under the terms of the swaps, the Company would (i) receive on the $375.0 million notional amount a 5.0% annual interest payment that is paid in two installments on the 1st business day of every January and July, commencing January 1, 2010 through and ending on the maturity date; and (ii) pay on the $375.0 million notional amount an annual three months LIBOR plus 2.05% interest payment, payable in four installments on the 1st business day of every January, April, July and October, commencing on October 1, 2009 and ending on the maturity date. The LIBOR-based rate was set quarterly three months prior to the date of the interest payment. The Company designated these swaps as fair value hedges. The fair value of the swaps at inception was zero and subsequent changes in the fair value of the interest rate swaps were reflected in the carrying value of the interest rate swaps on the balance sheet. The carrying value of the debt on the balance sheet was adjusted by an equal and offsetting amount. The gain or loss on the hedged item (that is, the fixed-rate borrowings) attributable to the hedged benchmark interest rate risk and the offsetting gain or loss on the related interest rate swaps for fiscal year 2012 and fiscal year 2011 were as follows:

Statement of Income Classification	November 3, 2012			October 29, 2011		
	Loss on Swaps	Gain on Note	Net Income Effect	Loss on Swaps	Gain on Note	Net Income Effect
Other income	$(769)	$769	$—	$(4,614)	$4,614	$—

The amounts earned and owed under the swap agreements were accrued each period and were reported in interest expense. There was no ineffectiveness recognized in any of the periods presented. In the second quarter of fiscal 2012, the Company terminated the interest rate swap agreement. The Company received $19.8 million in cash proceeds from the swap termination, which included $1.3 million in accrued interest. The proceeds, net of interest received, are disclosed in cash flows from financing activities in the consolidated statements of cash flows. As a result of the termination, the carrying value of the 5.0% Notes was adjusted for the change in the fair value of the interest component of the debt up to the date of the termination of the swap in an amount equal to the fair value of the swap, and will be amortized to earnings as a reduction of interest expense over the remaining life of the debt. During fiscal year 2012, $5.3 million was amortized into earnings as a reduction of interest expense related to the swap termination. This amortization is reflected in the consolidated statements of cash flows within operating activities.

The market risk associated with the Company's derivative instruments results from currency exchange rate or interest rate movements that are expected to offset the market risk of the underlying transactions, assets and liabilities being hedged. The counterparties to the agreements relating to the Company's derivative instruments consist of a number of major international financial institutions with high credit ratings. Based on the credit ratings of the Company's counterparties as of November 3, 2012, nonperformance is not perceived to be a significant risk. Furthermore, none of the Company's derivatives are subject to collateral or other security arrangements and none contain provisions that are dependent on the Company's credit ratings from any credit rating agency. While the contract or notional amounts of derivative financial instruments provide one measure of the volume of these transactions, they do not represent the amount of the Company's exposure to credit risk. The amounts potentially subject to credit risk (arising from the possible inability of counterparties to meet the terms of their contracts) are generally limited to the amounts, if any, by which the counterparties' obligations under the contracts exceed the obligations of the Company to the counterparties. As a result of the above considerations, the Company does not consider the risk of counterparty default to be significant.

The Company records the fair value of its derivative financial instruments in the consolidated financial statements in other current assets, other assets or accrued liabilities, depending on their net position, regardless of the purpose or intent for holding the derivative contract. Changes in the fair value of the derivative financial instruments are either recognized periodically in earnings or in shareholders' equity as a component of OCI. Changes in the fair value of cash flow hedges are recorded in OCI and reclassified into earnings when the underlying contract matures. Changes in the fair values of derivatives not qualifying for hedge accounting are reported in earnings as they occur.

The total notional amounts of derivative instruments designated as hedging instruments was $151.8 million and $153.7 million, respectively, of cash flow hedges denominated in Euros, British Pounds, Philippine Pesos and Japanese Yen as of November 3, 2012 and October 29, 2011, respectively. The Company also had $375.0 million of interest rate swap agreements accounted for as fair value hedges as of October 29, 2011. The fair values of these hedging instruments in the Company's consolidated balance sheets as of November 3, 2012 and October 29, 2011 were as follows:

| | | Fair Value At | |
	Balance Sheet Location	November 3, 2012	October 29, 2011
Interest rate swap agreements	Other assets	$ —	$22,187
Forward foreign currency exchange contracts	Prepaid expenses and other current assets	$1,161	$ 2,038

The effect of derivative instruments designated as cash flow hedges on the consolidated statements of income for fiscal 2012 and 2011 were as follows:

	November 3, 2012	October 29, 2011
(Gain) loss recognized in OCI on derivatives (net of tax of $1,233 in 2012 and $539 in 2011)	$(7,923)	$ 3,347
Loss (gain) reclassified from OCI into income (net of tax of $1,160 in 2012 and $1,171 in 2011)	$ 7,401	$(7,793)

The amounts reclassified into earnings before tax are recognized in cost of sales and operating expenses for fiscal 2012 and fiscal 2011 were as follows:

	November 3, 2012	October 29, 2011
Cost of sales	$3,096	$(4,363)
Research and development	$2,344	$(2,264)
Selling, marketing, general and administrative	$3,121	$(2,337)

All derivative gains and losses included in OCI will be reclassified into earnings within the next 12 months. There was no ineffectiveness during fiscal years ended November 3, 2012 and October 29, 2011.

Accumulated Derivative Gains or Losses

The following table summarizes activity in accumulated other comprehensive (loss) income related to derivatives classified as cash flow hedges held by the Company during the period from October 31, 2010 through November 3, 2012:

	2012	2011
Balance at beginning of year	$ 1,687	$ 6,133
Changes in fair value of derivatives—(loss) gain, net of tax	(7,923)	3,347
Loss (gain) reclassified into earnings from other comprehensive income (loss), net of tax	7,401	(7,793)
Balance at end of year	$ 1,165	$ 1,687

CONSOLIDATED STATEMENTS OF COMPREHENSIVE INCOME (LOSS)

(In millions)	Year Ended December 31,		
	2012	**2011**	**2010**
Net (loss) income	$(4,068)	$441	$(1,065)
Other comprehensive (loss) income:			
Foreign currency translation adjustment	32	(8)	(58)
Net change in unrealized gains and losses on derivative financial instruments, net of tax	82	17	(28)
Net change in certain retirement plans	(9)	(18)	
Total other comprehensive (loss) income	105	(9)	(86)
Total comprehensive (loss) income	$(3,963)	$432	$(1,151)

See notes to the consolidated financial statements.

NOTES TO THE CONSOLIDATED FINANCIAL STATEMENTS

Note A—Significant Accounting Policies (in part)

Financial Instruments

We recognize all derivative financial instruments in our consolidated financial statements at fair value in accordance with ASC Topic 815, *Derivatives and Hedging*, and we present assets and liabilities associated with our derivative financial instruments on a gross basis in our financial statements. In accordance with Topic 815, for those derivative instruments that are designated and qualify as hedging instruments, the hedging instrument must be designated, based upon the exposure being hedged, as a fair value hedge, cash flow hedge, or a hedge of a net investment in a foreign operation. The accounting for changes in the fair value (i.e. gains or losses) of a derivative instrument depends on whether it has been designated and qualifies as part of a hedging relationship and, further, on the type of hedging relationship. Our derivative instruments do not subject our earnings or cash flows to material risk, as gains and losses on these derivatives generally offset losses and gains on the item being hedged. We do not enter into derivative transactions for speculative purposes and we do not have any non-derivative instruments that are designated as hedging instruments pursuant to Topic 815. Refer to *Note E—Fair Value Measurements* for more information on our derivative instruments.

Note E—Fair Value Measurements (in part)

Derivative Instruments and Hedging Activities

We develop, manufacture and sell medical devices globally and our earnings and cash flows are exposed to market risk from changes in foreign currency exchange rates and interest rates. We address these risks through a risk management program that includes the use of derivative financial instruments, and operate the program pursuant to documented corporate risk management policies. We recognize all derivative financial instruments in our consolidated financial statements at fair value in accordance with ASC Topic 815, *Derivatives and Hedging*. In accordance with Topic 815, for those derivative instruments that are designated and qualify as hedging instruments, the hedging instrument must be designated, based upon the exposure being hedged, as a fair value hedge, cash flow hedge, or a hedge of a net investment in a foreign operation. The accounting for changes in the fair value (i.e. gains or losses) of a derivative instrument depends on whether it has been designated and qualifies as part of a hedging relationship and, further, on the type of hedging relationship. Our derivative instruments do not subject our earnings or cash flows to material risk, as gains and losses on these derivatives generally offset losses and gains on the item being hedged. We do not enter into derivative transactions for speculative purposes and we do not have any non-derivative instruments that are designated as hedging instruments pursuant to Topic 815.

Currency Hedging

We are exposed to currency risk consisting primarily of foreign currency denominated monetary assets and liabilities, forecasted foreign currency denominated intercompany and third-party transactions and net investments in certain subsidiaries. We manage our exposure to changes in foreign currency exchange rates on a consolidated basis to take advantage of offsetting transactions. We use both derivative instruments (currency forward and option contracts), and non-derivative transactions (primarily European manufacturing and distribution operations) to reduce the risk that our earnings and cash flows associated with these foreign currency denominated balances and transactions will be adversely affected by foreign currency exchange rate changes.

Designated Foreign Currency Hedges

All of our designated currency hedge contracts outstanding as of December 31, 2012 and December 31, 2011 were cash flow hedges under Topic 815 intended to protect the U.S. dollar value of our forecasted foreign currency denominated transactions. We record the effective portion of any change in the fair value of foreign currency cash flow hedges in other comprehensive income (OCI) until the related third-party transaction occurs. Once the related third-party transaction occurs, we reclassify the effective portion of any related gain or loss on the foreign currency cash flow hedge to earnings. In the event the hedged forecasted transaction does not occur, or it becomes no longer probable that it will occur, we reclassify the amount of any gain or loss on the related cash flow hedge to earnings at that time. We had currency derivative instruments designated as cash flow hedges outstanding in the contract amount of $2.469 billion as of December 31, 2012 and $2.088 billion as of December 31, 2011.

We recognized net losses of $39 million during 2012 on our cash flow hedges, as compared to $95 million of net losses during 2011, and $30 million of net losses during 2010. All currency cash flow hedges outstanding as of December 31, 2012 mature within 36 months. As of December 31, 2012, $31 million of net gains, net of tax, were recorded in accumulated other comprehensive income (AOCI) to recognize the effective portion of the fair value of any currency derivative instruments that are, or previously were, designated as foreign currency cash flow hedges, as compared to net losses of $52 million as of December 31, 2011. As of December 31, 2012, $2 million of net losses, net of tax, may be reclassified to earnings within the next twelve months.

The success of our hedging program depends, in part, on forecasts of transaction activity in various currencies (primarily Japanese yen, Euro, British pound sterling, Australian dollar and Canadian dollar). We may experience unanticipated currency exchange gains or losses to the extent that there are differences between forecasted and actual activity during periods of currency volatility. In addition, changes in foreign currency exchange rates related to any unhedged transactions may impact our earnings and cash flows.

Non-designated Foreign Currency Contracts

We use currency forward contracts as a part of our strategy to manage exposure related to foreign currency denominated monetary assets and liabilities. These currency forward contracts are not designated as cash flow, fair value or net investment hedges under Topic 815; are marked-to-market with changes in fair value recorded to earnings; and are entered into for periods consistent with currency transaction exposures, generally less than one year. We had currency derivative instruments not designated as hedges under Topic 815 outstanding in the contract amount of $1.942 billion as of December 31, 2012 and $2.209 billion as of December 31, 2011.

Interest Rate Hedging

Our interest rate risk relates primarily to U.S. dollar borrowings, partially offset by U.S. dollar cash investments. We have historically used interest rate derivative instruments to manage our earnings and cash flow exposure to changes in interest rates by converting floating-rate debt into fixed-rate debt or fixed-rate debt into floating-rate debt.

We designate these derivative instruments either as fair value or cash flow hedges under Topic 815. We record changes in the value of fair value hedges in interest expense, which is generally offset by changes in the fair value of the hedged debt obligation. Interest payments made or received related to our interest rate derivative instruments are included in interest expense. We record the effective portion of any change in the fair value of derivative instruments designated as cash flow hedges as unrealized gains or losses in OCI, net of tax, until the hedged cash flow occurs, at which point the effective portion of any gain or loss is reclassified to earnings. We record the ineffective portion of our cash flow hedges in interest expense. In the event the hedged cash flow does not occur, or it becomes no longer probable that it will occur, we reclassify the amount of any gain or loss on the related cash flow hedge to interest expense at that time.

In the first quarter of 2011, we entered interest rate derivative contracts having a notional amount of $850 million to convert fixed-rate debt into floating-rate debt, which we designated as fair value hedges. We terminated these hedges during the third quarter of 2011 and received total proceeds of approximately $80 million, which included approximately $5 million of accrued interest receivable. We are amortizing the gains and losses of these derivative instruments upon termination into earnings over the term of the hedged debt. The carrying amount of certain of our senior notes included unamortized gains of $64 million as of December 31, 2012 and $73 million as of December 31, 2011, and unamortized losses of $3 million as of December 31, 2012 and $4 million as of December 31, 2011, related to the fixed-to-floating interest rate contracts. In addition, we had pre-tax net gains within AOCI related to terminated floating-to-fixed treasury locks of $4 million as of December 31, 2012 and $7 million as of December 31, 2011. The gains that we recognized in earnings related to previously terminated interest rate derivatives were $11 million in 2012 and were not material in 2011. As of December 31, 2012, $10 million of net gains may be reclassified to earnings within the next twelve months from amortization of our previously terminated interest rate derivative contracts.

Counterparty Credit Risk

We do not have significant concentrations of credit risk arising from our derivative financial instruments, whether from an individual counterparty or a related group of counterparties. We manage our concentration of counterparty credit risk on our derivative instruments by limiting acceptable counterparties to a diversified group of major financial institutions with investment grade credit ratings, limiting the amount of credit exposure to each counterparty, and by actively monitoring their credit ratings and outstanding fair values on an on-going basis. Furthermore, none of our derivative transactions are subject to collateral or other security arrangements and none contain provisions that are dependent on our credit ratings from any credit rating agency.

We also employ master netting arrangements that reduce our counterparty payment settlement risk on any given maturity date to the net amount of any receipts or payments due between us and the counterparty financial institution. Thus, the maximum loss due to credit risk by counterparty is limited to the unrealized gains in such contracts net of any unrealized losses should any of these counterparties fail to perform as contracted. Although these protections do not eliminate concentrations of credit risk, as a result of the above considerations, we do not consider the risk of counterparty default to be significant.

Fair Value of Derivative Instruments

The following presents the effect of our derivative instruments designated as cash flow hedges under Topic 815 on our accompanying consolidated statements of operations during 2012 and 2011 (in millions):

	Amount of Pre-tax Gain (Loss) Recognized in OCI (Effective Portion)	Amount of Pre-tax Gain (Loss) Reclassified From AOCI Into Earnings (Effective Portion)	Location in Statement of Operations
Year Ended December 31, 2012			
Interest rate hedge contracts		$ 2	Interest expense
Currency hedge contracts	$ 95	(39)	Cost of products sold
	$ 95	$(37)	
Year Ended December 31, 2011			
Interest rate hedge contracts		$ 1	Interest expense
Currency hedge contracts	$(66)	(95)	Cost of products sold
	$(66)	$(94)	

The amount of gain (loss) recognized in earnings related to the ineffective portion of our hedging relationships was de minimus in 2012. In 2011, we recognized a $5 million gain related to the ineffective portion of hedging relationships.

Net gains and losses on currency hedge contracts not designated as hedging instruments were offset by net losses and gains from foreign currency transaction exposures, as shown in the following table:

	Year Ended December 31,			Location in Statement of Operations
(In millions)	2012	2011	2010	
Gain (loss) on currency hedge contracts	$ 23	$ 12	$(77)	Other, net
Gain (loss) on foreign currency transaction exposures	(41)	(24)	68	Other, net
Net foreign currency gain (loss)	$(18)	$(12)	$ (9)	

Topic 815 requires all derivative instruments to be recognized at their fair values as either assets or liabilities on the balance sheet. We determine the fair value of our derivative instruments using the framework prescribed by ASC Topic 820, *Fair Value Measurements and Disclosures*, by considering the estimated amount we would receive or pay to transfer these instruments at the reporting date and by taking into account current interest rates, foreign currency exchange rates, the creditworthiness of the counterparty for assets, and our creditworthiness for liabilities. In certain instances, we may utilize financial models to measure fair value. Generally, we use inputs that include quoted prices for similar assets or liabilities in active markets; quoted prices for identical or similar assets or liabilities in markets that are not active; other observable inputs for the asset or liability; and inputs derived principally from, or corroborated by, observable market data by correlation or other means. As of December 31, 2012, we have classified all of our derivative assets and liabilities within Level 2 of the fair value hierarchy prescribed by Topic 820, as discussed below, because these observable inputs are available for substantially the full term of our derivative instruments.

The following are the balances of our derivative assets and liabilities as of December 31, 2012 and December 31, 2011:

		As of	
(In millions)	Location in Balance Sheet[1]	December 31, 2012	December 31, 2011
Derivative Assets:			
Designated Hedging Instruments			
Currency hedge contracts	Prepaid and other current assets	$ 25	$ 31
Currency hedge contracts	Other long-term assets	63	20
		88	51
Non-Designated Hedging Instruments			
Currency hedge contracts	Prepaid and other current assets	33	36
Total derivative assets		$121	$ 87
Derivative Liabilities:			
Designated hedging instruments			
Currency hedge contracts	Other current liabilities	$ 20	$ 69
Currency hedge contracts	Other long-term liabilities	10	49
		30	118
Non-Designated Hedging Instruments			
Currency hedge contracts	Other current liabilities	27	13
Total derivative liabilities		$ 57	$131

[1] We classify derivative assets and liabilities as current when the remaining term of the derivative contract is one year or less.

4.17 JABIL CIRCUIT, INC. (AUG)

CONSOLIDATED STATEMENTS OF COMPREHENSIVE INCOME

(In thousands)

	Fiscal Year Ended August 31,		
	2012	2011	2010
Net income	$396,089	$382,958	$170,766
Other comprehensive income:			
Foreign currency translation adjustment	(79,323)	60,026	(70,293)
Changes in fair value of derivative instruments, net of tax	2,637	4,260	(1,742)
Actuarial gains (loss), net of tax	(13,094)	7,709	(7,751)
Prior service cost, net of tax	(33)	(5)	342
Reclassification of net losses realized and included in net income related to derivative instruments, net of tax	1,382	654	4,534
Comprehensive income	$307,658	$455,602	$ 95,856
Comprehensive income attributable to noncontrolling interests	1,402	1,895	1,926
Comprehensive income attributable to Jabil Circuit, Inc	$306,256	$453,707	$ 93,930

See accompanying notes to Consolidated Financial Statements.

NOTES TO CONSOLIDATED FINANCIAL STATEMENTS

12. Derivative Financial Instruments and Hedging Activities

The Company is directly and indirectly affected by changes in certain market conditions. These changes in market conditions may adversely impact the Company's financial performance and are referred to as market risks. The Company, where deemed appropriate, uses derivatives as risk management tools to mitigate the potential impact of certain market risks. The primary market risks managed by the Company through the use of derivative instruments are foreign currency fluctuation risk and interest rate risk.

All derivative instruments are recorded gross on the Consolidated Balance Sheets at their respective fair values. The accounting for changes in the fair value of a derivative instrument depends on the intended use and designation of the derivative instrument. For derivative instruments that are designated and qualify as a fair value hedge, the gain or loss on the derivative and the offsetting gain or loss on the hedged item attributable to the hedged risk are recognized in current earnings. For derivative instruments that are designated and qualify as a cash flow hedge, the effective portion of the gain or loss on the derivative instrument is initially reported as a component of accumulated other comprehensive income ("AOCI"), net of tax, and is subsequently reclassified into the line item within the Consolidated Statements of Operations in which the hedged items are recorded in the same period in which the hedged item affects earnings. The ineffective portion of the gain or loss is recognized immediately in current earnings. For derivative instruments that are not designated as hedging instruments, gains and losses from changes in fair values are recognized in earnings.

For derivatives accounted for as hedging instruments, the Company formally designates and documents, at inception, the financial instruments as a hedge of a specific underlying exposure, the risk management objective and the strategy for undertaking the hedge transaction. In addition, the Company formally performs an assessment, both at inception and at least quarterly thereafter, to determine whether the financial instruments used in hedging transactions are effective at offsetting changes in the cash flows on the related underlying exposures.

a. Foreign Currency Risk Management

Forward contracts are put in place to manage the foreign currency risk associated with anticipated foreign currency denominated revenues and expenses. A hedging relationship existed with an aggregate notional amount outstanding of $199.7 million and $329.8 million at August 31, 2012 and 2011, respectively. The related forward foreign exchange contracts have been designated as hedging instruments and are accounted for as cash flow hedges. The forward foreign exchange contract transactions will effectively lock in the value of anticipated foreign currency denominated revenues and expenses against foreign currency fluctuations. The anticipated foreign currency denominated revenues and expenses being hedged are expected to occur between September 1, 2012 and January 31, 2013.

In addition to derivatives that are designated and qualify for hedge accounting, the Company also enters into forward contracts to economically hedge transactional exposure associated with commitments arising from trade accounts receivable, trade accounts payable, fixed purchase obligations and intercompany transactions denominated in a currency other than the functional currency of the respective operating entity. The aggregate notional amount of these outstanding contracts at August 31, 2012 and 2011 was $837.3 million and $591.6 million, respectively.

The following table presents the Company's assets and liabilities related to forward foreign exchange contracts measured at fair value on a recurring basis as of August 31, 2012, aggregated by the level in the fair-value hierarchy in which those measurements are classified (in thousands):

	Level 1	Level 2	Level 3	Total
Assets:				
Forward foreign exchange contracts	$—	$ 5,780	$—	$ 5,780
Liabilities:				
Forward foreign exchange contracts	—	(4,166)	—	(4,166)
Total	$—	$ 1,614	$—	$ 1,614

The Company's forward foreign exchange contracts are measured on a recurring basis at fair value, based on foreign currency spot rates and forward rates quoted by banks or foreign currency dealers.

The following tables present the fair value of the Company's derivative instruments located on the Consolidated Balance Sheets utilized for foreign currency risk management purposes at August 31, 2012 and 2011 (in thousands):

	Fair Values of Derivative Instruments At August 31, 2012			
	Asset Derivatives		Liability Derivatives	
	Balance Sheet Location	Fair Value	Balance Sheet Location	Fair Value
Derivatives Designated as Hedging Instruments:				
Forward foreign exchange contracts	Prepaid expenses and other current assets	$1,335	Other accrued expense	$1,190
Derivatives Not Designated as Hedging Instruments:				
Forward foreign exchange contracts	Prepaid expenses and other current assets	$4,445	Other accrued expense	$2,976

	Fair Values of Derivative Instruments At August 31, 2011			
	Asset Derivatives		Liability Derivatives	
	Balance Sheet Location	Fair Value	Balance Sheet Location	Fair Value
Derivatives Designated as Hedging Instruments:				
Forward foreign exchange contracts	Prepaid expenses and other current assets	$2,825	Other accrued expense	$2,798
Derivatives Not Designated as Hedging Instruments:				
Forward foreign exchange contracts	Prepaid expenses and other current assets	$3,517	Other accrued expense	$3,979

The following tables present the impact that changes in fair value of derivatives utilized for foreign currency risk management purposes and designated as hedging instruments had on AOCI and earnings during fiscal years 2012 and 2011 (in thousands):

Derivatives in Cash Flow Hedging Relationship for the Fiscal Year Ended August 31, 2012	Amount of Gain (Loss) Recognized in OCI on Derivative (Effective Portion)	Location of Gain (Loss) Reclassified From AOCI into Income (Effective Portion)	Amount of Gain (Loss) Reclassified From AOCI Into Income (Effective Portion)	Location of Gain (Loss) Recognized in Income on Derivative (Ineffective Portion and Amount Excluded From Effectiveness Testing)	Amount of Gain (Loss) Recognized in Income on Derivative (Ineffective Portion and Amount Excluded From Effectiveness Testing)
Forward foreign exchange contracts	$ 2,858	Revenue	$ 2,642	Revenue	$ —
Forward foreign exchange contracts	$ 1,644	Cost of revenue	$ 2,717	Cost of revenue	$(1,345)
Forward foreign exchange contracts	$(1,864)	Selling, general and administrative	$(2,790)	Selling, general and administrative	$ 194

Derivatives in Cash Flow Hedging Relationship for the Fiscal Year Ended August 31, 2011	Amount of Gain (Loss) Recognized in OCI on Derivative (Effective Portion)	Location of Gain (Loss) Reclassified From AOCI into Income (Effective Portion)	Amount of Gain (Loss) Reclassified From AOCI into Income (Effective Portion)	Location of Gain (Loss) Recognized in Income on Derivative (Ineffective Portion and Amount Excluded From Effectiveness Testing)	Amount of Gain (Loss) Recognized in Income on Derivative (Ineffective Portion and Amount Excluded From Effectiveness Testing)
Forward foreign exchange contracts	$1,021	Revenue	$1,494	Revenue	$ 398
Forward foreign exchange contracts	$3,937	Cost of revenue	$1,910	Cost of revenue	$(349)
Forward foreign exchange contracts	$ (698)	Selling, general and administrative	$ 49	Selling, general and administrative	$ 322

As of August 31, 2012, the Company estimates that it will reclassify into earnings during the next 12 months existing gains related to foreign currency risk management hedging arrangements of approximately $10.0 thousand from the amounts recorded in AOCI as the anticipated cash flows occur.

The following tables present the impact that changes in fair value of derivatives utilized for foreign currency risk management purposes and not designated as hedging instruments had on earnings during fiscal years 2012 and 2011 (in thousands):

Derivatives Not Designated as Hedging Instruments	Location of Gain (Loss) Recognized in Income on Derivative	Amount of Gain (Loss) Recognized in Income on Derivative for the Fiscal Year Ended August 31, 2012
Forward foreign exchange contracts	Cost of revenue	$5,912

Derivatives Not Designated as Hedging Instruments	Location of Gain (Loss) Recognized in Income on Derivative	Amount of Gain (Loss) Recognized in Income on Derivative for the Fiscal Year Ended August 31, 2011
Forward foreign exchange contracts	Cost of revenue	$(812)

b. Interest Rate Risk Management

The Company periodically enters into interest rate swaps to manage interest rate risk associated with the Company's borrowings.

Fair Value Hedges

During the second quarter of fiscal year 2011, the Company entered into a series of interest rate swaps with an aggregate notional amount of $200.0 million designated as fair value hedges of a portion of the Company's 7.750% Senior Notes. Under these interest rate swaps, the Company received fixed rate interest payments and paid interest at a variable rate based on LIBOR plus a spread. The effect of these swaps was to convert fixed rate interest expense on a portion of the 7.750% Senior Notes to floating rate interest expense. Gains and losses related to changes in the fair value of the interest rate swaps were recorded to interest expense and offset changes in the fair value of the hedged portion of the underlying 7.750% Senior Notes.

During the fourth quarter of fiscal year 2011, the Company terminated the interest rate swaps entered into in connection with the 7.750% Senior Notes with a fair value of $12.2 million, including accrued interest of $0.6 million at August 31, 2011. The portion of the fair value that is not accrued is recorded as a hedge accounting adjustment to the carrying amount of the 7.750% Senior Notes and is being amortized as a reduction to interest expense over the remaining term of the 7.750% Senior Notes. The Company recorded $2.4 million in amortization as a reduction to interest expense for the fiscal year ended August 31, 2012. At August 31, 2012, the unamortized hedge accounting adjustment recorded is $9.2 million in the Consolidated Balance Sheets.

Cash Flow Hedges

During the fourth quarter of fiscal year 2007, the Company entered into forward interest rate swap transactions to hedge the fixed interest rate payments for an anticipated debt issuance, which was the issuance of the 8.250% Senior Notes. The swaps were accounted for as a cash flow hedge and had a notional amount of $400.0 million. Concurrently with the pricing of the 8.250% Senior Notes, the Company settled the swaps by its payment of $43.1 million. The ineffective portion of the swaps was immediately recorded to interest expense within the Consolidated Statements of Operations. The effective portion of the swaps is recorded on the Company's Consolidated Balance Sheets as a component of AOCI and is being amortized to interest expense within the Company's Consolidated Statements of Operations over the life of the 8.250% Senior Notes, which is through March 15, 2018.

The following tables present the impact that changes in the fair value of the derivative utilized for interest rate risk management and designated as a hedging instrument had on AOCI and earnings during fiscal years 2012 and 2011 (in thousands):

Derivatives in Cash Flow Hedging Relationship for the Fiscal Year Ended August 31, 2012	Amount of Gain (Loss) Recognized in OCI on Derivative (Effective Portion)	Location of Gain (Loss) Reclassified From Accumulated OCI into Income (Effective Portion)	Amount of Gain or (Loss) Reclassified From Accumulated OCI into Income (Effective Portion)	Location of Gain or (Loss) Recognized in Income on Derivative (Ineffective Portion and Amount Excluded From Effectiveness Testing)	Amount of Gain or (Loss) Recognized in Income on Derivative (Ineffective Portion and Amount Excluded From Effectiveness Testing)
Interest rate swap	$—	Interest expense	$(3,950)	Interest expense	$—

Derivatives in Cash Flow Hedging Relationship for the Fiscal Year Ended August 31, 2011	Amount of Gain (Loss) Recognized in OCI on Derivative (Effective Portion)	Location of Gain (Loss) Reclassified From Accumulated OCI into Income (Effective Portion)	Amount of Gain or (Loss) Reclassified From Accumulated OCI into Income (Effective Portion)	Location of Gain or (Loss) Recognized in Income on Derivative (Ineffective Portion and Amount Excluded From Effectiveness Testing)	Amount of Gain or (Loss) Recognized in Income on Derivative (Ineffective Portion and Amount Excluded From Effectiveness Testing)
Interest rate swap	$—	Interest expense	$(3,950)	Interest expense	$—

As of August 31, 2012, the Company estimates that it will reclassify into earnings during the next 12 months existing losses related to interest rate risk management hedging arrangements of approximately $4.0 million from the amounts recorded in AOCI as the anticipated cash flows occur.

The changes related to cash flow hedges (both forward foreign exchange contracts and interest rate swaps) included in AOCI net of tax are as follows (in thousands):

Accumulated comprehensive loss August 31, 2010	$(16,086)
Changes in fair value of derivative instruments	4,260
Adjustment for net losses (gains) realized and included in net income related to derivative instruments	654
Accumulated comprehensive loss, August 31, 2011	$(11,172)
Changes in fair value of derivative instruments	2,637
Adjustment for net losses (gains) realized and included in net income related to derivative instruments	1,382
Accumulated comprehensive loss, August 31, 2012	$ (7,153)

4.18 EASTMAN CHEMICAL COMPANY (DEC)

CONSOLIDATED STATEMENTS OF EARNINGS, COMPREHENSIVE INCOME AND RETAINED EARNINGS (in part)

	For Years Ended December 31,		
(Dollars in millions, except per share amounts)	2012	2011	2010
Comprehensive Income			
Net earnings including noncontrolling interest	$444	$647	$427
Other comprehensive income (loss), net of tax			
Change in cumulative translation adjustment	41	(15)	2
Defined benefit pension and other postretirement benefit plans:			
Amortization of unrecognized prior service credits included in net periodic costs	(13)	(21)	(26)
Derivatives and hedging:			
Unrealized (loss) gain during period	(36)	(20)	18
Reclassification adjustment for gains included in net income	(7)	—	(28)
Total other comprehensive loss, net of tax	(15)	(56)	(34)
Comprehensive income including noncontrolling interest	$429	$591	$393
Comprehensive income attributable to noncontrolling interest	7	1	2
Comprehensive income attributable to Eastman	422	590	391

NOTES TO THE AUDITED CONSOLIDATED FINANCIAL STATEMENTS

1. Significant Accounting Policies (in part)

Derivative Financial Instruments

Derivative financial instruments are used by the Company when appropriate to manage its exposures to fluctuations in foreign currency exchange rates, certain contract sales prices, raw material and energy costs, and interest rates. Such instruments are used to mitigate the risk that changes in exchange rates, sales prices, raw material and energy costs, or interest rates will adversely affect the eventual dollar cash flows resulting from the hedged transactions.

The Company from time to time enters into currency option and forward contracts to hedge anticipated, but not yet committed, export sales and purchase transactions expected within no more than five years and denominated in foreign currencies (principally the euro, British pound and the Japanese yen); and forward exchange contracts to hedge certain firm commitments denominated in foreign currencies. To mitigate short-term fluctuations in market prices for propane, ethane, paraxylene, and natural gas (major raw material and energy used in the manufacturing process) and selling prices for ethylene, the Company from time to time enters into option and forward contracts. From time to time, the Company also utilizes interest rate derivative instruments, primarily swaps, to hedge the Company's exposure to movements in interest rates.

The Company's qualifying option and forward contracts are accounted for as hedges because the derivative instruments are designated and effective as hedges and reduce the Company's exposure to identified risks. Gains and losses resulting from effective hedges of existing liabilities, firm commitments, or anticipated transactions are deferred and recognized when the offsetting gains and losses are recognized on the related hedged items and are reported as a component of operating earnings. Derivative assets and liabilities are recorded at fair value.

The gains or losses on nonqualifying derivatives or derivatives that are not designated as hedges are marked to market and immediately recorded into earnings from continuing operations.

Deferred currency option premiums are included in the fair market value of the hedges. The related obligation for payment is generally included in other liabilities and is paid in the period in which the options are exercised or expire.

For additional information see Note 12, "Derivatives".

12. Derivatives (in part)

Hedging Programs

The Company is exposed to market risk, such as changes in currency exchange rates, commodity prices, and interest rates. The Company uses various derivative financial instruments when appropriate pursuant to the Company's hedging policies to mitigate these market risk factors and their effect on the cash flows of the underlying transactions. Designation is performed on a specific exposure basis to support hedge accounting. The changes in fair value of these hedging instruments are offset in part or in whole by corresponding changes in the cash flows of the underlying exposures being hedged. The Company does not hold or issue derivative financial instruments for trading purposes.

Currency Rate Hedging

The Company manufactures and sells its products in a number of countries throughout the world and, as a result, is exposed to changes in foreign currency exchange rates. To manage the volatility relating to these exposures, the Company nets the exposures on a consolidated basis to take advantage of natural offsets. To manage the remaining exposure, the Company enters into currency options and forwards to hedge probable anticipated, but not yet committed, export sales and purchase transactions expected within no more than five years and denominated in foreign currencies (principally the euro, British pound, and Japanese yen) and forward exchange contracts to hedge certain firm commitments denominated in foreign currencies. These contracts are designated as cash flow hedges. The MTM gains or losses on qualifying hedges are included in accumulated other comprehensive income (loss) to the extent effective, and reclassified into sales in the period during which the hedged transaction affects earnings.

Commodity Hedging

Raw material and energy sources used by the Company and sales of certain commodity products by the Company are subject to price volatility caused by weather, supply conditions, economic variables and other unpredictable factors. To mitigate short-term fluctuations in market prices for propane, ethane, paraxylene, natural gas, and ethylene, the Company enters into option and forward contracts. These contracts are designated as cash flow hedges. The mark-to-market gains or losses on qualifying hedges are included in accumulated other comprehensive income (loss) to the extent effective, and reclassified into cost of sales (for commodity purchases) and sales (for commodity sales) in the period during which the hedged transaction affects earnings.

Interest Rate Hedging

The Company's policy is to manage interest expense using a mix of fixed and variable rate debt. To manage this mix effectively, the Company from time to time enters into interest rate swaps in which the Company agrees to exchange the difference between fixed and variable interest amounts calculated by reference to an agreed upon notional principal amount. These swaps are designated as hedges of the fair value of the underlying debt obligations and the interest rate differential is reflected as an adjustment to interest expense over the life of the swaps. As these instruments are 100 percent effective, there is no impact on earnings due to hedge ineffectiveness.

From time to time, the Company also utilizes interest rate derivative instruments, primarily forwards, to hedge the Company's exposure to movements in interest rates prior to anticipated debt offerings. These instruments are designated as cash flow hedges and are typically 100 percent effective. As a result, there is no current impact on earnings due to hedge ineffectiveness.

The MTM gains or losses on these hedges are included in accumulated other comprehensive income (loss) to the extent effective, and are reclassified into interest expense over the term of the related debt instruments.

Fair Value Hedges

Fair value hedges are defined as derivative or non-derivative instruments designated as and used to hedge the exposure to changes in the fair value of an asset or a liability or an identified portion thereof that is attributable to a particular risk. For derivative instruments that are designated and qualify as a fair value hedge, the gain or loss on the derivative as well as the offsetting loss or gain on the hedged item attributable to the hedged risk are recognized in current earnings. As of December 31, 2012 and December 31, 2011, the Company had no fair value hedges.

Cash Flow Hedges

Cash flow hedges are derivative instruments designated as and used to hedge the exposure to variability in expected future cash flows that is attributable to a particular risk. For derivative instruments that are designated and qualify as a cash flow hedge, the effective portion of the gain or loss on the derivative is reported as a component of other comprehensive income, net of income taxes and reclassified into earnings in the same period or periods during which the hedged transaction affects earnings. Gains and losses on the derivatives representing either hedge ineffectiveness or hedge components excluded from the assessment of effectiveness are recognized in current earnings.

As of December 31, 2012, the total notional amounts of the Company's foreign exchange forward and option contracts were €480 million (approximately $635 million equivalent) and ¥3.2 billion (approximately $35 million equivalent), respectively, the total notional volume for contract ethylene sales was approximately 3 million barrels, and the total notional volume hedged for feedstock was approximately 3 million barrels. The Company had no hedges for energy or interest rate swaps for the future issuance of debt ("forward starting interest rate swaps") at December 31, 2012.

As of December 31, 2011, the total notional amounts of the Company's foreign exchange forward and option contracts were €270 million (approximately $350 million equivalent) and ¥13.7 billion (approximately $185 million equivalent), respectively, the total notional volume hedged for energy was approximately 1 million mmbtu (million british thermal units), and the total notional volume hedged for feedstock was approximately 2 million barrels. Additionally, the total notional value of the interest rate swaps for the future issuance of debt ("forward starting interest rate swaps") was $200 million.

Derivatives' Hedging Relationships

(Dollars in millions) Derivatives in Fair Value Hedging Relationships	Location of Gain/(Loss) Recognized in Income on Derivatives	Amount of Gain/ (Loss) Recognized in Income on Derivatives	
		December 31, 2012	December 31, 2011
Interest rate contracts	Net interest expense	$—	$1
		$—	$1

(Dollars in millions) Derivatives' Cash Flow Hedging Relationships	Amount of After Tax of Gain/(Loss) Recognized in Other Comprehensive Income on Derivatives (Effective Portion)		Location of Gain/(Loss) Reclassified From Accumulated Other Comprehensive Income into Income (Effective Portion)	Pre-Tax Amount of Gain/(Loss) Reclassified From Accumulated Other Comprehensive Income into Income (Effective Portion)	
	December 31, 2012	December 31, 2011		December 31, 2012	December 31, 2011
Commodity contracts	$—	$ (6)	Cost of sales	$(22)	$—
Foreign exchange contracts	(15)	12	Sales	38	—
Forward starting interest rate swap contracts	(28)	(26)	Interest Expense	(5)	—
	$(43)	$(20)		$ 11	$—

Hedging Summary

At December 31, 2012 and 2011, pre-tax monetized positions and mark-to-market gains and losses from raw materials and energy, currency, and certain interest rate hedges that were included in accumulated other comprehensive income totaled approximately $75 million in losses and $4 million in losses, respectively. In 2012, losses on forward starting interest rate swaps included settlement of those related to the issuance of debt for the Solutia acquisition. Included in accumulated other comprehensive loss at December 31, 2011 are losses associated with forward starting interest rate swaps monetized in fourth quarter 2011. In 2011, losses on forward starting interest rate swaps and commodity contracts more than offset gains on foreign exchange contracts. If realized, approximately $11 million in pre-tax losses will be reclassified into earnings during the next 12 months due to losses amortized into earnings from forward-starting interest rate swaps and losses on commodity contracts, partially offset by gains on foreign exchange contracts. Ineffective portions of hedges are immediately recognized in cost of sales or other charges (income), net. For 2012, the ineffective portion of the Company's qualifying hedges was $2 million. There were no material gains or losses related to the ineffective portion of hedges recognized in 2011.

The gains or losses on nonqualifying derivatives or derivatives that are not designated as hedges are marked to market in the line item "Other charges (income), net" of the Statements of Earnings, and, in all periods presented, represent foreign exchange derivatives denominated in multiple currencies and are transacted and settled in the same quarter. The Company recognized approximately $5 million and $1 million net gain on nonqualifying derivatives during 2012 and 2011, respectively.

18. Stockholders' Equity (in part)

Accumulated Other Comprehensive Income (Loss), Net of Tax

(Dollars in millions)	Cumulative Translation Adjustment $	Benefit Plans Unrecognized Prior Service Credits $	Unrealized Gains (Losses) on Cash Flow Hedges $	Unrealized Losses on Investments $	Accumulated Other Comprehensive Income (Loss) $
Balance at December 31, 2010	79	99	17	(1)	194
Period change	(15)	(21)	(20)	—	(56)
Balance at December 31, 2011	64	78	(3)	(1)	138
Period change	41	(13)	(43)	—	(15)
Balance at December 31, 2012	105	65	(46)	(1)	123

Amounts of other comprehensive income (loss) are presented net of applicable taxes. The Company records deferred income taxes on the cumulative translation adjustment related to branch operations and other entities included in the Company's consolidated U.S. tax return. No deferred income taxes are provided on the cumulative translation adjustment of subsidiaries outside the United States, as such cumulative translation adjustment is considered to be a component of permanently invested, unremitted earnings of these foreign subsidiaries.

Components of other comprehensive income recorded in the Consolidated Statements of Earnings, Comprehensive Income and Retained Earnings are presented below, before tax and net of tax effects:

| (Dollars in millions) | For Year Ended December 31, | | | | | |
| | 2012 | | 2011 | | 2010 | |
	Before Tax	Net of Tax	Before Tax	Net of Tax	Before Tax	Net of Tax
Other comprehensive income (loss)						
Change in cumulative translation adjustment	$ 42	$ 41	$(15)	$(15)	$ 4	$ 2
Defined benefit pension and other postretirement benefit plans:						
Amortization of unrecognized prior service credits included in net periodic costs	(20)	(13)	(37)	(21)	(41)	(26)
Derivatives and hedging:						
Unrealized (loss) gain	(59)	(36)	(31)	(20)	29	18
Reclassification adjustment for gains included in net income	(11)	(7)	—	—	(45)	(28)
Total other comprehensive income (loss)	$(48)	$(15)	$(83)	$(56)	$(53)	$(34)

Format of Stockholders' Equity in Annual Filings

PRESENTATION

5.01 *Equity* (sometimes referred to as net assets) is the residual interest in the assets of an entity that remains after deducting its liabilities. As discussed in Financial Accounting Standards Board (FASB) *Accounting Standards Codification* (ASC) 505-10-50-2 if both financial position and results of operations are presented, disclosure of changes in (*a*) the separate accounts comprising stockholders' equity (in addition to retained earnings) and (*b*) the number of shares of equity securities during at least the most recent annual fiscal period and any subsequent interim period presented is required in order to make the financial statements sufficiently informative. Disclosure of such changes may take the form of separate statements or may be made in the basic financial statements or notes thereto. Most public entities present a statement of stockholders' equity to conform with Rule 3-04 of Securities and Exchange Commission (SEC) Regulation S-X.

5.02 FASB ASC 505-10-25-1 explains that additional paid-in capital, however created, should not be used to relieve income of the current or future years of charges that would otherwise be made to the income statement.

5.03 As discussed in FASB ASC 505-20-30-3, in accounting for a stock dividend, a corporation should transfer from retained earnings to the category of capital stock and additional paid-in capital an amount equal to the fair value of the additional shares issued.

5.04 Rule 5 02 of Regulation S-X requires separate captions for additional paid-in capital, other additional capital, and retained earnings. If appropriate, additional paid-in capital and other additional capital may be combined with the stock caption to which it applies.

DISCLOSURE

5.05 FASB ASC 505-10-50-3 states that an entity should explain the pertinent rights and privileges of the various securities outstanding. Examples are dividend and liquidation preferences; contractual rights of security holders to receive dividends or returns from the security issuer's profits, cash flows, or returns on investments; participation rights; call prices and dates; conversion or exercise prices or rates and pertinent dates; sinking-fund requirements; unusual voting rights; and significant terms of contracts to issue additional shares.

5.06 FASB ASC 505-10-50-2 also requires disclosure of changes in the separate accounts comprising shareholders' equity (in addition to retained earnings) and of the changes in the number of shares of equity securities during at least the most recent annual fiscal period. Disclosure of such changes may take the form of separate statements or may be made in the basic financial statements or notes thereto.

PRESENTATION AND DISCLOSURE EXCERPTS

ISSUANCE OF COMMON STOCK FOR A BUSINESS COMBINATION

5.07 FLOWERS FOODS, INC. (DEC)
CONSOLIDATED STATEMENTS OF CHANGES IN STOCKHOLDERS' EQUITY (in part)

| | Common Stock | | Capital in | | Accumulated Other | Treasury Stock | | Non- | |
(Amounts in thousands, except share data)	Number of Shares Issued	Par Value	Excess of Par Value	Retained Earnings	Comprehensive Loss	Number of Shares	Cost	controlling Interest	Total
Balances at December 31, 2011	152,488,008	$199	$544,065	$547,997	$(112,047)	(16,506,822)	$(221,246)	$—	$758,968
Net income				136,121					136,121
Derivative instruments, net of tax					10,808				10,808
Pension and postretirement plans, net of tax					(13,428)				(13,428)
Shares issued for acquisition			16,628			2,178,648	29,259		45,887
Stock repurchases						(935,742)	(18,726)		(18,726)
Exercise of stock options			(329)			1,047,297	14,210		13,881
Issuance of deferred stock awards			(610)			45,405	610		—

(continued)

(Amounts in thousands, except share data)	Common Stock Number of Shares Issued	Par Value	Capital in Excess of Par Value	Retained Earnings	Accumulated Other Comprehensive Loss	Treasury Stock Number of Shares	Cost	Non-controlling Interest	Total
Amortization of share-based compensation awards			9,373						9,373
Income tax benefits related to share-based payments			2,225						2,225
Performance-contingent restricted stock awards forfeitures and cancellations			606			(45,252)	(606)		—
Issuance of deferred compensation			(34)			1,647	34		—
Dividends paid on vested performance-contingent restricted stock awards and deferred share awards				(255)					(255)
Dividends paid—$0.63 per common share				(86,234)					(86,234)
Balances at December 29, 2012	152,488,008	$199	$571,924	$597,629	$(114,667)	(14,214,819)	$(196,465)	$—	$858,620

NOTES TO CONSOLIDATED FINANCIAL STATEMENTS

Note 7. Acquisitions (in part)

Lepage Acquisition (in part)

On July 21, 2012, we completed the acquisition of Lepage Bakeries, Inc. ("Lepage") in two separate but concurrent transactions. Pursuant to the Acquisition Agreement dated May 31, 2012 (the "Acquisition Agreement"), by and among Flowers, Lobsterco I, LLC, a Maine single-member limited liability company and direct wholly owned subsidiary of Flowers ("Lobsterco I"), Lepage, RAL, Inc., a Maine corporation ("RAL"), Bakeast Company, a Maine general partnership ("Bakeast Partnership"), Bakeast Holdings, Inc., a Delaware corporation ("Bakeast Holdings," and collectively with Lepage, RAL and Bakeast Partnership, the "Acquired Entities"), and the equityholders of the Acquired Entities named in the Acquisition Agreement (collectively, the "Equityholders"), Lobsterco I purchased from the Equityholders all of the issued and outstanding shares of the Acquired Entities in exchange for approximately $318.4 million in cash and $17.7 million in deferred obligations, which is the fair value of gross payments of $20.0 million.

Pursuant to the Agreement and Plan of Merger dated May 31, 2012 (the "Merger Agreement"), by and among Flowers, Lobsterco II, LLC, a Maine single-member limited liability company and direct wholly owned subsidiary of Flowers ("Lobsterco II"), Aarow Leasing, Inc., a Maine corporation ("Aarow"), The Everest Company, Incorporated, a Maine corporation ("Everest," and together with Aarow, the "Acquired Companies"), and certain equityholders of Lepage, the Acquired Companies merged with and into Lobsterco II (the "Merger") and all of the issued and outstanding shares of common stock of the Acquired Companies were exchanged for 2,178,648 shares of Flowers common stock.

Lepage operates three bakeries, two in Lewiston, Maine, and one in Brattleboro, Vermont. Lepage serves customers in the New England and New York markets making fresh bakery products under the *Country Kitchen* and *Barowsky's* brands. This acquisition provides a DSD platform to accelerate penetration of *Nature's Own* and *Tastykake* brands in the Northeast. The Lepage acquisition has been accounted for as a business combination. The results of Lepage's operations are included in the company's consolidated financial statements beginning on July 21, 2012 and are included in the company's DSD operating segment.

The preliminary aggregate purchase price was $381.9 million as described in the table below. We incurred $7.1 million in acquisition-related costs during 2012 for Lepage. These expenses are included in the selling, distribution and administrative line item in the company's consolidated statement of income for the fifty-two weeks ending on December 29, 2012.

The following table summarizes the consideration transferred to acquire Lepage and the amounts of identified assets acquired and liabilities assumed based on the estimated fair value at the acquisition date (amounts in thousands):

Fair Value of Consideration Transferred:	
Cash	$300,000
Cash paid for preliminary tax adjustment	18,426
Net working capital adjustment estimate	(55)
Deferred payment obligations	17,663
Flowers Foods, Inc. common stock	45,887
Total fair value of consideration transferred	$381,921
Recognized Amounts of Identifiable Assets Acquired and Liabilities Assumed:	
Financial assets	$ 11,658
Inventories	4,537
Property, plant, and equipment	59,970
Assets Held for sale—Distributor routes	16,161
Identifiable intangible assets estimate	256,400
Deferred income taxes, net	(1,137)
Financial liabilities	(15,617)
Net recognized amounts of identifiable assets acquired	$331,972
Goodwill	$ 49,949

The $18.4 million cash payment for the preliminary tax adjustment is the amount paid to the Lepage equityholders at the closing of the acquisition in connection with certain incremental tax liabilities that will be incurred by those equityholders if the parties jointly make an election under Section 338(h)(10) of the Internal Revenue Code. In the event the parties decide not to make such an election, the payment will be returned to the company. There is an additional $2.1 million preliminary tax adjustment (recorded in the financial liabilities figure in the table above) the company will pay for entity level state taxes.

The $17.7 million obligation for the deferred payments represents the fair value of the fixed payments of $1,250,000 beginning on the first business day of each of the sixteen calendar quarters following the fourth anniversary of the closing of the acquisition (total of $20.0 million in gross payments). The first payment will be made by Flowers on October 1, 2016 and the final payment will be made on July 1, 2020. The difference between the fair value and the gross payments of $2.3 million is recorded as a reduction to the liability and is being amortized to interest expense over eight years.

We issued 2,178,648 shares of Flowers common stock to certain equityholders of Lepage with a fair value of $45.9 million. The number of shares issued was calculated by dividing $50.0 million by the average closing price of Flowers Foods, Inc. common stock for the twenty consecutive trading day period ending five trading days prior to the closing. The shares issued to the equityholders were separated into five categories with each category having a different holding period requirement. As a result, each holding period had a fair value assignment based on an implied fair value which was determined using the Black-Scholes call option formula for an option expiring on each restriction lapse date. The estimated exercise price is equal to the stock price on the last trading day before the closing on July 21, 2012 of $20.48. The table below outlines the determination of fair value and provides the assumptions used in the calculation:

Restriction Lapse Year	2012	2013	2014	2015	2016	Total
Value of Flowers shares issued (thousands)	$25,000	$10,000	$5,000	$5,000	$5,000	$50,000
Implied Fair Value of Restricted shares (thousands)	$23,626	$ 9,154	$4,447	$4,363	$4,297	$45,887
Exercise price (per share)	$ 20.48	$ 20.48	$20.48	$20.48	$20.48	
Expected term (yrs)	0.37	1.00	2.00	3.00	4.00	
Volatility (%)	25.0%	25.0%	25.0%	25.0%	25.0%	
Risk-free rate (%)	0.1%	0.2%	0.2%	0.3%	0.4%	
Dividend Yield (%)	3.0%	3.0%	3.0%	3.0%	3.0%	

SETTLEMENT OF WARRANTS

5.08 EMC CORPORATION (DEC)
CONSOLIDATED STATEMENTS OF SHAREHOLDERS' EQUITY (in part)

(In thousands)

	Common Stock		Additional Paid-in Capital	Retained Earnings	Accumulated Other Comprehensive Loss	Non-controlling Interest in VMware	Shareholders' Equity
	Shares	Par Value					
Balance, December 31, 2011	2,048,890	20,489	3,405,513	16,120,621	(235,009)	968,089	20,279,703
Stock issued through stock option and stock purchase plans	41,972	420	559,855	—	—	—	560,275
Tax benefit from stock options exercised	—	—	267,122	—	—	—	267,122
Restricted stock grants, cancellations and withholdings, net	10,819	109	(126,180)	—	—	—	(126,071)
Repurchase of common stock	(27,067)	(271)	(699,729)	—	—	—	(700,000)
EMC purchase of VMware stock	—	—	(258,296)	—	—	(41,704)	(300,000)
Stock options issued in business acquisitions	—	—	20,382	—	—	—	20,382
Stock-based compensation	—	—	897,617	—	—	—	897,617
Impact from equity transactions of VMware, Inc.	—	—	(435,766)	—	—	85,943	(349,823)
Actuarial loss on pension plan, net of tax benefit of $5,490	—	—	—	—	(14,064)	—	(14,064)
Change in market value of investments	—	—	—	—	47,026	895	47,921
Change in market value of derivatives	—	—	—	—	(8,220)	21	(8,199)
Translation adjustment	—	—	—	—	1,994	—	1,994
Convertible debt conversions and warrant settlement	32,345	323	(1,027)	—	—	—	(704)
Reclassification of convertible debt (to)/from mezzanine (Note E)	—	—	61,621	—	—	—	61,621
Net income	—	—	—	2,732,613	—	153,404	2,886,017
Balance as of December 31, 2012	2,106,959	$21,070	$3,691,112	$18,853,234	$(208,273)	$1,166,648	$23,523,791

NOTES TO CONSOLIDATED FINANCIAL STATEMENTS

E. Convertible Debt (in part)

The holders of the 2013 Notes may convert their 2013 Notes at their option on any day prior to the close of business on the scheduled trading day immediately preceding September 1, 2013 only under the following circumstances: (1) during the five business-day period after any five consecutive trading-day period (the "measurement period") in which the price per 2013 Note for each day of that measurement period was less than 98% of the product of the last reported sale price of our common stock and the conversion rate on each such day; (2) during any calendar quarter, if the last reported sale price of our common stock for 20 or more trading days in a period of 30 consecutive trading days ending on the last trading day of the immediately preceding calendar quarter exceeds 130% of the applicable conversion price in effect on the last trading day of the immediately preceding calendar quarter; or (3) upon the occurrence of certain events specified in the 2013 Notes. Additionally, the 2013 Notes will become convertible during the last three months prior to their maturity.

Upon conversion, we will pay cash up to the principal amount of the debt converted. With respect to any conversion value in excess of the principal amount of the 2013 Notes converted, we have the option to settle the excess with cash, shares of our common stock, or a combination of cash and shares of our common stock based on a daily conversion value, determined in accordance with the indenture, calculated on a proportionate basis for each day of the relevant 20-day observation period. The initial conversion rate for the 2013 Notes will be 62.1978 shares of our common stock per one thousand dollars of principal amount of 2013 Notes, which represents a 27.5% conversion premium from the date the 2013 Notes were issued and is equivalent to a conversion price of approximately $16.08 per share of our common stock. The conversion price is subject to adjustment in some events as set forth in the indenture. In addition, if a "fundamental change" (as defined in the indenture) occurs prior to the maturity date, we will in some cases increase the conversion rate for a holder of 2013 Notes that elects to convert its 2013 Notes in connection with such fundamental change.

At December 31, 2012 and 2011, the contingent conversion thresholds on the 2013 Notes were exceeded. As a result, the 2013 Notes became convertible at the option of the holder. Accordingly, since the terms of the 2013 Notes require the principal to be settled in cash, we reclassified from shareholders' equity the portion of the 2013 Notes attributable to the conversion feature which had not yet been accreted to its face value, and the 2013 Notes were classified as a current liability. Contingencies continue to exist regarding the holders' ability to convert the 2013 Notes in future quarters. The determination of whether the 2013 Notes are convertible will be performed on a quarterly basis. Consequently, the 2013 Notes might not be convertible in future quarters. Approximately $14.9 million of the 2013 Notes have been converted as of December 31, 2012.

The carrying amount of the 2013 Notes reported in the consolidated balance sheets as a current liability as of December 31, 2012 was $1,652.4 million and the fair value was $2,665.7 million. The carrying amount of the equity component of the 2013 Notes was $325.1 million at December 31, 2012. As of December 31, 2012, the unamortized discount on the 2013 Notes consists of $57.7 million, which will be fully amortized by December 1, 2013.

In connection with the issuance of the 2011 Notes and 2013 Notes, we entered into separate convertible note hedge transactions with respect to our common stock (the "Purchased Options"). The Purchased Options allow us to receive shares of our common stock and/or cash related to the excess conversion value that we would pay to the holders of the 2011 Notes and 2013 Notes upon conversion. The Purchased Options will cover, subject to customary anti-dilution adjustments, approximately 215 million shares of our common stock. We paid an aggregate amount of $669.1 million of the proceeds from the sale of the 2011 Notes and 2013 Notes for the Purchased Options that was recorded as additional paid-in-capital in shareholders' equity. In the fourth quarter of 2011, we exercised 107.5 million of the Purchased Options in conjunction with the planned settlements of the 2011 Notes, and we received 29.5 million shares of net settlement on January 9, 2012, representing the excess conversion value of the options. The remaining 107.5 million of the Purchased Options expire on December 1, 2013.

We also entered into separate transactions in which we sold warrants to acquire, subject to customary anti-dilution adjustments, approximately 215 million shares of our common stock at an exercise price of approximately $19.55 per share of our common stock. We received aggregate proceeds of $391.1 million from the sale of the associated warrants. Upon exercise, the value of the warrants is required to be settled in shares. Half of the associated warrants were exercised between February 15, 2012 and March 14, 2012 and the remaining half of the associated warrants have expiration dates between February 18, 2014 and March 18, 2014. During the first quarter of 2012, the exercised warrants were settled with 32.3 million shares of our common stock.

The Purchased Options and associated warrants will generally have the effect of increasing the conversion price of the 2013 Notes to approximately $19.55 per share of our common stock, representing an approximate 55% conversion premium based on the closing price of $12.61 per share of our common stock on November 13, 2006, which was the issuance date of the 2013 Notes.

STOCK COMPENSATION PLANS

5.09 ZIMMER HOLDINGS, INC. (DEC)

CONSOLIDATED STATEMENTS OF STOCKHOLDERS' EQUITY (in part)

	Zimmer Holdings, Inc. Stockholders								
	Common Shares		Paid-in	Retained	Accumulated Other Comprehensive	Treasury Shares		Noncontrolling	Total Stockholders'
(In millions)	Number	Amount	Capital	Earnings	Income	Number	Amount	Interest	Equity
Balance December 31, 2011	255.9	2.5	3,399.2	6,426.8	271.4	(77.9)	(4,592.7)	7.6	5,514.8
Net earnings	—	—	—	755.0	—	—	—	(2.1)	752.9
Other comprehensive income	—	—	—	—	72.5	—	—	(0.1)	72.4
Cash dividend declared of $0.54 per share of common stock	—	—	—	(93.3)	—	—	—	—	(93.3)
Stock compensation plans, including tax benefits	1.2	0.1	101.4	(2.6)	—	0.1	6.2	—	105.1
Share repurchases	—	—	—	—	—	(7.7)	(485.6)	—	(485.6)
Balance December 31, 2012	257.1	$2.6	$3,500.6	$7,085.9	$343.9	(85.5)	$(5,072.1)	$5.4	$5,866.3

3. Share-Based Compensation

Our share-based payments primarily consist of stock options, restricted stock, restricted stock units (RSUs), and an employee stock purchase plan. Share-based compensation expense is as follows (in millions):

For the Years Ended December 31,	2012	2011	2010
Stock options	$32.4	$41.7	$47.6
RSUs and other	22.6	18.8	14.4
Total expense, pre-tax	55.0	60.5	62.0
Tax benefit related to awards	(16.6)	(17.8)	(16.2)
Total expense, net of tax	$38.4	$42.7	$45.8

Share-based compensation cost capitalized as part of inventory for the years ended December 31, 2012, 2011 and 2010 was $6.1 million, $8.8 million, and\ $12.2 million, respectively. As of December 31, 2012 and 2011, approximately $3.3 million and $4.8 million of capitalized costs remained in finished goods inventory.

Stock Options

We had two equity compensation plans in effect at December 31, 2012: the 2009 Stock Incentive Plan (2009 Plan) and the Stock Plan for Non-Employee Directors. The 2009 Plan succeeds the 2006 Stock Incentive Plan (2006 Plan) and the TeamShare Stock Option Plan (TeamShare Plan). No further awards have been granted under the 2006 Plan or under the TeamShare Plan since May 2009, and shares remaining available for grant under those plans have been merged into the 2009 Plan. Vested and unvested stock options and unvested restricted stock and RSUs previously granted under the 2006 Plan, the TeamShare Plan and another prior plan, the 2001 Stock Incentive Plan, remained outstanding as of December 31, 2012. We have reserved the maximum number of shares of common stock available for award under the terms of each of these plans. We have registered 57.9 million shares of common stock under these plans. The 2009 Plan provides for the grant of nonqualified stock options and incentive stock options, long-term performance awards in the form of performance shares or units, restricted stock, RSUs and stock appreciation rights. The Compensation and Management Development Committee of the Board of Directors determines the grant date for annual grants under our equity compensation plans. The date for annual grants under the 2009 Plan to our executive officers is expected to occur in the first quarter of each year following the earnings announcements for the previous quarter and full year. The Stock Plan for Non-Employee Directors provides for awards of stock options, restricted stock and RSUs to non-employee directors. It has been our practice to issue shares of common stock upon exercise of stock options from previously unissued shares, except in limited circumstances where they are issued from treasury stock. The total number of awards which may be granted in a given year and/or over the life of the plan under each of our equity compensation plans is limited. At December 31, 2012, an aggregate of 8.7 million shares were available for future grants and awards under these plans.

Stock options granted to date under our plans generally vest over four years and generally have a maximum contractual life of 10 years. As established under our equity compensation plans, vesting may accelerate upon retirement after the first anniversary date of the award if certain criteria are met. We recognize expense related to stock options on a straight-line basis over the requisite service period, less awards expected to be forfeited using estimated forfeiture rates. Due to the accelerated retirement provisions, the requisite service period of our stock options range from one to four years. Stock options are granted with an exercise price equal to the market price of our common stock on the date of grant, except in limited circumstances where local law may dictate otherwise.

A summary of stock option activity for the year ended December 31, 2012 is as follows (options in thousands):

	Stock Options	Weighted Average Exercise Price	Weighted Average Remaining Contractual Life	Intrinsic Value (In Millions)
Outstanding at January 1, 2012	16,748	$68.04		
Options granted	1,720	64.26		
Options exercised	(933)	46.05		
Options cancelled	(239)	60.21		
Options expired	(658)	75.43		
Outstanding at December 31, 2012	16,638	$68.74	4.8	$64.2
Vested or expected to vest as of December 31, 2012	16,169	$68.94	4.7	$61.9
Exercisable at December 31, 2012	12,977	$71.34	3.9	$38.0

We use a Black-Scholes option-pricing model to determine the fair value of our stock options. Expected volatility was derived from the implied volatility of traded options on our stock that were actively traded around the grant date of the stock options with exercise prices similar to the stock options and maturities of over one year. The expected term of the stock options has been derived from historical employee exercise behavior. The risk-free interest rate was determined using the implied yield currently available for zero-coupon U.S. government issues with a remaining term approximating the expected life of the options. We began paying dividends in 2012. Accordingly, prior to 2012 we assumed no dividend yield. Starting in 2012, the dividend yield was determined by using an estimated annual dividend and dividing it by the market price of our stock on the grant date.

The following table presents information regarding the weighted average fair value for stock options granted, the assumptions used to determine fair value, and the intrinsic value of options exercised in the indicated year:

For the Years Ended December 31,	2012	2011	2010
Dividend yield	1.1%	—%	—%
Volatility	25.6%	26.1%	26.3%
Risk-free interest rate	1.5%	2.2%	2.8%
Expected life (years)	6.1	6.1	5.9
Weighted average fair value of options granted	$15.40	$18.33	$18.17
Intrinsic value of options exercised (in millions)	$17.1	$27.5	$ 8.5

As of December 31, 2012, there was $38.4 million of unrecognized share-based payment expense related to nonvested stock options granted under our plans. That expense is expected to be recognized over a weighted average period of 2.5 years.

RSUs

We have awarded RSUs to our employees. The terms of the awards have been three to five years. Some of the awards have only service conditions while some have performance and market conditions as well. The service condition awards vest ratably on the anniversary date of the award. The awards that have performance and market conditions vest all at once on the third anniversary date. Future service conditions may be waived if an employee retires after the first anniversary date of the award, but performance and market conditions continue to apply. Accordingly, the requisite service period used for share-based payment expense ranges from one to five years.

A summary of nonvested RSU activity for the year ended December 31, 2012 is as follows (in thousands):

	RSUs	Weighted Average Grant Date Fair Value
Outstanding at January 1, 2012	1,187	$56.25
Granted	685	65.91
Vested	(299)	52.92
Forfeited	(363)	64.58
Outstanding at December 31, 2012	1,210	60.03

For the RSUs with service conditions only, the fair value of the awards was determined based upon the fair market value of our common stock on the date of grant. For the RSUs with market conditions, a Monte Carlo valuation technique was used to simulate the market conditions of the awards. The outcome of the simulation was used to determine the fair value of the awards.

We are required to estimate the number of RSUs that will vest and recognize share-based payment expense on a straight-line basis over the requisite service period. As of December 31, 2012, we estimate that approximately 1,113,000 outstanding RSUs will vest. If our estimate were to change in the future, the cumulative effect of the change in estimate will be recorded in that period. Based upon the number of RSUs that we expect to vest, the unrecognized share-based payment expense as of December 31, 2012 was $38.9 million and is expected to be recognized over a weighted-average period of 2.3 years. The fair value of RSUs vesting during the years ended December 31, 2012, 2011 and 2010 based upon our stock price on the date of vesting was $18.9 million, $11.8 million and $3.2 million, respectively.

ISSUANCE OF PREFERRED STOCK

5.10 THE PNC FINANCIAL SERVICES GROUP, INC. (DEC)

CONSOLIDATED STATEMENT OF CHANGES IN EQUITY

(In millions)	Shares Outstanding Common Stock	Common Stock	Capital Surplus— Preferred Stock	Capital Surplus— Common Stock and Other	Retained Earnings	Accumulated Other Comprehensive Income (Loss)	Treasury Stock	Non-controlling Interests	Total Equity
Balance at December 31, 2009[a]	462	$2,354	$7,974	$8,945	$13,144	$(1,962)	$(513)	$2,625	$32,567
Cumulative effect of adopting ASU 2009–17					(92)	(13)			(105)
Balance at January 1, 2010	462	$2,354	$7,974	$8,945	$13,052	$(1,975)	$(513)	$2,625	$32,462
Net income (loss)					3,412			(15)	3,397
Other comprehensive income (loss), net of tax						1,544			1,544
Cash dividends declared									
Common					(204)				(204)
Preferred					(146)				(146)
Redemption of preferred stock and noncontrolling interest Series N (TARP)			(7,579)						(7,579)
Preferred stock discount accretion			252		(252)				
Other				(1)	(3)				(4)
Common stock activity[b]	65	328		3,113					3,441
Treasury stock activity	(1)			(62)			(59)		(121)
Other				62				(14)	48
Balance at December 31, 2010[a]	526	$2,682	$647	$12,057	$15,859	$(431)	$(572)	$2,596	$32,838
Net income					3,056			15	3,071
Other comprehensive income (loss), net of tax						326			326
Cash dividends declared									
Common					(604)				(604)
Preferred					(56)				(56)
Preferred stock discount accretion			2		(2)				
Common stock activity	1	1		10					11
Treasury stock activity[c]				(36)			85		49
Preferred stock issuance—Series O[d]			988						988
Other				41				582	623
Balance at December 31, 2011[a]	527	$2,683	$1,637	$12,072	$18,253	$(105)	$(487)	$3,193	$37,246
Net income					3,013			(12)	3,001
Other comprehensive income (loss), net of tax						939			939
Cash dividends declared									
Common					(820)				(820)
Preferred					(177)				(177)
Preferred stock discount accretion			4		(4)				
Common stock activity	1	7		45					52
Treasury stock activity[c]				51			(82)		(31)
Preferred stock issuance—Series P[e]			1,482						1,482
Preferred stock issuance—Series Q[f]			467						467
Other				25				(419)	(394)
Balance at December 31, 2012[a][g]	528	$2,690	$3,590	$12,193	$20,265	$834	$(569)	$2,762	$41,765

[a] The par value of our preferred stock outstanding was less than $.5 million at each date and, therefore, is excluded from this presentation.
[b] Includes 63.9 million common shares issuance, the net proceeds of which were used together with other available funds to redeem the Series N (TARP) Preferred Stock, for a $3.4 billion net increase in total equity.
[c] Net treasury stock activity totaled less than .5 million shares issued or redeemed.
[d] 10,000 Series O preferred shares with a $1 par value were issued on July 20, 2011.
[e] 15,000 Series P preferred shares with a $1 par value were issued on April 24, 2012.
[f] 4,500 Series Q preferred shares with a $1 par value were issued on September 21, 2012 and 300 shares were issued on October 9, 2012.
[g] 5,001 Series M preferred shares with a $1 par value were issued and redeemed on December 10, 2012.

NOTES TO CONSOLIDATED FINANCIAL STATEMENTS

Note 19 Equity (in part)

Preferred Stock

The following table provides the number of preferred shares issued and outstanding, the liquidation value per share and the number of authorized preferred shares that are available for future use.

December 31 Shares in Thousands	Liquidation Value Per Share	Preferred Shares	
		2012	2011
Authorized			
$1 par value		16,588	16,588
Issued and outstanding			
Series B	$ 40	1	1
Series K	10,000	50	50
Series L	100,000	2	2
Series O	100,000	10	10
Series P	100,000	15	
Series Q	100,000	5	
Total issued and outstanding		83	63

Our Series B preferred stock is cumulative and is not redeemable at our option. Annual dividends on Series B preferred stock total $1.80 per share. Holders of Series B preferred stock are entitled to 8 votes per share, which is equal to the number of full shares of common stock into which the Series B Preferred Stock is convertible.

Our Series K preferred stock was issued in May 2008 in connection with our issuance of $500 million of Depositary Shares, each representing a fractional interest in a share of the Fixed-to-Floating Non-Cumulative Perpetual Preferred Stock, Series K. Dividends are payable if and when declared each May 21 and November 21 until May 21, 2013. After that date, dividends will be payable each 21 st of August, November, February and May. Dividends will be paid at a rate of 8.25% prior to May 21, 2013 and at a rate of three-month LIBOR plus 422 basis points beginning May 21, 2013. The Series K preferred stock is redeemable at our option on or after May 21, 2013.

Our 9.875% Fixed-to-Floating Rate Non-Cumulative Preferred Stock, Series L was issued in connection with the National City transaction in exchange for National City's Fixed-to-Floating Rate Non-Cumulative Preferred Stock, Series F. Dividends on the Series L preferred stock are payable if and when declared each 1 st of February, May, August and November. Dividends will be paid at a rate of 9.875% prior to February 1, 2013 and at a rate of three-month LIBOR plus 633 basis points beginning February 1, 2013. The Series L is redeemable at PNC's option, subject to Federal Reserve approval, if then applicable, on or after February 1, 2013 at a redemption price per share equal to the liquidation preference plus any declared but unpaid dividends.

Our Series O preferred stock was issued on July 27, 2011, when we issued one million depositary shares, each representing a 1/100 th interest in a share of our Fixed-to-Floating Rate Non-Cumulative Perpetual Preferred Stock, Series O for gross proceeds before commissions and expenses of $1 billion. Dividends are payable when, as, and if declared by our board of directors or an authorized committee of our board, semi-annually on February 1 and August 1 of each year until August 1, 2021 at a rate of 6.75%. After that date, dividends will be payable on February 1, May 1, August 1 and November 1 of each year beginning on November 1, 2021 at a rate of three-month LIBOR plus 3.678% per annum. The Series O preferred stock is redeemable at our option on or after August 1, 2021 and at our option within 90 days of a regulatory capital treatment event as defined in the designations.

Our Series P preferred stock was issued on April 24, 2012, when we issued 60 million depositary shares, each representing a 1/4,000 th interest in a share of our Fixed-to-Floating Rate Non-Cumulative Perpetual Preferred Stock, Series P for gross proceeds before commissions and expenses of $1.5 billion. Dividends are payable when, as, and if declared by our board of directors or an authorized committee of our board, quarterly on February 1, May 1, August 1 and November 1 of each year. Dividends are paid for each dividend period to, but excluding, May 1, 2022 at a rate of 6.125% and for each dividend period from and including May 1, 2022 at a rate of three-month LIBOR plus 4.0675% per annum. The Series P preferred stock is redeemable at our option on or after May 1, 2022 and at our option within 90 days of a regulatory capital treatment event as defined in the designations.

Our Series Q preferred stock was issued on September 21, 2012, when we issued 18 million depositary shares, each representing a 1/4,000 th interest in a share of our 5.375% Non-Cumulative Perpetual Preferred Stock, Series Q for gross proceeds before commissions and expenses of $450 million. Dividends are payable when, as, and if declared by our board of directors or an authorized committee of our board, quarterly on March 1, June 1, September 1 and December 1 of each year at a rate of 5.375%. The Series Q preferred stock is redeemable at our option on or after December 1, 2017 and at our option within 90 days of a regulatory capital treatment event as defined in the designations. We issued additional Series Q Preferred Stock on October 9, 2012, in connection with the issuance of an additional 1.2 million depositary shares for gross proceeds before commissions and expenses of $30 million, when the underwriters exercised a portion of their over-allotment option.

We have authorized but unissued Series H, I, and J preferred stock. As described in Note 14 Capital Securities of Subsidiary Trusts and Perpetual Trust Securities, under the terms of two of the hybrid capital vehicles we issued that currently qualify as capital for regulatory purposes (the Trust II Securities and the Trust III Securities), these Trust Securities are automatically exchangeable into shares of PNC preferred stock (Series I and Series J, respectively) in each case under certain conditions relating to the capitalization or the financial condition of PNC Bank, N.A. and upon the direction of the Office of the Comptroller of the Currency. The Series preferred stock of PNC REIT Corp. is also automatically exchangeable under similar conditions into shares of PNC Series H preferred stock.

As a part of the National City transaction, we established the PNC Non-Cumulative Perpetual Preferred Stock, Series M (the Series M Preferred Stock), which mirrored in all material respects the former National City Non-Cumulative Perpetual Preferred Stock, Series E. On December 10, 2012, PNC issued $500.1 million (5,001 shares) of the Series M Preferred Stock as required under a Stock Purchase Contract Agreement between PNC and National City Preferred Capital Trust I (the "Trust") dated January 30, 2008. PNC immediately redeemed all $500.1 million of the Series M Preferred Stock from the Trust and the Trust in turn redeemed all $500.0 million outstanding of its 12% Fixed-to-Floating Rate Normal APEX and all $.1 million of its Common Securities.

The replacement capital covenants with respect to the Normal APEX Securities, our Series M shares and our 6,000,000 of Depositary Shares (each representing 1/4,000th of an interest in a share of our 9.875% Fixed-to-Floating Rate Non-Cumulative Preferred Stock, Series L) were terminated on November 5, 2010 as a result of a successful consent solicitation.

In connection with the redemption of the Series N Preferred Stock, we accelerated the accretion of the remaining issuance discount on the Series N Preferred Stock, recorded a corresponding reduction in retained earnings of $250 million during the first quarter of 2010 and paid dividends of $89 million to the US Treasury. This resulted in a noncash reduction in net income attributable to common shareholders and related basic and diluted earnings per share.

ISSUED AND OUTSTANDING CAPPED CALLS

5.11 MICRON TECHNOLOGY, INC. (AUG)
CONSOLIDATED STATEMENTS OF CHANGES IN EQUITY

(In millions)

| | Micron Shareholders | | | | | | | |
| | Common Stock | | Additional Capital | Accumulated Deficit | Accumulated Other Comprehensive Income (Loss) | Total Micron Shareholders' Equity | Non-controlling Interests in Subsidiaries | Total Equity |
	Number of Shares	Amount						
Balance at September 3, 2009	848.7	$ 85	$7,257	$(2,385)	$(4)	$4,953	$1,986	$6,939
Net income				1,850		1,850	50	1,900
Other comprehensive income (loss), net					15	15	(1)	14
Stock issued in acquisition of Numonyx	137.7	14	1,098			1,112		1,112
Stock-based compensation expense			93			93		93
Stock issued under stock plans	6.6		8			8		8
Distributions to noncontrolling interests, net						—	(229)	(229)
Repurchase and retirement of common stock	(2.4)		(20)	(1)		(21)		(21)
Exercise of stock rights held by Intel	3.9					—		—
Acquisition of noncontrolling interests in TECH			10			10	(10)	—
Balance at September 2, 2010	994.5	$99	$8,446	$ (536)	$ 11	$8,020	$1,796	$9,816
Net income				167		167	23	190
Other comprehensive income (loss), net					121	121	6	127
Issuance and repurchase of convertible debts			211			211		211
Stock-based compensation expense			76			76		76
Stock issued under stock plans	11.1	1	27			28		28
Distributions to noncontrolling interests, net						—	(217)	(217)
Repurchase and retirement of common stock	(21.3)	(2)	(160)	(1)		(163)		(163)
Acquisition of noncontrolling interests in TECH			67			67	(226)	(159)
Purchase of capped calls			(57)			(57)		(57)
Balance at September 1, 2011	984.3	$98	$8,610	$ (370)	$132	$8,470	$1,382	$9,852
Net loss				(1,032)		(1,032)	1	(1,031)
Other comprehensive income (loss), net					(52)	(52)	(6)	(58)
Issuance of convertible debts			191			191		191
Conversion of 2013 Notes	27.3	3	135			138		138
Stock-based compensation expense			87			87		87
Stock issued under stock plans	7.1	1	5			6		6
Acquisition of noncontrolling interest in IMFS						—	(466)	(466)
Distributions to noncontrolling interests, net						—	(194)	(194)
Purchase and settlement of capped calls			(102)			(102)		(102)
Repurchase and retirement of common stock	(1.0)	—	(6)	—		(6)		(6)
Balance at August 30, 2012	1,017.7	$102	$8,920	$(1,402)	$ 80	$7,700	$ 717	$8,417

NOTES TO CONSOLIDATED FINANCIAL STATEMENTS

(All tabular amounts in millions except per share amounts)

Debt (in part)

Convertible Notes With Debt and Equity Components (in part)

The accounting standards for convertible debt instruments that may be fully or partially settled in cash upon conversion require the debt and equity components to be separately accounted for in a manner that reflects our nonconvertible borrowing rate when interest expense is recognized in subsequent periods. The amount recorded as debt is based on the fair value of the debt component as a standalone instrument, determined using an average interest rate for similar nonconvertible debt issued by entities with credit ratings comparable to ours at the time of issuance. The difference between the debt recorded at inception and its principal amount is to be accreted to principal through interest expense through the estimated life of the note.

The debt and equity components of all of our convertible notes outstanding as of August 30, 2012 were required to be accounted for separately. The debt and equity components of our 2013 Notes were not required to be stated separately.

2032C and 2032D Notes

On April 18, 2012, we issued $550 million of the 2032C Notes and $450 million of the 2032D Notes (collectively referred to as the "2032 Notes"), each due May 2032. Issuance costs for the 2032 Notes totaled $21 million. The initial conversion rate for the 2032C Notes is 103.8907 shares of common stock per $1,000 principal amount, equivalent to an initial conversion price of approximately $9.63 per share of common stock. The initial conversion rate for the 2032D Notes is 100.1803 shares of common stock per $1,000 principal amount, equivalent to an initial conversion price of approximately $9.98 per share of common stock. Interest is payable in May and November of each year.

Upon issuance of the 2032 Notes, we recorded $805 million of debt, $191 million of additional capital and $17 million of deferred debt issuance costs (included in other noncurrent assets). The amount recorded as debt is based on the fair value of the debt component as a standalone instrument and was determined using an average interest rate for similar nonconvertible debt issued by entities with credit ratings comparable to ours at the time of issuance (Level 2). The difference between the debt recorded at inception and the principal amount ($104 million for the 2032C Notes and $92 million for the 2032D Notes) is being accreted to principal as interest expense through May 2019 for the 2032C Notes and May 2021 for the 2032D Notes, the expected life of the notes.

Conversion Rights: Holders may convert their 2032 Notes under the following circumstances: (1) if the 2032 Notes are called for redemption; (2) during any calendar quarter if the closing price of our common stock for at least 20 trading days in the 30 consecutive trading days ending on the last trading day of the preceding calendar quarter is more than 130% of the conversion price (approximately $12.52 per share for the 2032C Notes and $12.97 per share for the 2032D Notes) of the 2032C or 2032D Notes; (3) during the five business day period immediately after any five consecutive trading day period in which the trading price of the 2032C or 2032D Notes is less than 98% of the product of the closing price of our common stock and the conversion rate of the 2032C or 2032D Notes; (4) if specified distributions or corporate events occur, as set forth in the indenture for the 2032 Notes; or (5) at any time after February 1, 2032.

We have the option to pay cash, issue shares of common stock or any combination thereof for the aggregate amount due upon conversion. It is our current intent to settle the principal amount of the 2032 Notes in cash upon conversion. As a result, upon conversion of the 2032 Notes, only the amounts payable in excess of the principal amounts of the 2032 Notes are considered in diluted earnings per share under the treasury stock method.

Cash Redemption at Our Option: We may redeem for cash the 2032C Notes on or after May 1, 2016 and the 2032D Notes on or after May 1, 2017 if the volume weighted average price of our common stock has been at least 130% of the conversion price (approximately $12.52 per share for the 2032C Notes and $12.97 per share for the 2032D Notes) for at least 20 trading days during any 30 consecutive trading day period. The redemption price will equal the principal amount plus accrued and unpaid interest. If we redeem the 2032C Notes prior to May 4, 2019, or the 2032D Notes prior to May 4, 2021, we will also pay a make-whole premium in cash equal to the present value of all remaining scheduled payments of interest from the redemption date to May 4, 2019 for the 2032C Notes, or to May 4, 2021 for the 2032D Notes, using a discount rate equal to 150 basis points.

Cash Repurchase at the Option of the Holder: We may be required by the holders of the 2032 Notes to repurchase for cash all or a portion of the 2032C Notes on May 1, 2019 and all or a portion of the 2032D Notes on May 1, 2021. The repurchase price is equal to the principal amount plus accrued and unpaid interest. Upon a change in control or a termination of trading, as defined in the indenture, holders of the 2032 Notes may require us to repurchase for cash all or a portion of their 2032 Notes at a repurchase price equal to the principal amount plus accrued and unpaid interest.

2031A and 2031B Notes

On July 26, 2011, we issued $345 million of the 2031A Notes and $345 million of 2031B Notes (collectively referred to as the "2031 Notes"), each due August 2031. The initial conversion rate for the 2031 Notes is 105.2632 shares of common stock per $1,000 principal amount, equivalent to an initial conversion price of approximately $9.50 per share of common stock. Interest is payable in February and August of each year.

Conversion Rights: Holders may convert their 2031 Notes under the following circumstances: (1) during any calendar quarter if the closing price of our common stock for at least 20 trading days in the 30 consecutive trading days ending on the last trading day of the preceding calendar quarter is more than 130% of the conversion price of the 2031 Notes (approximately $12.35 per share); (2) if the 2031 Notes are called for redemption; (3) if specified distributions or corporate events occur, as set forth in the indenture for the 2031 Notes; (4) if the trading price of the 2031 Notes is less than 98% of the product of the closing price of our common stock and the conversion rate of the 2031 Notes during the periods specified in the indenture; or (5) at any time after May 1, 2031.

Upon conversion, we will pay cash up to the aggregate principal amount and cash, shares of common stock or a combination of cash and shares of common stock, at our option, for any remaining conversion obligations. As a result of the conversion provisions in the indenture, upon conversion of the 2031 Notes, only the amounts payable in excess of the principal amounts of the 2031 Notes are considered in diluted earnings per share under the treasury stock method.

Cash Redemption at Our Option: We may redeem for cash the 2031A Notes on or after August 5, 2013 and the 2031B Notes on or after August 5, 2014 if the last reported sale price of our common stock has been at least 130% of the conversion price (approximately $12.35 per share) for at least 20 trading days during any 30 consecutive trading day period. The redemption price will equal the principal amount plus accrued and unpaid interest. If we redeem the 2031A Notes prior to August 5, 2015, or the 2031B Notes prior to August 5, 2016, we will also pay a make-whole premium in cash equal to the present value of all remaining scheduled payments of interest on the 2031 Notes, using a discount rate equal to 150 basis points.

Cash Repurchase at the Option of the Holder: We may be required by the holders of the 2031 Notes to repurchase for cash all or a portion of the 2031A Notes on August 1, 2018 and all or a portion of the 2031B Notes on August 1, 2020. The repurchase price is equal to the principal amount, plus accrued and unpaid interest. Upon a change in control or a termination of trading, as defined in the indenture, we may be required by the holders of the 2031 Notes to repurchase for cash all or a portion of their 2031 Notes at a repurchase price equal to the principal amount plus accrued and unpaid interest.

Shareholders' Equity (in part)

Capped Calls

Issued and Outstanding Capped Calls: Concurrent with the offering of the 2032C and 2032D Notes, in April 2012, we entered into capped call transactions (the "2012C Capped Calls" and "2012D Capped Calls," collectively the "2012 Capped Calls") that have an initial strike price of approximately $9.80 and $10.16 per share, respectively, subject to certain adjustments, which was set to be slightly higher than the initial conversion prices of approximately $9.63 for the 2032C Notes and $9.98 for the 2032D Notes. The 2012C Capped Calls are in four tranches, with cap prices of $14.26, $14.62, $15.33 and $15.69 per share, and cover, subject to anti-dilution adjustments similar to those contained in the 2032C Notes, an approximate combined total of 56.3 million shares of common stock. The 2012C Capped Calls expire on various dates between May 2016 and November 2017. The 2012D Capped Calls are in four tranches, with cap prices of $14.62, $15.33, $15.69 and $16.04 per share, and cover, subject to anti-dilution adjustments similar to those contained in the 2032D Notes, an approximate combined total of 44.3 million shares of common stock. The 2012D Capped Calls expire on various dates between November 2016 and May 2018. The 2012 Capped Calls are intended to reduce the potential dilution upon conversion of the 2032 Notes. The 2012 Capped Calls may be settled in shares or cash, at our election. Settlement of the 2012 Capped Calls in cash on their respective expiration dates would result in us receiving an amount ranging from zero, if the market price per share of our common stock is at or below $9.80, to a maximum of $551 million. We paid $103 million to purchase the 2012 Capped Calls, which was charged to additional capital.

Concurrent with the offering of the 2031 Notes, in July 2011, we entered into capped call transactions (the "2011 Capped Calls") that have an initial strike price of approximately $9.50 per share, subject to certain adjustments, which was set to equal the initial conversion price of the 2031 Notes. The 2011 Capped Calls are in four equal tranches, with cap prices of $11.40, $12.16, $12.67 and $13.17 per share, and cover, subject to anti-dilution adjustments similar to those contained in the 2031 Notes, an approximate combined total of 72.6 million shares of common stock. The 2011 Capped Calls expire on various dates between July 2014 and February 2016. The 2011 Capped Calls are intended to reduce the potential dilution upon conversion of the 2031 Notes. Settlement of the 2011 Capped Calls in cash on their respective expiration dates would result in us receiving an amount ranging from zero if the market price per share of our common stock is at or below $9.50 to a maximum of $207 million. We paid $57 million to purchase the 2011 Capped Calls, which was charged to additional capital.

Concurrent with the offering of the 2013 Notes in April 2009, we entered into capped call transactions (the "2009 Capped Calls") that have an initial strike price of approximately $5.08 per share, subject to certain adjustments, which was set to equal the initial conversion price of the 2013 Notes. The 2009 Capped Calls have a cap price of $6.64 per share and cover, subject to anti-dilution adjustments similar to those contained in the 2013 Notes, an approximate combined total of 45.2 million shares of common stock, and are subject to standard adjustments for instruments of this type. The 2009 Capped Calls expire in October 2012 and November 2012. We elected to settle the 2009 Capped Calls in cash and the amount we will receive will depend on the market price per share of our common stock on the expiration dates. We paid $25 million to purchase the 2009 Capped Calls, which was charged to additional capital.

Settlement and Expiration of the 2007 Capped Calls: Concurrent with the offering of the 2014 Notes, we purchased capped calls with a strike price of approximately $14.23 per share and various expiration dates between November 2011 and December 2012 (the "2007 Capped Calls"). In the first six months of 2012, 2007 Capped Calls covering 30.4 million shares expired according to their terms. In April 2012, we settled the remaining 2007 Capped Calls, covering 60.9 million shares, and received a de minimis payment.

BENEFICIAL CONVERSION FEATURE ON CONVERTIBLE BOND

5.12 SPRINT NEXTEL CORPORATION (DEC)

CONSOLIDATED STATEMENTS OF SHAREHOLDERS' EQUITY (in part)

(In millions)

| | Common Shares | | | Treasury Shares | | Accumulated | Accumulated Other Comprehensive | |
	Shares[1]	Amount	Paid-in Capital	Shares	Amount	Deficit	Loss	Total
Balance, December 31, 2011	2,996	$5,992	$46,716	—	$—	$(40,489)	$ (792)	$11,427
Net loss						(4,326)		(4,326)
Other comprehensive loss, net of tax							(341)	(341)
Issuance of common shares, net	14	27	2					29
Share-based compensation expense			44					44
Beneficial conversion feature on convertible bond			254					254
Balance, December 31, 2012	3,010	$6,019	$47,016	—	$—	$(44,815)	$(1,133)	$ 7,087

[1] See note 14 for information regarding common shares.

NOTES TO THE CONSOLIDATED FINANCIAL STATEMENTS

Note 3. Proposed Business Transactions and Acquisitions (in part)

SoftBank Transaction

On October 15, 2012, Sprint entered into an Agreement and Plan of Merger (Merger Agreement) with SOFTBANK CORP., a *kabushiki kaisha* organized and existing under the laws of Japan, and certain of its wholly-owned subsidiaries (together, "SoftBank"). In addition, on October 15, 2012, Sprint and SoftBank entered into a Bond Purchase Agreement (Bond Agreement).

Bond Agreement

Pursuant to the Bond Agreement, on October 22, 2012, Sprint issued a convertible bond (Bond) to New Sprint, with a face amount of $3.1 billion, stated interest rate of 1%, and maturity date of October 15, 2019, which is convertible into 590,476,190 shares of Sprint common stock at $5.25 per share, or approximately 16.4% upon conversion of the Bond (based on Sprint common shares outstanding as of December 31, 2012), subject to adjustment in accordance with the terms of the Bond Agreement. This conversion feature remains in effect in the event the merger does not close. Interest on the Bond will be due and payable in cash semiannually in arrears on April 15 and October 15 of each year, commencing on April 15, 2013. Upon receipt of regulatory approval, the Bond will be converted into Sprint shares immediately prior to consummation of the SoftBank Merger and may not otherwise be converted prior to the termination of the Merger Agreement. Conversion of the Bond is subject in any case to receipt of any required approvals and, subject to certain exceptions, receipt of waivers under the Company's existing credit facilities. Subject to certain exceptions, SoftBank may not transfer the Bond without Sprint's consent.

Merger Agreement

Upon consummation of the SoftBank Merger, which is subject to various conditions, including Sprint shareholder and regulatory approval, SoftBank will fund New Sprint with additional capital of approximately $17.0 billion, of which approximately $12.1 billion will be distributed to Sprint shareholders as merger consideration with the remaining $4.9 billion held in the cash balance of New Sprint for general corporate purposes, including but not limited to the Clearwire Acquisition. Pursuant to the terms and subject to the conditions described in the Merger Agreement, upon consummation of the SoftBank Merger, outstanding shares of Sprint common stock, except as otherwise provided for in the Merger Agreement, will be converted, at the election of Sprint shareholders, into (i) cash in an amount equal to $7.30 for each share of Sprint common stock or (ii) one share of New Sprint common stock for each share of Sprint common stock, subject in each case to proration such that a stockholder may receive a combination of cash and New Sprint common stock.

Upon consummation of the SoftBank Merger, SoftBank will receive a five -year warrant to purchase 54,579,924 shares in New Sprint at $5.25 per share which would yield approximately $300 million in proceeds upon exercise. Upon consummation of the SoftBank Merger, (i) Sprint will become a wholly-owned subsidiary of New Sprint, (ii) New Sprint will be a publicly traded company, (iii) SoftBank will indirectly own approximately 70% of New Sprint on a fully diluted basis, and (iv) the former shareholders and other equityholders of Sprint will own approximately 30% of the fully diluted equity of New Sprint. The SoftBank Merger is subject to various conditions, including receipt of required regulatory approvals and approval of Sprint's shareholders, and is expected to close in mid-2013.

Under the terms of the Export Development Canada (EDC) facility, the secured equipment credit facility and our revolving credit facility, consummation of the SoftBank Merger would constitute a change of control that would require repayment of all outstanding balances thereunder. Amounts outstanding under the EDC facility and secured equipment credit facility, which were approximately $796 million in the aggregate at December 31, 2012, would become due and payable at the time of closing. In addition, our $2.2 billion revolving bank credit facility would expire upon a change of control, of which approximately

$925 million was outstanding as of December 31, 2012 through letters of credit, including the letter of credit required by the Report and Order (see note 13). Sprint is currently in discussions with existing lenders and intends to amend these facilities to, among other things, exclude the SoftBank Merger from the change of control provisions.

As of the date the Merger Agreement was entered into, approximately $8.8 billion of our senior notes and guaranteed notes provided holders with the right to require us to repurchase the notes if a change of control triggering event (as defined in our indentures and supplemental indentures governing applicable notes) occurred, which included both a change of control and a ratings decline of the applicable notes by each of Moody's Investor Services and Standard & Poor's Rating Services. On November 20, 2012, Sprint announced that it had obtained the necessary consents to amend the applicable provisions of the outstanding indentures such that the SoftBank Merger would not constitute a change of control and, as a result indebtedness outstanding under Sprint's applicable indentures will not become payable by reason of completion of the SoftBank Merger.

Note 8. Long-Term Debt, Financing and Capital Lease Obligations (in part)

Debt Issuances (in part)

On October 22, 2012, the Company issued a convertible bond (Bond) to Starburst II, Inc., a Delaware corporation and a wholly-owned subsidiary of SoftBank, with a face amount of $3.1 billion, stated interest rate of 1%, and maturity date of October 15, 2019, which is convertible into 590,476,190 shares of Sprint common stock at $5.25 per share, or approximately 16.4% upon conversion of the Bond (based on Sprint common shares outstanding as of December 31, 2012), subject to adjustment in accordance with the terms of the Bond Agreement. The closing price of Sprint's common stock at the date of the bond issuance was $5.68, which was greater than the conversion price. This resulted in an initial beneficial conversion feature at an intrinsic value of $254 million which was recognized as a discount on the debt and additional paid-in capital. This discount will be accreted through the stated redemption date of the debt. If the bonds are converted prior to the bond redemption date, any unamortized discount will be recorded as interest expense immediately upon conversion. Interest on the Bond will be due and payable in cash semiannually in arrears on April 15 and October 15 of each year, commencing on April 15, 2013. Upon receipt of regulatory approval, the Bond will be converted into Sprint shares immediately prior to consummation of the merger and may not otherwise be converted prior to the termination of the Merger Agreement. Conversion of the Bond is subject in any case to receipt of any required approvals and, subject to certain exceptions, to receipt of waivers under the Company's existing credit facilities. Subject to certain exceptions, SoftBank may not transfer the Bond without Sprint's consent.

CONVERSION OF SHARES

5.13 BEAM INC. (DEC)
CONSOLIDATED STATEMENT OF EQUITY

(In millions)	$2.67 Convertible Preferred Stock	Common Stock	Paid-In Capital	Accumulated Other Comprehensive Income (Loss)	Retained Earnings	Treasury Stock, at Cost	Non-controlling Interests	Total Equity
Balance at December 31, 2009	$5.2	$734.0	$755.6	$(211.8)	$7,135.4	$(3,326.0)	$13.3	$5,105.7
Net income	—	—	—	—	487.6	—	8.4	496.0
Other comprehensive income	—	—	—	39.8	—	—	—	39.8
Dividends paid to noncontrolling interests	—	—	—	—	—	—	(4.8)	(4.8)
Dividends	—	—	—	—	(116.2)	—	—	(116.2)
Shares issued from treasury stock for benefit plans	—	—	5.7	—	—	61.4	—	67.1
Stock-based compensation	—	—	55.2	—	(7.5)	46.6	—	94.3
Tax benefit on exercise of stock options	—	—	6.1	—	—	—	—	6.1
Conversion of preferred stock	(0.3)	—	(2.4)	—	—	2.7	—	—
Balance at December 31, 2010	$4.9	$734.0	$820.2	$(172.0)	$7,499.3	$(3,215.3)	$16.9	$5,688.0
Net income	—	—	—	—	911.4	—	4.1	915.5
Other comprehensive loss	—	—	—	(239.9)	—	—	—	(239.9)
Dividends paid to noncontrolling interests	—	—	—	—	—	—	(0.8)	(0.8)
Dividends	—	—	—	—	(117.8)	—	—	(117.8)
Stock-based compensation	—	—	54.8	—	(3.4)	103.4	—	154.8
Tax benefit on exercise of stock options	—	—	9.2	—	—	—	—	9.2
Conversion of preferred stock	(0.2)	—	(1.8)	—	—	2.0	—	—
Sale of Acushnet Company	—	—	—	—	—	—	(16.6)	(16.6)
Spin-off of Fortune Brands Home & Security, Inc.	—	—	—	107.8	(2,396.9)	—	(3.6)	(2,292.7)
Balance at December 31, 2011	$4.7	$734.0	$882.4	$(304.1)	$5,892.6	$(3,109.9)	$ —	$4,099.7
Net income	—	—	—	—	382.4	—	—	382.4
Other comprehensive income	—	—	—	118.1	—	—	—	118.1
Dividends	—	—	—	—	(130.1)	—	—	(130.1)
Stock-based compensation	—	—	13.2	—	(3.2)	126.1	—	136.1
Tax benefit on exercise of stock options	—	—	12.8	—	—	—	—	12.8
Conversion of preferred stock	(3.4)	—	(31.2)	—	—	34.5	—	(0.1)
Redemption of preferred stock	(1.3)	—	(0.4)	—	—	—	—	(1.7)
Spin-off of Fortune Brands Home & Security, Inc.	—	—	(3.1)	—	(2.0)	—	—	(5.1)
Balance at December 31, 2012	$—	$734.0	$873.7	$(186.0)	$6,139.7	$(2,949.3)	$ —	$4,612.1

19. $2.67 Convertible Preferred Stock (in part)

On November 20, 2012, we completed the previously announced redemption of all outstanding shares (49,590 shares) of our $2.67 Convertible Preferred Stock that had not been converted in accordance with their terms into shares of our common stock. As a result of such redemption, there are no longer any issued and outstanding shares of our $2.67 Convertible Preferred Stock. Pursuant to the redemption, stockholders tendered the outstanding shares for payment at an aggregate redemption price of $31.02 per share ($30.50 per share plus accrued and unpaid dividends of $0.52 per share). We paid the aggregate redemption price for the shares in cash during the fourth quarter of 2012. There were 153,710 shares of the $2.67 Convertible Preferred Stock outstanding at December 31, 2011.

FAIR VALUE OF EQUITY AWARDS

5.14 LSI CORPORATION (DEC)
CONSOLIDATED STATEMENTS OF STOCKHOLDERS' EQUITY (in part)

(In thousands)

	Common Stock		Additional Paid-in Capital	Accumulated Deficit	Accumulated Other Comprehensive Income/(Loss)	Total
	Shares	Amount				
Balances at December 31, 2011	561,767	5,618	5,623,581	(4,037,031)	(533,228)	1,058,940
Net income	—	—	—	196,228	—	196,228
Other comprehensive loss	—	—	—	—	(45,102)	(45,102)
Fair value of partially vested SandForce equity awards	—	—	19,089	—	—	19,089
Issuance under employee equity incentive plans, net	25,088	251	97,079	—	—	97,330
Repurchase of shares	(35,961)	(360)	(272,225)	—	—	(272,585)
Stock-based compensation	—	—	105,724	—	—	105,724
Balances at December 31, 2012	550,894	$5,509	$5,573,248	$(3,840,803)	$(578,330)	$1,159,624

NOTES TO CONSOLIDATED FINANCIAL STATEMENTS

Note 6—Business Combinations (in part)

Information about the acquisition made during 2012 is presented below. There were no business acquisitions during 2011 or 2010.

Acquisition of SandForce (in part)

On January 3, 2012, the Company acquired SandForce, a provider of flash storage processors for enterprise and client flash solutions and solid state drives. The Company acquired SandForce to enhance its competitive position in the PCIe® flash adapter market where LSI's products already used SandForce flash storage processors. Additionally, the combination of LSI's custom capability and SandForce's standard product offerings allows the Company to offer a full range of products aimed at the growing flash storage processor market for ultrabook, notebook and enterprise solid state drives and flash solutions. Total consideration consisted of the following (in thousands):

Cash paid, net of cash acquired	$319,231
Fair value of partially vested equity awards	19,089
Fair value of LSI's previous investment in SandForce	8,120
Total	$346,440

In connection with the SandForce acquisition, the Company assumed stock options and RSUs originally granted by SandForce and converted them into LSI stock options and RSUs. The portion of the fair value of partially vested equity awards associated with prior service of SandForce employees represents a component of the total consideration for the SandForce acquisition, as presented above. Stock options assumed were valued using a binomial lattice model calibrated to the exercise behavior of LSI's employees. RSUs were valued based on LSI's stock price as of the acquisition date.

Prior to the acquisition, the Company held an equity interest in SandForce. The Company determined the fair value of this equity interest by applying the per share value of the contractual cash consideration to the SandForce shares held by the Company immediately prior to the acquisition. The fair value of the Company's pre-acquisition investment in SandForce represents a component of total consideration, as presented above. As a result of re-measuring the pre-acquisition equity interest in SandForce to fair value, the Company recognized a gain of $5.8 million, which was included in interest income and other, net, in 2012.

The allocation of the purchase price to SandForce's tangible and identified intangible assets acquired and liabilities assumed was based on their estimated fair values.

The purchase price has been allocated as follows (in thousands):

Accounts receivable	$ 10,711
Inventory	24,268
Identified intangible assets	172,400
Goodwill	182,628
Net deferred tax liabilities	(42,365)
Other, net	(1,202)
Total	$346,440

SHARE REPURCHASE PROGRAM

5.15 EXPRESS SCRIPTS HOLDING COMPANY (DEC)

CONSOLIDATED STATEMENT OF CHANGES IN STOCKHOLDERS' EQUITY (in part)

	Number of Shares	Amount						
	Common Stock	Common Stock	Additional Paid-in Capital	Accumulated Other Comprehensive Income	Retained Earnings	Treasury Stock	Non-controlling Interest	Total
(In millions)								
Balance at December 31, 2011	690.7	$6.9	$ 2,438.2	$17.0	$6,645.6	$(6,634.0)	$ 1.6	$ 2,475.3
Net income	—	—	—	—	1,312.9	—	17.2	1,330.1
Other comprehensive income	—	—	—	1.9	—	—	—	1.9
Cancellation of treasury shares in connection with Merger activity	(204.7)	(2.0)	(728.5)	—	(5,890.3)	6,620.8	—	—
Issuance of common shares in connection with Merger activity	318.0	3.2	18,841.6	—	—	—	—	18,844.8
Common stock issued under employee plans, net of forfeitures and stock redeemed for taxes	14.1	0.1	(104.8)	—	—	—	—	(104.7)
Amortization of unearned compensation under employee plans	—	—	410.0	—	—	—	—	410.0
Exercise of stock options	—	—	387.9	—	—	13.2	—	401.1
Tax benefit relating to employee stock compensation	—	—	45.3	—	—	—	—	45.3
Distributions to non-controlling interest	—	—	—	—	—	—	(8.1)	(8.1)
Balance at December 31, 2012	818.1	$8.2	$21,289.7	$18.9	$2,068.2	$ —	$10.7	$23,395.7

NOTES TO CONSOLIDATED FINANCIAL STATEMENTS

3. Changes in Business (in part)

Acquisitions (in part). As a result of the Merger on April 2, 2012, Medco and ESI each became 100% owned subsidiaries of Express Scripts and former Medco and ESI stockholders became owners of stock in Express Scripts, which is listed on the Nasdaq stock exchange. Upon closing of the Merger, former ESI stockholders owned approximately 59% of Express Scripts and former Medco stockholders owned approximately 41%. Per the terms of the Merger Agreement, upon consummation of the Merger on April 2, 2012, each share of Medco common stock was converted into (i) the right to receive $28.80 in cash, without interest and (ii) 0.81 shares of Express Scripts stock. Holders of Medco stock options, restricted stock units and deferred stock units received replacement awards at an exchange ratio of 1.3474 Express Scripts stock awards for each Medco award owned, which is equal to the sum of (i) 0.81 and (ii) the quotient obtained by dividing (1) $28.80 (the cash component of the Merger consideration) by (2) an amount equal to the average of the closing prices of ESI common stock on the Nasdaq for each of the 15 consecutive trading days ending with the fourth complete trading day prior to the completion of the Merger.

9. Common Stock (in part)

On May 27, 2011, ESI entered into agreements to repurchase shares of its common stock for an aggregate purchase price of $1,750.0 million under an Accelerated Share Repurchase ("ASR") agreement. The ASR agreement consisted of two agreements, providing for the repurchase of shares of ESI's common stock worth $1.0 billion and $750.0 million, respectively. Upon payment of the purchase price on May 27, 2011, ESI received 29.4 million shares of ESI's common stock at a price of $59.53 per share. During the third quarter of 2011, we settled the $1.0 billion portion of the ASR agreement and received 1.9 million shares at a final forward price of $53.51 per share. During the fourth quarter of 2011, we settled $725.0 million of the $750.0 million portion of the ASR agreement and received 2.1 million shares at a weighted-average final forward price of $50.69.

On April 27, 2012, we settled the remaining portion of the ASR agreement and received 0.1 million additional shares, resulting in a total of 33.5 million shares received under the agreement.

The ASR agreement was accounted for as an initial treasury stock transaction and a forward stock purchase contract. The forward stock purchase contract was classified as an equity instrument under applicable accounting guidance and was deemed to have a fair value of zero at the effective date. The initial repurchase of shares resulted in an immediate reduction of the outstanding shares used to calculate the weighted-average common shares outstanding for basic and diluted net income per share on the effective date of the agreements. The remaining 4.0 million shares and 0.1 million shares received for the portions of the ASR agreement that were settled during 2011 and 2012, respectively, reduced weighted-average common shares outstanding for the years ended December 31, 2011 and 2012, respectively.

ESI had a stock repurchase program, originally announced on October 25, 1996. Treasury shares were carried at first in, first out cost. In addition to the shares repurchased through the ASR, ESI repurchased 13.0 million shares under its existing stock repurchase program during the second quarter of 2011 for $765.7 million.

On May 5, 2010, ESI announced a two-for-one stock split for stockholders of record on May 21, 2010 effective June 8, 2010. The split was effected in the form of a dividend by issuance of one additional share of common stock for each share of common stock outstanding.

Upon consummation of the Merger on April 2, 2012, all ESI shares held in treasury were no longer outstanding and were cancelled and retired and ceased to exist. Express Scripts eliminated the value of treasury shares, at cost, immediately prior to the Merger as a reduction to retained earnings and paid-in capital.

The Board of Directors of Express Scripts has not yet adopted a stock repurchase program to allow for the repurchase of shares of Express Scripts.

Common Stock

DISCLOSURE

5.16 Rule 5–02 of Regulation S-X requires stating on the face of the balance sheet the number of shares issued or outstanding, as appropriate, and the dollar amount. The number of shares authorized should be disclosed on the balance sheet or in the notes.

Preferred Stock

PRESENTATION

5.17 FASB ASC 505-10-50-4 requires that if preferred stock or other senior stock has a preference in involuntary liquidation, the entity should disclose the liquidation preference of the stock (the relationship between the preference in liquidation and the par or stated value of the shares). That disclosure should be made in the "Equity" section of the balance sheet in the aggregate, either parenthetically or in short.

5.18 FASB ASC 480-10-05-1 requires that an issuer classify certain financial instruments with characteristics of both liabilities and equity as liabilities. Some issuances of stock, such as mandatorily redeemable preferred stock, impose unconditional obligations requiring the issuer to transfer assets or issue its equity shares.

DISCLOSURE

5.19 FASB ASC 505-10-50-4 requires disclosure of both of the following either on the face of the statement of financial position or in the notes thereto:
- The aggregate or per-share amounts at which preferred stock may be called or is subject to redemption through sinking-fund operations or otherwise
- The aggregate and per-share amounts of arrearages in cumulative preferred dividends

Rule 5-02 of SEC Regulation S-X also calls for disclosure of the number of shares authorized and the number of shares issued or outstanding, as appropriate.

PREFERRED STOCK

5.20 THE INTERPUBLIC GROUP OF COMPANIES, INC. (DEC)
CONSOLIDATED BALANCE SHEETS (in part)

(Amounts in Millions)

	December 31, 2012	December 31, 2011
Stockholders' Equity:		
Preferred stock, no par value, shares authorized: 20.0		
Series B shares issued and outstanding: 2012—0.2; 2011—0.2	221.5	221.5
Common stock, $0.10 par value, shares authorized: 800.0 shares issued: 2012—492.1;		
2011—491.4 shares outstanding: 2012—417.5; 2011—449.5	48.8	48.2
Additional paid-in capital	2,465.4	2,427.5
Retained earnings	738.3	405.1
Accumulated other comprehensive loss, net of tax	(288.0)	(225.7)
	3,186.0	2,876.6
Less: Treasury stock, at cost: 2012—74.6 shares; 2011—41.9 shares	(765.4)	(414.9)
Total IPG stockholders' equity	2,420.6	2,461.7
Noncontrolling interests	36.0	35.6
Total stockholders' equity	2,456.6	2,497.3

CONSOLIDATED STATEMENTS OF STOCKHOLDERS' EQUITY

(Amounts in Millions)

	Preferred Stock	Common Stock Shares	Common Stock Amount	Additional Paid-in Capital	Retained Earnings (Accumulated Deficit)	Accumulated Other Comprehensive Loss, Net of Tax	Treasury Stock	Total IPG Stockholders' Equity	Non-Controlling Interests	Total Stock-Holders' Equity
Balance at December 31, 2009	$525.0	486.5	$47.1	$2,441.0	$(324.8)	$(176.6)	$(14.0)	$2,497.7	$38.6	$2,536.3
Net income					261.1			261.1	20.1	281.2
Other comprehensive income						57.6		57.6	1.9	59.5
Reclassifications related to redeemable noncontrolling interests				3.5				3.5	(1.5)	2.0
Noncontrolling interest transactions				(28.1)				(28.1)	0.2	(27.9)
Distributions to noncontrolling interests									(21.5)	(21.5)
Change in redemption value of redeemable noncontrolling interests				(11.0)				(11.0)		(11.0)
Repurchase of preferred stock	(303.5)			35.9				(267.6)		(267.6)
Capped call transaction costs				(22.8)				(22.8)		(22.8)
Preferred stock dividends				(15.6)				(15.6)		(15.6)
Stock-based compensation		2.7	0.4	55.4				55.8		55.8
Shares withheld for taxes		(0.2)	(0.1)	(11.8)				(11.9)		(11.9)
Tax effect from stock-based compensation				4.5				4.5		4.5
Other		0.5	0.1	5.8			(0.1)	5.8	0.1	5.9
Balance at December 31, 2010	$221.5	489.5	$47.5	$2,456.8	$ (63.7)	$(119.0)	$(14.1)	$2,529.0	$37.9	$2,566.9
Net income					532.3			532.3	19.2	551.5
Other comprehensive loss						(106.7)		(106.7)	(2.5)	(109.2)
Reclassifications related to redeemable noncontrolling interests				2.7				2.7	7.7	10.4
Noncontrolling interest transactions				0.4	0.6			1.0	(2.6)	(1.6)
Distributions to noncontrolling interests									(23.0)	(23.0)
Change in redemption value of redeemable noncontrolling interests				(10.6)	(3.5)			(14.1)		(14.1)
Repurchase of common stock							(400.8)	(400.8)		(400.8)
Common stock dividends				(56.8)	(54.3)			(111.1)		(111.1)
Preferred stock dividends				(5.8)	(5.8)			(11.6)		(11.6)
Stock-based compensation		1.5	0.8	47.9				48.7		48.7
Exercise of stock options		1.3	0.1	11.9				12.0		12.0
Shares withheld for taxes		(0.9)	(0.2)	(26.8)				(27.0)		(27.0)
Tax effect from stock-based compensation				8.4				8.4		8.4
Other				(0.6)	(0.5)			(1.1)	(1.1)	(2.2)

(continued)

	Preferred Stock	Common Stock Shares	Common Stock Amount	Additional Paid-in Capital	Retained Earnings (Accumulated Deficit)	Accumulated Other Comprehensive Loss, Net of Tax	Treasury Stock	Total IPG Stockholders' Equity	Non-Controlling Interests	Total Stock-Holders' Equity
Balance at December 31, 2011	$221.5	491.4	$48.2	$2,427.5	$405.1	$(225.7)	$(414.9)	$2,461.7	$35.6	$2,497.3
Net income					446.7			446.7	17.9	464.6
Other comprehensive loss						(62.3)		(62.3)	(1.1)	(63.4)
Reclassifications related to redeemable noncontrolling interests				12.0				12.0	(1.1)	10.9
Noncontrolling interest transactions									(2.2)	(2.2)
Distributions to noncontrolling interests									(17.0)	(17.0)
Change in redemption value of redeemable noncontrolling interests					2.7			2.7		2.7
Repurchase of common stock							(350.5)	(350.5)		(350.5)
Common stock dividends					(103.4)			(103.4)		(103.4)
Preferred stock dividends					(11.6)			(11.6)		(11.6)
Stock-based compensation		1.6	0.7	31.3				32.0		32.0
Exercise of stock options		1.1	0.1	10.8				10.9		10.9
Shares withheld for taxes		(2.1)	(0.2)	(23.5)				(23.7)		(23.7)
Tax effect from stock-based compensation				14.8				14.8		14.8
Other				(7.5)	(1.2)			(8.7)	3.9	(4.8)
Balance at December 31, 2012	$221.5	492.0	$48.8	$2,465.4	$738.3	$(288.0)	$(765.4)	$2,420.6	$36.0	$2,456.6

NOTES TO CONSOLIDATED FINANCIAL STATEMENTS

(Amounts in Millions, Except Per Share Amounts)

Note 3: Convertible Preferred Stock

Each share of our 5¼% Series B Cumulative Convertible Perpetual Preferred Stock (the "Series B Preferred Stock") has a liquidation preference of $1,000 per share and is convertible at the option of the holder at any time into shares of our common stock, subject to adjustment upon the occurrence of certain events, including the payment of cash dividends on our common stock. The Series B Preferred Stock may be converted at our option if the closing price of our common stock multiplied by the conversion rate in effect at that time equals or exceeds 130% of the liquidation preference for 20 trading days during any consecutive 30 trading day period. Holders of the Series B Preferred Stock will be entitled to an adjustment to the conversion rate if they convert their shares in connection with a fundamental change satisfying certain specified conditions. The Series B Preferred Stock is junior to all of our existing and future debt obligations and senior to our common stock with respect to payments of dividends and rights upon liquidation, winding up or dissolution, to the extent of the liquidation preference.

The number of shares outstanding, conversion rates and corresponding conversion prices and conversion shares for our Series B Preferred Stock are listed below.

	December 31,		
	2012	2011	2010
Shares outstanding (actual number)	221,474	221,474	221,474
Conversion rate per share	76.2197	74.4500	73.1904
Conversion price	$ 13.12	$ 13.43	$ 13.66
Conversion shares	16.9	16.5	16.2

During 2012 and 2011, the conversion rate per share for our Series B Preferred Stock was adjusted as a result of the cumulative effect of certain cash dividends declared and paid on our common stock during the year, which resulted in a corresponding adjustment of the conversion price and conversion shares. In 2010, we launched a tender offer and purchased 303,526 shares (actual number) of our Series B Preferred Stock for cash for an aggregate purchase price of $267.6. The aggregate purchase price was calculated as the number of shares tendered multiplied by the purchase price of $869.86 per share plus unpaid dividends of $1.9, which were prorated for the period the tendered shares were outstanding, and transaction costs directly associated with the repurchase. The carrying value of the tendered shares was $293.3 and was determined based on the number of shares tendered multiplied by the liquidation preference, less the pro-rata amount of issuance costs associated with the original issuance of the preferred stock. A benefit of $25.7, representing the excess carrying value of the tendered shares over consideration from the repurchase, was recorded as an adjustment to additional paid-in capital. Additionally, the pro-rata amount of issuance costs of $10.2 was recorded as an adjustment to additional paid-in capital.

The terms of our Series B Preferred Stock do not permit us to pay dividends on our common stock unless all accumulated and unpaid dividends on the Series B Preferred Stock have been or contemporaneously are declared and paid, or provision for the payment thereof has been made. We declared annual dividends of $52.50 per share, or $11.6, $11.6 and $15.6, on our Series B Preferred Stock during 2012, 2011 and 2010, respectively. Regular quarterly dividends, if declared, are $13.125 per share. Dividends on each share of Series B Preferred Stock are payable quarterly in cash or, if certain conditions are met, in common stock, at our option on January 15, April 15, July 15 and October 15, or the next business date if these dates fall on the weekend or a holiday, of each year. Dividends on our Series B Preferred Stock are cumulative from the date of issuance and are payable on each payment date to the extent that we have assets that are legally available to pay dividends and our Board of Directors, or an authorized committee of our Board, declares a dividend payable.

The terms of the Series B Preferred Stock include an embedded derivative instrument, the fair value of which as of December 31, 2012 and 2011 was negligible. The Series B Preferred Stock is not considered a security with participation rights in earnings available to IPG common stockholders due to the contingent nature of the conversion feature of these securities.

Note 4: Earnings Per Share

The following sets forth basic and diluted earnings per common share available to IPG common stockholders.

	Years Ended December 31,		
	2012	2011	2010
Net income available to IPG common stockholders—basic	$435.1	$520.7	$271.2
Adjustments: Effect of dilutive securities			
Interest on 4.25% Notes[1]	0.3	1.4	1.4
Interest on 4.75% Notes	4.1	4.1	4.0
Dividends on preferred stock	11.6	11.6	0.0
Benefit from preferred stock repurchased[2]	0.0	0.0	(21.7)
Net income available to IPG common stockholders—diluted	$451.1	$537.8	$254.9
Weighted-average number of common shares outstanding—basic	432.5	465.5	473.6
Add: Effect of dilutive securities			
Restricted stock, stock options and other equity awards	7.2	9.1	11.3
4.25% Notes[1]	7.9	33.0	32.2
4.75% Notes	16.9	16.5	16.1
Preferred stock outstanding	16.9	16.5	0.0
Preferred stock repurchased	0.0	0.0	8.9
Weighted-average number of common shares outstanding—diluted	481.4	540.6	542.1
Earnings per share available to IPG common stockholders—basic	$ 1.01	$ 1.12	$ 0.57
Earnings per share available to IPG common stockholders—diluted	$ 0.94	$ 0.99	$ 0.47

[1] We retired all of our outstanding 4.25% Notes in March 2012. For purposes of calculating diluted earnings per share for 2012, the potentially dilutive shares are pro-rated based on the period they were outstanding.

[2] For the year ended December 31, 2010, the benefit from the preferred stock repurchased is excluded from net income available to IPG common stockholders for purposes of calculating diluted earnings per share since the associated common shares, if converted, were dilutive. In addition, the benefit is also net of $4.0 of preferred dividends that were declared during the first quarter of 2010 and associated with the preferred stock repurchased.

The following table presents the potential shares excluded from the diluted earnings per share calculation because the effect of including these potential shares would be antidilutive.

	Years Ended December 31,		
	2012	2011	2010
Preferred stock outstanding	0.0	0.0	16.2
Securities excluded from the diluted earnings per share calculation because the exercise price was greater than the average market price:			
Stock options[1]	6.6	8.9	15.6

[1] These options are outstanding at the end of the respective periods. In any period in which the exercise price is less than the average market price, these options have the potential to be dilutive, and application of the treasury stock method would reduce this amount.

Dividends

PRESENTATION

5.21 For public entities with respect to any dividends, Rule 3-04 of Regulation S-X requires the amount per share and in the aggregate for each class of shares to be stated. This may be stated on the financial statements or within the note disclosures. Further, Rule 4-08 of Regulation S-X requires disclosure of any restrictions that limit the payment of dividends.

5.22 An entity may distribute certain stock purchase rights that enable the holders of such rights to purchase additional equity in an entity if an outside party acquires or tenders for a substantial minority interest in the subject entity. These are commonly referred to as "poison pill arrangements."

PRESENTATION AND DISCLOSURE EXCERPTS

CASH DIVIDENDS

5.23 CENTURYLINK, INC. (DEC)
CONSOLIDATED STATEMENTS OF STOCKHOLDERS' EQUITY

(Dollars in millions)	2012	2011	2010
		Years Ended December 31,	
Common Stock (represents dollars and shares)			
Balance at beginning of period	$ 619	305	299
Issuance of common stock to acquire Qwest, including shares issued in connection with share-based compensation awards	—	294	—
Issuance of common stock to acquire Savvis, including shares issued in connection with share-based compensation awards	—	14	—
Issuance of common stock through dividend reinvestment, incentive and benefit plans	8	6	6
Shares withheld to satisfy tax withholdings	(1)	—	—
Balance at end of period	626	619	305
Additional Paid-In Capital			
Balance at beginning of period	18,901	6,181	6,020
Issuance of common stock to acquire Qwest, including assumption of share-based compensation awards	—	11,974	—
Issuance of common stock to acquire Savvis, including assumption of share-based compensation awards	—	601	—
Issuance of common stock through dividend reinvestment, incentive and benefit plans	102	97	124
Shares withheld to satisfy tax withholdings	(34)	(30)	(16)
Share-based compensation and other, net	110	78	53
Balance at end of period	19,079	18,901	6,181
Accumulated Other Comprehensive (Loss) Income			
Balance at beginning of period	(1,012)	(141)	(85)
Other comprehensive (loss) income	(689)	(871)	(56)
Balance at end of period	(1,701)	(1,012)	(141)
Retained Earnings			
Balance at beginning of period	2,319	3,302	3,233
Net income	777	573	948
Dividends declared	(1,811)	(1,556)	(879)
Balance at end of period	1,285	2,319	3,302
Total Stockholders' Equity	$19,289	20,827	9,647

NOTES TO CONSOLIDATED FINANCIAL STATEMENTS

(18) Dividends

Our Board of Directors declared the following dividends payable in 2012 and 2011:

Date Declared	Record Date	Dividend Per Share	Total Amount (In millions)	Payment Date
November 13, 2012	December 11, 2012	.725	$454	December 21, 2012
August 21, 2012	September 11, 2012	.725	$452	September 21, 2012
May 24, 2012	June 5, 2012	.725	$453	June 15, 2012
February 12, 2012	March 6, 2012	.725	$452	March 16, 2012
November 15, 2011	December 6, 2011	.725	$449	December 16, 2011
August 23, 2011	September 6, 2011	.725	$449	September 16, 2011
May 18, 2011	June 6, 2011	.725	$436	June 16, 2011
January 24, 2011	February 18, 2011	.725	$222	February 25, 2011

CONSOLIDATED STATEMENTS OF CHANGES IN SHAREHOLDERS' EQUITY (in part)

(In thousands of dollars)	Series B 6.75% Convertible Perpetual Preferred Stock	Common Stock	Retained Earnings	Accumulated Other Comprehensive Income (Loss)	Non-controlling Interests	Total Shareholders' Equity
Fiscal Year Ended March 31, 2012						
Balance at beginning of year	$213,023	$191,608	$825,751	$(44,776)	$13,799	$1,199,405
Changes in preferred and common stock						
Issuance of common stock	—	259	—	—	—	259
Repurchase of common stock	—	(661)	—	—	—	(661)
Accrual of stock-based compensation	—	5,987	—	—	—	5,987
Withholding of shares from stock-based compensation for grantee income taxes	—	(1,584)	—	—	—	(1,584)
Dividend equivalents on RSUs	—	526	—	—	—	526
Changes in retained earnings						
Net income	—	—	92,057	—	8,762	100,819
Cash dividends declared						
Series B 6.75% convertible perpetual preferred stock ($67.50 per share)	—	—	(14,850)	—	—	(14,850)
Common stock ($1.94 per share)	—	—	(44,951)	—	—	(44,951)
Repurchase of common stock	—	—	(2,827)	—	—	(2,827)
Dividend equivalents on RSUs	—	—	(526)	—	—	(526)
Other comprehensive income (loss)						
Foreign currency translation adjustments, net of income taxes	—	—	—	(8,239)	81	(8,158)
Foreign currency hedge adjustment, net of income taxes	—	—	—	(3,424)	—	(3,424)
Interest rate hedge adjustment, net of income taxes	—	—	—	(727)	—	(727)
Pension and other postretirement benefit plan adjustments, net of income taxes	—	—	—	(23,195)	—	(23,195)
Other changes in noncontrolling interests						
Dividends paid to noncontrolling shareholders	—	—	—	—	(103)	(103)
Balance at end of year	$213,023	$196,135	$854,654	$(80,361)	$22,539	$1,205,990

NOTES TO CONSOLIDATED FINANCIAL STATEMENTS

(All dollar amounts are in thousands, except per share amounts or as otherwise noted.)

Note 1. Nature of Operations and Significant Accounting Policies (in part)

Earnings per Share

The Company calculates basic earnings per share based on earnings available to common shareholders after payment of dividends on the Company's Series B 6.75% Convertible Perpetual Preferred Stock. The calculation uses the weighted average number of common shares outstanding during each period. Diluted earnings per share is computed in a similar manner using the weighted average number of common shares and dilutive potential common shares outstanding. Dilutive potential common shares are outstanding dilutive stock options and stock appreciation rights that are assumed to be exercised, unvested restricted stock units and performance share awards that are assumed to be fully vested and paid out in shares of common stock, and shares of convertible perpetual preferred stock that are assumed to be converted when the effect is dilutive. In periods when the effect of the convertible perpetual preferred stock is dilutive and these shares are assumed to be converted into common stock, dividends paid on the preferred stock are excluded from the calculation of diluted earnings per share.

Calculations of earnings per share for the fiscal years ended March 31, 2012, 2011, and 2010, are provided in Note 4.

Note 4. Earnings Per Share

The following table sets forth the computation of basic and diluted earnings per share:

	Fiscal Year Ended March 31,		
	2012	2011	2010
Basic Earnings Per Share			
Numerator for basic earnings per share			
Net income attributable to Universal Corporation	$92,057	$156,565	$168,397
Less: Dividends on convertible perpetual preferred stock	(14,850)	(14,850)	(14,850)
Earnings available to Universal Corporation common shareholders for calculation of basic earnings per share	77,207	141,715	153,547
Denominator for basic earnings per share			
Weighted average shares outstanding	23,228	23,859	24,732
Basic earnings per share	$ 3.32	$ 5.94	$ 6.21

(continued)

	Fiscal Year Ended March 31,		
	2012	**2011**	**2010**
Diluted Earnings Per Share			
Numerator for diluted earnings per share			
Earnings available to Universal Corporation common shareholders	$77,207	$141,715	$153,547
Add: Dividends on convertible perpetual preferred stock (if conversion assumed)	14,850	14,850	14,850
Earnings available to Universal Corporation common shareholders for calculation of diluted earnings per share	92,057	156,565	168,397
Denominator for diluted earnings per share			
Weighted average shares outstanding	23,228	23,859	24,732
Effect of dilutive securities (if conversion or exercise assumed)			
Convertible perpetual preferred stock	4,772	4,750	4,733
Employee share-based awards	339	279	197
Denominator for diluted earnings per share	28,339	28,888	29,662
Diluted earnings per share	$ 3.25	$ 5.42	$ 5.68

For the fiscal years ended March 31, 2012, 2011, and 2010, certain stock appreciation rights and certain stock options outstanding were not included in the computation of diluted earnings per share because their effect would have been antidilutive. These shares totaled 348,451 at a weighted-average exercise price of $56.75 for the fiscal year ended March 31, 2012, 622,801 at a weighted-average exercise price of $53.44 for the fiscal year ended March 31, 2011, and 404,800 at a weighted-average exercise price of $58.96 for the fiscal year ended March 31, 2010.

Note 12. Common and Preferred Stock (in part)

Common Stock (in part)

At March 31, 2012, the Company's shareholders had authorized 100,000,000 shares of its common stock, and 23,257,175 shares were issued and outstanding. Holders of the common stock are entitled to one vote for each share held on all matters requiring a vote. Holders of the common stock are also entitled to receive dividends when, as, and if declared by the Company's Board of Directors. The Board of Directors customarily declares and pays regular quarterly dividends on the outstanding common shares; however, such dividends are at the Board's full discretion, and there is no obligation to continue them. If dividends on the Company's Series B 6.75% Convertible Perpetual Preferred Stock (the "Preferred Stock" or "Preferred Shares") are not declared and paid for any dividend period, then the Company may not pay dividends on the common stock or repurchase common shares until the dividends on the Preferred Stock have been paid for a period of four consecutive quarters.

Preferred Stock (in part)

The Company is also authorized to issue up to 5,000,000 shares of preferred stock, 500,000 shares of which have been reserved for Series A Junior Participating Preferred Stock and 220,000 shares of which have been reserved for Series B 6.75% Convertible Perpetual Preferred Stock. No Series A Junior Participating Preferred Stock has been issued. In 2006, 220,000 shares of Series B 6.75% Convertible Perpetual Preferred Stock (the "Preferred Stock" or "Preferred Shares") were issued under this authorization. At March 31, 2012, 219,999 shares were issued and outstanding. The Preferred Stock has a liquidation preference of $1,000 per share. Holders of the Preferred Shares are entitled to receive quarterly dividends at the rate of 6.75% per annum on the liquidation preference when, as, and if declared by the Company's Board of Directors. Dividends are not cumulative in the event the Board of Directors does not declare a dividend for one or more quarterly periods. Under the terms of the Preferred Stock, the Board of Directors is prohibited from declaring regular dividends on the Preferred Shares in any period in which the Company fails to meet specified levels of shareholders' equity and net income; however, in that situation, the Board of Directors may instead declare such dividends payable in shares of the Company's common stock or from net proceeds of common stock issued during the ninety-day period prior to the dividend declaration. The Preferred Shares have no voting rights, except in the event the Company fails to pay dividends for four consecutive or non-consecutive quarterly dividend periods or fails to pay the redemption price on any date that the Preferred Shares are called for redemption, in which case the holders of Preferred Shares will be entitled to elect two additional directors to the Company's Board to serve until dividends on the Preferred Stock have been fully paid for four consecutive quarters.

The Preferred Shares are convertible, at any time at the option of the holder, into shares of the Company's common stock at a conversion rate that is adjusted each time the Company pays a dividend on its common stock that exceeds $0.43 per share. The conversion rate at March 31, 2012, was 21.7365 shares of common stock per preferred share, which represents a conversion price of approximately $46.01 per common share. Upon conversion, the Company may, at its option, satisfy all or part of the conversion value in cash.

5.25 IRON MOUNTAIN INCORPORATED (DEC)
CONSOLIDATED STATEMENTS OF EQUITY (in part)

(In thousands, except share data)

| | | Iron Mountain Incorporated Stockholders' Equity | | | | | |
| | | Common Stock | | Additional Paid-in Capital | Retained Earnings | Accumulated Other Comprehensive Items, Net | Noncontrolling Interests |
	Total	Shares	Amounts				
Balance, December 31, 2011	1,254,256	172,140,966	1,721	343,603	902,567	(2,203)	8,568
Issuance of shares under employee stock purchase plan and option plans and stock-based compensation, including tax benefit of $1,045	73,453	1,958,690	20	73,433	—	—	—
Shares issued in connection with special dividend (see Note 13)	—	17,009,281	170	559,840	(560,010)	—	—
Stock repurchases	(34,688)	(1,103,149)	(11)	(34,677)	—	—	—
Parent cash dividends declared	(328,707)	—	—	—	(328,707)	—	—
Currency translation adjustment	23,186	—	—	—	—	22,517	669
Net income (loss)	174,834	—	—	—	171,708	—	3,126
Noncontrolling interests equity contributions	836	—	—	—	—	—	836
Noncontrolling interests dividends	(1,722)	—	—	—	—	—	(1,722)
Purchase of noncontrolling interests	1,000	—	—	—	—	—	1,000
Balance, December 31, 2012	$1,162,448	190,005,788	$1,900	$942,199	$185,558	$20,314	$12,477

NOTES TO CONSOLIDATED FINANCIAL STATEMENTS

(In thousands, except share and per share data)

13. Stockholders' Equity Matters (in part)

In February 2010, our board of directors adopted a dividend policy under which we have paid, and in the future intend to pay, quarterly cash dividends on our common stock. Declaration and payment of future quarterly dividends is at the discretion of our board of directors. In 2011 and 2012, our board of directors declared the following dividends:

Declaration Date	Dividend Per Share	Record Date	Total Amount	Payment Date
March 11, 2011	$0.1875	March 25, 2011	$ 37,601	April 15, 2011
June 10, 2011	0.2500	June 24, 2011	50,694	July 15, 2011
September 8, 2011	0.2500	September 23, 2011	46,877	October 14, 2011
December 1, 2011	0.2500	December 23, 2011	43,180	January 13, 2012
March 8, 2012	0.2500	March 23, 2012	42,791	April 13, 2012
June 5, 2012	0.2700	June 22, 2012	46,336	July 13, 2012
September 6, 2012	0.2700	September 25, 2012	46,473	October 15, 2012
October 11, 2012	4.0600	October 22, 2012	700,000	November 21, 2012
December 14, 2012	0.2700	December 26, 2012	51,296	January 17, 2013

On October 11, 2012, we announced the declaration by our board of directors of a special dividend of $700,000 (the "Special Dividend"), payable, at the election of the stockholders, in either common stock or cash to stockholders of record as of October 22, 2012 (the "Record Date"). The Special Dividend, which is a distribution to stockholders of a portion of our accumulated earnings and profits, was paid in a combination of common stock and cash. The Special Dividend was paid on November 21, 2012 (the "Distribution Date") to stockholders as of the Record Date. Stockholders elected to be paid their pro rata portion of the Special Dividend in all common stock or cash. The total amount of cash paid to all stockholders associated with the Special Dividend was approximately $140,000 (including cash paid in lieu of fractional shares). Our shares of common stock were valued for purposes of the Special Dividend based upon the average closing price on the three trading days following November 14, 2012, or $32.87 per share, and as such, the number of shares of common stock we issued in the Special Dividend was approximately 17,000 and the total amount of common stock paid to all stockholders associated with the Special Dividend was approximately $560,000. These shares impact weighted average shares outstanding from the date of issuance, thus impacting our earnings per share data prospectively from the Distribution Date.

Stock Splits

RECOGNITION AND MEASUREMENT

5.26 The FASB ASC glossary defines a *stock split* as an issuance by a corporation of its own common shares to its common shareholders without consideration and under conditions indicating that such action is prompted mainly by a desire to increase the number of outstanding shares for the purpose of effecting a reduction in their unit market price and, thereby, of obtaining wider distribution and improved marketability of the shares. It is also sometimes called a stock split-up.

5.27 FASB ASC 505-20 addresses the accounting for stock splits, as well as stock dividends, and provides guidance on determining whether a stock dividend or stock split should be accounted for according to its form or whether it should be accounted for differently.

PRESENTATION AND DISCLOSURE EXCERPTS

STOCK SPLIT

5.28 DONALDSON COMPANY, INC. (JUL)

CONSOLIDATED STATEMENTS OF CHANGES IN SHAREHOLDERS' EQUITY (in part)

(Thousands of dollars, except per share amounts)	Common Stock	Additional Paid-in Capital	Retained Earnings	Stock Compensation Plans	Accumulated Other Comprehensive Income (Loss)	Treasury Stock	Total
Balance July 31, 2011	443,216	—	925,542	24,736	40,027	(498,810)	934,711
Comprehensive income							
Net earnings			264,301				264,301
Foreign currency translation					(98,723)		(98,723)
Pension liability adjustment, net of deferred taxes					(42,520)		(42,520)
Net loss on cash flow hedging derivatives					(672)		(672)
Comprehensive income							122,386
Treasury stock acquired						(130,233)	(130,233)
Stock options exercised		(9,834)	(5,116)			27,698	12,748
Deferred stock and other activity		(2,158)	312	213		1,926	293
Performance awards			(9)	(1)			(10)
Stock option expense			7,800				7,800
Tax reduction—employee plans		11,992					11,992
Two-for-one Stock split	315,000		(776,369)			461,369	—
Dividends ($0.335 per share)			(49,673)				(49,673)
Balance July 31, 2012	$758,216	$ —	$366,788	$24,948	$(101,888)	$(138,050)	$910,014

NOTES TO CONSOLIDATED FINANCIAL STATEMENTS

NOTE A Summary of Significant Accounting Policies (in part)

Earnings Per Share. The Company's basic net earnings per share are computed by dividing net earnings by the weighted average number of outstanding common shares. The Company's diluted net earnings per share is computed by dividing net earnings by the weighted average number of outstanding common shares and common equivalent shares relating to stock options and stock incentive plans. Certain outstanding options were excluded from the diluted net earnings per share calculations because their exercise prices were greater than the average market price of the Company's common stock during those periods. There were 1,063,135 options, 988,698 options, and 1,691,654 options excluded from the diluted net earnings per share calculation for the fiscal year ended July 31, 2012, 2011, and 2010, respectively.

The following table presents information necessary to calculate basic and diluted earnings per share:

(Thousands of dollars, except per share amounts)	2012	2011	2010
Weighted average shares—basic	150,286	154,393	155,697
Diluted share equivalents	2,655	2,804	2,659
Weighted average shares—diluted	152,941	157,197	158,356
Net earnings for basic and diluted earnings per share computation	$264,301	$225,291	$166,163
Net earnings per share—basic	$ 1.76	$ 1.46	$ 1.07
Net earnings per share—diluted	$ 1.73	$ 1.43	$ 1.05

On January 27, 2012, the Company announced that its Board of Directors declared a two-for-one stock split effected in the form of a 100 percent stock dividend. The stock split was distributed March 23, 2012, to stockholders of record as of March 2, 2012. Earnings and dividends per share and weighted average shares outstanding are presented in this Form 10-K after the effect of the 100 percent stock dividend. The two-for-one stock split is reflected in the share amounts in all periods presented in the table above and elsewhere in this annual Form 10-K.

Treasury Stock. Repurchased common stock is stated at cost and is presented as a separate reduction of shareholders' equity.

Note I Shareholders' Equity (in part)

Treasury Stock. The Company believes that the share repurchase program is a way of providing return to its shareholders. The Board of Directors authorized the repurchase, at the Company's discretion, of up to 16.0 million shares of common stock under the stock repurchase plan dated March 26, 2010. As of July 31, 2012, the Company had remaining authorization to repurchase 5.6 million shares under this plan. Following is a summary of treasury stock share activity for Fiscal 2012 and 2011:

	2012	2011
Balance at beginning of year	13,245,864	12,222,381
Stock repurchases	4,503,587	1,956,648
Net issuance upon exercise of stock options	(1,270,526)	(862,981)
Issuance under compensation plans	(89,528)	(62,304)
Stock split and other activity	(12,408,565)	(7,880)
Balance at end of year	3,980,832	13,245,864

NOTE Q Quarterly Financial Information (Unaudited)

(In thousands)	First Quarter	Second Quarter	Third Quarter	Fourth Quarter
2012				
Net sales	$608,295	$580,883	$647,237	$656,833
Gross margin	214,934	200,817	228,229	229,783
Net earnings	68,553	53,821	70,946	70,981
Basic earnings per share	0.46	0.36	0.47	0.47
Diluted earnings per share	0.45	0.35	0.46	0.47
Dividends declared per share	0.075	0.080	0.090	0.090
Dividends paid per share	0.075	0.075	0.080	0.090
2011				
Net sales	$536,909	$537,105	$594,565	$625,450
Gross margin	188,090	189,543	209,158	227,005
Net earnings	53,134	44,579	61,811	65,767
Basic earnings per share	0.34	0.29	0.40	0.43
Diluted earnings per share	0.34	0.28	0.39	0.42
Dividends declared per share	—	0.130	—	0.150
Dividends paid per share	0.063	0.065	0.065	0.075

Note: the above table reflects the Impact of the two-for-one stock split that occurred on March 23, 2012.

The first quarter of Fiscal 2011 included restructuring charges after-tax of $0.6 million or $0.01 per share.

REVERSE STOCK SPLIT

5.29 TENET HEALTHCARE CORPORATION (DEC)
MARKET FOR REGISTRANT'S COMMON EQUITY, RELATED STOCKHOLDER MATTERS AND ISSUER PURCHASES OF EQUITY SECURITIES

Common Stock (in part). Our common stock is listed on the New York Stock Exchange ("NYSE") under the symbol "THC." On October 11, 2012, our common stock began trading on the NYSE on a split-adjusted basis following a one-for-four reverse stock split we announced on October 1, 2012. Every four shares of our issued and outstanding common stock were exchanged for one issued and outstanding share of common stock, without any change in the par value per share, and our authorized shares of common stock were proportionately decreased from 1,050,000,000 shares to 262,500,000 shares. No fractional shares were issued in connection with the stock split. The following table sets forth, for the periods indicated, the high and low sales prices per share of our common stock on the NYSE, as adjusted to reflect the reverse stock split:

	High	Low
Year Ended December 31, 2012		
First Quarter	$24.20	$18.36
Second Quarter	22.56	17.32
Third Quarter	25.76	17.24
Fourth Quarter	33.86	22.86
Year Ended December 31, 2011		
First Quarter	$30.20	$26.28
Second Quarter	30.80	23.56
Third Quarter	26.16	16.08
Fourth Quarter	21.20	13.84

Note 1. Significant Accounting Policies (in part)

Basis of Presentation (in part)

Our Consolidated Financial Statements include the accounts of Tenet and its wholly owned and majority-owned subsidiaries. We eliminate intercompany accounts and transactions in consolidation, and we include the results of operations of businesses that are newly acquired in purchase transactions from their dates of acquisition. We account for significant investments in other affiliated companies using the equity method. Unless otherwise indicated, all financial and statistical data included in these notes to our Consolidated Financial Statements relate to our continuing operations, with dollar amounts expressed in millions (except per-share amounts). Certain balances in the accompanying Consolidated Financial Statements and these notes have been reclassified to give retrospective presentation for the discontinued operations described in Note 4. Furthermore, all amounts related to shares, share prices and earnings per share have been restated to give retrospective presentation for the reverse stock split described in Note 2.

Note 2. Equity (in part)

Reverse Stock Split

On October 11, 2012, our common stock began trading on the New York Stock Exchange on a split-adjusted basis following a one-for-four reverse stock split we announced on October 1, 2012. Every four shares of our issued and outstanding common stock were exchanged for one issued and outstanding share of common stock, without any change in the par value per share, and our authorized shares of common stock were proportionately decreased from 1,050,000,000 shares to 262,500,000 shares. No fractional shares were issued in connection with the stock split. All current and prior period amounts in the accompanying Consolidated Financial Statements and these notes related to shares, share prices and earnings per share have been restated to give retrospective presentation for the reverse stock split.

Changes to Retained Earnings

RECOGNITION AND MEASUREMENT

5.30 The retained earnings account is affected by direct charges and credits. The most frequent direct charges to retained earnings are net loss for the year, losses on treasury stock transactions, and cash or stock dividends. The most common direct credit to retained earnings is net income for the year.

PRESENTATION

5.31 In addition to direct charges and credits, the retained earnings account is also affected by opening balance adjustments. Reasons for which the opening balance of retained earnings is properly restated include certain changes in accounting principles, changes in the reporting entity, and corrections of an error in previously issued financial statements.

5.32 FASB ASC 250-10-05-2 requires, unless impracticable or otherwise specified by applicable authoritative guidance, retrospective application to prior periods' financial statements of a change in accounting principle. *Retrospective application* is the application of a different accounting principle to prior accounting periods as if that principle had always been used. More specifically, FASB ASC 250-10-45-6 explains that retrospective application involves the following:

- The cumulative effect of the change on periods prior to those presented should be reflected in the carrying amount of assets and liabilities as of the beginning of the first period presented.
- An offsetting adjustment, if any, shall be made to the opening balance of retained earnings or other appropriate component of equity or net assets in the statement of financial position for that period.
- Financial statements for each individual prior period presented should be adjusted to reflect the period-specific effects of applying the new accounting principle.

5.33 FASB ASC 250-10-45-23 also requires any accounting error in the financial statements of a prior period discovered after the financial statements are issued or available to be issued to be reported as an error correction by restating the prior period financial statements. Restatement involves similar requirements as those specified for retrospective application of a change in accounting principle.

5.34 SEC Staff Accounting Bulletin (SAB) No. 108 provides guidance on the consideration of the effects of prior year misstatements in quantifying current year misstatements for the purpose of assessing materiality. SAB No. 108 requires that registrant entities determine the quantitative effect of a financial statement misstatement by using both an income statement ("rollover") and a balance sheet ("iron curtain") approach and evaluate whether, under either approach, the error is material after considering all relevant quantitative and qualitative factors.

CHANGE IN ACCOUNTING PRINCIPLE

5.35 AMERICAN INTERNATIONAL GROUP, INC. (DEC)
CONSOLIDATED STATEMENT OF EQUITY

(In millions)	Preferred Stock	Common Stock	Treasury Stock	Additional Paid-In Capital	Retained Earnings (Accumulated Deficit)	Accumulated Other Comprehensive Income	Total AIG Share-holders' Equity	Non-redeemable Noncontrolling Interests	Total Equity
Balance, January 1, 2010	$69,784	$ 354	$ (874)	$ 5,030	$(11,491)	$ 7,021	$ 69,824	$28,252	$ 98,076
Cumulative effect of change in accounting principle, net of tax	—	—	—	—	(8,415)	(932)	(9,347)	—	(9,347)
SeriesF drawdown	2,199	—	—	—	—	—	2,199	—	2,199
Common stock issued	—	2	—	(20)	—	—	(18)	—	(18)
Equity unit exchange	—	12	—	3,645	—	—	3,657	—	3,657
Net income attributable to AIG or other noncontrolling interests[a]	—	—	—	—	10,058	—	10,058	336	10,394
Net income attributable to noncontrolling nonvoting, callable, junior and senior preferred interests	—	—	—	—	—	—	—	1,818	1,818
Other comprehensive income[b]	—	—	—	—	—	2,782	2,782	176	2,958
Deferred income taxes	—	—	—	(332)	—	—	(332)	—	(332)
Net decrease due to deconsolidation	—	—	—	—	—	—	—	(2,740)	(2,740)
Contributions from noncontrolling interests	—	—	—	—	—	—	—	253	253
Distributions to noncontrolling interests	—	—	—	—	—	—	—	(175)	(175)
Other	—	—	1	32	—	—	33	—	33
Balance, December 31, 2010	$71,983	$ 368	$ (873)	$ 8,355	$ (9,848)	$ 8,871	$ 78,856	$27,920	$106,776
SeriesF drawdown	20,292	—	—	—	—	—	20,292	—	20,292
Repurchase of SPV preferred interests in connection with Recapitalization[c]	—	—	—	—	—	—	—	(26,432)	(26,432)
Exchange of consideration for preferred stock in connection with Recapitalization[c]	(92,275)	4,138	—	67,460	—	—	(20,677)	—	(20,677)
Common stock issued	—	250	—	2,636	—	—	2,886	—	2,886
Purchase of common stock	—	—	(70)	—	—	—	(70)	—	(70)
Settlement of equity unit stock purchase contract	—	9	—	2,160	—	—	2,169	—	2,169
Net income attributable to AIG or other noncontrolling interests[a]	—	—	—	—	20,622	—	20,622	82	20,704
Net income attributable to noncontrolling nonvoting, callable, junior and senior preferred interests	—	—	—	—	—	—	—	74	74
Other comprehensive loss[b]	—	—	—	—	—	(2,483)	(2,483)	(119)	(2,602)
Deferred income taxes	—	—	—	2	—	—	2	—	2
Acquisition of noncontrolling interest	—	—	—	(164)	—	93	(71)	(489)	(560)
Net decrease due to deconsolidation	—	—	—	—	—	—	—	(123)	(123)
Contributions from noncontrolling interests	—	—	—	—	—	—	—	120	120
Distributions to noncontrolling interests	—	—	—	—	—	—	—	(128)	(128)
Other	—	1	1	10	—	—	12	(50)	(38)
Balance, December 31, 2011	$ —	$4,766	$ (942)	$80,459	$10,774	$ 6,481	$101,538	$ 855	$102,393
Common stock issued under stock plans	—	18	—	(15)	—	—	3	—	3
Purchase of common stock	—	—	(13,000)	—	—	—	(13,000)	—	(13,000)
Net income attributable to AIG or other noncontrolling interests[a]	—	—	—	—	3,438	—	3,438	40	3,478
Other comprehensive income (loss)[b]	—	—	—	—	—	6,093	6,093	(1)	6,092
Deferred income taxes	—	—	—	(9)	—	—	(9)	—	(9)
Net decrease due to deconsolidation	—	—	—	—	—	—	—	(27)	(27)
Contributions from noncontrolling interests	—	—	—	—	—	—	—	80	80
Distributions to noncontrolling interests	—	—	—	—	—	—	—	(167)	(167)
Other	—	—	—	(25)	(36)	—	(61)	(113)	(174)
Balance, December 31, 2012	$ —	$4,766	$(13,924)	$80,410	$14,176	$12,574	$ 98,002	$ 667	$ 98,669

[a] Excludes gains of $222 million, $552 million and $73 million in 2012, 2011 and 2010, respectively, attributable to redeemable noncontrolling interests and net income attributable to noncontrolling nonvoting, callable, junior and senior preferred interests held by the Federal Reserve Bank of New York of $0, $74 million and $1.8 billion in 2012, 2011 and 2010, respectively.

[b] Excludes $4 million, $(2) million and $5 million attributable to redeemable noncontrolling interests for the year ended December 31, 2012, 2011 and 2010, respectively.

[c] See Notes 18 and 25 to Consolidated Financial Statements.

See Accompanying Notes to Consolidated Financial Statements, which include a summary of revisions to prior year balances in connection with a change in accounting principle.

Accounting Standards Adopted During 2012 (in part)

We adopted the following accounting standards on January 1, 2012.

Accounting for Costs Associated With Acquiring or Renewing Insurance Contracts

In October 2010, the FASB issued an accounting standard update that amends the accounting for costs incurred by insurance companies that can be capitalized in connection with acquiring or renewing insurance contracts. The standard clarifies how to determine whether the costs incurred in connection with the acquisition of new or renewal insurance contracts qualify as DAC. We adopted the standard retrospectively on January 1, 2012.

Deferred policy acquisition costs represent those costs that are incremental and directly related to the successful acquisition of new or renewal insurance contracts. We defer incremental costs that result directly from, and are essential to, the acquisition or renewal of an insurance contract. Such costs generally include agent or broker commissions and bonuses, premium taxes, and medical and inspection fees that would not have been incurred if the insurance contract had not been acquired or renewed. Each cost is analyzed to assess whether it is fully deferrable. We partially defer costs, including certain commissions, when we do not believe the entire cost is directly related to the acquisition or renewal of insurance contracts.

We also defer a portion of employee total compensation and payroll-related fringe benefits directly related to time spent performing specific acquisition or renewal activities, including costs associated with the time spent on underwriting, policy issuance and processing, and sales force contract selling. The amounts deferred are those that resulted in successful policy acquisition or renewal for each distribution channel and/or cost center from which the cost originates.

Advertising costs related to the issuance of insurance contracts that meet the direct-advertising criteria are deferred and amortized as part of DAC.

The method we use to amortize DAC for either short- or long-duration insurance contracts did not change as a result of the adoption of the standard.

The adoption of the standard resulted in a reduction to beginning of period retained earnings for the earliest period presented and a decrease in the amount of capitalized costs in connection with the acquisition or renewal of insurance contracts. Accordingly, we revised our historical financial statements and accompanying notes to the consolidated financial statements for the changes in DAC and associated changes in acquisition expenses and income taxes for affected entities and segments, including divested entities presented in continuing and discontinued operations.

The following table presents amounts previously reported as of December 31, 2011, to reflect the effect of the change due to the retrospective adoption of the standard, and the adjusted amounts that are reflected in our Consolidated Balance Sheet.

| | December 31, 2011 | | |
(In millions)	As Previously Reported	Effect of Change	As Currently Reported
Balance Sheet:			
Deferred income taxes	$ 17,897	$ 1,718	$ 19,615
Deferred policy acquisition costs	14,026	(5,089)	8,937
Other assets	11,705	(42)	11,663
Total assets	556,467	(3,413)	553,054
Retained earnings	14,332	(3,558)	10,774
Accumulated other comprehensive income	6,336	145	6,481
Total AIG shareholders' equity	104,951	(3,413)	101,538

CORRECTION OF AN ERROR OR MISSTATEMENT

5.36 THE L.S. STARRETT COMPANY (JUN)
CONSOLIDATED BALANCE SHEETS (in part)

(In thousands except share data)

	June 30, 2012	June 30, 2011
Liabilities and Stockholders' Equity		
Stockholders' equity:		
Class A common stock $1 par (20,000,000 shares authorized; 6,017,227 outstanding at June 30, 2012 and 5,933,059 outstanding at June 30, 2011)	6,017	5,933
Class B common stock $1 par (10,000,000 shares authorized; 753,307 outstanding at June 30, 2012 and 800,868 outstanding at June 30, 2011)	753	801
Additional paid-in capital, as adjusted (Note 17)	51,941	51,411
Retained earnings, as adjusted (Note 17)	94,661	96,477
Accumulated other comprehensive loss	(25,534)	(1,961)
Total stockholders' equity	127,838	152,661

CONSOLIDATED STATEMENTS OF STOCKHOLDERS' EQUITY AND COMPREHENSIVE INCOME (LOSS)

(In thousands except per share data)

	Common Stock Outstanding		Additional Paid-in Capital	Retained Earnings	Accumulated Other Comprehensive Loss	Total
	Class A	Class B				
Balance, June 27, 2009	$5,770	$869	$49,984	$103,027	$(16,772)	$142,878
Corrections in accounting for stock-based compensation and income taxes (Note 17)			548	(1,225)		(677)
Balance, June 27, 2009, as adjusted	$5,770	$869	$50,532	$101,802	$(16,772)	$142,201
Comprehensive income (loss):						
Net loss				(8,021)		(8,021)
Unrealized net gain (loss) on investments					2	2
Pension and postretirement plans					(3,444)	(3,444)
Translation gain (loss), net					2,537	2,537
Total comprehensive loss						(8,926)
Dividends ($0.30 per share)				(2,000)		(2,000)
Issuance of stock under ESOP	38		302			340
Issuance of stock under ESPP		3	20			23
Stock-based compensation			67			67
Conversion	51	(51)				—
Balance, June 26, 2010	$5,859	$821	$50,921	$ 91,781	$(17,677)	$131,705
Comprehensive income (loss):						
Net earnings				6,845		6,845
Pension and postretirement plans					5,938	5,938
Translation gain (loss), net					9,778	9,778
Total comprehensive income						22,561
Dividends ($0.32 per share)				(2,149)		(2,149)
Repurchase of shares			(1)			(1)
Issuance of stock under ESOP	21		209			230
Issuance of stock under ESPP		33	220			253
Stock-based compensation			62			62
Conversion	53	(53)				—
Balance, June 30, 2011	$5,933	$801	$51,411	$ 96,477	$ (1,961)	$152,661
Comprehensive income (loss):						
Net earnings				888		888
Pension and postretirement plans					(8,898)	(8,898)
Translation gain (loss), net					(14,675)	(14,675)
Total comprehensive loss						(22,685)
Dividends ($0.40 per share)				(2,704)		(2,704)
Issuance of stock under ESOP	27		287			314
Issuance of stock under ESPP		9	72			81
Stock-based compensation			171			171
Conversion	57	(57)				—
Balance, June 30, 2012	$6,017	$753	$51,941	$ 94,661	$(25,534)	$127,838
Cumulative balance:						
Translation gain (loss), net					$(15,905)	
Pension and postretirement plans, net of taxes					(9,629)	
					$(25,534)	

NOTES TO CONSOLIDATED FINANCIAL STATEMENTS

17. Prior Period Adjustments

During the first quarter of fiscal 2012, the Company identified a prior period error in the method of calculating compensation expense imputed under the Employee Stock Purchase Plan (ESPP) which had accumulated over a period of years. This error, which was immaterial to previously issued financial statements, resulted in an understatement of compensation expense in the Consolidated Statement of Operations for prior periods. The recorded balance of additional paid-in capital was likewise understated in the consolidated balance sheets for prior periods. The Company evaluated the effects of this error on prior periods' consolidated financial statements, individually and in the aggregate, in accordance with the guidance in ASC Topic 250, Accounting Changes and Error Corrections, ASC Topic 250-10-S99-1, Assessing Materiality, and ASC Topic 250-10-S99-2, Considering the Effects of Prior Year Misstatements when Quantifying Misstatements in Current Year Financial Statements ("ASC 250"), and concluded that no prior period is materially misstated. In order to correct this immaterial error, the Company has revised the accompanying statements of stockholders' equity and comprehensive income (loss) as of the earliest period presented (June 27, 2009) to decrease retained earnings by $548,000 and to increase additional paid-in capital by the same amount. We made no adjustments to the accompanying fiscal 2011 and 2010 statements of operations and cash flows due to the de minimis impact of the errors to those statements.

During the fourth quarter of fiscal 2012, the Company identified a prior period error in the estimate of a potential income tax exposure arising in fiscal 2008. This error, which was immaterial to previously issued financial statements, resulted in an understatement of income tax expense in the consolidated statement of operations for such fiscal year. The recorded balance of other tax obligations was likewise understated in the consolidated balance sheets for since fiscal 2008.

The Company evaluated the effects of this error on prior periods' consolidated financial statements, individually and in the aggregate, in accordance with the guidance in ASC 250 and concluded that no prior period financial statements are materially misstated. In order to correct this immaterial error, the Company has revised the accompanying statements of stockholders' equity and comprehensive income (loss) as of the earliest period presented (June 27, 2009) to decrease retained earnings by $677,000 and to increase other tax obligations by the same amount. No adjustments were required to be made to the accompanying fiscal 2011 and 2010 statements of operations and cash flows.

OTHER CHANGES IN RETAINED EARNINGS—SHARE REPURCHASE PROGRAMS

5.37 VISA INC. (SEP)

CONSOLIDATED STATEMENTS OF CHANGES IN EQUITY (in part)

(In millions, except per share data)	Common Stock Class A	Class B	Class C	Additional Paid-in Capital	Treasury Stock	Accumulated Income (Deficit)	Accumulated Other Comprehensive Income (Loss)	Non-Controlling Interest	Total Equity (Deficit)
Balance as of September 30, 2011	520	245	47	$19,907	$—	$6,706	$(176)	$—	$26,437
Net income attributable to Visa Inc.						2,144			2,144
Loss attributable to non-controlling interest								(2)	(2)
Other comprehensive income, net of tax							5		5
Comprehensive income including non-controlling interest									2,147
Issuance of restricted share awards	1								—
Conversion of class C common stock upon sale into public market	16		(16)						—
Share-based compensation (Note 17)				147					147
Excess tax benefit for share-based compensation				71					71
Cash proceeds from exercise of stock options	4			174					174
Restricted stock instruments settled in cash for taxes[1]				(40)					(40)
Cash dividends declared and paid, at a quarterly amount of $0.22 per as-converted share (Note 15)						(595)			(595)
Repurchase of class A common stock (Note 15)	(6)			(264)		(446)			(710)
Purchase of non-controlling interest				(3)				2	(1)
Balance as of September 30, 2012	535	245	31	$19,992	$—	$7,809	$(171)	$—	$27,630

[1] Decrease in class A common stock is less than 1 million shares.

NOTES TO CONSOLIDATED FINANCIAL STATEMENTS

Note 15—Stockholders' Equity (in part)

Reduction in as-converted shares. During fiscal 2012, total as-converted class A common stock was reduced by 22.8 million shares, using $2.4 billion of operating cash on hand. Of the $2.4 billion, $710 million was used to repurchase class A common stock in the open market. In addition, the Company made deposits totaling $1.7 billion of operating cash into the litigation escrow account previously established under the retrospective responsibility plan. These deposits have the same economic effect on earnings per share as repurchasing the Company's class A common stock, because they reduce the class B conversion rate and consequently the as-converted class A common stock share count.

In July 2012, the Company's board of directors authorized a $1 billion share repurchase program to be in effect through July 2013. As of September 30, 2012, the program had remaining authorized funds of $865 million. In October 2012, the Company's board of directors authorized an additional $1.5 billion share repurchase program to be in effect through October 2013. All share repurchase programs authorized prior to July 2012 have been completed.

The following table presents share repurchases in the open market during the following fiscal years:

(In millions, except per share data)	2012	2011
Shares repurchased in the open market[1]	6.2	26.6
Weighted-average repurchase price per share	$114.87	$76.08
Total cost	$ 710	$2,024

[1] All shares repurchased in the open market have been retired and constitute authorized but unissued shares.

5.38 JOHNSON & JOHNSON (DEC)
CONSOLIDATED STATEMENTS OF EQUITY

(Dollars in Millions) (Note 1)

	Total	Retained Earnings	Accumulated Other Comprehensive Income	Common Stock Issued Amount	Treasury Stock Amount
Balance, January 3, 2010	$50,588	70,306	(3,058)	3,120	(19,780)
Net earnings attributable to Johnson & Johnson	13,334	13,334			
Cash dividends paid	(5,804)	(5,804)			
Employee compensation and stock option plans	1,731	(63)			1,794
Repurchase of common stock	(2,797)				(2,797)
Other comprehensive income, net of tax:	(473)		(473)		
Balance, January 2, 2011	$56,579	77,773	(3,531)	3,120	(20,783)
Net earnings attributable to Johnson & Johnson	9,672	9,672			
Cash dividends paid	(6,156)	(6,156)			
Employee compensation and stock option plans	1,760	111			1,649
Repurchase of common stock	(2,525)				(2,525)
Other	(149)	(149)			
Other comprehensive income, net of tax:	(2,101)		(2,101)		
Balance, January 1, 2012	$57,080	81,251	(5,632)	3,120	(21,659)
Net earnings attributable to Johnson & Johnson	10,853	10,853			
Cash dividends paid	(6,614)	(6,614)			
Employee compensation and stock option plans	3,269	19			3,250
Issuance of common stock associated with the acquisition of Synthes, Inc.	13,335	483			12,852
Repurchase of common stock[1]	(12,919)				(12,919)
Other comprehensive income, net of tax:	(178)		(178)		
Balance, December 30, 2012	$64,826	85,992	(5,810)	3,120	(18,476)

[1] Includes repurchase of common stock associated with the acquisition of Synthes, Inc.

NOTES TO CONSOLIDATED FINANCIAL STATEMENTS

12. Capital and Treasury Stock

Changes in treasury stock were:

	Treasury Stock	
(Amounts in millions except treasury stock shares in thousands)	Shares	Amount
Balance at January 3, 2010	365,522	$19,780
Employee compensation and stock option plans	(28,866)	(1,794)
Repurchase of common stock	45,090	2,797
Balance at January 2, 2011	381,746	20,783
Employee compensation and stock option plans	(26,007)	(1,649)
Repurchase of common stock	39,741	2,525
Balance at January 1, 2012	395,480	21,659
Employee compensation and stock option plans	(55,170)	(3,250)
Issuance of common stock associated with the acquisition of Synthes, Inc.	(203,740)	(12,852)
Repurchase of common stock[1]	204,784	12,919
Balance at December 30, 2012	341,354	$18,476

[1] Includes repurchase of common stock associated with the acquisition of Synthes, Inc.

Aggregate shares of Common Stock issued were approximately 3,119,843,000 shares at the end of 2012, 2011 and 2010.

Cash dividends paid were $2.40 per share in 2012, compared with dividends of $2.25 per share in 2011, and $2.11 per share in 2010.

20. Business Combinations and Divestitures (in part)

Certain businesses were acquired for $17,821 million in cash and stock and $1,204 million of liabilities assumed during 2012. These acquisitions were accounted for by the purchase method and, accordingly, results of operations have been included in the financial statements from their respective dates of acquisition.

The 2012 acquisitions included: Synthes Inc., a global developer and manufacturer of orthopaedics devices; Guangzhou Biosesal Biotech Co. Ltd, a developer of biologic combinations addressing moderate to severe hemostasis; Angiotech Pharmaceuticals, Inc., intellectual property and know how related to the Quill TM Knotless Tissue-Closure Device; CorImmun Inc., a developer of a phase II treatment for CHF; Calibra Medical, Inc., developer of a unique, wearable three-day insulin patch for convenient and discreet mealtime dosing for people with diabetes who take multiple daily injections of insulin; Spectrum Vision LLC, a full service distributor of contact lenses serving Russia with facilities in the Ukraine and Kazakhstan; marketing authorizations, trademarks, and patents extending ZYRTEC® related market rights in Australia and Canada.

During the fiscal second quarter, the Company completed the acquisition of Synthes, Inc., a global developer and manufacturer of orthopaedics devices, for a purchase price of $20.2 billion in cash and stock. The net acquisition cost of the transaction is $17.5 billion based on cash on hand at closing of $2.7 billion.

Under the terms of the agreement, each share of Synthes, Inc. common stock was exchanged for CHF 55.65 in cash and 1.717 shares of Johnson & Johnson common stock, based on the calculated exchange ratio. The exchange ratio was calculated on June 12, 2012 and based on the relevant exchange rate and closing price of Johnson & Johnson common stock on that date, the total fair value of consideration transferred was $19.7 billion. When the acquisition was completed on June 14, 2012, based on the relevant exchange rate and closing price of Johnson & Johnson common stock on that date, the total fair value of the consideration transferred was $20.2 billion. Janssen Pharmaceutical, a company organized under the laws of Ireland and a wholly-owned subsidiary of Johnson & Johnson, used cash on hand to satisfy the cash portion of the merger consideration.

The stock portion of the merger consideration consisted of shares of Johnson & Johnson common stock purchased by Janssen Pharmaceutical, from two banks, pursuant to two accelerated share repurchase (ASR) agreements dated June 12, 2012. On June 13, 2012, Janssen Pharmaceutical purchased an aggregate of approximately 203.7 million shares of Johnson & Johnson common stock at an initial purchase price of $12.9 billion under the ASR agreements, with all of the shares delivered to Janssen Pharmaceutical on June 13, 2012. Final settlement of the transactions under each ASR agreement is expected to occur in the first half of 2013, and may occur earlier at the option of the two banks, as applicable, or later under certain circumstances. Based on the theoretical settlement of the ASR agreements, an additional 19.3 million shares would be issued to settle the ASR agreements as of December 30, 2012.

In addition, while the Company believes that the transactions under each ASR agreement and a series of related internal transactions were consummated in a tax efficient manner in accordance with applicable law, it is possible that the Internal Revenue Service could assert one or more contrary positions to challenge the transactions from a tax perspective. If challenged, an amount up to the total purchase price for the Synthes shares could be treated as subject to applicable U.S. tax at approximately the statutory rate to the Company, plus interest.

The following table summarizes the consideration transferred to acquire Synthes, Inc. valued on the acquisition date of June 14, 2012:

(Dollars in millions)	
Cash (multiply 55.65CHF by shares of Synthes common stock outstanding by the exchange rate)[A]	$ 6,902
Common Stock (multiply 1.717 by shares of Synthes common stock outstanding by J&J stock price)[B]	$13,335
Total fair value of consideration transferred	$20,237

[A] Synthes common stock outstanding of 118.7 million shares as of the acquisition date and CHF/USD exchange rate of .95674.

[B] Johnson & Johnson closing stock price on the New York Stock Exchange as of acquisition date of $65.45 per share.

The Company is still finalizing the allocation of the purchase price to the individual assets acquired and liabilities assumed. The allocation of the purchase price included in the current period balance sheet is based on the best estimate of management. To assist management in the allocation, the Company engaged valuation specialists to prepare independent appraisals. Certain estimated values surrounding litigation loss contingencies are not yet finalized and are subject to change. We will finalize the amounts recognized as we obtain the information necessary to complete the analysis. We expect to finalize these amounts as soon as possible but no later than one year from the acquisition date.

Spinoffs

RECOGNITION AND MEASUREMENT

5.39 The distributions of nonmonetary assets that constitute a business to owners of an entity are commonly referred to as spinoffs. A *business* is defined as an integrated set of activities and assets that is capable of being conducted and managed for the purpose of providing a return in the form of dividends, lower costs, or other economic benefits directly to investors or other owners, members, or participants. Spinoffs are discussed in FASB ASC 505-60.

5.40 FASB ASC 505-60-25-2 requires that the accounting for the distribution of nonmonetary assets to owners of an entity in a spinoff should be based on the recorded amount (after reduction, if appropriate, for an indicated impairment of value). An entity's distribution of the shares of a wholly owned or consolidated subsidiary to its shareholders should be recorded based on the carrying value of the subsidiary. Regardless of whether the spun-off operations will be sold immediately after the spinoff, the transaction should not be accounted for as a sale of the accounting spinnee followed by a distribution of the proceeds. In order to determine the required accounting and reporting in a spinoff transaction, an entity needs to determine which party is the accounting spinnor and which is the accounting spinnee. The accounting spinnee should be reported as a discontinued operation by the accounting spinnor if the spinnee is a component of an entity and meets the conditions for such reporting.

PRESENTATION AND DISCLOSURE EXCERPT

SPINOFFS

5.41 IDT CORPORATION (JUL)
CONSOLIDATED STATEMENTS OF EQUITY (in part)

| | IDT Corporation Stockholders | | | | | | | | | | Noncontrolling Interests | | |
| | Common Stock | | Class A Commonn Stock | | Class B Common Stock | | Additional Paid-In Capital | Treasury Stock | Accumulated Other Comprehensive Income (Loss) | Accumu-lated Deficit | Non-controlling Interests | Receivable for Issuance of Equity | Total Equity |
	Shares	Amount	Shares	Amount	Shares	Amount							
Balance at July 31, 2011	—	$—	3,272	$33	23,586	$236	$520,732	$(94,941)	$3,027	$(219,992)	$(4,305)	$(1,000)	$203,790
Dividends declared ($0.66 per share)	—	—	—	—	—	—	—	—	—	(15,014)	—	—	(15,014)
Restricted Class B common stock purchased from employee	—	—	—	—	—	—	—	(210)	—	—	—	—	(210)
Repurchases of Class B common stock through repurchase program	—	—	—	—	—	—	—	(2,606)	—	—	—	—	(2,606)
Stock-based compensation	—	—	—	—	—	—	3,605	—	—	—	—	—	3,605
Restricted stock issued to employees and directors	—	—	—	—	432	4	(4)						
Stock issued for matching contributions to the 401(k) Plan	—	—	—	—	94	1	910	—	—	—	—	—	911
Sale of stock of subsidiary	—	—	—	—	—	—	(78)	—	—	—	211	—	133
Distributions to noncontrolling interests	—	—	—	—	—	—	—	—	—	—	(1,580)	—	(1,580)
Other	—	—	—	—	—	—	—	—	—	—	225	—	225
Genie Spin-Off	—	—	—	—	—	—	(129,296)	—	(438)	—	5,688	1,000	(123,046)
Other comprehensive loss	—	—	—	—	—	—	—	—	(2,387)	—	119	—	(2,268)
Net income for the year ended July 31, 2012	—	—	—	—	—	—	—	—	—	38,648	137	—	38,785
Balance at July 31, 2012	—	$—	3,272	$33	24,112	$241	$395,869	$(97,757)	$ 202	$(196,358)	$ 495	$ —	$102,725

NOTES TO CONSOLIDATED FINANCIAL STATEMENTS

Note 1—Description of Business and Summary of Significant Accounting Policies (in part)

Description of Business (in part)

On October 28, 2011, the Company completed a pro rata distribution of the common stock of the Company's subsidiary, Genie Energy Ltd. ("Genie"), to the Company's stockholders of record as of the close of business on October 21, 2011 (the "Genie Spin-Off") (see Note 2). Genie and subsidiaries met the criteria to be reported as discontinued operations and accordingly, their assets, liabilities, results of operations and cash flows are classified as discontinued operations for all periods presented.

Note 2—Discontinued Operations (in part)

Genie Energy Ltd.

On October 28, 2011, the Company completed a pro rata distribution of the common stock of the Company's subsidiary, Genie Energy Ltd., to the Company's stockholders of record as of the close of business on October 21, 2011. At the time of the Genie Spin-Off, Genie owned 99.3% of Genie Energy International Corporation, which owned 100% of IDT Energy and 92% of Genie Oil and Gas, Inc. As of October 28, 2011, each of the Company's stockholders received one share of Genie Class A common stock for every share of the Company's Class A common stock and one share of Genie Class B common stock for every share of the Company's Class B common stock held of record as of the close of business on October 21, 2011. Genie and subsidiaries met the criteria to be reported as discontinued operations and accordingly, their assets, liabilities, results of operations and cash flows are classified as discontinued operations for all periods presented.

The Company has received a ruling from the Internal Revenue Service ("IRS") substantially to the effect that, for U.S. federal income tax purposes, the distribution of shares of Genie common stock will qualify as tax-free for Genie, the Company and the Company's stockholders under Section 355 of the Internal Revenue Code of 1986 (the "Code"). In addition to obtaining the IRS ruling, the Company has received an opinion from PricewaterhouseCoopers LLP on the three requirements for a tax-free distribution that are not addressed in the IRS ruling. Specifically, the opinion concludes that the distribution (i) should satisfy the business purpose requirement of the Code for a tax-free distribution, (ii) should not be viewed as being used principally as a device for the distribution of earnings and profits of the distributing corporation or the controlled corporation or both, and (iii) should not be viewed as part of a plan (or series of related transactions) pursuant to which one or more persons will acquire directly or indirectly stock representing a 50 percent or greater interest in the distributing corporation or controlled corporation within the meaning of the relevant section of the Code.

In October 2011, prior to the Genie Spin-Off, the Company committed to fund Genie with a total of $106.0 million in aggregate cash and cash equivalents, including restricted cash. The Company funded Genie with $70.3 million at the time of the Genie Spin-Off so that Genie held $94.0 million in cash and cash equivalents and $0.1 million in restricted cash. Subsequent to the Genie Spin-Off, in November and December 2011, the Company funded Genie with the final remaining $11.9 million.

Treasury Stock

PRESENTATION

5.42 Repurchased common stock is often referred to as treasury stock or treasury shares. FASB ASC 505-30-45-1 discusses the balance sheet presentation of treasury stock and states that if a corporation's stock is acquired for purposes other than retirement (formal or constructive), or if ultimate disposition has not yet been decided, the cost of acquired stock may be shown separately as a deduction from the total of capital stock, additional paid-in capital, and retained earnings or may be accorded the accounting treatment appropriate for retired stock.

5.43 A repurchase of shares at a price significantly in excess of the current market price creates a presumption that the repurchase price includes amounts attributable to items other than the shares repurchased. FASB ASC 505-30-30-2 explains that a repurchase of shares at a price significantly in excess of the current market price may require an entity to allocate amounts to other elements of the transaction.

PRESENTATION AND DISCLOSURE EXCERPT

TREASURY STOCK

5.44 MUELLER INDUSTRIES, INC. (DEC)
MARKET FOR REGISTRANT'S COMMON EQUITY, RELATED STOCKHOLDER MATTERS AND ISSUER PURCHASES OF EQUITY SECURITIES (in part)

Issuer Purchases of Equity Securities (in part)

The Company's Board of Directors has extended, until October 2013, the authorization to repurchase up to ten million shares of the Company's common stock through open market transactions or through privately negotiated transactions. The Company has no obligation to purchase any shares and may cancel, suspend, or extend the time period for the purchase of shares at any time. Any purchases will be funded primarily through existing cash and cash from operations. The Company may hold any shares purchased in treasury or use a portion of the repurchased shares for its stock-based compensation plans, as well as for other corporate purposes. From its initial authorization in 1999 through December 29, 2012, the Company had repurchased approximately 2.4 million shares under this authorization. The Company's repurchase transaction with Leucadia National Corporation in September 2012 was completed outside of this authorization. Below is a summary of the Company's stock repurchases for the quarter ended December 29, 2012.

	(a) Total Number of Shares Purchased	(b) Average Price Paid per Share	(c) Total Number of Shares Purchased as Part of Publicly Announced Plans or Programs	(d) Maximum Number of Shares That May Yet Be Purchased Under the Plans or Programs 7,644,530[1]
September 30—October 27, 2012	315,353[2]	$49.78	—	
October 28—November 24, 2012	4,251[2]	43.67	—	
November 25—December 29, 2012	20,621[2]	49.49	—	

[1] Shares available to be purchased under the Company's ten million share repurchase authorization until October 2013. The extension of the authorization was announced on October 26, 2012.

[2] Shares tendered to the Company by holders of stock based awards in payment of purchase price and/or withholding taxes upon exercise. In addition, includes restricted stock forfeitures.

CONSOLIDATED BALANCE SHEETS (in part)

(In thousands, except share data)	2012	2011
Equity		
Mueller Industries, Inc. stockholders' equity:		
Preferred stock—$1.00 par value; shares authorized 5,000,000; none outstanding	—	—
Common stock—$.01 par value; shares authorized 100,000,000; issued 40,091,502; outstanding 28,099,635 in 2012 and 38,236,568 in 2011	401	401
Additional paid-in capital	267,826	266,936
Retained earnings	749,777	682,380
Accumulated other comprehensive loss	(42,623)	(49,409)
Treasury common stock, at cost	(468,473)	(44,620)
Total Mueller Industries, Inc. stockholders' equity	506,908	855,688
Noncontrolling interest	31,058	29,074
Total equity	537,966	884,762

CONSOLIDATED STATEMENTS OF CHANGES IN EQUITY

(In thousands)	2012 Shares	2012 Amount	2011 Shares	2011 Amount	2010 Shares	2010 Amount
Common Stock:						
Balance at beginning of year	40,092	$ 401	40,092	$ 401	40,092	$ 401
Balance at end of year	40,092	$ 401	40,092	$ 401	40,092	$ 401
Additional Paid-in Capital:						
Balance at beginning of year		$ 266,936		$263,233		$262,166
Issuance of shares under incentive stock option plans		(4,303)		2,340		(394)
Stock-based compensation expense		6,136		3,482		2,877
Income tax benefit from exercise of stock options		2,528		853		145
Issuance of restricted stock		(3,471)		(2,972)		(1,561)
Balance at end of year		$ 267,826		$266,936		$263,233
Retained Earnings:						
Balance at beginning of year		$ 682,380		$611,279		$540,218
Net income attributable to Mueller Industries, Inc.		82,395		86,321		86,171
Dividends paid or payable to stockholders of Mueller Industries, Inc.		(14,998)		(15,220)		(15,110)
Balance at end of year		$ 749,777		$682,380		$611,279
Accumulated Other Comprehensive (Loss) Income:						
Balance at beginning of year		$ (49,409)		$ (37,046)		$ (36,104)
Total other comprehensive income (loss) attributable to Mueller Industries, Inc.		6,786		(12,363)		(942)
Balance at end of year		$ (42,623)		$ (49,409)		$ (37,046)
Treasury Stock:						
Balance at beginning of year	1,855	$ (44,620)	2,237	$ (49,131)	2,442	$(53,514)
Issuance of shares under incentive stock option plans	(576)	20,881	(464)	10,637	(149)	3,240
Repurchase of common stock	10,855	(448,205)	214	(9,098)	15	(418)
Issuance of restricted stock	(142)	3,471	(132)	2,972	(71)	1,561
Balance at end of year	11,992	$(468,473)	1,855	$ (44,620)	2,237	$ (49,131)
Noncontrolling Interest:						
Balance at beginning of year		$ 29,074		$ 27,161		$ 25,775
Net income attributable to noncontrolling interest		1,278		765		1,364
Dividends paid to noncontrolling interests		—		—		(741)
Foreign currency translation		706		1,148		763
Balance at end of year		$ 31,058		$ 29,074		$ 27,161

NOTES TO CONSOLIDATED FINANCIAL STATEMENTS

Note 5—Debt (in part)

On September 24, 2012, the Company entered into an agreement with Leucadia National Corporation (Leucadia) to repurchase 10.4 million shares of the Company's common stock at a total cost of $427.3 million. The Company funded the purchase price with available cash on hand and borrowings of $200.0 million under its $350.0 revolving credit facility (the Revolving Credit Facility) provided by its credit agreement (the Agreement) dated March 7, 2011. On December 11, 2012, the Company amended the Agreement to add a $200.0 million term loan facility (the Term Loan Facility), after which the total borrowing capacity under the Agreement was increased to $550.0 million. The Company used the borrowings under the Term Loan Facility to replace the amounts previously advanced under the Revolving Credit Facility. The amendment also adjusted the pricing and extended the maturity date to December 11, 2017 for all borrowings under the Agreement. Borrowings under the Agreement bear interest, at the Company's option, at LIBOR or Base Rate as defined by the Agreement, plus a variable premium. LIBOR advances may be based upon the one, three, or six-month LIBOR. The variable premium is based upon the Company's debt to total capitalization ratio, and can range from 112.5 to 162.5 basis points for LIBOR based loans and 12.5 to 62.5 basis points for Base Rate loans. At December 29, 2012, the premium was 137.5 basis points for LIBOR loans and 37.5 basis points for Base Rate loans. Additionally, a facility fee is payable quarterly on the total commitment and varies from 25.0 to 37.5 basis points based upon the Company's debt to total capitalization ratio. Availability of funds under the Revolving Credit Facility is reduced by the amount of certain outstanding letters of credit, which are used to secure the Company's payment of insurance deductibles and certain retiree health benefits, totaling approximately $10.9 million at December 29, 2012. Terms of the letters of credit are generally one year but are renewable annually.

Note 6—Equity (in part)

The Company's Board of Directors has extended, until October 2013, its authorization to repurchase up to ten million shares of the Company's common stock through open market transactions or through privately negotiated transactions. The Company has no obligation to purchase any shares and may cancel, suspend, or extend the time period for the purchase of shares at any time. Any purchases will be funded primarily through existing cash and cash from operations. The Company may hold any shares purchased in treasury or use a portion of the repurchased shares for its stock-based compensation plans, as well as for other corporate purposes.From its initial authorization in 1999 through December 29, 2012, the Company had repurchased approximately 2.4 million shares under this authorization.

The Company entered into an agreement with Leucadia pursuant to which the Company repurchased from Leucadia 10.4 million shares of the Company's common stock on September 24, 2012 at a total cost of $427.3 million. The Company's repurchase transaction with Leucadia was completed outside of the repurchase authorization previously approved by the Board of Directors.

Other Components of Stockholders' Equity

PRESENTATION

5.45 For public entities, Rule 3-04 of Regulation S-X requires that an analysis of the changes in each caption of stockholders' equity and noncontrolling interests presented in the balance sheets should be given in a note or separate statement. This analysis should be presented in the form of a reconciliation of the beginning balance to the ending balance for each period for which an income statement is required to be filed, with all significant reconciling items described by appropriate captions and contributions from, and distributions to, owners shown separately.

5.46 Many of the survey entities present accounts other than capital stock, additional paid-in capital, retained earnings, accumulated other comprehensive income, and treasury stock in the "Stockholders' Equity" section of the balance sheet. Other stockholders' equity accounts appearing on the balance sheets of the survey entities include, but are not limited to, guarantees of employee stock ownership plan debt, unearned or deferred compensation related to employee stock award plans, and amounts owed to an entity by employees for loans to buy company stock, in each instance pursuant to relevant FASB ASC requirements. Other items, such as foreign currency translation adjustments, unrealized gains and losses on certain investments in debt and equity securities, and defined benefit postretirement plan adjustments, are considered components of other comprehensive income. FASB ASC 220-10-45-14 provides guidance for reporting other comprehensive income in the "Equity" section of a statement of financial position.

DISCLOSURE

5.47 Rule 3-04 of SEC Regulation S-X requires an SEC registrant to disclose an analysis of the changes in each caption of other stockholders' equity and noncontrolling interests presented in the balance sheets in a note or separate statement (see also FASB ASC 505-10-S99-1).

5.48 FASB ASC 810, *Consolidation*, establishes accounting and reporting standards for the noncontrolling interest in a subsidiary. It clarifies that a *noncontrolling interest in a subsidiary* is an ownership interest in the consolidated entity that should be reported as equity in the consolidated financial statements but separate from the parent's equity, and clearly identified and labeled. In addition, FASB ASC 810 requires expanded disclosures in the consolidated financial statements that clearly identify and distinguish between the interests of the parent's owners and the interests of the noncontrolling owners of a subsidiary. Those expanded disclosures include a reconciliation of the beginning and ending balances of the equity attributable to the parent and noncontrolling owners and a schedule showing the effects of changes in a parent's ownership interest in a subsidiary on the equity attributable to the parent.

PRESENTATION AND DISCLOSURE EXCERPTS

UNEARNED COMPENSATION

5.49 DARDEN RESTAURANTS, INC. (MAY)
CONSOLIDATED BALANCE SHEETS (in part)

(In millions)

	May 27, 2012	May 29, 2011
Liabilities and Stockholders' Equity		
Stockholders' equity:		
Common stock and surplus, no par value. Authorized 500.0 shares; issued 289.0 and 287.2 shares, respectively; outstanding 129.0 and 134.6 shares, respectively	2,518.8	2,408.8
Preferred stock, no par value. Authorized 25.0 shares; none issued and outstanding	—	—
Retained earnings	3,172.8	2,921.9
Treasury stock, 160.0 and 152.6 shares, at cost, respectively	(3,695.8)	(3,325.3)
Accumulated other comprehensive income (loss)	(146.6)	(59.8)
Unearned compensation	(7.2)	(9.4)
Total stockholders' equity	$1,842.0	$1,936.2

CONSOLIDATED STATEMENTS OF CHANGES IN STOCKHOLDERS' EQUITY (in part)

(In millions, except per share data)

	Common Stock and Surplus	Retained Earnings	Treasury Stock	Accumulated Other Comprehensive Income (Loss)	Unearned Compensation	Officer Notes Receivable	Total Stockholders' Equity
Balances at May 29, 2011	$2,408.8	$2,921.9	$(3,325.3)	$(59.8)	$(9.4)	$—	$1,936.2
Net earnings	—	475.5	—	—	—	—	475.5
Other comprehensive income	—	—	—	(86.8)	—	—	(86.8)
Cash dividends declared ($1.72 per share)	—	(224.6)	—	—	—	—	(224.6)
Stock option exercises (2.2 shares)	59.4	—	3.5	—	—	—	62.9
Stock-based compensation	26.5	—	—	—	—	—	26.5
ESOP note receivable repayments	—	—	—	—	2.1	—	2.1
Income tax benefits credited to equity	17.9	—	—	—	—	—	17.9
Purchases of common stock for treasury (8.2 shares)	—	—	(375.1)	—	—	—	(375.1)
Issuance of treasury stock under Employee Stock Purchase Plan and other plans (0.2 shares)	6.2	—	1.1	—	0.1	—	7.4
Balances at May 27, 2012	$2,518.8	$3,172.8	$(3,695.8)	$(146.6)	$(7.2)	$—	$1,842.0

NOTES TO CONSOLIDATED FINANCIAL STATEMENTS

Note 9—Long-Term Debt (in part)

The components of long-term debt are as follows:

(In millions)	May 27, 2012	May 29, 2011
5.625% senior notes due October 2012	$ 350.0	$ 350.0
7.125% debentures due February 2016	100.0	100.0
6.200% senior notes due October 2017	500.0	500.0
4.500% senior notes due October 2021	400.0	—
6.000% senior notes due August 2035	150.0	150.0
6.800% senior notes due October 2037	300.0	300.0
ESOP loan with variable rate of interest (0.59% at May 27, 2012) due December 2018	5.9	8.0
Total long-term debt	$1,805.9	$1,408.0
Fair value hedge	3.2	3.7
Less issuance discount	(5.5)	(4.4)
Total long-term debt less issuance discount	$1,803.6	$1,407.3
Less current portion	(349.9)	—
Long-term debt, excluding current portion	$1,453.7	$1,407.3

Note 17—Retirement Plans (in part)

Defined Contribution Plan (in part)

ESOP shares are included in weighted-average common shares outstanding for purposes of calculating net earnings per share. At May 27, 2012, the ESOP's debt to us had a balance of $5.9 million with a variable rate of interest of 0.59 percent and is due to be repaid no later than December 2014. The number of our common shares held in the ESOP at May 27, 2012 approximated 4.9 million shares, representing 3.7 million allocated shares and 1.2 million suspense shares.

At the end of fiscal 2005, the ESOP borrowed $1.6 million from us at a variable interest rate and acquired an additional 0.05 million shares of our common stock, which were held in suspense within the ESOP at May 29, 2005. The loan, which had a variable interest rate of 0.59 percent at May 27, 2012, is due to be repaid no later than December 2018. The shares acquired under this loan are accounted for in accordance with FASB ASC Subtopic 718-40, Employee Stock Ownership Plans. Fluctuations in our stock price are recognized as adjustments to common stock and surplus when the shares are committed to be released. These ESOP shares are not considered outstanding until they are committed to be released and, therefore, have been excluded for purposes of calculating basic and diluted net earnings per share at May 27, 2012. The fair value of these shares at May 27, 2012 was $2.1 million.

DEFERRED COMPENSATION

5.50 NVR, INC. (DEC)
CONSOLIDATED BALANCE SHEETS (in part)

(In thousands, except share and per share data)

	December 31,	
	2012	**2011**
Liabilities and Shareholders' Equity		
Shareholders' equity:		
Common stock, $0.01 par value; 60,000,000 shares authorized; 20,556,198 shares issued as of both December 31, 2012 and 2011	206	206
Additional paid-in-capital	1,169,699	1,072,779
Deferred compensation trust—152,223 and 152,964 shares of NVR, Inc. common stock as of December 31, 2012 and 2011, respectively	(25,331)	(25,581)
Deferred compensation liability	25,331	25,581
Retained earnings	4,339,080	4,158,492
Less treasury stock at cost—15,642,068 and 15,578,565 shares as of December 31, 2012 and 2011, respectively	(4,028,508)	(3,856,678)
Total shareholders' equity	1,480,477	1,374,799

CONSOLIDATED STATEMENTS OF SHAREHOLDERS' EQUITY

(In thousands)

	Common Stock	Additional Paid-in-Capital	Retained Earnings	Treasury Stock	Deferred Compensation Trust	Deferred Compensation Liability	Total
Balance, December 31, 2009	$206	$ 830,531	$3,823,067	$(2,896,542)	$(40,799)	$40,799	$1,757,262
Net income	—	—	206,005	—	—	—	206,005
Deferred compensation activity	—	—	—	—	13,217	(13,217)	—
Purchase of common stock for treasury	—	—	—	(417,079)	—	—	(417,079)
Equity-based compensation	—	53,136	—	—	—	—	53,136
Tax benefit from equity benefit plan activity	—	63,558	—	—	—	—	63,558
Proceeds from stock options exercised	—	77,492	—	—	—	—	77,492
Treasury stock issued upon option exercise and restricted share vesting	—	(73,483)	—	73,483	—	—	—
Balance, December 31, 2010	206	951,234	4,029,072	(3,240,138)	(27,582)	27,582	1,740,374
Net income	—	—	129,420	—	—	—	129,420
Deferred compensation activity	—	—	—	—	2,001	(2,001)	—
Purchase of common stock for treasury	—	—	—	(689,302)	—	—	(689,302)
Equity-based compensation	—	64,473	—	—	—	—	64,473
Tax benefit from equity benefit plan activity	—	22,835	—	—	—	—	22,835
Proceeds from stock options exercised	—	106,999	—	—	—	—	106,999
Treasury stock issued upon option exercise and restricted share vesting	—	(72,762)	—	72,762	—	—	—
Balance, December 31, 2011	206	1,072,779	4,158,492	(3,856,678)	(25,581)	25,581	1,374,799
Net income	—	—	180,588	—	—	—	180,588
Deferred compensation activity	—	—	—	—	250	(250)	—
Purchase of common stock for treasury	—	—	—	(227,281)	—	—	(227,281)
Equity-based compensation	—	64,841	—	—	—	—	64,841
Tax benefit from equity benefit plan activity	—	14,319	—	—	—	—	14,319
Proceeds from stock options exercised	—	73,211	—	—	—	—	73,211
Treasury stock issued upon option exercise and restricted share vesting	—	(55,451)	—	55,451	—	—	—
Balance, December 31, 2012	$206	$1,169,699	$4,339,080	$(4,028,508)	$(25,331)	$25,331	$1,480,477

(Dollars in thousands, except per share data)

10. Equity-Based Compensation, Profit Sharing and Deferred Compensation Plans (in part)

Deferred Compensation Plans

The Company has two deferred compensation plans ("Deferred Comp Plans"). The specific purpose of the Deferred Comp Plans is to i) establish a vehicle whereby named executive officers may defer the receipt of salary and bonus that otherwise would be nondeductible for Company tax purposes into a period where the Company would realize a tax deduction for the amounts paid, and ii) to enable certain of our employees who are subject to the Company's stock holding requirements to acquire shares of our common stock on a pre-tax basis in order to more quickly meet, and maintain compliance with those stock holding requirements. Amounts deferred into the Deferred Comp Plans are invested in NVR common stock, held in a rabbi trust account, and are paid out in a fixed number of shares upon expiration of the deferral period.

The rabbi trust account held 152,223 and 152,964 shares of NVR common stock as of December 31, 2012 and 2011, respectively. During 2012, 741 shares of NVR common stock were issued from the rabbi trust related to deferred compensation for which the deferral period ended. There were no shares of NVR common stock contributed to the rabbi trust in 2012 or 2011. Shares held by the Deferred Comp Plans are treated as outstanding shares in the Company's earnings per share calculation for each of the years ended December 31, 2012, 2011 and 2010.

WARRANTS

5.51 LAS VEGAS SANDS CORP. (DEC)
CONSOLIDATED STATEMENTS OF EQUITY

| | Las Vegas Sands Corp. Stockholder's Equity | | | | | | |
(In thousands)	Preferred Stock	Common Stock	Capital in Excess of Par Value	Accumulated Other Comprehensive Income	Retained Earnings	Non-controlling Interests	Total
Balance at January 1, 2010	$234,607	$660	$5,114,851	$ 26,748	$473,833	$1,089,888	$6,940,587
Net income	—	—	—	—	599,394	182,209	781,603
Currency translation adjustment	—	—	—	102,771	—	(4,253)	98,518
Exercise of stock options	—	2	16,453	—	—	—	16,455
Tax shortfall from stock-based compensation	—	—	(195)	—	—	—	(195)
Stock-based compensation	—	—	58,120	—	—	2,698	60,818
Exercise of warrants	(27,251)	46	252,719	—	—	—	225,514
Acquisition of remaining shares of noncontrolling interest	—	—	2,345	—	—	(2,345)	—
Deemed contribution from Principal Stockholder	—	—	412	—	—	—	412
Dividends declared, net of amounts previously accrued	—	—	—	—	(86,546)	—	(86,546)
Accumulated but undeclared dividend requirement on preferred stock issued to Principal Stockholder's family	—	—	—	—	(6,854)	—	(6,854)
Accretion to redemption value of preferred stock issued to Principal Stockholder's family	—	—	—	—	(92,545)	—	(92,545)
Preferred stock inducement premium	—	—	—	—	(6,579)	—	(6,579)
Balance at December 31, 2010	207,356	708	5,444,705	129,519	880,703	1,268,197	7,931,188
Net income	—	—	—	—	1,560,123	322,996	1,883,119
Currency translation adjustment	—	—	—	(35,415)	—	2,622	(32,793)
Exercise of stock options	—	2	24,223	—	—	1,280	25,505
Stock-based compensation	—	—	60,363	—	—	2,927	63,290
Issuance of restricted stock	—	1	(1)	—	—	—	—
Exercise of warrants	(68,380)	22	80,870	—	—	—	12,512
Disposition of interest in majority owned subsidiary	—	—	—	—	—	829	829
Repurchase and redemption of preferred stock	(138,976)	—	—	—	(128,845)	—	(267,821)
Dividends declared, net of amounts previously accrued	—	—	—	—	(68,443)	—	(68,443)
Distributions to noncontrolling interests	—	—	—	—	—	(10,388)	(10,388)
Accretion to redemption value of preferred stock issued to Principal Stockholder's family	—	—	—	—	(80,975)	—	(80,975)
Preferred stock inducement premium	—	—	—	—	(16,871)	—	(16,871)
Balance at December 31, 2011	—	733	5,610,160	94,104	2,145,692	1,588,463	9,439,152
Net income	—	—	—	—	1,524,093	357,720	1,881,813
Currency translation adjustment, net of reclassification adjustment	—	—	—	168,974	—	3,814	172,788
Exercise of stock options	—	2	40,038	—	—	6,200	46,240
Stock-based compensation	—	—	63,102	—	—	3,264	66,366
Issuance of restricted stock	—	1	(1)	—	—	—	—
Exercise of warrants	—	88	528,820	—	—	—	528,908
Acquisition of remaining shares of noncontrolling interest	—	—	(4,631)	—	—	4,631	—
Dividends declared	—	—	—	—	(3,090,757)	(357,056)	(3,447,813)
Distributions to noncontrolling interests	—	—	—	—	—	(10,466)	(10,466)
Deemed distribution to Principal Stockholder	—	—	—	—	(18,576)	—	(18,576)
Balance at December 31, 2012	$ —	$824	$6,237,488	$263,078	$560,452	$1,596,570	$8,658,412

Note 9—Equity (in part)

Preferred Stock and Warrants (in part)

In November 2008, the Company issued 10,446,300 shares of its 10% Series A Cumulative Perpetual Preferred Stock (the "Preferred Stock") and warrants to purchase up to an aggregate of approximately 174,105,348 shares of common stock at an exercise price of $6.00 per share and an expiration date of November 16, 2013 (the "Warrants"). Units consisting of one share of Preferred Stock and one Warrant to purchase 16.6667 shares of common stock were sold for $100 per unit. As described further below, the outstanding Preferred Stock was redeemed in whole by the Company on November 15, 2011, at a redemption price of $110 per share. Holders of the Preferred Stock had no rights to exchange or convert such shares into any other securities.

Under Nevada law, the Company had the ability to declare or pay dividends on the Preferred Stock only to the extent by which the total assets exceeded the total liabilities and so long as the Company was able to pay its debts as they became due in the usual course of its business. When declared by the Company's Board of Directors, holders of the Preferred Stock were entitled to receive cumulative cash dividends quarterly on each February 15, May 15, August 15 and November 15, which began on February 15, 2009.

Preferred Stock Issued to Public

Of the 10,446,300 shares of Preferred Stock issued, the Company issued 5,196,300 shares to the public together with Warrants to purchase up to an aggregate of approximately 86,605,173 shares of its common stock and received gross proceeds of $519.6 million ($503.6 million, net of transaction costs). The allocated carrying values of the Preferred Stock and Warrants on the date of issuance (based on their relative fair values) were $298.1 million and $221.5 million, respectively.

During the year ended December 31, 2012, 39,070 Warrants were exercised to purchase an aggregate of 655,496 shares of the Company's common stock at $6.00 per share and $3.9 million in cash was received as settlement of the Warrant exercise price.

During the year ended December 31, 2011, holders of preferred stock exercised 1,317,220 Warrants to purchase an aggregate of 21,953,704 shares of the Company's common stock at $6.00 per share and tendered 1,192,100 shares of preferred stock and $12.5 million in cash as settlement of the Warrant exercise price. In conjunction with certain of these transactions, the Company paid $16.9 million in premiums to induce the exercise of Warrants with settlement through tendering preferred stock. During the year ended December 31, 2011, the Company also repurchased and retired 736,629 shares of preferred stock for $82.3 million.

During the year ended December 31, 2010, holders of preferred stock exercised 2,730,209 Warrants to purchase an aggregate of 45,503,562 shares of the Company's common stock at $6.00 per share and tendered 475,076 shares of preferred stock and $225.5 million in cash as settlement of the Warrant exercise price. In conjunction with certain of these transactions, the Company paid $6.6 million in premiums to induce the exercise of Warrants with settlement through tendering preferred stock.

Preferred Stock Issued to Principal Stockholder's Family (in part)

Of the 10,446,300 shares of Preferred Stock issued, the Company issued 5,250,000 shares to the Principal Stockholder's family together with Warrants to purchase up to an aggregate of approximately 87,500,175 shares of its common stock and received gross proceeds of $525.0 million ($523.7 million, net of transaction costs). The allocated carrying values of the Preferred Stock and Warrants on the date of issuance (based on their relative fair values) were $301.1 million and $223.9 million, respectively. The Preferred Stock amount had been recorded as mezzanine equity as the Principal Stockholder and his family have a greater than 50% ownership of the Company and therefore had the ability to require the Company to redeem their Preferred Stock beginning November 15, 2011.

On March 2, 2012, the Principal Stockholder's family exercised all of their outstanding Warrants to purchase 87,500,175 shares of the Company's common stock for $6.00 per share and paid $525.0 million in cash as settlement of the Warrant exercise price.

Rollfoward of Shares of Common Stock and Preferred Stock Issued to Public

A summary of the outstanding shares of common stock and preferred stock issued to the public is as follows:

	Preferred Stock	Common Stock
Balance as of January 1, 2010	4,089,999	660,322,749
Exercise of stock options	—	1,667,636
Issuance of restricted stock	—	15,765
Forfeiture of unvested restricted stock	—	(1,730)
Exercise of warrants	(475,076)	45,503,562
Balance as of December 31, 2010	3,614,923	707,507,982
Exercise of stock options	—	2,549,131
Issuance of restricted stock	—	1,250,381
Forfeiture of unvested restricted stock	—	(11,500)
Exercise of warrants	(1,192,100)	21,953,704
Repurchases and redemption of preferred stock	(2,422,823)	—
Balance as of December 31, 2011	—	733,249,698
Exercise of stock options	—	2,387,831
Issuance of restricted stock	—	516,556
Forfeiture of unvested restricted stock	—	(12,000)
Exercise of warrants	—	88,155,671
Balance as of December 31, 2012	—	824,297,756

Note 16—Related Party Transactions (in part)

On November 15, 2011, the Company paid $577.5 million to redeem all of the Preferred Stock held by the Principal Stockholder's family. On March 2, 2012, the Principal Stockholder's family exercised all of their outstanding Warrants to purchase 87,500,175 shares of the Company's common stock for $6.00 per share and paid $525.0 million in cash as settlement of the Warrant exercise price. See "—Note 9—Equity—Preferred Stock Issued to Principal Stockholder's Family."

NONCONTROLLING INTEREST

5.52 CF INDUSTRIES HOLDINGS, INC. (DEC)
CONSOLIDATED BALANCE SHEETS (in part)

	December 31, 2012	December 31, 2011
	(In millions, except share and per share amounts)	
Liabilities and Equity		
Equity:		
Stockholders' equity:		
Preferred stock—$0.01 par value, 50,000,000 shares authorized	—	—
Common stock—$0.01 par value, 500,000,000 shares authorized, 2012—62,961,628 shares issued and 2011—71,935,838 shares issued	0.6	0.7
Paid-in capital	2,492.4	2,804.8
Retained earnings	3,461.1	2,841.0
Treasury stock—at cost, 2012—10,940 shares and 2011—6,515,251 shares	(2.3)	(1,000.2)
Accumulated other comprehensive loss	(49.6)	(99.3)
Total stockholders' equity	5,902.2	4,547.0
Noncontrolling interest	380.0	385.9
Total equity	6,282.2	4,932.9

CONSOLIDATED STATEMENTS OF EQUITY

(In millions)	$0.01 Par Value Common Stock	Treasury Stock	Paid-in Capital	Retained Earnings	Accumulated Other Comprehensive Income (Loss)	Total Stockholders' Equity	Non-controlling Interest	Total Equity
	Common Stockholders							
Balance at December 31, 2009	$0.5	$ —	$ 723.5	$1,048.1	$(43.2)	$1,728.9	$ 16.0	$1,744.9
Net earnings	—	—	—	349.2	—	349.2	91.5	440.7
Other comprehensive income								
Foreign currency translation adjustment	—	—	—	—	22.8	22.8	1.4	24.2
Unrealized (loss) on securities—net of taxes	—	—	—	—	(14.6)	(14.6)	—	(14.6)
Defined benefit plans—net of taxes	—	—	—	—	(18.3)	(18.3)	—	(18.3)
Comprehensive income						339.1	92.9	432.0
Acquisition of Terra Industries Inc.	—	—	—	—	—	—	373.0	373.0

(continued)

| | Common Stockholders | | | | | | | |
(In millions)	$0.01 Par Value Common Stock	Treasury Stock	Paid-in Capital	Retained Earnings	Accumulated Other Comprehensive Income (Loss)	Total Stockholders' Equity	Non-controlling Interest	Total Equity
Issuance of $0.01 par value common stock in connection with acquisition of Terra Industries Inc.	0.1	—	881.9	—	—	882.0	—	882.0
Issuance of $0.01 par value common stock in connection with equity offering, net of costs of $41.4 million	0.1	—	1,108.5	—	—	1,108.6	—	1,108.6
Acquisition of treasury stock under employee stock plans	—	(0.7)	—	—	—	(0.7)	—	(0.7)
Issuance of $0.01 par value common stock under employee stock plans	—	0.7	4.6	(0.3)	—	5.0	—	5.0
Stock-based compensation expense	—	—	7.9	—	—	7.9	—	7.9
Excess tax benefit from stock-based compensation	—	—	5.8	—	—	5.8	—	5.8
Cash dividends ($0.40 per share)	—	—	—	(26.2)	—	(26.2)	—	(26.2)
Distributions declared to noncontrolling interest	—	—	—	—	—	—	(101.1)	(101.1)
Effect of exchange rates changes	—	—	—	—	—	—	2.2	2.2
Balance at December 31, 2010	$0.7	$—	$2,732.2	$1,370.8	$(53.3)	$4,050.4	$383.0	$4,433.4
Net earnings	—	—	—	1,539.2	—	1,539.2	221.8	1,761.0
Other comprehensive income								
Foreign currency translation adjustment	—	—	—	—	(7.0)	(7.0)	(0.6)	(7.6)
Unrealized gain on securities—net of taxes	—	—	—	—	1.9	1.9	—	1.9
Defined benefit plans—net of taxes	—	—	—	—	(40.9)	(40.9)	—	(40.9)
Comprehensive income						1,493.2	221.2	1,714.4
Purchases of treasury stock	—	(1,000.2)	—	—	—	(1,000.2)	—	(1,000.2)
Acquisition of treasury stock under employee stock plans	—	(0.4)	—	—	—	(0.4)	—	(0.4)
Issuance of $0.01 par value common stock under employee stock plans	—	0.4	15.5	(0.3)	—	15.6	—	15.6
Stock-based compensation expense	—	—	9.9	—	—	9.9	—	9.9
Excess tax benefit from stock-based compensation	—	—	47.2	—	—	47.2	—	47.2
Cash dividends ($1.00 per share)	—	—	—	(68.7)	—	(68.7)	—	(68.7)
Distributions declared to noncontrolling interest	—	—	—	—	—	—	(213.9)	(213.9)
Effect of exchange rates changes	—	—	—	—	—	—	(4.4)	(4.4)
Balance at December 31, 2011	$0.7	$(1,000.2)	$2,804.8	$2,841.0	$(99.3)	$4,547.0	$385.9	$4,932.9
Net earnings	—	—	—	1,848.7	—	1,848.7	74.7	1,923.4
Other comprehensive income								
Foreign currency translation adjustment	—	—	—	—	46.0	46.0	0.7	46.7
Unrealized gain on hedging derivatives—net of taxes	—	—	—	—	4.6	4.6	—	4.6
Unrealized gain on securities—net of taxes	—	—	—	—	2.6	2.6	—	2.6
Defined benefit plans—net of taxes	—	—	—	—	(3.5)	(3.5)	—	(3.5)
Comprehensive income						1,898.4	75.4	1,973.8
Purchases of treasury stock	—	(500.0)	—	—	—	(500.0)	—	(500.0)
Retirement of treasury stock	(0.1)	1,500.2	(374.2)	(1,125.9)	—	—	—	—
Acquisition of treasury stock under employee stock plans	—	(2.3)	—	—	—	(2.3)	—	(2.3)
Issuance of $0.01 par value common stock under employee stock plans	—	—	14.6	—	—	14.6	—	14.6
Stock-based compensation expense	—	—	11.1	—	—	11.1	—	11.1
Excess tax benefit from stock-based compensation	—	—	36.1	—	—	36.1	—	36.1
Cash dividends ($1.60 per share)	—	—	—	(102.7)	—	(102.7)	—	(102.7)
Distributions declared to noncontrolling interest	—	—	—	—	—	—	(83.1)	(83.1)
Effect of exchange rates changes	—	—	—	—	—	—	1.8	1.8
Balance at December 31, 2012	$0.6	$(2.3)	$2,492.4	$3,461.1	$(49.6)	$5,902.2	$380.0	$6,282.2

NOTES TO CONSOLIDATED FINANCIAL STATEMENTS

2. Summary of Significant Accounting Policies (in part)

Consolidation and Noncontrolling Interest

The consolidated financial statements of CF Holdings include the accounts of CF, all majority-owned subsidiaries and variable interest entities in which CF Holdings or a subsidiary is the primary beneficiary. All significant intercompany transactions and balances have been eliminated.

CFL is a variable interest entity that is consolidated in the financial statements of CF Holdings. CFL owns a nitrogen fertilizer complex in Medicine Hat, Alberta, Canada and supplies fertilizer products to CF and Viterra Inc. (Viterra). CF Industries, Inc. owns 49% of CFL's voting common shares and 66% of CFL's nonvoting preferred shares. Viterra owns 34% of the voting common stock and non-voting preferred stock of CFL. The remaining 17% of the voting common stock is owned by GROWMARK, Inc. and La Coop fédérée. Viterra's 34% interest in the distributed and undistributed earnings of CFL is included in noncontrolling interest reported in the consolidated statement of operations. The interests of Viterra and the holders of 17% of CFL's common shares are included in noncontrolling interest reported on the consolidated balance sheet. During the second half of 2012, we entered into agreements to purchase all of the noncontrolling interests in CFL. For additional information, see Note 4—Noncontrolling Interest.

TNCLP is a master limited partnership that is consolidated in the financial statements of CF Holdings. TNCLP owns the nitrogen manufacturing facility in Verdigris, Oklahoma. Through the acquisition of Terra in April 2010, we own an aggregate 75.3% of TNCLP and outside investors own the remaining 24.7%. Partnership interests in TNCLP are traded on the NYSE. As a result, TNCLP files separate financial reports with the Securities Exchange Commission (SEC). The outside investors' limited partnership interests in the partnership are included in noncontrolling interest in the consolidated financial statements. This noncontrolling interest represents the noncontrolling unitholders' interest in the partners' capital of TNCLP.

4. Noncontrolling Interest

Canadian Fertilizers Limited (CFL)

CFL owns a nitrogen fertilizer complex in Medicine Hat, Alberta, Canada which supplies fertilizer products to CF Industries, Inc. and Viterra Inc. (Viterra). CFL's Medicine Hat complex is the largest nitrogen fertilizer complex in Canada, with two world-scale ammonia plants, a world-scale granular urea plant and on-site storage facilities for both ammonia and urea.

CF Industries, Inc. owns 49% of CFL's voting common shares and 66% of CFL's nonvoting preferred shares. Viterra owns 34% of the voting common shares and non-voting preferred shares of CFL. The remaining 17% of the voting common shares are owned by GROWMARK, Inc. and La Coop fédérée. CFL is a variable interest entity that we consolidate in our financial statements.

General creditors of CFL do not have direct recourse to the assets of CF Industries, Inc. However, the product purchase agreement between CF Industries, Inc. and CFL does require CF Industries, Inc. to advance funds to CFL in the event that CFL is unable to meet its obligations as they become due. The amount of each advance would be at least 66% of the deficiency and would be more in any year in which CF Industries, Inc. purchased more than 66% of Medicine Hat's production. A similar purchase agreement and obligation also exists for Viterra. CF Industries, Inc. and Viterra currently manage CFL such that each party is responsible for its share of CFL's fixed costs and that CFL's production volume is managed to meet the parties' combined requirements. Based on the contractual arrangements, CF Industries, Inc. is the primary beneficiary of CFL as CF Industries, Inc. directs the activities that most significantly impact CFL's economic performance and receives at least 66% of the economic risks and rewards of CFL.

CFL's net sales were $217.1 million and $709.6 million and $454.0 million, for 2012, 2011 and 2010, respectively. CFL's net sales in 2012 were impacted by the selling price modification discussed further below. CFL's assets and liabilities at December 31, 2012 were $108.1 million and $57.6 million, respectively, and at December 31, 2011 were $528.5 million and $479.5 million, respectively.

Because CFL's functional currency is the Canadian dollar, consolidation of CFL results in a cumulative foreign currency translation adjustment, which is reported in other comprehensive income (loss). In accordance with CFL's governing agreements, CFL's net earnings are distributed to its members annually based on approval by CFL's shareholders. A portion of the amounts reported as noncontrolling interest in the consolidated statements of operations represents Viterra's 34% interest in the earnings of CFL, while a portion of the amounts reported as noncontrolling interest on our consolidated balance sheets represent the interests of Viterra and the holders of 17% of CFL's common shares.

CF Industries, Inc. operates the Medicine Hat facility pursuant to a management agreement and purchases approximately 66% of the facility's ammonia and granular urea production pursuant to a product purchase agreement. Viterra has the right, but not the obligation, to purchase the remaining 34% of the facility's production under a similar product purchase agreement. To the extent that Viterra does not purchase its 34% of the facility's production, CF Industries, Inc. is obligated to purchase any remaining amounts. However, since 1995, Viterra has purchased at least 34% of the facility's production each year. Both the management agreement and the product purchase agreement can be terminated by either CF Industries, Inc. or CFL upon a twelve-month notice.

Under the product purchase agreements that were in effect until the fourth quarter of 2012, both CF Industries, Inc. and Viterra paid the greater of production cost or market price for purchases. An initial portion of the selling price was paid based upon production cost plus an agreed-upon margin once title passes as the products were shipped. The remaining portion of the selling price, representing the difference between the market price and production cost plus an agreed-upon margin, was paid after the end of the year. The sales revenue attributable to this remaining portion of the selling price was accrued on an interim basis. In the Company's consolidated financial statements, the net sales and accounts receivable attributable to CFL are solely generated by transactions with Viterra, as all transactions with CF Industries are eliminated in consolidation. At December 31, 2012 and December 31, 2011, the net receivable due from Viterra related to the product purchases that was reflected on our consolidated balance sheets was $2.0 million and $141.0 million, respectively. See further discussion below regarding a modification to the CFL selling prices which reduced the net receivable due from Viterra.

The product purchase agreements also provide that CFL will distribute its net earnings to CF Industries, Inc. and Viterra annually based on the respective quantities of product purchased from CFL. The net earnings attributable to Viterra that are reported in noncontrolling interest on the consolidated balance sheets at December 31, 2012 and December 31, 2011 were approximately $5.3 million and $149.7 million, respectively. The annual distribution is paid after the end of the year. The distributions to Viterra are reported as financing activities in the consolidated statements of cash flows, as we consider these payments to be similar to dividends.

In August 2012, CF Industries Holdings, Inc. entered into an agreement to acquire Viterra's interest in CFL for a total purchase price of C$0.9 billion, subject to certain adjustments. In October 2012, we entered into an agreement with each of GROWMARK, Inc. and La Coop fédérée to acquire the common shares of CFL owned by those parties. As a result of these transactions, we will own 100% of CFL and will be entitled to purchase 100% of CFL's nitrogen fertilizer production. The completion of these transactions is subject to the receipt of regulatory approvals in Canada and other terms and conditions in the definitive agreements.

In the fourth quarter of 2012, the CFL Board of Directors approved an amendment to the product purchase agreements. The amendment modified the selling prices that CFL charges for products sold to Viterra and CF Industries. The modified selling prices are based on production cost plus an agreed-upon margin and are effective retroactive to January 1, 2012. As a result of the January 1, 2012 effective date, the Company has recognized in its fourth quarter 2012 consolidated statement of operations a reduction in net sales to Viterra of $129.7 million and a corresponding reduction in earnings attributable to the noncontrolling interest to reverse the interim market price accruals recognized in the first three quarters of 2012. The net effect of this change had no impact on the Company's net earnings attributable to common stockholders, but did reduce the Company's reported net sales, gross margin, operating earnings and earnings before income taxes by $129.7 million in the fourth quarter. The selling price modification also had no impact on the Company's net cash flows as the selling price modification was entirely offset by a change in the distributions payable to the noncontrolling interest.

Terra Nitrogen Company, L.P. (TNCLP)

TNCLP is a master limited partnership that owns a nitrogen manufacturing facility in Verdigris, Oklahoma. We own an aggregate 75.3% of TNCLP through general and limited partnership interests. Outside investors own the remaining 24.7% of the limited partnership. For financial reporting purposes, the assets, liabilities and earnings of the partnership are consolidated into our financial statements. The outside investors' limited partnership interests in the partnership have been recorded as part of noncontrolling interest in our consolidated financial statements. The noncontrolling interest represents the noncontrolling unitholders' interest in the equity of TNCLP. An affiliate of CF Industries is required to purchase all of TNCLP's fertilizer products at market prices as defined in the Amendment to the General and Administrative Services and Product Offtake Agreement, dated September 28, 2010.

TNCLP makes cash distributions to the general and limited partners based upon formulas defined within its Agreement of Limited Partnership. Cash available for distribution is defined in the agreement generally as all cash receipts less all cash disbursements, less certain reserves (including reserves for future operating and capital needs) established as the general partner determines in its reasonable discretion to be necessary or appropriate. Changes in working capital impact available cash, as increases in the amount of cash invested in working capital items (such as accounts receivable or inventory) reduce available cash, while declines in the amount of cash invested in working capital increase available cash. Cash distributions to the limited partners and general partner vary depending on the extent to which the cumulative distributions exceed certain target threshold levels set forth in the Agreement of Limited Partnership.

In each of the applicable quarters of 2012, 2011 and 2010, the minimum quarterly distributions were satisfied, which entitled us, as the general partner, to receive increased distributions on our general partner interests as provided for in the Agreement of Limited Partnership. The earnings attributed to our general partner interest in excess of the threshold levels for the years ended December 31, 2012, 2011, and 2010 were $234.0 million, $214.2 million and $49.0 million, respectively.

At December 31, 2012, Terra Nitrogen GP Inc. (TNGP), the general partner of TNCLP (and an indirect wholly-owned subsidiary of CF Industries), and its affiliates owned 75.3% of TNCLP's outstanding units. When not more than 25% of TNCLP's issued and outstanding units are held by non-affiliates of TNGP, TNCLP, at TNGP's sole discretion, may call, or assign to TNGP or its affiliates, TNCLP's right to acquire all such outstanding units held by non-affiliated persons. If TNGP elects to acquire all outstanding units, TNCLP is required to give at least 30 but not more than 60 days notice of TNCLP's decision to purchase the outstanding units. The purchase price per unit will be the greater of (1) the average of the previous 20 trading days' closing prices as of the date five days before the purchase is announced or (2) the highest price paid by TNGP or any of its affiliates for any unit within the 90 days preceding the date the purchase is announced.

A reconciliation of the beginning and ending balances of noncontrolling interest and distributions payable to the noncontrolling interests on our consolidated balance sheets is provided below.

| | | | | Year Ended December 31, | | | | | |
| | 2012 | | | 2011 | | | 2010 | | |
(In millions)	CFL	TNCLP	Total	CFL	TNCLP	Total	CFL	TNCLP	Total
Noncontrolling Interest:									
Beginning balance	$ 16.7	$369.2	$ 385.9	$ 17.4	$365.6	$ 383.0	$ 16.0	$ —	$ 16.0
Terra acquistion	—	—	—	—	—	—	—	373.0	373.0
Earnings attributable to noncontrolling interest	3.5	71.2	74.7	154.0	67.8	221.8	75.8	15.7	91.5
Declaration of distributions payable	(5.3)	(77.8)	(83.1)	(149.7)	(64.2)	(213.9)	(78.0)	(23.1)	(101.1)
Effect of exchange rate changes	2.5	—	2.5	(5.0)	—	(5.0)	3.6	—	3.6
Ending balance	$ 17.4	$362.6	$ 380.0	$ 16.7	$369.2	$ 385.9	$ 17.4	$365.6	$ 383.0
Distributions Payable to Noncontrolling Interest									
Beginning balance	$149.7	$ —	$ 149.7	$ 78.0	$ —	$ 78.0	$ 92.1	$ —	$ 92.1
Declaration of distributions payable	5.3	77.8	83.1	149.7	64.2	213.9	78.0	23.1	101.1
Distributions to noncontrolling interest	(154.0)	(77.8)	(231.8)	(81.5)	(64.2)	(145.7)	(93.9)	(23.1)	(117.0)
Effect of exchange rate changes	4.3	—	4.3	3.5	—	3.5	1.8	—	1.8
Ending balance	$ 5.3	$ —	$ 5.3	$149.7	$ —	$ 149.7	$ 78.0	$ —	$ 78.0

General

PRESENTATION

6.01 Financial Accounting Standards Board (FASB) *Accounting Standards Codification* (ASC) 230, *Statement of Cash Flows*, requires entities to present a statement of cash flows that classifies cash receipts and payments by operating, investing, and financing activities. The information provided in a statement of cash flows, if used with related disclosures and information in the other financial statements, should help investors, creditors, and others do the following:
- Assess the entity's ability to generate positive future net cash flows
- Assess the entity's ability to meet its obligations, its ability to pay dividends, and its needs for external financing
- Assess the reasons for differences between net income and associated cash receipts and payments
- Assess the effects on an entity's financial position of both its cash and noncash investing and financing transactions during the period

6.02 Paragraphs 4–6 of FASB ASC 230-10-45 provide that the statement of cash flows explains the change in cash and cash equivalents during a period. *Cash equivalents* are defined by the FASB ASC glossary to be short-term, highly liquid investments that have both of the following characteristics:
- Readily convertible to known amounts of cash
- So near their maturity that they present an insignificant risk of changes in value because of changes in interest rates

Generally, only investments with original maturities of three months or less qualify under that definition. *Original maturity* means original maturity to the entity holding the investment.

6.03 FASB ASC 230-10-45-4 states that the amount of cash and cash equivalents at the beginning and end of the period reported on a statement of cash flows should agree with the amount of cash and cash equivalents reported on a statement of financial position. Because not all investments that qualify are required to be treated as cash equivalents, an entity should establish a policy concerning which short-term, highly liquid investments that satisfy the definition of *cash equivalents* are treated as such.

6.04 Paragraphs 7–9 of FASB ASC 230-10-45 explain that generally, cash receipts and payments should be reported separately and not netted. For certain items, the turnover is quick, the amounts are large, and the maturities are short. For certain other items, such as demand deposits of a bank and customer accounts payable of a broker-dealer, the entity is substantively holding or disbursing cash on behalf of its customers. Only the net changes during the period in assets and liabilities with those characteristics need be reported because knowledge of the gross cash receipts and payments related to them may not be necessary to understand the entity's operating, investing, and financing activities. Specifically, provided that the original maturity of the asset or liability is three months or less, cash receipts and payments pertaining to investments (other than cash equivalents), loans receivable, and debt qualify for net reporting based on this rationale.

6.05 FASB ASC 830-230-45-1 specifies that the effect of exchange rate changes on cash balances held in foreign currencies be reported as a separate part of the reconciliation of the change in cash and cash equivalents during the period in the statement of cash flows. Further, a statement of cash flows of an entity with foreign exchange transactions or foreign operations should report the reporting currency equivalent of foreign currency cash flows using the exchange rates in effect at the time of the cash flows. An appropriately weighted average exchange rate for the period may be used for translation if the result is substantially the same as if the rates at the dates of the cash flows were used.

DISCLOSURE

6.06 FASB ASC 230-10-50-1 explains that an entity should disclose its policy regarding cash equivalent classification, and any change to that policy is a change in accounting principle that should be affected by restating financial statements for earlier years presented for comparative purposes. FASB ASC 230-10-50-2 specifies that if the indirect method is used, amounts of interest (net of capitalized amounts) and income tax payments during the period are required to be disclosed.

6.07 Paragraphs 3–6 of FASB ASC 230-10-50 require the disclosure of information about noncash investing and financing activities. Examples of noncash investing and financing transactions include converting debt to equity; acquiring assets by assuming directly-related liabilities, such as purchasing a building by incurring a mortgage to the seller: obtaining an asset by entering into a capital lease; obtaining a building or investment asset by receiving a gift; and exchanging noncash assets or liabilities for other noncash assets or liabilities. If only a few noncash transactions exist, it may be convenient to include them on the same page as the statement of cash flows. Otherwise, the transactions may be reported elsewhere in the financial statements and clearly referenced to the statement of cash flow.

CASH AND CASH EQUIVALENTS

6.08 LAM RESEARCH CORPORATION (JUN)
CONSOLIDATED BALANCE SHEETS (in part)

(In thousands, except per share data)

	June 24, 2012	June 26, 2011
Assets		
Cash and cash equivalents	$1,564,752	$1,492,132
Short-term investments	1,297,931	630,115
Accounts receivable, less allowance for doubtful accounts of $5,248 as of June 24, 2012 and $4,720 as of June 26, 2011	765,818	590,568
Inventories	632,853	396,607
Deferred income taxes	47,782	78,435
Prepaid expenses and other current assets	105,973	85,408
Total current assets	4,415,109	3,273,265

NOTES TO CONSOLIDATED FINANCIAL STATEMENTS

Note 4: Financial Instruments (in part)

Fair Value

The Company defines fair value as the price that would be received from selling an asset or paid to transfer a liability in an orderly transaction between market participants at the measurement date. When determining the fair value measurements for assets and liabilities required or permitted to be recorded at fair value, the Company considers the principal or most advantageous market in which it would transact, and it considers assumptions that market participants would use when pricing the asset or liability.

A fair value hierarchy has been established that prioritizes the inputs to valuation techniques used to measure fair value. The level of an asset or liability in the hierarchy is based on the lowest level of input that is significant to the fair value measurement. Assets and liabilities carried at fair value are classified and disclosed in one of the following three categories:

Level 1: Valuations based on quoted prices in active markets for identical assets or liabilities with sufficient volume and frequency of transactions.

Level 2: Valuations based on observable inputs other than Level 1 prices such as quoted prices for similar assets or liabilities, quoted prices in markets that are not active, or model-derived valuations techniques for which all significant inputs are observable in the market or can be corroborated by, observable market data for substantially the full term of the assets or liabilities.

Level 3: Valuations based on unobservable inputs to the valuation methodology that are significant to the measurement of fair value of assets or liabilities and based on non-binding, broker-provided price quotes and may not have been corroborated by observable market data.

The following table sets forth the Company's financial assets and liabilities measured at fair value on a recurring basis:

(In thousands)	Total	Fair Value Measurement at June 24, 2012 Quoted Prices in Active Markets for Identical Assets (Level 1)	Significant Other Observable Inputs (Level 2)	Significant Unobservable Inputs (Level 3)
Assets				
Short-Term Investments				
Money Market Funds	$1,318,812	$1,318,812	$ —	$—
Municipal Notes and Bonds	322,567	—	322,567	—
US Treasury and Agencies	137,446	130,624	6,822	—
Government-Sponsored Enterprises	123,268	—	123,268	—
Foreign Government Bonds	6,358	—	6,358	—
Corporate Notes and Bonds	768,901	164,885	604,016	—
Mortgage Backed Securities—Residential	25,972	—	25,972	—
Mortgage Backed Securities—Commercial	84,853	—	84,853	—
Total Short-Term Investments	$2,788,177	$1,614,321	$1,173,856	$—
Equities	5,913	5,913	—	—
Mutual Funds	17,754	17,754	—	—
Derivatives Assets	5,020		5,020	—
Total	$2,816,864	$1,637,988	$1,178,876	$—
Liabilities				
Derivative liabilities	$ 4,529	$ —	$ 4,328	$201

The amounts in the table above are reported in the consolidated balance sheet as of June 24, 2012 as follows:

Reported As:	Total	(Level 1)	(Level 2)	(Level 3)
			(In thousands)	
Cash equivalents	$1,325,361	$1,318,812	$ 6,549	$—
Short-term investments	1,297,931	130,624	1,167,307	—
Restricted cash and investments	164,885	164,885	—	—
Prepaid expenses and other current assets	5,020	—	5,020	—
Other assets	23,667	23,667	—	—
Total	$2,816,864	$1,637,988	$1,178,876	$—
Accrued expenses and other current liabilities	$ 4,529	$ —	$ 4,328	$201

The following table sets forth the Company's financial assets and liabilities measured at fair value on a recurring basis:

(In thousands)	Total	Fair Value Measurement at June 26, 2011		
		Quoted Prices in Active Markets for Identical Assets (Level 1)	Significant Other Observable Inputs (Level 2)	Significant Unobservable Inputs (Level 3)
Assets				
Short-Term Investments				
Money Market Funds	$1,300,098	$1,300,098	$ —	$—
Municipal Notes and Bonds	321,339	—	321,339	—
US Treasury and Agencies	8,496	8,496	—	—
Government-Sponsored Enterprises	19,868	—	19,868	—
Foreign Government Bonds	1,005	—	1,005	—
Corporate Notes and Bonds	382,432	164,885	217,547	—
Mortgage Backed Securities—Residential	2,633	—	2,633	—
Mortgage Backed Securities—Commercial	60,729	—	60,729	—
Total Short-Term Investments	$2,096,600	$1,473,479	$623,121	$—
Equities	7,443	7,443	—	—
Mutual Funds	19,467	19,467	—	—
Derivatives Assets	1,994	—	1,994	—
Total	$2,125,504	$1,500,389	$625,115	$—
Liabilities				
Derivative liabilities	$ 1,924	$ —	$ 1,924	$—

The amounts in the table above are reported in the consolidated balance sheet as of June 26, 2011 as follows:

Reported As:	Total	(Level 1)	(Level 2)	(Level 3)
			(In thousands)	
Cash equivalents	$1,301,600	$1,300,098	$ 1,502	$—
Short-term investments	630,115	8,496	621,619	—
Restricted cash and investments	164,885	164,885	—	—
Prepaid expenses and other current assets	1,994	—	1,994	—
Other assets	26,910	26,910	—	—
Total	$2,125,504	$1,500,389	$625,115	$—
Accrued expenses and other current liabilities	$ 1,924	$ —	$ 1,924	$—

The Company's primary financial instruments include its cash, cash equivalents, short-term investments, restricted cash and investments, long-term investments, accounts receivable, accounts payable, long-term debt and capital leases, and foreign currency related derivatives. The estimated fair value of cash, accounts receivable and accounts payable approximates their carrying value due to the short period of time to their maturities. The estimated fair values of capital lease obligations approximate their carrying value as the substantial majority of these obligations have interest rates that adjust to market rates on a periodic basis. Refer to Note 13 of the Notes to the Condensed Consolidated Financial Statements for additional information regarding the fair value of the Company's convertible notes.

Investments

The acquisition of Novellus during the quarter ended June 24, 2012 resulted in increases to cash and cash equivalents, short-term investments, and restricted cash and investments of $419 million, $641 million, and $1 million, respectively. The following tables summarize the Company's investments (in thousands):

	June 24, 2012				June 26, 2011			
	Cost	Unrealized Gain	Unrealized (Loss)	Fair Value	Cost	Unrealized Gain	Unrealized (Loss)	Fair Value
Cash	$ 240,841	$ —	$ —	$ 240,841	$ 190,903	$ —	$ —	$ 190,903
Fixed Income Money Market Funds	1,318,812	—	—	1,318,812	1,300,098	—	—	1,300,098
Municipal Notes and Bonds	321,001	1,574	(8)	322,567	319,913	1,510	(84)	321,339
US Treasury and Agencies	137,516	43	(113)	137,446	8,462	34	—	8,496
Government-Sponsored Enterprises	123,269	67	(68)	123,268	19,864	6	(2)	19,868
Foreign Government Bonds	6,315	43	—	6,358	1,004	1	—	1,005

(continued)

	June 24, 2012				June 26, 2011			
	Cost	Unrealized Gain	Unrealized (Loss)	Fair Value	Cost	Unrealized Gain	Unrealized (Loss)	Fair Value
Corporate Notes and Bonds	$ 767,847	$1,443	$ (389)	$ 768,901	$ 380,992	$1,498	$ (58)	$ 382,432
Mortgage Backed Securities—Residential	25,857	121	(6)	25,972	2,521	144	(32)	2,633
Mortgage Backed Securities—Commercial	84,682	555	(384)	84,853	60,639	277	(187)	60,729
Total Cash and Short-Term Investments	$3,026,140	$3,846	$ (968)	$3,029,018	$2,284,396	$3,470	$ (363)	$2,287,503
Publicly Traded Equity Securities	$ 9,320	$ —	$(3,407)	$ 5,913	$ 9,320	$ —	$(1,877)	$ 7,443
Private Equity Securities	5,000	—	—	5,000	—	—	—	—
Mutual Funds	17,459	366	(71)	17,754	17,975	1,492	—	19,467
Total Financial Instruments	$3,057,919	$4,212	$(4,446)	$3,057,685	$2,311,691	$4,962	$(2,240)	$2,314,413
As Reported								
Cash and Cash Equivalents	$1,564,752	$ —	$ —	$1,564,752	$1,492,132	$ —	$ —	$1,492,132
Short-Term Investments	1,295,053	3,846	(968)	1,297,931	627,008	3,470	(363)	630,115
Restricted Cash and Investments	166,335	—	—	166,335	165,256	—	—	165,256
Other Assets	31,779	366	(3,478)	28,667	27,295	1,492	(1,877)	26,910
Total	$3,057,919	$4,212	$(4,446)	$3,057,685	$2,311,691	$4,962	$(2,240)	$2,314,413

The Company accounts for its investment portfolio at fair value. Realized gains (losses) for investment sales and pay-downs are specifically identified. Management assesses the fair value of investments in debt securities that are not actively traded through consideration of interest rates and their impact on the present value of the cash flows to be received from the investments. The Company also considers whether changes in the credit ratings of the issuer could impact the assessment of fair value. Net realized gains (losses) on investments included other-than-temporary impairment charges of $1.7 million, $0 million and $0.9 million in fiscal years 2012, 2011 and 2010, respectively. Additionally, gross realized gains/(losses) from sales of investments were approximately $1.4 million and $(1.0) million in fiscal year 2012, $0.7 million and $(0.3) million in fiscal year 2011, $0.8 million and $(0.2) million in fiscal year 2010, respectively.

The following is an analysis of the Company's fixed income securities in unrealized loss positions (in thousands):

	June 24, 2012					
	Unrealized Losses Less Than 12 Months		Unrealized Losses 12 Months or Greater		Total	
	Fair Value	Unrealized	Fair Value	Unrealized	Fair Value	Unrealized
Fixed Income Securities						
Municipal Notes and Bonds	$ 28,970	$ (8)	$ —	$ —	$ 28,970	$ (8)
US Treasury and Agencies	$ 72,260	$(113)	—	—	72,260	(113)
Government-Sponsored Enterprises	83,962	(68)	—	—	83,962	(68)
Corporate Notes and Bonds	205,979	(377)	2,378	(12)	208,357	(389)
Mortgage Backed Securities—Residential	4,969	(2)	175	(4)	5,144	(6)
Mortgage Backed Securities—Commercial	43,445	(345)	1,596	(39)	45,041	(384)
Total Fixed Income	$439,585	$(913)	$4,149	$(55)	$443,734	$(968)

The amortized cost and fair value of cash equivalents, short-term investments, and restricted cash and investments with contractual maturities are as follows:

	June 24, 2012		June 26, 2011	
(In thousands)	Cost	Estimated Fair Value	Cost	Estimated Fair Value
Due in less than one year	$1,819,712	$1,820,089	$1,606,390	$1,606,925
Due in more than one year	965,587	968,088	487,103	489,675
	$2,785,299	$2,788,177	$2,093,493	$2,096,600

Management has the ability, if necessary, to liquidate any of its cash equivalents and short-term investments in order to meet the Company's liquidity needs in the next 12 months. Accordingly, those investments with contractual maturities greater than one year from the date of purchase nonetheless are classified as short-term on the accompanying Consolidated Balance Sheets.

FOREIGN CURRENCY CASH FLOWS

6.09 CONSTELLATION BRANDS, INC. (FEB)

CONSOLIDATED STATEMENTS OF CASH FLOWS (in part)

	For the Years Ended		
(In millions)	February 29, 2012	February 28, 2011	February 28, 2010
Net cash provided by operating activities	$ 784.1	$ 619.7	$ 402.6
Net cash (used in) provided by investing activities	(135.1)	188.1	256.6
Net cash used in financing activities	(575.1)	(846.1)	(623.1)
Effect of exchange rate changes on cash and cash investments	2.7	4.0	(5.7)
Net Increase (Decrease) in Cash and Cash Investments	76.6	(34.3)	30.4
Cash and Cash Investments, beginning of year	9.2	43.5	13.1
Cash and Cash Investments, end of year	$ 85.8	$ 9.2	$ 43.5

1. Summary of Significant Accounting Policies (in part)

Foreign Currency Translation—

The "functional currency" of the Company's subsidiaries outside the U.S. is the respective local currency. The translation from the applicable foreign currencies to U.S. dollars is performed for balance sheet accounts using exchange rates in effect at the balance sheet date and for revenue and expense accounts using a weighted average exchange rate for the period. The resulting translation adjustments are recorded as a component of Accumulated Other Comprehensive Income (Loss) ("AOCI"). As a result of the January 2011 CWAE Divestiture (as defined in Note 7), the Company reclassified $657.1 million, net of income tax effect, from AOCI to selling, general and administrative expenses on the Company's Consolidated Statements of Operations (see Note 7, Note 19). Gains or losses resulting from foreign currency denominated transactions are also included in selling, general and administrative expenses on the Company's Consolidated Statements of Operations. The Company engages in foreign currency denominated transactions with customers and suppliers, as well as between subsidiaries with different functional currencies. Aggregate foreign currency transaction net losses were $0.7 million, $2.3 million and $4.6 million for the years ended February 29, 2012, February 28, 2011, and February 28, 2010, respectively.

Derivative Instruments—

As a multinational company, the Company is exposed to market risk from changes in foreign currency exchange rates and interest rates that could affect the Company's results of operations and financial condition. The amount of volatility realized will vary based upon the effectiveness and level of derivative instruments outstanding during a particular period of time, as well as the currency and interest rate market movements during that same period.

The Company enters into derivative instruments, primarily interest rate swaps and foreign currency forward and option contracts, to manage interest rate and foreign currency risks. In accordance with the Financial Accounting Standards Board ("FASB") guidance for derivatives and hedging, the Company recognizes all derivatives as either assets or liabilities on its consolidated balance sheet and measures those instruments at fair value (see Note 5, Note 6). The fair values of the Company's derivative instruments change with fluctuations in interest rates and/or currency rates and are expected to offset changes in the values of the underlying exposures. The Company's derivative instruments are held solely to hedge economic exposures. The Company follows strict policies to manage interest rate and foreign currency risks, including prohibitions on derivative market-making or other speculative activities.

To qualify for hedge accounting treatment under the FASB guidance for derivatives and hedging, the details of the hedging relationship must be formally documented at inception of the arrangement, including the risk management objective, hedging strategy, hedged item, specific risk that is being hedged, the derivative instrument, how effectiveness is being assessed and how ineffectiveness will be measured. The derivative must be highly effective in offsetting either changes in the fair value or cash flows, as appropriate, of the risk being hedged. Effectiveness is evaluated on a retrospective and prospective basis based on quantitative measures.

Certain of the Company's derivative instruments do not qualify for hedge accounting treatment under the FASB guidance for derivatives and hedging; for others, the Company chooses not to maintain the required documentation to apply hedge accounting treatment. These undesignated instruments are used to economically hedge the Company's exposure to fluctuations in the value of foreign currency denominated receivables and payables; foreign currency investments, primarily consisting of loans to subsidiaries; and cash flows related primarily to repatriation of those loans or investments. Foreign currency contracts, generally less than 12 months in duration, are used to hedge some of these risks. The Company's derivative policy permits the use of undesignated derivatives when the derivative instrument is settled within the fiscal quarter or offsets a recognized balance sheet exposure. In these circumstances, the mark to fair value is reported currently through earnings in selling, general and administrative expenses on the Company's Consolidated Statements of Operations. As of February 29, 2012, and February 28, 2011, the Company had undesignated foreign currency contracts outstanding with a notional value of $148.6 million and $160.0 million, respectively. The Company had no undesignated interest rate swap agreements outstanding as of February 29, 2012, and February 28, 2011.

Furthermore, when the Company determines that a derivative instrument which qualified for hedge accounting treatment has ceased to be highly effective as a hedge, the Company discontinues hedge accounting prospectively. The Company also discontinues hedge accounting prospectively when (i) a derivative expires or is sold, terminated, or exercised; (ii) it is no longer probable that the forecasted transaction will occur; or (iii) management determines that designating the derivative as a hedging instrument is no longer appropriate.

Cash Flow Hedges:

The Company is exposed to foreign denominated cash flow fluctuations in connection with third party and intercompany sales and purchases and, historically, third party financing arrangements. The Company primarily uses foreign currency forward and option contracts to hedge certain of these risks. In addition, the Company utilizes interest rate swaps to manage its exposure to changes in interest rates. Derivatives managing the Company's cash flow exposures generally mature within three years or less, with a maximum maturity of five years. Throughout the term of the designated cash flow hedge relationship, but at least quarterly, a retrospective evaluation and prospective assessment of hedge effectiveness is performed. All components of the Company's derivative instruments' gains or losses are included in the assessment of hedge effectiveness. In the event the relationship is no longer effective, the Company recognizes the change in the fair value of the hedging derivative instrument from the date the hedging derivative instrument became no longer effective immediately in the Company's Consolidated Statements of Operations. In conjunction with its effectiveness testing, the Company also evaluates ineffectiveness associated with the hedge relationship. Resulting ineffectiveness, if any, is recognized immediately on the Company's Consolidated Statements of Operations in selling, general and administrative expenses.

The Company records the fair value of its foreign currency and interest rate swap contracts qualifying for cash flow hedge accounting treatment on its consolidated balance sheet with the effective portion of the related gain or loss on those contracts deferred in stockholders' equity (as a component of AOCI). These deferred gains or losses are recognized in the Company's Consolidated Statements of Operations in the same period in which the underlying hedged items are recognized and on the same line item as the underlying hedged items. However, to the extent that any derivative instrument is not considered to be highly effective in offsetting the change in the value of the hedged item, the hedging relationship is terminated and the amount related to the ineffective portion of such derivative instrument is immediately recognized on the Company's Consolidated Statements of Operations in selling, general and administrative expenses.

As of February 29, 2012, and February 28, 2011, the Company had cash flow designated foreign currency contracts outstanding with a notional value of $353.7 million and $166.4 million, respectively. In addition, as of February 29, 2012, and February 28, 2011, the Company had cash flow designated interest rate swap agreements outstanding with a notional value of $500.0 million (see Note 11). The Company expects $3.1 million of net losses, net of income tax effect, to be reclassified from AOCI to earnings within the next 12 months.

Fair Value Hedges:

Fair value hedges are hedges that offset the risk of changes in the fair values of recorded assets and liabilities, and firm commitments. The Company records changes in fair value of derivative instruments which are designated and deemed effective as fair value hedges, in earnings offset by the corresponding changes in the fair value of the hedged items. The Company did not designate any derivative instruments as fair value hedges for the years ended February 29, 2012, February 28, 2011, and February 28, 2010.

Net Investment Hedges:

Net investment hedges are hedges that use derivative instruments or non-derivative instruments to hedge the foreign currency exposure of a net investment in a foreign operation. Historically, the Company has managed currency exposures resulting from certain of its net investments in foreign subsidiaries principally with debt denominated in the related foreign currency. Accordingly, gains and losses on these instruments were recorded as foreign currency translation adjustments in AOCI. The Company did not designate any derivative or non-derivative instruments as net investment hedges for the years ended February 29, 2012, February 28, 2011, and February 28, 2010. As a result of the January 2011 CWAE Divestiture, the Company reclassified $17.8 million of net gains, net of income tax effect, from AOCI to earnings related to its prior net investment hedges of its U.K. subsidiary (see Note 5).

5. Derivative Instruments:

The fair value and location of the Company's derivative instruments on its Consolidated Balance Sheets are as follows (see Note 6):

Balance Sheet Location (In millions)	February 29, 2012	February 28, 2011
Derivative Instruments Designated as Hedging Instruments		
Foreign currency contracts:		
Prepaid expenses and other	$ 7.9	$11.0
Other accrued expenses and liabilities	$ 2.7	$ 3.4
Other assets, net	$ 3.6	$ 2.8
Other liabilities	$ 2.2	$ 0.9
Interest rate swap contracts:		
Other accrued expenses and liabilities	$15.0	$ 6.1
Other assets, net	—	$ 1.7
Other liabilities	$30.7	$ —
Derivative Instruments Not Designated as Hedging Instruments		
Foreign currency contracts:		
Prepaid expenses and other	$ 1.4	$ 3.2
Other accrued expenses and liabilities	$ 1.1	$ 1.0
Other assets, net	$ 0.3	$ —
Other liabilities	$ 0.4	$ —

The effect of the Company's derivative instruments designated in cash flow hedging relationships on its Consolidated Statements of Operations, as well as its Other Comprehensive Income ("OCI"), net of income tax effect, for the years ended February 29, 2012, February 28, 2011, and February 28, 2010, is as follows. As a result of the CWAE Divestiture, the Company recognized net gains of $6.3 million, net of income tax effect, for the year ended February 28, 2011, related to the discontinuance of cash flow hedge accounting due to the probability that the original forecasted transaction would not occur by the end of the originally specified time period (or within the two months following). There were no such amounts recognized for the years ended February 29, 2012, and February 28, 2010.

Derivative Instruments in Designated Cash Flow Hedging Relationships (In millions)	Net Gain (Loss) Recognized in OCI (Effective Portion)	Location of Net Gain (Loss) Reclassified From AOCI to Income (Effective Portion)	Net Gain (Loss) Reclassified From AOCI to Income (Effective Portion)
For the Year Ended February 29, 2012			
Foreign currency contracts	$ 5.8	Sales	$ 6.4
Foreign currency contracts	3.1	Cost of product sold	1.6
Interest rate swap contracts	(27.2)	Interest expense, net	(3.8)
Total	$(18.3)	Total	$ 4.2
For the Year Ended February 28, 2011			
Foreign currency contracts	$ 11.2	Sales	$ 13.6
Foreign currency contracts	0.6	Cost of product sold	9.5
Interest rate swap contracts	(2.7)	Interest expense, net	—
Total	$ 9.1	Total	$ 23.1
For the Year Ended February 28, 2010			
Foreign currency contracts	$ 39.3	Sales	$ 18.6
Foreign currency contracts	13.2	Cost of product sold	(4.6)
Foreign currency contracts	12.4	Selling, general and administrative expenses	22.8
Interest rate swap contracts	(4.7)	Interest expense, net	(27.7)
Total	$ 60.2	Total	$ 9.1

Derivative Instruments in Designated Cash Flow Hedging Relationships (In millions)	Location of Net Gain Recognized in Income (Ineffective Portion)	Net Gain Recognized in Income (Ineffective Portion)
For the Year Ended February 29, 2012		
Foreign currency contracts	Selling, general and administrative expenses	$2.2
For the Year Ended February 28, 2011		
Foreign currency contracts	Selling, general and administrative expenses	$1.4
For the Year Ended February 28, 2010		
Foreign currency contracts	Selling, general and administrative expenses	$2.5

Non-Derivative Instruments in Designated Net Investment Hedging Relationships (In millions)	Net Gain (Loss) Recognized in OCI (Effective Portion)	Location of Net Gain Reclassified From AOCI to Income (Effective Portion)	Net Gain Reclassified From AOCI to Income (Effective Portion)
For the Year Ended February 28, 2011			
Sterling Senior Debt Instrument	$—	Selling, general and administrative expenses	$17.8

The effect of the Company's undesignated derivative instruments on its Consolidated Statements of Operations for the years ended February 29, 2012, February 28, 2011, and February 28, 2010, is as follows:

Derivative Instruments Not Designated as Hedging Instruments (In millions)	Location of Net (Loss) Gain Recognized in Income	Net (Loss) Gain Recognized in Income
For the Year Ended February 29, 2012		
Foreign currency contracts	Selling, general and administrative expenses	$ (1.9)
For the Year Ended February 28, 2011		
Foreign currency contracts	Selling, general and administrative expenses	$ 4.3
For the Year Ended February 28, 2010		
Foreign currency contracts	Selling, general and administrative expenses	$12.8
Interest rate swap contracts	Interest expense, net	(0.4)
	Total	$12.4

INTEREST AND INCOME TAX PAYMENTS

6.10 SPX CORPORATION (DEC)
CONSOLIDATED STATEMENTS OF CASH FLOWS (in part)

(In millions)

	Year Ended December 31,		
	2012	**2011**	**2010**
Net cash from continuing operations	84.7	252.5	218.1
Net cash from (used in) discontinued operations	(14.9)	70.1	35.5
Net cash from operating activities	69.8	322.6	253.6

(continued)

	Year Ended December 31,		
	2012	**2011**	**2010**
Cash Flows From (used in) Investing Activities:			
Net cash used in continuing operations	(97.6)	(893.8)	(172.9)
Net cash from (used in) discontinued operations (includes net cash proceeds from dispositions of $1,133.4 and $10.1 in 2012 and 2010, respectively)	1,128.3	(50.5)	(10.2)
Net cash from (used in) investing activities	1,030.7	(944.3)	(183.1)
Cash Flows From (used in) Financing Activities:			
Net cash from (used in) continuing operations	(669.6)	713.9	(145.3)
Net cash used in discontinued operations	—	—	(1.7)
Net cash from (used in) financing activities	(669.6)	713.9	(147.0)
Change in cash and equivalents due to changes in foreign currency exchange rates	2.2	3.4	9.0
Net change in cash and equivalents	433.1	95.6	(67.5)
Consolidated cash and equivalents, beginning of period	551.0	455.4	522.9
Consolidated cash and equivalents, end of period	$ 984.1	$ 551.0	$ 455.4
Cash and equivalents of continuing operations	$ 984.1	$ 551.0	$ 455.4
Supplemental Disclosure of Cash Flow Information:			
Interest paid	$ 102.0	$ 90.1	$ 73.9
Income taxes paid, net of refunds of $10.3, $54.7 and $25.9 in 2012, 2011 and 2010, respectively	$ 59.3	$ —	$ 30.0
Non-Cash Investing and Financing Activity:			
Debt assumed	$ 61.5	$ 19.9	$ 3.9

6.11 TIME WARNER INC. (DEC)

CONSOLIDATED STATEMENT OF CASH FLOWS (in part)

(Millions)

	2012	**2011**	**2010**
Cash provided by operations from continuing operations	3,476	3,448	3,314
Cash used by operations from discontinued operations	(34)	(16)	(24)
Cash provided by operations	3,442	3,432	3,290
Cash used by investing activities	(1,246)	(1,086)	(1,436)
Cash used by financing activities	(2,831)	(2,533)	(2,924)
Decrease in cash and equivalents	(635)	(187)	(1,070)
Cash and equivalents at beginning of period	3,476	3,663	4,733
Cash and equivalents at end of period	$ 2,841	$ 3,476	$ 3,663

NOTES TO CONSOLIDATED FINANCIAL STATEMENTS

18. Additional Financial Information (in part)

Additional financial information with respect to cash payments and receipts, Interest expense, net, Other loss, net, Accounts payable and accrued liabilities and Other noncurrent liabilities is as follows (millions):

	Year Ended December 31,		
	2012	**2011**	**2010**
Cash Flows			
Cash payments made for interest	$(1,262)	$(1,119)	$(1,086)
Interest income received	42	40	26
Cash interest payments, net	$(1,220)	$(1,079)	$(1,060)
Cash payments made for income taxes	$(1,346)	$(1,174)	$ (961)
Income tax refunds received	78	95	90
TWC tax sharing payments[a]	(6)	—	(87)
Cash tax payments, net	$(1,274)	$(1,079)	$ (958)

[a] Represents net amounts paid to TWC in accordance with a tax sharing agreement with TWC.

NONCASH ACTIVITIES

6.12 HOVNANIAN ENTERPRISES, INC. (OCT)

CONSOLIDATED STATEMENTS OF CASH FLOWS (in part)

	Year Ended		
(In thousands)	October 31, 2012	October 31, 2011	October 31, 2010
Net cash (used in) provided by operating activities	(66,998)	(207,415)	32,487
Net cash (used in) provided by investing activities	(1,500)	1,195	(16)
Net cash provided by (used in) financing activities	90,990	89,780	(91,983)
Net increase (decrease) in cash and cash equivalents	22,492	(116,440)	(59,512)
Cash and cash equivalents balance, beginning of year	250,740	367,180	426,692
Cash and cash equivalents balance, end of year	$273,232	$ 250,740	$367,180
Supplemental disclosures of cash flows:			
Cash received during the year for income taxes	$ 103	$ 28,008	$253,425

Supplemental disclosure of noncash investing activities:

During fiscal 2012, we purchased our partners' interest in one of our unconsolidated homebuilding joint ventures. The consolidation of this entity resulted in increases in inventory, other assets, non-recourse land mortgages and accounts payables and other liabilities of $34.3 million, $5.0 million, $20.6 million and $15.8 million, respectively.

In fiscal 2012, we completed several debt for equity exchanges and a debt for debt exchange. See Notes 9 and 10 for further information.

In fiscal 2011, our partner in a land development joint venture transferred its interest in the venture to us. The consolidation resulted in increases in inventory and non-recourse land mortgages of $9.5 million and $18.5 million, respectively, and a decrease in other liabilities of $9.0 million.

NOTES TO CONSOLIDATED FINANCIAL STATEMENTS

9. Senior Secured, Senior, Senior Amortizing, Senior Exchangeable and Senior Subordinated Amortizing Notes (in part)

On November 3, 2003, K. Hovnanian issued $215.0 million 6.5% Senior Notes due 2014. The notes are redeemable in whole or in part at our option at 100% of their principal amount upon payment of a make-whole price. The net proceeds of the issuance were used for general corporate purposes. These notes were the subject of a November 2011 exchange offer discussed below.

On March 18, 2004, K. Hovnanian issued $150.0 million 6.375% Senior Notes due 2014. The notes are redeemable in whole or in part at our option at 100% of their principal amount upon payment of a make-whole price. The net proceeds of the issuance were used to redeem all of our $150 million outstanding 9.125% Senior Notes due 2009, which occurred on May 3, 2004, and for general corporate purposes. Also on March 18, 2004, we paid off our $115 million Term Loan with available cash. These notes were the subject of a November 2011 exchange offer discussed below.

On November 30, 2004, K. Hovnanian issued $200.0 million 6.25% Senior Notes due 2015. The notes are redeemable in whole or in part at our option at 100% of their principal amount upon payment of a make-whole price. The net proceeds of the issuance were used to repay the outstanding balance on our revolving credit facility and for general corporate purposes. These notes were the subject of a November 2011 exchange offer discussed below.

On August 8, 2005, K. Hovnanian issued $300.0 million 6.25% Senior Notes due 2016. The 6.25% Senior Notes were issued at a discount to yield 6.46% and have been reflected net of the unamortized discount in the accompanying Consolidated Balance Sheets. The notes are redeemable in whole or in part at our option at 100% of their principal amount plus the payment of a make-whole amount. The net proceeds of the issuance were used to repay the outstanding balance under our revolving credit facility as of August 8, 2005, and for general corporate purposes, including acquisitions. These notes were the subject of a November 2011 exchange offer discussed below.

On February 27, 2006, K. Hovnanian issued $300.0 million of 7.5% Senior Notes due 2016. The notes are redeemable in whole or in part at our option at 100% of their principal amount plus the payment of a make-whole amount. The net proceeds of the issuance were used to repay a portion of the outstanding balance under our revolving credit facility as of February 27, 2006. These notes were the subject of a November 2011 exchange offer discussed below.

On June 12, 2006, K. Hovnanian issued $250.0 million of 8.625% Senior Notes due 2017. The notes are redeemable in whole or in part at our option at 100% of their principal amount plus the payment of a make-whole amount. The net proceeds of the issuance were used to repay a portion of the outstanding balance under our revolving credit facility as of June 12, 2006. These notes were the subject of a November 2011 exchange offer discussed below.

On May 27, 2008, K. Hovnanian issued $600.0 million ($594.4 million net of discount) of 11.5% Senior Secured Notes due 2013. The notes were secured, subject to permitted liens and other exceptions, by a second-priority lien on substantially all of the assets owned by us, K. Hovnanian and the guarantors to the extent such assets secured obligations under the 10.625% Senior Secured Notes due 2016. A portion of the net proceeds of the issuance were used to repay the outstanding balance under the then existing amended credit facility. These second lien notes were the subject of tender offers, and notes that remained outstanding following such tender offers were subsequently redeemed, as discussed below.

On December 3, 2008, K. Hovnanian issued $29.3 million of 18.0% Senior Secured Notes due 2017 in exchange for $71.4 million of various series of our unsecured senior notes. This exchange resulted in a recognized gain on extinguishment of debt of $41.3 million, net of the write-off of unamortized discounts and fees. The notes were secured, subject to permitted liens and other exceptions, by a third-priority lien on substantially all of the assets owned by us, K. Hovnanian, and the guarantors to the extent such assets secured obligations under our 10.625% Senior Secured Notes due 2016 and 11.5% Senior Secured Notes due 2013. These third lien notes were the subject of tender offers, and notes that remained outstanding following such tender offers were subsequently redeemed, as discussed below.

On October 20, 2009, K. Hovnanian issued $785.0 million ($770.9 million net of discount) of 10.625% Senior Secured Notes due October 15, 2016. The notes were secured, subject to permitted liens and other exceptions, by a first-priority lien on substantially all of the assets owned by us, K. Hovnanian and the guarantors. The net proceeds from this issuance, together with cash on hand, were used to fund certain cash tender offers for our then outstanding 11.5% Senior Secured Notes due 2013 and 18.0% Senior Secured Notes due 2017 and certain series of our unsecured notes. In May 2011, we issued $12.0 million of additional 10.625% Senior Secured Notes as discussed below. The 10.625% Senior Secured Notes due 2016 were the subject of a tender offer in October 2012, and the notes that were not tendered in the tender offer were redeemed, as discussed below.

On January 15, 2010, the remaining $13.6 million principal amount of our 6.0% Senior Subordinated Notes due 2010 matured and was paid. During the year ended October 31, 2010, we repurchased in open market transactions $27.0 million principal amount of 6.5% Senior Notes due 2014, $54.5 million principal amount of 6.375% Senior Notes due 2014, $29.5 million principal amount of 6.25% Senior Notes due 2015, $1.4 million principal amount of 8.875% Senior Subordinated Notes due 2012, and $11.1 million principal amount of 7.75% Senior Subordinated Notes due 2013. The aggregate purchase price for these repurchases was $97.9 million, plus accrued and unpaid interest. These repurchases resulted in a gain on extinguishment of debt of $25.0 million during the year ended October 31, 2010, net of the write-off of unamortized discounts and fees.

On February 14, 2011, K. Hovnanian issued $155.0 million aggregate principal amount of 11.875% Senior Notes due 2015, which are guaranteed by us and substantially all of our subsidiaries. The Senior Notes bear interest at a rate of 11.875% per annum, which is payable semi-annually on April 15 and October 15 of each year, beginning on April 15, 2011, and mature on October 15, 2015. The 11.875% Senior Notes are redeemable in whole or in part at our option at any time at 100% of their principal amount plus an applicable "Make-Whole Amount." In addition, we may redeem up to 35% of the aggregate principal amount of the 11.875% Senior Notes prior to April 15, 2014 with the net cash proceeds from certain equity offerings at 111.875% of principal. These notes were the subject of a November 2011 exchange offer discussed below.

The net proceeds from the issuances of the 11.875% Senior Notes due in 2015, Class A Common Stock (see Note 3) and 7.25% Tangible Equity Units (see Note 10) were approximately $286.2 million, a portion of which were used to fund the purchase through tender offers, on February 14, 2011, of the following series of K. Hovnanian's senior and senior subordinated notes: approximately $24.6 million aggregate principal amount of 8.0% Senior Notes due 2012, $44.1 million aggregate principal amount of 8.875% Senior Subordinated Notes due 2012 and $29.2 million aggregate principal amount of 7.75% Senior Subordinated Notes due 2013 (the "2013 Notes" and, together with the 2012 Senior Notes and the 2012 Senior Subordinated Notes, the "Tender Offer Notes"). On February 14, 2011, K. Hovnanian called for redemption on March 15, 2011 all Tender Offer Notes that were not tendered in the tender offers for an aggregate redemption price of approximately $60.1 million. Such redemptions were funded with proceeds from the offerings of the Class A Common Stock, the Tangible Equity Units and the Senior Notes.

On May 4, 2011, K. Hovnanian issued $12.0 million of additional 10.625% Senior Secured Notes due 2016 resulting in net proceeds of approximately $11.6 million. On June 3, 2011 we used these net proceeds together with cash on hand, to fund the redemption of the remaining outstanding principal amount ($0.5 million) of our 11.5% Senior Secured Notes due 2013 and the remaining outstanding principal amount ($11.7 million) of our 18.0% Senior Secured Notes due 2017. These transactions, along with the tender offers and redemptions in February and March 2011 discussed above, resulted in a loss of $3.1 million during the year ended October 31, 2011.

During the three months ended October 31, 2011 we completed a number of open market repurchases. These included $24.6 million principal amount of 11.875% Senior Notes due 2015, and $1.0 million principal amount of 6.5% Senior Notes due 2014. The aggregate purchase price for these repurchases was $14.0 million, plus accrued and unpaid interest. These repurchases resulted in a gain on extinguishment of debt of $10.6 million, net of the write-off of unamortized discounts and fees. The gains from the repurchases are included in the Consolidated Statement of Operations as "(Loss) gain on extinguishment of debt".

On November 1, 2011, K. Hovnanian issued $141.8 million aggregate principal amount of 5.0% Senior Secured Notes due 2021 (the "5.0% 2021 Notes") and $53.2 million aggregate principal amount of 2.0% Senior Secured Notes due 2021 (the "2.0% 2021 Notes and, together with the 5.0% 2021 Notes, the "2021 Notes") in exchange for $195.0 million of K. Hovnanian's unsecured senior notes with maturities ranging from 2014 through 2017. Holders of the senior notes due 2014 and 2015 that were exchanged in the exchange offer also received an aggregate of approximately $14.2 million in cash payments and all holders of senior notes that were exchanged in the exchange offer received accrued and unpaid interest (in the aggregate amount of approximately $3.3 million). Costs associated with this transaction were $4.7 million. The 5.0% 2021 Notes and the 2.0% 2021 Notes were issued as separate series under an indenture, but have substantially the same terms other than with respect to interest rate and related redemption provisions, and vote together as a single class. The 2021 Notes are redeemable in whole or in part at our option at any time, at 100.0% of the principal amount plus the greater of 1% of the principal amount and an applicable "Make-Whole Amount." In addition, we may redeem up to 35% of the aggregate principal amount of the notes before November 1, 2014 with the net cash proceeds from certain equity offerings at 105.0% (in the case of the 5.0% Secured Notes) and 102.0% (in the case of the 2.0% Secured Notes) of principal. The accounting for the debt exchange was treated as a troubled debt restructuring. Under this accounting, the Company did not recognize any gain or loss on extinguishment of debt and the costs associated with the debt exchange were expensed as incurred as shown in "Other operations" in the Consolidated Statement of Operations.

The guarantees with respect to the 2021 Notes of the Secured Group are secured, subject to permitted liens and other exceptions, by a first-priority lien on substantially all of the assets of the members of the Secured Group. As of October 31, 2012, the collateral securing the guarantees primarily included (1) $51.1 million of cash and cash equivalents and (2) equity interests in guarantors that are members of the Secured Group. Subsequent to such date, cash uses include general business operations and real estate and other investments. The aggregate book value of the real-property of the Secured Group collateralizing the 2021 Notes was approximately $37.5 million as of October 31, 2012 (not including the impact of inventory investments, home deliveries, or impairments thereafter and which may differ from the appraised value). Members of the Secured Group also own equity in joint ventures, either directly or indirectly through ownership of joint venture holding companies, with a book value of $45.9 million as of October 31, 2012; this equity is not pledged to secure, and is not collateral for, the 2021 Notes. Members of the Secured Group are "unrestricted subsidiaries" under K. Hovnanian's other senior notes, senior secured notes, senior amortizing notes, senior exchangeable notes and senior subordinated amortizing notes, and thus have not guaranteed such indebtedness.

In addition, on November 1, 2011, K. Hovnanian entered into a Second Supplemental Indenture (the "11.875% Notes Supplemental Indenture"), among K. Hovnanian, the Company, as guarantor, the other guarantors party thereto and Wilmington Trust Company, as trustee, amending and supplementing that certain Indenture dated February 14, 2011 (the "Base Indenture") by and among K. Hovnanian, the Company, as guarantor, and Wilmington Trust Company, as trustee, as amended by the First Supplemental Indenture dated as of February 14, 2011 (the "First Supplemental Indenture"), by and among K. Hovnanian, the Company, as guarantor, the other guarantors party thereto and Wilmington Trust Company, as trustee (the Base Indenture as amended by the First Supplemental Indenture, the "Existing Indenture"). The 11.875% Notes Supplemental Indenture was executed and delivered following the receipt by K. Hovnanian of consents from a majority of the holders of K. Hovnanian's 11.875% Senior Notes due 2015. The 11.875% Notes Supplemental Indenture provides for the elimination of substantially all of the restrictive covenants and certain of the default provisions contained in the Existing Indenture and the 11.875% Senior Notes due 2015.

On October 2, 2012, K. Hovnanian issued $577.0 million aggregate principal amount of 7.25% senior secured first lien notes due 2020 (the "First Lien Notes") and $220.0 million aggregate principal amount of 9.125% senior secured second lien notes due 2020 (the "Second Lien Notes" and, together with the First Lien Notes, the "2020 Secured Notes") in a private placement (the "2020 Secured Notes Offering"). The net proceeds from the 2020 Secured Notes Offering, together with the net proceeds of the Units offering discussed below, and cash on hand, were used to fund the tender offer and consent solicitation with respect to the Company's then outstanding 10.625% Senior Secured Notes due 2016 and the redemption of the remaining notes that were not purchased in the tender offer as described below.

The First Lien Notes are secured by a first-priority lien and the Second Lien Notes are secured by a second-priority lien, in each case, subject to permitted liens and other exceptions, on substantially all the assets owned by us, K. Hovnanian and the guarantors of such notes. At October 31, 2012, the aggregate book value of the real property that would constitute collateral securing the 2020 Secured Notes was approximately $572.4 million, which does not include the impact of inventory investments, home deliveries, or impairments thereafter and which may differ from the value if it were appraised. In addition, cash collateral that would secure the 2020 Secured Notes was $236.8 million as of October 31, 2012, which includes $30.7 million of restricted cash collateralizing certain letters of credit. Subsequent to such date, cash uses include general business operations and real estate and other investments.

The First Lien Notes are redeemable in whole or in part at our option at any time prior to October 15, 2015 at 100% of the principal amount plus an applicable "Make-Whole Amount." We may also redeem some of all of the First Lien Notes at 105.438% of principal commencing October 15, 2015, at 103.625% of principal commencing October 15, 2016, at 101.813% of principal commencing October 15, 2017 and 100% of principal commencing October 15, 2018. In addition, we may redeem up to 35% of the aggregate principal amount of the First Lien Notes prior to October 15, 2015 with the net cash proceeds from certain equity offerings at 107.25% of principal.

The Second Lien Notes are redeemable in whole or in part at our option at any time prior to November 15, 2015 at 100% of the principal amount plus an applicable "Make-Whole Amount." We may also redeem some of all of the Second Lien Notes at 106.844% of principal commencing November 15, 2015, at 104.563% of principal commencing November 15, 2016, at 102.281% of principal commencing November 15, 2017 and 100% of principal commencing November 15, 2018. In addition, we may redeem up to 35% of the aggregate principal amount of the Second Lien Notes prior to November 15, 2015 with the net cash proceeds from certain equity offerings at 109.125% of principal.

Also on October 2, 2012, the Company and K. Hovnanian issued $100,000,000 aggregate stated amount of 6.0% Exchangeable Note Units (the "Units") (equivalent to 100,000 Units). Each $1,000 stated amount of Units initially consists of (1) a zero coupon senior exchangeable note due December 1, 2017 (the "Exchangeable Note") issued by K. Hovnanian, which bears no cash interest and has an initial principal amount of $768.51 per Exchangeable Note, and that will accrete to $1,000 at maturity and (2) a senior amortizing note due December 1, 2017 (the "Senior Amortizing Note") issued by K. Hovnanian, which has an initial principal amount of $231.49 per Senior Amortizing Note, bears interest at a rate of 11.0% per annum, and has a final installment payment date of

December 1, 2017. Each Unit may be separated into its constituent Exchangeable Note and Senior Amortizing Note after the initial issuance date of the Units, and the separate components may be combined to create a Unit.

Each Exchangeable Note had an initial principal amount of $768.51 (which will accrete to $1,000 over the term of the Exchangeable Note at an annual rate of 5.17% from the date of issuance, calculated on a semi-annual bond equivalent yield basis). Holders may exchange their Exchangeable Notes at their option at any time prior to 5:00 p.m., New York City time, on the business day immediately preceding December 1, 2017. Each Exchangeable Note will be exchangeable for shares of Class A Common Stock at an initial exchange rate of 185.5288 shares of Class A Common Stock per Exchangeable Note (equivalent to an initial exchange price, based on $1,000 principal amount at maturity, of approximately $5.39 per share of Class A Common Stock). The exchange rate will be subject to adjustment in certain events. Following certain corporate events that occur prior to the maturity date, the Company will increase the applicable exchange rate for any holder who elects to exchange its Exchangeable Notes in connection with such corporate event. In addition, holders of Exchangeable Notes will also have the right to require K. Hovnanian to repurchase such holders' Exchangeable Notes upon the occurrence of certain of these corporate events.

On each June 1 and December 1 commencing on June 1, 2013 (each, an "installment payment date") K. Hovnanian will pay holders of Senior Amortizing Notes equal semi-annual cash installments of $30.00 per Senior Amortizing Note (except for the June 1, 2013 installment payment, which will be $39.83 per Senior Amortizing Note), which cash payment in the aggregate will be equivalent to 6.0% per year with respect to each $1,000 stated amount of Units. Each installment will constitute a payment of interest (at a rate of 11.0% per annum) and a partial repayment of principal on the Senior Amortizing Note. Following certain corporate events that occur prior to the maturity date, holders of the Senior Amortizing Notes will have the right to require K. Hovnanian to repurchase such holders' Senior Amortizing Notes.

The net proceeds of the Units Offering, along with the net proceeds from the 2020 Secured Notes Offering previously discussed, and cash on hand, were used to fund the tender offer and consent solicitation with respect to the Company's then outstanding 10.625% Senior Secured Notes due 2016 and redemption of the remaining notes that were not purchased in the tender offer as described below.

On October 2, 2012, pursuant to a cash tender offer and consent solicitation, we purchased in a fixed-price tender offer approximately $637.2 million aggregate principal amount of 10.625% Senior Secured Notes due 2016 for approximately $691.3 million, plus accrued and unpaid interest. Subsequently, all 10.625% Senior Secured Notes due 2016 that were not tendered in the tender offer (approximately $159.8 million) were redeemed for an aggregate redemption price of approximately $181.8 million. The tender offer and redemption resulted in a loss on extinguishment of debt of $87.0 million, including of the write-off of unamortized discounts and fees.

During the year ended October 31, 2012, we repurchased for cash in the open market and privately negotiated transactions $21.0 million principal amount of our 6.25% Senior Notes due 2016, $61.1 million principal amount of our 7.5% Senior Notes due 2016, $37.4 million principal amount of our 8.625% Senior Notes due 2017 and $2.0 million principal amount of our 11.875% Senior Notes due 2015. No such repurchases were made during the quarter ended October 31, 2012. The aggregate purchase price for these repurchases was $72.2 million, plus accrued and unpaid interest. These repurchases resulted in a gain on extinguishment of debt of $48.4 million for the year ended October 31, 2012, net of the write-off of unamortized discounts and fees. The gain is included in the Consolidated Statement of Operations as "(Loss) gain on extinguishment of debt." Certain of these repurchases were funded with the proceeds from our April 11, 2012 issuance of 25,000,000 shares of our Class A Common Stock (see Note 3).

In addition, during the year ended October 31, 2012, pursuant to agreements with bondholders we exchanged $7.8 million principal amount of our 6.25% Senior Notes due 2016, $4.0 million principal amount of our 7.5% Senior Notes due 2016 and $18.3 million of our outstanding 8.625% Senior Notes due 2017 for shares of our Class A Common Stock, as discussed in Note 3. These transactions were treated as a substantial modification of debt, resulting in a gain on extinguishment of debt of $9.3 million for the year ended October 31, 2012. No such exchanges were made during the quarter ended October 31, 2012. The gain is included in the Consolidated Statement of Operations as "(Loss) gain on extinguishment of debt."

10. Tangible Equity Units

On February 9, 2011, we issued an aggregate of 3,000,000 7.25% Tangible Equity Units (the "Units"), and on February 14, 2011, we issued an additional 450,000 Units pursuant to the over-allotment option granted to the underwriters. Each Unit initially consists of (i) a prepaid stock purchase contract (each a "Purchase Contract") and (ii) a senior subordinated amortizing note due February 15, 2014 (each, a "Senior Subordinated Amortizing Note"). As of October 31, 2012 and 2011, we had an aggregate principal amount of $6.1 million and $13.3 million, respectively, of Senior Subordinated Amortizing Notes outstanding. On each February 15, May 15, August 15 and November 15, K. Hovnanian will pay holders of Senior Subordinated Amortizing Notes equal quarterly cash installments of $0.453125 per Senior Subordinated Amortizing Note, which cash payments in the aggregate will be equivalent to 7.25% per year with respect to each $25 stated amount of Units. Each installment constitutes a payment of interest (at a rate of 12.072% per annum) and a partial repayment of principal on the Senior Subordinated Amortizing Notes, allocated as set forth in the amortization schedule provided in the indenture under which the Senior Subordinated Amortizing Notes were issued. The Senior Subordinated Amortizing Notes have a scheduled final installment payment date of February 15, 2014. If we elect to settle the Purchase Contracts early, holders of the Senior Subordinated Amortizing Notes will have the right to require K. Hovnanian to repurchase such holders' Senior Subordinated Amortizing Notes, except in certain circumstances as described in the indenture governing Senior Subordinated Amortizing Notes.

Unless settled earlier, on February 15, 2014 (subject to postponement under certain circumstances), each Purchase Contract will automatically settle and we will deliver a number of shares of Class A Common Stock based on the applicable market value, as defined in the purchase contract agreement, which will be between 4.7655 shares and 5.8140 shares per Purchase Contract (subject to adjustment). Each Unit may be separated into its constituent Purchase Contract and Senior Subordinated Amortizing Note after the initial issuance date of the Units, and the separate components may be combined to create a Unit. The Senior Subordinated Amortizing Note component of the Units is recorded as debt, and the Purchase Contract component of the Units is recorded in equity as additional paid in capital. We have recorded $68.1 million, the initial fair value of the Purchase Contracts, as additional paid in capital. As of October 31, 2012, 1.6 million Purchase Contracts have been converted into 7.7 million shares of our Class A Common Stock.

During the second quarter of fiscal 2012, we exchanged pursuant to agreements with bondholders approximately $3.1 million aggregate principal amount of our Senior Subordinated Amortizing Notes for shares of our Class A Common Stock, as discussed in Note 3. These transactions resulted in a gain on extinguishment of debt of $0.2 million for the year ended October 31, 2012.

Cash Flows From Operating Activities

PRESENTATION

6.13 FASB ASC 230-10-45 defines those transactions and events that constitute operating cash receipts and payments. Cash inflows from operating activities include the following:
- Cash receipts from sales of goods or services, including receipts from the collection or sale of accounts and both short- and long-term notes receivable from customers arising from those sales. Goods include certain loans and other debt and equity instruments of other entities that are acquired specifically for resale.
- Cash receipts from returns on loans, other debt instruments of other entities, and equity securities—interest and dividends.
- All other cash receipts that do not stem from transactions defined as investing or financing activities, such as amounts received to settle lawsuits; proceeds of insurance settlements, except for those that are directly related to investing or financing activities, such as destruction of a building; and refunds from suppliers.
- Cash outflows from operating activities include the following: Cash payments to acquire materials for manufacture or goods for resale, including principal payments on accounts and both short- and long-term notes payable to suppliers for those materials or goods. Goods include certain loans and other debt and equity instruments of other entities that are acquired specifically for resale.
- Cash payments to other suppliers and employees for other goods or services.
- Cash payments to governments for taxes, duties, fines, and other fees or penalties and the cash that would have been paid for income taxes if increases in the value of equity instruments issued under share-based payment arrangements that are not included in the cost of goods or services recognizable for financial reporting purposes also had not been deductible in determining taxable income.
- Cash payments to lenders and other creditors for interest.
- Cash payment made to settle an asset retirement obligation.
- All other cash payments that do not stem from transactions defined as investing or financing activities, such as payments to settle lawsuits, cash contributions to charities, and cash refunds to customers.

6.14 Entities can present operating activities using either the direct or indirect method. However, FASB ASC 230-10-45-30 also requires entities using the direct method to provide a reconciliation of net income to net cash flow from operating activities in a separate schedule.

6.15 FASB ASC 230-10-45-28 also notes that when reconciling net income to net cash flow from operating activities, a business entity should adjust net income to remove past operating cash receipts and payments and accruals of expected future operating cash receipts and payments, including changes during the period in inventory and receivables and payables pertaining to operating activities. Additionally, all items that are included in net income, such as depreciation and amortization expense, that do not affect net cash provided from, or used for, operating activities should be adjusted for.

DIRECT METHOD

6.16 CVS CAREMARK CORPORATION (DEC)
CONSOLIDATED STATEMENTS OF CASH FLOWS

(In millions)	2012	2011	2010
Cash Flows From Operating Activities:			
Cash receipts from customers	$113,205	$ 97,688	$ 94,503
Cash paid for inventory and prescriptions dispensed by retail network pharmacies	(90,032)	(75,148)	(73,143)
Cash paid to other suppliers and employees	(13,643)	(13,635)	(13,778)
Interest received	4	4	4
Interest paid	(581)	(647)	(583)
Income taxes paid	(2,282)	(2,406)	(2,224)
Net cash provided by operating activities	6,671	5,856	4,779
Cash Flows From Investing Activities:			
Purchases of property and equipment	(2,030)	(1,872)	(2,005)
Proceeds from sale-leaseback transactions	529	592	507
Proceeds from sale of property and equipment	23	4	34
Acquisitions (net of cash acquired) and other investments	(378)	(1,441)	(177)
Purchase of available-for-sale investments	—	(3)	—
Maturity of available-for-sale investments	—	60	1
Proceeds from sale of subsidiary	7	250	—
Net cash used in investing activities	(1,849)	(2,410)	(1,640)
Cash Flows From Financing Activities:			
Increase (decrease) in short-term debt	(60)	450	(15)
Proceeds from issuance of long-term debt	1,239	1,463	991
Repayments of long-term debt	(1,718)	(2,122)	(2,103)
Purchase of noncontrolling interest in subsidiary	(26)	—	—
Dividends paid	(829)	(674)	(479)
Derivative settlements	—	(19)	(5)
Proceeds from exercise of stock options	836	431	285
Excess tax benefits from stock-based compensation	28	21	28
Repurchase of common stock	(4,330)	(3,001)	(1,500)
Other	—	(9)	—
Net cash used in financing activities	(4,860)	(3,460)	(2,798)
Net increase (decrease) in cash and cash equivalents	(38)	(14)	341
Cash and cash equivalents at the beginning of the year	1,413	1,427	1,086
Cash and cash equivalents at the end of the year	$ 1,375	$ 1,413	$ 1,427
Reconciliation of Net Income to Net Cash Provided by Operating Activities:			
Net income	$ 3,875	$ 3,457	$ 3,424
Adjustments required to reconcile net income to net cash provided by operating activities:			
Depreciation and amortization	1,753	1,568	1,469
Stock-based compensation	132	135	150
Loss on early extinguishment of debt	348	—	—
Gain on sale of subsidiary	—	(53)	—
Deferred income taxes and other noncash items	(106)	144	30
Change in operating assets and liabilities, net of effects from acquisitions:			
Accounts receivable, net	(387)	(748)	532
Inventories	(858)	607	(352)
Other current assets	3	(420)	(4)
Other assets	(99)	(49)	(210)
Accounts payable and claims and discounts payable	1,147	1,128	(40)
Accrued expenses	753	85	(176)
Other long-term liabilities	110	2	(44)
Net cash provided by operating activities	$ 6,671	$ 5,856	$ 4,779

6.17 IDT CORPORATION (JUL)
CONSOLIDATED STATEMENTS OF CASH FLOWS

(In thousands)	Year Ended July 31 2012	2011	2010
Operating Activities			
Net income	$ 38,785	$ 23,371	$ 20,273
Adjustments to reconcile net income to net cash provided by operating activities:			
Net income from discontinued operations	(3,015)	(945)	(13,701)
Depreciation and amortization	16,648	20,952	33,341
Severance and other payments	—	(2,978)	(2,457)
Deferred income taxes	(37,925)	(2,130)	(690)
Provision for doubtful accounts receivable	2,098	3,310	3,769
Gain on sale of wireless spectrum	(5,330)	—	—
Net realized gains from marketable securities	—	(5,379)	(336)
Gain on proceeds from insurance	—	(2,637)	—
Gain on sales of buildings	—	—	(675)
Interest in the equity of investments	(1,157)	57	1,865
Stock-based compensation	3,325	4,081	2,226
Change in assets and liabilities:			
Trade accounts receivable	8,754	(25,017)	28,636
Prepaid expenses, other current assets and other assets	(2,105)	(1,784)	(10,293)
Trade accounts payable, accrued expenses, other current liabilities and other liabilities	9,947	38,657	(27,320)
Customer deposits	9,057	130	(200)
Income taxes payable	(4,701)	(1,430)	1,904
Deferred revenue	6,780	8,115	3,003
Net cash provided by operating activities	41,161	56,373	39,345
Investing Activities			
Capital expenditures	(10,830)	(13,300)	(8,163)
(Repayment) collection of notes receivable, net	—	(88)	130
Increase in investments	—	(3,015)	(400)
Proceeds from sales and redemptions of investments	3,169	2,446	2,762
(Increase) decrease in restricted cash and cash equivalents	(5,733)	(5,011)	44,165
Proceeds from sale of wireless spectrum	6,800	—	—
Proceeds from sales of buildings	—	100	5,270
Proceeds from insurance	—	3,524	500
Proceeds from marketable securities	—	5,731	4,618
Purchases of certificates of deposit	—	(5,503)	—
Proceeds from maturities of certificates of deposit	3,540	2,258	—
Net cash (used in) provided by investing activities	(3,054)	(12,858)	48,882
Financing Activities			
Cash of subsidiaries deconsolidated as a result of spin-offs	(104,243)	—	(9,775)
Dividends paid	(15,014)	(15,178)	—
Distributions to noncontrolling interests	(1,580)	(2,010)	(1,939)
Proceeds from sales of stock of subsidiary	133	—	290
Proceeds from exercise of stock options	—	1,674	90
Repayments of capital lease obligations	(1,781)	(4,821)	(5,955)
Repayments of borrowings	(332)	(4,602)	(622)
Repurchases of Class B common stock from Howard S. Jonas	—	(7,499)	—
Repurchases of common stock and Class B common stock	(2,816)	(205)	(1,879)
Net cash used in financing activities	(125,633)	(32,641)	(19,790)
Discontinued Operations			
Net cash (used in) provided by operating activities	(889)	5,476	17,788
Net cash (used in) provided by investing activities	(2,048)	(3,786)	6,815
Net cash provided by financing activities	—	8,472	4,929
Net cash (used in) provided by discontinued operations	(2,937)	10,162	29,532
Effect of exchange rate changes on cash and cash equivalents	(2,334)	1,512	(598)
Net (decrease) increase in cash and cash equivalents	(92,797)	22,548	97,371
Cash and cash equivalents (including discontinued operations) at beginning of year	244,301	221,753	124,382
Cash and cash equivalents (including discontinued operations) at end of year	151,504	244,301	221,753
Less cash and cash equivalents of discontinued operations at end of year	—	(23,875)	(13,142)
Cash and cash equivalents (excluding discontinued operations) at end of year	$ 151,504	$ 220,426	$ 208,611
Supplemental Disclosure of Cash Flow Information			
Cash payments made for interest	$ 3,621	$ 5,008	$ 4,822
Cash payments made for income taxes	$ 1,049	$ 4,235	$ 4,898
Supplemental Schedule of Non-Cash Financing and Investing Activities			
Mortgage notes payable settled in connection with the sales of buildings	$ —	$ —	$ 8,837
Net assets excluding cash and cash equivalents of subsidiaries deconsolidated as a result of spin-offs	$ 18,803	$ —	$ 6,011

6.18 ALLIANT TECHSYSTEMS INC. (DEC)

CONSOLIDATED STATEMENTS OF CASH FLOWS (in part)

	Years Ended March 31		
(Amounts in thousands)	2012	2011	2010
Operating Activities			
Net income	$ 263,204	$ 313,711	$278,944
Adjustments to net income to arrive at cash provided by operating activities:			
Depreciation	98,037	100,041	93,739
Amortization of intangible assets	10,848	11,145	6,091
Amortization of debt discount	12,293	17,168	19,867
Amortization of deferred financing costs	4,764	5,157	2,839
Trade name impairments	—	—	38,008
Other asset impairment	—	—	11,405
Deferred income taxes	7,518	23,018	(3,338)
(Gain) loss on disposal of property	(2,928)	2,281	5,756
Share-based plans expense	6,724	9,740	16,664
Excess tax benefits from share-based plans	(23)	(540)	(1,691)
Changes in assets and liabilities:			
Net receivables	(207,451)	(153,723)	(81,279)
Net inventories	(16,466)	(6,400)	57
Accounts payable	42,557	20,065	(16,221)
Contract advances and allowances	(2,103)	15,108	20,739
Accrued compensation	(25,063)	(53,616)	800
Accrued income taxes	19,801	(40,164)	59,154
Pension and other postretirement benefits	37,547	86,955	(241,560)
Other assets and liabilities	123,048	71,124	(16,312)
Cash provided by operating activities	372,307	421,070	193,662

ADJUSTMENTS TO RECONCILE NET INCOME—GAIN/LOSS ON DISCONTINUED OPERATIONS/SALE OF BUSINESS

6.19 CABOT CORPORATION (SEP)

CONSOLIDATED STATEMENTS OF CASH FLOWS (in part)

	Years Ended September 30		
(In millions)	2012	2011	2010
Cash Flows From Operating Activities:			
Net income	$406	$258	$169
Adjustments to reconcile net income to cash provided by operating activities:			
Depreciation and amortization	156	144	143
Deferred tax provision	(6)	(25)	(2)
Gain on sale of business, net of tax	(191)	—	—
Impairment charges	—	—	2
Loss on disposal of property, plant and equipment	1	2	6
Equity in earnings of affiliated companies	(11)	(8)	(7)
Non-cash compensation	18	19	27
Other non-cash (income) charges, net	3	(3)	(5)
Changes in assets and liabilities:			
Accounts and notes receivable	6	(111)	(116)
Inventories	(30)	(79)	(7)
Prepaid expenses and other current assets	26	(17)	(18)
Accounts payable and accrued liabilities	100	23	47
Income taxes payable	(13)	1	7
Other liabilities	(38)	(12)	(7)
Cash dividends received from equity affiliates	6	4	6
Other	(18)	(1)	4
Cash provided by operating activities	415	195	249

ADJUSTMENTS TO RECONCILE NET INCOME—RESTRUCTURING EXPENSE

6.20 SPECTRUM BRANDS HOLDINGS, INC. (SEP)
CONSOLIDATED STATEMENTS OF CASH FLOWS (in part)

Years ended September 30, 2012, 2011 and 2010

(In thousands)

	2012	2011	2010
Cash Flows From Operating Activities:			
Net income (loss)	$48,572	$(75,171)	$(190,107)
Loss from discontinued operations, net of tax	—	—	(2,735)
Income (loss) from continuing operations	48,572	(75,171)	(187,372)
Adjustments to reconcile net income (loss) to net cash provided by operating activities:			
Depreciation	40,950	47,065	54,822
Amortization of intangibles	63,666	57,695	45,920
Amortization of unearned restricted stock compensation	29,164	30,389	16,676
Amortization of debt issuance costs	9,922	13,198	9,030
Intangible asset impairment	—	32,450	—
Administrative related reorganization items	—	—	3,646
Payments for administrative related reorganization items	—	—	(47,173)
Non-cash increase to cost of goods sold due to fresh-start reporting inventory valuation	—	—	34,865
Non-cash interest expense on 12% Notes	—	—	24,555
Write off of unamortized (premium) discount on retired debt	(466)	8,950	59,162
Write off of debt issuance costs	2,946	15,420	6,551
Non-cash restructuring and related charges	5,195	15,143	16,359
Non-cash debt accretion	722	4,773	18,302
Changes in assets and liabilities:			
Accounts receivable	22,892	12,969	12,702
Inventories	(11,642)	96,406	(66,127)
Prepaid expenses and other current assets	561	815	2,025
Accounts payable and accrued liabilities	1,424	(60,505)	86,497
Deferred taxes and other	40,909	27,792	(21,881)
Net cash provided by operating activities of continuing operations	254,815	227,389	68,559
Net cash used by operating activities of discontinued operations	—	—	(11,221)
Net cash provided by operating activities	254,815	227,389	57,338

ADJUSTMENTS TO RECONCILE NET INCOME—CASH SURRENDER VALUE

6.21 JACK IN THE BOX INC. (SEP)
CONSOLIDATED STATEMENTS OF CASH FLOWS (in part)

(Dollars in thousands)

	Fiscal Year		
	2012	2011	2010
Cash Flows From Operating Activities:			
Net earnings	$ 57,651	$ 80,600	$ 70,210
Adjustments to reconcile net earnings to net cash provided by operating activities:			
Depreciation and amortization	97,958	96,147	101,514
Deferred finance cost amortization	2,695	2,554	1,658
Deferred income taxes	(6,615)	(12,832)	(27,554)
Share-based compensation expense	6,883	8,062	10,605
Pension and postretirement expense	33,526	23,845	29,140
Losses (gains) on cash surrender value of company-owned life insurance	(12,137)	1,094	(6,199)
Gains on the sale of company-operated restaurants	(29,145)	(61,125)	(54,988)
Gains on the acquisition of franchise-operated restaurants	—	(426)	—
Losses on the disposition of property and equipment	6,281	7,650	10,757
Impairment charges and other	9,403	1,367	12,970
Loss on early retirement of debt	—	—	513
Changes in assets and liabilities, excluding acquisitions and dispositions:			
Accounts and other receivables	3,497	(26,116)	(8,174)
Inventories	4,334	(1,540)	284
Prepaid expenses and other current assets	(12,849)	19,163	(22,967)
Accounts payable	(3,264)	1,498	(2,219)
Accrued liabilities	247	2,446	(36,934)
Pension and postretirement contributions	(20,318)	(4,790)	(24,072)
Other	(1,417)	(13,337)	7,322
Cash flows provided by operating activities	136,730	124,260	61,866

ADJUSTMENTS TO RECONCILE NET INCOME—DEFERRED TAXES

6.22 THE BON-TON STORES, INC. (JAN)
CONSOLIDATED STATEMENTS OF CASH FLOWS (in part)

(In thousands)	Fiscal Year Ended		
	January 28, 2012	January 29, 2011	January 30, 2010
Cash Flows From Operating Activities:			
Net (loss) income	$(12,128)	$ 21,494	$ (4,055)
Adjustments to reconcile net (loss) income to net cash provided by operating activities:			
Depreciation and amortization	95,033	102,202	111,635
Amortization of lease-related interests	4,747	4,555	4,866
Impairment charges	3,690	1,738	5,883
Share-based compensation expense	5,261	7,795	5,082
(Gain) loss on sale of property, fixtures and equipment	(91)	(2,064)	101
Reclassifications of other comprehensive loss	3,216	7,470	10,651
(Gain) loss on extinguishment of debt	(8,729)	—	678
Amortization of deferred financing costs	8,690	9,323	5,551
Amortization of deferred gain on sale of proprietary credit card portfolio	(2,414)	(2,414)	(2,414)
Deferred income tax (benefit) provision	(2,500)	1,605	4,183
Changes in operating assets and liabilities:			
(Increase) decrease in merchandise inventories	(17,180)	(22,926)	6,683
Decrease in prepaid expenses and other current assets	9,386	9,272	25,751
Decrease in other long-term assets	396	2,617	1,655
Increase in accounts payable	23,405	6,045	22,655
Decrease in accrued payroll and benefits and accrued expenses	(21,307)	(1,391)	(5,071)
(Decrease) increase in income taxes payable	(137)	137	(62)
Increase (decrease) in other long-term liabilities	10,459	(4,323)	262
Net cash provided by operating activities	99,797	141,135	194,034

ADJUSTMENTS TO RECONCILE NET INCOME—PROVISION FOR LOSSES ON ACCOUNTS RECEIVABLE

6.23 VALASSIS COMMUNICATIONS, INC. (DEC)
CONSOLIDATED STATEMENTS OF CASH FLOWS (in part)

(U.S. dollars in thousands)

	Year Ended December 31,		
	2012	2011	2010
Cash Flows From Operating Activities:			
Net earnings	$118,985	$113,430	$385,405
Adjustments to reconcile net earnings to net cash provided by operating activities:			
Depreciation and amortization	57,955	60,708	61,446
Amortization of debt issuance costs	1,847	3,028	2,353
Provision for losses on accounts receivable	821	4,024	10,138
Goodwill impairment	7,585	—	—
Loss on extinguishment of debt	—	5,748	3,429
(Gain) loss on derivatives, net	(1,251)	6,326	18,816
Loss (gain) on sale of property, plant and equipment	727	72	(47)
Stock-based compensation expense	13,908	12,908	32,125
Deferred income taxes	(9,448)	(7,951)	(3,520)
Intangible asset impairment	—	7,134	—
Changes in assets and liabilities:			
Accounts receivable, net	26,148	7,608	(41,254)
Inventories	(2,133)	867	(1,515)
Prepaid expenses and other	2,299	(221)	4,297
Other assets	448	(532)	(1,259)
Accounts payable	(54,769)	4,776	(8,817)
Progress billings	(380)	(13,026)	12,469
Accrued expenses	(8,225)	(7,194)	(18,262)
Other non-current liabilities	(8,478)	2,536	7,522
Total adjustments	27,054	86,811	77,921
Net cash provided by operating activities	146,039	200,241	463,326

6.24 AIR PRODUCTS AND CHEMICALS, INC. (SEP)

CONSOLIDATED STATEMENTS OF CASH FLOWS (in part)

		Year Ended 30 September	
(Millions of dollars)	2012	2011	2010
Operating Activities			
Net Income	$1,193.3	$1,261.5	$1,054.5
Less: Net income attributable to noncontrolling interests	26.0	37.3	25.4
Net income attributable to Air Products	1,167.3	1,224.2	1,029.1
Income from discontinued operations	(168.1)	(89.9)	(87.5)
Income from continuing operations attributable to Air Products	999.2	1,134.3	941.6
Adjustments to reconcile income to cash provided by operating activities:			
Depreciation and amortization	840.8	834.3	826.8
Deferred income taxes	65.2	185.7	89.1
Benefit from Spanish tax ruling	(58.3)	—	—
Gain on previously held equity interest	(85.9)	—	—
Undistributed earnings of unconsolidated affiliates	(53.6)	(47.5)	(50.6)
Gain on sale of assets and investments	(8.4)	(14.6)	(16.4)
Share-based compensation	43.8	44.8	48.6
Noncurrent capital lease receivables	(282.5)	(272.5)	(85.6)
Net loss on Airgas transaction	—	48.5	96.0
Payment of Airgas acquisition-related costs	—	(156.2)	(12.0)
Write-down of long-lived assets associated with restructuring/customer bankruptcy	80.2	—	—
Other adjustments	124.5	68.2	10.1
Working capital changes that provided (used) cash, excluding effects of acquisitions and divestitures:			
Trade receivables	(55.1)	(53.8)	(104.9)
Inventories	1.3	(107.5)	(62.9)
Contracts in progress, less progress billings	(42.9)	16.7	(33.9)
Other receivables	(18.3)	8.0	35.2
Payables and accrued liabilities	249.7	(29.8)	(281.3)
Other working capital	(34.6)	51.8	85.2
Cash provided by operating activities	1,765.1	1,710.4	1,485.0

Cash Flows From Investing Activities

PRESENTATION

6.25 FASB ASC 230 defines those transactions and events that constitute investing cash receipts and payments. Investing activities include making and collecting loans and acquiring and disposing of debt or equity instruments and property, plant, and equipment (PPE) and other productive assets. FASB ASC 230-10-45-20 explains that investing activities exclude acquiring and disposing of certain loans or other debt or equity instruments that are acquired specifically for resale. Cash flows from purchases, sales, and maturities of available-for-sale securities should be classified as cash flows from investing activities and reported gross in the statement of cash flows. The following are considered cash receipts and payments from investing activities:

- Receipts from collections or sales of loans made by the entity and of other entities' debt instruments, other than cash equivalents and certain debt instruments that are acquired specifically for resale, that were purchased by the entity.
- Receipts from sales of equity instruments of other entities, other than certain equity instruments carried in a trading account, and from returns of investment in those instruments.
- Receipts from sales of PPE and other productive assets.
- Receipts from sales of loans that were not specifically acquired for resale. If loans were acquired as investments, cash receipts from sales of those loans shall be classified as investing cash inflows, regardless of a change in the purpose for holding those loans.
- Disbursements for loans made by the entity and payments to acquire debt instruments of other entities, other than cash equivalents and certain debt instruments that are acquired specifically for resale.
- Payments to acquire equity instruments of other entities, other than certain equity instruments carried in a trading account.
- Payments at the time of purchase or soon before or after purchase to acquire PPE and other productive assets, including interest capitalized as part of the cost of those assets. Generally, only advance payments, the down payment, or other amounts paid at the time of purchase or soon before or after the purchase of PPE and other productive assets are investing cash outflows. However, incurring directly-related debt to the seller is a financing transaction; thus, subsequent payments of principal on that debt are financing cash outflows.

6.26 CARPENTER TECHNOLOGY CORPORATION (JUN)
CONSOLIDATED STATEMENTS OF CASH FLOWS (in part)

For the Years Ended June 30, 2012, 2011 and 2010

($ in millions)	2012	2011	2010
Investing Activities			
Purchases of property, equipment and software	(171.9)	(79.6)	(44.2)
Proceeds from disposals of property and equipment	1.2	1.1	1.0
Acquisition of businesses, net of cash acquired	(12.9)	(45.4)	—
Capital contributions to equity method investment	(1.8)	(6.2)	—
Purchases of marketable securities	—	(91.3)	(145.0)
Proceeds from sales and maturities of marketable securities	30.5	166.0	55.3
Net cash used for investing activities	(154.9)	(55.4)	(132.9)

NOTES TO CONSOLIDATED FINANCIAL STATEMENTS

2. Acquisition and Strategic Partnership (in part)

Fiscal Year 2012 Acquisitions

Latrobe Specialty Metals, Inc.

On February 29, 2012, the Company completed its previously announced acquisition of Latrobe Specialty Metals, Inc ("Latrobe") for a total purchase price of $427.0 million, net of cash acquired (the "Latrobe Acquisition"). The purchase price includes the issuance of 8.1 million shares of the Company's common stock to former Latrobe stockholders in exchange for their Latrobe capital stock and $11.5 million of cash paid at closing, net of cash acquired of $2.5 million, to satisfy certain costs of the sellers. The fair value of the shares issued as part of the consideration paid for Latrobe was determined based on the closing market price of the Company's shares on the acquisition date. The Company also assumed $153.7 million of indebtedness which was paid off in cash concurrently with the closing of the acquisition.

Latrobe manufacturers and distributes high-performance specialty metals serving customers across end-use markets including the aerospace and defense, energy and industrial markets. The manufacturing operations of Latrobe are based principally in Latrobe, Pennsylvania.

The following is a summary of the preliminary purchase price allocation in connection with the Latrobe Acquisition. The amounts in the preliminary purchase price allocation are not yet final and are subject to change. The final allocation of the purchase price is expected to be completed during the first half of fiscal year 2013 when all the necessary information is obtained to the complete the analysis.

($ in millions)	
Accounts receivable	$ 67.3
Inventory	241.2
Property, plant and equipment	172.4
Intangible assets	87.1
Other	10.6
Accounts Payable and accrued liabilities	(63.9)
Long-term debt	(153.7)
Pension and other postretirement liabilities	(100.8)
Deferred income taxes	(47.7)
Total identifiable net assets	212.5
Goodwill	214.5
Total purchase price, net of cash acquired	$ 427.0

The goodwill recognized in connection with the Latrobe Acquisition consists of the value associated with the immediate increase in the Company's premium melt capacity to meet strong customer demand, improvements in the Company's position in attractive end use markets such as aerospace and defense and energy, the complementary asset capabilities which the Company expects will lead to enriched, higher margin product mix and operating cost synergies as well as the capabilities for commercialization of new Carpenter products under development. None of the goodwill recognized is deductible for income tax purposes.

In connection with the Latrobe Acquisition, the Company incurred approximately $11.7 million and $2.4 million of acquisition-related costs during the fiscal year ended June 30, 2012 and 2011, respectively. These costs are included in the consolidated statements of income and represent incremental legal, accounting and investment banking fees incurred in connection with the transaction as well as approximately $5.2 million of liability for costs associated with the sale of certain Latrobe assets necessary to obtain approval for the transaction from the Federal Trade Commission ("FTC"). As part of the FTC approval, the

Company entered into a consent decree to transfer assets and technical knowledge to Eramet S.A. and its subsidiaries, Aubert & Duval and Brown Europe, which will allow them to become a second manufacturer of two specific alloys in order to provide customers with a supply alternative in the marketplace.

The consolidated net sales for the fiscal year ended June 30, 2012 includes approximately $163.2 million of net sales related to the Latrobe business since the Latrobe Acquisition. The Company's operating income for the fiscal year ended June 30, 2012 includes approximately $10.5 million related to the operations of the Latrobe business since the Latrobe Acquisition, net of approximately $11.6 million recorded in connection with the fair value cost inventory adjustments.

The unaudited pro forma results presented below include the effects of the Latrobe Acquisition as if it had occurred as of July 1, 2010. The unaudited pro forma results reflect certain adjustments related to the acquisition, such as the depreciation and amortization associated with estimates for the fair value of the property and equipment and acquired intangible assets and the impacts of the elimination of Latrobe debt that was repaid at closing. The supplemental proforma earnings were adjusted to exclude acquisition related costs in the fiscal year 2012 and 2011 periods and the proforma earnings in the fiscal 2010 period were adjusted to include acquisition related costs related to the Latrobe Acquisition.

| ($ in millions) | June 30, | | |
	2012	2011	2010
Revenue	$2,339.6	$2,125.3	$1,504.8
Earnings	$ 160.1	$ 93.5	$ (0.4)
Earnings per Common Share			
Basic	$ 3.04	$ 1.78	$ (0.02)
Diluted	$ 3.01	$ 1.77	$ (0.02)

The pro forma results do not include any anticipated synergies or other expected benefits of the acquisition. Accordingly, the unaudited pro forma financial information above is not necessarily indicative of either future results of operations or results that might have been achieved had the acquisition been completed on the dates indicated.

Arwin Machining Plus, Ltd.

On December 15, 2011, the Company acquired substantially all of the assets of Arwin Machining Plus, Ltd. ("Arwin") for a cash purchase price of $1.4 million. The Arwin assets, consisting principally of machinery and equipment, have been integrated into the Canadian operations of Amega West Services ("Amega West"), a wholly owned subsidiary of the Company. The Company believes the acquisition enhances Amega West's machining capabilities by adding the expertise and positions necessary to increase responsiveness to customers and to assist with the development of new directional drilling applications. The purchase price was allocated $0.7 million to machinery and equipment and $0.7 million to goodwill, most of which is expected to be deductible for tax purposes.

INVESTMENTS

6.27 WELLPOINT, INC. (DEC)
CONSOLIDATED STATEMENTS OF CASH FLOWS (in part)

| (In millions) | Years Ended December 31 | | |
	2012	2011	2010
Investing Activities			
Purchases of fixed maturity securities	(15,040.4)	(11,914.8)	(10,567.2)
Proceeds from fixed maturity securities:			
Sales	13,675.9	10,446.2	7,215.1
Maturities, calls and redemptions	1,781.5	1,891.3	3,321.7
Purchases of equity securities	(292.6)	(355.6)	(350.9)
Proceeds from sales of equity securities	422.7	287.4	197.9
Purchases of other invested assets	(303.7)	(207.9)	(91.4)
Proceeds from sales of other invested assets	35.5	29.4	34.5
Changes in securities lending collateral	307.9	28.9	(504.8)
Purchases of subsidiaries, net of cash acquired	(4,597.0)	(600.0)	(0.3)
Purchases of property and equipment	(544.9)	(519.5)	(451.4)
Proceeds from sales of property and equipment	0.4	3.7	0.8
Other, net	3.1	(31.1)	(75.5)
Net cash used in investing activities	(4,551.6)	(942.0)	(1,271.5)

5. Investments (in part)

A summary of current and long-term investments, available-for-sale, at December 31, 2012 and 2011 is as follows:

	Cost or Amortized Cost	Gross Unrealized Gains	Gross Unrealized Losses		Estimated Fair Value	Non-Credit Component of Other-Than-Temporary Impairments Recognized in AOCI
			Less Than 12 Months	12 Months or Greater		
December 31, 2012:						
Fixed maturity securities:						
United States Government securities	$ 330.3	$ 13.1	$ (0.2)	$ —	$ 343.2	$ —
Government sponsored securities	153.6	2.6	—	—	156.2	—
States, municipalities and political subdivisions—tax-exempt	5,501.3	388.2	(5.7)	(1.6)	5,882.2	—
Corporate securities	7,642.0	387.0	(17.0)	(8.0)	8,004.0	(1.7)
Options embedded in convertible debt securities	67.2	—	—	—	67.2	—
Residential mortgage-backed securities	2,204.7	103.1	(1.1)	(1.9)	2,304.8	(0.4)
Commercial mortgage-backed securities	323.2	22.5	—	—	345.7	—
Other debt securities	236.8	7.6	(0.2)	(3.1)	241.1	(1.3)
Total fixed maturity securities	16,459.1	924.1	(24.2)	(14.6)	17,344.4	$ (3.4)
Equity securities	897.0	358.0	(12.5)	—	1,242.5	
Total investments, available-for-sale	$17,356.1	$1,282.1	$ (36.7)	$(14.6)	$18,586.9	
December 31, 2011:						
Fixed maturity securities:						
United States Government securities	$ 564.9	$ 39.9	$ (0.1)	$ —	$ 604.7	$ —
Government sponsored securities	173.1	2.5	—	—	175.6	—
States, municipalities and political subdivisions—tax-exempt	4,994.2	352.3	(3.9)	(15.0)	5,327.6	(0.5)
Corporate securities	6,588.0	305.3	(88.4)	(6.9)	6,798.0	(0.4)
Options embedded in convertible debt securities	79.7	—	—	—	79.7	—
Residential mortgage-backed securities	2,471.4	112.1	(7.6)	(10.9)	2,565.0	(6.2)
Commercial mortgage-backed securities	363.2	14.9	(1.0)	(1.7)	375.4	—
Other debt securities	239.9	3.1	(2.0)	(7.1)	233.9	(3.2)
Total fixed maturity securities	15,474.4	830.1	(103.0)	(41.6)	16,159.9	$(10.3)
Equity securities	966.1	277.0	(26.2)	—	1,216.9	
Total investments, available-for-sale	$16,440.5	$1,107.1	$(129.2)	$(41.6)	$17,376.8	

At December 31, 2012, we owned $2,650.5 of mortgage-backed securities and $207.3 of asset-backed securities out of a total available-for-sale investment portfolio of $18,586.9. These securities included sub-prime and Alt-A securities with fair values of $44.4 and $133.7, respectively. These sub-prime and Alt-A securities had accumulated net unrealized gains of $1.1 and $6.2, respectively. The average credit rating of the sub-prime and Alt-A securities was "BB" and "CCC", respectively.

The following tables summarize for fixed maturity securities and equity securities in an unrealized loss position at December 31, 2012 and 2011, the aggregate fair value and gross unrealized loss by length of time those securities have been continuously in an unrealized loss position.

	Less Than 12 Months			12 Months or Greater		
(Securities are whole amounts)	Number of Securities	Estimated Fair Value	Gross Unrealized Loss	Number of Securities	Estimated Fair Value	Gross Unrealized Loss
December 31, 2012:						
Fixed maturity securities:						
United States Government securities	17	$ 48.5	$ (0.2)	—	$ —	$ —
States, municipalities and political subdivisions—tax-exempt	184	420.1	(5.7)	1	46.9	(1.6)
Corporate securities	457	1,066.5	(17.0)	74	52.6	(8.0)
Residential mortgage-backed securities	79	211.0	(1.1)	44	25.5	(1.9)
Commercial mortgage-backed securities	4	10.1	—	3	4.1	—
Other debt securities	7	5.4	(0.2)	21	28.9	(3.1)
Total fixed maturity securities	748	1,761.6	(24.2)	143	158.0	(14.6)
Equity securities	961	149.6	(12.5)	—	—	—
Total fixed maturity and equity securities	1,709	$1,911.2	$ (36.7)	143	$158.0	$(14.6)

(continued)

(Securities are whole amounts)	Less Than 12 Months			12 Months or Greater		
	Number of Securities	Estimated Fair Value	Gross Unrealized Loss	Number of Securities	Estimated Fair Value	Gross Unrealized Loss
December 31, 2011:						
Fixed maturity securities:						
United States Government securities	3	$ 7.1	$ (0.1)	—	$ —	$ —
States, municipalities and political subdivisions—tax-exempt	19	86.6	(3.9)	84	195.2	(15.0)
Corporate securities	1,047	1,798.1	(88.4)	36	35.4	(6.9)
Residential mortgage-backed securities	91	170.4	(7.6)	65	78.0	(10.9)
Commercial mortgage-backed securities	14	27.7	(1.0)	5	15.6	(1.7)
Other debt securities	41	118.5	(2.0)	31	32.7	(7.1)
Total fixed maturity securities	1,215	2,208.4	(103.0)	221	356.9	(41.6)
Equity securities	1,137	271.6	(26.2)	—	—	—
Total fixed maturity and equity securities	2,352	$2,480.0	$(129.2)	221	$356.9	$(41.6)

The amortized cost and fair value of fixed maturity securities at December 31, 2012, by contractual maturity, are shown below. Expected maturities may be less than contractual maturities because the issuers of the securities may have the right to prepay obligations without prepayment penalties.

	Amortized Cost	Estimated Fair Value
Due in one year or less	$ 968.2	$ 985.4
Due after one year through five years	4,900.0	5,108.9
Due after five years through ten years	4,545.6	4,868.2
Due after ten years	3,517.4	3,731.4
Mortgage-backed securities	2,527.9	2,650.5
Total available-for-sale fixed maturity securities	$16,459.1	$17,344.4

BUSINESS COMBINATIONS

6.28 ELECTRONIC ARTS INC. (MAR)
CONSOLIDATED STATEMENTS OF CASH FLOWS (in part)

(In millions)	Year Ended March 31,		
	2012	2011	2010
Investing Activities			
Capital expenditures	(172)	(59)	(72)
Purchase of headquarters facilities	—	—	(233)
Proceeds from sale of property	26	—	—
Purchase of short-term investments	(468)	(514)	(611)
Proceeds from maturities and sales of short-term investments	526	442	710
Proceeds from sale of marketable equity securities	—	132	17
Acquisition of subsidiaries, net of cash acquired	(676)	(16)	(283)
Acquisition-related restricted cash	75	—	(100)
Net cash used in investing activities	(689)	(15)	(572)

NOTES TO CONSOLIDATED FINANCIAL STATEMENTS

(5) Business Combinations

Fiscal Year 2012 Acquisitions

PopCap Games Inc.

In August 2011, we acquired all of the outstanding shares of PopCap for an aggregate purchase price of approximately (1) $645 million in cash and (2) $87 million in privately-placed shares of our common stock to the founders and chief executive officer of PopCap. In addition, we agreed to grant over a four year period to PopCap's employees up to $50 million in long-term equity retention arrangements in the form of restricted stock unit awards and options to acquire our common stock. These awards and options are accounted for as stock-based compensation in accordance with ASC 718, Compensation—Stock Compensation. PopCap is a leading developer of games for mobile phones, tablets, PCs, and social network sites. This acquisition strengthens our participation in casual gaming and contributes to the growth of our digital product offerings.

The following table summarizes the acquisition date fair value of the consideration transferred which consisted of the following (in millions):

Cash	$645
Equity	87
Total purchase price	$732

The equity included in the consideration above consisted of privately-placed shares of our common stock, whose fair value was determined based on the quoted market price of our common stock on the date of acquisition.

In addition, we may be required to pay additional variable cash consideration that is contingent upon the achievement of certain performance milestones through December 31, 2013 and is limited to a maximum of $550 million based on achievement of certain non-GAAP earnings targets before interest and tax. At the upper end of the earn-out, the performance targets for earnings before income and taxes ("EBIT") are approximately $343 million in aggregate PopCap stand-alone EBIT generated over the two-year period ending December 31, 2013. The estimated fair value of the contingent consideration arrangement at the acquisition date was $95 million. We estimated the fair value of the contingent consideration using probability assessments of expected future cash flows over the period in which the obligation is expected to be settled, and applied a discount rate that appropriately captures a market participant's view of the risk associated with the obligation.

The final allocation of the purchase price was completed during the third quarter of fiscal year 2012. The following table summarizes the fair values of assets acquired and liabilities assumed at the date of acquisition (in millions):

Current assets	$ 62
Property and equipment, net	6
Goodwill	563
Finite-lived intangible assets	302
Contingent consideration	(95)
Deferred income taxes, net	(51)
Other liabilities	(55)
Total purchase price	$732

All of the goodwill is assigned to our EA Labels operating segment. None of the goodwill recognized upon acquisition is deductible for tax purposes. See Note 6 for additional information related to the changes in the carrying amount of goodwill and Note 18 for segment information.

Finite-lived intangible assets acquired in this transaction are being amortized on a straight-line basis over their estimated lives ranging from three to nine years. The intangible assets as of the date of the acquisition include:

	Gross Carrying Amount (In millions)	Weighted-Average Useful Life (In years)
Developed and core technology	$245	6
Trade names and trademarks	40	9
In-process research and development	15	5
Other intangibles	2	4
Total finite-lived intangibles	$302	6

In connection with our acquisition of PopCap, we acquired in-process research and development assets valued at approximately $15 million in relation to game software that had not reached technical feasibility as of the date of acquisition. The fair value of PopCap's products under development was determined using the income approach, which discounts expected future cash flows from the acquired in-process technology to present value. The discount rates used in the present value calculations were derived from an average weighted average cost of capital of 13 percent.

There were six in-process research and development projects acquired as of the acquisition date each with $4 million or less of assigned fair value and $15 million of aggregate fair value. Additionally each project had less than $2 million of estimated costs to complete and $5 million aggregate cost to complete. As of the acquisition date, the weighted-average estimated percentage completion of all six projects combined was 36 percent. Benefits from the development efforts have begun to be received in the fourth quarter of fiscal year 2012 and the remaining development efforts are expected to be completed in fiscal year 2013.

The results of operations of PopCap and the estimated fair market values of the assets acquired and liabilities assumed have been included in our Consolidated Financial Statements since the date of acquisition. Pro forma results of operations have not been presented because the effect of the acquisition was not material to our Consolidated Statements of Operations.

KlickNation and Other Fiscal 2012 Acquisitions

In November 2011, we acquired KlickNation, a developer of social role-playing games. During the fiscal year ended March 31, 2012, we completed three other acquisitions. These business combinations were completed for total cash consideration of approximately $55 million. These acquisitions were not material to our Consolidated Balance Sheets and Statements of Operations. The results of operations and the estimated fair value of the acquired assets and assumed liabilities have been included in our Consolidated Financial Statements since the date of the acquisitions. See Note 6 for information regarding goodwill and acquisition-related intangible assets. Pro forma results of operations have not been presented because the effect of the acquisitions was not material to our Consolidated Statements of Operations.

Fiscal Year 2011 Acquisition

In October 2010, we acquired all of the outstanding shares of Chillingo in cash. Chillingo publishes games and software for various mobile platforms. In addition, in connection and with the acquisition, we will pay additional variable cash contingent upon the achievement of certain performance milestones through March 31, 2014. We paid $4 million related to this arrangement during the first quarter of fiscal year 2013. This acquisition did not have a significant impact on our Consolidated Financial Statements.

Fiscal Year 2010 Acquisitions

Playfish

In November 2009, we acquired all of the outstanding shares of Playfish for an aggregate purchase price of approximately $308 million in cash and equity. Playfish is a developer of free-to-play social games that can be played on social networking platforms. The following table summarizes the acquisition date fair value of the consideration transferred which consisted of the following (in millions):

Cash	$297
Equity	11
Total purchase price	$308

The equity included in the consideration above consisted of restricted stock and restricted stock units, using the quoted market price of our common stock on the date of grant.

In addition, we were required to pay additional variable cash consideration that was contingent upon the achievement of certain performance milestones through December 31, 2011 and was limited to a maximum of $100 million based on tiered revenue targets. In connection with this arrangement, we paid $25 million during the fourth quarter of fiscal year 2012. We expect to pay an additional $25 million during the second quarter of fiscal year 2013.

The following table summarizes the fair values of assets acquired and liabilities assumed at the date of acquisition (in millions):

Current assets	$ 32
Deferred income taxes, net	20
Property and equipment, net	1
Goodwill	274
Finite-lived intangibles assets	53
Contingent consideration	(63)
Other liabilities	(9)
Total purchase price	$308

All of the goodwill was initially assigned to our Playfish operating segment, and subsequently assigned to our EA Labels operating segment. None of the goodwill recognized upon acquisition is deductible for tax purposes. See Note 6 for additional information related to the changes in the carrying amount of goodwill and Note 18 for segment information.

Finite-lived intangible assets acquired in this transaction are being amortized on a straight-line basis over their estimated lives ranging from two to five years. The intangible assets as of the date of the acquisition include:

	Gross Carrying Amount (In millions)	Weighted-Average Useful Life (In years)
Registered user base	$ 33	2
Developed and core technology	13	5
Trade names and trademarks	4	5
Other intangibles	3	4
Total finite-lived intangibles	$53	3

The results of operations of Playfish and the estimated fair market values of the assets acquired and liabilities assumed have been included in our Consolidated Financial Statements since the date of acquisition. Pro forma results of operations have not been presented because the effect of the acquisition was not material to our Consolidated Statements of Operations.

Other Fiscal Year 2010 Acquisitions

During the fiscal year ended March 31, 2010, we completed three additional acquisitions that did not have a significant impact on our Consolidated Financial Statements.

6.29 GENERAL ELECTRIC COMPANY (DEC)

STATEMENT OF CASH FLOWS (in part)

For the Years Ended December 31	General Electric Company and Consolidated Affiliates		
(In millions)	2012	2011	2010
Cash Flows—Investing Activities			
Additions to property, plant and equipment	(15,126)	(12,650)	(9,800)
Dispositions of property, plant and equipment	6,200	5,896	7,208
Net decrease (increase) in GECC financing receivables	6,872	14,630	21,758
Proceeds from sales of discontinued operations	227	8,950	2,510
Proceeds from principal business dispositions	3,618	8,877	3,062
Payments for principal businesses purchased	(1,456)	(11,202)	(1,212)
All other investing activities	11,064	6,095	10,262
Cash from (used for) investing activities—continuing operations	11,399	20,596	33,788
Cash from (used for) investing activities—discontinued operations	(97)	(714)	(1,352)
Cash from (used for) investing activities	11,302	19,882	32,436

NOTES TO CONSOLIDATED FINANCIAL STATEMENTS

Note 2. Assets And Liabilities of Businesses Held For Sale and Discontinued Operations (in part)

Other Financial Services (in part)

In the first quarter of 2012, we announced the planned disposition of Consumer Ireland and classified the business as discontinued operations. We completed the sale in the third quarter of 2012 for proceeds of $227 million. Consumer Ireland revenues and other income (expense) from discontinued operations were $7 million, $13 million and $25 million in 2012, 2011 and 2010, respectively. Consumer Ireland losses from discontinued operations, net of taxes, were $195 million (including a $121 million loss on disposal), $153 million and $96 million in 2012, 2011 and 2010, respectively.

In the second quarter of 2011, we entered into an agreement to sell our Australian Home Lending operations and classified it as discontinued operations. As a result, we recognized an after-tax loss of $148 million in 2011. We completed the sale in the third quarter of 2011 for proceeds of approximately $4,577 million. Australian Home Lending revenues and other income (expense) from discontinued operations were $4 million, $250 million and $510 million in 2012, 2011 and 2010, respectively. Australian Home Lending earnings (loss) from discontinued operations, net of taxes, were $6 million, $(65) million and $70 million in 2012, 2011 and 2010, respectively.

CAPITALIZED SOFTWARE

6.30 THE HERSHEY COMPANY (DEC)

CONSOLIDATED STATEMENTS OF CASH FLOWS (in part)

	For the Years Ended December 31,		
(In thousands of dollars)	2012	2011	2010
Cash Flows Provided From (Used by) Investing Activities			
Capital additions	(258,727)	(323,961)	(179,538)
Capitalized software additions	(19,239)	(23,606)	(21,949)
Proceeds from sales of property, plant and equipment	453	312	2,201
Proceeds from sale of trademark licensing rights	—	20,000	—
Loan to affiliate	(23,000)	(7,000)	—
Business acquisitions	(172,856)	(5,750)	—
Net Cash (Used by) Investing Activities	(473,369)	(340,005)	(199,286)

NOTES TO CONSOLIDATED FINANCIAL STATEMENTS

1. Summary of Significant Accounting Policies (in part)

Computer Software

We capitalize costs associated with software developed or obtained for internal use when both the preliminary project stage is completed and it is probable that computer software being developed will be completed and placed in service. Capitalized costs include only (i) external direct costs of materials and services consumed in developing or obtaining internal-use software, (ii) payroll and other related costs for employees who are directly associated with and who devote time to the internal-use software project and (iii) interest costs incurred, when material, while developing internal-use software. We cease capitalization of such costs no later than the point at which the project is substantially complete and ready for its intended purpose.

The unamortized amount of capitalized software was $50.5 million as of December 31, 2012 and was $49.4 million as of December 31, 2011. We amortize software costs using the straight-line method over the expected life of the software, generally 3 to 5 years. Accumulated amortization of capitalized software was $256.1 million as of December 31, 2012 and $232.8 million as of December 31, 2011.

We review the carrying value of software and development costs for impairment in accordance with our policy pertaining to the impairment of long-lived assets. Generally, we measure impairment under the following circumstances:

- When internal-use computer software is not expected to provide substantive service potential;
- A significant change occurs in the extent or manner in which the software is used or is expected to be used;
- A significant change is made or will be made to the software program; and
- Costs of developing or modifying internal-use computer software significantly exceed the amount originally expected to develop or modify the software.

RESTRICTED CASH

6.31 WYNDHAM WORLDWIDE CORPORATION (DEC)
CONSOLIDATED STATEMENTS OF CASH FLOWS (in part)

(In millions)

	Year Ended December 31,		
	2012	**2011**	**2010**
Investing Activities			
Property and equipment additions	(208)	(239)	(167)
Net assets acquired, net of cash acquired	(263)	(27)	(236)
Development advances	(14)	(5)	(10)
Equity investments and loans	(42)	(12)	—
Proceeds from asset sales	1	31	20
Decrease/(increase) in securitization restricted cash	11	6	(5)
Increase in escrow deposit restricted cash	(5)	(5)	(12)
Other, net	1	(5)	(8)
Net cash used in investing activities	(519)	(256)	(418)

NOTES TO CONSOLIDATED FINANCIAL STATEMENTS

(Unless otherwise noted, all amounts are in millions, except share and per share amounts)

2. Summary of Significant Accounting Policies (in part)

Restricted Cash

The largest portion of the Company's restricted cash relates to securitizations. The remaining portion is comprised of cash held in escrow related to the Company's vacation ownership business and cash held in all other escrow accounts.

Securitizations: In accordance with the contractual requirements of the Company's various vacation ownership contract receivable securitizations, a dedicated lockbox account, subject to a blocked control agreement, is established for each securitization. At each month end, the total cash in the collection account from the previous month is analyzed and a monthly servicer report is prepared by the Company, which details how much cash should be remitted to the noteholders for principal and interest payments, and any cash remaining is transferred by the trustee back to the Company. Additionally, as required by various securitizations, the Company holds an agreed-upon percentage of the aggregate outstanding principal balances of the VOI contract receivables collateralizing the asset-backed notes in a segregated trust (or reserve) account as credit enhancement. Each time a securitization closes and the Company receives cash from the noteholders, a portion of the cash is deposited in the reserve account. Such amounts were $121 million and $132 million as of December 31, 2012 and 2011, respectively, of which $65 million and $71 million is recorded within other current assets as of December 31, 2012 and 2011, respectively, and $56 million and $61 million is recorded within other non-current assets as of December 31, 2012 and 2011, respectively, on the Consolidated Balance Sheets.

Escrow Deposits: Laws in most U.S. states require the escrow of down payments on VOI sales, with the typical requirement mandating that the funds be held in escrow until the rescission period expires. As sales transactions are consummated, down payments are collected and are subsequently placed in escrow until the rescission period has expired. Depending on the state, the rescission period can be as short as 3 calendar days or as long as 15 calendar days. In certain states, the escrow laws require that 100% of VOI purchaser funds (excluding interest payments, if any), be held in escrow until the deeding process is complete. Where possible, the Company utilizes surety bonds in lieu of escrow deposits. Escrow deposit amounts were $56 million and $53 million as of December 31, 2012 and 2011, respectively, which is recorded within other current assets on the Consolidated Balance Sheets.

6.32 LEAR CORPORATION (DEC)
CONSOLIDATED STATEMENTS OF CASH FLOWS (in part)

(In millions, except share data)

	For the Year Ended December 31,		
	2012	2011	2010
Cash Flows From Investing Activities:			
Additions to property, plant and equipment	(458.3)	(329.5)	(193.3)
Insurance proceeds	19.2	3.5	—
Cash paid for acquisitions, net of cash acquired	(243.9)	(8.4)	—
Other, net	(4.9)	31.2	1.2
Net cash used in investing activities	(687.9)	(303.2)	(192.1)

NOTES TO CONSOLIDATED FINANCIAL STATEMENTS

(12) Commitments and Contingencies (in part)

Insurance Recoveries

The Company has incurred losses and incremental costs related to the destruction of assets caused by a fire at one of its European production facilities in the third quarter of 2011. During the fourth quarter of 2012, the Company reached a settlement for the recovery of such costs under applicable insurance policies. Anticipated proceeds from insurance recoveries related to losses and incremental costs that have been incurred ("loss recoveries") are recognized when receipt is probable. Anticipated proceeds from insurance recoveries in excess of the net book value of destroyed property, plant and equipment ("insurance gain contingencies") are recognized when all contingencies related to the claim have been resolved. Loss recoveries related to the destruction of inventory and incremental costs are included in costs of sales, and loss recoveries and insurance gain contingencies related to the destruction of property, plant and equipment are included in other expense, net. Cash proceeds related to the destruction of inventory and incremental costs are included in cash flows from operating activities, and cash proceeds related to the destruction of property, plant and equipment are included in cash flows from investing activities.

Since the fire in the third quarter of 2011, the Company incurred cumulative losses and incremental costs of $58.4 million ($34.4 million incurred in 2012). The Company also recognized in cost of sales cumulative recoveries of $59.1 million ($49.0 million recognized in 2012) and in other expense cumulative recoveries and gains of $29.9 million ($26.5 million recognized in 2012). In addition, the Company received cumulative cash proceeds of $79.0 million ($66.4 million received in 2012), of which $56.3 million ($47.2 million in 2012) has been reflected in cash flows from operating activities and $22.7 million ($19.2 million in 2012) has been reflected in cash flows from investing activities.

Cash Flows From Financing Activities

PRESENTATION

6.33 FASB ASC 230-10-45 defines those transactions and events that constitute financing cash receipts and payments. The following are considered cash receipts and payments from financing activities:

- Proceeds from issuing equity instruments.
- Proceeds from issuing bonds, mortgages, and notes and from other short- or long-term borrowing.
- Receipts from contributions and investment income that, by donor stipulation, are restricted for the purposes of acquiring, constructing, or improving PPE or other long-lived assets or establishing or increasing a permanent or term endowment.
- Proceeds received from derivative instruments that include financing elements at inception, regardless of whether the proceeds were received at inception or over the term of the derivative instrument, other than a financing element inherently included in an at-the-market derivative instrument with no prepayments.
- Cash that is recognizable for financial reporting purposes because it is retained as a result of the tax deductibility of increases in the value of equity instruments issued under share-based payment arrangements that are not included in the cost of goods or services. For this purpose, excess tax benefits should be determined on an individual award (or portion thereof) basis.
- Payments of dividends or other distributions to owners, including outlays to reacquire the entity's equity instruments.
- Repayments of borrowed amounts.
- Other principal payments to creditors who have extended long-term credit.
- Distributions to counterparties of derivative instruments that include financing elements at inception, other than a financing element inherently included in an at-the-market derivative instrument with no prepayments. The distributions may be either at inception or over the term of the derivative instrument.
- Payments for debt issue costs.

6.34 ASHLAND INC. (SEP)

STATEMENTS OF CONSOLIDATED CASH FLOWS (in part)

(In millions)	Years Ended September 30		
	2012	**2011**	**2010**
Cash Flows Provided (Used) by Financing Activities From Continuing Operations			
Proceeds from issuance of long-term debt	502	2,910	334
Repayment of long-term debt	(1,023)	(1,513)	(780)
Proceeds from short-term debt, net	261	12	48
Repurchase of common stock	—	(71)	—
Debt issuance/modification costs	(10)	(82)	(13)
Cash dividends paid	(63)	(51)	(35)
Proceeds from exercise of stock options	4	3	6
Excess tax benefits related to share-based payments	12	4	5
	(317)	1,212	(435)

NOTES TO CONSOLIDATED FINANCIAL STATEMENTS

Note I—Debt (in part)

The following table summarizes Ashland's current and long-term debt at September 30, 2012 and 2011.

(In millions)	2012	2011
Term loan A, due 2016[a]	$1,425	$1,500
Term loan B, due 2018[a]	1,036	1,400
4.750% notes, due 2022	500	—
9.125% notes, due 2017	76	633
6.50% junior subordinated notes, due 2029[b]	129	128
6.60% notes, due 2027[b]	12	12
Accounts receivable securitization	300	—
Medium-term notes, due 2013–2019, interest at a weighted-average rate of 8.4% at September 30, 2012 (7.7% to 9.4%)	21	21
8.80% debentures, due 2012	20	20
Other international loans, interest at a weighted-average rate of 6.5% at September 30, 2012 (2.1% to 11.9%)	69	116
Other	2	2
Total debt	3,590	3,832
Short-term debt	(344)	(83)
Current portion of long-term debt	(115)	(101)
Long-term debt (less current portion)	$3,131	$3,648

[a] Senior credit facilities.
[b] Retained instrument from the Hercules acquisition.

At September 30, 2012 Ashland's total debt had an outstanding principal balance of $3,748 million and discounts of $158 million. The scheduled aggregate maturities of debt for the next five fiscal years are as follows: $158 million in 2013, $163 million in 2014, $459 million in 2015, $1,050 million in 2016 and $78 million in 2017.

Senior Credit Facilities

On August 23, 2011, in conjunction with the ISP acquisition closing, Ashland entered into a $3.9 billion Senior Credit Facility. The Senior Credit Facility is comprised of (i) a $1.5 billion term loan A facility, (ii) a $1.4 billion term loan B facility and (iii) a $1.0 billion revolving credit facility. Proceeds from borrowings under the term loan A facility and the term loan B facility were used, together with cash on hand, to finance the cash consideration paid for the ISP acquisition, as well as to finance the repayment of existing indebtedness of ISP in connection with the acquisition.

The Senior Credit Facility is guaranteed by Ashland's existing and future subsidiaries (other than certain immaterial subsidiaries, joint ventures, special purpose financing subsidiaries, regulated subsidiaries, certain foreign subsidiaries and certain other subsidiaries), and is secured by a first-priority security interest in substantially all the personal property assets, and certain real property assets, of Ashland and the guarantors, including all or a portion of the equity interests of certain of Ashland's domestic subsidiaries and first-tier foreign subsidiaries and, in certain cases, a portion of the equity interests of other foreign subsidiaries. The term loan A facility was drawn in full at closing and is required to be repaid by Ashland in consecutive quarterly installments which began on December 31, 2011, with an aggregate amount equal to 5% of the original principal amount of such facility due in each of the first and second years after August 23, 2011 (the closing date), an aggregate amount equal to 10% of the original principal amount due in each of the third and fourth years after the closing date, an aggregate amount equal to 15% of the original principal amount due in the fifth year after the closing date, and a final payment of all outstanding principal and interest due on August 23, 2016. The term loan B facility was also drawn in full at closing and is required to be repaid by Ashland in consecutive quarterly installments which began on December 31, 2011, with an aggregate amount equal to 1% of the original principal amount of such facility due in each of the seven years after the closing date, and a final payment of all outstanding principal and interest due on August 23, 2018. Total borrowing capacity remaining under the $1.0 billion revolving credit facility was $905 million, representing a reduction of $95 million for letters of credit outstanding at September 30, 2012.

At Ashland's option, loans issued under the credit agreement carry interest rates of LIBOR or an alternate base rate, in each case plus the applicable interest rate margin. Loans in respect of the term loan B facility carry interest rates of LIBOR plus 2.75%, in the case of LIBOR borrowings, or at the alternate base rate plus 1.75%, and is subject to a 1% LIBOR floor. Loans in respect of the term loan A facility and the revolving credit facility carried an initial interest rate of LIBOR plus 2.25%, in the case of LIBOR borrowings, or at the alternate base rate plus 1.25%, through and including February 19, 2012, and thereafter the interest rate will fluctuate between LIBOR plus 1.75% and LIBOR plus 2.50% (or between the alternate base rate plus 0.75% and the alternate base rate plus 1.50%), based upon Ashland's corporate credit ratings or the consolidated gross leverage ratio (as defined in the credit agreement) (whichever yields a lower applicable interest rate margin) at such time. In addition, Ashland initially was required to pay fees of 0.40% on the daily unused amount of the revolving credit facility through and including February 19, 2012, and thereafter the fee rate will fluctuate between 0.30% and 0.50%, based upon Ashland's corporate credit ratings or the consolidated gross leverage ratio. In order to manage the variable interest rate risk associated with term loans A and B, Ashland entered into interest rate swap agreements. As of September 30, 2012, the total notional value of interest rate swaps related to term loans A and B equaled $1.4 billion and $650 million, respectively, whereas the total notional values were $1.5 billion and $650 million, respectively, as of September 30, 2011. These interest rate swaps effectively fixed the interest rates for approximately 84% and 75%, respectively, of the term loan A and term loan B principal in the aggregate for 2012 and 2011. See Note G for additional information on the interest rate swap instruments.

The term loan A facility and the revolving credit facility may be prepaid at any time without premium. If within one year of the closing date, Ashland refinances, or voluntarily prepays loans in respect of, the term loan B facility through the incurrence of other long-term bank debt that has a lower effective yield than the yield on the term loan B facility, then Ashland is required to pay a prepayment premium equal to 1.0% of the aggregate principal amount of the term loan B facility so refinanced or prepaid. In addition, Ashland is required to make mandatory prepayments in respect of the Senior Credit Facility with specified percentages of the net cash proceeds of certain asset dispositions, casualty events and debt and equity issuances and with specified percentages of excess cash flow, in each case subject to certain conditions.

During 2012, Ashland prepaid $350 million of principal on its term loan B facility, using proceeds from its newly issued accounts receivable securitization facility. As a result, Ashland recognized a $6 million charge for the debt issuance costs associated with the principal prepayment, which is included in the net interest and other financing expense caption in the Statements of Consolidated Income.

Former Senior Credit Facility

During March 2011, Ashland terminated its previous term loan A facility due 2014, paying off the outstanding balance of $289 million with funds received from the sale of Distribution. As a result of the termination of this facility, Ashland recognized an $11 million charge for the remaining debt issuance costs related to the loan, which is included in the net interest and other financing expense caption in the Statements of Consolidated Income.

On March 31, 2010, as part of a refinancing of its then-existing senior credit facilities, Ashland entered into a credit agreement with a group of lenders. The credit agreement provided for an aggregate principal amount of $850 million in senior secured credit facilities, consisting of a $300 million four-year term loan A facility and a $550 million revolving credit facility. The proceeds from the borrowings from the term loan A facility were used, together with proceeds from the prior accounts receivable securitization facility described further within this note, and cash on hand, to repay all amounts outstanding under Ashland's previous senior secured facilities and to pay for fees and expenses incurred in connection with the credit facilities and the related transactions. As discussed above, the term loan A facility was terminated and repaid in March 2011, and the revolving credit facility was replaced with a new $1.0 billion revolving credit facility as part of the August 23, 2011 current Senior Credit Facility.

9.125% Senior Notes and 4.750% Senior Notes

In May 2009, Ashland issued $650 million aggregate principal amount of 9.125% senior unsecured notes due 2017. The notes were issued at 96.577% of the aggregate principal amount to yield 9.75%. In connection with the current Senior Credit Facility, these notes were secured on an equal and ratable basis with indebtedness under the Senior Credit Facility. These notes were also guaranteed by the same guarantors under the Senior Credit Facility. Ashland may redeem outstanding notes at any time on or after June 1, 2013 at certain fixed redemption prices. The notes will mature on June 1, 2017 and rank equally with other unsecured and unsubordinated senior obligations.

In July 2012, Ashland commenced a tender offer to purchase for cash any and all of the premium $650 million aggregate principal of the 9.125% senior notes. In conjunction with this tender offer, Ashland issued $500 million aggregate principal amount of 4.750% senior unsecured, unsubordinated notes due 2022. The proceeds of the new notes, together with available cash, were used to pay the consideration, accrued and unpaid interest and related fees and expenses in connection with Ashland's cash tender offer of the 9.125% senior notes. At the close of the tender offer, $572 million aggregate principal amount of the 9.125% senior notes was redeemed by Ashland, representing 88% of the 9.125% senior notes. Ashland recognized a $24 million charge for debt issuance costs and original issue discount related to the portion of the 9.125% senior notes that were redeemed early, as well as a $67 million charge related to an early redemption premium payment, both of which are included in the net interest and other financing expense caption in the Statements of Consolidated Income for 2012.

Accounts Receivable Securitization

On August 31, 2012, Ashland entered into a $350 million accounts receivable securitization facility pursuant to (i) a Sale Agreement, among Ashland and certain of its direct and indirect subsidiaries (each an Originator and collectively, the Originators) and CVG Capital III LLC, a wholly-owned "bankruptcy remote" special purpose subsidiary of the Originators (CVG) and (ii) a Transfer and Administration Agreement, among CVG, each Originator, Ashland, as Master Servicer, certain Conduit Investors, Uncommitted Investors, Letter of Credit Issuers, Managing Agents, Administrators and Committed Investors, and The Bank of Nova Scotia, as agent for various secured parties (the Agent).

Under the Sale Agreement, each Originator will transfer, on an ongoing basis, substantially all of its accounts receivable, certain related assets and the right to the collections on those accounts receivable to CVG. Under the terms of the Transfer and Administration Agreement, CVG may, from time to time, obtain up to $350 million (in the form of cash or letters of credit for the benefit of Ashland and its subsidiaries) from the Conduit Investors, the Uncommitted Investors and/or the Committed Investors through the sale of an undivided interest in such accounts receivable, related assets and collections. The Transfer and Administration Agreement has a term of three years, but is extendable at the discretion of the Investors. Ashland will account for the Securitization Facility as secured borrowings, and the receivables sold pursuant to the facility are included in the Consolidated Balance Sheet as accounts receivable. Fundings under the Transfer and Administration Agreement will be repaid as accounts receivable are collected, with new fundings being advanced (through daily reinvestments) as new accounts receivable are originated by the Originators and transferred to CVG, with settlement generally occurring monthly. Ashland continues to classify any borrowings under this facility as a short-term debt instrument within the Consolidated Balance Sheets. Once sold to CVG, the accounts receivable, related assets and rights to collection described above will be separate and distinct from each Originator's own assets and will not be available to its creditors should such Originator become insolvent. Substantially all of CVG's assets have been pledged to the Agent in support of its obligations under the Transfer and Administration Agreement. In addition, the Originators' equity interests in CVG have been pledged to the lenders under the Senior Credit Facility.

At September 30, 2012, the outstanding amount of accounts receivable transferred by Ashland to CVG was $616 million. Ashland had drawn $300 million under the facility as of September 30, 2012 in available funding from qualifying receivables. Funds drawn at the inception of the accounts receivable securitization facility were used to prepay $350 million of principal on Ashland's term loan B facility. The weighted-average interest rate for this instrument was 1.0% for the period issued during 2012.

Hercules Retained Instruments

Upon completion of the Hercules acquisition in 2009, Ashland assumed the following Hercules debt facilities: 6.60% notes due 2027, 6.50% junior subordinated deferrable interest debentures due 2029, and term loans of Hercules Tianpu at rates ranging from 2.10% to 5.47% through 2011. The term loans of Hercules Tianpu were fully repaid during 2011.

The 6.50% junior subordinated deferrable interest debentures due 2029 (the 6.50% debentures) had an initial issue price of $741.46 and have a redemption price of $1,000. The 6.50% debentures were initially issued to Hercules Trust II (Trust II), a subsidiary trust established in 1999. Trust II had issued, in an underwritten public offering, 350,000 CRESTS SM Units, each consisting of a 6.50% preferred security of Trust II and a warrant (exercisable through 2029) to purchase 23.4192 shares of the Hercules Common Stock for the equivalent of $42.70 per share. The preferred securities and the warrants were separable and were initially valued at $741.46 and $258.54, respectively. In connection with the Hercules dissolution and liquidation of Trust II in December 2004, Trust II distributed the 6.50% debentures to the holders of the preferred securities and the preferred securities were cancelled. The CRESTS SM Units now consist of the 6.50% debentures and the warrants, both of which were fair valued in conjunction with the Hercules acquisition. Ashland will accrete the difference between the $282 million par value and the $124 million recorded fair value at the time of the acquisition of the 6.50% debentures over the remaining term. The effective rate for this instrument was 15.6% during 2012 and 2011.

6.35 THE GOLDMAN SACHS GROUP, INC. (DEC)

CONSOLIDATED STATEMENTS OF CASH FLOWS (in part)

(In millions)	Year Ended December		
	2012	**2011**	**2010**
Cash Flows From Financing Activities			
Unsecured short-term borrowings, net	(1,952)	(3,780)	1,196
Other secured financings (short-term), net	1,540	(1,195)	12,689
Proceeds from issuance of other secured financings (long-term)	4,687	9,809	5,500
Repayment of other secured financings (long-term), including the current portion	(11,576)	(8,878)	(4,849)
Proceeds from issuance of unsecured long-term borrowings	27,734	29,169	20,231
Repayment of unsecured long-term borrowings, including the current portion	(36,435)	(29,187)	(22,607)
Derivative contracts with a financing element, net	1,696	1,602	1,222
Deposits, net	24,015	7,540	(849)
Preferred stock repurchased	—	(3,857)	—
Common stock repurchased	(4,640)	(6,048)	(4,183)
Dividends and dividend equivalents paid on common stock, preferred stock and restricted stock units	(1,086)	(2,771)	(1,443)
Proceeds from issuance of preferred stock, net of issuance costs	3,087	—	—
Proceeds from issuance of common stock, including stock option exercises	317	368	581
Excess tax benefit related to share-based compensation	130	358	352
Cash settlement of share-based compensation	(1)	(40)	(1)
Net cash provided by/(used for) financing activities	7,516	(6,910)	7,839

NOTES TO CONSOLIDATED FINANCIAL STATEMENTS

Note 19. Shareholders' Equity (in part)

Common Equity

Dividends declared per common share were $1.77 in 2012, $1.40 in 2011 and $1.40 in 2010. On January 15, 2013, Group Inc. declared a dividend of $0.50 per common share to be paid on March 28, 2013 to common shareholders of record on February 28, 2013.

The firm's share repurchase program is intended to help maintain the appropriate level of common equity. The repurchase program is effected primarily through regular open-market purchases, the amounts and timing of which are determined primarily by the firm's current and projected capital positions (i.e., comparisons of the firm's desired level and composition of capital to its actual level and composition of capital), but which may also be influenced by general market conditions and the prevailing price and trading volumes of the firm's common stock. Any repurchase of the firm's common stock requires approval by the Federal Reserve Board.

During 2012, 2011 and 2010, the firm repurchased 42.0 million shares, 47.0 million shares and 25.3 million shares of its common stock at an average cost per share of $110.31, $128.33 and $164.48, for a total cost of $4.64 billion, $6.04 billion and $4.16 billion, respectively, under the share repurchase program. In addition, pursuant to the terms of certain share-based compensation plans, employees may remit shares to the firm or the firm may cancel restricted stock units (RSUs) to satisfy minimum statutory employee tax withholding requirements. Under these plans, during 2012, 2011 and 2010, employees remitted 33,477 shares, 75,517 shares and 164,172 shares with a total value of $3 million, $12 million and $25 million, and the firm cancelled 12.7 million, 12.0 million and 6.2 million of RSUs with a total value of $1.44 billion, $1.91 billion and $972 million, respectively.

Preferred Equity

The table below presents perpetual preferred stock issued and outstanding as of December 2012.

Series	Shares Authorized	Shares Issued	Shares Outstanding	Dividend Rate	Redemption Value (In millions)
A	50,000	30,000	29,999	3 month LIBOR + 0.75%, with floor of 3.75% per annum	$ 750
B	50,000	32,000	32,000	6.20% per annum	800
C	25,000	8,000	8,000	3 month LIBOR + 0.75%, with floor of 4.00% per annum	200
D	60,000	54,000	53,999	3 month LIBOR + 0.67%, with floor of 4.00% per annum	1,350
E	17,500	17,500	17,500	3 month LIBOR + 0.77%, with floor of 4.00% per annum	1,750
F	5,000	5,000	5,000	3 month LIBOR + 0.77%, with floor of 4.00% per annum	500
I	34,500	34,000	34,000	5.95% per annum	850
	242,000	180,500	180,498		$6,200

Each share of non-cumulative Series A Preferred Stock, Series B Preferred Stock, Series C Preferred Stock and Series D Preferred Stock issued and outstanding has a par value of $0.01, has a liquidation preference of $25,000, is represented by 1,000 depositary shares and is redeemable at the firm's option, subject to the approval of the Federal Reserve Board, at a redemption price equal to $25,000 plus declared and unpaid dividends. On October 24, 2012, Group Inc. issued 34,000 shares of non-cumulative Series I Preferred Stock, par value $0.01 per share. Each share of Series I Preferred Stock issued and outstanding has a liquidation preference of $25,000, is represented by 1,000 depositary shares and is redeemable at the firm's option beginning November 10, 2017, subject to the approval of the Federal Reserve Board, at a redemption price equal to $25,000 plus accrued and unpaid dividends.

In 2007, the Board of Directors of Group Inc. (Board) authorized 17,500 shares of Series E Preferred Stock, and 5,000 shares of Series F Preferred Stock, in connection with the APEX Trusts. On June 1, 2012, Group Inc. issued 17,500 shares of Series E Preferred Stock to Goldman Sachs Capital II pursuant to the stock purchase contracts held by Goldman Sachs Capital II. On September 4, 2012, Group Inc. issued 5,000 shares of Series F Preferred Stock to Goldman Sachs Capital III pursuant to the stock purchase contracts held by Goldman Sachs Capital III. Each share of Series E and Series F Preferred Stock issued and outstanding has a par value of $0.01, has a liquidation preference of $100,000 and is redeemable at the option of the firm at any time subject to approval from the Federal Reserve Board and to certain covenant restrictions governing the firm's ability to redeem or purchase the preferred stock without issuing common stock or other instruments with equity-like characteristics, at a redemption price equal to $100,000 plus declared and unpaid dividends. See Note 16 for further information about the APEX Trusts.

All series of preferred stock are pari passu and have a preference over the firm's common stock on liquidation. Dividends on each series of preferred stock, if declared, are payable quarterly in arrears. The firm's ability to declare or pay dividends on, or purchase, redeem or otherwise acquire, its common stock is subject to certain restrictions in the event that the firm fails to pay or set aside full dividends on the preferred stock for the latest completed dividend period.

In March 2011, the firm provided notice to Berkshire Hathaway Inc. and certain of its subsidiaries (collectively, Berkshire Hathaway) that it would redeem in full the 50,000 shares of the firm's 10% Cumulative Perpetual Preferred Stock, Series G (Series G Preferred Stock) held by Berkshire Hathaway for the stated redemption price of $5.50 billion ($110,000 per share), plus accrued and unpaid dividends. In connection with this notice, the firm recognized a preferred dividend of $1.64 billion (calculated as the difference between the carrying value and the redemption value of the preferred stock), which was recorded as a reduction to earnings applicable to common shareholders for the first quarter of 2011. The redemption also resulted in the acceleration of $24 million of preferred dividends related to the period from April 1, 2011 to the redemption date, which was included in the firm's results during the three months ended March 2011.

The Series G Preferred Stock was redeemed on April 18, 2011. Berkshire Hathaway continues to hold a five-year warrant, issued in October 2008, to purchase up to 43.5 million shares of common stock at an exercise price of $115.00 per share.

On January 9, 2013, Group Inc. declared dividends of $234.38, $387.50, $250.00, $250.00 and $437.99 per share of Series A Preferred Stock, Series B Preferred Stock, Series C Preferred Stock, Series D Preferred Stock and Series I Preferred Stock, respectively, to be paid on February 11, 2013 to preferred shareholders of record on January 27, 2013. In addition, the firm declared dividends of $977.78 per each share of Series E Preferred Stock and Series F Preferred Stock, to be paid on March 1, 2013 to preferred shareholders of record on February 14, 2013.

The table below presents preferred dividends declared on preferred stock.

	Year Ended December					
	2012		2011		2010	
	Per share	In millions	Per share	In millions	Per share	In millions
Series A	$ 960.94	$ 29	$ 950.51	$ 28	$ 950.51	$ 28
Series B	1,550.00	50	1,550.00	50	1,550.00	50
Series C	1,025.01	8	1,013.90	8	1,013.90	8
Series D	1,025.01	55	1,013.90	55	1,013.90	55
Series E	2,055.56	36	—	—	—	—
Series F	1,000.00	5	—	—	—	—
Series G[1]	—	—	2,500.00	125	10,000.00	500
Total		$183		$266		$641

[1] Amount for the year ended December 2011 excludes preferred dividends related to the redemption of the firm's Series G Preferred Stock.

6.36 LENNAR CORPORATION (NOV)

CONSOLIDATED STATEMENTS OF CASH FLOWS (in part)

(Dollars in thousands)	2012	2011	2010
Cash Flows From Financing Activities:			
Net borrowings under Lennar Financial Services debt	$ 47,860	138,456	54,121
Proceeds from senior notes	750,000	—	247,323
Proceeds from convertible senior notes	50,000	350,000	722,500
Debt issuance costs of senior notes and convertible senior notes	(9,118)	(7,438)	(18,415)
Redemption of senior notes	—	(113,242)	(251,943)
Partial redemption of senior notes	(210,862)	—	(222,711)
Principal repayments on Rialto Investments notes payable	(191,221)	—	—
Proceeds from other borrowings	41,500	4,287	5,676
Principal payments on other borrowings	(97,891)	(136,147)	(141,505)
Exercise of land option contracts from an unconsolidated land investment venture	(50,396)	(40,964)	(39,301)
Receipts related to noncontrolling interests	1,659	5,822	14,088
Payments related to noncontrolling interests	(480)	(7,137)	(4,848)
Excess tax benefits from share-based awards	10,814	—	—
Common stock:			
Issuances	32,174	6,751	2,238
Repurchases	(17,149)	(5,724)	(1,806)
Dividends	(30,394)	(29,906)	(29,577)
Net cash provided by financing activities	326,496	164,758	335,840

NOTES TO CONSOLIDATED FINANCIAL STATEMENTS

13. Share-Based Payments

The Company has share-based awards outstanding under one plan which provides for the granting of stock options and stock appreciation rights and awards of restricted common stock ("nonvested shares") to key officers, associates and directors. These awards are primarily issued in the form of new shares. The exercise prices of stock options and stock appreciation rights may not be less than the market value of the common stock on the date of the grant. Exercises are permitted in installments determined when options are granted. Each stock option and stock appreciation right will expire on a date determined at the time of the grant, but not more than ten years after the date of the grant.

Cash flows resulting from tax benefits related to tax deductions in excess of the compensation expense recognized for those options (excess tax benefits) are classified as financing cash flows. For the year ended November 30, 2012 there was $10.8 million of excess tax benefits from share based awards. For the years ended November 30, 2011 and 2010 there was an immaterial amount of excess tax benefits from share-based awards.

Compensation expense related to the Company's share-based awards was as follows:

	Years Ended November 30,		
(In thousands)	2012	2011	2010
Stock options	$ 2,433	4,382	5,985
Nonvested shares	29,312	19,665	22,090
Total compensation expense for share-based awards	$31,745	24,047	28,075

Cash received from stock options exercised during the years ended November 30, 2012, 2011 and 2010 was $26.5 million, $6.2 million, and $2.0 million, respectively. The tax deductions related to stock options exercised during the years ended November 30, 2012, 2011, and 2010 were $14.8 million, $0.8 million and $0.2 million, respectively.

The fair value of each of the Company's stock option awards is estimated on the date of grant using a Black-Scholes option-pricing model that uses the assumptions noted in the table below. The fair value of the Company's stock option awards, which are subject to graded vesting, is expensed on a straight-line basis over the vesting life of the stock options. Expected volatility is based on historical volatility of the Company's stock over the most recent period equal to the expected life of the award. The risk-free rate for periods within the contractual life of the stock option award is based on the yield curve of a zero-coupon U.S. Treasury bond on the date the stock option award is granted with a maturity equal to the expected term of the stock option award granted. The Company uses historical data to estimate stock option exercises and forfeitures within its valuation model. The expected life of stock option awards granted is derived from historical exercise experience under the Company's share-based payment plans and represents the period of time that stock option awards granted are expected to be outstanding.

The fair value of these options was determined at the date of the grant using the Black-Scholes option-pricing model. The significant weighted average assumptions for the years ended November 30, 2012, 2011 and 2010 were as follows:

	2012	2011	2010
Dividends yield	0.6%	0.9%	0.9%–1.1%
Volatility rate	47.0%	46.7%	80%–112%
Risk-free interest rate	0.2%	0.6%	0.2%–0.6%
Expected option life (years)	1.5	1.5	1.5

A summary of the Company's stock option activity for the year ended November 30, 2012 was as follows:

	Stock Options	Weighted Average Exercise Price	Weighted Average Remaining Contractual Life	Aggregate Intrinsic Value (In thousands)
Outstanding at November 30, 2011	3,861,286	$18.43		
Grants	17,500	$25.75		
Forfeited or expired	(636,412)	$42.97		
Exercises	(1,962,302)	$13.52		
Outstanding at November 30, 2012	1,280,072	$13.85	0.7 years	$30,969
Vested and expected to vest in the future at November 30, 2012	1,280,072	$13.85	0.7 years	$30,969
Exercisable at November 30, 2012	1,280,072	$13.85	0.7 years	$30,969
Available for grant at November 30, 2012	11,819,055			

The weighted average fair value of options granted during the years ended November 30, 2012, 2011 and 2010 was $5.72, $4.01 and $8.66, respectively. The total intrinsic value of options exercised during the years ended November 30, 2012, 2011, and 2010 was $38.1 million, $2.1 million and $0.6 million, respectively.

The fair value of nonvested shares is determined based on the trading price of the Company's common stock on the grant date. The weighted average fair value of nonvested shares granted during the years ended November 30, 2012, 2011 and 2010 was $30.62, $18.40 and $15.21, respectively. A summary of the Company's nonvested shares activity for the year ended November 30, 2012 was as follows:

	Shares	Weighted Average Grant Date Fair Value
Nonvested restricted shares at November 30, 2011	2,963,750	$16.48
Grants	1,335,087	$30.62
Vested	(1,728,056)	$15.95
Forfeited	—	$ —
Nonvested restricted shares at November 30, 2012	2,570,781	$24.18

At November 30, 2012, there was $56.7 million of unrecognized compensation expense related to unvested share-based awards granted under the Company's share-based payment plans, of which none relates to stock options and $56.7 million relates to nonvested shares. The unrecognized expense related to nonvested shares is expected to be recognized over a weighted-average period of 2.4 years. During the years ended November 30, 2012, 2011 and 2010, 1.7 million nonvested shares, 1.4 million nonvested shares and 1.3 million nonvested shares, respectively, vested. For the year ended November 30, 2012, the Company recorded a tax benefit related to nonvested share activity of $11.7 million. For the years ended November 30, 2011 and 2010, there was no tax provision related to nonvested share activity because the Company had recorded a full valuation allowance against its deferred tax assets.

DIVIDENDS

6.37 CA, INC. (MAR)
CONSOLIDATED STATEMENTS OF CASH FLOWS (in part)

	Year Ended March 31,		
(In millions)	2012	2011	2010
Financing Activities From Continuing Operations:			
Dividends paid	$ (192)	$ (82)	$ (83)
Purchases of common stock, including accelerated share repurchase	(1,053)	(235)	(227)
Debt borrowings	476	260	744
Debt repayments	(599)	(273)	(1,205)
Debt issuance costs	(2)	—	(6)
Proceeds from call spread option	—	—	61
Exercise of common stock options and other	40	10	11
Net cash used in financing activities—continuing operations	$(1,330)	$(320)	$ (705)

Note 13—Stockholders' Equity (in part)

Dividends: In January 2012, the Board of Directors approved a $2.5 billion capital allocation program through fiscal year 2014 that includes an increase in the Company's annual dividend from $0.20 to $1.00 per share of common stock as and when declared by the Board of Directors.

The Company's Board of Directors declared the following dividends during fiscal years 2012 and 2011:

Year Ended March 31, 2012:

(In millions, except per share amounts) Declaration Date	Dividend Per Share	Record Date	Total Amount	Payment Date
May 12, 2011	$0.05	May 23, 2011	$ 25	June 16, 2011
August 3, 2011	$0.05	August 16, 2011	$ 25	September 14, 2011
November 9, 2011	$0.05	November 22, 2011	$ 25	December 14, 2011
January 23, 2012	$0.25	February 14, 2012	$117	March 13, 2012

Year Ended March 31, 2011:

(In millions, except per share amounts) Declaration Date	Dividend Per Share	Record Date	Total Amount	Payment Date
May 12, 2010	$0.04	May 31, 2010	$21	June 16, 2010
July 28, 2010	$0.04	August 9, 2010	$20	August 19, 2010
December 2, 2010	$0.04	December 13, 2010	$20	December 22, 2010
February 2, 2011	$0.04	February 14, 2011	$21	March 14, 2011

DEBT ISSUANCE COSTS

6.38 JDS UNIPHASE CORPORATION (JUN)
CONSOLIDATED STATEMENTS OF CASH FLOWS (in part)

(In millions)

	Years Ended		
	June 30, 2012	July 2, 2011	July 3, 2010
Financing Activities:			
Payment of financing obligations	(11.6)	(6.8)	(8.6)
Proceeds from financing obligations	6.9	—	—
Redemption of convertible debt	(13.2)	(0.2)	—
Payment of debt issuance costs	(1.9)	—	—
Proceeds from exercise of employee stock options and employee stock purchase plan	17.9	38.1	9.6
Net cash (used in) provided by financing activities	(1.9)	31.1	1.0

NOTES TO CONSOLIDATED FINANCIAL STATEMENTS

Note 11. Debts and Letters of Credit (in part)

1% Senior Convertible Notes

On June 5, 2006, the Company completed an offering of $425 million aggregate principal amount of 1% Senior Convertible Notes due 2026. Proceeds from the notes amounted to $415.9 million after issuance costs. The notes bear interest at a rate of 1.00% per year and are convertible into a combination of cash and shares of the Company's common stock at a conversion price of $30.30 per share. Interest on the notes is payable semi-annually in arrears on May 15 and November 15 of each year, beginning on November 15, 2006. The notes mature on May 15, 2026.

The holders of the notes may require the Company to purchase all or a portion of the notes on each of May 15, 2013, May 15, 2016 and May 15, 2021 at a price equal to 100% of the principal amount of the notes to be purchased plus any accrued and unpaid interest to, but excluding, the purchase date. In addition, upon certain fundamental changes, holders may require the Company to purchase for cash the notes at a price equal to 100% of the principal amount of the notes to be purchased plus any accrued and unpaid interest to, but excluding, the purchase date. The Company may not redeem the notes before May 20, 2013. On or after that date, the Company may redeem all or part of the notes for cash at 100% of the principal amount of the notes to be redeemed, plus accrued and unpaid interest to, but excluding, the redemption date.

Upon adoption of the authoritative guidance which applies to the 1% Senior Convertible Notes, the Company calculated the carrying value of the liability component at issuance as the present value of its cash flows using a discount rate of 8.1%, based on the 7-year swap rate plus credit spread as of the issuance date. The credit spread for JDSU is based on the historical average "yield to worst" rate for BB-rated issuers. The carrying value of the liability component was determined to be $266.5 million. The equity component, or debt discount, of the notes was determined to be $158.5 million. The debt discount is being amortized using the effective interest rate of 8.1% over the period from issuance date through May 15, 2013 as a non-cash charge to interest expense. As of June 30, 2012, the remaining term of the 1% Senior Convertible Notes is less than one year and accordingly is classified as short-term debt.

The $9.1 million of costs incurred in connection with the issuance of the notes were capitalized and bifurcated into debt issuance cost of $5.7 million and equity issuance cost of $3.4 million. The debt issuance cost is being amortized to interest expense using the effective interest method from issuance date through May 15, 2013.

During fiscal 2012, the Company repurchased $14.0 million aggregate principal amount of the notes for $13.9 million in cash. In connection with the repurchase, a loss of $0.7 million was recognized in interest and other income (loss), net in compliance with the authoritative guidance. After giving effect to the repurchase, the total amount of 1% Senior Convertible Notes outstanding as of June 30, 2012 was $292.8 million.

As of June 30, 2012, the unamortized portion of the debt issuance cost related to the notes is $0.7 million and is included in Other current assets on the Consolidated Balance Sheets.

The following table presents the carrying amounts of the liability and equity components *(in millions)* :

	Years Ended	
	June 30, 2012	July 2, 2011
Carrying amount of equity component	$158.3	$158.5
Principal amount of 1% Senior Coupon Notes	311.0	325.0
Unamortized discount of liability component	(18.2)	(39.2)
Carrying amount of liability component	$292.8	$285.8

Based on quoted market prices, as of June 30, 2012 and July 2, 2011, the fair market value of the 1% Senior Convertible Notes was approximately $307.3 million and $332.1 million, respectively. Changes in fair market value reflect the change in the market price of the notes. The 1% Senior Convertible Notes are classified within level 2 as they are not actively traded in markets; and the bond parity derivatives related to the convertible notes are classified within level 1 since the quoted market price for identical instrument are available in active markets. The fair value of the bond parity derivatives is approximately zero as of June 30, 2012 and July 2, 2011.

The following table presents the effective interest rate and the interest expense for the contractual interest and the accretion of debt discount (in millions, except for the effective interest rate):

	Years Ended	
	June 30 2012	July 2 2011
Effective interest rate	8.1%	8.1%
Interest expense-contractual interest	$ 3.2	$ 3.3
Accretion of debt discount	20.1	18.7

The increase of the debt related to the interest accretion is treated as a non-cash transaction and the repayment of the carrying amount of the debt is classified as a financing activity within the Consolidated Statement of Cash Flows.

Revolving Credit Facility

On January 20, 2012, the Company entered into an agreement (the "Credit Agreement") for a five-year $250.0 million revolving credit facility that matures in January 2017. At the Company's option, the principal amount available under the facility may be increased by up to an additional $100 million. Borrowings under the credit facility bear an annual interest rate, at the Company's option, equal to either (i) the Alternate Base Rate (as defined in the Credit Agreement) plus the applicable margin for base rate loans, which ranges between 0.75% and 2.00%, based on the Company's leverage ratio or (ii) the Adjusted LIBO Rate (as defined in the Credit Agreement) plus the applicable margin for Eurocurrency loans, which ranges between 1.75% and 3.00%, based on the Company's leverage ratio. The Company is required to pay a commitment fee on the unutilized portion of the facility of between 0.25% and 0.50%, based on the Company's leverage ratio.

Obligations under the Credit Agreement are guaranteed by certain wholly owned domestic subsidiaries of the Company ("the Guarantors"). The Company's obligations under the Credit Agreement have been secured by a pledge of substantially all assets of the Company and the Guarantors (subject to certain exclusions), full pledges of equity interests in certain domestic subsidiaries and partial pledges of equity interests in certain foreign subsidiaries. The Company has also agreed to maintain at least $200 million of cash and permitted investments in accounts which are subject to a control agreement.

The Credit Agreement contains certain affirmative and negative covenants applicable to the Company and its subsidiaries, which include, among other things, restrictions on their ability to (i) incur additional indebtedness, (ii) make certain investments, (iii) acquire other entities, (iv) dispose of assets, (v) incur liens and (vi) make certain payments including those related to dividends or repurchase of equity. The Credit Agreement also contains financial maintenance covenants, including a maximum senior secured leverage ratio, a maximum total leverage ratio, a minimum interest coverage ratio and the requirement to maintain minimum liquidity.

The $1.9 million of costs incurred in connection with the issuance of the revolving credit facility were capitalized and are being amortized to interest expense on a straight-line basis over five years based on the contractual term of the revolving credit facility. As of June 30, 2012, the unamortized portion of debt issuance cost related to the revolving credit facility was $1.7 million, and was included in Other current assets and Other non-current assets on the Consolidated Balance Sheets.

There was no drawdown under the facility during fiscal 2012, and the outstanding balance as of June 30, 2012 is zero.

FINANCIAL INSTRUMENT SETTLEMENTS

6.39 DEAN FOODS COMPANY (DEC)
CONSOLIDATED STATEMENTS OF CASH FLOWS (in part)

	Year Ended December 31		
(In thousands)	2012	2011	2010
Cash Flows From Financing Activities:			
Proceeds from issuance of debt	—	—	400,000
Repayment of Dean Foods Company senior secured term loan debt	(1,350,275)	(209,885)	(514,189)
Proceeds from senior secured revolver	2,481,800	3,274,390	4,006,680
Payments for senior secured revolver	(2,316,500)	(3,627,690)	(4,068,880)
Proceeds from receivables-backed facility	2,834,551	4,246,006	2,220,267
Payments for receivables-backed facility	(3,072,961)	(4,007,598)	(2,220,267)
Proceeds from subsidiary senior secured credit facility	1,019,200	—	—
Payments for subsidiary senior secured credit facility	(238,650)	—	—
Payments of financing costs	(12,278)	(600)	(52,720)
Proceeds from sale of subsidiary shares in initial public offering, net of offering costs	367,540	—	—
Issuance of common stock, net of share repurchases for withholding taxes	6,434	3,623	3,415
Tax savings on share-based compensation	571	33	278
Capital contribution from non-controlling interest	—	6,754	7,992
Net cash used in financing activities—continuing operations	(280,568)	(314,967)	(217,424)
Net cash provided by (used in) financing activities—discontinued operations	(21,895)	21,369	(268)
Net cash used in financing activities	(302,463)	(293,598)	(217,692)

NOTES TO CONSOLIDATED FINANCIAL STATEMENTS

10. Debt (in part)

	December 31, 2012		December 31, 2011	
(In thousands, except percentages)	Amount Outstanding	Interest Rate	Amount Outstanding	Interest Rate
Dean Foods Company debt obligations:				
Senior secured credit facility	$1,292,197	4.82%*	$2,477,160	3.00%*
Senior notes due 2016	499,167	7.00	498,959	7.00
Senior notes due 2018	400,000	9.75	400,000	9.75
	2,191,364		3,376,119	
Subsidiary debt obligations:				
WhiteWave senior secured credit facilities	780,550	2.20*	—	—
Senior notes due 2017	130,879	6.90	129,117	6.90
Receivables-backed facility	—	—	238,410	1.31**
Capital lease obligations and other	—		281	
Alpro revolving credit facility	—			
	911,429		367,808	
	3,102,793		3,743,927	
Less current portion	(25,535)		(202,292)	
Total long-term portion	$3,077,258		$3,541,635	

* Represents a weighted average rate, including applicable interest rate margins, for the senior secured revolving credit facility, term loan A and term loan B.
** Represents a weighted-average rate, including applicable interest rate margins, for indebtedness outstanding under the receivables securitization facility.

The scheduled maturities of long-term debt at December 31, 2012, were as follows (in thousands):

	Total	Dean Foods Term Loan B	Other Dean Foods Company Debt*	WhiteWave Senior Secured Credit Facilities
2013	$ 25,535	$ 10,535	$ —	$ 15,000
2014	290,535	10,535	265,000	15,000
2015	31,786	10,536	—	21,250
2016	992,173	470,923	500,000	21,250
2017	1,137,218	524,668	142,000	470,550
Thereafter	637,500	—	400,000	237,500
Subtotal	3,114,747	1,027,197	1,307,000	780,550
Less discounts	(11,954)	—	(11,954)	—
Total outstanding debt	$3,102,793	$1,027,197	$1,295,046	$780,550

* Includes the Dean Foods revolving credit facility, receivables-backed facility, Dean Foods Company senior notes and the subsidiary senior notes.

Dean Foods Senior Secured Credit Facility—Our senior secured credit facility consists of an original combination of a $1.5 billion five-year revolving credit facility, a $1.5 billion five-year term loan A and a $1.8 billion seven-year term loan B. In June 2010, we amended and restated the agreement governing the senior secured credit facility, and entered into a further amendment in December 2010, which included extension of the maturity dates for certain principal amounts, amendment of the maximum permitted leverage ratio and minimum interest coverage ratio and the addition of a senior secured leverage ratio (each as defined in our credit agreement), and the amendment of certain other terms. At December 31, 2012, there were outstanding borrowings of $1.03 billion under the term loan B and $265 million under the revolving credit facility. Our average daily balance under the revolving credit facility during the year ended December 31, 2012 was $107.2 million. Letters of credit in the aggregate amount of $1.0 million were issued under the revolving credit facility but undrawn.

Effective April 2, 2012, pursuant to the terms of our amended and restated credit agreement dated June 30, 2010, the total commitment amount available to us under the senior secured revolving credit facility decreased from $1.5 billion to $1.275 billion, and any principal borrowings on a pro rata basis related to the $225 million of non-extended revolving credit facility commitments were reallocated to the remaining portion of the facility. Additionally, in connection with the WhiteWave IPO discussed in Note 2, effective October 31, 2012, we voluntarily reduced the total commitment amount available to us under the revolving credit facility from $1.275 billion to $1.0 billion. No principal payments are due on these revolving credit facility commitments until April 2, 2014. The amended and restated senior secured revolving credit facility is available for the issuance of up to $350 million of letters of credit and up to $150 million of swing line loans. Our credit agreement requires mandatory principal prepayments upon the occurrence of certain asset sales (provided that such sales, in total, exceed $250 million in any fiscal year), recovery events or as a result of exceeding certain leverage limits.

Our credit agreement permits us to complete acquisitions that meet all of the following conditions without obtaining prior approval: (1) the acquired company is involved in the manufacture, processing and distribution of food or packaging products or any other line of business in which we were engaged as of April 2007; (2) the net cash purchase price for any single acquisition is not greater than $500 million and not greater than $100 million if our leverage ratio is greater than 4.50 times on a pro-forma basis; (3) we acquire at least 51% of the acquired entity; (4) the transaction is approved by the board of directors or shareholders, as appropriate, of the target; and (5) after giving effect to such acquisition on a pro-forma basis, we would have been in compliance with all financial covenants. All other acquisitions must be approved in advance by the required lenders.

The senior secured credit facility contains limitations on liens, investments and the incurrence of additional indebtedness, prohibits certain dispositions of property and restricts certain payments, including dividends. There are no restrictions on these certain payments, including dividends, when our leverage ratio is below 4.50 times consolidated EBITDA (as defined in the credit agreement) on a pro-forma basis. The senior secured credit facility is secured by liens on substantially all of our domestic assets, including the assets of our domestic subsidiaries, but excluding all assets of WhiteWave and its subsidiaries, the capital stock of subsidiaries of the former Dean Foods Company ("Legacy Dean") and the capital stock of WhiteWave and its subsidiaries, the real property owned by Legacy Dean and its subsidiaries, and accounts receivable associated with the receivables-backed facility. In connection with the WhiteWave IPO, WhiteWave and its subsidiaries have been released from their obligations as guarantors of Dean Foods' senior secured credit facility and designated as unrestricted subsidiaries thereunder.

The credit agreement governing our senior secured credit facility contains standard default triggers, including without limitation: failure to maintain compliance with the financial and other covenants contained in the credit agreement, default on certain of our other debt, a change in control and certain other material adverse changes in our business. The credit agreement does not contain any requirements to maintain specific credit rating levels.

As discussed in Note 3, on January 3, 2013, we completed the sale of our Morningstar division to a third party and we received net proceeds of approximately $1.45 billion, a portion of which was used for the full repayment of $480 million in outstanding 2016 Tranche B term loan borrowings, $547 million in outstanding 2017 Tranche B term loan borrowings and $265 million in revolver borrowings outstanding as of December 31, 2012. As a result of these principal repayments, we expect to write off $1.5 million in previously deferred financing costs related to Dean Foods' senior secured credit facility in the first quarter of 2013.

Additionally, we repatriated approximately €55 million ($71 million) from our foreign operations during the second quarter of 2012 and utilized approximately $70 million of those funds to prepay a portion of our then-outstanding 2014 tranche A term loan borrowings.

WhiteWave Senior Secured Credit Facilities—On October 12, 2012, in connection with the WhiteWave IPO discussed in Note 2, WhiteWave entered into senior secured credit facilities, consisting of a five-year $850 million revolving credit facility, a five-year $250 million term loan A-1 and a seven-year $250 million term loan A-2. The revolving credit facility will be available for the issuance of up to $75 million of letters of credit and up to $75 million of swing line loans.

As of December 31, 2012, WhiteWave had total outstanding borrowings of $780.6 million under its senior secured credit facility, which consisted of $500 million in term loan borrowings and $280.6 million drawn under its revolving credit facility.

The terms of WhiteWave's senior secured credit facilities include the following:
- maturity on October 31, 2017 for the term loan A-1 and revolving credit facility and October 31, 2019 for the $250 million term loan A-2 facility;
- required amortization repayment in quarterly installments of the following amounts on the $250 million term loan A-1 facility: $12.5 million in 2013 and 2014, $18.75 million in 2015 and 2016, and $25.0 million in 2017, with the balance at maturity, and in the case of the $250 million term loan A-2 facility, $2.5 million in 2013 through 2019, with the balance at maturity;

- an accordion feature allowing, under certain circumstances, the maximum principal amount of the senior secured credit facilities to be increased by up to $500 million, subject to lender commitments;
- mandatory prepayments in the event of certain asset sales and receipt of insurance proceeds;
- customary representations and warranties that are made at closing and upon each borrowing under the senior secured credit facilities;
- customary affirmative and negative covenants for agreements of this type, including delivery of financial and other information, compliance with laws, further assurances, and limitations with respect to indebtedness, liens, fundamental changes, restrictive agreements, dispositions of assets, acquisitions and other investments, sale leaseback transactions, conduct of business, transactions with affiliates, and restricted payments; and
- financial covenants establishing (a) a maximum consolidated net leverage ratio initially set at 4.25 to 1.00 and stepping down to 4.00 to 1.00 beginning March 31, 2014 and then to 3.75 to 1.00 beginning March 31, 2015 and thereafter (subject to WhiteWave's right to increase such ratio by 0.50 to 1.00, but not to exceed 4.50 to 1.00, for the next four fiscal quarters following any permitted acquisition for which the purchase consideration equals or exceeds $50 million) and (b) a minimum consolidated interest coverage ratio set at 3.00 to 1.00.

WhiteWave's senior secured credit facilities are secured by security interests and liens on substantially all of its assets and the assets of its material domestic subsidiaries. The senior secured credit facilities are guaranteed by its material domestic subsidiaries. Dean Foods Company does not guarantee WhiteWave's senior secured credit facilities. Borrowings under the senior secured credit facilities currently bear interest at a rate of LIBOR plus 1.75% per annum or, in the case of the $250 million term loan A-2 facility, LIBOR plus 2.00% per annum, and are subject to adjustment based on WhiteWave's consolidated net leverage ratio.

WhiteWave incurred financing costs of approximately $12 million in connection with the execution of its senior secured credit facilities, which have been deferred and will be recognized over the terms of the respective debt agreements using the effective interest method.

Use of Net Proceeds from WhiteWave IPO and Initial Borrowing under WhiteWave Senior Secured Credit Facilities—On October 31, 2012, WhiteWave incurred approximately $885 million in new indebtedness under its senior secured credit facilities. Substantially all of the net proceeds of the borrowing and $282 million of the net proceeds from the WhiteWave IPO, totaling approximately $1.16 billion, were contributed to WWF Opco, which then paid such proceeds to Dean Foods to repay then-outstanding obligations under intercompany notes owed to Dean Foods. On October 31, 2012, we utilized those funds to repay in full the then-outstanding $480 million aggregate principal amount of our 2014 Tranche A term loan and the then-outstanding $675 million aggregate principal amount of our outstanding 2014 Tranche B term loan borrowings. As a result of these principal repayments, $3.5 million in previously deferred financing costs related to Deans Foods' senior secured credit facility were written off in the fourth quarter of 2012.

Dean Foods Receivables-Backed Facility—We have a $600 million receivables securitization facility pursuant to which certain of our subsidiaries sell their accounts receivable to four wholly-owned entities intended to be bankruptcy-remote. The entities then transfer the receivables to third-party asset-backed commercial paper conduits sponsored by major financial institutions. The assets and liabilities of these four entities are fully reflected in our Consolidated Balance Sheets, and the securitization is treated as a borrowing for accounting purposes. The receivables-backed facility is available for the issuance of letters of credit of up to $300 million.

In connection with the WhiteWave IPO, effective September 1, 2012, WWF Opco and its subsidiaries were no longer participants in the Dean Foods receivables securitization program. Receivables sold by WWF Opco to these entities on or prior to August 31, 2012 will continue to be collected by us; however, any receivables generated by WhiteWave or WWF Opco subsequent to September 1, 2012 will not be sold into the receivables securitization program, and no WWF Opco receivables previously sold into the facility will be included in the determination of our ability to re-borrow under the facility. Additionally, effective November 1, 2012, Morningstar Foods and its subsidiaries were no longer participants in the Dean Foods receivables securitization program. Receivables sold by Morningstar to these entities prior to October 31, 2012 will continue to be collected by us; however, any receivables generated by Morningstar or its subsidiaries subsequent to November 1, 2012 will not be sold into the receivables securitization program, and no Morningstar receivables previously sold into the facility will be included in the determination of our ability to re-borrow under the facility as described below. See Note 2 and Note 3, respectively, for more information regarding the WhiteWave IPO and the Morningstar divestiture.

The total amount of receivables sold to the receivables securitization entities as of December 31, 2012 was $748.5 million. During the year ended December 31, 2012, we borrowed $2.83 billion and subsequently repaid $3.07 billion under the facility with no remaining drawn balance at December 31, 2012, excluding letters of credit in the aggregate amount of $230.6 million that were issued but undrawn. Our average daily balance under this facility during the year ended December 31, 2012 was $148.5 million. The receivables-backed facility bears interest at a variable rate based upon commercial paper and one-month LIBOR rates plus an applicable margin. Our ability to re-borrow under this facility is subject to a monthly borrowing base formula. Based on this formula, we had the ability to borrow up to $572.4 million of the $600 million total commitment amount as of December 31, 2012.

6.40 CHESAPEAKE ENERGY CORPORATION (DEC)

CONSOLIDATED STATEMENTS OF CASH FLOWS (in part)

	Years Ended December 31,		
($ in millions)	2012	2011	2010
Cash Flows From Financing Activities:			
Proceeds from credit facilities borrowings	20,318	15,509	15,117
Payments on credit facilities borrowings	(21,650)	(17,466)	(13,303)
Proceeds from issuance of term loans, net of discount and offering costs	5,722	—	—
Proceeds from issuance of senior notes, net of discount and offering costs	1,263	1,614	1,967
Proceeds from issuance of preferred stock, net of offering costs			2,562
Cash paid to purchase debt	(4,000)	(2,015)	(3,434)
Cash paid for common stock dividends	(227)	(207)	(189)
Cash paid for preferred stock dividends	(171)	(172)	(92)
Cash (paid) received on financing derivatives	(37)	1,043	621
Proceeds from sales of noncontrolling interests	1,077	1,348	—
Proceeds from other financings	257	300	—
Distributions to noncontrolling interest owners	(218)	(9)	—
Net increase (decrease) in outstanding payments in excess of cash balance	(172)	353	20
Other	(79)	(140)	(88)
Cash provided by financing activities	2,083	158	3,181

NOTES TO CONSOLIDATED FINANCIAL STATEMENTS

8. Stockholders' Equity, Restricted Stock, Stock Options and Noncontrolling Interests (in part)

Noncontrolling Interests

Cleveland Tonkawa Financial Transaction. We formed CHK Cleveland Tonkawa, L.L.C. (CHK C-T) in March 2012 to continue development of a portion of our natural gas and oil assets in our Cleveland and Tonkawa plays. CHK C-T is an unrestricted subsidiary under our corporate credit facility agreement and is not a guarantor of, or otherwise liable for, any of our indebtedness or other liabilities, including under our indentures. In exchange for all of the common shares of CHK C-T, we contributed to CHK C-T approximately 245,000 net acres of leasehold and the existing wells within an area of mutual interest in the Cleveland and Tonkawa plays covering Ellis and Roger Mills counties in western Oklahoma. In March 2012, in a private placement, third-party investors contributed $1.25 billion in cash to CHK C-T in exchange for (i) 1.25 million preferred shares, and (ii) our obligation to deliver a 3.75% overriding royalty interest (ORRI) in the existing wells and up to 1,000 new net wells to be drilled on certain of our Cleveland and Tonkawa play leasehold. Subject to customary minority interest protections afforded the investors by the terms of the CHK C-T limited liability company agreement (the CHK C-T LLC Agreement), as the holder of all the common shares and the sole managing member of CHK C-T, we maintain voting and managerial control of CHK C-T and therefore include it in our consolidated financial statements. Of the $1.25 billion of investment proceeds, we allocated $225 million to the ORRI obligation and $1.025 billion to the preferred shares based on estimates of fair values. The ORRI obligation is included in other current and long-term liabilities and the preferred shares are included in noncontrolling interests on our consolidated balance sheet. Pursuant to the CHK C-T LLC Agreement, CHK C-T is currently required to retain an amount of cash (measured quarterly) equal to (i) the next two quarters of preferred dividend payments plus (ii) its projected operating funding shortfall for the next six months. The amount so retained, approximately $57 million as of December 31, 2012, is reflected as restricted cash on our consolidated balance sheet.

Dividends on the preferred shares are payable on a quarterly basis at a rate of 6% per annum based on $1,000 per share. This dividend rate is subject to increase in limited circumstances in the event that, and only for so long as, any dividend amount is not paid in full for any quarter. As the managing member of CHK C-T, we may, at our sole discretion and election at any time after March 31, 2014, distribute certain excess cash of CHK C-T, as determined in accordance with the CHK C-T LLC Agreement. Any such optional distribution of excess cash is allocated 75% to the preferred shares (which is applied toward redemption of the preferred shares) and 25% to the common shares unless we have not met our drilling commitment at such time, in which case an optional distribution would be allocated 100% to the preferred shares (and applied toward redemption thereof). We may also, at our sole discretion and election, in accordance with the CHK C-T LLC Agreement, cause CHK C-T to redeem all or a portion of the CHK C-T preferred shares for cash. The preferred shares will be redeemed at a valuation equal to the greater of a 9% internal rate of return or a return on investment of 1.35 x, in each case inclusive of dividends paid through redemption at the rate of 6% per annum and optional distributions made through the applicable redemption date. In the event that redemption does not occur on or prior to March 31, 2019, the optional redemption valuation will increase to provide a 15% internal rate of return to the investors. The preferred shares are redeemed on a pro-rata basis in accordance with the then-applicable redemption valuation formula. As of December 31, 2012, the redemption price and the liquidation preference were each $1,305 per preferred share.

We have committed to drill, for the benefit of CHK C-T in the area of mutual interest, a minimum of 37.5 net wells per six-month period through 2013, inclusive of wells drilled in 2012, and 25 net wells per six-month period in 2014 through 2016, up to a minimum cumulative total of 300 net wells. If we fail to meet the then-current cumulative drilling commitment in any six-month period, any optional cash distributions would be distributed 100% to the investors. If we fail to meet the then-current cumulative drilling commitment in two consecutive six-month periods, the then-applicable internal rate of return to investors at redemption would increase by 3% per annum. In addition, if we fail to meet the then-current cumulative drilling commitment in four consecutive six-month periods, the then-applicable internal rate of return to investors at redemption would be increased by an additional 3% per annum. Any such increase in the internal rate of return would be effective only until the end of the first succeeding six-month period in which we have met our then-current cumulative drilling commitment. CHK C-T is responsible for all capital and operating costs of the wells drilled for the benefit of the entity.

The CHK C-T investors' right to receive, proportionately, a 3.75% ORRI in up to 1,000 new net wells and the contributed wells, on our Cleveland and Tonkawa leasehold is subject to an increase to 5% on net wells drilled in any year following a year in which we do not meet our commitment to drill the wells subject to the ORRI obligation, which runs from 2012 through the first quarter of 2025. However, in no event would we deliver to investors more than a total ORRI of 3.75% in existing wells and 1,000 new net wells. If at any time we hold fewer net acres than would enable us to drill all then-remaining net wells on 160-acre spacing, the investors have the right to require us to repurchase their right to receive ORRIs in the remaining net wells at the then-current fair market value of such remaining net wells. We retain the right to repurchase the investors' right to receive ORRIs in the remaining net wells at the then-current fair market value of such remaining net wells once we have drilled a minimum of 867 net wells. The obligation to deliver future ORRIs has been recorded as a liability which will be settled through the conveyance of the underlying ORRIs to the investors on a net-well basis, at which time the associated liability will be reversed and the sale of the ORRIs reflected as an adjustment to the capitalized cost of our natural gas and oil properties.

As of December 31, 2012, $1.015 billion was recorded as noncontrolling interests on our consolidated balance sheet representing the third-party investments in CHK C-T. For 2012, income of $57 million was attributable to the noncontrolling interests of CHK C-T. Under the development agreement, approximately 85 qualified net wells were added in 2012. Under the ORRI obligation, we delivered an ORRI in approximately 76 new net wells. For 2012, we met all commitments associated with the CHK C-T transaction.

Utica Financial Transaction. We formed CHK Utica, L.L.C. (CHK Utica) in October 2011 to develop a portion of our Utica Shale natural gas and oil assets. CHK Utica is an unrestricted subsidiary under our corporate credit facility agreement and is not a guarantor of, or otherwise liable for, any of our indebtedness or other liabilities, including under our indentures. In exchange for all of the common shares of CHK Utica, we contributed to CHK Utica approximately 700,000 net acres of leasehold and the existing wells within an area of mutual interest in the Utica Shale play covering 13 counties located primarily in eastern Ohio. During November and December 2011, in private placements, third-party investors contributed $1.25 billion in cash to CHK Utica in exchange for (i) 1.25 million preferred shares, and (ii) our obligation to deliver a 3% ORRI in 1,500 net wells to be drilled on certain of our Utica Shale leasehold. Subject to customary minority interest protections afforded the investors by the terms of the CHK Utica limited liability company agreement (the CHK Utica LLC Agreement), as the holder of all the common shares and the sole managing member of CHK Utica, we maintain voting and managerial control of CHK Utica and therefore include it in our consolidated financial statements. Of the $1.25 billion of investment proceeds, we allocated $300 million to the ORRI obligation and $950 million to the preferred shares based on estimates of fair values. The ORRI obligation is included in other current and long-term liabilities and the preferred shares are included in noncontrolling interests on our consolidated balance sheets. Pursuant to the CHK Utica LLC Agreement, CHK Utica is required to retain a cash balance equal to the next two quarters of preferred dividend payments. The amount reserved for paying such dividends, approximately $44 million, is reflected as restricted cash on our consolidated balance sheet as of December 31, 2012. In addition, pursuant to the CHK Utica LLC Agreement, with respect to any sales proceeds as defined by the agreement, CHK Utica is required to separately account for, and dedicate all of such sales proceeds to either (i) capital expenditures made by CHK Utica in connection with its assets or (ii) the redemption of CHK Utica preferred shares. As a result of the sale of non-core Utica Shale assets in 2012, the amount reserved for paying capital expenditures, approximately $155 million, is reflected as restricted cash in other long-term assets on our consolidated balance sheet as of December 31, 2012. See Note 11 for further discussion of the sale of non-core Utica Shale assets.

Dividends on the preferred shares are payable on a quarterly basis at a rate of 7% per annum based on $1,000 per share. This dividend rate is subject to increase in limited circumstances in the event that, and only for so long as, any dividend amount is not paid in full for any quarter. If we fail to meet the then-current drilling commitment in any year, we must pay CHK Utica $5 million for each well we are short of such drilling commitment. As the managing member of CHK Utica, we may, at our sole discretion and election at any time after December 31, 2013, distribute certain excess cash of CHK Utica, as determined in accordance with the CHK Utica LLC Agreement. Any such optional distribution of excess cash is allocated 70% to the preferred shares (which is applied toward redemption of the preferred shares) and 30% to the common shares unless we have not met our drilling commitment during a liquidated damages period, in which case an optional distribution would be allocated 100% to the preferred shares (and applied toward redemption thereof). We may also, at our sole discretion and election, in accordance with the CHK Utica LLC Agreement, cause CHK Utica to redeem the CHK Utica preferred shares for cash, in whole or in part. The preferred shares will be redeemed at a valuation equal to the greater of a 10% internal rate of return or a return on investment of 1.4 x, in each case inclusive of dividends paid at the rate of 7% per annum and optional distributions made through the applicable redemption date. In the event that redemption does not occur on or prior to October 31, 2018, the optional redemption valuation will increase to the greater of a 17.5% internal rate of return or a return on investment of 2.0 x. The preferred shares are redeemed on a pro-rata basis in accordance with the then-applicable redemption valuation formula. As of December 31, 2012, the redemption price and the liquidation preference were each approximately $1,322 per preferred share.

We have committed to drill, for the benefit of CHK Utica in the area of mutual interest, a minimum of 50 net wells per year from 2012 through 2016, up to a minimum cumulative total of 250 net wells. CHK Utica is responsible for all capital and operating costs of the wells drilled for the benefit of the entity. CHK Utica also receives its proportionate share of the benefit of the drilling carry associated with our joint venture with Total in the Utica Shale. See Note 11 for further discussion of the joint venture.

The CHK Utica investors' right to receive, proportionately, a 3% ORRI in the first 1,500 net wells drilled on our Utica Shale leasehold is subject to an increase to 4% on net wells drilled in any year following a year in which we do not meet our commitment to drill the wells subject to the ORRI obligation, which runs from

2012 through 2023. However, in no event would we deliver to investors more than a total ORRI of 3% in 1,500 net wells. If at any time we hold fewer net acres than would enable us to drill all then-remaining net wells on 150-acre spacing, the investors have the right to require us to repurchase their right to receive ORRIs in the remaining net wells at the then-current fair market value of such remaining net wells. We retain the right to repurchase the investors' right to receive ORRIs in the remaining net wells at the then-current fair market value of such remaining net wells once we have drilled a minimum of 1,300 net wells. The obligation to deliver future ORRIs has been recorded as a liability which will be settled through the future conveyance of the underlying ORRIs to the investors on a net-well basis, at which time the associated liability will be reversed and the sale of the ORRIs reflected as an adjustment to the capitalized cost of our natural gas and oil properties.

As of December 31, 2012 and 2011, $950 million was recorded as noncontrolling interests on our consolidated balance sheets representing the third-party investments in CHK Utica. For 2012 and 2011, income of approximately $88 million and $10 million was attributable to the noncontrolling interests of CHK Utica. Under the development agreement, approximately 66 qualified net wells were added in 2012. Under the ORRI obligation, we delivered an ORRI in approximately 34 new net wells. For 2012, we met our drilling commitment associated with the CHK Utica transaction, but did not meet our ORRI commitment. The ORRI will increase to 4% for wells drilled in 2013, and the ultimate number of wells in which we must assign an interest will be reduced accordingly.

Chesapeake Granite Wash Trust. In November 2011, Chesapeake Granite Wash Trust (the Trust) sold 23,000,000 common units representing beneficial interests in the Trust at a price of $19.00 per common unit in its initial public offering. The common units are listed on the New York Stock Exchange and trade under the symbol "CHKR". We own 12,062,500 common units and 11,687,500 subordinated units, which in the aggregate represent an approximate 51% beneficial interest in the Trust. The Trust has a total of 46,750,000 units outstanding.

In connection with the initial public offering of the Trust, we conveyed royalty interests to the Trust that entitle the Trust to receive (i) 90% of the proceeds (after deducting certain post-production expenses and any applicable taxes) that we receive from the production of hydrocarbons from 69 producing wells, and, (ii) 50% of the proceeds (after deducting certain post-production expenses and any applicable taxes) in 118 development wells that have been or will be drilled on approximately 45,400 gross acres (29,000 net acres) in the Colony Granite Wash play in Washita County in the Anadarko Basin of western Oklahoma. Pursuant to the terms of a development agreement with the Trust, we are obligated to drill, or cause to be drilled, the development wells at our own expense prior to June 30, 2016, and the Trust will not be responsible for any costs related to the drilling of the development wells or any other operating or capital costs of the Trust properties. In addition, we granted to the Trust a lien on our remaining interests in the undeveloped properties that are subject to the development agreement in order to secure our drilling obligation to the Trust, although the maximum amount that may be recovered by the Trust under such lien could not exceed $263 million initially and is proportionately reduced as we fulfill our drilling obligation over time. As of December 31, 2012, we had drilled or caused to be drilled 55 development wells, as calculated under the development agreement, and the maximum amount recoverable under the drilling support lien was approximately $140 million.

The subordinated units we hold in the Trust are entitled to receive pro rata distributions from the Trust each quarter if and to the extent there is sufficient cash to provide a cash distribution on the common units that is not less than the applicable subordination threshold for such quarter. If there is not sufficient cash to fund such a distribution on all of the Trust units, the distribution to be made with respect to the subordinated units will be reduced or eliminated for such quarter in order to make a distribution, to the extent possible, of up to the subordination threshold amount on the common units. In exchange for agreeing to subordinate a portion of our Trust units, and in order to provide additional financial incentive to us to satisfy our drilling obligation and perform operations on the underlying properties in an efficient and cost-effective manner, Chesapeake is entitled to receive incentive distributions equal to 50% of the amount by which the cash available for distribution on the Trust units in any quarter exceeds the applicable incentive threshold for such quarter. The remaining 50% of cash available for distribution in excess of the applicable incentive threshold will be paid to Trust unitholders, including Chesapeake, on a pro rata basis. At the end of the fourth full calendar quarter following our satisfaction of our drilling obligation with respect to the development wells, the subordinated units will automatically convert into common units on a one-for-one basis and our right to receive incentive distributions will terminate. After such time, the common units will no longer have the protection of the subordination threshold, and all Trust unitholders will share in the Trust's distributions on a pro rata basis.

On November 7, 2012, the Trust declared a cash distribution of $0.63 per common unit and $0.22 per subordinated unit for the three-month period ended September 30, 2012 and covering production for the period from June 1, 2012 to August 31, 2012. The distribution paid to third-party unitholders on November 29, 2012 was approximately $15 million.

On August 10, 2012, the Trust declared a cash distribution of $0.61 per common unit and $0.48 per subordinated unit for the three-month period ended June 30, 2012 and covering production for the period from March 1, 2012 to May 31, 2012. The distribution paid to third-party unitholders on August 30, 2012 was approximately $14 million.

On May 10, 2012, the Trust declared a cash distribution of $0.66 per unit for the three-month period ended March 31, 2012 and covering production for the period from December 1, 2011 to February 29, 2012. The distribution paid to third-party unitholders on May 31, 2012 was approximately $15 million.

On February 8, 2012, the Trust declared a cash distribution of $0.73 per unit for the three-month period ended December 31, 2011 and covering production for the period from September 1, 2011 to November 30, 2011. The distribution paid to third-party unitholders on March 1, 2012 was approximately $17 million.

We have determined that the Trust constitutes a VIE and that Chesapeake is the primary beneficiary. As a result, the Trust is included in our consolidated financial statements. As of December 31, 2012 and 2011, $356 million and $381 million, respectively, were recorded as noncontrolling interests on our consolidated balance sheets representing the public unitholders' investment in common units of the Trust. For 2012 and 2011, approximately $35 million and $5 million of income was attributable to the Trust's noncontrolling interests in our consolidated statement of operations. See Note 13 for further discussion of VIEs.

Cardinal Gas Services, L.L.C. Cardinal Gas Services, L.L.C. (Cardinal), an unrestricted, non-guarantor consolidated subsidiary, was formed in December 2011 to acquire, develop, operate and own midstream assets in the Utica Shale. In exchange for the contribution of approximately $14 million in midstream assets to Cardinal, we received 66% of the outstanding membership units of Cardinal. In exchange for approximately $5 million, Total E&P USA, Inc. (Total) received 25% of the outstanding membership units and in exchange for approximately $2 million, CGAS Properties, L.P. (CGAS), an affiliate of EnerVest, Ltd., received 9% of the membership units. Each member was responsible for its proportionate share of capital costs. We determined that Cardinal constituted a VIE and that Chesapeake was the primary beneficiary. As a result, Cardinal was included in our consolidated financial statements until December 2012, and the contributions from Total and CGAS were recorded as noncontrolling interests. In December 2012, we sold our interest in this consolidated entity in connection with the sale of CMO. See Note 11. As of December 31, 2012 and 2011, the noncontrolling interest balances on the consolidated balance sheets associated with the contributions from Total and CGAS were $0 and approximately $7 million, respectively.

Wireless Seismic, Inc. We have a controlling 57% equity interest in Wireless Seismic, Inc. (Wireless), a privately owned company engaged in research, development and eventual production of wireless seismic systems and any related technology that deliver seismic information obtained from standard geophones in real time to laptop and desktop computers. As a result of our control, Wireless is included in our consolidated financial statements. As of December 31, 2012, $5 million was recorded as noncontrolling interests on our consolidated balance sheet representing third-party investments in Wireless. For 2012, $4 million of Wireless' loss was attributable to noncontrolling interests of Wireless in our consolidated statement of operations.

Big Star Crude Co., LLC. Oilfield Trucking Solutions, LLC, a wholly owned subsidiary of Chesapeake, entered into a joint venture to form Big Star Crude Co., LLC, which engages in commercial trucking. We have determined that Big Star is a VIE because our voting rights are disproportionate to our economic interests and the activities of the entity involve and are conducted on our behalf. We have also determined that Chesapeake is the primary beneficiary, since it has the power to direct the activities of this VIE, has the obligation to absorb losses and has the right to receive benefits from the VIE. As a result, Big Star is included in our consolidated financial statements. As of December 31, 2012, $1 million was recorded as noncontrolling interests on our consolidated balance sheets representing our joint venture partner's equity investment in Big Star. For 2012, a nominal amount of Big Star's loss was attributable to noncontrolling interests of Big Star in our consolidated statement of operations.

Author's Note
In this section, readers will find guidance for both nonissuers, the audits of which are performed under generally accepted auditing standards (GAAS) issued by the Auditing Standards Board (ASB), and issuers, the audits of which are performed under standards issued by the Public Company Accounting Oversight Board (PCAOB). Under each topic within this section, guidance for both nonissuers and issuers is presented separately, unless noted otherwise. All illustrative reporting excerpts are from the survey entities included in this edition (all of which are public companies) and are, thus, based on PCAOB standards. Illustrative reporting examples based on GAAS can be found in the AICPA's *Audit and Accounting Manual* and *The Auditor's Report: Comprehensive Guidance and Examples.*

In an effort to make GAAS easier to read, understand, and apply, the ASB launched the Clarity Project in 2011. As a result of this project, all existing AU sections within the AICPA's *Professional Standards* have been redrafted and are effective for audits of financial statements for periods ending on or after December 15, 2012. The issuance of the clarified standards reflects the ASB's established clarity drafting conventions that include, among other improvements, more clearly stated objectives of the auditor and the requirements with which the auditor has to comply when conducting an audit in accordance with GAAS. As the ASB redrafted the standards for clarity, it also converged the standards with International Standards on Auditing issued by the International Auditing and Assurance Standards Board.

Given the effective date of the clarified auditing standards, the following guidance for nonissuers is based on the clarified standards.

Presentation in Annual Report

PRESENTATION

7.01 This section reviews the format and content of independent auditors' reports appearing in the annual reports of the 350 survey entities. AU section 508, *Reports on Audited Financial Statements* (AICPA, *PCAOB Standards and Related Rules,* Interim Standards), applies to auditors' reports of issuers issued in connection with audits of historical financial statements that are intended to present the financial position, results of operations, and cash flows in conformity with generally accepted accounting principles (GAAP).

7.02 With the adoption of the clarified auditing standards, the following AU-C sections are applicable to the auditor's report:
- AU-C section 560, *Subsequent Events and Subsequently Discovered Facts* (AICPA, *Professional Standards*)
- AU-C section 600, *Special Considerations—Audits of Group Financial Statements (Including the Work of Component Auditors* (AICPA, *Professional Standards*)
- AU-C section 700, *Forming an Opinion and Reporting on Financial Statements* (AICPA, *Professional Standards*)
- AU-C section 705, *Modifications to the Opinion in the Independent Auditor's Report* (AICPA, *Professional Standards*)
- AU-C section 706, *Emphasis-of-Matter Paragraphs and Other-Matter Paragraphs in the Independent Auditor's Report* (AICPA, *Professional Standards*)
- AU-C section 708, *Consistency of Financial Statements* (AICPA, *Professional Standards*)
- AU-C section 800, *Special Considerations—Audits of Financial Statements Prepared in Accordance With Special Purpose Frameworks* (AICPA, *Professional Standards*)
- AU-C section 805, *Special Considerations—Audits of Single Financial Statements and Specific Elements, Accounts, or Items of a Financial Statement* (AICPA, *Professional Standards*)
- AU-C section 810, *Engagements to Report on Summary Financial Statements* (AICPA, *Professional Standards*)
- AU-C section 905, *Alert That Restricts the Use of the Auditor's Written Communication* (AICPA, *Professional Standards*)
- AU-C section 910, *Financial Statements Prepared in Accordance With a Financial Reporting Framework Generally Accepted in Another Country* (AICPA, *Professional Standards*)

As stated, AICPA professional standards apply to audits of nonissuers. PCAOB Auditing Standards apply to audits of issuers.

7.03 Section 103(a) of the Sarbanes-Oxley Act of 2002 authorized the PCAOB to establish auditing and related professional practice standards to be used by public accounting firms registered with the PCAOB. PCAOB Rule 3100, *Compliance With Auditing and Related Professional Practice Standards* (AICPA, *PCAOB Standards and Related Rules*, Select Rules of the Board), requires auditors to comply with all applicable auditing and related professional practice standards of the PCAOB. On an initial, transitional basis, the PCAOB adopted, as interim standards, the generally accepted auditing standards described in AU section 150, *Generally Accepted Auditing Standards* (AICPA, *Professional Standards*), in existence on April 16, 2003, to the extent not superseded or amended by the PCAOB.

Auditors' Reports
PRESENTATION
NONISSUERS

7.04 AU-C section 700 explains and provides examples of the unmodified auditor's report. The report should be written and include
- title,
- addressee,
- introductory paragraph,
- paragraph explaining management's responsibilities for the financial statements,
- auditor's responsibility,
- auditor's opinion,
- other reporting responsibilities (if applicable),
- signature of the auditor,
- auditor's address, and
- the date of the auditor's report.

7.05 Paragraph .23 of AU-C section 700 states that the auditor's report should have a title that includes the word *independent* to clearly indicate that it is the report of an independent auditor.

7.06 Paragraph .24 of AU-C section 700 states that the auditor's report should be addressed as required by the circumstances of the engagement.

7.07 The introductory paragraph, as described by paragraph .25 of AU-C section 700, should
- identify the entity whose financial statements have been audited,
- state that the financial statements have been audited,
- identify the title of each statement that the financial statements comprise, and
- specify the date or period covered by each financial statement that the financial statements comprise.

7.08 Paragraphs .26–.28 of AU-C section 700 describe what should be included in the paragraph explaining management's responsibilities for the financial statements. These responsibilities include management's responsibility for the preparation and fair presentation of the financial statements in accordance with the applicable financial reporting framework. The description of management's responsibilities should not reference a separate statement by management if such a statement is included in a document containing the auditor's report.

7.09 Paragraphs .29–.33 of AU-C section 700 explain what should be included in the auditor's responsibility portion of the auditor's report. Included in these responsibilities is that the audit was conducted in accordance with GAAS and determining whether the audit evidence obtained is sufficient and appropriate to provide a basis for the auditor's opinion.

7.10 Paragraphs .34–.36 of AU-C section 700 describe the opinion paragraph of the auditor's report. This paragraph should state that the financial statements present fairly, in all material respects, the financial position of the entity as of the balance sheet date and the results of its operations and its cash flows for the period then ended, in accordance with the applicable financial reporting framework. The auditor's opinion should also identity the applicable financial reporting framework and its origin.

7.11 Paragraph .A58 of AU-C section 700 presents examples of the auditor's standard reports for single year financial statements and comparative two year financial statements. Two of these examples follow.

An Auditor's Report on a Single Year Prepared in Accordance With Accounting Principles Generally Accepted in the United States of America

Circumstances include the following:
- Audit of a complete set of general purpose financial statements (single year).
- The financial statements are prepared in accordance with accounting principles generally accepted in the United States of America.

INDEPENDENT AUDITOR'S REPORT

[Appropriate Addressee]

Report on the Financial Statements[1]

We have audited the accompanying financial statements of ABC Company, which comprise the balance sheet as of December 31, 20X1, and the related statements of income, changes in stockholders' equity, and cash flows for the year then ended, and the related notes to the financial statements.

Management's Responsibility for the Financial Statements

Management is responsible for the preparation and fair presentation of these financial statements in accordance with accounting principles generally accepted in the United States of America; this includes the design, implementation, and maintenance of internal control relevant to the preparation and fair presentation of financial statements that are free from material misstatement, whether due to fraud or error.

Auditor's Responsibility

Our responsibility is to express an opinion on these financial statements based on our audit. We conducted our audit in accordance with auditing standards generally accepted in the United States of America. Those standards require that we plan and perform the audit to obtain reasonable assurance about whether the financial statements are free from material misstatement.

An audit involves performing procedures to obtain audit evidence about the amounts and disclosures in the financial statements. The procedures selected depend on the auditor's judgment, including the assessment of the risks of material misstatement of the financial statements, whether due to fraud or error. In making those risk assessments, the auditor considers internal control relevant to the entity's preparation and fair presentation of the financial statements in order to design audit procedures that are appropriate in the circumstances, but not for the purpose of expressing an opinion on the effectiveness of the entity's internal control.[2] Accordingly, we express no such opinion. An audit also includes evaluating the appropriateness of accounting policies used and the reasonableness of significant accounting estimates made by management, as well as evaluating the overall presentation of the financial statements.

We believe that the audit evidence we have obtained is sufficient and appropriate to provide a basis for our audit opinion.

Opinion

In our opinion, the financial statements referred to above present fairly, in all material respects, the financial position of ABC Company as of December 31, 20X1, and the results of its operations and its cash flows for the year then ended in accordance with accounting principles generally accepted in the United States of America.

Report on Other Legal and Regulatory Requirements

[Form and content of this section of the auditor's report will vary depending on the nature of the auditor's other reporting responsibilities.]

[Auditor's signature]
[Auditor's city and state]
[Date of the auditor's report]

An Auditor's Report on Consolidated Comparative Financial Statements Prepared in Accordance With Accounting Principles Generally Accepted in the United States of America

Circumstances include the following:
- Audit of a complete set of general purpose consolidated financial statements (comparative).
- The financial statements are prepared in accordance with accounting principles generally accepted in the United States of America.

---

[1] The subtitle "Report on the Financial Statements" is unnecessary in circumstances when the second subtitle, "Report on Other Legal and Regulatory Requirements," is not applicable.

[2] In circumstances when the auditor also has responsibility to express an opinion on the effectiveness of internal control in conjunction with the audit of the financial statements, this sentence would be worded as follows: "In making those risk assessments, the auditor considers internal control relevant to the entity's preparation and fair presentation of the financial statements in order to design audit procedures that are appropriate in the circumstances." In addition, the next sentence, "Accordingly, we express no such opinion." would not be included.

[Appropriate Addressee]

Report on the Financial Statements[3]

We have audited the accompanying consolidated financial statements of ABC Company and its subsidiaries, which comprise the consolidated balance sheets as of December 31, 20X1 and 20X0, and the related consolidated statements of income, changes in stockholders' equity, and cash flows for the years then ended, and the related notes to the financial statements.

<u>Management's Responsibility for the Financial Statements</u>

Management is responsible for the preparation and fair presentation of these consolidated financial statements in accordance with accounting principles generally accepted in the United States of America; this includes the design, implementation, and maintenance of internal control relevant to the preparation and fair presentation of consolidated financial statements that are free from material misstatement, whether due to fraud or error.

<u>Auditor's Responsibility</u>

Our responsibility is to express an opinion on these consolidated financial statements based on our audits. We conducted our audits in accordance with auditing standards generally accepted in the United States of America. Those standards require that we plan and perform the audit to obtain reasonable assurance about whether the consolidated financial statements are free from material misstatement.

An audit involves performing procedures to obtain audit evidence about the amounts and disclosures in the consolidated financial statements. The procedures selected depend on the auditor's judgment, including the assessment of the risks of material misstatement of the consolidated financial statements, whether due to fraud or error. In making those risk assessments, the auditor considers internal control relevant to the entity's preparation and fair presentation of the consolidated financial statements in order to design audit procedures that are appropriate in the circumstances, but not for the purpose of expressing an opinion on the effectiveness of the entity's internal control.[4] Accordingly, we express no such opinion. An audit also includes evaluating the appropriateness of accounting policies used and the reasonableness of significant accounting estimates made by management, as well as evaluating the overall presentation of the consolidated financial statements.

We believe that the audit evidence we have obtained is sufficient and appropriate to provide a basis for our audit opinion.

<u>Opinion</u>

In our opinion, the consolidated financial statements referred to above present fairly, in all material respects, the financial position of ABC Company and its subsidiaries as of December 31, 20X1 and 20X0, and the results of their operations and their cash flows for the years then ended in accordance with accounting principles generally accepted in the United States of America.

Report on Other Legal and Regulatory Requirements

[Form and content of this section of the auditor's report will vary depending on the nature of the auditor's other reporting responsibilities.]

[Auditor's signature]
[Auditor's city and state]
[Date of the auditor's report]

7.12 If statements of income, retained earnings, and cash flows are presented on a comparative basis for one of more periods, but the balance sheet(s) as of the end of one or more of the prior period(s) is not presented, the phrase "for the years then ended" should be changed to indicate that the auditor's opinion applies to each period for which statements of income, retained earnings, and cash flows are presented, such as "for each of the three years in the period ended [date of latest balance sheet]."

---

[3] The subtitle "Report on the Financial Statements" is unnecessary in circumstances when the second subtitle, "Report on Other Legal and Regulatory Requirements," is not applicable.
[4] In circumstances when the auditor also has responsibility to express an opinion on the effectiveness of internal control in conjunction with the audit of the financial statements, this sentence would be worded as follows: "In making those risk assessments, the auditor considers internal control relevant to the entity's preparation and fair presentation of the financial statements in order to design audit procedures that are appropriate in the circumstances." In addition, the next sentence, "Accordingly, we express no such opinion." would not be included.

7.13 Financial Accounting Standards Board (FASB) *Accounting Standards Codification* (ASC) 220, *Comprehensive Income*, permits entities to report components of comprehensive income in either a separate financial statement or a combined statement of income and comprehensive income.

7.14 FASB ASC 505-10-50-2 allows for changes in the separate accounts comprising stockholders' equity to be presented either on the face of the basic financial statements or in the form of a separate statement, such as a statement of changes in stockholders' equity.

ISSUERS

7.15 Paragraph .08(a) of AU section 508 states that the title of an auditor's report should include the word *independent*.

7.16 Paragraph .09 of AU section 508 states the following:

The report may be addressed to the company whose financial statements are being audited or to its board of directors or stockholders. A report on the financial statements of an unincorporated entity should be addressed as circumstances dictate, for example, to the partners, to the general partner, or to the proprietor. Occasionally, an auditor is retained to audit the financial statements of a company that is not a client; in such a case, the report is customarily addressed to the client and not to the directors or stockholders of the company whose financial statements are being audited.

7.17 For audits of public entities (that is, *issuers*, as defined by the Sarbanes-Oxley Act of 2002, and other entities, when prescribed by the rules of the Securities and Exchange Commission [SEC]), PCAOB Auditing Standard No. 1, *References in Auditors' Reports to the Standards of the Public Company Accounting Oversight Board* (AICPA, *PCAOB Standards and Related Rules*, Auditing Standards), directs auditors to state that the engagement was conducted in accordance with "the standards of the Public Company Accounting Oversight Board (United States)" whenever the auditor has performed the engagement in accordance with the PCAOB's standards. An example of a standard independent registered auditor's report presented in the appendix, "Illustrative Reports," of Auditing Standard No. 1 follows:

REPORT OF INDEPENDENT REGISTERED PUBLIC ACCOUNTING FIRM

We have audited the accompanying balance sheets of X Company as of December 31, 20X3 and 20X2, and the related statements of operations, stockholders' equity, and cash flows for each of the three years in the period ended December 31, 20X3. These financial statements are the responsibility of the Company's management. Our responsibility is to express an opinion on these financial statements based on our audits.

We conducted our audits in accordance with the standards of the Public Company Accounting Oversight Board (United States). Those standards require that we plan and perform the audit to obtain reasonable assurance about whether the financial statements are free of material misstatement. An audit includes examining, on a test basis, evidence supporting the amounts and disclosures in the financial statements. An audit also includes assessing the accounting principles used and significant estimates made by management, as well as evaluating the overall financial statement presentation. We believe that our audits provide a reasonable basis for our opinion.

In our opinion, the financial statements referred to above present fairly, in all material respects, the financial position of the company as of [at] December 31, 20X3 and 20X2, and the results of its operations and its cash flows for each of the three years in the period ended December 31, 20X3, in conformity with U.S. generally accepted accounting principles.

[*Signature*]
[*City and State or Country*]
[*Date*]

7.18 For audit requirements on reporting on internal controls over financial reporting, refer to paragraph 7.63.

PRESENTATION AND DISCLOSURE EXCERPTS

PRICEWATERHOUSECOOPERS LLP AUDITORS' REPORT

> **Author's Note**
> Although most audit reports use the exact format and order of paragraphs, PricewaterhouseCoopers uses a variation of the standard auditor's report that rearranges the standard auditor report.

7.19 BRIGGS & STRATTON CORPORATION (JUN)
REPORT OF INDEPENDENT REGISTERED PUBLIC ACCOUNTING FIRM

To the Board of Directors and Shareholders of
Briggs & Stratton Corporation:

In our opinion, the consolidated financial statements listed in the index appearing under Item 15(a)(1) present fairly, in all material respects, the financial position of Briggs & Stratton Corporation and its subsidiaries at July 1, 2012 and July 3, 2011 and the results of their operations and their cash flows for each of the three fiscal years in the period ended July 1, 2012 in conformity with accounting principles generally accepted in the United States of America. In addition, in our opinion, the financial statement schedules listed in the index appearing under Item 15 (a)(2) presents fairly, in all material respects, the information set forth therein when read in conjunction with the related consolidated financial statements. Also in our opinion, the Company maintained, in all material respects, effective internal control over financial reporting as of July 1, 2012, based on criteria established in *Internal Control—Integrated Framework* issued by the Committee of Sponsoring Organizations of the Treadway Commission (COSO). The Company's management is responsible for these financial statements and financial statement schedules, for maintaining effective internal control over financial reporting and for its assessment of the effectiveness of internal control over financial reporting, included in Management's Report on Internal Control over Financial Reporting appearing under Item 9 (a). Our responsibility is to express opinions on these financial statements, on the financial statement schedules, and on the Company's internal control over financial reporting based on our integrated audits. We conducted our audits in accordance with the standards of the Public Company Accounting Oversight Board (United States). Those standards require that we plan and perform the audits to obtain reasonable assurance about whether the financial statements are free of material misstatement and whether effective internal control over financial reporting was maintained in all material respects. Our audits of the financial statements included examining, on a test basis, evidence supporting the amounts and disclosures in the financial statements, assessing the accounting principles used and significant estimates made by management, and evaluating the overall financial statement presentation. Our audit of internal control over financial reporting included obtaining an understanding of internal control over financial reporting, assessing the risk that a material weakness exists, and testing and evaluating the design and operating effectiveness of internal control based on the assessed risk. Our audits also included performing such other procedures as we considered necessary in the circumstances. We believe that our audits provide a reasonable basis for our opinions.

A company's internal control over financial reporting is a process designed to provide reasonable assurance regarding the reliability of financial reporting and the preparation of financial statements for external purposes in accordance with generally accepted accounting principles. A company's internal control over financial reporting includes those policies and procedures that (i) pertain to the maintenance of records that, in reasonable detail, accurately and fairly reflect the transactions and dispositions of the assets of the company; (ii) provide reasonable assurance that transactions are recorded as necessary to permit preparation of financial statements in accordance with generally accepted accounting principles, and that receipts and expenditures of the company are being made only in accordance with authorizations of management and directors of the company; and (iii) provide reasonable assurance regarding prevention or timely detection of unauthorized acquisition, use, or disposition of the company's assets that could have a material effect on the financial statements.

Because of its inherent limitations, internal control over financial reporting may not prevent or detect misstatements. Also, projections of any evaluation of effectiveness to future periods are subject to the risk that controls may become inadequate because of changes in conditions, or that the degree of compliance with the policies or procedures may deteriorate.

STATEMENT OF OPERATIONS AND COMPREHENSIVE INCOME

7.20 SYSCO CORPORATION (JUN)
REPORT OF INDEPENDENT REGISTERED PUBLIC ACCOUNTING FIRM ON CONSOLIDATED FINANCIAL STATEMENTS

To the Board of Directors and Shareholders
Sysco Corporation

We have audited the accompanying consolidated balance sheets of Sysco Corporation (a Delaware Corporation) and subsidiaries (the "Company") as of June 30, 2012 and July 2, 2011, and the related consolidated results of operations, statements of comprehensive income, shareholders' equity, and cash flows for each of the three years in the period ended June 30, 2012. These financial statements are the responsibility of the Company's management. Our responsibility is to express an opinion on these financial statements based on our audits.

We conducted our audits in accordance with the standards of the Public Company Accounting Oversight Board (United States). Those standards require that we plan and perform the audit to obtain reasonable assurance about whether the financial statements are free of material misstatement. An audit includes examining, on a test basis, evidence supporting the amounts and disclosures in the financial statements. An audit also includes assessing the accounting principles used and significant estimates made by management, as well as evaluating the overall financial statement presentation. We believe that our audits provide a reasonable basis for our opinion.

In our opinion, the financial statements referred to above present fairly, in all material respects, the consolidated financial position of the Company at June 30, 2012 and July 2, 2011, and the consolidated results of its operations and its cash flows for each of the three years in the period ended June 30, 2012, in conformity with U.S. generally accepted accounting principles.

We also have audited, in accordance with the standards of the Public Company Accounting Oversight Board (United States), the Company's internal control over financial reporting as of June 30, 2012, based on criteria established in Internal Control-Integrated Framework issued by the Committee of Sponsoring Organizations of the Treadway Commission and our report dated August 27, 2012 expressed an unqualified opinion thereon.

STATEMENT OF CHANGES IN SHAREHOLDERS' EQUITY

7.21 THE KROGER CO. (JAN)
REPORT OF INDEPENDENT REGISTERED PUBLIC ACCOUNTING FIRM

To the Shareowners and Board of Directors of
The Kroger Co.

In our opinion, the accompanying consolidated balance sheets and the related consolidated statements of operations, cash flows and changes in shareowners' equity present fairly, in all material respects, the financial position of The Kroger Co. and its subsidiaries at January 28, 2012 and January 29, 2011, and the results of their operations and their cash flows for each of the three years in the period ended January 28, 2012 in conformity with accounting principles generally accepted in the United States of America. Also in our opinion, the Company maintained, in all material respects, effective internal control over financial reporting as of January 28, 2012, based on criteria established in *Internal Control—Integrated Framework* issued by the Committee of Sponsoring Organizations of the Treadway Commission (COSO). The Company's management is responsible for these financial statements, for maintaining effective internal control over financial reporting and for its assessment of the effectiveness of internal control over financial reporting, included in Management's Report on Internal Control over Financial Reporting appearing under Item 9A. Our responsibility is to express opinions on these financial statements and on the Company's internal control over financial reporting based on our integrated audits. We conducted our audits in accordance with the standards of the Public Company Accounting Oversight Board (United States). Those standards require that we plan and perform the audits to obtain reasonable assurance about whether the financial statements are free of material misstatement and whether effective internal control over financial reporting was maintained in all material respects. Our audits of the financial statements included examining, on a test basis, evidence supporting the amounts and disclosures in the financial statements, assessing the accounting principles used and significant estimates made by management, and evaluating the overall financial statement presentation. Our audit of internal control over financial reporting included obtaining an understanding of internal control over financial reporting, assessing the risk that a material weakness exists, and testing and evaluating the design and operating effectiveness of internal control based on the assessed risk. Our audits also included performing such other procedures as we considered necessary in the circumstances. We believe that our audits provide a reasonable basis for our opinions.

A company's internal control over financial reporting is a process designed to provide reasonable assurance regarding the reliability of financial reporting and the preparation of financial statements for external purposes in accordance with generally accepted accounting principles. A company's internal control over financial reporting includes those policies and procedures that (i) pertain to the maintenance of records that, in reasonable detail, accurately and fairly reflect the transactions and dispositions of the assets of the company; (ii) provide reasonable assurance that transactions are recorded as necessary to permit preparation of financial statements in accordance with generally accepted accounting principles, and that receipts and expenditures of the company are being made only in accordance with authorizations of management and directors of the company; and (iii) provide reasonable assurance regarding prevention or timely detection of unauthorized acquisition, use, or disposition of the company's assets that could have a material effect on the financial statements.

Because of its inherent limitations, internal control over financial reporting may not prevent or detect misstatements. Also, projections of any evaluation of effectiveness to future periods are subject to the risk that controls may become inadequate because of changes in conditions, or that the degree of compliance with the policies or procedures may deteriorate.

Reference to the Report of Other Auditors

PRESENTATION

NONISSUERS

7.22 AU-C section 600 *Special Considerations—Audits of Group Financial Statements (Including the Work of Component Auditors)* (AICPA, *Professional Standards*), establishes requirements and provides guidance for the independent auditor in deciding (*a*) whether he or she may use the work and reports of component auditors who have audited the financial statements of one or more subsidiaries, divisions, branches, components, or investments included in the financial statements presented and (*b*) the form and content of the principal auditor's report in these circumstances.

7.23 Paragraph .25 of AU-C section 600 explains that when the group engagement partner decides to make reference to the component auditor, the following should be true:
- The component's financial statements are prepared using the same financial reporting framework as the group financial statements.
- The component auditor has performed an audit of the financial statements of the component in accordance with generally accepted accounting standards.
- The component auditor has issued an auditor's report that is not restricted as to use.

7.24 As described in paragraph .27 of AU-C section 600, the group financial statements should clearly indicate that the component was not audited by the auditor of the group financial statements but was audited by the component auditor and should include the magnitude of the portion of the financial statement audited by the component auditor. The disclosure of the magnitude of the portion of the financial statements audited by a component auditor may be achieved by stating either the dollar amounts or percentages (whichever most clearly describes the portion of the financial statements audited by a component auditor) of one or more of the following: total assets, total revenues, or other appropriate criteria. When two or more component auditors participate in the audit, the dollar amounts or the percentages covered by the component auditors may be stated in the aggregate. If the group engagement partner decides to name a component auditor in the auditor's report on the group financial statements, then the component auditor's express permission should be obtained and the component's auditor's report should be presented together with that of the auditor's report on the group financial statements as explained in paragraph .28 of AU-C section 600.

7.25 Exhibit A of AU-C section 600 contains an example of appropriate reporting in the auditor's report on the group financial statements when reference is made to the audit of a component auditor.

ISSUERS

7.26 Paragraphs C8–C11 of PCAOB Auditing Standard No. 5, *An Audit of Internal Control Over Financial Reporting That Is Integrated with An Audit of Financial Statements* (AICPA, *PCAOB Standards and Related Rules*, Auditing Standards), provide guidance on opinions based, in part, on the report of another auditor in an audit of internal control over financial reporting. Paragraphs C8–C11 of Auditing Standard No. 5 state the following:
- If the auditor decides it is appropriate to serve as the principal auditor of the financial statements, then that auditor also should be the principal auditor of the company's internal control over financial reporting. When serving as the principal auditor of internal control over financial reporting, the auditor should decide whether to make reference in the report on internal control over financial reporting to the audit of internal control over financial reporting performed by the other auditor. In these circumstances, the auditor's decision is based on factors analogous to those of the auditor who uses the work and reports of other independent auditors when reporting on a company's financial statements.
- The decision about whether to make reference to another auditor in the report on the audit of internal control over financial reporting might differ from the corresponding decision as it relates to the audit of the financial statements. For example, the audit report on the financial statements may make reference to the audit of a significant equity investment performed by another independent auditor, but the report on internal control over financial reporting might not make a similar reference because management's assessment of internal control over financial reporting ordinarily would not extend to controls at the equity method investee.
- When the auditor decides to make reference to the report of the other auditor as a basis, in part, for his or her opinion on the company's internal control over financial reporting, the auditor should refer to the report of the other auditor when describing the scope of the audit and expressing the opinion.

7.27 When the principal auditor decides not to make reference to the audit of the other auditor, he or she must obtain and review and retain the following information from the other auditor, as prescribed in PCAOB AU section 508, *Reports on Audited Financial Statements* (AICPA, *PCAOB Standards and Related Rules*, Interim Standards):
- An engagement completion document consistent with paragraphs 12–13 of PCAOB Auditing Standard No. 3, *Audit Documentation* (AICPA, *PCAOB Standards and Related Rules,* Auditing Standards). This engagement completion document should include all cross-referenced supporting audit documentation.
- A list of significant risks, the auditor's responses, and the results of the auditor's related procedures.

- Sufficient information relating to significant findings or issues that are inconsistent with or contradict the auditor's final conclusions, as described in paragraph 8 of Auditing Standard No. 3.
- Any findings affecting the consolidating or combining of accounts in the consolidated financial statements.
- Sufficient information to enable the office issuing the auditor's report to agree or reconcile the financial statement amounts audited by the other firm to the information underlying the consolidated financial statements.
- A schedule of accumulated misstatements, including a description of the nature and cause of each accumulated misstatement, and an evaluation of uncorrected misstatements, including the quantitative and qualitative factors the auditor considered to be relevant to the evaluation.
- All significant deficiencies and material weaknesses in internal control over financial reporting, including a clear distinction between those two categories.
- Letters of representations from management.
- All matters to be communicated to the audit committee.

7.28 The reference to other auditors in this report is related to investments in unconsolidated affiliates.

PRESENTATION AND DISCLOSURE EXCERPT

REFERENCE TO OTHER AUDITORS

7.29 SPX CORPORATION (DEC)
REPORT OF INDEPENDENT REGISTERED PUBLIC ACCOUNTING FIRM

To the Shareholders and Board of Directors of
SPX Corporation:

We have audited the accompanying Consolidated Balance Sheets of SPX Corporation and subsidiaries (the "Company") as of December 31, 2012 and 2011, and the related Consolidated Statements of Operations, Comprehensive Income, Equity, and Cash Flows for each of the three years in the period ended December 31, 2012. These financial statements are the responsibility of the Company's management. Our responsibility is to express an opinion on these financial statements based on our audits. We did not audit the consolidated financial statements of EGS Electrical Group, LLC and subsidiaries ("EGS") for the fiscal years ended September 30, 2012, 2011 and 2010, the Company's investment that is accounted for by use of the equity method (see Note 9 to the Company's consolidated financial statements). The Company's equity in income of EGS for the fiscal years ended September 30, 2012, 2011 and 2010 was $39.0 million, $28.7 million and $28.8 million, respectively. The consolidated financial statements of EGS were audited by other auditors whose report has been furnished to us, and our opinion, insofar as it relates to the amounts included for EGS, is based solely on the report of the other auditors.

We conducted our audits in accordance with the standards of the Public Company Accounting Oversight Board (United States). Those standards require that we plan and perform the audit to obtain reasonable assurance about whether the financial statements are free of material misstatement. An audit includes examining, on a test basis, evidence supporting the amounts and disclosures in the financial statements. An audit also includes assessing the accounting principles used and significant estimates made by management, as well as evaluating the overall financial statement presentation. We believe that our audits and the report of the other auditors provide a reasonable basis for our opinion.

In our opinion, based on our audits and the report of the other auditors, such consolidated financial statements present fairly, in all material respects, the financial position of SPX Corporation and subsidiaries at December 31, 2012 and 2011, and the results of their operations and their cash flows for each of the three years in the period ended December 31, 2012, in conformity with accounting principles generally accepted in the United States of America.

We have also audited, in accordance with the standards of the Public Company Accounting Oversight Board (United States), the Company's internal control over financial reporting as of December 31, 2012, based on the criteria established in Internal Control—Integrated Framework issued by the Committee of Sponsoring Organizations of the Treadway Commission and our report dated February 22, 2013 expressed an unqualified opinion on the Company's internal control over financial reporting based on our audit.

Uncertainties

PRESENTATION

NONISSUERS

7.30 Paragraph .A13 of AU-C section 705 explains that an audit includes an assessment of whether the audit evidence related to uncertainties supports management's analysis. Absence of the existence of information related to the outcome of an uncertainty does not necessarily lead to a conclusion that the audit evidence supporting management's assertion is not sufficient. Rather, the auditor's professional judgment regarding the sufficiency of the audit evidence is based on the audit evidence that is, or should be, available. This does not apply to uncertainties related to going concern situations, for which AU-C section 570, *The Auditor's Consideration of an Entity's Ability to Continue as a Going Concern* (AICPA, *Professional Standards*), provides guidance.

ISSUERS

7.31 Paragraph .30 of AU section 508 does not require an explanatory paragraph for *uncertainties*, as defined in paragraph .29 of AU section 508. This does not apply to uncertainties related to going concern situations, for which AU section 341, *The Auditor's Consideration of an Entity's Ability to Continue as a Going Concern* (AICPA, *PCAOB Standards and Related Rules*, Interim Standards), provides guidance.

PRESENTATION AND DISCLOSURE EXCERPTS

GOING CONCERN

7.32 W. R. GRACE & CO. (DEC)
REPORT OF INDEPENDENT REGISTERED PUBLIC ACCOUNTING FIRM

To the Shareholders and Board of Directors of
W. R. Grace & Co.:

In our opinion, the accompanying consolidated balance sheets and the related consolidated statements of operations, comprehensive income, equity (deficit), and cash flows present fairly, in all material respects, the financial position of W.R Grace & Co. and its subsidiaries (the "Company") at December 31, 2012 and December 31, 2011, and the results of their operations and their cash flows for each of the three years in the period ended December 31, 2012 in conformity with accounting principles generally accepted in the United States of America. In addition, in our opinion, the financial statement schedule listed in the accompanying index presents fairly, in all material respects, the information set forth therein when read in conjunction with the related consolidated financial statements. Also in our opinion, the Company maintained, in all material respects, effective internal control over financial reporting as of December 31, 2012, based on criteria established in *Internal Control—Integrated Framework* issued by the Committee of Sponsoring Organizations of the Treadway Commission (COSO). The Company's management is responsible for these financial statements and financial statement schedule, for maintaining effective internal control over financial reporting and for its assessment of the effectiveness of internal control over financial reporting, included in the accompanying management's Report on Internal Control over Financial Reporting. Our responsibility is to express opinions on these financial statements, on the financial statement schedule, and on the Company's internal control over financial reporting based on our integrated audits. We conducted our audits in accordance with the standards of the Public Company Accounting Oversight Board (United States). Those standards require that we plan and perform the audits to obtain reasonable assurance about whether the financial statements are free of material misstatement and whether effective internal control over financial reporting was maintained in all material respects. Our audits of the financial statements included examining, on a test basis, evidence supporting the amounts and disclosures in the financial statements, assessing the accounting principles used and significant estimates made by management, and evaluating the overall financial statement presentation. Our audit of internal control over financial reporting included obtaining an understanding of internal control over financial reporting, assessing the risk that a material weakness exists, and testing and evaluating the design and operating effectiveness of internal control based on the assessed risk. Our audits also included performing such other procedures as we considered necessary in the circumstances. We believe that our audits provide a reasonable basis for our opinions.

The accompanying consolidated financial statements have been prepared assuming that the Company will continue as a going concern. As discussed in Note 1 to the consolidated financial statements, on April 2, 2001, the Company and substantially all of its domestic subsidiaries voluntarily filed for protection under Chapter 11 of the United States Bankruptcy Code, which raises substantial doubt about the Company's ability to continue as a going concern in its present form. Management's intentions with respect to this matter are described in Note 2. The accompanying consolidated financial statements do not include any adjustments that might result from the outcome of this uncertainty.

A company's internal control over financial reporting is a process designed to provide reasonable assurance regarding the reliability of financial reporting and the preparation of financial statements for external purposes in accordance with generally accepted accounting principles. A company's internal control over financial reporting includes those policies and procedures that (i) pertain to the maintenance of records that, in reasonable detail, accurately and fairly reflect the transactions and dispositions of the assets of the company; (ii) provide reasonable assurance that transactions are recorded as necessary to permit preparation of financial statements in accordance with generally accepted accounting principles, and that receipts and expenditures of the company are being made only in accordance with authorizations of management and directors of the company; and (iii) provide reasonable assurance regarding prevention or timely detection of unauthorized acquisition, use, or disposition of the company's assets that could have a material effect on the financial statements.

Because of its inherent limitations, internal control over financial reporting may not prevent or detect misstatements. Also, projections of any evaluation of effectiveness to future periods are subject to the risk that controls may become inadequate because of changes in conditions, or that the degree of compliance with the policies or procedures may deteriorate.

NOTES TO CONSOLIDATED FINANCIAL STATEMENTS

1. Basis of Presentation and Summary of Significant Accounting and Financial Reporting Policies (in part)

Voluntary Bankruptcy Filing. During 2000 and the first quarter of 2001, Grace experienced several adverse developments in its asbestos-related litigation, including: a significant increase in personal injury claims, higher than expected costs to resolve personal injury and certain property damage claims, and class action lawsuits alleging damages from ZONOLITE® Attic Insulation ("ZAI"), a former Grace attic insulation product.

After a thorough review of these developments, Grace's Board of Directors concluded that a federal court-supervised bankruptcy process provided the best forum available to achieve fairness in resolving these claims and on April 2, 2001 (the "Filing Date"), Grace and 61 of its United States subsidiaries and affiliates, (collectively, the "Debtors"), filed voluntary petitions for reorganization (the "Filing") under Chapter 11 of the United States Bankruptcy Code in the United States Bankruptcy Court for the District of Delaware (the "Bankruptcy Court"). The cases were consolidated and are being jointly administered under case number 01-01139 (the "Chapter 11 Cases"). Grace's non-U.S. subsidiaries and certain of its U.S. subsidiaries were not included in the Filing.

Under Chapter 11, the Debtors have continued to operate their businesses as debtors-in-possession under court protection from creditors and claimants, while using the Chapter 11 process to develop and implement a plan for addressing the asbestos-related claims. Since the Filing, all motions necessary to conduct normal business activities have been approved by the Bankruptcy Court. (See Note 2 for Chapter 11 Information.)

2. Chapter 11 Information (in part)

Accounting Impact. The accompanying Consolidated Financial Statements have been prepared in accordance with ASC 852, "Reorganizations". ASC 852 requires that financial statements of debtors-in-possession be prepared on a going concern basis, which contemplates continuity of operations and realization of assets and liquidation of liabilities in the ordinary course of business. However, as a result of the Filing, the realization of certain of the Debtors' assets and the liquidation of certain of the Debtors' liabilities are subject to significant uncertainty. While operating as debtors-in-possession, the Debtors may sell or otherwise dispose of assets and liquidate or settle liabilities for amounts other than those reflected in the Consolidated Financial Statements. Further, the ultimate plan of reorganization could materially change the amounts and classifications reported in the Consolidated Financial Statements.

Pursuant to ASC 852, Grace's pre-petition and future liabilities that are subject to compromise are required to be reported separately on the balance sheet at an estimate of the amount that will ultimately be allowed by the Bankruptcy Court. As of December 31, 2012, such pre-petition liabilities include fixed obligations (such as debt and contractual commitments), as well as estimates of costs related to contingent liabilities (such as asbestos-related litigation, environmental remediation and other claims). Obligations of Grace subsidiaries not covered by the Filing continue to be classified on the Consolidated Balance Sheets based upon maturity dates or the expected dates of payment. ASC 852 also requires separate reporting of certain expenses, realized gains and losses, and provisions for losses related to the Filing as reorganization items. Grace presents reorganization items as "Chapter 11 expenses, net of interest income," a separate caption in its Consolidated Statements of Operations.

Grace has not recorded the benefit of any assets that may be available to fund asbestos-related and other liabilities under the Fresenius Settlement and the Sealed Air Settlement, as under the Joint Plan, these assets will be transferred to the PI Trust and the PD Trust. The estimated fair value available under the Fresenius Settlement and the Sealed Air Settlement as measured at December 31, 2012, was $1,307 million composed of $115 million in cash from Fresenius and $1,192 million in cash and stock from Cryovac under the Joint Plan. Payments under the Sealed Air Settlement will be made directly to the PI Trust and the PD Trust by Cryovac.

Grace's Consolidated Balance Sheets separately identify the liabilities that are "subject to compromise" as a result of the Chapter 11 proceedings. In Grace's case, "liabilities subject to compromise" represent both pre-petition and future liabilities as determined under U.S. GAAP. Changes to pre-petition liabilities subsequent to the Filing Date reflect: (1) cash payments under approved court orders; (2) the terms of the Joint Plan, as discussed above and in Note 3, including the accrual of interest on pre-petition debt and other fixed obligations; (3) accruals for employee-related programs; and (4) changes in estimates related to other pre-petition contingent liabilities. The accounting for the asbestos-related liability component of "liabilities subject to compromise" is described in Note 3.

Components of liabilities subject to compromise are as follows:

(In millions)	December 31, 2012	December 31, 2011	Filing Date (Unaudited)
Asbestos-related contingencies	$2,065.0	$1,700.0	$1,002.8
Pre-petition bank debt plus accrued interest	937.2	907.3	511.5
Environmental contingencies	140.5	149.9	164.8
Unfunded special pension arrangements	134.3	129.0	70.8
Income tax contingencies	87.6	69.3	242.1
Postretirement benefits other than pension	63.9	64.6	185.4
Drawn letters of credit plus accrued interest	36.1	34.5	—
Accounts payable	31.3	31.3	43.0
Retained obligations of divested businesses	29.0	28.4	43.5
Other accrued liabilities	102.3	89.8	102.1
Reclassification to current liabilities[1]	(10.1)	(8.4)	—
Total liabilities subject to compromise	$3,617.1	$3,195.7	$2,366.0

[1] As of December 31, 2012 and 2011, approximately $10.1 million and $8.4 million, respectively, of certain pension and postretirement benefit obligations subject to compromise have been presented in "other current liabilities"in the Consolidated Balance Sheets in accordance with ASC 715 "Compensation—Retirement Benefits."

Note that the unfunded special pension arrangements reflected above exclude non-U.S. pension plans and qualified U.S. pension plans that became underfunded subsequent to the Filing. Contributions to qualified U.S. pension plans are subject to Bankruptcy Court approval.

Change in Liabilities Subject to Compromise

The following table is a reconciliation of the changes in pre-filing date liability balances for the period from the Filing Date through December 31, 2012.

(In millions) (Unaudited)	Cumulative Since Filing
Balance, Filing Date April 2, 2001	$2,366.0
Cash Disbursements and/or Reclassifications Under Bankruptcy Court Orders:	
Payment of environmental settlement liability	(252.0)
Freight and distribution order	(5.7)
Trade accounts payable order	(9.1)
Resolution of contingencies subject to Chapter 11	(130.0)
Other court orders for payments of certain operating expenses	(378.2)
Expense (Income) Items:	
Interest on pre-petition liabilities	549.8
Employee-related accruals	127.5
Provision for asbestos-related contingencies	1,109.8
Provision for environmental contingencies	355.2
Provision for income tax contingencies	(80.4)
Balance sheet reclassifications	(35.8)
Balance, end of period	$3,617.1

Additional liabilities subject to compromise may arise due to the rejection of executory contracts or unexpired leases, or as a result of the Bankruptcy Court's allowance of contingent or disputed claims.

For the holders of pre-petition bank credit facilities, beginning January 1, 2006, Grace agreed to pay interest on pre-petition bank debt at the prime rate, adjusted for periodic changes, and compounded quarterly. The effective rate for the twelve months ended December 31, 2012 and 2011, was 3.25%. From the Filing Date through December 31, 2005, Grace accrued interest on pre-petition bank debt at a negotiated fixed annual rate of 6.09%, compounded quarterly. The pre-petition bank debt holders have argued that they are entitled to post-petition interest at the default rate specified under the terms of the underlying credit agreements, which they asserted was approximately an additional $185 million as of December 31, 2012, and growing (Grace believes that if default interest was ultimately determined to be payable, the additional amount of accrued interest would be substantially less than that asserted by the pre-petition bank debt holders). The Bankruptcy Court and the District Court have overruled this assertion and the pre-petition bank debt holders have appealed these rulings to the Third Circuit.

For the holders of claims who, but for the Filing, would be entitled under a contract or otherwise to accrue or be paid interest on such claim in a non-default (or non-overdue payment) situation under applicable non-bankruptcy law, Grace accrues interest at the rate provided in the contract between the Grace entity and the claimant or such rate as may otherwise apply under applicable non-bankruptcy law.

For all other holders of allowed general unsecured claims, Grace accrues interest at a rate of 4.19% per annum, compounded annually, unless otherwise negotiated during the claim settlement process.

Chapter 11 Expenses

(In millions)	Year Ended December 31,		
	2012	2011	2010
Legal and financial advisory fees	$17.4	$20.6	$18.2
Interest (income) expense	(0.8)	(0.6)	(0.5)
Chapter 11 expenses, net of interest income	$16.6	$20.0	$17.7

Pursuant to ASC 852, interest income earned on the Debtors' cash balances must be offset against Chapter 11 expenses.

Condensed Financial Information of the Debtors

W. R. Grace & Co.—Chapter 11 Filing Entities
Debtor-in-Possession Statements of Operations

(In millions) (Unaudited)	Year Ended December 31,		
	2012	2011	2010
Net sales, including intercompany	$1,512.6	$1,479.4	$1,211.4
Cost of goods sold, including intercompany, exclusive of depreciation and amortization shown separately below	899.1	889.9	741.4
Selling, general and administrative expenses	245.2	267.8	244.8
Defined benefit pension expense	50.6	43.6	57.3
Depreciation and amortization	67.3	68.3	66.9
Chapter 11 expenses, net of interest income	16.6	20.0	17.7
Libby medical program settlement	19.6	—	—
Provision for asbestos-related contingencies	365.0	—	—
Research and development expenses	35.9	39.7	34.8
Interest expense and related financing costs	41.5	40.0	39.7
Restructuring expenses	2.5	0.6	3.5
Provision for environmental remediation	2.4	17.7	3.5
Other income, net	(98.1)	(93.6)	(90.7)
	1,647.6	1,294.0	1,118.9
Income (loss) before income taxes and equity in net income of non-filing entities	(135.0)	185.4	92.5
Benefit from (provision for) income taxes	39.3	(70.8)	(38.0)
Income (loss) before equity in net income of non-filing entities	(95.7)	114.6	54.5
Equity in net income of non-filing entities	189.8	154.8	152.6
Net income attributable to W. R. Grace & Co. shareholders	$ 94.1	$ 269.4	$ 207.1

W. R. Grace & Co.—Chapter 11 Filing Entities
Debtor-in-Possession Statements of Cash Flows

(In millions) (Unaudited)	Year Ended December 31,		
	2012	2011	2010
Operating Activities			
Net income attributable to W. R. Grace & Co. shareholders	$ 94.1	$ 269.4	$ 207.1
Reconciliation to Net Cash Provided by Operating Activities:			
Depreciation and amortization	67.3	68.3	66.9
Provision for asbestos-related contingencies	365.0	—	—
Equity in net income of non-filing entities	(189.8)	(154.8)	(152.6)
(Benefit from) provision for income taxes	(39.3)	70.8	38.0
Income taxes (paid), net of refunds	(33.9)	(13.2)	12.9
Tax benefits from stock-based compensation	(36.8)	—	—
Defined benefit pension expense	50.6	43.6	57.3
Payments under defined benefit pension arrangements	(114.9)	(251.4)	(51.4)
Repatriation of cash from foreign entities	21.6	30.3	116.8
Changes in assets and liabilities, excluding the effect of foreign currency translation:			
Trade accounts receivable	(7.1)	(26.2)	(24.7)
Inventories	53.7	(56.2)	(17.3)
Accounts payable	(15.1)	37.5	14.6
All other items, net	108.6	18.9	(52.9)
Net cash provided by operating activities	324.0	37.0	214.7
Investing Activities			
Capital expenditures	(82.6)	(77.7)	(55.1)
Transfer to restricted cash and cash equivalents	(35.4)	(8.4)	(74.5)
Other	—	10.0	(25.3)
Net cash used for investing activities	(118.0)	(76.1)	(154.9)
Net cash provided by financing activities	69.6	40.5	41.9
Net increase in cash and cash equivalents	275.6	1.4	101.7
Cash and cash equivalents, beginning of period	788.6	787.2	685.5
Cash and cash equivalents, end of period	$1,064.2	$ 788.6	$ 787.2

| (In millions) (Unaudited) | December 31, | |
	2012	2011
Assets		
Current assets		
Cash and cash equivalents	$1,064.2	$ 788.6
Restricted cash and cash equivalents	118.3	82.9
Trade accounts receivable, net	132.6	125.5
Accounts receivable—unconsolidated affiliate	14.1	10.2
Receivables from non-filing entities, net	160.5	143.1
Inventories	106.3	160.0
Other current assets	58.5	67.3
Total current assets	1,654.5	1,377.6
Properties and equipment, net	433.5	418.8
Deferred income taxes	935.5	752.7
Asbestos-related insurance	500.0	500.0
Loans receivable from non-filing entities, net	282.1	362.3
Investment in non-filing entities	449.5	333.6
Investment in unconsolidated affiliate	85.5	70.8
Other assets	47.2	63.7
Total assets	$4,387.8	$3,879.5
Liabilities and Equity		
Liabilities not subject to compromise		
Current liabilities (including $6.0 due to unconsolidated affiliate) (2011—$3.5)	$ 244.7	$ 250.7
Underfunded defined benefit pension plans	161.0	215.5
Other liabilities (including $22.4 due to unconsolidated affiliate) (2011—$18.3)	56.5	58.1
Total liabilities not subject to compromise	462.2	524.3
Liabilities subject to compromise	3,617.1	3,195.7
Total liabilities	4,079.3	3,720.0
Total W. R. Grace & Co. Shareholders' equity	308.4	159.4
Noncontrolling interests in Chapter 11 filing entities	0.1	0.1
Total equity	308.5	159.5
Total liabilities and equity	$4,387.8	$3,879.5

In addition to Grace's financial reporting obligations as prescribed by the SEC, the Debtors are also required, under the rules and regulations of the Bankruptcy Code, to periodically file certain statements and schedules with the Bankruptcy Court. This information is available to the public through the Bankruptcy Court. This information is prepared in a format that may not be comparable to information in Grace's quarterly and annual financial statements as filed with the SEC. These statements and schedules are not audited and do not purport to represent the financial position or results of operations of Grace on a consolidated basis.

3. Asbestos-Related Litigation (in part)

Asbestos-Related Liability. The recorded asbestos-related liability as of December 31, 2012, and December 31, 2011, was $2,065.0 million and $1,700.0 million respectively, and is included in "liabilities subject to compromise" in the accompanying Consolidated Balance Sheets. Grace increased its asbestos-related liability by $365.0 million in the fourth quarter of 2012 to reflect an updated estimate of the value of the consideration payable to the PI Trust and the PD Trust (the "Trusts") under the Joint Plan, assuming emergence from bankruptcy at the end of 2013. As discussed in Note 2, Grace reached an agreement in October 2012 to cash settle the warrant to be issued to the PI Trust at emergence. As a result of this settlement, as well as an updated valuation estimate of the deferred payment obligations and other consideration payable to the Trusts, Grace concluded that the previously recorded liability of $1,700.0 million was no longer in the reasonable range of possible valuations of the consideration payable to the Trusts.

The components of the consideration payable to the Trusts under the Joint Plan are as follows:
- The warrant to acquire 10 million shares of the Company's common stock for $17.00 per share which will be recorded at fair value on the effective date of the Joint Plan. Under the agreement to cash settle the warrant, the warrant will have a value between $375 million and $490 million. Based on the current trading range of Company common stock and other valuation factors, at December 31, 2012, Grace estimates the value of the warrant at emergence will be the maximum value of $490 million.
- The deferred payment obligation of $110 million per year for five years beginning January 2, 2019, and of $100 million per year for ten years beginning January 2, 2024, which will be recorded at fair value on the effective date of the Joint Plan. At December 31, 2012, Grace estimates the value of the deferred payment obligation at emergence will be $547 million, which assumes a discount rate of approximately 10%. The value of the deferred payment obligation is affected by (i) interest rates; (ii) the Company's credit standing and the payment period of the deferred payments; (iii) restrictive covenants and terms of the Company's other credit facilities; (iv) assessment of the risk of a default, which if default were to occur would require Grace to issue shares of Company common stock; and (v) the subordination provisions of the deferred payment agreement.
- The cash payable by Grace to fund the PI and PD Trusts as discussed in Note 2, which will be recorded at fair value on the effective date of the Joint Plan. Grace estimates the fair value to be $528 million at December 31, 2012.

- As discussed in Note 2, proceeds with respect to all of Grace's insurance policies that provide coverage for asbestos-related claims would be transferred to the PI Trust under the Joint Plan. The recorded asbestos-related insurance receivable and related liability of $500.0 million at December 31, 2012, is within the reasonable range of possible valuations of these policies at emergence.

Grace periodically evaluates the recorded amount of its asbestos-related liability and may further adjust the liability prior to the effective date of the Joint Plan if it determines that the currently recorded amount no longer represents a reasonable estimate of the value of the consideration payable to the Trusts under the Joint Plan. The ultimate cost of settling the asbestos-related liability will be based on the value of the consideration transferred to the Trusts at emergence and will vary from the current estimate.

FRESH-START ACCOUNTING

7.33 VISTEON CORPORATION (DEC)
REPORT OF INDEPENDENT REGISTERED PUBLIC ACCOUNTING FIRM

To the Board of Directors and Stockholders of
Visteon Corporation

In our opinion, the accompanying consolidated balance sheet as of December 31, 2011 and the related consolidated statement of operations, comprehensive income, shareholders' equity (deficit) and cash flows for the year ended December 31, 2011 and the three months ended December 31, 2010 present fairly, in all material respects, the financial position of Visteon Corporation and its subsidiaries (Successor Company) at December 31, 2011, and the results of their operations and their cash flows for the year ended December 31, 2011 and the three months ended December 31, 2010 in conformity with accounting principles generally accepted in the United States of America. In addition, in our opinion, the financial statement schedule listed in the index appearing under Item 15 (a) (2) for the year ended December 31, 2011 and the three months ended December 31, 2010 presents fairly, in all material respects, the information set forth therein when read in conjunction with the related consolidated financial statements. The Company's management is responsible for these financial statements and financial statement schedule. Our responsibility is to express an opinion on these financial statements and financial statement schedule based on our audits. We conducted our audits in accordance with the standards of the Public Company Accounting Oversight Board (United States). Those standards require that we plan and perform the audits to obtain reasonable assurance about whether the financial statements are free of material misstatement. Our audits of the financial statements included examining, on a test basis, evidence supporting the amounts and disclosures in the financial statements, assessing the accounting principles used and significant estimates made by management, and evaluating the overall financial statement presentation. Our audits also included performing such other procedures as we considered necessary in the circumstances. We believe that our audits provide a reasonable basis for our opinion.

As discussed in Note 1 to the consolidated financial statements, Visteon Corporation and certain of its U.S. subsidiaries (the "Debtors") voluntarily filed a petition on May 28, 2009 with the United States Bankruptcy Court for the District of Delaware for reorganization under Chapter 11 of the Bankruptcy Code. The Company's Fifth Amended Joint Plan of Reorganization (the "Plan") was confirmed on August 31, 2010. Confirmation of the Plan resulted in the discharge of certain claims against the Debtors that arose before May 28, 2009 and substantially alters rights and interests of equity security holders as provided for in the Plan. The Plan was substantially consummated on October 1, 2010 and the Company emerged from bankruptcy. In connection with its emergence from bankruptcy, the Company adopted fresh start accounting on October 1, 2010.

As discussed in Note 4 to the consolidated financial statements, in March 2012, the Company entered into an agreement to sell certain assets and liabilities of the Lighting operation. As the Lighting operation represents a component of the Company's business, the results of operations for the Lighting business have been reclassified to Income (Loss) from Discontinued Operations for the year ended December 31, 2011 and the three-months ended December 31, 2010.

/s/ PricewaterhouseCoopers LLP
Detroit, Michigan
February 27, 2012, except with respect to our opinion on the consolidated financial statements insofar as it relates to the effects of the presentation of discontinued operations discussed in Note 4 and the adoption of the new comprehensive income disclosures discussed in Note 1, as to which the date is May 2, 2012 and the change in the presentation of the segment disclosures as discussed in Note 22, as to which the date is February 28, 2013.

NOTES TO CONSOLIDATED FINANCIAL STATEMENTS

Note 1. Description of Business (in part)

On May 28, 2009, Visteon and certain of its U.S. subsidiaries (the "Debtors") filed voluntary petitions for reorganization relief under chapter 11 of the United States Bankruptcy Code (the "Bankruptcy Code") in the United States Bankruptcy Court for the District of Delaware (the "Court") in response to sudden and severe declines in global automotive production during the latter part of 2008 and early 2009 and the resulting adverse impact on the Company's cash flows and liquidity. On August 31, 2010 (the "Confirmation Date"), the Court entered an order (the "Confirmation Order") confirming the Debtors' joint plan of reorganization (as amended and supplemented, the "Plan"). On October 1, 2010 (the "Effective Date"), all conditions precedent to the effectiveness of the Plan and related documents were satisfied or waived and the Company emerged from bankruptcy. Additional details regarding the status of the Company's Chapter 11 Proceedings are included herein under Note 3, "Voluntary Reorganization under Chapter 11 of the United States Bankruptcy Code."

The Company adopted fresh-start accounting upon emergence from the Chapter 11 Proceedings and became a new entity for financial reporting purposes as of the Effective Date. Therefore, the consolidated financial statements for the reporting entity subsequent to the Effective Date (the "Successor") are not comparable to the consolidated financial statements for the reporting entity prior to the Effective Date (the "Predecessor"). Additional details regarding the adoption of fresh-start accounting are included herein under Note 3, "Voluntary Reorganization under Chapter 11 of the United States Bankruptcy Code."

Note 3. Voluntary Reorganization under Chapter 11 of the United States Bankruptcy Code

The Chapter 11 Proceedings were initiated in response to sudden and severe declines in global automotive production during the latter part of 2008 and early 2009 and the adverse impact on the Company's cash flows and liquidity. The reorganization cases are being jointly administered as Case No. 09-11786 under the caption "In re Visteon Corporation, et al." On August 31, 2010, the Court entered the Confirmation Order confirming the Debtors' Plan and on the Effective Date all conditions precedent to the effectiveness of the Plan and related documents were satisfied or waived and the Company emerged from bankruptcy.

Plan of Reorganization

A plan of reorganization determines the rights and satisfaction of claims of various creditors and security holders, but the ultimate settlement of certain claims will be subject to the uncertain outcome of litigation, negotiations and Court decisions up to and for a period of time after a plan of reorganization is confirmed. The following is a summary of the substantive provisions of the Plan and related transactions and is not intended to be a complete description of, or a substitute for a full and complete reading of, the Plan.

- Cancellation of any shares of Visteon common stock and any options, warrants or rights to purchase shares of Visteon common stock or other equity securities outstanding prior to the Effective Date.
- Issuance of approximately 45,000,000 shares of Successor common stock to certain investors in a private offering (the "Rights Offering") exempt from registration under the Securities Act for proceeds of approximately $1.25 billion.
- Execution of an exit financing facility including $500 million in funded, secured debt and a $200 million asset-based, secured revolver that was undrawn at the Effective Date.
- Application of proceeds from such borrowings and sales of equity along with cash on hand to make settlement distributions contemplated under the Plan, including cash settlement of the pre-petition seven-year secured term loan claims of approximately $1.5 billion, along with interest of approximately $160 million; cash settlement of the U.S. asset-backed lending facility ("ABL") and related letters of credit of approximately $128 million; establishment of a professional fee escrow account of $68 million; and, cash settlement of other claims and fees of approximately $119 million.
- Issuance of approximately 2,500,000 shares of Successor common stock to holders of pre-petition notes, including 7% Senior Notes due 2014, 8.25% Senior Notes due 2010, and 12.25% Senior Notes due 2016; holders of the 12.25% senior notes also received warrants to purchase up to 2,355,000 shares of reorganized Visteon common stock at an exercise price of $9.66 per share.
- Issuance of approximately 1,000,000 shares of Successor common stock and warrants to purchase up to 1,552,774 shares of Successor common stock at an exercise price of $58.80 per share for Predecessor common stock interests.
- Issuance of approximately 1,700,000 shares of restricted stock to management under a post-emergence share-based incentive compensation program.
- Reinstatement of certain pre-petition obligations including certain OPEB liabilities and administrative, general and other unsecured claims.

Transactions with Ford Motor Company

On September 29, 2010, the Company entered into a Global Settlement and Release Agreement (the "Release Agreement") with Ford and Automotive Components Holdings, LLC ("ACH") conditioned on the effectiveness of the Company's Plan. The Release Agreement provides, among other things, for: (i) the termination of the Company's future obligations to reimburse Ford for certain pension and retiree benefit costs; (ii) the resolution of and release of claims and causes of actions against the Company and certain claims, liabilities, or actions against the Company's non-debtor affiliates; (iii) withdrawal of all proofs of claim, with a face value of approximately $163 million, including a claim for pension and retiree benefit liabilities described above, filed against the Company by Ford and/or ACH and an agreement to not assert any further claims against the estates, other than with respect to preserved claims; (iv) the rejection of all purchase orders under which the Company is not producing component parts and other agreements which would not provide a benefit to the reorganized Company and waiver of any claims against the Company arising out of such rejected agreements; (v) the reimbursement by Ford of up to $29 million to the Company for costs associated with restructuring initiatives in various parts of the world; and (vi) a commitment by Ford and its affiliates to source the Company new and replacement business totaling approximately $600 million in annual sales for vehicle programs launching through 2013.

In exchange for these benefits, the Company assumed all outstanding purchase orders and related agreements under which the Company was producing parts for Ford and/or ACH and agreed to continue to produce and deliver component parts to Ford and ACH in accordance with the terms of such purchase orders to ensure Ford continuity of supply. The Company also agreed to release Ford and ACH from any claims, liabilities, or actions that the Company may potentially assert against Ford and/or ACH.

On July 26, 2010, the Company, Visteon Global Technologies, Inc., ACH and Ford entered into an agreement (the "ACH Termination Agreement") to terminate each of (i) the Master Services Agreement, dated September 30, 2005 (as amended); (ii) the Visteon Salaried Employee Lease Agreement, dated October 1, 2005 (as amended); and, (iii) the Visteon Hourly Employee Lease Agreement, dated October 1, 2005 (as amended). On August 17, 2010, the Court approved the ACH

Termination Agreement, pursuant to which Ford released Visteon from certain OPEB obligations related to employees previously leased to ACH resulting in a $9 million gain during the third quarter of 2010.

Financial Reporting Under the Chapter 11 Proceedings

Financial reporting applicable to a company in chapter 11 of the Bankruptcy Code generally does not change the manner in which financial statements are prepared. However, financial statements for periods including and subsequent to a chapter 11 bankruptcy filing must distinguish between transactions and events that are directly associated with the reorganization proceedings and the ongoing operations of the business. Reorganization gains, net included in the consolidated financial statements, including the amounts associated with the Company's discontinued operations, are comprised of the following:

(Dollars in millions)	Nine Months Ended October 1, 2010
Gain on settlement of liabilities subject to compromise	$(956)
Professional fees and other direct costs, net	129
Gain on adoption of fresh-start accounting	(106)
	$(933)
Cash payments for reorganization expenses	$ 111

In connection with the Plan, on the Effective Date, the Company recorded a pre-tax gain of approximately $1.1 billion for reorganization related items. This gain included $956 million related to the cancellation of certain pre-petition obligations previously recorded as liabilities subject to compromise in accordance with terms of the Plan. Additionally, on the Effective Date, the Company became a new entity for financial reporting purposes and adopted fresh-start accounting, which requires, among other things, that all assets and liabilities be recorded at fair value resulting in a gain of $106 million.

Fresh Start Accounting

The application of fresh-start accounting results in the allocation of reorganization value to the fair value of assets and is permitted only when the reorganization value of assets immediately prior to confirmation of a plan of reorganization is less than the total of all post-petition liabilities and allowed claims and the holders of voting shares immediately prior to the confirmation of the plan of reorganization receive less than 50% of the voting shares of the emerging entity. The Company adopted fresh-start accounting as of the Effective Date, which represents the date that all material conditions precedent to the Plan were resolved, because holders of existing voting shares immediately before filing and confirmation of the plan received less than 50% of the voting shares of the emerging entity and because its reorganization value is less than post-petition liabilities and allowed claims, as shown below:

(Dollars in millions)	October 1, 2010
Post-petition liabilities	$ 2,763
Liabilities subject to compromise	3,121
Total post-petition liabilities and allowed claims	5,884
Reorganization value of assets	(5,141)
Excess post-petition liabilities and allowed claims	$ 743

Reorganization Value

The Company's reorganization value includes an estimated enterprise value of approximately $2.4 billion, which represents management's best estimate of fair value within the range of enterprise values contemplated by the Court of $2.3 billion to $2.5 billion. The range of enterprise values considered by the Court was determined using certain financial analysis methodologies including the comparable companies analysis, the precedent transactions analysis and the discounted cash flow analysis. The application of these methodologies requires certain key judgments and assumptions, including financial projections, the amount of cash available to fund operations and current market conditions.

The comparable companies analysis estimates the value of a company based on a comparison of such company's financial statistics with the financial statistics of publicly-traded companies with similar characteristics. Criteria for selecting comparable companies for this analysis included, among other relevant characteristics, similar lines of business, geographic presence, business risks, growth prospects, maturity of businesses, market presence, size and scale of operations. The comparable companies analysis established benchmarks for valuation by deriving financial multiples and ratios for the comparable companies, standardized using common metrics of (i) EBITDAP (Earnings Before Interest, Taxes, Depreciation, Amortization and Pension expense) and (ii) EBITDAP minus capital expenditures. EBITDAP based metrics were utilized to ensure that the analysis allowed for valuation comparability between companies which sponsor pensions and those that do not. The calculated range of multiples for the comparable companies was used to estimate a range which was applied to the Company's projected EBITDAP and projected EBITDAP minus capital expenditures to determine a range of enterprise values. The multiples ranged from 4.6 to 7.8 depending on the comparable company for EBITDAP and from 6.1 to 14.6 for EBITDAP minus capital expenditures. Because the multiples derived excluded pension expense, the analysis further deducted an estimated amount of pension underfunding totaling $455 million from the resulting enterprise value.

The precedent transactions analysis is based on the enterprise values of companies involved in public or private merger and acquisition transactions that have operating and financial characteristics similar to Visteon. Under this methodology, the enterprise value of such companies is determined by an analysis of the consideration paid and the debt assumed in the merger, acquisition or restructuring transaction. As in a comparable companies valuation analysis, the precedent transactions analysis establishes benchmarks for valuation by deriving financial multiples and ratios, standardized using common variables such as revenue or EBITDA (Earnings Before Interest, Taxes, Depreciation and Amortization). In performing the precedent transactions analysis an EBITDAP metric was not able to be used due to the unavailability of pension expense information for the transactions analyzed. Therefore, the precedent transactions analysis relied on derived EBITDA multiples, which were then applied to the Company's operating statistics to determine enterprise value. Different than the comparable companies analysis in that the EBITDA metric is already burdened by pension costs, the precedent transactions analysis did not need to separately deduct pension underfunding in order to calculate enterprise value. The calculated multiples used to estimate a range of enterprise values for the Company, ranged from 4.0 to 7.1 depending on the transaction.

The discounted cash flow analysis estimates the value of a business by calculating the present value of expected future cash flows to be generated by such business. This analysis discounts the expected cash flows by an estimated discount rate. This approach has three components: (i) calculating the present value of the projected unlevered after-tax free cash flows for a determined period of time, (ii) adding the present value of the terminal value of the cash flows and (iii) subtracting the present value of projected pension payments in excess of the terminal year pension expense through 2017, due to the underfunded status of such pension plans. These calculations were performed on unlevered after-tax free cash flows, using an estimated tax rate of 35%, for the period beginning July 1, 2010 through December 31, 2013 (the "Projection Period"), discounted to the assumed effective date of June 30, 2010.

The discounted cash flow analysis was based on financial projections as included in the Fourth Amended Disclosure Statement (the "Financial Projections") and included assumptions for the weighted average cost of capital (the "Discount Rate"), which was used to calculate the present value of future cash flows and a perpetuity growth rate for the future cash flows, which was used to determine the enterprise value represented by the time period beyond the Projection Period. The Discount Rate was calculated using the capital asset pricing model resulting in Discount Rates ranging from 14% to 16%, which reflects a number of Company and market-specific factors. The perpetuity growth rate was calculated using the perpetuity growth rate method resulting in a perpetuity growth rate for free cash flow of 0% to 2%. Projected pension payments were discounted on a similar basis as the overall discounted cash flow Discount Rate range.

The estimated enterprise value was based upon an equally weighted average of the values resulting from the comparable companies, precedent transactions and discounted cash flow analyses, as discussed above, and was further adjusted for the estimated value of non-consolidated joint ventures and the estimated amounts of available cash (i.e. cash in excess of estimated minimum operating requirements). The value of non-consolidated joint ventures was calculated using a discounted cash flow analysis of the dividends projected to be received from these operations and also includes a terminal value based on the perpetuity growth method, where the dividend is assumed to continue into perpetuity at an assumed growth rate. This discounted cash flow analysis utilized a discount rate based on the cost of equity range of 13% to 21% and a perpetuity growth rate after 2013 of 2% to 4%. Application of this valuation methodology resulted in an estimated value of non-consolidated joint ventures of $195 million, which was incremental to the estimated enterprise value. Projected global cash balances were utilized to determine the estimated amount of available cash of $242 million, which was incremental to the estimated enterprise value. Amounts of cash expected to be used for settlements under the terms of the Plan and the estimated minimum level of cash required for ongoing operations were deducted from total projected cash to arrive at an amount of remaining or available cash. The estimated enterprise value, after adjusting for the estimated fair values of non-debt liabilities, is intended to approximate the reorganization value, or the amount a willing buyer would pay for the assets of the company immediately after restructuring.

A reconciliation of the reorganization value is provided in the table below.

Components of Reorganization Value

(Dollars in millions)	October 1, 2010
Enterprise value	$2,390
Non-debt liabilities	2,751
Reorganization value	$5,141

The value of a business is subject to uncertainties and contingencies that are difficult to predict and will fluctuate with changes in factors affecting the prospects of such a business. As a result, the estimates set forth herein are not necessarily indicative of actual outcomes, which may be significantly more or less favorable than those set forth herein. These estimates assume that the Company will continue as the owner and operator of these businesses and related assets and that such businesses and assets will be operated in accordance with the business plan, which is the basis for Financial Projections. The Financial Projections are based on projected market conditions and other estimates and assumptions including, but not limited to, general business, economic, competitive, regulatory, market and financial conditions, all of which are difficult to predict and generally beyond the Company's control. Depending on the actual results of such factors, operations or changes in financial markets, these valuation estimates may differ significantly from that disclosed herein.

The Company's reorganization value was first allocated to its tangible assets and identifiable intangible assets and the excess of reorganization value over the fair value of tangible and identifiable intangible assets was recorded as goodwill. Liabilities existing as of the Effective Date, other than deferred taxes, were recorded at the present value of amounts expected to be paid using appropriate risk adjusted interest rates. Deferred taxes were determined in conformity with applicable income tax accounting standards. Accumulated depreciation, accumulated amortization, retained deficit, common stock and accumulated other comprehensive loss attributable to the predecessor entity were eliminated.

Lack of Consistency

PRESENTATION

NONISSUERS

7.34 As required by paragraph .08 of AU-C section 708, if there has been a change in accounting principles or the method of their application that has a material effect on the comparability of the company's financial statements, the auditor should refer to the change in an emphasis-of-matter paragraph in the report. Such paragraph should follow the opinion paragraph and identify the nature of the change and refer the reader to the note in the financial statements that discusses the change in detail.

7.35 Paragraph .09 of AU-C section 708 states that the auditor should include an emphasis-of-matter paragraph relating to a change in accounting principle in reports on financial statements in the period of the change, and in subsequent periods, until the new accounting principle is applied in all periods presented. If the change in accounting principle is accounted for by retrospective application to the financial statements of all prior periods presented, the emphasis-of-matter paragraph is needed only in the period of such change.

ISSUERS

7.36 Although the information in paragraphs 7.34–.35 apply to issuers as well, PCAOB Auditing Standard No. 6, *Evaluating Consistency of Financial Statements* (AICPA, *PCAOB Standards and Related Rules*, Auditing Standards), further states that the auditor should evaluate a change in accounting principle to determine whether the
- newly adopted accounting principle is a generally accepted accounting principle (GAAP).
- method of accounting for the effect of the change is in conformity with GAAP.
- disclosures related to the accounting change are adequate.
- company has justified that the alternative accounting principle is preferable.

7.37 Auditing Standard No. 6 further states that if the auditor concludes that the criteria in paragraph 7.36 for a change in accounting principle are not met, the auditor should consider the matter to be a departure from GAAP and, if the effect of the change in accounting principle is material, should issue a qualified or an adverse opinion.

7.38 In addition to a change in accounting principle, a lack of consistency can also be the result of a correction of a material misstatement in previously issued financial statements. Paragraphs .18A–.18C of PCAOB AU section 508 state that the correction of a material misstatement in previously issued financial statements should be recognized in the auditor's report on the audited financial statements through the addition of an explanatory paragraph following the opinion paragraph.

7.39 The explanatory paragraph should include a
- statement that the previously issued financial statements have been restated for the correction of a misstatement in the respective period.
- reference to the company's disclosure of the correction of the misstatement.

7.40 This type of explanatory paragraph in the auditor's report should be included in reports on financial statements when the related financial statements are restated to correct the prior material misstatement. The paragraph need not be repeated in subsequent years.

PRESENTATION AND DISCLOSURE EXCERPTS

REVENUE RECOGNITION

7.41 JDS UNIPHASE CORPORATION (JUN)
REPORT OF INDEPENDENT REGISTERED PUBLIC ACCOUNTING FIRM

To the Board of Directors and Stockholders of
JDS Uniphase Corporation:

In our opinion, the consolidated financial statements listed in the index appearing under Item 15(a)(1) present fairly, in all material respects, the financial position of JDS Uniphase Corporation and its subsidiaries at June 30, 2012 and July 2, 2011, and the results of their operations and their cash flows for each of the three years in the period ended June 30, 2012 in conformity with accounting principles generally accepted in the United States of America. Also in our opinion, the Company maintained, in all material respects, effective internal control over financial reporting as of June 30, 2012, based on criteria established in

Internal Control—Integrated Framework issued by the Committee of Sponsoring Organizations of the Treadway Commission (COSO). The Company's management is responsible for these financial statements, for maintaining effective internal control over financial reporting and for its assessment of the effectiveness of internal control over financial reporting, included in Management's Report on Internal Control over Financial Reporting appearing under Item 9A. Our responsibility is to express opinions on these financial statements and on the Company's internal control over financial reporting based on our integrated audits. We conducted our audits in accordance with the standards of the Public Company Accounting Oversight Board (United States). Those standards require that we plan and perform the audits to obtain reasonable assurance about whether the financial statements are free of material misstatement and whether effective internal control over financial reporting was maintained in all material respects. Our audits of the financial statements included examining, on a test basis, evidence supporting the amounts and disclosures in the financial statements, assessing the accounting principles used and significant estimates made by management, and evaluating the overall financial statement presentation. Our audit of internal control over financial reporting included obtaining an understanding of internal control over financial reporting, assessing the risk that a material weakness exists, and testing and evaluating the design and operating effectiveness of internal control based on the assessed risk. Our audits also included performing such other procedures as we considered necessary in the circumstances. We believe that our audits provide a reasonable basis for our opinions.

As discussed in Note 1 to the consolidated financial statements, the Company adopted the authoritative guidance which applies to revenue arrangements with multiple deliverables and to certain software arrangements on a prospective basis for applicable transactions originating or materially modified on or after July 4, 2010.

A company's internal control over financial reporting is a process designed to provide reasonable assurance regarding the reliability of financial reporting and the preparation of financial statements for external purposes in accordance with generally accepted accounting principles. A company's internal control over financial reporting includes those policies and procedures that (i) pertain to the maintenance of records that, in reasonable detail, accurately and fairly reflect the transactions and dispositions of the assets of the company; (ii) provide reasonable assurance that transactions are recorded as necessary to permit preparation of financial statements in accordance with generally accepted accounting principles, and that receipts and expenditures of the company are being made only in accordance with authorizations of management and directors of the company; and (iii) provide reasonable assurance regarding prevention or timely detection of unauthorized acquisition, use, or disposition of the company's assets that could have a material effect on the financial statements.

Because of its inherent limitations, internal control over financial reporting may not prevent or detect misstatements. Also, projections of any evaluation of effectiveness to future periods are subject to the risk that controls may become inadequate because of changes in conditions, or that the degree of compliance with the policies or procedures may deteriorate.

NOTES TO CONSOLIDATED FINANCIAL STATEMENTS

Note 1. Description of Business and Summary of Significant Accounting Policies (in part)

Multiple-Element Arrangements

In October 2009, the FASB issued authoritative guidance that applies to arrangements with multiple deliverables. The guidance eliminates the residual method of revenue recognition, on non-software arrangements, and allows the use of management's best estimate of selling price ("BESP") for individual elements of an arrangement when vendor-specific objective evidence ("VSOE") or third-party evidence ("TPE") is unavailable. In addition, the FASB issued authoritative guidance which removes non-software components of tangible products and certain software components of tangible products from the scope of existing software revenue guidance, resulting in the recognition of revenue similar to that for other tangible products. The Company adopted these standards at the beginning of its first quarter of fiscal year 2011 on a prospective basis for applicable transactions originating or materially modified on or after July 3, 2010.

When a sales arrangement contains multiple deliverables, such as sales of products that include services, the multiple deliverables are evaluated to determine the units of accounting, and the entire fee from the arrangement is allocated to each unit of accounting based on the relative selling price. Under this approach, the selling price of a unit of accounting is determined by using a selling price hierarchy which requires the use of VSOE of fair value if available, TPE if VSOE is not available, or BESP if neither VSOE nor TPE is available. Revenue is recognized when the revenue recognition criteria for each unit of accounting are met.

The Company establishes VSOE of selling price using the price charged for a deliverable when sold separately and, in remote circumstances, using the price established by management having the relevant authority. TPE of selling price is established by evaluating similar and interchangeable competitor goods or services in sales to similarly situated customers. When VSOE or TPE are not available the Company then uses BESP. Generally, the Company is not able to determine TPE because its product strategy differs from that of others in our markets, and the extent of customization varies among comparable products or services from its peers. The Company establishes BESP using historical selling price trends and considering multiple factors including, but not limited to, geographies, market conditions, competitive landscape, internal costs, gross margin objectives, and pricing practices. When determining BESP, the Company applies significant judgment in establishing pricing strategies and evaluating market conditions and product lifecycles.

The determination of BESP is made through consultation with and approval by the segment management. Segment management may modify or develop new pricing practices and strategies in the future. As these pricing strategies evolve, we may modify our pricing practices in the future, which may result in changes in BESP. The aforementioned factors may result in a different allocation of revenue to the deliverables in multiple element arrangements from fiscal 2011, which may change the pattern and timing of revenue recognition for these elements but will not change the total revenue recognized for the arrangement.

To the extent that a deliverable(s) in a multiple-element arrangement is subject to specific guidance (for example, software that is subject to the authoritative guidance on software revenue recognition) the Company allocates the fair value of the units of accounting using relative selling price and that unit of accounting is accounted for in accordance with the specific guidance. Some product offerings include hardware that are integrated with or sold with software that delivers the functionality of the equipment. The Company believes that this equipment is not considered software related and would therefore be excluded from the scope of the authoritative guidance on software revenue recognition.

If the transactions entered into or materially modified on or after July 3, 2010 were subject to the previous accounting guidance, the reported net revenue amount during the year ended July 2, 2011, would decrease by approximately $7 million.

INVENTORY

7.42 OWENS-ILLINOIS, INC. (DEC)
REPORT OF INDEPENDENT REGISTERED PUBLIC ACCOUNTING FIRM

The Board of Directors and Share Owners of
Owens-Illinois, Inc.

We have audited the accompanying consolidated balance sheets of Owens-Illinois, Inc. as of December 31, 2012 and 2011, and the related consolidated statements of results of operations, comprehensive income, share owners' equity, and cash flows for each of the three years in the period ended December 31, 2012. Our audits also included the financial statement schedule listed in the Index at Item 15. These financial statements and schedule are the responsibility of the Company's management. Our responsibility is to express an opinion on these financial statements and schedule based on our audits.

We conducted our audits in accordance with the standards of the Public Company Accounting Oversight Board (United States). Those standards require that we plan and perform the audit to obtain reasonable assurance about whether the financial statements are free of material misstatement. An audit includes examining, on a test basis, evidence supporting the amounts and disclosures in the financial statements. An audit also includes assessing the accounting principles used and significant estimates made by management, as well as evaluating the overall financial statement presentation. We believe that our audits provide a reasonable basis for our opinion.

In our opinion, the financial statements referred to above present fairly, in all material respects, the consolidated financial position of Owens-Illinois, Inc. at December 31, 2012 and 2011, and the consolidated results of their operations and their cash flows for each of the three years in the period ended December 31, 2012, in conformity with U.S. generally accepted accounting principles. Also, in our opinion, the related financial statement schedule, when considered in relation to the basic financial statements taken as a whole, presents fairly in all material respects the information set forth therein.

As discussed in Note 1 to the consolidated financial statements, the Company has elected to change its method of valuing its U.S. inventories from the last-in, first-out method to the average cost method, effective January 1, 2012.

We also have audited, in accordance with the standards of the Public Company Accounting Oversight Board (United States), Owens-Illinois, Inc.'s internal control over financial reporting as of December 31, 2012, based on criteria established in Internal Control—Integrated Framework issued by the Committee of Sponsoring Organizations of the Treadway Commission and our report dated February 13, 2013 expressed an unqualified opinion thereon.

NOTES TO CONSOLIDATED FINANCIAL STATEMENTS

Tabular data dollars in millions, except per share amounts

1. Significant Accounting Policies (in part)

Change in Accounting Method. Effective January 1, 2012, the Company elected to change the method of valuing U.S. inventories to the lower of the average cost method or market, while in prior years these inventories were valued using the lower of the last-in, first-out ("LIFO") method or market. The Company believes the average cost method is preferable as it conforms the inventory costing methods globally, improves comparability with industry peers and better reflects the current value of inventory on the consolidated balance sheets. All prior periods presented have been adjusted to apply the new method retrospectively.

The effect of the change on the Consolidated Results of Operations for the years ended December 31, 2011 and 2010 is as follows:

	As Originally Reported Under LIFO	Effect of Change	As Adjusted
2011			
Manufacturing, shipping and delivery expense	$(5,979)	$10	$(5,969)
Amounts attributable to the Company:			
Net loss from continuing operations	(511)	10	(501)
Basic loss per share	(3.12)	0.06	(3.06)
Diluted loss per share	(3.12)	0.06	(3.06)
2010			
Manufacturing, shipping and delivery expense	$(5,283)	$ 2	$(5,281)
Amounts attributable to the Company:			
Net earnings from continuing operations	258	2	260
Basic earnings per share	1.57	0.01	1.58
Diluted earnings per share	1.55	0.01	1.56

The effect of the change on the Consolidated Balance Sheet as of December 31, 2011 is as follows:

	As Originally Reported Under LIFO	Effect of Change	As Adjusted
Assets:			
Inventories	$1,012	$49	$1,061
Share owners' equity:			
Retained earnings (loss)	(428)	49	(379)

The effect of the change on the consolidated share owners' equity as of January 1, 2010 is as follows:

	As Originally Reported Under LIFO	Effect of Change	As Adjusted
Retained earnings	$129	$37	$166

The effect of the change on the Consolidated Statement of Cash Flows for the years ended December 31, 2011 and 2010 is as follows:

	As Originally Reported Under LIFO	Effect of Change	As Adjusted
2011			
Net earnings (loss)	$(490)	$ 10	$(480)
Change in components of working capital	(107)	(10)	(117)
2010			
Net earnings (loss)	$ (5)	$ 2	$ (3)
Change in components of working capital	(71)	(2)	(73)

Had the Company not made this change in accounting method, manufacturing, shipping and delivery expense for the year ended December 31, 2012 would have been lower by $4 million and net earnings attributable to the Company would have been higher by $4 million than reported in the Consolidated Results of Operations. In addition, both basic and diluted earnings per share would have been higher by $0.03 for the year ended December 31, 2012.

EMPLOYEE BENEFITS

7.43 CONAGRA FOODS, INC. (MAY)
NOTES TO CONSOLIDATED FINANCIAL STATEMENTS

Columnar Amounts in Millions Except Per Share Amounts

1. Summary of Significant Accounting Policies (in part)

Employment-Related Benefits— Employment-related benefits associated with pensions, postretirement health care benefits, and workers' compensation are expensed as such obligations are incurred. The recognition of expense is impacted by estimates made by management, such as discount rates used to value these liabilities, future health care costs, and employee accidents incurred but not yet reported. We use third-party specialists to assist management in appropriately measuring the obligations associated with employment-related benefits.

In May 2012, we elected to change our method of accounting for pension benefits. Historically, we have recognized actuarial gains and losses in accumulated other comprehensive income (loss) in the consolidated balance sheets upon each plan remeasurement, amortizing them into operating results over the average future service period of active employees in these plans, to the extent such gains and losses were in excess of 10% of the greater of the market-related value of plan assets or the plan's projected benefit obligation ("the corridor"). We have elected to immediately recognize actuarial gains and losses in our operating results in the year in which they occur, to the extent they exceed the corridor, eliminating the amortization. Actuarial gains and losses outside the corridor, to the extent they occur, will be recognized annually as of our measurement date, which is our fiscal year-end, or when measurement is required otherwise under generally accepted accounting principles. Additionally, for purposes of calculating the expected return on plan assets, we will no longer use the market-related value of plan assets, an averaging technique permitted under generally accepted accounting principles, but instead will use the fair value of plan assets. These changes are intended to improve the transparency of our operating results by more quickly recognizing the effects of changes in plan asset values and the impact of current interest rates on plan obligations.

These changes have been reported through retrospective application of the new policies to all periods presented, by recalculating all actuarial gains and losses under the new method back to a reasonable period of time when actuarial gains and losses recognized were immaterial. The Company also considered the impact of the revised pension expense on cost of goods sold in its assessment of the impact of all adjustments in application of the new policy. The impacts of all adjustments made to the financial statements are summarized below:

Consolidated Statement of Operations

	Fiscal Year Ended May 29, 2011			Fiscal Year Ended May 30, 2010		
	Previously Reported	Revised	Effect of Change	Previously Reported	Revised	Effect of Change
Selling, general and administrative expenses	$1,511.1	$1,509.9	$(1.2)	$1,819.4	$1,987.7	$ 168.3
Cost of goods sold	9,389.6	9,389.6	—	8,953.7	8,966.3	12.6
Income tax expense	421.0	421.6	0.6	360.9	292.3	(68.6)
Income from continuing operations	830.3	830.9	0.6	742.6	630.3	(112.3)
Net income	818.8	819.4	0.6	723.3	611.0	(112.3)
Net income attributable to ConAgra Foods, Inc.	817.0	817.6	0.6	725.8	613.5	(112.3)
Earnings per share from continuing operations-basic	$ 1.92	$ 1.92	$ —	$ 1.68	$ 1.43	$ (0.25)
Earnings per share attributable to ConAgra Foods-basic	$ 1.90	$ 1.90	$ —	$ 1.63	$ 1.38	$ (0.25)
Earnings per share from continuing operations-diluted	$ 1.90	$ 1.90	$ —	$ 1.66	$ 1.41	$ (0.25)
Earnings per share attributable to ConAgra Foods-diluted	$ 1.88	$ 1.88	$ —	$ 1.62	$ 1.37	$ (0.25)

Consolidated Balance Sheet

	May 29, 2011		
	Previously Reported*	Revised	Effect of Change
Retained earnings	$4,821.8	$4,690.3	$(131.5)
Accumulated other comprehensive loss	(222.7)	(91.2)	131.5

Consolidated Statement of Cash Flows

	Fiscal Year Ended May 29, 2011			Fiscal Year Ended May 30, 2010		
	Previously Reported	Revised	Effect of Change	Previously Reported	Revised	Effect of Change
Cash flows from operating activities:						
Net income	$ 818.8	$ 819.4	$ 0.6	$ 723.3	$ 611.0	$(112.3)
Income from continuing operations	830.3	830.9	0.6	742.6	630.3	(112.3)
Pension expense	—	54.0	54.0	—	227.4	227.4
Other items	267.5	212.9	(54.6)	89.7	(25.4)	(115.1)
Net cash flows from operating activities	1,352.3	1,352.3	—	1,472.7	1,472.7	—

Consolidated Statement of Common Stockholders' Equity

	Fiscal Year Ended May 29, 2011			Fiscal Year Ended May 30, 2010		
	Previously Reported*	Revised	Effect of Change	Previously Reported*	Revised	Effect of Change
Retained earnings:						
Beginning balance	$4,385.3	$4,253.2	$(132.1)	$4,010.7	$3,990.9	$ (19.8)
Net income	817.0	817.6	0.6	725.8	613.5	(112.3)
Ending balance	4,821.8	4,690.3	(131.5)	4,385.3	4,253.2	(132.1)
Accumulated other comprehensive loss:						
Beginning balance	(285.3)	(153.2)	132.1	(103.7)	(83.9)	19.8
Pensions and postretirement healthcare benefits	24.2	23.6	(0.6)	(178.1)	(65.8)	112.3
Ending balance	(222.7)	(91.2)	131.5	(285.3)	(153.2)	132.1
Total equity	4,676.7	4,676.7	—	4,897.1	4,897.1	—

* Retained earnings also reflects the impact of the change related to income taxes as discussed in Note 16.

Consolidated Statement of Comprehensive Income

	Fiscal Year Ended May 29, 2011			Fiscal Year Ended May 30, 2010		
	Previously Reported	Revised	Effect of Change	Previously Reported	Revised Revised	Effect of Change
Net income	$818.8	$819.4	$ 0.6	$ 723.3	$611.0	$(112.3)
Pension and postretirement healthcare liabilities, net of tax	24.2	23.6	(0.6)	(178.1)	(65.8)	112.3

The Board of Directors and Stockholders
ConAgra Foods, Inc.:

We have audited the accompanying consolidated balance sheets of ConAgra Foods, Inc. and subsidiaries (the Company) as of May 27, 2012 and May 29, 2011, and the related consolidated statements of earnings, comprehensive income, common stockholders' equity, and cash flows for each of the years in the three-year period ended May 27, 2012. These consolidated financial statements are the responsibility of the Company's management. Our responsibility is to express an opinion on these consolidated financial statements based on our audits.

We conducted our audits in accordance with the standards of the Public Company Accounting Oversight Board (United States). Those standards require that we plan and perform the audit to obtain reasonable assurance about whether the financial statements are free of material misstatement. An audit includes examining, on a test basis, evidence supporting the amounts and disclosures in the financial statements. An audit also includes assessing the accounting principles used and significant estimates made by management, as well as evaluating the overall financial statement presentation. We believe that our audits provide a reasonable basis for our opinion.

In our opinion, the consolidated financial statements referred to above present fairly, in all material respects, the financial position of ConAgra Foods, Inc. and subsidiaries as of May 27, 2012 and May 29, 2011, and the results of their operations and cash flows for each of the years in the three-year period ended May 27, 2012, in conformity with U.S. generally accepted accounting principles.

As discussed in Note 1 to the consolidated financial statements, the Company elected to change its method of accounting for pension benefits in 2012. This method has been applied retrospectively to all periods presented.

We also have audited, in accordance with the standards of the Public Company Accounting Oversight Board (United States), the Company's internal control over financial reporting as of May 27, 2012, based on the criteria established in *Internal Control—Integrated Framework* issued by the Committee of Sponsoring Organizations of the Treadway Commission (COSO), and our report dated July 20, 2012 expressed an unqualified opinion on the effectiveness of the Company's internal control over financial reporting.

LETTER ON CHANGE IN ACCOUNTING PRINCIPLES

July 20, 2012

ConAgra Foods, Inc.
1 Conagra Drive
Omaha, Nebraska 68102

Ladies and Gentlemen:

We have audited the consolidated balance sheets of ConAgra Foods, Inc. and subsidiaries (the Company) as of May 27, 2012 and May 29, 2011, and the related consolidated statements of earnings, comprehensive income, common stockholders' equity, and cash flows for each of the years in the three-year period ended May 27, 2012, and have reported thereon under date of July 20, 2012. The aforementioned consolidated financial statements and our audit report thereon are included in the Company's annual report on Form 10-K for the year ended May 27, 2012. As stated in Note 1 to those financial statements, the Company changed its method of accounting for pension benefits to immediately recognize actuarial gains and losses in its operating results in the year in which they occur, to the extent they exceed 10 percent of the greater of the market related value of plan assets or the plans' projected benefit obligation ("the corridor"), and to use the fair value of plan assets for purposes of calculating the expected return on plan assets. Note 1 also states that the newly adopted accounting principles are intended to improve the transparency of the Company's operating results by more quickly recognizing the effects of changes in plan asset values and the impact of current interest rates on plan obligations. In accordance with your request, we have reviewed and discussed with Company officials the circumstances and business judgment and planning upon which the decision to make this change in the method of accounting was based.

With regard to the aforementioned accounting changes, authoritative criteria have not been established for evaluating the preferability of one acceptable method of accounting over another acceptable method. However, for purposes of the Company's compliance with the requirements of the Securities and Exchange Commission, we are furnishing this letter.

Based on our review and discussion, with reliance on management's business judgment and planning, we concur that the newly adopted methods of accounting are preferable in the Company's circumstances.

Very truly yours,
/s/ KPMG LLP

COMPREHENSIVE INCOME

7.44 COHERENT, INC. (SEP)

REPORT OF INDEPENDENT REGISTERED PUBLIC ACCOUNTING FIRM

To the Board of Directors and Stockholders of Coherent, Inc.:

We have audited the accompanying consolidated balance sheets of Coherent, Inc. and its subsidiaries (collectively, the "Company") as of September 29, 2012 and October 1, 2011, and the related consolidated statements of operations, comprehensive income, stockholders' equity, and cash flows for each of the three years in the period ended September 29, 2012. These consolidated financial statements are the responsibility of the Company's management. Our responsibility is to express an opinion on these consolidated financial statements based on our audits.

We conducted our audits in accordance with the standards of the Public Company Accounting Oversight Board (United States). Those standards require that we plan and perform the audit to obtain reasonable assurance about whether the financial statements are free of material misstatement. An audit includes examining, on a test basis, evidence supporting the amounts and disclosures in the financial statements. An audit also includes assessing the accounting principles used and significant estimates made by management, as well as evaluating the overall financial statement presentation. We believe that our audits provide a reasonable basis for our opinion.

In our opinion, such consolidated financial statements present fairly, in all material respects, the financial position of the Company as of September 29, 2012 and October 1, 2011, and the results of its operations and its cash flows for each of the three years in the period ended September 29, 2012, in conformity with accounting principles generally accepted in the United States of America.

As discussed in Note 2 to the consolidated financial statements, the Company has retrospectively adopted new accounting guidance related to the presentation of comprehensive income.

We have also audited, in accordance with the standards of the Public Company Accounting Oversight Board (United States), the Company's internal control over financial reporting as of September 29, 2012, based on the criteria established in *Internal Control—Integrated Framework* issued by the Committee of Sponsoring Organizations of the Treadway Commission and our report dated November 28, 2012 expressed an unqualified opinion on the Company's internal control over financial reporting.

CONSOLIDATED STATEMENTS OF COMPREHENSIVE INCOME

(In thousands)

	Year Ended		
	September 29, 2012	October 1, 2011	October 2, 2010
Net income	$ 62,962	$ 93,238	$ 36,916
Other comprehensive income (loss):			
Translation adjustments	(10,796)	(10,842)	(18,259)
Changes in unrealized gains (losses) on available-for-sale securities, net of taxes	30	(21)	(11)
Net loss realized on derivative instruments, net of tax	—	—	85
Other comprehensive income (loss), net of tax[1]	(10,766)	(10,863)	(18,185)
Total comprehensive income	$ 52,196	$ 82,375	$ 18,731

[1] Tax expense (benefit) of $(166), $(2,283) and $756 was provided on translation adjustments during fiscal 2012, 2011 and 2010, respectively. Tax expense (benefit) on changes in unrealized gains (losses) on available-for-sale securities and on net loss realized on derivative instruments was insignificant.

NOTES TO CONSOLIDATED FINANCIAL STATEMENTS

2. Significant Accounting Policies (in part)

Adoption of New Accounting Pronouncement and Update to Significant Accounting Policies (in part)

In June 2011, the FASB issued a final standard requiring the presentation of net income and other comprehensive income in either a single continuous statement or in two separate, but consecutive, statements of net income and other comprehensive income. The new standard eliminated the option previously elected by the Company to present items of other comprehensive income in the annual statement of changes in stockholders' equity. The new requirements did not change the components of comprehensive income recognized in net income or other comprehensive income, or when an item of other comprehensive income must be reclassified to net income. Earnings per share computations do not change. We adopted this standard on a full retrospective basis, as required, in the second quarter of fiscal 2012. As this standard relates only to the presentation of other comprehensive income, the adoption of this accounting standard did not have an impact on our consolidated financial position, results of operations and cash flows.

7.45 PRUDENTIAL FINANCIAL, INC. (DEC)

REPORT OF INDEPENDENT REGISTERED PUBLIC ACCOUNTING FIRM

To the Board of Directors and Stockholders of
Prudential Financial, Inc.:

In our opinion, the consolidated financial statements listed in the accompanying index present fairly, in all material respects, the financial position of Prudential Financial, Inc. and its subsidiaries at December 31, 2012 and December 31, 2011, and the results of their operations and their cash flows for each of the three years in the period ended December 31, 2012 in conformity with accounting principles generally accepted in the United States of America. In addition, in our opinion, the financial statement schedules listed in the index appearing under Item 15.2 present fairly, in all material respects, the information set forth therein when read in conjunction with the related consolidated financial statements. Also in our opinion, the Company maintained, in all material respects, effective internal control over financial reporting as of December 31, 2012, based on criteria established in *Internal Control—Integrated Framework* issued by the Committee of Sponsoring Organizations of the Treadway Commission ("COSO"). The Company's management is responsible for these financial statements and financial statement schedules, for maintaining effective internal control over financial reporting and for its assessment of the effectiveness of internal control over financial reporting, included in Management's Annual Report on Internal Control over Financial Reporting, listed in the accompanying index. Our responsibility is to express opinions on these financial statements, on the financial statement schedules, and on the Company's internal control over financial reporting based on our integrated audits. We conducted our audits in accordance with the standards of the Public Company Accounting Oversight Board (United States). Those standards require that we plan and perform the audits to obtain reasonable assurance about whether the financial statements are free of material misstatement and whether effective internal control over financial reporting was maintained in all material respects. Our audits of the financial statements included examining, on a test basis, evidence supporting the amounts and disclosures in the financial statements, assessing the accounting principles used and significant estimates made by management, and evaluating the overall financial statement presentation. Our audit of internal control over financial reporting included obtaining an understanding of internal control over financial reporting, assessing the risk that a material weakness exists, and testing and evaluating the design and operating effectiveness of internal control based on the assessed risk. Our audits also included performing such other procedures as we considered necessary in the circumstances. We believe that our audits provide a reasonable basis for our opinions.

Our audits were conducted for the purpose of forming an opinion on the consolidated financial statements taken as a whole. The accompanying supplemental combining financial information is presented for the purposes of additional analysis of the consolidated financial statements rather than to present the financial position and results of operations of the individual components. Such supplemental information has been subjected to the auditing procedures applied in the audits of the consolidated financial statements and, in our opinion, is fairly stated in all material respects in relation to the consolidated financial statements taken as a whole.

As described in Note 2 of the consolidated financial statements, on January 1, 2012 and in December 2012, the Company adopted, retrospectively, i) a change to the method of accounting for the deferral of acquisition costs for new or renewed insurance contracts and ii) a change in the method of applying an accounting principle for pension plans, respectively.

A company's internal control over financial reporting is a process designed to provide reasonable assurance regarding the reliability of financial reporting and the preparation of financial statements for external purposes in accordance with generally accepted accounting principles. A company's internal control over financial reporting includes those policies and procedures that (i) pertain to the maintenance of records that, in reasonable detail, accurately and fairly reflect the transactions and dispositions of the assets of the company; (ii) provide reasonable assurance that transactions are recorded as necessary to permit preparation of financial statements in accordance with generally accepted accounting principles, and that receipts and expenditures of the company are being made only in accordance with authorizations of management and directors of the company; and (iii) provide reasonable assurance regarding prevention or timely detection of unauthorized acquisition, use, or disposition of the company's assets that could have a material effect on the financial statements.

Because of its inherent limitations, internal control over financial reporting may not prevent or detect misstatements. Also, projections of any evaluation of effectiveness to future periods are subject to the risk that controls may become inadequate because of changes in conditions, or that the degree of compliance with the policies or procedures may deteriorate.

NOTES TO CONSOLIDATED FINANCIAL STATEMENTS

2. Significant Accounting Policies and Pronouncements (in part)

Adoption of New Accounting Pronouncements (in part)

Effective January 1, 2012, the Company adopted, retrospectively, new authoritative guidance to address diversity in practice regarding the interpretation of which costs relating to the acquisition of new or renewal insurance contracts qualify for deferral. Under the amended guidance, acquisition costs are to include only those costs that are directly related to the acquisition or renewal of insurance contracts by applying a model similar to the accounting for loan origination costs. An entity may defer incremental direct costs of contract acquisition with independent third parties or employees that are essential to the contract transaction, as well as the portion of employee compensation, including payroll fringe benefits and other costs directly related to underwriting, policy issuance and processing, medical inspection, and contract selling for successfully negotiated contracts. Prior period financial information presented in these financial statements has been adjusted to reflect the retrospective adoption of the amended guidance. Retained earnings and AOCI previously reported for December 31, 2009 were reduced $2,358 million and $90 million, respectively, as a result of this retrospective adoption. The lower level of costs now qualifying for deferral will be only partially offset by a lower level of amortization of "Deferred policy acquisition costs", and, as such, will initially result in lower earnings in future periods, primarily within the International Insurance and Individual Annuities segments. The impact to the International Insurance segment largely reflects lower deferrals of allocated costs of its proprietary distribution system, while the impact to the Individual Annuities segment mainly reflects lower deferrals of its wholesaler costs. This amended guidance is effective for fiscal years, and interim periods within those years, beginning after December 15, 2011 and permits, but does not require, retrospective application. The Company adopted this guidance effective January 1, 2012 and applied the retrospective method of adoption. While the adoption of this amended guidance changes the timing of when certain costs are reflected in the Company's results of operations, it has no effect on the total acquisition costs to be recognized over time and has no impact on the Company's cash flows.

The following tables present amounts as previously reported for the periods indicated, the effect on those amounts of the change due to the retrospective adoption of the amended guidance related to the deferral of acquisition costs as described above, as well as the effect of retrospective application of a change in accounting principle for the Company's pension plans as also discussed above.

Consolidated Statement of Financial Position:

| (In millions) | December 31, 2011 | | | |
	As Previously Reported	Effect of DAC Change	Effect of Pension Accounting Change	As Currently Reported
Deferred policy acquisition costs	$ 16,790	$(4,273)	$ 0	$ 12,517
Other assets	12,215	(4)	0	12,211
Total assets	624,521	(4,277)	0	620,244
Future policy benefits	170,459	212	0	170,671
Policyholders' account balances	134,552	6	0	134,558
Income taxes	8,083	(1,525)	0	6,558
Total liabilities	586,710	(1,307)	0	585,403
Accumulated other comprehensive income (loss)	5,563	(145)	(173)	5,245
Retained earnings	19,281	(2,825)	173	16,629
Total Prudential Financial, Inc. equity	37,223	(2,970)	0	34,253
Total equity	37,811	(2,970)	0	34,841
Total liabilities and equity	$624,521	$(4,277)	$ 0	$620,244

Consolidated Statement of Operations:

| (In millions) | Year Ended December 31, 2011 | | | |
	As Previously Reported	Effect of DAC Change	Effect of Pension Accounting Change	As Currently Reported
Revenues				
Premiums	$24,338	$ (37)	$ 0	$24,301
Asset management fees and other income	4,828	22	0	4,850
Total revenues	49,045	(15)	0	49,030
Benefits and Expenses				
Amortization of deferred policy acquisition costs	3,292	(597)	0	2,695
General and administrative expenses	9,815	827	(37)	10,605
Total benefits and expenses	43,928	230	(37)	44,121
Income (loss) from continuing operations before income taxes and equity in earnings of operating joint ventures	5,117	(245)	37	4,909
Income tax expense	1,599	(124)	13	1,488
Income (loss) from continuing operations before equity in earnings of operating joint ventures	3,518	(121)	24	3,421
Equity in earnings of operating joint ventures, net of tax	185	(3)	0	182
Income (loss) from continuing operations	3,703	(124)	24	3,603
Net income (loss)	3,738	(124)	24	3,638
Net income (loss) attributable to prudential financial, inc.	$ 3,666	$ (124)	$ 24	$ 3,566
Earnings Per Share				
Financial Services Businesses				
Basic earnings per share—Common Stock:				
Income from continuing operations attributable to Prudential Financial, Inc.	$ 7.23	$(0.27)	$0.05	$ 7.01
Net income attributable to Prudential Financial, Inc.	$ 7.31	$(0.28)	$0.05	$ 7.08
Diluted earnings per share—Common Stock:				
Income from continuing operations attributable to Prudential Financial, Inc.	$7.14	$(0.27)	$0.05	$6.92
Net income attributable to Prudential Financial, Inc.	$7.22	$(0.28)	$0.05	$6.99
Closed Block Business				
Basic and Diluted earnings per share—Class B Stock:				
Income from continuing operations attributable to Prudential Financial, Inc.	$ 55.50	$ 5.50	$ 0	$ 61.00
Net income attributable to Prudential Financial, Inc.	$ 55.50	$ 5.50	$ 0	$ 61.00

(continued)

(In millions)	As Previously Reported	Effect of DAC Change	Effect of Pension Accounting Change	As Currently Reported
			Year Ended December 31, 2010	
Revenues				
Premiums	$18,260	$ (22)	$ 0	$18,238
Policy charges and fee income	3,321	2	0	3,323
Asset management fees and other income	3,704	37	0	3,741
Total revenues	38,200	17	0	38,217
Benefits and Expenses				
Amortization of deferred policy acquisition costs	1,437	(352)	0	1,085
General and administrative expenses	7,688	630	(9)	8,309
Total benefits and expenses	33,808	278	(9)	34,077
Income (loss) from continuing operations before income taxes and equity in earnings of operating joint ventures	4,392	(261)	9	4,140
Income tax expense	1,303	(63)	3	1,243
Income (loss) from continuing operations before equity in earnings of operating joint ventures	3,089	(198)	6	2,897
Equity in earnings of operating joint ventures, net of tax	84	(2)	0	82
Income (loss) from continuing operations	3,173	(200)	6	2,979
Net income (loss)	3,206	(200)	6	3,012
Net income (loss) attributable to prudential financial, inc.	$ 3,195	$(200)	$ 6	$ 3,001
Earnings Per Share				
Financial Services Businesses				
Basic earnings per share—Common Stock:				
Income from continuing operations attributable to Prudential Financial, Inc.	$ 5.75	$(0.45)	$0.01	$ 5.31
Net income attributable to Prudential Financial, Inc.	$ 5.82	$(0.46)	$0.02	$ 5.38
Diluted earnings per share—Common Stock:				
Income from continuing operations attributable to Prudential Financial, Inc.	$ 5.68	$(0.44)	$0.01	$ 5.25
Net income attributable to Prudential Financial, Inc.	$ 5.75	$(0.45)	$0.02	$ 5.32
Closed Block Business				
Basic and Diluted earnings per share—Class B Stock:				
Income from continuing operations attributable to Prudential Financial, Inc.	$222.00	$ 7.00	$0.00	$229.00
Net income attributable to Prudential Financial, Inc.	$222.50	$ 7.00	$0.00	$229.50

Consolidated Statement of Cash Flows:

(In millions)	As Previously Reported	Effect of DAC Change	Effect of Pension Accounting Change	As Currently Reported
			Year Ended December 31, 2011	
Cash Flows From Operating Activities				
Net income	$ 3,738	$(124)	$ 24	$ 3,638
Adjustments to reconcile net income to net cash provided by operating activities:				
Change in:				
Deferred policy acquisition costs	(605)	229	0	(376)
Future policy benefits and other insurance liabilities	6,761	38	0	6,799
Other, net	1,676	(143)	(24)	1,509
Cash flows from operating activities	$12,377	$ 0	$ 0	$12,377

(In millions)	As Previously Reported	Effect of DAC Change	Effect of Pension Accounting Change	As Currently Reported
			Year Ended December 31, 2010	
Cash Flows From Operating Activities				
Net income	$ 3,206	$(200)	$ 6	$ 3,012
Adjustments to reconcile net income to net cash provided by operating activities:				
Policy charges and fee income	(976)	(2)	0	(978)
Change in:				
Deferred policy acquisition costs	(1,654)	278	0	(1,376)
Future policy benefits and other insurance liabilities	4,475	22	0	4,497
Other, net	714	(98)	(6)	610
Cash flows from operating activities	$ 6,542	$ 0	$ 0	$ 6,542

Emphasis of A Matter

PRESENTATION

NONISSUERS

7.46 Paragraph .06 of AU-C section 706 explains that if the auditor considers it necessary to draw users' attention to a matter appropriately presented or disclosed in the financial statements, the auditor should include an emphasis-of-matter paragraph. Paragraph .07 of AU-C section 706 states that the emphasis-of-matter paragraph should
- be included immediately after the opinion paragraph in the auditor's report,
- use the heading "Emphasis of Matter" or other appropriate heading,
- include in the paragraph a clear reference to the matter being emphasized and where relevant disclosures that fully describe the matter can be found in the financial statements, and
- indicate that the auditor's opinion is not modified with respect to the matter emphasized.

7.47 Other-matter paragraphs should be included in the auditor's report when the auditor considers it necessary to communicate matters other than those that are presented or disclosed in the financial statements, as described in paragraph .08 of AU-C section 706. The paragraph should be included immediately after the opinion paragraph and any emphasis-of-matter paragraph or elsewhere in the auditor's report if the content of the other-matter paragraph is relevant to the "Other Reporting Responsibilities" section.

ISSUERS

7.48 Paragraph .19 of AU section 508 states the following:

In any report on financial statements, the auditor may emphasize a matter regarding the financial statements. Such explanatory information should be presented in a separate paragraph of the auditors' report. Phrases such as "with the foregoing [following] explanation" should not be used in the opinion paragraph if an emphasis paragraph is included in the auditors' report. Emphasis paragraphs are never required; they may be added solely at the auditors' discretion. Examples of matters the auditor may wish to emphasize are—
- That the entity is a component of a larger business enterprise.
- That the entity has had significant transactions with related parties.
- Unusually important subsequent events.
- Accounting matters, other than those involving a change or changes in accounting principles, affecting the comparability of the financial statements with those of the preceding period.

Several survey entities included emphasis-of-matter paragraphs explaining items contained in the financial statements.

PRESENTATION AND DISCLOSURE EXCERPT

EMPHASIS OF A MATTER

7.49 DEAN FOODS COMPANY (DEC)
NOTES TO CONSOLIDATED FINANCIAL STATEMENTS

3. Discontinued Operations and Divestitures (in part)

Discontinued Operations—Morningstar

On December 2, 2012, we entered into an agreement to sell our Morningstar division to a third party. Morningstar is a leading manufacturer of dairy and non-dairy extended shelf-life and cultured products, including creams and creamers, ice cream mixes, whipping cream, aerosol whipped toppings, iced coffee, half and half, value-added milks, sour cream and cottage cheese. The sale closed on January 3, 2013 and we received net proceeds of approximately $1.45 billion, a portion of which was used to retire outstanding debt under our senior secured credit facility. We expect to record a net pre-tax gain of approximately $850 million on the sale of our Morningstar division, excluding $22.9 million of transaction costs recognized in discontinued operations during 2012. The operating results of our Morningstar division, previously reported within the Morningstar segment, have been reclassified as discontinued operations in our Consolidated Financial Statements for the years ended December 31, 2012, 2011 and 2010 and as of December 31, 2012 and 2011.

The following is a summary of Morningstar's assets and liabilities classified as discontinued operations as of December 31, 2012 and 2011:

	December 31	
	2012	2011
Assets		
Current assets	$154,211	$147,091
Property, plant and equipment, net	176,582	178,145
Goodwill	306,095	306,095
Identifiable intangibles and other assets, net	36,101	37,342
Assets of discontinued operations	$672,989	$668,673
Liabilities		
Accounts payable and accrued expenses	$ 94,188	$105,252
Debt	97	22,001
Other long-term liabilities	7,047	5,949
Liabilities of discontinued operations	$101,332	$133,202

The following is a summary of Morningstar's operating results and certain other directly attributable expenses, including interest expense, which are included in discontinued operations for the years ended December 31, 2012, 2011 and 2010:

	Year Ended December 31		
(In thousands)	2012	2011	2010
Operations:			
Net sales	$1,438,371	$1,414,302	$1,302,650
Income before income taxes	69,513	87,443	73,577
Income tax	(23,832)	(32,777)	(27,329)
Net income	$ 45,681	$ 54,666	$ 46,248

Transaction Costs

During the years ended December 31, 2012, 2011 and 2010, we recorded expenses of approximately $23.6 million, $1.5 million and $9.8 million, respectively, in connection with the Morningstar, Mountain High, private label yogurt, Waukesha and Rachel's sales, as well as other transactional activities, excluding the transaction costs associated with the WhiteWave IPO discussed in Note 2. Of this amount, $22.9 million, $0.0 million and $3.6 million was recorded in discontinued operations during the years ended December 31, 2012, 2011 and 2010, respectively. The remaining amount is recorded in general and administrative expenses in our Consolidated Statements of Operations.

REPORT OF INDEPENDENT REGISTERED PUBLIC ACCOUNTING FIRM

To the Board of Directors and Stockholders of
Dean Foods Company
Dallas, Texas

We have audited the accompanying consolidated balance sheets of Dean Foods Company and subsidiaries (the "Company") as of December 31, 2012 and 2011, and the related consolidated statements of operations, comprehensive income (loss), stockholders' equity (deficit) and cash flows for each of the three years in the period ended December 31, 2012. Our audits also included the financial statement schedule listed in the Index at Item 15. These financial statements and financial statement schedule are the responsibility of the Company's management. Our responsibility is to express an opinion on the financial statements and financial statement schedule based on our audits.

We conducted our audits in accordance with the standards of the Public Company Accounting Oversight Board (United States). Those standards require that we plan and perform the audit to obtain reasonable assurance about whether the financial statements are free of material misstatement. An audit includes examining, on a test basis, evidence supporting the amounts and disclosures in the financial statements. An audit also includes assessing the accounting principles used and significant estimates made by management, as well as evaluating the overall financial statement presentation. We believe that our audits provide a reasonable basis for our opinion.

In our opinion, such consolidated financial statements present fairly, in all material respects, the financial position of Dean Foods Company and subsidiaries as of December 31, 2012 and 2011 and the results of their operations and their cash flows for each of the three years in the period ended December 31, 2012, in conformity with accounting principles generally accepted in the United States of America. Also, in our opinion, such financial statement schedule, when considered in relation to the basic consolidated financial statements taken as a whole, presents fairly, in all material respects, the information set forth therein.

As discussed in Note 3 to the consolidated financial statements, the Company discontinued its operations of the Morningstar division when it entered into an agreement to sell the division on December 2, 2012. The operating results of the Morningstar division have been reclassified as discontinued operations in the consolidated financial statements.

We have also audited, in accordance with the standards of the Public Company Accounting Oversight Board (United States), the Company's internal control over financial reporting as of December 31, 2012, based on the criteria established in Internal Control—Integrated Framework issued by the Committee of Sponsoring Organizations of the Treadway Commission and our report dated February 27, 2013 expressed an unqualified opinion on the Company's internal control over financial reporting.

Departures From Unmodified (Unqualified) Opinions

PRESENTATION

> **Author's Note**
> The clarified auditing standards use the term *unmodified opinions*, and the extant standards as adopted by the PCAOB use the term *unqualified opinions*.

NONISSUERS

7.50 Paragraph .07 of AU-C section 705 states that the auditor should modify the opinion in the auditor's report when the auditor concludes the financial statements as a whole are materially misstated or the auditor is unable to obtain sufficient appropriate audit evidence to conclude that the financial statements as a whole are free from material misstatements.

ISSUERS

7.51 AU section 508 does not require auditors to express qualified opinions about the effects of uncertainties or lack of consistency. Under AU section 508, departures from unqualified opinions include opinions qualified because of a scope limitation or departure from GAAP, including inadequate disclosures; adverse opinions; and disclaimers of opinion. Paragraphs .20–.63 of AU section 508 discuss these departures. None of the auditors' reports issued in connection with the financial statements of the survey entities contained a *departure*, as defined by AU section 508.

Reports on Comparative Financial Statements

PRESENTATION

NONISSUERS

7.52 AU-C section 700 discusses reports on comparative statements. Paragraph .53 of AU-C section 700 states that when reporting on prior period financial statements in connection with the current period's audit, if the auditor's opinion on such prior period financial statements differs from the opinion the auditor expresses, the auditor should disclose the following in an emphasis-of-matter or other-matter paragraph, in accordance with AU-C section 706:
- The date of the auditor's previous report
- The type of opinion previously expressed
- The substantive reasons for the different opinion
- That the auditor's opinion on the amended financial statements is different from the auditor's previous opinion.

ISSUERS

7.53 Paragraphs .65–.74 of AU section 508 discuss reports on comparative financial statements.

COMPARATIVE FINANCIAL STATEMENTS

7.54 PILGRIM'S PRIDE CORPORATION (DEC)
REPORT OF INDEPENDENT REGISTERED PUBLIC ACCOUNTING FIRM

The Board of Directors and Stockholders
Pilgrim's Pride Corporation

We have audited the accompanying consolidated balance sheet of Pilgrim's Pride Corporation (the "Company") as of December 30, 2012, and the related consolidated statements of operations, comprehensive income (loss), stockholders' equity, and cash flows for the fifty-three weeks ended December 30, 2012. In connection with our audit of the consolidated financial statements, we have also audited financial statement schedule II, Valuation and Qualifying Accounts, as of and for the fifty-three weeks ended December 30, 2012. These consolidated financial statements and financial statement schedule are the responsibility of the Company's management. Our responsibility is to express an opinion on these consolidated financial statements and schedule based on our audits.

We conducted our audit in accordance with the standards of the Public Company Accounting Oversight Board (United States). Those standards require that we plan and perform the audit to obtain reasonable assurance about whether the financial statements are free of material misstatement. An audit includes examining, on a test basis, evidence supporting the amounts and disclosures in the financial statements. An audit also includes assessing the accounting principles used and significant estimates made by management, as well as evaluating the overall financial statement presentation. We believe that our audit provides a reasonable basis for our opinion.

In our opinion, the consolidated financial statements referred to above present fairly, in all material respects, the consolidated financial position of Pilgrim's Pride Corporation as of December 30, 2012, and the consolidated results of its operations and its cash flows for the fifty-three weeks ended December 30, 2012, in conformity with U.S. generally accepted accounting principles. Also, in our opinion, the related financial statement schedule, when considered in relation to the basic consolidated financial statements taken as a whole, presents fairly, in all material respects, the information set forth therein.

We also have audited the retrospective adjustments applied to earnings per share in the 2011 and 2010 consolidated financial statements as described in "Note 15. Stockholder's Equity" under the section "Rights Offering." In our opinion, such adjustments are appropriate and have been properly applied. We were not engaged to audit, review, or apply any procedures to the 2011 and 2010 consolidated financial statements of the Company other than with respect to the adjustments and, accordingly, we do not express an opinion or any other form of assurance on the 2011 and 2010 consolidated financial statements taken as a whole.

We also have audited, in accordance with the standards of the Public Company Accounting Oversight Board (United States), Pilgrim's Pride Corporation's internal control over financial reporting as of December 30, 2012, based on criteria established in *Internal Control—Integrated Framework* issued by the Committee of Sponsoring Organizations of the Treadway Commission (COSO), and our report dated February 15, 2013 expressed an unqualified opinion on the effectiveness of the Company's internal control over financial reporting.

/s/ KPMG LLP
Denver, Colorado
February 15, 2013

REPORT OF INDEPENDENT REGISTERED PUBLIC ACCOUNTING FIRM

The Board of Directors and Stockholders
Pilgrim's Pride Corporation

We have audited, before the effects of the adjustments to retrospectively apply the change in accounting described in "Note 15. Stockholder's Equity," the accompanying consolidated balance sheet of Pilgrim's Pride Corporation (the "Company") as of December 25, 2011, and the related consolidated statements of operations, comprehensive income, stockholders' equity, and cash flows for the years ended December 25, 2011 and December 26, 2010 (the 2011 and 2010 consolidated financial statements before the effects of the adjustments discussed in "Note 15. Stockholders' Equity" are not presented herein). Our audits also include the financial statement schedule listed in the index at Item 15(a). These financial statements and schedule are the responsibility of the Company's management. Our responsibility is to express an opinion on these financial statements and schedule based on our audits.

We conducted our audits in accordance with the standards of the Public Company Accounting Oversight Board (United States). Those standards require that we plan and perform the audit to obtain reasonable assurance about whether the financial statements are free of material misstatement. An audit includes examining, on a test basis, evidence supporting the amounts and disclosures in the financial statements. An audit also includes assessing the accounting principles used and significant estimates made by management, as well as evaluating the overall financial statement presentation. We believe that our audits provide a reasonable basis for our opinion.

In our opinion, the financial statements, before the effects of the adjustments to retrospectively apply the change in accounting described in "Note 15. Stockholder's Equity," present fairly, in all material respects, the consolidated financial position of Pilgrim's Pride Corporation at December 25, 2011, and the consolidated results of its operations and its cash flows for the years ended December 25, 2011 and December 26, 2010, in conformity with U.S. generally accepted accounting principles. Also, in our opinion, the related financial statement schedule, when considered in relation to the basic financial statements taken as a whole, presents fairly, in all material respects, the information set forth therein.

We were not engaged to audit, review, or apply any procedures to the adjustments to retrospectively apply the change in accounting described in "Note 15. Stockholder's Equity," and, accordingly, we do not express an opinion or any other form of assurance about whether such adjustments are appropriate and have been properly applied. Those adjustments were audited by KPMG LLP.

/s/ Ernst & Young LLP
Denver, Colorado
February 17, 2012

NOTES TO CONSOLIDATED FINANCIAL STATEMENTS

15. Stockholders' Equity (in part)

Rights Offering

In January 2012, Pilgrim's commenced the Rights Offering for stockholders of record as of January 17, 2012 (the "Record Date"). The basic subscription privilege gave stockholders the option to purchase 0.2072 shares of Pilgrim's common stock, rounded up to the next largest whole number, at a subscription price of $4.50 per share for each share of Pilgrim's common stock they owned as of the Record Date. The multiplier was determined by dividing the 44,444,444 shares being offered in the Rights Offering by the total number of shares owned by all stockholders on the Record Date. Those stockholders that exercised their basic subscription privilege in full also received an over-subscription privilege that afforded them the opportunity to purchase additional shares at the subscription price of $4.50 per share from a pool of the shares left over had all stockholders not elected to exercise their basic subscription privileges in full. JBS USA committed to participate in the Rights Offering and exercise its basic and over-subscription privileges in full. The last day a stockholder could exercise either their basic subscription rights or their over-subscription rights was February 29, 2012. On March 7, 2012, the Company issued 44,444,444 shares of common stock to stockholders that exercised their basic subscription privileges and over-subscription privileges under the Rights Offering. Gross proceeds received under the Rights Offering totaled $200.0 million. The Company incurred costs directly attributable to the Rights Offering of $1.7 million that it deferred and charged against the proceeds of the Rights Offering in *Additional Paid-in Capital* on the Consolidated Balance Sheet. The Company used the net proceeds of $198.3 million for additional working capital to improve its capital position and for general corporate purposes. Pilgrim's also used a portion of the net proceeds to repay the outstanding principal amount of $50.0 million, plus accrued interest, of its subordinated debt owed to JBS USA and to repay indebtedness under the U.S. Credit Facility.

The Rights Offering contained a subscription price that was less than the fair value of the Company's common stock on the last day the rights could be exercised. This price discount is considered a bonus element similar to a stock dividend. Because of this bonus element, the Company adjusted both the weighted average basic and diluted shares outstanding as reported in the Quarterly Report on Form 10-Q filed with the SEC on April 29, 2011 by multiplying those weighted average shares by an adjustment factor that represented the $6.40 fair value of a share of the Company's common stock immediately prior to the exercise of the basic and over-subscription privileges under the Rights Offering divided by the $6.07 theoretical ex-rights fair value of a share of the Company's common stock immediately prior to the exercise of the basic and over-subscription privileges under the Rights Offering. Weighted average basic and diluted shares outstanding and net loss per weighted average basic and diluted share for 2011 as originally reported and as adjusted for this bonus element were as follows:

(In thousands, except per share data)	As Originally Reported	As Adjusted	Effect of Change
2011:			
Weighted average basic shares outstanding	214,282	224,996	10,714
Weighted average diluted shares outstanding	214,282	224,996	10,714
Net loss per weighted average basic share	$ (2.32)	$ (2.21)	$ 0.11
Net loss per weighted average diluted share	$ (2.32)	$ (2.21)	$ 0.11
2010:			
Weighted average basic shares outstanding	214,282	224,996	10,714
Weighted average diluted shares outstanding	214,282	224,996	10,714
Net income per weighted average basic share	$ 0.41	$ 0.39	$ (0.02)
Net income per weighted average diluted share	$ 0.41	$ 0.39	$ (0.02)

7.55 ATMEL CORPORATION (DEC)

REPORT OF INDEPENDENT REGISTERED PUBLIC ACCOUNTING FIRM

To the Board of Directors and Stockholders
Atmel Corporation:

We have audited the accompanying consolidated balance sheet of Atmel Corporation and subsidiaries (the Company) as of December 31, 2012, and the related consolidated statements of operations, comprehensive income, stockholders' equity, and cash flows for the year then ended. In connection with our audit of the consolidated financial statements, we also have audited the financial statement schedule of valuation and qualifying accounts as set forth under Item 15(a)(2). We also have audited the Company's internal control over financial reporting as of December 31, 2012, based on criteria established in *Internal Control—Integrated Framework* issued by the Committee of Sponsoring Organizations of the Treadway Commission (COSO). The Company's management is responsible for these consolidated financial statements and financial statement schedule, for maintaining effective internal control over financial reporting, and for its assessment of the effectiveness of internal control over financial reporting, included in the accompanying *Management's Report on Internal Control over Financial Reporting* appearing under Item 9A. Our responsibility is to express an opinion on these consolidated financial statements, financial statement schedule, and an opinion on the Company's internal control over financial reporting based on our audit.

We conducted our audit in accordance with the standards of the Public Company Accounting Oversight Board (United States). Those standards require that we plan and perform the audit to obtain reasonable assurance about whether the financial statements are free of material misstatement and whether effective internal control over financial reporting was maintained in all material respects. Our audit of the consolidated financial statements included examining, on a test basis, evidence supporting the amounts and disclosures in the financial statements, assessing the accounting principles used and significant estimates made by management, and evaluating the overall financial statement presentation. Our audit of internal control over financial reporting included obtaining an understanding of internal control over financial reporting, assessing the risk that a material weakness exists, and testing and evaluating the design and operating effectiveness of internal control based on the assessed risk. Our audit also included performing such other procedures as we considered necessary in the circumstances. We believe that our audit provides a reasonable basis for our opinion.

A company's internal control over financial reporting is a process designed to provide reasonable assurance regarding the reliability of financial reporting and the preparation of financial statements for external purposes in accordance with generally accepted accounting principles. A company's internal control over financial reporting includes those policies and procedures that (1) pertain to the maintenance of records that, in reasonable detail, accurately and fairly reflect the transactions and dispositions of the assets of the company; (2) provide reasonable assurance that transactions are recorded as necessary to permit preparation of financial statements in accordance with generally accepted accounting principles, and that receipts and expenditures of the company are being made only in accordance with authorizations of management and directors of the company; and (3) provide reasonable assurance regarding prevention or timely detection of unauthorized acquisition, use, or disposition of the company's assets that could have a material effect on the financial statements.

Because of its inherent limitations, internal control over financial reporting may not prevent or detect misstatements. Also, projections of any evaluation of effectiveness to future periods are subject to the risk that controls may become inadequate because of changes in conditions, or that the degree of compliance with the policies or procedures may deteriorate.

In our opinion, the consolidated financial statements referred to above present fairly, in all material respects, the financial position of Atmel Corporation and subsidiaries as of December 31, 2012, and the results of their operations and their cash flows for the year then ended, in conformity with U.S. generally accepted accounting principles. Also in our opinion, the related financial statement schedule, when considered in relation to the basic consolidated financial statements taken as a whole, presents fairly, in all material respects, the information set forth therein. Also in our opinion, Atmel Corporation maintained, in all material respects, effective internal control over financial reporting as of December 31, 2012, based on criteria established in *Internal Control—Integrated Framework* issued by the Committee of Sponsoring Organizations of the Treadway Commission.

/s/ KPMG LLP
Santa Clara, California
February 26, 2013

REPORT OF INDEPENDENT REGISTERED PUBLIC ACCOUNTING FIRM

The Board of Directors and Stockholders of
Atmel Corporation:

In our opinion, the consolidated balance sheet as of December 31, 2011 and the related consolidated statements of operations, comprehensive income, stockholders' equity and cash flows for each of the two years in the period ended December 31, 2011 present fairly, in all material respects, the financial position of Atmel Corporation and its subsidiaries (the "Company") at December 31, 2011, and the results of their operations and their cash flows for each of the two years in the period ended December 31, 2011, in conformity with accounting principles generally accepted in the United States of America. In addition, in our opinion, the financial statement schedule listed in the index appearing under Item 15(a)(2) for each of the two years in the period ended December 31, 2011 presents fairly, in all material respects, the information set forth therein when read in conjunction with the related consolidated financial statements. These financial statements and financial statement schedule are the responsibility of the Company's management. Our responsibility is to express an opinion on these financial statements and financial statement schedule based on our audits. We conducted our audits of these statements in accordance with the standards of the Public Company Accounting Oversight Board (United States). Those standards require that we plan and perform the audit to obtain reasonable assurance about whether the financial statements are free of material misstatement. An audit includes examining, on a test basis, evidence supporting the amounts and disclosures in the financial statements, assessing the accounting principles used and significant estimates made by management, and evaluating the overall financial statement presentation. We believe that our audits provide a reasonable basis for our opinion.

/s/ PricewaterhouseCoopers LLP
San Jose, California
February 28, 2012

Opinion Expressed on Supplementary Financial Information

PRESENTATION

> **Author's Note**
> Because the report on supplementary financial information is applicable only for issuers, the following guidance is not intended for nonissuers.

7.56 Annual reports to security holders may be combined with the required information of SEC Form 10-K and are suitable for filing with the SEC if certain conditions are satisfied. Accordingly, many survey entities prepare an integrated annual report or simply provide to stockholders a copy of Form 10-K in lieu of the annual report. Form 10-K requires inclusion of certain supplementary financial information, including schedules (Article 12 of Regulation S-X), that must be audited. The report on the audit of schedules may be a separate report or combined with the report on the audit of the basic financial statements.

PRESENTATION AND DISCLOSURE EXCERPTS

SUPPLEMENTARY FINANCIAL INFORMATION

7.57 AUTODESK, INC. (JAN)
REPORT OF ERNST & YOUNG LLP, INDEPENDENT REGISTERED PUBLIC ACCOUNTING FIRM

The Board of Directors and Stockholders of Autodesk, Inc.

We have audited the accompanying consolidated balance sheets of Autodesk, Inc. as of January 31, 2012 and 2011, and the related consolidated statements of operations, cash flows and stockholders' equity for each of the three years in the period ended January 31, 2012. Our audits also included the financial statement schedule listed in the Index at Item 15(a)(2). These financial statements and schedule are the responsibility of the Company's management. Our responsibility is to express an opinion on these financial statements and schedule based on our audits.

We conducted our audits in accordance with the standards of the Public Company Accounting Oversight Board (United States). Those standards require that we plan and perform the audit to obtain reasonable assurance about whether the financial statements are free of material misstatement. An audit includes examining, on a test basis, evidence supporting the amounts and disclosures in the financial statements. An audit also includes assessing the accounting principles used and significant estimates made by management, as well as evaluating the overall financial statement presentation. We believe that our audits provide a reasonable basis for our opinion.

In our opinion, the financial statements referred to above present fairly, in all material respects, the consolidated financial position of Autodesk, Inc. at January 31, 2012 and 2011, and the consolidated results of its operations and its cash flows for each of the three years in the period ended January 31, 2012, in conformity with U.S. generally accepted accounting principles. Also, in our opinion, the related financial statement schedule, when considered in relation to the basic financial statements taken as a whole, presents fairly in all material respects the information set forth therein.

We also have audited, in accordance with the standards of the Public Company Accounting Oversight Board (United States), Autodesk, Inc.'s internal control over financial reporting as of January 31, 2012, based on criteria established in *Internal Control—Integrated Framework* issued by the Committee of Sponsoring Organizations of the Treadway Commission and our report dated March 15, 2012 expressed an unqualified opinion thereon.

Financial Statement Schedule II

Description	Balance at Beginning of Year	Additions Charged to Costs and Expenses or Revenues	Deductions and Write-Offs	Balance at End of Year
		(In millions)		
Fiscal Year Ended January 31, 2012				
Allowance for doubtful accounts	$ 4.2	$ 2.4	$ 1.1	$ 5.5
Product returns reserves	10.6	32.7	37.5	5.8
Restructuring	8.6	—	6.2	2.4
Fiscal Year Ended January 31, 2011				
Allowance for doubtful accounts	$ 4.6	$ (0.3)	$ 0.1	$ 4.2
Product returns reserves	11.8	38.9	40.1	10.6
Restructuring	19.4	13.7	24.5	8.6
Fiscal Year Ended January 31, 2010				
Allowance for doubtful accounts	$ 8.6	$ 1.7	$ 5.7	$ 4.6
Product returns reserves	12.5	42.9	43.6	11.8
Restructuring	43.9	48.9	73.4	19.4

7.58 JOHNSON & JOHNSON (DEC)

REPORT OF INDEPENDENT REGISTERED PUBLIC ACCOUNTING FIRM ON FINANCIAL STATEMENT SCHEDULE

To the Board of Directors of
Johnson & Johnson:

Our audits of the consolidated financial statements and of the effectiveness of internal control over financial reporting referred to in our report dated February 21, 2013 appearing in the 2012 Annual Report to Shareholders of Johnson & Johnson (which report and consolidated financial statements are incorporated by reference in this Annual Report on Form 10-K) also included an audit of the financial statement schedule listed in Item 15(a)2 of this Form 10-K. In our opinion, this financial statement schedule presents fairly, in all material respects, the information set forth therein when read in conjunction with the related consolidated financial statements.

EXHIBITS AND FINANCIAL STATEMENT SCHEDULES

Schedule II—Valuation And Qualifying Accounts

Fiscal Years Ended December 30, 2012, January 1, 2012 and January 2, 2011

(Dollars in Millions)

	Balance at Beginning of Period	Accruals	Payments/ Other	Balance at End of Period
2012				
Accrued Rebates[1]	$2,215	8,973	(8,722)	2,466
Accrued Returns	682	549	(521)	710
Accrued Promotions	396	1,583	(1,544)	435
Subtotal	$3,293	11,105	(10,787)	3,611
Reserve for doubtful accounts	361	127	(22)	466
Reserve for cash discounts	99	1,010	(1,004)	105
Total	$3,753	12,242	(11,813)	4,182
2011				
Accrued Rebates[1]	$2,146	8,331	(8,262)	2,215
Accrued Returns	640	560	(518)	682
Accrued Promotions	427	1,774	(1,805)	396
Subtotal	$3,213	10,665	(10,585)	3,293
Reserve for doubtful accounts	340	77	(56)	361
Reserve for cash discounts	110	960	(971)	99
Total	$3,663	11,702	(11,612)	3,753
2010				
Accrued Rebates[1]	$1,639	8,400	(7,893)	2,146
Accrued Returns	689	517	(566)	640
Accrued Promotions	429	2,664	(2,666)	427
Subtotal	$2,757	11,581	(11,125)	3,213
Reserve for doubtful accounts	333	130	(123)	340
Reserve for cash discounts	101	1,112	(1,103)	110
Total	$3,191	12,823	(12,351)	3,663

[1] Includes reserve for customer rebates of $642 million, $656 million and $701 million at December 30, 2012, January 1, 2012 and January 2, 2011, respectively.

Dating of Report

PRESENTATION

NONISSUERS

7.59 Dating of the auditor's report is discussed in both AU-C section 700 and AU-C section 560. Paragraph .41 of AU-C section 700 states that the auditor's report should be dated no earlier than the date on which the auditors has obtained sufficient appropriate audit evidence on which to base the auditor's opinion, including evidence that
- the audit documentation has been reviewed;
- all statements that the financial statements comprise, including related notes, have been prepared; and
- management has asserted that it has taken responsibility for those financial statements.

7.60 Paragraph .13 of AU-C section 560 states that if management revises the financial statements, the auditor should perform the audit procedures necessary in the circumstances on the revision. The auditor also should either
- date the auditor's report as of a later date or
- include an additional date in the auditor's report on the revised financial statements that is limited to the revision (that is, dual-date the auditor's report for that revision), thereby indicating that the auditor's procedures subsequent to the original date of the auditor's report are limited solely to the revision of the financial statements described in the relevant note to the financial statements.

ISSUERS

7.61 Paragraphs .01 and .05 of PCAOB AU section 530, *Dating of the Independent Auditor's Report* (AICPA, *PCAOB Standards and Related Rules*, Interim Standards), state the following:

.01 The auditor should date the audit report no earlier than the date on which the auditor has obtained sufficient appropriate evidence to support the auditor's opinion. Paragraph .05 describes the procedure to be followed when a subsequent event occurring after the report date is disclosed in the financial statements.

Note: When performing an integrated audit of financial statements and internal control over financial reporting, the auditor's reports on the company's financial statements and on internal control over financial reporting should be dated the same date.

Note: If the auditor concludes that a scope limitation will prevent the auditor from obtaining the reasonable assurance necessary to express an opinion on the financial statements, then the auditor's report date is the date that the auditor has obtained sufficient appropriate evidence to support the representations in the auditor's report.

.05 The independent auditor has two methods for dating the report when a subsequent event disclosed in the financial statements occurs after the auditor has obtained sufficient appropriate evidence on which to base his or her opinion, but before the issuance of the related financial statements. The auditor may use "dual dating," for example, "February 16, 20___, except for Note___, as to which the date is March 1, 20___," or may date the report as of the later date. In the former instance, the responsibility for events occurring subsequent to the original report date is limited to the specific event referred to in the note (or otherwise disclosed). In the latter instance, the independent auditor's responsibility for subsequent events extends to the later report date and, accordingly, the procedures outlined in section 560.12 generally should be extended to that date.

PRESENTATION AND DISCLOSURE EXCERPT

DATING OF REPORT

7.62 AXIALL CORPORATION (DEC)
REPORT OF INDEPENDENT REGISTERED PUBLIC ACCOUNTING FIRM

To the Board of Directors and Stockholders of
Axiall Corporation
Atlanta, Georgia

We have audited the accompanying consolidated statements of income, comprehensive income, stockholders' equity, and cash flows of Axiall Corporation (formerly known as Georgia Gulf Corporation) and subsidiaries (the "Company") for the year ended December 31, 2010. Our audit also included the 2010 information in the financial statement schedule listed in the Index at Item 15. These financial statements and financial statement schedule are the responsibility of the Company's management. Our responsibility is to express an opinion on the financial statements and financial statement schedule based on our audit.

We conducted our audit in accordance with the standards of the Public Company Accounting Oversight Board (United States). Those standards require that we plan and perform the audit to obtain reasonable assurance about whether the financial statements are free of material misstatement. An audit includes examining, on a test basis, evidence supporting the amounts and disclosures in the financial statements. An audit also includes assessing the accounting principles used and significant estimates made by management, as well as evaluating the overall financial statement presentation. We believe that our audit provides a reasonable basis for our opinion.

In our opinion, such consolidated financial statements present fairly, in all material respects, the results of the Company's operations and their cash flows for the year ended December 31, 2010, in conformity with accounting principles generally accepted in the United States of America. Also, in our opinion, the related financial statement schedule, when considered in relation to the basic consolidated financial statements taken as a whole, presents fairly, in all material respects, the information set forth therein.

/s/ DELOITTE & TOUCHE LLP
Atlanta, Georgia
March 10, 2011
(February 24, 2012 as to the consolidated statement of comprehensive income for the year ended December 31, 2010 and February 28, 2013 as to comprehensive income for the year ended December 31, 2010 as presented within Note 19)

Auditors' Reports on Internal Control Over Financial Reporting

PRESENTATION

> *Author's Note*
> Because the report on internal control over financial reporting is required only for issuers, the following guidance is not applicable for nonissuers.

7.63 Section 404(a) of the Sarbanes-Oxley Act of 2002 requires that management of a public entity assess the effectiveness of the entity's internal control over financial reporting as of the end of the entity's most recent fiscal year and include in the entity's annual report management's conclusions about the effectiveness of the entity's internal control structure and procedures. Management is required to state a direct conclusion about whether the entity's internal control over financial reporting is effective. Management's report on internal control over financial reporting is required to include the following:
- A statement of management's responsibility for establishing and maintaining adequate internal control over financial reporting for the entity
- A statement identifying the framework used by management to conduct the required assessment of the effectiveness of the entity's internal control over financial reporting
- An assessment of the effectiveness of the entity's internal control over financial reporting as of the end of the entity's most recent fiscal year, including an explicit statement about whether that internal control over financial reporting is effective
- A statement that the registered public accounting firm that audited the financial statements included in the annual report has issued an attestation report on management's assessment of the entity's internal control over financial reporting

7.64 Under Section 404(b) of the Sarbanes-Oxley Act of 2002, the auditor who audits the public entity's financial statements included in the annual report is required to audit the entity's internal control over financial reporting. In addition, the auditor is required to audit and report on management's assessment of the effectiveness of internal control over financial reporting. Under PCAOB Auditing Standard No. 5, *An Audit of Internal Control Over Financial Reporting That is Integrated with an Audit of Financial Statements* (AICPA, *PCAOB Standards and Related Rules*, Auditing Standards), the auditor's objective in an audit of internal control over financial reporting is to express an opinion on the effectiveness of the entity's internal control over financial reporting. The audit of internal control over financial reporting should be integrated with the audit of the financial statements. Accordingly, independent auditors engaged to audit the financial statements of such entities also are required to audit and report on the entity's internal control over financial reporting as of the end of such fiscal year. Further, if the auditor determines that elements of management's annual report on internal control over financial reporting are incomplete or improperly presented, the auditor should modify the report to include an explanatory paragraph describing the reasons for this determination and identify and fairly describe any material weakness. Paragraph 86 of Auditing Standard No. 5 allows the auditor to issue a combined report (that is, one report containing both an opinion on the financial statements and an opinion on internal control over financial reporting) or separate reports on the entity's financial statements and internal control over financial reporting.

7.65 In September 2010, the SEC approved a final rule related to the Dodd-Frank Wall Street Reform and Consumer Protection Act (Dodd-Frank Act). The Dodd-Frank Act provides that Section 404(b) of the Sarbanes-Oxley Act of 2002 shall not apply with respect to any audit report prepared for an issuer that is neither an accelerated filer nor a large accelerated filer. Prior to the Dodd-Frank Act, a nonaccelerated filer would have been required, under existing SEC rules, to include an attestation report of its registered public accounting firm on internal control over financial reporting in the filer's annual report filed with the SEC for fiscal years ending on or after June 15, 2010.

PRESENTATION AND DISCLOSURE EXCERPTS

SEPARATE REPORT ON INTERNAL CONTROL

7.66 TOLL BROTHERS, INC. (OCT)

REPORT OF INDEPENDENT REGISTERED PUBLIC ACCOUNTING FIRM

The Board of Directors and Stockholders of Toll Brothers, Inc.

We have audited Toll Brothers, Inc.'s internal control over financial reporting as of October 31, 2012, based on criteria established in Internal Control—Integrated Framework issued by the Committee of Sponsoring Organizations of the Treadway Commission (the COSO criteria). Toll Brothers, Inc.'s management is responsible for maintaining effective internal control over financial reporting, and for its assessment of the effectiveness of internal control over financial reporting included in the accompanying Management's Annual Report on Internal Control Over Financial Reporting. Our responsibility is to express an opinion on the company's internal control over financial reporting based on our audit.

We conducted our audit in accordance with the standards of the Public Company Accounting Oversight Board (United States). Those standards require that we plan and perform the audit to obtain reasonable assurance about whether effective internal control over financial reporting was maintained in all material respects. Our audit included obtaining an understanding of internal control over financial reporting, assessing the risk that a material weakness exists, testing and evaluating the design and operating effectiveness of internal control based on the assessed risk, and performing such other procedures as we considered necessary in the circumstances. We believe that our audit provides a reasonable basis for our opinion.

A company's internal control over financial reporting is a process designed to provide reasonable assurance regarding the reliability of financial reporting and the preparation of financial statements for external purposes in accordance with generally accepted accounting principles. A company's internal control over financial reporting includes those policies and procedures that (1) pertain to the maintenance of records that, in reasonable detail, accurately and fairly reflect the transactions and dispositions of the assets of the company; (2) provide reasonable assurance that transactions are recorded as necessary to permit preparation of financial statements in accordance with generally accepted accounting principles, and that receipts and expenditures of the company are being made only in accordance with authorizations of management and directors of the company; and (3) provide reasonable assurance regarding prevention or timely detection of unauthorized acquisition, use or disposition of the company's assets that could have a material effect on the financial statements.

Because of its inherent limitations, internal control over financial reporting may not prevent or detect misstatements. Also, projections of any evaluation of effectiveness to future periods are subject to the risk that controls may become inadequate because of changes in conditions, or that the degree of compliance with the policies or procedures may deteriorate.

In our opinion, Toll Brothers, Inc. maintained, in all material respects, effective internal control over financial reporting as of October 31, 2012, based on the COSO criteria.

We also have audited, in accordance with the standards of the Public Company Accounting Oversight Board (United States), the consolidated balance sheets of Toll Brothers, Inc. as of October 31, 2012 and 2011, and the related consolidated statements of operations, changes in equity, and cash flows for each of the three years in the period ended October 31, 2012 of Toll Brothers, Inc. and our report dated December 28, 2012 expressed an unqualified opinion thereon.

REPORT OF INDEPENDENT REGISTERED PUBLIC ACCOUNTING FIRM

The Board of Directors and Stockholders of Toll Brothers, Inc.

We have audited the accompanying consolidated balance sheets of Toll Brothers, Inc. as of October 31, 2012 and 2011, and the related consolidated statements of operations, changes in equity, and cash flows for each of the three years in the period ended October 31, 2012. These financial statements are the responsibility of the Company's management. Our responsibility is to express an opinion on these financial statements based on our audits.

We conducted our audits in accordance with the standards of the Public Company Accounting Oversight Board (United States). Those standards require that we plan and perform the audit to obtain reasonable assurance about whether the financial statements are free of material misstatement. An audit includes examining, on a test basis, evidence supporting the amounts and disclosures in the financial statements. An audit also includes assessing the accounting principles used and significant estimates made by management, as well as evaluating the overall financial statement presentation. We believe that our audits provide a reasonable basis for our opinion.

In our opinion, the financial statements referred to above present fairly, in all material respects, the consolidated financial position of Toll Brothers, Inc. at October 31, 2012 and 2011, and the consolidated results of its operations and its cash flows for each of the three years in the period ended October 31, 2012, in conformity with U.S. generally accepted accounting principles.

We also have audited, in accordance with the standards of the Public Company Accounting Oversight Board (United States), Toll Brothers Inc.'s internal control over financial reporting as of October 31, 2011, based on criteria established in Internal Control-Integrated Framework issued by the Committee of Sponsoring Organizations of the Treadway Commission and our report dated December 28, 2012 expressed an unqualified opinion thereon.

COMBINED REPORT ON FINANCIAL STATEMENTS AND INTERNAL CONTROL

7.67 VISA INC. (SEP)
REPORT OF INDEPENDENT REGISTERED PUBLIC ACCOUNTING FIRM

The Board of Directors and Stockholders
Visa Inc.:

We have audited the accompanying consolidated balance sheets of Visa Inc. and subsidiaries as of September 30, 2012 and 2011, and the related consolidated statements of operations, comprehensive income, changes in equity, and cash flows for each of the years in the three-year period ended September 30, 2012. We also have audited Visa Inc.'s internal control over financial reporting as of September 30, 2012, based on criteria established in *Internal Control—Integrated Framework* issued by the Committee of Sponsoring Organizations of the Treadway Commission (COSO). Visa Inc.'s management is responsible for these consolidated financial statements, for maintaining effective internal control over financial reporting, and for its assessment of the effectiveness of internal control over financial reporting, included in the accompanying Management's Report on Internal Control Over Financial Reporting. Our responsibility is to express an opinion on these consolidated financial statements and an opinion on the Company's internal control over financial reporting based on our audits.

We conducted our audits in accordance with the standards of the Public Company Accounting Oversight Board (United States). Those standards require that we plan and perform the audits to obtain reasonable assurance about whether the financial statements are free of material misstatement and whether effective internal control over financial reporting was maintained in all material respects. Our audits of the consolidated financial statements included examining, on a test basis, evidence supporting the amounts and disclosures in the financial statements, assessing the accounting principles used and significant estimates made by management, and evaluating the overall financial statement presentation. Our audit of internal control over financial reporting included obtaining an understanding of internal control over financial reporting, assessing the risk that a material weakness exists, and testing and evaluating the design and operating effectiveness of internal control based on the assessed risk. Our audits also included performing such other procedures as we considered necessary in the circumstances. We believe that our audits provide a reasonable basis for our opinions.

A company's internal control over financial reporting is a process designed to provide reasonable assurance regarding the reliability of financial reporting and the preparation of financial statements for external purposes in accordance with generally accepted accounting principles. A company's internal control over financial reporting includes those policies and procedures that (1) pertain to the maintenance of records that, in reasonable detail, accurately and fairly reflect the transactions and dispositions of the assets of the company; (2) provide reasonable assurance that transactions are recorded as necessary to permit preparation of financial statements in accordance with generally accepted accounting principles, and that receipts and expenditures of the company are being made only in accordance with authorizations of management and directors of the company; and (3) provide reasonable assurance regarding prevention or timely detection of unauthorized acquisition, use, or disposition of the company's assets that could have a material effect on the financial statements.

Because of its inherent limitations, internal control over financial reporting may not prevent or detect misstatements. Also, projections of any evaluation of effectiveness to future periods are subject to the risk that controls may become inadequate because of changes in conditions, or that the degree of compliance with the policies or procedures may deteriorate.

In our opinion, the consolidated financial statements referred to above present fairly, in all material respects, the financial position of Visa Inc. and subsidiaries as of September 30, 2012 and 2011, and the results of their operations and their cash flows for each of the years in the three-year period ended September 30, 2012, in conformity with U.S. generally accepted accounting principles. Also in our opinion, Visa Inc. maintained, in all material respects, effective internal control over financial reporting as of September 30, 2012, based on criteria established in *Internal Control—Integrated Framework* issued by the Committee of Sponsoring Organizations of the Treadway Commission.

REPORT ON INTERNAL CONTROL NOT PRESENTED

7.68 THE STANDARD REGISTER COMPANY (DEC)
REPORT OF INDEPENDENT REGISTERED PUBLIC ACCOUNTING FIRM

Board of Directors and Shareholders
The Standard Register Company
Dayton, Ohio

We have audited the accompanying consolidated balance sheets of The Standard Register Company and subsidiaries as of December 30, 2012 and January 1, 2012, and the related consolidated statements of income, comprehensive income, cash flows, and shareholders' (deficit) equity for each of the three fiscal years in the period ended December 30, 2012. These financial statements are the responsibility of the Company's management. Our responsibility is to express an opinion on these financial statements based on our audits.

We conducted our audits in accordance with the standards of the Public Company Accounting Oversight Board (United States). Those standards require that we plan and perform the audit to obtain reasonable assurance about whether the financial statements are free of material misstatement. An audit includes examining, on a test basis, evidence supporting the amounts and disclosures in the financial statements, assessing the accounting principles used and significant estimates made by management, as well as evaluating the overall financial statement presentation. We believe that our audits provide a reasonable basis for our opinion.

The Company is not required to have, nor were we engaged to perform, an audit of its internal control over financial reporting as of December 30, 2012. Our audits included the consideration of internal control over financial reporting as a basis for designing audit procedures that are appropriate in the circumstances, but not for the purpose of expressing an opinion on the effectiveness of the Company's internal control over financial reporting. Accordingly, we express no such opinion.

In our opinion, the consolidated financial statements referred to above present fairly, in all material respects, the financial position of The Standard Register Company and subsidiaries as of December 30, 2012 and January 1, 2012, and the results of their operations and their cash flows for each of the three fiscal years in the period ended December 30, 2012, in conformity with accounting principles generally accepted in the United States of America.

AUDIT REPORT WITH SPECIFIC ITEMS EXCLUDED

7.69 AIR PRODUCTS AND CHEMICALS, INC. (SEP)
REPORT OF INDEPENDENT REGISTERED PUBLIC ACCOUNTING FIRM

The Board of Directors and Shareholders of
Air Products and Chemicals, Inc.:

We have audited the accompanying consolidated balance sheets of Air Products and Chemicals, Inc. and Subsidiaries (the Company) as of 30 September 2012 and 2011, and the related consolidated income statements and consolidated statements of equity, comprehensive income, and cash flows for each of the years in the three-year period ended 30 September 2012. In connection with our audits of the consolidated financial statements, we also have audited the financial statement schedule referred to in Item 15(a)(2) in this Form 10-K. We also have audited the Company's internal control over financial reporting as of 30 September 2012, based on criteria established in Internal Control—Integrated Framework issued by the Committee of Sponsoring Organizations of the Treadway Commission. The Company's management is responsible for these consolidated financial statements and financial statement schedule, for maintaining effective internal control over financial reporting, and for its assessment of the effectiveness of internal control over financial reporting, included in the accompanying "Management's Report on Internal Control over Financial Reporting." Our responsibility is to express an opinion on these consolidated financial statements and financial statement schedule and an opinion on the Company's internal control over financial reporting based on our audits.

We conducted our audits in accordance with the standards of the Public Company Accounting Oversight Board (United States). Those standards require that we plan and perform the audits to obtain reasonable assurance about whether the financial statements are free of material misstatement and whether effective internal control over financial reporting was maintained in all material respects. Our audits of the consolidated financial statements included examining, on a test basis, evidence supporting the amounts and disclosures in the financial statements, assessing the accounting principles used and significant estimates made by management, and evaluating the overall financial statement presentation. Our audit of internal control over financial reporting included obtaining an understanding of internal control over financial reporting, assessing the risk that a material weakness exists, and testing and evaluating the design and operating effectiveness of internal control based on the assessed risk. Our audits also included performing such other procedures as we considered necessary in the circumstances. We believe that our audits provide a reasonable basis for our opinions.

A company's internal control over financial reporting is a process designed to provide reasonable assurance regarding the reliability of financial reporting and the preparation of financial statements for external purposes in accordance with generally accepted accounting principles. A company's internal control over financial reporting includes those policies and procedures that (1) pertain to the maintenance of records that, in reasonable detail, accurately and fairly reflect the transactions and dispositions of the assets of the company; (2) provide reasonable assurance that transactions are recorded as necessary to permit preparation of financial statements in accordance with generally accepted accounting principles, and that receipts and expenditures of the company are being made only in accordance with authorizations of management and directors of the company; and (3) provide reasonable assurance regarding prevention or timely detection of unauthorized acquisition, use, or disposition of the company's assets that could have a material effect on the financial statements.

Because of its inherent limitations, internal control over financial reporting may not prevent or detect misstatements. Also, projections of any evaluation of effectiveness to future periods are subject to the risk that controls may become inadequate because of changes in conditions, or that the degree of compliance with the policies or procedures may deteriorate.

In our opinion, the consolidated financial statements referred to above present fairly, in all material respects, the financial position of Air Products and Chemicals, Inc. and Subsidiaries as of 30 September 2012 and 2011, and the results of their operations and their cash flows for each of the years in the three-year period ended 30 September 2012, in conformity with U.S. generally accepted accounting principles. Also in our opinion, the related financial statement schedule, when considered in relation to the basic consolidated financial statements taken as a whole, presents fairly, in all material respects, the information set forth therein. Also in our opinion, Air Products and Chemicals, Inc. and Subsidiaries maintained, in all material respects, effective internal control over financial reporting as of 30 September 2012, based on criteria established in Internal Control—Integrated Framework issued by the Committee of Sponsoring Organizations of the Treadway Commission.

The Company acquired a controlling equity interest in the outstanding shares of Indura S.A. on 1 July 2012 and management excluded Indura S.A.'s internal control over financial reporting from its assessment of the effectiveness of the Company's internal control over financial reporting as of 30 September 2012. The Company's consolidated financial statements included $1,747 million in total assets (10%) and $140 million in total sales (less than 2%) associated with Indura S.A. as of and for the year ended 30 September 2012. Our audit of internal control over financial reporting of Air Products and Chemicals, Inc. also excluded an evaluation of the internal control over financial reporting of Indura S.A.

INEFFECTIVE INTERNAL CONTROLS & MANAGEMENT'S REPORT ON INTERNAL CONTROL OVER FINANCIAL REPORTING

7.70 URS CORPORATION (DEC)
REPORT OF INDEPENDENT REGISTERED PUBLIC ACCOUNTING FIRM

To the Board of Directors and Stockholders of
URS Corporation:

In our opinion, the accompanying consolidated financial statements listed in the index appearing under Item 15(a)1 present fairly, in all material respects, the financial position of URS Corporation and its subsidiaries at December 28, 2012 and December 30, 2011 and the results of their operations and their cash flows for each of the three years in the period ended December 28, 2012 in conformity with accounting principles generally accepted in the United States of America. Also in our opinion, the Company did not maintain, in all material respects, effective internal control over financial reporting as of December 28, 2012, based on criteria established in *Internal Control—Integrated Framework* issued by the Committee of Sponsoring Organizations of the Treadway Commission (COSO) because a material weakness in internal control over financial reporting related to some key accounting personnel who have the ability to prepare and post journal entries without an independent review by someone without the ability to prepare and post journal entries existed as of that date. A material weakness is a deficiency, or a combination of deficiencies, in internal control over financial reporting, such that there is a reasonable possibility that a material misstatement of the annual or interim financial statements will not be prevented or detected on a timely basis. The material weakness referred to above is described in Management's Annual Report on Internal Control over Financial Reporting appearing under Item 9A. We considered this material weakness in determining the nature, timing, and extent of audit tests applied in our audit of the December 28, 2012 consolidated financial statements, and our opinion regarding the effectiveness of the Company's internal control over financial reporting does not affect our opinion on those consolidated financial statements. The Company's management is responsible for these financial statements, for maintaining effective internal control over financial reporting and for its assessment of the effectiveness of internal control over financial reporting included in management's report referred to above. Our responsibility is to express opinions on these financial statements and on the Company's internal control over financial reporting based on our integrated audits. We conducted our audits in accordance with the standards of the Public Company Accounting Oversight Board (United States). Those standards require that we plan and perform the audits to obtain reasonable assurance about whether the financial statements are free of material misstatement and whether effective internal control over financial reporting was maintained in all material respects. Our audits of the financial statements included examining, on a test basis, evidence supporting the amounts and disclosures in the financial statements, assessing the accounting principles used and significant estimates made by management, and evaluating the overall financial statement presentation. Our audit of internal control over financial reporting included obtaining an understanding of internal control over financial reporting, assessing the risk that a material weakness exists, and testing and evaluating the design and operating effectiveness of internal control based on the assessed risk. Our audits also included performing such other procedures as we considered necessary in the circumstances. We believe that our audits provide a reasonable basis for our opinions.

A company's internal control over financial reporting is a process designed to provide reasonable assurance regarding the reliability of financial reporting and the preparation of financial statements for external purposes in accordance with generally accepted accounting principles. A company's internal control over financial reporting includes those policies and procedures that (i) pertain to the maintenance of records that, in reasonable detail, accurately and fairly reflect the transactions and dispositions of the assets of the company; (ii) provide reasonable assurance that transactions are recorded as necessary to permit preparation of financial statements in accordance with generally accepted accounting principles, and that receipts and expenditures of the company are being made only in accordance with authorizations of management and directors of the company; and (iii) provide reasonable assurance regarding prevention or timely detection of unauthorized acquisition, use, or disposition of the company's assets that could have a material effect on the financial statements.

Because of its inherent limitations, internal control over financial reporting may not prevent or detect misstatements. Also, projections of any evaluation of effectiveness to future periods are subject to the risk that controls may become inadequate because of changes in conditions, or that the degree of compliance with the policies or procedures may deteriorate.

As described in Management's Annual Report on Internal Control over Financial Reporting, management has excluded Flint Energy Services, Ltd. ("Flint") from its assessment of internal control over financial reporting as of December 28, 2012 because it was acquired by the Company in a business combination during 2012. We have also excluded Flint from our audit of internal control over financial reporting. Flint is a wholly-owned subsidiary whose total assets and total revenues represent 12% and 13% respectively, of the related consolidated financial statement amounts as of and for the year ended December 28, 2012.

CONTROLS AND PROCEDURES (in part)

Management's Annual Report on Internal Control over Financial Reporting

Our management is responsible for establishing and maintaining adequate internal control over financial reporting, as that term is defined in Exchange Act Rules 13a-15(f) and 15d-15(f). Internal control over financial reporting is a process designed to provide reasonable assurance regarding the reliability of our financial reporting and the preparation of financial statements for external purposes in accordance with generally accepted accounting principles (GAAP). Internal control over financial reporting includes those policies and procedures that (i) pertain to the maintenance of records that in reasonable detail accurately and fairly reflect the transactions and dispositions of the assets of the company; (ii) provide reasonable assurance that transactions are recorded as necessary to permit preparation of financial statements in accordance with GAAP, and that receipts and expenditures of the company are being made only in accordance with authorizations of management and directors of the company; and (iii) provide reasonable assurance regarding prevention or timely detection of unauthorized acquisition, use or disposition of the company's assets that could have a material effect on the financial statements.

Management, with the participation of our CEO and CFO, assessed our internal control over financial reporting as of December 28, 2012, the end of our fiscal year. Management based its assessment on criteria established in *Internal Control—Integrated Framework* issued by the Committee of Sponsoring Organizations of the Treadway Commission. Management's assessment included evaluation and testing of the design and operating effectiveness of key financial reporting controls, process documentation, accounting policies, and our overall control environment.

Based on management's assessment, management has concluded that the Company did not maintain effective control over financial reporting as of December 28, 2012 because of the material weakness described below. A material weakness is a deficiency, or combination of deficiencies, in internal control over financial reporting, such that there is a reasonable possibility that a material misstatement of the annual or interim financial statements will not be prevented or detected on a timely basis.

Material Weakness Related to Journal Entries. We did not maintain effective internal control over financial reporting as some key accounting personnel have the ability to prepare and post journal entries without an independent review by someone without the ability to prepare and post journal entries. Specifically, our internal controls over journal entries were not designed effectively to provide reasonable assurance that journal entries were appropriately recorded or that they were properly reviewed for validity, accuracy, and completeness for substantially all of the key accounts and disclosures. While this control deficiency did not result in any audit adjustments or misstatements, it could result in a misstatement of the aforementioned account balances or disclosures that would result in a material misstatement to the annual or interim consolidated financial statements that would not be prevented or detected.

Management has elected to exclude Flint from its assessment of internal control over financial reporting as of December 28, 2012 because we acquired Flint in a business combination on May 14, 2012. Flint is a wholly-owned subsidiary of URS, whose total assets and total revenues represented 12% and 13%, respectively, of the related consolidated financial statement amounts as of and for the year ended December 28, 2012.

Our independent registered public accounting firm, PricewaterhouseCoopers LLP, audited the effectiveness of the company's internal control over financial reporting at December 28, 2012 as stated in their report appearing under Item 8 of this report.

Remediation Plan

We are currently reviewing our journal entry process. We intend to modify access to our accounting systems to assure that, prior to posting of journal entries to our ledgers, individuals without prepare-and-post access review all journal entries for validity, accuracy and completeness, particularly related to accounts where the person who prepares the journal entries is the same person who reconciles the corresponding accounts.

General Management and Special-Purpose Committee Reports

PRESENTATION

7.71 Some survey entities presented a report of management on financial statements. These reports may include the following:
- Description of management's responsibility for preparing the financial statements
- Identification of independent auditors
- Statement about management's representations to the independent auditors
- Statement about financial records and related data made available to the independent auditors
- Description of special-purpose committees of the board of directors
- General description of the entity's system of internal control
- Description of the entity's code of conduct

Occasionally, survey entities presented a report of a special-purpose committee, such as the audit committee or compensation committee.

PRESENTATION AND DISCLOSURE EXCERPTS

REPORT OF MANAGEMENT ON FINANCIAL STATEMENTS

7.72 PEPSICO, INC. (DEC)
MANAGEMENT'S RESPONSIBILITY FOR FINANCIAL REPORTING

To Our Shareholders:

At PepsiCo, our actions—the actions of all our associates—are governed by our Global Code of Conduct. This Code is clearly aligned with our stated values—a commitment to sustained growth, through empowered people, operating with responsibility and building trust. Both the Code and our core values enable us to operate with integrity—both within the letter and the spirit of the law. Our Code of Conduct is reinforced consistently at all levels and in all countries. We have maintained strong governance policies and practices for many years.

The management of PepsiCo is responsible for the objectivity and integrity of our consolidated financial statements. The Audit Committee of the Board of Directors has engaged independent registered public accounting firm, KPMG LLP, to audit our consolidated financial statements, and they have expressed an unqualified opinion.

We are committed to providing timely, accurate and understandable information to investors. Our commitment encompasses the following:

Maintaining strong controls over financial reporting. Our system of internal control is based on the control criteria framework of the Committee of Sponsoring Organizations of the Treadway Commission published in their report titled *Internal Control—Integrated Framework*. The system is designed to provide reasonable assurance that transactions are executed as authorized and accurately recorded; that assets are safeguarded; and that accounting records are sufficiently reliable to permit the preparation of financial statements that conform in all material respects with accounting principles generally accepted in the U.S. We maintain disclosure controls and procedures designed to ensure that information required to be disclosed in reports under the Securities Exchange Act of 1934 is recorded, processed, summarized and reported within the specified time periods. We monitor these internal controls through self-assessments and an ongoing program of internal audits. Our internal controls are reinforced through our Global Code of Conduct, which sets forth our commitment to conduct business with integrity, and within both the letter and the spirit of the law.

Exerting rigorous oversight of the business. We continuously review our business results and strategies. This encompasses financial discipline in our strategic and daily business decisions. Our Executive Committee is actively involved—from understanding strategies and alternatives to reviewing key initiatives and financial performance. The intent is to ensure we remain objective in our assessments, constructively challenge our approach to potential business opportunities and issues, and monitor results and controls.

Engaging strong and effective Corporate Governance from our Board of Directors. We have an active, capable and diligent Board that meets the required standards for independence, and we welcome the Board's oversight as a representative of our shareholders. Our Audit Committee is comprised of independent directors with the financial literacy, knowledge and experience to provide appropriate oversight. We review our critical accounting policies, financial reporting and internal control matters with them and encourage their direct communication with KPMG LLP, with our General Auditor, and with our General Counsel. We also have a Compliance & Ethics Department, led by our Chief Compliance & Ethics Officer, to coordinate our compliance policies and practices.

Providing investors with financial results that are complete, transparent and understandable. The consolidated financial statements and financial information included in this report are the responsibility of management. This includes preparing the financial statements in accordance with accounting principles generally accepted in the U.S., which require estimates based on management's best judgment.

PepsiCo has a strong history of doing what's right. We realize that great companies are built on trust, strong ethical standards and principles. Our financial results are delivered from that culture of accountability, and we take responsibility for the quality and accuracy of our financial reporting.

February 21, 2013

REPORT OF THE AUDIT COMMITTEE

7.73 HARLEY-DAVIDSON, INC. (DEC)
REPORT OF THE AUDIT COMMITTEE

The Audit Committee of the Board of Directors reviews the Company's financial reporting process and the audit process. All of the Audit Committee members are independent in accordance with the Audit Committee requirements of the New York Stock Exchange, Inc.

The Audit Committee of the Board of Directors has reviewed and discussed with management its assessment of the effectiveness of the Company's internal control system over financial reporting as of December 31, 2012. Management has concluded that the internal control system was effective. Additionally, the Company's internal control over financial reporting as of December 31, 2012 was audited by Ernst & Young LLP, the Company's independent registered public accounting firm for the 2012 fiscal year. The Audit Committee has reviewed and discussed the audited financial statements of the Company for the 2012 fiscal year with management as well as with representatives of Ernst & Young LLP. The Audit Committee has also discussed with Ernst & Young LLP matters required to be discussed under Statement on Auditing Standards No. 61, Communications with Audit Committees (SAS 61), as amended (AICPA, Professional Standards, Vol. 1, AU section 380) and adopted by the Public Company Accounting Oversight Board in Rule 3200T. The Audit Committee has received written disclosures from Ernst & Young LLP regarding their independence as required by PCAOB Ethics and Independence Rule 3526, Communication with Audit Committees Concerning Independence, and has discussed with representatives of Ernst & Young LLP the independence of Ernst & Young LLP. Based on the review and discussions referred to above, the Audit Committee has recommended to the Board of Directors that the audited financial statements for the 2012 fiscal year be included in the Company's Annual Report on Form 10-K for the 2012 fiscal year.

REPORT ON ETHICAL STANDARDS

7.74 WAL-MART STORES, INC. (JAN)
REPORT ON ETHICAL STANDARDS

Our Company was founded on the belief that open communications and the highest standards of ethics are necessary to be successful. Our long-standing "Open Door" communication policy helps management be aware of and address issues in a timely and effective manner. Through the open door policy all associates are encouraged to inform management at the appropriate level when they are concerned about any matter pertaining to Walmart.

Walmart has adopted a Statement of Ethics to guide our associates in the continued observance of high ethical standards such as honesty, integrity and compliance with the law in the conduct of Walmart's business. Familiarity and compliance with the Statement of Ethics is required of all associates who are part of management. The Company also maintains a separate Code of Ethics for our senior financial officers. Walmart also has in place a Related-Party Transaction Policy. This policy applies to Walmart's senior officers and directors and requires material related-party transactions to be reviewed by the Audit Committee. The senior officers and directors are required to report material related-party transactions to Walmart. We maintain a global ethics office which oversees and administers an ethics helpline. The ethics helpline provides a channel for associates to make confidential and anonymous complaints regarding potential violations of our statements of ethics, including violations related to financial or accounting matters.

MANAGEMENT'S REPORT ON INTERNAL CONTROL OVER FINANCIAL REPORTING

7.75 MUELLER INDUSTRIES, INC. (DEC)
MANAGEMENT'S REPORT ON INTERNAL CONTROL OVER FINANCIAL REPORTING

The Company's management is responsible for establishing and maintaining adequate internal control over financial reporting as defined in Rules 13a-15(f) under the Securities Exchange Act of 1934. Pursuant to the rules and regulations of the SEC, internal control over financial reporting is a process designed by, or under the supervision of, the Company's principal executive and principal financial officers, and effected by the Company's board of directors, management and other personnel, to provide reasonable assurance regarding the reliability of financial reporting and the preparation of financial statements for external purposes in accordance with accounting principles generally accepted in the United States and includes those policies and procedures that (i) pertain to the maintenance of records that in reasonable detail accurately and fairly reflect the transactions and dispositions of the Company's assets; (ii) provide reasonable assurance that transactions are recorded as necessary to permit preparation of financial statements in accordance with generally accepted accounting principles, and that receipts and expenditures of the issuer are being made only in accordance with authorizations of the Company's management and directors;

and (iii) provide reasonable assurance regarding prevention or timely detection of unauthorized acquisition, use or disposition of the Company's assets that could have a material effect on the financial statements. Due to inherent limitations, internal control over financial reporting may not prevent or detect misstatements. Further, because of changes in conditions, effectiveness of internal control over financial reporting may vary over time.

The Company's management, with the participation of the Company's Chief Executive Officer and Chief Financial Officer, has evaluated the effectiveness of the Company's internal control over financial reporting as of December 29, 2012 based on the control criteria established in a report entitled *Internal Control—Integrated Framework*, issued by the Committee of Sponsoring Organizations of the Treadway Commission (COSO). Based on such evaluation management has concluded that our internal control over financial reporting is effective as of December 29, 2012.

Ernst & Young LLP (E&Y), the independent registered public accounting firm that audited the Company's financial statements included in this Annual Report on Form 10-K, has issued an attestation report on the Company's internal control over financial reporting, which is included herein.

CHANGES IN INTERNAL CONTROL OVER FINANCIAL REPORTING

During the fourth quarter of 2012, the Company determined that control deficiencies in its internal control over financial reporting at one of its divisions, the Standard Products Division (SPD), existed as of December 31, 2011. These control deficiencies related to a combination of appropriate review of significant manual journal entries as well as financial review monitoring controls. The Company and E&Y have concluded that, had it and they been aware of the combination of these control deficiencies in the Company's internal control over financial reporting at February 28, 2012, the date of its and their reports on internal control over financial reporting as of December 31, 2011, both would have concluded that a material weakness existed and that the Company's internal control over financial reporting was ineffective at that date.

The material weakness did not result in a material misstatement in the Company's financial position, results of operations, or cash flows as of and for the period ended December 31, 2011. Furthermore, during the fourth quarter of 2012, the Company designed and implemented remediation measures to address the material weakness described above and enhance the Company's internal control over financial reporting. The following actions which the Company believes have remediated the material weakness in internal control over financial reporting were completed as of the date of this filing:
- The Company reorganized the accounting function of SPD that was in place when the control deficiencies occurred and supplemented that function with a finance team that has more public company accounting and finance experience; and
- The finance team effectively added monitoring practices concerning the review of manual journal entries and reported financial results.

List of 350 Survey Entities and Where in the Text Excerpts From Their Annual Reports Can Be Found

The following table lists the 350 entities surveyed in alphabetical order, as well as where in the text their annual reports are excerpted.

Company Name	Month of Fiscal Year End	Accounting Technique Illustration
3M Company	December	
A. O. Smith Corporation	December	
Abbott Laboratories	December	
ABM Industries Incorporated	October	1.100
Acuity Brands, Inc.	August	
AGCO Corporation	December	1.23
Air Products and Chemicals, Inc.	September	6.24, 7.69
Airgas, Inc.	March	1.78
AK Steel Holding Corporation	December	
Alcoa Inc.	December	1.34, 2.100
Allegheny Technologies Incorporated	December	
Allergan, Inc.	December	3.32
Alliance One International, Inc.	March	1.20, 2.91
Alliant Techsystems Inc.	March	6.18
Altria Group, Inc.	December	
American Greetings Corporation	Feburary	
American International Group, Inc.	December	1.18, 1.50, 5.35
AMETEK, Inc.	December	
Amkor Technology, Inc.	December	
Amphenol Corporation	December	
Anadarko Petroleum Corporation	December	2.24, 3.22, 3.69
Analog Devices, Inc.	October	4.15
Ann Inc.	January	3.20
Apache Corporation	December	3.29
Apple Inc.	September	2.120
Applied Materials, Inc.	October	3.59
Archer Daniels Midland Company	June	3.38
Arden Group, Inc.	December	
Arkansas Best Corporation	December	
Armstrong World Industries, Inc.	December	1.75
Arrow Electronics, Inc.	December	
Ashland Inc.	September	6.34
AT&T Inc.	December	
Atmel Corporation	December	7.55
Autodesk, Inc.	January	7.57
Automatic Data Processing, Inc.	June	
AutoNation, Inc.	December	
AutoZone, Inc.	August	
Avnet, Inc.	June	2.35, 3.13
Avon Products, Inc.	December	1.101
Axiall Corporation	December	1.117, 4.10, 7.62
B/E Aerospace, Inc.	December	
Badger Meter, Inc.	December	
Baker Hughes Incorporated	December	
Ball Corporation	December	3.67

Company Name	Month of Fiscal Year End	Accounting Technique Illustration
Barnes & Noble, Inc.	April	1.120
Bassett Furniture Industries, Incorporated	November	
Beam Inc.	December	3.93, 5.13
Becton, Dickinson and Company	September	
Berkshire Hathaway Inc.	December	1.22, 1.51
Best Buy Co., Inc.	Feburary	
BMC Software, Inc.	March	
Boeing Company, The	December	2.108, 3.68
Bon-Ton Stores, Inc., The	January	3.18, 6.22
Boston Scientific Corporation	December	4.16
Briggs & Stratton Corporation	June	7.19
Brink's Company, The	December	
Brown Shoe Company, Inc.	January	
Brown-Forman Corporation	April	4.09
Brunswick Corporation	December	1.48, 2.152
CA, Inc.	March	6.37
Cablevision Systems Corporation	December	2.139
Cabot Corporation	September	2.72, 6.19
CACI International Inc	June	2.90, 3.79
Campbell Soup Company	July	1.118
Cardinal Health, Inc.	June	
Career Education Corporation	December	1.49, 2.146
Carlisle Companies Incorporated	December	
Carpenter Technology Corporation	June	6.26
Caterpillar Inc.	December	1.35
CBS Corporation	December	
CenturyLink, Inc.	December	5.23
Cenveo, Inc.	December	
CF Industries Holdings, Inc.	December	5.52
Chesapeake Energy Corporation	December	1.121, 6.40
Chevron Corporation	December	3.24
Children's Place Retail Stores, Inc., The	January	
Cisco Systems, Inc.	July	1.24, 4.08
Citigroup Inc.	December	1.53, 2.19, 3.63
Cliffs Natural Resources Inc.	December	3.48
Clorox Company, The	June	
Coach, Inc.	June	
Coca-Cola Company, The	December	1.26, 1.125, 2.67
Coca-Cola Enterprises Inc.	December	
Coherent, Inc.	September	7.44
Collective Brands, Inc.	January	
Commercial Metals Company	August	
Computer Sciences Corporation	March	
ConAgra Foods, Inc.	May	7.43
ConocoPhillips	December	1.88, 1.122, 3.49, 3.88
Constellation Brands, Inc.	Feburary	2.115, 6.09
Convergys Corporation	December	
Cooper Tire & Rubber Company	December	4.13
Corning Incorporated	December	3.35
Covance Inc.	December	
Crane Co.	December	2.28
Cummins Inc.	December	
CVS Caremark Corporation	December	1.46, 6.16
Dana Holding Corporation	December	
Danaher Corporation	December	
Darden Restaurants, Inc.	May	5.49
Dean Foods Company	December	2.50, 2.128, 3.31, 6.39, 7.49
Deere & Company	October	1.21
Dell Inc.	January	3.07
DIRECTV	December	1.52
Discovery Communications, Inc.	December	2.66
Domino's Pizza, Inc.	December	
Donaldson Company, Inc.	July	5.28
Dover Corporation	December	3.61
Dow Chemical Company, The	December	1.89, 2.34
Dun & Bradstreet Corporation, The	December	

Company Name	Month of Fiscal Year End	Accounting Technique Illustration
E. W. Scripps Company, The	December	
Eastman Chemical Company	December	1.45, 4.18
eBay Inc.	December	
Ecolab Inc.	December	
Electronic Arts Inc.	March	2.137, 6.28
Eli Lilly and Company	December	
EMC Corporation	December	5.08
EMCOR Group, Inc.	December	2.121
Emerson Electric Co.	September	
Energizer Holdings, Inc.	September	2.06, 4.06
Equifax Inc.	December	2.125
Estee Lauder Companies Inc., The	June	4.11
Exide Technologies	March	
Express Scripts Holding Company	December	2.155, 5.15
Exxon Mobil Corporation	December	
FedEx Corporation	May	
Fidelity National Information Services, Inc.	December	
First Solar, Inc.	December	2.156
Flowers Foods, Inc.	December	1.70, 3.34, 5.07
Fluor Corporation	December	
FMC Corporation	December	2.157
Foot Locker, Inc.	January	
Ford Motor Company	December	1.66, 2.27
Fred's, Inc.	January	
Freeport-McMoRan Copper & Gold Inc.	December	2.158, 3.17
Furniture Brands International, Inc.	December	2.81, 2.136
GameStop Corp.	January	
GenCorp Inc.	November	1.115, 3.92
General Cable Corporation	December	
General Dynamics Corporation	December	
General Electric Company	December	3.08, 6.29
General Mills, Inc.	May	
Genuine Parts Company	December	1.54
Goldman Sachs Group, Inc., The	December	1.82, 6.35
Goodyear Tire & Rubber Company, The	December	
Google Inc.	December	4.14
Greif, Inc.	October	1.55
Griffon Corporation	September	
Guess?, Inc.	January	2.145, 3.50
H.J. Heinz Company	April	2.124
Halliburton Company	December	
Hanesbrands Inc.	December	
Harley-Davidson, Inc.	December	7.73
Harman International Industries, Incorporated	June	
Harris Corporation	June	3.26, 3.87
Hasbro, Inc.	December	
Health Net, Inc.	December	
Hershey Company, The	December	6.30
Hess Corporation	December	
Hewlett-Packard Company	October	2.80
Hill-Rom Holdings, Inc.	September	
Hormel Foods Corporation	October	
Hovnanian Enterprises, Inc.	October	6.12
Humana Inc.	December	
Huntsman Corporation	December	3.91
IAC/InterActiveCorp	December	2.68
IDT Corporation	July	5.41, 6.17
Illinois Tool Works Inc.	December	
Ingram Micro Inc.	December	
Ingredion Incorporated	December	1.102
Insperity, Inc.	December	1.83
Intel Corporation	December	
International Business Machines Corporation	December	2.83
International Flavors & Fragrances Inc.	December	
International Paper Company	December	1.17
Interpublic Group of Companies, Inc., The	December	5.20

Company Name	Month of Fiscal Year End	Accounting Technique Illustration
Iron Mountain Incorporated	December	1.86, 3.28, 3.33, 5.25
ITT Corporation	December	
J. C. Penney Company, Inc.	January	
J. M. Smucker Company, The	April	
Jabil Circuit, Inc.	August	4.17
Jack in the Box Inc.	September	6.21
Jarden Corporation	December	
JDS Uniphase Corporation	June	6.38, 7.41
Johnson & Johnson	December	3.21, 5.38
Johnson Controls, Inc.	September	
Jones Group Inc., The	December	1.77
Joy Global Inc.	October	
JPMorgan Chase & Co.	December	1.116
Juniper Networks, Inc.	December	2.86
KB Home	November	
Kellogg Company	December	
KLA-Tencor Corporation	June	
Kohl's Corporation	January	
Kroger Co., The	January	3.51, 7.21
L.S. Starrett Company, The	June	1.56, 5.36
L-3 Communications Holdings, Inc.	December	2.26
Lam Research Corporation	June	1.71, 1.76, 6.08
Las Vegas Sands Corp.	December	2.62, 2.161, 5.51
La-Z-Boy Incorporated	April	
Lear Corporation	December	2.135, 6.32
Lee Enterprises, Incorporated	September	
Leggett & Platt, Incorporated	December	
Lennar Corporation	November	1.67, 6.36
Lockheed Martin Corporation	December	2.118, 3.80
Louisiana-Pacific Corporation	December	1.84, 2.109
Lowe's Companies, Inc.	January	2.162
LSI Corporation	December	5.14
Manitowoc Company, Inc., The	December	
Marriott International, Inc.	December	
MasterCard Incorporated	December	2.53
McClatchy Company, The	December	1.85
McKesson Corporation	March	2.42, 2.119
Medtronic, Inc.	April	2.99
Merck & Co., Inc.	December	3.11
Meritor, Inc.	September	
MetLife, Inc.	December	3.41
Micron Technology, Inc.	August	5.11
Microsoft Corporation	June	
Molex Incorporated	June	
Molson Coors Brewing Company	December	2.160
Monsanto Company	August	2.33
Morgan Stanley	December	1.108, 3.58
Mosaic Company, The	May	1.19, 2.131
Motorola Solutions, Inc.	December	3.75
Mueller Industries, Inc.	December	3.14, 5.44, 7.75
Murphy Oil Corporation	December	2.61, 2.89
NACCO Industries, Inc.	December	
Nash-Finch Company	December	2.82
National Oilwell Varco, Inc.	December	
NetApp, Inc.	April	
New York Times Company, The	December	
Newell Rubbermaid Inc.	December	
NewMarket Corporation	December	4.07
News Corporation	June	1.47, 3.76
Noble Energy, Inc.	December	3.15
Northrop Grumman Corporation	December	
NVR, Inc.	December	5.50
Office Depot, Inc.	December	
Oracle Corporation	May	
Owens-Illinois, Inc.	December	2.159, 2.166, 7.42
PACCAR Inc	December	

Company Name	Month of Fiscal Year End	Accounting Technique Illustration
Parker-Hannifin Corporation	June	1.25
Peabody Energy Corporation	December	1.90, 2.107, 3.03, 3.36
PepsiCo, Inc.	December	3.39, 7.72
PerkinElmer, Inc.	December	3.74
Pfizer Inc.	December	
Pilgrim's Pride Corporation	December	
Pitney Bowes Inc.	December	
Plum Creek Timber Company, Inc.	December	7.54
PNC Financial Services Group, Inc., The	December	2.21, 5.10
Polaris Industries Inc.	December	
PolyOne Corporation	December	
PPG Industries, Inc.	December	
Precision Castparts Corp.	March	3.60
priceline.com Incorporated	December	3.40
Procter & Gamble Company, The	June	
Prudential Financial, Inc.	December	7.45
PulteGroup, Inc.	December	
PVH Corp.	January	2.44
RadioShack Corporation	December	
Ralph Lauren Corporation	March	3.23
Raytheon Company	December	2.55
Regal Beloit Corporation	December	
Regal Entertainment Group	December	2.140
Republic Services, Inc.	December	2.126
Reynolds American Inc.	December	
Rite Aid Corporation	Feburary	
Robbins & Myers, Inc.	August	
Rock-Tenn Company	September	
Rockwell Automation, Inc.	September	2.130
Rockwell Collins, Inc.	September	
Safeway Inc.	December	
Schnitzer Steel Industries, Inc.	August	
Scotts Miracle-Gro Company, The	September	
Seaboard Corporation	December	
Sealed Air Corporation	December	1.103, 3.12, 3.30
Sealy Corporation	November	2.95
Service Corporation International	December	3.43
Shaw Group Inc., The	August	2.129, 3.81
Sherwin-Williams Company, The	December	3.62
Smithfield Foods, Inc.	April	
Snap-on Incorporated	December	2.41, 2.73
Spectrum Brands Holdings, Inc.	September	3.77, 6.20
Sprint Nextel Corporation	December	1.73, 5.12
SPX Corporation	December	1.27, 6.10, 7.29
St. Jude Medical, Inc.	December	2.117
Standard Pacific Corp.	December	
Standard Register Company, The	December	7.68
Stanley Black & Decker, Inc.	December	2.49
Steel Dynamics, Inc.	December	2.25
Steelcase Inc.	Feburary	2.92
SYNNEX Corporation	November	
Sysco Corporation	June	3.52, 7.20
Target Corporation	January	
Teleflex Incorporated	December	1.29, 2.127
Tenet Healthcare Corporation	December	5.29
Tenneco Inc.	December	2.47
Terex Corporation	December	2.43
Texas Instruments Incorporated	December	2.69
Textron Inc.	December	
Thermo Fisher Scientific Inc.	December	
Tiffany & Co.	January	
Time Warner Inc.	December	6.11
Toll Brothers, Inc.	October	2.112, 7.66
TRW Automotive Holdings Corp.	December	3.54
Tupperware Brands Corporation	December	3.42
Tutor Perini Corporation	December	2.51, 3.57

Company Name	Month of Fiscal Year End	Accounting Technique Illustration
Unifi, Inc.	June	
Unisys Corporation	December	
United Continental Holdings, Inc.	December	2.52
United Parcel Service, Inc.	December	2.93
United States Steel Corporation	December	
UnitedHealth Group Incorporated	December	2.20
Universal Corporation	March	1.87, 2.48, 5.24
Universal Forest Products, Inc.	December	
Universal Health Services, Inc.	December	2.122, 2.154, 3.25
URS Corporation	December	2.94, 7.70
Valassis Communications, Inc.	December	1.74, 6.23
Valero Energy Corporation	December	3.70
Varian Medical Systems, Inc.	September	
VeriSign, Inc.	December	3.27
Verizon Communications Inc.	December	2.85, 2.147
Viacom Inc.	September	
Visa Inc.	September	7.67
Vishay Intertechnology, Inc.	December	1.28, 3.95
Visteon Corporation	December	7.33
Vulcan Materials Company	December	
W. R. Grace & Co.	December	7.32
Wal-Mart Stores, Inc.	January	2.45, 7.74
Walter Energy, Inc.	December	2.164
Washington Post Company, The	December	4.12
Waste Management, Inc.	December	2.123, 3.37
Weis Markets, Inc.	December	1.44
WellPoint, Inc.	December	3.16, 6.27
Wendy's Company, The	December	3.09
Werner Enterprises, Inc.	December	
Western Union Company, The	December	2.84
Weyerhaeuser Company	December	2.165
Williams-Sonoma, Inc.	January	2.54
Winnebago Industries, Inc.	August	2.153
Worthington Industries, Inc.	May	
Wyndham Worldwide Corporation	December	6.31
Wynn Resorts, Limited	December	
Xerox Corporation	December	
Xilinx, Inc.	March	
Yahoo! Inc.	December	3.73
YUM! Brands, Inc.	December	
Zimmer Holdings, Inc.	December	3.56, 5.09

A

D

F

reports on comparative financial statements, 7.53
uncertainties, 7.31

J

Joint ventures
  balance sheets, 2.63–2.69
  cost method, 2.68
  disclosure, 2.65
  fair value, 2.69
  presentation, 2.64
  presentation and disclosure excerpts, 2.66–2.69
  recognition and measurement, 2.63

L

Lack of consistency in independent auditors' report
  comparative financial statements, 7.52–7.55
  comprehensive income, 7.44
  correction of errors and restatement, 7.34–7.40
  deferred policy acquisition costs, 7.45
  employee benefits, 7.43
  inventory, 7.42
  issuers, 7.36–7.40
  nonissuers, 7.35–7.35
  presentation, 7.35–7.40
  presentation and disclosure excerpts, 7.41–7.45
  revenue recognition, 7.41

Land, 2.87. See also Property, plant, and equipment

Last-in, first-out (LIFO) inventory, 2.39–2.40, 2.42

Lawsuits. See Litigation

Leases
  leasing commitments, 1.76
  lessee leases, 2.145–2.146
  lessor leases, 2.147
  long-term. See Long-term leases
  operating leases, 2.141, 2.143, 2.144

Legal matters, contingencies, 1.82

Lessee leases, 2.145–2.146

Lessor leases, 2.147

Letters of credit, 1.72

Liabilities
  contingent liabilities, 2.151
  current liabilities, 2.104, 2.132
  employee compensatory plans, 3.55
  fair value measurement, 1.106, 1.107
  income taxes, disclosure, 3.72
  noncurrent liabilities, 2.104
  offsetting with assets, 1.12
  other current. See Other current liabilities
  other noncurrent. See Other noncurrent liabilities
  pension plan disclosures, 3.45
  preferred stock classified as, 5.18
  servicing liabilities, fair value, 2.30, 2.32

Licenses and licensing, 1.77, 2.85

Life insurance cash surrender value, 2.92

LIFO. See Last-in, first-out (LIFO) inventory

Line of credit, 1.100

Liquidity, 1.20

Litigation
  expenses and losses, 3.35
  other current liabilities, 2.128
  other noncurrent liabilities, 2.159
  revenues and gains, 3.14
  subsequent events, 1.116

Loans. See also Credit agreements; Debt
  due-on-demand arrangements, 2.96, 2.113
  loans payable, 2.98
  related party transactions, 1.122

Long-term assets held for sale. See Held for sale

Long-term debt
  balance sheet, 2.132–2.137
  collateralized, 2.136
  convertible, 2.137
  covenants, 2.137
  current amount, 2.113–2.115
  disclosure, 2.133–2.134
  presentation, 2.132
  presentation and disclosure excerpts, 2.135–2.137
  unsecured, 2.135

Long-term leases
  balance sheet, 2.141–2.147
  commitments, 1.72
  disclosure, 2.144
  lessee leases, 2.145–2.146
  lessor leases, 2.147
  presentation, 2.142–2.143
  presentation and disclosure excerpts, 2.145–2.147
  recognition and measurement, 2.141

Long-term prepayments, 2.87

Long-term receivables, 1.122, 2.72

Loss carryforward, contingencies, 1.90, 3.76–3.77

Loss contingencies, 1.79, 1.80

Losses. See also Expenses and losses
  actuarial gains, pension plan disclosures, 3.46
  adjustments to reconcile net income, 6.19
  debt extinguishment, 3.43
  defined, 3.19
  derivatives, 1.97, 1.98
  derivatives held as cash flow hedges, 4.15–4.16
  discontinued operations, 3.83, 3.85, 6.19
  impairment of investments, 2.11
  provision for, 3.25
  sale of business, 6.19
  unrealized, net change on available-for-sale securities, 4.14
  unrealized, on marketable securities, 2.10

M

Management's discussion and analysis (MD&A), financial condition and results of operations, 1.09

Management's reports
  on financial statements, 7.16, 7.72
  general management committee reports, 7.71–7.75
  on internal control, 7.70, 7.75
  segment reporting approaches, 1.32

Management's responsibilities, auditors' report, 7.04, 7.08, 7.11

Mandatorily redeemable preferred stock, 2.149, 5.18

Powerful Online Research Tools

The AICPA Online Professional Library offers the most current access to comprehensive accounting and auditing literature, as well business and practice management information, combined with the power and speed of the Web. Through your online subscription, you'll get:

- Cross-references within and between titles — smart links give you quick access to related information and relevant materials
- First available updates — no other research tool offers access to new AICPA standards and conforming changes more quickly, guaranteeing that you are always current with all of the authoritative guidance!
- Robust search engine — helps you narrow down your research to find your results quickly
- And much more...

Choose from two comprehensive libraries or select only the titles you need!

With the *Essential A&A Research Collection*, you gain access to the following:
- AICPA Professional Standards
- AICPA Technical Practice Aids
- PCAOB Standards & Related Rules
- All current AICPA Audit and Accounting Guides
- All current Audit Risk Alerts
One-year individual online subscription
Item # ORS-XX

OR

***Premium A&A Research Collection* and get everything from the *Essential A&A Research Collection* plus:**
- AICPA Audit & Accounting Manual
- All current Checklists & Illustrative Financial Statements
- eXacct: Financial Reporting Tools & Techniques
- IFRS Accounting Trends & Techniques
One-year individual online subscription
Item # WAL-BY

You can also add the FASB *Accounting Standards Codification*™ and the GASB Library to either collection.

Take advantage of a 30-day free trial!
See for yourself how these powerful online libraries can improve your productivity and simplify your accounting research.

Visit **cpa2biz.com/library** for details or to subscribe.

Additional Publications

Audit Risk Alerts/Financial Reporting Alerts
Find out about current economic, regulatory and professional developments before you perform your audit engagement. AICPA industry-specific Audit Risk Alerts will make your audit planning process more efficient by giving you concise, relevant information that shows you how current developments may impact your clients and your audits. For financial statement preparers, AICPA also offers a series of Financial Reporting Alerts. For a complete list of Audit Risk Alerts available from the AICPA, please visit **cpa2biz.com/ara**.

Checklists and Illustrative Financial Statements
Updated to reflect recent accounting and auditing standards, these industry-specific practice aids are invaluable tools to both financial statement preparers and auditors. For a complete list of Checklists available from the AICPA, please visit **cpa2biz.com/checklists**.